A Powerful Learning Tool

You can use *Learning Biological Psychology* to enhance your understanding of this book in a variety of ways.

Reinforce your knowledge of the chapter material with comprehensive study questions.

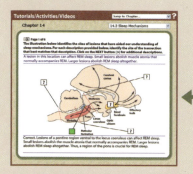

Learn complex concepts and processes through animated tutorials, activities, and videos.

Use the interactive terminology quiz to learn key terms from each chapter.

Test your overall understanding of each chapter with self-quizzes.

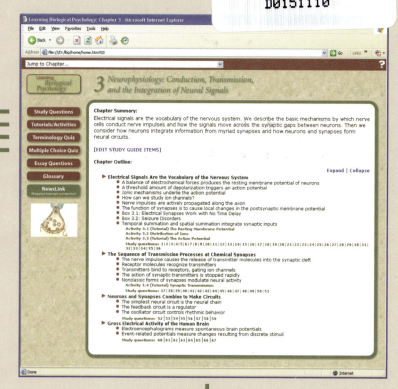

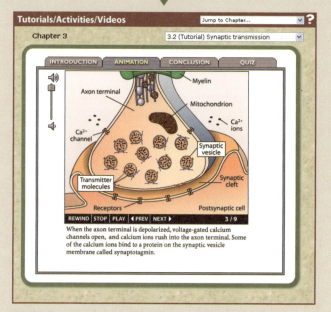

Link directly from a chapter outline to related study questions, tutorials, and activities.

Biological Psychology

DON JUAN: . . . Will you not agree with me
. . . that it is inconceivable that Life,
having once produced [birds],
should, if love and beauty were her
object, start off on another line
and labor at the clumsy elephant
and hideous ape, whose grandchildren
we are?

THE DEVIL: You conclude then, that Life
was driving at clumsiness and
ugliness?

DON JUAN: No, perverse devil that you
are, a thousand times no. Life was
driving at brains—at its darling
object: an organ by which it can
attain not only self-consciousness
but self-understanding.

George Bernard Shaw
Man and Superman, Act III

The brain is wider than the sky,
  For, put them side by side,
The one the other will include
  With ease, and you beside.

The brain is deeper than the sea,
  For, hold them, blue to blue,
The one the other will absorb,
  As sponges, buckets do.

The brain is just the weight of God,
  For, lift them, pound for pound,
And they will differ, if they do,
  As syllable from sound.

Emily Dickinson

Biological Psychology

AN INTRODUCTION TO BEHAVIORAL AND COGNITIVE NEUROSCIENCE

FOURTH EDITION

Mark R. Rosenzweig
University of California, Berkeley

S. Marc Breedlove
Michigan State University

Neil V. Watson
Simon Fraser University

Sinauer Associates, Inc • *Publishers*
Sunderland, Massachusetts

About the Cover   A Brain On the Ceiling of the Sistine Chapel?

In one of the panels of the ceiling of the Sistine Chapel, Michelangelo Buonarroti's masterpiece "The Creation of Adam" (painted 1508–1512) depicts God reaching out to bestow the gift of life upon humanity, through Adam. But the oddly shaped drapery behind God, and the arrangement of his attendants, has prompted speculation that Michelangelo was conveying a hidden message: God and attendants appear to be part of a human brain (Meshberger, 1990).

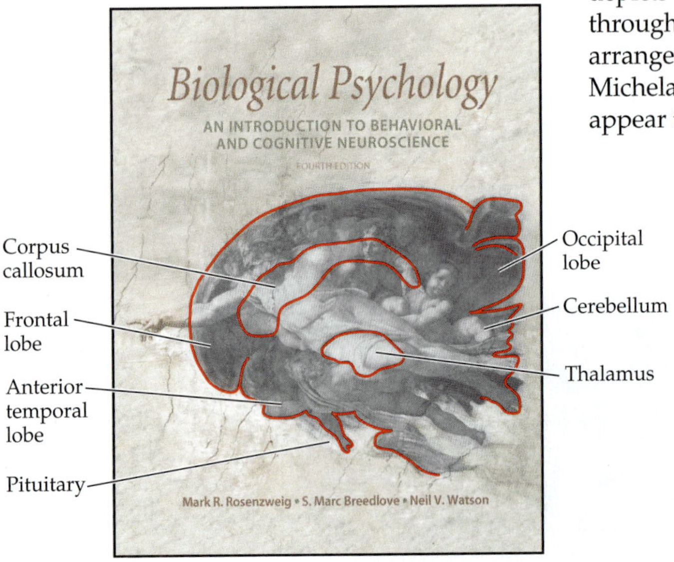

As illustrated here, it requires only a little imagination to identify the broad outlines of a brain in Michelangelo's depiction of God (compare it with the midsagittal section of a human brain in Figure 2.7). During the Renaissance, when this fresco was created, the all-powerful Church forbade depiction of the dissected human body, considering it to be a desecration. But there is no doubt that Michelangelo engaged in extensive dissections of cadavers, gaining the detailed knowledge of human anatomy that informs his sculpture and paintings. It is highly likely that he knew perfectly well what a dissected human brain looks like. So was Michelangelo making a subtle commentary about the origins of behavior? We probably will never know. But it is now clear that our uniquely human qualities—language, reason, emotion, and the rest—are products of the brain.

Biological Psychology, Fourth Edition

For information, address
   Sinauer Associates, 23 Plumtree Road, Sunderland, MA 01375 U.S.A.
   FAX: 413-549-1118
   E-mail: publish@sinauer.com
   Internet: www.sinauer.com

Library of Congress Cataloging-in-Publication Data

Rosenzweig, Mark R.
   Biological psychology : an introduction to behavioral and cognitive
   neuroscience / Mark R. Rosenzweig.-- 4th ed.
      p. cm.
   Includes bibliographical references and index.
   ISBN 0-87893-754-4
  1. Psychobiology. 2. Cognitive neuroscience. I. Title.
QP360.R658 2005
612.8--dc22   2004010301

5 4 3 2

We dedicate this book affectionately to our wives, children, and grandchildren.
We appreciate their support and patience over the years of this project.

M.R.R.			**S.M.B.**					**N.V.W.**		
	Janine			*Cindy*					*Maria*	
Anne	*Suzanne*	*Philip*	*Ben*	*Nick*	*Tessa*	*Kit*		*Bix*	*Sophie*	*Lia*
Jim	*Kent*	*Laura*								
	Lauren	*Thomas*								
	David	*Caroline*								
	Gregory									
	Elise									

Brief Contents

Contents

4 The Chemical Bases of Behavior: Neurotransmitters and Neuropharmacology 90

5 Hormones and the Brain 122

Part II Evolution and Development of the Nervous System

6 Evolution of Brain and Behavior 154

7 Life-Span Development of the Brain and Behavior 182

Part III *Perception and Action*

14 *Biological Rhythms, Sleep, and Dreaming* 424

Biological Rhythms 425

Sleeping and Waking 433

PART V *Emotions and Mental Disorders*

15 *Emotions, Aggression, and Stress* 458

16 *Psychopathology: Biological Basis of Behavioral Disorders* 488

PART VI Cognitive Neuroscience

Preface

These days, the newspapers, magazines, and TV are chock full of intriguing and sometimes astonishing stories about how the brain functions. On any given day, our website (www.biopsychology.com) posts three or more biopsychology news stories, all drawn from the wire services and major newsfeeds. Neuroscience seems poised to answer so many formerly mysterious questions:

- Does stem-cell research hold the promise of treatments for neurological disorders like Alzheimer's disease and Parkinson's disease?
- Does the brain make new neurons throughout life, in numbers large enough to make a functional difference? Can we control this process?
- Can we improve memory performance by manipulating genes, or diets, or drugs?
- Does strong liking for sweet foods involve the same brain mechanisms as addiction to drugs?
- How can recent discoveries about the neural control of appetite help us to curb the obesity epidemic?
- Does a gene that predisposes for Alzheimer's disease impair memory even in those who do not develop the disease?

These are important questions, but the basic issues surrounding them cannot be reduced to "sound bites." A meaningful approach to questions like these requires an understanding of the bodily systems that underlie behavior and experience. Our aim in *Biological Psychology* is to provide a foundation that places these and other important problems in a unified scientific context.

This book explores the biological bases of our experience and behavior: the ways in which bodily states and processes produce and control behavior and cognition, and—just as important—the ways in which behavior, cognition, and the environment exert their influence on bodily systems. We treat biology in a broad sense. As in most textbooks of this sort, there is substantial coverage of the proximate, physiological underpinnings of behavior, but we have also related these systems to their ultimate, evolutionary origins whenever possible. The focus of the book is human behavior, but we include numerous discussions of other species' solutions to the problems of survival as well.

Many scientific disciplines contribute to these themes, so we draw upon the research of psychologists, anatomists, biochemists, endocrinologists, engineers, geneticists, immunologists, neurologists, physiologists, evolutionary biologists, and zoologists. In order to gain a panoramic view of the questions that concern biological psychologists, we have tried to rise above the limits of any single specialty. Throughout the book we employ a five-fold approach to biological psychology—

descriptive, comparative/evolutionary, developmental, mechanistic, and applied/clinical. We also emphasize the remarkable plasticity of the nervous system; it is increasingly evident that this malleability is a general feature of neural tissue.

In our experience, students enrolled in biological psychology courses can be quite diverse in terms of their academic backgrounds and their personal interests, so we have taken pains to make the subject as accessible as possible to the widest spectrum of students by providing both the behavioral and biological foundations for each main topic. Some students will feel comfortable skipping or skimming some of this background material, but others will benefit from studying it carefully before moving on to the core of each chapter.

We have adopted an ordering of chapters that seems logical to us, but we realize that some instructors may prefer to teach topics in a different order or to omit some chapters entirely, so we have written each chapter as a relatively self-contained unit. Recognizing that courses also vary in length from a single quarter or semester to two semesters, we wrote the text with the intent that it could be reasonably covered in a single quarter by omitting a few chapters, but the text provides enough material for a two-quarter or even a two-semester course. We have successfully taught the course using the book in each of these settings. Specific suggestions for creating syllabi with different emphases can be found in the Instructor's Manual, along with detailed outlines for lectures and other helpful material. In addition, the Instructor's Resource CD contains many resources for use in the lecture, such as animations, videos, and PowerPoint® slides of every figure in the book. (For more information on the media and supplements, turn to page XVIII.)

Many features of the text are designed to enhance students' mastery of the material:

- We have continued to develop what we believe is the finest full-color illustration program in any biological psychology text. This acclaimed art program has undergone hundreds of additions and refinements, always with a clear pedagogical goal in mind. Data from original sources have been recast in ways that are designed to aid the student's understanding. All-new photographs and drawings —clear, detailed, and consistent—are another feature of this edition.
- Each chapter opens with a vivid vignette that places the chapter content in a real-world context, serving to draw the reader into the relevant research issues from the outset; the vignette is eventually resolved within the body of the chapter. Each chapter concludes with a Summary and list of Recommended Reading.
- Key terms are set in boldface type where first defined, and are also included in an improved, more comprehensive Glossary.
- "Boxes" describe interesting applications, important methods, sidelights, or refreshers on theoretical concepts relevant to biological psychology, or place the findings in the chapter in a historical perspective.
- Icons in the margins call attention to six special aspects of the text:

COMPETING HYPOTHESES

We frequently underscore the point that science is a process, and that it advances by continually testing competing hypotheses to account for observations. As examples in the text illustrate, sometimes further research indicates which of a group of hypotheses is correct; sometimes all the hypotheses are rejected for a new, more adequate hypothesis.

IMPORTANT METHOD

Many of the stunning advances in neuroscience in recent years are due to the introduction of powerful new methods that have made it possible to make progress on previously intractable problems. This icon highlights these new methods as well as more venerable research techniques. Important animal models used in research are also highlighted with this icon.

GENES AND BEHAVIOR

The revolution in molecular biology is clarifying many of the mechanisms involved in genetic influences on behavior, and this icon highlights important examples.

EVOLUTION AT WORK

Evolution is a major theme of current research on neuroscience and behavior, and we highlight many examples.

NEURAL PLASTICITY

As noted above, plasticity of the nervous system is an important theme in the text. This icon calls attention to particularly robust examples of plasticity.

CLINICAL ISSUE

Discussion of clinical issues occurs frequently in the text, and this icon points out discussions of important disorders of the nervous system.

Learning Biological Psychology, our comprehensive electronic study guide revised and updated by Raymond Kesner and David Vago of the University of Utah, is a powerful companion to the textbook that enhances the learning experience with a variety of multimedia resources. The CD icon appears wherever the student can make use of the interactive activities or animations included in *Learning Biological Psychology* to clarify important concepts.

Some of the most satisfying experiences in writing—and revising—this book have been the lively and creative discussions among the authors. Each of us has a different research focus, and each of us is involved in certain fields more fully than the others. Pooling our experiences and discussing the relevance of findings in one area to other aspects of biological psychology has been a rewarding experience, and we believe that this integration of knowledge from diverse but complementary fields has enriched the book.

Acknowledgments

In preparing this book we benefited from the help of many highly skilled people. These include members of the staff of Sinauer Associates: Graig Donini, Editor; Kathaleen Emerson, Production Editor; Jason Dirks, Media and Supplements Editor; Jennifer Garrett, Editoral Assistant; Christopher Small, Production Manager; Jefferson Johnson, Book Designer; Joan Gemme, Electronic Book Production. Copy Editor Stephanie Hiebert once again skillfully edited the text, and Photo Researcher David McIntyre sought out many of the photographs. Maria Watson painstakingly scrutinized drafts of many of the chapters and provided many helpful comments. Mike Demaray, Craig Durant and colleagues at Dragonfly Media Group transformed our rough sketches and wish list into the handsome and dynamic art program of this text. Many anatomical depictions of the human nervous system seen in this book were adapted from drawings originally rendered for Hal Blumenfeld's Neuroanatomy through Clinical Cases (Blumenfeld, 2002), and we are grateful for this source of expertise in helping to make our illustrations aesthetically pleasing and neuroanatomically accurate.

We also want to thank our past undergraduate and graduate students ranging back to the 1950s for their helpful responses to our instruction, and the colleagues who provided information and critical comments about our manuscript: Brian Derrick, Karen De Valois, Russell De Valois, Jack Gallant, Ervin Hafter, Richard Ivry, Lucia Jacobs, Dacher Keltner, Raymond E. Kesner, Joe L. Martinez, Jr., James L. McGaugh, Frederick Seil, Arthur Shimamura, and Irving Zucker.

We remain grateful to the reviewers whose comments helped shape the first and second editions, including: Duane Albrecht, University of Texas; Anne E. Powell Anderson, Smith College; Mark S. Blumberg, University of Iowa; Eliot A. Brenowitz, The University of Washington; Peter C. Brunjes, University of Virginia; Rebecca D. Burwell, Brown University; Catherine P. Cramer, Dartmouth College; Loretta M. Flanagan-Cato, University of Pennsylvania; Francis W. Flynn, University of Wyoming; John D. E. Gabrieli, Stanford University; Diane C. Gooding, University of Wisconsin; Janet M. Gray, Vassar College; James Gross, Stanford University; Mary E. Harrington, Smith College; Wendy Heller, University of Illinois; Mark Hollins, University of North Carolina; Janice Juraska, University of Illinois; Keith R. Kluender, University of Wisconsin; Leah A. Krubitzer, University of California-Davis; Joseph E. LeDoux, New York University; Michael A. Leon, University of California, Irvine; Simon LeVay; Stephen A. Maren, University of Michigan; Robert J. McDonald, University of Toronto; Robert L. Meisel, Purdue University; Jeffrey S. Mogil, University of Illinois; Randy J. Nelson, The Ohio State University; Miguel Nicolelis, Duke University; Lee Osterhout, The University of Washington; James Pfaus, Concordia University; Helene S. Porte, Cornell University; George V. Rebec, Indiana University; Scott R. Robinson, University of Iowa; David A. Rosenbaum, Pennsylvania State University; Martin F. Sarter, The Ohio State University; Jeffrey D. Schall, Vanderbilt University; Stan Schein, University of California-Los Angeles; Dale R. Sengelaub, Indiana University; Matthew Shapiro, McGill University; Rae Silver, Columbia University; Cheryl L. Sisk, Michigan State University; Laura Smale, Michigan State University; Robert L. Spencer, University of Colorado; Steven K. Sutton, University of Miami; Franco J. Vaccarino, University of Toronto; Cyma Van Petten, University of Arizona; Charles J. Vierck, University of Florida; Neil V. Watson, Simon Fraser University; Robert Wickesberg, University of Illinois; Walter Wilczynski, University of Texas; S. Mark Williams, Duke University; and Mark C. Zrull, Appalachian State University.

The following reviewers read and critiqued drafts of the third edition text, and we are grateful for their assistance:

Eliot Brenowitz, University of Washington

David J. Bucci, University of Vermont

Judith Byrnes-Enoch, Empire State College

S. Tiffany Cunningham, University of Massachusetts Boston

Colin Ellard, University of Waterloo

Rick Gilmore, Pennsylvania State University

Janet M. Gray, Vassar College

Janice M. Juraska, University of Illinois

Theresa M. Lee, University of Michigan

Sheri Mizumori, University of Washington

Joseph H. Porter, Virginia Commonwealth University

Beth Powell, Smith College

George V. Rebec, Indiana University

Stan Schein, University of California, Los Angeles

Carol Seger, Colorado State University

Jerome M. Siegel, University of California at Los Angeles Medical Center

Wendy Sternberg, Haverford College

David R. Vago, University of Utah

Sheree Watson, University of Southern Mississippi

Robert West, University of Notre Dame

Finally, we would like to thank all our colleagues who contribute research in the behavioral neurosciences.

MARK R. ROSENZWEIG • S. MARC BREEDLOVE • NEIL V. WATSON

Supplements to accompany *Biological Psychology, Fourth Edition*

For the Student

Learning Biological Psychology CD-ROM
Study Material by Raymond Kesner and David Vago, *University of Utah*; Animated Tutorials by Sumanas, Inc. *Learning Biological Psychology*, included in every copy of the textbook, is an interactive CD study guide designed to help the student grasp the material introduced in the textbook. Combining the best features of a study guide with the advantages of the electronic medium, *Learning Biological Psychology* offers a wealth of comprehensive study material.

The CD includes (see the front endpapers for more):

- Chapter outline organizational structure
- Comprehensive interactive study questions
- Animated tutorials and activities
- Essay questions
- Terminology quizzes
- Multiple-choice quizzes
- Complete glossary

Biological Psychology NewsLink (www.biopsychology.com)
Available free to all users, this website is an invaluable resource for current news articles in the field. Updated daily, the site links to thousands of news items from a wide variety of sources, all referenced to textbook chapters and keywords.

For the Instructor

The following supplements are available to qualified adopters of the textbook.

Instructor's Resource CD (ISBN 0-87893-715-3)
This expanded resource includes all the figures and tables from the textbook in JPEG format, reformatted and relabeled for optimal readability. Also included are ready-to-use PowerPoint® presentations of all figures and tables, as well as other resources for both lecture and assessment. The IRCD includes:

- All textbook figures and tables, in both high- and low-resolution format, including all numbered photos (new for the Fourth Edition)
- PowerPoint presentations of all textbook figures and tables
- All the animations from the student CD
- Videos with accompanying notes
- Electronic version of the Instructor's Manual & Test Bank (PDF format)
- Computerized test bank using Brownstone's Diploma software (included)

Instructor's Manual & Test Bank (ISBN 0-87893-716-1)
Raymond Kesner and David Vago, *University of Utah*
The Instructor's Manual includes the following for each chapter of the textbook: Chapter Overview, Chapter Outline, Key Concepts, Lecture Outline, and References. The Test Bank includes over 2,100 questions of the following types: essay/discussion, multiple choice, fill-in-the-blank, matching, term definition, and paragraph development.

Overhead Transparencies (ISBN 0-87893-718-8)
This set includes 125 figures (approximately 175 transparencies), selected from throughout the textbook for teaching purposes. These are relabeled and optimized for projection in class.

Biological Psychology

1

Biological Psychology: Scope and Outlook

Who's in Charge?

A dreadful accident befalls "protocol android" C-3PO in the movie Star Wars Episode II: Attack of the Clones. *The robot, designed to communicate and handle situations diplomatically, has its head knocked off and attached to the body of a battle droid. Meanwhile the head of a battle droid is attached to C-3PO's body. The scene offers an important lesson in robotics: How will the two mismatched robots behave? Will the robot with C-3PO's head behave diplomatically while the robot with the battle head fights? Or vice versa? The answer is that both robots show a mixture of behaviors, polite and hostile.*

So now we know how robots work in the imaginary world of Star Wars: *Behavior is controlled by circuits in the head* and *in the body. But what about real organisms on Earth? If we could transplant heads between people, which would have the biggest effect on behavior: the head or the body?*

Until the 1600s almost everyone would have predicted that the body has more of an effect on personality and behavior than the head, because the heart was considered the place where the "in-ner person" or soul resided. But the English physician Thomas Willis (1621–1675) convinced most scientists that the brain is the organ that receives sensations, stores our memories, and generates our behavior. This view still predominates, so you probably predicted that the head would have more influence over behavior than the body. Most scientists today would agree, but that doesn't mean the body has no influence.

If you kept your brain, but your tall, athletic, attractive body was exchanged overnight for a perfectly functional but short, weak, unattractive body, would you behave the same? You would be unable to do some things that you could do before, so those behaviors would change. Your body would feel different; wouldn't that affect your emotions? Other people would respond differently to you, and that change would leave its mark too. In all these respects, your new body would exert changes in your old brain. Likewise your brain, striving to regain athletic form, would change the new body. You see, the separation of brain and body isn't all that clear-cut. Maybe Star Wars *has it right.*

In this book we explore the many ways in which the structures and actions of the brain produce mind and behavior. But that is only half of our task. We are also interested in the ways in which behavior in turn modifies the structures and actions of the brain. One of the most important lessons we hope to convey is that interactions between brain and behavior are reciprocal. The brain controls behavior, and in turn, behavior alters the brain.

We hope to give an interesting account of the main ideas and research in biological psychology, which is of great popular as well as scientific interest. Because there are so many pieces to tie together, we try to introduce a given piece of information when it makes a difference to the understanding of a subject—especially when it forms part of a story. Most importantly, we seek to communicate our own interest and excitement about the mysteries of mind and body.

What Is Biological Psychology?

No treaty or trade union agreement has ever defined the boundaries of biological psychology. It is a field that includes many players who come from quite different backgrounds—psychologists, biologists, physiologists, engineers, neurologists, psychiatrists, and many others. It also shares concepts and research approaches with many other disciplines.

Biological psychology is the field that relates behavior to bodily processes, especially the workings of the brain. Because study of the brain is known as **neuroscience** (the root *neuro-* comes from the Greek word *neuron,* meaning "nerve" or "cord"), biological psychology is also known as **behavioral neuroscience.** The main goal of this area of study is to understand behavior and experience in terms of their biological substrates. Like other sciences, biological psychology is dedicated to improving the human condition. As Einstein once said in an address to students, concern for humanity and its fate must always form the chief interest of all scientific endeavors "in order that the creations of our minds shall be a blessing and not a curse." Figure 1.1 maps the relations of biological psychology to other disciplines. Clearly, the biological psychology umbrella is very wide.

Five Viewpoints Explore the Biology of Behavior

In our pursuit to understand the biological bases of behavior, we use several different perspectives. Because each one yields information that complements the others, the combination of perspectives is especially powerful. The five major perspectives are

1. *Describing* behavior
2. Studying the *evolution* of behavior
3. Observing the *development* of behavior and its biological characteristics over the life span
4. Studying the biological *mechanisms* of behavior
5. Studying *applications* of biological psychology—for example, its applications to dysfunctions of human behavior

Gerry Bergstein, Illustrated Man #2, 1999, oil on canvas, 72" × 29"

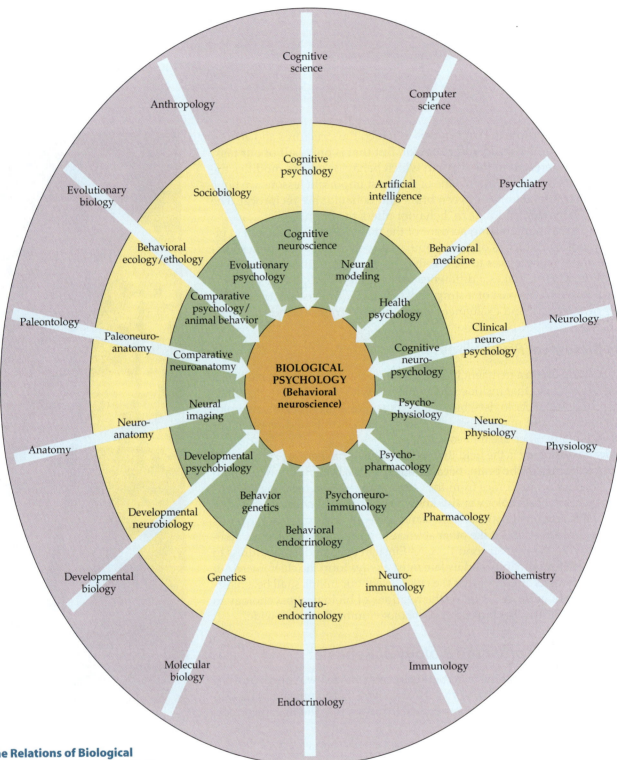

1.1 The Relations of Biological Psychology to Other Fields of Study
In this graphical representation of the relationships among biological psychology and other scientific disciplines, fields toward the center of the map are closest to biological psychology in their history, outlook, aims, and/or methods.

These perspectives are discussed in the sections that follow, and Table 1.1 shows how each perspective can be applied to three kinds of behavior.

Behavior can be described according to different criteria

Until we describe what we want to study, we cannot get far. Depending on the goals of our investigation, we may describe behavior in terms of detailed acts or processes,

TABLE 1.1 *Five Research Perspectives Applied to Three Kinds of Behavior*

| Research perspective | Kind of behavior | | |
	Sexual behavior	Learning and memory	Language and communication
1. Description			
Structural description	What are the main patterns of reproductive behavior and sex differences in behavior?	In what main ways does behavior change as a consequence of experience—for example, conditioning?	How are the sounds of speech patterned?
Functional description	How do specialized patterns of behavior contribute to mating and to care of young?	How do certain behaviors lead to rewards or avoidance of punishment?	What behavior is involved in making statements or asking questions?
2. Evolutionary	How does mating depend on hormones in different species?	How do different species compare in kinds and speed of learning?	How did the human speech apparatus evolve?
3. Development	How do reproductive and secondary sex characteristics develop over the life span?	How do learning and memory change over the life span?	How do children learn to speak?
4. Mechanisms	What neural circuits and hormones are involved in reproductive behavior?	What anatomical and chemical changes in the brain hold memories?	What brain regions are particularly involved in language?
5. Applications	Low doses of testosterone restore libido in some postmenopausal women.	Gene therapy and behavioral therapy improve memory in some senile patients.	Speech therapy, in conjunction with amphetamine treatment, speeds language recovery following stroke.

or in terms of results or functions. An analytical description of arm movements might record the successive positions of the limb or the contraction of different muscles. A functional behavioral description, on the other hand, would state whether the limb was being used in walking, running, hopping, swimming, or shooting dice. To be useful for scientific study, a description must be precise and reveal the essential features of the behavior, using accurately defined terms and units.

We compare species to learn how the brain and behavior have evolved

Darwin's theory of evolution through natural selection is central to all modern biology and psychology. From this perspective emerge two rather different emphases: (1) the *continuity* of behavior and biological processes among species because of common ancestry and (2) the species-specific *differences* in behavior and biology that have evolved as adaptations to different environments. At some points in this book we will concentrate on continuity—that is, features of behavior and its biological mechanisms that are common to many species. At other points, we will look at species-specific behaviors.*

EVOLUTION AT WORK

Continuity of behaviors and mechanisms   Nature is conservative. Body or behavior inventions, once evolved, may be maintained for millions of years and may be seen in animals that otherwise appear very different. For example, the nerve impulse (see Chapter 3) is essentially the same in a jellyfish, a cockroach, and a human being. Some of the chemical compounds that transmit messages through the bloodstream (hormones) are also the same in diverse animals. Species share such **conserved** characteristics because the features first arose in a shared ancestor (Box 1.1). But mere similarity of a feature between species does not guarantee that the feature came from

---

* The icons that appear in the margins throughout the book are explained in the preface.

BOX 1.1 We Are All Alike, and We Are All Different

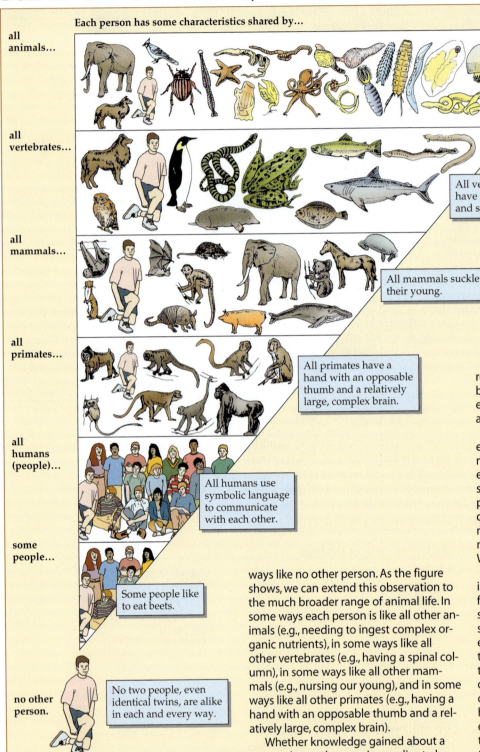

Each person has some characteristics shared by…

all animals…

All animals use DNA to store genetic information.

all vertebrates…

All vertebrates have a backbone and spinal cord.

all mammals…

All mammals suckle their young.

all primates…

All primates have a hand with an opposable thumb and a relatively large, complex brain.

all humans (people)…

All humans use symbolic language to communicate with each other.

some people…

Some people like to eat beets.

no other person.

No two people, even identical twins, are alike in each and every way.

How do similarities and differences among people and animals fit into biological psychology? The anthropologist Clyde Kluckhohn (1949) observed that each person is in some ways like all other people, in some ways like some other people, and in some ways like no other person. As the figure shows, we can extend this observation to the much broader range of animal life. In some ways each person is like all other animals (e.g., needing to ingest complex organic nutrients), in some ways like all other vertebrates (e.g., having a spinal column), in some ways like all other mammals (e.g., nursing our young), and in some ways like all other primates (e.g., having a hand with an opposable thumb and a relatively large, complex brain).

Whether knowledge gained about a process in another species applies to humans depends on whether we are like that species in regard to that process. The fundamental research on the mechanisms of inheritance in the bacterium *Escherichia coli* proved so widely applicable that some molecular biologists proclaimed, "What is true of *E. coli* is true of the elephant." To a remarkable extent, that statement is true, but there are also some important differences in the genetic mechanisms of *E. coli* and mammals.

With respect to each biological property, researchers must determine how animals are identical and how they are different. When we seek animal models for studying human behavior or biological processes, we must ask the following question: Does the proposed animal model really have some things in common with the process at work in humans? We will see many cases in which it does.

Even within the same species, however, individuals differ from one another: cat from cat, blue jay from blue jay, and person from person. Biological psychology seeks to understand individual differences as well as similarities. This interest in the individual is one of the most important differences between psychology and other approaches to behavior. The lottery of heredity ensures that each individual has a unique genetic makeup (the only exception being identical twins). The way the individual's unique genetic composition is translated into body form and behavioral capacities is part of our story. Furthermore, each individual has a unique set of personal experiences. Therefore, the way in which each person is able to process information and store the memories of these experiences is another part of our story.

a common ancestral species. Similar solutions to a problem may have evolved independently in different classes of animals.

Species-specific behaviors   Different species have evolved some specific ways of dealing with their environments. An earthworm's sensory endowments, for example, are quite different from those of a robin. Certain species of bats rely almost exclusively on hearing to navigate and find their prey; these species have become nearly blind. Other species of bats, however, are visually oriented, depending on their eyes to find their way around and to secure their food. Human beings use both vision and hearing. However, we ignore electrical fields in the environment, while certain kinds of fish detect them to guide locomotion.

The body and behavior develop over the life span

Ontogeny is the process by which an individual changes in the course of its lifetime—grows up and grows old. Observing the way in which a particular behavior changes during ontogeny may give us clues to its functions and mechanisms. For example, we know that learning ability in monkeys increases over several years of development. Therefore, we can speculate that prolonged maturation of brain circuits is required for complex learning tasks. In rodents the ability to form long-term memories lags somewhat behind the maturation of learning ability. So young rodents learn well but forget more quickly than older ones, suggesting that learning and memory involve different processes. Studying the development of reproductive capacity and of differences in behavior between the sexes, along with changes in body structures and processes, enables us to throw light on body mechanisms of sex behaviors.

Biological mechanisms underlie all behavior

The history of a species tells us the evolutionary determinants of its behavior; the history of an individual tells us the developmental determinants. To learn about the mechanisms of an individual's behavior, we study how his or her present body works. To understand the underlying mechanisms of behavior, we must regard the organism (with all due respect) as a "machine," made up of billions of nerve cells, or **neurons** (the Greek word for "nerve"). We must ask the question, How is this thing constructed to be able to do all that?

Our major aim in biological psychology is to examine body mechanisms that make particular behaviors possible. In the case of learning and memory, for example, we would like to know the sequence of electrical and biochemical processes that occur when we learn something and retrieve it from memory. What parts of the nervous system are involved in that process? In the case of reproductive behavior, we would like to know how the body grows to produce the capacity for sexual behavior. We also want to understand the neuronal and hormonal processes that underlie reproductive behavior.

Research can be applied to human problems

A major goal of biological psychology is to use research findings to improve the health and well-being of humans and other animals. Numerous human diseases involve malfunctioning of the brain. Many of these are already being alleviated as a result of research in the neurosciences, and the prospects for continuing advances are good. Attempts to apply knowledge also benefit basic research. For example, the study of memory disorders in humans has pushed investigators to extend our knowledge of the brain regions involved in different kinds of memory (see Chapter 17).

**CLINICAL
ISSUE**

Three Approaches Relate Brain and Behavior

Biological psychologists use three approaches to understand the relationship between brain and behavior: somatic intervention, behavioral intervention, and correlation. In

(*a*) **Manipulating the body may affect behavior**

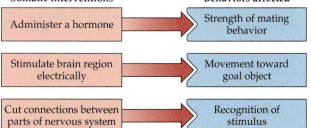

(*b*) **Experience affects the body (including the brain)**

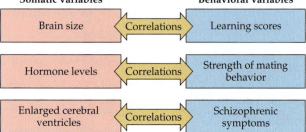

(*c*) **Bodily and behavioral measures covary**

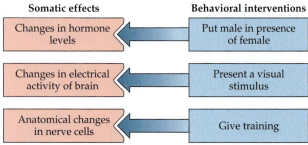

(*d*) **Biological psychology seeks to understand all these relationships**

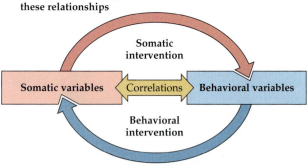

1.2 Three Main Approaches to Studying the Neuroscience of Behavior (*a*) In somatic intervention, investigators change the body structure or chemistry of an animal in some way and observe and measure any resulting behavioral effects. (*b*) Conversely, in behavioral intervention, researchers change an animal's behavior or its environment and try to ascertain whether the change results in physiological or anatomical changes. (*c*) Measurements of both kinds of variables allow researchers to arrive at correlations between somatic changes and behavioral changes. (*d*) Each approach enriches and informs the others.

the most commonly employed approach, **somatic intervention** (Figure 1.2*a*), we alter a structure or function of the brain or body to see how this changes behavior. In this approach, somatic intervention is the independent variable, and the behavioral effect is the dependent variable; that is, the resulting behavior depends on how the brain has been altered. For example, in response to mild electrical stimulation of one part of her brain, not only did one patient laugh, but she found whatever she happened to be looking at amusing (Fried et al., 1998).

In later chapters we describe many kinds of somatic intervention with both humans and other animals—for example:

- A hormone is administered to some animals but not to others; various behaviors of the two groups are later compared.
- A part of the brain is stimulated electrically, and behavioral effects are observed.
- A connection between two parts of the nervous system is cut, and changes in behavior are measured.

The approach opposite to somatic intervention is psychological or **behavioral intervention** (Figure 1.2*b*). In this approach, the scientist intervenes in the behavior of an organism and looks for resulting changes in body structure or function. Here behavior is the independent variable, and change in the body is the dependent variable. Among the examples that we will consider in later chapters are the following:

- Putting two adults of opposite sex together may lead to increased secretion of certain hormones.
- Exposing a person or animal to a visual stimulus provokes changes in electrical activity and blood flow in parts of the brain.
- Training of animals in a maze is accompanied by electrical, biochemical, and anatomical changes in parts of their brains.

The third approach to brain–behavior relations, **correlation** (Figure 1.2*c*), consists of finding the extent to which a given body measure varies with a given behavioral measure. Some questions we will examine later are as follows:

- Are people with large brains more intelligent than people with smaller brains?
- Are individual differences in sexual behavior correlated with levels of certain hormones in the individuals?
- Is the severity of schizophrenia correlated with the magnitude of changes in brain structure?

Such correlations should not be taken as proof of causal relationship. For one thing, even if a causal relation exists, the correlation does not reveal its direction—that is, which variable is independent and which is dependent. For another, two factors might be correlated only because a third, unknown factor affects the two factors measured. What a correlation does indicate is that the two variables are linked in some way—directly or indirectly. Such a correlation often stimulates investigators to formulate hypotheses and to test them by somatic or behavioral intervention.

Combining these three approaches yields the circle diagram of Figure 1.2*d*. This diagram incorporates the basic approaches to studying relationships between bodily processes and behavior. It also emphasizes the theme (brought out in the case of the switched heads described at the beginning of this chapter) that the relations between brain and body are reciprocal: Each affects the other in an ongoing cycle of bodily and behavioral interactions. We will see examples of this reciprocal relationship throughout the book.

Neural Plasticity: Behavior Can Change the Brain

**NEURAL
PLASTICITY**

The idea that there is a reciprocal relationship between brain and behavior has embedded within it a concept that is, for most people, startling. When we say that behavior and experience affect the brain, we mean that they, literally, physically alter the brain. The brain of a child growing up in a French-speaking household assembles itself into a configuration that is different from the brain of a child who hears only English. That's why the first child, as an adult, understands French effortlessly while the second does not. In this case we cannot tell you what the structural differences are exactly, but we do know one part of the brain that is being altered by these different experiences (see Chapter 19).

There are numerous examples, almost all in the animal literature, in which experience has been demonstrated to affect the number or size of neurons, or the number or size of connections between neurons. This ability of the brain, both in development and in adulthood, to be changed by the environment and by experience, is called **neural plasticity.**

Today when we hear the word *plastic,* we think of the class of materials found in so many modern products. But originally *plastic* meant "flexible, malleable" (from the Greek *plassein,* "to mold or form"), and the modern materials were named plastics because they can be molded into nearly any shape. William James (1890) described plasticity as the possession of a structure weak enough to yield to an influence, but strong enough not to yield all at once:

**William James
(1842–1910)**

> Nervous tissue seems endowed with a very extraordinary degree of plasticity of this sort; so that we may without hesitation lay down as our first proposition the following, that the phenomena of habit in living beings are due to the plasticity of the organic materials of which their bodies are composed. (p. 110)

In the ensuing years, research has shown that the brain is even more plastic than James suspected. For example, parts of neurons known as dendritic spines (see Chapter 2) appear to be in constant motion, changing shape in the course of seconds (Fischer et al., 1998). We will see many examples in which experience alters the structure and/or function of the brain. In Chapter 5, hearing a baby cry will cause the mother's brain to secrete a hormone; in Chapter 7, visual experience in kittens will direct the formation of connections in the brain; in Chapter 12, a mother rat's grooming of her pups will affect the survival of spinal cord neurons; and in Chapter 18, a sea slug learning a task will strengthen the connections between two particular neurons.

Biological and social psychology are related

The plasticity of the human brain has a remarkable consequence: Other individuals can have an effect on the physical structure of your brain! Indeed, the whole point of coming to a lecture hall is to have the instructor use words and figures to alter your brain, so that you can retrieve that information in the future (in other words, she is teaching you something). Many of these alterations in your brain last only until you take an exam, but every once in a while the instructor may tell you something that you'll remember for the rest of your life. Most aspects of our social behavior are learned—from the language we speak to the clothes we wear and the kinds of food

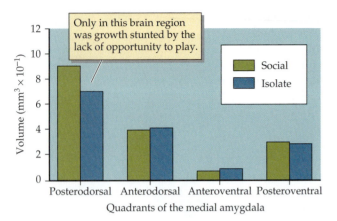

Only in this brain region was growth stunted by the lack of opportunity to play.

1.3 The Role of Play in Brain Development A brain region involved in processing odors (the posterodorsal portion of the medial amygdala) was smaller in male rats housed individually compared to males housed together and allowed to play. Other nearby regions were identical in the two groups. (After Cooke et al., 2000.)

we eat—so our examination of the mechanisms of learning and memory (see Chapters 17 and 18) is important for understanding social behavior.

For an example from an animal model, consider the fact that rats spend a lot of time investigating the smells around them, including those coming from other rats. Cooke et al. (2000) took young rats, just weaned from their mother, and either raised each male in a cage alone, or raised them with other males to play with. Examination of these animals as adults revealed a very specific difference between the groups: A region of the brain known to process odors was smaller in the isolated males than in the males raised with playmates (Figure 1.3). Was it the lack of play (Gordon et al., 2003), the lack of odors to investigate, or the stress of isolation that made the region smaller? Whatever the mechanism, social experience affects this brain structure. In Chapter 18 we'll see that social experience also enhances the effects of environmental enrichment on brain growth.

Here's an example of how social influences can affect the human brain. When people were asked to put a hand into moderately hot water (47°C), part of the brain became active, presumably because of the discomfort involved (Rainville et al., 1997). But subjects who were led to believe the water would be *very* hot had a more activated brain than subjects who were led to believe the discomfort would be minimal (Figure 1.4), even though the water was the same temperature for all subjects. The socially induced psychological expectation affected the magnitude of the brain response, even though the physical stimulus was exactly the same. (By the way, the people with the more activated brains also reported that their hands hurt more.)

In most cases, biological and social factors continuously interact and affect each other in an ongoing series of events as behavior unfolds. For example, the level of the hormone testosterone in a man's circulation affects his dominance behavior and aggression (see Chapter 15). The dominance may be exhibited in a great variety of social settings, ranging from playing chess to physical aggression. In humans and other primates, the level of testosterone correlates positively with the degree of dominance and with the amount of aggression exhibited. Winning a contest, whether a game of chess or a boxing match, raises the level of testosterone; losing a contest lowers the levels. Thus at any moment the level of testosterone is determined, in part, by recent dominant–submissive social experience, and the level of testosterone determines, in part, the degree of dominance and aggression in the future. Of course,

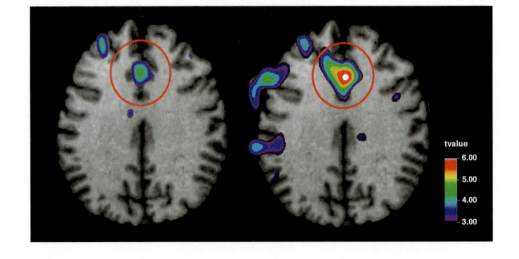

1.4 Pictures of Pain Subjects told to expect only mild discomfort from putting a hand into 47°C water (*left*) showed less activation in a particular brain region (the anterior cingulate cortex) than subjects expecting more discomfort (*right*) from water of the very same temperature. Areas of high activation are indicated by orange, red, and white. (From Rainville et al., 1997; courtesy of Pierre Rainville.)

social and cultural factors also help determine the frequency of aggression; cross-cultural differences in rates of aggression exist that cannot be correlated with hormonal levels, and ways of expressing aggression and dominance are influenced by sociocultural factors.

Perhaps nothing distinguishes biological psychology from other neurosciences more clearly than the fascination with neural plasticity and the role of experience. Biological psychologists have a pervasive interest in how experience physically alters the brain and therefore affects future behavior. We will touch on this theme in almost every chapter and review some of these examples again in the afterword.

Biological Psychologists Use Several Levels of Analysis

Finding explanations for behavior often involves dealing with several levels of biological analysis. The units of each level of analysis are simpler in structure and organization than those of the level above. Figure 1.5 shows how the **levels of analysis** range from social interactions to the brain, continuing to successively less-complex units until we arrive at single nerve cells and their even simpler, molecular constituents.

Scientific explanations usually involve analysis on a simpler or more basic level of organization than that of the structure or function to be explained. This approach is known as **reductionism.** In principle it is possible to reduce each explanatory series down to the molecular or atomic level, though for practical reasons this extent of reductionism is rare. For example, organic chemists and neurochemists usually deal with large, complex molecules and the laws that govern them; seldom do they seek explanations in terms of atoms.

IMPORTANT METHOD

1.5 Levels of Analysis in Biological Psychology The scope of biological psychology ranges from the level of the individual interacting with others, to the level of the molecule. Depending on the question at hand, investigators use different techniques to focus on these many levels, but always with an eye toward how their findings apply to behavior.

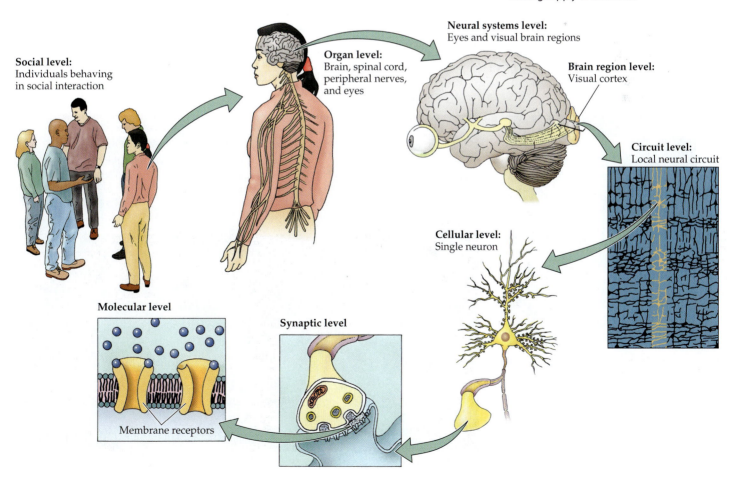

Social level:
Individuals behaving in social interaction

Organ level:
Brain, spinal cord, peripheral nerves, and eyes

Neural systems level:
Eyes and visual brain regions

Brain region level:
Visual cortex

Circuit level:
Local neural circuit

Cellular level:
Single neuron

Molecular level

Membrane receptors

Synaptic level

Naturally, in all fields different problems are carried to different levels of analysis, and fruitful work is often being done simultaneously by different workers at several levels. Thus in their research on visual perception, cognitive psychologists advance analytical descriptions of behavior. They try to determine how the eyes move while looking at a visual pattern, or how the contrast among parts of the pattern determines its visibility. Meanwhile, other biological psychologists study the differences in visual endowments among species and try to determine the adaptive significance of these differences. For example, how is the presence (or absence) of color vision related to the life of a species? At the same time, other investigators trace out brain structures and networks involved in different kinds of visual discrimination. Still other scientists try to ascertain the electrical and chemical events that occur at synapses in the brain during vision.

A Preview of the Book: Fables and Facts about the Brain

Here are some examples of research topics considered in this book:

- How does the brain grow, maintain, and repair itself over the life span, and how are these capacities related to the growth and development of the mind and behavior from the womb to the tomb?
- How does the nervous system capture, process, and represent information about the environment? For example, sometimes brain damage causes a person to lose the ability to identify other people's faces; what does that tell us about how the brain recognizes faces?
- How does sexual orientation develop? Some brain regions are different in heterosexual versus homosexual men; what do such studies tell us about the development of human sexual orientation?
- What brain sites and activities underlie feelings and emotional expression? Are particular parts of the brain active in romantic love, for example (Figure 1.6a)?
- Some people suffer damage to the brain and afterward seem alarmingly unconcerned about dangerous situations and unable to judge the emotions of other people; what parts of the brain are damaged to cause such changes?

1.6 "Tell Me, Where Is Fancy Bred?"
(a) The parts of the brain highlighted here become especially active when a person thinks about his or her romantic partner. (b) Different brain regions are activated when people perform four different language tasks. The techniques used to generate such images are described in Chapter 2. (Part a from Bartels and Zeki, 2000; part b courtesy of Marcus Raichle.)

(a)

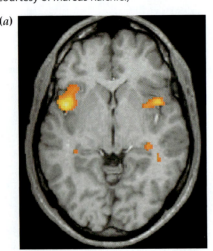

(b)

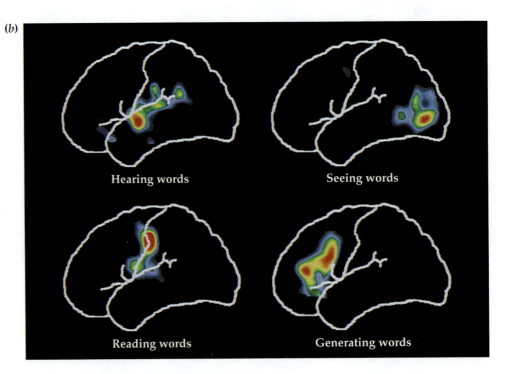

Hearing words   Seeing words

Reading words   Generating words

- The ability to recollect and use the past is critical for the survival of any animal, from the most simple to the most complex. How does the brain manage to change during learning, and how are memories retrieved?
- What are the neurobiological bases of language in humans?
- Why are different brain regions active during different language tasks (Figure 1.6b)?

The relationship between the brain and behavior is on the one hand very mysterious because it is difficult to understand how a physical device, the brain, could be responsible for our subjective experiences of fear, love, and awe. Yet despite this mystery, we all use our brains every day. Perhaps it is the "everyday miracle" aspect of the topic that has generated so much folk wisdom about the brain.

Sometimes these popular ideas about the brain are in line with our current knowledge, but in many cases we know they are false. For example, the notion that we normally use only a tenth (or a third, or a half, or some other fraction) of our brain is commonplace, but patent nonsense. Brain scans make it clear that the entire brain is activated by even fairly mundane tasks. Indeed, although the areas of activation shown in Figure 1.6 appear to be rather small and discrete, we will show in Box 2.2 that experimenters must work very hard to create images that separate activation related to a particular task from the background of widespread, ongoing brain activity.

In fact, it's fairly easy to reel off a host of commonly held beliefs about the relationships between the brain and behavior. Table 1.2 on the following page presents a list of such beliefs (many of which you may have heard) interspersed with some claims that are true but may sound improbable to you.

Neuroscience Contributes to Our Understanding of Psychiatric Disorders

One of the great promises of biological psychology is that it can help us understand brain disorders and devise treatment strategies. Like any other complex mechanism, the brain is subject to a variety of malfunctions and breakdowns. People afflicted by disorders of the brain are not an exotic few. At least one person in five around the world currently suffers from neurological and/or psychiatric disorders that vary in severity from complete disability to significant changes in quality of life.

Figure 1.7a shows the estimated numbers of U.S. residents afflicted by some of the main neurological disorders. Figure 1.7b gives estimates of the numbers of U.S. adults who suffer from certain major psychiatric disorders. The percentage of U.S. adults suffering from mental illness may be increasing (Torrey, 2002).

The toll of these disorders is enormous, both in terms of individual suffering and in social costs. The National Foundation for Brain Research estimated that direct and indirect costs of behavioral and brain disorders amount to $400 billion a year in the United States. For example, $160 billion a year is spent on the treatment of alcohol and substance abuse, and the cost for treatment of dementia (severely disordered thinking) exceeds the costs of treating cancer and heart disease combined. The high cost in suffering and expense has compelled researchers to try to understand the mechanisms involved in these disorders and to try to alleviate or even prevent them.

(a) **Prevalence of neurological disorders**

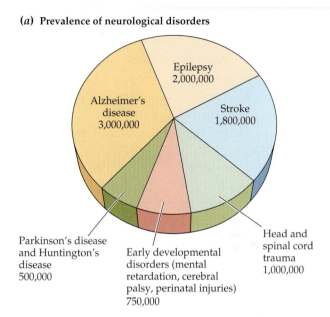

(b) **Incidence of psychiatric disorders**

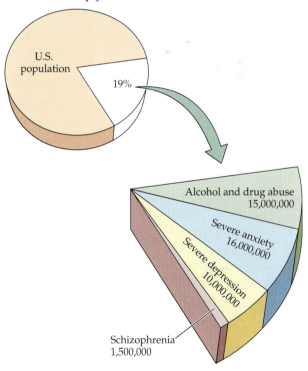

1.7 The Toll of Brain Disorders As these pie charts show, neurological (a) and psychiatric (b) disorders are quite common in the United States. As brain research progresses, the distinction between psychiatric and neurological disorders begins to seem artificial or arbitrary.

TABLE 1.2 *Facts or Fables of Biological Psychology?*

Statement	True/False/Uncertain	Chapter where discussed
Some human nerve cells are 3 feet long.	True	2
Nerve impulses travel at the speed of light.	False	3
More people die each year from the use of legal drugs than illegal ones.	True	4
Only humans ingest mind-altering substances.	False	4
Our bodies make chemicals that are similar in structure to heroin and marijuana and act on the same sites in the brain.	True	4
Testosterone is made only by males, and estrogen is made only by females.	False	5
Only humans have created cultures.	False	6
Once our brains are developed, we can never grow new nerve cells.	False	7
Some people are incapable of feeling pain.	True	8
Different parts of the tongue are specialized to recognize certain tastes.	False	9
The brightness and color of the objects we see are creations of our perceptual systems, not properties of the objects themselves.	True	10
Dogs are color-blind.	False	10
Each side of the brain controls the muscles on the opposite side of the body.	True	11
There are no anatomical differences between men's and women's brains.	False	12
In some animal species every individual is female. In some other species, individuals can change sex during their lifetimes.	True	12
Some people are "born gay."	Uncertain	12
Most of our energy is expended just maintaining our body temperature.	True	13
We can lose weight permanently by surgically removing fat from our bodies.	False	13
The peaks in cases of depression and suicide occur around Christmas holidays.	False	14
During sleep the brain is relatively inactive.	Not always	14
Sleepwalkers are acting out dreams.	False	14
Prolonged sleep deprivation will make you temporarily crazy.	False	14
Some animals can have half their brain asleep and the other half awake.	True	14
The left side of the face is more emotionally expressive than the right side.	True	15
Prolonged stress can cause heart disease.	True	15
All cultural groups recognize the same facial expressions for various emotions.	Uncertain	15
It is possible to scientifically determine whether someone is lying.	False (for now)	15
Scientists are not sure why antidepressant drugs work.	True	16
People in northern countries are more susceptible to seasonal depression.	Uncertain	16
Some people are incapable of producing any new memories.	True	17
We never really forget anything we have experienced.	Uncertain	17
Each memory is stored in its own brain cells.	False (probably)	18
We can change the structure of an animal's brain by raising it in a more stimulating environment.	True	18
People are "right-brained" or "left-brained": Dominance of the left or right hemisphere of the brain accounts for major differences in people's cognitive styles or personalities.	False	19
Some brain disorders cause people to lose the ability to recognize faces. In other disorders, patients are unable to name only certain kinds of animals or certain kinds of food.	True	19
A child can have half of the brain removed and still develop normal intelligence.	True	19
Chimpanzees can use symbols to communicate.	True	19

(*a*) Person with schizophrenia

(*b*) Normal

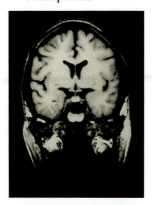 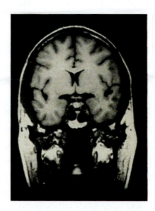

1.8 Identical Twins but Nonidentical Brains and Behavior In these images of the brains of identical twins, the fluid-filled cerebral ventricles are prominent as dark "butterfly" shapes. The twin whose brain is imaged in (*a*) suffers from schizophrenia and has the enlarged cerebral ventricles that some researchers believe are characteristic of this disorder. The other twin does not suffer from schizophrenia; his brain (*b*) clearly has smaller ventricles. (Courtesy of E. Fuller Torrey.)

The following are examples of research that is providing relief from some of these grave disorders—examples that will be discussed further in later chapters:

- Antipsychotic drugs, introduced in the 1950s, allow many people suffering from schizophrenia to lead fuller lives, less haunted by crippling, intense symptoms. Differences in brain structure between patients with schizophrenia and other people (Figure 1.8) suggest certain mechanisms that might someday provide a new treatment approach.
- Discoveries that reveal the modes of action of habit-forming drugs and their effects on the nervous system give hope that effective cures will be found for people addicted to drugs.
- The fastest-growing affliction in industrialized societies is Alzheimer's disease, a profound loss of cognitive abilities that strikes especially older people. Researchers are actively pursuing the causes and brain mechanisms of this devastating condition.

Laboratory and Clinical Approaches Complement Each Other

Basic research and clinical practice influence each other. Basic research provides concepts and techniques that clinicians use to understand and help people with malfunctioning brains. At the same time, clinical observation of these patients provides data and stimulates the development of theories about brain mechanisms. This exchange is mutually beneficial, and the boundaries between laboratory and clinic are disappearing.

Two brains in one head

Research on the functions of the two cerebral hemispheres illustrates the productive interplay between laboratory and clinic. Suppose that each time a right-handed person buttoned a shirt, the person's left hand sought to unbutton it. Two separate controllers would seem to be involved, but is this possible? Most of us are saved from such frustration because information from the right and left sides of the body is integrated by pathways that connect the two sides of the brain. But what happens when these connections are severed? Can we then observe two different types of consciousness?

Although the structures of the left and right sides of the brain seem very much alike, functional differences between the cerebral hemispheres of human brains become evident after brain damage such as that resulting from a stroke. For instance, injury to certain parts of the left cerebral hemisphere can produce striking changes in speech and language, whereas injury to the right hemisphere rarely affects speech.

CLINICAL ISSUE

This situation used to be described as *cerebral dominance,* implying that a talkative left cerebral hemisphere dominated a mute right hemisphere.

New information about hemispheric specialization of function has come from studies of patients in whom the connections between the right and left cerebral hemispheres have been cut; these people are referred to as **split-brain individuals.** Early work with such patients in the 1930s did not reveal clear differences between the functions of the two hemispheres, because of a lack of appropriate methods of behavioral assessment.

**Roger Sperry
(1913–1995)**

Coming from a background of animal research, however, Roger Sperry (1974) and his collaborators (e.g., Gazzaniga, 1992) understood how to test separately the functioning of the two hemispheres, and they found remarkable differences in humans. These results prompted Sperry to speak of separate forms of consciousness in the two hemispheres of the brain. The patients seemed literally to be of two minds. Indeed, one of Sperry's patients was seen to button a shirt with one hand and try to unbutton it with the other. For his research with split-brain subjects and other contributions, Sperry was awarded the 1981 Nobel Prize in Physiology or Medicine. We'll discuss split-brain studies further in Chapter 19.

Animal Research Makes Vital Contributions

Because we will draw on animal research throughout this book, we should comment on some of the ethical issues of experimentation on animals. Human beings' involvement and concern with other species predates recorded history. Early humans had to study animal behavior and physiology in order to escape some species and hunt others. To study biological bases of behavior inevitably requires research on animals of other species as well as on human beings.

Because of the importance of carefully regulated animal research for both human and animal health and well-being, the National Research Council (NRC Commission on Life Science, 1988; NRC Committee on Animals as Monitors of Environmental Hazards, 1991) undertook a study on the many uses of animals in research. The study notes that 93% of the mammals used in research are laboratory-reared rodents. It also reports that most Americans believe that animal research should continue. Of course, researchers have an obligation to minimize the discomfort of their animal subjects, and ironically enough, animal research has provided us with the drugs and techniques to make most research painless for the animal subjects.

Nevertheless, a very active minority of people believe that research with animals, even if it does lead to lasting benefits, is immoral. For example, Peter Singer (1975) asserts that research with animals can be justified only if it actually produces benefits, and he notes that most experiments do not yield such positive results. Unfortunately, he offers no guidance on how to predict which experiments will produce important breakthroughs. In the meantime, animal rights groups have vandalized labs, burned down buildings, and, as recently as 2003, exploded bombs in laboratories.

**IMPORTANT
METHOD**

Psychology students usually underestimate the contributions of animal research to all the main fields of psychology because, as one study found, the most widely used introductory psychology textbooks obscure the contributions of animal research, and they present major findings from animal research as if they had been obtained with human subjects (Domjan and Purdy, 1995).

The History of Research on the Brain and Behavior Begins in Antiquity

Although the brain has long been studied, only recently have scientists recognized the central role of the brain in controlling behavior. When Egyptian pharaoh Tutankhamen was mummified (about 1300 B.C.E.), four important organs were preserved in alabaster jars in his tomb: liver, lungs, stomach, and intestines. The heart was preserved in its place within the body. All these organs were considered necessary to ensure the pharaoh's continued existence in the afterlife. The brain, however, was removed from the skull and discarded. Although the Egyptian version of the afterlife entailed considerable struggle, the brain was not considered an asset.

Neither the Hebrew Bible (written from the twelfth to the second century B.C.E.) nor the New Testament ever mentions the brain. However, the Bible mentions the heart hundreds of times and makes several references each to the liver, the stomach, and the bowels as the seats of passion, courage, and pity, respectively. "Get thee a heart of wisdom," said the prophet.

The heart is also where Aristotle (about 350 B.C.E.), the most prominent scientist of ancient Greece, located mental capacities. We still reflect this ancient notion when we call people *kind-hearted, open-hearted, hard-hearted, faint-hearted,* or *heartless,* and when we speak of learning *by heart.* Aristotle considered the brain to be only a cooling unit to lower the temperature of the hot blood from the heart. Around 400 B.C.E. the great Greek physician Hippocrates was expressing the minority view when he wrote,

> Not only our pleasure, our joy and our laughter but also our sorrow, pain, grief, and tears rise from the brain, and the brain alone. With it we think and understand, see and hear, and we discriminate between the ugly and the beautiful, between what is pleasant and what is unpleasant and between good and evil.

Around 350 B.C.E., the Greek physician Herophilus (called the "Father of Anatomy") advanced our knowledge of the nervous system by dissecting bodies of both people and animals. Among other investigations, he traced nerves from muscles and skin into the spinal cord. He also noted that each region of the body is connected to separate nerves.

A second-century Greco-Roman physician, Galen (the "Father of Medicine"), treated the injuries of gladiators. His reports of behavioral changes caused by injuries to the heads of gladiators drew attention to the brain as the controller of behavior. Galen advanced the idea that animal spirits—a mysterious fluid—passed along nerves to all regions of the body. But Galen's ideas about the anatomy of the human brain were very inaccurate because he refused to dissect humans.

Renaissance scientists began to understand brain anatomy and physiology

The eminent Renaissance painter and scientist Leonardo da Vinci (1452–1519) studied the workings of the human body and laid the foundations of anatomical drawing. He especially pioneered in providing views from different angles and cross-sectional representations. His artistic renditions of the body included portraits of the nerves in the arm and the fluid-filled ventricles of the brain (Figure 1.9).

Renaissance anatomists emphasized the shape and appearance of the external surfaces of the brain because these were the parts that were easiest to see when the skull was removed. It was immediately apparent to anyone who looked that the brain has an extraordinarily complex shape. To Renaissance artists, this marvelous structure was God's greatest gift to humankind. So in Michelangelo's (1475–1564) painting on the ceiling of the Sistine Chapel, God seems to ride the form of the human brain when bestowing life to Adam (see the cover of this book).

In 1633, René Descartes wrote an influential book (*De Homine* [*On Man*]), in which he tried to explain how the behavior of animals, and to some extent of humans, could be like the workings of a machine. In addition to tackling other topics, Descartes proposed the concept of spinal reflexes and a neural pathway for them (Figure 1.10).

Attempting to relate the mind to the body, he suggested that the two come into contact in the pineal gland, located within the brain. He suggested the pineal gland for this role because (1) whereas most brain structures are double, located symmetrically in the two hemispheres, the pineal gland is single, like consciousness; and (2)

**René Descartes
(1596–1650)**

(*a*) **Early drawing**

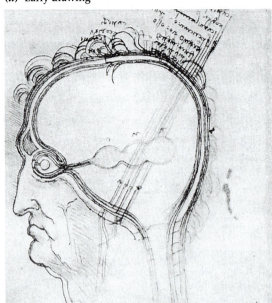

(*b*) **Later drawing based on observation**

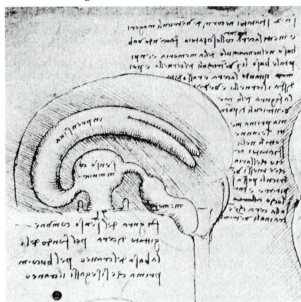

1.9 Leonardo da Vinci's Changing View of the Brain   (*a*) In an early representation, Leonardo simply copied old schematic drawings that represented the cerebral ventricles as a linear series of chambers. (*b*) Later he made a drawing based on direct observation: After making a cast of the ventricles of an ox brain by pouring melted wax into the brain and letting it set, he cut away the tissue to reveal the true shape of the ventricles.

1.10 An Early Account of Reflexes   In this depiction of an explanation by Descartes, when a person's toe touches fire, the heat causes nervous activity to flow up the nerve to the brain. There the nervous activity is "reflected" back down to the leg muscles, which contract, pulling the foot away from the fire; the idea of activity being reflected back is what gave rise to the word *reflex*. In Descartes's time, the difference between sensory and motor nerves had not yet been discovered, nor was it known that nerve fibers normally conduct in only one direction. Nevertheless, Descartes promoted thinking about bodily processes in scientific terms, and this focus led to steadily more accurate knowledge and concepts.

Descartes believed, erroneously, that the pineal gland exists only in humans and not in animals.

As Descartes was preparing to publish his book, he learned that the Pope had forced Galileo to renounce his teaching that Earth revolves around the sun, threatening to execute him if he did not recant. Fearful that his own speculations about mind and body could also incur the wrath of the church, Descartes withheld his book from publication, and it did not appear in print until 1662, after his death.

Descartes believed that if people were nothing more than intricate machines, they could have about as much free will as a pocket watch and no opportunity to make the moral choices that were so important to the church. He asserted that humans, at least, had a nonmaterial soul as well as a material body. This notion of **dualism** spread widely and left other philosophers with the task of determining how a nonmaterial soul could exert influence over a material body and brain. Biological psychologists reject dualism and insist that all the workings of the mind can also, in theory, be understood as purely physical processes in the material world, specifically in the brain.

The concept of localization of function arose in the nineteenth century

By the end of the 1600s, the English physician Thomas Willis, with his detailed descriptions of the structure of the human brain and his systematic study of brain disorders, convinced educated people in the Western world that the brain is the organ that coordinates and controls behavior (Zimmer, 2004). A popular notion of the nineteenth century, called **phrenology,** elaborated on this idea by asserting that the cerebral cortex consisted of separate functional areas, and that each area was responsible for a behavioral faculty such as love of family, perception of color, or curiosity. Investigators assigned functions to brain regions anecdotally, by observing the behavior of individuals and noting, from the shape of the skull, which underlying regions of the brain were more or less developed (Figure 1.11*a*).

(a)

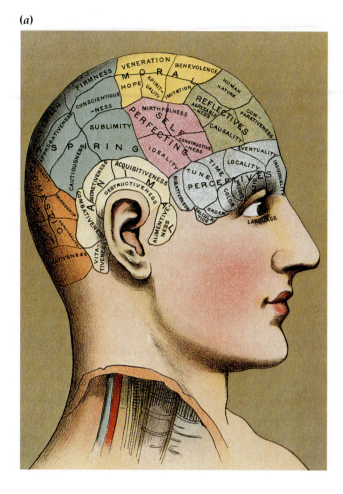

(b)

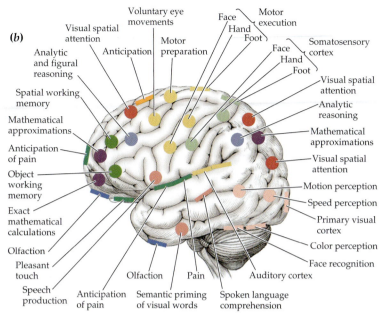

1.11 Old and New Phrenology (a) In the early nineteenth century, certain "faculties," such as skill at mathematics or a tendency toward aggression, were believed to be directly associated with particular brain regions. Phrenologists used diagrams like this one to measure bumps on the skull, which they took as an indication of how fully developed each brain region was in an individual, and hence how fully that person should display particular qualities. (b) Today, technology allows us to roughly gauge how active different parts of the brain are when a person is performing various tasks (see Chapter 2). But virtually the entire brain is active during any task, so the localization of function that such studies provide is really a measure of where *peak* activity occurs, rather than a suggestion of a single region that is involved in a particular task. (Part b after Nichols and Newsome, 1999.)

Undoubtedly some phrenologists were hucksters. In Mark Twain's childhood memories, phrenologists who came to town and felt the heads of paying clients usually wrote "character charts that would compare favorably with George Washington's." The adult Twain, in disguise, visited a phrenologist who noted from the shape of Twain's skull that he lacked any sense of humor (Twain, 1990). But many phrenologists were sincere and capable scientists trying to make sense of the variations they found in the shapes of people's heads.

Opponents rejected the entire concept of localization of brain function, insisting that the brain, like the mind, functions as a whole. Today we know that the whole brain is indeed active when we are doing almost any task. On the other hand, as we saw earlier in this chapter, when we are performing particular tasks, certain brain regions become even more activated. Different tasks activate different brain regions. Modern brain maps of these places where *peaks* of activation occur (Figure 1.11b) bear a passing resemblance to their phrenological predecessors, differing only in the specific locations of functions. But unlike the phrenologists, we can find confirmation of these modern maps by other methods, such as examining what happens after brain damage.

Even as far back as the 1860s, the French surgeon Paul Broca (1824–1880) argued that language ability was not a property of the entire brain but rather was localized in a restricted brain region. Broca presented a postmortem analysis of a patient who had been unable to talk for several years. The only portion of the patient's brain that appeared damaged was a small region within the frontal portions of the brain on

**CLINICAL
ISSUE**

1.12 A Nineteenth-Century Anatomist's Look at Nerve Cells
These drawings of brain cells, still cited today, were made by the great Spanish anatomist Santiago Ramón y Cajal (1852–1934) on the basis of his careful observations with the microscope.

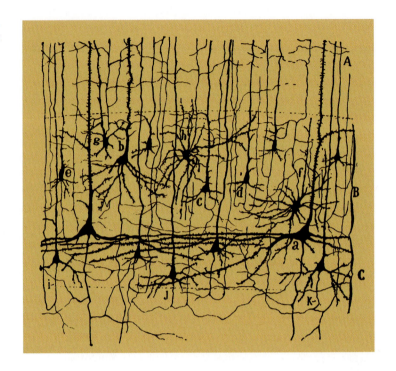

the left side—a region now known as *Broca's area* (labeled "Speech production" in Figure 1.11*b*). The study of additional patients further convinced Broca that language expression is mediated by this specific brain region rather than reflecting activities of the entire brain.

These nineteenth-century observations form the background for a continuing theme of research in biological psychology—notably the search for distinguishing differences among brain regions on the basis of their structure, and the effort to relate different kinds of behavior to different brain regions (Kemp, 2001). An additional theme emerging from these studies is the relation of brain size to ability (Box 1.2). Nineteenth-century microscope studies of sections of the brain revealed for the first time the shapes, sizes, and identity of nerve cells of the brain (Figure 1.12).

In 1890, William James's book *Principles of Psychology* signaled the beginnings of a modern approach to biological psychology. The strength of the ideas described in this book is evident by the continuing frequent citation of the work, especially by contemporary cognitive neuroscientists. In James's work, psychological ideas such as consciousness and other aspects of human experience came to be seen as properties of the nervous system. A true biological psychology began to emerge from this approach.

Modern biological psychology arose in the twentieth century

The end of the nineteenth century brought many important developments for biological psychology. German psychologist Hermann Ebbinghaus showed in 1885 how to measure learning and memory in humans. In 1898, American psychologist Edward L. Thorndike demonstrated in his doctoral thesis how to measure learning and memory in animal subjects. Early in the twentieth century, Russian physiologist Ivan P. Pavlov announced research in his laboratory on the conditioned reflex in animals.

American psychologist Shepard I. Franz (1902) sought the site of learning and memory in the brain, combining Thorndike's training procedures with localized brain lesions in animal subjects. This work started a search for the traces of experience in the brain—a quest that Karl S. Lashley referred to as the "search for the engram." Lashley studied with Franz and took over the problem of investigating the locations and mechanisms of memory functions in the brain. His approach was primarily anatomical, and he focused on assessing the behavioral effects of brain le-

**Karl S. Lashley
(1890–1958)**

BOX 1.2 Is Bigger Better? The Case of the Brain and Intelligence

Does a bigger brain indicate greater intelligence? This question has been the subject of lively controversy for at least two centuries. Sir Francis Galton (1822–1911), the scientist who invented the correlation coefficient, stated that the greatest disappointment in his life was his failure to find a significant relationship between head size and intelligence. But Galton didn't have the proper tools to conduct this investigation. He had to use head size when he really wanted to measure brain size. In addition, at the time he undertook this study, there were no good measures of intelligence. Galton had to rely on teachers' estimates of their students' intelligence, and every student knows that teachers can be quite wrong. Other investigators in the nineteenth century measured the volumes of skulls (Figure A) of various groups and estimated intelligence on the basis of occupations or other doubtful criteria.

The development and standardization of intelligence tests in the twentieth century provided invaluable help for one side of the question, but until recently, measures of head size still had to be used to estimate brain size for any sample of living subjects. Such studies usually showed positive but small correlations between brain size and intelligence. In one review of several such studies, the correlations ranged from +0.08 to +0.22 (van Valen, 1974).

The invention of noninvasive techniques to visualize and measure the brains of living subjects has made possible a direct approach to the question of relations between brain size and intelligence. Brain size is measured for each subject by magnetic resonance imaging (MRI) (this technique is discussed in more detail in Chapter 2); intelligence is measured by standard IQ tests. In one study the overall result was a significant correlation coefficient of about 0.26 (Posthuma et al., 2002). In another study, 67 normal adult subjects were recruited through newspaper advertising and screened for neurological or psychiatric disorders, then given IQ tests. MRI scans such as those shown in Figure B were used for accurate measurement of the size of different brain regions. After correction for body size, the correlation between brain size and IQ scores was 0.38 (Andreasen et al., 1993).

Thus, on the basis of modern techniques, the long-standing controversy appears to have been settled in favor of a significant correlation between brain size and intelligence. Note, however, that the

(A) A nineteenth-century apparatus for head measurement

modest size of the correlation, while statistically significant, indicates that only about 10% of variability in IQ is accounted for by brain size. Thus there is plenty of room for other factors to contribute to overall intelligence. Plus there is still plenty of dispute about whether IQ tests really measure a general property of intelligence (Sternberg, 2000).

Historically, scientists have misused information about brain size in racially or ethnically prejudicial ways (S. J. Gould, 1981). In fact, however, all racial groups show overlapping and widely varying intelligence and brain size. (Figure A from the Bettmann Archive; Figure B courtesy of Nancy Andreasen.)

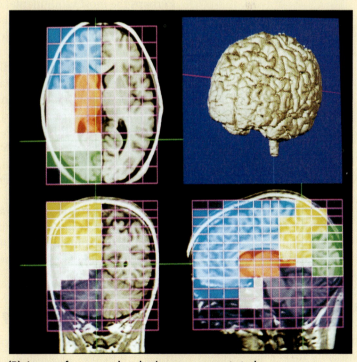

(B) Images from a modern brain measurement study

sions. In a long career, Lashley contributed many important findings and trained many students to study the biological mechanisms not only of learning and memory, but also of perception and motivation.

Biological psychology bears the strong imprint of Canadian psychologist Donald O. Hebb (1904–1985), a student of Lashley (Brown and Milner, 2003). In his book *The Organization of Behavior* (1949), Hebb showed in principle how complex cognitive behavior could be accomplished by networks of active neurons. He suggested how brain cell connections that are initially more or less random could become organized by sensory input and stimulation into strongly interconnected groups that he called *cell assemblies.* His hypothesis about how neurons strengthen their connections through use became known as the *Hebbian synapse,* a topic much studied by current neuroscientists (see Chapter 18).

Consciousness is a thorny problem

Almost anyone using this book has at some time wondered about **consciousness:** the personal, private awareness of our emotions, intentions, thoughts, and movements, and of the sensations that impinge upon us. How is it possible that you are aware of the words on this page, the room you are occupying, the goals you have in life?

In his review of theories of consciousness, Adam Zeman (2002) notes that almost all scientists agree on some aspects of consciousness:

- Consciousness matters; it permits us to do certain important things, like planning and mentally "simulating" what might happen in the future.
- Consciousness is bound up somehow with the activity of the brain.
- We are not aware of all of our brain's activities. Some brain activity, and therefore some of our behavior, is unconscious.
- The deepest parts of our brain (the brainstem) are important for arousal.
- The topmost parts of the brain (the cortex and thalamus) are responsible for whatever we experience from moment to moment.

We will see many examples of experiments that demonstrate these properties of consciousness in the chapters to come. Yet important questions remain unanswered. Perhaps the most fundamental question is, How does consciousness work? Any satisfying theory about consciousness would be able, for example, to explain why a certain pattern of activity in your brain causes you to experience the sensation of blue when looking at the sky, or the smell of cinnamon when entering a bakery. A good theory would let us predict that by messing about with your brain, changing particular connections or activating particular neurons, you would now experience yellow when seeing the sky (and it's no fair putting colored goggles in front of your eyes, that's easy to understand). Unfortunately, we are nowhere near understanding consciousness this clearly. Thus in the rest of this book we will rarely use the words *conscious* or *consciousness.* Normally we cannot say anything about the particulars of what human or animal subjects are *experiencing,* but only whether, by their behavior, they give evidence that the brain detected a signal or event. So we are in no position to know whether complicated machines, like the android C-3PO that we discussed at the start of the chapter, are, or might one day be, conscious.

Some people even doubt whether our "merely human" brains will ever be able to understand something as complicated as consciousness. Nevertheless, any gains we make in understanding how the brain works, which is the subject of this book, will get us closer to that goal.

Recommended Reading

Finger, S. (1994). *Origins of neuroscience.* New York: Oxford University Press.

Howard, P. J. (2000). *Owner's manual for the brain: Everyday applications from mind-brain research* (2nd ed.). Austin, TX: Bard Press.

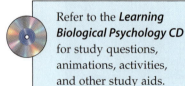
Refer to the *Learning Biological Psychology CD* for study questions, animations, activities, and other study aids.

Pechura, C. M., and Martin, J. B. (Eds.). (1991). *Mapping the brain and its functions.* Washington, DC: National Academy Press.

Zeman, A. (2002). *Consciousness: A user's guide.* New Haven, CT: Yale University Press.

Zimmer, C. (2004). *The soul made flesh: The discovery of the brain—and how it changed the world.* New York: Basic Books.

To keep in touch with progress in this field, look for reviews and evaluations of research in the following publications:

Annual Review of Neuroscience. Palo Alto, CA: Annual Reviews.

Annual Review of Psychology. Palo Alto, CA: Annual Reviews.

Nature Neuroscience. New York: Nature America.

The Neuroscientist. Baltimore: Williams & Wilkins.

Trends in Neurosciences. Amsterdam: Elsevier.

I Biological Foundations of Behavior

Within your head and spinal cord lies the essence of your identity—the central nervous system—containing at least 100 billion nerve cells. Connected together in highly varied and intricate networks, individual nerve cells may receive connections from thousands of others. These networks are information-processing systems, integrating and analyzing the diverse information encoded within the electrochemical impulses that are the basic units of nervous communication. Connected to every part of the body via an extensive web of nerve fibers, the central nervous system monitors, regulates, and modulates the functions of every body structure and system. This vast assembly is the source of all behavior, making possible our perceptions, thoughts, movements, motives, and feelings. Our objective in this section is to become acquainted with the structure and basic functioning of this amazing apparatus.

Ivan Lee Sanford, *Cubist Brain*

2

Functional Neuroanatomy: The Nervous System and Behavior

Mapping the Human Brain

It is perhaps the most dramatic of all medical procedures: While you remain conscious and aware of your surroundings, the surface of your brain is exposed and electrically stimulated in various locations, and your behavioral responses are carefully noted. With procedures perfected during the mid-twentieth century by neurosurgeon Wilder Penfield, thousands of people have undergone electrical-stimulation mapping of the brain as a prelude to surgery. By using stimulation to evaluate sites surrounding a tumor or other abnormality, the surgeon can remove diseased tissue from the brain without encroaching on regions critical for important functions like speech or movement. But Penfield and others realized that, beyond its importance in guiding surgery, stimulation mapping offered a way to ask more-profound questions about the organization of the brain.

Penfield found that stimulation of some brain regions reliably provoked specific movements, whereas stimulation of other regions produced specific sensations, like a tingling hand or flashes of blue light. Elsewhere, stimulations could evoke clear and nuanced vignettes of past experiences: the smell of a childhood haunt, a fragment of a song, the view from the back porch. Some regions were organized identically in different individuals; other regions defied attempts to create functional maps that could be generalized to other people.

Although we now know quite a bit about the organization of basic functions, the brain's control of complex cognition mostly remains a tantalizing mystery. However, the advent of sophisticated brain-imaging technology has infused new vigor into the search for answers to fundamental questions about brain organization. Does each brain region control a specific behavior? Conversely, can every behavior be linked to a particular brain region? Or do some regions act as general-purpose processors? How do the brains of men and women differ? Is everybody's brain organized in the same way?

Thoughts, feelings, perceptions, and acts—from the simplest movements to the most complex ideas—these are the products of the 3-pound organ inside your head. Beneath the convoluted surface of the human brain lies a structure of staggering complexity. We must begin our efforts to understand the biological bases of behavior by surveying the major structures and basic functioning of this most complicated organ.

In this chapter we will discuss the physical architecture of the nervous system, starting with its cellular building blocks. We will then look at the larger structures and subdivisions that are made up of these cells, as well as some of the accessory structures that support them. In Chapter 3 we will delve into the workings of nerve cells, especially the creation and transmission of the electrochemical signals that convey neural information. Chapter 4 extends our discussion of neural activity by reviewing the experimental, medical, and recreational use of chemicals to change the functioning of the nervous system, a field known as *psychopharmacology*. Chapter 5 concludes our survey of the structure and function of the nervous system, discussing the hormonal interface between the nervous system and the rest of the body.

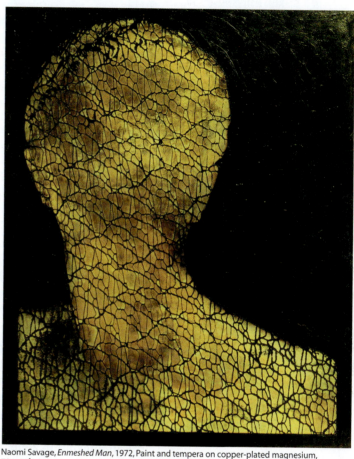

Naomi Savage, *Enmeshed Man*, 1972, Paint and tempera on copper-plated magnesium, 70 × 55½ in.

The Nervous System Is Composed of Cells

The nervous system extends throughout the body, contacting every organ and muscle. The building blocks of the entire nervous system are cells, the most important of which are the **nerve cells, or neurons.** Each human being has about 100 billion to 150 billion neurons; the assembly of these building blocks into circuits is what underlies the simplest and the most complex of our abilities and talents. Each neuron receives inputs from many other nerve cells, integrates those inputs, and then distributes the processed information to many other nerve cells. This is the vital job your brain must accomplish: the integration and analysis of information.

The neuron doctrine defines neurons and their connections

In the late nineteenth century, anatomists sought to understand the differences between human and animal brains by using microscopes to study brain cells. Using special stains to make the normally transparent cells visible, they found that brains contain a large assembly of oddly shaped neurons. Unlike the cells of other organs, neurons are enormously varied in size and form.

Some nineteenth-century anatomists thought that neurons were continuous with one another, forming a nearly endless series of interconnected tubes. According to this view, information in

**Santiago Ramón y Cajal
(1852–1934)**

the nervous system was shunted through these continuous channels. However, the brilliant Spanish anatomist Santiago Ramón y Cajal offered a convincing alternative. He presented elegant studies of nerve cells and patiently drew portraits of neurons that are still appreciated today (see Figure 1.12). Ramón y Cajal was convinced that although neurons come very close to one another (i.e., they are *contiguous*), they are not quite *continuous* with one another. He insisted that at each point of contact between neurons is a tiny gap that keeps the cells separate.

From these studies emerged a new perspective—the **neuron doctrine.** According to this doctrine, (1) the brain is composed of separate neurons and other cells that are independent structurally, metabolically, and functionally; and (2) information is transmitted from cell to cell across tiny gaps, which were later named **synapses.** By the 1950s, the high-resolution abilities of the electron microscope had fully confirmed the neuron doctrine. Nerve cells are indeed separate from each other.

Another important class of cells in the nervous system consists of the **glial cells** (also sometimes called *glia* or *neuroglia*). We will discuss the main types of glial cells and their functions later in the chapter, but because neurons are generally larger and produce readily measured electrical signals, we know much more about them than about glial cells.

The neuron has four basic functional and structural divisions

The typical neuron collects signals from several sources, integrates and transforms all of this information, and distributes the processed information to other cells by means of its own electrochemical output signals.

Because they are cells, neurons contain the usual cellular components that are common to all cells of the body, including **mitochondria** (singular *mitochondrion*) that produce energy, the **cell nucleus** that contains genetic instructions, and the **ribosomes** and related machinery that translate genetic instructions into proteins. In addition, however, all neurons share some distinctive structural parts that are directly related to information processing. These are illustrated in Figure 2.1:

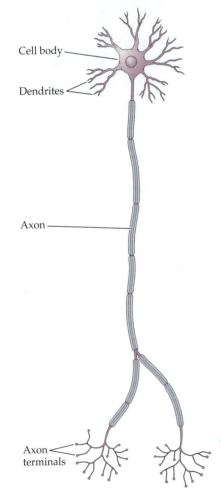

Cell body

Dendrites

Axon

Axon
terminals

- Cellular extensions called **dendrites** (from the Greek *dendron*, "tree") serve as an **input zone,** receiving information from other neurons. Dendrites may be elaborately branched, to accommodate contacts from many other neurons.
- A **cell body** region (or **soma,** plural *somata*), which is defined by the presence of the cell's nucleus, may receive additional synaptic contacts. In most types of neurons, inputs are combined and transformed by specialized structures that serve as an **integration zone.** This zone is typically part of the cell body.
- A single extension, the **axon,** leads away from the cell body and serves as a **conduction zone,** transmitting the cell's electrical impulse away from the cell body.
- Specialized swellings at the ends of the axon, the **axon terminals** (sometimes called *synaptic boutons*), are a functional **output zone.** They communicate the cell's activity to other cells.

In many neurons the axon is only a few micrometers (µm) long, but for the neurons that connect the spinal cord to the rest of the body, axons may reach more than a meter in length.* For example, the giraffe has axons that are, incredibly, several meters long. In order for you to wiggle your toes, individual axons must carry the instructions from the spinal cord to muscles in your foot. Long fibers of sensory neurons then carry messages back to the spinal cord. We will return to cellular neuroanatomy later in the chapter, following our discussion of the major components of the nervous system. The relative sizes of some of the neural structures that we will be discussing throughout the book are illustrated in Figure 2.2.

---

* The meter (m), the basic unit of length in the metric system, equals 39.37 inches. A centimeter (cm) is one-hundredth of a meter (10^{-2} m); a millimeter (mm) is one-thousandth of a meter (10^{-3} m); a micrometer, or micron, (µm) is one-millionth of a meter (10^{-6} m); and a nanometer (nm) is one-billionth of a meter (10^{-9} m).

2.1 The Major Parts of the Neuron

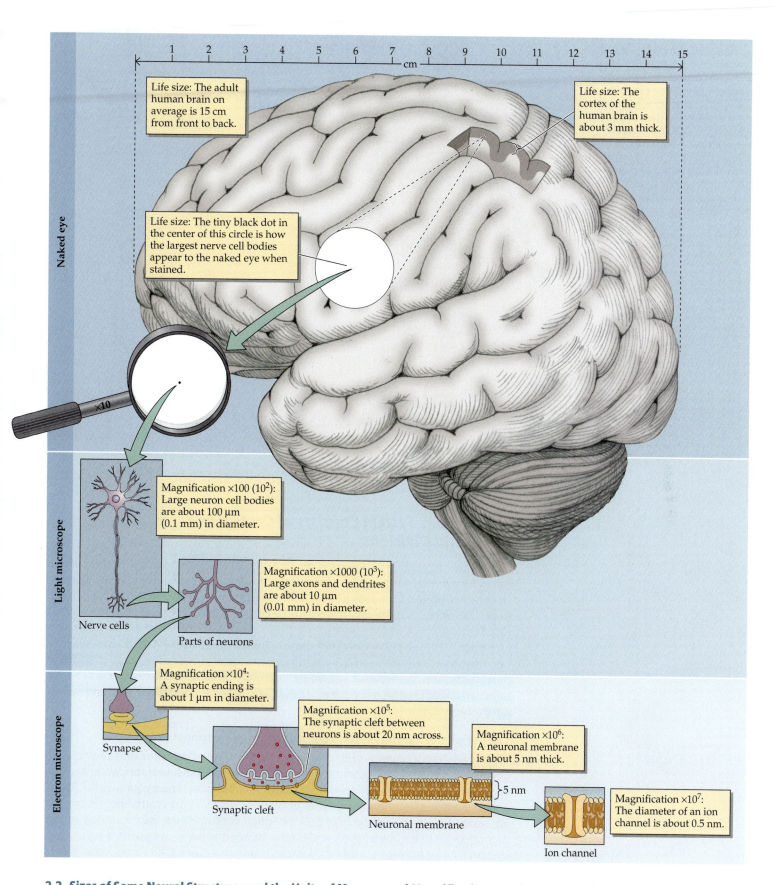

cm

Life size: The adult human brain on average is 15 cm from front to back.

Life size: The cortex of the human brain is about 3 mm thick.

Life size: The tiny black dot in the center of this circle is how the largest nerve cell bodies appear to the naked eye when stained.

×10

Naked eye

Light microscope

Magnification ×100 (10^2): Large neuron cell bodies are about 100 µm (0.1 mm) in diameter.

Nerve cells

Magnification ×1000 (10^3): Large axons and dendrites are about 10 µm (0.01 mm) in diameter.

Parts of neurons

Electron microscope

Magnification ×10^4: A synaptic ending is about 1 µm in diameter.

Synapse

Magnification ×10^5: The synaptic cleft between neurons is about 20 nm across.

Synaptic cleft

Magnification ×10^6: A neuronal membrane is about 5 nm thick.

5 nm

Neuronal membrane

Magnification ×10^7: The diameter of an ion channel is about 0.5 nm.

Ion channel

2.2 Sizes of Some Neural Structures and the Units of Measure and Magnification Used in Studying Them

2.3 The Central and Peripheral Nervous Systems (*a*) This view of the nervous system is a composite of two drawings. A modern view of the central nervous system (the brain and spinal cord) is shown in blue and is superimposed on a rendering of the peripheral nervous system by the great sixteenth-century anatomist Andreas Vesalius. The peripheral nervous system, shown in yellow, courses through the body and connects all body organs and systems to the central nervous system. (*b*) The brain and spinal cord together form the central nervous system.

(*a*)

(*b*)

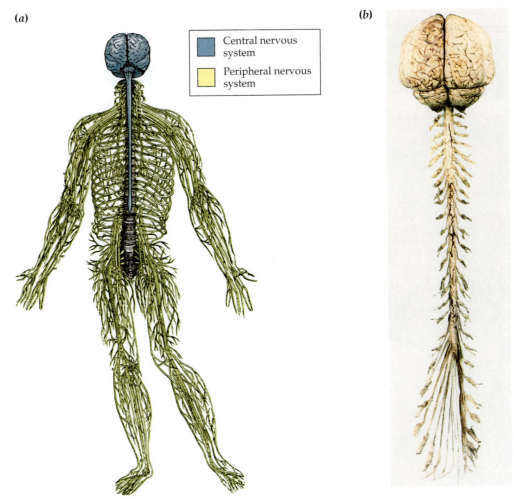

	Central nervous system
	Peripheral nervous system

The Nervous System Consists of Central and Peripheral Divisions

Neuroscience research proceeds at many different levels of analysis. In this section we'll describe the large-scale components of the human nervous system, viewing the brain with the unaided eye. We will resume our discussion of the cells of the nervous system in more detail toward the end of this chapter and in chapters that follow.

Figure 2.3*a* presents a view of the entire human nervous system. Examining the nervous system from this viewpoint reveals a natural subdivision into a **peripheral nervous system** (all nervous system parts that are outside the bony skull and spinal column) and a **central nervous system (CNS)**, consisting of the brain and spinal cord (Figure 2.3*b*).

The peripheral nervous system consists of three components

The peripheral nervous system consists of **nerves**—collections of axons bundled together—that extend throughout the body. These nerves transmit information to muscles (in motor pathways) or arise from sensory surfaces (in sensory pathways). Three components make up the peripheral nervous system: (1) the cranial nerves, which are connected directly to the brain; (2) the spinal nerves, which are connected at regular intervals to the spinal cord; and (3) the autonomic nervous system, a regulatory system that primarily controls the viscera (internal organs). All three components communicate sensory information to the CNS and transmit commands from the CNS to the body.

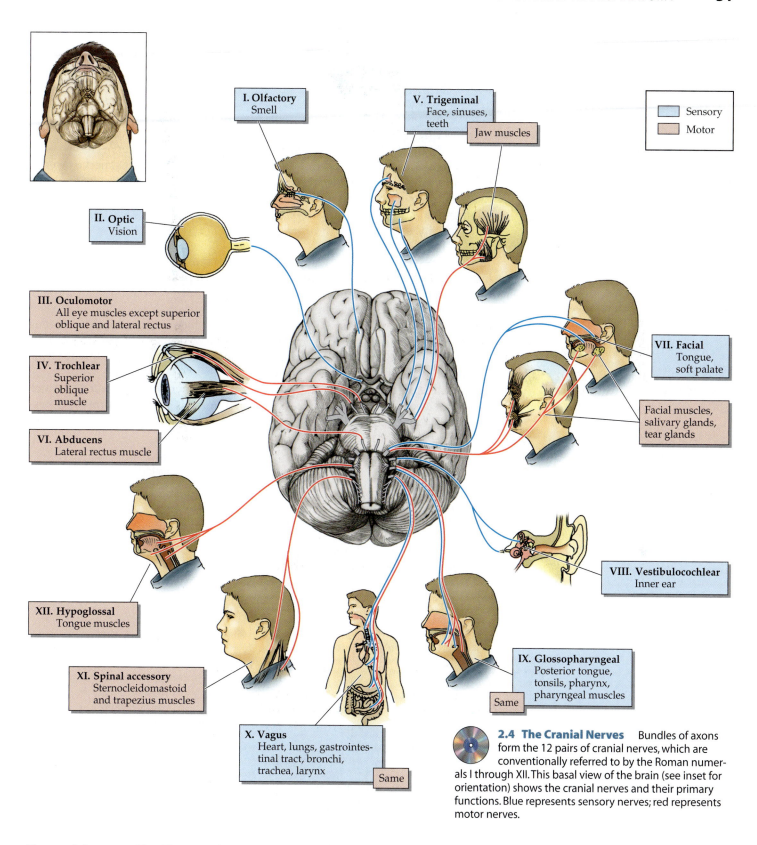

I. Olfactory
Smell

II. Optic
Vision

III. Oculomotor
All eye muscles except superior
oblique and lateral rectus

IV. Trochlear
Superior
oblique
muscle

VI. Abducens
Lateral rectus muscle

XII. Hypoglossal
Tongue muscles

XI. Spinal accessory
Sternocleidomastoid
and trapezius muscles

X. Vagus
Heart, lungs, gastrointestinal tract, bronchi,
trachea, larynx

Same

V. Trigeminal
Face, sinuses,
teeth

Jaw muscles

Sensory

Motor

VII. Facial
Tongue,
soft palate

Facial muscles,
salivary glands,
tear glands

VIII. Vestibulocochlear
Inner ear

IX. Glossopharyngeal
Posterior tongue,
tonsils, pharynx,
pharyngeal muscles

Same

2.4 The Cranial Nerves   Bundles of axons
form the 12 pairs of cranial nerves, which are
conventionally referred to by the Roman numer-
als I through XII. This basal view of the brain (see inset for
orientation) shows the cranial nerves and their primary
functions. Blue represents sensory nerves; red represents
motor nerves.

The cranial nerves   The 12 pairs of cranial nerves in the human brain chiefly serve
sensory and motor systems of the head (Figure 2.4). These nerves pass through small
openings in the skull to enter or leave the brain. The cranial nerves are known both
by name and by Roman numeral. Three cranial nerves are exclusively sensory pathways to the brain: the olfactory (I), optic (II), and auditory (or vestibulocochlear; VIII)

nerves. Five are exclusively motor pathways from the brain: The oculomotor (III), trochlear (IV), and abducens (VI) nerves innervate muscles to move the eye; the spinal accessory (XI) nerves control neck muscles; and the hypoglossal (XII) nerves control the tongue.

The remaining cranial nerves have both sensory and motor functions. The trigeminal (V), for example, serves facial sensation through some axons, and it controls chewing movements through other axons. The facial (VII) nerves control facial muscles and receive taste sensation, and the glossopharyngeal (IX) nerves receive sensation from the throat and control the muscles there. The vagus (X) nerve extends far from the head, running to the heart, liver, and intestines. Its long, convoluted route is the reason for its name, which is Latin for "wandering." The vagus and some other cranial nerves are also part of the parasympathetic nervous system, which we'll describe shortly.

The spinal nerves   Along the length of the spinal cord are 31 pairs of **spinal nerves** (also called *somatic nerves*), with one member of each pair for each side of the body (Figure 2.5). These nerves join the spinal cord at regularly spaced intervals through openings in the bony structures of the spinal column. Each spinal nerve consists of the fusion of two distinct branches, called *roots,* which are functionally different. The **dorsal** (back) **root** of each spinal nerve consists of sensory pathways from the body to the spinal cord. The **ventral** (front) **root** consists of motor pathways from the spinal cord to the muscles.

The name of a spinal nerve is the same as the segment of spinal cord to which it is connected: There are 8 **cervical** (neck), 12 **thoracic** (trunk), 5 **lumbar** (lower

2.5 The Spinal Cord and Spinal Nerves (*Middle*) The spinal column runs from the base of the brain to the sacrum; a pair of nerves emerges from each level (see Figure 2.3*b*). (*Bottom right*) The spinal cord is surrounded by bony vertebrae and is enclosed in three membrane layers (the meninges). Each vertebra has an opening on each side through which the spinal nerves pass. (*Top right*) The spinal cord gray matter is located in the center of the cord and is surrounded by white matter. In the gray matter are interneurons and the motoneurons that send axons to the muscles. The white matter consists of myelinated axons that run up and down the spinal column. (*Left*) These stained cross sections show the spinal cord at the cervical, thoracic, lumbar, and sacral levels. (Photographs from Hanaway et al., 1998.)

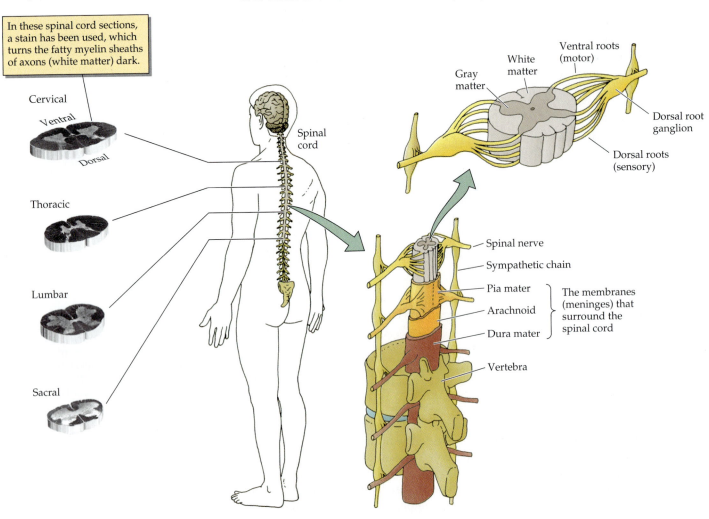

In these spinal cord sections, a stain has been used, which turns the fatty myelin sheaths of axons (white matter) dark.

Cervical
Ventral
Dorsal

Thoracic

Lumbar

Sacral

Spinal cord

Gray matter
White matter
Ventral roots (motor)
Dorsal root ganglion
Dorsal roots (sensory)

Spinal nerve
Sympathetic chain
Pia mater
Arachnoid
Dura mater
} The membranes (meninges) that surround the spinal cord

Vertebra

back), 5 **sacral** (pelvic), and 1 **coccygeal** (bottom) spinal segments. Thus the T12 spinal nerve is the spinal nerve that is connected to the twelfth segment of the thoracic portion of the spinal cord. Fibers from different spinal nerves join to form peripheral nerves, usually at some distance from the spinal cord.

The autonomic nervous system   Ancient anatomists found collections of neurons outside the CNS, which we call **ganglia** (singular *ganglion*). Because they were outside the CNS, these neuron aggregates were named **autonomic** ("independent") **ganglia.** Today we know that the autonomic ganglia are controlled by neurons in the CNS; the autonomic nervous system actually spans both the central and the peripheral nervous systems.

Autonomic neurons within the brain and spinal cord send out their axons to innervate neurons in the ganglia. These neurons, which have their cell bodies within the ganglia, in turn send their axons out to innervate all the major organs. The central neurons that innervate the ganglia are known as **preganglionic** autonomic cells; the ganglionic neurons that innervate the body are known as **postganglionic** autonomic cells.

The autonomic nervous system has three major divisions: the sympathetic nervous system, the parasympathetic nervous system, and the enteric nervous system. The preganglionic cells of the **sympathetic nervous system** are found exclusively in the spinal cord, specifically in the thoracic and lumbar regions. These cells send their axons a short distance to innervate a chain of ganglia running along each side of the spinal column; this chain is called the **sympathetic chain** (Figure 2.6 *left*). Cells of the sympathetic chain innervate smooth muscles in organs and in the walls of blood vessels. A convenient, if somewhat oversimplified, summary of the effects of sympathetic activation is that it prepares the body for action: Blood pressure increases, the pupils of the eyes widen, and the heart quickens.

The **parasympathetic nervous system** (from the Greek *para*, "around") gets its name because its preganglionic neurons are found above and below those of the sympathetic system—in the brain and the sacral spinal cord (Figure 2.6 *right*). These preganglionic cells also innervate ganglia, but parasympathetic ganglia are not collected in a chain as sympathetic ganglia are. Rather, parasympathetic ganglia are dispersed throughout the body, usually near the organ affected.

For many body functions, the sympathetic and parasympathetic divisions act in opposite directions, and the result is very accurate control. For example, the heartbeat is quickened by the activity of sympathetic nerves during exercise, but it is slowed by the vagus nerve (part of the parasympathetic system) during rest. Sympathetic activation constricts blood vessels, raising blood pressure, while parasympathetic activation relaxes vessel walls; sympathetic activation inhibits digestion, while parasympathetic stimulates it. The simplified view of the parasympathetic division is thus that it prepares the body for rest.

CLINICAL ISSUE

Resembling a mesh embedded within the walls of the digestive organs, the **enteric nervous system** is a local network of sensory and motor neurons that regulates the functioning of the gut. It is innervated by both sympathetic and parasympathetic neurons, and thus it is ordinarily under the control of the CNS. Because it regulates digestive activities of the gut, the enteric nervous system plays a key role in maintaining fluid and nutrient balances in the body (discussed in Chapter 13).

The sympathetic, parasympathetic, and enteric nervous systems are "autonomous" also in another sense: Their functions are not subject to conscious "voluntary" control in the same way that we can control our movements.

The central nervous system consists of the brain and spinal cord

The spinal cord is a conduit that funnels sensory information from the body up to the brain and conveys brain motor commands out to the body. Thus we will discuss the spinal cord later when we are examining sensation (in Chapter 8) and movement (in Chapter 11). Here we will deal with the executive portion of the CNS: the brain.

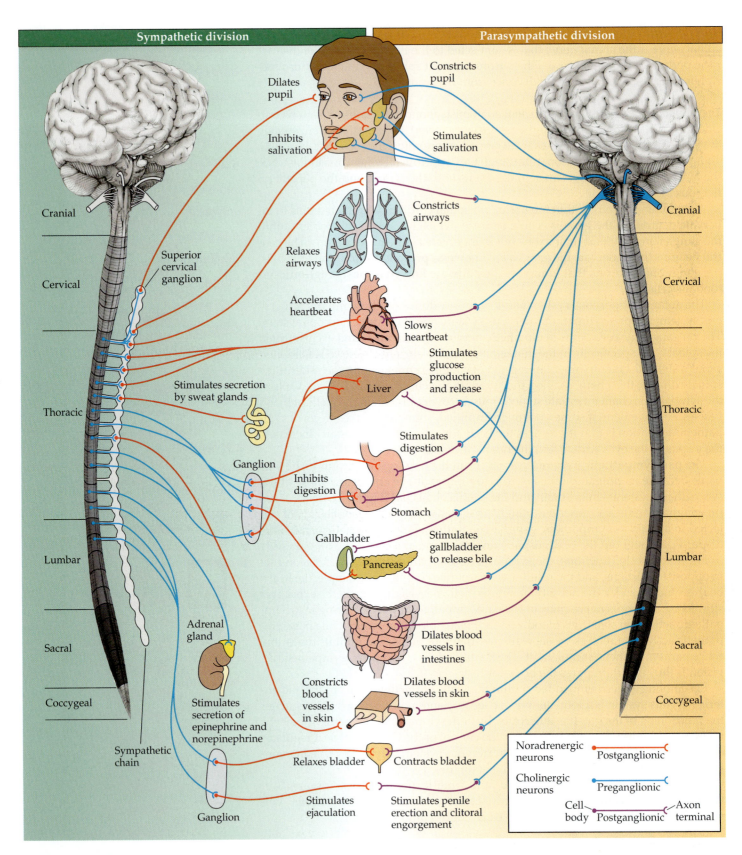

| Sympathetic division | Parasympathetic division |

Dilates pupil

Inhibits salivation

Constricts pupil

Stimulates salivation

Cranial

Cervical

Superior cervical ganglion

Constricts airways

Relaxes airways

Accelerates heartbeat

Slows heartbeat

Stimulates glucose production and release

Liver

Thoracic

Stimulates secretion by sweat glands

Ganglion

Inhibits digestion

Stimulates digestion

Stomach

Gallbladder

Stimulates gallbladder to release bile

Pancreas

Lumbar

Dilates blood vessels in intestines

Sacral

Adrenal gland

Stimulates secretion of epinephrine and norepinephrine

Constricts blood vessels in skin

Dilates blood vessels in skin

Coccygeal

Sympathetic chain

Relaxes bladder

Contracts bladder

Stimulates ejaculation

Stimulates penile erection and clitoral engorgement

Ganglion

Cranial

Cervical

Thoracic

Lumbar

Sacral

Coccygeal

Noradrenergic neurons	•—— Postganglionic
Cholinergic neurons	•—— Preganglionic
Cell body •—— Postganglionic	Axon terminal

2.6 The Autonomic Nervous System (*Left*) The sympathetic division of the autonomic nervous system consists of the sympathetic chains and the nerve fibers that flow from them. (*Right*) The parasympathetic division arises from both the cranial and the sacral parts of the spinal cord. All preganglionic axons, whether sympathetic or parasympathetic, release acetylcholine as a neurotransmitter, as do parasympathetic postganglionic cells. Sympathetic postganglionic cells use norepinephrine (noradrenaline) as a neurotransmitter. The two different postganglionic transmitters are what allow the autonomic nervous system to have two opposing effects on target organs. Neurotransmitters are discussed in detail in Chapter 4.

Brain features that are visible to the naked eye   Given the importance of the adult human brain, it is surprising that on average it weighs a mere 1400 g, just 2% of the average body weight. However, even gross inspection reveals that what the brain lacks in weight it makes up for in intricacy. Figure 2.7 offers three views of the human

2.7 Three Views of the Human Brain   (a) Lateral view (from the side). (b) Midsagittal (midline) view. (c) Basal view (from below). On the right is a postmortem brain specimen seen from each view. (Photographs courtesy of S. Mark Williams and Dale Purves, Duke University Medical Center.)

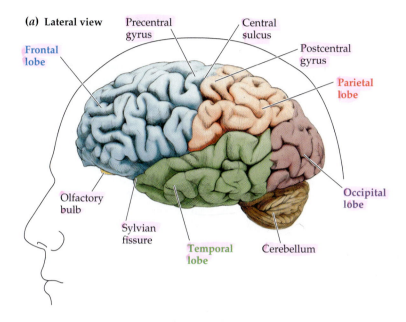

(*a*) **Lateral view**

Precentral gyrus · Central sulcus · Frontal lobe · Postcentral gyrus · Parietal lobe · Olfactory bulb · Occipital lobe · Sylvian fissure · Temporal lobe · Cerebellum

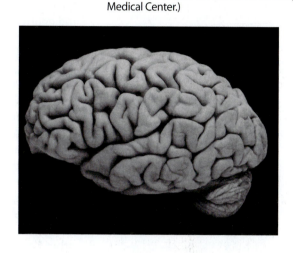

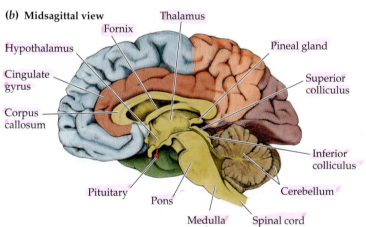

(*b*) **Midsagittal view**

Fornix · Thalamus · Hypothalamus · Pineal gland · Cingulate gyrus · Superior colliculus · Corpus callosum · Inferior colliculus · Pituitary · Pons · Medulla · Spinal cord · Cerebellum

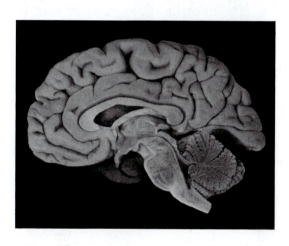

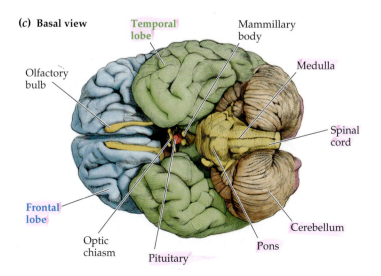

(*c*) **Basal view**

Temporal lobe · Mammillary body · Olfactory bulb · Medulla · Frontal lobe · Spinal cord · Optic chiasm · Pituitary · Pons · Cerebellum

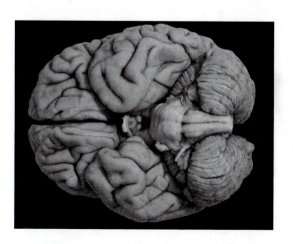

brain in standard orientations. These views will be helpful in our future discussions. Viewed from the side (see Figure 2.7*a*) or from the top, the human brain is dominated by the **cerebral hemispheres,** which sit atop and surround the brainstem, which is continuous with the spinal cord.

The convolutions of the paired cerebral hemispheres are the result of elaborate folding together of tissue. The resulting ridges of tissue, called **gyri** (singular *gyrus*), are separated from each other by furrows called **sulci** (singular *sulcus*). Such folding enormously increases the cerebral surface area; about two-thirds of the cerebral surface is hidden in the depths of these folds.

The major sectors of the cerebral hemispheres are the **frontal, parietal, temporal,** and **occipital** regions, or lobes. These lobes, named after the bones of the skull that overlie them, are distinguished by colors in Figure 2.7. Some of the boundaries defined by folds are clearly marked; for example, the lateral sulcus, or **Sylvian fissure** (which demarcates the temporal lobe), and the **central sulcus** (which divides frontal from parietal lobes) are quite prominent. The boundaries dividing parietal from occipital lobes, and occipital from temporal lobes, are less well defined. The outer shell of the hemispheres is the **cerebral cortex,** sometimes referred to as simply the *cortex* (the word *cortex,* Latin for "bark of a tree," refers to the outermost layers of a structure).

In general, the cortex may be regarded as the seat of complex cognition; damage to the cortex may impair "higher" functions such as speech, memory, or visual processing. In contrast, "lower" parts of the brain regulate respiration, heart rate, and other basic functions. The four lobes of the brain perform different tasks. For example, the occipital lobes receive and process information from the eyes, giving rise to the sense of sight. Auditory information is directed to the temporal lobes, and damage there can impair hearing. The sense of touch is mediated by a strip of parietal cortex just behind the central sulcus (called the **postcentral gyrus**), while in front of the central sulcus, the **precentral gyrus** of the frontal lobe is crucial for motor control. In fact, Wilder Penfield's experiments with stimulation mapping of the brain, which we discussed at the beginning of the chapter, revealed that the precentral gyrus contains an orderly map of the muscles of the other side of the body (see Figure 11.12). Similarly, the postcentral gyrus contains a sensory map of the body (Penfield and Rasmussen, 1950). A large C-shaped bundle of axons called the **corpus callosum** (see Figure 2.7*b*) crosses the midline and allows communication between the right and left cerebral hemispheres.

To get the most out of our discussion of these systems, you will need to understand the conventions that anatomists use for describing various viewpoints of the body and the brain. These conventions are described in Box 2.1.

No matter what plane is used to section the brain, two distinct shades of color are evident (Figure 2.8). The light-colored **white matter** consists mostly of fiber tracts. It gains its appearance from a whitish fatty substance called **myelin,** which ensheathes and insulates the axons of many neurons. The darker-colored **gray matter** is dominated more by nerve cell bodies and dendrites, which are devoid of myelin.

Developmental subdivisions of the brain   The complex form of the adult human brain makes it hard to understand why anatomists use terms the way they do. For example, the part of your brain closest to the back of your head is labeled as part of the forebrain. How can we make sense of this terminology? The clue to how the brain is subdivided lies in the way it develops early in life. In Chapter 7 we will consider brain development as a subject in its own right. For now we will discuss brain development in the context of categorizing brain structures.

In a very young embryo of any vertebrate, the CNS looks like a tube. The walls of this **neural tube** are made of cells, and the interior is filled with fluid. A few weeks after conception, the human neural tube begins to show three separate swellings at the head end (Figure 2.9*a*): the **forebrain** (or *prosencephalon*), the **midbrain** (or *mesencephalon*), and the **hindbrain** (or *rhombencephalon*). (The term *encephalon,* meaning "brain," comes from the Greek *en,* "in," and *kephale,* "head.")

**Wilder Penfield
(1891–1976)**

(a) **Lateral view showing planes of section**

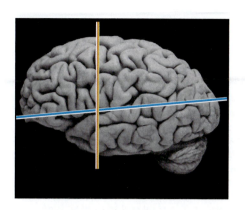

(b) **Horizontal section**

Basal ganglia · Thalamus · Gray matter (cortex) · White matter

Frontal poles

Occipital poles

Third ventricle

Posterior horn of lateral ventricle

(c) **Coronal or transverse section**

Basal ganglia

Corpus callosum · Caudate nucleus · Putamen

Lateral ventricle · Amygdala · Temporal lobe

2.8 Inside the Brain (a) The colored lines here indicate the planes of section shown in (b) and (c). The light color of the white matter is from the fatty myelin surrounding the axons in the major fiber tracts. Gray matter consists of cell bodies that form the outer layers of the brain and nuclei within the brain. (Photographs courtesy of S. Mark Williams and Dale Purves, Duke University Medical Center.)

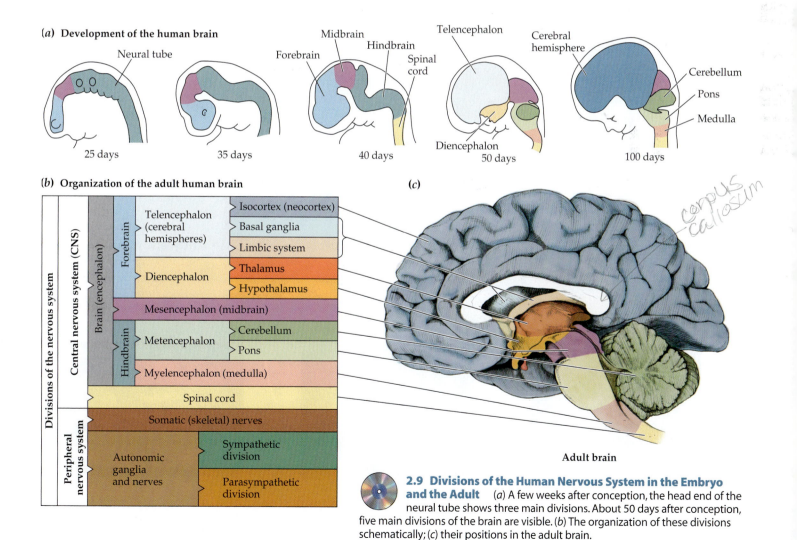

(a) **Development of the human brain**

Neural tube

25 days — 35 days

Midbrain · Hindbrain

Forebrain · Spinal cord

40 days

Telencephalon

Diencephalon

50 days

Cerebral hemisphere · Cerebellum · Pons · Medulla

100 days

(b) **Organization of the adult human brain**

Divisions of the nervous system				
Central nervous system (CNS)	Brain (encephalon)	Forebrain	Telencephalon (cerebral hemispheres)	Isocortex (neocortex)
				Basal ganglia
				Limbic system
			Diencephalon	Thalamus
				Hypothalamus
		Mesencephalon (midbrain)		
		Hindbrain	Metencephalon	Cerebellum
				Pons
			Myelencephalon (medulla)	
	Spinal cord			
Peripheral nervous system	Somatic (skeletal) nerves			
	Autonomic ganglia and nerves		Sympathetic division	
			Parasympathetic division	

(c)

corpus callosum

Adult brain

2.9 Divisions of the Human Nervous System in the Embryo and the Adult (a) A few weeks after conception, the head end of the neural tube shows three main divisions. About 50 days after conception, five main divisions of the brain are visible. (b) The organization of these divisions schematically; (c) their positions in the adult brain.

BOX 2.1 Three Customary Orientations for Viewing the Brain and Body

Because the nervous system is a three-dimensional structure, two-dimensional illustrations and diagrams cannot represent it completely. The brain is usually cut in one of three main planes to obtain a two-dimensional section from this three-dimensional object. It is useful to know the terminology and conventions that apply to these sections, which are shown in the figure.

The plane that bisects the body into right and left halves is called the **sagittal plane** (from the Latin *sagitta*, "arrow"). The plane that divides the body into a front (anterior) and a back (posterior) part is called by several names: **coronal plane** (from the Latin *corona*, "crown"), *frontal plane,* or *transverse plane.* For clarity, we will view coronal sections from behind so that the right side of the figure represents the right side of the brain. (In medicine, coronal sections are viewed as if you were facing the patient, with the patient's left on your right.) The third main plane,

which divides the brain into upper and lower parts, is called the **horizontal plane.**

In addition, several directional terms are used. **Medial** means "toward the middle" and is contrasted with **lateral,** "toward the side." Relative to one location, a second location is **ipsilateral** if it is on the same side of the body and **contralateral** if on the opposite side of the body. The head end is referred to by any of several terms: **anterior, cephalic** (from the Greek *kephale,* "head"), or **rostral** (from the Latin *rostrum,* "prow of a ship"). The tail end is called **posterior** or **caudal** (from the Latin *cauda,* "tail"). **Proximal** (from the Latin *proximus,* "nearest") means "near the trunk or center," and **distal** means "toward the periphery" or "toward the end of a limb" (distant from the origin or point of attachment).

Dorsal means "toward or at the back," and **ventral** means "toward or at the belly or front." In four-legged animals, such as

the cat or the rat, *dorsal* refers to both the back of the body and the top of the head and brain. For consistency in comparing brains among species, this term is also used to refer to the top of the brain of a human or of a chimpanzee, even though in such two-legged animals the top of the brain is not at the back of the body. Similarly, *ventral* is understood to designate the bottom of the brain of a two-legged as well as of a four-legged animal.

Although these terms may seem strange at first, they provide a means of describing anatomy without ambiguity. If you want to become adept with these terms, you might find it helpful to get together with a friend and quiz each other about anatomical relations. "Where's the navel? In a medial position on the ventral surface, caudal to the rib cage, and rostral to the pelvis." (Photographs courtesy of S. Mark Williams and Dale Purves, Duke University Medical Center.)

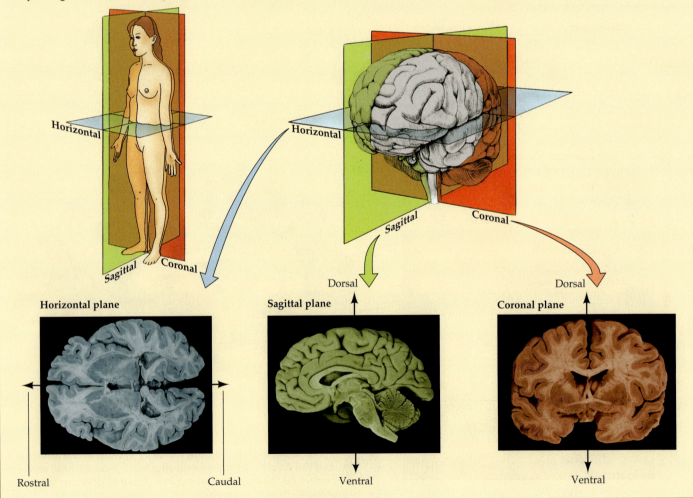

About 50 days after conception, the forebrain and hindbrain have already developed clear subdivisions. At the very front of the developing brain is the **telencephalon,** which will become the cerebral hemispheres (consisting of cortex plus some deeper structures belonging to two functionally related groups: the basal ganglia and the limbic system). The other part of the forebrain is the **diencephalon** (or "between brain"), which will include regions called the *thalamus* and the *hypothalamus.*

The midbrain (**mesencephalon**) comes next. Behind it the hindbrain has two divisions: the **metencephalon,** which will develop into the **cerebellum** ("little brain") and the **pons** ("bridge"); and the **myelencephalon,** or **medulla.** The term **brainstem** usually refers to the midbrain, pons, and medulla combined. Figure 2.9*c* shows the positions of these main structures and their relative sizes in the adult human brain. Even when the brain achieves its adult form, it is still a fluid-filled tube, but a tube of very complicated shape.

Each of the five main sections (telencephalon, diencephalon, mesencephalon, metencephalon, and myelencephalon) can be subdivided in turn. We can work our way from the largest, most-general divisions of the nervous system on the left of the schematic in Figure 2.9*b* to more-specific ones on the right.

Within each region are aggregations of neurons called **nuclei** (singular *nucleus*) and bundles of axons called **tracts.** Recall that in the periphery, aggregations of neurons are called *ganglia,* and bundles of axons are called *nerves.* Unfortunately, the same word *nucleus* can mean either "a collection of nerve cell bodies" or "the spherical center of a single cell," so you must rely on the context to understand which meaning is intended. Because these nuclei and tracts are the same from individual to individual, and often from species to species, they have names too.

You are probably more interested in the functions of all these parts of the brain than in their names, but each region serves more than one function, and ideas about function are constantly being revised by new data. Having now oriented you to the general organization of the brain, we will embark on just a brief look at the functions of specific parts, leaving the detailed discussion for later chapters.

Brain Structures Can Be Described on the Basis of Function

Although we give simple, capsule statements about functions here, later chapters take them up more fully, so we concentrate now on understanding the physical layout of the parts rather than their functions. We'll look briefly at each of the five basic parts of the brain in turn and then examine the cerebral cortex in a little more detail. Although there are some single structures around the midline—such as the corpus callosum, pineal gland, and pituitary gland (see Figure 2.7*b*)—each of the structures we'll describe next is found in both the right and the left sides of the brain. An intriguing aspect of this bilateral symmetry is that each hemisphere of the brain controls, and receives inputs from, the other (contralateral) side of the body.

Within the cerebral hemispheres are the basal ganglia and the limbic system

The **basal ganglia** include the **caudate nucleus,** the **putamen,** and the **globus pallidus** in the telencephalon under the cerebral cortex, and the **substantia nigra** in the midbrain (Figure 2.10*a*; see also Figure 2.8*b* and *c*). These four nuclei (not really ganglia, despite the unfortunate name *basal ganglia*) send axons back and forth to innervate one another, forming a neural system. The basal ganglia are very important in motor control, as we will see in Chapter 11.

The **limbic system** is a loosely defined, widespread network of structures (Figure 2.10*b*) that are involved in emotion and learning. The **amygdala** (Latin for "almond," which it resembles in shape) consists of several subdivisions with quite diverse functions, including emotional regulation (Chapter 15) and the perception of odor (Chapter 9). The **hippocampus** (plural *hippocampi;* from the Greek *hippokampos,* "sea horse," which it resembles in shape) and the **fornix** (plural *fornices*) are important for learn-

(*a*) **Basal ganglia**

(*b*) **Limbic system**

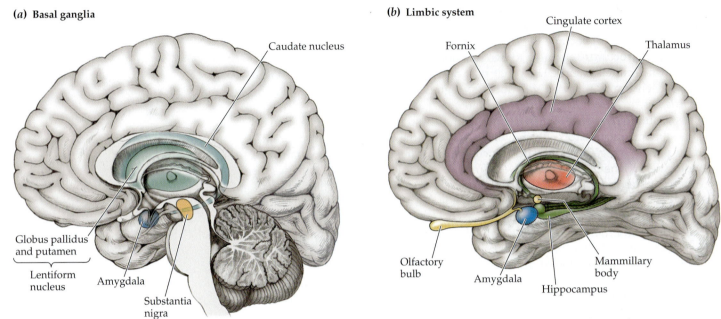

2.10 Two Important Brain Systems   (*a*) The basal ganglia—caudate nucleus, putamen, globus pallidus, and substantia nigra—are important in movement. (The substantia nigra is not visible here because it is buried deep within the midbrain.) (*b*) The limbic system—hippocampus, thalamus, cingulate cortex, fornix, olfactory bulb, amygdala, and mammillary bodies—is important for emotion, learning, and memory.

ing (Chapter 17). Other components of the limbic system include a strip of cortex called the **cingulate gyrus,** which is implicated in diverse functions including the direction of attention, and the **olfactory bulb,** involved in the sense of smell. The rest of the limbic system is found in the diencephalon (see the next section), including the hypothalamus and the breast-shaped **mammillary bodies** (see Figure 2.10*b*).

The diencephalon is divided into thalamus and hypothalamus

The uppermost portion of the diencephalon is the **thalamus** (plural *thalami*), seen in the center of the adult brain in Figures 2.7*b*, 2.8*b*, and 2.10*b*. The thalamus is a complex cluster of nuclei that act as way stations to the cerebral cortex. Almost all sensory information enters the thalamus, where neurons send that information to the overlying cortex. The cortical cells in turn innervate the thalamus, perhaps to control which sensory information is transmitted.

Because it is under the thalamus, the second part of the diencephalon is known as the **hypothalamus** (see Figure 2.7*b*). The hypothalamus is relatively small, but it is packed with many distinct nuclei that have vital functions. It has been implicated in hunger, thirst, temperature regulation, reproductive behaviors, and much more. The hypothalamus also controls the pituitary gland, which in turn controls almost all hormone secretion, as we'll learn in Chapter 5.

The midbrain has sensory and motor systems

The most prominent features of the midbrain are two pairs of bumps on the dorsal surface. The more rostral pair are the **superior colliculi** (singular *colliculus*), and the caudal pair are the **inferior colliculi** (see Figure 2.7*b*). The superior colliculi receive visual information; the inferior colliculi receive information about sound.

Two important motor centers are embedded within the midbrain. One is the **substantia nigra,** which we mentioned as part of the basal ganglia, containing neurons that release the transmitter dopamine into the caudate (loss of this dopamine leads to Parkinson's disease, discussed in Chapter 11). The other motor center is the **red nucleus** (because it looks red in freshly dissected tissue), which communicates with motoneurons in the spinal cord. The midbrain also contains several nuclei that send their axons out to form cranial nerves. Other such cranial nerve nuclei are found throughout the brainstem.

Also found in the midbrain is a distributed network of neurons collectively referred to as the **reticular formation** (from the Latin *reticulum*, "network"). The reticular formation stretches from the midbrain down to the medulla. Many varied functions have been attributed to different parts of this loose aggregation of neurons, including sleep and arousal, temperature regulation, and motor control.

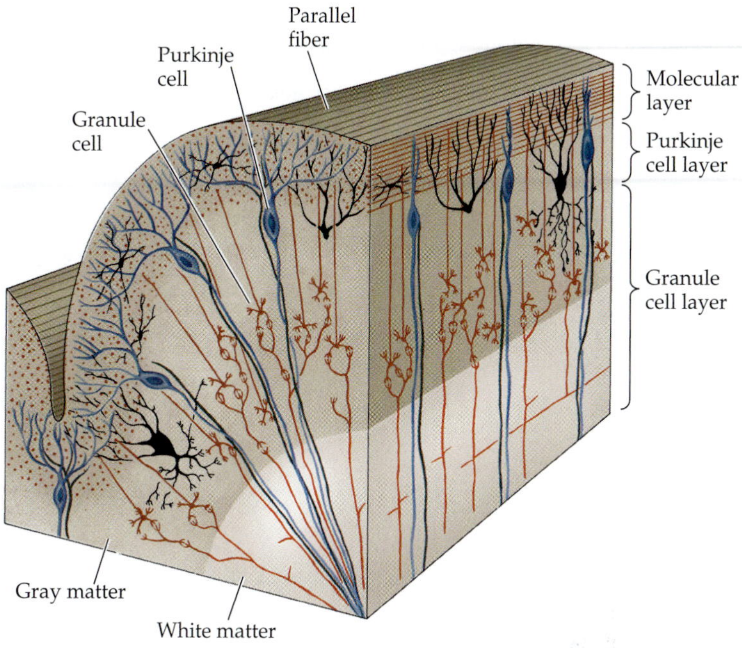

The cerebellum is attached to the pons

The lateral, midline, and basal views of the brain in Figure 2.7 show the cerebellum. Like the cerebral hemispheres, the surface of the cerebellum is elaborately folded. The arrangement of cells within this folded sheet is relatively simple, consisting of three layers (Figure 2.11). A middle layer is composed of a single row of large neurons called **Purkinje cells** after the anatomist who first described their elaborate fan-shaped dendritic patterns. Axons from the small neurons of the **granule cell** layer, lying below the Purkinje cells, rise to the surface of the cerebellum to form the **parallel fibers** of the outermost layer (called the *molecular layer*). The cerebellum is particularly important for motor coordination and control.

Immediately below (ventral to) the cerebellum lies the pons (see Figure 2.7*b* and *c*), a part of the brainstem. Within the pons are important motor control and sensory nuclei, including several cranial nerve nuclei. Information from the ear first enters the brain in the pons, via the nucleus of the vestibulocochlear (VIII) nerve.

2.11 The Arrangement of Cells within the Cerebellum Large Purkinje cells dominate the cerebellum. Innervation between the various types of cells in the cerebellum forms a very consistent pattern. Cells depicted here in black inhibit the actions of other cells.

The medulla maintains vital body functions

The medulla is the most caudal portion of the brainstem and marks the transition from brainstem to spinal cord. Within the medulla are the nuclei of cranial nerves XI and XII—cell bodies of neurons that control the neck and tongue muscles, respectively. The reticular formation, which we first saw in the midbrain, stretches through the pons and ends in the medulla. Because the medulla contains nuclei that regulate breathing and heart rate, tissue damage there is often fatal. All axons passing between the brain and spinal cord necessarily course through the medulla, and several medullary nuclei add their own axons to the descending fiber tracts.

The cerebral cortex performs complex cognitive processing

Neuroscientists have long argued that understanding human cognition depends on unraveling the structure and fundamental functions of the cerebral cortex. In fact, by accepting electrical silence of the cortex as a definition for death, many governments now define human life in terms of a functional cerebral cortex. If the cerebral cortex were unfolded, it would occupy an area of about 2000 cm² (315 square inches), more than three times the area of this book's cover. How are these cells arranged? And how do the arrangements allow for particular feats of human information processing?

The neurons of the cerebral cortex are arranged in six distinct layers (Figure 2.12*a*). Tissue with this six-layered organization is referred to as **isocortex** (from the Greek

2.12 Layers of the Cerebral Cortex (*a*) The six layers of cortex can be distinguished with stains that reveal all cell bodies (*left*), or with stains that reveal a few neurons in their entirety (*right*). (*b*) This pyramidal cell has been enlarged about 100 times.

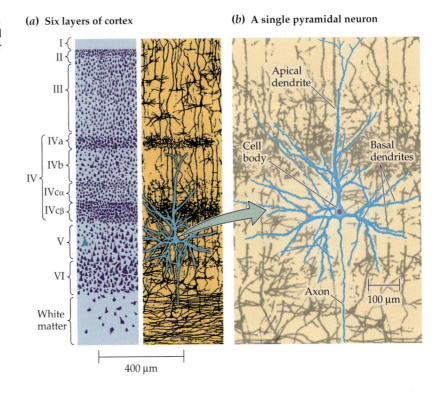

(*a*) Six layers of cortex

(*b*) A single pyramidal neuron

iso, "same," and the Latin *cortex,* "bark of a tree"). (This tissue has historically been called **neocortex,** but that term is no longer favored because it implies that this tissue evolved more recently—the Greek *neos* means "new"—a supposition for which there is no evidence.). Other telencephalic structures are made up of **allocortex** (from the Greek *allos,* "other"), tissue with three layers or unlayered organization, previously known as *archi-* or *paleocortex* (Carpenter and Sutin, 1983). Each cortical layer is distinct because it consists either of groups of cells of particular sizes, or of patterns of dendrites or axons. For example, the outermost layer, layer I, is distinct because it has few cell bodies, while layer III stands out because of its many neurons with large cell bodies.

The most prominent kind of neuron in the cerebral cortex—the **pyramidal cell** (Figure 2.12*b*)—usually has its cell body in layer III or V. One dendrite of each pyramidal cell (called the **apical dendrite**) extends to the outermost surface of the cortex. The pyramidal cell also has several dendrites (called **basal dendrites**) that spread out horizontally from the cell body. Frequently neurons of the cortex appear to be arranged in columns perpendicular to the layers.

Cortical columns In some regions of the cerebral cortex, neurons are organized into regular columns that serve as cohesive information-processing units. These **cortical columns** extend through the entire thickness of the cortex, from the white matter to the surface. Within each column, most of the synaptic interconnections of neurons are vertical, although there are some horizontal connections as well. The human cerebral cortex contains about 1 million cortical columns, each about 3 mm deep and 400 to 1000 μm in diameter (Mountcastle, 1979). In Chapter 10 we will discuss in some detail the cortical columns that analyze visual stimuli.

Cortical regions communicate with one another via tracts of axons looping through the underlying white matter (Figure 2.13). Some of these connections are short pathways to nearby cortical regions; others travel longer distances through the cerebral hemispheres. Earlier we mentioned the largest of these pathways, the corpus callosum, through which run connections between corresponding points on the two hemispheres. Longer links between cortical regions involve multisynaptic

Vernon Mountcastle

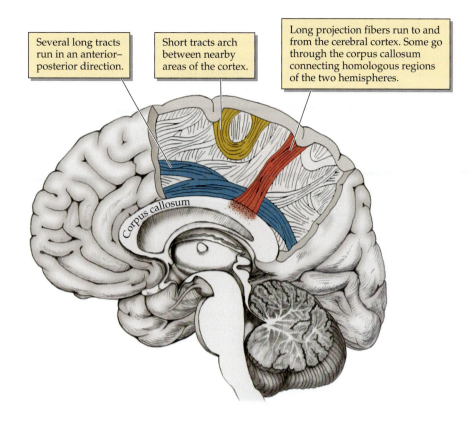

Several long tracts run in an anterior–posterior direction.

Short tracts arch between nearby areas of the cortex.

Long projection fibers run to and from the cerebral cortex. Some go through the corpus callosum connecting homologous regions of the two hemispheres.

Corpus callosum

2.13 Cortical-Tract Connections between Cortical Regions

chains of neurons that loop through subcortical regions such as the thalamus and the basal ganglia.

The Brain is Well Protected and Has an Abundant Blood Supply

Within the bony skull and vertebrae, the brain and spinal cord are surrounded by three protective membranes called **meninges** (see Figure 2.5). The outermost sheet is a tough envelope, formed from extensions of specialized astrocytes, called the **dura mater** (in Latin, literally "hard mother"). The innermost layer, the delicate **pia mater** ("tender mother"), adheres tightly to the surface of the brain and follows all its contours. (The term *mater*, "mother," reflects the medieval belief that these tissues gave birth to the brain.) The delicate, weblike membrane between the dura mater and the pia mater is called the **arachnoid** (literally, "spiderweb-like"). Space within the arachnoid is filled with **cerebrospinal fluid** (**CSF**), a clear, colorless liquid. **Meningitis** is an inflammation of the meninges that results from viral or bacterial infection, producing a characteristic set of symptoms that includes fever, rash, and stiff neck, progressing to death or lasting disability if unchecked.

CLINICAL ISSUE

The cerebral ventricles are chambers filled with fluid

Inside the brain is a series of chambers filled with CSF (Figure 2.14). These cavities form what is known as the **ventricular system.** The CSF circulating through the ventricular system has at least two main functions. First, CSF acts mechanically as a shock absorber for the brain: Floating in CSF, the brain is protected from sudden movements of the head that would otherwise cause contact with the inside of the skull. Second, CSF provides a medium for the exchange of materials, including nutrients, between blood vessels and brain tissue.

Each hemisphere of the brain contains a **lateral ventricle**—a complexly shaped chamber that extends into all four lobes of the hemisphere. The lateral ventricles are lined with a specialized membrane called the **choroid plexus,** which produces cerebrospinal fluid by filtering blood. CSF flows from the lateral ventricles into the **third ventricle,** which is located in the midline, and continues down a narrow passage to

(a) Cerebral ventricles of the brain

(b) A closer view

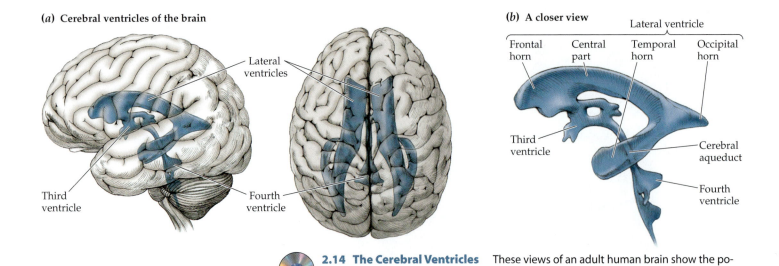

2.14 The Cerebral Ventricles These views of an adult human brain show the position of the cerebral ventricles within it. Cerebrospinal fluid is made in the lateral ventricles and exits from the fourth ventricle to surround the brain and spinal cord.

the **fourth ventricle,** which lies anterior to the cerebellum. Just below the cerebellum are three small openings through which CSF leaves the ventricular system to circulate over the outer surface of the brain and spinal cord. CSF is absorbed back into the circulatory system through large veins beneath the top of the skull.

The brain has an elaborate vascular system

Although it accounts for only 2% of the weight of the average human body, the brain consumes more than 20% of the body's energy. However, the brain has very little reserve of the basic metabolic fuels, oxygen and glucose, and thus depends critically on its blood supply to provide them. Two pairs of arteries—the carotid arteries and the vertebral arteries—supply blood to the brain (Figure 2.15). The common **carotid arteries** ascend the left and right sides of the neck and branch into external and internal carotid arteries. The internal carotid artery enters the skull and branches into anterior and middle cerebral arteries, which supply blood to large regions of the cerebral hemispheres. The **vertebral arteries** ascend along the bony vertebrae and enter the base of the skull. They fuse to form the **basilar artery,** which runs along the ventral surface of the brainstem. Branches of the basilar artery supply blood to the brainstem and to posterior portions of the cerebral hemispheres.

At the base of the brain, the carotid and basilar arteries join to form a structure called the **circle of Willis** (see Figure 2.15a). This joining of arterial paths may provide some needed "backup" if any of the main arteries to the brain should be damaged or blocked by disease. The common term **stroke** refers to changes in the flow of blood in the brain produced by the blockage or rupture of blood vessels, or by reduced flow due to heart impairment. Stroke is among the most common life-threatening disorders of humans; the five most common warning signs of stroke are sudden numbness or weakness, dim vision, dizziness, severe headache, and confusion or difficulty speaking. Effective treatments are available to help restore blood flow and minimize the effects of a stroke, but only if the victim is treated immediately after the onset of symptoms; obtaining medical attention as soon as possible is essential.

CLINICAL ISSUE

Fine arterioles branch off from the main arteries and in turn give rise to the very fine capillaries that deliver nutrients and other substances to brain cells and remove waste products. This exchange in the brain is quite different from exchanges between blood vessels and cells in other body organs. Capillaries in the brain offer much-greater resistance to the passage of molecules across their walls than do capillaries elsewhere. The brain is thus protected from exposure to some substances found in

(*a*) **Basal view of brain**

Circle of Willis

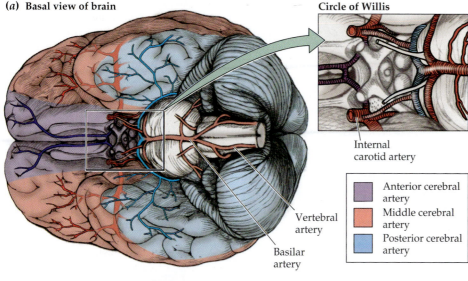

Internal
carotid artery

Vertebral
artery

Basilar
artery

| | Anterior cerebral artery |
| Middle cerebral artery |
| Posterior cerebral artery |

2.15 The Blood Supply of the Human Brain The anterior, middle, and posterior cerebral arteries—the three principal arteries that provide blood to the cerebral hemispheres—are depicted here in views of the basal (*a*), midsagittal (*b*), and lateral (*c*) surfaces of the brain. The basilar and internal carotid arteries form a circle at the base of the brain known as the *circle of Willis*.

(*b*) **Midsagittal view**

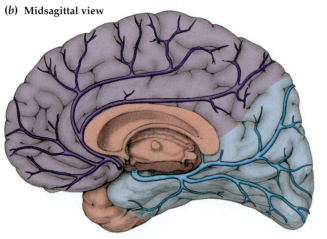

(*c*) **Lateral view**

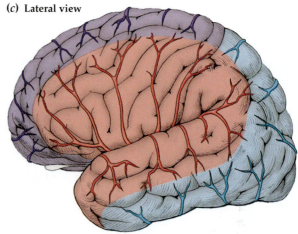

the blood. We refer to this protective mechanism as the **blood–brain barrier.** This barrier results from the tight fit between the cells that make up the walls of capillaries (endothelial cells) in the brain, preventing the passage of large molecules. The blood–brain barrier may have evolved to protect the brain from substances that other organs can tolerate, but it also makes the delivery of drugs to the brain more difficult.

Newer Imaging Techniques Allow Us to Look into the Living Human Brain

Researchers have long sought ways to peer into the living human brain to see structures and how they work during different behaviors. Initial attempts using X-rays of the head proved to be of limited usefulness because X-rays cannot resolve the brain's small variations in density: X-ray photos of the brain are featureless. Of several techniques subsequently devised to improve contrast in brain X-rays, one—the **angiogram** (from the Greek *angeion,* "blood vessel," and *gramma,* "record" or "picture")—remains particularly useful. In angiography, a radiopaque (X-ray–blocking) dye is injected into the brain's blood supply, allowing detailed visualization of the cerebral blood vessels. Angiography is helpful in diagnosing vascular diseases such as stroke.

• Advances in computing technology have led to the development of imaging techniques in which a computer-generated view of the brain is created by the mathematical integration of masses of raw data. The raw data that are processed are collected by specialized scanners that focus on different properties of the brain and thus reveal different aspects of the brain's structure and function: In **computerized axial tomography** (**CAT** or **CT;** from the Greek *tomos,* "cross-cut" or "section"), X-ray energy is used to generate images. In a CT scanner, an X-ray source is moved by steps in an arc around the head. At each point, detectors on the opposite side of the head measure the amount of X-ray radiation that is absorbed; this value is proportional to the density of the tissue through which the X-rays passed. When this process is repeated from many angles, and the results are mathematically combined, an anatomical map of the brain based on tissue density can be computer-generated (Figure 2.16a). CT scans are medium-resolution images, useful for visualizing problems such as hemorrhages, strokes, tumors, or cortical atrophy. In studies of the organization of the human brain, CT scanning has

(a) Computerized tomography (CT)

Normal (horizontal view)   Victim of stroke

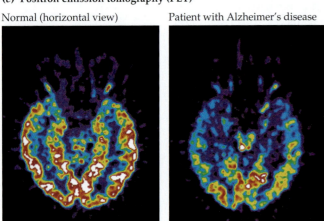

(b) Magnetic resonance imaging (MRI)

Horizontal view   Coronal view

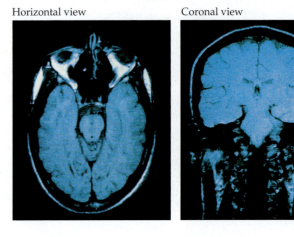

(c) Positron emission tomography (PET)

Normal (horizontal view)   Patient with Alzheimer's disease

(d) Functional magnetic resonance imaging (fMRI)

Anterior 3-D view   Lateral 3-D view of right hemisphere

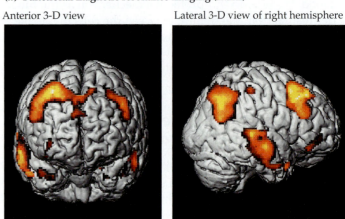

2.16 Visualizing the Living Human Brain The images obtained from some important brain-imaging techniques. (a) CT scans from a normal individual and from a patient who suffered a stroke; the stroke lesion is visible as a large yellow area. (b) Horizontal and coronal MRI images of a normal human brain. Note the clarity in the definition of gyri and sulci of the cerebral cortex. (c) PET scans from a normal human and a patient with Alzheimer's, showing levels of metabolic activity in the brain. Note the greater level of activity in the normal brain. (d) Functional-MRI images showing changes in regional brain metabolism recorded during the presentation of visual or auditory stimuli. The images are three-dimensional renderings showing areas where brain activity changed in subjects viewing images of their romantic partner (see Figure 1.6). (Images in *d* courtesy of Semir Zeki.)

helped researchers identify brain regions that, when damaged, produce disorders of memory, language, attention, and other major cognitive functions.

- A more recent approach to structural imaging, **magnetic resonance imaging (MRI)**, provides higher-resolution images that have supplanted CTs for many applications. MRI images are derived from radio frequency energy, so an additional benefit is that patients are not exposed to potentially damaging X-rays. An MRI scan involves three main steps. First the patient's head is placed in a powerful magnet (the magnet in an MRI machine is 30,000 to 80,000 times stronger than Earth's magnetic field, and could easily lift an automobile). The magnet causes all the protons in the brain's tissues to line up in parallel, instead of in their usual random orientations. (The brain contains a lot of protons; they are the nuclei of hydrogen atoms and thus are present in water molecules.) Next the protons are knocked over by a powerful pulse of radio waves. Then, when this pulse is turned off, the protons relax back to their original configuration, emitting radio waves as they do so.

    CLINICAL ISSUE

    The emitted radio waves are measured by detectors around the head. Different tissues exhibit different rates of proton relaxation, so a computer program can use a map of these radio wave emissions to create an image of the brain based on density (Figure 2.16b) (Elster and Burdette, 2001). With their higher resolution, MRI images can reveal subtle changes in the brain, such as the local demyelination that is characteristic of multiple sclerosis.

- In **positron emission tomography (PET)** (Figure 2.16c) the objective is to obtain images of the brain's *activity*, rather than details of its *structure*. Short-lived radioactive chemicals are injected into the bloodstream, and a ring of detectors maps the destination of these chemicals in the brain by sensing their emissions of radiation. The most common PET technique employs a radioactive form of glucose, the metabolic fuel that is especially taken up and used by highly active brain regions. A computer-generated image in which color is used to distinguish different levels of radioactive emissions yields a striking portrait of the activity of the brain from moment to moment (see Figure 2.16c) (Roland, 1993).

    By controlling a subject's behavior while the scanning takes place, and using special mathematical techniques as outlined in Box 2.2, we can generate metabolic maps of the brain that identify which brain regions contribute to specific functions. This approach has yielded new insights into the neural control of diverse activities, such as the control of movement, visual processing, verbal behavior, selective attention, decision making, and so on. PET is also clinically useful for identifying regions that are metabolically abnormal despite being structurally intact.

    IMPORTANT METHOD

- First introduced in the 1990s, **functional MRI (fMRI)** has revolutionized cognitive neuroscience research, producing the startling high-resolution three-dimensional images of brain activity that frequently appear in newspapers and magazines (Figure 2.16d). Compared to other imaging technologies, fMRI exhibits improved speed (temporal resolution) and sharpness (spatial resolution). Although the basic technology is the same as for MRI scanning (described above), it is applied differently. In fMRI scanning, high-powered, rapidly oscillating magnetic-field gradients are used to detect small changes in brain metabolism, particularly oxygen use, rather than structural information.

    As with PET, scientists can use fMRI data to create images that reflect the activity of different parts of the brain while people engage in various experimental tasks, with excellent spatial resolution. The detailed activity maps provided by fMRI allow researchers to overcome the limitations of invasive procedures like surgical stimulation mapping, which we discussed at the outset of the chapter, and are revealing how networks of brain structures collaborate on complex cognitive processes. Interestingly, current research coupling fMRI imaging with electrical recordings of single cells in nonhuman primates indicates that the fMRI image generally reflects synaptic inputs and local processing, rather than the production of neural impulses (Logothetis, 2003).

BOX 2.2 Isolating Specific Brain Activity

Many illustrations in this and later chapters show scans of brain activity that are specifically related to brain disorders or cognitive processes. Usually most of the brain is active, so isolating specific activity requires special procedures. The PET scan shown here beneath the box labeled "Visual stimulus" was made while a person looked at a fixation point surrounded by a flickering checkerboard ring. The scan next to it (beneath the box labeled "Control") was made while a person looked at a fixation point alone. In a comparison of the two, it is hard to see differences, but subtracting the control values from the stimulation values yields an image such as that shown at the upper right ("Difference image"); in this scan it is easy to see that the main difference in activity is in the posterior part of the brain (the visual cortex).

The PET scans shown in the bottom row are difference images for five individuals who performed the same two stimulation and control tasks. Averaging these five scans yields the mean difference image for all five subjects that is shown at far right. Averaged images yield more-reliable results than individual images, but they lack some of the specificity of the individual images.

All the PET and fMRI images in this book are difference images, usually made from scans of a single individual's brain. When you see brain function images in this book or in the popular press, note whether they are direct scans or difference images; if the latter, note whether they show values for an individual or for the mean of a group. (PET scans courtesy of Marcus Raichle.)

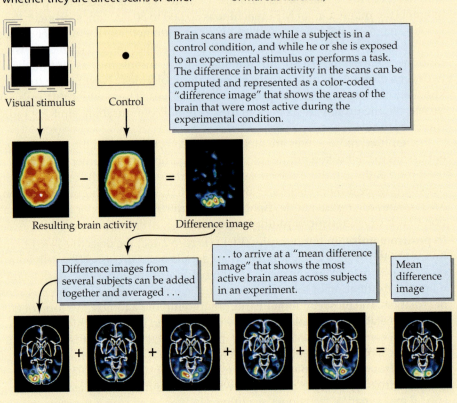

Visual stimulus   Control

Brain scans are made while a subject is in a control condition, and while he or she is exposed to an experimental stimulus or performs a task. The difference in brain activity in the scans can be computed and represented as a color-coded "difference image" that shows the areas of the brain that were most active during the experimental condition.

Resulting brain activity   Difference image

Difference images from several subjects can be added together and averaged . . .

. . . to arrive at a "mean difference image" that shows the most active brain areas across subjects in an experiment.

Mean difference image

- Other investigators are using light to make images of brain activity within the head (Gratton and Fabiani, 2001; Villringer and Chance, 1997). In **optical imaging,** near-infrared light (wavelengths of 700 to 1000 nm) passes through skin, scalp, and skull and penetrates a short distance into the cortex. When such light is transmitted into the brain and detectors pick up the reflections through the scalp, the responses reflect the activity of cortical regions. Some components of the optical responses reflect the electrical signals of neurons, and other components reflect blood flow.

  The relatively low expense and small size of the optical imaging apparatus may allow many more laboratories to use brain imaging in their research. Optical studies could be done with young children or children with attention deficits who will not lie still in an MRI magnet or a PET scanner. And because optical imaging is based on light, it is ideal for simultaneous use with other techniques: optical imaging has been coupled with **transcranial magnetic stimulation** (Figure 2.17), in which focal magnetic currents are used to stimulate the cortex of alert normal subjects directly, without having to make a hole in the scalp or skull (Noguchi et al., 2003). This approach allows experimenters to stimulate a discrete area of the brain while simultaneously mapping the resulting pattern of activation.

To investigate many problems of biological psychology, imaging provides evidence that converges with studies of naturally occurring or experimental brain lesions. Each of these kinds of investigation helps overcome limitations on the other sources of evidence. Furthermore, "remarkable progress in brain imaging techniques does not compete with the psychological analysis of behavior but instead places a new premium upon the thoughtfulness and accuracy of such analysis" (Gabrieli, 1998, p. 89). We will see many examples of brain imaging in later chapters.

The Cells of the CNS Are Specialized for Processing and Transmitting Information

At the beginning of this chapter we introduced the cells of the nervous system and the main structures of a neuron. Because they are the basic information-processing units of the nervous system, the ability to see and measure CNS cells and trace their connections is vital to solving many problems in biological psychology and neuroscience, ranging from following the fetal growth of neurons to determining ways to repair damage in the adult nervous system (Box 2.3).

However, neurons and glial cells are difficult to examine and measure for several reasons. First, they are small, and their extensions are even smaller (1 to 3 μm in diameter). Furthermore, if you cut a thin slice of brain tissue and look at it under a microscope, you will find it hard to see any brain cells because they don't contrast with surrounding areas. The ability to see details of cells requires special chemical agents to make cells or parts of cells stand out from the background. These various techniques for visualizing neurons and for tracing pathways in the nervous system will appear in almost every chapter in this book.

Compared to glial cells, of which there are only four basic types, neurons are remarkably diverse in shape; at least 200 geometrically distinguishable types of nerve cells are found in the brains of mammals. Figure 2.18 offers a small sample of the many different shapes that neurons may take. These differences in size and shape reflect the different ways in which neurons process and transmit information.

Neurons can be classified by shape, size, or function

Anatomists use the shapes of cell bodies, dendrites, and axons to classify the many varieties of nerve cells into three principal types: multipolar, bipolar, and monopolar. These different types of neurons are specialized for particular kinds of infor-

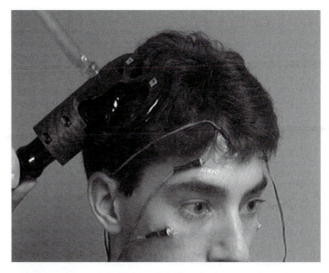

2.17 Transcranial Magnetic Stimulation Magnetic fields induced by electromagnetic coils stimulate neurons of the underlying cortical surface.

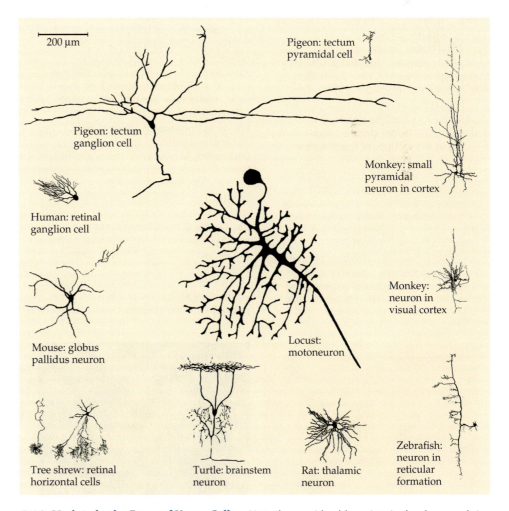

200 μm

Pigeon: tectum pyramidal cell

Pigeon: tectum ganglion cell

Monkey: small pyramidal neuron in cortex

Human: retinal ganglion cell

Mouse: globus pallidus neuron

Monkey: neuron in visual cortex

Locust: motoneuron

Tree shrew: retinal horizontal cells

Turtle: brainstem neuron

Rat: thalamic neuron

Zebrafish: neuron in reticular formation

2.18 Variety in the Form of Nerve Cells Note the considerable variety in the shape and size of these neurons (drawn to scale) from the brain or spinal cord of different animals.

BOX 2.3 Neuroanatomical Methods Provide Ways to Make Sense of the Brain

Visualizing Structures in the Brain

In the middle of the nineteenth century, dyes used to color fabrics provided a breakthrough in anatomical analysis. Dead, preserved nerve cells treated with these dyes, known in histology (the study of tissue slices under the microscope) as *stains,* suddenly become vivid, and hidden parts become evident. Different dyes have special affinities for different parts of the cell, such as membranes, the cell body, or the sheaths surrounding axons.

Golgi stains outline the whole cell, including details such as dendritic spines (Figure A). Golgi staining is often used to characterize the variety of cell types in a region. For reasons that remain a mystery, this technique stains only a small number of cells, each of which stands out in dramatic contrast to adjacent unstained cells. Injecting fluorescent molecules directly into a neuron provides a Golgi stain–like view of its dendrites (Figure B).

Nissl stains outline all cell bodies because the dyes are attracted to RNA, which encircles the nucleus. Nissl stains allow us to measure cell body size and the density of cells in particular regions (Figure C). Other stains are absorbed by myelin, the fatty sheaths that surround some axons (see, for example, the sections of spinal cord shown in Figure 2.5). Improved microscopes have also broadened our understanding of the fine structure of cells. Modern light microscopy provides detailed resolution of features as small as 1 to 2 μm. The wavelengths of visible light are too long to resolve smaller details, but because electrons have shorter wavelengths than photons, electron microscopy extends the range of microscopy by a hundredfold, revealing some of the smallest details within cells (e.g., see Figures 2.20 and 2.21).

In a procedure known as **autoradiography,** cells are manipulated into taking photographs of themselves. For example, in order to identify the parts of the brain that are affected by a newly discovered drug, experimenters might inject animals with a radioactively labeled form of the drug. Time is then allowed for the radioactive drug to reach its target (in many cases, drugs act at postsynaptic receptors in discrete brain regions). To create an autoradiogram, the experimenters sacrifice the animal, cut thin sections of brain tissue, and place the sections on slides, which they cover with photographic emulsion. Radioactivity emitted by the labeled drug in the tissue causes silver to be deposited—the same effect that light has on film. The silver deposition produces fine, dark grains immediately above the regions where the drug has become selectively concentrated (see Box 5.1 and Figure 14.3).

Another approach to marking cells of the brain is to apply immunological techniques. These techniques allow neuroanatomists to mark groups of cells that have an attribute in common, such as particular membrane components or particular proteins within a cell. This approach is known as **immunocytochemistry** (**ICC**) because it uses immune system molecules (antibodies) to label cells chemically. The brain is sliced up and exposed to antibodies. After allowing time for the antibodies to attach to molecules of the target protein, unattached antibodies are rinsed off and chemical treatments make the antibodies visible. Cells that were making the protein will be labeled from the chemical treatments (Figure D).

This technique can even tell us where, within the cell, the protein is found. For example, if the protein is a neurotransmit-ter, the antibodies will detect it in axon terminals. A conceptually related procedure called **in situ hybridization** (Figure E) goes a step further and, using radioactively labeled lengths of nucleic acid (RNA or DNA), identifies those neurons that contain a specific mRNA message (see the appendix). This is equivalent to identifying the cells in which a gene of interest has been turned on.

When neurons become more active, they tend to express **immediate early genes** (**IEGs**), such as *c-fos.* Using ICC to label the IEG product has become a very popular method for determining which neurons are active in particular functions. In this technique, animals are sacrificed shortly after performing a behavior of interest, and the distribution of IEG product in brain slices taken from these animals corresponds to the regions of the brain that were most likely involved in that behavior (Figure F). The use of IEG ICC has largely replaced older techniques that used radioactive versions of metabolic fuels to localize brain activation.

Tracing Pathways in the Brain

The cells of the brain are interconnected through a complex web of pathways. Gaining an understanding of neuronal circuitry required the development of techniques that clearly identify the origins or destinations of axonal tracts. Tracing pathways in the nervous system is difficult for several reasons: (1) Axons have an even smaller diameter than cell bodies; (2) axons from different sources look alike; and (3) fibers with different destinations often travel together over parts of their routes, making it hard to disentangle one set from the rest. Although at first glance this

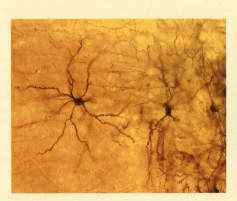

(A) Golgi stain

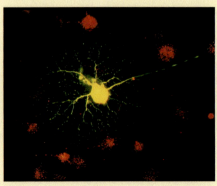

(B) Neuron injected with fluorescent dye

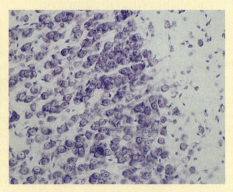

(C) Nissl stain

BOX 2.3 *(continued)*

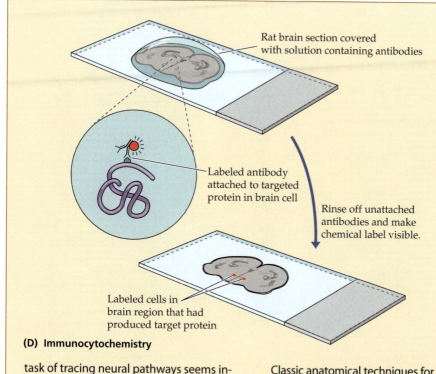

Rat brain section covered with solution containing antibodies

Labeled antibody attached to targeted protein in brain cell

Rinse off unattached antibodies and make chemical label visible.

Labeled cells in brain region that had produced target protein

(D) Immunocytochemistry

the injection of radioactively labeled amino acids into a collection of cell bodies. These radioactive molecules are taken up by the cell, incorporated into proteins, and transported to the tips of the axons. Autoradiographic procedures, as described earlier in this box, are then used to visualize the locations of the transported substances, making the whole pathway known.

A powerful technique for determining the cells of origin of a particular set of axons employs a tracer such as **horseradish peroxidase** (**HRP**), an enzyme found in the roots of horseradish. HRP catalyzes certain chemical reactions that leave a visible reaction product of dark granules. HRP acts as a tracer of pathways because it is taken up into the axon at the terminals and transported back to the cell body. After HRP is injected into one part of the nervous system, any neurons that have axon terminals there transport the HRP back to the cell body, which can be made visible by means of certain chemical reactions (Figure G). All along the way, visible reaction products are formed—akin to footprints along a pathway. (Figure A courtesy of Timothy DeVoogd; Figure B courtesy of Carla Shatz; Figure E courtesy of Brian Sauer and Suzanne Pham.)

task of tracing neural pathways seems insurmountable—remember, our brain contains many billions of neurons—anatomists were not daunted.

Classic anatomical techniques for tracing pathways rely on visualization of the products of degenerating axons. Newer procedures accomplish the same goal by

(E) In situ hybridization: enkephalin gene expression

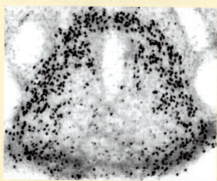

(F) Expression of c-fos in activated cells

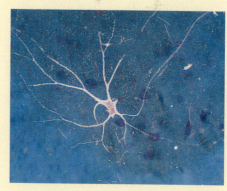

(G) HRP-filled motoneuron

mation processing. **Multipolar neurons** are nerve cells that have many dendrites and a single axon (Figure 2.19*a*). Most of the neurons of the vertebrate brain are multipolar. **Bipolar neurons** have a single dendrite at one end of the cell and a single axon at the other end (Figure 2.19*b*). This type of nerve cell is found in some sensory systems, including the retina and the olfactory (smell) system. **Monopolar neurons** have a single branch (usually thought of as an axon) that, after leaving the cell body, extends in two directions (Figure 2.19*c*). One end is the receptive pole (the input zone); the other, the output zone. Such cells transmit touch information from the body into the spinal cord. In all three types of neurons, the dendrites are in the input zone; and in multipolar and bipolar cells, the cell body is part of the input zone.

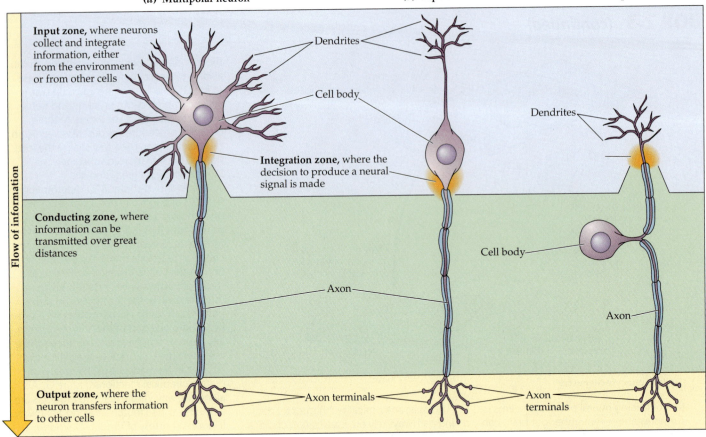

(a) Multipolar neuron

(b) Bipolar neuron

(c) Monopolar neuron

Input zone, where neurons collect and integrate information, either from the environment or from other cells

Integration zone, where the decision to produce a neural signal is made

Conducting zone, where information can be transmitted over great distances

Output zone, where the neuron transfers information to other cells

Flow of information

Dendrites

Cell body

Dendrites

Cell body

Axon

Axon

Axon terminals

Axon terminals

2.19 A Classification of Neurons into Three Principal Types   (*a*) A multipolar neuron has many dendrites extending from the cell body, and a single axon. (*b*) A bipolar neuron has a single dendrite extending from the cell body, and a single axon. (*c*) A monopolar neuron has a single branch that emerges from the cell body and extends in two directions. Note the four functional zones (input, integration, conducting, and output), which are common to all neurons.

Another common way of classifying nerve cells is by size. Examples of small nerve cells are the types called *granule* ("grain"), *spindle,* and *stellate* ("star-shaped"). Large cells include the types called *pyramidal, Golgi type I,* and *Purkinje.* Each region of the brain is a collection of both large and small neurons. Vertebrate nerve cell bodies range from as small as 10 μm to as large as 100 μm in diameter; the diversity in neuronal sizes is evident in Figure 2.18.

In a third simple scheme, neurons are classified by function. The axon terminals of some neurons contact muscles or glands, and the job of these neurons is to make the muscle contract or to change the activity of the gland. Such neurons are called **motoneurons** (or *motor neurons*). Other neurons are directly affected by environmental stimuli; they respond to light, a particular odor, or touch. These cells are **sensory neurons.** The remaining neurons, which constitute the vast majority, receive input from and send their output to other neurons; thus they are called **interneurons.**

Glial cells support neural activity

Glial cells are named after the original conception of their function—that they serve as something like glue (the Greek *glia* means "glue"). Clearly, structural support—or some aspects of it—is one biological role of glial cells. Glial cells may also directly affect neuronal functioning, by providing neurons with raw materials and chemical signals that alter neuronal structure and excitability. Unlike nerve cells, glial cells are produced throughout life, and they substantially outnumber neurons in the adult brain. Although many aspects of the functional roles of glial cells

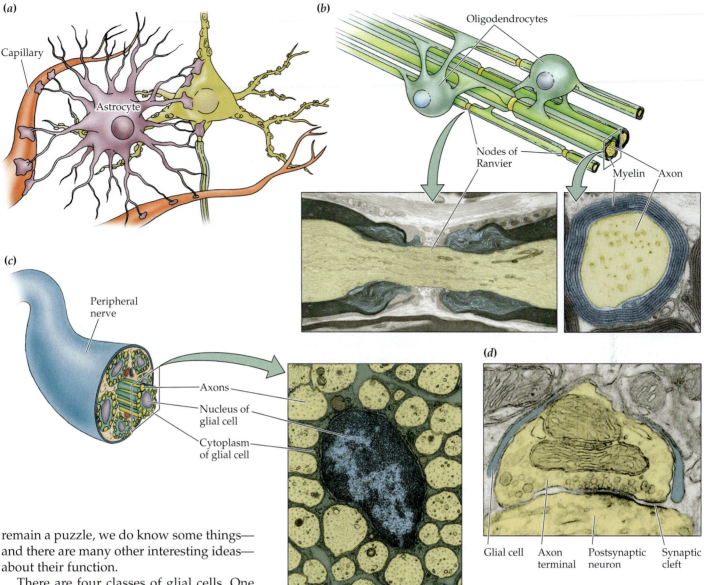

2.20 Representative Glial Cells   (*a*) One type of astrocyte—the protoplasmic astrocyte—contacts capillaries and is adjacent to nerve cell membranes. (*b*) Extensions of oligodendrocytes form myelin wrapping (blue) on axons (yellow); four axons are shown in this view. The colorized electron micrograph of a myelinated axon (at right) shows the many layers of the myelin sheath. The longitudinal micrograph of an axon (*left*) shows a Node of Ranvier, the gap between adjacent myelinated segments. (*c*) Axons that lack this wrapping, called *unmyelinated axons,* are embedded in the troughs of glial cells. In the magnified cross section shown here, the light-colored circular shapes are unmyelinated axons. The large dark area in the center of the photograph is the nucleus of a glial cell, the cytoplasm of which surrounds the axons. (*d*) Processes from astrocytes (in blue) surround and insulate synapses, and directly modify synaptic activity. (Micrographs *b* (*left*) and *d* courtesy of Mark Ellisman and the National Center for Microscopy and Imaging Research; *b* (*right*) and *c* from Peters et al., 1991.)

remain a puzzle, we do know some things—and there are many other interesting ideas—about their function.

There are four classes of glial cells. One type, called an **astrocyte** (from the Greek *astron,* "star"), is a star-shaped cell with numerous extensions (or processes) in all directions (Figure 2.20*a*), weaving among neurons and axons. Some astrocytes form end feet on the blood vessels of the brain. These end feet look as though they are attached to the vessels by suckerlike extensions. Recent research indicates that astrocytes and neurons are in surprisingly close two-way communication, acting in concert to regulate diverse neural processes.

Synaptic transmission and neurotransmitter metabolism, neuronal remodeling and the formation of new synapses, and the dynamic control of local blood flow are all directly coordinated by neurons and astrocytes working together. Although they are not capable of generating their own electrical impulses, astrocytes receive synapses directly from neurons and also monitor the activity of nearby neuronal synapses. They then communicate among themselves and with the neighboring neurons to modulate the neurons' responses (Fields and Stevens-Graham, 2002; Mauch et al., 2001; Zonta et al., 2003).

A second type of glial cell is the **microglial cell.** As the name suggests, microglial cells are very small. They migrate in large numbers to sites of injury or disease in the nervous system, apparently to remove debris from injured or dead cells.

The third and fourth types of glial cells—*oligodendrocytes* and *Schwann cells*—perform a vital function for nerve cells, as the next section describes.

Some glial cells wrap around axons, forming myelin sheaths

All along the length of the axons of many neurons, nearby glial cells wrap adjacent sections of the axon in sheaths of myelin, giving the axon the appearance of a string of slender beads. The process of ensheathing axons is termed **myelination.** Between each pair of myelinated segments is a small gap where the axonal membrane is exposed, called a **node of Ranvier** (see Figure 2.20b). As we will see in Chapter 3, the myelin sheathing and nodes of Ranvier greatly increase the speed at which neural impulses are conducted. Therefore, it's not surprising that anything that interferes with the myelin sheath, such as the demyelinating disease **multiple sclerosis,** can have catastrophic consequences for the individual.

Within the brain and spinal cord, the myelin sheath is formed by a type of glial cell called an **oligodendrocyte** (see Figure 2.20b). This cell is much smaller than an astrocyte and has fewer extensions (the Greek *oligos* means "few"). A single oligodendrocyte typically contributes sheathing to numerous adjacent axons (see Figure 2.20b), and oligodendrocytes are also commonly associated with nerve cell bodies. The regularity of the wrapping is nicely illustrated in cross sections of the axon (Figure 2.20b). The myelination performed by oligodendrocytes continues for extended periods of time in human beings—in some brain regions up to 10 to 15 years after birth, and possibly throughout life.

For axons outside the brain and spinal cord, myelin is provided by another type of glial cell—the **Schwann cell.** A single Schwann cell ensheathes a limited length of a single axon.

Many axons of very thin diameter have no close wrapping of myelin; they are commonly referred to as unmyelinated fibers or axons. Although these fibers do not have an elaborate coating, they still have a relationship with oligodendrocytes and Schwann cells, which segregate the unmyelinated axons (Figure 2.20c). Furthermore, the manner in which these glial cells surround some synaptic contacts suggests that one of their roles is to insulate and isolate synapses to prevent interference (Figure 2.20d).

**CLINICAL
ISSUE**

Glial cells are of clinical interest because they form many of the tumors that arise in the brain. Furthermore, some glial cells, especially astrocytes, respond to brain injury by changing in size—that is, by swelling. This **edema** damages neurons and is responsible for many symptoms of brain injuries.

The neuronal cell body and dendrites receive information across synapses

The diversity of neuronal shapes arises especially from the variation in the form and shape of dendrites, the extensions that arise from the nerve cell body and branch out in highly complex ways (see Figure 2.18). The overall arrangement of a neuron's dendrites—its **arborization**—provides clues about the cell's information-processing function. The surfaces of the dendrites are covered with contacts from other neurons, the synapses. Most neurons receive thousands of synapses. Through the synapses, information is transmitted from one neuron to another. A synapse, or synaptic region, has three principal components (Figure 2.21):

1. The **presynaptic membrane,** located on the axon terminal of the presynaptic neuron
2. A specialized **postsynaptic membrane** on the surface of the dendrite or cell body of the postsynaptic neuron

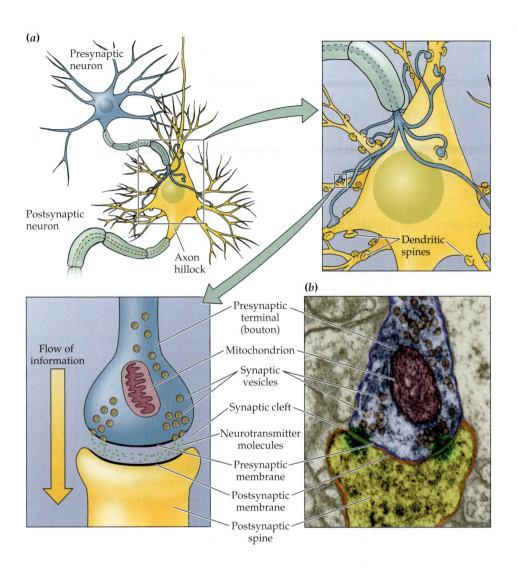

2.21 Synapses (*a*) Axons typically form a synapse on the cell body or dendrites of a neuron. On dendrites, synapses may form on dendritic spines or on the shaft of a dendrite. A transmission electron micrograph (*b*) provides a view of the fine structure of a synapse.

3. A **synaptic cleft,** a gap of about 20 to 40 nm that separates the presynaptic and postsynaptic membranes

Detailed electron microscopic examination of the presynaptic terminal shows that it contains many small spheres, called **synaptic vesicles.** They range in size from 30 to 140 nm. These vesicles contain a chemical substance that can be released into the synaptic cleft, and this release is triggered by electrical activity in the axon. The released chemical, called a **synaptic transmitter,** or **neurotransmitter,** flows across the cleft and produces electrical changes in the postsynaptic membrane. Many different substances, such as acetylcholine, dopamine, and glutamate, have been confirmed to act as neurotransmitters. Many more candidates are under active investigation. We will discuss neurotransmitters in depth in Chapter 4.

The local electrical changes in the postsynaptic membrane may be either excitatory or inhibitory. The surface of the postsynaptic membrane is different from adjacent regions of the membrane. It contains special **receptor molecules** (often referred to simply as *receptors*) that capture and react to molecules of the transmitter agent (see Figure 1.5). Numerous synapses cover the surfaces of dendrites and of the cell body. The high number of synapses is possible because these synaptic junctions are very small—less than 1 µm^2 each. Some individual cells of the brain receive as many as 100,000 synaptic contacts, although the more common number for larger cells is about 5000 to 10,000. Synaptic contacts are particularly numerous in nerve cells that have elaborate dendrites.

Studding the dendrites of many neurons are outgrowths called **dendritic spines** (see Figure 2.21), which, by effectively increasing the surface area of the dendrites, allow for extra synaptic contacts. Both the number and structure of dendritic spines may be rapidly altered by experience, such as training or exposure to sensory stimuli (see Chapter 18). This property of dendritic spines, a form of **neuroplasticity,** has made them the focus of intensive research efforts. Recent evidence indicates that the neuroplastic changes of dendritic spines may range from minute-by-minute fluctuations to lifelong stable changes (Grutzendler et al., 2002; Trachtenberg et al., 2002).

The axon is a specialized output zone

A typical axon has several regions that are structurally and functionally distinguishable (see Figure 2.19). In multipolar neurons the axon arises from the **axon hillock,** a cone-shaped projection from the cell body (see Figure 2.21*a*). The axon hillock is the neuron's integration zone, giving rise to the electrical impulses that carry the neuron's message along the axon toward its targets (see Chapter 3). The axon beyond the hillock is tubular, with a diameter ranging from 0.5 to 20 µm in mammals and up to 500 µm in the "giant" axons of some invertebrates.

With very few exceptions, nerve cells have only one axon. But axons often divide into several branches, called **axon collaterals.** Because of this branching, a single nerve cell can exert influence over a wide array of other cells. Toward its ending, an axon or a collateral typically divides into numerous fine branches. At the ends of these branches are found the axon terminals that make synaptic contacts on other cells, or **innervate** them. Table 2.1 compares the main structural features of axons and dendrites. An additional pair of words is important for describing axons: We call axons **afferents** if they carry information *into* a region that we are interested in, and **efferents** if they carry information *away* from the region (a handy way to remember this is that *e*fferents *e*xit but *a*fferents *a*rrive, relative to the region of interest).

The cell body manufactures proteins under the guidance of the DNA (deoxyribonucleic acid) contained in the cell nucleus (see the appendix). Therefore, proteins that are needed for the cell to function properly must be transported from the cell body to distant regions in the axon, and recycled materials must be returned to the cell body. The movement of materials within the axon is referred to as **axonal transport** (Figure 2.22). Some molecules are transported along axons at a "slow" rate (less than 8 mm per day); others are transported by a "fast" system (200–400 mm per day).

TABLE 2.1 *Distinctions between Axons and Dendrites*

Axons	Dendrites
Usually one per neuron, with many terminal branches	Usually many per neuron
Diameter is uniform until start of terminal branching	Diameter tapers progressively toward its ending
Join cell body at a distinct region called the axon hillock	No hillock-like region
Usually covered with myelin	No myelin covering
Lengths from practically nonexistent to several meters	Usually much shorter than axons
Along length, branches tend to be perpendicular	Along lengths, branches occur over wide range of acute angles

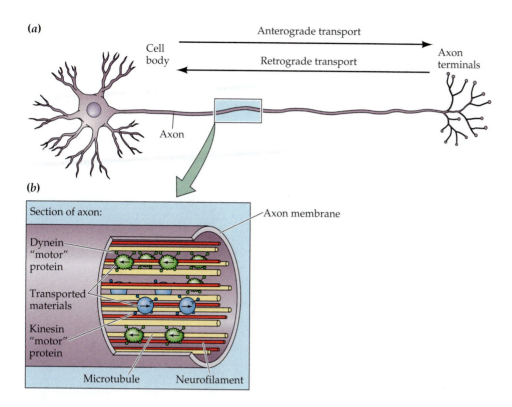

2.22 Axonal Transport (*a*) Axons transport proteins via microtubules and neurofilaments in both anterograde (from cell body to axon terminals) and retrograde (from axon terminals to cell body) directions. (*b*) A view of the cytoskeleton of an axon shows microtubules and neurofilaments with specialized "protein motors"—dynein and kinesin—moving material.

How do substances move in axons? The shape of a neuron is determined by its **cytoskeleton** ("cell skeleton"), which is made up of three kinds of structural elements (the Greek *kytos*, from which we get the prefix *cyto-*, means "hollow vessel"; *cyto-* is used to mean "cells"). Tiny **microfilaments** (7 nm in diameter), which are found in all cells, form a mesh under the cell membrane. Intermediate-sized rods (10 nm in diameter) called **neurofilaments**, and larger cylindrical **microtubules** (20 to 26 nm in diameter), are arranged longitudinally within the axon (see Figure 2.22*b*) and provide it with mechanical strength. Investigators have observed that these rods are also involved in axonal transport, working in conjunction with several types of "motor" proteins that have been identified (Amos and Cross, 1997; Schnapp, 1997). Movement of substances toward the axon terminals is termed **anterograde** transport and relies primarily on the motor protein **kinesin.** Movement of substances toward the cell body is termed **retrograde** transport and depends on the motor protein **dynein.**

Neurons and glial cells form information-processing circuits

Supported and influenced by glial cells, and sharing information across synapses, neurons form ensembles that perform intricate processing of information (Figure 2.23). For complicated high-level processes, these cell assemblies may involve vast numbers of cells and synaptic contacts. In most cases the pattern of connections between neurons is not immutable, and it undergoes adaptive changes in form and function in response to experiences. In Chapter 3 we will turn to the incredible processes by which the basic units of information—neural impulses—are formed, modified, and transmitted.

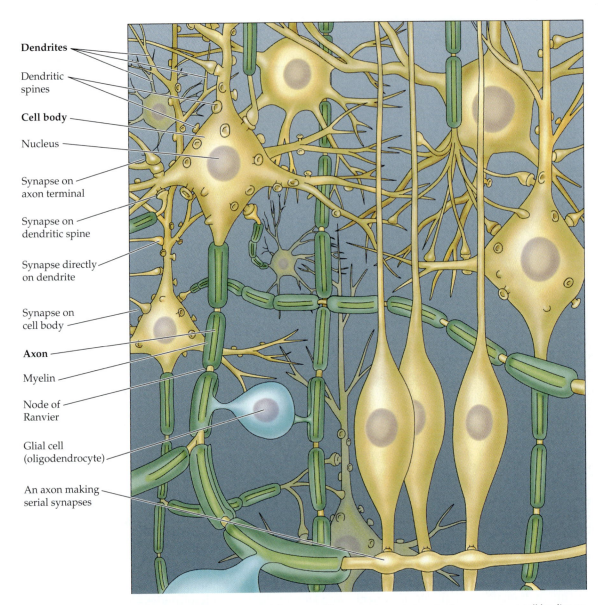

Dendrites

Dendritic
spines

Cell body

Nucleus

Synapse on
axon terminal

Synapse on
dendritic spine

Synapse directly
on dendrite

Synapse on
cell body

Axon

Myelin

Node of
Ranvier

Glial cell
(oligodendrocyte)

An axon making
serial synapses

2.23 Neurons and Glial Cells Work Together to Process Information   Many axon terminals contact dendritic spines; others contact dendrites directly. Note that the many dendritic spines shown here would probably be occupied by axon terminals, but for clarity they have been left empty. Alternatively, axon terminals may contact cell bodies or may even synapse on the axons or terminals of postsynaptic neurons, extending the range of information-processing possibilities.

Refer to the *Learning Biological Psychology CD* for study questions, animations, activities, and other study aids.

Summary

1. The nervous system is extensive—monitoring, regulating, and modulating the activities of all parts and organs of the body.

2. At the microscopic level, neurons are the basic units of the nervous system. The typical neuron of most vertebrate species has four main parts: (1) the cell body, which contains the nucleus; (2) dendrites, which receive information; (3) an axon, which carries impulses from the neuron; and (4) axon terminals, which transmit the neuron's impulses to other cells. Because of the variety of functions they serve, neurons are extremely varied in size, shape, and chemical activity.

3. At the gross anatomical level (i.e., to the naked eye), the nervous system of vertebrates is divided into peripheral and central nervous systems.

4. The peripheral nervous system includes the cranial nerves, spinal nerves, and autonomic ganglia. The autonomic nervous system consists of the sympathetic nervous sys-

tem, which tends to ready the body for action; the parasympathetic nervous system, which tends to have an effect opposite to that of the sympathetic system; and the enteric nervous system, which innervates the gut.

5. The central nervous system (CNS) consists of the brain and spinal cord. The main divisions of the brain can be seen most clearly in the embryo. These divisions are the forebrain (telencephalon and diencephalon), the midbrain (mesencephalon), and the hindbrain (metencephalon and myelencephalon).

6. The human brain is dominated by the cerebral hemispheres, which include the cerebral cortex, an extensive sheet of folded tissue. The cerebral cortex is responsible for higher-order functions such as vision, language, and memory. Other neural systems include the basal ganglia, which regulate movement; the limbic system, which controls emotional behaviors; and the cerebellum, which aids motor control.

7. The brain and spinal cord, surrounded and protected by the meninges, float in cerebrospinal fluid (CSF), which surrounds and infiltrates the brain (via cerebral ventricles).

8. The vascular system of the brain is an elaborate array of blood vessels that deliver nutrients and other substances to the brain. The walls of the blood vessels in the brain provide a barrier to the flow of large, potentially harmful molecules into the brain.

9. Modern imaging techniques make it possible to visualize the anatomy of the living human brain and regional metabolic differences. These techniques include computerized axial tomography (CT), positron emission tomography (PET), magnetic resonance imaging (MRI), functional MRI (fMRI), and infrared optical imaging.

10. In order to process information, neurons arrange themselves into computational ensembles. Neurons make functional contacts with other neurons, or with muscles or glands, at specialized junctions called synapses. Synapses may be made onto dendritic spines, which exhibit neuroplasticity, changing shape in response to experience.

11. At most synapses a chemical transmitter liberated by the presynaptic terminal diffuses across the synaptic cleft and binds to special receptor molecules in the postsynaptic membrane.

12. The axon is generally tubular, branching at the end into many collaterals. Axonal transport is the movement of materials within the axon.

13. Glial cells serve many functions, including the breakdown of transmitters, the production of myelin sheaths around axons, the exchange of nutrients and other materials with neurons, the direct regulation of the interconnections and activity of neurons, and the removal of cellular debris.

Recommended Reading

Blumenfeld, H. (2002). *Neuroanatomy through clinical cases.* Sunderland, MA: Sinauer Associates.

Brodal, P. (2003). *The central nervous system: Structure and function.* New York: Oxford University Press.

Cabeza, R., and Kingstone, A. (2001). *Handbook of functional neuroimaging of cognition.* Cambridge MA: MIT Press.

Carter, R. (2000). *Mapping the mind.* Berkeley, CA: University of California Press.

Duvernoy, H. M., Bourgoin, P., Cabanis, E. A., Cattin, F., et al. (1999). *The human brain: Surface, three-dimensional sectional anatomy with MRI, and blood supply.* Heidelberg, Germany: Springer.

Mai, J. K., Assheuer, J., and Paxinos, G. (1997). *Atlas of the human brain.* San Diego, CA: Academic Press.

Nolte, J. (2002). *The human brain: An introduction to its functional neuroanatomy.* St. Louis MO: Mosby.

Peters, A., Palay, S. L., and Webster, H. D. (1991). *The fine structure of the nervous system: Neurons and their supporting cells.* Oxford, England: Oxford University Press.

Posner, M. I., and Raichle, M. E. (1997). *Images of mind.* San Francisco: Freeman.

Woolsey, T. A., Hanaway, J., and Gado, M. H. (2002). *The brain atlas: A visual guide to the human central nervous system.* Bethesda, MD: Fitzgerald Science.

3

Neurophysiology: Conduction, Transmission, and the Integration of Neural Signals

Finding an Answer in a Heartbeat

In the early twentieth century, debate raged over the basic nature of neural communication. The discovery that individual nerve cells contacted each other at thousands of points was fresh knowledge. What happened at these synapses? Did an electrical current pass between the cells? Might information instead be encoded in a mysterious substance, wafting across the synapse from one cell to the other? A definitive answer to these questions seemed beyond the reach of the available technology.

A solution came to Otto Loewi in a dream, one night in 1921—a simple experiment that would definitively discriminate between the two candidate modes of transmission: chemical versus electrical. In excitement, Loewi sat up in bed and scribbled a few notes on a tiny slip of paper, but in the morning he was disappointed to find the notes indecipherable. When the dream came

again at 3:00 AM the following night, Loewi just got up and went straight to the lab, where he performed the experiment while it was still fresh in his mind.

An eminent pharmacologist and anatomist, Loewi had recently been studying cardiac function in frogs. So he electrically stimulated the vagus nerve of a frog, which he knew would decrease its heart rate, and collected a sample of the fluid that bathed the frog's heart. Then he bathed a second frog's heart with the sample from the first frog. When the second frog's heart also slowed, Loewi knew that he had a solution to the riddle of synaptic transmission. The stimulation of the first heart must have caused the release of a diffusible chemical—what Loewi initially called Vagusstoff (substance from the vagus)—into the fluid. It was a breakthrough for which Loewi would receive a Nobel Prize in 1936.

As you read this page, light stimulates your eye and starts a barrage of signals that race along nerve cells to your brain. As these impulses spread through your cerebral circuitry, larger-scale bursts of neural activity produce the conscious experience of reading. The simultaneous activation of related thoughts and memories stored within your brain produces your unique response to the information that the page contains. In this chapter we delve into the electrochemical properties of neurons that allow them to encode information in the form of neural impulses. We then turn to the transmission of information across synapses, and some of the basic forms of information processing accomplished by ensembles of neurons.

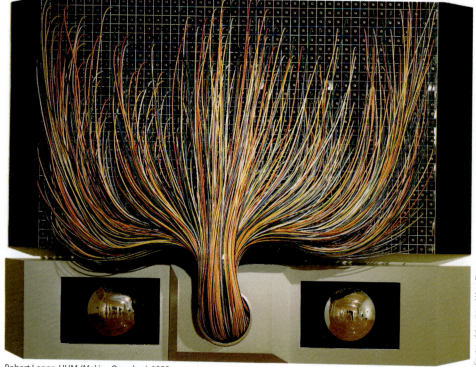

Robert Longo, HUM *(Making Ourselves)*, 1988

Courtesy of the artist and Metro Pictures.

Electrical Signals Are the Vocabulary of the Nervous System

All living cells possess an electrical charge—they are more negative on the inside than on the outside—that is a legacy of their evolutionary origins. The first, single-celled, organisms contained lots of negatively charged proteins, which conferred overall negative polarity. Long ago, nerve cells began to exploit this property to communicate with one another. In this chapter we'll learn how one neuron transmits information to another neuron by producing a local, temporary change in the target neuron's polarity. The target neuron integrates a multitude of these inputs to decide whether to fire its own signal, ultimately altering the polarity of yet other neurons.

This electrical communication system works in much the same way in animals as diverse as human beings, insects, and jellyfish. These neural signals underlie the whole range of thought and action, from composing music or solving a mathematical problem to feeling an itch on the skin and swatting a mosquito. To understand this system, we'll first review the physical forces at work, then discuss some details of why nerve cells are electrically polarized, how one neuron influences the polarity of others, and how a change of polarity in one part of a neuron can spread throughout that cell.

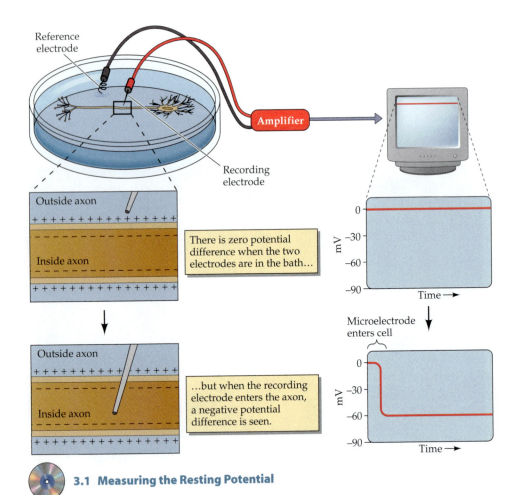

Reference electrode

Recording electrode

Amplifier

Outside axon
+ + + + + + + + + + + + + + + +
- - - - - - - - - - - - - - - -

Inside axon

- - - - - - - - - - - - - - - -
+ + + + + + + + + + + + + + + +

There is zero potential difference when the two electrodes are in the bath...

Outside axon
+ + + + + + + + + + + + + +
- - - - - - - - - - - - - -

Inside axon
- - - - - - - - - - - - - -
+ + + + + + + + + + + + + + +

...but when the recording electrode enters the axon, a negative potential difference is seen.

0
-30
-60
-90
mV
Time →

Microelectrode enters cell

0
-30
-60
-90
mV
Time →

3.1 Measuring the Resting Potential

A balance of electrochemical forces produces the resting membrane potential of neurons

Let's start by considering a neuron at rest, neither perturbed by other neurons nor producing its own signals. A neuron contains many **anions** (negatively charged ions; an **ion** is a charged molecule dissolved in fluid), especially large protein anions that cannot exit the cell. It contains relatively fewer **cations** (positively charged ions). All of these ions are dissolved in an **intracellular fluid,** which is separated from the **extracellular fluid** by a **cell membrane.**

If we insert a fine glass **microelectrode** into the interior of a neuron, and use an instrument to compare it with an electrode located in the extracellular fluid (as illustrated in Figure 3.1), we find that the neuron is more negative on the inside than on the outside. Specifically, a neuron at rest exhibits a characteristic **resting membrane potential** (an electrical-potential difference across the membrane) of about −50 to −80 thousandths of a volt (−50 to −80 **millivolts [mV];** the negative sign indicates the **negative polarity** of the cell's interior).

To fully understand the basis of this membrane potential, we have to consider some special properties of the cell membrane, and two forces that act to drive ions across it.

Cell membranes are made up of a **lipid bilayer**—two layers of linked fatty molecules (see Figure 3.4)—within which many sorts of specialized proteins "float." One important type of membrane-spanning protein is the **ion channel,** a tubelike pore that allows ions of a specific type to pass through the membrane. As we'll see later, some types of ion channels are **gated** and can open and close rapidly in response to changes in voltage, to the presence of certain chemicals, or to mechanical deflection of the cell membrane. But some ion channels stay open all the time, and the cell membrane of a neuron contains many such channels that selectively allow only potassium (K^+) ions to cross the membrane. Because it is studded with these K^+ channels, we say that the cell membrane of a neuron exhibits **selective permeability** (Figure 3.2a) to potassium; that is, K^+ ions (but not other types of ions) can enter or exit the cell fairly freely, unimpeded by the cell membrane.

The resting potential of the neuron reflects a balancing act between two opposing forces that drive ions in and out of the neuron. The first of these is the **concentration gradient** (Figure 3.2b), which is the force that causes molecules of a substance to diffuse from regions of high concentration to regions of low concentration. If a drop of food coloring is placed in a glass of water, the molecules of dye move from the drop, where they are highly concentrated, to the rest of the glass, where they are

(a) Diffusion through semipermeable membranes

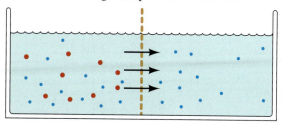

Certain membranes, including those found in cells, permit some substances to pass through, but not others.

(b) Diffusion

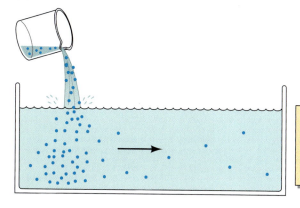

Particles move from areas of high concentration to areas of low concentration. That is, they move down their concentration gradient.

(c) Electrostatic forces

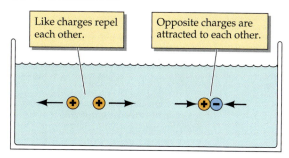

Like charges repel each other.

Opposite charges are attracted to each other.

less concentrated. In other words, molecules tend to move down their concentration gradient until they are evenly distributed.

The second force at work is **electrostatic pressure** (Figure 3.2c), which arises from the distribution of electrical charges rather than the distribution of molecules. Charged particles exert electrical force on one another: Like charges repel, and opposite charges attract. Positively charged cations are thus attracted to the negatively charged interior of the cell; and conversely, anions are repelled by the cell interior and so tend to exit to the extracellular fluid.

Let's consider the situation across a neuron's cell membrane (recall that at rest it is selectively permeable to K^+). Electrostatic pressure tends to pull positively charged K^+ ions into the neuron's negatively charged interior. As a result, however, the concentration of K^+ ions on the inside of the cell steadily increases relative to the outside, and thus the concentration gradient for K^+ increasingly pushes K^+ ions *out* of the cell. Eventually the opposing forces exerted by the K^+ concentration gradient and by electrostatic pressure reach **equilibrium**, exactly balancing each other: Any

3.3 The Ionic Basis of the Resting Potential

(a) Membrane permeability to ions

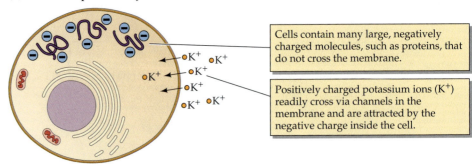

Cells contain many large, negatively charged molecules, such as proteins, that do not cross the membrane.

Positively charged potassium ions (K^+) readily cross via channels in the membrane and are attracted by the negative charge inside the cell.

Equilibrium potential

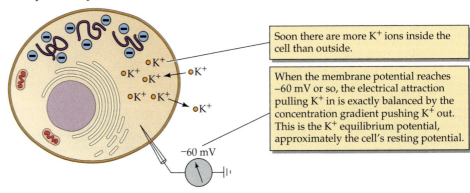

Soon there are more K^+ ions inside the cell than outside.

When the membrane potential reaches −60 mV or so, the electrical attraction pulling K^+ in is exactly balanced by the concentration gradient pushing K^+ out. This is the K^+ equilibrium potential, approximately the cell's resting potential.

−60 mV

(b) The sodium–potassium pump

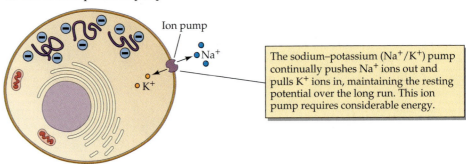

Ion pump

Na^+

The sodium–potassium (Na^+/K^+) pump continually pushes Na^+ ions out and pulls K^+ ions in, maintaining the resting potential over the long run. This ion pump requires considerable energy.

K^+

further movement of K^+ ions into the cell is perfectly matched by the flow of K^+ ions out of the cell. This point corresponds to the cell's resting membrane potential of about −60 mV (values may range between −50 and −80 mV). Figure 3.3a depicts this process.

The **Nernst equation** is a mathematical function describing the voltage that develops when a semipermeable membrane separates different concentrations of ions. The equation's prediction of the resting membrane potential of neurons is *almost* perfect, but it yields a slight overestimation. What is the basis of the discrepancy? The predicted value differs from the observed value because the membrane is not absolutely impermeable to sodium (Na^+) ions. Small numbers of Na^+ ions leak in, drawn to the cell's negatively charged interior.

If left unchecked, this Na^+ leakage would eventually reduce the membrane potential to zero, and the cell would become incapable of generating electrical signals. But the neuron prevents this with a mechanism, the **sodium–potassium pump,** that

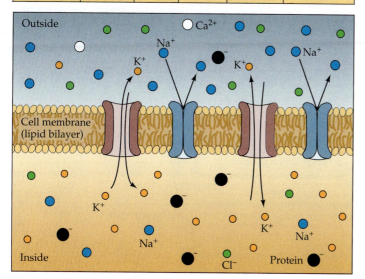

Units of concentration					
	● Na⁺	● K⁺	● Cl⁻	○ Ca²⁺	● Protein
Outside cell	440	20	560	10	few
Inside cell	50	400	40–150	0.0001	many

3.4 The Distribution of Ions Inside and Outside of a Neuron   Most potassium ions (K^+) are found inside the neuron; most sodium (Na^+) and chloride (Cl^-) ions are in the extracellular space. These ions are exchanged through specialized channels in the cell membrane. The large, negatively charged protein molecules stay inside the neuron and account for much of the negative resting potential.

actively pumps Na^+ out of the cell and K^+ in, just rapidly enough to counter the leakage (Figure 3.3*b*). This action consumes energy because the pump is working against both the concentration gradient and electrostatic pressure. In fact, a large fraction of the energy consumed by the brain—whether waking or sleeping—is used to maintain the ionic differences across neuronal membranes. This distribution of ions is illustrated in Figure 3.4. Notice the high intracellular concentration of K^+ and the high extracellular concentration of Na^+.

The resting potential of a neuron provides a baseline level of polarization. What distinguishes neurons from most other cells is that they routinely undergo a brief but radical change in polarization, sending an electrical signal from one end of the neuron to the other, as we'll discuss next.

A threshold amount of depolarization triggers an action potential

Nerve impulses, or **action potentials,** are very brief but large changes in neuronal polarization that arise initially at the axon hillock (the specialized membrane located at the site where the axon emerges from the cell body; see Figure 2.19) and are then propagated rapidly along the axon; neuroscientists often refer to action potentials informally as "spikes" of electrical activity. The information that a neuron sends to its postsynaptic targets is encoded in patterns of these action potentials, so we need to understand their properties—where they come from, how they shoot down the axon, and how they communicate their information across synapses to other cells. Let's turn first to the creation of the action potential.

Two concepts are central to understanding how action potentials are triggered. **Hyperpolarization** is an increase in membrane potential (i.e., the neuron becomes even more negative on the inside, relative to the outside). So if the neuron already has a resting membrane potential, of say, –60 mV, hyperpolarization makes it *even more* negative, maybe –70 mV. **Depolarization** is the reverse, referring to a decrease in membrane potential. The depolarization of a neuron from a resting potential of –60 mV to, say, –50 mV makes the inside of the neuron more like the outside. In

(a)

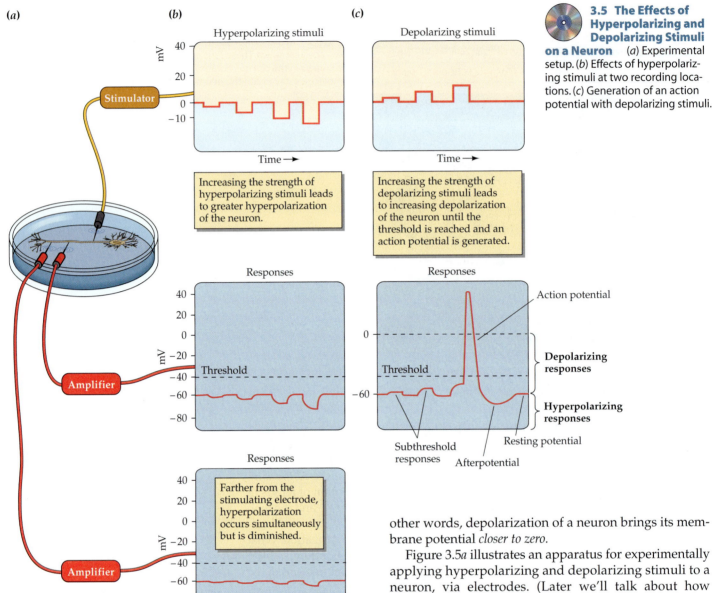

(b)

Hyperpolarizing stimuli

Increasing the strength of hyperpolarizing stimuli leads to greater hyperpolarization of the neuron.

Responses

Threshold

Responses

Farther from the stimulating electrode, hyperpolarization occurs simultaneously but is diminished.

(c)

Depolarizing stimuli

Increasing the strength of depolarizing stimuli leads to increasing depolarization of the neuron until the threshold is reached and an action potential is generated.

Responses

Threshold

Action potential

Depolarizing responses

Hyperpolarizing responses

Subthreshold responses

Afterpotential

Resting potential

3.5 The Effects of Hyperpolarizing and Depolarizing Stimuli on a Neuron (a) Experimental setup. (b) Effects of hyperpolarizing stimuli at two recording locations. (c) Generation of an action potential with depolarizing stimuli.

other words, depolarization of a neuron brings its membrane potential *closer to zero.*

Figure 3.5*a* illustrates an apparatus for experimentally applying hyperpolarizing and depolarizing stimuli to a neuron, via electrodes. (Later we'll talk about how synapses from other neurons produce similar hyperpolarizations and depolarizations.) Applying a *hyperpolarizing* stimulus to the membrane produces an immediate response that passively follows the *shape* of the stimulus pulse (Figure 3.5*b;* the distortions at the beginning and end of the neuron's response are attributable to the membrane's ability to store electricity, known as *capacitance*). The greater the stimulus, the greater the response, so the neuron's change in potential is called a **graded response.**

If we measured the membrane response using a series of electrodes placed at successive distances from the location where the stimulation is applied, we would see another way in which the membrane response seems passive. Like the ripples spreading from a pebble dropped in a pond, the **local potentials** produced by stimulation of the membrane diminish as they spread away from the point of stimulation. A simple law of physics describes this phenomenon: As it spreads across the membrane, the size of a local potential decays as a function of the square of the distance.

Up to a point, the application of *depolarizing* pulses to the membrane follows the same pattern as for hyperpolarizing stimuli, producing local, graded responses.

However, the situation changes suddenly if the stimulus depolarizes the cell to −40 mV or so (the exact value varies slightly among neurons). At this point, known as the **threshold,** a sudden and brief (0.5–2.0 ms) response is provoked: the action potential, or nerve impulse (Figure 3.5*c*). An action potential is a nearly instantaneous reversal of the membrane potential that momentarily makes the inside of the membrane *positive* with respect to the outside. Unlike the passive graded potentials we have been discussing, the action potential is actively propagated (or regenerated) down the axon, through ionic mechanisms that we'll discuss shortly.

Applying strong stimuli to produce depolarizations that far exceed the neuron's threshold reveals another important property of action potentials: Larger depolarizations do not produce larger action potentials. In other words, the size (or *amplitude*) of the action potential is independent of stimulus magnitude. This characteristic is referred to as the **all-or-none property** of the nerve impulse: Either it fires at its full amplitude, or it doesn't fire at all. It turns out that stimulus strength is encoded by changes in the *frequency* of nerve impulses rather than in their *amplitude.* With strong stimuli, more nerve impulses are produced, but the size of each impulse remains the same.

A closer look at the form of the action potential shows that the return to baseline membrane potential is not simple. Many axons exhibit electrical oscillations immediately following the spike; these changes are called **afterpotentials** (see Figure 3.5*c*), and they are also related to ion movements.

Ionic mechanisms underlie the action potential

What events explain the action potential? To answer this question, English neurophysiologists Alan Hodgkin and Andrew Huxley took advantage of the giant axon of the squid, part of a neuron involved in the animal's emergency escape behavior. At more than 500 μm in diameter, the giant axon of the squid is readily apparent to the naked eye, and therefore much better suited to experimentation than mammalian axons, which range in size from 0.5 to 20 μm in diameter. Microelectrodes with tips about 0.2 μm in diameter can be inserted into a giant axon without its properties or activity being altered; it is even possible to push the intracellular fluid out of the squid axon and replace it with other fluids to monitor the effect on the action potential.

**Alan Hodgkin
(1914–1998)**

Experimental evidence revealed that the action potential is created by the movement of sodium ions (Na^+) into the cell, through the membrane (Hodgkin and Katz, 1949). At its peak, the action potential approaches the equilibrium potential for Na^+ as predicted by the Nernst equation: about +40 mV. At this point, the concentration gradient pushing Na^+ ions into the cell is exactly balanced by the positive charge pushing them out. In recognition of these discoveries, Hodgkin and Huxley were awarded a Nobel Prize in 1963.

Andrew Huxley

In its resting state the neural membrane can be thought of as a potassium membrane because it is permeable only to K^+ and the potential is approximately that of the potassium equilibrium potential. In generating the action potential, however, the axonal membrane is a sodium membrane, permeable mainly to Na^+, so the membrane potential briefly tends toward the sodium equilibrium potential. Thus the action potential occurs during a sudden shift in membrane properties, which revert quickly to the resting state. How is this accomplished? The action potential depends on a very special ion channel: the voltage-gated Na^+ channel.

**IMPORTANT
METHOD**

Like other ion channels, the voltage-gated Na^+ channel is a tubular, membrane-spanning protein, but its central Na^+-selective pore is ordinarily closed. When the cell membrane becomes depolarized to threshold levels, however, the channel's shape changes and the Na^+ channel opens. Consider what happens when a patch of axonal

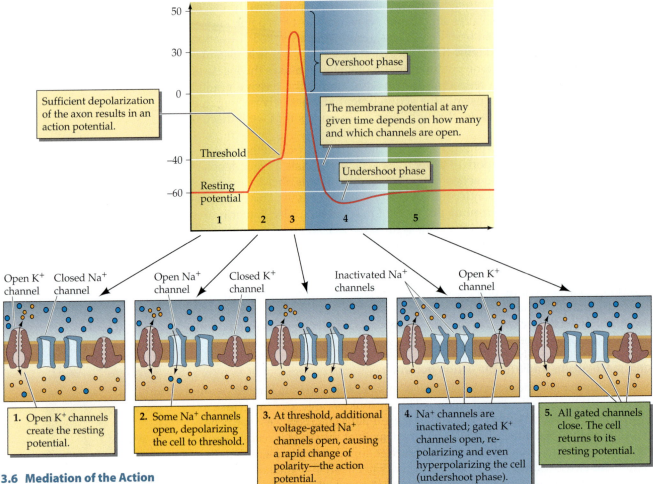

Sufficient depolarization of the axon results in an action potential.

Overshoot phase

The membrane potential at any given time depends on how many and which channels are open.

Threshold

Undershoot phase

Resting potential

Open K⁺ channel   Closed Na⁺ channel

Open Na⁺ channel   Closed K⁺ channel

Inactivated Na⁺ channels

Open K⁺ channel

1. Open K⁺ channels create the resting potential.

2. Some Na⁺ channels open, depolarizing the cell to threshold.

3. At threshold, additional voltage-gated Na⁺ channels open, causing a rapid change of polarity—the action potential.

4. Na⁺ channels are inactivated; gated K⁺ channels open, re-polarizing and even hyperpolarizing the cell (undershoot phase).

5. All gated channels close. The cell returns to its resting potential.

3.6 Mediation of the Action Potential by Voltage-Gated Sodium Channels

membrane depolarizes (Figure 3.6). As the depolarization approaches threshold, some of these Na⁺ channels open. As Na⁺ ions start to enter the neuron, the membrane potential is further reduced, causing still more Na⁺ channels to open. Thus the process accelerates until all barriers to the entry of Na⁺ are removed, and Na⁺ ions rush in.

The voltage-gated Na⁺ channels stay open for a little less than a millisecond; then they close again. By this time the membrane potential has reached the sodium equilibrium potential of about +40 mV. Now, positive charges inside the nerve cell tend to push K⁺ ions out, and voltage-gated K⁺ channels open, increasing the permeability to K⁺, so the resting potential is soon restored.

The application of very strong stimuli reveals another important property of axonal membranes. As we offer the beleaguered axon ever-greater stimuli, an upper limit to the frequency of action potentials becomes apparent at about 1200 impulses per second. (Many neurons have even slower maximum rates of response.) Similarly, applying pairs of stimuli that are spaced closer and closer together reveals a related phenomenon: Beyond a certain point, only the first stimulus is able to elicit an action potential. The axonal membrane is said to be **refractory** (unresponsive) to the second stimulus.

Refractoriness has two phases: During the **absolute refractory phase,** a brief period immediately following the production of an action potential, no amount of stimulation can induce another action potential. The absolute phase is followed by a period of reduced sensitivity, the **relative refractory phase,** during which only a very strong stimulation can produce another action potential. The overall length of the refractory phase is what determines a neuron's maximal rate of firing.

The absolute and relative refractory phases can be related to changes in membrane permeability to Na⁺ as well. When the voltage-gated Na⁺ channels have opened completely during the rise of the nerve impulse, further stimulation does not affect the course of events. The Na⁺ channels, having opened during the action potential and then closed again, refuse to open again for a short time. Thus, during the rising and falling phases of an action potential, the neuron is *absolutely* refractory to elicitation of a second impulse. While K⁺ ions are flowing out and the resting potential is being restored, the neuron is *relatively* refractory, partly because some Na⁺ channels are still refractory, and partly because the cell is slightly hyperpolarized and therefore farther from threshold.

This tiny protein molecule, the voltage-gated Na⁺ channel, is really a quite complicated machine. It monitors the axon's polarity, and at threshold the channel changes its shape to open the pore. But the channel also has a timing device that shuts the pore about a millisecond later. Finally, the channel somehow "remembers" that it was open lately and refuses to open again for a short time. These properties produce and enforce the properties of the action potential.

In general, the transmission of action potentials is limited to axons. Because of the kinds of membrane channels they contain, cell bodies and most dendrites do not conduct action potentials. The cell body and dendrites have ion channels that are gated by certain chemicals, and they can therefore be stimulated chemically, as we'll discuss later in this chapter. But cell bodies and dendrites usually have few voltage-gated Na⁺ channels. For this reason, a change in electrical potential cannot regenerate itself over the surface of the cell body by affecting voltage-gated channels in the adjacent stretch of cell membrane. The same is true for most dendrites, but in an interesting exception to this rule, some dendrites actively propagate a potential to the cell body (Martina et al., 2000). The voltage-gated ion channels of axons are what make them electrically excitable.

How can we study ion channels?

Let's look briefly at present concepts of the structure of ion channels and then consider how investigators have been able to determine these structures. As we mentioned earlier, the cell membrane is made up of fatty molecules, so it tends to repel water. Because ions in water or body fluids are usually surrounded by clusters of water molecules, they cannot easily pass through neuronal membranes.

Recent research has begun to reveal some of the functional details of the channels through which ions must pass, such as K⁺ channels (Berneche and Roux 2001; Morais-Cabral et al., 2001; Zhou et al., 2001). The inner surfaces of the K⁺ channel are lined with oxygen atoms that mimic water molecules. With these oxygen atoms substituting for their usual escort of water molecules, K⁺ ions fit exactly into this *selectivity filter* (Figure 3.7a). Other ions, such as the smaller Na⁺ ions, do not fit as comfortably and thus remain outside, in solution. The end result is a ten-thousandfold selectivity for K⁺ ions and extremely rapid conduction of K⁺ into the cell.

The ion channels in neuronal membranes are too tiny to be seen in detail, even with the electron microscope. How, then, can investigators determine their structures and modes of operation? Several techniques have been used, providing more complete knowledge about ion channels. Molecular genetic analysis of potassium and sodium channels in a variety of cells, including muscle cells and neurons, has yielded a detailed portrait of ion chan-

3.7 Potassium Channels

(a) Passive K⁺ channel

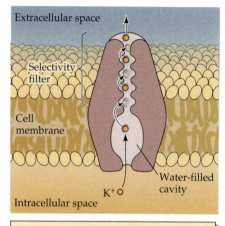

For some passive channels, K⁺ ions enter the water-filled cavity, and can pass through the selectivity filter because oxygen atoms lining the channel are exactly far enough apart to mimic a water-filled environment for K⁺ ions, but not for other smaller ions, such as Na⁺.

(b) Voltage-gated K⁺ channel

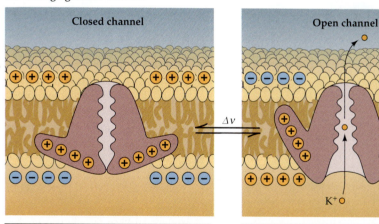

Voltage gated K⁺ channels have positively charged voltage-sensing "paddles," which are normally attracted to the negatively charged interior of the neuron, mechanically closing the channel's gate.

When the membrane depolarizes, the paddles are attracted to negative charges on the outside of the cell, and repelled by the now-positive interior. This movement pops open the channel gate, allowing ions to enter the selectivity filter.

nel structure and function. Some of these studies have come from the scrutiny of abnormalities in sodium and potassium channel function that underlie particular human diseases. For example, some heritable muscle disorders characterized by loss of muscle tone or paralysis involve abnormalities in the sodium channels of muscle (S. C. Cannon, 1996). These studies reveal that multiple genes encode the structure and function of ion channel proteins. Other studies make use of pharmacology, patch clamp techniques, or X-ray crystallography, which we will describe next.

X-ray crystallography   In this technique, billions of copies of a protein molecule are induced to crystallize, and X-rays are bounced off the resulting structure. The identity and location of the atoms that make up the protein can be inferred from the pattern of reflection, and through mathematical modeling, the overall configuration of the protein can be reconstructed. In addition to establishing how K$^+$ channels selectively admit K$^+$ ions at high rates (described earlier), Rod MacKinnon and his collaborators have used this technique to make breakthrough discoveries about the gating mechanisms of voltage-gated K$^+$ channels (Jiang et al., 2003).

Apparently, K$^+$ channels employ electrically charged "paddles," located within the lipid bilayer of the cell membrane, that act as voltage sensors. Attracted to membrane charges, these paddles mechanically pop open the ion channel when the membrane potential changes appropriately (see Figure 3.7b). Because these channels belong to a large and diverse family, it is likely that similar mechanisms will be described for other varieties of voltage-gated channels. MacKinnon's work was recognized with the 2003 Nobel Prize in Chemistry.

Pharmacological techniques   In pharmacological experiments, certain toxins are used to block specific ion channels—some affecting the outer end of the channel, and others inhibiting the inner end. By specifically blocking only some channels, these toxins provide information about those channels, as well as about the remaining, unblocked channels.

Two animal toxins are known to block sodium channels when applied to the outer surface of the membrane; they do not affect other kinds of channels. These toxins are **tetrodotoxin** (**TTX**) and **saxitoxin** (**STX**). The size and structure of TTX and STX, together with those of other molecules that do or do not alter Na$^+$ permeability, indicate the dimensions of the sodium channel. Tetrodotoxin is found in the ovaries of the puffer fish, which is esteemed as a delicacy in Japan. If the ovaries of the puffer fish are not removed properly and if the fish is not cleaned with great care, people who eat it may be poisoned by TTX, which prevents their neurons from producing action potentials. Two kinds of scorpions have also evolved venoms that block the sodium channel.

Patch clamp recordings   In the patch clamp technique, a small patch of membrane is sealed by suction to the end of a micropipette, enabling investigators to record currents through single ion channels (Figure 3.8). Erwin Neher and Bert Sakmann were awarded the 1991 Nobel Prize in Physiology or Medicine for devising this technique. Patch clamp recordings have been made not only in nerve cells but also in glial cells and mus-

3.8 Patch Clamp Recording from a Single Ion Channel

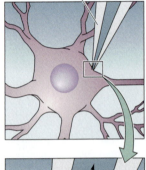

Patch-clamping pipette

A recording pipette filled with an electricity-conducting solution is placed in contact with a neuron's membrane.

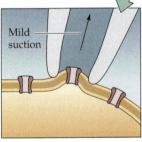

Mild suction

Slight suction clamps a patch of the membrane to the pipette tip.

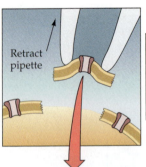

Retract pipette

Retracting the pipette removes the membrane patch, often with one or more ion channels in it; the opening and closing of ion channels can be recorded electrically through the pipette.

Closed

200 ms

Flow of electrical current as ion channel opens

cle cells. The recordings show that gated channels open abruptly and remain open only briefly (see Figure 3.8, bottom).

Opening of some channels is made more likely by changes in voltage; one example is the voltage-activated Na^+ channel that is responsible for the rising phase of the nerve impulse. This type of channel responds extremely rapidly. Another major family of gated channels respond to chemical substances applied to the surface of the cell; their responses are slower than those of the voltage-gated channels. Examples of these chemically gated channels will be given a little later in this chapter, when we discuss what happens at synapses.

Erwin Neher (*left*)
Bert Sakmann (*right*)

Nerve impulses are actively propagated along the axon

We have explored the characteristics of an action potential and the voltage-gated channels that mediate it. Now we can ask how the action potential spreads down the length of the axon. To examine this process, we place recording electrodes at several points along the axon (Figure 3.9). The nerve impulse is initiated at one end of the axon, and recordings are made with electrodes placed along the length of the axon. These recordings show that the nerve impulse travels along the length of the axon. The nerve impulse initiated at one location on the axon spreads in a sort of chain reaction along the length, traveling at speeds that range from less than 1 meter per second (m/s) in some fibers to more than 100 m/s in others.

How does the nerve impulse travel? It is important to understand that the action potential is *regenerated* at successive locations along the length of the axon. It spreads

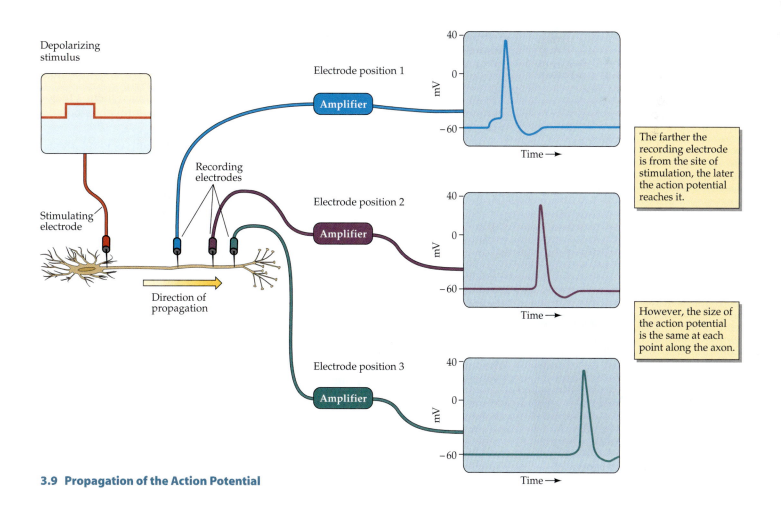

3.9 Propagation of the Action Potential

from one region to another because the flow of current associated with the action potential depolarizes, and thus stimulates, adjacent axon segments. An analogy is the spread of fire along a row of closely spaced match heads. When one match is lit, the heat associated with its flame can be hot enough to start fire in an adjacent match and so on along the row. Voltage-gated Na^+ channels open when the axon is depolarized to threshold. In turn, the influx of Na^+ ions—the movement into the cell of positive charges—depolarizes the adjacent segment of axonal membrane and therefore opens new gates for the movement of Na^+ ions.

The axon normally conducts impulses in only one direction because the action potential starts at the axon hillock. Here voltage-gated Na^+ channels span the membrane, and as the action potential progresses along the axon, it leaves in its wake a stretch of refractory membrane (Figure 3.10a). Propagated activity does not spread from the hillock back over the cell body and dendrites, because the membrane there does not possess voltage-gated Na^+ channels, so it does not produce a regenerated impulse.

If we record the speed of action potentials along axons that differ in diameter, we see that **conduction velocity** varies with the diameter of the axon. Larger axons allow the depolarization to spread faster through the interior. In mammals, relatively large, heavily myelinated fibers are found in sensory and motor nerves. In these neurons, conduction velocity ranges from about 5 m/s for axons that are 2 μm in diameter to 120 m/s for axons that are 20 μm in diameter. Although not as fast as the speed of light, as it was once believed to be, neural conduction is nevertheless very fast: up to about one-third the speed of sound in air. This relatively high rate of conduction ensures rapid sensory and motor processing.

EVOLUTION AT WORK

The myelin sheathing on larger mammalian nerve fibers greatly speeds conduction. As we described in Chapter 2, the myelin sheath is interrupted by **nodes of Ranvier,** small gaps spaced about every millimeter along the axon (see Figure 2.20). Because the myelin insulation offers considerable resistance to the flow of ionic currents across the membrane, the impulse jumps from node to node. This process is called **saltatory conduction** (from the Latin *saltare,* "to leap or jump") (Figure 3.10b). The evolution of rapid saltatory conduction in vertebrates has given them a major behavioral advantage over invertebrates, in which axons are unmyelinated and mostly small in diameter, and thus slower in conduction.

One exception to this rule is that many invertebrates have a few giant axons, which mediate essential motor responses, such as escape behavior. In the invertebrate, as in the vertebrate, conduction velocity increases with axon diameter. The giant axon of the squid has an unusually high rate of conduction for an invertebrate, but the rate still is only about 20 m/s, about the rate of small myelinated axons only 5 μm in diameter.

To conduct impulses as fast as a myelinated vertebrate axon does, an unmyelinated invertebrate axon would have to be 100 times larger in volume. It has been estimated that at least 10% of the volume of the human brain is occupied by myelinated axons. To maintain the conduction velocity of our cerebral neurons without the help of myelin, our brains would have to be ten times as large as they are. This helps explain why myelination is an important index of maturation of the developing nervous system (see Chapter 7).

The function of synapses is to cause local changes in the postsynaptic membrane potential

At the beginning of the chapter, we related the tale of Otto Loewi's discovery of chemical signaling between neurons. Through painstaking experimentation, Loewi eventually proved that the chemical inhibiting the heart (which he called *Vagusstoff*) was actually acetylcholine. Acetylcholine was thus the first demonstrated **neurotransmitter** (or **transmitter**), a chemical released by a neuron to affect a postsynaptic cell. We will discuss transmitters later in this chapter and in Chapter 4. Although

Otto Loewi (1873–1961)

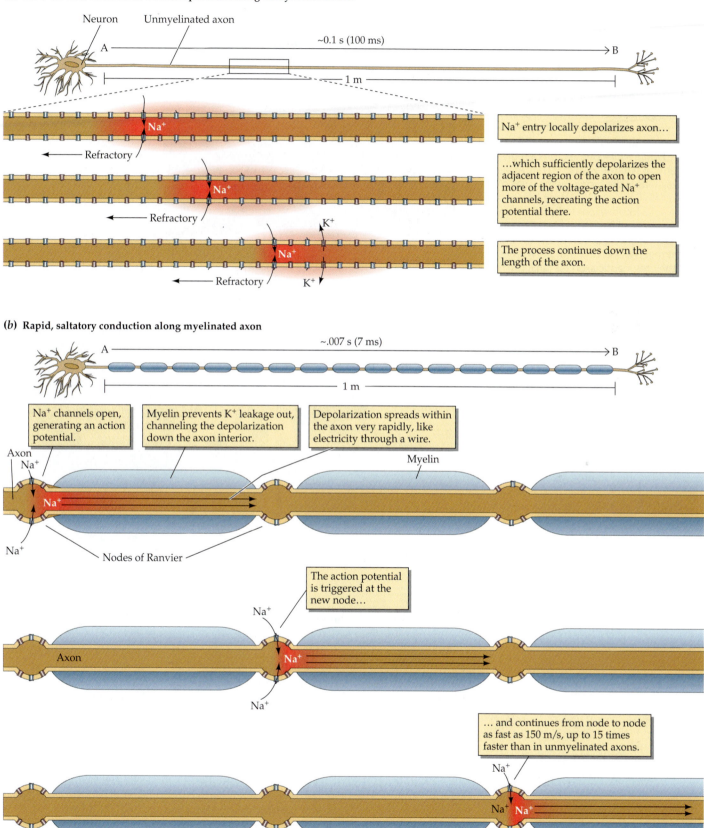

(*a*) **Slow (10 m/s) conduction of action potential along unmyelinated axon**

Neuron   Unmyelinated axon

A   ~0.1 s (100 ms)   → B

1 m

Na⁺

Na⁺ entry locally depolarizes axon…

← Refractory

Na⁺

…which sufficiently depolarizes the adjacent region of the axon to open more of the voltage-gated Na⁺ channels, recreating the action potential there.

← Refractory

K⁺

Na⁺   K⁺

The process continues down the length of the axon.

← Refractory   K⁺

(*b*) **Rapid, saltatory conduction along myelinated axon**

A   ~.007 s (7 ms)   → B

1 m

Na⁺ channels open, generating an action potential.

Myelin prevents K⁺ leakage out, channeling the depolarization down the axon interior.

Depolarization spreads within the axon very rapidly, like electricity through a wire.

Axon
Na⁺   Myelin

Na⁺

Na⁺   Nodes of Ranvier

The action potential is triggered at the new node…

Na⁺

Axon   Na⁺

Na⁺

… and continues from node to node as fast as 150 m/s, up to 15 times faster than in unmyelinated axons.

Na⁺

Na⁺   Na⁺

3.10 Conduction along Unmyelinated versus Myelinated Axons

BOX 3.1   Electrical Synapses Work with No Time Delay

Although most synapses require a chemical substance to mediate synaptic transmission, electrical synapses are also widespread in the brain (M. V. Bennett, 2000). At **electrical synapses** the presynaptic membrane comes even closer to the postsynaptic membrane than it does at chemical synapses; the gap measures only 2 to 4 nm (see Figure A). In contrast, the cleft of a chemical synapse is 20 to 40 nm. At electrical synapses, the facing membranes of the two cells have relatively large channels arranged to allow ions to flow from one neuron directly into the other (Figure B). As a consequence, the flow of electrical current that is associated with nerve impulses in the presynaptic axon terminal can travel across the presynaptic and the postsynaptic membranes.

Transmission at these synapses closely resembles conduction along the axon. Electrical synapses therefore work with practically no time delay, in contrast to chemical synapses, where the delay is on the order of a millisecond—slow in terms of neurons. Because of the speed of their transmission, electrical synapses are frequently found in neural circuits that mediate escape behaviors in invertebrates. They are also found where many fibers must be activated synchronously, as in the vertebrate oculomotor system, and they are found in mammalian isocortex (Gibson et al., 1999); clinically, it is suspected that electrical synapses contribute to the spread of synchronized seizure discharges in epilepsy (Szente et al., 2002). (Figure A courtesy of Constantino Sotelo.)

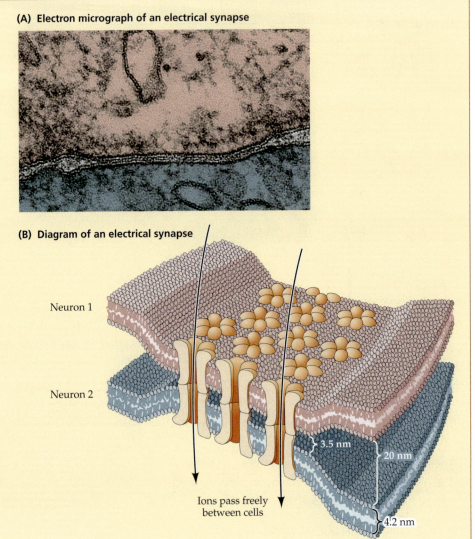

(A) Electron micrograph of an electrical synapse

(B) Diagram of an electrical synapse

Neuron 1

Neuron 2

3.5 nm

20 nm

4.2 nm

Ions pass freely between cells

most synapses use a chemical signal such as acetylcholine, eventually it was found that the nervous system also employs electrical synapses (Box 3.1).

What all neurotransmitters have in common is that they briefly alter the resting potential of the postsynaptic cell. We call these brief changes **postsynaptic potentials.** A given neuron, receiving synapses from hundreds of other cells, is subject to hundreds of postsynaptic potentials. When integrated, these hundreds of local potentials determine whether this neuron will reach threshold and therefore generate an action potential.

We can study postsynaptic potentials with a setup like that shown in Figure 3.11. This setup allows us to compare the effects of activity of excitatory (red) versus inhibitory (blue) presynaptic cells on the local membrane potential of a postsynaptic cell (in yellow). The responses of the presynaptic and postsynaptic cells are shown on the same graphs in Figure 3.11 for easy comparison of their time relations. It is important to remember that excitatory and inhibitory neurons get their names from their actions on postsynaptic neurons, not from their effects on behavior.

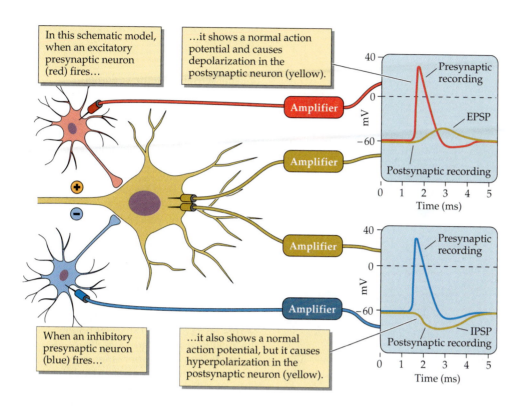

In this schematic model, when an excitatory presynaptic neuron (red) fires…

…it shows a normal action potential and causes depolarization in the postsynaptic neuron (yellow).

When an inhibitory presynaptic neuron (blue) fires…

…it also shows a normal action potential, but it causes hyperpolarization in the postsynaptic neuron (yellow).

Stimulation of an excitatory presynaptic neuron first leads to an all-or-none action potential in the presynaptic cell. In the postsynaptic cell, after a brief synaptic delay, a small local depolarization is seen. This postsynaptic membrane depolarization is known as an **excitatory postsynaptic potential** (**EPSP**) because it pushes the postsynaptic cell a little closer to the threshold for an action potential.

Generally the combined effect of many excitatory synapses is required to elicit an action potential in a postsynaptic neuron. If EPSPs are elicited almost simultaneously by many neurons that converge on the postsynaptic cell, these potentials can sum and produce a depolarization large enough to reach threshold and trigger an action potential. Note that there is a delay: In the fastest cases, the postsynaptic depolarization begins about half a millisecond after the presynaptic impulses arrive at the axon terminals. This delay reflects the time needed for the release of neurotransmitter and its diffusion across the synaptic cleft, as we'll discuss later.

The action potential of an inhibitory presynaptic neuron looks exactly like that of the excitatory presynaptic neuron; all neurons use the same kind of propagated signal (see Figure 3.11). But the effect mediated on the *postsynaptic* side is quite different. When the inhibitory neuron is stimulated, the postsynaptic effect is an *increase* of the resting membrane potential. This hyperpolarization moves the cell membrane potential away from threshold—it *decreases* the probability that the neuron will fire an impulse—so it is called an **inhibitory postsynaptic potential** (**IPSP**).

Usually IPSPs result from the opening of channels that permit chloride (Cl⁻) ions to enter the cell. Because Cl⁻ ions are much more concentrated outside the cell than inside (see Figure 3.4), they are driven inside the cell, making it even more negative. Although in this discussion we have been paying more attention to excitation, inhibition also plays a vital role in neural processing of information. Just as driving a car requires brakes as well as an accelerator, neural switches must be turned off as well as on. The nervous system treads a narrow path between overexcitation, which leads to seizures (Box 3.2), and underexcitation which leads to coma and death.

BOX 3.2   Seizure Disorders

Epilepsy (from the Greek *epilepsia,* a form of the verb meaning "to seize") has provoked wonder and worry since the dawn of civilization. Through the ages the seizures that accompany this disease have spawned much speculation about the cause—from demons to gods. About 30 million people, worldwide, suffer from epilepsy.

Seizures are an unfortunate manifestation of the electrical character of the nervous system. Because of the extensive connections among its nerve cells, the brain can generate massive waves of intense nerve cell activity that seem to involve almost the entire brain. A **seizure** is the synchronized excitation of large groups of nerve cells, evident in EEGs as an abnormal pattern of brain activity. Many abnormalities of the brain, such as trauma, injury, or metabolic problems, can predispose brain tissue to produce synchronized *epileptiform* activity, which can easily spread. Some heritable forms of epilepsy seem to be caused by mutations in ion channels (McNamara, 1999).

There are several major categories of seizure disorders. Generalized seizures are characterized by loss of consciousness and symmetrical involvement of body musculature. In **grand mal seizures,** abnormal EEG activity is evident all over the brain (Figure A). The person loses consciousness and makes characteristic movements: an enduring *tonic* contraction of the muscles for 1 or 2 minutes, followed by jerky, rhythmic *clonic* contractions and relaxations. Minutes or hours of confusion and sleep follow the seizure.

Petit mal seizures are a more subtle variant of generalized seizures, in which characteristic "spike-and-wave" EEG activity is evident for 5 to 15 s at a time (Figure B), sometimes occurring many times per

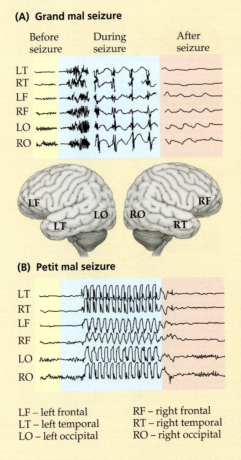

(A) Grand mal seizure

	Before seizure	During seizure	After seizure
LT			
RT			
LF			
RF			
LO			
RO			

(B) Petit mal seizure

LT		
RT		
LF		
RF		
LO		
RO		

LF – left frontal   RF – right frontal
LT – left temporal   RT – right temporal
LO – left occipital   RO – right occipital

day. During these periods the person is unaware of the environment, and later the person cannot recall events that occurred during the petit mal episode. Behaviorally, the person does not show unusual muscle activity, except for a cessation of ongoing activity and sustained staring.

Complex partial seizures do not involve the entire brain and thus can produce a wide variety of symptoms, often preceded by an unusual sensation or **aura.** In one example, a woman felt an unusual sensation in the abdomen, a sense of foreboding, and tingling in both hands before the seizure spread. At the height of it, she was unresponsive and rocked her body back and forth while speaking nonsensically, twisting her left arm, and looking toward the right. Figure C is a three-dimensional reconstruction showing where the seizures occurred in her brain. In some individuals, complex partial seizures may be provoked by environmental stimuli and may produce strikingly abnormal behavior.

Seizures affect nonhuman animals, too, and such cases are studied as a model of human epilepsy. In **kindling** (McNamara, 1984), animals receive repeated electrical stimulation that is too weak to cause a seizure on its own. Eventually, although the individual stimuli are small, the accumulated effect is that spontaneous seizures appear. In other words, the kindling stimulations somehow change the tissue and make it more epilepsy-prone. Interestingly, after years of epilepsy, some human patients develop multiple foci for the initiation of seizures, perhaps because of a kindling process (Morrell, 1991). (Figure C courtesy of Hal Blumenfeld, Rik Stokking, Susan Spencer, and George Zubal, Yale School of Medicine.)

(C) Complex partial seizure

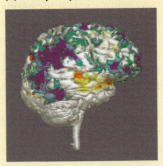

What determines whether a synapse excites or inhibits the postsynaptic cell? One factor is the particular neurotransmitter released by the presynaptic cell. Some transmitters generate an EPSP in the postsynaptic cells; others generate an IPSP. Whether a neuron fires an action potential at any given moment is decided by the relation between the number of excitatory and the number of inhibitory signals it is receiving, and it receives many signals of both types at all times.

Temporal summation and spatial summation integrate synaptic inputs

Synaptic transmission and impulse conduction not only communicate signals, but also integrate and transform messages in ways that make complex behavior possible. This means that the nerve cell, with its myriad synaptic inputs, is able both to add and to subtract input signals. These operations are possible because of the characteristics of synaptic inputs, the way in which the neuron integrates the postsynaptic potentials, and the trigger mechanism that determines whether a neuron will fire an impulse.

As we have seen, the postsynaptic potentials that are caused by transmitter chemicals can be either depolarizing (excitatory) or hyperpolarizing (inhibitory). From their points of origin on the dendrites and cell body, these EPSPs and IPSPs spread passively over the neuron, decreasing in strength over time and distance. Whether the postsynaptic neuron will fire an action potential is determined by whether depolarization sufficient to exceed threshold reaches the axon hillock, the trigger zone in mammalian multipolar neurons.

The conceptual model in Figure 3.12 illustrates the process of information processing by a neuron. For simplicity, no dendrites are shown, and all inputs synapse on the cell body. The presynaptic terminals are represented as simple electrical contacts through which excitatory (depolarizing) or inhibitory (hyperpolarizing) current may be applied to the postsynaptic cell membrane. The axon hillock contains a voltmeter; if the membrane potential rises (depolarizes) above a threshold level, an action potential is fired.

Suppose that two excitatory endings are activated, as shown in Figure 3.12a, causing local depolarizations (in red) of the cell body. These depolarizations spread out over the neuron, dissipating as they spread, so that only a small proportion of the original depolarization reaches the axon hillock. Taken alone, neither would be sufficient to reach threshold depolarization, but when combined, the two depolarizations add together to push the hillock region to threshold.

Figure 3.12b shows what happens when inhibitory synapses also are active, creating postsynaptic hyperpolarizations. These hyperpolarizations also spread passively, dissipating as they travel. Because some potentials excite and others inhibit the hillock, these effects partially cancel each other. Thus the net effect is the difference between the two: The neuron subtracts the IPSPs from the EPSPs.

The observation that the EPSPs produced by two excitatory terminals sum to yield a greater depolarization than either would produce by itself—and the related observation that simultaneous IPSPs sum to an extra-large hyperpolarization—suggests a further refinement. When summed, EPSPs and IPSPs tend to cancel each other out. This summation of potentials originating from different physical locations across the cell body is called **spatial summation.** Only if the overall sum of *all* the potentials—both EPSPs and IPSPs—is sufficient to depolarize the cell to threshold at the axon hillock, is an action potential triggered (Figure 3.12c). Usually the convergence of excitatory messages from many presynaptic fibers (and not a lot of inhibitory inputs) is required for a neuron to fire an action potential.

Postsynaptic effects that are not absolutely simultaneous can also be summed, because the postsynaptic potentials last a few milliseconds before fading away. The closer they are in time, the greater is the overlap and the more complete is the summation, which in this case is called **temporal summation.** Temporal summation is easily understood if you imagine a neuron with only one input. If EPSPs arrive one right after the other, they sum and the postsynaptic cell eventually reaches threshold and produces an action potential.

It should now be clear that, although nerve impulses are all-or-none phenomena, the overall postsynaptic effect is graded in size and determined by the processing of numerous inputs occurring close together in time. The membrane potential at the axon hillock thus reflects the moment-to-moment integration of all of its inputs, which the hillock encodes into an ongoing pattern of action potentials.

Dendrites have been omitted from Figure 3.12 for simplicity, but they add to the story. In reality, a vast number of synaptic inputs, arrayed across the dendrites and cell body, can induce postsynaptic potentials. Dendrites therefore augment the receptive surface of the neuron and increase the amount of input information the neuron can handle. All other things being equal, the farther out on a dendrite that a potential is produced, the less effect the potential should have at the axon hillock,

(*a*) **Excitatory inputs cause the cell to fire**

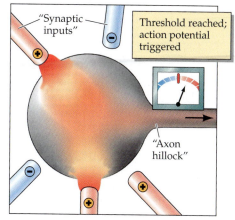

"Synaptic inputs"

Threshold reached; action potential triggered

"Axon hillock"

(*b*) **Inhibition also plays a role**

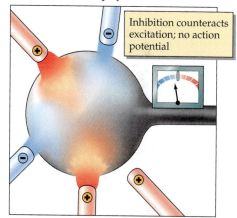

Inhibition counteracts excitation; no action potential

(*c*) **The cell integrates excitation and inhibition**

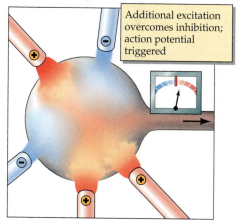

Additional excitation overcomes inhibition; action potential triggered

3.12 A Physical Model of Spatial Summation in a Postsynaptic Cell

TABLE 3.1 *Characteristics of Electrical Signals of Nerve Cells*

Type of signal	Signaling role	Typical duration (ms)	Amplitude	Character	Mode of propagation	Ion channel opening	Channel sensitive to:
Action potential (neural impulse)	Conduction along a neuron	1–2	Overshooting, 100 mV	All-or-none, digital	Actively propagated, regenerative	First Na^+, then K^+, in different channels	Voltage (depolarization)
Excitatory postsynaptic potential (EPSP)	Transmission between neurons	10–100	Depolarizing, from less than 1 to more than 20 mV	Graded, analog	Local, passive spread	Na^+–K^+	Chemical (neurotransmitter)
Inhibitory postsynaptic potential (IPSP)	Transmission between neurons	10–100	Hyperpolarizing, from less than 1 to about 15 mV	Graded, analog	Local, passive spread	K^+–Cl^-	Chemical (neurotransmitter)

because the potential decreases in amplitude (i.e., strength) as it passively spreads. When the potential arises at a dendritic spine, its effect is further reduced because it has to spread down the shaft of the spine. Thus, information arriving at various parts of the neuron is weighted in terms of the distance and path resistance to the axon hillock.

Interestingly, recent research has revealed that in some types of neurons (but not all), synapses that are distant from the axon hillock compensate by producing larger local potentials. The effect is that the synaptic inputs to the cell are normalized; distant synapses can have as much effect at the axon hillock as nearer synapses. Furthermore, some neurons have *dendritic* integration zones, featuring voltage-gated ion channels, that serve to sum and amplify local postsynaptic potentials, increasing their eventual impact at the axon hillock (S. R. Williams and Stuart, 2003).

Finally, glial cells also play a role in synaptic transmission: They increase the strength of the postsynaptic potential (Pfrieger and Barres, 1997), overlying the presynaptic terminal and thereby preventing neurotransmitter leakage out of the synaptic cleft.

Table 3.1 summarizes the many properties of action potentials and synaptic potentials, noting the principal similarities and differences among the three kinds of neural potentials.

The Sequence of Transmission Processes at Chemical Synapses

The sequence of events during chemical synaptic transmission, shown in Figure 3.13, includes the following main steps:

1. The action potential is propagated into the presynaptic axon terminal.
2. Voltage-gated calcium channels in the axon terminal open, and calcium (Ca^{2+}) ions enter the axon terminal.
3. Calcium causes synaptic vesicles, filled with neurotransmitter, to fuse with the presynaptic membrane and burst, releasing the transmitter molecules into the synaptic cleft.
4. Some transmitter molecules bind to special receptor molecules in the postsynaptic membrane, leading—directly or indirectly—to the opening of ion channels in the postsynaptic membrane. The resulting flow of ions creates a local EPSP or IPSP in the postsynaptic neuron.
5. The IPSPs and EPSPs in the postsynaptic cell spread toward the axon hillock. If the depolarization there is sufficient to reach threshold, the neuron will fire an action potential.

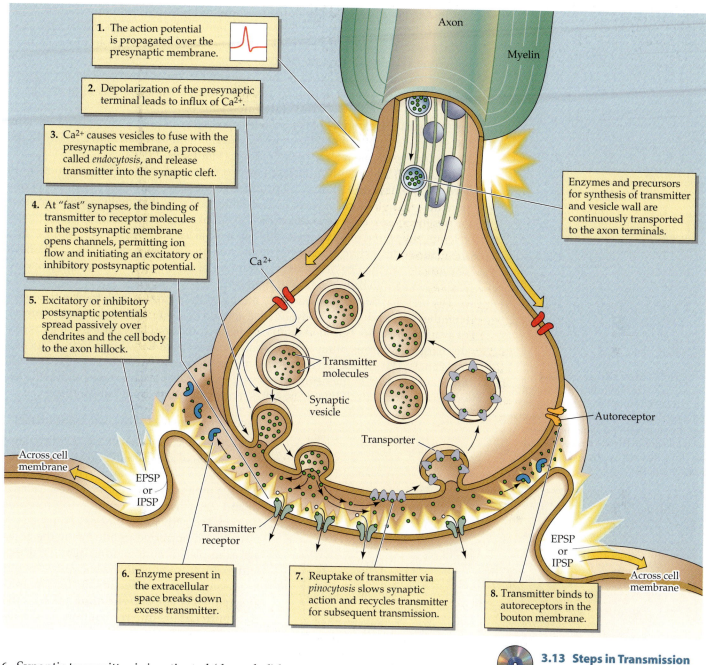

1. The action potential is propagated over the presynaptic membrane.

2. Depolarization of the presynaptic terminal leads to influx of Ca^{2+}.

3. Ca^{2+} causes vesicles to fuse with the presynaptic membrane, a process called *endocytosis*, and release transmitter into the synaptic cleft.

4. At "fast" synapses, the binding of transmitter to receptor molecules in the postsynaptic membrane opens channels, permitting ion flow and initiating an excitatory or inhibitory postsynaptic potential.

5. Excitatory or inhibitory postsynaptic potentials spread passively over dendrites and the cell body to the axon hillock.

Enzymes and precursors for synthesis of transmitter and vesicle wall are continuously transported to the axon terminals.

Axon

Myelin

Ca^{2+}

Transmitter molecules

Synaptic vesicle

Transporter

Autoreceptor

Across cell membrane

EPSP or IPSP

Transmitter receptor

EPSP or IPSP

Across cell membrane

6. Enzyme present in the extracellular space breaks down excess transmitter.

7. Reuptake of transmitter via *pinocytosis* slows synaptic action and recycles transmitter for subsequent transmission.

8. Transmitter binds to autoreceptors in the bouton membrane.

3.13 Steps in Transmission at a Chemical Synapse

6. Synaptic transmitter is inactivated (degraded) by enzymes, or
7. Synaptic transmitter is removed rapidly from the synaptic cleft by transporters, so the transmission is brief and accurately follows the presynaptic input signal.
8. Synaptic transmitter may also activate presynaptic autoreceptors, resulting in a decrease in transmitter release.

The nerve impulse causes the release of transmitter molecules into the synaptic cleft

When a nerve impulse reaches a presynaptic terminal, how does it cause vesicles near the presynaptic membrane to discharge their contents into the synaptic cleft, where the transmitter molecules quickly diffuse to the receptor molecules on the other side? The arrival of action potentials at the presynaptic terminal causes calcium ions (Ca^{2+}) to enter the terminal. The higher the frequency of action potentials, the greater the influx of Ca^{2+}, and the greater the number of vesicles that discharge their contents into the synapse. If the concentration of Ca^{2+} in the extracellular fluid is reduced, fewer Ca^{2+} ions enter the terminal and less transmitter is released. Most synaptic delay is caused by the time needed for Ca^{2+} to enter the terminal. Diffusion of the transmitter across the cleft, and interaction of transmitter molecules with their receptors, also introduce some delay.

Synaptic vesicles are about 50 nm in diameter, and all the vesicles for a given transmitter in a synapse appear to contain about the same number of molecules of transmitter chemical. The structural components of the synaptic-vesicle membrane are complex; one component is a protein called *synaptotagmin* that can bind calcium. Other vesicle components deal with the mechanism that places the vesicle in the right position for the release of its contents (Matthews, 1996).

Because all the synaptic vesicles in an axon terminal contain the same number of molecules of transmitter, they all produce about the same change in postsynaptic potential when they rupture and release their contents. Normally a nerve impulse causes the release of several hundred vesicles at a time. But if the concentration of calcium is lowered at a synapse, only a few vesicles are released per impulse, and the magnitude of change in postsynaptic potential associated with the contents of one vesicle can then be deduced. The number of molecules of transmitter per vesicle is estimated to be in the tens of thousands.

The presynaptic terminal normally produces and stores enough transmitter to ensure that it is ready for activity. Intense activity of the neuron reduces the number of available vesicles, but soon more vesicles are produced to replace those that were discharged. Neurons differ in their ability to keep pace with a rapid rate of incoming signals. The production of the transmitter chemical is governed by enzymes that are manufactured in the neuronal cell body and transported actively down the axons to the terminals. If they were not, synaptic function could not continue.

3.14 A Nicotinic Acetylcholine Receptor   Each nicotinic ACh receptor consists of five subunits. The two ligand-binding sites normally bind ACh molecules, but they also bind nicotine and other nicotinic drugs. The ACh molecule and Na^+ ions are enlarged here for diagrammatic purposes.

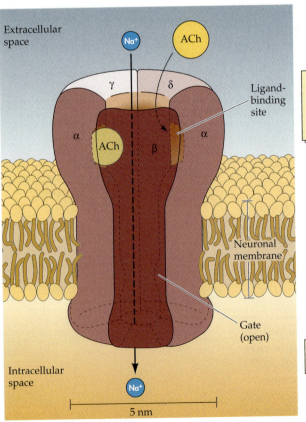

Extracellular space

Na+

ACh

γ

δ

Ligand-binding site

α

α

ACh

β

When ACh molecules occupy both binding sites, the sodium channel opens…

Neuronal membrane

Gate (open)

Intracellular space

Na+

5 nm

…depolarizing the postsynaptic cell.

Receptor molecules recognize transmitters

The action of a key in a lock is a good analogy to the action of a transmitter on a receptor protein. Just as a particular key can open different doors, a molecule of the correct shape, called a **ligand** (see Chapter 4), can fit into a receptor protein and activate or block it. Neurotransmitters and hormones made inside the body are examples of **endogenous ligands;** drugs and toxins from outside the body that are put inside are **exogenous ligands.** So, for example, at synapses where **acetylcholine** (**ACh**) is the transmitter, it fits into recognition sites in **receptor molecules** located in the postsynaptic membrane (Figure 3.14).

The nature of the postsynaptic receptors at a given synapse determines the action of the transmitter (see Chapter 4). For example, ACh can function as either an inhibitory or an excitatory neurotransmitter, at different synapses. At excitatory synapses, binding of ACh opens channels for Na^+ and K^+ ions. At inhibitory synapses, ACh opens channels that allow chloride ions (Cl^-) to enter, thereby increasing the potential across the membrane (hyperpolarizing it).

The lock-and-key analogy is strengthened by the observation that various chemicals can fit onto receptor proteins and block the entrance of the key. Some of the preparations used in this research resemble the ingredients of a witch's brew. Two blocking agents for ACh are poisons: curare and bungaro-toxin. **Curare** is the arrowhead poison used by native South Americans. Extracted from a plant, it greatly increases the efficiency of hunting: If the hunter hits any part of the prey, the arrow's poison soon paralyzes the animal. **Bungarotoxin** is a lethal poison produced by the bungarus snake of Taiwan. This toxin has proved very use-ful in studies of acetylcholine receptors because a radioactive label can be attached to it without its action being altered. With such labeling, it is possible to investigate the number and distribution of receptor molecules at synapses, as well as details of the binding of transmitter to receptors.

Another poison, muscarine, mimics the action of ACh at some synapses. This poi-son is extracted from the mushroom *Amanita muscaria*. Molecules such as muscarine and nicotine that act like a transmitter at a receptor are called **agonists** (from the Greek *agon*, "contest, struggle") of that transmitter. Conversely, molecules that in-terfere with or prevent the action of a transmitter, in such a manner as curare or bun-garotoxin block the action of ACh, are called **antagonists.**

Just as there are master keys that fit many different locks, there are submaster keys that fit a certain group of locks, and keys that fit only a single lock. Similarly, each chemical transmitter binds to several different receptor molecules. ACh acts on at least four kinds of **cholinergic** receptors. Nicotinic and muscarinic are the two main kinds of cholinergic receptors.

Nicotinic cholinergic receptors are found at synapses on skeletal muscles and in autonomic ganglia. Muscarinic cholinergic receptors are found on organs innervated by the parasympathetic division of the autonomic system (e.g., the heart muscle, the intestines, and the salivary gland). Most ACh receptors in the brain, too, are mus-carinic. Most nicotinic sites are excitatory, but there are also inhibitory nicotinic synapses, and there are both excitatory and inhibitory muscarinic synapses, mak-ing at least four kinds of acetylcholine receptors. The existence of many types of re-ceptors for each transmitter agent appears to be an evolved device to provide speci-ficity of transmitter action in the nervous system.

The nicotinic ACh receptor resembles a lopsided dumbbell with a tube running down its central axis (see Figure 3.14). The handle of the dumbbell spans the cell membrane (which is about 6 nm thick); the larger sphere extends about 5 nm above the surface of the membrane into the extracellular space, and the smaller sphere ex-tends about 2 nm into the cell. The sides of the ion channel (the tube that runs through the handle) consist of five protein subunits arranged like staves in a bar-rel. Two subunits are alike and, in conjunction with neighboring subunits, provide two recognition sites for ACh (Karlin, 2002); the other three subunits are all differ-ent. Both ACh-binding sites must be occupied for the channel to open. The genes for each of the four subunits have been isolated (Mishina et al., 1984), and neuro-scientists have been able to assemble complete or incomplete receptors to study how they work.

After the structure of the nicotinic ACh receptor was determined, similar analyses were carried out for other receptors, including receptors for some of the synaptic trans-mitter molecules that we will be considering later, such as GABA (gamma-aminobu-tyric acid), glycine, and glutamate. Several of these receptors resemble each other, sug-gesting that they all belong to the same family and have a common evolutionary origin.

The coordination of different transmitter systems of the brain is incredibly com-plex. Each type of neurotransmitter receptor has a unique pattern of distribution within the brain. Different receptor systems become active at different times in fetal life. The number of any given type of receptor remains plastic in adulthood: Not only are there seasonal variations, but many kinds of receptors show a regular daily variation of 50% or more in number, affecting the sensitivity of cells to that variety of transmitter. Similarly, the numbers of some receptors have been found to vary with the use of drugs (see Chapter 4). In general, an increase in receptor numbers is referred to as **up-regulation,** and a process that decreases receptor density is called **down-regulation** of that receptor type.

NEURAL PLASTICITY

Transmitters bind to receptors, gating ion channels

The recognition of transmitter molecules by receptor molecules may lead to gating of ion channels in two different ways. **Ionotropic receptors** (Figure 3.15*a*) directly control an ion channel. When bound by the transmitter, the ion channel opens and ions flow across the membrane. (Ionotropic receptors are also known as chemically gated or **ligand-gated ion channels.**) **Metabotropic receptors** (Figure 3.15*b*) recognize the synaptic transmitter, but they do not directly control ion channels. Instead they activate molecules known as **G proteins.**

G protein is a convenient designation for proteins that bind the compounds guanosine diphosphate (GDP), guanosine triphosphate (GTP), and other guanine nucleotides. Sometimes the G protein itself acts to open ion channels, but in other cases the G protein activates another, internal chemical signal to affect ion channels. If we think of the transmitter-activated G protein as the first messenger inside the postsynaptic cell, then the next chemical activated within the cell is a **second messenger.** There are several different second messengers, such as cyclic AMP, diacylglycerol, or arachidonic acid, that amplify the effect of the first messenger and can initiate processes that lead to changes in electrical potential at the membrane. Second messengers can also produce longer-lasting biochemical changes within the neuron.

About 80% of the known neurotransmitters and hormones activate cellular signal mechanisms through receptors coupled to G proteins, so this coupling device is very important (Birnbaumer et al., 1990). The G protein is located on the inner side of the neural membrane. When a transmitter molecule binds to a receptor that is coupled to a G protein, parts of the G protein complex separate from each other. One part, called the *alpha subunit,* migrates away within the cell and modulates the activity of its target molecules. Depending on the type of cell and receptor, the target may be a second-messenger system, an enzyme that works on an ion channel, or an ion pump. Many combinations of different receptors with different G proteins have already been identified, and more are being discovered at a rapid pace (Fredriksson et al., 2003; Gudermann et al., 1997).

3.15 Two Types of Chemical Synapses

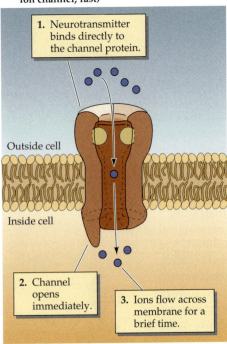

(a) **Ionotropic receptor (ligand-gated ion channel; fast)**

1. Neurotransmitter binds directly to the channel protein.

Outside cell

Inside cell

2. Channel opens immediately.

3. Ions flow across membrane for a brief time.

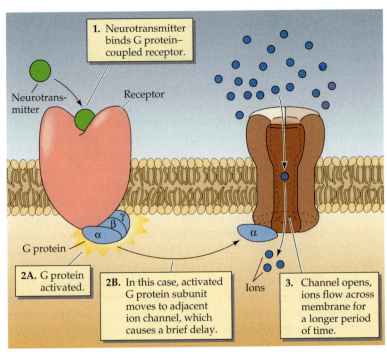

(b) **Metabotropic receptor (G protein–coupled receptor; slow)**

1. Neurotransmitter binds G protein–coupled receptor.

Neurotransmitter

Receptor

G protein

2A. G protein activated.

2B. In this case, activated G protein subunit moves to adjacent ion channel, which causes a brief delay.

Ions

3. Channel opens, ions flow across membrane for a longer period of time.

The action of synaptic transmitters is stopped rapidly

When a chemical transmitter such as ACh is released into the synaptic cleft, its post-synaptic action is not only prompt, but usually very brief as well. This brevity ensures that the message is repeated faithfully. Accurate timing of synaptic transmission is necessary in many neural systems—for example, to drive the rapid cycles of muscle contraction and relaxation essential to many coordinated behaviors.

The prompt cessation of transmitter effects is achieved in one of two ways (see Figure 3.13):

1. Transmitter can be rapidly broken down and thus inactivated by a special enzyme—a process known as **degradation.** For example, the enzyme that inactivates ACh is acetylcholinesterase (AChE). Acetylcholinesterase breaks down ACh very rapidly into choline and acetic acid, and these products are recycled (at least in part) to make more ACh in the end bouton. AChE is found especially at synapses, but also elsewhere in the nervous system. Thus, if any ACh escapes from a synapse where it is released, it is unlikely to reach other synapses intact, where it could start false messages.

2. Alternatively, transmitter molecules may be rapidly cleared from the synaptic cleft by being taken up into the presynaptic terminal—a process known as **reuptake.** The repackaging of released transmitter molecules into vesicles is called **pinocytosis** (see Figure 3.13), and allows for recycling the transmitter chemical. Norepinephrine, dopamine, and serotonin are examples of transmitters whose activity is terminated mainly by reuptake. In these cases, special receptors for the transmitter are located on the presynaptic axon terminal. Once taken up into the presynaptic terminal, some of the transmitter molecules are inserted into vesicles and can be released in response to further nerve impulses. Malfunction of reuptake mechanisms has been suspected to cause some kinds of mental illness, such as depression (see Chapter 16).

In many cases, neurons are also influenced by neuromodulators, substances that by themselves do not produce significant neural effects but that bind to receptors to change how they respond to a transmitter (see Chapter 4).

Nonclassic forms of synapses modulate neural activity

For simplicity, we have been focusing on the classic, directed **axo-dendritic** synapse. However, many nonclassic forms of chemical synapses exist in the nervous system. As the name implies, **axo-axonic** synapses form on axons, often near the axon terminal, allowing the presynaptic neuron to strongly facilitate or inhibit the activity of the postsynaptic axon.

Similarly, neurons may form **dendro-dendritic** contacts, allowing coordination of their activities. At a **retrograde synapse**, transmission starts with classic axo-dendritic synaptic activity, but the postsynaptic cell subsequently releases a gas neurotransmitter, such as carbon monoxide or nitric oxide (see Chapter 4), which signals the presynaptic cell to release more transmitter. And throughout the brain are found axons with regular swellings, called **varicosities**, along their length; these **nondirected synapses** steadily release neurotransmitter, like a drip-irrigation system, to affect surrounding areas.

Neurons and Synapses Combine to Make Circuits

Now that we have discussed the basic properties of neurons and synapses, it is time for an initial look at how they can be connected into circuits to perform important functions. The use of the term *circuit* for an assemblage of neurons and their synaptic interconnections is an analogy to electrical or electronic circuits, in which an arrangement of components (e.g., resistors, capacitors, transistors, and their connecting wires) accomplishes a particular function, such as amplification, oscillation, or filtering.

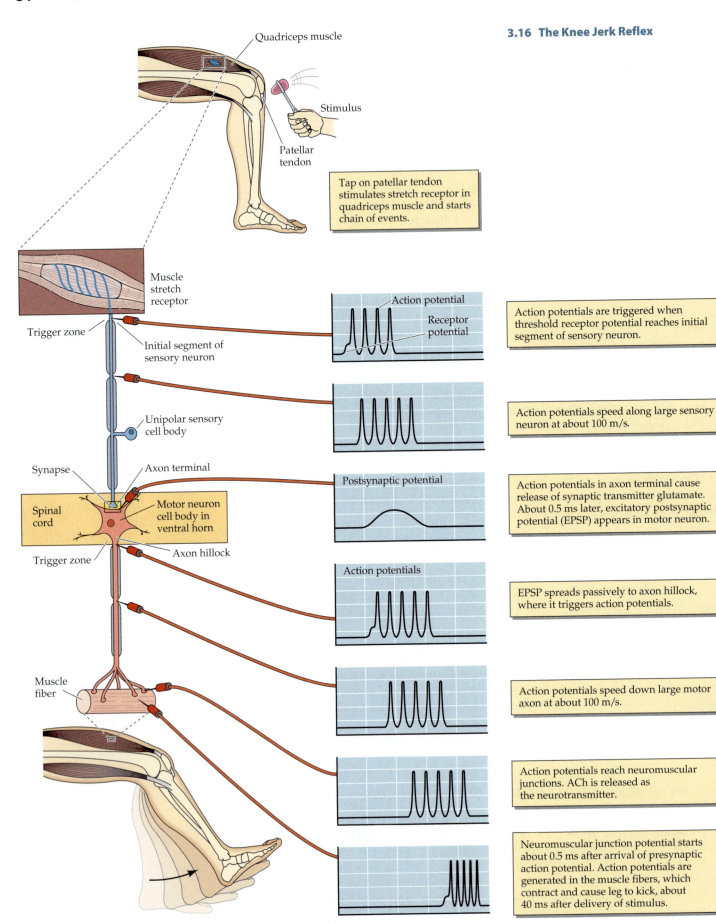

Quadriceps muscle

Stimulus

Patellar tendon

Tap on patellar tendon stimulates stretch receptor in quadriceps muscle and starts chain of events.

Muscle stretch receptor

Action potential

Receptor potential

Action potentials are triggered when threshold receptor potential reaches initial segment of sensory neuron.

Trigger zone

Initial segment of sensory neuron

Action potentials speed along large sensory neuron at about 100 m/s.

Unipolar sensory cell body

Synapse

Axon terminal

Postsynaptic potential

Action potentials in axon terminal cause release of synaptic transmitter glutamate. About 0.5 ms later, excitatory postsynaptic potential (EPSP) appears in motor neuron.

Spinal cord

Motor neuron cell body in ventral horn

Trigger zone

Axon hillock

Action potentials

EPSP spreads passively to axon hillock, where it triggers action potentials.

Action potentials speed down large motor axon at about 100 m/s.

Muscle fiber

Action potentials reach neuromuscular junctions. ACh is released as the neurotransmitter.

Neuromuscular junction potential starts about 0.5 ms after arrival of presynaptic action potential. Action potentials are generated in the muscle fibers, which contract and cause leg to kick, about 40 ms after delivery of stimulus.

Electrical or electronic circuits can represent signals in either analog or digital ways—that is, in terms of continuously varying values or in terms of integers. Neurons also have both analog signals (graded potentials) and digital signals (all-or-none action potentials). The nervous system comprises many different types of neural circuits that accomplish basic functions in cognition, emotion, and action—all the categories of behavior and experience. For now we will look at just three basic types of neural circuits: (1) the neural chain, (2) the feedback circuit, and (3) the oscillator circuit.

The simplest neural circuit is the neural chain

The first neural circuit that investigators proposed was the linking of neurons in a chain. From the seventeenth century until well into the twentieth century, most attempts to understand behavior in neural terms were based on chains of neurons, which do account for some behaviors. For example, the basic circuit for the stretch reflex, such as the **knee jerk reflex,** consists of a sensory neuron, a motor neuron, and a single synapse where the sensory neuron joins the motor neuron. Hundreds or thousands of such circuits work in parallel to enable the stretch reflex.

Figure 3.16 shows the sequence and timing of events in the knee jerk reflex. Note that this reflex is extremely rapid: Only about 40 ms elapse between the stimulus and the initiation of the response. Several factors account for this rapidity: (1) Both the sensory and the motor axons involved are myelinated and of large diameter, and thus conduct rapidly; (2) the sensory cells synapse directly on the motor neurons; and (3) both the central synapse and the neuromuscular junction are fast, ionotropic synapses.

For some purposes the afferent (input) parts of the visual system can be represented as a neural chain (Figure 3.17a; in reality, however, the retina contains many kinds of neural circuits, which we will discuss in Chapter 10). A more accurate schematic diagram of the visual system (Figure 3.17b) brings out two other features of many neural circuits: **convergence** and **divergence.** Note that in these circuits multiple units are arranged in parallel; such systems often feature additional circuitry that connects across the parallel cells to provide **lateral interaction.** This type of initial processing tends to emphasize patterns of activity across a large array.

(a) **The visual system represented as a neural chain**

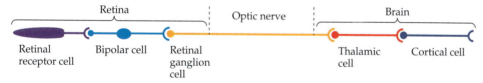

Retina   Optic nerve   Brain

Retinal receptor cell   Bipolar cell   Retinal ganglion cell   Thalamic cell   Cortical cell

(b) **A more realistic representation, showing convergence and divergence**

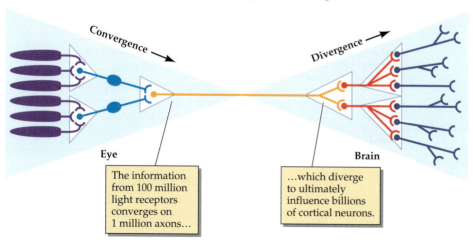

Convergence   Divergence

Eye   Brain

The information from 100 million light receptors converges on 1 million axons...

...which diverge to ultimately influence billions of cortical neurons.

3.17 Two Representations of Neural Circuitry (a) This simple representation shows the input part of the visual system. (b) This more complex representation illustrates convergence and divergence.

In many parts of the nervous system, the axons from large numbers of neurons converge on certain cells. In the human eye, about 100 million receptor cells concentrate their information down on about 1 million ganglion cells; these ganglion cells convey the information from the eye to the brain (see Figure 3.17*b*). Higher in the visual system there is much divergence: The 1 million axons of the optic nerve communicate to billions of neurons in several different specialized regions of the cerebral cortex.

The feedback circuit is a regulator

In a feedback circuit, part of the output is *fed back* to the input. There are two types of feedback circuits: positive and negative. In **positive feedback circuits,** the effect of the output is to sustain or increase the activity of the initial input; in **negative feedback circuits,** the output inhibits the activity of the initial input. In some feedback circuits, a branch of the axon of a neuron loops back and contacts the same neuron (Figure 3.18*a*). In others, one or more intermediate neurons (interneurons) form the feedback loop.

Feedback circuits were first discovered in the nervous system in the 1940s, and psychologist Donald O. Hebb (1949) pointed out their relevance for psychological and neuroscience theory. For example, a positive feedback circuit can be used to sustain neural activity, which can contribute to maintaining a motivational state or to forming the cellular basis of memory. Negative feedback circuits help regulate many body functions by maintaining relatively constant conditions.

A thermostat is an example of a negative feedback device; many neural circuits in the body function in the same basic manner. The stretch reflex (an example of which is the knee jerk reflex illustrated in Figure 3.16) serves as part of a negative feedback system in maintaining posture as you stand. Swaying a little to the front causes muscles in the back of the leg to stretch; the leg muscles respond by contracting, bringing the body again to the vertical. Similarly, swaying to the back stretches muscles in the front, and again the stretch reflex brings about the necessary compensation.

The oscillator circuit controls rhythmic behavior

Many kinds of behavior—from beating of the heart, breathing, walking, sleeping, and waking, to annual migration—are rhythmic, and their cycles differ in duration from short to long. Some neurons, mostly in invertebrates, show inherent spontaneous rhythmicity of activity: The frequency of neural impulses of such *pacemaker* cells waxes and wanes in regular alternation. Rhythmic

3.18 Negative Feedback Circuits
(*a*) A circuit within a single cell. (*b*) A simple oscillator circuit, in which a continuous series of action potentials from neuron A is modulated by inhibitory output from cell C to cell B, which ultimately causes rhythmic output from cells B and C.

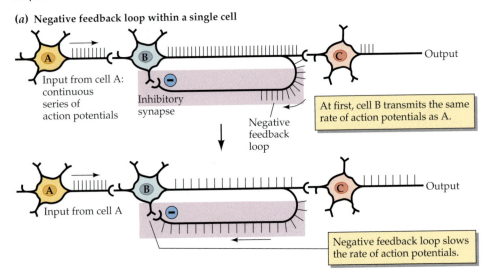

(*a*) **Negative feedback loop within a single cell**

Input from cell A: continuous series of action potentials

Inhibitory synapse

Negative feedback loop

At first, cell B transmits the same rate of action potentials as A.

Input from cell A

Output

Negative feedback loop slows the rate of action potentials.

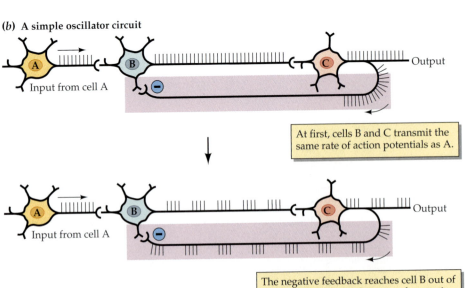

(*b*) **A simple oscillator circuit**

Input from cell A

Output

At first, cells B and C transmit the same rate of action potentials as A.

Input from cell A

Output

The negative feedback reaches cell B out of phase with the input, because of synaptic delays, causing rhythmic output.

wing beating in some insects is controlled by such oscillation. In both invertebrates and vertebrates, however, oscillatory activity usually depends on circuits of neurons. Figure 3.18*b* shows a simple **oscillator circuit**.

Gross Electrical Activity of the Human Brain

The electrical activity of millions of cells working together combines to produce electrical potentials large enough to be recorded at the surface of the skull. Recordings of electrical activity in the brain that are made with large electrodes either on the scalp or within the brain can provide useful glimpses of the simultaneous workings of large populations of neurons. Investigators divide these gross brain potentials into two principal classes: those that appear spontaneously without specific stimulation and those that are evoked by particular stimuli.

Electroencephalograms measure spontaneous brain potentials

A recording of spontaneous brain potentials, or *brain waves*, is called an **electroencephalogram** (**EEG**) (Figure 3.19*a*). As we will see in Chapter 14, EEG recordings of a sleeping person allow investigators to distinguish different kinds and stages of sleep. Brain potentials also provide significant diagnostic data—for example, in dis-

(*a*) Multichannel EEG recording

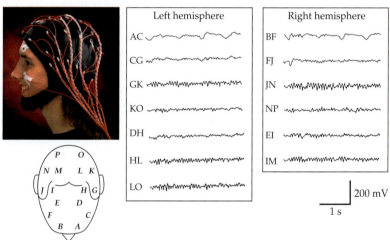

(*b*) Event-related potentials (average of many stimulus presentations)

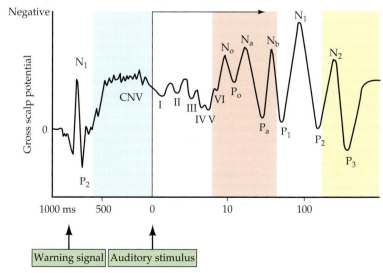

3.19 Gross Potentials of the Human Nervous System (*a*) (*Top left*) Electrode array for EEG recording. (*Bottom left*) Each electrode can be assigned a letter on a map of the scalp. (*Right*) Typical EEG records showing potential measured between various points on the scalp. (*b*) Event-related potentials (average of many stimulus presentations). Following stimulus presentation, a fixed sequence of processing-related potentials is generated. Early components (labeled I–VI) are associated with brainstem activity, followed by large-amplitude negative- and positive-voltage events (labeled N_0–N_2 and P_0–P_3). The longer-latency components are associated with cognitive processing of task demands.

tinguishing forms of seizure disorders (Box 3.2). In addition, they provide prognostic data, such as predictions of the functional effects of brain injury. In most of the United States, EEGs are used to determine death according to the legal definition.

Event-related potentials measure changes resulting from discrete stimuli

Gross potential changes evoked by discrete stimuli—usually sensory stimuli, such as light flashes or clicks—are called **event-related potentials** (**ERPs**) (Figure 3.19*b*). Typically in experiments that exploit this phenomenon, many ERPs are averaged to obtain a reliable estimate of stimulus-elicited brain activity. Sensory-evoked potentials have very distinctive characteristics of wave shape and latency that reflect the type of stimulus, the state of the subject, and the site of recording. Subtler psychological processes, such as expectancy (anticipation that something is about to happen), also appear to influence some characteristics of evoked potentials.

Computer techniques enable researchers to record brain potentials using electrodes that are located a significant distance from the sites at which the potentials are generated. An example that has attracted considerable research and clinical attention is *auditory-evoked brainstem potentials* (see Figure 3.19*b*). The neural generators of these waves are located far from the site of recording—in the auditory nerve and successive levels of the auditory pathway in the brainstem. These ERPs provide a way to assess the integrity and functioning of the brainstem and especially its auditory pathways. For example, decreases in the amplitude of certain waves or increases in their latency have been valuable in detecting hearing impairments in very young children and noncommunicative persons. Infants with impaired hearing produce reduced auditory ERPs or no ERP at all in response to sounds. Another use of ERPs is in the assessment of brainstem injury or damage.

The long-latency components of scalp-recorded ERPs tend to reflect the impact of endogenous information-processing variables, such as attention, decision making, and other complex cognitive processes. In contrast, short-latency responses are determined more by exogenous factors, such as the physical characteristics of the stimulus. For example, dimensions like stimulus intensity have a far more profound effect on early components of ERPs than on longer-latency components.

Although it is usually difficult to localize which brain region has produced a given component of the ERP, such changes are detected quickly, within a fraction of a second. In contrast, computer-coordinated imaging of brain activity, such as functional MRI (fMRI) (see Chapter 2), indicates clearly which brain region is active, but because such imaging techniques must average activity over seconds or minutes, they are slower than ERPs. Perhaps the greatest promise for future research is a melding of the two techniques—using ERPs to detect changes in brain activity rapidly, and using fMRI or PET scans to indicate where those electrical changes originate within the brain (e.g., Liebenthal et al., 2003).

Summary

1. Nerve cells are specialized for receiving, processing, and transmitting signals.

2. Neurons exhibit a small electrical potential across the cell membrane; neural signals are changes in this potential.

3. The different concentrations of ions inside and outside the neuron—especially potassium ions (K^+), to which the resting membrane is selectively permeable—account for the resting potential. At equilibrium, the electrostatic pressure driving K^+ ions into the neuron is balanced by the concentration gradient driving K^+ ions out; at this point, the membrane potential is about –60 mV, the resting potential.

4. Much of the energy of the brain is expended in maintaining ionic gradients, through the operation of sodium–potassium pumps.

5. A propagated nerve impulse, called an action potential, travels the length of the axon without diminishing in amplitude; the impulse is regenerated by successive segments of the axon.

6. Reduction of the resting potential (depolarization) opens voltage-gated Na⁺ channels of the axonal membrane. If this depolarization reaches a threshold value, the membrane becomes completely permeable to sodium, and the axon becomes briefly more positive inside than outside; that is, an action potential is generated. Depolarization of a segment of membrane stimulates the adjacent segment of membrane to depolarize, so the action potential sweeps along the axon.

7. Postsynaptic (local) potentials spread very rapidly, but they are not propagated. They diminish in amplitude as they spread passively along dendrites and the cell body.

8. Excitatory postsynaptic potentials (EPSPs) are depolarizing (they decrease the resting potential) and increase the likelihood that the neuron will generate an action potential. Inhibitory postsynaptic potentials (IPSPs) are hyperpolarizing (they increase the resting potential) and decrease the likelihood that the neuron will fire.

9. Cell bodies process information by integrating (adding algebraically) postsynaptic potentials across their surfaces. Postsynaptic potentials are integrated through both spatial summation (summing potentials that occur in different locations) and temporal summation (summing potentials across time).

10. An action potential is initiated at the axon hillock when the excess of EPSPs over IPSPs reaches threshold.

11. During the action potential, the neuron cannot be excited by a second stimulus; it is absolutely refractory. For a few milliseconds thereafter the neuron is relatively refractory, requiring a stronger stimulation than usual in order to fire.

12. Some synapses use electrical transmission and do not require a chemical transmitter. At these electrical synapses, the cleft between presynaptic and postsynaptic cells is extremely small.

13. At most synapses, the transmission of information from one neuron to another requires a chemical transmitter that diffuses across the synaptic cleft and binds to receptor molecules in the postsynaptic membrane. A substance that binds to a receptor is called a ligand.

14. At some synapses, the receptor molecule responds to recognition of a transmitter by opening an ion channel within its own structure. At other synapses, the binding of a transmitter molecule to a receptor molecule leads to opening of channels through the activity of G proteins and second messengers.

15. Neurons and synapses can be assembled into circuits that process information. Three basic kinds of neural circuits are the neural chain, the feedback circuit, and the oscillator circuit.

16. The summation of electrical changes over millions of nerve cells can be detected by electrodes on the scalp. Electroencephalograms (EEGs) can reveal rapid changes in brain function, especially in response to a brief, controlled stimulus that evokes an event-related potential (ERP).

Recommended Reading

Cowan, W. M., Sudhof, T. C., and Stevens, C. F. (Eds.). (2003). *Synapses*. Baltimore: Johns Hopkins University Press.

Hall, Z. W. (Ed.). (1992). *An introduction to molecular neurobiology*. Sunderland, MA: Sinauer Associates.

Hille, B. (2001). *Ion channels of excitable membranes*. Sunderland, MA: Sinauer Associates.

Kandel, E. R., Schwartz, J. H., and Jessell, T. M. (2000). *Principles of neural science* (4th ed.). New York: McGraw-Hill.

Nicholls, J. G., Martin, A. R., Wallace, B. G., and Fuchs, P. A. (2000). *From neuron to brain* (4th ed.). Sunderland, MA: Sinauer Associates.

Purves, D., Augustine, G. J., Fitzpatrick, D., Hall, W. C., et al. (2004). *Neuroscience* (3rd ed.). Sunderland, MA: Sinauer Associates.

Shepherd, G. M. (Ed.). (2003). *The synaptic organization of the brain* (5th ed.). New York: Oxford University Press.

Smith, C. U. M. (2002). *Elements of molecular neurobiology* (2nd ed.). New York: Wiley.

Refer to the *Learning Biological Psychology CD* for study questions, animations, activities, and other study aids.

4

The Chemical Bases of Behavior: Neurotransmitters and Neuropharmacology

The Birth of a Pharmaceutical Problem Child

In the 1930s and 1940s, Swiss pharmacologist Albert Hofmann was working for Sandoz Pharmaceuticals and studying ergot, a fungus that grows on grain, in the hope of synthesizing new and useful drugs from it. Compounds generated in these studies were administered to animals, and if no useful properties were detected, they were subsequently set aside. But for some reason, in 1943 Dr. Hofmann chose to restart his investigations with one of these previously discarded compounds. Then one day in April of that year, he appeared to be coming down with a cold and left work to go home, only to begin experiencing bizarre visual phenomena: "an uninterrupted stream of fantastic pictures, extraordinary shapes with intense, kaleidoscopic play of colors" (Hofmann, 1981). When he closed his eyes, the luridly colored, oddly shifting forms seemed to surge toward him. The state lasted about 2 hours. Suspecting that he had accidentally ingested a small amount of the experimental compound, Hofmann began to experiment with it again.

Although one could debate the wisdom of testing unknown drugs on himself, Hofmann was breaking no laws in force at the time. When he self-administered even a seemingly tiny dose, he nonetheless experienced incapacitating changes in brain function and astonishing, sometimes frightening, visual apparitions. In addition to the visual phenomena, he reported sometimes feeling that his sense of self was "loosened." Careful analyses later revealed the new drug to be amazingly potent: A few millionths of a gram was enough to induce substantial effects. What was this substance? By what mechanisms did it affect the brain?

Most drugs affect the brain and behavior by changing synaptic transmission. To begin our discussion about drugs and the nervous system, we expand on the discussion of neurotransmitters that we began in Chapter 3. Then we review some of the major classes of drugs that affect the nervous system and behavior, and we look at some of the ways in which they interact with neural systems. Finally, we turn to mechanisms of drug abuse and dependency.

As far back as we can trace human history, people have tasted, sipped, chewed, or swallowed all kinds of substances—animal, vegetable, and mineral. From these experiences, people have learned to consume some substances and shun others. Social customs and dietary codes evolved to protect people from consuming harmful substances. This long history of seeking, testing, and using different substances came not only from the need for nourishment but also from the desire to relieve pain, control anxiety, and pursue pleasure. But we are not alone in this activity: "Almost every species of animal has engaged in the natural pursuit of intoxicants" (R. K. Siegel, 1989, p. viii).

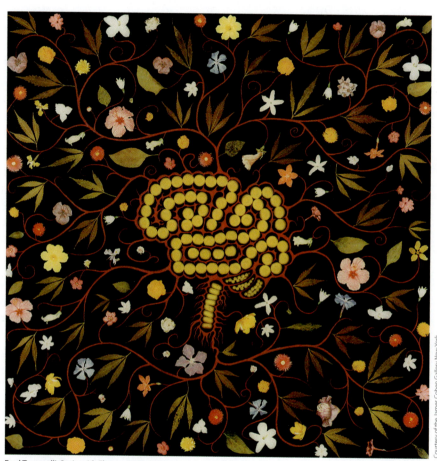

Fred Tomaselli, *Brain with Flowers*, 1990–1997
Cannabis leaves, LSD, photos, acrylic, and resin on wood

Courtesy of the James Cohen Gallery, New York.

Many Chemical Neurotransmitters Have Been Identified

We learned in Chapter 3 that neurons release a chemical known as a *neurotransmitter* (or simply *transmitter*) to communicate with target cells, usually other neurons. Identifying neurotransmitters and understanding how they act are continuing quests.

TABLE 4.1 *Some Synaptic Transmitters and Families of Transmitters*

Family and subfamily	Transmitter(s)
AMINES	
Quaternary amines	Acetylcholine (ACh)
Monoamines	*Catecholamines*
	Norepinephrine (NE)
	Epinephrine (adrenaline)
	Dopamine (DA)
	Indoleamines
	Serotonin (5-hydroxytryptamine; 5-HT)
	Melatonin
AMINO ACIDS	Gamma-aminobutyric acid (GABA)
	Glutamate
	Glycine
	Histamine
NEUROPEPTIDES	
Opioid peptides	*Enkephalins*
	Met-enkephalin
	Leu-enkephalin
	Endorphins
	β-endorphin
	Dynorphins
	Dynorphin A
PEPTIDE HORMONES	Oxytocin
	Substance P
	Cholecystokinin (CCK)
	Vasopressin
	Neuropeptide Y (NPY)
	Hypothalamic releasing hormones
GASES	Nitric oxide
	Carbon monoxide

What does it take for a substance to be considered a transmitter? The criteria come from the view of synaptic transmission that we discussed in Chapter 3. To prove that a particular substance acts as a neurotransmitter, we must demonstrate the following:

- The substance exists in the presynaptic axon terminals.
- The presynaptic cell contains appropriate enzymes for synthesizing the substance.
- The substance is released in significant quantities when nerve impulses reach the terminals.
- Specific receptors that recognize the released substance exist on the postsynaptic membrane.
- Experimental application of the substance produces changes in postsynaptic potentials.
- Blocking release of the substance prevents presynaptic nerve impulses from altering the activity of the postsynaptic cell.

Table 4.1 summarizes the major categories of the many neurotransmitters that we already know about. Substances that satisfy the criteria for transmitters include various **amine neurotransmitters,** such as acetylcholine, dopamine, and serotonin; **amino acid neurotransmitters** like GABA and glutamate; and a wide variety of **peptide neurotransmitters,** made up of short chains of amino acids (see Table 4.1). As the search continues, the number of probable synaptic transmitters continues to grow, bringing with it surprises such as the existence of **gas neurotransmitters.**

Even if a substance is known to be a transmitter in one location, it may be hard to prove that it acts as a transmitter at another location where it is found. For example, acetylcholine was long accepted as a transmitter agent in the peripheral nervous system (remember Otto Loewi's discoveries recounted in Chapter 3), but it was harder to prove that acetylcholine serves as a transmitter in the central nervous system as well. Now it is recognized that acetylcholine is widely distributed in the brain, and its possible relationship to the cognitive deficits seen in Alzheimer's disease is the subject of much current work. Considering the rate at which these substances are being discovered and characterized, it would not be surprising if there turned out to be several hundred different peptides conveying information at synapses in different subsets of neurons.

As we discussed in Chapter 3, neurotransmitters affect their targets by interacting with **receptors,** protein molecules embedded in the postsynaptic membrane that recognize the transmitter. The transmitter molecule binds to the receptor, changing its shape to open an ion channel (fast, **ionotropic** receptors), or altering chemical reactions within the target cell (slow, **metabotropic** receptors) (see Figure 3.15). Receptors add to the complexity of neural signaling because there may be a wide variety of different kinds of receptors for a given transmitter. The different **receptor subtypes** may trigger very different responses in target cells, and they also often have different anatomical distributions within the nervous system (Figure 4.1).

A substance that binds to a receptor is termed a **ligand,** and ligands typically have one of three effects: (1) When bound to a receptor, a ligand classified as an **agonist** initiates the normal effects of the receptor. (2) A receptor **antagonist** is a ligand that binds to a receptor and does not activate it, thereby blocking it from being activated

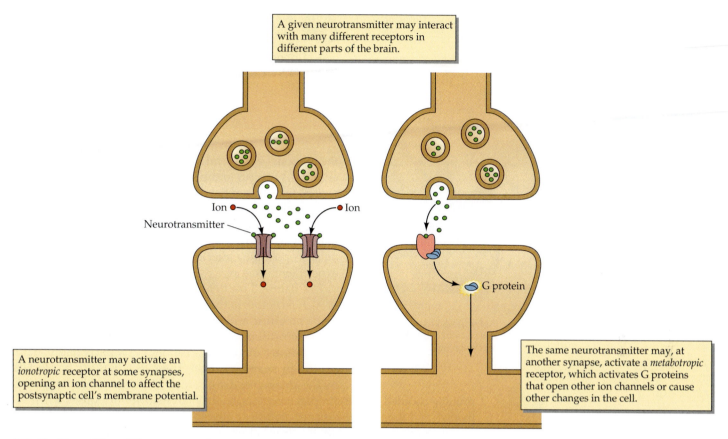

A given neurotransmitter may interact with many different receptors in different parts of the brain.

Ion

Neurotransmitter

Ion

G protein

A neurotransmitter may activate an *ionotropic* receptor at some synapses, opening an ion channel to affect the postsynaptic cell's membrane potential.

The same neurotransmitter may, at another synapse, activate a *metabotropic* receptor, which activates G proteins that open other ion channels or cause other changes in the cell.

4.1 The Versatility of Neurotransmitters   A single neurotransmitter may interact with many different receptors in different parts of the brain—binding to fast, ionotropic receptors on some target cells, and to slow, metabotropic receptors on other cells. Either type of receptor may either excite or inhibit the target cell.

by other ligands. (3) An **inverse agonist**—a less common type of ligand—binds to the receptor and initiates an effect that is the *reverse* of the normal function of the receptor. We will look at some of the ligands that the brain produces—the classic neurotransmitters—and then turn to the major categories of drugs that affect the brain.

Neurotransmitter Systems Form a Complex Array in the Brain

The neurochemical complexity of the brain has become more evident as techniques such as immunocytochemistry (see Box 2.3) have provided a more complete appreciation of the location of these substances within the nervous system, and the multiplicity of ways in which they interact. Although at one time in the recent past it was thought that each nerve cell contained only one transmitter, we now know that some nerve cells contain more than one transmitter—a phenomenon known as neurotransmitter **co-localization** or *co-release*. In this section we discuss the distribution of a few of the major neurotransmitters, and their receptors.

Acetylcholine was the first neurotransmitter to be identified

Acetylcholine (ACh), the chemical at work in Otto Loewi's classic experiment (see Chapter 3), was the first chemical substance to be known as a neurotransmitter. The distribution of ACh in the brain was subsequently determined by mapping of the enzymes involved in its synthesis; Figure 4.2 shows the distribution of ACh-containing (**cholinergic**) nerve cell bodies and their projections.

Several distinct clusters of cholinergic cells are apparent. The basal forebrain includes major groups of cholinergic cells in the medial septal nucleus, the nucleus of

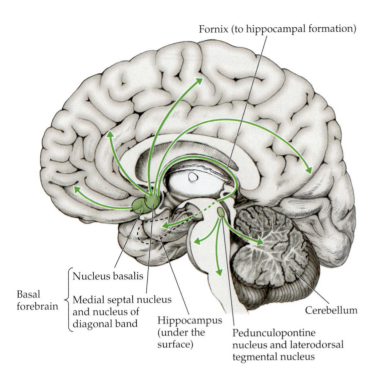

Fornix (to hippocampal formation)

Basal forebrain
- Nucleus basalis
- Medial septal nucleus and nucleus of diagonal band

Hippocampus (under the surface)

Pedunculopontine nucleus and laterodorsal tegmental nucleus

Cerebellum

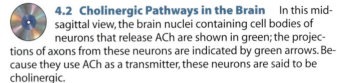

4.2 Cholinergic Pathways in the Brain   In this midsagittal view, the brain nuclei containing cell bodies of neurons that release ACh are shown in green; the projections of axons from these neurons are indicated by green arrows. Because they use ACh as a transmitter, these neurons are said to be cholinergic.

the diagonal band, and the nucleus basalis. These cholinergic cells project to the hippocampus and amygdala, as well as throughout the cerebral cortex. Widespread loss of cholinergic neurons is evident in Alzheimer's disease, suggesting that cholinergic systems are crucial for learning and memory (see Chapter 18). Similarly, the cholinergic antagonist scopolamine interferes with learning and memory in experimental settings.

In Chapter 3 we noted that there are two broad classes of ACh receptors in the peripheral and central nervous systems: **nicotinic** and **muscarinic** receptors. Within each of these two groups are subtypes of receptors. Most nicotinic receptors are ionotropic, responding rapidly and usually having an excitatory effect. These receptors can be blocked by the antagonist drug curare. Muscarinic receptors are G protein–coupled (metabotropic) receptors, so they have slower responses when activated, and they can be either excitatory or inhibitory (see Figure 3.15b). Muscarinic receptors can be blocked by the drugs atropine or scopolamine.

Five monoamines act as neurotransmitters

There are two principal classes of **monoamines:** catecholamines and indoleamines. The **catecholamine** neurotransmitters are dopamine, epinephrine, and norepinephrine. The **indoleamines** are melatonin and serotonin. Box 4.1 describes how neurons synthesize the monoamines and ACh. In the sections that follow, we will take a closer look at three important monoamines: dopamine, norepinephrine, and serotonin.

Dopamine   About a million nerve cells in the human brain contain **dopamine (DA)**. The locations of these cells and their projections in the brain are shown in Figure 4.3. Dopaminergic neurons are found in several main groups; Figure 4.3 focuses on two of these groups: the mesostriatal system and the mesolimbocortical pathway. Several subtypes of DA receptors have been discovered and have been labeled D_1, D_2, D_3, D_4, and D_5, numbered in the order of their discovery.

The **mesostriatal pathway,** as the name indicates, originates from the mesencephalon (midbrain)—specifically the **substantia nigra** and nearby areas—and ascends as part of the medial forebrain bundle to innervate the **striatum:** the caudate nucleus and putamen (see Figure 4.3). Although this group contains relatively few nerve cells, a single axon can give rise to thousands of synapses. Significant loss of these neurons re-

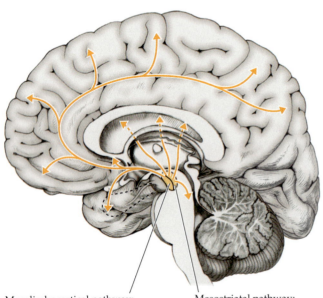

Mesolimbocortical pathway: ventral tegmental area to nucleus accumbens, cortex, and hippocampus

Mesostriatal pathway: substantia nigra to striatum (caudate and putamen)

4.3 Dopaminergic Pathways in the Brain   The neurons in the pathways represented in this midsagittal view release dopamine and thus are called *dopaminergic.*

BOX 4.1 Pathways for Neurotransmitter Synthesis

Here we provide reference information on the chemical pathways by which the classic neurotransmitters are synthesized. By understanding these pathways, pharmacologists can target drug discoveries toward affecting specific transmitter systems. Furthermore, because enzyme action is crucial for transmitter synthesis, neuroanatomists can use the anatomical distribution of these enzymes to determine which transmitters are used by different brain regions. For example, the enzyme **choline acetyltransferase (ChAT)** catalyzes the synthesis of ACh from its precursor, choline:

Acetyl CoA + choline

    ChAT

ACh + coenzyme A

The enzyme **acetylcholinesterase (AChE)** breaks down the ACh, leaving choline and acetic acid:

ACh

    AChE

Choline + acetic acid

As it turns out, AChE is very widely distributed, but ChAT is found primarily in the nuclei shown in Figure 4.2.

All of the catecholamine transmitters (norepinephrine, epinephrine, and dopamine) are synthesized from the amino acid tyrosine, in a succession of metabolic steps:

Tyrosine

    Tyrosine hydroxylase

L-dopa

    Aromatic L-amino acid decarboxylase

Dopamine

    Dopamine β-hydroxylase

Norepinephrine

    Phenylethanolamine N-methyltransferase

Epinephrine

Note that only neurons that possess the enzyme tyrosine hydroxylase have the capacity to produce any catecholamine transmitter, and that L-dopa is a precursor for all three.

The indoleamine serotonin is produced from the amino acid tryptophan in two chemical steps:

Tryptophan

    Tryptophan hydroxylase

5-Hydroxytryptophan (5-HTP)

    Aromatic L-amino acid decarboxylase

5-Hydroxytryptamine (5-HT; serotonin)

The monoamines (dopamine, norepinephrine, epinephrine, serotonin, and melatonin) are inactivated through a combination of presynaptic reuptake and enzymatic breakdown. Most of this enzymatic action is performed by a class of enzymes called **monoamine oxidases (MAOs)**.

Neuropeptides are synthesized like any other peptide or protein—through transcription of a gene and translation of messenger RNA (mRNA)—so we can find neurons making those transmitters by looking for the appropriate mRNA transcript (see the appendix).

---

sults in the resting tremors or even complete paralysis of Parkinson's disease (see Chapter 11), which can be treated for a time by the provision of more L-dopa precursor molecules (see Box 4.1). Therefore, the mesostriatal DA system is thought normally to play a crucial role in motor control.

The **mesolimbocortical pathway** also originates in the midbrain, in the ventral tegmental area (see Figure 4.3), and projects to the limbic system (amygdala, nucleus accumbens, hippocampus) and the cortex. Overactivity in this pathway is involved in schizophrenia. A rich research literature (e.g., Nader et al., 1997) connects activity in this system, especially via the dopamine D$_2$ receptor subtype, to reward and reinforcement; we revisit this topic at the end of this chapter. In humans, dopamine released from mesolimbocortical neurons in the amygdala appears to participate in the performance of specific cognitive functions, such as verbal learning (Fried et al., 2001).

CLINICAL ISSUE

Norepinephrine   Neurons that release **norepinephrine (NE)** are organized into three main clusters in the brainstem: the **locus coeruleus** complex in the pons, the lateral tegmental system of the midbrain, and the dorsal medullary group (Figure 4.4). Because norepinephrine is also known as *noradrenaline,* NE-producing cells are said to be **noradrenergic.**

The output of the noradrenergic locus coeruleus cells extends broadly throughout the cerebrum, including the cerebral cortex and thalamic nuclei. In addition, the output of these cells projects prominently to the cerebellum and spinal cord. Because of this wide distribution of projection paths, noradrenergic cells of the locus

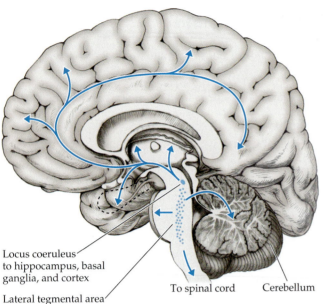

4.4 Noradrenergic Pathways in the Brain   The neurons in the pathways shown in this midsagittal view release norepinephrine as a transmitter.

Locus coeruleus to hippocampus, basal ganglia, and cortex

Lateral tegmental area

To spinal cord   Cerebellum

coeruleus are believed to modulate many behavioral and physiological processes. The CNS contains four subtypes of NE receptors—α_1-, α_2-, β_1- and β_2-adrenoceptors—all of which are metabotropic receptors. Noradrenergic activity has been implicated in many diverse functions, including mood, overall arousal, and sexual behavior.

Serotonin   Because its chemical name is 5-hydroxytryptamine, **serotonin** is abbreviated **5-HT.** Large areas of the brain are innervated by **serotonergic** fibers, although 5-HT cell bodies are relatively few and are concentrated in the **raphe nuclei** (pronounced "ra-FAY"; Latin for "seam") of the midbrain and brainstem, along the midline. Figure 4.5 shows the distribution of serotonergic cell bodies and their fiber projections. Only about 200,000 of the 100 billion neurons of the human brain are serotonergic, but they exert widespread influence throughout the rest of the brain, especially the projection emanating from the **dorsal raphe.**

Serotonin has been implicated in the control of sleep states (see Chapter 14), mood, anxiety, and many other functions. Drugs that globally increase 5-HT activity are effective antidepressants; Prozac is an example (see Chapter 16). At least 15 types of 5-HT receptors ($5HT_1$, $5HT_2$, and so on) have been described.

CLINICAL ISSUE

Some amino acids act as neurotransmitters

The most common transmitters in the brain are based on amino acids. In this group are two prominent excitatory neurotransmitters (**glutamate** and **aspartate**) and two prominent inhibitory transmitters (**gamma-aminobutyric acid [GABA]** and **glycine**). These transmitters are distributed throughout the central nervous system. Glutamate is the most common excitatory transmitter, and GABA is the major inhibitory transmitter in the brain.

Glutamate transmission employs a group of ionotropic receptors referred to as *AMPA, kainate,* and *NMDA* receptors (their names refer to drugs that act as selective agonists). Because NMDA-type glutamate receptors are active in a fascinating model of learning and memory (see Chapter 18), they have been studied very closely (Box 4.2). There are also several metabotropic glutamate receptors (mGluR) which act more slowly because they work through second messengers.

Glutamate is associated with **excitotoxicity,** a phenomenon in which neural injury, such as a stroke or trauma, provokes an excessive release of glutamate that produces prolonged depolarization of postsynaptic cells. This overexcitation ultimately kills the postsynaptic neurons, exacerbating the effects of the brain injury. Another interesting fea-

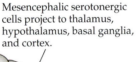
Mesencephalic serotonergic cells project to thalamus, hypothalamus, basal ganglia, and cortex.

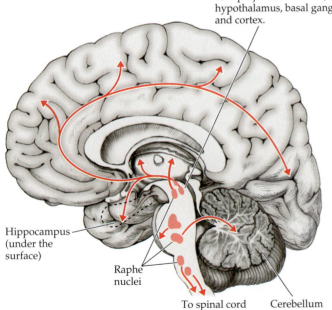

Hippocampus (under the surface)

Raphe nuclei

To spinal cord   Cerebellum

4.5 Serotonergic Pathways in the Brain   The neurons in the nuclei shown in this midsagittal view release serotonin (5-HT) and thus are said to be *serotonergic.*

BOX 4.2 A Receptor with a Long Memory

Because they have been implicated in the basic processes of memory formation, NMDA receptors are currently being subjected to intense scrutiny by researchers. The **NMDA receptor** is one of the two main kinds of receptors activated by glutamate, which is a major excitatory synaptic transmitter found in all parts of the nervous system. The name *NMDA receptor* reflects the fact that this receptor is especially sensitive to the glutamate agonist **N-m**ethyl-**D**-**a**spartate. The other main kind of glutamate receptor is called the **AMPA receptor** because it is particularly sensitive to α-**a**mino-3-hydroxy-5-**m**ethyl-4-isoxazole**p**ropionic **a**cid. AMPA receptors and NMDA receptors often work in conjunction to produce long-lasting changes in synaptic functioning; it is hypothesized that this action encodes basic units of new memories.

The NMDA receptor acts differently from most receptor molecules because it is both ligand-gated and voltage-sensitive. When the NMDA receptor is activated, Ca^{2+} ions flow through its central channel into the neuron. But only very small amounts of Ca^{2+} flow through the

NMDA receptor at the resting potential of –75 mV or at any membrane potential between –75 and –35 mV. The reason for the low Ca^{2+} conductance at these membrane potentials is that magnesium ions (Mg^{2+}) block the NMDA receptor's central Ca^{2+} channel, as the *left-hand panel* of the figure illustrates.

AMPA receptor activation allows Na^+ ions to flow into the neuron, so sufficient activation of AMPA receptors can partially depolarize the membrane to less than –35 mV. This depolarization removes the Mg^{2+} block (*middle panel* of the figure); the NMDA receptor now responds strongly and admits large amounts of Ca^{2+} through the channel. The Ca^{2+} starts a cascade of effects (described in more detail in Chapter 18) that results in more AMPA receptors (*right-hand panel*). Thus the NMDA receptor is fully active only when it is gated by a *combination* of voltage and ligand. Patch clamp studies show that the activation of NMDA receptors usually has a relatively slow onset and a prolonged effect (up to 500 ms), whereas non-NMDA receptors at the same synapse act rapidly, and their channels remain open only a few milliseconds at a time.

We can study the contributions of NMDA receptors by observing which functions are impaired or abolished by an NMDA antagonist. One such agent is aminophosphonovalerate (APV), which antagonizes the binding of glutamate to the NMDA receptor. Experiments with APV demonstrate that NMDA receptors are not needed for the normal flow of synaptic messages. But when the activity of other receptors reaches a relatively high level and partially depolarizes the membrane, NMDA receptors amplify and prolong the synaptic activity. These special properties allow the NMDA receptors to play a wide variety of important roles, especially in memory formation.

The search for new drugs that affect the NMDA receptor complex is intense (Kemp and McKernan, 2002). Because NMDA receptors are involved in so many functions, new drugs may provide benefits ranging from improvements in cognitive function—because NMDA receptors are involved in memory processes—to minimizing the extent of neural damage following a stroke by countering glutamate's neurotoxic effects.

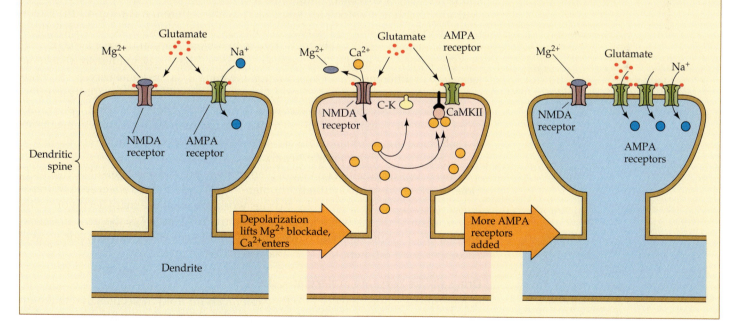

ture of glutaminergic synapses is that nearby astrocytes seem to be responsible for taking up glutamate, clearing it from the cleft after synaptic transmission (Rothstein, 2000).

GABA receptors are divided into three large classes (designated $GABA_A$, $GABA_B$, and $GABA_C$), each exhibiting quite different properties. By mixing and matching various subunits, the brain may normally make hundreds of different GABA receptors. GABA$_A$ receptors are ionotropic (they are ligand-gated chloride channels; see Figure 4.1), and when activated they produce fast inhibitory postsynaptic potentials. Each GABA$_A$ receptor contains several distinct binding sites, as we'll see later.

**CLINICAL
ISSUE**

GABA$_B$ receptors are metabotropic receptors, in contrast to the ionotropic GABA$_A$ receptors. GABA$_B$ receptors are associated with a slow-occurring type of inhibitory postsynaptic potential, which is probably mediated by a special kind of interneuron called a *neurogliaform cell* (Tamás et al., 2003). GABA$_C$ receptors are ionotropic with a chloride channel, but they differ in subunit structure from other GABA receptors. Given GABA's inhibitory actions, it is not surprising that some GABA agonists are potent tranquilizers (e.g., Valium), and that inverse agonists of GABA receptors can provoke seizures by decreasing the important inhibitory influence of GABA.

Many peptides function as neurotransmitters

Many different peptides are found in the brain; those that have a prominent role as neurotransmitters include (1) **opioid peptides** (peptides that can mimic opiate drugs such as morphine), including met-enkephalin, leu-enkephalin, β-endorphin, and dynorphin; (2) a group of peptides found in the gut and spinal cord or brain, including substance P, cholecystokinin (CCK), neurotensin, neuropeptide Y (NPY), and others; and (3) pituitary hormones such as oxytocin and vasopressin, among others. Many of these peptides act as neurotransmitters at certain synapses, but they also act as hormones in other systems (see Chapter 5). Peptide transmitters are often co-localized with other neurotransmitters, especially monoamines.

Research on Drugs Ranges from Molecular Processes to Effects on Behavior

The subject of **neuropsychopharmacology**—how drugs affect the nervous system and behavior—is vast and changing at a rapid pace. The range and complexity of neuropsychopharmacology are suggested by the different meanings of the Greek word *pharmakon*, which is the root of the word *pharmacology*. *Pharmakon* has three principal meanings: (1) "a charm"—that is, an object thought to have a magical effect; (2) "a poison"; and (3) "a remedy or medicine." Similarly, in English we use the term *drug* in different ways. One common meaning is "a medicine used in the treatment of a disease" (as in *prescription drug* or *over-the-counter drug*). Quite a different meaning of *drug,* but also a common one, is "a psychoactive agent," especially an addictive one—that is, a drug of abuse. The common element of these meanings is a substance that, taken in relatively small amounts, has clear effects on experience, mood, emotion, activity, and/or health.

Some drugs originally evolved in plants, often as a defense against being eaten. Other modern drugs are **synthetic** (human-made) and tuned to affect specific transmitter systems. To understand how drugs work, we must use many levels of analysis—from molecules to behavior and experience (see Figure 1.5). Because drugs exert their effects at the molecular level but have profound effects on behavior, we will encounter these different levels of analysis in this chapter.

Drugs fit like keys into molecular locks

Some drugs are effective because they interact with lipid molecules that make up the membrane, or because they directly alter the activity of particular enzymes, but most drugs of interest to biological psychology are ligands that interact with specific receptor molecules. These receptors may be located either in the cell membrane or in the interior of the neuron.

Recall that any given neurotransmitter interacts with a variety of different subtypes of receptors. This principle is crucial to neuropharmacology because, unlike the transmitter, which will act on all its receptor subtypes, a drug can be targeted to interact with just one or a few receptor subtypes. Different subtypes of receptors generally differ in their distribution within the brain, and they also serve very different cellular functions, so selectively activating or blocking specific subtypes of receptors can have widely varying effects. For example, treating someone with doses of serotonin would activate all of her serotonin receptors, regardless of subtype, and produce a variety of nonspecific effects. But treatments with drugs that are selective antagonists of $5HT_3$ receptors, with little activity at other types of serotonin receptors, produce a powerful and specific anti-nausea effect. We have also discussed how a single transmitter, GABA, may act on hundreds of different receptors. Apparently evolution tinkers with the structure of receptors more than transmitters.

Drug molecules do not seek out particular receptor molecules; rather, drug molecules spread widely throughout the body, and when they come in contact with receptor molecules possessing the specific shape that fits the drug molecule, the two molecules bind together briefly and begin a chain of events. The lock-and-key analogy is often used for this binding action, as mentioned in Chapter 3. In the case of receptor-selective drugs, though, we have to think of keys (drug molecules) trying to insert themselves in all the locks (receptor molecules) in the neighborhood; each such key fits into only a particular subset of the locks. Once the drug (the key) binds to the receptor (the lock), it alters the activity of the receptor, activating it or blocking it. But the binding is usually temporary, and when the drug or transmitter breaks away from the receptor, the receptor resumes its unbound shape and functioning.

Occasionally researchers stumble upon a substance that appears to fit specific receptors for which no endogenous ligand is known (the word **endogenous** means "occurring naturally within the body." Drugs are **exogenous** substances; that is, they are introduced from outside the body.) This scenario, in which an "orphan" receptor is discovered, usually touches off a major research effort to discover the unknown endogenous substance. As we'll discuss later in the chapter, this process spurred the discovery of naturally occurring opiates, anxiolytics, and other compounds.

EVOLUTION AT WORK

Drug–receptor interactions vary in specificity and activity

The tuning of drug molecules to a receptor is not absolutely specific. That is, a particular drug molecule will generally bind strongly with one kind of receptor molecule, more weakly with some others, and not at all with many others. A drug molecule that has more than one kind of action in the body exhibits this flexibility because it affects more than one kind of receptor molecule. For example, some drugs combat anxiety at low doses without producing sedation (relaxation, drowsiness), but at higher doses they cause sedation, probably because at those doses they activate another type of receptor molecule.

IMPORTANT METHOD

4.6 Using Binding Affinity to Compare Drug Effectiveness

The degree of chemical attraction between a ligand and a receptor is termed **binding affinity** (or simply **affinity**). A drug with high affinity for a particular type of receptor will selectively bind to that type of receptor even at low doses, and will stay bound for a relatively long time. Lower-affinity receptors will attract and bind fewer molecules of the drug. The measurement of binding affinity is described in Figure 4.6.

Once bound, the propensity of a ligand to *activate* the receptor to which it is bound is termed its **efficacy** (or **intrinsic activity**). As you might guess, agonists have high effi-

Receptor   Lower-affinity drug   Higher-affinity drug

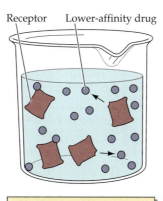

If a particular drug has a low affinity for a receptor, then it will quickly uncouple from the receptor. To bind half the receptors at any given time, a higher concentration of the drug is needed.

If a drug has a high affinity for a receptor, the two will stay together for a longer time, and a lower concentration of drug will be sufficient to bind half the receptors.

If equal concentrations of the two drugs are present, the high-affinity drug will be bound to more receptors at any given time. If the drugs activate the receptor equally, then the higher-affinity drug will have a more potent effect.

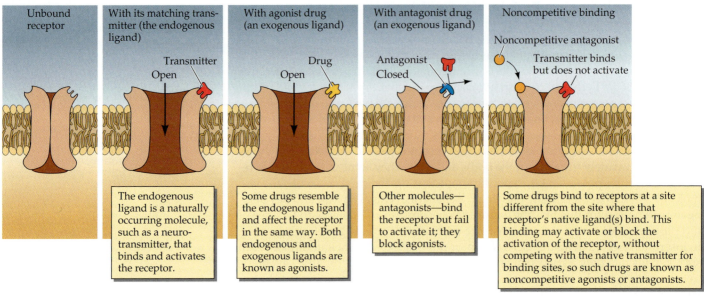

| Unbound receptor | With its matching transmitter (the endogenous ligand) | With agonist drug (an exogenous ligand) | With antagonist drug (an exogenous ligand) | Noncompetitive binding |

Transmitter Open

The endogenous ligand is a naturally occurring molecule, such as a neurotransmitter, that binds and activates the receptor.

Drug Open

Some drugs resemble the endogenous ligand and affect the receptor in the same way. Both endogenous and exogenous ligands are known as agonists.

Antagonist Closed

Other molecules—antagonists—bind the receptor but fail to activate it; they block agonists.

Noncompetitive antagonist

Transmitter binds but does not activate

Some drugs bind to receptors at a site different from the site where that receptor's native ligand(s) bind. This binding may activate or block the activation of the receptor, without competing with the native transmitter for binding sites, so such drugs are known as noncompetitive agonists or antagonists.

4.7 The Agonistic and Antagonistic Actions of Drugs

cacy and antagonists have low efficacy (Figure 4.7). **Partial agonists** are drugs that produce a middling response regardless of dose. So it is a combination of affinity and efficacy—where it binds and what it does—that determines the overall action of a drug. To some extent you can compare the effectiveness of different drugs by comparing their affinity for the receptor of interest (see Figure 16.8 for an example).

So far we have been talking about drugs that are **competitive** ligands: drugs that bind to the same receptor sites as the endogenous transmitter. To complicate things a bit further, some drugs bind to a part of the receptor complex that does not normally bind the transmitter (see Figure 4.7). In such cases the drug does not compete with the transmitter for its binding site, so we say that the drug is a **noncompetitive** ligand, binding to a **modulatory site** on the receptor. Noncompetitive ligands may either activate the receptor, thereby acting as noncompetitive agonists, or prevent the receptor from being activated by the transmitter, thus acting as noncompetitive antagonists. We'll discuss modulatory sites on the GABA receptor later in this chapter.

Dose–response relationships reflect the potency and safety of drugs

As you would probably guess, administering larger doses of a drug increases the concentration of drug that is in circulation, and ultimately increases the proportion of receptors that are bound and affected by the drug. Within certain limits, this increase in receptor binding also increases the response to the drug; in other words, bigger doses tend to produce bigger effects. When plotted as a graph, the relationship between drug doses and observed effects is called a **dose–response curve** (**DRC**) (Figure 4.8). Careful analysis of DRCs reveals many aspects of a drug's activity and is one of the main tools for understanding **pharmacodynamics** (the functional relationships between drugs and their targets).

The DRC is a fairly simple graph. Increasing doses of the test drug are plotted along the *x*-axis (by convention a logarithmic scale is used), and increasing response strength is ordered along the *y*-axis. For most drugs, and most responses, the DRC has a characteristic slanted S shape. This shape arises because at very low doses too little drug is available to provoke a measurable response, and at higher doses so many high-affinity receptors are bound that adding more drug cannot provoke any further response. At *very* high doses, most of the receptors are occupied, and we say that the receptors are **saturated.** Note that maximal response and saturation are not the same thing; a maximal response to a drug is often reached before the receptors

IMPORTANT METHOD

(a)

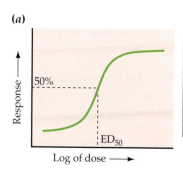

The basic dose response curve (DRC) plots increasing drug doses against increasing strength of the response being studied. The dose at which the drug has a half-maximal effect is termed the ED_{50} (for Effective Dose 50%).

(b)

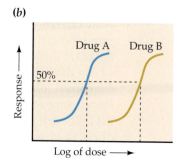

The relative potencies of two drugs can be directly assessed by comparing their ED_{50} values. In this example, both test drugs have comparable effects, but Drug A has the effects at substantially lower doses and is thus more potent than Drug B. This sort of analysis is particularly useful for comparing chemically related drugs, or *congeners*.

(c)

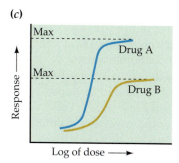

Drug efficacies are compared by evaluating maximal responses, rather than doses. Here, Drug A has a much greater maximal effect than Drug B, no matter what dose of Drug B is used. A drug of only moderate efficacy is termed a *partial agonist* (or, equivalently, a *partial antagonist*).

(d)

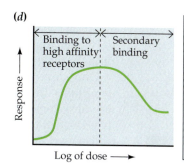

The shape of a *nonmonotonic* DRC is normal up to a point but then it reverses, and the measured response begins to decrease (or fluctuate) with increasing doses. At that point, the drug has reached sufficiently high concentrations in the body that it is starting to have effects elsewhere than at the drug's highest affinity receptors.

(e)

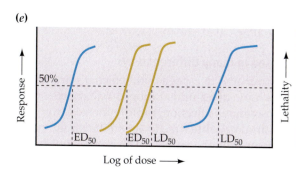

The therapeutic index is the separation between effective doses of a drug, and toxic doses. Classically, it is defined by comparing a drug's ED_{50} with the dose at which 50% of treated animals die (termed the Lethal Dose 50%, or LD_{50}). In this example, Drug A (in blue) exhibits a wide therapeutic index: its ED_{50} and LD_{50} values are far apart, and the drug is considered to be relatively safe. Drug B (yellow) is much more dangerous, because its ED_{50} and LD_{50} are close together and the risk of accidentally giving a lethal dose is high. In fact, because the two curves slightly overlap, a dose that is effective in some individuals would be lethal to others. LD_{50} experiments are controversial, and methods have been developed to estimate LD_{50} with less actual lethality.

4.8 Dose–Response Relationships

are saturated. The slanted middle portion of the curve therefore corresponds to the range of potentially useful doses.

Figure 4.8 illustrates how DRCs can be used to assess several important characteristics of drugs. For example, the DRC reveals the effective dose range of a drug, and allows comparison of the potencies of different drugs on the basis of the **ED_{50}**—the dose at which a 50% response is produced (see Figure 4.8*a* and *b*). The maximal response of a drug corresponds to its efficacy (Figure 4.8*c*). Side effects that may appear with larger doses often reflect **secondary binding** of the drug after the high-affinity receptors have been saturated (Figure 4.8*d*). An important application of the DRC is evaluation of the safety of the drug, expressed as the **therapeutic index** (Figure 4.8*e*).

Repeated treatments can reduce the effectiveness of drugs

Our bodies are impressively adaptable. Many body systems change their functioning in order to accommodate environmental challenges, and in most ways drug treatments can be viewed as changes in the body's chemical environment. This adaptability is evident in the development of drug **tolerance,** in which successive treatments with a particular drug have decreasing effects.

Drug tolerance can develop in several different ways. Some drugs provoke **metabolic tolerance,** in which the body's metabolic organ systems (such as the liver) become increasingly effective at eliminating the drug before it has a chance to affect the brain (or other target).

Alternatively, the target tissue itself may show altered sensitivity to the drug, or **functional tolerance.** In neuropharmacology, an important source of functional tolerance is the regulation of receptor proteins—changing the number of receptors present in the cell membrane. This receptor regulation alters neuronal sensitivity in the direction opposite to the drug's effect. Thus, over the course of repeated exposures to an *agonist* drug, target neurons often **down-regulate** (decrease the available receptors to which the drug can bind), thereby countering the drug effect. If the drug is an *antagonist,* target neurons may instead **up-regulate** (increase the number of receptors). Tolerance to a drug often generalizes to other drugs belonging to the same chemical class; this effect is termed **cross-tolerance.** For example, people who have developed tolerance to morphine tend to exhibit a degree of tolerance to all the other drugs in the opiate category, including codeine, heroin, and methadone.

Once developed, drug tolerance is believed to be a major cause of **withdrawal symptoms,** the unpleasant sensations associated with cessation of drug use, while neural systems re-regulate. As we will discuss later, many researchers believe that avoidance of the physical discomfort of withdrawal symptoms is an important aspect of drug addiction. Furthermore, some drug responses can become *stronger* with repeated treatments, rather than weaker. Termed **sensitization,** this effect is thought to contribute to the drug craving that addicts experience. This heightened sensitivity may last for a prolonged period, and it seems to reflect long-term brain changes in response to drugs of abuse (Peris et al., 1990).

NEURAL PLASTICITY

CLINICAL ISSUE

Drugs are administered and eliminated in many different ways

The amount of drug that reaches the brain and the speed with which it starts acting are determined in part by the drug's route of administration. Some routes of administration, such as smoking or intravenous injection, rapidly increase the concentration of drug in the body that is **bioavailable** (free to act on the target tissue, and therefore not bound to other proteins or in the process of being metabolized or excreted). With other routes, such as oral ingestion, the concentration of drug builds up more slowly over longer periods of time. Furthermore, the duration of a drug effect is largely determined by the manner in which the drug is metabolized and excreted from the body—via the kidneys, liver, lungs, and other routes. In some cases, the metabolites of drugs are themselves active; this **biotransformation** of drugs can be a source of unwanted side effects. Factors that affect the movement of a drug into, through, and out of the body are collectively referred to as **pharmacokinetics.**

Humans have devised a remarkable array of techniques for introducing substances into the body; these are summarized in Table 4.2. In Chapter 2 we discussed the **blood–brain barrier:** the tight junctions between the endothelial cells of blood vessels within the CNS that inhibit the movement of larger molecules out of the bloodstream and into the brain. This barrier poses a major challenge for neuropharmacology because many drugs that might be clinically or experimentally useful are too large to pass the blood–brain barrier to enter the brain. To a limited extent this problem can be circumvented by the administration of drugs directly into the brain, but that is a drastic step. Alternatively, some drugs can take advantage of **active transport** systems that normally move nutrients out of the bloodstream and into the brain.

Drugs Affect Each Stage of Neural Conduction and Synaptic Transmission

Almost all the behavioral effects that we discuss in this chapter are caused by the activities of drugs on synaptic events and processes and on neural conduction.

TABLE 4.2 *The Relationship between Routes of Administration and Effects of Drugs*

Route of administration	Examples and mechanisms	Typical speed of effects
INGESTION Tablets and capsules Syrups Infusions and teas Suppositories	Many sorts of drugs and remedies; depends on absorption by the gut, which is somewhat slower than most other routes	Slow to moderate
INHALATION Smoking Nasal absorption Inhaled powders and sprays	Nicotine, cocaine, and other drugs of abuse; also used for a variety of prescription drugs and hormone treatments. Inhalation methods take advantage of the rich vascularization of the nose and lungs to convey drugs directly into the bloodstream.	Moderate to fast
PERIPHERAL INJECTION Subcutaneous Intramuscular Intraperitoneal (abdominal) Intravenous	Many drugs; subcutaneous (under the skin) injections tend to have the slowest effects because they must diffuse into nearby tissue in order to reach the bloodstream; intravenous injections have very rapid effects because the drug is placed directly into circulation.	Moderate to very fast
CENTRAL INJECTION Intracerebroventricular (into ventricular system) Intrathecal (into spinal CSF) Epidural (under the dura mater) Intracerebral (directly into a brain region)	Central methods involve injection directly into the CNS; used in order to circumvent the blood–brain barrier, to rule out peripheral effects, or to directly affect a discrete brain location.	Fast to very fast

Figure 4.9 illustrates how certain drugs affect the major steps in neural conduction and synaptic transmission (see also Figure 3.13). In the discussion that follows we'll comment on some of these agents and their effects, as well as on related effects of other drugs.

Drugs affect presynaptic events

If axonal transport is inhibited by a drug (e.g., colchicine has this activity), enzymes that are manufactured in the cell body are not replaced in the presynaptic terminals. Because enzymes are needed to manufacture transmitter chemicals and vesicles, drugs that inhibit axonal transport prevent replenishment of the transmitter agent as it is used up, and synaptic transmission fails. The drug reserpine interferes with the storage of catecholamine transmitters in vesicles by making the vesicles leaky. And even if a presynaptic terminal has an adequate supply of transmitter stored in vesicles, various agents or conditions can prevent the release of transmitter when a nerve impulse reaches the terminal. A low extracellular calcium (Ca^{2+}) concentration, or pharmacological blockade of Ca^{2+} channels at the axon terminals, inhibits transmitter release by preventing the Ca^{2+} influx that is required for transmitter release.

Some toxins prevent the release of specific kinds of transmitters (see Figure 4.9 for examples) (de Paiva et al., 1993). For instance, botulinum toxin, which is formed by bacteria that multiply in improperly canned food, poisons many people each year by blocking the release of ACh. The toxin binds to specialized receptors in nicotinic cholinergic neural membranes and is transported into the cell, where it blocks the Ca^{2+}-dependent release of transmitter (McMahon et al., 1992), resulting in muscle paralysis. In much-diluted form, botulinum toxin is marketed as Botox, which inhibits facial wrinkling by locally paralyzing facial muscles into which it has been injected. Tetanus (lockjaw) bacteria produce an often fatal toxin that blocks activity at inhibitory synapses and causes strong involuntary contractions of muscles.

Other agents stimulate or facilitate the release of certain transmitters. **Neuromodulators** are not transmitters themselves, but they modulate the effectiveness of

CLINICAL ISSUE

(a) Presynaptic mechanisms

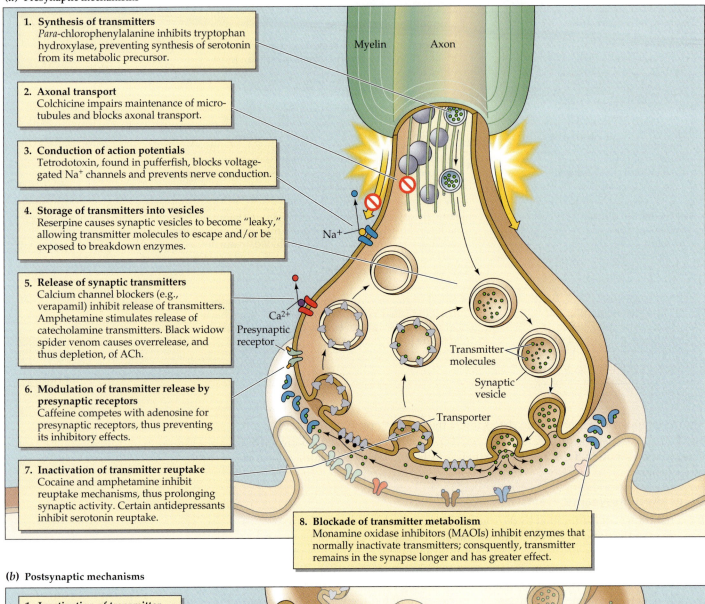

1. Synthesis of transmitters
Para-chlorophenylalanine inhibits tryptophan hydroxylase, preventing synthesis of serotonin from its metabolic precursor.

2. Axonal transport
Colchicine impairs maintenance of micro-tubules and blocks axonal transport.

3. Conduction of action potentials
Tetrodotoxin, found in pufferfish, blocks voltage-gated Na⁺ channels and prevents nerve conduction.

4. Storage of transmitters into vesicles
Reserpine causes synaptic vesicles to become "leaky," allowing transmitter molecules to escape and/or be exposed to breakdown enzymes.

5. Release of synaptic transmitters
Calcium channel blockers (e.g., verapamil) inhibit release of transmitters. Amphetamine stimulates release of catecholamine transmitters. Black widow spider venom causes overrelease, and thus depletion, of ACh.

6. Modulation of transmitter release by presynaptic receptors
Caffeine competes with adenosine for presynaptic receptors, thus preventing its inhibitory effects.

7. Inactivation of transmitter reuptake
Cocaine and amphetamine inhibit reuptake mechanisms, thus prolonging synaptic activity. Certain antidepressants inhibit serotonin reuptake.

8. Blockade of transmitter metabolism
Monamine oxidase inhibitors (MAOIs) inhibit enzymes that normally inactivate transmitters; consquently, transmitter remains in the synapse longer and has greater effect.

Myelin   Axon

Na⁺

Ca²⁺
Presynaptic receptor

Transmitter molecules

Synaptic vesicle

Transporter

(b) Postsynaptic mechanisms

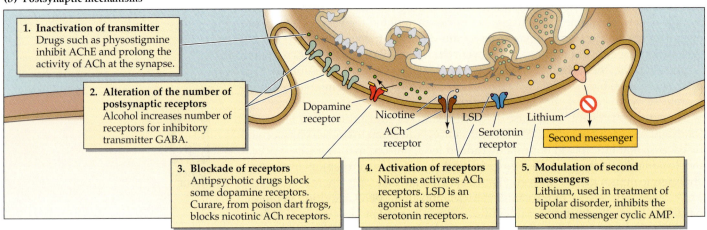

1. Inactivation of transmitter
Drugs such as physostigmine inhibit AChE and prolong the activity of ACh at the synapse.

2. Alteration of the number of postsynaptic receptors
Alcohol increases number of receptors for inhibitory transmitter GABA.

3. Blockade of receptors
Antipsychotic drugs block some dopamine receptors. Curare, from poison dart frogs, blocks nicotinic ACh receptors.

4. Activation of receptors
Nicotine activates ACh receptors. LSD is an agonist at some serotonin receptors.

5. Modulation of second messengers
Lithium, used in treatment of bipolar disorder, inhibits the second messenger cyclic AMP.

Dopamine receptor

Nicotine
ACh receptor

LSD

Serotonin receptor

Lithium

Second messenger

4.9 Steps in Synaptic Transmission That Are Affected by Drugs

synaptic transmission. The noncompetitive ligands discussed earlier (see Figure 4.7) are neuromodulators. In general, neuromodulators affect either the release of the transmitter or the receptor response to the transmitter. For example, black widow spider venom exaggerates the release of ACh.

Perhaps the most beloved of all neuromodulators is the **caffeine** that we obtain from drinking coffee and other caffeinated beverages (worldwide, we consume about 400 *billion* cups of coffee each year). Caffeine acts as an exogenous neuromodulator, by blocking the effect of an endogenous neuromodulator, **adenosine.** By competing with adenosine for access to adenosine A_{2A} receptors on the surfaces of neurons, caffeine produces long-lasting changes in an internal signaling pathway mediated by a protein called DARPP-32 (which, incredibly, is short for *d*opamine- and cyclic *A*MP–*r*egulated *p*hospho*p*rotein of molecular mass *32*,000) (Lindskog et al., 2002). Because adenosine normally acts on presynaptic terminals to inhibit the release of catecholamine transmitters, caffeine increases catecholamine release, causing arousal. (Interestingly, by a different route the stimulant drug amphetamine shares the action of facilitating catecholamine release.)

Where does adenosine normally come from? It appears that at least some catecholaminergic synapses co-release adenosine with the neurotransmitter. The adenosine binds to receptors on the same presynaptic terminal that released it, so we say that the adenosine acts on **autoreceptors.** It may seem odd that a neuron that is releasing transmitter would also release a neuromodulator to inhibit transmitter release, but this type of complicated modulation of transmitter release is probably the rule, not the exception.

Drugs affect postsynaptic events

As we've discussed, postsynaptic receptor molecules can be blocked or activated by various drugs. For example, curare blocks nicotinic ACh receptors. Because the synapses between nerves and skeletal muscles are nicotinic, curare paralyzes all skeletal muscles, including those used in breathing. We discussed several other drugs that affect postsynaptic receptors when we described the different neurotransmitter systems at the start of this chapter. Behavior can be disrupted not only when transmitter–receptor action is blocked, but also when it is prolonged. Agents that inhibit the enzyme acetylcholinesterase (AChE) allow ACh to remain active at the synapse and alter the timing of synaptic transmission. Effects can range from mild to severe, depending on the anti-AChE agent and its dosage.

Drugs That Affect the Brain Can Be Divided into Functional Classes

The many drugs that affect the brain are classified on the basis of both their specific effects on behavior and their physiological actions in the brain. In the sections that follow, we will briefly review some of the major categories of psychoactive substances.

Antipsychotic drugs relieve the symptoms of schizophrenia

Originally thought to be an antihistamine in the 1950s, chlorpromazine was accidentally discovered to reduce some of the symptoms of schizophrenia. Subsequent intense research activity identified several other **antipsychotic drugs** (known as **neuroleptics**). The neuroleptics revolutionized the treatment of schizophrenia because they greatly reduce many of the symptoms that prevent patients with this condition from living on their own. These first-generation drugs, classified as **typical neuroleptics,** all share one key feature: They act as selective antagonists of dopamine D_2 receptors. One of the best-known typical neuroleptics, haloperidol (Haldol), exhibits a nearly 100-fold selectivity for D_2 over D_1 receptors.

The 1990s saw the advent of second-generation antipsychotics, know as **atypical neuroleptics.** These newer drugs are just as effective in treating schizophrenia, but

CLINICAL ISSUE

they are less likely to cause unwanted side effects, especially the movement disorders that tend to accompany the long-term use of typical neuroleptics. Some atypical neuroleptics, particularly clozapine, also block certain serotonin receptors; one unique feature of clozapine is that it reduces additional symptoms (termed *negative* symptoms; see Table 16.2) that typical neuroleptics generally do not relieve. Unfortunately, despite progress in its treatment, schizophrenia remains a major health problem. We return to the topic of schizophrenia and its treatment in Chapter 16.

Antidepressants relieve chronic mood problems

CLINICAL ISSUE

Disturbances of mood, or **affective disorders,** are among the most common of all psychiatric complaints. In the span of one year, about 5.8% of men and 9.5% of women will experience a significant episode of depression, which is the most prevalent affective disorder (World Health Organization, 2001).

The first generation of effective **antidepressant** medications, developed in the 1950s, were the **monoamine oxidase inhibitors** (**MAOIs**); modern MAOI antidepressants include tranylcypromine (Parnate) and isocarboxazid (Marplan). Recall that one of the major activities of MAOs is to break down monoamine neurotransmitters at synapses, thereby reducing transmitter activity (see Figure 4.9). By inhibiting monoamine oxidase, MAOI drugs allow monoamine neurotransmitters to accumulate at synapses, with an associated improvement in mood.

Increasing synaptic monoamine availability appears to be a key activity of all antidepressants. The second generation of antidepressants—the **tricyclics**—combat depression by increasing the synaptic content of norepinephrine and serotonin. Named after their molecular three-ringed structure, tricyclics such as imipramine (Tofranil) act by blocking the reuptake of neurotransmitters into presynaptic axon terminals. More recently developed antidepressants, such as fluoxetine (Prozac), sertraline (Zoloft) and citalopram (Celexa), are classified as **selective serotonin reuptake inhibitors** (**SSRIs**); as the name indicates, these drugs alleviate depression by selectively allowing serotonin to accumulate in synapses. These newer antidepressants lack some of the undesirable side effects of tricyclics, but they can take as long as 6 to 8 weeks to have full effect. We will discuss the causes and treatment of affective disorders in more detail in Chapter 16.

Anxiolytics combat anxiety

Most of us occasionally suffer feelings of vague dissatisfaction or apprehension that we call anxiety, but here we will be concerned with the disabling emotional distress that resembles abject fear and terror. Severe anxiety that prevents people from carrying on normal daily activities is estimated to afflict about 8% of adult Americans. These clinical states of anxiety include panic attacks, phobias (such as the fear of taking an airplane or even of leaving the house), and generalized anxiety (see Chapter 16).

Humans have long sought relief from anxiety through the ingestion of **anxiolytics** (from the word *anxiety* and the Greek *lytikos,* "able to loosen"). Sometimes also called *tranquilizers,* anxiolytics belong to the general category of **depressants:** drugs that depress or reduce nervous system activity. Alcohol is perhaps the original anxiolytic, but its anxiety-fighting properties come at the cost of intoxication, addiction potential, and neuropsychological impairment with long-term abuse. Opiates and barbiturates have also been used to relieve anxiety, but they have strongly sedative effects, strong addiction potential, and, in the case of barbiturates, significant risk of accidental overdose.

First discovered in the 1960s, **benzodiazepine** agonists have proven to be safe and effective anxiolytics, and they are among the most heavily prescribed drugs. We mentioned earlier the benzodiazepine diazepam (trade name Valium), which binds to specific sites on GABA$_A$ receptors and enhances the activity of GABA (Walters et al., 2000). Because GABA$_A$ receptors are inhibitory, benzodiazepines help GABA to produce larger inhibitory postsynaptic potentials than would be caused by GABA alone.

In fact, GABA$_A$ receptors have several different binding sites—some that facilitate and some that inhibit the effect of GABA (Figure 4.10).

Note that benzodiazepines do not bind to the same site on the receptor as the transmitter GABA does; rather, the drug binds to a modulatory site on the receptor. The benzodiazepine-binding site is an **orphan receptor**—a receptor for which an endogenous ligand has not been conclusively identified—and the hunt for its endogenous ligand has been intense. A possible endogenous ligand is **allopregnanolone,** a steroid derived from the hormone progesterone. This neurohormone is induced and released as a consequence of stress; it has a calming effect. Alcohol ingestion also increases brain concentrations of allopregnanolone (VanDoren et al., 2000), so this steroid may mediate some of the calming influence of alcohol.

New generations of anxiolytics that are under development affect other transmitter systems, notably serotonin. The serotonergic anxiolytic buspirone (Buspar) is an effective anxiolytic that lacks the sedative effects of benzodiazepines. Although it is known to be a 5HT$_{1A}$ agonist and, to a lesser extent, a partial agonist of dopamine D$_2$ receptors, the exact mechanism of buspirone's anxiolytic action remains unknown.

Alcohol has several effects

Alcohol has traveled the full route of human history, no doubt because it is so easily produced by the fermentation of fruit or grains, and thus is an ingredient of many types of pleasant beverages. Taken in moderation, alcohol is harmless or even beneficial to the health of adults; for example, consumption of one drink or so per day is associated with reduced risk of cardiovascular and Alzheimer's diseases, and with improved control of blood sugar levels (Davies et al., 2002; Leroi et al., 2002; Mukamal et al., 2003). *Excessive* alcohol consumption, however, is very damaging and linked to more than 60 disease processes.

The psychoactive effect of alcohol in the nervous system is biphasic: An initial stimulant phase is followed by a more prolonged depressant phase. GABA plays an important role in mediating the effects of alcohol in the brain. In a similar manner to the benzodiazepines, but acting via a different receptor site, alcohol activates the GABA$_A$ receptor–coupled chloride channel and thus increases postsynaptic inhibition. Alcohol also affects other transmitters. For example, low doses of alcohol stimulate dopamine pathways, and the resulting increase in dopamine may be related to the euphoriant properties of alcohol.

Chronic abuse of alcohol can damage nerve cells. Cells of the superior frontal cortex, Purkinje cells of the cerebellum, and hippocampal pyramidal cells show particularly prominent pathological changes. Some of these degenerative effects of chronic alcohol use may be due to a secondary consequence of alcoholism: poor diet. Chronic alcoholism is accompanied by severe thiamine deficiency, which can lead to neural degeneration and Korsakoff's syndrome (see Chapter 17). And alcohol abuse by expectant mothers can cause grievous permanent brain damage to the developing fetus (termed **fetal alcohol syndrome**), a topic to which we will return in Chapter 7 (see Figure 7.24). In fact, it is not clear whether it is safe for pregnant women to consume *any* alcohol, even small quantities (Day et al., 2002).

Kril et al. (1997) reported that the frontal lobes of people suffering from alcoholism—especially the superior frontal association cortex—are the brain areas that are most affected by chronic alcohol use. However, some of the anatomical changes that are evident in the brains of people suffering from chronic alcoholism may be reversible with abstinence. For example, chronic exposure to alcohol in experimental rats reduces the number of synapses on cerebellar neurons, but this number is restored to control levels after a period of recovery (Dlugos and Pentney, 1997). In

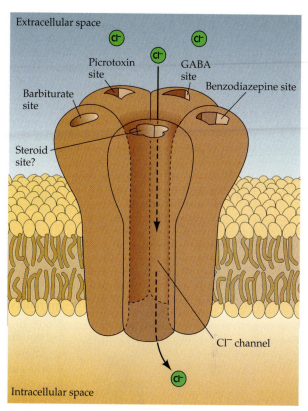

4.10 The GABA$_A$ Receptor Has Many Different Binding Sites

CLINICAL ISSUE

4.11 The Effects of Alcohol on the Brain MRI studies of humans who suffer from alcoholism show that abstaining from alcohol for 30 days increases the volume of cortical gray matter (*a*) and decreases the volume of the lateral ventricles (*b*). (After Pfefferbaum et al., 1995.)

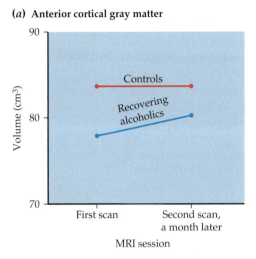

(*a*) Anterior cortical gray matter

Controls

Recovering alcoholics

First scan   Second scan, a month later

MRI session

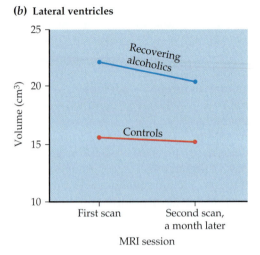

(*b*) Lateral ventricles

Recovering alcoholics

Controls

First scan   Second scan, a month later

MRI session

GENES AND BEHAVIOR

humans suffering from alcoholism, MRI studies of short-term effects of abstinence show an increase in the volume of cortical gray matter and a reduction in ventricular volume (Figure 4.11) (Pfefferbaum et al., 1995).

There is a strong hereditary component to alcoholism, as indicated by human studies and selective breeding experiments in rats. In humans, 20% to 50% of the sons of people who suffer from alcoholism and 3% to 8% of the daughters eventually suffer from alcoholism themselves. Rates of alcoholism in the first-degree relatives of people who suffer from alcoholism are several times higher than are rates for the general population (Schuckit and Smith, 1997). Some evidence suggests that a genetic vulnerability combined with a stressful environment can result in alcoholism (McGue, 1999).

Even in the absence of clear-cut alcoholism, periodic overconsumption of alcohol—*bingeing*—may cause brain damage. Fulton Crews and coworkers have reported that in as little as 4 days, rats bingeing on alcohol exhibit neural degeneration in several areas of the brain. Damage is especially evident in the olfactory bulbs and in limbic structures connected with the hippocampus, and it is associated with impairments of cognitive ability (Obernier et al., 2002). Alcohol bingeing also significantly reduces the rate of neurogenesis—the formation of new neurons—in the adult hippocampus (Nixon and Crews, 2002).

Opiates help relieve pain

Opium, extracted from poppy flower seedpods (Figure 4.12), has been used by humans since at least the Stone Age. Morphine, the major active substance in opium, is a very effective **analgesic** (painkiller) that has brought relief from severe pain to many millions of people. Unfortunately, morphine also has a strong potential for addiction, as does its close relative, **heroin** (diacetylmorphine).

In 1973, pharmacologists Candace Pert and Solomon Snyder found that opiate drugs such as morphine bind to specific receptor molecules that are concentrated in certain regions of the brain. Opiate receptors are found especially in the limbic and hypothalamic areas of the brain, and they are particularly rich in the

4.12 The Source of Opium and Morphine The opium poppy has a distinctive flower and seedpod. The bitter flavor and CNS actions of opium may provide the poppy plant a defense against being eaten.

Olfactory bulb

Caudate nucleus

Medial thalamus

Hippo-campus

Periaque-ductal gray

Inferior colliculus

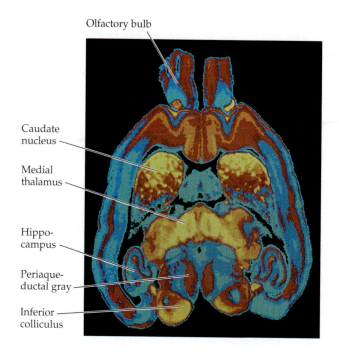

4.13 The Distribution of Opiate Receptors in the Rat Brain This horizontal section (rostral is at the top) shows opiate receptors widely distributed in the brain (the areas of highest binding are shown in yellow, orange, and red). They are concentrated in the medial thalamus and in some brainstem areas: the periaqueductal gray and the inferior colliculus. (Courtesy of Miles Herkenham, National Institute of Mental Health.)

locus coeruleus and in the gray matter that surrounds the aqueduct in the brainstem (known as the **periaqueductal gray**) (Figure 4.13). Injection of morphine directly into the periaqueductal gray produces strong analgesia, indicating that this is a region where morphine acts to reduce pain perception (see Chapter 8). After the discovery of these orphan opiate receptors, investigators began an intensive search for endogenous opiate receptor ligands.

A pair of endogenous peptides that bind to opiate receptors were eventually identified and named **enkephalins** (from the Greek *en*, "in," and *kephale*, "head") (Hughes et al., 1975). Research with animal subjects demonstrated that, like morphine, enkephalins relieve pain and are addictive. Physically, however, only a small part of the enkephalin molecule is the same as the morphine molecule, but this common part is what binds to the opioid receptor. Further research uncovered additional families of **endogenous opioids**—that is, opioids that are found naturally in the brain. One of these families consists of compounds called **endorphins,** a contraction of *endogenous morphine*—literally, "the brain's own morphine."

There are three main kinds of opioid receptors—the δ, κ, and μ opioid receptors—differing in their affinity for various *opiatergic* drugs (C. J. Evans et al., 1992; J. B. Wang et al., 1993; Yasuda et al., 1993). All three opiate receptor subtypes are G protein–coupled metabotropic receptors.

Marijuana has a wide array of effects

Marijuana and related preparations, such as hashish, are obtained from the *Cannabis sativa* (Figure 4.14) plant and are the most widely used of all illicit drugs. Typically ingested via smoking, marijuana contains dozens of active ingredients, chief among which is the compound **Δ9-tetrahydrocannabinol** (**THC**) (Gaoni and Mechoulam, 1964). The subjective experience of marijuana use is quite variable among individuals: Relaxation and mood alteration are the most frequent effects; but stimulation, hallucination, and paranoia also occur in some cases. Sustained use of marijuana can cause addiction (Maldonado and Rodríguez de Fonseca, 2002), and frequent smoking of marijuana, like tobacco, can contribute to respiratory diseases.

In studying the actions of marijuana, investigators deciphered the structure of the relevant receptor molecules before they discovered the endogenous ligand—the body's own marijuana-like compound, or **cannabinoid.** Subsequent research

Candace Pert

Solomon Snyder

4.14 An Indoor Marijuana Farm Although growing the marijuana plant (*Cannabis sativa*) is illegal in the United States, this plant has been estimated to be the largest cash crop in several states. Growers have developed techniques for growing highly potent strains of cannabis indoors under "grow lights."

showed that cannabinoid receptors are concentrated in the substantia nigra, the hippocampus, the cerebellar cortex, and the cerebral cortex (Figure 4.15) (Devane et al., 1988); other regions, such as the brainstem, show few of these receptors. There are at least two subtypes of cannabinoid receptors—CB_1 and CB_2 (Gerard et al., 1991; Pertwee, 1997)—both of which are G protein–coupled metabotropic receptors. Genetic disruption of CB_1 receptors is sufficient to make mice unresponsive to the rewarding properties of cannabinoid drugs (Ledent et al., 1999). Only the CB_1 receptor is found in the nervous system; CB_2 receptors are especially prominent in the immune system.

Several probable endogenous ligands—termed **endocannabinoids**—have been identified. Interestingly, endocannabinoids can function as **retrograde messengers,** conveying messages from the postsynaptic cell to the presynaptic cell. This retrograde signal is thought to modulate the release of neurotransmitter by the presynaptic nerve terminal (R. I. Wilson and Nicoll, 2002). The first to be identified and most widely studied of the endocannabinoids is **anandamide** (from the Sanskrit *ananda*, "bliss") (Devane et al., 1992), which has diverse functional effects, including alterations of memory formation, appetite stimulation, reduced sensitivity to pain, and protection from excitotoxic brain damage (Marsicano et al., 2003; P. B. Smith et al., 1994). Other endocannabinoids under active investigation include 2-arachidonylglycerol (2-AG) (Stella et al., 1997) and oleamide (Leggett et al., 2004).

The study of endogenous cannabinoid ligands will aid the search for drugs that have the beneficial effects of marijuana (relieving pain, lowering blood pressure, combating nausea, lowering eye pressure in glaucoma, and so on), without the harmful aspects. Ironically, because any newly developed synthetic cannabinoid drug could be patented by a pharmaceutical company, it could be legally prescribed to patients, such as those trying to combat the nausea of chemotherapy. Presently such patients break the law in the United States when using "medical marijuana." In a real sense, marijuana use is not legalized in these cases because no Wall Street company stands to profit from it. You can't file a patent for a plant that's already been in use for centuries.

Stimulants increase the activity of the nervous system

The degree of activity of the nervous system is determined by competing excitatory and inhibitory influences. Stimulants are drugs that tip the balance toward the excitatory side; they therefore have an alerting, activating effect. Many naturally occurring and artificial stimulants are widely used; examples include amphetamine, nicotine, caffeine, and cocaine. Some stimulants act directly by increasing excitatory synaptic potentials. Others act by blocking normal in-

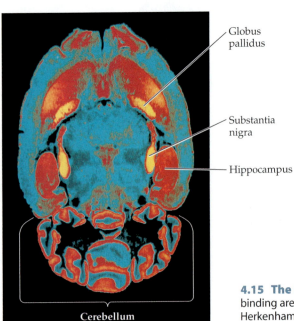

Globus pallidus

Substantia nigra

Hippocampus

Cerebellum

4.15 The Distribution of Cannabinoid Receptors in the Rat Brain The areas of highest binding are indicated by yellow, orange, and red in this horizontal section. (Courtesy of Miles Herkenham, National Institute of Mental Health.)

hibitory processes; one example we've seen already is the blocking of adenosine by caffeine. Paradoxically, stimulants such as methylphenidate (Ritalin) have a calming effect in humans with attention deficit hyperactivity disorder (ADHD); this activity may be mediated by changes in serotonergic activity (Gainetdinov et al., 1999).

**CLINICAL
ISSUE**

Nicotine   Tobacco is native to the Americas, where European explorers first encountered smoking; these explorers brought tobacco back to Europe with them. Tobacco use subsequently became much more widespread, especially following technological innovations that made tobacco easier to smoke, in the form of cigarettes (W. Bennett, 1983). Exposed to the large surface of the lungs, the **nicotine** from cigarettes enters the blood and brain much more rapidly than does nicotine from snuff, chewing tobacco, or smoke that is not deeply inhaled, such as pipe and cigar smoke.

The stimulant nicotine activates one class of ACh receptors, which, as we learned earlier, are called *nicotinic receptors*. Most nicotinic receptors are found at neuromuscular junctions and in neurons of the autonomic ganglia, but many are also present in the central nervous system and likewise are directly stimulated by nicotine. When nicotine enters the bloodstream, it increases the heart rate—both directly (by stimulating sympathetic ganglia) and indirectly (by stimulating the adrenal gland to release the hormone epinephrine). Nicotine also increases blood pressure, secretion of hydrochloric acid in the stomach, and motor activity of the bowel. These neural effects, quite apart from the effects of tobacco tar on the lungs, contribute to the unhealthful consequences of heavy and prolonged use of tobacco products.

Cocaine   For hundreds of years, people in Bolivia, Colombia, and Peru have been using the leaves of the coca shrub—either chewed or brewed as a tea—to increase endurance, alleviate hunger, and promote a sense of well-being. This use of coca leaves does not seem to cause problems. The artificially purified coca extract (**cocaine**), however, is a potently addictive alkaloid stimulant that has harmed millions of lives.

First isolated in 1859, cocaine was added to beverages and tonics for its stimulant qualities, and subsequently it was used as a local anesthetic (it is in the same chemical family as procaine, trade name Novocain) and to relieve depression. In addition, it was widely used as a psychostimulant until 1932, when it gave way to amphetamine, which acts much like cocaine but was easier to obtain (amphetamine was sold in inhalers for nasal congestion, and some people cracked open inhalers to get the drug). When legal restrictions on amphetamine raised its price in the 1960s, cocaine use rose again. Many users snort cocaine powder, which rapidly enters the bloodstream via the nasal route (see Table 4.2).

Crack is a smokable form of cocaine that appeared in the mid-1980s. Because cocaine in this form enters the blood and the brain more rapidly, crack cocaine is even more addictive than cocaine powder. Like other psychostimulants, cocaine acts by blocking monoamine transporters, especially those for dopamine (Figure 4.16), thereby blocking reuptake of the transmitters and therefore boosting their effects. Cocaine may have neurotoxic effects, and an overdose can provoke marked changes in cerebral blood flow, including strokes (Holman et al., 1993). As a consequence of sensitization, which we discussed earlier, chronic cocaine use can provoke symptoms similar to psychosis. Cessation of cocaine use often produces very uncomfortable withdrawal symptoms: initial agitation and powerful drug cravings, followed by depression and an in-

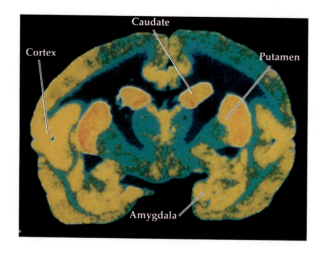

4.16 Cocaine-Binding Sites in the Monkey Brain   This autoradiograph of a coronal section shows the distribution of cocaine-binding sites. The areas of the highest binding are shown by orange and yellow. (Courtesy of Bertha K. Madras.)

ability to enjoy anything else in life. Decreases in cerebral glucose metabolism are evident for several months after cocaine use is discontinued.

Some children are initially exposed to cocaine while in the womb, and there has been widespread fear that exposure during fetal life might produce irreversible harm to the development of brain and behavior (Vogel, 1997). Although the home environment of children who were exposed to cocaine prenatally has potent effects on intellectual development, fetal exposure to cocaine also impairs intellectual growth to some extent. One cocaine-related developmental effect on infants is a decreased ability to focus attention, an effect that is also seen in rats exposed to prenatal cocaine (Gendle et al., 2003).

Amphetamine The molecular structure of the synthetic psychostimulant **amphetamine** resembles that of the catecholamine transmitters (norepinephrine, epinephrine, and dopamine). Amphetamine and the even more potent methamphetamine (*speed*) cause the release of these transmitters from the presynaptic terminals even in the absence of action potentials, and when action potentials *do* reach the axon terminals, amphetamine also potentiates the subsequent release of transmitter. Furthermore, once transmitter has been released, amphetamine enhances activity in two ways: (1) by blocking the reuptake of catecholamines into the presynaptic terminal, and (2) by competing with the catecholamines for the enzyme that inactivates them (monoamine oxidase).

Because amphetamine stimulates and enhances the activity of the catecholamine transmitters, it has a variety of behavioral effects. On a short-term basis, it produces heightened alertness and even euphoria, and it wards off boredom. Its short-term use can promote sustained effort without rest or sleep and with lowered fatigue. However, although a person may be able to accomplish more work and feel more confident by using amphetamine, most studies show that the quality of work is not improved by the drug; it increases motivation but not cognitive ability.

As a consequence of the rapid development of tolerance to amphetamine, chronic users take larger and larger doses, leading to sleeplessness, severe weight loss, and general deterioration of mental and physical condition. Prolonged use of amphetamine may lead to symptoms that closely resemble those of paranoid schizophrenia: compulsive, agitated behavior and irrational suspiciousness. In fact, some amphetamine users have been misdiagnosed as having schizophrenia (see Chapter 16). Amphetamine acts on the autonomic nervous system to produce high blood pressure, tremor, dizziness, sweating, rapid breathing, and nausea. Worst of all, people who chronically abuse speed display symptoms of brain damage long after they quit using the drug (Ernst et al., 2000).

Cocaine and amphetamine treatments each induce the brain to produce a peptide called, naturally enough, **cocaine- and amphetamine-regulated transcript (CART)**. Injections of CART in a particular brain region (the ventral tegmental area, which we'll discuss a little later in the chapter) is very rewarding for rats (Kimmel et al., 2000), so the peptide may mediate some of the pleasurable effects of these drugs. The CART system also seems to be involved in the regulation of appetite (see Chapter 13).

Hallucinogenic drugs alter sensory perception

Drugs classified as **hallucinogens** alter sensory perceptions, often in striking or dramatic ways, and produce peculiar experiences. But the term *hallucinogen* is probably a misnomer because, whereas a hallucination is a novel perception that takes place in the absence of sensory stimulation (hearing voices, or seeing something that isn't there), the drugs in this category tend to alter or distort existing perceptions. The effects of lysergic acid diethylamide (**LSD**, or *acid*) and related substances like mescaline (*peyote*) and psilocybin (*magic mushrooms*), are predominantly visual. Users often see fantastic pictures with intense colors, and they are often aware that these strangely altered perceptions are not real events.

Hallucinogenic agents are chemically diverse; several have been found to affect one or another of the amine synaptic transmitter systems. For example, mescaline, the drug extracted from the peyote plant, affects noradrenergic and serotonergic systems. Many hallucinogens, including LSD, mescaline, psilocybin, and others, tend to act as serotonin receptor agonists or partial agonists, especially at subtypes of $5HT_2$ receptors. Other hallucinogens, such as muscarine, found in some mushrooms, affect the ACh system.

You may have guessed that Albert Hofmann, whose story opened this chapter, was the discoverer of LSD. In fact, the study of LSD's activities became the focus of his professional career, summarized in his 1981 book, *LSD: My Problem Child*. Following its discovery, LSD was intensively studied as a possible psychiatric treatment. Starting in the 1950s, many investigators worked on LSD, hoping it would provide a useful model of psychosis that would suggest clues about the biochemical processes in mental illnesses. The structure of LSD resembles that of serotonin, and LSD was soon found to act on serotonin receptors, probably evoking visual phenomena by activating serotonin receptors of the visual cortex. Former users of LSD sometimes report experiencing flashbacks—that is, experiences as if they had taken a dose of drug, even though they are drug-free. These episodes can follow even brief use of LSD, but it is not yet clear whether they reflect permanent neural changes or a special form of memory.

Phencyclidine (commonly known as **PCP** or *angel dust*) was developed in 1956 as a potent analgesic and anesthetic agent. It was soon dropped from use as an anesthetic because patients reported effects such as agitation, excitement, delirium, hostility, and disorganization of perceptions, but PCP continues to be used as a street drug, principally because of its hallucinogenic actions. Even at relatively low doses, PCP produces numerous undesirable effects, including combativeness and catatonia (stupor and immobility). Higher doses or repeated use can lead to long-lasting profound confusion, or convulsions and coma. The similarity between PCP's effects and psychosis has led some researchers to propose PCP as a chemical model of schizophrenia (see Chapter 16). In animal models, PCP causes degeneration in the hippocampus and the cingulate gyrus.

PCP antagonizes the NMDA receptor (see Figure 16.9), perhaps at a special binding site, and it stimulates release of the transmitter dopamine (Gorelick and Balster, 1995). Ketamine is a less potent NMDA antagonist that is used as an anesthetic agent. PET studies of the effects of ketamine on the brains of healthy volunteers showed focal increases of metabolic activity in the prefrontal cortex (Breier, Malhotra, et al., 1997), so perhaps PCP also acts there. Like PCP, ketamine produced transient psychotic symptoms in these volunteers.

Some "recreational" drugs may have long-term effects

The dangers of drug use widely heralded in public health campaigns usually focus on short-term changes. We all know about the heroin *rush,* the cocaine *high,* and the many other relatively short-term effects of recreational drugs described in newspapers, magazines, and textbooks. But do these drugs have enduring effects that persist well beyond a period of hours or days? Some ominous findings indicate that brain changes produced by recreational drugs may persist for months (McCann et al., 1997).

For example, *Ecstasy* is the street name for the hallucinogenic amphetamine derivative **MDMA** (3,4-methylenedioxymethamphetamine). In nonhumans, this drug produces persistent effects on serotonin-producing neurons: prolonged reduction in serotonin metabolites and the serotonin transporter. In addition, fine serotonergic axons are damaged, but cell bodies in the brainstem appear to be spared. Figure 4.17 shows a marked reduction in

Albert Hofmann

4.17 Long-Term Effects of a Single Dose of Ecstasy on the Monkey Brain Serotonin axons in the dorsal cortex of a control squirrel monkey (*a*) and a squirrel monkey treated with a single dose of MDMA (Ecstasy) 18 months earlier (*b*). (Fischer et al., 1995; photo courtesy of George Ricaurte.)

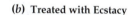

(*a*) Control

(*b*) Treated with Ecstacy

serotonin axons in the cortex and hippocampus of a squirrel monkey treated with MDMA 18 months earlier (C. Fischer et al., 1995). Humans who take MDMA also display reduced serotonin binding in the cortex (Semple et al., 1999). These changes may be related to the persistent psychiatric and cognitive effects, including memory disturbances, seen after MDMA use (Wareing et al., 2000).

Drug Abuse Is Pervasive

CLINICAL ISSUE

Substance abuse and addiction have become a social problem that afflicts many millions of people and disrupts the lives of their families, friends, and associates. The whole community is affected because (1) many people who use tobacco, alcohol, and other drugs run up medical expenses and die prematurely (the toll from smoking and alcohol abuse far outweighs that of illegal drugs, with smoking alone accounting for about 20% of all U.S. deaths each year); (2) substance abusers commit crimes and cause traffic accidents, fires, and other social disorders; (3) the costs of helping addicts control their dependence and abuse, and of controlling drug trafficking, are high; and (4) many babies whose mothers used psychoactive substances (including alcohol and nicotine) during pregnancy are born with brain impairments. In the discussion that follows, we will examine the mechanisms of drug abuse, the different approaches to understanding drug abuse, how individuals vary in their vulnerability to drug abuse, and how drug abuse can be prevented and treated.

The mechanisms of drug abuse have been studied extensively

Investigators have advanced a variety of physiological, behavioral, and environmental explanations for dependence on various substances (M. Glantz and Pickens, 1992). We will focus primarily on addiction to cocaine, the opiate drugs (such as morphine and heroin), nicotine, and alcohol because these substances have been studied the most thoroughly. Specific terminology related to substance dependence (addiction) and substance abuse is clarified in Box 4.3. In the United States alone, some 22 million people suffer from substance-related disorders, according to the 2002 National Survey of Drug Use and Health (Substance Abuse and Mental Health Services Administration, 2003).

COMPETING HYPOTHESES

   Although we are concerned mainly with substance abuse by humans, self-administration of addictive substances by wild animals is well documented (R. K. Siegel, 1989). For example, elephants have been observed becoming repeatedly intoxicated by eating fermented fruits. When confined to game preserves, elephants accept alcohol, and when their space is restricted—causing what is assumed to be a stressful condition for them—they increase their drinking of alcoholic substances. Baboons consume tobacco in the wild, and intoxicating mushrooms are eaten by cattle, reindeer, and rabbits. These observations suggest that the propensity for drug use, and possibly even addiction, is widespread among animals.

   Because addictive substances are no exception to the general rule that drugs produce multiple effects, it is difficult to determine which mechanisms are most important in producing dependence. For example, we have already noted that cocaine has the following major characteristics: (1) It is a local anesthetic; (2) it produces intensely pleasurable feelings, so it is a rewarding agent; and (3) it is a psychomotor stimulant. The opiate drugs, like morphine and heroin, also produce intensely rewarding sensations, but they are depressants, not stimulants. Like cocaine, the opiates produce a strong physical dependence and powerful withdrawal symptoms on cessation of use. But opiates tend to produce only tolerance, whereas at least some of the actions of cocaine induce sensitization. So in order to be comprehensive, a theory of drug abuse and addiction must be able to account for dependence across a wide variety of compounds with very different effects.

BOX 4.3 The Terminology of Substance-Related Disorders

For definitions of mental disorders, psychiatrists, psychologists, and neuroscientists rely on the *Diagnostic and Statistical Manual of Mental Disorders* (4th edition, revised), often called *DSM IV-R* (American Psychiatric Association, 1994). What the public usually calls *addiction*, the *DSM IV-R* calls **substance-related disorders.** Within this category, **dependence** (commonly called *addiction*) is a more severe disorder than **abuse.**

The essential feature of dependence on psychoactive substances (e.g., alcohol, tobacco, cocaine, marijuana) is "a cluster of cognitive, behavioral, and physiological symptoms indicating that the individual continues use of the substance despite significant substance-related problems." To be diagnosed as dependent, a person must meet at least three of seven criteria relating to patterns of consumption, craving, expenditure of time and energy in serving the addiction, and impact on the other aspects of the person's life. The diagnosed severity of this dependence varies from mild to moderate to severe, depending on how many of the seven criteria have been met.

When the minimum criteria for dependence have not been met but there is evidence of maladaptive patterns of substance use that have persisted at least 1 month or have occurred repeatedly, the diagnosis is substance abuse. Some examples of situations in which a diagnosis of abuse is appropriate are as follows:

1. A student has substance-related absences, suspensions, or expulsion from school.
2. A person is repeatedly intoxicated with alcohol in situations that are hazardous—for example, when driving a car, operating machinery, or engaging in risky recreations such as swimming or rock climbing.
3. A person has recurrent substance-related legal problems—for example, arrests for disorderly conduct, assault and battery, or driving under the influence.

Several perspectives help us understand drug abuse

Several major models of drug abuse and addiction, and their remediation, have arisen during the last two centuries. Some explanations are better suited to one or another phase of drug abuse, as we'll see. Each of the models we discuss next continues to find favor with some authorities.

The moral model   The earliest approach to explaining drug abuse was to blame the drug user for lack of moral character or lack of self-control. Explanations of this sort often have a religious character and hold that only divine help will free a person from addiction. Applications based on the moral model can be effective. For example, the temperance movement in the United States, beginning around the 1830s, is estimated to have cut per capita consumption of alcohol to about one-third its level in the period from 1800 to 1820 (Rorabaugh, 1976).

COMPETING HYPOTHESES

The disease model   In this view, the person who abuses drugs requires medical treatment rather than moral exhortation or punishment. This view also justifies spending money to research drug abuse in the same way that money is spent to research other diseases. It is still not clear, however, what kind of a disease addiction is, and the model is mute regarding the process by which the addiction gets started.

Usually the term *disease* is reserved for a state in which we can identify an abnormal physical or biochemical condition. Investigators have not been able to find such an abnormal physical or biochemical condition in the case of drug addiction (although mounting evidence suggests that some people are more susceptible to addiction than others, as we'll see a little later). Nevertheless, this model continues to appeal to many. In 1995, the director of the U.S. National Institute on Alcohol Abuse and Alcoholism stated that ultimately scientific research will lead to "better treatment, better diagnosis, better prevention, and the putting to rest of the notion that alcoholism isn't a disease" (Azar, 1995).

The physical dependence model   The physical dependence model, sometimes called the *withdrawal avoidance model*, is based on the unpleasant withdrawal symptoms that occur when a person stops taking a drug that he or she has used frequently. The

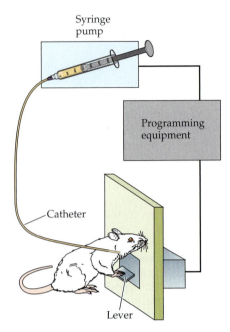

Syringe
pump

Programming
equipment

Catheter

Lever

4.18 Experimental Setup for Self-Administration of a Drug by an Animal

Charles R. Schuster

**IMPORTANT
METHOD**

specific withdrawal symptoms depend on the drug, but they are often the opposite of the effects produced by the drug itself. For example, the withdrawal symptoms of morphine include irritability, tremor, and elevated heart rate and blood pressure. Waves of goosebumps occur, and the skin resembles that of a plucked turkey, which is why abrupt withdrawal without any treatment is called *cold turkey*. Whereas most drugs of abuse produce pleasurable feelings, withdrawal usually induces the opposite: dysphoria. Withdrawal symptoms can be suppressed quickly (within 15 to 20 minutes in the case of morphine) by administration of the withdrawn drug, or a related compound (e.g., heroin withdrawal symptoms can be attenuated by its chemical cousin methadone). This model provides one explanation of why addicts work compulsively to get drugs: to avoid or overcome withdrawal effects.

Withdrawal symptoms are so striking that some investigators have proposed the idea that development of dependence is the basic characteristic of addiction. But it is clear that people can become dependent on drugs, like cocaine, that do not produce any dramatic withdrawal symptoms (Wise, 1996). Are these people *psychologically* addicted rather than *physically* addicted? So far, such a distinction seems irrelevant because either form of addiction can have disastrous, even fatal, consequences. Indeed, the entire theme of this book is that *psychological* processes all have a physical basis in the brain, which is just as real as the muscular contractions that produce shivering or nausea. Clearly a better explanation is needed.

Positive reward model   The positive reward model of addictive behavior arose from animal research that was started in the 1950s (McKim, 1991). Before that time, researchers believed that animals could not become addicted to drugs, thinking (incorrectly) that animals were not capable of learning an association between the time a drug is injected and the onset of its effects. The subsequent development of a drug self-administration apparatus (Figure 4.18) made it possible to quantify the motivation of animals to consume drugs.

Early studies by psychopharmacologist Charles R. Schuster and his collaborators demonstrated that morphine-dependent rats or monkeys quickly learn to repeatedly press a lever to receive a small morphine injection; the drug infusion therefore acted like any other experimental reward, such as food or water (T. Thompson and Schuster, 1964). And animals that had not been made morphine-dependent prior to the experiment would happily self-administer doses of morphine so low that no physical dependence ever developed (Schuster, 1970). Animals would also furiously press a lever to self-administer cocaine and other stimulants that do not produce marked withdrawal symptoms (Koob, 1995; Pickens and Thompson, 1968; Tanda et al., 2000); indeed, cocaine supports some of the highest rates of lever pressing ever recorded.

These and other studies contradict the assumptions of both the disease model and the physical dependence model of drug addiction. Although physical dependence may be an important factor in the consumption of some drugs, it is not necessary for self-administration and cannot serve as the sole explanation for drug addiction. Furthermore, these studies indicate that drug self-administration can be interpreted as a behavior controlled by positive rewards (operant conditioning theory; see Box 17.1), without the need to implicate a disease process.

A wide variety of addictive drugs cause the release of dopamine in the **nucleus accumbens,** just as more-conventional reinforcers, such as food or sex, do (Di Chiara et al., 1999). As we mentioned previously, dopamine released from axons originating from the ventral tegmental area (Figure 4.19), part of the mesolimbocortical dopaminergic pathway illustrated in Figure 4.3, has been widely implicated in the perception of reward. In discussing cocaine we noted that injection of the peptide CART to the ventral tegmental area is rewarding for rats. If the dopaminergic pathway from the ventral tegmental area to the nucleus accumbens serves as a reward system for a wide variety of experiences, then the addictive power of drugs may

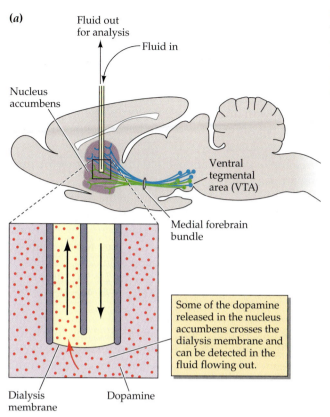

(a)

Fluid out for analysis

Fluid in

Nucleus accumbens

Ventral tegmental area (VTA)

Medial forebrain bundle

Some of the dopamine released in the nucleus accumbens crosses the dialysis membrane and can be detected in the fluid flowing out.

Dialysis membrane

Dopamine

4.19 A Neural Pathway Implicated in Drug Abuse The microdialysis technique makes use of a small, permanently implanted probe to monitor neurochemical changes in awake, behaving animals. (a) A microdialysis probe inserted into the nucleus accumbens can detect changes in dopamine levels in response to drug administration. (b) Dopamine levels in the nucleus accumbens rise sharply in rats during self-administration (begins at arrow) of cocaine. (Part b after Pettit and Justice, 1991.)

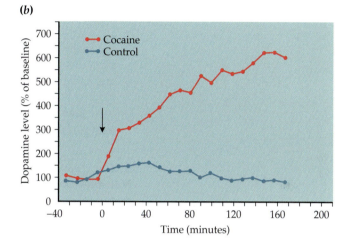

(b)

come from their artificial stimulation of this pathway. Acting on this assumption, Pilla et al. (1999) found that a weak DA agonist reduced cocaine craving in rats; perhaps the mild DA stimulation produced by the agonist filled in for the DA that would have been released by cocaine.

Similarly, socially dominant rhesus monkeys reportedly have increased numbers of dopamine D_2 receptors compared to subordinate monkeys, and are less susceptible to the reinforcing properties of cocaine than are the subordinates (Morgan et al., 2002). Interestingly, a single dose of cocaine is able to produce long-lasting changes in dopaminergic circuitry (Ungless et al., 2001); perhaps rapid changes like this are what allow addiction to get started.

People differ in their vulnerability to drug abuse

Not everyone who uses an addictive drug becomes addicted. For example, very few hospitalized patients treated with opiates for pain relief go on to abuse opiates after release (Brownlee and Schrof, 1997). Of Vietnam veterans who had become addicted to heroin overseas, only 12% relapsed to dependence within 3 years after their return. The individual and environmental differences that account for this differential susceptibility are the subject of active investigation (M. Glantz and Pickens, 1992). Because these factors interact throughout life, longitudinal studies engaging in long-term tracking of subjects have been especially valuable. Factors that have been demonstrated to be significant, at least for some drugs, fall into several categories:

- *Biological factors.* Sex is a significant variable; males are more likely to abuse drugs than are females. There is also evidence for genetic predisposition. For example, having a biological parent who suffers from alcoholism makes drug abuse more likely, even for children adopted away soon after birth (Cadoret et al., 1986); a tendency to use opiates and cocaine also appears to be heritable (Kendler et al., 2000). And in genetically modified mice, variation in a gene regulating the hormonal response to stress contributes to increased intake of alcohol following stressful events (Sillaber et al., 2002); a similar mechanism could explain why some humans tip over into alcoholism at stressful times in their lives.

- *Personal characteristics.* Certain traits, such as aggressiveness and poor emotional control, are especially associated with drug abuse. Strong educational goals, maturity, and personal responsibilities are associated with lower likelihood of drug abuse.

- *Family situation.* Family breakup, a poor relationship with parents, or the presence of an antisocial sibling are associated with drug abuse.

- *Social and community factors.* A high prevalence of drug use in the community, and especially in the peer group, predisposes an individual toward drug abuse. The effect of social factors is particularly marked with respect to the incidence of smoking: Although 7 of 10 adult smokers in the United States say they want to quit, according to the U.S. Centers for Disease Control, their success in doing so directly correlates with race and educational status. Poorer, less-educated adults are the least successful in giving up smoking, as are black and Hispanic Americans.

The greater the number of risk factors that apply, the more likely an individual will abuse alcohol or marijuana (Brook et al., 1992). Furthermore, these risk factors do not necessarily operate independently; in some cases they interact to produce a more severe addiction that is resistant to interventions.

CLINICAL ISSUE

Drug use, abuse, and dependence can be prevented or treated in multiple ways

Given the health and social costs of substance abuse, the development of effective treatment programs is a pressing concern. Many approaches are related to the models of drug abuse we described earlier. In keeping with the moral model, many people abstain, or do not go beyond initial experimentation with potentially addictive substances. And many of those who become dependent are able to overcome their addiction without outside help: More than 90% of ex-smokers and about half of those who recover from alcoholism appear to have quit on their own (S. Cohen et al., 1989; Institute of Medicine, 1990).

For those who require medical intervention, several categories of medication are available (Nathan and Gorman, 1998), including the following:

- *Drugs for detoxification.* Included in this category are benzodiazepines and drugs that suppress central adrenergic activity (e.g., clonidine). These drugs help reduce withdrawal symptoms during the early drug-free period.

- *Agonist or partial agonist analogs of the addictive drug.* Analogs partially activate the same mechanisms as the addictive drug, to help wean the individual. For example, the opiate receptor agonist methadone reduces heroin appetite and lessens withdrawal symptoms; similarly, nicotine patches provide reduced doses of the addictive compound, without the other harmful components of cigarette smoke.

- *Antagonists to the addictive drug.* Specific antagonists block the effects of an abused drug (for example, the opiate antagonist naloxone blocks heroin's actions), but they also may produce harsh withdrawal symptoms.

- *Medications that alter drug metabolism.* Patients on disulfiram (trade name Antabuse) accumulate acetaldehyde, a toxic metabolite of alcohol that can be quite unpleasant. Drinking then produces illness that counteracts the rewarding aspects of alcohol abuse.

- *Reward-blocking medications.* Researchers are looking at ways to block the positive reward associated with drugs of abuse, primarily by using dopamine receptor blockers to reduce the activity of the mesolimbocortical dopamine reward system that we discussed earlier. One problem with this approach that must be overcome is the tendency of treatments to produce a general *anhedonia:* a generalized loss of pleasurable feelings.

- *Anticraving medications.* These medications reduce the appetite for the abused substance; for example, naltrexone (trade name ReVia) blocks the rewarding aspects of consuming alcohol or other abused substances, and acamprosate (trade name Campral) eases alcohol-associated withdrawal symptoms.

Could people be immunized against drug abuse? Vaccines against such drugs as cocaine, heroin, and nicotine have been synthesized, and they have improved to the point that they are now in clinical trials (Bonese et al., 1974; Kantak, 2003). Here the strategy is to prompt the individual's immune system to produce antibodies that remove the targeted drugs from circulation before they ever reach the brain. Similarly, injections of purified antibodies can help overdose victims by removing circulating drug molecules (Proksch et al., 2000).

Many of these types of treatment help at least some substance abusers; but no single approach appears to be uniformly effective, and rates of relapse remain high. Research breakthroughs are therefore badly needed to overcome the painful and costly problems of drug abuse and dependence.

Refer to the ***Learning Biological Psychology CD*** for study questions, animations, activities, and other study aids.

CLINICAL ISSUE

Summary

1. New compounds that meet the criteria for classification as neurotransmitters are continually being identified. The major categories of neurotransmitters are amine neurotransmitters, amino acid neurotransmitters, peptide neurotransmitters, and soluble gas neurotransmitters.

2. Because many drugs work by acting on receptor molecules, investigators search for the receptor molecules and for the endogenous substances that work on the receptors. A given neurotransmitter may normally bind several different receptors.

3. A ligand is any substance that binds to a receptor. Agonists activate transmitter pathways, antagonists block transmitter pathways, and inverse agonists have active effects that are opposite to a transmitter's normal effects.

4. The classic neurotransmitters are found in segregated regions that project widely throughout the brain.

5. Drugs vary in their binding affinity for different types of receptors, and also in efficacy—their ability to produce effects—once they are bound. Some ligands classified as neuromodulators bind to modulatory sites on receptors rather than competing for neurotransmitter-binding sites.

6. The relationship between concentrations of a drug and its physiological effects is formally studied by use of a dose–response curve. Dose–response relationships reveal a drug's activity, specificity, potency, and safety.

7. Repeated treatments with a drug can produce tolerance to its effects, often through the process of up- or down-regulation of receptors. This compensatory mechanism is responsible for withdrawal symptoms. However, repeated use of some drugs produces sensitization, in which the drug's effects increase with use of the same dosage.

8. Effective drug treatments revolutionized the management of schizophrenia. Most antipsychotic medications block dopamine D_2 receptors, but some also block serotonin receptors.

9. The main categories of antidepressants are MAO inhibitors, tricyclics, and selective serotonin reuptake inhibitors. All share the basic action of increasing the availability of monoamine transmitters in synapses.

10. Substances that are used to combat anxiety, such as the benzodiazepines, are called anxiolytic drugs. The benzodiazepines synergize the activity of the inhibitory transmitter GABA at some of its receptors.

11. Alcohol in moderation has beneficial effects; but in higher doses it is very harmful, damaging neurons in many areas of the brain. Alcohol acts on GABA receptors to produce some of its effects.

12. Opiates are potent painkillers; endogenous opiates include the endorphins, and exogenous opiates include morphine and heroin.

13. The active ingredient in marijuana, THC, acts on cannabinoid receptors to produce its effects. A probable endogenous cannabinoid, anandamide, serves as a retrograde transmitter in some synapses.

14. Some stimulants, such as nicotine, imitate an excitatory synaptic transmitter. Others, such as amphetamine, cause the release of excitatory synaptic transmitters and block the reuptake of transmitters. Still others, such as caffeine, block the activity of an inhibitory neuromodulator.

15. Some drugs are called hallucinogens because they alter sensory perception and produce peculiar experiences. Different hallucinogens act on different kinds of synaptic receptors, and it is not yet clear what causes the hallucinogenic effects.

16. Drug abuse and addiction are being studied intensively, and several models have been proposed: the moral model, the disease model, the physical dependence model, and the positive reward model.

17. People differ in their vulnerability to drug abuse according to several factors: genetic predisposition, personality characteristics, and family and social context.

18. There are several medicinal approaches to treating drug addiction, including antiwithdrawal and anticraving medication and immunization.

Recommended Reading

Cooper, J. R., Bloom, F. E., and Roth, R. H. (2002). *The biochemical basis of neuropharmacology* (8th ed.). New York: Oxford University Press.

Davis, K. L., Charney, D., Coyle, J. T., and Nemeroff, C. (Eds.). (2002). *Psychopharmacology: The fifth generation of progress.* New York: Lippincott, Williams & Wilkins.

Feldman, R. S., Meyer, J. S., and Quenzer, L. F. (1997). *Principles of neuropsychopharmacology.* Sunderland, MA: Sinauer Associates.

Julien, R. J. (2000). *A primer of drug action* (9th ed.). New York: Freeman.

Nestler, E. J., Hyman, S. E., and Malenka, R. C. (2001). *Molecular neuropharmacology: A foundation for clinical neuroscience.* New York: McGraw-Hill.

Schatzberg, A. F., and Nemeroff, C. B. (Eds.). (2004). *Textbook of psychopharmacology.* Arlington, VA: American Psychiatric Publishing.

Stahl, S. M., and Munter, N. (2000). *Essential psychopharmacology: Neuroscientific basis and practical applications.* Cambridge, England: Cambridge University Press.

5

Hormones and the Brain

Life-Threatening Lethargy

"Chuck's" mother finally got frightened and called 911. She told the emergency room doctors that Chuck, a man in his 50s, had been lying on the sofa for weeks, watching TV and refusing to get up or do much else. He was sleepy most of the time, forgot appointments, and failed to finish chores that he started. This situation may sound familiar, but additional observations suggested that Chuck's problem was more than depression or mere laziness. His speech was slurred, his movements and heart rate were slow, and his cognitive abilities were so compromised that he couldn't name the month or the current president. In counting backward from 100 by sevens, he stalled at 93.

Chuck denied using drugs recreationally, and although he recalled taking some unknown medication previously, he was not currently taking any prescription drugs. Blood tests indicated no alcohol and no chronic infections that would affect the CNS; brain scans found no stroke, tumor, or other brain injuries. In the end, his diagnosis was suggested by one of the simplest and most familiar of tests: the knee jerk reflex in response to the tap of a rubber mallet. Chuck's knee jerk reflex was abnormally slow. A mysterious process appeared to be impeding the flow of information in his neurons, not only in the knee jerk circuitry but also, by extension, in the rest of his CNS (Jauhar, 2003). What was wrong with Chuck?

The cells in our body communicate via chemicals, including an extensive array of hormones. Deficiency or excess of some hormones can result in striking changes in our cognitive and emotional behavior. Tiny amounts of some hormones can markedly modify our moods and actions, our inclination to eat or drink, our aggressiveness or submissiveness, and our reproductive and parental behavior. Furthermore, hormones do more than influence adult behavior. Early in life, thyroid hormones drive brain development. Later in life, the changing outputs of endocrine glands and the body's changing sensitivity to hormones are prominent aspects of adolescence and aging.

In this chapter we consider the mechanisms of hormone action, the main endocrine glands and their hormones, and examples of hormonal influences on physiology and on behavior. After presenting a brief history of discoveries relevant to hormones and their actions, we compare the ways in which the endocrine and nervous systems communicate and coordinate function. Later chapters will include detailed discussion of hormonal effects on sexual behavior (Chapter 12), body weight (Chapter 13), stress, and emotion (Chapter 15).

Nachume Miller, Untitled, 1995, 10'6" × 18'2"

Hormones Act in a Great Variety of Ways throughout the Body

Hormones (from the Greek *horman*, "to excite") are chemicals secreted by one group of cells and carried through the bloodstream to other parts of the body, where they act on specific target tissues to produce specific physiological effects. Specialists who study hormones are known as endocrinologists because many hormones are produced by **endocrine glands** (from the Greek *endon*, "within," and *krinein*, "to secrete"), so called because they release their hormones within the body. Endocrine glands are sometimes contrasted with *exocrine glands* (tear glands, salivary glands, sweat glands), which use ducts to secrete fluid outside the body (the Greek *exo* means "out").

Our current understanding of hormones developed in stages

The importance of hormones was anticipated in several ancient civilizations in which endocrine glands were eaten to modify health (a Chinese scholar of 100 A.C.E. recommended eating dog testes to combat impotence). Ancient societies also noted some of the behavioral and physiological changes from obvious endocrine pathology, such as the disfiguring enlargement of the thyroid

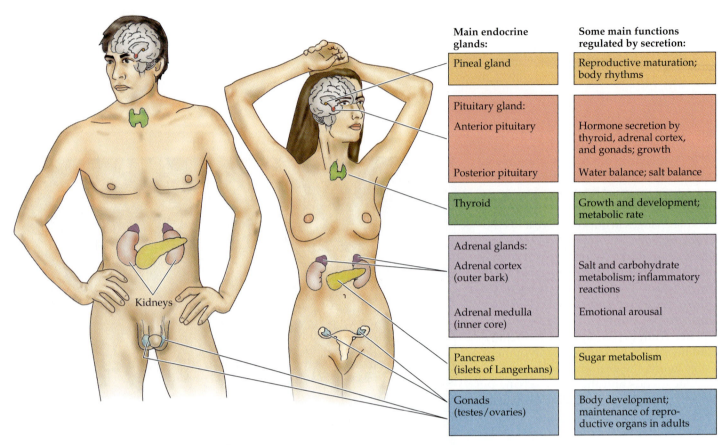

Main endocrine glands:	Some main functions regulated by secretion:
Pineal gland	Reproductive maturation; body rhythms
Pituitary gland: Anterior pituitary	Hormone secretion by thyroid, adrenal cortex, and gonads; growth
Posterior pituitary	Water balance; salt balance
Thyroid	Growth and development; metabolic rate
Adrenal glands: Adrenal cortex (outer bark)	Salt and carbohydrate metabolism; inflammatory reactions
Adrenal medulla (inner core)	Emotional arousal
Pancreas (islets of Langerhans)	Sugar metabolism
Gonads (testes/ovaries)	Body development; maintenance of reproductive organs in adults

 5.1 Major Endocrine Glands and Their Functions Table 5.2 lists the hormones secreted by the glands shown here and the effects of those hormones in the body.

**A. A. Berthold
(1803–1861)**

called *goiter*. In the fourth century B.C.E., Aristotle accurately described the effects of **castration** (removal of the testes) in birds, and he compared the behavioral and bodily effects with those seen in eunuchs (castrated men). Although he did not know what mechanism was involved, clearly the testes were important for the reproductive capacity and sexual characteristics of the male.

The ancient Greeks emphasized body *humors,* or fluids, as an explanation of temperament and emotions. It was believed that these fluids—phlegm, blood, black bile, and yellow bile (also known as *choler*)—all interacted to produce health or disease. The notion of body fluids as the basis of human temperament lingers in our language in many now-seldom-used terms, such as *phlegmatic* ("sluggish"), *sanguine* ("cheerful"; *sanguis* is Latin for "blood"), *bilious* ("irritable"), and *choleric* ("hot-tempered") to describe personalities.

Today we know there are far more than four hormones. Endocrine glands come in a variety of sizes, shapes, and locations in the body (Figure 5.1). Although the endocrine glands and their hormones are important, the definition of *hormone* is more inclusive than it used to be, recognizing that other tissues, such as the heart and kidneys, secrete compounds known as hormones. Even plants, which have no endocrine glands, use chemical signals that are considered to be hormones.

The first major endocrine experiment was carried out in 1849 by German physician Arnold Adolph Berthold. When Berthold castrated young roosters, they showed declines in both reproductive behavior and secondary sexual characteristics, such as the rooster's comb (Figure 5.2). Berthold observed that if he placed one testis into

Group 1	Group 2	Group 3
Left undisturbed, young roosters grow up to have large red wattles and combs, to mount and mate with hens readily, and to fight one another and crow loudly.	Animals whose testes were removed during development displayed neither the appearance nor the behavior of normal roosters as adults.	However, if one of the testes was reimplanted into the abdominal cavity immediately after its removal, the rooster developed normal wattles and normal behavior.

	Group 1	Group 2	Group 3
Comb and wattles:	Large	Small	Large
Mount hens?	Yes	No	Yes
Aggressive?	Yes	No	Yes
Crowing?	Normal	Weak	Normal

Conclusion
Because the reimplanted testis in group 3 was in an abnormal body site, disconnected from normal innervation, and yet still affected development, Berthold reasoned that the testes release a hormonal signal that has widespread effects.

5.2 The First Experiment in Behavioral Endocrinology Berthold's nineteenth-century experiment demonstrated the importance of hormones for behavior.

the body cavity of these castrates, sometimes it received a blood supply and restored both the normal behavior of these roosters and their combs. They began crowing and showed usual sexual behaviors. Because the nerve supply to the testis had not been reestablished, Berthold concluded that the testes release a chemical into the blood that affects both male behavior and male body structures. Today we know that the testes make and release the hormone testosterone, which exerts these effects.

The French physiologist Claude Bernard helped set the stage in the nineteenth century for the emergence of endocrinology as a science. Bernard stressed the importance of the internal environment ("internal milieu") in which cells exist and emphasized that this environment must be carefully regulated. He regarded a constant internal body environment as necessary for independent activity in the external environment.

This idea was later embedded in the concept of homeostasis advanced by American physiologist Walter B. Cannon in the 1920s. **Homeostasis** is the maintenance of a relatively constant internal environment by an array of mechanisms in the body. Clinical and experimental observations starting in the late nineteenth century showed the importance of several glands—including the thyroid, the adrenal cortex, and the pituitary—for maintaining this constant environment inside our bodies.

Techniques that were developed in the twentieth century enabled scientists to identify many different hormones. Several Nobel Prizes have been awarded for the

**Claude Bernard
(1813–1878)**

**Vincent du Vigneaud
(1901–1978)**

Rosalyn Yalow

determination of the structure of hormones. For example, Vincent du Vigneaud received the 1955 Nobel Prize in Chemistry for synthesizing the hormones oxytocin and vasopressin. The discovery of a sensitive technique (called *radioimmunoassay*, or *RIA*) for measuring small quantities of hormones earned Rosalyn Yalow the 1977 Nobel Prize in Physiology or Medicine.

Organisms use several types of chemical communication

By reviewing the several categories of chemical signals used by the body, we can see how hormonal communication by endocrine glands compares to other methods of communication:

* *Synaptic communication.* This form of communication was described in Chapters 3 and 4. In synaptic transmitter function (sometimes called **neurocrine** function), the released chemical signal diffuses across the synaptic cleft and causes a change in polarization of the postsynaptic membrane (Figure 5.3a). Typically, synaptic transmitter function is highly localized.
* *Autocrine communication.* In **autocrine** communication a released chemical acts on the releasing cell itself and thereby affects its own activity (Figure 5.3b). An example of autocrine function is seen in nerve cells containing autoreceptors that are affected by the released synaptic transmitter molecules and thus monitor their own activity. In this case, the signal molecule serves both an autocrine and a synaptic transmitter function.
* *Paracrine communication.* In **paracrine** communication, the released chemical signal diffuses to nearby target cells (Figure 5.3c). The strongest impact is on the nearest cells.
* *Endocrine communication.* In **endocrine** communication, the chemical signal is a hormone released into the bloodstream and taken up selectively by target organs, which may be quite far away (Figure 5.3d).

(*a*) **Neurocrine function (synaptic transmission)**

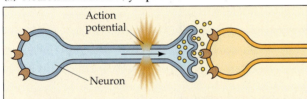

(*d*) **Endocrine function**

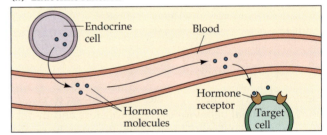

(*b*) **Autocrine function**

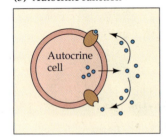

(*c*) **Paracrine function**

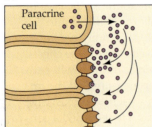

(*e*) **Pheromone function**

(*f*) **Allomone function**

5.3 Chemical Communication Systems   (*a*) In synaptic transmitter (neurocrine) communication, a chemical signal is released from the presynaptic terminal of the neuron and binds to receptor molecules on a postsynaptic target cell. (*b*) In autocrine communication, the chemical signal secreted by a cell affects the very cell that released it. Some synaptic transmitters are also autocrine signals in that they affect receptors on the presynaptic terminal (autoreceptors). (*c*) In paracrine communication, chemical signals diffuse through extracellular space to nearby target cells. The strongest effects are produced in the nearest cells. (*d*) Endocrine glands produce chemical signals and release them into the bloodstream. Effects are produced in the body wherever receptors for the hormone are found. (*e*) Pheromones carry a message from one individual to other individuals of the same species. Often pheromones indicate whether the individual emitting them is ready to mate. (*f*) Allomones are produced by individuals of one species to communicate with (and affect the behavior of) individuals of other species. Some plants communicate with animals via scented allomones.

- *Pheromone communication.* Hormones can be used for communication not only within an individual, but also between individuals. **Pheromones** (from the Greek *pherein,* "to carry") are hormones produced by one individual and then released outside the body to affect other individuals of the same species (Figure 5.3*e*). For example, many species of ants produce a variety of pheromones that are used to communicate the presence of intruders in the nest, or to mark the trail that leads to a rich food source. Dogs and wolves urinate on various landmarks to designate their territory; other members of the species smell the pheromones in the urine and either respect or challenge the territory. In Chapters 9 and 12 we'll discuss pheromones in more detail.
- *Allomone communication.* Some chemical signals are released by members of one species and affect the behavior of individuals of *another* species (W. L. Brown, 1968). These hormones are called **allomones** (from the Greek *allos,* "other"). Allomones can carry messages between animal species or from plants to animals (Figure 5.3*f*). Flowers exude scented allomones to attract insects and birds in order to distribute pollen. Skunks produce what may be the best-known allomone of all.

Hormone actions can be organized according to nine general principles

Although there are some exceptions, the following rules are general principles of hormone action:

1. Hormones frequently act in a *gradual* fashion, activating behavioral and physiological responses hours or weeks after entering the bloodstream. The responses may persist for days after hormone release is over.
2. When hormones alter behavior, they tend to act by changing the intensity or probability of evoked behaviors, rather than acting as a switch to turn behaviors on or off regardless of context (Box 5.1).
3. Both the quantities and the types of hormones released are influenced by environmental factors. Therefore *the relationship between behavior and hormones is clearly reciprocal;* that is, hormones change behaviors and behaviors change hormone levels. For example, high levels of testosterone are related to aggression, and in some species males who lose in aggressive encounters show a reduction in testosterone levels, while the winners in these bouts show little change in testosterone levels. This example shows the reciprocal relation between behavioral and somatic (body) events that we discussed in Chapter 1 (see Figure 1.2).
4. Each hormone has multiple effects on different tissues, organs, and behaviors; conversely, a single type of behavior or physiological change can be affected by many different hormones (Figure 5.4).

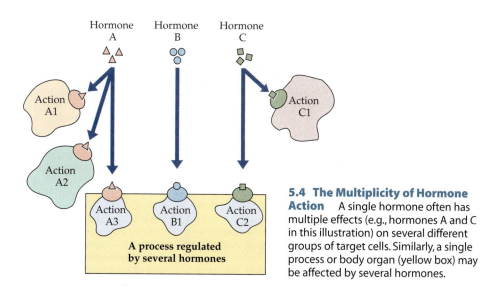

5.4 The Multiplicity of Hormone Action A single hormone often has multiple effects (e.g., hormones A and C in this illustration) on several different groups of target cells. Similarly, a single process or body organ (yellow box) may be affected by several hormones.

BOX 5.1 Techniques of Modern Behavioral Endocrinology

To establish that a particular hormone affects behavior, investigators usually begin with the type of experiment that Berthold performed in the nineteenth century: observing the behavior of the intact animal, then removing the endocrine gland and looking for a change in behavior (see Figure 5.2). Berthold was limited to this type of experiment, but modern scientists have many additional options available. Let's imagine we are investigating a particular effect of hormones on behavior to see how we might proceed.

Which Hormones Affect Which Behaviors?

First we must carefully observe the behavior of several individuals, seeking ways to classify and quantify the different types of behavior and to place them in the context of the behavior of other individuals. For example, most adult male rats will try to mount and copulate with a female placed in their cage. If the testes are removed from the male rat, he will eventually stop copulating with females. We know that one of the hormones produced by the testes is testosterone. Is it the loss of testosterone that causes the loss of male copulatory behavior?

To explore this question, we purchase some synthetic testosterone, inject it into castrated males, and observe whether the copulatory behavior returns. (It does.) Another way to ask whether a steroid hormone is affecting a particular behavior is to examine the behavior of animals that lack the receptors for that steroid. We can delete the gene for a given hormone receptor, making a **knockout mouse** (because the gene for the receptor has been "knocked out"), and ask which behaviors are different in the knockouts versus normal animals (see Box 7.3).

Next we might examine individual male rats and ask whether the ones that copulate a lot have more testosterone circulating in their blood than those who copulate only a little. To investigate this question, we measure individual differences in the amount of copulatory behavior, take a sample of blood from each individual, and measure levels of testosterone. To take this measure we use **radioimmunoassay** (**RIA**), a technique using an antibody that binds to a particular hormone. By adding many such antibodies to each blood sample and measuring how many of the antibodies find a hormone molecule to bind, we can estimate the total number of molecules of

the hormone per unit volume of blood. (We won't go into detail here about how we determine the number of antibodies that bind to hormone.)

It turns out that individual differences in the sexual behavior of normal male rats (and normal male humans) do *not* correlate with differences in testosterone levels in the blood. In both rats and humans, a drastic loss of testosterone, as after castration, results in a gradual decline in sexual behavior. All normal males, however, appear to make more than enough testosterone to maintain sexual behavior, so something else must modulate this behavior. In other words, the hormone acts in a permissive manner: It permits the display of the behavior, but something else determines how much of the behavior each individual exhibits.

Where Are the Target Cells?

What does testosterone do to permit sexual behavior? One step toward answering this question is to ask another question: Which parts of the brain are normally affected by this hormone? We have two methods at our disposal for investigating this question.

First, we might inject a castrated animal with testosterone that has been radioactively labeled (i.e., one or more of the atoms in the molecule has been replaced with a radioactive atom). After waiting about an hour for the testosterone to accumulate in the brain regions that have receptors for the hormone, we would sacrifice the animal, remove the brain, freeze it, cut thin sections from it, and place the thin sections on photographic film. If the tissue were left in place for a few months, enough radioactive par-

ticles from the testosterone would hit the film to expose it. We would then develop the film to learn which brain regions had accumulated testosterone. This method is known as **autoradiography** because the tissue "takes its own picture" with radioactivity (Figure A).

When the labeled hormone is a steroid like testosterone, the radioactivity accumulates in the nuclei of neurons and leaves small black specks on the film (Figure B). When the radiolabeled hormone is a protein hormone such as oxytocin, the radioactivity accumulates in the mem-

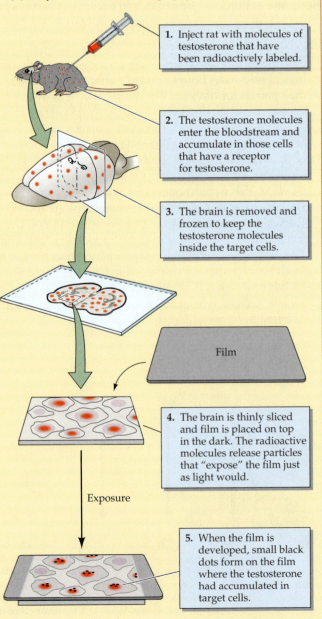

(A) Steps in steroid autoradiography

1. Inject rat with molecules of testosterone that have been radioactively labeled.

2. The testosterone molecules enter the bloodstream and accumulate in those cells that have a receptor for testosterone.

3. The brain is removed and frozen to keep the testosterone molecules inside the target cells.

Film

Exposure

4. The brain is thinly sliced and film is placed on top in the dark. The radioactive molecules release particles that "expose" the film just as light would.

5. When the film is developed, small black dots form on the film where the testosterone had accumulated in target cells.

BOX 5.1 *(continued)*

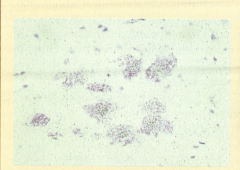

(B) An autoradiogram showing that spinal motoneurons (purple shapes) accumulate radioactive testosterone (small dots)

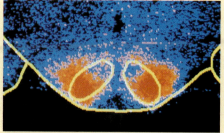

(C) An oxytocin autoradiogram showing the concentration of oxytocin receptors in the ventromedial hypothalamus (oval outlines)

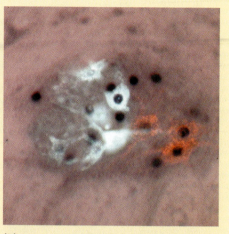

(D) Immunocytochemistry revealing testosterone receptors (dark circles over cell nuclei) in neurons labeled with fluorogold (white-filled somata) or fluororuby (red cells)

branes of cells and appears in particular layers of the brain. Computers can generate color maps that highlight regions with high densities of receptors (Figure C).

The second method for detecting hormone receptors is **immunocytochemistry.** In this method (which is described in more detail in Box 2.3), we use antibodies that recognize either the hormone or the hormone receptor (Figure D). This method allows us to map the distribution of hormone receptors in the brain. We put the antibodies on slices of brain tissue, wait for them to bind to the receptors, wash off the unbound antibodies, and use chemical methods to visualize the antibodies by creating a tiny dark spot at each one. When the antibodies recognize a steroid receptor, chemical reactions cause a dark coloration in the nuclei of target brain cells. We can also use **in situ hybridization** (see Box 2.3) to look for the neurons that make the mRNA for the steroid receptor. Because these cells make the transcript for the receptor, they are likely to possess the receptor protein itself.

What Happens at the Target Cells?

Once we have used autoradiography, immunocytochemistry, or in situ hybridization (or, better yet, all three) to identify brain regions that have receptors for the hormone, those regions become candidates for the places at which the hormone works to change behavior. Now we can take castrated males and implant tiny pellets of testosterone into one of those brain regions. We use RIA to ensure that the pellets are small enough that they have no effect on hormone levels in the blood. Then we ask whether the small implant in that brain region restores the behavior. If not, then in other animals we can implant pellets in a different region or try placing implants in a combination of brain sites.

It turns out that such implants can restore male sexual behavior in rats only if they are placed in the medial preoptic area (mPOA) of the hypothalamus. Thus we have found so far that testosterone does something to the mPOA to permit individual males to display sexual behavior. Now we can examine the mPOA in detail to learn what changes in the anatomy, physiology, or protein production of this region are caused by testosterone. We have more or less caught up to modern-day scientists who work on this very question. Some of the preliminary answers suggested by their research will be discussed in Chapter 12. (Figure C courtesy of Bruce McEwen; Figure D courtesy of Cynthia Jordan.)

5. Hormones are produced in small amounts and often are secreted in bursts. This *pulsatile* secretion pattern is sometimes crucial for the small amount of hormone to be effective.

6. The levels of many hormones vary rhythmically throughout the day, and many hormone systems are controlled by circadian "clocks" in the brain, as we'll see in Chapter 14.

7. Hormones interact; the effects of one hormone can be markedly changed by the actions of another hormone.

8. The chemical structure of a given hormone is similar in all vertebrates, but the *functions* served by that hormone can vary across species.

9. Hormones can affect only cells that possess a receptor protein that recognizes the hormone and alters cell function. Among different vertebrates, the same brain regions often possess the same hormone receptors.

Neural versus hormonal communication   There are four main differences between neural and hormonal communication:

1. *Neural communication* works somewhat like a telephone system: Messages travel over fixed channels to precise destinations. The anatomical connections between

neurons determine the transmission of information from one cell to another. In contrast, *hormonal communication* works more like a TV broadcasting system: Many different endocrine messages spread throughout the body and can then be picked up by scattered cells that have receptors for them. Some hormones broadcast rather locally; for instance, the hypothalamus sends hormones only a few millimeters through the blood vessels to the anterior pituitary gland. Other hormones broadcast throughout the body, but because cells in only a particular organ have the proper receptors, these hormones influence only that organ.

2. Whereas neural messages are rapid and are measured in milliseconds, hormonal messages are slower and are measured in seconds and minutes.

3. Most neural messages are *digitized* (all-or-none) impulses. Hormonal messages are *analog*—that is, graded in strength.

4. Neural and hormonal communication also differ in terms of voluntary control. You cannot, on command, increase or decrease the output of a hormone or a response mediated by the endocrine system, but you can voluntarily lift your arm, blink your eyelids, or perform many other acts under neuromuscular control. This distinction between neural and hormonal systems, however, is not absolute. Many muscular responses cannot be performed or changed at will, even though they are under neural control. An example is heart rate, which is regulated by the vagus nerve and can meet changing demands during exercise or stress, but which only very few people can alter promptly and directly on command. Later in this chapter we will note examples of a conditioned response that is controlled by hormones: the milk letdown reflex mediated by oxytocin during breast-feeding.

Similarities in neural and hormonal communication In spite of the differences outlined in the previous section, the neural and hormonal systems have important similarities. The nervous system uses specialized biochemical substances (neurotransmitters) to communicate across synaptic junctions in much the same way that the endocrine system uses hormones (Figure 5.5). Of course, the distance traveled by the chemical messengers differs enormously in the two cases: The synaptic cleft is only about 30 nm (30×10^{-9} m) wide, but hormones may travel a meter or so from the site of secretion to the target organ. Nevertheless, the analogy between chemical transmission at synapses and hormonal communication holds up in several specific respects. For example, the neuron produces particular transmitter chemicals and stores them for later release, just as an endocrine gland stores its hormones for secretion.

Another similarity between the two systems is that both neurotransmitters and hormones, upon binding to receptor molecules on the cell surface, often activate a **second messenger** within the target cell to bring about changes within it. Neurotransmitters also often activate second messengers inside postsynaptic cells. Whether activated by a hormone or a neurotransmitter, the sec-

(a) **Neurocrine communication (synaptic transmission)**

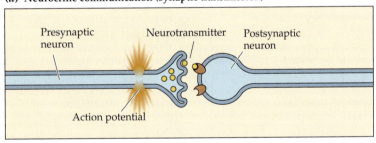

(b) **Endocrine communication**

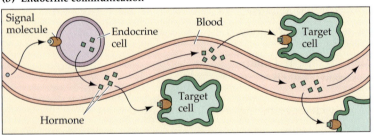

(c) **Neuroendocrine communication**

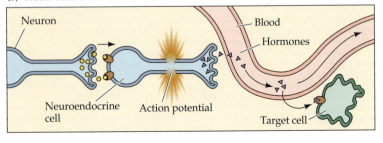

5.5 Neuroendocrine Cells Blend Neuronal and Endocrine Mechanisms (*a*) Neurons communicate with other neurons or with muscle cells or glands, and signal transmission is determined by the pattern of anatomical connections. (*b*) Endocrine signals are transmitted through the bloodstream and are recognized by appropriate receptors in specific locations in the body. (*c*) Neuroendocrine (neurosecretory) cells are the interface between neurons and endocrine glands. They receive neural signals from other neurons and secrete a hormone into the bloodstream. In this way electrical signals are converted into hormonal signals.

ond messengers are chemicals that can affect a variety of chemical processes inside the target cell, and thereby alter its function. Moreover, the same chemicals act as second messengers in both the nervous and the endocrine systems.

A look at the specialized neurons in the hypothalamus that synthesize hormones and release them into the bloodstream will highlight the similarities between neuronal and hormonal communication. These so-called **neurosecretory** (or **neuroendocrine**) **cells** make it hard to draw a firm line between neurons and endocrine cells (see Figure 5.5c). In fact, some investigators believe that the endocrine glands may have evolved from neurosecretory cells (Norman and Litwack, 1987).

Findings that certain chemicals in vertebrates—either hormonal peptides or **neuropeptides** (peptides used by neurons)—are also found in single-celled organisms suggest that both the nervous system and the endocrine system are derived from chemical communication systems in our remote single-celled ancestors (LeRoith et al., 1992). Some neuropeptides are used as neurotransmitters, but sometimes neuropeptides act as **neuromodulators** (see Chapter 4), substances that alter the reactivity of cells to specific transmitters. Neuromodulators tend to have a slower onset of effect and a longer duration of action than do neurotransmitters. So neuromodulators are something of a blend of neurotransmitter (because they're released into synapses) and hormone (because they act gradually).

EVOLUTION AT WORK

Hormones can be classified by chemical structure

Most hormones fall into one of three categories: protein hormones, amine hormones, or steroid hormones. Like all other proteins, **protein hormones** are composed of strings of amino acids (Figure 5.6a). (Recall that a peptide is simply a small protein— i.e., a short string of amino acids. In this chapter we will refer to both protein and

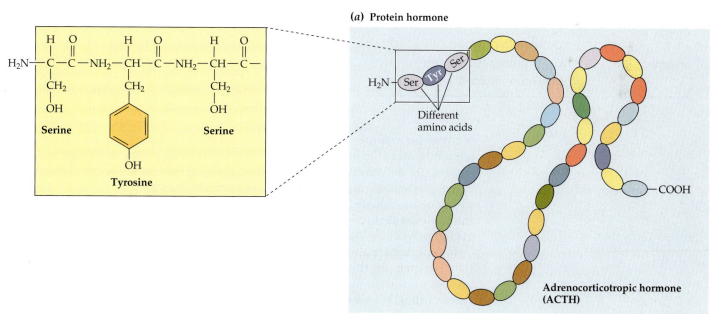

(a) Protein hormone

5.6 Chemical Structures of the Three Main Hormone Types (a) Protein hormones consist of strings of amino acids. If the string of amino acids is short, as it is in adrenocorticotropic hormone (ACTH), it may be referred to as a peptide hormone. (b) Amine hormones, such as thyroxine, are modified single amino acids. (c) Steroid hormones, such as estradiol, are derived from cholesterol and consist of four interconnected rings of carbon atoms, to which are attached different numbers and types of atoms.

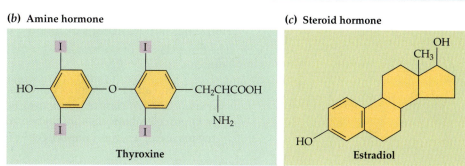

(b) Amine hormone

(c) Steroid hormone

TABLE 5.1   *Major Classes of Hormones*

Class	Hormone
PROTEIN HORMONES	Adrenocorticotropic hormone (ACTH)
	Follicle-stimulating hormone (FSH)
	Luteinizing hormone (LH)
	Thyroid-stimulating hormone (TSH)
	Growth hormone (GH)
	Prolactin
	Insulin
	Glucagon
	Oxytocin
	Vasopressin (arginine vasopressin, AVP; antidiuretic hormone, ADH)
	Releasing hormones, such as: Corticotropin-releasing hormone (CRH) Gonadotropin-releasing hormone (GnRH)
AMINE HORMONES	Epinephrine (adrenaline)
	Norepinephrine (NE)
	Thyroid hormones
	Melatonin
STEROID HORMONES	
Gonadal	Estrogens (e.g., estradiol)
	Progestins (e.g., progesterone)
	Androgens (e.g., testosterone, dihydrotestosterone)
Adrenal	Glucocorticoids (e.g., cortisol)
	Mineralocorticoids (e.g., aldosterone)

peptide hormones as *protein hormones.*) Different protein hormones consist of different combinations of amino acids. **Amine hormones** have a simpler structure, each one consisting of a single amino acid (hence their alias, *monoamine* hormones) that has been modified into a related molecule (Figure 5.6*b*). **Steroid hormones** are composed not of amino acids, but of four interconnected rings of carbon atoms (Figure 5.6*c*). Different steroid hormones vary in the number and kinds of atoms attached to the rings. This structure allows steroids to dissolve readily in lipids, so they can cross cell membranes easily.

The distinction between protein or amine hormones and steroid hormones is important because these two hormone classes interact with different types of receptors and by different mechanisms. Table 5.1 gives examples of each class of hormones.

Hormones Act on a Wide Variety of Cellular Mechanisms

In later chapters we will be considering the effects of specific hormones on behavior. In preparation for that discussion, let's look briefly at three aspects of hormonal activity: the effects of hormones on cells, the mechanisms by which hormones exercise these effects, and the regulation of hormone secretion.

Hormones affect cells by influencing their growth and activity

By influencing cells in various tissues and organs, hormones affect many everyday behaviors in humans and other animals. Hormones exert these far-reaching effects by (1) promoting the proliferation, growth, and differentiation of cells, and (2) modulating cell activity. Early developmental processes are promoted by various hormones—for example, the thyroid hormones. Without these hormones, fewer cells are produced in the brain, and mental development is stunted. Although cells proliferate and differentiate mainly during early development in the brain, hormones cause cells in some organs to divide and grow at later stages of life, too. For example, male and female hormones cause secondary sex characteristics to appear during adolescence: breasts and broadening of the hips in women, and facial hair and enlargement of the Adam's apple in men.

In cells that are already differentiated, hormones can modulate the rate of function. For example, thyroid hormones and insulin promote the metabolic activity of most of the cells in the human body. Other hormones modulate activity in certain types of cells. For example, luteinizing hormone (a hormone from the anterior pituitary gland) promotes the secretion of sex hormones by the testes and ovaries.

Hormones initiate actions by binding to receptor molecules

The three classes of hormones exert their influences on target organs in two different ways:

1. Protein and amine hormones bind to specific receptors (proteins that recognize only one hormone or class of hormones). Such receptors are usually found *on the surface* of target cell membranes and, when stimulated by the appropriate hormone, cause the release of a second messenger in the cell. (As we saw in Chapter 3, the release

of a second messenger can also be caused by some synaptic transmitters.) Protein hormones exert their effects by using this mechanism to alter proteins that already exist within the cell.

2. Steroid hormones pass through the membrane and bind to specific receptor proteins *inside* the cell. The steroid–receptor complex then binds to DNA in the nucleus of the cell. This binding affects the transcription of specific genes, increasing the production of some proteins and decreasing the production of others. Hence these hormones act by affecting gene expression and thereby altering the production of proteins (see the appendix).

Let's look at these two main modes of action in a little more detail and examine the ways in which hormones affect cells.

Protein and amine hormones act rapidly   What determines whether a cell responds to a particular protein hormone? Only those cells that produce the appropriate receptor proteins for a hormone and insert them into the membrane can respond to that hormone. Part of the receptor protein faces the outside of the cell to interact with the hormone, while other parts of the receptor dangle inside the cell and affect processes there. When a hormone binds to the extracellular portion of the receptor, the receptor molecule changes its overall shape. The alteration in the intracellular portion of the receptor then changes the internal chemistry of the cell, often by activating a second messenger (Figure 5.7*a*).

One second-messenger compound—cyclic adenosine monophosphate, commonly referred to as **cyclic AMP** or **cAMP**—transmits the messages of many of the peptide and amine hormones. It may seem surprising that the same second messenger can mediate the effects of many different hormones, but recall from Chapter 3 that the same kind of neural impulses can convey all sorts of neural messages. This situation is similar: A change in cAMP levels can cause very different outcomes, depending on which cells are affected, on which part of a cell is affected, and on the prior biochemical activity inside the cell. Other widespread second-messenger compounds include **cyclic guanosine monophosphate (cGMP)** and **phosphoinositides.**

The specificity of hormonal effects is determined in part by the selectivity of receptors; only a few cells produce the receptor that recognizes and reacts to the hormone, and only those cells respond. For example, adrenocorticotropic hormone

(*a*) **Protein hormone action**

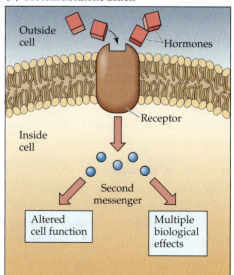

(*b*) **Steroid hormone action**

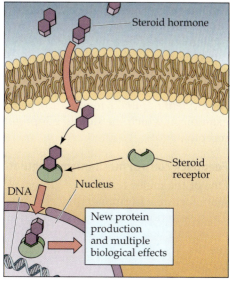

5.7 Two Main Mechanisms of Hormone Action   (*a*) Protein hormone receptors are found in the cell membrane. When the hormone binds to the receptor, a second-messenger system is activated, which affects various cellular processes. (*b*) Steroid hormones diffuse passively into cells. Inside the target cells are large receptor molecules that bind to the steroid hormone. The steroid–receptor complex then binds to DNA, causing an increase in the production of some gene products and a decrease in the production of others. This is the mechanism by which steroids exert a genomic effect, which is distinct from the nongenomic effects mentioned in the text.

(ACTH) interacts with receptors on the membranes of cells in the adrenal cortex, and in these cells an increase in cAMP leads to the synthesis and release of other hormones.

Protein hormones usually act relatively rapidly, within seconds to minutes. (Although rapid for a hormone, this action is much slower than neural activity.) There can also be prolonged effects. For example, ACTH promotes the proliferation and growth of adrenal cortical cells, thereby increasing the long-term capacity to sustain production of their hormones. A cell may increase or decrease the number of hormone receptors it makes, and these changes are sometimes referred to as up-regulation and down-regulation, respectively.

Steroid hormones act slowly   Steroid hormones typically act more slowly than protein or amine hormones, requiring hours to take effect. The specificity of action of steroid hormones is determined by the receptors that reside *inside* target cells.

Steroid hormones pass in and out of many cells in which they have no effect. If appropriate receptor proteins are inside, however, these receptors bind to the hormone, and the receptor–steroid complex then binds to DNA, so the complexes become concentrated in the nuclei of target cells (Figure 5.7*b*). Thus, as Box 5.1 describes, we can study where a steroid hormone is active by observing where radioactively tagged molecules of the steroid accumulate. For example, when tagged estradiol is administered into the circulatory system, it accumulates not only in the reproductive tract (as you might expect), but also in the nuclei of some neurons throughout the hypothalamus.

By altering protein production, steroids have a slow but long-lasting effect on the development or adult function of cells. We will discuss such effects of steroids further in Chapter 12. Within our DNA is a large "superfamily" of steroid receptor genes (Ribeiro et al., 1995), and some steroids act on more than one receptor. For example, Jan-Ake Gustafsson and colleagues found a second estrogen receptor, which they named estrogen receptor β (Kuiper et al., 1996) to distinguish it from the previously discovered estrogen receptor α. Both estrogen receptors are found in the brain—one more prominent in some regions, the other more prominent in others. Scientists are trying to tease apart their separate effects on behavior.

When a cell possesses a steroid receptor, it *may* respond to the steroid hormone, but just having the steroid receptor is not enough to guarantee a response. Recently discovered **steroid receptor cofactors** are a variety of proteins that a cell may also make. In addition to the steroid receptor, some cofactors appear to be needed for a cell to respond. Two different cells containing the same steroid receptors may respond quite differently to the steroid hormone if they are producing different steroid receptor cofactors (Tetel, 2000). These cofactors seem to determine which genes will be regulated when the steroid hormone and its receptor reach the nucleus.

Steroids may be able to affect cells in other ways. For example, estradiol, in addition to its slow, long-lasting action on gene expression, can have a rapid, brief effect on some neurons without affecting gene expression. This rapid **nongenomic effect** of steroids may involve a separate class of receptors in the neuronal *membrane* (Wehling, 1997), modulating neural excitability. In Chapter 4 we discussed an example in which the steroid allopregnanolone modulates activity of the $GABA_A$ receptor.

Jan-Ake Gustafsson

Feedback control mechanisms regulate the secretion of hormones

One of the major features of almost all hormonal systems is that they don't just manufacture a hormone; they also detect and evaluate the effects of the hormone. Thus, secretion is usually monitored and regulated so that the rate is appropriate to ongoing activities and needs of the body. The basic control used is a **negative feedback** system: Output of the hormone *feeds back* to inhibit the drive for more hormone.

(*a*) **Autocrine feedback**

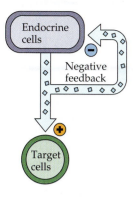

(*b*) **Target cell feedback**

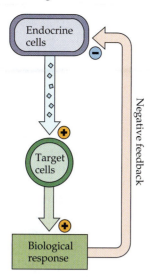

5.8 Endocrine Feedback Loops (*a*) In the simplest type of negative feedback control, an endocrine gland releases a hormone that not only acts on a target, but also feeds back in an autocrine fashion to inhibit further hormone secretion. (*b*) The hormone from the endocrine gland acts on target cells to produce a specific set of biological effects. The consequences of these effects may be detected by the endocrine gland, inhibiting further hormone release. (*c*) In many feedback systems the brain becomes involved. The hypothalamic region drives the endocrine gland via either neural or hormonal signals. The target organ signals the brain to inhibit this drive. (*d*) Highly complex feedback mechanisms involve the hypothalamus and the anterior pituitary, as well as the endocrine gland. Feedback regulation may involve a variety of routes and hormones.

(*c*) **Brain regulation**

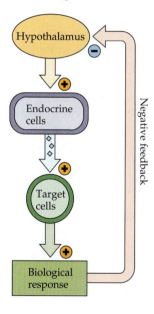

(*d*) **Brain and pituitary regulation**

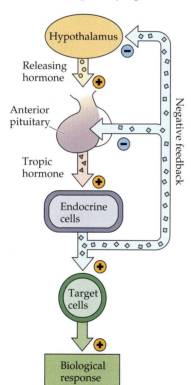

Figure 5.8*a* diagrams the simplest kind of system that regulates hormones: An endocrine cell releases a hormone that acts on target cells, but the same hormone also feeds back to inhibit the gland that released it. This is an autocrine response.

In other cases, the endocrine cell reacts not to its own hormone, but to the biological response that the hormone elicits from the target cells (Figure 5.8*b*). If the initial effect is too small, additional hormone is released; if the effect is sufficient, no further hormone is released. For example, we release the hormone insulin to control the level of glucose circulating in our blood. After a meal, glucose from the food

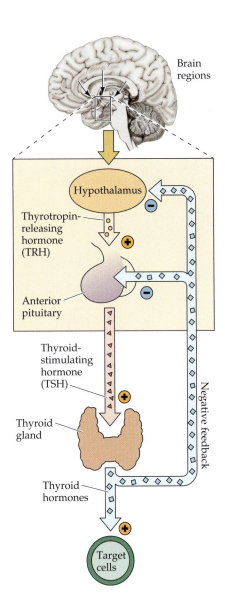

Brain regions

Hypothalamus

Thyrotropin-releasing hormone (TRH)

Anterior pituitary

Thyroid-stimulating hormone (TSH)

Thyroid gland

Thyroid hormones

Negative feedback

Target cells

5.9 An Example of Complex Endocrine Regulation   The brain funnels information to the hypothalamus, which then controls the anterior pituitary, which in turn stimulates the thyroid gland. Note that three hormones and at least four cell groups are interacting in this instance.

enters the bloodstream, causing insulin to be released from the pancreas. The insulin causes glucose to enter muscle and fat cells. As the level of glucose in the blood falls, the pancreas secretes less insulin, so a balance tends to be maintained.

Thus, insulin is normally self-limiting: The more insulin that is secreted, the more glucose is pulled out of circulation and the lower the call for insulin. This negative feedback action of a hormone system is like that of a thermostat, and just as the thermostat can be set to different temperatures at different times, the set points of a person's endocrine feedback systems can be changed to meet varying circumstances. We'll encounter negative feedback effects again in Chapter 13.

A more complex endocrine system includes the brain, usually the hypothalamus, as part of the circuit that controls an endocrine gland (Figure 5.8c). When we are alarmed, for example, the hypothalamus directs the adrenal medulla to secrete the hormone epinephrine, which affects many target cells. The brain detects these effects (racing heart, trembling knees) and exerts negative feedback on the hypothalamus to reduce further hormone output.

An even greater degree of complexity is encountered when the anterior pituitary becomes involved (Figure 5.8d). As we'll see, several anterior pituitary hormones affect the secretion of other endocrine glands; all of these pituitary hormones are called **tropic hormones.** (*Tropic,* pronounced with a long *o* as in *toe,* means "directed toward.") The hypothalamus uses another set of hormones, called **releasing hormones,** to control the pituitary release of tropic hormones. Thus the brain's releasing hormones affect the pituitary's tropic hormones, which affect the release of hormone from another endocrine gland. Negative feedback in this case goes from the hormone of the endocrine gland to both the hypothalamus and the anterior pituitary (Figure 5.9).

Each Endocrine Gland Secretes Specific Hormones

We will restrict our account in this chapter to some of the main endocrine glands because a thorough treatment would fill an entire book (e.g., Hadley, 2000). Table 5.2 gives a fuller but far from complete listing of hormones and their functions. Keep in mind that most hormones have more functions than are mentioned here and that several hormones may act together to produce effects in the same target cells.

The pituitary gland releases many important hormones

Resting in a depression in the base of the skull is the **pituitary gland** (see Figure 5.1), about 1 cm^3 in volume and weighing about 1 g. The hypothalamus sits just above it. The term *pituitary* comes from the Latin *pituita,* "mucus," reflecting the outmoded belief that waste products dripped down from the brain into the pituitary, which secreted them out through the nose. (The ancients may have thought you could literally sneeze your brains out!) The pituitary used to be referred to as the *master gland,* a reference to its regulatory role with regard to several other endocrine glands. But this gland is itself enslaved by the hypothalamus above it, as we'll see.

The pituitary gland consists of two main parts: the **anterior pituitary** (adenohypophysis) and the **posterior pituitary** (neurohypophysis). The anterior and posterior pituitary are completely separate in function. The pituitary is connected to the

TABLE 5.2 *Main Endocrine Glands, Their Hormone Products, and Principal Effects of Their Hormones*

Gland	Hormones	Principal effects
Posterior pituitary (storage organ for certain hormones produced by hypothalamus)	Oxytocin	Stimulates contraction of uterine muscles; stimulates release of milk by mammary glands
	Vasopressin (AVP; antidiuretic hormone, ADH)	Stimulates increased water reabsorption by kidneys; stimulates constriction of blood vessels
Anterior pituitary	Growth hormone (GH)	Stimulates growth
	Thyroid-stimulating hormone (TSH)	Stimulates the thyroid
	Adrenocorticotropic hormone (ACTH)	Stimulates the adrenal cortex
	Follicle-stimulating hormone (FSH)	Stimulates growth of ovarian follicles and of seminiferous tubules of the testes
	Luteinizing hormone (LH)	Stimulates conversion of follicles into corpora lutea; stimulates secretion of sex hormones by gonads
	Prolactin	Stimulates milk secretion by mammary glands
Hypothalamus	Releasing hormones	Regulate hormone secretion by anterior pituitary
	Oxytocin; vasopressin	*See under* Posterior pituitary
Pineal	Melatonin	Regulates seasonal changes; regulates puberty
Adrenal cortex	Glucocorticoids (corticosterone, cortisol, hydrocortisone, etc.)	Inhibit incorporation of amino acids into protein in muscle; stimulate formation and storage of glycogen; help maintain normal blood sugar level
	Mineralocorticoids (aldosterone, deoxycorticosterone, etc.)	Regulate metabolism of sodium and potassium
	Sex hormones (especially androstenedione)	Regulate facial and body hair
Gonads		
Testes	Androgens (testosterone, dihydrotestosterone, etc.)	Stimulate development and maintenance of male primary and secondary sexual characteristics and behavior
Ovaries	Estrogens (estradiol, estrone, etc.)	Stimulate development and maintenance of female secondary sexual characteristics and behavior
	Progestins (progesterone)	Stimulate female secondary sexual characteristics and behavior; maintain pregnancy
Thyroid	Thyroxine, triiodothyronine	Stimulate oxidative metabolism
	Calcitonin	Prevents excessive rise in blood calcium
Pancreas	Insulin	Stimulates glycogen formation and storage
	Glucagon	Stimulates conversion of glycogen into glucose
Stomach	Secretin	Stimulates secretion of pancreatic juice
	Cholecystokinin (CCK)	Stimulates release of bile by gallbladder
	Enterogastrone	Inhibits secretion of gastric juice
	Gastrin	Stimulates secretion of gastric juice
	Ghrelin	Stimulates the anterior pituitary to release growth hormone
Heart	Atrial natriuretic peptide	Promotes salt loss in urine

hypothalamus by a thin piece of tissue called the pituitary stalk (Figure 5.10). The stalk contains many axons and is richly supplied with blood vessels. The axons extend only to the posterior pituitary, which we will consider next. The blood vessels, as we will see later, transmit information exclusively to the anterior pituitary.

The posterior pituitary The posterior pituitary gland contains two principal hormones: **oxytocin** and **arginine vasopressin** (**AVP**), often called just **vasopressin.** Neurons in various hypothalamic nuclei, especially the supraoptic nucleus and

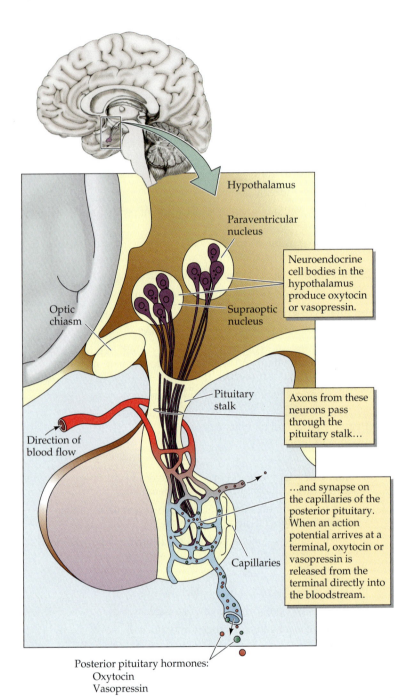

Neuroendocrine cell bodies in the hypothalamus produce oxytocin or vasopressin.

Hypothalamus

Paraventricular nucleus

Supraoptic nucleus

Optic chiasm

Pituitary stalk

Axons from these neurons pass through the pituitary stalk...

Direction of blood flow

...and synapse on the capillaries of the posterior pituitary. When an action potential arrives at a terminal, oxytocin or vasopressin is released from the terminal directly into the bloodstream.

Capillaries

Posterior pituitary hormones:
Oxytocin
Vasopressin

5.10 Hormone Production by the Posterior Pituitary

NEURAL PLASTICITY

the paraventricular nucleus, synthesize these two hormones and transport them along their axons to the axon terminals (see Figure 5.10). Nerve impulses in these hypothalamic neurosecretory cells travel down the axons in the pituitary stalk and reach the axon terminals in the posterior pituitary, causing release of the hormone from the terminals into the rich vascular bed of the neurohypophysis. The axon terminals abut capillaries (small blood vessels), allowing the hormone to enter circulation immediately.

Some of the signals that activate the nerve cells of the supraoptic and paraventricular nuclei are related to thirst and water regulation, which we will discuss in Chapter 13. Secretion of AVP increases blood pressure by causing blood vessels to contract. AVP also inhibits the formation of urine, so it is sometimes called antidiuretic hormone (ADH) (a *diuretic* is a food or drug that promotes urination). This action of AVP helps conserve water. In fact, the major physiological role of AVP is its potent antidiuretic activity; it exerts this effect with less than one-thousandth of the dose needed to alter blood pressure.

Oxytocin is involved in many aspects of reproductive and parental behavior. One of its functions is to stimulate contractions of the uterine muscles and thus hasten birth (the word *oxytocin* is derived from the Greek *oxys*, "rapid," and *tokos*, "childbirth"). In fact, injections of oxytocin (or the synthetic version, Pitocin) are frequently used to accelerate delivery when prolonged labor threatens the health of the fetus.

Oxytocin also triggers the **milk letdown reflex,** the contraction of cells in the mammary glands. The mechanism that mediates this phenomenon is a good example of the interaction of behavior and hormone release. When an infant or young animal first begins to suckle, the arrival of milk at the nipple is delayed by 30 to 60 s. This delay is caused by the sequence of steps that precede letdown. Stimulation of the nipple activates receptors in the skin, which transmit this information through a chain of neurons and synapses to hypothalamic cells that contain oxytocin. Once these cells have been sufficiently stimulated, the hormone is released from the posterior pituitary and travels via the bloodstream to the mammary glands, where it produces a contraction of the tissues storing milk, making the milk available at the nipple (Figure 5.11).

For mothers this reflex response to suckling frequently becomes conditioned to baby cries, so milk appears promptly at the start of nursing. Because the mother learns to release oxytocin *before* the suckling begins, sometimes the cries of someone else's baby in public may trigger an inconvenient release of milk. Oxytocin and vasopressin also serve as neurotransmitters from hypothalamic cells (Figure 5.12), projecting widely through the nervous system. Oxytocin and AVP have been implicated in social behaviors, a topic we will discuss at the end of this chapter.

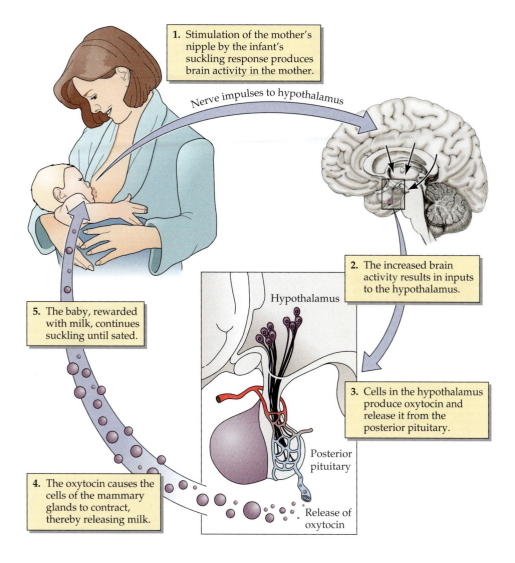

1. Stimulation of the mother's nipple by the infant's suckling response produces brain activity in the mother.

Nerve impulses to hypothalamus

5. The baby, rewarded with milk, continues suckling until sated.

4. The oxytocin causes the cells of the mammary glands to contract, thereby releasing milk.

2. The increased brain activity results in inputs to the hypothalamus.

Hypothalamus

3. Cells in the hypothalamus produce oxytocin and release it from the posterior pituitary.

Posterior pituitary

Release of oxytocin

The anterior pituitary Different cells of the anterior lobe of the pituitary synthesize and release different tropic hormones, which we'll discuss in the next section. Synthesis and release of the tropic hormones, however, are under the control of releasing hormones, as mentioned earlier. The releasing hormones are made by cells of the hypothalamus. We will briefly note some of the properties of these hypothalamic releasing hormones before further considering anterior pituitary actions.

Hypothalamic releasing hormones govern the anterior pituitary

Neurons that synthesize different releasing hormones reside in different regions of the hypothalamus; like the neurons that produce oxytocin and vasopressin, these cells are considered neuroendocrine, or neurosecretory, cells. The axons of the neuroendocrine cells converge on the median eminence just above the pituitary stalk. This region contains an elaborate profusion of capillaries that form the **hypothalamic–pituitary portal system**.

Axons in this area contain large granules filled with hormones, which are released not into a synapse, but into the capillaries, where blood carries the releasing hormone a short distance into the anterior pituitary. The blood supply of the anterior pituitary thus contains many different releasing hormones that cause various an-

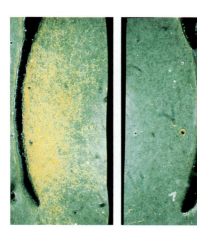

5.12 Vasopressin Can Serve as a Neurotransmitter Revealed here by immunocytochemistry are vasopressin-filled axonal fibers in the septum of intact (*left*) and castrated (*right*) male rats. (Courtesy of Geert DeVries.)

5.13 Hormone Release by the Anterior Pituitary

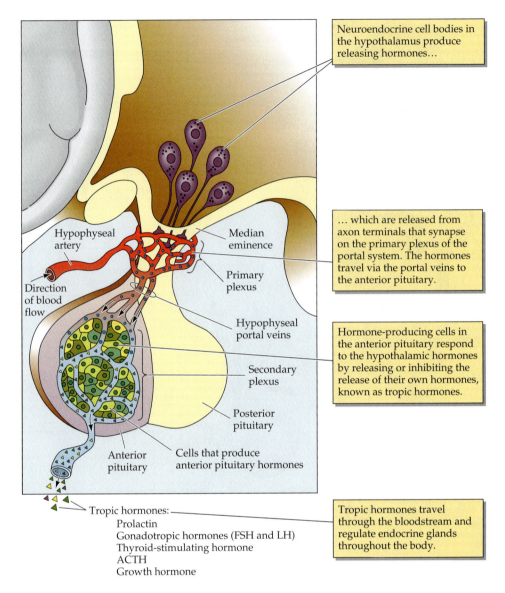

Neuroendocrine cell bodies in the hypothalamus produce releasing hormones…

Hypophyseal artery

Median eminence

Primary plexus

Direction of blood flow

… which are released from axon terminals that synapse on the primary plexus of the portal system. The hormones travel via the portal veins to the anterior pituitary.

Hypophyseal portal veins

Secondary plexus

Hormone-producing cells in the anterior pituitary respond to the hypothalamic hormones by releasing or inhibiting the release of their own hormones, known as tropic hormones.

Posterior pituitary

Anterior pituitary

Cells that produce anterior pituitary hormones

Tropic hormones:
Prolactin
Gonadotropic hormones (FSH and LH)
Thyroid-stimulating hormone
ACTH
Growth hormone

Tropic hormones travel through the bloodstream and regulate endocrine glands throughout the body.

terior pituitary cells to change the rate at which they release their tropic hormone (Figure 5.13).

These types of controls apply to all the anterior pituitary hormones. Neuroendocrine cells in the hypothalamus make one releasing hormone or another, transport it down their axons to the median eminence, and when an action potential arrives at the terminals, dump the releasing hormone into the hypothalamic–pituitary portal system. When the releasing hormones reach the anterior pituitary, they cause the cells there to release more or less tropic hormone into the bloodstream. Thus the hypothalamic releasing hormones are an important control element in the regulation of secretions of endocrine organs throughout the body. Cutting the pituitary stalk interrupts the blood vessels and the flow of releasing hormones and leads to profound atrophy of the pituitary.

The neuroendocrine cells that synthesize the releasing hormones are themselves subject to two kinds of influences:

1. They receive *neural impulses* (either excitatory or inhibitory) from other brain regions via the synaptic contacts of these cells in the hypothalamus. In this manner a wide range of neural signals reflecting both internal and external events influence

the endocrine system. Thus the outputs of endocrine glands can be regulated in accordance with ongoing events and can be conditioned by learning.

2. They are directly affected by *circulating messages,* such as other hormones (especially hormones that have themselves been secreted in response to tropic hormones), and by blood sugar and products of the immune system. In other words, these neuroendocrine cells are not shielded by the blood–brain barrier that we discussed in Chapter 2.

Tropic hormones of the anterior pituitary The anterior pituitary gland secretes six main tropic hormones (Figure 5.14; see also Table 5.2). Two of these regulate the function of the adrenal cortex and thyroid gland:

1. **Adrenocorticotropic hormone (ACTH)** controls the production and release of hormones of the adrenal cortex. The adrenal cortex in turn releases steroid hormones. The levels of ACTH and adrenal steroids show a marked rhythm in the course of a day (see Chapter 14).
2. **Thyroid-stimulating hormone (TSH)** increases the release of thyroid hormones from the thyroid gland and markedly affects thyroid gland size.

Two other tropic hormones of the anterior pituitary influence the gonads:

3. **Luteinizing hormone (LH)** stimulates the release of eggs from the ovaries in females and prepares the uterine lining for the implantation of a fertilized egg. In males, LH stimulates interstitial cells of the testes to produce testosterone.
4. **Follicle-stimulating hormone (FSH)** stimulates the secretion of estrogens in females and of testosterone in males. It also influences both egg and sperm production.

5.14 Secretions of the Anterior Pituitary Hormones produced in the anterior pituitary include tropic hormones, which control endocrine glands and directly affect other body organs, such as bones.

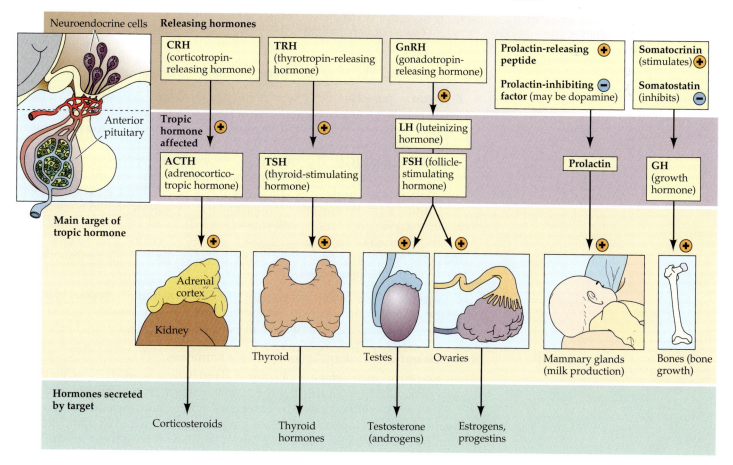

BOX 5.2 Stress and Growth: Psychosocial Dwarfism

Genie had a horrifically deprived childhood. For over 10 years, starting from the age of 20 months, she was isolated in a small, closed room, and much of the time she was tied to a potty chair. Her disturbed parents provided food, but nobody held Genie or spoke to her. When she was released from her confinement and observed by researchers at the age of 13, her size made her appear only 6 or 7 years old (Rymer, 1993).

Other less horrendous forms of family deprivation have also been shown to result in failure of growth. This syndrome is referred to as **psychosocial dwarfism** to emphasize that the growth failure arises from psychological and social factors mediated through the CNS and its control over endocrine functions (W. H. Green et al., 1984). When children suffering from psychosocial dwarfism are removed from stressful circumstances, many begin to grow rapidly. The growth rates of three such children, before and after periods of emotional deprivation, are shown in the figure (arrows indicate when each child was removed from the abusive situation). These children seem to have compensated for much of the growth deficit that occurred during prolonged stress periods.

How do stress and emotional deprivation impair growth? Growth impairments appear to be mediated by changed outputs of several hormones, including growth hormone (GH), cortisol, and other hormones, known as **somatomedins** (which are normally released by the liver in response to GH). GH and the somatomedins normally stimulate cell growth; high levels of cortisol inhibit growth.

Some children with psychosocial dwarfism show almost a complete lack of release of GH, which may be caused by an absence of the releasing hormone somatocrinin from the hypothalamus (Albanese et al., 1994). Disturbed sleep has also been suggested as a cause of this failure because GH is typically released during certain stages of sleep, as we will see in Chapter 14, and children under stress show disturbed sleep patterns (L. I. Gardner, 1972). Other children who exhibit psychosocial dwarfism show normal levels of GH but low levels of somatomedins, and these hormones, along with GH, appear to be necessary for normal growth. Still other children with this condition show elevated levels of cortisol, probably as a result of stress, that inhibit growth. Some affected children show none of these hormonal disturbances, so there must also be other routes through which emotional experiences affect growth.

Growth is an example of a process that involves many factors—hormonal, metabolic, and dietary—and can therefore malfunction in a variety of ways. Cases of psychosocial dwarfism are more common than once was thought, and investigators who study this syndrome are calling for further awareness of and attention to it (W. H. Green et al., 1984). For Genie, relief came in time to restore much of her *body* growth, but her mental development remained severely limited; she never learned to say more than a few words, and, now in her 40s, she lives in an institution.

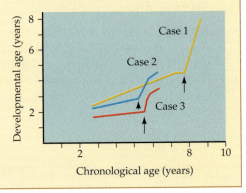

The two remaining tropic hormones control milk production and body growth:

5. **Prolactin** is named after its role of promoting mammary development for lactation in female mammals. In other vertebrates, prolactin plays other roles; in ringdoves of both sexes, for example, it promotes the secretion of crop milk, which parents feed to their chicks.

6. **Growth hormone** (GH; also known as *somatotropin* or *somatotropic hormone*) acts throughout the body to influence the growth of cells and tissues by affecting protein metabolism. The daily production and release of GH are especially prominent during sleep. Several other factors inhibit the release of growth hormone, including starvation, exercise, and stress (Box 5.2). In addition to hypothalamic factors that affect GH release, the stomach secretes a hormone, called *ghrelin* (from the proto-Indo-European root for "grow"), that evokes GH release from the anterior pituitary (Kojima et al., 1999).

Let's consider three of the target organs stimulated by tropic hormones of the anterior pituitary: the adrenal gland, the thyroid gland, and the gonads. Each of these glands secretes hormones of its own in response to the pituitary tropic hormones.

Two divisions of the adrenal gland produce hormones

Resting on top of each kidney is an **adrenal gland,** which secretes a large variety of hormones (Figure 5.15; see also Figure 5.1). In mammals, the adrenal structure is divided into two major portions. The outer bark of the gland, the **adrenal cortex,** is composed of distinct layers of cells, each producing different steroid hormones; this portion is about 80% of the gland. The core of the gland is the **adrenal medulla,** really a portion of the sympathetic nervous system because it is richly supplied with nerves from the autonomic ganglia.

The adrenal medulla releases amine hormones—**epinephrine** (adrenaline) and **norepinephrine** (noradrenaline)—in response to nerve impulses of the sympathetic nervous system. In Chapter 4 we saw that epinephrine and norepinephrine are also synaptic transmitters at certain sites in the nervous system.

The adrenal cortex produces and secretes a variety of steroid hormones, collectively called the **adrenocorticoids** (or adrenal steroids). One subgroup is the **glucocorticoids,** so named because of their effects on the metabolism of carbohydrates, including glucose. Hormones of this type, such as **cortisol,** increase the level of blood glucose and accelerate the breakdown of proteins. In high concentrations, glucocorticoids have a marked anti-inflammatory effect; that is, they inhibit the swelling around injuries or infections. This action normally results in the temporary decrease of bodily responses to tissue injury. However, high levels of glucocorticoids can destroy brain cells, as we'll see in Chapter 15 when we discuss stress.

A second subgroup of adrenal steroids is the **mineralocorticoids,** so named because of their effects on minerals such as sodium and potassium. The primary mineralocorticoid hormone is **aldosterone,** which acts on the kidneys to retain sodium and thus reduces the amount of urine produced, conserving water. This action helps maintain a homeostatic equilibrium of ions in blood and extracellular fluids.

The adrenal cortex also produces **sex steroids.** The molecular structure of these hormones is very similar to that of the other adrenal steroids. The chief sex hormone secreted by the human adrenal cortex is **androstenedione;** it contributes to the adult pattern of body hair in men and women. In some females the adrenal cortex produces more than the normal amounts of sex hormones, causing a more masculine appearance (see Chapter 12).

The level of circulating adrenal cortical hormones is regulated in several steps (see Figure 5.15). The pituitary hormone ACTH promotes steroid synthesis in the adrenal gland. Adrenal steroids in turn exert a negative feedback effect on ACTH release. As the level of adrenal cortical hormones increases, the secretion of ACTH is suppressed, so the output of hormones from the adrenal cortex diminishes. When the levels of adrenal steroids fall, the pituitary ACTH-secreting cells are released from suppression, and the concentration of ACTH in the blood rises, leading to increased output of adrenal cortical hormones.

Thyroid hormones regulate growth and metabolism

Situated just below the vocal apparatus in the throat is the **thyroid gland** (see Figure 5.1). This gland produces and secretes several hormones. Two of these—**thyroxine** and **triiodothyronine**—are usually referred to as thyroid hormones; a third—calcitonin—promotes calcium deposition in bones and will not be discussed further.

The thyroid is unique among endocrine glands because it stores large amounts of hormone and releases it slowly; normally the thyroid has at least a 100-day supply of hormones. Although thyroid hormones are amines—derived from amino acids—they behave like steroids. They bind to specialized receptors (part of the steroid receptor superfamily) found inside cells. The thyroid hormone–receptor complex then binds to DNA and regulates gene expression.

Figure 5.9 shows the control network for regulating thyroxine levels in blood. The major control is exerted by thyroid-stimulating hormone (TSH) from the anterior pituitary gland. The secretion of TSH by the pituitary is controlled by two factors. The dominant factor is the negative feedback from thyroid hormones circulating in the blood; they directly inhibit the pituitary, reducing TSH release. The second factor is the production (by the hypothalamus) of **thyrotropin-releasing hormone (TRH)**,

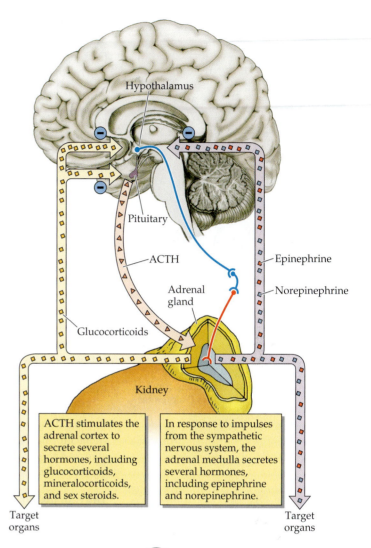

Hypothalamus
Pituitary
ACTH
Epinephrine
Norepinephrine
Adrenal gland
Glucocorticoids
Kidney

ACTH stimulates the adrenal cortex to secrete several hormones, including glucocorticoids, mineralocorticoids, and sex steroids.

In response to impulses from the sympathetic nervous system, the adrenal medulla secretes several hormones, including epinephrine and norepinephrine.

Target organs   Target organs

5.15 Regulation of Hormones Produced by the Adrenal Glands Situated above the kidneys, each adrenal gland consists of an outer layer (the cortex, shown in yellow) and an inner layer (the medulla, shown in blue). The main hormones of the cortical portion are glucocorticoids, mineralocorticoids, and sex steroids (androgens and estrogens). The level of circulating adrenal steroids is regulated in several steps that involve both corticotropin-releasing hormone from the hypothalamus and adrenocorticotropic hormone (ACTH) secreted by the anterior pituitary. The cells of the adrenal medulla release epinephrine and norepinephrine as a result of stimulation by the sympathetic nervous system.

5.16 Isn't That a Stylish Collar?
Because there is little iodine in the soil around Bern, Switzerland, vegetables grown there provide insufficient iodine even for prosperous people like the novelist Jeremias Gotthelf (1797–1854). He suffered from a large goiter that he routinely concealed behind elaborate collars. (Painted by Friedrich Dietler.)

which stimulates the release of TSH from the pituitary. When the level of circulating thyroid hormone falls, both TRH and TSH are secreted; when TSH reaches the thyroid gland, it stimulates the production and release of thyroid hormones.

Thyroid hormones are the only substances produced by the body that contain iodine, and their manufacture is critically dependent on the supply of iodine. In parts of the world where foods contain little iodine, many people suffer from hypothyroidism. In such cases the thyroid gland enlarges, driven by higher and higher TSH levels. In the attempt to produce more thyroid hormones, the gland swells, producing a **goiter.** The soil in Switzerland has little iodine, so even well-fed citizens there often had goiters through the nineteenth century (Figure 5.16). Today the addition of a small amount of iodine to salt—producing *iodized salt*—ensures that we won't develop goiters even if we get insufficient iodine in our vegetables.

Remember Chuck at the start of this chapter? His problem was acute hypothyroidism. He had been diagnosed years before and given thyroid hormone pills, but the prescription ran out and he neglected to refill it. Six months later, when he showed up in the ER, he had not yet developed a goiter, but he was suffering. Thyroid hormones have a general effect on the nervous system, maintaining alertness and reflexes. Chuck's cognitive function became so impaired he couldn't even remember that he had taken thyroid hormone before. But the slow knee jerk reflex suggested hypothyroidism, and blood tests confirmed that he had almost no thyroid hormone. Chuck was lucky that doctors caught his problem before he slipped into hypothyroid coma, which is fatal about 20% of the time, even when treated (Jauhar, 2003). People with less-severe hypothyroidism may appear depressed, so the hormonal imbalance may be overlooked.

Thyroid hormones also influence growth; this function is especially evident when thyroid deficiency starts early in life. Besides stunted body growth and characteristic facial malformation, thyroid deficiency produces a marked reduction in brain size and the branching of axons and dendrites. This state, called **cretinism** or *congenital hypothyroidism*, is accompanied by mental retardation.

The gonads produce steroid hormones, regulating reproduction

Almost all aspects of reproductive behavior, including mating and parental behavior, depend on hormones. Since Chapter 12 is devoted to reproductive behavior and physiology, at this point we will only briefly note relevant hormones and some pertinent aspects of anatomy and physiology. Female and male **gonads** (ovaries and testes, respectively; see Figure 5.1) consist of two different subcompartments—one to produce hormones (the sex steroids we mentioned earlier) and another to produce gametes (eggs or sperm). The gonadal hormones are critical for triggering both reproductive behavior controlled by the brain, and gamete production.

The testes   Within the **testes** are sperm-producing cells (the Sertoli cells) and Leydig cells, which produce and secrete the sex steroid called **testosterone.** Testosterone and other male hormones are called **androgens** (from the Greek *andro-*, "man," and *gennan*, "to produce"). The production and release of testosterone are regulated by luteinizing hormone from the anterior pituitary. LH in turn is controlled by a hypothalamic releasing hormone called **gonadotropin-releasing hormone (GnRH).**

Testosterone controls a wide range of body changes that become visible at puberty, including changes in voice, hair growth, and genital size. In species that breed only in certain seasons of the year, testosterone has especially marked effects on appearance and behavior—for example, the antlers and fighting between males that are displayed by many species of deer (Figure 5.17). Figure 5.18*a* summarizes the regu-

5.17 The Influence of a Hormone   The antlers and combative behavior of male red deer, a subspecies of the North American elk, are both seasonally affected by testosterone.

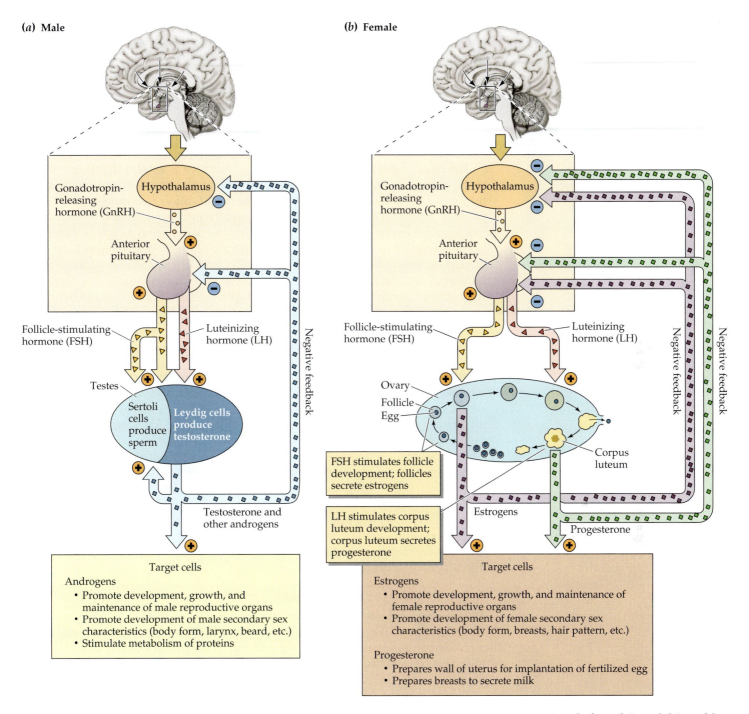

(a) Male

Gonadotropin-releasing hormone (GnRH)

Hypothalamus

Anterior pituitary

Follicle-stimulating hormone (FSH)

Luteinizing hormone (LH)

Negative feedback

Testes

Sertoli cells produce sperm

Leydig cells produce testosterone

Testosterone and other androgens

Target cells

Androgens
- Promote development, growth, and maintenance of male reproductive organs
- Promote development of male secondary sex characteristics (body form, larynx, beard, etc.)
- Stimulate metabolism of proteins

(b) Female

Gonadotropin-releasing hormone (GnRH)

Hypothalamus

Anterior pituitary

Follicle-stimulating hormone (FSH)

Luteinizing hormone (LH)

Negative feedback

Negative feedback

Ovary

Follicle

Egg

Corpus luteum

FSH stimulates follicle development; follicles secrete estrogens

LH stimulates corpus luteum development; corpus luteum secretes progesterone

Estrogens

Progesterone

Target cells

Estrogens
- Promote development, growth, and maintenance of female reproductive organs
- Promote development of female secondary sex characteristics (body form, breasts, hair pattern, etc.)

Progesterone
- Prepares wall of uterus for implantation of fertilized egg
- Prepares breasts to secrete milk

5.18 Regulation of Gonadal Steroid Hormones (*a*) In males the principal gonadal steroid secreted is testosterone. (*b*) The female gonads produce two classes of steroids: estrogens and progestins.

lation of testosterone secretion. As men age, testosterone levels tend to decline. Although elderly men who happen to maintain high levels of circulating testosterone perform better on tests of memory and attention than those with low levels (Yaffe et al., 2002), there have been too few studies to tell whether taking supplemental testosterone actually helps aging men (Harder, 2003). Furthermore, taking supplemental testosterone can sometimes increase aggressive or manic behaviors (Pope et al., 2000).

The ovaries The paired female gonads, the **ovaries,** also produce both the mature gametes—called *ova* (singular *ovum*) or eggs—and sex steroid hormones. However, hormonal secretion by the ovaries is more complicated than by the testes. Ovarian hormones are produced in cycles, the duration of which varies with the species. Human ovarian cycles last about 4 weeks; rat cycles last only 4 days.

The ovary produces two major classes of steroid hormones: **progestins** (from the Latin *pro,* "favoring," and *gestare,* "to bear," because these hormones help to maintain pregnancy) and **estrogens** (from the Latin *oestrus,* "gadfly or frenzy," and the Greek *gennan,* "to produce"). If you suspect sexism in the naming of estrogens as though they induce frenzy, you're right. This term borrowed from the now discredited idea that women suffered hysteria because of secretions from their uterus. In fact, estrogens may improve cognitive functioning (Maki and Resnick, 2000), although this topic is still debated (Dohanich, 2003). Estrogens may also protect the brain from some of the effects of stress and stroke (Behl, 2002).

CLINICAL ISSUE

The most important naturally occurring estrogen is **estradiol,** but many synthetic estrogens are tested in search of drugs that produce only the beneficial effects of the hormone, without increasing the risk of cancer (Christensen, 1999). The primary progestin is **progesterone.** Interestingly, estrogens make the brain sensitive to progesterone by promoting the production of progestin receptors there. Like hormone release in the testes, the ovarian release of hormones is controlled by two tropic hormones of the anterior pituitary: FSH and LH. The release of these tropic hormones is controlled by GnRH from the hypothalamus (Figure 5.18b). **Oral contraceptives** contain steroids that exert a negative feedback effect on the hypothalamus, inhibiting the release of GnRH. The lack of GnRH prevents the release of FSH and LH from the pituitary, and therefore the ovary fails to release an egg for fertilization.

Relations among gonadal hormones All three classes of sex hormones—androgens, estrogens, and progestins—have closely related chemical structures. They and the adrenal steroids are all derived from cholesterol, and they all have the basic structure of four interconnected carbon rings (see Figure 5.6c). Furthermore, progestins can be converted to androgens, and androgens in turn can be converted into estrogens. Each of these conversions is controlled by specific protein enzymes. The structural similarity among steroids reflects their evolutionary history; as enzymes evolved to modify old steroids, a new steroid was available for signaling.

Different organs differ in the relative amounts of these hormones that they produce. For example, whereas the testis converts only a relatively small proportion of testosterone into estradiol, the ovary converts most of the testosterone it makes into estradiol. *No steroid is found exclusively in either males or females;* rather the two sexes differ in the proportion of these steroids.

The pineal gland secretes melatonin

The **pineal gland** sits atop the brainstem and in mammals is overlaid by the cerebral hemispheres (Figure 5.19a; see also Figure 5.1). Whereas most other brain structures are paired (present on both left and right), the pineal gland is a single structure. This unusual aspect of the pineal may explain why the seventeenth-century philosopher René Descartes proposed that it could contain the soul.

Today we know that the pineal is innervated by the sympathetic nervous system, specifically by the superior cervical ganglion (see Figure 5.19a). In response to the activity of cells in this ganglion, the pineal releases an amine hormone called **melatonin.** The melatonin receptor is a G-coupled protein residing in cell membranes and is similar to receptors for peptide hormones. In many vertebrate species, the pineal secretion of melatonin controls whether animals are in breeding condition. Melatonin is released almost exclusively at night (Figure 5.19b).

In seasonally breeding mammals such as hamsters, the lengthening nights of autumn affect activity in the superior cervical ganglion, which in turn causes the pineal to prolong its nocturnal release of melatonin. The hypothalamus responds to the prolonged exposure to melatonin by becoming extremely sensitive to the negative feedback effects of gonadal steroids. Consequently, less and less GnRH is released, resulting in less gonadotropin release, as well as atrophy of the gonads. Lesion of the pineal prevents such regression, whereas prolonged treatment of normal ani-

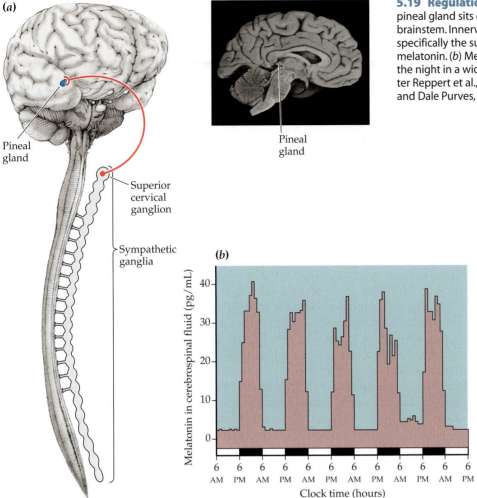

5.19 Regulation of the Pineal Gland (*a*) The pea-shaped pineal gland sits close to the floor of the third ventricle, atop the brainstem. Innervated by the sympathetic nervous system, specifically the superior cervical ganglion, the pineal releases melatonin. (*b*) Melatonin is released almost exclusively during the night in a wide variety of vertebrates, including humans. (After Reppert et al., 1979; photograph courtesy of S. Mark Williams and Dale Purves, Duke University Medical Center.)

mals with melatonin induces gonadal regression. In fact, one of the earliest hints of pineal function was the report that a boy who had a tumor that was destroying his pineal reached puberty early in life.

In birds, light from the environment penetrates the thin skull and reaches the pineal gland directly. Photosensitive cells in the bird pineal gland monitor daily light durations. In several reptile species the pineal is close to the skull and even has an extension of photoreceptors providing a "third eye" in the back of the head. (You may have noticed that the teacher who seemed to see everything that happened behind his back had a rather reptilian appearance.) The reptile pineal photoreceptors do not form images but act as simple photocells, monitoring day length to regulate seasonal functions.

Humans are not, strictly speaking, seasonal breeders, but melatonin has been implicated in our daily cycles, such as sleep rhythms. Like other vertebrates, we release melatonin at night, and administering melatonin has been reported to induce sleep sooner at night. In fact, many studies indicate a role for melatonin in the timing of sleep. For example, melatonin has been used for treatment of jet lag (Lewy et al., 1992; Sack et al., 1992).

The pancreas secretes two main hormones

Throughout the **pancreas** (which is located in the back of the abdominal cavity; see Figure 5.1) are clusters of cells called **islets of Langerhans,** which secrete hormones directly into the bloodstream. These endocrine cells are intermingled with other cells that perform an exocrine function, secreting digestive enzymes (such as bile) into ducts leading to the gastrointestinal tract. Hormones secreted by the islets of Langerhans include **insulin** and **glucagon,** both of which have potent and frequently reciprocal effects on glucose utilization. Insulin is produced in one type of cell within the islets (beta cells), and glucagon is secreted by another type (alpha cells). We'll discuss these hormones further in Chapter 13.

Hormones Affect Behavior in Many Different Ways

As mentioned at the start of this chapter, we will discuss specific examples of the role of hormones in reproductive behavior (Chapter 12), eating and drinking (Chapter 13), biological rhythms (Chapter 14), and stress (Chapter 15). Hormonal effects on growth are considered in Box 5.2. For now, to get an idea of how hormones affect behavior, let's briefly consider the role of hormones in modulating memory formation, and the psychopathology that can result from too much or too little hormone.

Hormones can affect social behavior

We've already seen the role that the hormone oxytocin plays in the interaction of nursing babies and their mothers (see Figure 5.11). It turns out that this hormone is involved in several other social behaviors too. For one thing, both men and women release a pulse of oxytocin during orgasm (Carmichael et al., 1994), where the hormone adds to the pleasurable feelings accompanying sexual encounters.

In nonhuman animals, oxytocin and vasopressin have been shown to modulate many social processes. Rodents given supplementary doses of oxytocin spend more time in physical contact with each other (Carter, 1992). Male mice with the oxytocin gene knocked out are unable to produce the hormone and they display social amnesia: They seem unable to recognize the scent of female mice that they have met before (Ferguson et al., 2000). You can cure these oxytocin knockout males of their social amnesia simply by infusing oxytocin into a brain region known as the *medial amygdala* (Winslow and Insel, 2002). In female mice, evidence suggests that the oxytocin released during delivery and lactation may improve the mother's ability to navigate a maze (Tomizawa et al., 2003).

In another rodent, the prairie vole (*Microtus ochrogaster*), in which couples form stable monogamous pair-bonds, oxytocin infusions in the brains of females help them bond to their mates. In male prairie voles, it is vasopressin rather than oxytocin that facilitates their forming a preference for their female partners. In fact, the distribution of vasopressin receptors in the brains of male prairie voles may be what makes them monogamous.

For example, in the closely related meadow voles (*M. pennsylvanicus*), which do not form pair-bonds and have multiple mating partners, the males have far fewer vasopressin receptors in certain brain regions than do prairie voles (Figure 5.20; Lim et al., in press). And if laboratory mice are genetically engineered to produce vasopressin receptors in their brains in the same pattern seen in prairie vole males, then the mice are much more interested in associating with females, almost as if they were trying to form a pair-bond.

Thus it appears that oxytocin and vasopressin regulate a range of social behaviors, and that natural selection sometimes alters the social behaviors of a species through changes in the brain distribution of receptors for these two peptides.

Endocrine pathology can produce extreme effects on human behavior

Both deficient and excessive hormone secretion are associated with a variety of human physiological, anatomical, and behavioral disorders (Erhardt and Goldman, 1992). Some of these disorders have long been known, especially those that include either marked behavioral changes or anatomical abnormalities.

Many hormonal disorders resemble psychiatric disorders (Table 5.3). For example, parathyroid deficiency results in calcium deposition in the basal ganglia and

(a)

(b)

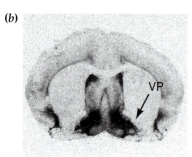

(c)

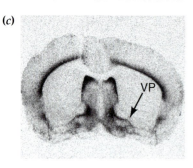

Figure 5.20 Vasopressin and the Monogamous Brain   (*a*) Prairie voles form long-lasting pair bonds. (*b*) Monogamy in male prairie voles seems to be due to the dense concentration of vasopressin receptors in the ventral pallidum (VP). (*c*) Males of the closely related meadow vole species have fewer vasopressin receptors in the VP, which may explain why they are not monogamous. (Photographs courtesy of Miranda Lim and Larry Young.)

TABLE 5.3 *Hormonal Disorders and Associated Cognitive, Emotional, and Psychiatric Disorders*

Hormonal disorder	Impaired cognition	Anxiety	Depression	Psychosis and delirium
Hyperthyroidism	+	++	+	+
Hypothyroidism	+	+	++	++
Hypercortisolism	+	++	++	++
Hypocortisolism	—	+	++	++
Panhypopituitarism[a]	—	+	++	++
Hyperparathyroidism	+	+	++	++
Hypoparathyroidism	?	++	++	++
Hyperinsulinism	+	++	—	++
Hypoinsulinism	+	—	—	+

Note: +, sometimes; ++, often.

[a]Undersecretion of all or nearly all anterior pituitary hormones.

symptoms that resemble schizophrenia. Patients with excessive thyroid release frequently appear intensely anxious; we mentioned earlier that people with decreased thyroid release may show cognitive impairments and depression. An inherited form of attention deficit disorder in children involves decreased sensitivity to thyroid hormone (P. Hauser et al., 1993).

Excessive release of glucocorticoids by the adrenal cortex, **Cushing's syndrome,** is accompanied by many bodily and psychological changes, including fatigue, depression, unusual distribution of hair, and other autonomic changes. Several studies have indicated that affective changes, especially depression, frequently long precede other physiological effects of excessive cortisol secretion. In some people who take excessive amounts of glucocorticoids, such as athletes, psychiatric symptoms can emerge that include periods of intense psychotic behavior.

CLINICAL ISSUE

Hormonal and Neural Systems Interact to Produce Integrated Responses

Although we have focused on the endocrine system in this chapter, the endocrine system participates in interactions with many organs of the body, including, of course, the brain. Let's examine some of these relations.

Incoming sensory stimuli elicit nerve impulses that go to several brain regions, including the cerebral cortex, cerebellum, and hypothalamus. Behavioral responses bring further changes in stimulation. For example, a person may approach or go away from the original source of stimulation, and this action alters the size of a visual image, the loudness of a sound, and so forth. Meanwhile the endocrine system is altering the response characteristics of the person. If the stimulus calls for action, energy is mobilized through hormonal routes. The state of some sensory receptor organs may also be altered, thus modifying further processing of stimuli.

Many behaviors require neural and hormonal coordination. For example, when a stressful situation is perceived through neural sensory channels, hormonal secretions prepare the individual to make energetic responses. The muscular movements for the fight-or-flight response (see Chapter 2) are controlled neurally, but the required energy is mobilized through hormonal routes. Another example of neural and hormonal coordination is the milk letdown reflex (see Figure 5.11).

Four kinds of signals are possible between nerve cells and endocrine cells: neural-to-neural, neural-to-endocrine, endocrine-to-endocrine, and endocrine-to-neural. All four kinds of signals can be found in the courtship behavior of the ring-dove. The visual stimulation and perception of a male dove that sees a female in-

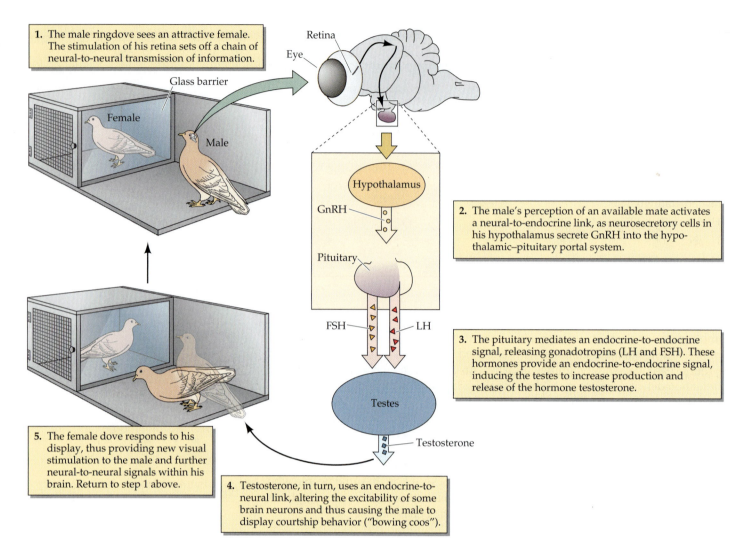

1. The male ringdove sees an attractive female. The stimulation of his retina sets off a chain of neural-to-neural transmission of information.

2. The male's perception of an available mate activates a neural-to-endocrine link, as neurosecretory cells in his hypothalamus secrete GnRH into the hypothalamic–pituitary portal system.

3. The pituitary mediates an endocrine-to-endocrine signal, releasing gonadotropins (LH and FSH). These hormones provide an endocrine-to-endocrine signal, inducing the testes to increase production and release of the hormone testosterone.

4. Testosterone, in turn, uses an endocrine-to-neural link, altering the excitability of some brain neurons and thus causing the male to display courtship behavior ("bowing coos").

5. The female dove responds to his display, thus providing new visual stimulation to the male and further neural-to-neural signals within his brain. Return to step 1 above.

5.21 Four Kinds of Signals between the Nervous System and the Endocrine System

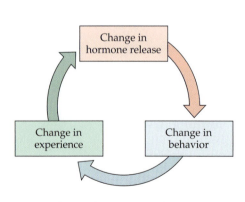

5.22 The Reciprocal Relations between Hormones and Behavior

volve (1) neural-to-neural transmission (Figure 5.21). The particular visual stimulus activates (2) a neural-to-endocrine link, which causes neurosecretory cells in the male's hypothalamus to secrete GnRH. (3) Endocrine-to-endocrine signals cause increased production and release of the hormone testosterone. Testosterone, in turn, alters the excitability of neurons in the male's brain through (4) an endocrine-to-neural link and thus causes the male to display courtship behavior. The female dove responds to this display, thus providing new visual stimulation to the male and further neural-to-neural signals within his brain.

The circle schema in Figure 5.22 depicts the cyclical interactions between endocrine activity and behavior. We saw earlier how Chuck's lack of thyroid hormone drastically affected his behavior and therefore what he experienced (i.e., not much except television). The level of circulating hormones can also be altered by experience, which in turn can affect future behavior and future experience. For example, starting to exercise or stepping out in the cold increases the level of thyroxine in the circulation. Men rooting for a sports team will produce more testosterone if their team wins (Bernhardt et al., 1998). Physical stresses, pain, and unpleasant emotional situations decrease thyroid output and trigger the release of adrenal glucocorticoids (see Chapter 15).

Conversely, each of these hormonal events will affect the brain, shaping the person's behavior, which will once more affect their future hormone production. Any thorough understanding of the relationship between hormones and behavior must come to grips with these reciprocal interactions. In Chapter 15 we will learn that the neural and endocrine systems also interact extensively with the immune system.

Summary

1. Hormones are chemical compounds that act as signals in the body. They are secreted by endocrine glands into the bloodstream and are taken up by receptor molecules in target cells.

2. Neural communication differs from hormonal communication in that neural signals travel rapidly over fixed pathways, whereas hormonal signals spread more slowly and throughout the body.

3. Neural and hormonal communication systems have several characteristics in common: Both utilize chemical messages; some substances act as a hormone in some locations and as a synaptic transmitter in others. Both systems manufacture, store, and release chemical messengers. Both use specific receptors and may employ second messengers.

4. Some hormones have receptors in a wide variety of cells and can therefore influence the activity of most cells in the body. Others have receptors in only certain special cells or organs.

5. Hormones act by promoting the proliferation and differentiation of cells and by modulating the activity of cells that have already differentiated.

6. Protein and amine hormones bind to specific receptor molecules at the surface of the target cell membrane and activate second-messenger molecules inside the cell. Steroid hormones pass through the membrane and bind to receptor molecules inside the cell.

7. A negative feedback system monitors and controls the rate of secretion of each hormone. In the simplest case the hormone acts on target cells, leading them to change the amount of a substance they release; this change in turn regulates the output of the endocrine gland.

8. Several hormones are controlled by a more complex feedback system: A releasing hormone from the hypothalamus regulates the release of an anterior pituitary tropic hormone, which in turn controls secretion by an endocrine gland. In these cases, feedback of the endocrine hormone acts mainly at the hypothalamus and anterior pituitary.

9. Endocrine influences on structures and functions often involve more than one hormone, as in growth, homeostasis, metabolism, and learning and memory.

10. Many behaviors require the coordination of neural and hormonal components. Messages may be transmitted in the body via neural-to-neural, neural-to-endocrine, endocrine-to-endocrine, or endocrine-to-neural links. There are continuous, reciprocal influences between the endocrine system and the nervous system: Experience affects hormone secretion, and hormones affect behavior and therefore future experiences.

Recommended Reading

Becker, J. B., Breedlove, S. M., Crews, D., and McCarthy, M. M. (Eds.). (2002). *Behavioral endocrinology* (2nd ed.). Cambridge, MA: MIT Press.

Hadley, M. E. (2000). *Endocrinology* (5th ed.). Englewood Cliffs, NJ: Prentice Hall.

Litwack, G., and Norman, A. W. (1997). *Hormones* (2nd ed.). San Diego, CA: Academic Press.

Nelson, R. J. (2000). *An introduction to behavioral endocrinology* (2nd ed.). Sunderland, MA: Sinauer Associates.

Williams, R. H., and Larsen, P. R. (2002). *Williams textbook of endocrinology* (10th ed.). Philadelphia: Saunders.

Refer to the *Learning Biological Psychology CD* for study questions, animations, activities, and other study aids.

II Evolution and Development of the Nervous System

Part 2 presents two viewpoints and two timescales for the development of the nervous system and behavior. Chapter 6 considers the *evolution* of the brain and behavior over millions of years. Chapter 7 takes up the growth of the *individual* over the months and years of the life span. Both viewpoints help us understand development, somewhat as an architect and a contractor make different but essential contributions to building a house.

The architect brings to the construction of houses the sort of perspective that evolution brings to the construction of animals. The information in the architect's plan is analogous to the information in the genome. In preparing plans, the architect calls on a long history of hard-won knowledge about structures that meet basic human needs. The contractor's perspective is more like that of the developing individual, using the plans to construct a particular house—translating the abstract information of the blueprints into a practical, working structure. The contractor's judgment and interpretation are necessary, so two houses built by different contractors from the same blueprint will not be identical, just as identical twins differ slightly.

The architect tries to foresee some of the problems of construction and to build safety factors into the plans, so that small deviations or errors will not seriously impair the safety or utility of the building. But the architect also relies on the contractor to fill in details and to improvise when external conditions require it. So, too, does evolutionary wisdom, distilled in the genome, rely on the environment and experience to guide the construction of the developing brain.

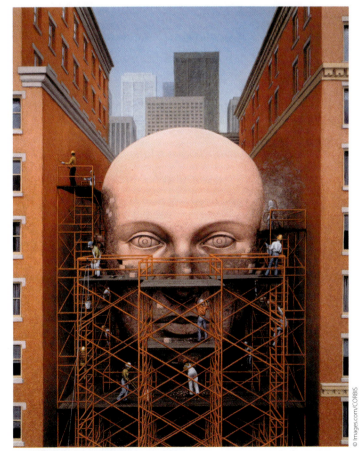

John Martin, *Head Being Built Between Buildings*

6

Evolution of Brain and Behavior

We Are Not so Different Are We?

If you have spent any length of time at the primate enclosure at the zoo, it will come as no surprise to learn that our closest animal relatives are the chimpanzees. After all, so many of their expressions and behaviors seem oddly, well, human. But despite the apparent similarities, humans and chimps are also strikingly dissimilar in many fundamental ways. Humans have complex languages, whereas chimps make only a small variety of vocal sounds. Humans walk erect and have long legs, whereas chimps locomote mostly on all fours and have relatively long arms. The human brain is about twice the size of the chimp's. Humans have relatively little body hair, whereas chimps are covered with fur. Humans sleep in fairly large shelters that are long-lasting, whereas chimps tend to improvise a new bed each night. Humans have spread wide from their origins in Africa, overpopulating the globe, whereas chimps have remained in Africa, their numbers dwindling at an alarming rate.

Given the many differences between humans and chimps, you might be surprised to learn that genetic material differs by only about 1.2% between the two species. One prominent scientist recently suggested that, since the genes of chimps and humans differ so little, the social context provided during the rearing of human children must be what causes them to come out so differently from chimpanzees (Rose, 2004). If that suggestion strikes you as unlikely, you are probably right. Several people have tried to rear chimpanzees like human children (see Chapter 19), and none of the chimps ever won a spelling bee or got a driver's license (not even a learner's permit).

Of course, social rearing is crucial for human development, but it cannot explain the vast differences between chimps and humans. So the problem remains: If human and chimp DNA is nearly 99% identical, how can we explain the striking differences in behavior, anatomy, and neurobiology? In other words, what makes humans human?

O ur major objective in this chapter is to explore the intriguing story of how brains and behavior have evolved. We also consider why brain size in primates, especially in humans, increased so rapidly in our recent evolution.

The quest to understand the nervous system has led to the study of a wide variety of animals, not only mammals and other vertebrates but also invertebrates. But describing the relationships between the nervous system and behavior in even a small fraction of Earth's inhabitants would be an awesome (and dull) task unless we had a rationale beyond mere completeness. If we choose the right species to compare, however, we can learn a good deal about the principles of nervous system organization.

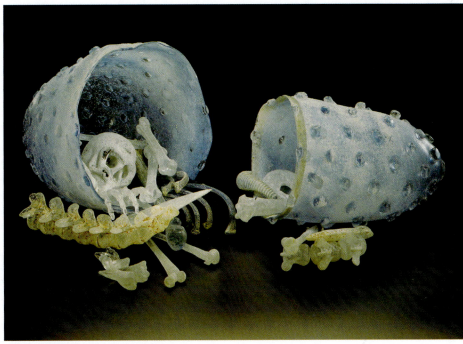

William Morris, *Artifact Series #9 (Burial)*, 1989

Why Should We Study Other Species?

One old-fashioned reason for comparing species was human-centered, based on the question, Why does the human being end up on top of the animal order? This human-centered perspective was properly criticized because it implicitly pictured other animals as incomplete "little humans," a view that no modern scientists see as valid. It also embraced the old idea that animals vary along a single scale from simple to complex, whereas scientists now see animal evolution as a multi-branching set of radiations. Today we use comparisons of different species to gather clues about evolutionary history.

A **phylogeny** (from the Greek *phylon*, "tribe, kind," and *genes*, "born") is the evolutionary history of a particular group of organisms; it is often represented as a *family tree* that shows which species may have given rise to others. (Some scientists prefer to say *bush* rather than *tree* because the phylogeny branches so extensively.) Comparisons among extant animals, coupled with fragmentary but illuminating data from fossils, allow us to hypothesize about the history of the body and brain, and the forces that shaped them (Pennisi, 2003).

Figure 6.1 shows a recent attempt by Wildman et al. (2003) to reconstruct the family tree of apes and humans. Their diagram depicts humans and chimpanzees as more closely related to each other than either one is to the gorilla. Not all investigators agree about that particular point, but they do all agree that humans, chimpanzees, and gorillas are closely related. We will say more about phylogenies a little later in the chapter.

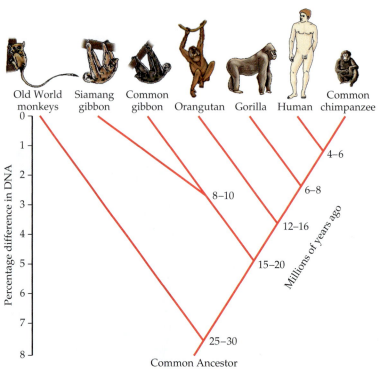

6.1 Family Tree of Apes and Humans   This tree was derived from measurements of differences between pairs of species in samples of their genetic material—molecules of deoxyribonucleic acid (DNA). To see how different two species are in their genetic endowments, trace the lines from the two members of a pair to the point that connects them, and match the point with the scale on the left. For example, the line from humans and the line from chimpanzees converge at a point indicating that human DNA differs from chimpanzee DNA by only about 1.6%. The DNA of humans and of chimpanzees, in turn, differs from that of the gorilla by about 2.3%. The scale on the right gives the estimated amount of time, in millions of years, since any pair of species shared a common ancestor. For example, humans and chimpanzees diverged from a common ancestor about 4 million to 6 million years ago. (After Wildman et al., 2003.)

No animal is simply sitting around providing researchers with the details of human biological history; rather, each species is busily evolving adaptations to survive in its present environment. Species with varying biological histories show different solutions to the dilemmas of survival and reproduction. In many cases, adaptations to particular ecological niches have led to changes in brain structure. One important adaptation is the ability to learn in order to successfully predict how to find food and to avoid danger. This adaptation must have arisen early in evolution, because relatively simple animals show changes in behavior that arise from experience. Understanding how the nervous systems of these simpler animals form and store memories provides insights into the mechanisms of memory in more-complex animals, including human beings, as we will see in Chapter 18.

How Closely Related Are Two Species?

The attempt to construct the tree of life raises the question, How can we find out how closely related two species are? Some basic knowledge of this topic is important for the examples that we will consider later in this chapter and in other chapters.

Early views of classification and evolution

People have probably always classified the animals around them and realized that some forms resemble each other more closely than others. The contact between Eu-

TABLE 6.1 *Classification of Some Species of Animals*

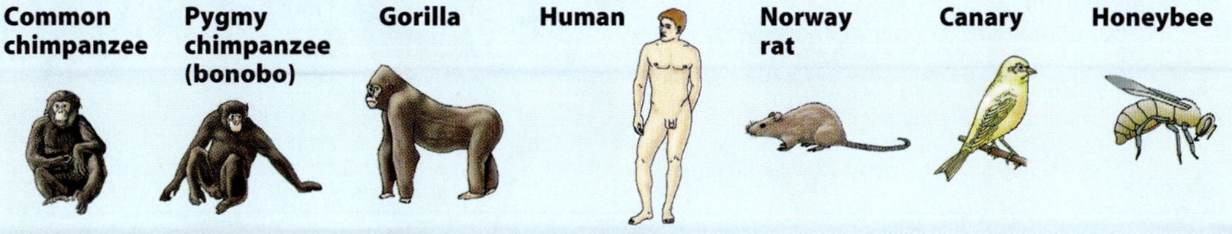

Taxonomic category	Common chimpanzee	Pygmy chimpanzee (bonobo)	Gorilla	Human	Norway rat	Canary	Honeybee
Kingdom	Animalia →						
Phylum	Chordata →						Arthropoda
Class	Mammalia →					Aves	Insecta
Order	Primates →				Rodentia	Passeriformes	Hymenoptera
Family	Pongidae →			Hominidae	Muridae	Fringillidae	Apidae
Genus	*Pan* →		*Gorilla*	*Homo*	*Rattus*	*Serinus*	*Apis*
Species	*Pan troglodytes*	*Pan paniscus*	*Gorilla gorilla*	*Homo sapiens*	*Rattus norvegicus*	*Serinus canarius*	*Apis mellifera*

rope and the Americas beginning in 1492 prompted European scholars to question how best to classify the many newly discovered animals.

The Swedish biologist Carolus Linnaeus (1707–1778) proposed the basic system that we use today. In Linnaeus's system, each species is assigned two names—the first name identifying the **genus** (plural *genera*), the second name indicating the **species.** Both names are always italicized, and the genus name is capitalized. According to this system, the modern human species is *Homo sapiens.* Table 6.1 shows the classifications of some other species.

The different levels of classification in Table 6.1 are illustrated and defined in Figure 6.2. The main trunk, the animal kingdom, includes all animal species. As branches divide and subdivide toward the crown of the tree, each successive category includes fewer species, and the species are more closely related. The order of categories, from most broad to most narrow, is this: kingdom, phylum (plural *phyla*), class, order, family, genus, species. (Here's an aid to remembering the succession of classifications from broadest to most specific: *K*indly *p*ut *c*lothes *o*n, *f*or *g*oodness' *s*ake.) Linnaeus classified animals mainly on the basis of gross anatomical similarities and differences; he did not mean to imply anything about evolution or common ancestry.

Until about 200 years ago, it was generally believed that each species had been created separately. Then, at about the time of Linnaeus, some **naturalists**—students of animal life and structure—began to have doubts. For example, some naturalists observed that the limb bones of all mammals, no matter what the animal's way of life, are remarkably similar in many details. If these species had been specifically created for different ways of locomotion, the naturalists reasoned, they should have been built on different plans rather than all being modifications of a single plan.

The idea of evolution slowly became more accepted among naturalists as nineteenth-century geologists showed that Earth has been changing for millions of years. The fossils discovered early in the nineteenth century provided additional evidence for **evolution**—the gradual changing of one species into another. But a plausible *mechanism* for evolution was lacking.

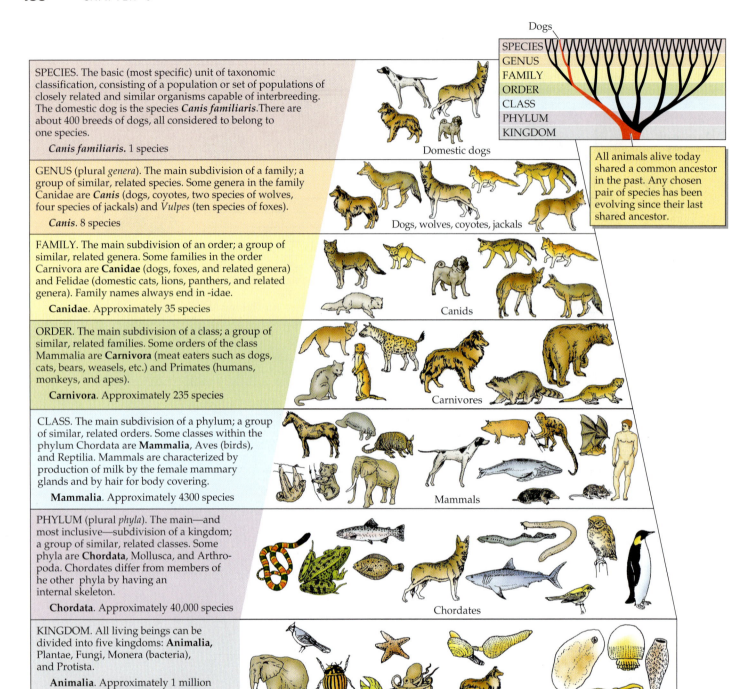

SPECIES. The basic (most specific) unit of taxonomic classification, consisting of a population or set of populations of closely related and similar organisms capable of interbreeding. The domestic dog is the species *Canis familiaris.* There are about 400 breeds of dogs, all considered to belong to one species.

Canis familiaris. 1 species

Domestic dogs

GENUS (plural *genera*). The main subdivision of a family; a group of similar, related species. Some genera in the family Canidae are *Canis* (dogs, coyotes, two species of wolves, four species of jackals) and *Vulpes* (ten species of foxes).

Canis. 8 species

Dogs, wolves, coyotes, jackals

FAMILY. The main subdivision of an order; a group of similar, related genera. Some families in the order Carnivora are **Canidae** (dogs, foxes, and related genera) and Felidae (domestic cats, lions, panthers, and related genera). Family names always end in -idae.

Canidae. Approximately 35 species

Canids

ORDER. The main subdivision of a class; a group of similar, related families. Some orders of the class Mammalia are **Carnivora** (meat eaters such as dogs, cats, bears, weasels, etc.) and Primates (humans, monkeys, and apes).

Carnivora. Approximately 235 species

Carnivores

CLASS. The main subdivision of a phylum; a group of similar, related orders. Some classes within the phylum Chordata are **Mammalia**, Aves (birds), and Reptilia. Mammals are characterized by production of milk by the female mammary glands and by hair for body covering.

Mammalia. Approximately 4300 species

Mammals

PHYLUM (plural *phyla*). The main—and most inclusive—subdivision of a kingdom; a group of similar, related classes. Some phyla are **Chordata**, Mollusca, and Arthropoda. Chordates differ from members of he other phyla by having an internal skeleton.

Chordata. Approximately 40,000 species

Chordates

KINGDOM. All living beings can be divided into five kingdoms: **Animalia,** Plantae, Fungi, Monera (bacteria), and Protista.

Animalia. Approximately 1 million species of animals are known. The total number of existing species has been estimated to be as high as 30 million.

Animals

Dogs

SPECIES
GENUS
FAMILY
ORDER
CLASS
PHYLUM
KINGDOM

All animals alive today shared a common ancestor in the past. Any chosen pair of species has been evolving since their last shared ancestor.

6.2 Linnaean Classification of the Domestic Dog

Early in the nineteenth century the French naturalist Jean-Baptiste de Lamarck (1744–1829) proposed that species evolve through the gradual accumulation of characteristics acquired by individuals throughout life as they exercise and stretch their bodies. If the ancestors to giraffes had short necks, perhaps individuals had to stretch their necks to reach leaves and this stretching caused their offspring to be born with slightly longer necks. Over generations, the necks of giraffes would become longer.

But this idea, called the *inheritance of acquired characteristics,* proved to be incompatible with later discoveries about genetic inheritance.

Half a century after Lamarck, in 1858, Charles Darwin and Alfred Russel Wallace announced the hypothesis of **evolution by natural selection.** Darwin and Wallace each had hit upon the idea independently. Darwin had been accumulating much evidence to support this hypothesis ever since, as a young naturalist in the 1830s, he had voyaged on the HMS *Beagle* to South America and the Galápagos Islands. In 1859 Darwin published his revolutionary book *On the Origin of Species by Means of Natural Selection.* The hypothesis he stated was based on three main observations and one important inference. The facts were these: (1) Individuals of a given species are not identical, (2) some of this variation can be inherited, and (3) not all offspring survive. The inference was that the variations among individuals affect the probabilities that they will survive, reproduce, and pass on their characteristics.

The concept of evolution by natural selection has become one of the major organizing principles in all the life sciences, directing the study of behavior and its mechanisms, as well as the study of morphology (form and structure). Darwin (1859) wrote, prophetically, that because of his work, "Psychology will be based on a new foundation, that of the necessary acquirement of each mental power and capacity by gradation" (p. 113); that is, psychology will be based on evolution.

Darwin later added another evolutionary principle, that of **sexual selection** (1871). This principle holds that members of each sex exert selective pressures on the other in terms of both anatomical and behavioral features that favor reproductive success. Thus, for example, female choices have led to the ornamental but costly tails of peacocks. We will discuss this principle at greater length in Chapter 12, and we will also call on it at the end of this chapter in relation to evolution of the human brain.

**Charles Darwin
(1809–1892)**

**Alfred Russel Wallace
(1823–1913)**

Modern evolutionary theory combines natural selection and genetics

A gap in Darwin's theory was that he could not specify the source of the variation upon which natural selection acts or the mechanism by which biological inheritance works. A major step to round out the theory of evolution was accomplished by the pioneering work of an Austrian monk and botanist named Gregor Johann Mendel (1822–1884). On the basis of his research with pea plants, Mendel published the laws of inheritance in an obscure journal in 1866 (Mendel, 1967). Only in 1900, when they were rediscovered independently by the Dutch biologist Hugo de Vries (1848–1935) and two other European biologists, were these laws brought into prominence and related to evolution. After conducting his experiments, de Vries searched the scientific literature and was surprised to find Mendel's forgotten papers. De Vries then heralded Mendel's discovery and reported his own work only as confirmation.

De Vries went beyond Mendel in an important respect: Working with primroses, he found that occasionally a new variety arose spontaneously and then passed its characteristics on to successive generations. In 1901 de Vries pointed out that in such cases, evolution could occur by sudden jumps, or **mutations,** as he called these changes. (Nowadays, scientists deliberately induce mutations in plants and animals, as we will discuss in Box 7.3.) Thus de Vries discovered that evolution is not only the slow process that Darwin hypothesized; it can also occur rapidly.

**GENES AND
BEHAVIOR**

Although **genetics,** the study of the mechanisms of inheritance, started with plants such as the pea and the primrose, investigators soon began to study organisms that reproduce more rapidly. An example is the fruit fly *Drosophila,* whose generation time is 10 days and whose salivary glands produce giant chromosomes that are visible under a light microscope. **Chromosomes** (from the Greek *chroma,* "color," and *soma,* "body") are rod-shaped assemblies of DNA in the nucleus of each cell that bear genetic information. Since 1882 it had been known that chromosomes replicate themselves during cell division, but the significance of this phenomenon did not become apparent until Mendel's work was rediscovered. Many of the findings about

Francis Crick (1916–2004) and James D. Watson

Rosalind Franklin (1920–1958)

genetic mechanisms made with *Drosophila* and even with bacteria hold true for larger organisms, such as humans, that reproduce much more slowly.

By the 1940s, scientists realized that nucleic acids are the instruments of genetic inheritance. In 1953 James D. Watson and Francis Crick announced that the structure of the DNA molecule, which forms chromosomes, is a double helix. This discovery led in turn to the cracking of the genetic code, a topic that will be taken up in the appendix. Francis Crick and James D. Watson were awarded the Nobel Prize in Physiology or Medicine in 1962. As a key to their discovery, Watson and Crick relied on X-ray photographs of DNA taken by chemist Rosalind Franklin, and some scientists believe that if she had not died prematurely she might have shared the Nobel Prize.

Both gradual changes within a species and the formation of new species can now be understood in the light of modern evolutionary theory, which combines Darwin's hypothesis of natural selection with modern genetics and molecular biology. Further insights continue to be added by research in these and related fields, such as developmental biology, paleontology, and systematic biology.

Newer methods aid in classifying animals and inferring evolution

The field of **taxonomy** (from the Greek *taxis,* "arrangement," and *nomos,* "law"), or *classification,* of animals is an ongoing endeavor. Taxonomists continue to be challenged as previously unknown animals are discovered, as new techniques become available, and as new concepts arise.

For example, some of the relationships among apes and humans are still being debated. You may have noticed that Figure 6.1 and Table 6.1 differ in their placement of human beings. Figure 6.1 is based mainly on comparisons between samples of DNA among species. It shows the chimpanzees closer to humans than to gorillas in their genes. This phylogeny has led Wildman et al. (2003) to propose that the genus *Homo* be enlarged to include the chimpanzees. Table 6.1, which is based on body measurements and on behavior—and on traditional thinking about the place of humans in nature—puts both chimpanzees and gorillas in the family Pongidae (the great apes), whereas humans are traditionally placed in their own family, Hominidae. Wildman and his associates point out that the small genetic divergence between humans and chimpanzees, and the fact that the two species separated apparently quite recently (sharing a common ancestor less than 6 million years ago), is within the limits for other species that are considered part of the same genus.

Both the fossil record and DNA analyses help us classify animals and make inferences about their evolution. Fossils can be used to trace the families of many living species into the remote past and to clarify some classifications. The fossil record has been invaluable, but it is still very incomplete; important fossils are being discovered every year. For example, an international group led by paleontologist Tim White discovered, in Ethiopia, the oldest *Homo sapiens* skulls (T. D. White et al., 2003). These skulls were dated from their rock environment to about 160,000 years ago (Clark et al., 2003)—just the age that had been estimated from DNA evidence for the emergence of the first modern humans. The fossil record also reveals many extinct species, including extinct members of the hominid line. For another example of extinctions, it is estimated that since birds first evolved about 150 million years ago, a total of about 150,000 species of birds have existed, but only about 9000 exist today (Sibley and Ahlquist, 1990).

We have already mentioned the development of molecular techniques that allow us to study genetic material and to measure genetic variation with precision. Analysis of genetic material—fragments of DNA molecules—from many species has confirmed many classifications and improved others. Furthermore, quantifying the difference between base pairs in DNA samples from two species allows investigators to estimate the genealogical distance between them. (The method used in this quantification—nucleic acid hybridization—is described briefly in the appendix.) Thus, DNA analyses and comparisons help in constructing phylogenetic trees such as the one in Figure 6.1.

In addition, DNA appears to change at a relatively steady average rate in all lineages of a given order of animals (Hillis et al., 1996). Thus the proportion of differences between DNA samples from two species can be used as a "molecular clock" to estimate how long ago they diverged from a common ancestor. The absolute times in Figure 6.1 should be considered with caution, however, because scientists disagree about the calibration of the molecular clocks. This debate does not lessen the value of the relative time periods; that is, the overall picture appears to be accurate even if future research expands or contracts the timescale.

Small fragments of DNA have been obtained from insects fossilized in amber as long as 40 million years ago, helping us to discriminate among possible lines of descent of some modern insects and to test further the "clock" of changes in DNA over time (Poinar, 1994). A fictionalized version of this technique helped make millions of dollars for the writers and producers of the *Jurassic Park* movies.

Estimates from fossil and DNA evidence do not always agree completely in dating branches of the evolutionary tree. Fossil dates tend to be too recent, because we can never find the first specimen of a given species. Molecular dates have tended to be too old, because of problems with calibrating rates of change of DNA over time. But Benton and Ayala (2003) show that examples of divergence are diminishing, and most paleontological and molecular dates now agree. The fact that human DNA overall resembles that of chimpanzees more than that of gorillas does not hold for every segment of DNA. The human genome can be thought of as a mosaic, with some segments resembling those of gorillas more than those of chimpanzees (Paabo, 2003).

Evolution may converge upon similar solutions

Adaptation to similar ecological features may bring about similarities in behavior or structure among animals that are only distantly related (that differ in genetic heritage). These similarities are referred to as examples of **convergent evolution.** For example, the body forms of a tuna and a dolphin resemble each other because they each evolved for efficient swimming, even though the tuna is a fish and the dolphin is a mammal descended from terrestrial ancestors. Such a resemblance is an example of **homoplasy,** a resemblance between features that is due to convergent evolution.

By contrast, a **homology** is a resemblance based on common *ancestry*, such as the similarities in forelimb structures of mammals that we described earlier (Figure 6.3). **Analogy** refers to similar *function*, although the structures may look different (e.g., the hand of a human and the trunk of an elephant are analogous).

IMPORTANT METHOD

COMPETING HYPOTHESES

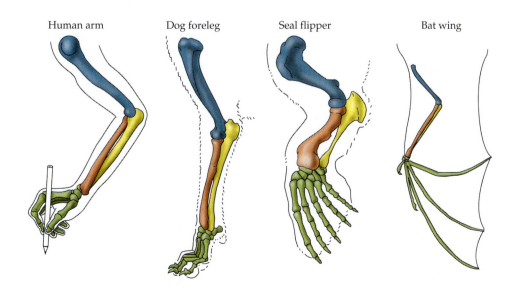

Human arm   Dog foreleg   Seal flipper   Bat wing

6.3 Homology of Forelimb Structures
Bones of the same sort are shown here in the same color in all species. The sizes and shapes of the bones of the forelimb have evolved so that they are adapted to widely different functions: skilled manipulation in humans, locomotion in dogs, swimming in seals, flying in bats. The similarities among the sets of bones reflect descent from a common ancestor.

Comparative Methods Help Us Study the Biological Mechanisms of Behavior

Comparing the behavior and neural mechanisms of different kinds of animals in different ecological niches is important in biological psychology. We use such comparisons in every chapter of this book. Although studying only one species may yield important information, comparing two or more carefully chosen species leads to a much deeper understanding of the phenomena because the evolutionary framework provides additional explanatory power. Let's look at a few examples.

Some ways of obtaining food require bigger brains than others

Most species of animals spend much of their time and energy in the pursuit of food, often using elaborate strategies. Researchers have found that the strategies that different species use to obtain food are correlated to brain size and structure. For example, mammals that eat food distributed in clusters that are difficult to find (such as ripe fruit) tend to have brains larger than those of related species whose food is rather uniformly distributed and easy to find (such as grass or leaves). This relationship has been found within families of rodents, insectivores (such as shrews and moles), lagomorphs (such as rabbits and pikas) (Clutton-Brock and Harvey, 1980), and primates (Mace et al., 1981).

Finding novel ways of getting food is related to the size of the forebrain in different orders of birds (Lefebvre et al., 1997). Investigators collected accounts of novel behavior from ornithological journals (e.g., magpies digging up potatoes, house sparrows searching car radiator grilles for insects, crows dropping palm nuts in the paths of cars that run over and open them). Separate data sets were prepared for North America and the British Isles. In both areas, more-innovative species have relatively larger forebrains. The results suggest selection for increased size of the forebrain to cope with environmental challenges and opportunities in new, flexible ways. Later in the chapter we will see an extension of this kind of study to species of primates, also showing that increased size of the forebrain is related to innovation (Reader and Laland, 2002).

Some behavioral adaptations have been related to differences in relative sizes of certain brain structures. For example, some species of bats find their way and locate prey by hearing; others rely almost entirely on vision. In the midbrain, the auditory center (the inferior colliculus) is much larger in bats that depend on hearing; bats that depend on sight have a larger visual center (the superior colliculus). Families of birds that store bits of food for later use (e.g., the acorn woodpecker, Clark's nutcracker, or the black-capped chickadee) have a larger hippocampus relative to the forebrain and to body weight than do families of birds that do not store food (Sherry, 1992). This difference has been found among both North American species (Figure 6.4) and European species.

We will see in Chapters 17 and 18 that the hippocampus is important for memory formation, and in some species especially for spatial memory, which is needed to recover stored food. The families of birds that store food are no more closely related to each other than they are to other, non-food-storing families and subfamilies of birds. Thus food storers are not all descended from an ancestral species that stored food and possessed a large hippocampus. Rather the evidence suggests that a large hippocampus is necessary for successful storage and recovery of food, and that several families of birds—in an example of convergent evolution—independently evolved a large hippocampus for these attributes (Sherry, 1992).

Investigators have expanded this analysis by asking, Among closely related species of birds that all store food,

NEURAL PLASTICITY

6.4 Food Storing in Birds as Related to Hippocampal Size Food-storing species of birds have twice as large a hippocampus in relation to their forebrain (the telencephalon) as do species that do not store food. Note that both axes on this graph are logarithmic. (After Sherry et al., 1989.)

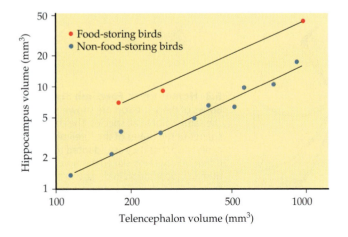

but in which some species depend more on stored food than others, is there a relationship between the amount of storing and the relative size of the hippocampus? The answer is yes for species of corvids (including jays and nutcrackers) (Basil et al., 1996) and for species of parids (including chickadees and titmice) (Hampton et al., 1995). So even within closely related species, reliance on storing and recovering food appears to have been a selection pressure that has led to larger hippocampal size.

Another example of independent evolution of behavior in birds is the learning of complex songs. Of the 23 orders of birds, only 3 orders learn their songs: the perching birds (Passeriformes), such as canaries, mockingbirds, and crows; the hummingbirds (Trochiliformes); and the parrots (Psittaciformes). Vocal learning in these species is necessary for reproduction—for example, for attracting mates and defending territory. This ability to learn song appears to have evolved independently in the three orders (Brenowitz, 1991). Interestingly, each of the three orders appears to have used the same brain regions to learn songs (Jarvis and Mello, 2000; Mello and Clayton, 1994; Nastiuk et al., 1994). We'll discuss neural circuits for birdsong learning more in Chapter 19.

Box 6.1 provides other examples of solutions that different species employ to solve the dilemmas of adaptation. As a general rule, the relative size of a brain region is a good guide to the importance of the function of that region for the adaptations of the species. In this sense more is better, but even small brains can produce complex behavior, as we will see in many instances in this book. Our understanding of how these differences in size and structure of the brain promote behavioral specializations should help us understand the neural basis of human behavior. For example, the sizes of some regions in the human temporal lobes seem related to language function (see Chapter 19).

Certain species are more suitable than others for comparative studies. Box 6.2 provides additional explanations for why we should study particular species.

Nervous Systems Differ Widely in Structure

Having compared aspects of the nervous systems of a few species, let's look more broadly at the variety of nervous systems of a few phyla of animals. Figure 6.5 shows the gross anatomy of the nervous systems of some representative animals.

A leading researcher in comparative neurosciences, Theodore H. Bullock (1984), asserted, "We cannot expect truly to comprehend either ourselves or how the nervous system works until we gain insight into this range of nervous systems, from nerve nets and simple ganglia in sea anemones and flatworms to the optic lobes of dragon flies, octopuses, and lizards to the cerebral cortex in primates" (p. 473). Faced with the enormous complexity of the vertebrate brain, with its billions of nerve cells, researchers have turned instead to the nervous systems of some invertebrates that have only hundreds or thousands of neurons. An exhaustive description of the "wiring diagram" of the nervous system and how it relates to behavior may some-

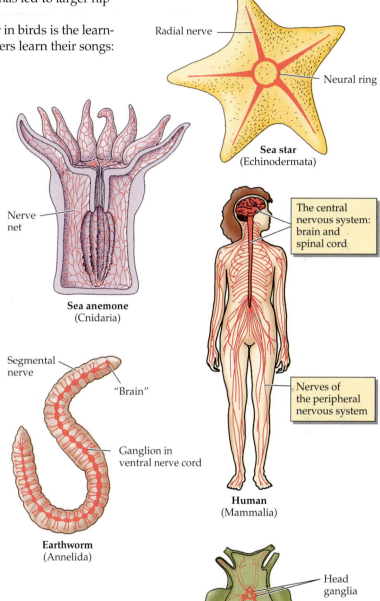

Radial nerve

Neural ring

Sea star
(Echinodermata)

Nerve net

Sea anemone
(Cnidaria)

The central nervous system: brain and spinal cord

Nerves of the peripheral nervous system

Human
(Mammalia)

Segmental nerve

"Brain"

Ganglion in ventral nerve cord

Earthworm
(Annelida)

Head ganglia

Abdominal ganglion

Aplysia
(Mollusca)

6.5 A Comparative View of Nervous Systems Gross anatomy of the nervous system in representative animals from five phyla shows some of the variety.

Theodore H. Bullock

day be possible with these invertebrates. First, however, let's start our comparison with brains closer to our own.

Mammals share main brain structures

A comparison of human and rat brains illustrates basic similarities and differences (Figure 6.6). Each of the main structures in the human brain has a counterpart in the rat brain. This comparison could be extended to much-greater detail, down to nuclei, fiber tracts, and types of cells. Even small structures in the brains of one mammalian species are found to have exact correspondence in the brains of others. All mammals also have similar types of neurons and similar organization of the cerebellar cortex and the cerebral cortex.

The differences between the brains of humans and the brains of other mammals are mainly quantitative; that is, they concern both actual and relative sizes of the whole brain, brain regions, and brain cells. Whereas the brain of an adult human be-

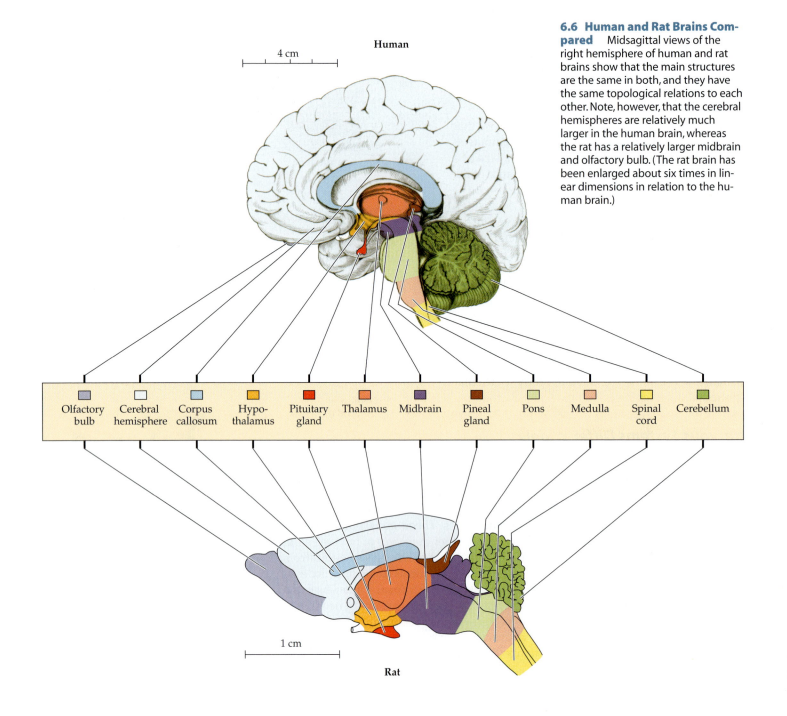

6.6 Human and Rat Brains Compared   Midsagittal views of the right hemisphere of human and rat brains show that the main structures are the same in both, and they have the same topological relations to each other. Note, however, that the cerebral hemispheres are relatively much larger in the human brain, whereas the rat has a relatively larger midbrain and olfactory bulb. (The rat brain has been enlarged about six times in linear dimensions in relation to the human brain.)

Human

4 cm

Olfactory bulb | Cerebral hemisphere | Corpus callosum | Hypo-thalamus | Pituitary gland | Thalamus | Midbrain | Pineal gland | Pons | Medulla | Spinal cord | Cerebellum

1 cm

Rat

BOX 6.1 To Each Its Own Sensory World

Lifestyle differences among mammals are related to the organization of the cerebral cortex, as the examples here show. The rat (*Rattus norvegicus*) is nocturnal and uses its whiskers to find its way in the dark. About 28% of the representation of the rat's body surface in the cortex is devoted to the whiskers (vibrissae), whereas only about 9% of the body surface representation of the squirrel (*Sciurus carolinensis*) is devoted to the whiskers (see Figure A) (Huffman et al., 1999). In addition, the nocturnal rat makes rather little use of vision, and its primary visual cortex (V1) is relatively small compared with that of the squirrel, which is diurnal.

The remarkable platypus (*Ornithorhynchus anatinus*) is an egg-laying mammal that lives in and around streams in eastern Australia and Tasmania. Because of its ducklike bill and webbed feet, some scientists thought it might be a hoax when the first skin preparations were brought to Europe at the beginning of the nineteenth century. The platypus is largely nocturnal and dives into murky waters, closing its eyes, ears, and nostrils as it hunts for invertebrates, including insects, shrimp, and crayfish. How it senses its prey remained a mystery until the 1980s, when investigators found that the main sensory organ of the platypus is its

bill, which is about 7 cm long in a 160-cm-long adult.

The bill has about 16 longitudinal stripes of receptors: stripes of touch receptors alternating with touch-electrical receptors (see Figure B) (Manger et al., 1998). As the platypus moves its bill underwater, it can detect prey by both the mechanical ripples and the changes in electrical fields that they cause. In keeping with the importance of the bill in locating prey, almost all of the somatosensory cortex (S1 and S2) in the platypus is devoted to the bill (see Figure B), and the primary visual (V1) and auditory (A1) areas are small (Krubitzer et al., 1995).

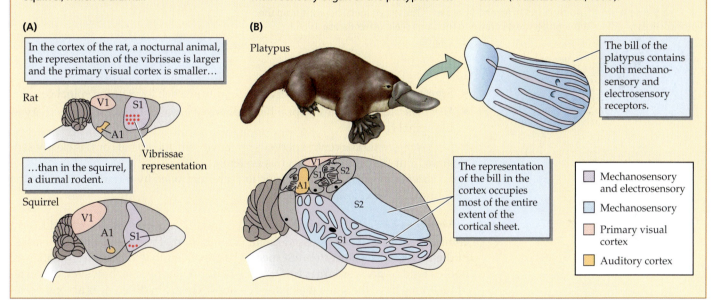

(A)

In the cortex of the rat, a nocturnal animal, the representation of the vibrissae is larger and the primary visual cortex is smaller…

Rat

…than in the squirrel, a diurnal rodent.

Vibrissae representation

Squirrel

(B) Platypus

The bill of the platypus contains both mechano-sensory and electrosensory receptors.

The representation of the bill in the cortex occupies most of the entire extent of the cortical sheet.

◻ Mechanosensory and electrosensory
◻ Mechanosensory
◻ Primary visual cortex
◻ Auditory cortex

ing weighs about 1400 g, that of an adult rat weighs a little less than 2 g. In each case, however, the brain represents about 2% of total body weight. The cerebral hemispheres occupy a much greater proportion of the brain in the human than in the rat, and the surface of the human brain shows prominent gyri and fissures, whereas the rat cerebral cortex is smooth and unfissured.

The rat has relatively larger olfactory bulbs than the human. This difference is probably related to the rat's much greater use of the sense of smell. The size of neurons also differs significantly between human and rat; in general, human neurons are much larger than rat neurons. In addition, there are great differences in the extent of dendritic trees. Figure 6.7 shows some examples of size differences among neurons of different species.

All vertebrate nervous systems share certain main features but differ in others

Now let's extend our view to the basic features of vertebrate nervous systems. The following are the main features of the vertebrate nervous system, some of which are illustrated for humans in Figure 6.5:

- *Development from a hollow dorsal neural tube* (see Chapters 2 and 7).
- *Bilateral symmetry.* The human cerebral hemispheres are almost mirror images. (We'll see some interesting exceptions in Chapter 19.)

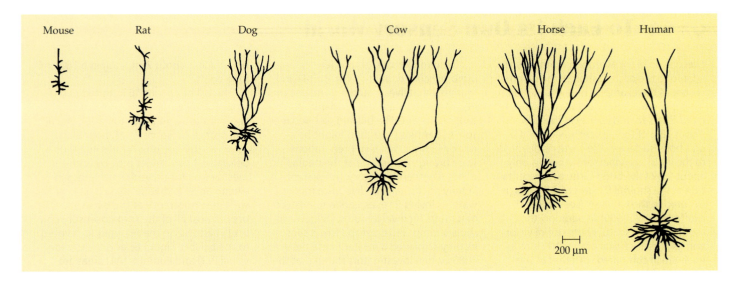

| Mouse | Rat | Dog | Cow | Horse | Human |

200 μm

6.7 The Same Kind of Neuron in Different Species These pyramidal neurons from the motor cortices of different mammals are all drawn to the same scale. (After Barasa, 1960.)

- *Segmentation.* Pairs of spinal nerves extend from each level of the spinal cord.
- *Hierarchical control.* The cerebral hemispheres control or modulate the activity of the spinal cord.
- *Separate systems.* The central nervous system (brain and spinal cord) is clearly separate from the peripheral nervous system.
- *Localization of function.* Certain functions are controlled by certain locations in the central nervous system.

Vertebrates have all of these features in common because they descended from a common ancestor that possessed them. Examination of the brains of many classes of the 10,000 to 20,000 vertebrate species has revealed that vertebrates with larger bodies tend to possess larger brains. No matter what the size, however, all vertebrate brains have the same major subdivisions. The main differences among vertebrates are the absolute and relative sizes of different regions.

Invertebrates show enormous diversity

Most of the animals on Earth are invertebrates, animals without backbones. (In fact, the order Coleoptera [the beetles] contains far more animal species than any other order has, so it's been said that, to a first approximation, every species is a beetle!) The invertebrates far exceed vertebrates in many ways, including number, diversity of appearance, and variety of habitat. Whereas invertebrates make up 17 phyla, the vertebrates are only a part of one phylum: Chordata (the chordates). The abundance of invertebrates is clearly demonstrated by the following estimate: For each person on Earth, there are at least 1 billion insects, which are just one type of invertebrate.

Neuroscientists focus on certain invertebrates because of the relative simplicity of their nervous systems and the great varieties of behavioral adaptation that they display. Simplicity of structure has not ruled out some forms of behavior, such as some types of learning and memory, that are also seen in more-complex organisms. Furthermore, invertebrates possess elaborate sensory systems that permit the detection of some stimuli with exquisite sensitivity. Every conceivable niche on land, sea, or air has been successfully exploited by one or more invertebrate species.

In the sections that follow we will describe some features of the nervous systems of mollusks and insects in preparation for our treatment of research on these animals in later chapters.

BOX 6.2 Why Should We Study Particular Species?

With all the species that are available, why should we choose certain ones for study? Investigators usually follow several criteria in selecting species for study. Here are some examples:

1. *Outstanding features.* Some species are champions at various behaviors and abilities, such as sensory discrimination (e.g., the acute auditory localization of the owl, or the extremely fine visual acuity of the eagle) or control of movement (e.g., the flight behavior of the housefly). These abilities are often linked to highly specialized neuronal structures. Such structures incorporate and optimize particular neuronal designs that may be less conspicuous in organisms that lack these superior capacities (Bullock, 1984, 1986). Study of such species may yield general principles that apply to other species. The female spotted hyena appears to have a penis and is dominant over the smaller male; this sex "reversal" is caused by unusual hormonal adaptations that help illuminate sexual development (see Box 12.2).

2. *Convenience.* Some species, such as the laboratory rat, are particularly convenient for study because they breed well in the laboratory, are relatively inexpensive to maintain, are not rare or endangered, have relatively short life spans, and have been studied extensively already, so

there is a good base of knowledge about them at the outset. In addition, they may serve as good models because their morphology and behavior show clear relationships to other species. Other species are convenient because they offer advantages for certain methods of study. For example, some mollusks have relatively simple nervous systems that aid in tracing neural circuits. The fruit fly *Drosophila* is excellent for genetic studies because it has a relatively simple genome and a short time period between generations; furthermore, investigators have been increasingly impressed by the large number of DNA sequences that *Drosophila* shares with mammals, including humans (R. Lewis, 1998).

3. *Comparison.* Close relationships between species that behave very differently enable the testing of hypotheses. For example, whereas in some closely related species of rodents the home ranges of males and females differ in size, in others they do not. Comparison of these species tests whether differences in maze-solving ability are associated with the size of the home range and with the size of the hippocampus (see Chapter 17).

4. *Preservation.* Studies of rare and/or endangered species can help set priorities

and assess options for the conservation of biodiversity (Mace et al., 2003). Endangered species are seldom studied in the laboratory, but they may be investigated in field studies or in zoos.

5. *Economic importance.* Species that are economically important include agricultural animals (e.g., sheep and cows), animals that furnish valuable products (e.g., fish), predators on agricultural animals (e.g., wolves), or destroyers of crops (e.g., elephants). Studying these animals can provide information that helps increase production and/or decrease losses.

6. *Treatment of disease.* Some species are subject to the same diseases as other species and therefore are valuable models for investigation (here we focus on diseases of the nervous system and endocrine [hormonal] system). Examples include certain kinds of mice, which provide a model for the behavior and anatomy of Down syndrome (see Chapter 7); baboons and certain breeds of dogs, which are prone to seizures (see Chapter 3); several breeds of dogs that are afflicted by narcolepsy (see Chapter 14); some strains of rodents that provide models for depression (see Chapter 16); and *Drosophila* and mice, which now provide models for investigations of Parkinson's disease (see Chapter 11).

The mollusk **Aplysia** Slugs, snails, clams, and octopuses are a few of the almost 100,000 species of mollusks. These soft-bodied animals display an enormous range of complexity in both body and behavior. Some mollusks, such as the octopus, show excellent problem-solving capabilities. The head end of a mollusk usually consists of a mouth, tentacles, and eyes. The typical structure also includes a footlike appendage and a visceral section that is frequently covered by a protective envelope called the *mantle*. A simple marine mollusk, *Aplysia*, has gained considerable notoriety because it has been used extensively in cellular studies of learning and memory (see Chapter 18). Here we will briefly review the principal structures of the nervous system of this organism.

The nervous system of *Aplysia* consists of four paired ganglia at the head end that form a ring around the esophagus (Figure 6.8*a*). Below these head ganglia is a fused abdominal ganglion. The ganglia are interconnected by tracts of axons. One head ganglion innervates the eyes and the tentacles; a second head ganglion innervates the mouth muscles. The other two paired ganglia innervate the foot. The abdominal ganglion controls such major visceral functions as circulation, respiration, and reproduction.

Comprehensive research by Eric Kandel and his collaborators has led to detailed maps of **identifiable neurons** in these ganglia, especially the abdominal ganglion. These cells are called *identifiable* because they are large and similar from one *Aplysia* to the next, so investigators can recognize them and give them code names. Because

(a) *Aplysia*, dorsal surface

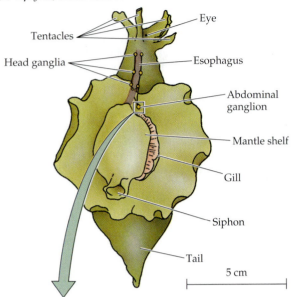

Tentacles

Eye

Head ganglia

Esophagus

Abdominal ganglion

Mantle shelf

Gill

Siphon

Tail

5 cm

(b) **Abdominal ganglion, dorsal surface**

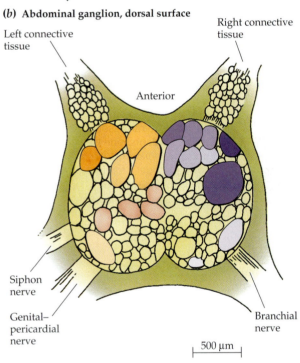

Left connective tissue

Right connective tissue

Anterior

Siphon nerve

Genital–pericardial nerve

Branchial nerve

500 μm

6.8 The Nervous System of *Aplysia* The sea snail *Aplysia* has a relatively simple nervous system with large identifiable neurons, which has made it a popular species for researching the neural basis of learning and memory. (a) In this dorsal view of the entire organism, the neural ganglia are shown in yellow and connecting nerve cords in black. (b) In this dorsal view of an abdominal ganglion, neurons in the circuit that is involved in habituation, a learned decreased response to a repeated stimulus, are shown in pink. (Part *a* after Kandel, 1976; *b* from Frazier et al., 1967.)

the nervous system of *Aplysia* includes many identifiable cells (Figure 6.8*b*), it has become possible to trace the circuits that mediate various behaviors in this animal. Work with *Aplysia* has also provided much detailed understanding of the molecular basis of learning (Carew, 2000; Squire and Kandel, 1999), supporting the view that simpler invertebrate nervous systems can provide useful models for examining complex features of the human brain.

Insect nervous systems Insects are remarkable for their variety of color, form, and presence in different habitats. The life cycle of many insects includes striking morphological changes (e.g., from caterpillar to butterfly) that not only affect the external form of the animal but also involve a resculpturing of the nervous system.

The sensory organs of insects display great variety and sensitivity. Success in the battle for survival has affected this group of animals in many distinctive ways, and it is easy to appreciate why neuroscientists have focused much research on the neural mechanisms of the behavior of insects. In spite of the diversity of insect body form (there are over a million living species), the central nervous systems of insects are remarkably similar: They vary "astonishingly little from the most primitive to the most advanced" (Edwards and Palka, 1991, p. 391).

The gross outline of the adult insect nervous system consists of a brain in the head end and ganglia in each body segment behind the head (Figure 6.9). Bundles of axons connect ganglia to the brain. The number of ganglia varies; in some insects all the ganglia of the chest and abdomen fuse into one major collection of cells. In other insects there are as many as eight ganglia in a chain. The brain itself contains three major compartments: two lobes of the protocerebrum and an optic lobe. The protocerebrum is the most complex part of the insect brain, and its right and left lobes are each continuous with the large optic lobe, an extension of the compound eye. Within the optic lobe are distinct masses of cells that receive input from the eye, as well as from the brain. Electrical stimulation of sites within the protocerebrum elicits complex behaviors.

The relative sizes of different components of the protocerebrum differ among insects, and some of these variations may be particularly relevant to behavioral variations. For example, a portion of the protocerebrum called the *corpus pedunculatum* is especially well developed in social insects, and the behavior of these animals tends to be more elaborate than that displayed by solitary insects.

One prominent feature of the nerve cord of insects is **giant axons**—fibers much bigger in diameter than most. The properties of these giant fibers have been explored in some interesting studies, using many different orders of insects (Edwards and Palka, 1991). These insects have receptive organs (the *cerci*, singular *cercus*) in the tail that detect air movement; these receptors connect to giant interneurons with very large axons that ascend the nerve cord to the head. Along the way, these axons excite some motoneurons.

6.9 The Nervous System of a Typical Insect, *Drosophila melanogaster*   In insects, such as this fruit fly, the brain with its subdivisions is linked via bundles of axons (connectives) to groups of ganglia in the thorax and abdomen. The brain, connectives, and ganglia are shown here in blue.

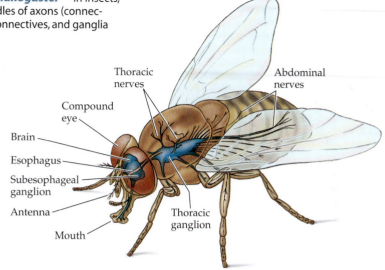

This system originated to allow insects to escape predation by retreating rapidly. In many insects (e.g., cockroaches) this system still functions as an escape system; in other insects the cerci and the connections of the giant interneurons have been modified so that they also play a role in reproductive behavior (in crickets) or help regulate flight maneuvers (in grasshoppers). Whatever its function in a particular species, the basic organization and cellular composition of this system appears to have remained the same for a very long time, perhaps as long as 400 million years (Edwards and Palka, 1991).

Vertebrate nervous systems differ from those of invertebrates

To summarize some of the features of vertebrate and invertebrate nervous systems that we have described up to now, let's compare them:

- *Basic plan.* All vertebrates and most invertebrates share a basic plan that consists of a central nervous system and a peripheral nervous system.
- *Brain.* All vertebrates and many invertebrates, including mollusks and insects, have brains. The general evolutionary trend in both vertebrates and invertebrates is toward increasing brain control over ganglia at lower levels of the body.
- *Number of neurons.* Whereas vertebrate brains usually have many neurons devoted to information processing, invertebrate brains usually have fewer but larger and more-complicated neurons that manage key integrative processes.
- *Identifiable neurons.* Some of the large invertebrate neurons are identifiable. In contrast, there are very few cases of identifiable neurons in vertebrates.
- *Ganglion structure.* Vertebrate ganglia have the cell bodies on the inside and the dendrites and axons on the outside. Ganglia in invertebrate nervous systems have a different structure: an outer rind of cell bodies and an inner core that consists of the extensions of the cell bodies forming a dense neuropil (a network of axons and dendrites).
- *Axons and neural conduction.* Many axons of mammalian neurons are surrounded by myelin, which helps them conduct impulses faster than unmyelinated axons can (see Chapter 3). Invertebrates have no myelin to speed nerve conduction, but many have a few giant axons to convey messages rapidly in escape systems.
- *Structural changes.* The structure of the nervous system undergoes large-scale changes in some invertebrates during metamorphosis. Vertebrates show important changes in neural structure during development, but these changes are not as dramatic as the changes during invertebrate metamorphoses.
- *Location in the body.* In vertebrates the central nervous system is encased in the bony skull and spinal column. In many invertebrates the nervous system is built around the digestive tract.
- *Constancy.* The basic structure and connections of the insect nervous system have remained similar throughout hundreds of millions of years, even though body forms have varied greatly. The vertebrate nervous system has also maintained the same basic structure for hundreds of millions of years of evolution. Although differences in body form are less extreme among vertebrates than among insects, nevertheless many evolutionary changes have taken place in vertebrate brains.

The Evolution of Vertebrate Brains Can Be Related to Changes in Behavior

During the course of evolution the characteristics of the nervous system have changed progressively. One especially prominent change in the last 100 million years has been a general tendency for the brain size of vertebrates to increase, and the brains of our human ancestors have shown a particularly striking increase in size during the last 2 million years. How, then, has the evolution of the brain been related to changes in behavioral capacity?

Present-day animals and fossils reveal evolution of the brain

Theoretically we could learn more about the evolution of the brain by studying the brains of fossil animals, but brains themselves do not fossilize—at least, not literally. Two methods of analysis have proved to be helpful. One is to use the cranial cavity of a fossil skull to make a cast of the brain that once occupied that space. These casts (called **endocasts;** the Greek *endon* means "within") give a reasonable indication of the size and shape of the brain, but no fine detail.

The other method is to study present-day animals, choosing species that show various degrees of similarity to (or difference from) ancestral forms. Although no modern animal is an ancestor of any other living form, some present-day species resemble ancestral forms more closely than others do. For example, present-day salamanders are much more similar to vertebrates of 300 million years ago than are any mammals. Among mammals, some species, such as the opossum, resemble fossil mammals of 50 million years ago more than do other species, such as the dog. Thus a species such as the opossum is said to retain primitive or ancestral states of particular anatomical features. Anatomists who study the brains of living species can obtain far more detailed information from such species than from endocasts because they can investigate the internal structure of the brain: its nuclei, fiber tracts, and the circuitry formed by connections of its neurons.

We must be careful not to interpret the evolutionary record as if it were a linear sequence. The main classes of vertebrates in Figure 6.10, for example, represent dif-

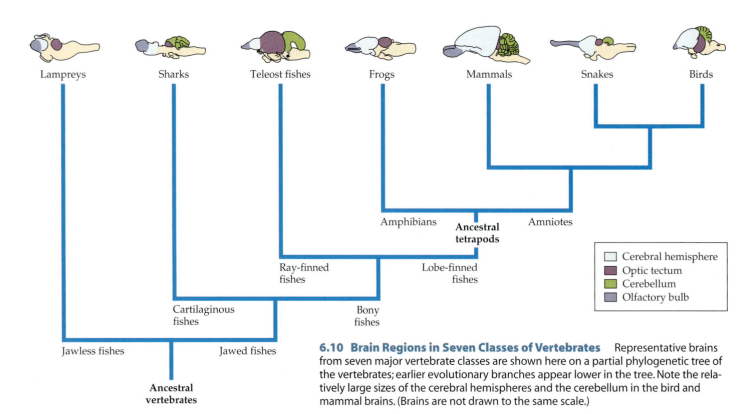

6.10 Brain Regions in Seven Classes of Vertebrates   Representative brains from seven major vertebrate classes are shown here on a partial phylogenetic tree of the vertebrates; earlier evolutionary branches appear lower in the tree. Note the relatively large sizes of the cerebral hemispheres and the cerebellum in the bird and mammal brains. (Brains are not drawn to the same scale.)

Legend:
- Cerebral hemisphere
- Optic tectum
- Cerebellum
- Olfactory bulb

Lampreys   Sharks   Teleost fishes   Frogs   Mammals   Snakes   Birds

Amphibians   **Ancestral tetrapods**   Amniotes

Ray-finned fishes   Lobe-finned fishes

Cartilaginous fishes   Bony fishes

Jawless fishes   Jawed fishes

Ancestral vertebrates

ferent lines or radiations of evolution that have been proceeding separately and simultaneously for at least 200 million years. For example, among the sharks, some complex forms long ago evolved much larger brains than primitive sharks had, but those large-brained sharks had nothing to do with the development of large brains in mammals. The line of descent that eventually led to mammals had separated from that of the sharks before the large-brained sharks evolved.

Through evolution, vertebrate brains have changed in both size and organization

Let's consider some examples of changes in the size and organization of vertebrate brains. Even the living vertebrate that has the most-primitive features—the lamprey (a jawless fish)—has a more complex brain than it used to be given credit for. The lamprey has not only the basic neural chassis of spinal cord, hindbrain, and midbrain, but also a diencephalon and a telencephalon. Its telencephalon has cerebral hemispheres and other subdivisions that are also found in the mammalian brain. So all vertebrate brains appear to have these regions.

One difference in basic brain structure between the lamprey and other vertebrates is that the cerebellum in the lamprey is very small. The evolution of large cerebellar hemispheres in birds and mammals appears to be a case of independent evolution from the small cerebellum in their common reptilian ancestor; the increased size of the cerebellum may be related to increased complexity of sensory processing and increased motor agility.

The differences among the brains of vertebrate species, then, lie not in the existence of basic subdivisions, but in their relative size and elaboration. At what stages of vertebrate evolution do various brain regions first become important? Large, paired optic lobes in its midbrain probably represent the lamprey's highest level of visual integration. In bony fishes, amphibians, and reptiles, the relatively large optic tectum in the midbrain is the main brain center for vision (see Figure 6.10). In birds and mammals, however, complex visual perception requires an enlarged telencephalon.

All mammals have a six-layered **isocortex** (from the Greek *iso,* "same," and the Latin *cortex,* "bark of a tree"). (This was formerly called the *neocortex,* but that term is outmoded.) In more-recent mammals the isocortex accounts for more than half the volume of the brain. In mammals the cortex is the structure mainly responsible for many complex functions, such as the perception of objects. Regions of the brain that were responsible for perceptual functions in less-encephalized animals—such as the midbrain optic lobes (in the lamprey) or the midbrain optic center (in the frog)—have in present-day mammals become visual reflex centers. (We will refer to the isocortex in almost every chapter in connection with perception and other complex cognitive functions.)

Reptiles were the first vertebrates to exhibit relatively large cerebral hemispheres. Reptiles were also the first vertebrates to have a cerebral cortex, but their cortex has only three layers, unlike the six-layered isocortex of mammals. Part of the cortex in reptiles appears to be homologous to the three-layered hippocampus in mammals.

Brain size evolved independently in multiple lineages

The brain is sometimes said to have increased in size with the appearance of each succeeding vertebrate class shown in Figure 6.10, but that statement is wrong in several respects. For one thing, there are exceptions among the present-day representatives of the various classes; for example, birds appeared later than mammals but do not have larger brains. For another, the generalization arose from the old way of viewing vertebrate evolution: as one linear series of increasing complexity rather than as a series of successive radiations.

If we compare animals of similar body size, we see considerable variation in brain size within each line of evolution. For example, within the ancient class of jawless fishes, the hagfishes, which are more-recent members of that class, have forebrains that are four times as large as those of lampreys of comparable body size. The increase of brain size in relation to behavioral capacity has been studied most thoroughly in the mammals.

The encephalization factor   The study of brain size is complicated by the wide range of body sizes, which raises the question, How are body size and brain size related? A general relationship was found first for present-day species and then applied successfully to fossil species. This function turns out to be useful in finding relationships between brain and behavior.

We humans long believed our own brains to be the largest, but this belief was upset in the seventeenth century when the elephant brain was found to weigh three times as much as our own. Later, whale brains were found to be even larger. These findings puzzled scholars, who took it for granted that human beings are the most intelligent of animals and therefore must have the largest brains. To address this apparent discrepancy, they proposed that brain weight should be expressed as a fraction of body weight. On this basis humans outrank elephants, whales, and all other animals of large or moderate body size. But a mouse has about the same ratio of brain weight to body weight as a human, and the tiny shrew outranks a human on this measure. Without trying to prove that one species or another is "brainiest," we would like to know how much brain is needed to control and serve a body of a given size. From a comparative point of view, what is the general relation between brain size and body size?

When we plot brain weights and body weights for a large sample of mammals, we see some generalities (Figure 6.11a). All the plot points fall within a narrow polygon. Since both scales are logarithmic, the graph encompasses a great variety of animal sizes, and departures from the general rule tend to be minimized. The line drawn through the center of the polygon has a slope of about 0.69 (Harvey and Krebs, 1990). When the sample of mammals is divided into orders, each order shows a graph roughly like that of the mammalian class in Figure 6.11a, but the slopes vary. The overall slope of Figure 6.11a is largely determined by the differences among mammalian orders in brain weight–body weight relations (Harvey and Pagel, 1991).

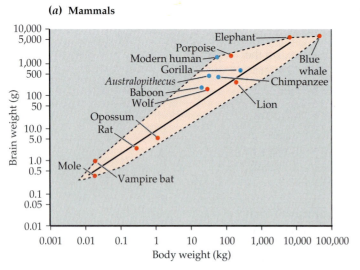

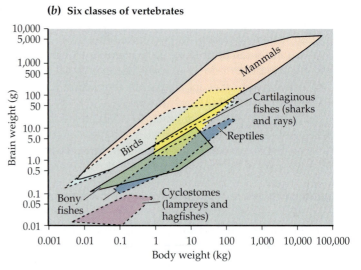

6.11   The Relation between Brain Weight and Body Weight
(*a*) Brain weight is related here to body weight in several mammalian species. Note that both axes are logarithmic, so the graph includes a wide range of brain weights and body weights. A polygon has been drawn to connect the extreme cases and include the whole sample. The diagonal line shows the basic relationship, with brain weight related to the 0.69 power of body weight. (*b*) Brain weight is plotted here against body weight for various species in six classes of vertebrates. Each class is represented by a polygon that includes a large sample of species in that class. The other classes of animals fall below the mammals, reflecting the fact that relative brain weight to body weight is smaller in those classes; they are less "brainy" than the mammals. (Part *a* after H. Stephan et al., 1981; *b* after Jerison, 1991.)

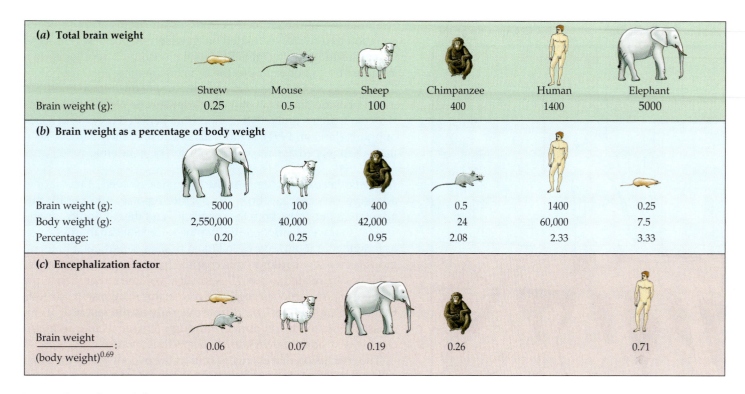

(a) Total brain weight						
	Shrew	Mouse	Sheep	Chimpanzee	Human	Elephant
Brain weight (g):	0.25	0.5	100	400	1400	5000

(b) Brain weight as a percentage of body weight						
Brain weight (g):	5000	100	400	0.5	1400	0.25
Body weight (g):	2,550,000	40,000	42,000	24	60,000	7.5
Percentage:	0.20	0.25	0.95	2.08	2.33	3.33

(c) Encephalization factor						
$\dfrac{\text{Brain weight}}{(\text{body weight})^{0.69}}$:	0.06	0.07	0.19	0.26		0.71

6.12 Who Is the Brainiest? For this sample of small to large mammals, the answer depends on what measure is used: total brain weight (*a*), brain weight as a percentage of body weight (*b*), or the encephalization factor (*c*). For each measure, the animals are ranked here from lowest value to highest.

Let's test the generality of this rule by examining the relation between brain weight and body weight for six vertebrate classes (Figure 6.11*b*). In each class except the mammals, the data yield a diagonal area with a slope of about three-fourths, so the relationship between brain weight and body weight is similar for all classes of vertebrates. But notice that the diagonal areas are displaced from each other vertically in Figure 6.11*b*: The mammals are highest, the bony fishes and reptiles clearly lower, and cyclostomes (e.g., the lamprey) the lowest. This configuration reflects the fact that these classes have successively less brain weight for a body of the same size. Thus a mammal or a bird that weighs about 100 g (e.g., a rat or blue jay) has a brain that weighs about 1 g, but a fish or a reptile of the same body weight has a brain that weighs only a little more than 0.1 g; a 100 g lamprey, for example, has a brain that weighs only about 0.03 g.

To take into account the variation both between classes and within classes, we need a measure of vertical distance above or below the diagonal line on the graph. This distance is usually called *k* and is different for each class and for each species. Because *k* indicates the relative amount of brain, it is called the **encephalization factor**. The greater the encephalization factor is for a species, the higher its value is above the diagonal line for its class. In Figure 6.11*a* the point for humans is farther from the black diagonal line than the point for any other species is. In terms of the encephalization factor, human beings rate higher than any other species. Figure 6.12*c* gives the values of the encephalization factor for several mammalian species.

Brain size has been studied in many species of vertebrates, both living and fossil. These studies have yielded clues about some selection pressures that have led to larger brains. For example, you may have heard the statement that dinosaurs became extinct because of the inadequacy of their small ("walnut-sized") brains (see Figure 6.13). Is this hypothesis correct?

THE FAR SIDE   By GARY LARSON

"The picture's pretty bleak, gentlemen... The world's climates are changing, the mammals are taking over, and we all have a brain about the size of a walnut."

6.13 Was the Dinosaur Being Too Modest?

Examination of the endocasts of dinosaur brains and use of the equation that relates estimated brain weight to body weight show that dinosaur brain weights fit the relationship for reptiles shown in Figure 6.11*b*. For example, the brain of *Tyrannosaurus rex* probably weighed about 700 g—only half the size of the human brain, but much heavier than a walnut and appropriate for a reptile of its size—so it seems unlikely that dinosaurs perished because of a lack of brains (Jerison, 1991). A more likely cause of their demise is climate change, perhaps caused by collision of an asteroid with Earth.

The evolution of brain size   As the brain has evolved, it has shown adaptive size changes both in specific regions and overall; this adaptation illustrates both the specificity and the continuity among species that we mentioned in Chapter 1. Certain capabilities, such as foraging for food, have been linked to sizes of particular brain regions, as we saw earlier in this chapter. In contrast, some other capabilities are related to overall isocortical volume rather than to the volume of any particular region of cortex; this relationship suggests that some capabilities could improve only as the result of an increase in total cortical volume, although this seems like an inefficient way to add tissue related to a specific function.

The conclusion that changes occur in the overall size of the brain rather than in specific brain regions is consistent with the concept that overall developmental factors and programs (which we will consider in Chapter 7) severely constrain the magnitude of local adaptations. Supporting this conclusion is the finding that if the weight of the brain of any mammalian species is known, the weight of each of its parts can be predicted (Finlay and Darlington, 1995).

To study this relationship, Finlay and Darlington used data published by H. Stephan et al. (1981) on sizes of the main parts of the brain in 131 species of mammals—insectivores, bats, prosimians, and simians (including *Homo sapiens*). Their data set has the advantages, for comparative study, of including a large number of species, a wide range of ecological niches (including terrestrial, arboreal [tree-dwelling], burrowing, amphibious, and flying), and a wide range of body weights (2 to 105,000 g) and brain sizes (60 to 1,252,000 mm^3). Another advantage is the fact that the 11 brain divisions measured constitute the entire brain.

In logarithmic scales, the size of each brain structure, except for the olfactory bulb, showed a highly linear relation to brain weight and correlated 0.96 or higher with total brain size. Thus for all parts of the brain except the olfactory bulb, a simple rule relates the size of the particular structure to total brain size.

Although the different parts of the brain increase roughly in proportion to total brain size increases, there are subtle differences in the rates of increase. As you compare mammalian brains from small to large, the medulla becomes smaller relative to brain weight, the cerebellum keeps pace with brain weight, and the isocortex grows more than any other part (Figure 6.14). Thus the proportion of brain devoted to each part differs in important ways from small to large brains.

The fact that the brain shows overall developmental constraints—with the size of most structures correlating highly with total brain size—does not contradict the existence of some specific size adaptations of brain structures. For one thing, the logarithmic scales used by Finlay and Darlington tend to obscure subtle differences, so even a threefold increase or decrease in size of a region is hardly noticed. For another thing, the brain divisions analyzed by Finlay and Darlington are relatively large, and most of them contain subdivisions that may vary in size. For example, one of the brain divisions in their study is the mesencephalon, which includes both the inferior colliculus and the superior colliculus; as we have mentioned, the infe-

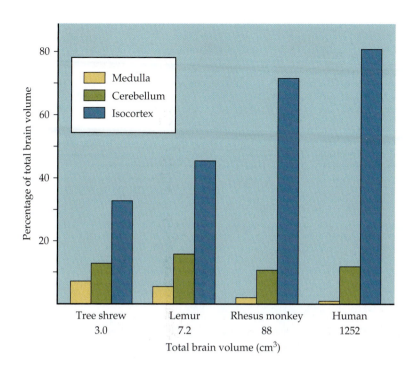

6.14 Changes in the Apportionment of Brain Regions among Primates This graph shows the percentage of brain volume occupied by three different parts of the brain in four different primates. As the size of the brain increases, the sizes of different parts of the brain increase at different rates. The size of the isocortex increases steadily as a proportion of brain size, while that of the cerebellum stays about the same, and the relative size of the medulla decreases. This generalization holds for all primates. (Data from H. Stephan et al., 1981.)

rior colliculus is larger in animals that depend mainly on audition, whereas the superior colliculus is larger in animals that rely on vision. So although general constraints on development are strong, different regions of the brain do exhibit specific adaptations.

The rapid evolution of hominid brains Valuable information about evolutionary relationships between brain and behavior comes from the study of hominids—primates of the family Hominidae—of which we humans are the only living species. Such studies shed light on our distant ancestors and help us understand how the body adapts to the environment through natural selection.

The structural and behavioral features that we consider characteristic of humans did not develop simultaneously (Falk, 1993). Our large brain is a relatively late development. According to one estimate, the trunk and arms of hominids reached their present form about 10 million years ago. Hominids began walking on two feet more than 4 million years ago, and the oldest manufactured stone tools date back to about 2.6 million years ago. (Note that the time span of human evolution and the dates of fossils have been altered by recent methods of dating. Not all authorities agree on these dates; they should be considered only approximate.)

The early toolmakers and users were bipedal hominids called **australopithecines.** Endocasts of their skulls show a brain volume of about 350 to 400 cm^3 (see Figure 6.15), about the size of the modern chimpanzee brain. Chimpanzees do not make tools from stone, although some collect stones to use as tools, and a captive chimpanzee has been taught to make stone tools. But the australopithecines made and used crude stone tools in hunting and in breaking animal bones to eat. The ability to use tools reduced the selection pressure to maintain large jaws and teeth, and hominid jaws and teeth thus became steadily smaller than the ape's and more like those of modern human beings. Smaller teeth may also be related to increasing social tolerance, since canine teeth are often used in fighting among primate groups.

Even though their brains did not grow much, never becoming larger than 600 cm^3, our australopithecine ancestors were successful animals, lasting—relatively unchanged—some 2 million years. Examination of ancient campsites suggests that these early hominids lived in nomadic groups of 20 to 50 individuals. They hunted and gathered plant foods—a new lifestyle that was continued by later hominids.

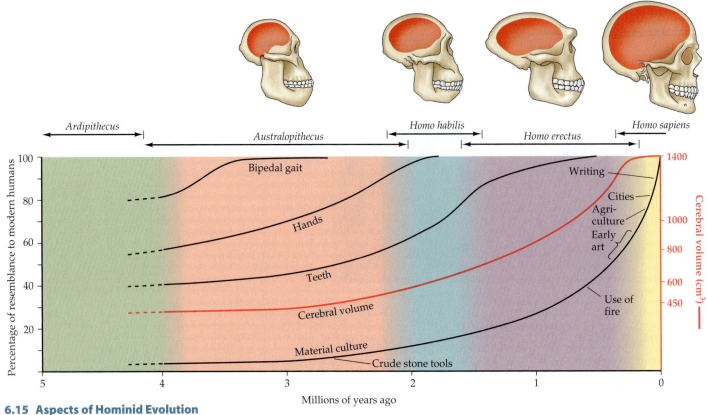

6.15 Aspects of Hominid Evolution
The bipedal (two-footed) gait was similar to that of modern humans even in *Australopithecus*, but cerebral volume reached its current size only in *Homo sapiens*. High culture (art, agriculture, cities, writing) emerged only relatively recently and was not associated with any further change in brain size. (After Tobias, 1980; updated with the assistance of Tim White.)

About 1.5 to 2 million years ago, when the australopithecines died out, *Homo erectus* appeared (Figure 6.15). This early representative of the genus *Homo* started with a cranial capacity of about 700 cm³ and a smaller face than *Australopithecus* had. As *Homo erectus* evolved, the brain became steadily larger, reaching the present-day volume of about 1400 cm³, and the face continued to become smaller. *Homo erectus* made elaborate stone tools, used fire, and killed large animals. Fossils and tools of *Homo erectus* are found throughout three continents, whereas those of the australopithecines are found only in Africa. *Homo erectus* may have represented a level of capacity and of cultural adaptation that allowed the hominids to expand into new environmental niches and to overcome barriers that kept earlier hominids in a narrower range.

Evolution of the brain and increased behavioral capacity advanced rapidly during the time of *Homo erectus* (see Figure 6.15). By the time *Homo sapiens* appeared, about 150,000 years ago, brain volume had reached the modern level. Thus, after remaining little changed in size during about 2 million years of tool use by the australopithecines, the hominid brain almost tripled in volume during the next 1.5 million years.

The size of the human brain now appears to be at a plateau. The recent changes in human lifestyle shown in Figure 6.15—such as the appearance of language, the introduction of agriculture and animal husbandry (about 10,000 years ago), and urban living (the last few thousand years)—have all been accomplished and assimilated by a brain that does not seem to have altered in size since *Homo sapiens* appeared. The lack of further increase in brain size may be related to the costs of a large brain, a topic we consider next.

The costs of a large brain   Having a large brain entails costs as well as benefits. Growth of a large brain requires a long gestation period, which is a burden on the mother, and childbirth is difficult because of the large size of the baby's head. Much of the growth of the brain continues during the years after birth, which means prolonged dependence of the infant and prolonged parental care. Although the brain makes up only about 2% of our total adult body weight, it requires about 15% of our cardiac output and metabolic budget when we are at rest. These percentages decrease when the body is active because muscles increase their demands, but even then the energy requirements of the brain remain high.

Construction of the human brain is so complex that more than half of our genes contribute to the task. The complex genetic messages that are generated are vulnerable to accidents; mutations of any of them are likely to lead to behavioral disorders. The evolution of large brains is especially remarkable when viewed in the context of these costs.

Selection pressures for increased brain size   A change in any organ during evolution suggests that the change confers advantages with respect to survival. A rapid increase, as in the size of the hominid brain, implies strong advantages for survival. What is the adaptive advantage of having such big brains?

Unfortunately, we cannot directly examine the brains of australopithecines. All we have is the information about overall size and external shape that endocasts afford. Chimpanzees have brains of about the same size and shape as australopithecine brains, but chimpanzees in the wild have never been seen to fashion a stone tool, even crudely. Chimps also catch small game, but not with the frequency that is suggested by the collections of bones of prey found in association with australopithecine remains. Thus, archaeological and behavioral evidence suggests that the australopithecine is our closer relative, further advanced toward human culture than the chimpanzee is.

However, chimpanzees show evidence of having some rudiments of culture: Groups at different sites in Africa show cultural differences. Researchers found 39 different behaviors that are frequent at one or more but not at all of seven locations examined (Whiten et al., 1999; see also de Waal, 1999, and Vogel, 1999). Most of these distinctive behaviors are related to obtaining food, including the use of stone and wooden tools (but not the *making* of stone tools); others are social behaviors such as grooming or mating displays. Even monkey groups have been observed to develop and transmit cultural differences (Figure 6.16).

Keeping in mind that the brain organization, as well as the behavior, of the australopithecine probably differed somewhat from that of the chimpanzee, let's look at how the modern human brain differs from the chimpanzee's brain to try to find some clues about the evolution of the hominid brain. Prominent differences between the organization of the brain of *Homo sapiens* and that of the chimpanzee include the following:

- The human brain has larger motor and sensory cortical areas devoted to the hands.

- In both the human brain and the chimpanzee brain, parts of the limbic system are involved in vocalization. The human brain, however, also shows large isocortical regions devoted to the production and perception of speech. Nonhuman primates have relatively smaller isocortical regions controlling vocalization.

- For speech, manual dexterity, and other functions, the human brain shows striking hemispheric specialization of func-

6.16 Transmitting Culture   Culture has been observed in nonhuman primates. For example, a population of Japanese macaques developed a set of behaviors that included washing food, playing in the water, and eating marine food items, and they transmitted this culture of water-related behaviors from generation to generation. (Courtesy of Frans B. M. de Waal.)

tions. In the chimpanzee the right and left hemispheres seem more equivalent in function.

* A controversial question is whether human prefrontal cortex (i.e., the cortex anterior to the motor cortex) is relatively larger in the human brain than would be predicted in an ape with a brain as large as ours. Deacon (1997) estimates that the prefrontal cortex is about twice as large in the human brain, and he suggests that the development of the prefrontal cortex permitted more-varied and more-elaborate processing of information and may have underlain the emergence of symbolic thinking. On the other hand, Semendeferi and colleagues (Semendeferi and Damasio, 2000; Semendeferi et al., 1997) measured brains of humans and of apes by magnetic resonance scanning and found that neither the frontal cortex as a whole nor its main regions are relatively larger in the human brain than in the ape brain.

In trying to account for the evolution of the human brain and for the special capabilities of *Homo sapiens*, different theorists have emphasized different behavioral traits: "Dexterity and tool use, language, group hunting, various aspects of social structure, and the ability to plan for the future have all been proposed as primary in the cascade of changes leading to the constellation of traits we now possess" (Finlay and Darlington, 1995, p. 1583).

From their analysis of the evolution of the mammalian brain, Finlay and Darlington suggest that the multiple facets and rapid rate of human evolution may be explained by the fact that large primates are on the part of the curve relating isocortex weight to brain weight where small increases in brain weight are associated with large increases in isocortex weight. Selection for any single cognitive ability might therefore cause, in parallel, greater processing capacity for all cognitive abilities. They suggest that the isocortex, as a general-purpose processor, may allow "the organism to take advantage of the extra brain structure in ways not directly selected for during evolution" (Finlay and Darlington, 1995, p. 1583). Charles Darwin (1888) made almost the same point:

> In many cases, the continued development of a part—for instance the beak of a bird or the teeth of a mammal—would not aid the species in gaining its food, or for any other object; but with man we can see no definite limit to the continual development of the brain and mental faculties, as far as advantage is concerned. (p. 169)

The survival advantage of larger brains does not hold only for human beings or primates. It would even be too limited to maintain that large brains are the specialty of the mammalian line. Within each line of vertebrate evolution, relative brain size varies: The more recently arrived species usually has the larger encephalization factor. Furthermore, in each vertebrate line it is the dorsal part of the telencephalon that has expanded and differentiated in the species with more elaborated capabilities. As we find more such common responses to selection pressures, they may reveal the "rules" of how nervous systems adapt and evolve.

Innovation, tool use, social learning, and enhanced brain size in primates   A major study correlated brain size in 116 species of primates with three different factors that have been proposed to account for the enhanced size of primate brains: (1) innovations in behavior, (2) use of tools, and (3) social learning—that is, learning by observing others (Reader and Laland, 2002). Rather than testing animals for these traits or observing them directly, Reader and Laland surveyed about 1000 articles in primate journals and other relevant literature and found 533 instances of innovation, 607 episodes of tool use, and 445 observations of social learning. The frequencies were corrected for the amount of research effort spent on each species. In addition to using total brain weights, Reader and Laland used the ratio of what has been called the *executive brain* (the sum of isocortex and striatum) to the brainstem (the sum of mesencephalon and medulla).

Both brain measures correlated positively with the frequency of each of the behavioral indices, indicating that each of the behavioral factors is related to expansion of the primate brain. Thus the results indicate that multiple sources of selection favored evolution of the large primate brain.

Sexual selection and brain size Using a different approach, we can evaluate the rapid expansion of the human brain over the last 1.5 million years in terms of Darwin's second evolutionary principle: sexual selection. Geoffrey Miller (2000) suggests that natural selection to obtain food and shelter is not likely to account completely for the large brain and complex intelligence of *Homo sapiens.* In fact, he notes, brain size tripled in our ancestors between 2.5 million years ago and 200,000 years ago, yet during this period our ancestors continued to make the same kind of stone axes. Only *after* the human brain stopped expanding did technological progress develop, so brain growth did not correlate well with the supposed survival benefit of enlarged brains.

COMPETING HYPOTHESES

Rather, Miller proposes an additional factor to account for large human brains: In humans, he postulates, much creativity, along with related brain growth, is due to sexual selection for abilities to attract attention, stimulate, and surprise a potential mate. This hypothesis, Miller claims, has the further value of presenting an evolutionary theory for such characteristic human traits as humor, art, music, language, and creativity.

The hypothesis that sexual selection for artistry and creativity may lead to increased brain size is supported by recent findings from the family of bowerbirds (Ptilonorhynchidae). To attract and impress females, male bowerbirds construct elaborate structures of twigs, decorated with colorful objects such as shiny beetles, shells, and petals (Figure 6.17). Zoologist Joah Madden found that bowerbirds have large brains, compared with other birds (Madden, 2001). Even within the bowerbirds, species that build more-elaborate bowers have larger brains.

Primate species differ in gene expression

At the start of this chapter we asked why humans and chimpanzees, which are identical in 99% of their genomic DNA sequences, differ in many morphological, behavioral, and cognitive aspects. One answer is that some genes affect brain development more than others. For example, the gene *ASPM* influences the size of the cerebral cortex, and the fact that the protein encoded by the gene differs considerably between humans and chimps suggests that *ASPM* evolved rapidly in the line leading to humans (P. D. Evans et al., 2004). So even moderate changes in just a few crucial genes may make a big difference.

Another means by which similar genomes can produce different brains is in the way the genes are *expressed.* Even small changes in DNA can result in big differences in when and where the gene is transcribed to pro-

6.17 Bowerbird Nests To attract mates, male bowerbirds build elaborate bowers of twigs, such as this structure, and decorate them with colorful objects. The architectural complexity and ornate decoration of the bowers may be the reason for the relatively large brains of bowerbirds. (Courtesy of Will Betz and Adrian Forsyth.)

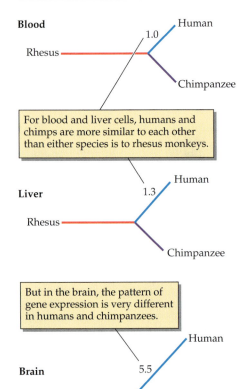

The distance between any two species indicates how different they are in the pattern of gene expression.

Blood

Human

Rhesus — 1.0

Chimpanzee

For blood and liver cells, humans and chimps are more similar to each other than either species is to rhesus monkeys.

Liver

Human

1.3

Rhesus —

Chimpanzee

But in the brain, the pattern of gene expression is very different in humans and chimpanzees.

Brain

Human

5.5

Rhesus —

Chimpanzee

6.18 Differences in Gene Expression in Various Tissues   The distance between any two species here indicates how different they are in the pattern of gene expression. (Enard et al., 2002.)

duce its encoded protein. Researchers report that humans differ considerably from other primates in gene expression in the brain (Enard et al., 2002). To study this question, the investigators measured mRNA and protein expression patterns in brain, liver, and blood cells in humans and other primates. They could then quantify how similar or different two species are in the pattern of genes expressed in particular tissues.

As Figure 6.18 shows, for blood cells and liver cells, humans and chimpanzees are more similar to each other than either species is to rhesus monkeys. These relationships probably reflect the well-documented evolutionary relationship among the three species. A comparison of the pattern of gene expression in the *brain*, however, shows that we are more different from chimpanzees than they are from monkeys. These results suggest that the pattern of gene expression in the brain has changed considerably, presumably under selective pressure, since we shared a common ancestor with chimpanzees. Thus the rate of evolutionary change in gene expression in the brain is accelerated in the human lineage relative to the chimpanzee and to other primates, whereas no such acceleration is evident in the liver or blood. The differences between humans and their closest relatives probably reflect not only differences in their DNA *sequences* but also in how those genes are *expressed* to construct a complex brain.

Even a small change in gene expression can cause a dramatic difference in brain development (Chenn and Walsh, 2002). In one case in mice, overexpression of one particular gene caused so much growth in the lateral dimension, but not the thickness of the cortex, that the normally smooth cortex of the mouse developed gyri and sulci (Figure 6.19). To answer the question we raised at the start of this chapter, the pattern of gene expression in the developing brain may be a major factor in making humans unique.

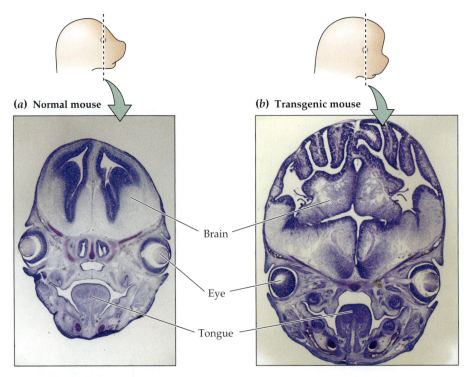

6.19 Over Your Head   Normally, mice at birth have a fairly simple cortex with no sulci or gyri (*a*), but increasing the expression of just one gene (that for β-catenin) in transgenic mice results in a monstrously complex, highly folded cortex (*b*). (From Chenn and Walsh 2002; photographs courtesy of Anjen Chenn.)

Summary

1. Studies of the classification of animals help determine how close the relationships between different species are. Knowing this relationship, in turn, helps us interpret similarities and differences in the behavior and structure of different species.

2. Comparative studies help us understand the evolution of the nervous system, including the human brain. They also provide a perspective for understanding species-typical behavioral adaptations.

3. The nervous systems of invertebrate animals range in complexity from a simple nerve net to the complex structures of the octopus. The nervous systems of certain invertebrates may provide a simplified model for understanding some aspects of vertebrate nervous systems.

4. Some of the distinctive features of invertebrate nervous systems include large, identifiable neurons and large axons that are frequently components of circuits mediating rapid escape behaviors.

5. The main divisions of the brain are the same in all vertebrates. Differences among these animals are largely quantitative, as reflected in differences in the relative sizes of nerve cells and brain regions.

6. Size differences in brain regions among various mammals are frequently related to distinctive forms of behavioral adaptation.

7. Evolutionary changes in brain size are apparent in comparisons of fossils and contemporary animals.

8. The brain size of a species must be interpreted in terms of body size. The overall rule for vertebrates is that brain weight is proportional to the 0.69 power of body weight.

9. Some animals have larger brains and some have smaller brains than is predicted by the general relation between brain and body weights; that is, they differ in encephalization factor. Humans, in particular, have larger brains than would be predicted from their body size.

10. Within each of the lines of vertebrate evolution, relative brain size varies, and the more recently evolved species usually have the larger encephalization factors.

11. The human brain, compared to the brains of nonhuman primates, has larger motor and sensory cortical areas devoted to the hands, larger cortical regions devoted to the production and perception of speech, a larger proportion of the brain devoted to varied and elaborate processing of information, and striking hemispheric specializations of function.

12. Not only natural selection, but also sexual selection, has been proposed to account for the large size of the human brain.

13. Differences between humans and their nearest evolutionary relatives, the chimpanzees, reflect not only the small differences in their genomic DNA sequences but also differences in gene expression patterns. Humans differ from other primates especially in the large number of genes expressed in the brain.

Refer to the *Learning Biological Psychology CD* for study questions, animations, activities, and other study aids.

Recommended Reading

Alcock, J. A. (2001). *Animal behavior: An evolutionary approach* (7th ed.). Sunderland, MA: Sinauer Associates.

de Waal, F. (2001). *The ape and the sushi master.* New York: Basic Books.

Futuyma, D. J. (1998). *Evolutionary biology* (3rd ed.). Sunderland, MA: Sinauer Associates.

Graur, D., and Li, W. (1999). *Fundamentals of molecular evolution* (2nd ed.). Sunderland, MA: Sinauer Associates.

Krebs, J. R., and Davies, N. B. (Eds.). (1997). *Behavioral ecology: An evolutionary approach.* Cambridge, MA: Blackwell Science.

Miller, G. F. (2000). *The mating mind: How sexual choice shaped the evolution of human nature.* New York: Doubleday.

Shettleworth, S. A. (1998). *Cognition, evolution, and behavior.* New York: Oxford University Press.

Striedter, G. F. (2005). *Principles of brain evolution.* Sunderland, MA: Sinauer Associates.

University of California Museum of Paleontology, Berkeley. 2004. *Understanding evolution: An evolution website for teachers* (http://evolution.berkeley.edu).

7

Life-Span Development of the Brain and Behavior

Overcoming Blindness

As a 3-year-old, Michael May was injured by a chemical explosion that destroyed his left eye and damaged the surface of his right eye so badly that he was blind. He could tell whether it was day or night, but otherwise he couldn't see anything. An early attempt to restore his sight with corneal transplants failed, but Michael seemed undaunted. He learned to play Ping-Pong using his hearing alone (but only using the table at his parent's house, where he learned to interpret the sound cues). Michael also enjoyed riding a bicycle, until his parents made him stop after he crashed his brother's and his sister's bikes. As an adult, Michael became a champion skier, marrying his instructor and raising two sons. He also started

his own company, making equipment to help blind people navigate on their own.

Then, when Michael was 46, technical advances made it possible to restore vision in his right eye. As soon as the bandages were removed, he could see his wife's blue eyes and blonde hair. But even 3 years later, he could not recognize her face unless she spoke to him, or recognize three-dimensional objects like a cube or a sphere unless they were moving. Of course Michael could still ski, but he found that he had to close his eyes to avoid falling over. On the slopes, seeing was more distracting than helpful. The doctors could tell that images were focusing properly on his retina, so why was his vision so poor?

… from hour to hour, we ripe and ripe,
And then, from hour to hour, we rot and rot …
  – William Shakespeare, As You Like It

A ge puts its stamp on the behavior of us all. Although the rate, progression, and orderliness of changes are especially prominent early in life, change is a feature of the entire span of life. In this chapter we describe the features of brains in terms of their progress through life from the womb to the tomb. The fertilization of an egg leads to a body with a brain that contains billions of neurons with an incredible number of connections. The pace of this process is extraordinary: During the height of prenatal growth of the human brain, more than 250,000 neurons are added per minute! We will describe the emergence of nerve cells, the formation of their connections, and the role of genes in shaping the nervous system. But we'll see that experience, gained through behavioral interactions with the environment, also sculpts the developing brain.

Growth and Development of the Brain Are Orderly Processes

Picture, if you can, the number of neurons in the mature human brain—about 100 billion. There are many types of neurons, each forming a vast array of hundreds or thousands of connections. The overall number of connections in the brain is about 100 trillion. Yet each of us began as a single microscopic cell—the fertilized egg. How can one cell divide and grow to form the most complicated machines on Earth, perhaps in the universe? Of course, some vital information was packed in the genes of that single cell, but we'll see that the developing nervous system also relies on its environment to guide the construction of this fabulous gadget between our ears.

One measure of brain development is weight, which is used to summarize many developmental processes. Figure 7.1 shows the changes with age in the weight of the brain, highlighting the rapid increase during the first 5 years. Let's explore at the cellular level what happens in the developing brain.

Mark Kostabi, *Bit by Bit,* 1992

7.1 Human Brain Weight as a Function of Age Note that the age scale on this graph has been expanded for the first 5 years to show this period of rapid growth more clearly. (After Dekaban and Sadowsky, 1978.)

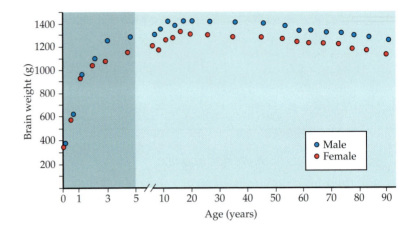

The brain emerges from the neural tube

A new human being begins when a sperm penetrates the wall of an egg cell. The fertilized egg, or **zygote,** has 46 chromosomes, which contain genetic recipes for the development of a new individual. (A summary of the life cycle of cells, including a discussion of the basic genetic materials and how they direct cell activities, is provided in the appendix.) Within 12 hours after conception the single cell begins dividing, so that after 3 days it has become a small mass of homogeneous cells, like a cluster of grapes, a mere 200 μm in diameter.

Within a week the emerging human embryo shows three distinct cell layers (Figure 7.2*a*). These layers are the beginnings of all the tissues of the embryo. The nervous system develops from the outer layer, called the **ectoderm** (from the Greek *ektos*, "out," and *derma*, "skin"). As the cell layers thicken, they grow into a flat oval plate. Uneven rates of cell division form a groove that will become the midline. At the head end of the groove, a thickened collection of cells forms 2 weeks after fertilization. Ridges of ectoderm continue to bulge on both sides of the middle position, forming the **neural groove** between them (Figure 7.2*b*).

The pace of events then increases. The tops of the neural ridges come together to form the **neural tube** (Figure 7.2*c*). At the anterior part of the neural tube, three subdivisions become apparent. These subdivisions correspond to the future **forebrain** (prosencephalon, consisting of the telencephalon and the diencephalon), **midbrain** (mesencephalon), and **hindbrain** (rhombencephalon, consisting of the metencephalon and the myelencephalon) (Figure 7.2*d*), which were discussed in Chapter 2. The interior of the neural tube becomes the cerebral ventricles of the brain, the central canal of the spinal cord, and the passages that connect them.

By the end of the eighth week, the human embryo shows the rudimentary beginnings of most body organs. The rapid development of the brain is reflected in the fact that by this time the head is one-half the total size of the embryo. (Note that the developing human is called an **embryo** during the first 10 weeks after fertilization; thereafter it is called a **fetus.**) Figure 7.2*e* shows the prenatal development of the human brain from weeks 10 through 41. Even after this period, there are dramatic local changes as some brain regions grow more than others, well into the teenage years (P. M. Thompson et al., 2000).

Development of the Nervous System Can Be Divided into Six Distinct Stages

From a cellular viewpoint it is useful to consider brain development as a sequence of distinct stages, most of which occur during prenatal life:

1. *Neurogenesis,* the mitotic division of nonneuronal cells to produce neurons
2. *Cell migration,* the massive movements of nerve cells or their precursors to estab-

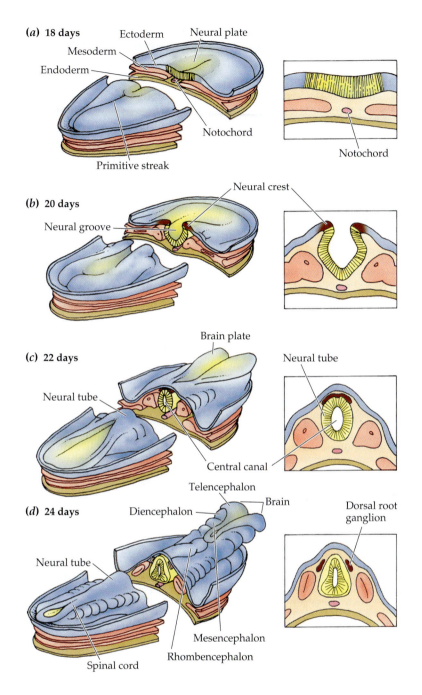

(a) **18 days**
Ectoderm
Neural plate
Mesoderm
Endoderm
Notochord
Primitive streak
Notochord

(b) **20 days**
Neural crest
Neural groove

(c) **22 days**
Brain plate
Neural tube
Neural tube
Central canal

(d) **24 days**
Telencephalon
Diencephalon
Brain
Neural tube
Dorsal root ganglion
Mesencephalon
Rhombencephalon
Spinal cord

7.2 Development of the Nervous System in the Human Embryo and Fetus (a) At 18 days the embryo has begun to implant in the uterine wall and consists of three layers of cells: endoderm, mesoderm, and ectoderm. A thickening of the ectoderm leads to the development of the neural plate (insets). (b) At 20 days the neural groove begins to develop. (c) At 22 days the neural groove has closed to form the neural tube with the rudimentary beginning of the brain at the anterior end. (d) A few days later, four major divisions of the brain—telencephalon, diencephalon, mesencephalon, and rhombencephalon—are discernible. (e) In these lateral views of the human brain (shown at one-third size) at several stages of fetal development, note the gradual emergence of gyri and sulci. (Part e from Larroche, 1977.)

(e)

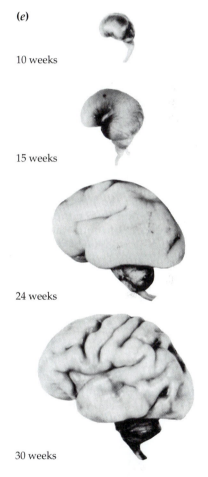

10 weeks

15 weeks

24 weeks

30 weeks

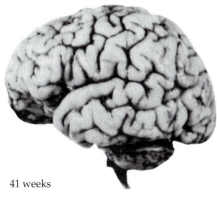

41 weeks

lish distinctive nerve cell populations (nuclei in the CNS, layers of the cerebral cortex, and so on)

3. *Differentiation* of cells into distinctive types of neurons or glial cells
4. *Synaptogenesis,* the establishment of synaptic connections as axons and dendrites grow
5. *Neuronal cell death,* the selective death of many nerve cells
6. *Synapse rearrangement,* the loss of some synapses and development of others, to refine synaptic connections

This sequence is portrayed in Figure 7.3. The six stages proceed at different rates and times in different parts of the nervous system. Some of the stages may overlap even within a region. In the discussion that follows, we will take up each stage in succession.

Cell proliferation produces cells that become neurons or glial cells

The production of nerve cells is called **neurogenesis.** Nerve cells themselves do not divide, but the cells that will give rise to neurons begin as a single layer of cells along the inner surface of the neural tube. These cells divide (in a process called **mitosis**) and gradually form a closely packed layer of cells called the **ventricular zone** (Figure 7.4). These cells continue to divide, giving rise to *daughter cells,* which also divide. All neurons and glial cells are derived from cells that originate from such ventricular mitosis. Eventually some daughter cells leave the ventricular zone and begin transforming into either a neuron or a glial cell. These two types of cells separate early in the ventricular zone. In most mammals, neural cells in the ventricular layer continue to form until birth; relatively few are added after birth.

Each part of an animal's brain has a species-characteristic "birth date." That is, there is an orderly chronological program for brain development, and it is possible to state the approximate days during development when particular cell groups stop dividing. Of course, given the complexity of vertebrate brains, it is difficult to trace individual cell development from the initial small population of ventricular cells. Descendants disappear in the crowd. However, in some simpler invertebrate nervous systems that have very few neurons, mitotic lineages can be traced more easily and completely.

A favorite animal of researchers who study the lineage of nerve cells is the nematode *Caenorhabditis elegans,* a tiny worm with fewer than a thousand cells, 302 of which are nerve cells. Because the body of *C. elegans* is almost transparent (Figure

7.3 The Six Stages of Neural Development

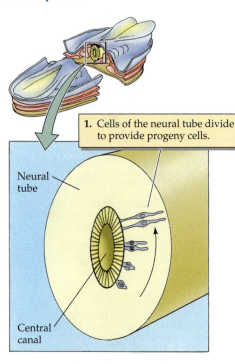

1. Cells of the neural tube divide to provide progeny cells.

Neural tube

Central canal

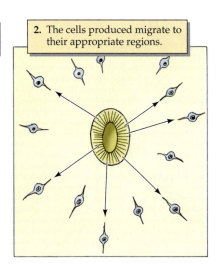

2. The cells produced migrate to their appropriate regions.

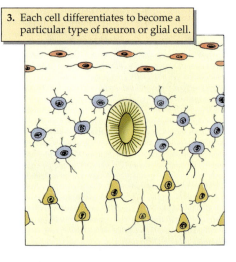

3. Each cell differentiates to become a particular type of neuron or glial cell.

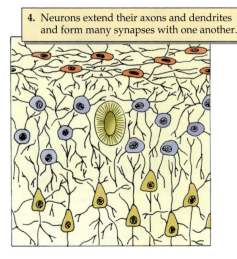

4. Neurons extend their axons and dendrites and form many synapses with one another.

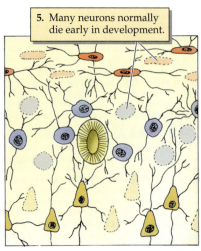

5. Many neurons normally die early in development.

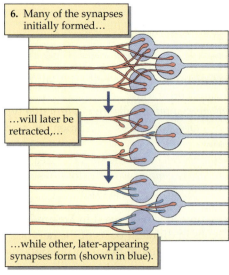

6. Many of the synapses initially formed…

…will later be retracted,…

…while other, later-appearing synapses form (shown in blue).

(a)

(b)

(c)

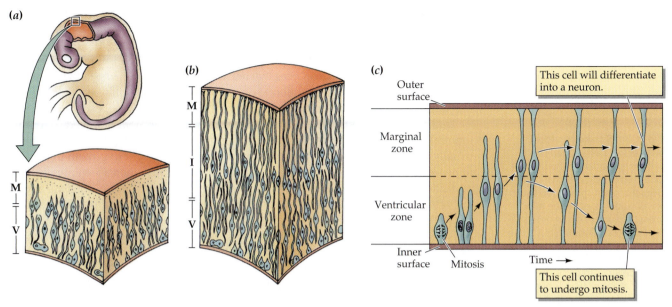

Outer
surface

Marginal
zone

Ventricular
zone

Inner
surface   Mitosis

M

I

V

M

V

This cell will differentiate
into a neuron.

Time →

This cell continues
to undergo mitosis.

7.5a), researchers have been able to map the origins of each nerve cell, and they have identified several of the genes that control the paths of this worm's neural development (Wolinsky and Way, 1990). By observing the successive cell divisions of a *C. elegans* zygote, investigators can predict exactly the fate of each cell in the adult—whether it will be a sensory neuron, muscle cell, skin cell, or other type of cell—on the basis of its mitotic "ancestors."

Whereas cell fate in *C. elegans* is a highly determined and stereotypical result of mitotic lineage (Figure 7.5b), in vertebrates the paths that cells take to form the completed

7.4 The Proliferation of Cellular Precursors of Neurons and Glial Cells (*a*) In this small section of the wall of the neural tube at an early stage of embryonic development, only ventricular (V) and marginal (M) layers are visible. (*b*) Later an intermediate (I) layer develops as the wall thickens. (*c*) Nuclei (within their cells) migrate from the ventricular layer to the outer layers. Some cells, however, return to the ventricular zone and divide, and the resulting daughter cells migrate to the outer layers, repeating the cycle.

(a)

7.5 Cell Fate in a Simple Organism (*a*) This montage of photomicrographs shows the transparent body of *Caenorhabditis elegans*. (*b*) In this mitotic lineage of cells that give rise to the body of the adult *C. elegans,* nervous system cells are highlighted in blue. The structure and function of every cell can be predicted from its mitotic lineage. Such mitotic determination of cell differentiation does not seem important to the development of vertebrates. (Part *a* courtesy of Paola Dal Santo and Erik M. Jorgensen, University of Utah; *b* after Pines, 1992.)

(b)

Zygote

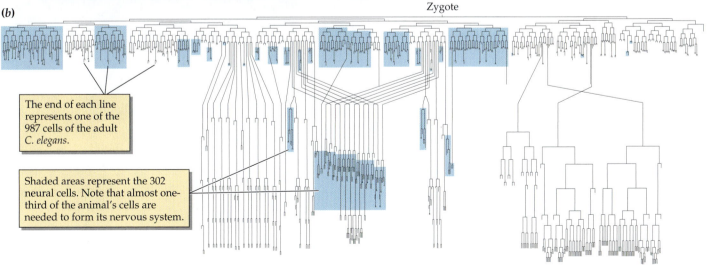

The end of each line represents one of the 987 cells of the adult *C. elegans.*

Shaded areas represent the 302 neural cells. Note that almost one-third of the animal's cells are needed to form its nervous system.

nervous system are more complex. Various techniques, such as the injection of substances that act as markers or the use of induced mutations, show that in vertebrates, the paths of development include more-local regulatory mechanisms. The hallmark of vertebrate development is that cell fate is affected by **cell–cell interactions** as cells sort themselves out and take on fates that are appropriate in the context of what neighboring cells are doing. Thus, vertebrate development is intrinsically less determined; that is, it is more subject to environmental signals and, as we'll see, experience.

Traditionally, investigators of nervous system development believed that most mammals had at birth all the nerve cells they would ever have. Researchers have usually attributed the postnatal growth of human brain weight to growth in the size of neurons, branching of dendrites, elaboration of synapses, increase in myelin, and addition of nonneuronal (glial) cells. But early reports that new neurons are added just after birth in some brain regions (Altman, 1969) have been supplemented with recent findings that new neurons are added even in adulthood in humans (Eriksson et al., 1998) and other animals (E. O., Reeves, et al., 1999; Magavi et al., 2000; Shingo et al., 2003). Likewise, nerve cells of the olfactory organ (which we use to detect odors) are normally replaced throughout life (Jacobson, 1991).

Furthermore, neurons are added to the adult nervous system in songbirds (discussed in Chapters 12 and 19). Elizabeth Gould and colleagues have found that enriched experience, such as learning, increases the rate of neurogenesis in adults (E. Gould, Beylin, et al., 1999; Praag et al., 2002). So by studying this chapter, you may be giving your brain a few more neurons to use on test day!

New nerve cells migrate

Neurons of the developing nervous system are always on the move. At some stage the cells that form in the ventricular layer through mitotic division move away, in a process known as **cell migration.** In primates, by the time of birth, almost all presumptive nerve cells have completed their migration, but in rats, cells that will become neurons continue to migrate in some regions for several weeks following birth.

Cells do not move in an aimless, haphazard manner. Many elegant studies by Pasko Rakic (1985) show that some cells in the developing brain move along the surface of a particular type of glial cell. Like spokes (radii) of a wheel, these **radial glial**

7.6 Glial Spokes Guide Migrating Cells Early in development, radial glial cells span the width of the emerging cerebral hemispheres. (*a*) Enlargement shows how radial glial cells act as guide wires for the migration of neurons. (*b*) Further enlargement shows a single neuron migrating out along a radial glial fiber. (*c*) Time-lapse video shows that, even when placed in tissue culture dishes, cerebellar granule cell neurons migrate up elongated cell bodies of glial cells (the long processes extending vertically). (Parts *a* and *b* after Cowan, 1979, based on Rakic, 1971; *c* from Hatten, 1990.)

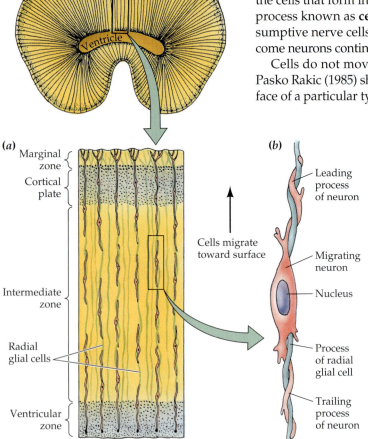

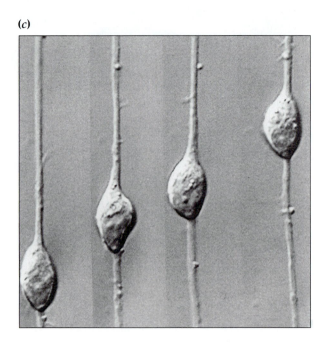

cells extend from the inner to the outer surfaces of the emerging nervous system (Figure 7.6). The radial glial cells act as a series of guide wires, and the newly formed cells creep along them, as if they were "riding the glial monorail" (Figure 7.6c) (Hatten, 1990). Some migrating cells move in a direction perpendicular to the radial glial cells (S. A. Anderson et al., 1997), like Tarzan swinging from vine to vine; others move in a rostral stream to produce the olfactory bulbs (C. M. Smith and Luskin, 1998).

Failures in the mechanism of cell migration result in either a vastly reduced population of neurons or a disorderly arrangement and, not surprisingly, behavioral disorders. The migration of cells and the outgrowth of nerve cell extensions (dendrites and axons) involve various chemicals. Molecules that promote the adhesion of developing elements of the nervous system, and thereby guide migrating cells and growing axons, are called **cell adhesion molecules** (**CAMs**) (Reichardt and Tomaselli, 1991). CAMs may also guide axons to regenerate when they are cut in adulthood (Box 7.1).

The single-file appearance of nerve cell precursors during cell migration (see Figure 7.6a) is followed by the aggregation, or grouping, of cells in a manner that foreshadows the nuclei of the adult brain that we discussed in Chapter 2. For example, cells of the cerebral cortex arrive in waves during fetal development, each successive wave forming a new outer layer, until the six layers of the adult cortex are formed, with the latest arrivals on the outside.

Cells in newly formed brain regions differentiate into neurons

Newly arrived cells in the brain bear no more resemblance to mature nerve cells than they do to the cells of other organs. Once they reach their destinations, however, the cells begin to use, or **express,** particular genes. This means that the cell transcribes a particular subset of genes to make the particular proteins it needs. This process of **differentiation** allows the cell to acquire the distinctive appearance of neurons characteristic of that particular region (Figure 7.7).

What controls differentiation is not completely understood, but two classes of influence are known. First, intrinsic self-organization is an important factor; cere-

Elizabeth Gould

Pasko Rakic

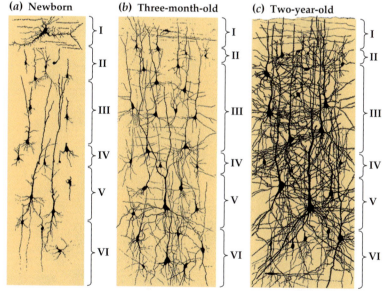

(a) Newborn   **(b) Three-month-old**   **(c) Two-year-old**

I II III IV V VI

7.7 Cerebral Cortex Tissue in the Early Development of Humans
These representations of cerebral cortex show the extent of neural connections and neuronal differentiation at birth (*a*), at 3 months of age (*b*), and at 2 years of age (*c*). Numerals refer to the six cortical layers. (From Conel, 1939, 1947, 1959.)

BOX 7.1   Degeneration and Regeneration of Nervous Tissue

When a mature nerve cell is injured, it can regrow in several ways. Complete replacement of injured nerve cells is rare in mammals, but Figures A and B illustrate two characteristic forms of degeneration and regeneration in the mammalian peripheral and central nervous systems. Injury close to the cell body of a neuron produces a series of changes that results in the eventual destruction of the cell; this process is called **retrograde degeneration** (see Figure A, 2 and 3). If the injured neuron dies, the target cells formerly innervated by that neuron may show signs of *transneuronal degeneration* (see Figure A, 4).

Cutting through the axon also produces loss of the distal part of the axon (the part that is separated from the cell body). This process is called wallerian degeneration, or **anterograde degeneration** (see Figure B, 2 and 3). The part of the axon that remains connected to the cell body may regrow. Severed axons in the peripheral nervous system regrow readily. Sprouts emerge from the part of the axon that is still connected to the nerve cell body and advance slowly toward the periphery (see Figure B, 4). Cell adhesion molecules (CAMs) help guide the regenerating axons. Some fish and amphibians have an enviable advantage over humans:

After an injury to the brain they can regenerate many of the lost connections. In these cases, CAMs appear to guide this regeneration (as we'll see in Box 7.2).

One interesting thing about regeneration of the nervous system is that it involves processes that seem similar to those that take place during an organism's original development. Studying regeneration, then, may increase our understanding of the original processes of growth of the nervous system, and vice versa. From a therapeutic viewpoint, these studies may help scientists learn how to induce repair and regrowth of damaged neural tissue in humans.

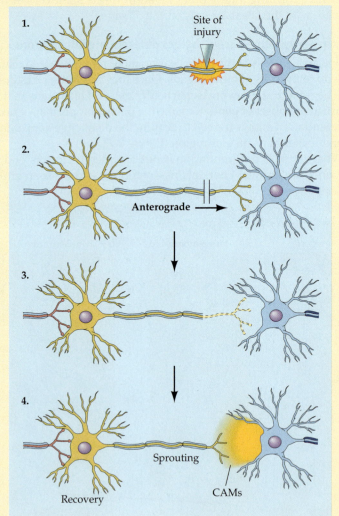

(A) Retrograde degeneration

1. Site of injury
2. ← Retrograde
3. Atrophy
4. Transneuronal degeneration   Transneuronal degeneration

(B) Anterograde degeneration

1. Site of injury
2. Anterograde →
3.
4. Sprouting   Recovery   CAMs

bellar Purkinje cells develop a very specific dendritic tree (Figure 7.8)—even **in vitro** (in a glass dish)—although they are deprived of some normal connections (Seil et al., 1974). When a cell shows characteristics that are independent of neighboring cells, we say that it is acting in a **cell-autonomous** manner. In cell-

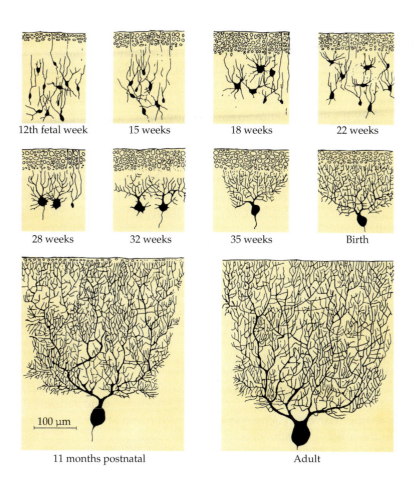

7.8 The Development of Purkinje Cells in the Human Cerebellum (After Zecevic and Rakic, 1976.)

12th fetal week 15 weeks 18 weeks 22 weeks

28 weeks 32 weeks 35 weeks Birth

100 µm

11 months postnatal Adult

7.9 The Induction of Spinal Motoneurons Spinal motoneurons normally cluster in the ventral region on either side of the spinal cord. In this cross section of embryonic chick spinal cord, the notochord (green circle at bottom) lies just beneath the spinal cord and secretes a protein called Sonic hedgehog. The concentration of this protein in the ventral spinal cord induces the cells there to develop as motoneurons (gold). Another protein (blue) is expressed only in the dorsal spinal cord. (Courtesy of Thomas Jessell.)

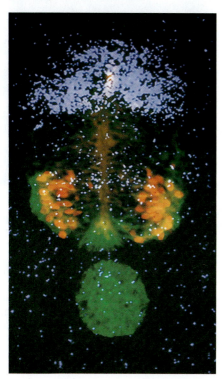

autonomous differentiation, presumably only the genes within that cell are directing events.

However, the neural environment also greatly influences nerve cell differentiation. In other words, neighboring cells are a second major influence on the differentiation of neurons. In vertebrates (unlike the nematode *C. elegans*), young neural cells seem to have the capacity to become many varieties of neurons, and the particular type of neuron that a cell becomes depends on where it happens to be and what its neighboring cells are. For example, consider spinal motoneurons—cells in the spinal cord that send their axons out to control muscles. Motoneurons are large, multipolar cells found in the left and right sides of the spinal cord in the ventral horn of gray matter. Motoneurons are among the first recognizable neurons in the spinal cord, and they send their axons out early in fetal development. How do these cells "know" they should express motoneuron-specific genes and differentiate into motoneurons?

Examination of the late divisions giving rise to motoneurons makes it clear that the cells are not attending to mitotic lineage (Leber et al., 1990). Instead, some spinal cells are directed to become motoneurons under the influence of other cells lying just ventral to the developing spinal cord—in the **notochord,** a rodlike structure that forms along the midline (see Figure 7.2*a*) (Roelink et al., 1994). The notochord releases a protein messenger (playfully named *Sonic hedgehog*) that diffuses to the spinal cord and directs some (but not all) cells to become motoneurons (Figure 7.9).

The influence of one set of cells on the fate of neighboring cells is known as **induction;** the notochord induces some spinal-cord cells to differentiate into motoneurons. Induction of this sort has been demonstrated many times in the developing vertebrate body and brain. Another way to describe the situation is that there is extensive cell–cell interaction, each cell taking cues from its neighbors. Because each cell influences the differentiation of others, neural development is very complex, but also very flexible.

For example, cells differentiate into the type of neuron that is appropriate for wherever they happen to be in the brain; thus, cell–cell interaction coordinates development—directing differentiation to provide the right type of neuron for each part of the brain. Another consequence of the reliance of development on cell–cell interactions such as induction is that if a few cells are injured or lost, other cells will "answer the call" of inducing factors and fill in for the missing cells.

This phenomenon can be observed in embryos from which some cells have been removed. For example, if cells are removed early enough from a developing limb bud in a chick embryo, other cells pitch in, and by the time the chick hatches, the limb looks normal—with no parts missing. Embryologists refer to such adaptive responses to early injury as **regulation:** The developing animal compensates for missing or injured cells. Because cell fate is so tightly coupled with mitotic lineage in *C. elegans,* this organism shows little or no regulation. If a cell in *C. elegans* is killed (with a laser through the microscope), no other cells take its place; the worm must do without that cell.

This system of cells taking cues from their neighbors as to what genes they should express and what function they should fulfill has another consequence: If cells that have not yet differentiated extensively can be obtained and placed into a particular brain region, they will differentiate in an appropriate way and become properly integrated. Such undifferentiated cells, called **stem cells,** are present throughout embryonic tissues, so they can be gathered from umbilical-cord blood or miscarried embryos.

It may be possible to take cells from adult tissue and, by treating them with various factors in a dish, transform them into "adult" stem cells (Palmer et al., 2001). We don't yet know whether placing stem cells in areas of brain degeneration, such as loss of myelination in multiple sclerosis, or of loss of dopaminergic neurons in Parkinson's disease, might reverse such degeneration as the implanted cells differentiate to fill in for the missing components (S. Liu et al., 2000).

NEURAL PLASTICITY

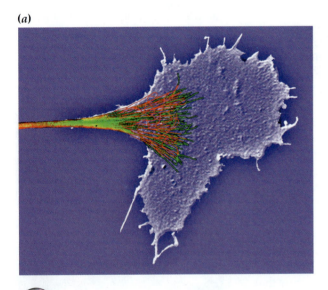

(a)

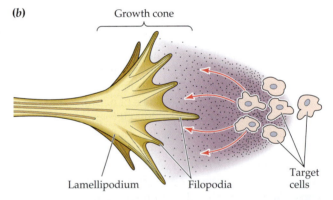

(b) Growth cone
Lamellipodium   Filopodia   Target cells

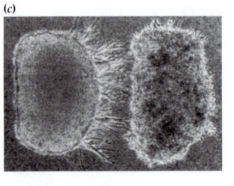

(c)

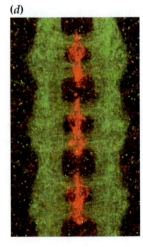

(d)

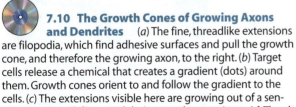

7.10 The Growth Cones of Growing Axons and Dendrites   (a) The fine, threadlike extensions are filopodia, which find adhesive surfaces and pull the growth cone, and therefore the growing axon, to the right. (b) Target cells release a chemical that creates a gradient (dots) around them. Growth cones orient to and follow the gradient to the cells. (c) The extensions visible here are growing out of a sensory ganglion (*left*) toward their normal target tissue. (d) The chemorepellent protein Slit (red), shown here in an embryo of the fruit fly, *Drosophila,* repels most axons (green), preventing them from crossing the midline. (Part *a* courtesy of Paul Bridgman; *b* after Tessier-Lavigne et al., 1988; *c* courtesy of Marc Tessier-Lavigne; *d* courtesy of Julie Simpson and Corey S. Goodman.)

The axons and dendrites of young neurons grow extensively and form synapses

The biggest change in brain cells early in life is the extensive growth of axons, dendrites, and synapses. This process is known as **synaptogenesis.** At the tips of both axons and dendrites are **growth cones,** swollen ends from which extensions emerge (Figure 7.10a). The very fine outgrowths, called **filopodia** (singular *filopodium,* from the Latin *filum,* "thread," and the Greek *pous,* "foot"), are spikelike; the sheetlike extensions are called **lamellipodia** (singular *lamellipodium,* from a form of the Latin *lamina,* "thin plate"). Both the filopodia and the lamellipodia seem to adhere to the extracellular environment, and then they contract to pull the growth cone in a particular direction (the growing axon or dendrite follows behind it). Dendrite growth cones in adults attest to the continued elongation and change in dendrites throughout life in response to experience.

What guides axons along the paths they take? Axons are guided by chemicals released by the target nerve cells or other tissues, such as muscles (C. S. Goodman, 1996; Tessier-Lavigne and Placzek, 1991). The axon growth cone responds to the concentration gradients of these chemicals that provide directional guidance, as illustrated in Figure 7.10b and c. Chemical signals that attract certain growth cones are called **chemoattractants** (Hiramoto et al., 2000); chemicals that repel growth cones are **chemorepellents** (Chen et al., 2000; Keynes and Cook, 1992). For example, because it is important for some axons to remain on one side of the body and for others to cross over, a protein called Slit repels some axons to prevent them from crossing the midline (Figure 7.10d) (Brose et al., 1999). Some secreted proteins act as chemoattractants to some growth cones and chemorepellents to others (Polleux et al., 2000).

Synapses can form rapidly on dendrites and dendritic spines (Figure 7.11). The spines themselves proliferate rapidly after birth. These connections can be affected by postnatal experience, as we will see in Chapter 18. To support the metabolic needs of the expanded dendritic tree, the nerve cell body greatly increases in volume.

Why is a synapse created at any single site on a neuron or other targets? Undoubtedly some type of chemical recognition bonds a presynaptic ending to a particular postsynaptic site; the molecular features of this recognition mechanism are slowly unfolding.

The death of many neurons is a normal part of development

As strange as it may seem, **neuronal cell death** is a crucial phase of brain development, especially during embryonic stages. This developmental stage is not unique to the nervous system. Naturally occurring cell death, also called **apoptosis** (from the Greek *apo,* "away from," and *ptosis,* "act of falling"), is evident as a kind of sculpting process in the emergence of other tissues in both animals and plants (Oppenheim, 1991).

These cells are not dying because of a defect. Rather, it appears that these cells have "decided" to die and are actively committing suicide. Among your chromosomes are **death genes**—genes that are expressed only when a cell undergoes apoptosis (Peter

(a) **Rat visual cortex**

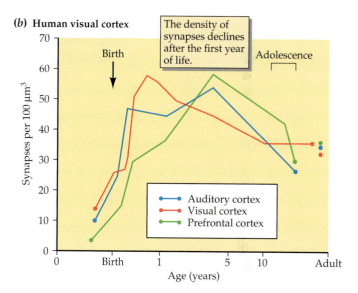

(b) **Human visual cortex**

> The density of synapses declines after the first year of life.

7.11 The Postnatal Development of Synapses The rate of synapse development in the visual cortex of rats (a) and humans (b). In humans, note the decline in the density of synapses after the first year of life. (Part a after Blue and Parnavelas, 1983; b from Huttenlocher et al., 1982.)

et al., 1997). For example, the **caspases** are a family of proteases (protein-dissolving enzymes) that cut up proteins and nuclear DNA. Apoptosis appears to begin with a sudden influx and release of Ca^{2+} ions that cause the mitochondria inside the cell to release a protein called, devilishly enough, **Diablo** (Verhagen et al., 2000).

Diablo binds to a family of proteins, the well-named **inhibitors of apoptosis proteins (IAPs)** (Earnshaw et al., 1999). The IAPs, in turn, have been inhibiting the caspases. So when Diablo binds the IAPs, the caspases are free to dismantle the cell. **Bcl-2** proteins block apoptosis by preventing Diablo release from the mitochondria. This intricate system of checks and balances, which determines whether a cell gives up the ghost (Figure 7.12), must have been established long ago in evolution, since homologs of the genes that produce these proteins function similarly in *C. elegans*.

In the nervous system, the number of cells that die during early development is quite large. In some regions of the brain and spinal cord, *most* of the nerve cells die during prenatal development. The proportion of nerve cells that die varies from region to region and ranges from 20% to 80% of the cells. Naturally occurring neuronal cell death was first described by Viktor Hamburger (1958) in chicks, in which nearly half the originally produced spinal motoneurons die before hatching (Figure 7.13).

Several factors influence this massive cell death in the nervous system. The extent of cell death is regulated in part by factors associated with the synaptic targets of cells. Reduction of the size of the synaptic target invariably reduces the number of surviving nerve cells. For example, if the leg of a tadpole is removed early in de-

Viktor Hamburger (1900–2001)

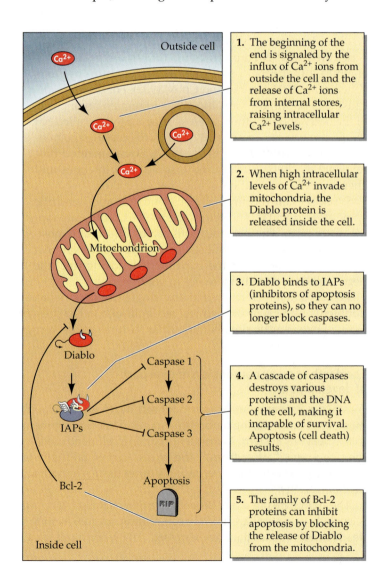

7.12 Death Genes Regulate Apoptosis

(*a*) **Chick spinal motoneurons**

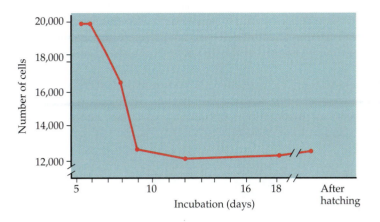

(*b*) **Human spinal motoneurons**

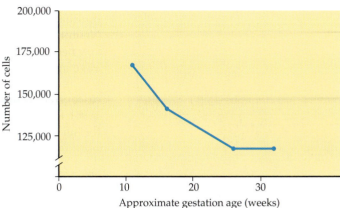

7.13 Many Neurons Die during Normal Early Development The pattern of neuronal cell death in spinal motoneurons of chicks (*a*) and humans (*b*). Many neuronal populations show a similar pattern of apoptosis. (Part *a* from Hamburger, 1975; *b* from Forger and Breedlove, 1987.)

velopment, many more developing spinal motoneurons die than if the leg had remained in position. Conversely, grafting on an extra leg—a technique that is possible with chicken embryos and tadpoles—reduces the usual loss of cells; in such cases the mature spinal cord has more than the usual number of motoneurons on that side.

One popular hypothesis is that neurons compete for connections to target structures (other nerve cells or end organs, such as muscle). Cells that make adequate synapses remain; those without a place to form synaptic connections die. Apparently the cells compete not just for synaptic sites, but for a chemical that the target structure makes and releases. Neurons that receive enough of the chemical survive; those that do not, die.

Such target-derived chemicals are called **neurotrophic factors** (or simply *trophic factors*) because they act as if they "feed" the neurons to help them survive (in Greek, *trophe* means "nourishment"). The neurotrophic factor that was the first to be identified prevents the death of developing sympathetic neurons, as we'll discuss next.

Neurotrophic factors allow neurons to survive and grow

More than 40 years ago, investigators discovered a substance—called **nerve growth factor** (**NGF**)—that markedly affects the growth of neurons in spinal ganglia and in the ganglia of the sympathetic nervous system (Levi-Montalcini, 1982). Administered to a chick embryo, NGF caused the formation of sympathetic ganglia with many more cells than usual. These cells were also larger and had many extensive processes (Figure 7.14).

The discovery of NGF earned Rita Levi-Montalcini and Stanley Cohen the 1986 Nobel Prize in Physiology or Medicine. Various target organs normally produce NGF during development. NGF is taken up by the axons of sympathetic neurons that innervate the organs and transported back to the cell body, and it prevents some of the sympathetic neurons from dying. The amount of NGF produced by targets during development is roughly correlated with the amount of sympathetic innervation that the targets receive in adulthood. This relationship suggests that differing extents of cell death, controlled by access to NGF, match the sympathetic innervation to each target.

Part of the interest in NGF arose from the possibility that there were more neurotrophic factors, each one affecting the survival of a particular cell type during a specific developmental period. After the discovery of NGF, investigators began searching for other neurotrophic factors. One such factor, purified from the brains of many animals, was named **brain-derived neurotrophic factor** (**BDNF**). The gene for BDNF turned out to be very similar to the gene for NGF. Investigators used molecular techniques to search for other NGF-related molecules and found several more.

Rita Levi-Montalcini

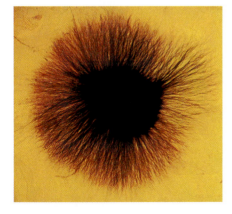

7.14 The Effects of Nerve Growth Factor If NGF is added to the solution bathing a spinal ganglion grown in vitro (in a glass dish), neuronal processes grow outward in an exuberant, radiating fashion. (From Levi-Montalcini, 1963.)

The family of NGF-like molecules was named the **neurotrophin** family, and its members are numbered: neurotrophin-1 (NGF), -2 (BDNF), -3, and -4/5 (it turned out that the fifth neurotrophin discovered was identical with the fourth—oops). Neurotrophic factors that are unrelated to NGF also have been found, including ciliary neurotrophic factor (named after its ability to keep neurons from ciliary ganglia alive in vitro).

The exact role of these various factors (and other neurotrophic factors yet to be discovered) is under intense scientific scrutiny (Kafitz et al., 1999; Lewin and Barde, 1996). Figure 7.15 depicts our current model of how neurotrophic factors influence the survival of neurons and/or their connections.

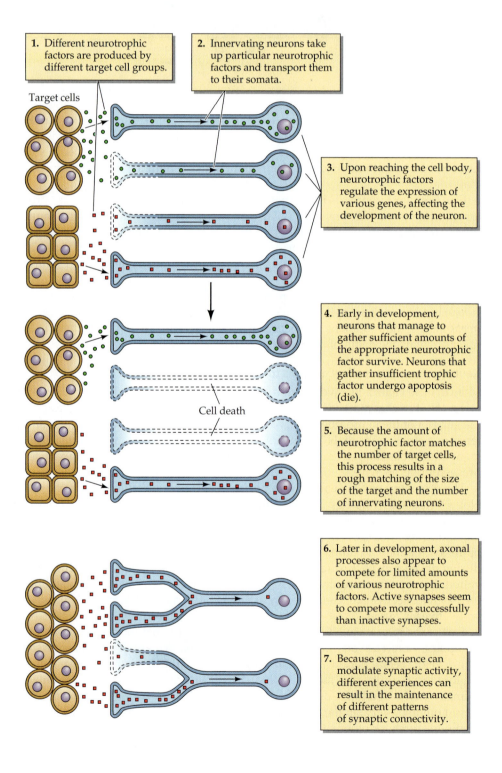

1. Different neurotrophic factors are produced by different target cell groups.

2. Innervating neurons take up particular neurotrophic factors and transport them to their somata.

Target cells

3. Upon reaching the cell body, neurotrophic factors regulate the expression of various genes, affecting the development of the neuron.

4. Early in development, neurons that manage to gather sufficient amounts of the appropriate neurotrophic factor survive. Neurons that gather insufficient trophic factor undergo apoptosis (die).

Cell death

5. Because the amount of neurotrophic factor matches the number of target cells, this process results in a rough matching of the size of the target and the number of innervating neurons.

6. Later in development, axonal processes also appear to compete for limited amounts of various neurotrophic factors. Active synapses seem to compete more successfully than inactive synapses.

7. Because experience can modulate synaptic activity, different experiences can result in the maintenance of different patterns of synaptic connectivity.

7.15 A Model for the Action of Neurotrophic Factors

Synaptic connections are refined by synapse rearrangement

Just as not all the neurons produced by a developing individual are kept into adulthood, some of the synapses formed early in development are later retracted. Originally this process was described as synapse elimination, but later studies found that although some original synapses are indeed lost, many new synapses are also formed. Thus a more accurate term is **synapse rearrangement,** or *synaptic remodeling*. In most cases, synapse rearrangement takes place after the period of cell death.

For example, as we learned already, about half of the spinal motoneurons that form die later (see Figure 7.13). By the end of the cell death period, each surviving motoneuron innervates many muscle fibers, and every muscle fiber is innervated by several motoneurons. But later the surviving motoneurons retract many of their axon collaterals, until each muscle fiber comes to be innervated by only one motoneuron.

Similar events have been documented in several neural regions, including the cerebellum (Mariani and Changeaux, 1981), the brainstem (Jackson and Parks, 1982), the visual cortex (Hubel et al., 1977), and several autonomic ganglia (Lichtman and Purves, 1980). In human cerebral cortex there seems to be a net loss of synapses from late childhood until midadolescence (see Figure 7.11*b*). What determines which synapses are kept and which are lost? Although we don't know all the factors, one important influence is neural activity (Box 7.2 shows an example). One theory is that active synapses take up some neurotrophic factor that maintains the synapse, while inactive synapses get too little trophic factor to remain stable (see Figure 7.15).

Later in this chapter we'll see specific examples in which active synapses are maintained and inactive synapses are retracted in the mammalian visual system. And in Chapter 8 we'll review evidence that synapse rearrangement in the cerebral cortex continues throughout life.

Glial Cells Provide Myelin, Which Is Vital for Brain Function

As already noted, glial cells develop from the same populations of immature cells as neurons. The factors that determine whether a cell differentiates into a neuron or a glial cell remain unknown. Glial cells continue to be added to the nervous system throughout life. (Sometimes the process becomes aberrant, resulting in glial tumors, or gliomas, of the brain.) In fact, the most intense phase of glial cell proliferation in many animals occurs *after* birth, when glial cells are added from immature cells located in the ventricular zone.

The development of sheaths around axons—the process of myelination (Figure 7.16)—greatly changes the rate at which axons conduct messages (see Figure 3.10). Myelination has a strong impact on behavior because it profoundly affects the velocity of the nerve impulse and thereby affects the temporal order of events in the nervous system. **Multiple sclerosis** is a disorder in which myelin is destroyed, probably by the patient's own immune system (Manova and Kostadinova, 2000), causing sometimes devastating disruptions of sensory and motor function.

In humans, the earliest myelination in the peripheral nervous system is evident in cranial and spinal nerves about 24 weeks after conception. But the most intense phase of myelination occurs shortly after birth. Furthermore, some investigators believe that myelin can be added to axons throughout life. The first nerve tracts in the human nervous system to become myelinated are in the spinal cord. Myelination then spreads successively into the hindbrain, midbrain, and forebrain. Within the cerebral cortex, sensory zones are myelinated before motor zones; correspondingly, sensory functions mature before motor functions.

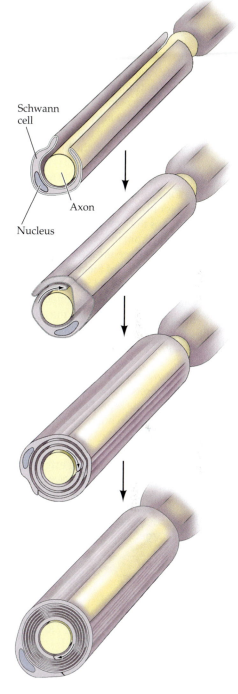

Schwann cell

Axon

Nucleus

7.16 Myelin Formation The repeated wrapping of a Schwann cell cytoplasm around an axon results in a many-layered sheath that insulates the axon electrically, speeding the conduction of electrical signals along its length.

Growth and Development of the Brain Reflect the Interaction of Intrinsic and Extrinsic Factors

Many factors influence the emergence of the form, arrangements, and connections of the developing brain. One influence is genes, which direct the production of every

BOX 7.2 The Frog Retinotectal System Demonstrates Intrinsic and Extrinsic Factors in Neural Development

In the 1940s Roger Sperry began a series of experiments that seemed to emphasize the importance of intrinsic factors, such as genes, for determining the pattern of connections in the brain. If the optic nerve that connects an eye to the brain is cut in an adult mammal, the animal is blinded in that eye and never recovers. In fish and amphibians such as frogs, however, the animal is only temporarily blinded; in a few months the axons from the eye (specifically, from the ganglion cells of the retina) reinnervate the brain (specifically the dorsal portion of the midbrain, called the *tectum*) and the animal recovers its eyesight. When food is presented on the left or right, above or below, the animal flicks its tongue accurately to retrieve it. Thus, either (1) the retina reestablishes the same pattern of connections to the tectum that was there before surgery and the brain interprets visual information as before, or (2) the retina reinnervates the tectum at random but the rest of the brain learns to interpret the information presented in this new pattern.

Several lines of evidence established that the first hypothesis is correct. One such piece of evidence is that the first-arriving retinal axons sometimes pass over uninnervated tectum to reach their original targets. In the classic case illus-

(A) Two possible mechanisms of chemoaffinity

Gradient 2

Gradient 1

Brain region

Projection fibers

Optic nerve

Retina

trating this phenomenon, the optic nerve was cut and the eye was rotated 180°; when the animal recovered eyesight, it behaved as if the visual image had been rotated 180°: It moved to the left when trying to get food presented on the right, and it flicked its tongue up when food was presented below. The only explanation for this behavior is that the retinal axons had grown back to their original posi-

tions on the tectum, ignoring the rotation of the eye. Furthermore, once the original connections had been reestablished, the brain interpreted the information as if the eye were in its original position. Even years later, animals that underwent this treatment had not learned to make sense of information from the rotated eye.

Sperry proposed the **chemoaffinity hypothesis** to explain how retinal axons

GENES AND BEHAVIOR

protein the cell can make. In the nematode *C. elegans,* genes are almost the only factors affecting development; the cells somehow keep track of their mitotic lineage and then simply express the genes that are appropriate for the cell fate that their lineage directs.

Genes are also a major influence on the development of the vertebrate brain. An animal that has inherited an altered gene will make an altered protein, which will affect any cell structure that includes that protein. Thus, every neuronal structure, and therefore every behavior, can be altered by changes in the appropriate gene(s). It is useful to think of genes as *intrinsic* factors—that is, factors that originate within the developing cell itself. All other influences we can consider *extrinsic*—that is, originating outside of the developing cell.

What are the extrinsic factors? One important extrinsic factor is whether the fetus is provided with the nutrients needed to carry out the genetic instructions. As we'll see, the lack of nutrients or the presence of chemicals that interfere with the delivery of nutrients can have a profound effect on brain development.

Another important class of extrinsic factors for all vertebrates is cell–cell interactions: Whether a cell expresses a particular gene, takes a particular shape, or per-

BOX 7.2 *(continued)*

know which part of the tectum to innervate. Suppose each retinal cell and each tectal cell had a specific chemical identity—an address of sorts. Then each retinal cell would need only to seek out the proper address in the tectum and the entire pattern would be reestablished; many chemical cues (represented by many colors in Figure A, left) or only a few (two colors in Figure A, right) may be involved.

Several preparations indicated that there are limits to how accurately retinal cells can find their original targets, but there is one dramatic demonstration: When retinal cells are placed in culture dishes, their axons grow and show preferences. The axons of ganglion cells from lateral retina prefer to grow over cell membranes from rostral tectum (their normal target) rather than over cell membranes from caudal tectum (F. Bonhoeffer

and Huf, 1985). Thus, apparently cell adhesion molecules (CAMs) in tectal membranes direct the retinal axons to the roughly appropriate region of tectum.

Having arrived at the roughly appropriate region of tectum, retinal connections are fine-tuned by extrinsic factors, specifically by experience. Normally each retina innervates only the tectum on the opposite side. When implantation of a third eye forces two retinas to innervate a single tectum (Figure B, left), they each do so in the same rough pattern, but they *segregate*; axons from one retina predominate in one area, and axons from the other retina predominate in neighboring tectum, so there are alternating stripes of innervation from the two eyes (Figure B, right).

This segregation depends on activity (Constantine-Paton et al., 1990). If neural activity in one eye is silenced (by injection

of drugs), the eye loses its connections to the tectum and the other eye takes over, innervating the entire tectum. If both eyes are silenced (by keeping the animals in the dark), neither eye predominates, their axons fail to segregate in the tectum, and the detailed pattern of innervation fails to appear. Presumably the two eyes are competing for limited supplies of a neurotrophic factor from the tectum, and active synapses take up more of the factor(s).

Thus the retinotectal system appears to reestablish the original pattern of innervation in two steps: (1) Chemical cues bring retinal axons to the approximately correct region of tectum. (2) The neural activity of the retinal cells, normally driven by visual experience, directs these axons to innervate or maintain innervation of the precise tectal region. (Figure B courtesy of Martha Constantine-Paton.)

(B) This three-eyed frog has two eyes innervating the left tectum.

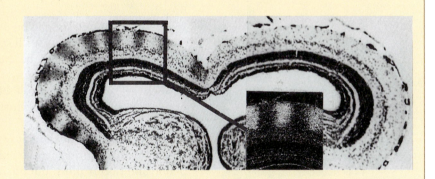

forms a particular task may depend on whether neighboring cells exert an inductive influence. The recognition that cell–cell interactions are very important for brain development led to the discovery of another extrinsic factor: neural activity driven by experience.

As we'll see, sometimes the electrical activity of a neuron can affect the fate of other cells (whether they live or die) and can determine whether or not synapses are maintained. In this way experience can alter the connections of the developing brain, thereby affecting an individual's behavior in adulthood.

Genes are the intrinsic factors that influence brain development

Psychologists have shown the importance of genetic factors in a variety of behaviors in many species, including humans (Rende and Plomin, 1995). Of course, genes do not work in isolation. Development should be viewed as the interaction of genetic instructions with the other, extrinsic influences.

The sum of all the intrinsic, genetic information an individual has is its **genotype,** or **genome.** The sum of all the physical characteristics that make up an individual is its **phenotype.** Your genotype was determined at the moment of fer-

TABLE 7.1 *Intrinsic and Extrinsic Factors That Affect Neural Development*

Factors	Examples of effects
INTRINSIC FACTORS (GENES)	
Chromosomal aberrations	Down syndrome, fragile X syndrome
Single-gene effects	Phenylketonuria, various *Drosophila* mutants, Tay-Sachs disease
EXTRINSIC FACTORS	
Nutrients	Malnutrition
Drugs, toxins	Fetal alcohol syndrome
Birth process in mammals	Hypoxia-induced mental retardation
Cell–cell interactions	
Induction directs differentiation	Motoneuron differentiation induced by notochord
Trophic factors direct cell death or synapse loss	NGF spares developing sympathetic neurons from death
Neural activity affects synapse maintenance and loss	
Non-sensory-driven	Eye segregation in layer IV cortex before birth
Sensory-driven (experience)	Ocular dominance outside layer IV after birth
	Increased IQ resulting from childhood enrichment

tilization and remains the same throughout your life. But your phenotype changes constantly, as you grow up and grow old and even, in a tiny way, as you take each breath.

Phenotype is determined by the interaction of genotype and extrinsic factors, including experience. Thus we'll see that twins who have identical genotypes do not have identical phenotypes, because they have not received identical extrinsic influences. Because their nervous system phenotypes are somewhat different, twins do not behave exactly the same. Table 7.1 lists intrinsic and extrinsic factors and some of the examples we'll use to illustrate each.

Identical genes, different nervous systems   One breeding technique produces genetically identical animals, called **clones,** which used to be known mainly in science fiction and horror films. But life imitates fiction. Although the sheep Dolly was the first successfully cloned mammal, she was not the first animal to be cloned. In grasshopper clones, the basic shape of larger cells was similar in all clones, but many neurons showed differences in neural connections among these genetically identical individuals (C. Goodman, 1979). Similar results were derived from clones of a tiny crustacean, the daphnia, well known to aquarium owners (Macagno et al., 1973).

GENES AND BEHAVIOR

Fish have identifiable neurons—Mauthner cells—and in some of these fish, females produce daughters that are genetically identical to each other and to their mother. Each fish has a single giant Mauthner cell on each side of the brain. Although the pattern of dendritic branching of the Mauthner cells is similar from individual to individual among clones, there are individual differences in the detail of branching and of synapses (Levinthal et al., 1976). Likewise, genetically identical cloned pigs show as much variation in behavior and temperament as do normal siblings (Archer et al., 2003).

Genetically identical mice raised in different laboratories behave in markedly different fashions on a variety of tests (Crabbe et al., 1999; Finch and Kirkwood, 2000). One source of variance in mice is in the mothering they receive. Genetically identical mice that are raised by different mothers show significant differences in behavior (Francis et al., 2003). For human identical twins, the branching pattern of nerve endings in the skin must differ, since even identical twins show some differences in their fingerprints (although their prints are more similar than are those of nonidentical twins). Indeed, in several places in this book we find that human identical twins do not always share such traits as schizophrenia (see Figure 1.8), sexual orientation, or depression, and these differences between twins cannot be attributed to the genome. Rather, the behavioral differences between twins (and between clones) are probably due to different experiences.

Basic research has revealed one important way in which experience affects the nervous system. Although nearly all of the cells in your body have a complete copy of your genome, each cell uses only a small subset of those genes at any one time. Recall that when a cell transcribes a particular gene and makes the encoded protein, we say the cell has *expressed* that gene. It turns out that neurons change which genes they are expressing in response to synaptic stimulation. Some genes, called immediate early genes, are expressed briefly by almost any neuron that has been stimulated (see Box 2.3).

Neuroscientists exploit this process by exposing an animal to, say, a sound of a particular frequency, and then examining the brain to see which neurons altered gene expression in response to different frequencies. Likewise, lights, odors, or touches will all affect neuronal expression of immediate early genes in particular regions of the brain and spinal cord that receive information about those sensations. Experience also affects the expression of many other genes (Mayfield et al., 2002), not just immediate early genes. So one reason why genetically identical individuals do not have the same brains or behavior is that they are inevitably exposed to different experiences, so they grow up expressing their identical genes in very nonidentical ways (Ridley, 2003).

Effects of mutations In rare instances an animal inherits a sudden change in genetic structure, a **mutation,** that is related to marked anatomical or physiological change. Researchers can increase the frequency of mutations by exposing animals to chemicals or radiation that produce changes in genes.

Mutants—animals that display these altered genes—are interesting to study because their changed genetic characteristics may be quite specific and striking. For example, Greenspan et al. (1980) described mutants of the fruit fly *Drosophila* that seemed normal in every way except that they had memory problems. These mutants—affectionately labeled *dunce, amnesiac,* and *turnip*—either failed to learn or could learn but forgot rapidly. Biochemical deficits in these mutants (due to mutations that render specific genes and therefore specific proteins ineffective) cause the failure of memory (Dudai, 1988).

Many mutations in mice affect the nervous system. Members of one group of mouse mutants that is especially intriguing to researchers all have single-gene mutations that affect postnatal development of the cerebellum (Tissir and Goffinet, 2003). The names of these mutant mice—*reeler, staggerer,* and *weaver*—reflect the locomotor impairment that characterizes them (Figure 7.17). Today scientists sometimes deliberately delete or

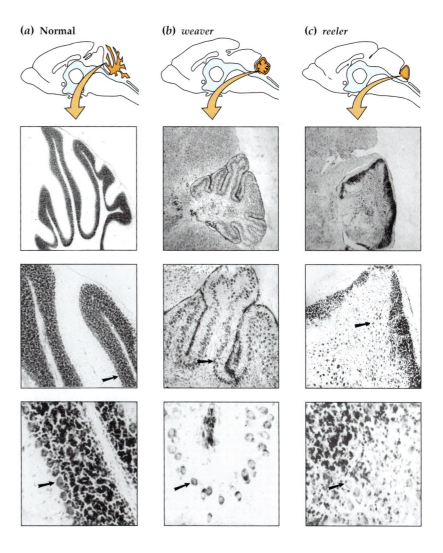

7.17 Cerebellar Mutants among Mice
(*a*) The cerebellum in a normal mouse at three levels of magnification (25×, 66×, and 250×, from top to bottom). (*b*) In the mutant *weaver,* note the almost complete absence of the tiny granule cells, while the alignment of the large Purkinje cells (arrows) is normal. (*c*) The mutant *reeler* shows marked derangement of the customary layering of cells. Both mutants show overall shrinkage of the cerebellum. (From A. L. Leiman, unpublished observations.)

(*a*) **Normal**   (*b*) *weaver*   (*c*) *reeler*

BOX 7.3 Transgenic and Knockout Mice

Animals with mutations in specific genes can offer clues about the role of genes in development and brain function. Until recently, the only types of mutants one could study were the very rare cases of spontaneous mutations or mutations caused by animals being treated with radiation or chemicals to increase the rate of mutation. Unless very small short-lived animals like *Drosophila* were the subject of the research, this process was tedious because very few of the induced mutations were in the gene of interest.

Among the many new tools brought to us by the revolution in molecular biology is *site-directed mutagenesis,* the ability to cause a mutation in a particular gene. Researchers using this technique must know the sequence of nucleotides in the gene of interest. Then they can use the tendency of complementary nucleotides to hybridize with that part of the gene to induce changes (see the appendix for a refresher on hybridization).

The easiest change to understand is total disruption of the gene, making it nonfunctional. If this is done in special embryonic mouse cells, there are ways to introduce the manipulated gene into the testes or ovaries of a developing mouse. That mouse can then produce offspring that are missing one copy of the gene and, through inbreeding, grandchildren missing both copies of the gene. We call the resulting animal a **knockout mouse** because the gene of interest has been *knocked out.*

By following the development of knockout mice, we can obtain clues about the roles of particular genes in normal animals. For example, the motoneurons of brain-derived neurotrophic factor (BDNF) knockout mice survive despite the absence of BDNF (Sendtner et al., 1996), so we know that trophic factor is not crucial for motoneuron survival. On the other hand, some parasympathetic ganglia fail to form in BDNF knockout mice (Erickson et al., 1996), suggesting that these neurons depend on BDNF for survival. As we'll see in Chapter 18, several genes suspected of playing a role in learning have been knocked out in mice, and the resulting animals indeed show deficits in learning.

There are some problems in interpreting such results, because the missing gene may have contributed only very indirectly to the learning process, or the animal's poor performance may have been due to a distraction caused by the knockout. For that matter, even normal behavior by animals missing the gene does not prove that the gene is unimportant for behavior. Perhaps the developing animal, in the absence of that gene, somehow has compensated for the loss and found a new way to solve the problem. This would be another example of the embryonic regulation that is so common in vertebrate development.

In other cases, a functional, manipulated copy of a gene can be introduced into the mouse. This animal is called a **transgenic mouse** because a gene has been *trans*ferred into its genome. Some-

times the introduction of just a single new gene can have a dramatic effect on brain development; for example, compare the brains of newborn mice that are normal with those of transgenic mice carrying a modified gene for β-catenin (see Figure 6.19). Modifying this one gene caused the mouse to make far too many neurons, so extra gyri and sulci developed to accommodate them (Chenn and Walsh, 2002).

The transgenic approach is often used as a method for improving our understanding of genetic disorders. For example, in Chapter 11 we'll learn that when a human gene that causes severe motor impairments is transferred into mice, the mice develop symptoms similar to those that appear in humans. It may be possible to study the disease more closely in these mice and test possible therapies.

So far, knockout and transgenic animals have one limitation: They possess the genetic manipulation from the moment of conception and in every cell in the body. More recently, molecular neurobiologists have begun knocking out or replacing a gene in an animal after it has reached adulthood (by injecting the animal with a triggering substance such as tetracycline), or by replacing or knocking out a gene in only one region of the brain. These manipulations allow the animals to develop with a normal genotype, thereby making it easier to interpret the result of the gene manipulation in adulthood. It may even be possible to knock out and then restore a gene in the same individual mouse.

introduce a particular gene in mice in order to study the effect of that gene on the nervous system (Box 7.3).

Despite the importance of genes for nervous system development, understanding the genome alone could never enable an understanding of the developing brain because, as we'll see next, experience also directs developing neurons.

Experience Is an Important Influence on Brain Development

The young of many species are born in a highly immature state, both anatomically and behaviorally. Varying an individual's experience during early development alters many aspects of behavior, brain anatomy, and brain chemistry in animal models (E. L. Bennett et al., 1964; Gottlieb, 1976; Rosenzweig and Bennett, 1977, 1978). Presumably, similar neural processes are affected by the early-childhood enrichment programs that produce a long-lasting increase in IQ in humans, especially those from deprived backgrounds (Ramey et al., 2000; Raine et al., 2002).

NEURAL PLASTICITY

Visual deprivation can lead to blindness

The role of experience in guiding neural development is best understood in the visual system. Some people do not see forms clearly with one of their eyes, even though the eye is intact and a sharp image is focused on the retina. Such impairments of vision are known as **amblyopia** (from the Greek *amblys*, "dull, blunt," and *ops*, "eye"). Some people with this disorder have a *lazy eye*, one that is turned inward (cross-eyed) or outward. Children born with such a misalignment see a double image rather than a single fused image. If the deviated eye is not surgically realigned early in childhood, vision becomes impaired. By the time an untreated person reaches the age of 7 or 8, pattern vision in the deviated eye is almost completely suppressed. Realignment of the eyes in adulthood does not restore acute vision to the turned eye.

**CLINICAL
ISSUE**

The inability to correct the problem in adulthood is quite striking in these cases, since throughout the person's development, light enters this eye in a normal manner and the nerve cells of the eye continue to be excited. Similar misalignment of the eyes, when it appears for the first time in adulthood, produces double vision, a condition that shows no change with further aging. These clinical observations of humans suggest that unusual positioning of the eyes during early development changes neural connections in the brain.

Understanding the cause of amblyopia in people has been greatly advanced by visual-deprivation experiments with animals. These experiments revealed startling changes related to disuse of the visual system during early critical periods. Depriving animals of light to both eyes (**binocular deprivation**) produces structural changes in visual cortical neurons: a loss of dendritic spines and a reduction in synaptic density.

If such deprivation is maintained for several weeks during development, when the animal's eyes are opened it will be blind. Although light enters its eyes and the cells of the eyes send messages to the brain, the brain seems to ignore the messages, and the animal is unable to detect visual stimuli. If the deprivation lasts long enough, the animal is *never* able to recover eyesight. Thus, early visual experience is crucial for the proper development of vision. There appears to be a **sensitive period** during which these manipulations of experience can exert long-lasting effects on the system. These effects are most extensive during the early period of synaptic development in the visual cortex (Figure 7.18). After the sensitive period, the manipulations have little or no effect.

Pioneering work by David Hubel and Torsten Wiesel, who shared the 1981 Nobel Prize in Physiology or Medicine, showed that depriving only one eye of light (**monocular deprivation**) produces profound structural and functional changes in

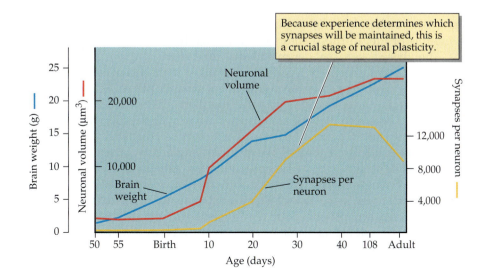

> Because experience determines which synapses will be maintained, this is a crucial stage of neural plasticity.

7.18 Brain Development in the Visual Cortex of Cats Synaptic development in cats is most intense from 8 to 37 days after birth, a period during which visual experience can have profound influence. Note that increases in brain weight and cell volume are parallel and precede synaptic development. Note also the decline in synapse numbers after 108 days of age—evidence of synapse rearrangement. (After Cragg, 1975.)

(a) Normal

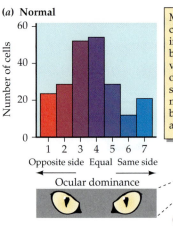

Most cells in visual cortex can be stimulated by light in either eye. This happens because, for most of the visual field, light from an object reaches corresponding spots on both retinas. So most cortical cells become binocular as the two eyes are stimulated by experience.

(b) Monocular deprivation

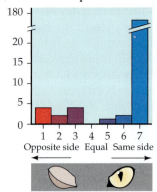

When one eye is closed in development, it quickly loses its connection to visual cortex. If deprived long enough, the animal will become blind in that eye. Similar deprivation in adulthood has virtually no effect on the connections from the eye or the ability of the cat to see.

(c) One eye deviated

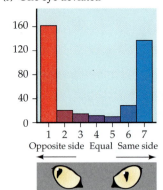

If the two eyes are not aligned properly, then light from the visual field may still reach both eyes, but it does not reach the *corresponding* parts of the two retinas. So each cortical cell comes to listen to only one eye or the other. This cat will have very poor depth perception.

(d) Binocular deprivation

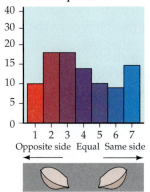

Ironically, briefly depriving *both* eyes during development may have less of an effect on the connections from the eye to the cortex than depriving one eye. The reason is that the two eyes are still evenly matched in their competition for connections to the cortex. However, *prolonged* binocular deprivation in development will lead to total blindness.

7.19 Ocular Dominance Histograms
These histograms show responses of cells in the visual cortex of cats in normal adults (a); after monocular deprivation through the early critical period (b); after early deviation of one eye—that is, squint (c); and after binocular deprivation (d). The numbers along the x-axis represent a gradation in response: Cells that respond *only* to stimulation of the opposite eye are class 1 cells. Cells that respond *mainly* to stimulation of the opposite eye are class 2. Cells that respond equally to either eye are class 4. Cells that respond only to stimulation of the eye on the same side are class 7, and so on. (After Hubel and Wiesel, 1965; Wiesel and Hubel, 1965.)

the thalamus and visual cortex. Monocular deprivation in an infant cat or monkey causes the deprived eye not to respond when the animal reaches adulthood.

The effect of visual deprivation can be illustrated graphically by an **ocular dominance histogram,** which portrays the strength of response of a brain neuron to stimuli presented to either the left or the right eye. Normally, most cortical neurons (except those in layer IV) are excited equally by light presented to either eye (Figure 7.19a).

Few neurons are activated solely by inputs to one eye. Monocular deprivation early in development, by keeping one eye closed or covered, results in a striking shift from the normal graph; most cortical neurons respond only to input from the nondeprived eye (Figure 7.19b). In cats the susceptible period for this effect is the first 4 months of life. In rhesus monkeys the sensitive period extends to age 6 months. After these ages visual deprivation has little effect.

During early development, synapses are rearranged in the visual cortex, and axons representing input from each eye "compete" for synaptic places. Active, effective synapses predominate over inactive synapses. Thus if one eye is "silenced," synapses carrying information from that eye are retracted while synapses derived from the other eye are maintained. Donald O. Hebb (1949) proposed that effective synapses (those that successfully drive the postsynaptic cell) might grow stronger at the expense of ineffective synapses. Thus, synapses that grow stronger or weaker depending on their effectiveness in driving their target cell are known as **Hebbian synapses** (Figure 7.20). In Chapter 18 we will see that the maintenance of active synapses and retraction of inactive synapses may also play a role in learning and memory.

Researchers offer a similar explanation for amblyopia produced by misalignment of the eyes. Hubel and Wiesel (1965) produced an animal replica of this human condition by surgically causing the eyes to diverge in kittens. The ocular dominance his-

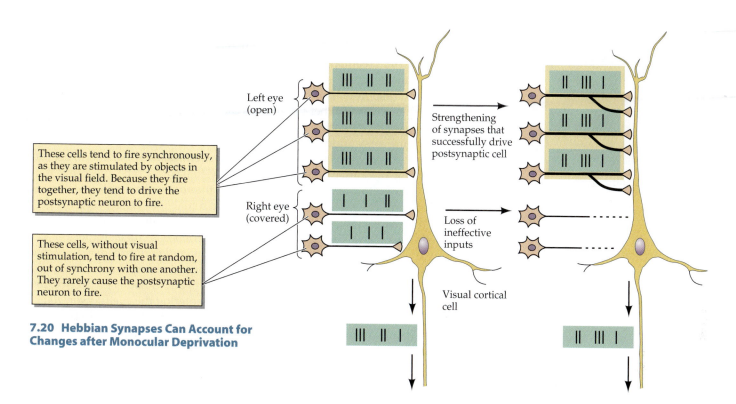

These cells tend to fire synchronously, as they are stimulated by objects in the visual field. Because they fire together, they tend to drive the postsynaptic neuron to fire.

Left eye (open)

Strengthening of synapses that successfully drive postsynaptic cell

These cells, without visual stimulation, tend to fire at random, out of synchrony with one another. They rarely cause the postsynaptic neuron to fire.

Right eye (covered)

Loss of ineffective inputs

Visual cortical cell

7.20 Hebbian Synapses Can Account for Changes after Monocular Deprivation

togram of these animals reveals that the normal binocular sensitivity of visual cortical cells is greatly reduced (see Figure 7.19c). A much larger proportion of visual cortical cells are excited by stimulation of either the right or the left eye in these animals than in control animals. The reason for this effect is that, after surgery, visual stimuli falling on the misaligned eyes no longer provide simultaneous, convergent input to the cells of the visual cortex.

The competitive interaction between the eyes results in a paradox: Brief deprivation of *both* eyes can have less of an effect on neuronal connections than an equal period of deprivation to only one eye has (compare panels *a, b,* and *d* in Figure 7.19). Presumably the binocular deprivation keeps both eyes on an equal footing for stimulating cells in the visual cortex, so the predominantly binocular input to the cortical cells is retained.

One popular notion is that neurotrophic factors may be playing a role in experience-driven synapse rearrangement. For example, if the postsynaptic cells are making a limited supply of a neurotrophic factor, and if active synapses take up more of the factor than inactive synapses do, then perhaps the inactive axons retract for lack of neurotrophic factor. If this were the case, then providing all the presynaptic axon terminals with excess neurotrophic factor might delay synapse rearrangement in response to manipulations of visual experience.

NEURAL PLASTICITY

Indeed, Cabelli et al. (1995) found that infusions of BDNF (neurotrophin-2) or neurotrophin-4 into the visual cortex of kittens inhibited the loss of synapses. Neither NGF (neurotrophin-1) nor neurotrophin-3 had this effect. Conversely, interfering with the action of BDNF causes the dendrites of neurons in visual cortex to shrink (McAllister et al., 1997), suggesting that this neurotrophic factor normally favors the retention of synapses. So perhaps presynaptic uptake of neurotrophic factors depends on synaptic activity, such that ineffective synapses wither for lack of neurotrophic factor.

Early exposure to visual patterns helps fine-tune connections in the visual system

At birth the visual cortex is quite immature, and most synapses have yet to form. Experiments in which visual patterns are manipulated early in an animal's life have

Colin Blakemore

used patterns such as horizontal or vertical lines (Blakemore, 1976), a field of such stripes seen through goggles (H. V. B. Hirsch and Spinelli, 1971), or small spots of light (Pettigrew and Freeman, 1973). In each case, experimenters try to ensure that the animals are exposed to visual stimuli of only one particular type. Then the animals' behavioral responses and/or their brain responses to the visual stimuli are recorded. The question is whether the animals can see stimuli to which they were exposed during a sensitive developmental period better than they see novel stimuli.

Although controversial (Movshon and van Sluyters, 1981), the results of such experiments suggest that visual experiences during the critical early periods of life can indeed modify the responses of nerve cells in the visual cortex. The effects are subtler than those seen with complete deprivation, but the ability of animals to detect visual stimuli of a particular, general pattern (e.g., horizontal lines versus vertical lines) depends on their exposure to such visual patterns during postnatal development.

Human disorders have also proven that early experience is crucial for vision. Babies born with cataracts (cloudy lenses) in industrialized countries usually have them removed a few months after birth and will have good vision. But if such a child grows up with the cataracts in place, removing them in adulthood is ineffective; the person never learns to make use of the information entering the eye (Bower, 2003). Early visual experience is known to be especially crucial for learning to perceive faces, because infants with cataracts that occlude vision for just the first 6 months of life are impaired at recognizing faces even 9 years later (Le Grand et al., 2001). These experience-dependent effects are probably mediated by synapse rearrangement within the visual cortex (Katz and Shatz, 1996; Ruthazer et al., 2003).

Why does Michael May, whom we met at the start of the chapter, have such poor vision despite the clear images entering his eye? Had the accident happened to him as an adult, the surgery to let light back into his eye would have restored normal vision. But like a kitten fitted with opaque contact lenses, Michael was deprived of form vision—in his case for over 40 years. Because this deprivation began when he was a child, synaptic connections within his visual cortex were not strengthened by the patterns of light moving across the retina. In the absence of patterned stimulation, synapses between the eye and the brain languished and disappeared.

In some sense, Michael was lucky that his blindness came as late as it did—he had normal form vision for the first three and a half years of his life. That stimulation may have been sufficient to maintain some synapses that would otherwise have been lost. These residual synapses are probably what allow him to make any sense whatsoever of his vision. Michael continues to learn to use sight more and more, even keeping a blog (Web log) of his experiences (http://www.senderogroup.com/mikejournal.htm). He loves having sight, but as he himself says, usually he has to "guess" what he's seeing.

One demonstration shows how visual experience in everyday life can affect our perception. In Figure 7.21, the numbers and letters along the bottom line appear more slanted than those above, but in fact the slant is the same. One theory is that our experience reading digital clock readouts and italic fonts may tune synapses in our brain to perceive them as more upright than they really are—an effect lost if the figures are backward (Whitaker and McGraw, 2000).

Experiences in other senses also affect neural development

Development of the brain also can be affected by early manipulation of nonvisual sensory inputs—a mouse's whiskers, for example. Thomas Woolsey and collaborators (T. A. Woolsey and Wann, 1976; T. A. Woolsey et al., 1981) found a unique clustering of nerve cells in a region of the cerebral cortex of the mouse that receives input from the whiskers.

The arrangement of whiskers on the skin is distinctive, and whiskers are arrayed similarly in all animals of the same species. The region of the cortex in which the whiskers are represented contains clusters of cells, called **whisker barrels** because their arrangement makes them look like barrels squeezed together in the cortex. The

Michael May

layout of these cortical barrels corresponds to the map of the whiskers. Only whiskers that continue to send neural impulses to the brain get to keep their place in the cortex (Figure 7.22).

There are many other examples of early experience altering brain sensory systems. For instance, restricting salt intake in developing rats alters their later sensitivity to salty fluids (Thaw et al., 2000). And closing one nostril in newborn rats prevents the developing olfactory receptors on that side from being stimulated by odors, causing the olfactory bulb on that side of the brain to be reduced by about 25% (Brunjes, 1994).

Maldevelopment of the Human Brain Impairs Behavior

Because the processes that guide development of the human brain are so varied and complex, there are many ways in which they can go wrong. For example, children who experience complicated delivery at birth, when a transient lack of oxygen (**hypoxia**) may affect the brain, are at greater risk for mental retardation than are children who have a problem-free birth. The many factors that control brain development—those that govern cell proliferation, migration, and differentiation, as well as

7.21 Which Line Is More Slanted? The numbers and letters on the lower line look more slanted than those on the upper line, but in fact the characters on the two lines are equally slanted. If you look at them in a mirror, the upper line will look more slanted. Is this optical illusion a result of the modification of synapses caused by a lifetime of looking at digital clocks and italic font?

Thomas Woolsey

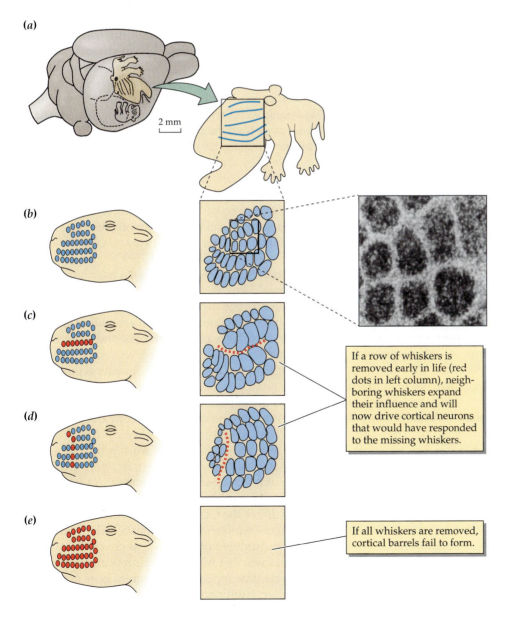

If a row of whiskers is removed early in life (red dots in left column), neighboring whiskers expand their influence and will now drive cortical neurons that would have responded to the missing whiskers.

If all whiskers are removed, cortical barrels fail to form.

7.22 Cortical Barrels in Mice (*a*) Representation of the body surface in mouse somatosensory cortex, showing the location of whisker barrels. (*b*) Each barrel (inset) receives its input from a single whisker on the opposite side of the mouse's snout. (*c, d*) If a row or column of whiskers is destroyed shortly after birth (as indicated by the red dots), the corresponding barrels in the cerebral cortex later will be missing and the adjoining barrels enlarged. (*e*) If all whiskers are destroyed, the entire group of barrels will disappear. (Part *a* and photograph courtesy of T. A. Woolsey; *b–e* after Cowan, 1979.)

the formation of synapses—are subject to failures that can have catastrophic consequences for adaptive behavior.

Some genetic disorders have widespread effects on the nervous system

Many genetic disorders affect metabolism and profoundly affect the developing brain. In this category are 100 to 200 different disorders involving disturbances in the metabolism of proteins, carbohydrates, or lipids. Characteristically, the genetic defect is the absence of a particular enzyme that controls a critical biochemical step in the synthesis or breakdown of a vital body product.

An example of the first type of deficit is **phenylketonuria** (**PKU**), a recessive hereditary disorder of protein metabolism that at one time resulted in many people with mental retardation. One out of 50 persons is a carrier; one in 10,000 births produces an affected victim. The basic defect is the absence of an enzyme necessary to metabolize phenylalanine, an amino acid that is present in many foods. The brain is damaged by an enormous buildup of phenylalanine.

The discovery of PKU marked the first time that an inborn error of metabolism was associated with mental retardation. Screening methods assess the level of phenylalanine in children a few days after birth. Early detection is important because brain impairment can be prevented by a diet low in phenylalanine. Such dietary control of phenylketonuria is critical during the early years of life, especially before age 2; after that, diet can be relaxed somewhat. Note this important example of the interaction of genes and the environment in PKU: The dysfunctional gene causes mental retardation *only* in the presence of phenylalanine. Reducing phenylalanine consumption reduces or prevents this effect of the gene.

A common form of cognitive disorder resulting from a chromosomal abnormality is **Down syndrome** (Figure 7.23*a*). People with Down syndrome usually have an extra chromosome 21, for a total of three rather than the typical two copies. This disorder is strikingly related to the age of the mother at the time of conception: For women over 45 years of age, the chance of having a baby with Down syndrome is nearly 1 in 40 (Karp, 1976). The behavioral dysfunctions are quite varied. Most individuals who have Down syndrome have a very low IQ, but some rare individuals attain an IQ as high as 80. Brain abnormalities in Down syndrome also vary. The cerebral cortex of patients with Down syndrome show abnormal formation of dendritic spines. A mouse model that involves an extra chromosome results in structural changes that appear analogous to Down syndrome in humans (C. J. Epstein, 1986; Siarey et al., 1997).

It is very likely that the most frequent cause of inherited mental retardation is the condition **fragile X syndrome** (Figure 7.23*b*). At the end of the long arm of the X chromosome is a site that seems fragile—prone to breaking because the DNA there is unstable (Yu et al., 1991). Persons with this abnormality have a modified facial appearance, including elongation of the face, large prominent ears, and a prominent chin. A wide range of cognitive impairments—from mild to severe retardation—are associated with this syndrome (Baumgardner et al., 1994). The disorder is more common in males than in females.

The molecular basis of fragile X syndrome provided a surprise for geneticists because it demonstrated that we don't always pass on a faithful copy of our DNA to our offspring. The fragile site in the DNA consists of three nucleotides (CGG; see the appendix for a review of nucleotides) repeated over and over. Most people have only 6 to 50 of these **trinucleotide repeats** at this site (Laxova, 1994). But during the production of sperm or eggs, the number of repeats sometimes changes, so a father who has only 50 trinucleotide repeats may provide 100 repeats to his daughter.

People who have between 51 and 200 of the CGG repeats are themselves unaffected, but any of their children who receive more than 200 repeats will display fragile X syndrome. No one knows why the number of repeats changes from one generation to the next, or what determines whether more or fewer repeats will appear (Paulson and Fischbeck, 1996). Trinucleotide repeats of a different gene are also at the heart of another behavioral disorder: Huntington's disease (see Chapter 11).

GENES AND BEHAVIOR

(*a*)

(*b*)

7.23 Atypical Chromosomes Have Widespread Effects   (*a*) A young woman with Down syndrome. (*b*) A young man with fragile X syndrome.

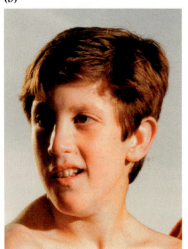

Exposure to drugs during pregnancy can impair neural development

Even in the protected environment of the womb, the embryo and fetus are not immune to outside influence; what is taking place in the mother's body directly affects them. Maternal conditions such as viral infection, exposure to drugs, and malnutrition are especially likely to result in developmental disorders in the unborn child. Concern with the maternal environment as a determinant of brain development spawned the field of **behavioral teratology** (*teratology*—from the Greek *teras*, "monster"—is the study of malformations). Investigators in this field are especially concerned with the pathological effects of drugs ingested during pregnancy.

There is a long history of concern about alcohol and pregnancy, dating back to classical times. Aristotle (cited in Abel, 1982) warned that "foolish, drunken … women … bring forth children like unto themselves, morose and languid." By now, the wisdom of this observation (if not the misogyny) is well supported by abundant research. About 40% of children born to alcoholic mothers show a distinctive profile of anatomical, physiological, and behavioral impairments known as **fetal alcohol syndrome** (**FAS**) (Abel, 1984; Colangelo and Jones, 1982).

Prominent anatomical effects of fetal exposure to alcohol include distinctive changes in facial features (e.g., a sunken nasal bridge and altered shape of the nose and eyelids) and stunted growth. Few of these children catch up in the years following birth. The most common problem associated with FAS is mental retardation, which varies in severity. No alcohol threshold has yet been established for this syndrome, but it can occur with relatively moderate intake during pregnancy.

In addition to mental retardation, children with fetal alcohol syndrome show other neurological abnormalities, such as hyperactivity, irritability, tremulousness, and other signs of motor instability. In some cases, they lack a corpus callosum (Figure 7.24). Even children of alcoholic mothers who do not show physical symptoms and are therefore not diagnosed as having FAS often have neurophysiological impairments (Mattson et al., 1998). This syndrome may not be restricted to alcohol; heavy use of marijuana seems to exert a similar effect on fetal growth and development (Hingson et al., 1982).

**CLINICAL
ISSUE**

Autism is a disorder of social competence

Autism is a life-long developmental disorder characterized by impaired social interactions and language, and a narrow range of interests and activities. Children with autism may or may not appear mentally deficient, but they tend to perseverate (such as by continually nodding the head or making stereotyped finger movements), and they have a difficult time judging other people's thoughts or feelings. Autism seems to represent a profound disorder in the ability to form and develop social relations. When shown photos of the faces of family members, autistic indi-

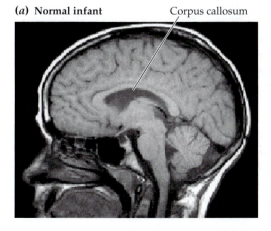

(*a*) **Normal infant**   Corpus callosum

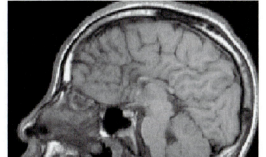

(*b*) **Infant with FAS**

7.24 Abnormal Brain Development Associated with Fetal Alcohol Syndrome   (*a*) The brain of a normal infant. (*b*) The brain of an infant of the same age with FAS. The brain of the infant with FAS shows microcephaly (abnormal smallness), fewer cerebral cortical gyri, and the absence of a corpus callosum connecting the two hemispheres. (Courtesy of E. Riley.)

(a) Control

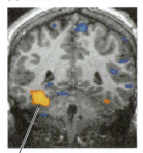

Fusiform gyrus

(b) Patient with autism

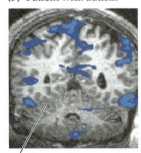

Fusiform gyrus

7.25 Organization of Facial Recognition (*a*) Control subjects display an activation (yellow) of the fusiform gyrus when viewing photos of family members. (*b*) Individuals with autism display a different pattern of brain response, which may contribute to their reduced social skills. (After Pierce et al., 2001; courtesy of Karen Pierce.)

viduals reveal a pattern of brain activation quite different from that exhibited by controls (Figure 7.25), suggesting a very different brain organization for the fundamental social skill of recognizing others. Autism is a heartbreaking disorder in which apparently normal toddlers begin regressing, losing language skills, and withdrawing from family interaction.

The disorder is found in about one to two children per thousand, is much more common in males than females, and has a strong heritability (Rapin and Katzman, 1998; Rodier, 2000). Unfortunately, at one time Freudian psychiatrist Bruno Bettelheim blamed autism on improper parental behavior, such as a "cold, distant" mother, but that idea has been almost universally discounted, and it is clear now that Bettelheim fabricated many of his case studies (Pollak, 1997).

Several structural differences between the brains of people with autism and controls have been reported, including a reduction in the size of the corpus callosum and certain cerebellar regions (Egaas et al., 1995). There is no cure, but many children with autism are helped a great deal by highly structured training in language and behavior. Despite a TV report that an autistic child benefited from treatment with a gastrointestinal hormone (secretin), placebo-controlled studies found the treatment ineffective (Sandler et al., 1999).

Autism may represent one end of a spectrum, because **Asperger's syndrome** is also characterized by difficulties in understanding social interactions, yet children with Asperger's do not lose their language capabilities, and they may indeed be quite articulate. They have difficulty interpreting other people's emotional facial expressions, but they tend to be very good at classifying objects and noting details (Baron-Cohen, 2003). Not surprisingly, individuals with Asperger's tend to become scientists and engineers. The number of children diagnosed with autism and Asperger's is increasing steadily, but no one knows why. One current hypothesis is that the mercury in childhood vaccines may act as a neurotoxin that increases the probability of autism disorders, but most studies find no evidence of such a link (Madsen et al., 2003).

The Brain Continues to Change As We Grow Older

The passage of time brings us an accumulation of joys and sorrows—perhaps riches and fame—and a progressive decline in many of our abilities. Although slower responses seem inevitable with aging, many of our cognitive abilities show little change during the adult years, until we reach an advanced age. What happens to brain structure from adolescence to the day when we all become a little forgetful and walk more hesitantly?

Changes in the structure of the brain with aging can be viewed at different levels, from subcellular structures to overall brain morphology. Brain weight declines with age, but some people have questioned the relevance of aging to these weight changes because it is hard to distinguish changes due to aging from changes that arise from disease states shortly before death.

An excellent study that eliminated such confounding factors showed that changes are very small up to the age of 45, after which time the weight of the brain begins to decline significantly (see Figure 7.1). The course of these changes is the same for men and women, even though women generally live 7 to 10 years longer than men. Data also emphasize that aging is a variable state. Declines are barely evident in many people, but they are exaggerated in some. This variability highlights the genetic contribution to aging and reinforces the idea that if you want to live long, choose parents and grandparents who lived a long time.

Another measure used in studies of brain aging is the number of neural and glial cells in particular volumes of tissue. Investigators map specific regions and count the number of cells in various areas, using tissue taken from people who have died at different ages. These studies suggest that cell changes begin as early as the third decade of life and are specific to particular regions. Even more noticeable than the decrease in the number of cells is the loss of synaptic connections, which is especially prominent in the frontal cortical regions.

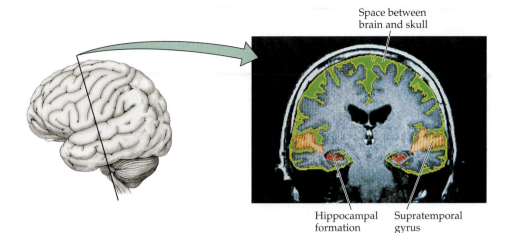

Space between
brain and skull

Hippocampal   Supratemporal
formation   gyrus

7.26 Hippocampal Shrinkage Correlates with Memory Decline in Aging
(*Left*) MRI images that illustrate the variables tested for correlation with memory decline in normal aged people are taken from the plane of section shown here. (*Right*) The hippocampal formation is shaded red, the supratemporal gyrus orange, and the space between brain and skull yellow-green. Only shrinkage of the hippocampal formation correlated with memory decline. (From Golomb et al., 1994; MRI courtesy of James Golomb.)

Memory impairment correlates with hippocampal shrinkage during aging

In a study of healthy and cognitively normal people, aged 55 to 87, investigators asked whether mild impairment in memory is specifically related to reduction in size of the hippocampal formation (HF) or is better explained by generalized shrinkage of brain tissue (Golomb et al., 1994). (In Chapter 18 we'll see that the hippocampus is implicated in memory.) Volunteers took a series of memory tests and were scored for both immediate recall and delayed recall. A series of ten coronal MRI images for each subject was measured for three variables (Figure 7.26): (1) volume of the HF; (2) volume of the supratemporal gyrus, a region that is close to the HF and is known to shrink with age but has not been implicated in memory; and (3) volume of the subarachnoid cerebrospinal fluid (i.e., the fluid-filled space between the interior of the skull and the surface of the brain), which yields a measure of overall shrinkage of the brain. Immediate memory showed very little decline with age, but delayed memory did decline. When effects of sex, age, IQ, and overall brain atrophy were eliminated statistically, HF volume was the only brain measure that correlated significantly with the delayed memory score.

Two regions of the motor system show how different the effects of aging can be. In the motor cortex a type of large neuron—the Betz cell—starts to decline in number by about age 50, and by the time a person reaches age 80, many of these cells have shriveled away (M. E. Scheibel et al., 1977). In contrast, other cells involved in motor circuitry—for example, those in an area of the brainstem called the *inferior olive*—remain about the same in number through at least eight decades of life.

PET scans of elderly people add a new perspective to aging-related changes. Studies of normal cases reveal that cerebral metabolism remains almost constant. This stability is in marked contrast to the decline of cerebral metabolism in Alzheimer's disease (see Figure 2.16), which we will consider next.

Alzheimer's disease is associated with a decline in cerebral metabolism

Since 1900, the population of elderly people in the United States has increased dramatically. Most people reaching this age lead happy, productive lives, although at a slower pace than they did in their earlier years. In a growing number of elderly people, however, age has brought a particular agony: the disorder called **Alzheimer's disease,** named after the neurologist who first described a type of **dementia** (drastic failure of cognitive ability, including memory failure and loss of orientation) appearing before the age of 65. Alzheimer's disease is sometimes called *senile dementia.*

Over 4 million Americans suffer from Alzheimer's disease, and the progressive aging of our population means that these ranks will continue to swell. This disorder is found worldwide with almost no geographic differences. The frequency of Alzheimer's increases with aging up to age 85 to 90 (Rocca et al., 1991), but people who reach that age *without* symptoms become increasingly *less* likely ever to develop them (Breitner et al., 1999).

**Alois Alzheimer
(1864–1915)**

(a) Normal   (b) Person with
             Alzheimer's

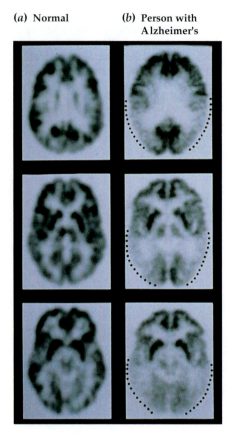

7.27 Patients with Alzheimer's Show Reduced Activity in the Brain When compared with normal elderly subjects (a), patients with Alzheimer's disease (b) show less-widespread brain activation in PET scans. The dots in the images in part b highlight regions where this difference is particularly apparent. (Courtesy of John Mazziotta.)

GENES AND BEHAVIOR

This last finding indicates that Alzheimer's is in fact a disease, and not simply the result of wear and tear in the brain. The fact that remaining physically and mentally active seems to reduce the risk of developing Alzheimer's disease (R. S. Wilson and Bennett, 2003) also refutes the notion that brains simply "wear out" with age. Extensive use of the brain makes Alzheimer's *less* likely.

Alzheimer's disease begins as a loss of memory of recent events. Eventually this memory impairment becomes all-encompassing, so extensive that Alzheimer's patients cannot maintain any form of conversation because both the context and prior information are rapidly lost. They cannot answer simple questions such as, What year is it? Who is the president of the United States? or Where are you now? Cognitive decline is progressive and relentless. In time, patients become disoriented and easily lose themselves in familiar surroundings.

Observations of whole brains of patients with Alzheimer's reveal striking cortical atrophy, especially in the frontal, temporal, and parietal areas. PET scans following the administration of a radioactive form of glucose show marked reduction of metabolism in posterior parietal cortex and some portions of the temporal lobe (Figure 7.27) (N. L. Foster et al., 1984). PET studies of the brain also indicate a correlation between the decline of dopamine receptors and memory in normal aging (Kaasinen and Rinne, 2002). The loss of dopamine receptors is especially prominent in the hippocampus of patients with Alzheimer's (Kemppainen et al., 2003).

The brains of individuals suffering from Alzheimer's reveal three characteristic changes at the cellular level (Figure 7.28):

1. Strange patches of degenerating axon terminals and dendrites, termed **senile plaques**, appear in frontal and temporoparietal cortex, the hippocampus, and associated limbic system sites. The plaques are formed by the buildup of a substance called β-**amyloid** (Selkoe, 1991), so they are sometimes called *amyloid plaques.*

2. Some cells show abnormalities called **neurofibrillary tangles,** which are abnormal whorls of neurofilaments, including a protein called **tau,** that form a tangled array in the cell. The number of senile plaques is directly related to the magnitude of cognitive impairment. Because neurofibrillary tangles appear in other brain disorders, in Alzheimer's they are probably a secondary response to amyloid plaques.

3. These degenerative events cause the basal forebrain nuclei to disappear in Alzheimer's patients, either because the cells die or because they stop producing their transmitter, acetylcholine. The latter possibility is more likely, because providing these neurons with NGF restores their cholinergic characteristics in aged monkeys (D. E. Smith et al., 1999).

If amyloid plaques are the primary cause of Alzheimer's disease, what causes the buildup of β-amyloid? **Amyloid precursor protein (APP)** is cleaved by two enzymes—β-**secretase** and **presenilin**—to form extracellular β-amyloid that builds up. Another enzyme, **apolipoproteinE (ApoE)**, works to break down β-amyloid. Mutations in each of the genes that produce these proteins have been associated with Alzheimer's disease, with presenilin mutations by far the most common cause (Selkoe, 1999).

This scenario, depicted in Figure 7.29, suggests several treatment strategies, such as injection of antibodies that will bind β-amyloid and slow the formation of plaques (Monsonego and Weiner, 2003). Chemicals that temporarily bind to amyloid plaques may permit the diagnosis of Alzheimer's disease *before* behavioral symptoms appear. In PET scans, the radioactively labeled chemicals accumulate over plaque sites to reveal whether buildup has begun (Bacskai et al., 2003).

Two Timescales Are Needed to Describe Brain Development

In the introduction to this part of the book, we warned that Chapters 6 and 7 would present two very different timescales for the development of brain and behavior—the eons of evolution versus the days and years of ontogeny. These different time-

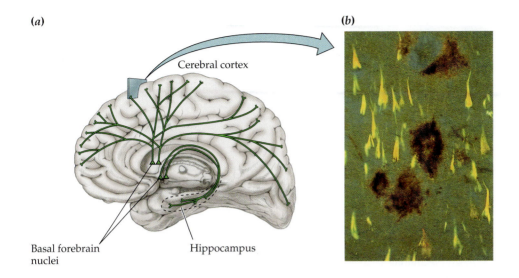

(a)

Cerebral cortex

Basal forebrain nuclei

Hippocampus

(b)

7.28 Patients with Alzheimer's Show Structural Changes in the Brain
(a) This representation of the brain shows the location of the basal forebrain nuclei and the distribution of their axons, which use acetylcholine as a neurotransmitter. These cells seem to disappear in Alzheimer's patients. (b) Neurofibrillary tangles (the flame-shaped objects) and senile plaques (the darkly stained clusters) are visible in this micrograph of the cerebral cortex of an aged patient with Alzheimer's. (From Roses, 1995; micrograph courtesy of Gary W. Van Hoesen.)

scales are analogous to the different but equally essential contributions of an architect and a contractor, respectively, in building a house.

In preparing his plans, the architect calls on a long history of human knowledge about structures that meet basic human needs. These plans incorporate hard-won information gathered over the centuries. Similarly, our genes carry a basic plan that has worked for millions of generations (absolutely every one of your millions of ancestors managed to reproduce!).

The contractor's perspective is more like that of a developing individual. He must use the general plans of the architect to construct a particular house here and now. As he builds, the contractor's judgment and interpretation are necessary, so two houses built from the same blueprints will not be identical, just as two monozygotic twins will show differences. In fact, even the best architects rely on contractors to adjust and improvise to make their plans work. Similarly, the information in our genome relies on extrinsic factors such as experience to determine the fine wiring of the nervous system.

Long ago, well before the common ancestor of all the vertebrates emerged, developing animals began relying on cell–cell interactions to adjust the fate of individual cells on the basis of their position in the organism as a whole. Once this strategy was adopted, it was only a matter of time before the fate of some neurons would be

7.29 One Hypothesis of Alzheimer's Disease

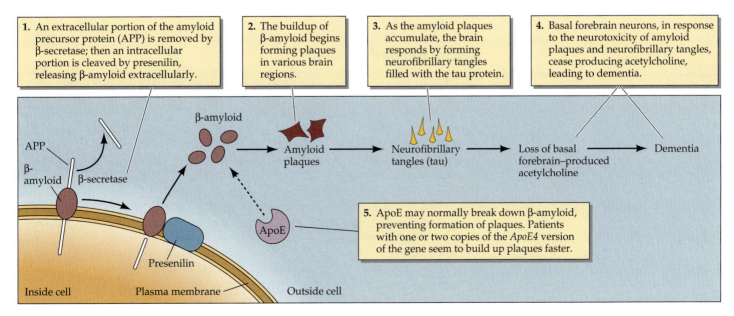

1. An extracellular portion of the amyloid precursor protein (APP) is removed by β-secretase; then an intracellular portion is cleaved by presenilin, releasing β-amyloid extracellularly.

2. The buildup of β-amyloid begins forming plaques in various brain regions.

3. As the amyloid plaques accumulate, the brain responds by forming neurofibrillary tangles filled with the tau protein.

4. Basal forebrain neurons, in response to the neurotoxicity of amyloid plaques and neurofibrillary tangles, cease producing acetylcholine, leading to dementia.

β-amyloid

APP

β-amyloid

β-secretase

Amyloid plaques → Neurofibrillary tangles (tau) → Loss of basal forebrain–produced acetylcholine → Dementia

ApoE

5. ApoE may normally break down β-amyloid, preventing formation of plaques. Patients with one or two copies of the *ApoE4* version of the gene seem to build up plaques faster.

Presenilin

Inside cell   Plasma membrane   Outside cell

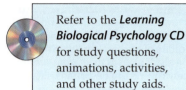

Refer to the *Learning Biological Psychology CD* for study questions, animations, activities, and other study aids.

affected by neural activity. So neural activity began determining which synapses and neurons would be retained and which would be eliminated. Eventually, it would be the neural activity derived from sensory neurons—experience itself—that would affect these decisions. That is how we humans came to have a nervous system so malleable, so plastic, that we can write, read, and think about our own origins.

Summary

1. Early embryological events in the formation of the nervous system include a sequence of six cellular processes: (1) neurogenesis, (2) cell migration, (3) cell differentiation, (4) synaptogenesis, (5) neuronal cell death, and (6) synapse rearrangement.

2. Fetal and postnatal changes in the brain include the myelination of axons by glial cells and the development of dendrites and synapses by neurons. Although in humans most neurons are present at birth, most synapses develop after birth and continue developing into adulthood.

3. In simple animals such as the nematode *Caenorhabditis elegans,* neural pathways and synapses form according to an innate, genetic plan that specifies the precise relations between growing axons and particular target cells. In more complicated animals, however—including all vertebrates—genes do not exert such rigid control on specific neural connections.

4. Among the many determinants of brain development are (1) genetic information and (2) a multitude of extrinsic factors, such as neurotrophic factors, nutrition, and experience.

5. Experience affects the growth and development of the nervous system. Experience can induce and modulate the formation of synapses, maintain synapses that are already formed, or determine which neurons and synapses will survive and which will be eliminated.

6. Maldevelopment of the brain can occur as a result of genetically controlled disorders. Some are metabolic disorders, such as phenylketonuria; others, such as Down syndrome, are related to disorders of chromosomes.

7. Impairments of fetal development that lead to mental retardation can be caused by the use of drugs such as alcohol or marijuana during pregnancy.

8. Autism appears to be a disruption in the development of cognitive processing about social interactions, which impairs development of language and other behaviors.

9. The brain continues to change throughout life. Old age is accompanied by the loss of neurons and synaptic connections in some regions of the brain. In some people the changes are more severe than in others; pathological changes characterize the condition known as Alzheimer's disease.

10. Alzheimer's seems to be caused by a buildup of β-amyloid, causing degenerative plaques and tangles through much of the cortex. Several genes, such as *presenilin* and *ApoE,* influence the rate of amyloid accumulation and therefore the risk of Alzheimer's.

Recommended Reading

Gilbert, S. F. (2003). *Developmental biology* (7th ed.). Sunderland, MA: Sinauer Associates.

Marcus, G. (2004). *The birth of the mind: How a tiny number of genes creates the complexities of human thought.* New York: Basic Books.

Nelson, C. A., and Luciana, M. (2001). *Handbook of developmental cognitive neuroscience.* Cambridge, MA: MIT Press.

Purves, D., and Lichtman, J. W. (1985). *Principles of neural development.* Sunderland, MA: Sinauer Associates.

Ridley, M. (2003). *Nature via nurture: Genes, experience and what makes us human.* New York: HarperCollins.

Sanes, D. H., Reh, T. A., and Harris, W. A. (2000). *Development of the nervous system.* San Diego, CA: Academic Press.

III Perception and Action

*L*ight from the sun warms our skin and stimulates our eyes. A chorus of sounds, ranging from the songs of insects to the hearty performances of opera singers, stimulates our ears. Winds bend the hairs on our skin and carry pleasant or unpleasant odors. The food we eat affects receptors in the mouth, the stomach, and the brain. All about us a wide range of energies and substances excites our senses and supplies our brains with a vast array of information about external and internal happenings.

The success of any animal—including humans—in dealing with the tasks of survival depends on its ability to construct reliable representations of the physical characteristics of its environment. In most cases, however, sensory systems are not slavish, passive copiers and reflectors of impinging stimuli—quite the contrary. Evolutionary success calls for far more selective action. For any species, sensory systems construct only partial and selective portraits of the world.

Sensory inputs to the brain do not merely provide "pictures in the head"; they often incite the individual to act. Consider the simple case of a sound that occurs suddenly: Our eyes almost automatically turn toward the source of the sound. Other movements are not directly triggered by sensory events, but are internally driven, with sensory inputs only modulating a complete motor program such as playing the piano. How information is processed in perceptual systems (the topic addressed in Chapters 8 through 10) and then used to choose particular motor responses (Chapter 11) is our theme in Part 3.

Sandra Dionisi, *Three Heads Seeing and Thinking*

8

General Principles of Sensory Processing, Touch, and Pain

What's Hot? What's Not?

It was a lovely warm summer evening, perfect for an after-dinner stroll. It was nice to see the neighbors out puttering in their yards, or sitting on the porch sipping cool drinks. When we came upon a woman in matching yellow shorts and blouse sprinkling something on her flowers, I noticed she was using what looked like a big salt shaker. I thought, "Gee, it's not very smart to put insecticide in a salt shaker. What if someone else in the house sprinkles it on food?"

Thinking I would sidle up to the topic to offer her my sage advice, I stopped to ask, "What are you putting on your flowers? Something to kill aphids?" She smiled and said, "No, it's red chili pepper flakes to keep the deer away." She assured me that her treatment worked. When she sprinkled the pepper flakes on the plants in the

evening, the flowers would be intact in the morning. If she neglected to treat them in the evening, she would find blossoms missing and telltale bite marks on the bushes come dawn. "Why sprinkle every evening? Do the flakes blow away?" I asked. "Well," she said, "the main problem is that tomorrow the birds come and eat up all the pepper seeds, so I have to put some more on in the evening."

So it turned out that she taught me something: Deer hate chili pepper flakes, and birds love them. I was pretty sure I understood why the deer avoid the chili peppers: They contain a chemical called capsaicin *that really burns my mouth when I eat spicy food. But why don't the birds avoid the peppers containing capsaicin? Doesn't it burn their mouths too?*

All around us are many different types of energy that affect us in various ways. Some molecules traveling through the air cause us to note particular odors. We detect waves of compression and expansion of air as sounds. Our abilities to detect, recognize, and appreciate these varied energies depend on the characteristics of sensory systems. These systems include receptors specialized to detect specific energies, as well as the neural pathways of the spinal cord and the brain that receive input from these receptors.

For each species, however, certain features of surrounding energies have become especially significant for adaptive success. For example, the bat darting through the evening sky is specially equipped to detect ultrasonic cries. Most humans, on the other hand, are hardly able to detect such sounds. Some snakes have infrared-sensing organs that enable them to generate an image of heat sources in their surroundings, thus enabling them to locate warm-blooded prey. How do animals, including humans, detect changes in the world around them?

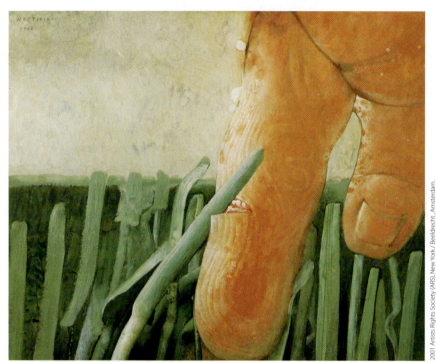

Co Westerik, *Cut by Grass* (1), 1966, oil and tempera on panel, 60 × 75 cm

2001 Artists Rights Society (ARS), New York / Beeldrecht, Amsterdam.

SENSORY PROCESSING

Each species has distinctive windows on the world based on the energy sensitivities of its receptors and on how its nervous system processes information from those receptors. In the first portion of this chapter we consider some of the basic principles of sensory processing. Then we look at how those principles apply to touch and pain sensation.

Sensory Receptor Organs Detect Energy or Substances

All animals have specialized body parts that are particularly sensitive to some forms of energy. These **sensory receptor organs** act as filters of the environment: They detect and respond to some events but not others. We call the event that affected the sensory organ a **stimulus** (plural *stimuli*). Stimuli may be sound waves reaching the ear, light entering the eye, or food touching the tongue. Receptors detect particular kinds of stimuli and convert them into the language of the nervous system: electrical signals. Eventually information from sensory receptor organs enters the brain as a series of action potentials traveling along millions of axons, and our brains must make sense of it all.

Across the animal kingdom, receptor organs offer enormous diversity. For some snakes, detectors of infrared radiation are essential, and several species of fish depend on receptors of electrical energy. Several migratory animals detect Earth's magnetic field (Diebel et al., 2000). These specialized sensors have evolved to detect signals that are crucial for particular environmental niches. Thus, receptor organs reflect strategies for success in particular worlds.

(a)

(b)

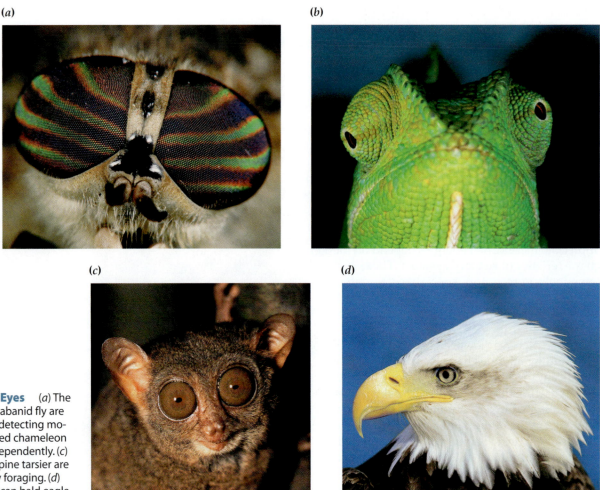

(c)

(d)

8.1 The Variety of Eyes (a) The compound eyes of a tabanid fly are specially adapted for detecting motion. (b) The flap-necked chameleon can move its eyes independently. (c) The eyes of the Philippine tarsier are specialized for nightly foraging. (d) The eyes of the American bald eagle demonstrate high acuity.

**EVOLUTION
AT WORK**

Even if we consider only a single receptor organ such as the eye, a wide array of sizes, shapes, and forms reflects the varying survival needs of different animals (Figure 8.1). Different kinds of energy, such as light and sound, need different receptors to convert them into neural activity, just as taking a photograph requires a camera, not an audiotape recorder.

Table 8.1 classifies sensory systems, identifying the kinds of stimuli detected by sensory receptor organs in each system. An **adequate stimulus** is the type of stimulus for which a given sensory organ is particularly adapted. The adequate stimulus for the eye is photic (light) energy; although mechanical pressure on the eye or an electrical shock can stimulate the retina and produce sensations of light, these are not considered adequate stimuli for the eye.

Sensory systems of particular animals have a restricted range of responsiveness

For any single form of physical energy, the sensory systems of a particular animal are quite selective. For example, humans do not hear sounds in the frequency range above 20,000 cycles per second (hertz, Hz)—a range we call *ultrasonic*. To a bat, however, air vibrations of 50,000 Hz would be sound waves, just as vibrations of 10,000 Hz would. The range of hearing of larger mammals is even lower than that of humans. Figure 8.2 compares the auditory ranges of some animals. In the visual realm, too, some animals can detect stimuli that humans cannot. For example, birds and bees see in the ultraviolet range of light.

TABLE 8.1 *Classification of Sensory Systems*

Type of sensory system	Modality	Adequate stimuli
Mechanical	Touch	Contact with or deformation of body surface
	Hearing	Sound vibrations in air or water
	Vestibular	Head movement and orientation
	Joint	Position and movement
	Muscle	Tension
Photic	Seeing	Visible radiant energy
Thermal	Cold	Decrement of skin temperature
	Warmth	Increment of skin temperature
Chemical	Smell	Odorous substances dissolved in air or water in the nasal cavity
	Taste	Substances in contact with the tongue or other taste receptor
	Common chemical	Changes in CO_2, pH, osmotic pressure
	Vomeronasal	Pheromones in air or water
Electrical	Electroreception	Differences in density of electrical currents

What Type of Stimulus Was That?

We may appreciate the poet who writes, "The dawn came up like thunder," but most of the time we want to know whether a sudden dramatic sensory event was auditory or visual, a touch or a smell. How do we know whether a sudden event was a noise, a flash, or a smack on the head?

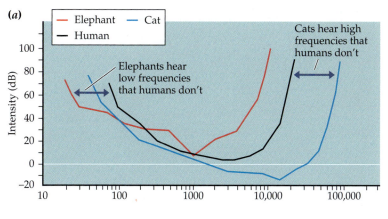

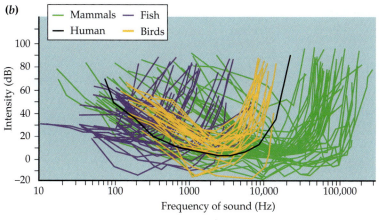

8.2 Do You Hear What I Hear? For comparison, the auditory sensitivity ranges of three mammals (*a*) and of many species of fish, birds, and mammals (*b*) are plotted here together. Note that the species within a class detect a similar range of frequencies. For a discussion of the measurement of sound, see Box 9.1. (After Fay, 1988.)

**Johannes Müller
(1801–1858)**

The physiologist Johannes Müller proposed the doctrine of **specific nerve energies,** which states that the receptors and neural channels for the different senses are independent and each uses a different nerve "energy." For example, no matter how the eye is stimulated—by light or mechanical pressure or by electrical shock—the resulting sensation is always visual. Müller formulated his hypothesis before anyone knew about action potentials. He imagined that different receptor organs might use a different type of energy to communicate with the brain, and that the brain knew which type of stimulus had happened depending on which type of energy was received.

Today, we know that the messages for the different senses—such as seeing, hearing, touching, sensing pain, and sensing temperature—all use the same type of "energy": action potentials. But the brain recognizes the modalities as separate and distinct because each modality sends its action potentials along separate nerve tracts. This is the concept of **labeled lines:** Particular nerve cells are, at the outset, labeled for distinctive sensory experiences. Neural activity in one line signals a sound, activity in another line signals a smell, and activity in other lines signals touch. We can even distinguish different types of touch because some lines signal light touch, others signal vibration, and yet other lines signal stretching of the skin (Figure 8.3).

You can demonstrate this effect right now. If you take your finger and *gently* press on your eyelid while your eye is open, you'll see a dark blob appear on the edge of your field of view (it helps to look at a blank white wall). Of course your skin also feels the touch of your finger, but why do you *see* a blob with your eye? The energy you applied, pressure, affected action potentials coming from your eye. Because your brain labels that line as always carrying visual information, what you *experienced* was a change in light.

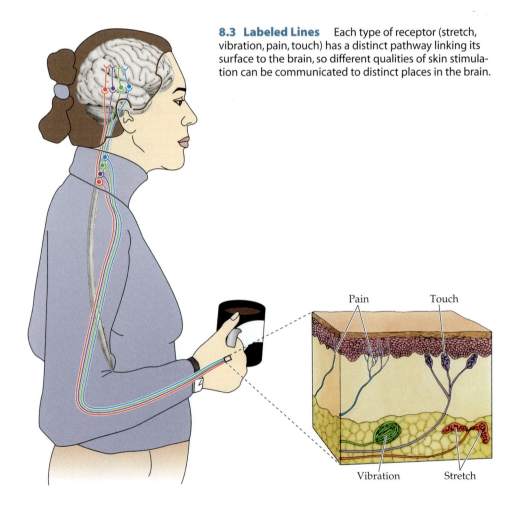

8.3 Labeled Lines   Each type of receptor (stretch, vibration, pain, touch) has a distinct pathway linking its surface to the brain, so different qualities of skin stimulation can be communicated to distinct places in the brain.

Pain   Touch

Vibration   Stretch

Sensory Processing Begins in Receptor Cells

Detection of energy starts with **receptor cells.** A given receptor cell is specialized to detect particular energies or chemicals. Upon exposure to a stimulus, a receptor cell converts the energy into a change in the electrical potential across its membrane. Changing the signal in this way is called **sensory transduction** (devices that convert energy from one form to another are known as *transducers,* and the process is called *transduction*). Receptors are transducers that convert energy around us into neural activity that leads to sensory perception. Figure 8.4 shows some different receptor cells in skin. We will look at these types in more detail later in the chapter.

Some receptor cells have axons to transmit information. Other receptor cells have no axons of their own but stimulate an associated nerve ending, either mechanically or chemically. For example, various kinds of corpuscles are associated with nerve endings in the skin. The eye has specialized receptor cells that convert photic energy (light) into electrical changes that cause neurotransmitter to be released on nearby neurons. The inner ear has specialized hair cells that transduce mechanical energy into electrical signals that stimulate the fibers of the auditory nerve.

The initial stage of sensory processing is a change in electrical potential in receptor cells

The structure of a receptor determines the forms of energy to which it will respond. In all cases the steps between the impact of energy at a receptor cell and the initiation of nerve impulses in a nerve fiber involve local changes of membrane potential; these are referred to as **generator potentials.** (In most instances, the generator potential resembles the excitatory postsynaptic potentials discussed in Chapter 3.) These electrical changes are the necessary and sufficient conditions for generating nerve impulses (action potentials).

One example of the generator potential can be studied in a receptor called the **Pacinian corpuscle** (Loewenstein, 1971). This receptor, which detects vibration, is found throughout the body in skin and muscle. It is made of a nerve fiber (an axon)

8.4 Receptors in Skin
The different functions of several of these receptors are compared in Figure 8.12.

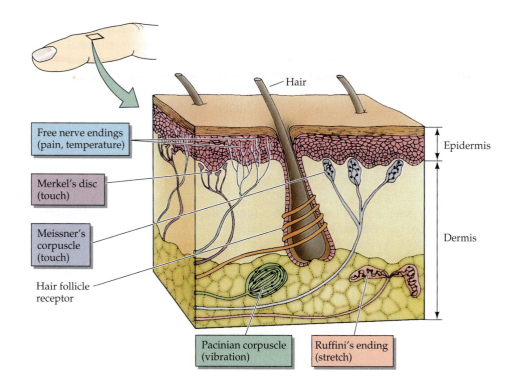

Hair

Free nerve endings (pain, temperature)

Merkel's disc (touch)

Meissner's corpuscle (touch)

Hair follicle receptor

Epidermis

Dermis

Pacinian corpuscle (vibration)

Ruffini's ending (stretch)

8.5 The Structure and Function of the Pacinian Corpuscle

(*a*) The Pacinian corpuscle surrounds an afferent nerve fiber ending. (*b*) When the nerve membrane is at rest, the ion channels are too narrow to admit sodium (Na⁺) ions. Vibration applied to the corpuscle stretches part of the neuronal membrane, enlarging the ion channels and permitting the entry of Na⁺, which initiates an action potential. (*c*) The neuron shows increasing response to stimuli of increasing intensity until it reaches threshold, triggering an action potential.

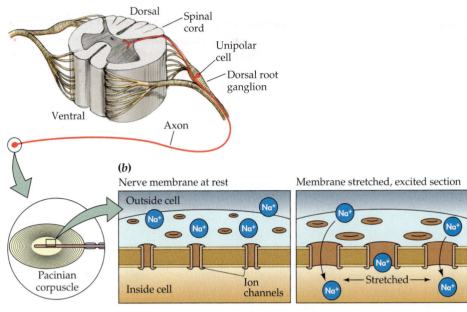

(*a*) **Innervation of a Pacinian corpuscle**

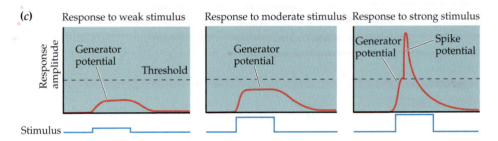

(*c*)

surrounded by a structure that resembles a tiny onion because it has concentric layers of tissue (Figure 8.5*a*).

Mechanical stimuli (in this case vibration) delivered to the corpuscle produce a graded electrical potential with an amplitude that is directly proportional to the strength of the stimulus. When this generator potential reaches sufficient amplitude, the nerve impulse is generated and we say the receptor has reached **threshold.** Careful dissection of the corpuscle, leaving the bared axon intact, shows that this graded potential—the generator potential—is initiated in the axon terminal itself. The sequence of excitatory events is as follows:

1. Mechanical stimulation deforms the corpuscle.
2. This deformation leads to mechanical stretch of the tip of the axon.
3. Stretching the axon enlarges pores in the membrane, allowing sodium ions to enter (Figure 8.5*b*.)
4. When the generator potential reaches threshold amplitude, the axon produces one or more nerve impulses (Figure 8.5*c*).

Sensory Information Processing Is Selective and Analytical

Thinkers in ancient Greece believed that the nerves were tubes through which tiny bits of stimulus objects traveled to the brain, to be analyzed and recognized there. (Imagine the nerves in your tongue sending minuscule chunks of garlic to your brain for analysis.) Even after learning about neural conduction in the twentieth century, many investigators thought that the sensory nerves simply transmitted accurate information about stimulation to the brain centers. Now, however, it is clear that the sensory organs and peripheral sensory pathways convey only limited—*even distorted*—information to the brain. A good deal of selection and analysis takes place in the peripheral sensory pathways. In the discussion that follows we will examine six aspects of sensory processing: coding, adaptation, pathways, suppression, receptive fields, and attention.

Coding: Sensory events are represented by action potentials

Information about the world is represented in the circuits of the nervous system by electrical potentials in cells. We have already considered the first step in this process—the transformation of energy at receptors (i.e., transduction) and the generator potential. But once action potentials have been produced, how do they represent the stimulus? In some manner, electrical events in nerve cells "stand for" (represent) stimuli impinging on an organism. This system of representation is often referred to as **coding**. (A *code* is a set of rules for translating information from one form to another. For example, we can code a message in English by using the set of rules that make up the short dots and long dashes of Morse code.) A limitation of neural codes is that each action potential is always the same size and duration.

Still, sensory information can be encoded by all-or-none action potentials through variation in the number and frequency of the impulses, and in the rhythm in which clusters of impulses occur. Let's examine neural representations of the intensity and location of stimuli.

Stimulus intensity   We respond to sensory stimuli over a wide range of intensities. Furthermore, within this range we can detect small differences of intensity. How are different intensities of a stimulus represented in the nervous system? A single nerve cell could represent the intensity of the stimulus by changing the frequency of nerve impulses transmitted (Figure 8.6a). However, only a limited range of different sensory intensities can be represented in this manner because neurons can fire only so fast.

As we noted in Chapter 3, the maximal rate of firing for a single nerve cell is about 1200 impulses per second, and most sensory fibers do not fire more than a few hundred impulses per second. But the number of differences in intensity that can be detected in vision and hearing is much, much greater than this code can offer. For example, we can see both in very dim light and when the light is 10 billionfold brighter. A single receptor that could change activity only a few hundredfold could never represent that entire range. Therefore, variations in the firing rate of a *single* cell simply cannot account for the full range of intensities we perceive.

Multiple nerve cells acting in a parallel manner provide a broader range for coding the intensity of a stimulus. As the strength of a stimulus increases, new nerve cells are "recruited"; thus, intensity can be represented by the number of active cells. A variant of this idea is the principle of intensity coding called **range fractionation** (Figure 8.6b). According to this hypothesis, a wide range of intensity values can be noted accurately in the nervous system by cells that are "specialists" in particular segments, or *fractions*, of an intensity scale.

8.6 Intensity Coding   (a) Each of the three nerve cells represented here has a different threshold—low, medium, or high—and thus a different rate of firing. Each cell varies its response over a *fraction* of the total *range* of stimulus intensities, an example of range fractionation. (b) Although none of these nerve cells can respond faster than 150 times per second, the sum of all three can vary in response rate from 0 to 450 impulses per second, accurately indicating the intensity of the stimulus.

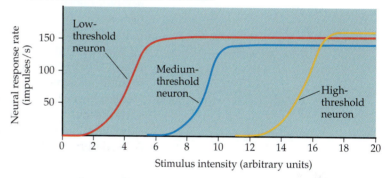

(a) **Response rate versus stimulus intensity for three neurons with different thresholds**

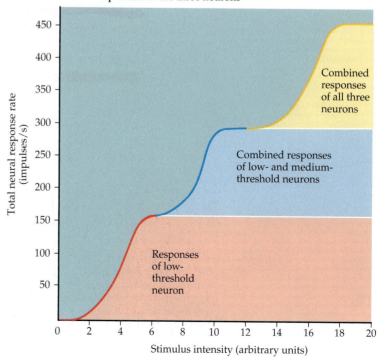

(b) **Simulation of responses for the three neurons**

This mode of stimulus coding requires an array of receptors and nerve cells that differ in threshold, the intensity of stimulus required to cause the sensory neuron to fire or change its rate of firing. Some sensory neurons have a very low threshold (so they are highly sensitive); others have much a higher threshold (so they are less sensitive). Thus, one clue to the intensity of a stimulus is whether it activated only low-threshold receptors, or both low- and high-threshold receptors.

Stimulus location   The position of an object or event, either outside or inside the body, is an important piece of information. Did something just poke my foot or my hand? Some sensory systems reveal this information by the position of excited receptors on the sensory surface. This feature is most evident in the **somatosensory** ("body sensation") system.

You know that an object is on your back if a receptor in the skin there is stimulated. If a receptor on your palm is stimulated, then the object must be there. Each receptor activates pathways that convey unique positional information. The spatial properties of a stimulus are represented by labeled lines that uniquely convey spatial information. Similarly, in the visual system an object's spatial location determines which receptors in the eye are stimulated.

In both the visual and the tactile system, cells at all levels of the nervous system—from the surface sheet of receptors to the cerebral cortex—are arranged in an orderly, maplike manner. The map at each level is not exact, but reflects both position and receptor density. More cells are allocated to the spatial representation of sensitive, densely innervated sites like the skin of the lips or the center of the eye, than to sites that are less sensitive, such as the skin of the back or the periphery of the eye.

With bilateral receptor systems—the two ears or the two nostrils—the relative time of arrival of the stimulus at the two receptors, or the relative intensity, is directly related to the location of the stimulus. For example, the only time when both ears are excited identically is when the sound source is equidistant from the ears, in the median plane of the head. As the stimulus moves to the left or right, receptors of the left and right sides are excited asymmetrically. Specialized nerve cells that receive inputs from both left and right ears to determine where sounds come from are discussed in Chapter 9.

Adaptation: Receptor response can decline even if the stimulus is maintained

Many receptors show progressive loss of response when stimulation is maintained. This process is called **adaptation**. We can demonstrate adaptation by recording nerve impulses in a fiber leading from a receptor. The frequency of nerve impulses progressively declines, even though the stimulus is continued (Figure 8.7). In terms of adaptation, there are two kinds of receptors: **Tonic receptors** show a slow or nonexistent decline in the frequency of nerve impulses as stimulation is maintained. In

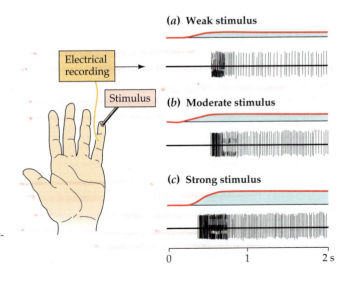

8.7 Sensory Adaptation   The rate of firing of the neuron represented here, the receptive field for which is located on the fifth finger, is rapid when the stimulus—whether weak (*a*), moderate (*b*), or strong (*c*)—is first applied, but then it adapts, slowing to a steady rate. (After Knibestol and Valbo, 1970.)

(*a*) Weak stimulus

Electrical recording

Stimulus

(*b*) Moderate stimulus

(*c*) Strong stimulus

0   1   2 s

other words, these receptors show relatively little adaptation. **Phasic receptors** display adaptation, rapidly decreasing the frequency of nerve impulses when the stimulus is maintained.

Adaptation means that there is a progressive shift in neural activity *away from accurate portrayal* of maintained physical events. Thus the nervous system may fail to register neural activity even though the stimulus continues. Such a striking discrepancy is no accident; sensory systems emphasize *change* in stimuli because changes are more likely to be significant for survival. Sensory adaptation is a form of information suppression that prevents the nervous system from becoming overwhelmed by stimuli that offer very little "news" about the world. For example, your pants may press a hair on your leg continuously, but you're saved from a constant neural barrage from this stimulus by several suppression mechanisms, including adaptation.

The bases of adaptation include both neural and nonneural events. For example, in some mechanical receptors, adaptation develops from the elasticity of the receptor cell itself. This situation is especially evident in the Pacinian corpuscle, which detects vibration (see Figure 8.5). Maintained vibration on the receptor results in an initial burst of neural activity and a rapid decrease to almost nothing. But when the corpuscle (which is a separate, accessory cell) is removed, the same constant stimulus applied to the uncovered sensory nerve fiber produces a continuing discharge of nerve impulses. So for this receptor, adaptation is a mechanical property of the nonneural component, the corpuscle.

Successive levels of the CNS process sensory information

Sensory information travels from the sensory surface to the highest levels of the brain, and each sensory system has its own distinctive pathway. Specifically, pathways from receptors lead into the spinal cord or brainstem, where they connect to distinct clusters of nerve cells. These cells, in turn, have axons that connect to other nerve cell groups. Each sensory modality—such as touch, vision, or hearing—has a distinct collection of tracts and stations in the brain that are collectively known as the **sensory pathway** for that modality.

Each station in the pathway is thought to accomplish a basic aspect of information processing. For example, painful stimulation of the finger leads to reflex withdrawal of the hand, which is mediated by spinal circuits. At the brainstem level, other circuits can turn the head toward the source of pain. Eventually sensory pathways terminate in the cerebral cortex, where the most complex aspects of sensory processing take place. For most senses, information reaches the **thalamus** before being relayed to the cortex (Figure 8.8). Information about each sensory modality is sent to a separate division of the thalamus.

Suppression: Sometimes we need receptors to be quiet

We have noted that successful survival does not depend on exact copying of external and internal stimuli. Rather, our success as a species demands that our sensory systems accentuate, from among the many things happening about us, the important *changes* of stimuli. We just discussed how sensory receptor adaptation can suppress a constant stimulus, but two other strategies are also available.

In many sensory systems, accessory structures can reduce the level of input in the sensory pathway. For example, closing the eyelids reduces the amount of light that reaches the retina. In the auditory system, contraction of the middle-ear muscles reduces the intensity of sounds that reach the inner ear. In this form of sensory control, the relevant mechanisms change the intensity of the stimulus before it reaches the receptors.

8.8 Levels of Sensory Processing
Sensory information enters the CNS through the brainstem or spinal cord, then reaches the thalamus. The thalamus shares the information with the cerebral cortex; the cortex directs the thalamus to supress some sensations. Primary sensory cortex swaps information with nonprimary sensory cortex. This organization is present in all sensory systems except smell (see Chapter 9).

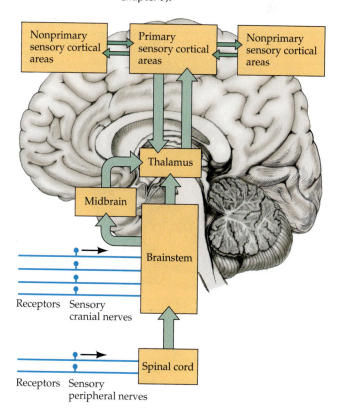

A second form of information control involves neural connections that descend from the brain to lower stations in the sensory pathway, in some cases as far as the receptor surface. For example, higher centers in the pain system (discussed later in this chapter) send axons down the spinal cord, where they can inhibit incoming pain signals. This **central modulation of sensory information** is also evident in the auditory system, where a small group of cells in the brainstem send axons along the auditory nerve to connect with the base of the receptor cells to dampen sounds selectively.

Receptive fields: What turns on this particular receptor cell?

The **receptive field** of a sensory neuron consists of the stimulus region and the features that cause that particular cell to alter its firing rate. To determine the receptive field of a neuron, investigators record its electrical responses to a variety of stimuli to see what makes the activity of the cell change from its resting rate (Figure 8.9). Such experiments show that somatosensory receptive fields have either an excitatory center and an inhibitory surround, or an inhibitory center and an excitatory surround. These receptive fields make it easier to detect edges and discontinuities on the objects we feel.

Receptive fields differ also in size and shape, and in the quality of stimulation that activates them. For example, some neurons respond preferentially to light touch, while others fire most rapidly in response to painful stimuli, and still others respond to cooling.

Following sensory information from the receptor cell in the periphery into the brain shows that neurons all along the pathway will respond to particular stimuli, so each of these cells has a receptive field. But as each successive neuron combines information from prior cells in the pathway, the receptive fields change considerably. Receptive fields have been studied for cells at all levels, from the periphery to the brain, and we will see many examples of receptive fields later in this chapter and in the next two chapters.

Receptive fields in the cerebral cortex For a given sensory modality we can find several different regions of cortex that receive information about that sense. Each of

IMPORTANT METHOD

8.9 Identifying Somatosensory Receptive Fields The procedures illustrated here are used to record from somatosensory neurons of the cerebral cortex. Changes in the position of the stimulus affect the rate of neural impulses. Neuron A responds to touch on a region of the forepaw; neuron B, only a few centimeters away in the somatosensory cortex, responds to stimulation of the tail. The receptive fields of these neurons include an excitatory center and an inhibitory surround, but other neurons have receptive fields with the reverse organization: inhibitory centers and excitatory surrounds.

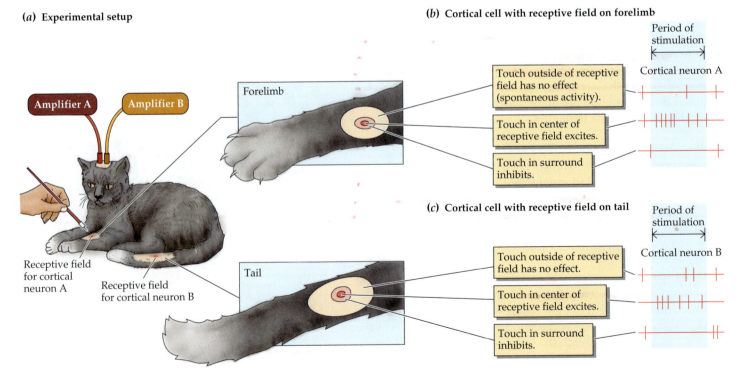

(a) **Experimental setup**

Amplifier A   Amplifier B

Receptive field for cortical neuron A

Receptive field for cortical neuron B

(b) **Cortical cell with receptive field on forelimb**

Forelimb

Period of stimulation

Touch outside of receptive field has no effect (spontaneous activity).

Touch in center of receptive field excites.

Touch in surround inhibits.

Cortical neuron A

(c) **Cortical cell with receptive field on tail**

Tail

Period of stimulation

Touch outside of receptive field has no effect.

Touch in center of receptive field excites.

Touch in surround inhibits.

Cortical neuron B

these cortical regions has a separate map of the same receptive surface, but the different cortical regions process the information differently and make different contributions to perceptual experiences (Miyashita, 1993; Zeki, 1993). For example, these areas receive fibers from different divisions of the thalamus, and the maps, although orderly, differ in internal arrangement.

By convention, one of the cortical maps is designated as **primary sensory cortex** for that particular modality. Thus there is primary somatosensory cortex, primary auditory cortex, and so on. The other cortical maps for a given modality are said to be **secondary sensory cortex** or **nonprimary sensory cortex** (see Figure 8.8). The primary cortical area is the main source of input to the other fields for the same modality, even though these other fields also have direct thalamic inputs. Information is sent back and forth between the primary and nonprimary sensory cortex through subcortical loops.

Clinton Woolsey and colleagues were the first to map primary somatosensory cortex, known as **somatosensory 1,** or **S1** (Figure 8.10). S1 in each hemisphere receives touch information from the opposite side of the body. Secondary somatosensory cortex (S2) maps both sides of the body in registered overlay; that is, the left-arm and right-arm representations occupy the same part of the map, and so forth.

Attention: How do we notice some stimuli but not others?

In 1890 William James wrote, "Everyone knows what attention is. It is the taking possession by the mind in clear and vivid form one out of what seem several simultaneous objects or trains of thought." In fact, however, not everyone agrees about the definition of **attention.** This important aspect of sensory processing has a multiplicity of meanings.

One view emphasizes the state of alertness or vigilance that enables animals to detect signals. In this view, attention is a generalized activation that attunes us to all inputs. According to another view, attention is the process that allows the selection of some sensory inputs from among many competing ones. Other investigators view attention as a "mental spotlight" that focuses on some stimuli, casting others in a "shadow." As you can see, this "self-evident" notion has considerable complexity.

**Clinton Woolsey
(1904–1993)**

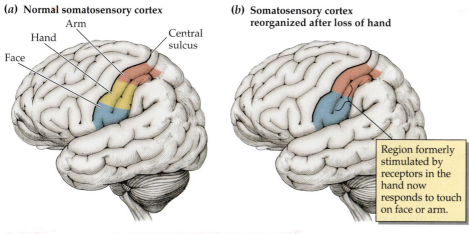

**NEURAL
PLASTICITY**

Region formerly stimulated by receptors in the hand now responds to touch on face or arm.

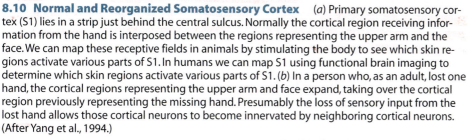

8.10 Normal and Reorganized Somatosensory Cortex   (a) Primary somatosensory cortex (S1) lies in a strip just behind the central sulcus. Normally the cortical region receiving information from the hand is interposed between the regions representing the upper arm and the face. We can map these receptive fields in animals by stimulating the body to see which skin regions activate various parts of S1. In humans we can map S1 using functional brain imaging to determine which skin regions activate various parts of S1. (b) In a person who, as an adult, lost one hand, the cortical regions representing the upper arm and face expand, taking over the cortical region previously representing the missing hand. Presumably the loss of sensory input from the lost hand allows those cortical neurons to become innervated by neighboring cortical neurons. (After Yang et al., 1994.)

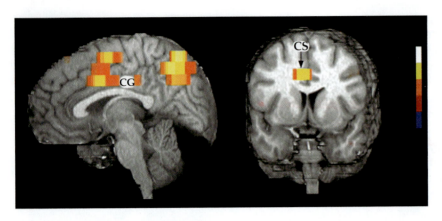

8.11 Brain Regions Activated When We Are Attending Functional-MRI images of a subject cued to expect a stimulus in a particular portion of the visual field show right-hemisphere activation in the cingulate cortex in midsagittal (*left*) and frontal (*right*) views. Areas of highest activation are shown in yellow. CG, cingulate gyrus; CS, cingulate sulcus. (Courtesy of Darren Gitelman.)

Certain regions of the cerebral cortex have been particularly implicated in attention, as evidenced by the impairment of attention in people and animals with localized cortical damage and by recordings of electrical activity of cells in different cortical regions while animals attend to stimuli or await stimuli in order to obtain rewards.

One cortical region that appears to play a special role in attention is a part of the posterior parietal lobe. Many cells here are polymodal. Some of them are especially responsive in a trained monkey that is expecting the appearance of a stimulus (Mountcastle et al., 1981). Lesions of this area in monkeys result in inattention or neglect of stimuli on the opposite side. (In Chapter 19 we will see that this symptom is especially severe in people with lesions of the right parietal lobe.) The frontal eye fields seem to be involved in attentive visual exploration of space. The cingulate cortex (the portion of cortex along and just above the corpus callosum; see Figure 2.10) has been implicated in motivational aspects of attention.

Figure 8.11 shows activation in the cingulate cortex during a task involving a shift in spatial orientation (Gitelman et al., 1996; Nobre et al., 1997). This region has been hypothesized to play a significant role in an "executive" attention system (Posner and Raichle, 1994).

Sensory systems influence one another

Often the use of one sensory system influences perception derived from another sensory system. For example, cats may not respond to birds unless they can both see and hear the birds; neither sense alone is sufficient to elicit a response (B. Stein and Meredith, 1993). Similarly, humans detect a visual signal more accurately if it is accompanied by a sound from the same part of space (McDonald et al., 2000).

Many sensory areas in the brain, so-called association areas, do not represent exclusively a single modality, but show a mixture of inputs from different modalities. Some "visual" cells, for instance, also respond to auditory or tactile stimuli. Perhaps loss of input from one modality allows these cells to analyze input from the remaining senses better, as happens, for example, in cases of people who become blind early in life and are better than sighted people at localizing auditory stimuli (Lessard et al., 1998). The normal stimulus convergence on such polymodal cells provides a mechanism for intersensory interactions (Fuster et al., 2000).

CLINICAL ISSUE

TOUCH: MANY SENSATIONS BLENDED TOGETHER

Skin envelops our bodies and provides a boundary with our surroundings. This delicate boundary harbors an array of receptors that enable us to detect many types of impinging stimuli. Among primates, an important aspect of skin sensations is the active manipulation of objects by the hands, which enables the identification and use of various shapes.

But touch is not just touch. Careful studies of skin sensations reveal qualitatively different sensory experiences: pressure, vibration, tickle, "pins and needles," and more complex dimensions, such as smoothness or wetness—all recorded by an array of receptors in the skin.

Skin Is a Complex Organ That Contains a Variety of Sensory Receptors

Because the average person has about 1 to 2 m^2 (10 to 20 square feet) of skin, skin is sometimes considered the largest human organ. Skin is made up of three separate

TABLE 8.2 *Fibers That Link Receptors to the CNS*

Sensory function(s)	Receptor type(s)	Axon type	Diameter (µm)	Conduction speed (m/s)
Proprioception (see Chapter 11)	Muscle spindle	Aα	13–20	80–120
Touch (see Figures 8.12 and 8.13)	Pacinian corpuscle, Ruffini's ending, Merkel's disc, Meissner's corpuscle	Aβ	6–12	35–75
Pain, temperature	Free nerve endings; VRL1	Aδ	1–5	5–30
Temperature, pain, itch	Free nerve endings; VR1, CMR1	C	0.02–1.5	0.5–2

layers; the relative thickness of each varies over the body surface. The outermost layer—the **epidermis**—is the thinnest. The middle layer—the **dermis**—contains a rich web of nerve fibers in a network of connective tissue and blood vessels.

Pain, heat, and cold at the skin is detected by free nerve endings (see Figure 8.4). Later in this chapter we'll discuss the details of these signals and their use of both fast and slow axons (Table 8.2).

Within the skin are four highly sensitive touch receptors (Figure 8.12). The Pacinian corpuscles are found deep within the dermis. As we mentioned earlier, the onionlike outer portion of the corpuscle acts as a filter, shielding the underlying nerve fiber from most stimulation. Only vibrating stimuli of more than 200 Hz will

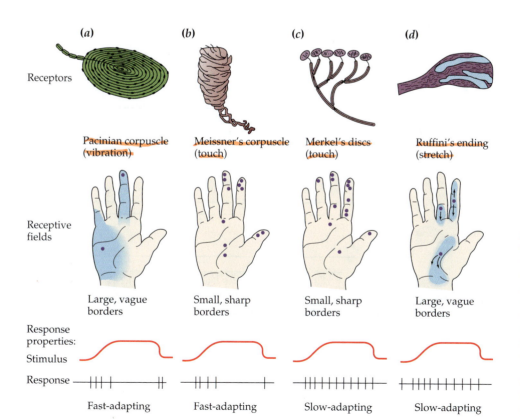

(a) Pacinian corpuscle (vibration)
(b) Meissner's corpuscle (touch)
(c) Merkel's discs (touch)
(d) Ruffini's ending (stretch)

Receptors

Receptive fields

Large, vague borders Small, sharp borders Small, sharp borders Large, vague borders

Response properties:

Stimulus

Response

Fast-adapting Fast-adapting Slow-adapting Slow-adapting

8.12 Properties of Skin Receptors Related to Touch Shown here for each skin receptor is the type of receptor (*top*), the size and type of the receptive field (*middle*), and the electrophysiological response (*bottom*). (*a*) Pacinian corpuscles activate fast-adapting fibers with large receptive fields. (*b*) Meissner's corpuscles are fast-adapting mechanoreceptors with small receptive fields. (*c*) Merkel's discs are slow-adapting receptors with small receptive fields. (*d*) Ruffini's endings are slow-adapting receptors with large receptive fields. (After Valbo and Johansson, 1984.)

pass through the corpuscle and stretch the nerve fiber to reach threshold. Normally the skin receives such rapid vibration when it is moving across the textured surface of an object. Pacinian corpuscles are fast-responding and fast-adapting receptors (see Figure 8.12a).

The touch receptors that mediate most of our ability to perceive form are the fast-adapting **Meissner's corpuscles** (see Figure 8.12b) and the slow-adapting, oval **Merkel's discs** (see Figure 8.12c). These receptors are especially densely distributed in skin regions where sensitive spatial discrimination is possible (fingertips, tongue, and lips).

The receptive fields of Merkel's discs usually have an inhibitory surround, which increases their spatial resolution. This field also makes them especially responsive to edges and to isolated points on a surface (such as the dots for Braille characters).

Meissner's corpuscles are more numerous than Merkel's discs but offer less spatial resolution. Meissner's corpuscles seem specialized to respond to *changes* in stimuli (as one would expect from rapidly adapting receptors) to detect localized movement between the skin and a surface. This sensitivity to change in stimuli provides detailed information about texture (K. O. Johnson and Hsiao, 1992). The low-threshold, rapidly adapting characteristics of Meissner's corpuscles may be due to a specialized Na$^+$ channel (M. P. Price et al., 2000).

The final touch receptors are the slow-adapting **Ruffini's endings**, which detect stretching of the skin when we move fingers or limbs (see Figure 8.12d).

Figure 8.13 compares how each of the four touch receptors respond when a finger is moved across the raised dots of Braille. All four of these touch receptors utilize moderately large (so-called Aβ) myelinated fibers, so they deliver information to the CNS rapidly (see Table 8.2).

8.13 Various Touch Receptors Responding to Braille
(After J. R. Phillips et al., 1990.)

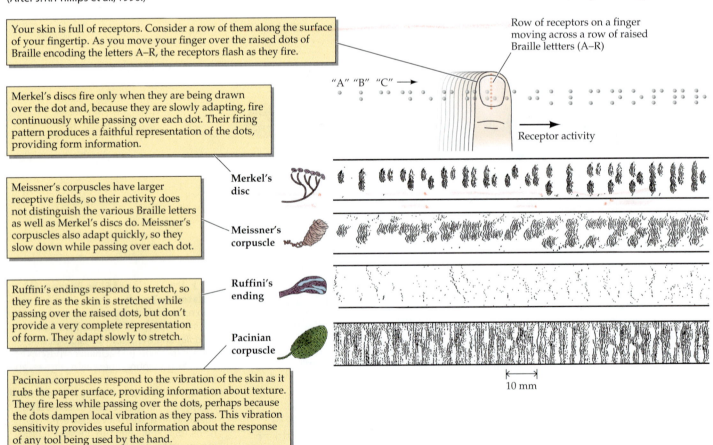

Your skin is full of receptors. Consider a row of them along the surface of your fingertip. As you move your finger over the raised dots of Braille encoding the letters A–R, the receptors flash as they fire.

Row of receptors on a finger moving across a row of raised Braille lettters (A–R)

"A" "B" "C" →

Receptor activity

Merkel's disc fire only when they are being drawn over the dot and, because they are slowly adapting, fire continuously while passing over each dot. Their firing pattern produces a faithful representation of the dots, providing form information.

Merkel's disc

Meissner's corpuscles have larger receptive fields, so their activity does not distinguish the various Braille letters as well as Merkel's discs do. Meissner's corpuscles also adapt quickly, so they slow down while passing over each dot.

Meissner's corpuscle

Ruffini's endings respond to stretch, so they fire as the skin is stretched while passing over the raised dots, but don't provide a very complete representation of form. They adapt slowly to stretch.

Ruffini's ending

Pacinian corpuscle

Pacinian corpuscles respond to the vibration of the skin as it rubs the paper surface, providing information about texture. They fire less while passing over the dots, perhaps because the dots dampen local vibration as they pass. This vibration sensitivity provides useful information about the response of any tool being used by the hand.

10 mm

The Dorsal Column System Carries Somatosensory Information from the Skin to the Brain

Nerve fibers from the skin surface run to the spinal cord. Within the cord, somatosensory fibers ascend to the brain by two major pathways. Later we will describe the spinothalamic system that carries information about pain and temperature. For now we will describe the system that gathers information about touch—the dorsal column system.

The touch receptors that we have described (Pacinian corpuscles, Merkel's discs, Meissner's corpuscles, and Ruffini's endings) send their axons to the spinal cord, where they enter the dorsal horn and turn up, traveling to the brain along the spinal cord's dorsal column of white matter, which is why this is called the **dorsal column system.** These axons go all the way up to the brainstem, where they synapse on neurons of the dorsal column nuclei in the medulla (Figure 8.14). The axons of these medullary neurons then cross the midline to the opposite side and ascend to a group of nuclei of the thalamus. Outputs of the thalamus are directed to postcentral cortical regions referred to as the *somatosensory cortex* or *S1.*

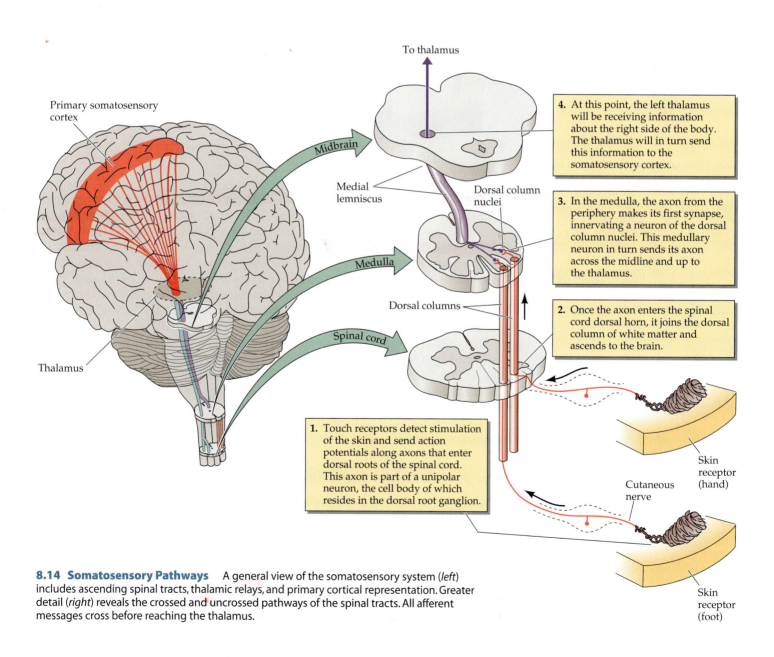

8.14 Somatosensory Pathways   A general view of the somatosensory system (*left*) includes ascending spinal tracts, thalamic relays, and primary cortical representation. Greater detail (*right*) reveals the crossed and uncrossed pathways of the spinal tracts. All afferent messages cross before reaching the thalamus.

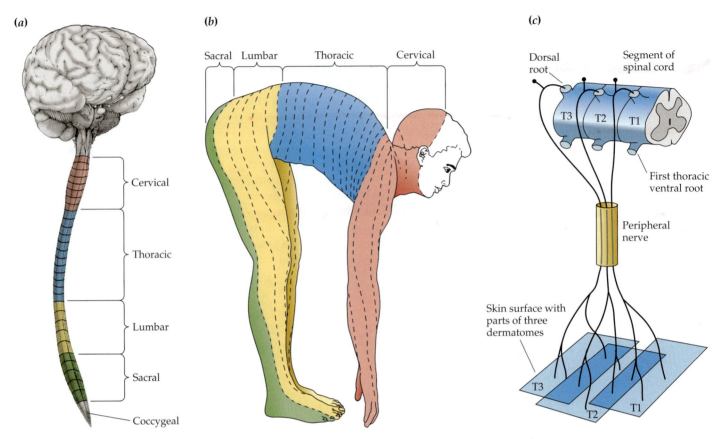

(a) (b) (c)

Sacral Lumbar Thoracic Cervical

Cervical

Thoracic

Lumbar

Sacral

Coccygeal

Dorsal root — Segment of spinal cord

T3 T2 T1

First thoracic ventral root

Peripheral nerve

Skin surface with parts of three dermatomes

T3 T2 T1

8.15 Dermatomes (*a*) Bands of skin send their sensory inputs to different dorsal roots of the spinal cord. Each dermatome is the section of the skin that is innervated primarily by a given dorsal root of the spinal cord. (*b*) In this side view of the human body in quadrupedal position, the pattern of dermatomes is color-coded to correspond to the spinal regions in *a*, and it appears more straightforward than it would in the erect posture. (*c*) Adjacent dorsal roots of the spinal cord collect sensory fibers from overlapping strips of skin, so the boundaries between the dermatomes overlap.

EVOLUTION AT WORK

The skin surface can be divided into bands called *dermatomes* according to which spinal nerve carries the most axons from each region (Figure 8.15*a*). A **dermatome** (from the Greek *derma*, "skin," and *tome*, "part, segment") is a strip of skin innervated by a particular spinal root. The pattern of dermatomes is hard to understand in an upright human, but remember that erect posture is a recent evolutionary development in mammals. The mammalian dermatomal pattern evolved among our quadrupedal (four-legged) ancestors. Thus the dermatomal pattern makes sense when depicted on a person in a quadrupedal posture (Figure 8.15*b*). There is also a modest amount of overlap between dermatomes (Figure 8.15*c*).

The cells in all brain regions concerned with somatic sensation are arranged according to the plan of the body surface. Each region is a map of the body in which the relative areas devoted to body regions reflect the density of body innervation. Because many fibers are involved with the sensory surface of the head, especially the lips, a particularly large number of cells are concerned with the head; in contrast, far fewer fibers innervate the trunk, so the number of cortical cells that represent the trunk is much smaller (Figure 8.16).

Cortical Columns Show Specificity for Modality and Location

We saw in Chapter 2 that the cerebral cortex is organized into vertical columns of neurons; here we will examine the functional significance of these cortical columns. In pioneering work begun in the 1950s, Mountcastle (1984) mapped the receptive fields of individual neurons in somatosensory cortex using microelectrodes.

Mountcastle found that each cortical cell not only has a precise receptive field, but also responds to only one submodality. For example, some cells respond only to a light touch, and others respond only to deep pressure. Furthermore, within a given column of neurons, all the cells respond to the same location and quality of stimu-

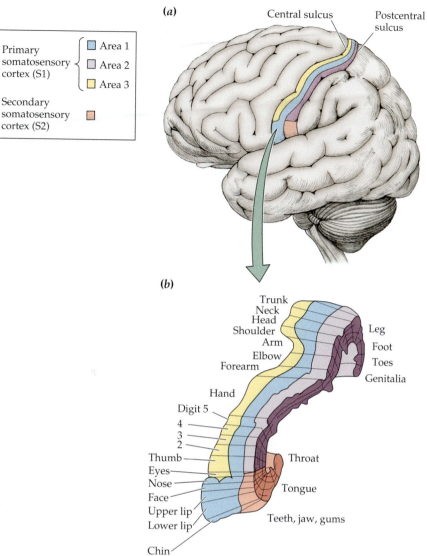

(a)

Central sulcus

Postcentral sulcus

Primary somatosensory cortex (S1)
- Area 1
- Area 2
- Area 3

Secondary somatosensory cortex (S2)

(b)

Trunk
Neck
Head
Shoulder
Arm
Elbow
Forearm
Hand
Digit 5
4
3
2
Thumb
Eyes
Nose
Face
Upper lip
Lower lip
Chin

Leg
Foot
Toes
Genitalia

Throat
Tongue
Teeth, jaw, gums

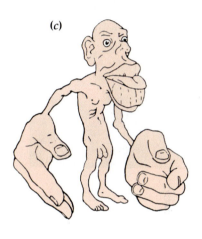

(c)

8.16 Representation of the Body Surface in Somatosensory Cortex   (a) The location of primary (S1) and secondary (S2) somatosensory cortical areas on the lateral surface of the human brain. (b) The order and size of cortical representations of different regions of skin. (c) The *homunculus* (literally, "little man") depicts the body surface with each area drawn in proportion to the size of its representation in the primary somatosensory cortex.

8.17 The Columnar Organization of the Somatosensory Cortex   The part of the somatosensory cortex shown here represents some of the fingers of the right hand. The different regions of somatosensory cortex—Brodmann's areas 3a, 3b, 1, and 2—receive their main inputs from different kinds of receptors. Area 3b receives most of its projections from the superficial skin, including both fast-adapting and slow-adapting receptors; these projections are represented in separate cortical columns or slabs. Area 3a receives input from receptors in the muscle spindles. The cortex is organized vertically in columns and horizontally in layers. Input from the thalamus arrives at layer IV, where neurons distribute information up and down layers. (After Kaas et al., 1979.)

lation. Cells in a band of columns respond to the same quality of stimulation, and another band of columns is devoted to another kind of stimulation (Figure 8.17).

Each column extends from the surface of the cortex (layer I in Figure 8.17) down to the base of the cortex (layer VI). Each type of receptor feeds information to a different cortical column. Moving the stimulation to a slightly different region on the

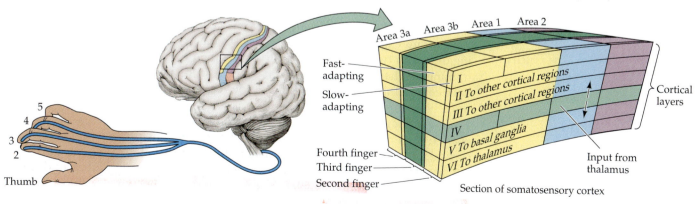

Area 3a   Area 3b   Area 1   Area 2

Fast-adapting

Slow-adapting

I
II *To other cortical regions*
III *To other cortical regions*
IV
V *To basal ganglia*
VI *To thalamus*

Cortical layers

Input from thalamus

5
4
3
2
Thumb

Fourth finger
Third finger
Second finger

Section of somatosensory cortex

(a)

(b)

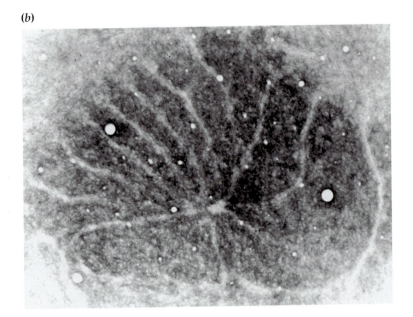

8.18 Hey There, You with the Star on Your Nose (a) The tip of the star-nosed mole's nose is a very delicate organ for touch. (b) Each of the 11 rays of the star projects to somatosensory cortex in a map that reflects the sensitivity of the various rays. (From Catania, 2001; photographs courtesy of Ken Catania.)

skin shifts the excitation to a different cortical column. Thus the columns code for both location and quality of stimulation.

Some mammals have a very different pattern of representation in somatosensory cortex. For example, the nose of the star-nosed mole is a very sensitive organ for touch, and a considerable portion of its somatosensory cortex is devoted to responding to each of the 11 rays of the "star" (Figure 8.18) (Catania, 2001).

Plasticity in cortical maps: Receptive fields can be changed by experience

At one time most researchers thought that cortical maps were fixed early in life and invariant among all members of the same species. But contemporary research shows that cortical maps can change with experience. Three experiments with monkeys illustrate the plasticity of sensory representation (Merzenich and Jenkins, 1993).

In the first experiment, the receptive field of a monkey's hand was mapped in detail in the somatosensory cortex (Figure 8.19a). Then the nerve to the thumb and index finger was severed. After a few weeks, remapping the same somatosensory cortex revealed that the area representing those fingers had shrunk, and stimulating the back of the hand activated the territory formerly held by the denervated fingers (Figure 8.19b).

In the second experiment, the middle finger was surgically removed. This treatment expanded the cortical representation of each adjacent finger (Figure 8.19c).

In a third experiment, the monkey was trained to maintain contact with a rotating disk with two fingers in order to obtain food rewards. After several weeks of training, the hand area was mapped again, and the trained fingers were found to have considerably enlarged representations compared to their previous areas (Figure 8.19d).

Similar findings were noted in rats exposed to differential tactile experience (Xerri et al., 1996). Professional musicians who play stringed instruments have expanded cortical representations of their left fingers, presumably because they have been using these fingers to depress the strings for precisely the right note (Elbert et al., 1995; Munte et al., 2002). Brain imaging also reveals cortical reorganization in people who lose a hand in adulthood (see Figure 8.10b).

NEURAL PLASTICITY

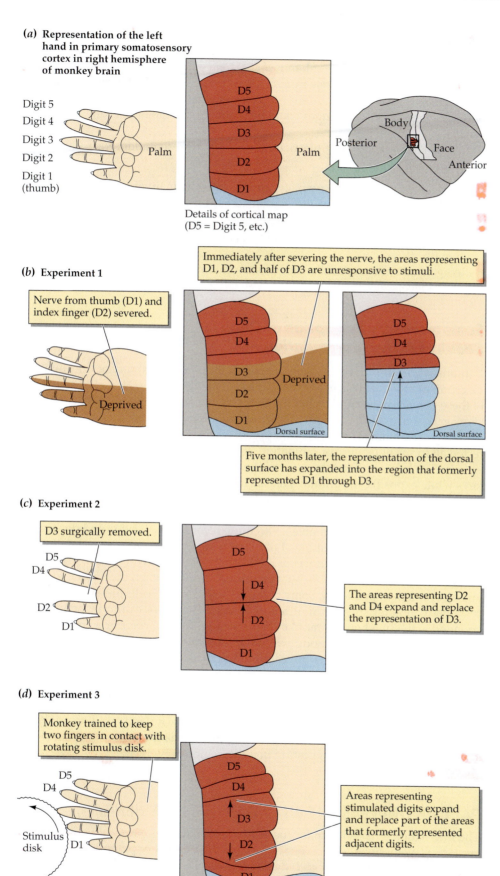

(a) Representation of the left hand in primary somatosensory cortex in right hemisphere of monkey brain

Digit 5
Digit 4
Digit 3
Digit 2
Digit 1 (thumb)

Palm

D5
D4
D3
D2
D1

Palm

Body
Posterior
Face
Anterior

Details of cortical map (D5 = Digit 5, etc.)

(b) Experiment 1

Nerve from thumb (D1) and index finger (D2) severed.

Deprived

Immediately after severing the nerve, the areas representing D1, D2, and half of D3 are unresponsive to stimuli.

D5
D4
D3   Deprived
D2
D1

Dorsal surface

D5
D4
D3

Dorsal surface

Five months later, the representation of the dorsal surface has expanded into the region that formerly represented D1 through D3.

(c) Experiment 2

D3 surgically removed.

D5
D4
D2
D1

D5
D4
D2
D1

The areas representing D2 and D4 expand and replace the representation of D3.

(d) Experiment 3

Monkey trained to keep two fingers in contact with rotating stimulus disk.

D5
D4
Stimulus disk
D1

D5
D4
D3
D2
D1

Areas representing stimulated digits expand and replace part of the areas that formerly represented adjacent digits.

8.19 The Plasticity of Somatosensory Representations These experiments demonstrate that the adult brain can be altered by experience. (After Merzenich and Jenkins, 1993.)

Some changes in cortical maps occur after weeks or months of use or disuse; they may arise from the production of new synapses (sprouting) (Florence et al., 1998) or the loss of others. On the other hand, some changes are so rapid, occurring within hours, that they probably arise from changes in the strength of existing synapses. Rapid changes in cortical maps may also result from a loss of sustained inhibition of some synapses; these changes could be thought of as the unmasking of "hidden synapses."

In a review of the topic of plasticity of sensory representation, Kaas (2000) concluded the following:

NEURAL PLASTICITY

- The detailed cortical sensory maps are dynamically maintained, capable of both rapid and gradual change with experience and use.
- Prolonged sensory manipulations can lead to activity-induced modifications in neurotransmitter expression, the growth of axons and dendrites, and synaptic strength.
- Reorganizations occur in all major sensory (and motor) systems at subcortical and cortical levels.

Somatosensory Perception of Objects Requires Active Manipulation

In monkeys, lesions of somatosensory cortex impaired the ability of the animal to discriminate the form, size, and roughness of tactile objects (Norsell, 1980). Each of these impairments could be localized to a subregion of somatosensory cortex: Lesions in one area affected mainly the discrimination of texture, lesions in a second area impaired mainly the discrimination of angles, and lesions in a third area affected all forms of tactile discrimination (Randolph and Semmes, 1974).

Scientists have recorded the activity of neurons in somatosensory cortex of monkeys while exposing the animal's hands to complex stimuli (Darian-Smith et al., 1980). Metal strips of varied widths and spacing were moved at different rates of speed under the fingertips of monkeys while recordings were made from sensory nerves. No single fiber could give an accurate record of each ridge and depression in the stimulus, but the ensemble of fibers provided an accurate representation.

Some somatosensory cortical cells could not be activated when the experimenter stimulated either skin or joints but responded strongly when the animal grasped an object and manipulated it. Some of these "active touch" cells had highly specific response characteristics (Iwamura and Tanaka, 1978). For example, one unit responded actively when the monkey felt a straight-edged ruler or a small rectangular block but did not respond when the monkey grasped a ball or bottle. The presence of two parallel edges appeared to be crucial for effective activation of this cell. Another cell responded best when the monkey grasped a ball or a bottle, but did not respond at all when the monkey manipulated a rectangular block.

PET studies have shown that, in humans, the posterior part of the parietal cortex is activated during exploration of objects by touch (Roland and Larson, 1976). Only when the subject explored an object by touch was the posterior parietal cortex specifically activated, suggesting that this region is particularly involved in active touch.

PAIN: AN UNPLEASANT BUT ADAPTIVE EXPERIENCE

EVOLUTION AT WORK

The International Association for the Study of Pain defines **pain** as "an unpleasant sensory and emotional experience associated with actual or potential tissue damage, or described in terms of such damage." Because pain is unpleasant and causes great suffering, it may be difficult to imagine a biological role for it. But clues to the adaptive significance of pain can be gleaned from the study of rare individuals who never experience pain. The **congenital insensitivity to pain** that such people exhibit is probably inherited, since the pain insensitivity syndrome is sometimes seen in siblings (E. Hirsch et al., 1995); and one version of insensitivity has been traced to a defect in a gene for a receptor to nerve growth factor (Indo et al., 1996), suggesting that pain fibers in these individuals fail to grow out for lack of response to a neurotrophic signal.

People who display this insensitivity can discriminate between the touch of the point or head of a pin but experience no pain when pricked with the point. The bodies of such people show extensive scarring from injuries to fingers, hands, and legs (Manfredi et al., 1981). One little girl insensitive to pain had deliberately pulled out most of her teeth by 8 years of age and had to be instructed to leave her teeth alone (P. Rasmussen, 1996). The first clinically reported person with congenital insensitivity to pain worked on the stage as a "human pincushion" (Figure 8.20) (Dearborn, 1932).

Many people with congenital insensitivity to pain die young, frequently from extreme trauma to the body. These cases suggest that pain guides adaptive behavior by indicating potential harm. Pain is so commonplace for most of us that we easily forget its guiding role: The experience of pain leads to behavior that removes the body from a source of injury.

Dennis and Melzack (1983) argue that pain serves three purposes:

1. Short-lasting pain causes us to withdraw from the source, often reflexively, thus preventing further damage.
2. Long-lasting pain promotes behaviors such as sleep, inactivity, grooming, feeding, and drinking that promote recuperation.
3. The expression of pain serves as a social signal to other animals. For example, screeching after a painful stimulus signals the potential harm to genetically related individuals, and elicits caregiving behavior from them, such as grooming, defending, and feeding.

Human Pain Can Be Measured

In some parts of the world people endure, with stoic indifference, rituals (including body mutilation) that would cause most other humans to cry out in pain. Incisions of the face, hands, arms, legs, or chest; walking on hot coals; and other treatments clearly harmful to the body can be part of the ritual. Comparable experiences are also seen in more ordinary circumstances, such as when a highly excited athlete continues to play a game with a broken arm or leg. Learning, experience, emotion, and culture all affect the perception of pain in striking ways.

Detailed psychological studies of the experience of pain further emphasize its complexity. The mere terms *mild* and *intense* are inadequate to describe the sensation that is distinctive to a particular disease or injury. Furthermore, assessment of the need for pain relief intervention requires some kind of quantitative measurement (Chapman et al., 1985). For example, Melzack (1984) has provided a detailed quantitative rating scale for pain.

This rating scale—called the *McGill Pain Questionnaire*—consists of a list of words arranged into classes that describe three different aspects of pain: (1) the *sensory–discriminative* quality (e.g., throbbing, gnawing, shooting), (2) the *motivational–affective* (emotional) quality (tiring, sickening, fearful), and (3) an overall *cognitive* evaluative quality (no pain, mild, excruciating). Patients are asked to select the set of words that best describes their pain. These three components reflect different aspects of pain perception (Figure 8.21).

THE HUMAN PINCUSHION WHO INCURS CONSTANT RISKS OF BLOOD POISONING.

8.20 Doesn't That Hurt? The earliest scientific report of a person with congenital insensitivity to pain was of a man working in the theater, like the man shown here, as a "human pincushion." (Photo by Culver Pictures, Inc.)

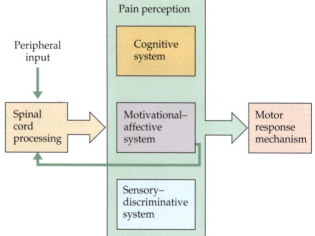

8.21 The Multifaceted Character of Pain

**CLINICAL
ISSUE**

One of the interesting aspects of the McGill scale is that it can distinguish among pain syndromes, meaning that patients use a distinctive constellation of words to describe a particular pain experience. For example, the pain of toothache is described differently from the pain of arthritis, which in turn is described differently from menstrual pain. The simple query by a physician "Is the pain still there?" has been replaced by a more detailed analysis that provides better clues about the effectiveness of pain control.

Pain information is transmitted through special neural systems

Contemporary studies of pain mechanisms have revealed receptors in the skin that transmit pain information and the relevant pathways of the central nervous system. In this section we will discuss some features of peripheral and central nervous system pathways that mediate pain.

Peripheral origins of pain information   In most cases the initial stimulus for pain is the partial destruction of or injury to tissue adjacent to certain nerve fibers. This tissue change results in the release of chemical substances that activate pain fibers in the skin. Various substances have been suggested as the chemical mediators of pain, including neuropeptides, serotonin, histamine, various proteolytic (protein-metabolizing) enzymes, and prostaglandins (a group of widespread hormones) (Figure 8.22).

It is now clear that some peripheral receptors and nerve fibers are specialized for signaling noxious stimulation. These receptors that respond to noxious stimulation are called **nociceptors.** **Free nerve endings** in the dermis display no specialized structures (they just look like naked nerve endings), but they have specialized receptors on the cell membrane that respond to temperatures and chemicals. Different free nerve endings produce different receptors, and so report different stimuli, such as pain and/or changes in temperature.

Hot, cold, or cool?   The best evidence for specialized pain fibers in the periphery came from studies of **capsaicin,** the chemical that makes chili peppers spicy hot. Investigators isolated a receptor found in free nerve endings that binds capsaicin, and found that the receptor also responds to sudden increases in temperature (Caterina et al., 1997). The receptor was cloned and named **vanilloid receptor 1** (**VR1**) because the crucial component of the capsaicin molecule is a chemical known as *vanilloid.* Mice lacking the gene for this receptor still responded to mechanosensory pain, but

8.22 Peripheral Mediation of Pain
When the skin is injured, activity of the peripheral nervous system causes the local release of various substances.

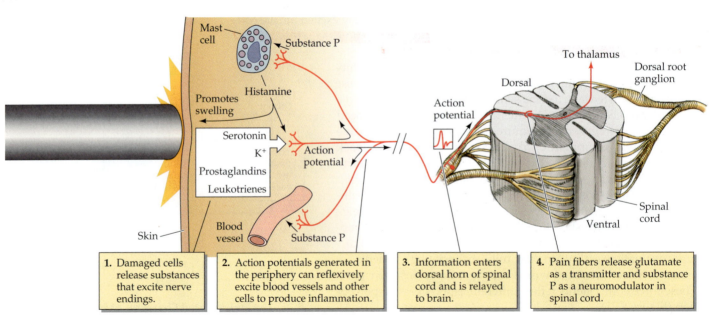

1. Damaged cells release substances that excite nerve endings.

2. Action potentials generated in the periphery can reflexively excite blood vessels and other cells to produce inflammation.

3. Information enters dorsal horn of spinal cord and is relayed to brain.

4. Pain fibers release glutamate as a transmitter and substance P as a neuromodulator in spinal cord.

not to mild heat or capsaicin (Caterina et al., 2000). So the reason that chili peppers taste "hot" is that the capsaicin in the peppers activates VR1 receptors in the body that normally detect noxious heat.

VR1's normal job is to detect a rise in temperature to warn us of danger. Chili peppers evolved the chemical capsaicin to ward off mammalian predators, as its ability to deter deer from eating prized flower bushes, which we learned about at the start of the chapter, suggests. Capsaicin molecules have the perfect shape to bind to VR1 and open its ion channel, just like heat normally does. Because the brain interprets action potentials from that nerve as signaling painful heat, we (and the deer) experience painful heat.

Why, though, aren't birds discouraged by capsaicin? The answer is that the bird version of VR1 is not affected by capsaicin (Tewksbury and Nabhan, 2001). In this case both the animal and the plant are benefited by capsaicin: The birds are able to get food from the plants—food that might not be there if other animals were not deterred from eating the plants—and in the process they spread the seeds of the plants far and wide. Clever, clever chili plants.

Why do our lips swell when we have overindulged in capsaicin? As Figure 8.22 illustrates, the action potentials generated by the chemical travel back out other branches of the axon to affect blood vessels and mast cells, triggering the swelling. Paradoxically, rubbing capsaicin into the skin overlying arthritic joints brings some pain relief, perhaps because overactivated pain fibers temporarily run out of transmitter.

A receptor that is similar to VR1 is called, confusingly enough, vanilloid receptor–like protein 1 (VRL1). This receptor detects even higher temperatures than does VR1 (Figure 8.23a). And VRL1 differs from VR1 in two other ways as well: VRL1 does *not* respond to capsaicin, and VRL1 receptors are found on larger nerve fibers than those carrying VR1. Recall from Chapter 3 that large axons conduct action potentials more rapidly than do small axons. VRL1 receptors are found on relatively large axons known as type **Aδ fibers:** large-diameter, myelinated axons (Figure 8.23b). Because of the relatively large axon diameter and myelination, these fibers report to the spinal cord very quickly. When you burn your finger on a hot skillet, the first, sharp pain you feel is conducted by these fat Aδ fibers that detected the heat with VRL1 receptors. In contrast, the nerve fibers that possess VR1 receptors consist of thin, unmyelinated fibers, called C fibers (see Figure 8.23b). These C fibers conduct slowly, and VR1 adapts slowly, providing the second wave of pain—the dull, lasting ache in that darned finger.

Why is there a slight delay between licking the cut surface of a chili pepper and feeling the burn? The reason is that only the VR1 fibers, with their slow conduction velocity, have been activated, not the fast Aδ fibers using VRL1. The free nerve endings that signal itch form another important class of signals from the skin that use slow C fibers (Andrew and Craig, 2001). These itch fibers respond to histamine released by mast cells near an injury (see Figure 8.22). Table 8.2 compares these different fibers.

Taking a cue from the success with capsaicin, another group tried looking for the "cool" receptor, reasoning that it should respond to the chemical menthol. They found and named the **cool-menthol receptor 1 (CMR1).** CMR1 responds to cool temperatures and is found on small C fibers, so it transmits information about cool temperatures rather slowly (see Figure 8.23a). Interestingly, sharks have evolved a completely different method of detecting temperature on their skin. They secrete a gel that surrounds nerve endings, and this gel changes voltage as temperatures vary, triggering an action potential in the underlying nerves (B. R. Brown, 2003).

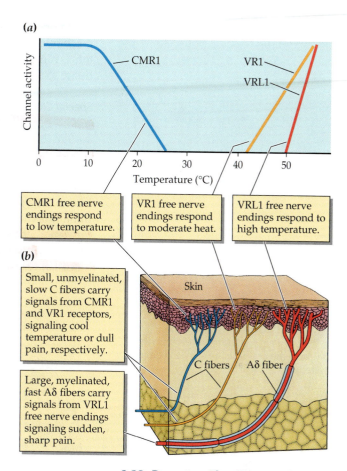

(a)

CMR1 free nerve endings respond to low temperature.

VR1 free nerve endings respond to moderate heat.

VRL1 free nerve endings respond to high temperature.

(b)

Small, unmyelinated, slow C fibers carry signals from CMR1 and VR1 receptors, signaling cool temperature or dull pain, respectively.

Large, myelinated, fast Aδ fibers carry signals from VRL1 free nerve endings signaling sudden, sharp pain.

8.23 Receptors That Detect Pain and Temperature (a) Free nerve endings with the cool-menthol receptor 1 (CMR1) are activated by temperatures below normal body temperature. Free nerve endings with the vanilloid receptor 1 (VR1) respond to moderate heat and the capsaicin found in chili peppers. Other free nerve endings, with the vanilloid receptor–like protein 1 (VRL1), detect high temperatures. (b) The VRL1 free nerve endings transmit a fast action potential along large, myelinated Aδ fibers to the spinal cord. CMR1 and VR1 receptors transmit along slower, unmyelinated C fibers.

EVOLUTION AT WORK

No one has yet isolated the receptor used by free nerve endings that detect only mechanical damage as opposed to temperature changes. The search for such receptors is hindered by the fact that no one is sure what chemical is released by damaged tissue to signal mechanical damage.

Special CNS pathways mediate pain   In the central nervous system, special pathways mediate pain and temperature information. Earlier we discussed the dorsal column system that carries touch information to the brain (see Figure 8.14). The sensation of pain and temperature is transmitted by the **anterolateral**, or **spinothalamic**, **system.** Free nerve endings in the skin send their axons to synapse on neurons in the dorsal horn of the spinal cord. These spinal-cord neurons send their axons across the midline to the opposite side and up the anterolateral column of the spinal cord to the thalamus (hence the term *spinothalamic*). So in the spinothalamic system, pain information crosses the midline in the spinal cord before ascending to the brain (Figure 8.24); recall that touch information, in contrast, first ascends to the brainstem and then crosses the midline (see Figure 8.14).

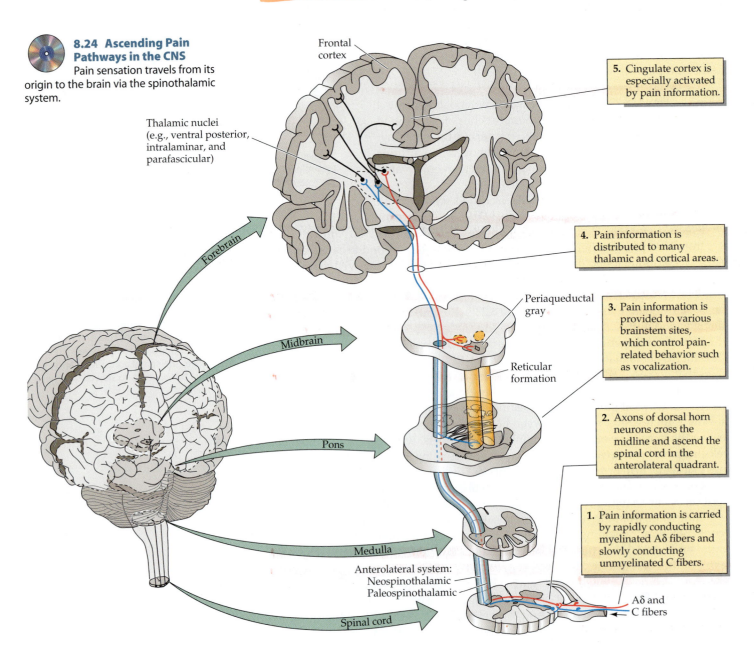

8.24 Ascending Pain Pathways in the CNS Pain sensation travels from its origin to the brain via the spinothalamic system.

Frontal cortex

Thalamic nuclei (e.g., ventral posterior, intralaminar, and parafascicular)

5. Cingulate cortex is especially activated by pain information.

4. Pain information is distributed to many thalamic and cortical areas.

Periaqueductal gray

3. Pain information is provided to various brainstem sites, which control pain-related behavior such as vocalization.

Reticular formation

2. Axons of dorsal horn neurons cross the midline and ascend the spinal cord in the anterolateral quadrant.

1. Pain information is carried by rapidly conducting myelinated Aδ fibers and slowly conducting unmyelinated C fibers.

Forebrain

Midbrain

Pons

Medulla

Anterolateral system: Neospinothalamic Paleospinothalamic

Spinal cord

Aδ and C fibers

The afferent fibers from the periphery that carry nociceptive information probably use **glutamate** as a neurotransmitter to excite spinal cells in the dorsal horn (S. Li and Tator, 2000), but they also release the neuromodulator **substance P.** Substance P is a neuropeptide (the *P* originally stood for *peptide*). Injection of capsaicin into the skin provides a specific painful stimulus that leads to the release of substance P in the dorsal horn. There the postsynaptic neurons take up the substance P and begin remodeling their dendrites; investigators have speculated that this neural plasticity later affects pain perception, as we'll see shortly (Mantyh et al., 1997).

Further evidence that substance P plays a role in pain comes from experiments with knockout mice that lack either the gene for the precursor to substance P (Cao et al., 1998) or a gene for the substance P receptor (De Felipe et al., 1998). (See Box 7.3 to review experimental techniques using knockout mice.) These mice are unresponsive to certain kinds of intense pain. Interestingly, they still respond to mildly painful stimuli, suggesting that other signals, perhaps the glutamate neurotransmitter, can carry that information. The dorsal-horn neurons that receive this information, part of the spinothalamic system we mentioned earlier, send their axons across the midline and up the spinal cord to terminate in several nuclei of the thalamus (see Figure 8.24).

Sometimes pain persists long after the injury that gave rise to it has healed. The most dramatic example is a person's continued perception of chronic pain coming from a missing limb after loss of an arm or leg. Called *phantom limb pain*, this sensation is an example of **neuropathic pain,** so called because the pain seems to be due to inappropriate signaling of pain by neurons (rather than to tissue damage). Such cases can be seen as a disagreeable manifestation of neural plasticity because the nervous system seems to have amplified its response to the pain signal (Woolf and Salter, 2000).

Cases of phantom limb pain are notoriously difficult to treat. In one type, the patient perceives that his missing limb is twisted and therefore hurts. Vilayanur Ramachandran has proposed a new treatment for this condition: The patient looks at himself in a mirror, positioned in such a way that the reflection of the intact limb seems to have filled in for the missing limb. The patient then repeatedly moves "both limbs" (by moving the remaining one), watching closely the whole while, and sometimes reports that the phantom limb feels as though it has straightened out and no longer hurts (Ramachandran and Rogers-Ramachandran, 2000). This result suggests that the brain interprets the signals coming from the limb stump as painful, but visual stimuli may lead to a reinterpretation.

Pain information is eventually integrated in the **cingulate cortex.** Recall from Chapter 1 that the cingulate cortex is much more activated by a stimulus if people are led to believe that the stimulus will be painful (see Figure 1.4) (Rainville et al., 1997). The extent of activation in the anterior cingulate (as well as the somatosensory cortex) also correlates with how much discomfort different people report in response to the same mildly painful stimulus (Coghill et al., 2003).

A sensory illusion further confirms the role of the cingulate cortex in pain perception: Placing your hand over alternating pipes of cool and warm (not hot) water produces the sensation of pain, as though the pipes were hot. Presumably this illusory pain sensation is produced by the unusual circumstance of CMR1 and VR1 receptors being stimulated at the same time. This is a wonderful illustration that "pain is in the brain" because no tissue is actually being damaged. The cingulate cortex is also activated in people experiencing this illusory pain (Craig et al., 1996).

Pain can be controlled by a variety of mechanisms and pathways

Relief from the suffering of pain has long been a dominant concern of humans. Throughout history, different remedies have been offered. One frustrating, puzzling aspect of pain pathways is that cutting the pathway reduces pain perception only temporarily. After a pathway in the spinal cord is cut, pain is initially diminished, but it returns in a few weeks or months.

NEURAL PLASTICITY

GENES AND BEHAVIOR

Vilayanur Ramachandran

Ronald Melzack

**P. D. Wall
(1925–2001)**

**CLINICAL
ISSUE**

The usual way that these data are interpreted is that nociceptive input from the remaining intact pathways becomes abnormally effective. In an enormously influential paper, Melzack and Wall (1965) suggested that pain is subject to many modulating influences, including some that can close spinal "gates" controlling the flow of pain information from the spinal cord to the brain. Maybe the spinal gates get stuck open in some people, sending pain signals continuously, and maybe we could find ways to close those gates to alleviate pain.

Soon after publication of this idea, scientists found that electrical stimulation of the brain could alleviate pain, which suggested that pain could be modulated not only by the spinal cord, but also by the brain. These discoveries inspired many new approaches to the alleviation of pain. In the sections that follow, we will discuss some of these strategies, which are prime examples of the interaction between basic research and application.

Opiate drugs Opium has been exploited for its pain-relieving effects for centuries. Modern researchers attempting to determine how opiates (drugs, such as morphine, that are derived from or related to opium) control pain finally showed that the brain contains natural opiate-like substances, or *opioids*. In effect, the brain modulates pain in a manner akin to how exogenous opiates such as morphine do. Several classes of **endogenous opioids,** such as **endorphin** and the **enkephalins,** have been discovered (see Chapter 4), and several classes of **opiate receptors** have been identified and designated by Greek letters. For example, the μ opiate receptor seems to be most affected by morphine.

Early observations showed that electrical stimulation of the **periaqueductal gray area** (see Figure 8.24) of the brainstem in rats produces potent **analgesia** (loss of pain sensation; from the Greek *an-*, "not," and *algesis*, "feeling of pain"). Injection of opiates into this area also relieves pain, suggesting that the region contains synaptic receptors for opiate-like substances. The periaqueductal gray area receives strong input from the spinal cord, which presumably delivers nociceptive information.

According to one model of the control of pain transmission in the spinal cord by the brainstem (Basbaum and Fields, 1978, 1984), periaqueductal gray neurons send endorphin-containing axons to stimulate neurons in the medulla. These medullary neurons send serotonin-containing axons to the spinal cord to inhibit the neurons that transmit information from the periphery. In this way, pain information is blocked by a direct gating action in the spinal cord. Electrical stimulation of the descending tract elicits inhibition of the response of spinal-cord sensory relay cells to noxious stimulation of the skin. Figure 8.25 shows both the ascending pain communication system and the descending pain control system.

In addition to their beneficial pain-relieving effects, opiates and other analgesics (painkillers) often produce side effects such as confusion, drowsiness, vomiting, constipation, and depression of the respiratory system. Now that we know the circuitry of the pain relief system, why give large doses of the drug systemically (i.e., throughout the body)? Instead, physicians can now administer very small doses of opiates directly to the spinal cord to relieve pain, thus avoiding many of the side effects. The drugs can be administered *epidurally* (just outside the spinal cord's dura mater) or *intrathecally* (between the dura mater and the spinal cord). Both routes are somewhat invasive and therefore are restricted to surgical anesthesia, childbirth, or the management of severe chronic pain (Landau and Levy, 1993).

There have been long-standing concerns about the use of morphine and other opiates for pain relief because of their addictive potential. Low doses and infrequent use were the common standard. However, the Agency for Healthcare Research and Quality urges swift use of painkillers after surgery. Once chronic pain develops, it is extremely difficult to overcome, so the best approach is to prevent the onset of chronic pain by early, aggressive treatment. The danger of addiction from the use of morphine to relieve surgical pain has been vastly overexaggerated (Melzack, 1990); it is no more than 0.04% (Brownlee and Schrof, 1997). In the media, people addicted to painkillers are often said to have "gotten hooked" when given a prescription for

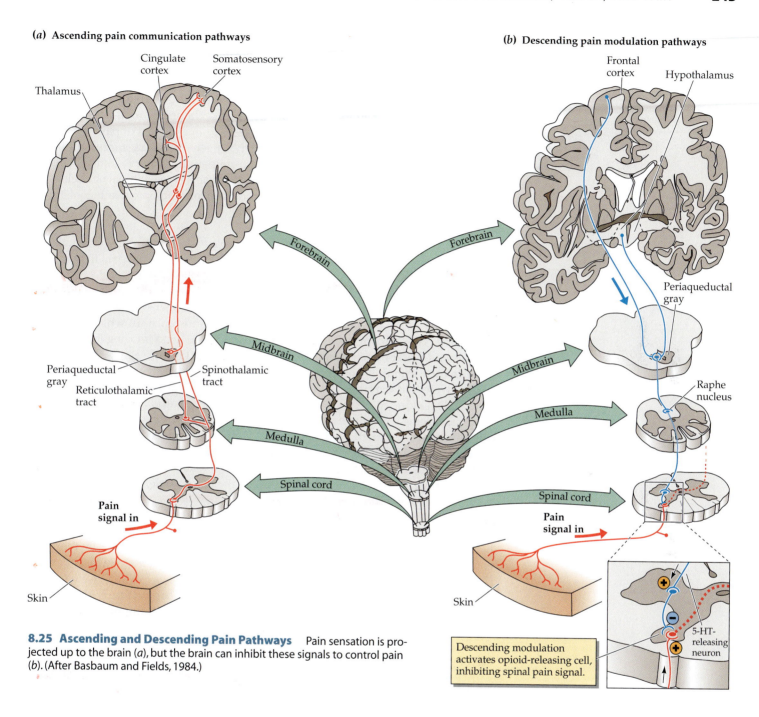

(a) Ascending pain communication pathways

Cingulate cortex
Somatosensory cortex
Thalamus
Forebrain
Periaqueductal gray
Spinothalamic tract
Reticulothalamic tract
Midbrain
Medulla
Spinal cord
Pain signal in
Skin

(b) Descending pain modulation pathways

Frontal cortex
Hypothalamus
Forebrain
Periaqueductal gray
Midbrain
Raphe nucleus
Medulla
Spinal cord
Pain signal in
Skin
5-HT-releasing neuron

Descending modulation activates opioid-releasing cell, inhibiting spinal pain signal.

8.25 Ascending and Descending Pain Pathways   Pain sensation is projected up to the brain (*a*), but the brain can inhibit these signals to control pain (*b*). (After Basbaum and Fields, 1984.)

pain. But further investigations reveal that almost all of these people had been drug abusers *before* they were given a prescription for pain (Szalavitz, 2004).

Other, nonopioid analgesics may be available soon. For example, two toxins—one isolated from frog skin (Bannon et al., 1998), the other from a marine snail (Sandall et al., 2003)—are very potent analgesics that seem to act on nicotinic cholinergic receptors. We do not yet know how this action would produce analgesia.

Stimulation of the skin   Humans have tried a lot of strange techniques to relieve pain. Centuries ago, for example, electric fish or eels were applied to sites of pain. More recently, a modern version of such treatment, called **transcutaneous electrical nerve stimulation (TENS)**, gained prominence as a way to suppress certain types of pain that are difficult to control. For some reason, stimulating the nerves around the source of pain provides relief, perhaps by closing the spinal "gate" for pain that

Melzack and Wall spoke of. Recall, for example, the last time you stubbed your toe. In addition to expelling a string of expletives, you may have vigorously rubbed the injured area, bringing a little relief. TENS is a more efficient way of stimulating those adjacent nerves.

In TENS treatment, electrical pulses delivered through electrodes attached to the skin excite nerves that supply the region that hurts. The stimulation itself produces a sense of tingling rather than pain. In some cases dramatic relief of pain can outlast the stimulation by a factor of hours. TENS has been especially successful in the treatment of patients whose pain is derived from peripheral nerve injuries such as arthritis or surgical incisions. We know that TENS acts at least in part by releasing endogenous opioids, because administration of **naloxone,** an opioid antagonist, partially blocks this analgesic action.

Placebos   The search for pain relief has led people to consume many unusual substances; even chemically inert pills have been reported to alleviate pain in many patients. The term **placebo** (Latin for "I shall please") refers to an inert substance (such as a sugar pill) or other treatment that has no obvious direct physiological effect. Whenever a placebo appears to alleviate pain, investigators try to determine the indirect effects of the placebo treatment or of the circumstances in which it was administered (W. A. Brown, 1998). For example, functional brain imaging indicates that opioids and placebos activate the same brain regions (Petrovic et al., 2002).

**CLINICAL
ISSUE**

In an early example, volunteer subjects who had just had their wisdom teeth extracted were told that they were being given an analgesic but were not told what kind (J. D. Levine et al., 1978). Some of these patients received morphine-based drugs, and some were given saline solutions—the placebo. One out of three patients given the placebo experienced pain relief. (Morphine produced relief in most of the patients, but not in all patients.)

The researchers gave the opioid antagonist naloxone to other patients who were also administered the placebo. Patients given the placebo *and* naloxone did not experience pain relief; this result implies that placebo relieves pain by causing the release of endogenous opioids. Grevert et al. (1983) found that naloxone reduced, but did not completely prevent placebo-induced analgesia. These results suggest that both opioid and nonopioid mechanisms contribute to placebo analgesia; the same conclusion comes from studies of other methods of analgesia that we discuss next.

Acupuncture   The earliest description of pain relief from **acupuncture** is at least 3000 years old. In some acupuncture procedures the needles are manipulated once they are in position; in other instances electrical or heat stimulation is delivered through the inserted needles. The points at which needles are inserted are related to the locus of pain and to some of the characteristics of the pain condition.

Acupuncture has gained popularity, but detailed clinical assessments indicate that only some people achieve continued relief from chronic pain. At least part of the pain-blocking character of acupuncture appears to be mediated by the release of endorphins (N. M. Tang et al., 1997). Administering opioid antagonists such as naloxone prior to acupuncture blocks or reduces its pain control effects. More research is needed in clinical settings to identify the limits of this type of pain control.

Stress   A deer fleeing from an encounter with a mountain lion would do well to ignore any pain from injuries for the moment. Sometimes people badly hurt in traumatic circumstances report little or no immediate pain, suggesting that the injured deer indeed feels no pain. Laboratory studies demonstrate the existence of pain control circuitry, but they don't tell us how the inhibitory systems are normally activated.

To answer this question, researchers have examined pain inhibition that arises in stressful circumstances. It appears that brain systems produce analgesia when pain threatens to overwhelm effective coping strategies. For example, researchers found that exposing rats to mild foot shock produced analgesia. Many other forms of stress, such as swimming in cold water, also inhibited pain responses.

For example, John Liebeskind—who was for many years a leading researcher in the area of pain—and his colleagues studied rats in stress situations that consisted of inescapable foot shock (Terman et al., 1984). Several different kinds of foot shock produced analgesia. Then these investigators assessed the role of endogenous opioids by administering an opiate antagonist: naltrexone. When analgesia is produced by *short* periods of foot shock, naltrexone reverses the analgesic response—a result demonstrating that the source of analgesia is an opioid system in the brain. However, naltrexone has little effect on stress-induced analgesia if the duration or intensity of foot shock is altered. This finding demonstrates that stress activates both an opioid-sensitive analgesic system and a pain control system that does *not* involve opioids. We know almost nothing about how the nonopioid analgesic system works.

**John Liebeskind
(1935–1997)**

Table 8.3 summarizes the many types of pain relief strategies and interventions, including surgical and pharmacological strategies, psychological brain and spinal-cord stimulation, and sensory stimulation. The elusive nature of pain is evident in this range of potential interventions, some of which reflect desperation in the face of great anguish. The persistence of pain often leads to the testing of new tools, some of which are readily denounced as quackery. However, some techniques that elicit initial skepticism may later be supported with better evidence.

TABLE 8.3 *Types of Pain Relief Intervention*

Measure	Mechanism	Limitations/comments
PSYCHOGENIC		
Placebo	May activate endorphin-mediated pain control system	Sometimes inhibited by opiate antagonists
Hypnosis	Alters brain's perception of pain	Control unaffected by opiate antagonists
Stress	Both opioid and nonopioid mechanisms	Clinically impractical and inappropriate
Cognitive (learning, coping strategies)	May activate endorphin-mediated pain control system	Limited usefulness in severe pain
PHARMACOLOGICAL		
Opiates	Bind to opioid receptors in peri-aqueductal gray and spinal cord	Severe side effects due to binding in other brain regions
Spinal block	Drugs block pain signals in spinal cord	Avoids side effects of systemic administration
Anti-inflammatory drugs	Block prostaglandin and leukotriene synthesis at site of injury	Major side effects
Aspirin	Blocks prostaglandin (see Figure 8.22) synthesis at site of injury	Does not block leukotriene synthesis
STIMULATION		
TENS/mechanical	Tactile or electrical stimulation of large fibers blocks or alters pain signal to brain	Segmental control; must be applied at site of pain
Acupuncture	Seems similar to TENS	Sometimes affected by opiate antagonists
Central gray	Electrical stimulation activates endorphin-mediated pain control systems, blocking pain signal in spinal cord	Control inhibited by opiate antagonists
SURGICAL		
Cut peripheral nerve cord Rhizotomy (cutting dorsal root) Cord hemisection Frontal lobotomy	Create physical break in pain pathway	Considerable risk of failure or return of pain

Refer to the *Learning Biological Psychology CD* for study questions, animations, activities, and other study aids.

For example, researchers examined the potential pain relief provided by magnets (Vallbona et al., 1997). Small magnets slightly stronger than the ones on your refrigerator door were strapped to sensitive pain-generating areas of the body. In other patients, inactive magnets were strapped over painful areas. A marked reduction in pain was reported by those who were exposed to the active rather than the inactive magnets. Other researchers have shown that somatosensory-evoked potentials elicited by painful stimuli are reduced when subjects are exposed to oscillating magnetic fields (Sartucci et al., 1997), so there may be magnetic pain relief treatments someday.

Summary

Sensory Processing

1. A sensory system furnishes selected information to the brain about internal and external events and conditions. It captures and processes only information that is significant for the particular organism.

2. Stimuli that some species detect readily have no effect on other species that lack the necessary receptors.

3. Some receptors are simple free nerve endings, but most include cells that are specialized to transduce particular kinds of energy.

4. Energy is transduced at sensory receptors by the production of a generator potential that stimulates the sensory neurons.

5. Coding translates receptor information into patterns of neural activity. The frequency and pattern of action potentials signal the intensity and type of stimulus encountered.

6. In adaptation, the rate of impulses progressively decreases as the same stimulation is maintained. This decline is slow in the case of tonic receptors but rapid for phasic receptors. Adaptation protects the nervous system from redundant stimulation.

7. The succession of levels in a sensory pathway is thought to allow for different, successively more elaborate, kinds of processing.

8. Mechanisms of information suppression include accessory structures that reduce the level of sensory input, and descending pathways that modulate sensory information centrally.

9. The receptive field of a cell is the stimulus region that changes the response of the cell. The receptive fields of neurons may be very different at successive levels of the sensory pathway.

10. Attention is the temporary enhancement of certain sensory messages during particular states of the individual. Attention is modulated at higher levels of the sensory pathway.

Touch: Many Sensations Blended Together

1. The skin contains several distinct types of receptors that have specific sensitivities. Inputs from the skin course through a distinct spinal pathway, the dorsal column system.

2. The surface of the body is represented at each level of the somatosensory system, and at the level of the cerebral cortex are multiple maps of the body surface.

Pain: An Unpleasant but Adaptive Experience

1. Pain guides adaptive behavior by providing indications of harmful stimuli. Pain is a complex state that is strongly influenced by cultural factors and many aspects of individual experience.

2. Pain, temperature, and itch information enters the spinal cord, crosses the midline and ascends through the anterolateral (spinothalamic) system to the brain.

3. Pain sensation is subject to many controlling or modulating conditions, including circuitry within the brain and spinal cord that employs opioid synapses. One component in the modulation of pain is made up of the descending pathways arising in the brain that inhibit incoming neural activity at synapses within the spinal cord.

4. Pain control has been achieved by the administration of drugs (including placebos), electrical and mechanical stimulation of the skin, acupuncture, and surgery, among other methods.

Recommended Reading

Fishman, S., and Berger, L. (2000). *The war on pain: How breakthroughs in the new field of pain medicine are turning the tide against suffering.* New York: HarperCollins.

Goldstein, E. B. (2001). *Sensation and perception* (6th ed.). Pacific Grove, CA: Wadsworth.

Johnson, K. O., Hsiao, S. S., and Twombly, I. A. (1995). Neural mechanisms of tactile form recognition. In M. S. Gazzaniga (Ed.), *The cognitive neurosciences* (pp. 253–269). Cambridge, MA: MIT Press.

Loeser, J. D., Butler, S. H., Chapman, C. R., and Turk, D. C. (Eds.) (2001). *Bonica's management of pain* (3rd ed.). Philadelphia: Lippincott.

Mogil, J. S., Yu, L., and Basbaum, A. I. (2000). Pain genes?: Natural variation and transgenic mutants. *Annual Review of Neuroscience, 23,* 777–811.

Vertosick, F. T. (2001). *Why we hurt: The natural history of pain.* New York: Harvest Books.

Wall, P. D., and Melzack, R. (Eds.). (1999). *Textbook of pain* (4th ed.). Edinburgh, Scotland: Churchill Livingstone.

Hearing, Vestibular Perception, Taste, and Smell

No Ear for Music

Chances are that if I give you the category "wedding music," you will immediately think of a tune or two that you can hear in your head: perhaps "The Wedding March" or, less fortunately, "The Chicken Dance." The same goes for Beethoven's Fifth Symphony, or the theme from Star Wars. These pieces of music, and others like them, are tunes that most people can identify right away, after hearing just a few bars.

But not Tony. He is completely flummoxed by music. His ability to understand pitch, and the relationships between chords, is nearly at chance levels. Although he is happy to try to belt out a song, he is unable to sing in tune and doesn't even recognize that he is singing off-key unless he is told so by a (grimacing) friend. He cannot identify

the tune to "Happy Birthday" unless he also hears the lyrics, in which case he can identify it immediately. And yet he has no problem with nonmusical uses of pitch, such as the rising tone at the end of a question.

Tony is a man of better-than-average intelligence, with perfectly normal cognitive functioning, except for his lifelong inability to appreciate music despite years of childhood music lessons. This highly specific difficulty with music is an affliction he has in common with many others; revolutionary Che Guevara and Nobel Prize–winning economist Milton Friedman are two noted examples. What is the nature of this mysterious problem? Is it a kind of hearing problem? A learning disability?

You exist only because your ancestors had keen senses that allowed them to find food and to avoid predators and other dangers. In this chapter we will continue our consideration of sensory worlds by discussing the perception of signals from distant sources, including hearing (audition) and smell (olfaction). We will also explore two related sensory systems: (1) the vestibular system, which detects orientation and movement of the body, and which is related to the auditory system; and (2) the sense of taste, which, like smell, is a chemical sense.

Recent discoveries have greatly expanded our understanding of both receptor mechanisms and central processing, especially in audition and olfaction. Both of these senses are extremely acute, and we will explore some of the special mechanisms that make them so sensitive. We begin with hearing because audition evolved from special mechanical receptors related to the somatosensory elements discussed in Chapter 8.

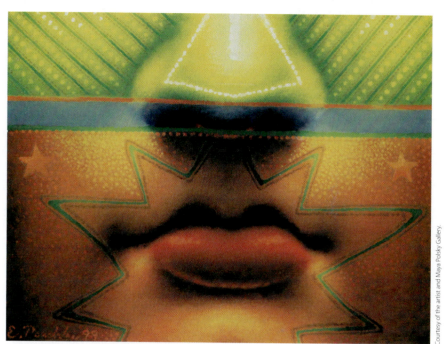

Ed Paschke, *Orange Star*, 1999, oil on canvas, 9" × 12"

HEARING

Hearing is an important part of the adaptive behavior of many animals. For humans, the sounds of speech form the basic elements of languages and therefore of social relations. Helen Keller, who was both blind and deaf, said, "Blindness deprives you of contact with things; deafness deprives you of contact with people."

The sounds of any single language are only a small subset of the enormous variety of sounds that can be produced by human vocal cavities. The sounds produced by animals—from insects to whales—also have a wide range of complexity, in keeping with their adaptive significance. For example, the melodic songs of male birds and the chirps of male crickets attract females of their species. The grunts, screeches, and burbly sounds of primates signal danger or the need for comfort or satisfaction. Elephants can recognize individuals by their calls (McComb et al., 2000). Owls and bats exploit the directional property of sound to locate prey and avoid obstacles in the dark, and whales employ sounds that can travel hundreds of miles in the ocean. Unlike visual stimuli, sounds can go around obstacles, and they work as well in the dark as in the light.

Your auditory system detects rapid changes of sound intensity (measured in **decibels, dB**) and frequency (measured in **hertz, Hz**). In fact, the speed of auditory information processing is so good that the analysis of frequency by the human ear rivals that of modern electronic gadgets. Your ear is also as sensitive as possible to weak sounds at frequencies in the range from 1000 to 2000 Hz. If it were any more sensitive, you would be distracted by the noise of air molecules bouncing against each other in your ear canal. Box 9.1 describes some basic properties of sound.

BOX 9.1 The Basics of Sound

We perceive a repetitive pattern of local increases and decreases in air pressure as sound. Usually, this oscillation is caused by a vibrating object, such as a tuning fork, or a person's larynx while speaking. A single alternation of compression and expansion of air is called one *cycle*.

Figure A illustrates the changes in pressure produced by a vibrating tuning fork. Because the sound produced by a tuning fork has only one frequency of vibration, it is called a *pure tone* and can be represented by a sine wave. A pure tone is described physically in terms of two measures:

1. **Frequency,** or the number of cycles per second, measured in hertz (Hz). For example, middle A on a piano has a frequency of 440 Hz (our perception of frequency is termed **pitch**).
2. **Amplitude,** or intensity—usually measured as sound pressure, or force per unit area, in dynes per square centimeter (dyn/cm^2) (our perception of amplitude is termed **loudness**).

Most sounds are more complicated than a pure tone. For example, a sound made by a musical instrument contains a fundamental frequency and harmonics. The **fundamental** is the basic frequency, and the **harmonics** are multiples of the fundamental. Thus if the fundamental is 440 Hz, the harmonics are 880, 1320, 1760, and so on. When different instruments play the same note, the notes differ in the relative intensities of the various harmonics; this difference is what gives each instrument its characteristic sound quality, or **timbre.**

Any complex sound can be decomposed into a sum of simple sine waves, through a mathematical process called **Fourier analysis.** (We will see in Chapter 10 that Fourier analysis can also be applied to visual patterns.) Figure B shows how several pure-tone sine waves can be summed to produce a complex waveform.

Because the ear is sensitive to a huge range of sound pressures, sound intensity (a measure of the difference between two pressures) is usually expressed in decibels (dB), a logarithmic scale. The common reference level, for human hearing is $0.0002\ dyn/cm^2$; this is the smallest amplitude at which an average human ear can detect a 1000 Hz tone. A faint whisper is about ten times as intense, and a jet airliner 500 feet overhead is about a million times as intense. The whisper is about 20 dB above threshold, and the jet-liner is about 120 dB above threshold. Normal conversation is about 60 dB above the reference level.

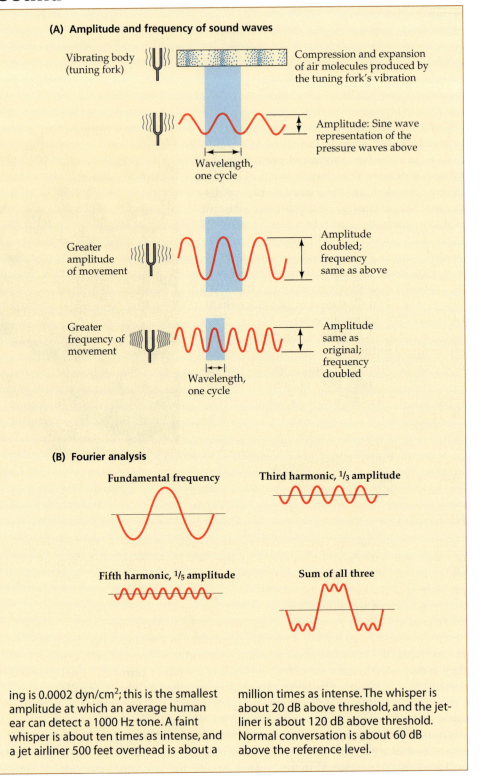

(A) Amplitude and frequency of sound waves

Vibrating body (tuning fork)

Compression and expansion of air molecules produced by the tuning fork's vibration

Amplitude: Sine wave representation of the pressure waves above

Wavelength, one cycle

Greater amplitude of movement

Amplitude doubled; frequency same as above

Greater frequency of movement

Amplitude same as original; frequency doubled

Wavelength, one cycle

(B) Fourier analysis

Fundamental frequency

Third harmonic, $1/3$ amplitude

Fifth harmonic, $1/5$ amplitude

Sum of all three

Each Part of the Ear Performs a Specific Function in Hearing

How do the small vibrations of air molecules become the speech, music, and other sounds we hear? The molecules exert mechanical force on auditory end organs, the peripheral components of the auditory system. In this section we will discuss these initial stages of auditory processing.

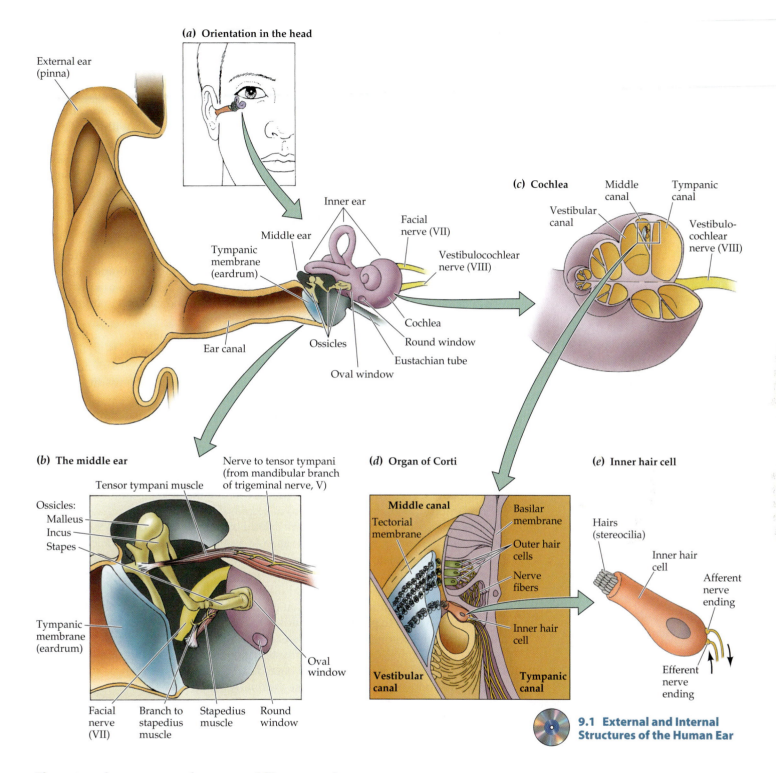

(a) Orientation in the head

External ear (pinna)

Inner ear

Middle ear

Tympanic membrane (eardrum)

Facial nerve (VII)

Vestibulocochlear nerve (VIII)

Ear canal

Ossicles

Cochlea

Round window

Eustachian tube

Oval window

(c) Cochlea

Vestibular canal

Middle canal

Tympanic canal

Vestibulo-cochlear nerve (VIII)

(b) The middle ear

Tensor tympani muscle

Nerve to tensor tympani (from mandibular branch of trigeminal nerve, V)

Ossicles:
Malleus
Incus
Stapes

Tympanic membrane (eardrum)

Oval window

Facial nerve (VII)

Branch to stapedius muscle

Stapedius muscle

Round window

(d) Organ of Corti

Middle canal

Tectorial membrane

Basilar membrane

Outer hair cells

Nerve fibers

Inner hair cell

Vestibular canal

Tympanic canal

(e) Inner hair cell

Hairs (stereocilia)

Inner hair cell

Afferent nerve ending

Efferent nerve ending

9.1 External and Internal Structures of the Human Ear

The external ear captures, focuses, and filters sound

Sound waves are collected by the **external ear,** which consists of the part we readily see, called the **pinna** (plural *pinnae;* Latin for "wing"), and a canal that leads to the eardrum (Figure 9.1*a* and *b*). The pinna is a distinctly mammalian characteristic, and mammals show a wide array of ear shapes and sizes. The acoustic properties of the external ear are important because its shape physically transforms sound energies.

The "hills and valleys" of the pinna modify the character of sound that reaches the middle and inner ear. Some frequencies of sound are enhanced; others are dimmed. For example, the shape of the human ear especially increases the reception of sounds in the frequency range of 2000 to 5000 Hz, a range that is important for speech perception. The shape of the external ear is also important in sound local-ization—that is, identifying the direction and distance of the source of a sound (discussed later in this chapter).

Although (some) humans can move their ears only enough to entertain children, many other mammals are able to dexterously shape and swivel their pinnae to help determine the source of a sound. Animals with acute auditory localization abilities, such as bats, may have especially mobile ears. Of course, animals with mobile ears have to take into account the position of the pinna when interpreting sounds around them. Information about the position of the external ear in such animals is conveyed to the auditory pathways in several forms, including feedback information from receptors in the muscles around the pinna.

The middle ear concentrates sound energies

Between the external ear and the receptor cells of the inner ear is a group of structures, including bones and muscles, that constitute the **middle ear** (see Figure 9.1b). A chain of three tiny bones, or **ossicles,** connects the **tympanic membrane** (eardrum) at the end of the ear canal to an opening of the inner ear called the **oval window.** These ossicles, the smallest bones in the body, are called the **malleus** (hammer), the **incus** (anvil), and the **stapes** (stirrup).

Small displacements of the tympanic membrane move the chain of ossicles. These bones help the minute mechanical forces of air particles perturb the fluid in the inner ear by focusing the pressures from the relatively large tympanic membrane onto the small oval window. This arrangement vastly amplifies sound pressure so that it is capable of stimulating the fluid-filled inner ear.

The mechanical linkage of the ossicles is not fixed; it is modulated by two muscles in ways that improve auditory perception and protect the delicate inner ear from loud, potentially damaging sounds. One of these muscles, the **tensor tympani** (see Figure 9.1b), is attached to the malleus, which is connected to the tympanic membrane. The other muscle of the middle ear is attached to the stapes and thus is called the **stapedius.** When activated, these muscles stiffen the linkages of the middle-ear bones, thus reducing the effectiveness of sounds.

The muscles of the middle ear are activated by sounds that are 80 to 90 dB above a person's hearing threshold—about as loud as a noisy street. When a loud sound reaches the ear, the stapedius muscle starts to contract about 200 ms later. The middle-ear muscles also attenuate self-made sounds; without this system, body movement, swallowing, vocalizations, and other internally produced sounds would be distractingly loud. In fact, species that produce especially loud calls, such as bats, rely on this system to protect their auditory receptors from physical damage (Avan et al., 1992). Interestingly, the middle-ear muscles contract just *before* the self-made sound occurs, demonstrating that the system is controlled in a complex manner. People whose middle-ear muscles have been damaged by disease complain about the annoying loudness of sounds that they formerly ignored.

The cochlea converts vibrational energy into waves of fluid

The complex structures of the **inner ear** (Figure 9.1c) ultimately convert sound into neural activity. In mammals the auditory portion of the inner ear is a coiled structure called the **cochlea** (from the Greek *kochlos,* "snail") (Figure 9.1c and d). Embedded in the temporal bone of the skull, the human cochlea is a marvel of miniaturization. In an adult, the cochlea measures only about 4 mm in diameter—about the size of a pea. Unrolled, the cochlea would measure about 35 to 40 mm in length.

The region nearest the oval-window membrane is the base of the spiral; the other end is referred to as the apex. The cochlea is a coil of three parallel canals: (1) the **vestibular canal,** (2) the **middle canal,** and (3) the **tympanic canal** (see Figure 9.1c). Because the entire structure is filled with noncompressible fluid, movement within the cochlea in response to a push on the oval window requires the presence of a movable outlet membrane. This membrane is the **round window,** which separates the tympanic canal from the middle ear (see Figure 9.1b).

The principal components that do the work of converting sounds into neural activity, collectively known as the **organ of Corti,** consist of three main structures: (1) the sensory cells (**hair cells**), (2) an elaborate framework of supporting cells, and (3) the terminations of the auditory fibers. The base of the organ of Corti is the **basilar membrane.** This flexible membrane separates the tympanic canal from the middle canal (see Figure 9.1*d*), and importantly, it vibrates in response to sound. The basilar membrane is about five times wider at the apex of the cochlea than at the base, even though the cochlea itself narrows toward its apex.

When the stapes moves in and out as a result of acoustic vibrations, it exerts varying pressure on the fluid of the vestibular canal, which in turn causes oscillating movements of the basilar membrane. Late in the nineteenth century, it was suggested that different parts of the basilar membrane might be affected by different frequencies of auditory stimulation. This property was eventually documented by the Nobel Prize–winning Hungarian scientist Georg von Békésy, who found that the site of the largest amplitude of displacement of the basilar membrane depends on the frequency of the stimulus (Figure 9.2). In other words, the membrane exhibits distinct "tuning." High frequencies cause maximal displacement of the basilar membrane near the base, where the membrane is narrow. For low-frequency stimuli, displacement of the basilar membrane is greatest in regions where the membrane is wider—toward the apex (Ashmore, 1994).

The hair cells transduce movements of the basilar membrane into electrical signals

Each human ear contains two sets of sensory cells within the organ of Corti: a single row of about 3500 **inner hair cells** (**IHCs;** called *inner* because they are closer to the central axis of the coiled cochlea) and about 12,000 **outer hair cells** (**OHCs**) in three rows (see Figure 9.1*d*). The IHCs are flask-shaped, and the OHCs are cylindrical, with a diameter of approximately 5 μm and a length of 20 to 70 μm.

From the upper end of each hair cell protrude tiny hairs whose length ranges from 2 to 6 μm (Figure 9.1*e*). Each hair cell has 50 to 200 of these relatively stiff hairs, called **stereocilia** (singular *stereocilium;* from the Greek *stereos,* "solid," and the Latin *cilium,* "eyelid") or simply *cilia.* The heights of the stereocilia increase progressively across the hair cell, so the tops approximate an inclined plane. Atop the organ of Corti is the **tectorial membrane** (see Figure 9.1*d*). The stereocilia of the OHCs extend into indentations in the bottom of this membrane.

Auditory nerve fibers contact the base of the hair cells (see Figure 9.1*e*). The organ of Corti has four kinds of synapses and nerve fibers. Two of these (1 and 3 in

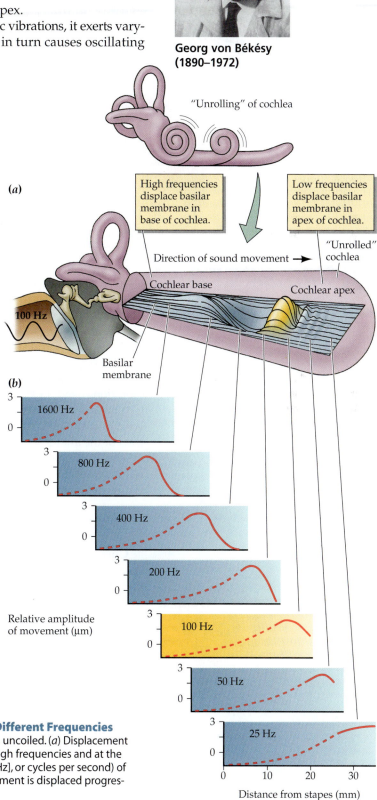

Georg von Békésy (1890–1972)

9.2 Basilar Membrane Movement for Sounds of Different Frequencies In this illustration the basilar membrane is represented as uncoiled. (*a*) Displacement of the basilar membrane peaks at the cochlear base for high frequencies and at the apex for low frequencies. (*b*) As the frequency (measured in hertz [Hz], or cycles per second) of stimulation decreases, the position of the peak of membrane movement is displaced progressively toward the apex of the cochlea.

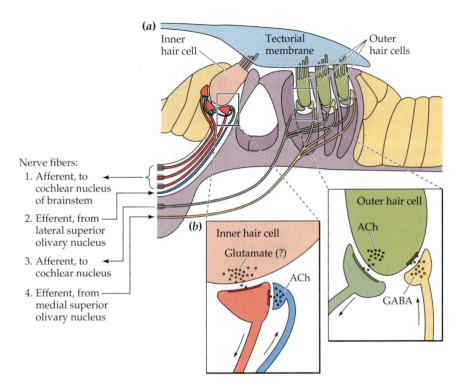

Nerve fibers:
1. Afferent, to cochlear nucleus of brainstem
2. Efferent, from lateral superior olivary nucleus
3. Afferent, to cochlear nucleus
4. Efferent, from medial superior olivary nucleus

9.3 Auditory Nerve Fibers and Synapses in the Organ of Corti (*a*) The inner and outer hair cells form synaptic connections to and from the brain. (*b*) Different synaptic transmitters are hypothesized to be active at the synapses of inner and outer hair cells in the organ of Corti.

Figure 9.3*a*) are afferents that convey messages from the hair cells to the brain; the other two (2 and 4 in Figure 9.3*a*) are efferents that convey messages from the brain to the hair cells. Different synaptic transmitters are active at each type of synapse (Figure 9.3*b*) (Eybalin, 1993). Each IHC is associated with 16 to 20 auditory nerve fibers; relatively few nerve fibers contact the many OHCs. In fact, the afferent nerve fibers running from the IHCs account for 90% to 95% of the afferent auditory fibers, and give rise to the perception of sound. These auditory afferents from the cochlea synapse on neurons in the cochlear nuclei of the pons.

The OHCs have a different function: modulating acoustic stimulation. Controlled by the CNS via their efferent nerve fibers, the OHCs can change their length (Zheng et al., 2000), thereby influencing the mechanics of the cochlea. Changes in length of the OHCs can stiffen or relax segments of the basilar membrane and thus actively sharpen its tuning to different frequencies, as we will see later in this chapter (Ashmore, 1994). The IHCs also receive efferent messages, probably to inhibit some of the input from loud sounds. Further evidence of the different roles of the inner and outer hair cells comes from studies of a mutant strain of mice that lack IHCs but have normal OHCs; these mice appear to be deaf (Deol and Gluecksohn-Waelsch, 1979).

How do hair cells turn movement into neural activity? Through the mechanisms we have already discussed, sounds induce vibrations of the basilar membrane. These vibrations bend the hair cell stereocilia that are inserted into the tectorial membrane (see Figure 9.1*d*). Very small displacements of hair bundles cause rapid changes in ionic channels of the stereocilia. These changes initiate excitation of the hair cells and then of the afferent axons (Hudspeth, 1989, 1992).

The ion channels in the stereocilia are believed to be gated by mechanical energy, as are those in touch receptors (see Chapter 8), but the gates in the channels for hearing are also specialized for rapid response: They can open and close thousands of times per second. This rapidity rules out the use of second messengers, which are found in receptors for smell, taste, and sight (as we'll see later in this chapter and in Chapter 10).

Current estimates suggest that each hair cell has only about 100 ion channels, about one or two per stereocilium. Comparing the recordings from different parts of the cell indicates that some ion channels are near the tops of the cilia. Fine, threadlike fibers called **tip links** run along the tips of the stereocilia (Figure 9.4*a*). These links mechanically coordinate the movements of the stereocilia (Eisen et al., 1999), but they also appear to be key elements in the generation of hair cell potentials. Studies by Hudspeth and colleagues (1997, 2000) suggest that a sound that makes the hair cells sway even only very slightly will increase the tension on the elastic tip links and pull open a "trapdoor," opening the ion channel, which closes again in a fraction of a millisecond as the hair cell sways back (Figure 9.4*b* and *c*).

Opening of the channels allows an inrush of potassium (K^+) ions and a rapid depolarization of the entire hair cell. This initial depolarization leads to a rapid influx of calcium ions (Ca^{2+}) at the *base* of the hair cell, which causes synaptic vesicles there to fuse with the presynaptic membrane and release their chemical contents—thought to be the synaptic transmitter glutamate—from the base of the hair cell, and stimulate the afferent nerve fiber (Figure 9.4*c*).

(a)

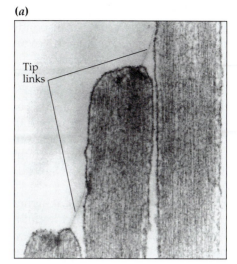

Tip links

 9.4 How Auditory Stimulation Affects the Stereocilia on Cochlear Hair Cells   (a) This micrograph of stereocilia shows the tip links as threadlike structures. (b) Hudspeth (1992) proposed the model of hair cell stimulation illustrated here. (c) Displacement of the stereocilia opens K⁺ channels. This depolarization opens Ca²⁺ channels in the cell's base, causing the release of neurotransmitter to excite afferent axons. (Micrograph courtesy of A. J. Hudspeth.)

(b)

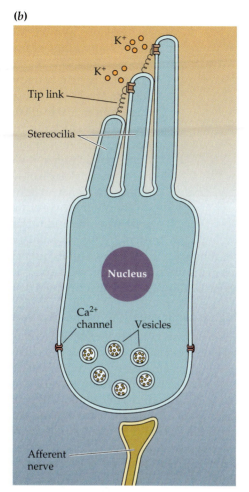

(c)

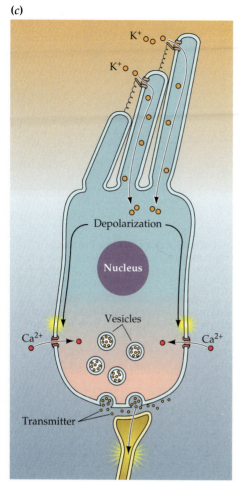

The ion pores in the cilia are large and do not discriminate different kinds of ions. They let even small organic molecules pass through, which is why some drugs, such as aspirin and antibiotics, can impair hair cells by attacking their mitochondria. Susceptibility to this kind of damage of the receptor is inherited maternally, as are the mitochondria themselves.

Active electromechanical processes in the cochlea enhance frequency discrimination

Humans can discriminate between sounds that differ in frequency by just 2 Hz. Early studies of the **tuning curves** of single auditory nerve fibers, recorded electrically from the vestibulocochlear (VIII) nerve, revealed much more precise tuning than Békésy had found in his measurements of the physical tuning of the basilar membrane. The fact that the basic physical characteristics of the basilar membrane cannot account for the sharpness of tuning found in the auditory nerve indicated that an additional sharpening process must be at work. We now know that the cochlea itself has a remarkable electromechanical system for enhancing its tuning.

We mentioned earlier that OHCs show the surprising property of changing length when they are stimulated electrically—an electromechanical response (Brownell et al., 1985). Hyperpolarization causes the OHCs to lengthen; depolarization causes them to shorten. These changes, which amount to as much as 4% of the length of the cell, occur almost instantaneously. Investigators hypothesize that these mechanical responses of the OHCs serve as a **cochlear amplifier,** amplifying the movements of the basilar membrane in some regions and damping basilar membrane movements in other regions. This active and ongoing modulation of the basilar membrane sharpens the tuning of the cochlea (Ashmore, 1994; Hubbard, 1993).

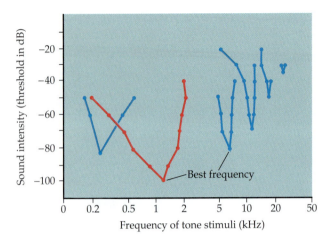

9.5 Examples of Tuning Curves of Auditory Nerve Cells   These curves are obtained by measurement of neural responses to sounds of different intensities and frequencies. Because they represent threshold measurements, the *lowest* point on each curve corresponds to that neuron's preferred frequency. Illustrated here are responses of six neural units recorded from the auditory nerve of the cat. (After Kiang, 1965.)

But whereas each neuron responds to a very precise frequency at its threshold, as more-intense stimuli are used the neuron responds to a broader range of frequencies. For example, the fiber whose responses are shown in red in Figure 9.5 has its *best frequency* at 1200 Hz; that is, it responds to a very weak tone at 1200 Hz. When sounds are 20 dB stronger, however, the fiber responds to any frequency from 500 to 1800 Hz. Thus although an auditory nerve fiber transmits exclusively auditory information, it does not respond to just one frequency of stimulation. If the brain received a signal from only one such fiber, it would not be able to tell whether the stimulus was a weak tone of 1200 Hz or a stronger tone of 500 or 1800 Hz, or any frequency in between.

The ability to discriminate frequencies is even sharper at higher stations of the auditory nervous system, as Békésy further hypothesized. At the medial geniculate nucleus and the auditory cortex, neurons are excited by certain frequencies and inhibited by neighboring frequencies. This interplay of excitation and inhibition further sharpens the frequency responses, allowing us to discriminate very small frequency differences.

The ears emit sounds as part of the hearing process

The cochlea is not only the first stage in the analysis of sounds; in most people it also *produces* sounds. If a brief sound—a click or a short burst of tone—is sent into the external ear canal, a few milliseconds later a similar sound comes back from the inner ear. This is not just an echo from the eardrum or middle ear, although such echoes exist. The cochlea produces this sound. The sounds that the cochlea produces in response to acoustic stimulation are called **evoked otoacoustic emissions (EOAEs)**. They occur in all people who have normal hearing, even in infants, and are thought to reflect the action of the cochlear amplifier discussed earlier, selectively boosting the response to particular frequencies. Alone or in combination with other techniques, the measurement of EOAEs is useful for detecting hearing impairments in newborns (Watkin, 2001).

In addition to evoked otoacoustic emissions, the ears of many people produce continuous low-level sounds at one or more frequencies; these sounds are called **spontaneous otoacoustic emissions (SOAEs)** (D. T. Kemp, 1979; Zurek, 1981). These spontaneous emissions are usually less than 20 dB above threshold; they can be detected by sensitive microphones in quiet environments, but the people who produce these sounds do not perceive them.

About two-thirds of women and half of men below the age of 60 produce SOAEs (McFadden, 1993a). Because they are observed in infants as well as in adults, SOAEs don't seem to require prior auditory experience. Usually people who produce SOAEs have more sensitive hearing than people who don't, a difference that is consistent with the idea that these emissions are part of the cochlear amplifier (McFadden, 1993b).

Surprisingly, women who have a twin brother produce significantly fewer SOAEs, and weaker EOAEs, than singleton females or females who have a female twin (McFadden, 1993b). A possible explanation for the lower incidence of SOAEs in females with male twins is that in the womb, the female is exposed to androgens secreted by the male—a prenatal masculinizing effect (see Chapter 12). Lesbians, on average, produce weaker EOAEs than heterosexual women (Loehlin and McFadden, 2003; McFadden and Pasanen, 1998); given the possible link between prenatal androgen exposure and SOAEs, perhaps there is also a link between prenatal androgen exposure and an increase in the probability of homosexuality in females.

Auditory System Pathways Run from the Brainstem to the Cortex

On each side of your head, about 30,000 to 50,000 auditory fibers from the cochlea make up the auditory part of the vestibulocochlear (VIII) cranial nerve. Recall that

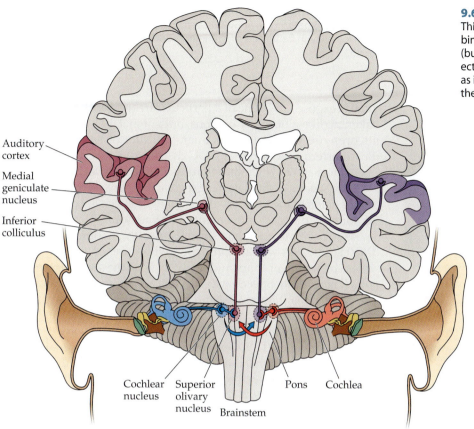

Auditory cortex

Medial geniculate nucleus

Inferior colliculus

Cochlear nucleus   Superior olivary nucleus   Pons   Cochlea

Brainstem

9.6 Auditory Pathways of the Human Brain
This view from the front of the head shows the first binaural afferent interactions in the brainstem. Most (but not all) of the information from each ear projects to the cortex on the opposite side of the brain, as illustrated here by the colors of the projections to the medial geniculate and cortex.

most of these afferent fibers are carrying messages from the IHCs, each of which stimulates several nerve fibers. Input from the auditory nerve is distributed in a complex manner to both sides of the brain, as depicted in Figure 9.6. Each auditory nerve fiber divides into two main branches as it enters the brainstem. Each branch then goes to separate groups of cells in the dorsal and ventral **cochlear nuclei.**

The output of the cochlear nuclei also travels via multiple paths. One path goes to the **superior olivary nuclei,** which receive inputs from both right and left cochlear nuclei. This bilateral input is the first stage in the CNS at which *binaural* (two-ear) effects are processed; as you might expect, this mechanism plays a key role in localizing sounds by comparing the two ears, as we'll discuss shortly. Several other parallel paths converge on the **inferior colliculus,** which is the auditory center of the midbrain. Outputs of the inferior colliculus go to the **medial geniculate nucleus** of the thalamus. At least two different pathways from the medial geniculate extend to several auditory cortical areas.

Electrical recordings from auditory projections reveal that at every level of the auditory system, from cochlea to auditory cortex, auditory neurons display **tonotopic organization;** that is, they are spatially arranged in an orderly map according to the auditory frequencies to which they respond. Tonotopic organization can be demonstrated by the mapping of auditory brain regions using 2-deoxyglucose (2-DG), as shown in Figure 9.7. Following 2-DG injection, an an-

9.7 Mapping Auditory Frequencies in the Cat Inferior Colliculus   (*a*) This lateral view of the cat brain shows the plane of the transverse section in (*b*) through the inferior colliculi. (*c, d*) Locations of the cells labeled with 2-DG via 2000 Hz stimulation (*c*) and 21,000 Hz stimulation (*d*) are indicated here by blue and red, respectively. (*e*) Complete tonotopic mapping shows the range of frequencies that can stimulate the cat's auditory system. (After Serviere et al., 1984.)

(*a*)

Inferior colliculi

(*b*)

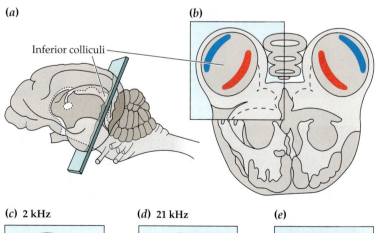

(*c*) **2 kHz**   (*d*) **21 kHz**   (*e*)

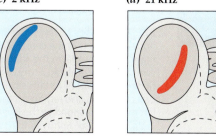

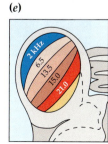

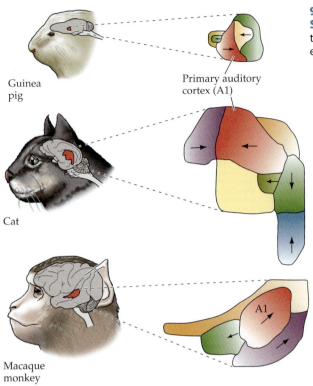

Guinea pig

Primary auditory cortex (A1)

Cat

Macaque monkey

A1

9.8 Tonotopic Organization of Auditory Cortical Regions in Three Species of Mammals The arrows show the direction of tonotopic representation, from low to high frequencies. A1, primary auditory cortex. (After Merzenich et al., 1993.)

imal is exposed to a tone of a particular frequency. Because 2-DG is taken up like glucose by neurons, but not metabolized, we can use its presence within neurons as an indicator of neuronal activity. Postmortem processing of 2-DG distribution reveals which cells were most active when the stimulus frequency was presented.

Most species of animals have several auditory cortical fields. Different fields of the auditory cortex may be specialized for location of sounds in space, movement of sound sources, perception of species-specific sounds, and so on (Figure 9.8). In humans, PET and fMRI studies show that stimulation with pure tones or noise activates chiefly the primary auditory cortex on the superior temporal lobe (Figure 9.9a). Speech activates this and other, more specialized auditory areas (Figure 9.9a and b). Interestingly, at least some of these regions are activated when normal subjects try to lip-read— that is, to understand someone by watching that person's lips without auditory cues (L. E. Bernstein et al., 2002; Calvert et al., 1997); this result suggests that the auditory cortex integrates other, nonauditory, information with sounds. We'll discuss the auditory cortex in more detail shortly.

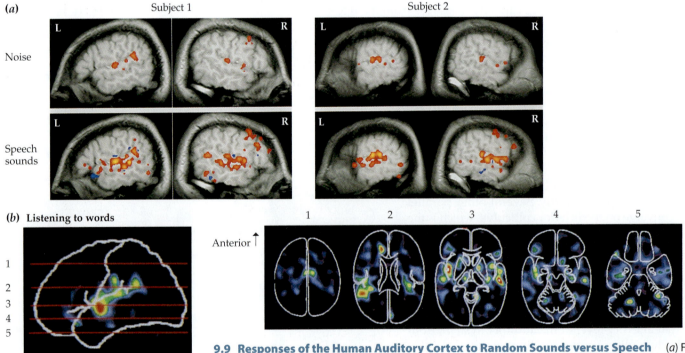

(a)

Subject 1   Subject 2

Noise

Speech sounds

(b) Listening to words

Anterior

9.9 Responses of the Human Auditory Cortex to Random Sounds versus Speech (a) Functional-MRI scans of the cerebral hemispheres show that pure tones or noise (*top*) activate chiefly the primary auditory area on the superior aspect of the temporal lobe, while listening to speech sounds (*bottom*) activates other auditory cortical regions, as well as the primary auditory area. (b) Lateral (*left*) and horizontal (*right*) PET scans show that listening to words activates not only several regions of the cerebral cortex but also regions of the thalamus and the cerebellum. The numbered horizontal lines in the left panel correspond to the levels of the horizontal sections in the right panel. (Part *a* from Binder et al., 1994, courtesy of Jeffrey Binder; *b* from Posner and Raichle, 1994, courtesy of Marcus Raichle.)

Two Main Theories Describe How We Discriminate Pitch

Most of us can discriminate very small differences in frequency of sound over the entire audible range—from 20 Hz to 15,000 or even 20,000 Hz. The ability to detect a change in frequency is usually measured as the **minimal discriminable frequency difference** between two tones. The detectable difference is about 2 Hz for sounds up to 2000 Hz; above these frequencies it grows larger.

Note that *frequency* and *pitch* are not synonymous terms. **Frequency** describes a physical property of sounds (see Box 9.1); **pitch** relates solely to the subjective sensory experience of sounds. This is an important distinction because frequency is not the sole determinant of perceived pitch (at some frequencies, higher-intensity sounds may seem higher-pitched), and changes in pitch do not precisely parallel changes in frequency.

How do we account for the ability to discriminate pitches? Two main theories have been offered. One, described as **place theory,** argues that our perception of pitch depends on where the sound causes maximal displacement of the basilar membrane. Recall that high frequencies displace the basilar membrane at the base of the cochlea, and low frequencies displace the basilar membrane in the apex of the cochlea. According to place theory, therefore, pitch is encoded in the physical location of the activated receptors along the length of the basilar membrane: Activation of receptors near the base of the cochlea signals "treble," and activation of receptors nearer the apex signals "bass."

COMPETING HYPOTHESES

The alternative idea, **volley theory,** emphasizes the relations between the frequency of auditory stimuli and the pattern or timing of action potentials. According to this perspective, the firing pattern of a single nerve cell reveals the frequency of the stimulus because each time the stimulus changes frequency, the pattern of neuronal discharge is altered. The crudest representation of this idea suggests a one-to-one relationship; that is, a 500 Hz tone is represented by 500 action potentials per second, and a 1000 Hz tone stimulating the same neuron is represented by a frequency of 1000 action potentials per second. In both cases the firing of the nerve impulse is *phase-locked* to the stimulus; that is, it occurs at a particular portion of the cycle. Such a phase-locked representation can be accomplished more accurately by several fibers than by a single fiber—hence the term *volley,* as in a volley of nerve impulses.

Are these views—place and volley theories—necessarily antagonistic? No. In fact, the contemporary view of pitch perception incorporates *both* perspectives.

As place theory predicts, a change in frequency is accompanied by a change in the region of maximal disturbance of the basilar membrane, as well as activation of associated auditory receptors. For complex sounds with components at several different frequencies, the cochlea accomplishes a sort of Fourier analysis (see Box 9.1), with the different frequencies mapped as peaks of vibration at different places along the basilar membrane. The accuracy of place representation of auditory frequency has improved over the course of evolution as the basilar membrane has lengthened and the number of hair cells and auditory nerve fibers has increased.

As volley theory predicts, temporal patterns of neural discharges appear to encode auditory frequencies. Direct recordings indicate that, for lower-frequency sounds, the frequency of action potentials often encodes the auditory frequency on a one-to-one basis. For higher-frequency sounds, the frequency of action potentials may instead encode an auditory frequency that is an integer multiple. Encoding a multiple, rather than one-to-one frequency allows the auditory system to overcome the maximal neuronal firing rate of about 1000 action potentials per second. In general, volley coding is emphasized at the lower end of the hearing range, up to about 4000 Hz.

So the frequency properties of a sound are coded in two ways: (1) according to the distribution of excitation among cells—that is, place coding or tonotopic representation—and (2) according to the temporal pattern (volley) of discharge in cells extending from the auditory nerve to the auditory cortex.

Some species are sensitive to sounds with very high frequencies (**ultrasound**) or very low frequencies (**infrasound**), and make use of them in special ways. For example, many species of bats produce loud vocalizations, in the range of 50,000 to 100,000 Hz, and listen to the echoes reflected back from objects in order to navigate and hunt in the dark. Their extraordinary sensitivity and accuracy is conferred by elaborate adaptations that adorn their bodies and brains.

At the other end of the spectrum, it has been observed that homing-pigeon races are severely disrupted if the birds encounter the sonic-boom shock wave of the Concorde jet (an infrasound pulse that can travel hundreds of miles), suggesting that the pigeons use infrasound cues to establish a navigational map (Hagstrum, 2000). Tigers may use infrasound to add impact to their roars (Walsh et al., 2003), and infrasound experimentally inserted into concerts heightens the music's emotional effect on human listeners, but it's not yet known how we detect infrasound.

By Comparing the Ears, We Can Localize Sounds

Normally we can locate the position of a sound source with great accuracy (within about 1°) by analyzing **binaural** (two-ear) differences in the sound. Two kinds of binaural cues signal the location of a sound source.

Intensity differences are differences in loudness at the two ears. In humans, intensity differences arise because the head casts a sound shadow, blocking sounds located to one side (off-axis sounds) from reaching both ears with equal loudness (this is less of a factor in species with different ear placement, such as dogs and cats). The head shadow is most pronounced for higher-frequency sounds. Low-frequency sounds have longer sound waves that reach around the head.

Latency differences are differences between the two ears in the time of arrival of sounds. They arise because one ear is always a little closer to an off-axis sound than is the other ear. Two kinds of latency differences are present in a sound: *onset disparity,* which is the difference between the two ears in hearing the beginning of the sound, and *ongoing phase disparity,* which is the continuous mismatch between the two ears in the arrival of all the peaks and troughs that make up the sound wave (these cues are illustrated in Figure 9.10).

We now know that sound localization involves processing of both intensity differences and latency differences; this is known as the **duplex theory.** At low frequencies, no matter where sounds are presented in *azimuth* (horizontally around your head), there are virtually no intensity differences between the ears. For these

9.10 Cues for Binaural Hearing
(*a*) The two ears receive somewhat different information from sound sources located to one side or the other of the observer's midline. (*b*) The head blocks frequencies greater than 1000 Hz, producing binaural differences in sound intensity. The resulting differences in perceived intensity are greater at higher frequencies. (*c*) Sounds also take longer to reach the more distant ear, resulting in binaural differences in time of arrival. Onset disparity is the latency difference between the two ears for the beginning of a sound. Ongoing phase disparity is the difference between the ears for the peaks and troughs of the sound wave.

(*a*)

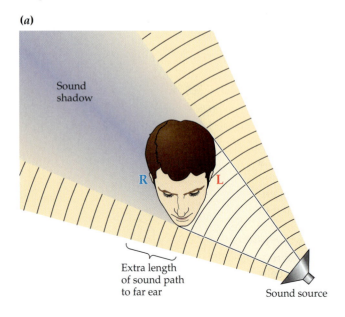

(*b*)

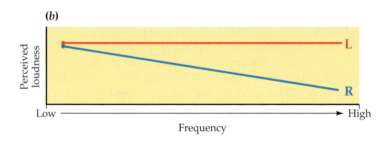

(*c*)

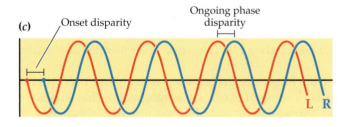

frequencies, differences in times of arrival are the principal cues for sound position (and at very low frequencies, neither cue is much help; this is why you can place the subwoofer of an audio system anywhere you want). At higher frequencies, however, the sound shadow cast by the head produces significant binaural intensity differences. Of course, you can't perceive which types of processing you're relying on for any given sound; in general, we are aware of the results of neural processing but not the processing itself.

What brain systems analyze binaural cues? Tympanate (eardrum) hearing appears to have evolved independently in birds and mammals (and others), and these groups of animals have evolved different solutions to particular auditory problems, such as the localization of sounds—a nice example of convergent evolution (see Chapter 6). Both birds and mammals have highly specialized brainstem mechanisms that receive information from the two ears, and they use arrays of bipolar neurons to derive sound location from the left and right auditory signals. These bipolar neurons are capable of making very precise timing calculations by comparing the inputs to their two dendrites (Agmon-Snir et al., 1998).

EVOLUTION AT WORK

In birds, the organization of neurons within the primary sound localization nucleus (called the *nucleus laminaris*) constitutes an auditory map of space: Each neuron is maximally excited by a particular latency difference between the two ears, corresponding to a particular place in space. This map is further developed at higher levels, especially the *tectum* (equivalent to the mammalian inferior colliculus), which contains a complete map of space.

Mammals apparently do things quite differently. The **superior olive** is the primary sound localization nucleus in the mammalian brain, and its two main divisions serve different functions. The *lateral superior olive* processes intensity differences. The *medial superior olive* (*MSO*) processes latency differences, but in contrast to birds, the MSO does not appear to contain a map of auditory space. Instead, sound location is encoded by the relative activity of the *entire* left MSO compared with the *entire* right MSO (Grothe, 2003; McAlpine et al., 2001).

So, for example, a sound on the midline would activate the left and right MSO equally, and the two signals would effectively cancel each other out. But an off-axis sound on the right would produce more excitation of the left MSO than the right MSO, and the converse would be true for sounds on the left. The bigger the difference between the left and right MSO, the farther the sound source is from the midline. This disparity is passed along for further processing at other levels of the auditory system, such as the inferior colliculus.

The structure of the external ear provides yet another sort of localization cue. As we mentioned earlier, the hills and valleys of the external ear selectively reinforce some frequencies in a complex sound, and diminish others. This process is known as **spectral filtering,** and the frequencies that are affected depend on where the sound originates (Kulkarni and Colburn, 1998).

The relationship between spectral cues and location is learned and calibrated during development. Spectral cues provide critical information about *elevation* (vertically around your head), and are especially important for sounds located on the midline where there are no intensity or latency differences between the ears. In fact, people who are deaf in one ear can utilize **monaural** (one-ear) spectral cues to localize sounds to some extent. Similarly, researchers can place a speaker directly in the ear canal and, by varying the spectral filtering of natural sounds, fool a person or animal into believing that the sound came from a particular point in space (Xu et al., 1999).

NEURAL PLASTICITY

As we mentioned earlier, neurons that respond to auditory localization are also found at a variety of levels above the brainstem, including the cortex, and single-cell recordings suggest that their selectivity varies widely. Some auditory neurons respond to a sound that originates almost anywhere in the opposite hemifield. Other, location-sensitive neurons have relatively small receptive fields that respond only to sounds at a particular location. Although there is no discrete spatial map in the mammalian auditory cortex, models suggest that combining the receptive fields of only 128 such cortical neurons would be sufficient to predict the source of a sound as well as the cat does (Furukawa et al., 2000). Orchestra conductors are especially good at localizing the sources of sounds (Münte et al., 2001), presumably because of extensive practice ("Mr. Donini, could you *please* play in tune?").

The Auditory Cortex Performs Complex Tasks in the Perception of Sound

The historical view of auditory function was that the various subcortical auditory areas performed only basic processing, serving mostly as stepping-stones in a pathway to the auditory cortex (Masterton, 1993). The cortex, it was believed, was where auditory sensation and discrimination really arose. But behavioral testing suggested otherwise; for example, cats retain the ability to discriminate different tones following surgical removal of auditory cortex (Raab and Ades, 1946; Rosenzweig, 1946; for a review, see Neff and Casseday, 1977). If the auditory cortex is not involved in these basic kinds of auditory discrimination, then what *does* it do?

Early studies relied on simple, but unnatural, pure tones (Masterton, 1993, 1997). Most of the sounds in nature, however—such as vocalizations of animals, footsteps, snaps, crackles, and pops—contain many frequencies and change rapidly, and the auditory nervous system likely evolved to deal with such sounds. Indeed, most central auditory neurons habituate rapidly to continuous sound, ceasing to respond after only a few milliseconds, but brief sounds or abrupt onsets of sound usually evoke responses from many neurons, from the cochlear nuclei to the auditory cortex. Ablation of the auditory cortex in cats does impair discrimination of temporal *patterns* of sound (Neff and Casseday, 1977). Similarly, bilateral ablation of the auditory cortex in monkeys impairs their ability to discriminate species-specific vocalizations (Heffner and Heffner, 1989). So auditory cortex is required to analyze complex sounds encountered in everyday life.

There seem to be two main streams of auditory processing in cortex (Kaas and Hackett, 1999): A dorsal stream, involving the parietal lobe, may be concerned with spatial location of sounds, while a ventral stream through the temporal lobe may analyze the various components of sounds (Romanski et al., 1999). Perhaps this distinction forms the basis of the *where* and *what* auditory processing streams; a similar processing scheme has been proposed for visual processing too (see Chapter 10).

Experience affects auditory perception and the auditory pathways

NEURAL PLASTICITY

Aspects of auditory discrimination, and the neural circuits involved in hearing, change as we grow. At birth the human infant has diverse hearing abilities. Postnatal developments involve elaborate structural changes throughout auditory pathways. Accompanying these changes are progressive improvements in the perception of complex sounds, such as speech. Because the world after birth is filled with a complex array of sounds, it is reasonable to ask whether experience shapes or modulates the forming of connections in the auditory system.

One demonstration of the role of early auditory experience comes from studies of musicians (Pantev et al., 1998). In these studies the evoked brain activity from musicians and nonmusicians was identical in response to pure tones. But if, instead of pure tones, the more complex and musically relevant sounds from a piano were used, musicians displayed a greater brain response than did nonmusicians. Now maybe these people became musicians because their brains were more responsive to complex tones to begin with. However, there was a significant correlation between the magnitude of brain response to piano tones and the age at which the musicians had begun studying music. The earlier the musician had begun her studies, the greater her brain response to piano tones, suggesting that early exposure to musical training affects brain auditory responsiveness.

Certainly there are big differences by adulthood: The portion of primary auditory cortex where music is first processed, called *Heschl's gyrus*, is more than twice as large in professional musicians as in nonmusicians, and more than twice as strongly activated by music (P. Schneider et al., 2002). Debate continues about the extent to which musical ability is hardwired, but the existence of disorders in which people cannot accurately discern tunes (called *amusia*; from the Greek *amousia*, "want of harmony") suggests that at least the rudiments of a musical sense are innate (Münte, 2002).

Tone-deaf Tony, whom we described at the beginning of the chapter, exemplifies this dyslexia-like problem. Whereas most infants clearly understand the basics of musical relationships almost from birth, people with congenital amusia never develop that ability (Peretz and Hyde, 2003). We assume that Tony was born with a problem that severely limited the ability of the relevant brain mechanisms, such as Heschl's gyrus, to comprehend music and respond to training.

The role of auditory experience in the development of sound localization is implied by observations in bilaterally deaf children who were fitted with different types of hearing aids (Beggs and Foreman, 1980). The children in one group were given a hearing aid that delivered the same sounds to both ears. In a second group children were fitted with a separate hearing aid for each ear so that they experienced dichotic stimuli. When examined years later, the children who had been fitted with dichotic hearing aids were able to localize sounds with significantly greater accuracy than the children who had experienced comparable overall levels of sounds but had been deprived of dichotic stimuli.

Eric Knudsen et al. (1984) have performed elegant studies using an especially acute binaural perceiver—the barn owl. When hunting, owls use both arrival differences and intensity differences to accurately localize sounds at night (Peña and Konishi, 2000). Cells of the avian tectum are arranged in a roughly spherical representation of space (Knudsen, 1984; Knudsen and Konishi, 1978). In the owl tectum, both auditory *and* visual space are represented, and the maps for the two senses correspond closely (Knudsen, 1982). In fact, most cells in the owl tectum respond to both auditory and visual stimuli, and it is thought that this close alignment of auditory and visual maps of space helps guide behavioral responses toward stimuli.

To assess the impact of early experience on the development of these maps, investigators plugged one ear of adult and baby owls. As a result, the birds made large errors in localizing sounds, with responses shifted in the direction of the open ear—presumably because the sound was more intense in that ear, which would normally mean that it had come from that side. Adult animals never seemed to adjust to the ear plug, but owls younger than 8 weeks at the time of plugging slowly began to compensate.

It turns out that vision is a key mediator in recalibrating auditory localization: The compensation did not occur if the owls were deprived of vision; and if they were fitted with prism glasses that deviated vision by 10° (Figure 9.11), the adjustment of

Eric Knudsen

NEURAL PLASTICITY

9.11 The Role of Vision in Auditory Localization   This young owl has had prisms fitted over its eyes to deviate vision by about 10° to the side. At first, the owl makes mistakes when reaching for a visual target, but eventually it learns to adapt to the prisms. The neurons in its tectum also adapt, so now neurons excited by a sound from a particular location in space are also excited by visual stimuli presented 10° to the left of that location. (Courtesy of Eric Knudsen.)

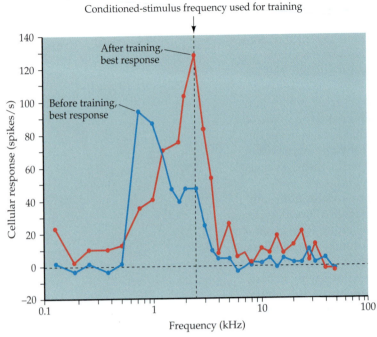

Conditioned-stimulus frequency used for training

After training, best response

Before training, best response

9.12 Long-Term Retention of a Trained Shift in Tuning of an Auditory Receptive Field Before training, the best frequency of the auditory cortex cell of an adult guinea pig that is represented on this graph was about 0.7 kHz. After training with a 1.1 kHz tone, the best frequency shifted to 1.1 kHz. After 2 and 4 weeks, the shift had remained stable. (From N. M. Weinberger, 1998.)

auditory localization was matched to this visual error (Knudsen and Knudsen, 1985). Apparently, the induced mismatch between the auditory and visual tectal maps provoked a remapping of auditory space in the baby owls that was no longer possible in the brains of the adult owls. These changes might arise either from structural modifications of growing neural circuits or from modulations of synaptic effectiveness (Knudsen, 1998).

Mammalian auditory areas also show plasticity, and unlike the case with owls, this plasticity persists into adulthood. In one example, monkeys were trained to discriminate sounds in order to receive a food reward. After several months of training, the cortical representation for the training frequencies had become substantially larger. Control subjects that just passively listened to the same tones did not show this response (Recanzone et al., 1993). Similarly, conditioning a guinea pig to tones of a particular frequency can cause cortical neurons to shift their response to favor that frequency (Figure 9.12) (N. M. Weinberger, 1998).

Intriguingly, it seems that reward may be a potent contributor to remodeling of auditory cortex. Each day for 20 days, Bao et al. (2001) presented rats with tones paired with microstimulation of the ventral tegmental area (VTA). VTA stimulation activates the brain's dopamine-based reward system (see Chapter 4). These investigators subsequently found that cortical representations were greatly increased for tones that occurred shortly before—but not after—the VTA stimulation. From an evolutionary perspective this sort of mechanism is highly adaptive because it specifically shapes the cortex to respond to stimuli that have previously signaled a reward.

Deafness Is a Major Disorder of the Nervous System

There are about 18 million cases of deafness or hearing impairment in the United States (Travis, 1992). These disabilities range in severity from occasional difficulties in speech perception (due to decreased sensitivity in the range of speech frequencies, about 500 to 2000 Hz) to a complete inability to hear. In this section, after looking at the different kinds of deafness, we will discuss a promising treatment for this disability.

There are three main causes of deafness

CLINICAL ISSUE

Many severe hearing impairments arise early in life and impair language acquisition. Others occur later in life as a consequence of environmental factors, such as exposure to loud sounds, infections, or side effects of certain drugs. There are three general categories of deafness—conduction, sensorineural, and central—the latter two of which involve compromised neural function.

Conduction deafness Conduction deafness arises when disorders of the outer or middle ear prevent vibrations produced by auditory stimuli from reaching the cochlea. In one common form of conduction deafness, the ossicles become fused and can no longer transmit sound vibrations effectively. Surgery to free up the ossicular chain is helpful in some cases. The nervous system is generally not involved in conduction deafness.

Sensorineural deafness An enormous variety of factors and conditions can cause sensorineural deafness: metabolic dysfunctions, infections, exposure to toxic substances, trauma, exposure to loud sounds, and hundreds of hereditary disorders (Pennisi, 1997). The end result is the same: Auditory nerve fibers are unable to become excited in a normal manner, and this hearing loss is usually permanent. Defects in certain genes governing hair cell structure and function are prominent genetic causes of sensorineural deafness (Littlewood and Muller, 2000; E. D. Lynch et al., 1997). It is estimated that mutations in a gene named *GJB2* may be responsible for as much as 50% of congenital or early-onset hearing impairment (Cryns and Van Camp, 2004); this gene encodes the protein connexin-26, which is involved in the formation of electrical synapses (*gap junctions*; see Chapter 3).

Drug-induced deafness sometimes results from the toxic properties of a group of antibiotics that includes streptomycin and gentamicin. The **ototoxic** (ear-damaging) properties of streptomycin were discovered when many patients that received it as treatment for tuberculosis subsequently developed cochlear and/or vestibular damage. In severe cases the hair cells of the cochlea were completely destroyed, producing total, irreversible loss of hearing.

Noise pollution and loud sounds—industrial noise, intense music, loud engines, and especially the firing of guns—can severely damage the cochlea in a short period of time. Once again, the hair cells suffer the brunt of the damage: In the affected part of the cochlea, the stereocilia appear shattered and broken, like a flattened forest.

The outer hair cells appear to be especially susceptible to sound trauma, but sustained exposure to intense sound will eventually lead to destruction of the organ of Corti in the relevant range of frequencies. Loud sounds coupled with the use of some over-the-counter drugs, such as aspirin, can also have profound effects on hearing (McFadden and Champlin, 1990), reducing sensitivity to certain tones by up to 40 dB, and/or leading to the development of **tinnitus,** a sensation of noises or ringing in the ears (Brien, 1993).

Can damaged hair cells be regrown? Although fish and amphibians produce new hair cells throughout life, mammals traditionally have been viewed as incapable of regenerating hair cells. This conclusion may have been too hasty, however. Through manipulation of certain genes, tissue cultures from the organ of Corti of young rats have been induced to produce new hair cells (Zheng and Gao, 2000). And a novel approach that uses a virus to insert a gene called *Math1* into cochlear epithelial cells reportedly causes those cells to turn into new hair cells (Kawamoto et al., 2003), raising hopes for a gene therapy to regenerate hair cells in deaf people someday.

GENES AND BEHAVIOR

Central deafness   Central deafness (hearing loss caused by brain lesions or impairments) is seldom a simple loss of sensitivity. An example of the complexity of changes in auditory perception following cerebral cortical damage is **word deafness,** a disorder in which people show normal speech and hearing for simple sounds but cannot recognize spoken words. Some researchers have suggested that the basis of word deafness is an abnormally slow analysis of auditory inputs. Another example of central deafness is **cortical deafness,** in which patients have difficulty recognizing both verbal and nonverbal auditory stimuli. Cortical deafness is a rare syndrome that arises from a bilateral destruction of inputs to the auditory cortex.

Strokes that interrupt all of the projection fibers from the medial geniculate nucleus to the various auditory cortical regions also cause deafness (Y. Tanaka et al., 1991). These patients still show various acoustic reflexes mediated by the brainstem—such as bodily responses to environmental sounds—although they deny hearing the sounds to which they are reacting. In contrast, patients with bilateral destruction of only the *primary* auditory cortex often have less-severe hearing loss, presumably because other auditory cortical regions contribute to hearing, as discussed earlier.

Electrical stimulation of the auditory pathway can alleviate deafness

Researchers have tried to restore hearing in profoundly deaf individuals by directly stimulating the auditory nerve with electrical currents (Loeb, 1990; J. M. Miller and

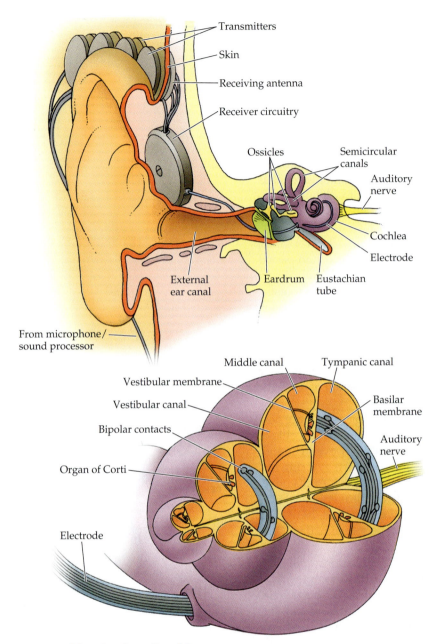

Transmitters

Skin

Receiving antenna

Receiver circuitry

Ossicles

Semicircular canals

Auditory nerve

Cochlea

Electrode

External ear canal

Eardrum

Eustachian tube

From microphone/ sound processor

Middle canal

Tympanic canal

Vestibular membrane

Basilar membrane

Vestibular canal

Bipolar contacts

Auditory nerve

Organ of Corti

Electrode

9.13 Cochlear Implants Provide Hearing in Some Deaf People
A microphone detects sound and directs the cochlear implant circuitry to stimulate the auditory nerve. Although this apparatus provides only a crude simulation of ordinary auditory nerve activity, the brain can learn to use the information to decipher speech.

Spelman, 1990). Progress in the development of **cochlear implants** that deliver such electrical stimulation has been rapid (Figure 9.13).

Who gains by the use of such devices? In several types of sensorineural hearing loss, including those caused by ototoxic drugs and childhood meningitis, the damage that produces deafness involves the hair cells. Although the hair cells may be completely destroyed, the electrical excitability of the auditory nerve often remains unchanged. Some of the most enthusiastic recipients of this clinical aid are patients who became deaf before acquiring language (Loeb, 1990). However, some deaf people and advocates of the deaf oppose the use of such prostheses (Crouch, 1997). They believe that deaf people should accept their disability and use sign language to communicate, rather than become imperfect hearers. Nevertheless, analytical studies reveal an increase in speech perception with continued use of cochlear prostheses (Skinner et al., 1997).

What kinds of sensory responses does electrical stimulation of the auditory nerve provoke? The usual technique employed in these studies is to insert a small group of wires through the cochlea to the endings of the auditory nerve. In these patients electrical stimulation produces pitch sensations that are partially related to the tonotopic organization of the cochlea. Unfortunately, the effective number of channels is limited by technical factors, so the range of frequencies that can be excited is also limited. With successive technical advances, the number has increased from 6 different frequencies to 32, but this range is still very limited compared to normal hearing. *Dynamic range*—the range of loudnesses within a sound—is also limited because intensities of electrical stimulation barely above the thresholds for detecting sound also produce discomfort.

Nevertheless, the pattern of electrical stimulation of the auditory nerve provided by cochlear implants can greatly facilitate acoustically mediated behaviors. For example, this treatment makes it possible to distinguish voiced and unvoiced speech sounds (e.g., "v" and "f"), which cannot be distinguished in lip-reading. In addition, thanks to cochlear implants, many formerly deaf people can converse over the telephone with absolutely no visual aids.

When a cochlear implant is turned on, functional imaging shows that the auditory cortex is activated (J. Ito et al., 1993; Klinke et al., 1999), and tonotopic organization of the activation is evident (Lazeyras et al., 2002), indicating that this region is processing the information. Cochlear implants also demonstrate the plasticity of the auditory cortex because patients must learn to interpret the signals provided by the implants. Furthermore, the earlier the implants are provided, the better the eventual performance (Rauschecker, 1999). The success of these implants is due mainly to the cleverness of the brain, not the implant.

A new generation of implantable aids, called **auditory brainstem implants** (**ABIs**), produce auditory sensations by directly stimulating the cochlear nuclei of the brainstem. By bypassing the ear altogether, ABI devices offer hope of hearing restoration even for those who lack a functional auditory nerve (Rauschecker and Shannon, 2002).

VESTIBULAR PERCEPTION

The vestibular system provides information about the force of gravity on the body and the acceleration of the head. When you go up in an elevator, you feel the acceleration clearly. When you turn your head or ride in a car going around a tight curve, you feel the change of direction. If you are not used to these kinds of stimulation, sensitivity to motion can make you "seasick." The receptors of the vestibular system inform the brain about mechanical forces that act on the body.

The Receptor Mechanisms for the Vestibular System Are in the Inner Ear

The receptors of the vestibular system lie within the inner ear next to the cochlea. (The term *vestibular* comes from the Latin *vestibulum,* "entrance hall," and reflects the fact that the system lies in hollow spaces in the temporal bone.) In mammals, one portion of the vestibular system consists of three **semicircular canals,** fluid-filled tubes that are each oriented in a different plane (Figure 9.14*a* and *b*). The three canals are connected at their ends to a saclike structure called the **utricle** (literally, "little uterus"). Lying below the utricle is another small fluid-filled sac, the **saccule** ("little sac").

Receptors in these structures, like those of the auditory system, are groups of hair cells whose bending leads to the excitation of nerve fibers. In each semicircular canal, the hair cells are in an enlarged region, the **ampulla** (plural *ampullae*), that lies at the junction between each canal and the utricle (Figure 9.14*b* and *f*). Here the cilia of the hair cells are embedded in a gelatinous mass. The orientation of the hairs is quite precise and determines the kind of mechanical force to which they are especially sensitive.

The three semicircular canals are at right angles to each other, so one or another detects rotational acceleration in any direction. The receptors in the saccule and utricle respond to vertical and horizontal linear forces, and thus signal static position as well (Figure 9.14*c*). Small bony crystals on the gelatinous membrane, called **otoliths** (from the Greek *ot-*, "ear," and *lithos,* "stone"), increase the sensitivity of these receptors to movement (Figure 9.14*d* and *e*). At the base of the hair cells in these receptors are nerve fibers connected much like those that connect auditory hair cells (Figure 9.14*g*).

Evolution Has Shaped the Auditory and Vestibular End Organs

The long evolutionary history of the auditory–vestibular system is better known than that of other sensory systems because the receptors are encased in bone, which can fossilize (van Bergeijk, 1967; E. G. Wever, 1974). It is generally accepted that the auditory end organ evolved from the vestibular system, although the ossicles probably evolved from parts of the jaw. Before that, the vestibular system evolved from the **lateral-line system,** a sensory system found in many kinds of fish and some amphibians. The lateral-line system consists of an array of receptors along the side of the body. Tiny hairs that emerge from sensory cells in the skin are embedded in small gelatinous columns called **cupulae** (singular *cupula*), like those in mammals (see Figure 9.14*f* and *g*).

EVOLUTION AT WORK

In aquatic animals with lateral-line systems, movements of water in relation to the body surface stimulate these receptors so that the animal can detect currents of

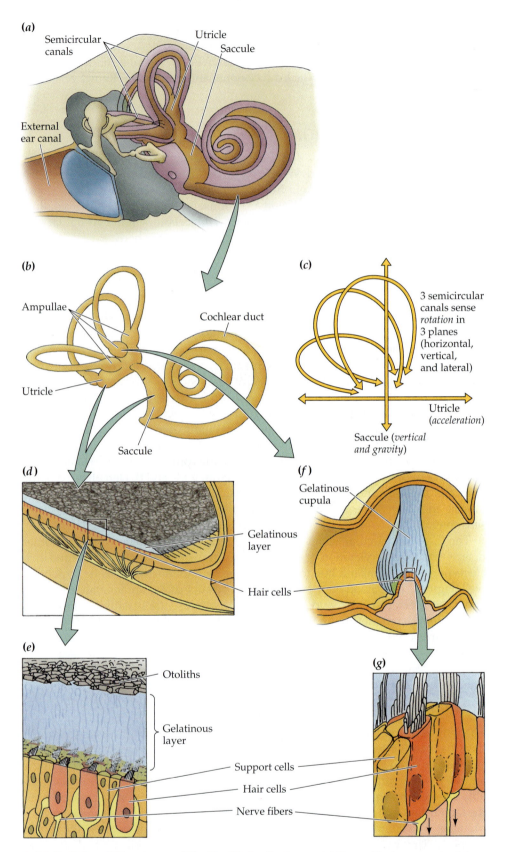

(a) Semicircular canals
Utricle
Saccule
External ear canal

(b) Ampullae
Cochlear duct
Utricle
Saccule

(c) 3 semicircular canals sense *rotation* in 3 planes (horizontal, vertical, and lateral)
Utricle *(acceleration)*
Saccule *(vertical and gravity)*

(d) Gelatinous layer
Hair cells

(f) Gelatinous cupula
Hair cells

(e) Otoliths
Gelatinous layer
Support cells
Hair cells
Nerve fibers

(g)

9.14 Peripheral Structures of the Vestibular System (*a*) The vestibular apparatus is located in the temporal bone. (*b*) The semicircular canals are connected through ampullae to the utricle, which connects to the saccule. (*c*) The semicircular canals detect rotation in three planes; the utricle and saccule detect linear acceleration and static position. (*d–g*) Embedded in a gelatinous layer, hair cells in the ampullae, utricle, and saccule are the receptors of the vestibular system. Otoliths increase the sensitivity of these hair cells to movement.

water and movements of other animals, prey, or predators. Information from the lateral line helps schools of fish stay in formation because each fish feels the currents made by the others. A specialized form of lateral-line organ is the lateral-line canal, a groove that partially encloses the cupulae. It is speculated that the first semicircular canals developed from a stretch of lateral-line canal that migrated into the body. This development gave the animal a sensor for turns to the right or left, and this receptor, being away from the surface of the body, was free of effects of stimulation of the skin. Sensitivity to change of direction was optimized when the canal developed into a roughly circular form.

From the vestibular system that arose out of the lateral-line system evolved the auditory system (Figure 9.15). Note that in birds the auditory receptor organ (the lagena) never coiled into a snail shape.

Nerve Fibers from the Vestibular Portion of the Vestibulocochlear (VIII) Nerve Synapse in the Brainstem

The structural arrangements of brain pathways dealing with the vestibular system reflect its importance to motor control and posture. Nerve fibers from the vestibular receptors enter lower levels of the brainstem and synapse in the **vestibular nuclei.** Some of the fibers bypass this structure and go directly to the cerebellum, contributing to its motor functions. The outputs of the vestibular nuclei are complex, as is appropriate, considering their influences on the motor system. These outputs go to the motor nuclei of the eye muscles, the thalamus, and the cerebral cortex, among others.

Some Forms of Vestibular Excitation Produce Motion Sickness

There is one aspect of vestibular activation that many of us would gladly do without. Certain types of body acceleration—as when riding in a boat, car, plane, or roller coaster—can produce the misery of **motion sickness.** Caloric stimulation—the pouring of warm or cold water into one ear canal—produces the same effect by initiating movements of inner ear fluids that simulate body movements. Motion sickness is caused especially by low-frequency movements that an individual cannot control. For example, passengers in a car are more likely to suffer from motion sickness than the driver.

One major theory of motion sickness—**sensory conflict theory**—argues that we feel bad when we receive contradictory sensory messages, especially a discrepancy between vestibular and visual information. When an airplane bounces around in turbulence, for instance, the vestibular system signals that various accelerations are occurring, but as far as the visual system is concerned, nothing is happening—the plane's interior is a constant. The resulting disorientation is distressing (Benson, 1990).

Why do we experience motion sickness? Michel Treisman (1977) hypothesized that the sensory conflict of some conditions of motion sets off responses that evolved to rid the body of swallowed poison. According to this hypothesis, discrepancies in sensory information normally signal danger and cause dizziness and vomiting to eliminate potentially toxic food. Such a response has obvious significance for preservation of life, although it is not helpful as a response to movements of vehicles.

THE CHEMICAL SENSES: TASTE AND SMELL

Sensitivity to chemical stimuli in the environment is vital for the survival of organisms throughout the animal kingdom. The sense of taste provides an immediate assessment of foods (Lindemann, 1995): Sweet indicates high-calorie foods; savory tastes signal a protein source; salty and sour relate to important aspects of homeostasis; bitter warns of toxic constituents. The sense of smell is critical for appreciating the rich and complex flavors of individual foods but has additional important

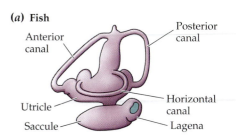

(*a*) **Fish**

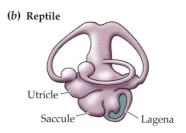

(*b*) **Reptile**

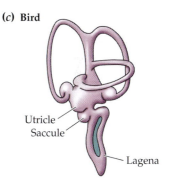

(*c*) **Bird**

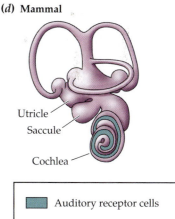

(*d*) **Mammal**

Auditory receptor cells

9.15 Evolution of the Vestibular and Auditory End Organs

functions as well, such as signaling the presence of prey, predators, or potential mates. This section will explore the many roles of the chemical senses—taste and smell—in guiding behavior.

Chemicals in Tastants Elicit Taste Sensations

We start our review of the chemical senses with taste, which is somewhat simpler than smell and in some ways has been more thoroughly investigated.

Humans detect five basic tastes

Because we recognize many substances by their distinct flavor, we tend to think that we can discriminate many tastes. But traditionally humans have been said to detect only four basic tastes: salty, sour, sweet, and bitter. Strong evidence now supports the inclusion of a fifth taste, called *umami,* which we will discuss in the next section. There also may be more than one kind of sweet taste. But in any case, there are only a few tastes.

The sensations uniquely aroused by an apple, a steak, or an olive are *flavors* rather than simple tastes; they involve smell as well as taste. Block your nose, and a potato tastes the same as an apple. Our ability to respond to many odors—it is estimated that humans can detect more than 10,000 different odors and can discriminate as many as 5000 (Ressler et al., 1994)—is what produces the complex array of flavors that we normally think of as tastes. Ordinarily, smell and taste work together, such that detecting certain tastes makes it easier to detect certain odors (Dalton et al., 2000). Although the taste system is very similar across different species of mammals, there is some variability; for example, cats are not sensitive to sweet.

The ability to taste many substances is already well developed in humans at birth. Even premature infants show characteristic responses to different tastes, sucking in response to a sweet substance but trying to spit out a bitter substance. Newborns seem to be relatively insensitive to salty tastes, but a preference for mildly salty substances develops in the first few months. This preference does not seem to be related to experience with salty tastes; rather it probably indicates maturation of the mechanisms of salt perception (Beauchamp et al., 1994).

Tastes excite specialized receptor cells on the tongue

In mammals, most taste receptor cells are located on small projections from the surface of the tongue; these little bumps are called **papillae** (singular *papilla;* Latin for "nipples"). Each papilla holds one or more **taste buds,** and each taste bud consists of a cluster of 50 to 150 cells (Figure 9.16*a*). At the surface end of the taste bud is an opening called the *taste pore.* The taste cells extend fine cilia into the taste pore, which come into contact with **tastants** (substances that can be tasted).

Not all the sensory cells in taste buds signal taste sensations; some are pain receptors, responding to stimuli such as "hot" red pepper, and others are touch receptors. With a life span of only 10 to 14 days, taste cells are constantly being replaced. A single taste bud has receptor cells that are at many different stages of development (Figure 9.16*b*).

There are three kinds of taste papillae; Figure 9.16*c* shows their distribution on the tongue. The most numerous are **fungiform papillae,** which resemble button mushrooms in shape (*fungus* is Latin for "mushroom"). The tongue contains hundreds of fungiform papillae, but the numbers vary greatly among individuals. A fungiform papilla usually contains only a single taste bud. Each of the few **circumvallate papillae** and **foliate papillae** contains several taste buds.

Many books show a map of the tongue indicating that each taste is perceived mainly in one region (sweet at the tip of the tongue, bitter at the back, and so on), but Linda Bartoshuk (1993), a specialist in taste psychophysics, states that this map is erroneous: "The [usual] tongue map has become an enduring scientific myth" (p. 253). Work of Collings (1974) and Yanagisawa et al. (1992) shows that all four ba-

Linda Bartoshuk

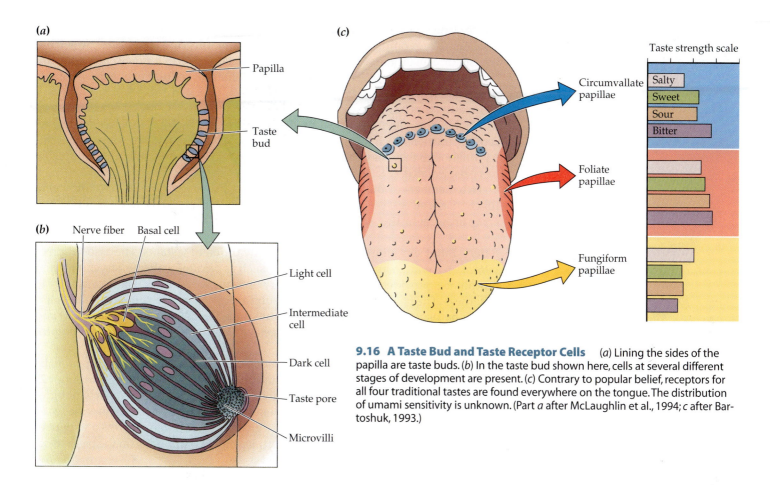

9.16 A Taste Bud and Taste Receptor Cells   (*a*) Lining the sides of the papilla are taste buds. (*b*) In the taste bud shown here, cells at several different stages of development are present. (*c*) Contrary to popular belief, receptors for all four traditional tastes are found everywhere on the tongue. The distribution of umami sensitivity is unknown. (Part *a* after McLaughlin et al., 1994; *c* after Bartoshuk, 1993.)

sic tastes can be perceived anywhere on the tongue where there are taste receptors. The areas do not differ greatly in the strength of taste sensations that they mediate (see Figure 9.16*c*). The distribution of umami sensitivity is not yet known.

Different cellular processes transduce the basic tastes

The tastes salty and sour are evoked when taste cells are stimulated by simple ions acting on ion channels in the membranes of the taste cells. Sweet and bitter tastes are perceived by specialized receptor molecules and communicated by second messengers.

Salty   Sodium ions (Na$^+$) are transported across the membranes of taste cells by sodium ion channels. Blocking these channels with a drug prevents the salty taste of sodium chloride in both humans and rats; facilitating the passage of Na$^+$ across the membrane with another drug intensifies salty tastes (Schiffman et al., 1986). The entry of sodium ions partially depolarizes the taste cells and causes them to release neurotransmitters that stimulate the afferent neurons that relay the information to the brain.

Sour   An acid tastes sour, whether it is a simple inorganic compound, such as hydrogen chloride, or a more complex organic compound, such as lactic acid. The property that all acids share is that each releases a hydrogen ion (H$^+$). The hydrogen ions block potassium channels in cell membranes, preventing the release of potassium ions (K$^+$) from taste cells. The buildup of K$^+$ in the cell leads to depolarization and to neurotransmitter release. The afferent fibers stimulated by these taste cells report the acidic stimulation to the brain.

**GENES AND
BEHAVIOR**

Sweet   The molecular mechanisms in the transduction of sweet, bitter, and umami tastes are more complex than those responsible for salty and sour tastes. Sweet, bitter, and umami tastants appear to stimulate specialized receptor molecules on membranes of the taste cells, causing a cascade of internal cellular events involving G proteins and second messengers.

Investigators have identified two important families of G protein–coupled taste receptors, designated **T1R** and **T2R,** that are expressed by some taste cells. These receptors function much like the slow metabotropic receptors we considered in Chapter 3, although they may employ a unique G protein α subunit, called *gustducin,* that has been isolated in taste cells (McLaughlin et al., 1994).

Two members of the T1R family—T1R2 and T1R3—combine (*heterodimerize*) to function as a sweet receptor in taste cells (G. Nelson et al., 2001), recognizing a wide array of sweet-tasting substances.

Bitter   Bitter sensations are evoked by many different tastants. The association of bitter tastes with many toxic substances—such as nicotine, caffeine, strychnine, and morphine—provided strong evolutionary pressure to develop a high sensitivity to bitterness. The fact that different bitter substances can be discriminated—as determined by psychophysical work with human tasters (McBurney et al., 1972) and with animal subjects (Lush, 1989)—suggested that there is more than one receptor for bitterness.

Indeed, members of the T2R family of G protein–coupled receptors appear to be bitter receptors (E. Adler et al., 2000; Chandrashekar et al., 2000). There are about 25 T2R family members, and this large number may reflect the wide variety of bitter substances encountered in the environment, as well as the adaptive importance of being able to detect and avoid them. Any given taste bud may express a variety of T2R receptors, so the brain probably identifies bitter compounds on the basis of activity patterns across an array of taste buds.

About 25% of people in the United States cannot taste the chemical phenylthiocarbamide (PTC) and the related compound 6-*n*-propylthiouracil (PROP), even though they can taste other bitter substances. Family studies indicate that there are genetic differences between tasters and nontasters. Furthermore, some people, referred to as *supertasters,* exhibit heightened sensitivity to some bitter tastes, suggesting that they are genetically different as well (Bartoshuk and Beauchamp, 1994). In fact, supertasters also enjoy stronger sweet sensations from some substances. Nontasters of PROP have the fewest taste buds (averaging 96 per square centimeter) on the tongue tip, medium tasters have an intermediate number (184), and supertasters have the most (425) (Reedy et al., 1993).

Umami   A probable fifth basic taste, **umami** (Japanese for "good taste") is described as a meaty, savory flavor. For most of the twentieth century, researchers argued about whether a distinct umami taste existed, but we now know about two types of receptors that appear to be specialized to respond to exactly this sort of tastant. The first of these, a variant of the metabotropic glutamate receptor, is expressed in certain taste buds (Chaudhari et al., 2000) and likely responds to the amino acid glutamate. Monosodium glutamate (MSG), which is used widely in cooking, undoubtedly stimulates this taste receptor.

Foods rich in protein will of course also be rich in amino acids, and this seems like useful information for an animal to detect. It turns out that a second probable umami receptor is a heterodimer of T1R1 and T1R3 receptors. Despite the similarity to the T1R2+T1R3-based sweet receptor described already, the T1R1+T1R3 receptor selectively responds to most of the 20 standard amino acids that might be encountered in the diet (G. Nelson et al., 2002).

In mice that lack the gene encoding the T1R3 receptor, sensitivity to sweet and umami tastants is greatly reduced, but not abolished (Damak et al., 2003). This implies that there must be additional receptor systems for these tastes that are T1R3-independent. The hunt for other types of taste receptors continues.

Taste information is transmitted to several parts of the brain

The **gustatory system** (from the Latin *gustare,* "to taste") extends from the taste receptor cells through brainstem nuclei and the thalamus to the cerebral cortex (Figure 9.17). Each taste cell transmits information to several afferent fibers, and each afferent fiber receives information from several taste cells. The afferent fibers run along three different cranial nerves—the facial (VII), glossopharyngeal (IX), and vagus (X) nerves (see Figure 2.4). The gustatory fibers in each of these nerves run to the brainstem. Here they synapse with second-order gustatory fibers that run to the ventral posterior medial nucleus of the thalamus. After another synapse, third-order gustatory fibers run to the cortical taste areas in the somatosensory cortex.

When you consider that individual taste cells may express more than one kind of taste receptor, and thus probably respond to more than one kind of tastant, it becomes clear that identification of the taste stimulus must rely on subsequent processing by the brain. According to one hypothesis, **pattern coding,** taste discrimination requires central processing based on relative activity coming from different afferent axons, originating from taste cells that are sensitive to differing complements of tastants.

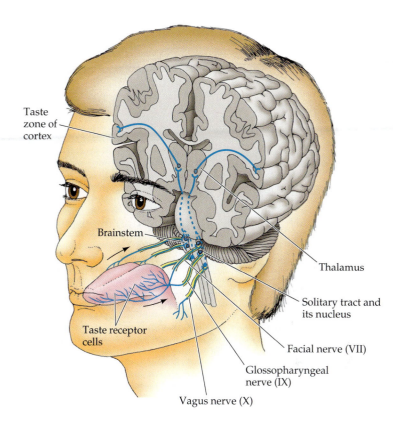

Taste zone of cortex

Brainstem

Thalamus

Solitary tract and its nucleus

Taste receptor cells

Facial nerve (VII)

Glossopharyngeal nerve (IX)

Vagus nerve (X)

9.17 Anatomy and Main Pathways of the Human Gustatory System

Chemicals in the Air Elicit Odor Sensations

In the 1980s, a survey of **olfaction** (smell sense) sponsored by *National Geographic* magazine elicited responses from more than 1.5 million individuals who smelled scents released when the surface of a piece of paper containing six different odors was scratched (Gilbert and Wysocki, 1987). Half of the respondents were able to detect all six odors presented, and only about 1% were unable to smell three or more samples. But there was widespread partial **anosmia** (odor blindness): A third of the respondents could not detect androsterone (sweat), and 29% could not detect galaxolide (musk). Women were slightly better than men in both detecting and identifying odors. The ability to detect odors declined somewhat with age. Smokers showed a dulled sense of smell; they found pleasant odors to be less pleasant and unpleasant odors less unpleasant than nonsmokers did.

Many aspects of an animal's world are determined by chemicals carried in the air. Olfactory sensitivity varies widely across species of mammals: Cats and mice, dogs and rabbits—all have a sharper sense of smell than humans, and dolphins don't have olfactory receptors at all (Freitag et al., 1998). These differences evolved because of variability in the importance of smell for survival and reproduction. Nevertheless, different species of mammals, including humans, accomplish olfaction in much the same way, as we describe next.

The sense of smell starts with receptor neurons in the nose

In humans, a sheet of cells called the **olfactory epithelium** (Figure 9.18) lines the dorsal portion of the nasal cavities and adjacent regions, including the septum that separates the left and right nasal cavities. Within the olfactory epithelium of the nasal cavity are three types of cells: receptor neurons, supporting cells, and basal cells. At least 6 million olfactory receptor neurons are found in the 2 cm^2 area of human olfactory epithelium. In many other mammals this number is an order of magnitude greater; for example, rabbits have about 40 million receptor neurons in the olfactory epithelium.

9.18 Anatomy and Main Pathways of the Human Olfactory System   The schematic diagram at lower right indicates the main olfactory pathways in the brain.

Each receptor cell has a long slender apical dendrite that extends to the outermost layer of the epithelium, the mucosal surface. There, numerous **cilia** (singular *cilium*) emerge from the **dendritic knob** and extend along the mucosal surface. At the opposite end of each bipolar olfactory receptor cell, a fine, unmyelinated axon, which is among the smallest-diameter axons in the nervous system, runs to the olfactory bulb (which we will discuss shortly).

In contrast with many other receptor neurons in the body, olfactory receptor neurons can be replaced in adulthood (Costanzo, 1991). One theory is that these receptor neurons normally degenerate after a few weeks because they are in direct contact with external irritants, such as chemicals and viruses, so they must constantly be replaced. It's clear that, if destroyed, an olfactory receptor cell will be replaced as an adjacent basal cell differentiates into a neuron and extends dendrites to the mucosal surface and an axon into the brain. What's not clear is whether receptor cells are *normally* "disposable," subject to constant turnover even in the absence of a particular trauma.

If the olfactory epithelium is damaged, it can be regenerated and will properly reconnect to the olfactory bulb. The functional capability of these new connections has been clearly demonstrated in both behavioral and electrophysiological studies of animals with completely regenerated olfactory epithelium. Investigators are trying to determine how these neurons can regenerate while those in most other parts of the nervous system cannot.

Odorants excite specialized receptor molecules on olfactory receptor cells

Odorants enter the nasal cavity during inhalation and especially during periods of sniffing; they also rise to the nasal cavity from the mouth when we chew food. The direction of airflow in the nose is determined by complex curved surfaces called **turbinates** that form the nasal cavity (see Figure 9.18). Airborne molecules initially encounter the fluids of the mucosal layer, which contain binding proteins that transport odorants to receptor surfaces (Farbman, 1994).

The odorant stimulus then interacts with receptor proteins located on the surface of the olfactory cilia and the dendritic knob of the receptor cells. Discovered and characterized by Linda Buck and Richard Axel (1991), these receptor proteins are members of a superfamily of G protein–linked receptors. Interactions of odorants with the receptor trigger the synthesis of second messengers, including cyclic AMP (cAMP) and inositol trisphosphate (IP_3). Cyclic AMP opens a cation channel (Brunet et al., 1996) to elicit the generator current that depolarizes the olfactory receptor cell, and the depolarization in turn leads to action potentials. For this and subsequent work, Buck and Axel were awarded the 2004 Nobel Prize in Physiology or Medicine.

This sensory transduction process, portrayed in Figure 9.19, is similar to the activation of other sensory systems, such as those for sweet and bitter tastes, and those in the eye (see Chapter 10). A specific G protein, named G_{olf} in recognition of its

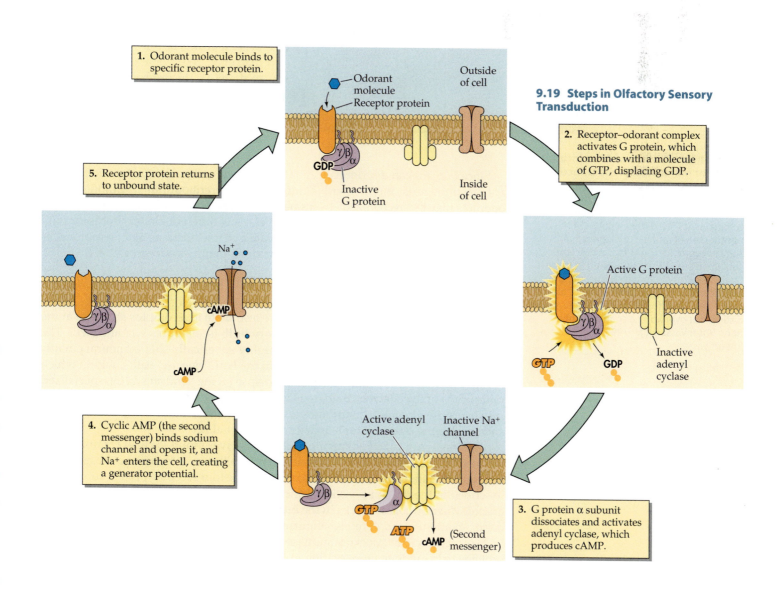

1. Odorant molecule binds to specific receptor protein.

9.19 Steps in Olfactory Sensory Transduction

2. Receptor–odorant complex activates G protein, which combines with a molecule of GTP, displacing GDP.

5. Receptor protein returns to unbound state.

Odorant molecule
Receptor protein
Outside of cell
GDP
Inactive G protein
Inside of cell

Na^+
cAMP
cAMP

Active G protein
GTP
GDP
Inactive adenyl cyclase

4. Cyclic AMP (the second messenger) binds sodium channel and opens it, and Na^+ enters the cell, creating a generator potential.

Active adenyl cyclase
Inactive Na^+ channel
GTP
ATP
cAMP (Second messenger)

3. G protein α subunit dissociates and activates adenyl cyclase, which produces cAMP.

(a)

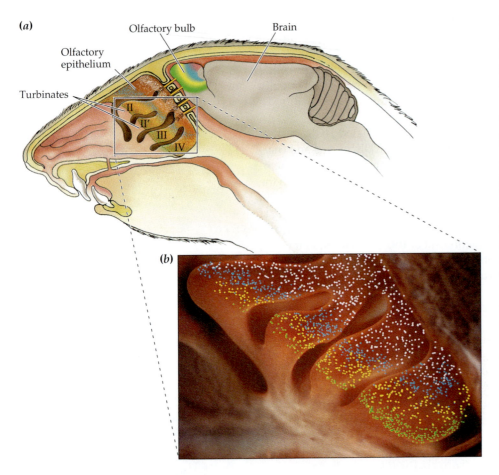

Olfactory epithelium

Turbinates

Olfactory bulb

Brain

II
II'
III
IV

(b)

9.20 Different Kinds of Olfactory Receptor Molecules on the Olfactory Epithelium   *(a)* In this diagram showing the anatomy of the rat olfactory organ, the Roman numerals designate different turbinates. *(b)* The different colors in this photograph of rat olfactory epithelium show receptor locations for four receptor subfamilies (and also correspond to those on the olfactory bulb, which illustrate the probable topographic innervation of that structure). The different receptor types have distinct but overlapping spatial distributions. (After Vassar et al., 1993; *b* courtesy of Robert Vassar.)

importance in olfaction, must be used by all the olfactory receptors because mice in which the gene that encodes G_{olf} is knocked out are generally anosmic (Belluscio et al., 1998).

Mice have about 2 million receptor cells, each of which expresses only one of about 1000 different receptor proteins. These receptor proteins can be divided into four different subfamilies of about 250 proteins each (Mori et al., 1999). Within each subfamily, members have a very similar structure and presumably recognize similar odorants. Each subfamily of receptors is synthesized in a separate band of the epithelium (Figure 9.20) (Vassar et al., 1993).

Now that it has been fully mapped, we know that the human genome contains some 900 apparent olfactory receptor genes, spread across almost all of the chromosomes, but only about 350 of these appear to be fully functional (Glusman et al., 2001; for a review, see Crasto et al., 2001). The rest have apparently accumulated mutations and become nonfunctional during the course of evolution, implying that whatever they detected ceased to be important to our ancestors' survival and reproduction.

Since humans can discriminate about 5000 odors, each of the 350 functional odorant receptors must interact with a number of different odorants. Although some odorants may be "recognized" by a single kind of receptor molecule, most odorants probably are recognized by a combination of a few different kinds of receptor molecules. In other words, most odorants activate a characteristic array of receptor cells (Duchamp-Viret et al., 1999), and pattern coding identifies odorants.

Olfactory axons connect with the olfactory bulb, which sends its output to several brain regions

The numerous axons of the olfactory nerve terminate in a complex structure at the anterior end of the brain called the **olfactory bulb** (see Figures 9.18 and 9.20). The olfactory bulb is organized into many roughly spherically shaped neural circuits called **glomeruli** (singular *glomerulus;* from the Latin *glomus,* "ball"), within which the axon terminals of olfactory neurons synapse on the dendrites of the specialized **mitral cells** of the olfactory bulb (see Figure 9.18). The intrinsic circuitry within and between these glomeruli contributes to an elaborate system for modulating, tuning, and sharpening olfactory bulb activity (Aungst et al., 2003).

Mice have about 1800 glomeruli. Each one receives inputs exclusively from olfactory neurons that are expressing the same type of olfactory receptor, and the glomeruli are organized in functional zones according to the four receptor protein subfamilies described in the previous section (Mori et al., 1999). So there appears to be a topographic distribution of smells in the bulb, and within each functional zone, neighboring glomeruli tend to receive inputs from receptors that are closely related.

Experiments with knockout mice (see Box 7.3) suggest that the olfactory receptor proteins help guide the innervating axons to the proper target when new olfactory receptors are generated. Disruptions of the receptor protein prevent newly generated olfactory receptor axons from reaching their normal glomerulus (F. Wang et al.,

1998). The olfactory bulb, in relation to the rest of the brain, is much smaller in humans than in animals such as rats that depend extensively on olfaction (compare Figures 9.18 and 9.20).

Outputs from the olfactory bulb, which are the axons of the mitral cells, extend to a variety of brain regions. These include the prepyriform and entorhinal cortex (note that smell is the only sensory modality that can synapse directly in the cortex rather than having to pass through the thalamus), the amygdala, and the hypothalamus. Using a "knock-in" mouse model, Linda Buck and coworkers (Zou et al., 2001) found that an olfactory map is maintained throughout the olfactory projections to the cortex.

In some of these mice, the gene for a substance called *barley lectin* was inserted right next to a particular gene encoding one type of olfactory receptor. In the other mice, the barley lectin gene was knocked in beside a different olfactory receptor gene, belonging to a different subfamily. Because of the proximity of the genes, any neuron that expressed the targeted olfactory receptor gene also made barley lectin. Barley lectin is a transsynaptic marker, meaning that it is transferred across synapses, from the originating receptor neuron to the connecting neurons, all the way to the cortex.

Tracing these connections by following the barley lectin marker in their mice (Figure 9.21*a*), the researchers found that two discrete glomeruli are labeled in the olfactory bulb—corresponding to the two different receptor types. Subsequent projections from these glomeruli to olfactory cortical sites maintained their high degree of segregation, and terminated in stereotyped, partially overlapping patterns in the cortex (Figure 9.21*b*). The pattern of results implies that an olfactory map exists throughout the olfactory system, including cortical sites, and may be innate to some extent.

Functional-MRI studies suggest that the human prepyriform cortex is activated during sniffing, whether or not an odor is present (Sobel et al., 1998), because the airflow induced by sniffing provides somatosensory stimulation. When an odor is present, primary olfactory cortex (prepyriform cortex) and secondary olfactory cortex (orbitofrontal cortex) are both activated during a sniff (Sobel et al., 2000). Furthermore, the same chemical mix may produce a different odor perception, depending on how fast the air enters during a sniff (Sobel et al., 1999). So the brain gauges the airflow rate during a sniff in order to properly interpret olfactory information.

Linda Buck

(a)

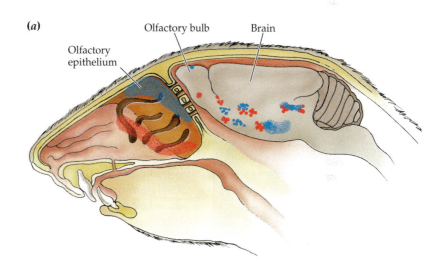

(b)

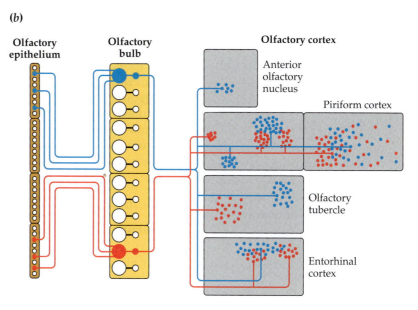

9.21 Organization of Odor Projections in the Brain
(*a*) Projections from two different types of olfactory receptors that were labeled with a barley lectin gene knock-in. Note that all of the olfactory neurons expressing one type of receptor terminate on the same glomerulus; all neurons expressing the other receptor terminate on a different glomerulus. This segregation is largely maintained in projections from the olfactory bulb to the cortex, terminating in a map of slightly overlapping fields. (*b*) Schematic display of the organization of the olfactory projections from the two types of receptors. (After Zou et al., 2001.)

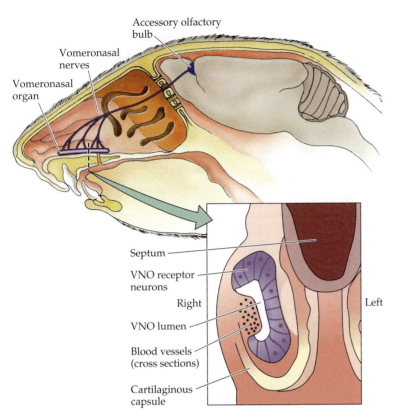

Catherine Dulac

9.22 The Vomeronasal System

Accessory olfactory bulb

Vomeronasal nerves

Vomeronasal organ

Septum

VNO receptor neurons

Right

VNO lumen

Blood vessels (cross sections)

Cartilaginous capsule

Left

Many vertebrates possess a vomeronasal system

Many vertebrates have a second chemical detection system that appears to specialize in detecting **pheromones,** the odor signals or trails that many animals secrete (see Chapter 5). This **vomeronasal system** (Figure 9.22), as it is called, is present in most terrestrial mammals, amphibians, and reptiles. The receptors for the system are found in a **vomeronasal organ** (**VNO**) of epithelial cells near the olfactory epithelium.

Rodents express two major families of vomeronasal receptors, termed the *V1Rs* and the *V2Rs*, that encode hundreds of different types of receptors (for a review, see Dulac and Torello, 2003). Although both are families of G protein–coupled receptors, they are quite different from each other; in fact, the V1Rs are more similar to the T2R bitter taste receptors (discussed earlier) than they are to the receptors of the main olfactory system. Interestingly, the distribution of certain V2Rs differs between male and female rats, in keeping with the critical role of pheromones in organizing rodent reproductive behavior (Herrada and Dulac, 1997). V2Rs are also sensitive to certain major histocompatibility complex (MHC) molecules (Loconto et al., 2003); detection of MHCs is thought to be one of the main ways in which animals can assess their degree of relatedness to other animals, which has implications for mating strategies (see Chapter 6). A VNO-specific ion channel called *TRP2* is also essential for VNO function (Stowers et al., 2002).

VNO receptors are remarkably sensitive, detecting extremely low concentrations of pheromone molecules (Leinders-Zufall et al., 2000). The receptors send their information to the accessory olfactory bulb (adjacent to the main olfactory bulb), which projects to the medial amygdala, which in turn projects to the hypothalamus. Relying in part on MHCs, hamsters (Mateo and Johnston, 2000) and mice (Isles et al., 2001) can distinguish relatives from nonrelatives just by smell, even if they were raised by foster parents. Presumably they compare whether other animals smell like themselves, perhaps to avoid mating with kin.

The VNO is usually said to be absent or vestigial in fishes, birds, and higher primates. (M. Halpern, 1987). And in humans, molecular and anatomical evidence for a functional VNO is scanty at best. Although humans have a structure that resembles a VNO, analysis of the genome indicates that almost all of the human variants of the genes that encode the V1R and V2R vomeronasal receptors are nonfunctional, as is the gene that encodes the TRP2 ion channel.

However, the report that extracts of human sweat, when applied to the upper lip of women, can adjust their menstrual cycle by 1 to 2 days (K. Stern and McClintock, 1998) suggests that humans do have the ability to detect certain pheromones. In this study the donor sweat was gathered from other women, and depending on where the donors were in their menstrual cycles, the recipients' cycles were either accelerated or retarded in response. Other studies have suggested that humans are sensitive to MHCs. The question of human sensitivity to pheromones therefore remains unresolved.

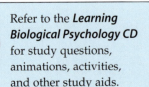

Refer to the *Learning Biological Psychology CD* for study questions, animations, activities, and other study aids.

Summary

Hearing

1. The external ear captures, focuses, and filters sound. The sound arriving at the tympanic membrane (eardrum) is focused by the ossicles of the middle ear onto the oval window to stimulate the fluid-filled inner ear (cochlea).

2. Sound arriving at the oval window causes traveling waves to sweep along the basilar membrane of the inner ear. For high-frequency sounds, the largest displacement of the basilar membrane is at the base of the cochlea, near the oval window; for low-frequency sounds, the largest amplitude is near the apex of the cochlea.

3. The organ of Corti has both inner hair cells (about 3500 in humans) and outer hair cells (about 12,000 in humans). The inner hair cells convey most of the information about sounds. The outer hair cells change their length under the control of the brain, amplifying the movements of the basilar membrane in response to sound and sharpening the frequency tuning of the cochlea.

4. Movement of the stereocilia of the hair cells causes the opening and closing of ion channels, thereby transducing mechanical movement into changes in electrical potential. These changes in potential stimulate the nerve cell endings that contact the hair cells.

5. At each level of the auditory system, sound frequencies are mapped in an orderly succession; this is called tonotopic mapping.

6. Two theories explain the discrimination of auditory frequency. According to place theory, our perception of pitch depends on where the sound causes maximal displacement of the basilar membrane. Volley theory argues that the relations between the frequencies of auditory stimuli and the pattern or timing of neural discharges are the important criteria for pitch discrimination. In practice, we appear to use both encoding systems to determine pitch.

7. Auditory localization depends on differences in the sounds arriving at the two ears. For low-frequency sounds, differences in time of arrival at the two ears are especially important. For high-frequency sounds, differences in intensity are especially important. Birds and mammals evolved different neural mechanisms for localizing sounds; in mammals the lateral superior olivary nucleus of the brainstem processes differences in intensity, and the medial superior olivary nucleus processes differences in time of arrival. Spectral filtering performed by the external ear provides elevation cues.

8. Primary auditory cortex is specialized for processing complex, biologically important sounds, rather than pure tones.

9. Experiences with sound early in life can influence later auditory localization and the responses of neurons in auditory pathways. Experiences later in life can also lead to changes in responses of auditory neurons.

10. Deafness can be caused by pathological changes at any level of the auditory system. Conduction deafness consists of impairments in the transmission of sound to the cochlea that are produced by changes in the external or middle ear. Sensorineural deafness arises in the cochlea, often because of the destruction of hair cells, or in the auditory nerve. Central deafness stems from brain damage.

11. Some forms of deafness may be alleviated by direct electrical stimulation of the auditory nerve (by a cochlear implant) or the brainstem cochlear nuclei (by an auditory brainstem implant). Genetic manipulations can induce new hair cell growth in laboratory animals, raising hope of a gene therapy for sensorineural deafness.

Vestibular Perception

1. The receptors of the vestibular system lie within the inner ear next to the cochlea. In mammals the vestibular system consists of three semicircular canals, plus the utricle and the saccule.

2. Within each of these structures, the receptors, like those of the auditory system, are groups of hair cells whose bending leads to the excitation of nerve fibers. The semicircular canals detect rotation of the body in three planes, and the utricle and saccule sense static positions and linear accelerations.

3. The vestibular system appears to have evolved from the lateral-line system, found in many kinds of fish and some amphibians. It is generally accepted that the auditory end organ evolved from the vestibular system.

The Chemical Senses: Taste and Smell

1. Humans detect only five main tastes: salty, sour, sweet, bitter, and umami.

2. In mammals, most taste receptor cells are located in clusters of cells called taste buds. Taste cells extend fine cilia into the taste pore of the bud, where tastants come into

contact with them. The taste buds are situated on small projections from the surface of the tongue called papillae.

3. The tastes of salty and sour are evoked by the action of simple ions on ion channels in the membranes of taste cells. Sweet and bitter tastes are perceived by specialized receptor molecules belonging to the T1R and T2R families, which are coupled to G proteins. A heterodimer of T1R2+T1R3 functions as a sweet receptor. About 25 different T2R receptors act as bitter receptors. Two candidate umami receptors are a specialized glutamate receptor and a T1R1+T1R3 heterodimer that responds to most amino acids.

4. Each taste axon responds most strongly to one taste but also to other tastes. Taste discrimination requires central processing based on relative activity coming from different afferent axons.

5. Each taste cell transmits information to several afferent fibers, and each afferent fiber receives information from several taste cells. The afferent fibers run along cranial nerves to brainstem nuclei. The gustatory system extends from the taste receptor cells through brainstem nuclei to the thalamus and then to the cerebral cortex.

6. In contrast to the ability to detect only a few tastes, humans can detect thousands of different odors. Many species depend more on smell than humans do; such species have more olfactory receptor cells and larger olfactory bulbs.

7. Each olfactory receptor cell is a small bipolar cell whose dendrites extend to the olfactory epithelium in the nose. The fine, unmyelinated axon runs to the olfactory bulb and synapses on the dendrites of mitral cells, within glomeruli. If an olfactory receptor cell dies, an adjacent cell will replace it.

8. There is a large family of odor receptor molecules. Each of these receptor molecules utilizes G proteins and second messengers.

9. Neurons that express the same receptor gene are not closely clustered in the olfactory epithelium; rather they are limited to distinct regions of the epithelium. Each subfamily of receptors is synthesized in a different band of the epithelium.

10. All olfactory neurons expressing a particular receptor synapse in the same glomerulus. The projection from the epithelium to the bulb maintains a zonal distribution for different kinds of receptor molecules.

11. Outputs from the olfactory bulb extend to prepyriform cortex, entorhinal cortex, the amygdala, and the hypothalamus, among other brain regions. Olfactory projections to the cortex maintain a stereotyped olfactory map of slightly overlapping projections from the glomeruli.

12. The vomeronasal organ contains receptors to detect pheromones released from other individuals of the species. These receptors transmit signals to the accessory olfactory bulb, which in turn communicates with the amygdala.

Recommended Reading

Bartoshuk, L. M., and Beauchamp, G. K. (1997). *Tasting and smelling*. New York: Academic Press.

Buck, L. B. (1996). Information coding in the vertebrate olfactory system. *Annual Review of Neuroscience, 19,* 517–545.

Doty, R. L. (2003). *Handbook of gustation and olfaction* (2nd ed.). New York: Dekker.

Finger, T. E., Silver, W. L., and Restrepo, D. (Eds.). (2000). *The neurobiology of taste and smell*. New York: Wiley-Liss.

Hildebrand, J. G., and Shepherd, G. M. (1997). Mechanisms of olfactory discrimination: Converging evidence for common principles across phyla. *Annual Review of Neuroscience, 20,* 595–631.

Murphy, C. (Ed.). (1998). *Olfaction and taste XII: An international symposium*. New York: New York Academy of Sciences.

Rouby, C., Schaal, B., Dubois, D., Gervais, R., et al. (eds.). (2002). *Olfaction, taste, and cognition*. Cambridge: Cambridge University Press.

Yost, W. A. (2000). *Fundamentals of hearing* (4th ed.). San Diego, CA: Academic Press.

10

Vision: From Eye to Brain

When Seeing Isn't Seeing

It was cold in the bathroom, so the young woman turned on a small heater before she got in the shower. She didn't know that the heater was malfunctioning, filling the room with deadly, odorless carbon monoxide gas. Her husband found her unconscious on the floor and called for an ambulance to rush her to the emergency room. When she regained consciousness, "D.F." seemed to have gotten off lightly, avoiding what could have been a fatal accident. She could understand the doctors' questions and reply sensibly, move all her limbs, and perceive touch on her skin, but something was wrong with her sight.

D.F. couldn't recognize faces, even her husband's, nor could she name any objects presented to her view. D.F. still cannot recognize objects today, more than 15 years after her accident. Yet she is not entirely blind. Show her a flashlight and she can tell you that it's made of shiny aluminum with some red plastic, but she doesn't recognize it ("Is it a kitchen utensil?"). Without telling her what it is, if you ask her to pick it up, D.F.'s hand goes directly to the flashlight and holds it exactly as one normally holds a flashlight. Show D.F. a slot in a piece of plastic and she cannot tell you whether the slot is oriented vertically, horizontally, or diagonally; but if you hand her a disk and ask her to put it through the hole, D.F. invariably turns the disk so that it goes smoothly through the slot (Goodale et al., 1991). Can she see or not?

Vision offers tremendous benefits for vital behaviors such as finding food, avoiding predators, finding a mate, and locating shelter. So a variety of visual systems have evolved, differing in some respects but similar in others. Beyond serving basic needs, vision affords most of us the pleasures of nature and art, reading and writing, and watching motion pictures and TV. Because vision is so important, much effort is expended to improve it, to prevent its deterioration, and even to restore vision to the blind.

However, the sheer volume of visual information poses a serious problem. Seeing the world around you has been compared to drinking from a waterfall. How does the visual system avoid being overwhelmed by the flood of information that enters the eyes? The answer seems to be that the visual perceptions of each species depend on how their eyes and brains evolved to process information about light and attend to the aspects likely to be important for their survival.

Different kinds of processing allow us to see the form, color, position, and distance of objects in the visual field and to recognize objects. Research on vision is one of the most active fields of biological psychology and neuroscience, as it should be, since about one-third of the human cerebral cortex is devoted to visual analysis and perception. Our aim in this chapter is to convey some of the challenges, accomplishments, and excitement of this field.

Vision Provides Information about the Form, Color, Location, Movement, and Identity of Objects

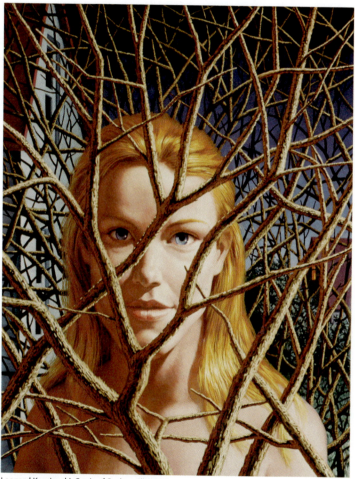

Leonard Koscianski, *Carrie of Cockeysville*, 1998

Although we're familiar with vision because we use it every day, some features of visual perception are not immediately apparent. A good grasp of the visual system will help us understand many of these surprising phenomena.

Perception of form and identification of objects are complex accomplishments

The whole area that you can see without moving your head or eyes is called your **visual field**. In a single glance, you can perceive the details of objects accurately only in the center of your visual field. We are usually not aware of this phenomenon because we move our gaze rapidly as we scan a scene or read text. Thus we build up a sort of collage of detailed views. But try keeping your eyes fixed on a letter in the center of a line and then attempt to read a word on the opposite page. You'll find it difficult because **visual acuity** (the sharpness of vision) falls off rapidly from the center of the visual field toward the periphery. This difference in acuity across the visual field is the reason your gaze has to jump from place to place in a line as you read.

If a stimulus suddenly appears away from the center of the visual field, we shift our direction of view, placing the new stimulus in the center of the visual field, where we can see it clearly. When we examine the circuitry of the retina and of higher stations of the visual system a little later, we will learn why vision is so much more acute in the center of the visual field.

If we examine the visual field of each eye separately, we find a **blind spot** about 16° to the temporal (lateral) side of the fixation point. This blind spot is relatively large, about 5° in diameter. (Because the eye is roughly spherical, it's conventional to refer to locations within it by using degrees.) Use Figure 10.1 to find the blind spot in the visual field of your right eye.

The retina, a sheet of tissue covering the inside of the eye, contains millions of light-sensitive receptors, and the reason for the blind spot is that there are no receptors in a region called the **optic disc** (Figure 10.2). The optic disc, located about 16° to the nasal (nose) side of the retinal center, is where the fibers of the optic nerve exit the eye. Because there are no receptors in this region, we can't see anything in the corresponding temporal part of the visual field. The optic disc on the nasal side of the retina causes the blind spot in the temporal side of the visual field because the eye reverses the retinal image, left to right, as Figure 10.2 shows; the retinal image is also inverted top to bottom.

The blind spot does not appear as a dark spot; it is simply a region from which we cannot obtain visual information. Find your blind spot again using Figure 10.1a

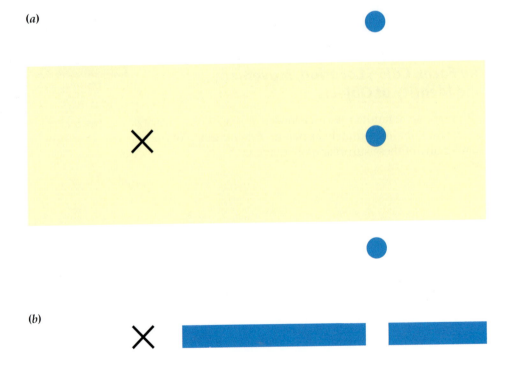

(a)

(b)

10.1 The Blind Spot   To locate your blind spot, hold the page about 10 to 12 cm (4 to 5 inches) away. Close your left eye and focus your right eye on the X. In (a), the middle dot on the right should disappear. In (b), when you place the gap at your blind spot, you will see a solid line rather than a broken line. (You may need to adjust the page closer or farther away to locate your blind spot.)

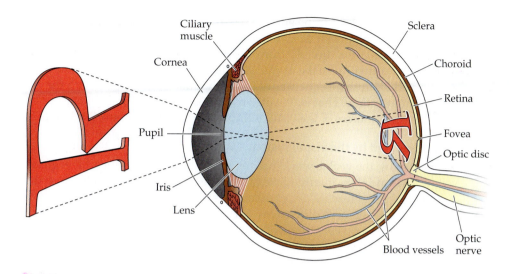

10.2 Structures of the Human Eye Here the right eye is viewed in cross section from above. The visual image focused on the retina is inverted top to bottom and reversed right to left. The gap in the retina where the optic nerve leaves the eyeball is the optic disc, where the absence of receptors causes the blind spot.

and place a pencil so that its center runs vertically through the blind spot. Do you see a gap in the pencil where it intersects the blind spot? No. You receive no information from the blind spot, yet you *perceive* a complete pencil; your perceptual system fills in from the surrounding area.

If you place the gap in the line in Figure 10.1*b* in your blind spot, you will see the line as complete because the gap is invisible. Similarly, if you keep your left eye closed and look at a uniform area or most patterns with your right eye, you will not be aware of any gap in your visual field. An isolated stimulus, however (such as the dot in Figure 10.1*a*), may disappear in the blind spot. King Charles I of England is said to have amused himself by "beheading" some courtiers in this way, before he was literally beheaded himself.

We perceive a simple form like a triangle or recognize the face of a friend so rapidly and easily that we do not appreciate that these are exceedingly complex events that require processing in several parts of the brain. Most of the forms we see are embedded in complicated fields of objects; separating out a particular form for attention and identification requires practice and skill. It has been very difficult to achieve even primitive recognition of objects with artificial systems. Furthermore, recognition requires more than the accurate perception of objects. For example, some people with brain damage lose their ability to recognize familiar faces or objects, even though they can still describe them accurately.

Consider the complexity of visual perception at the level of the nervous system. Each receptor in the retina is in a particular state of excitation at each instant. In effect, each receptor is signaling a level of excitation that can be represented by a number. About three times per second, the nervous system takes in a number from each of the approximately 100 million photoreceptors, and it faces the stupendous task of trying to figure out what in the outside world could have produced that particular array of values.

Figure 10.3 illustrates a simple example of such a task. The numbers in this array represent shades of gray from darkest (2) to lightest (9). As you inspect this grid, you may notice that the numbers representing lighter shades appear mainly in the upper half of the array, but you don't perceive a form.

Now look at Figure 10.4, which shows the shades of gray that correspond to the numbers in the array in Figure 10.3; the form and identity leap out. Your nervous system processes data such as those in Figure 10.3 to achieve the perception of the form in Figure 10.4 in an instant. How the nervous system processes so much data so quickly is the staggering problem that confronts anyone who tries to understand vision.

It appears that we have to learn how to recognize faces and objects. Furthermore, this ability can be lost after years without sight, as shown by the case of Michael May

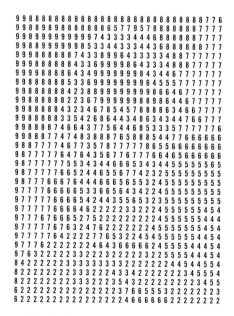

10.3 Can You Identify the Subject?
This array of numbers represents the point-to-point illumination of a picture, from darkest (2) to lightest (9).

10.4 The Subject of Figure 10.3

described in Chapter 7 (Fine et al., 2003). In fact, as we'll see, not only object recognition, but also color, brightness, motion, and other aspects of visual perception do not come directly from the retinal image. Rather, according to Purves and Lotto (2003), the retinal stimuli trigger responses that have been determined by the consequences of the individual's interactions with the environment over time. That is, "… the observer sees the probability distribution of the possible sources of the visual stimulus" (Purves and Lotto, 2003, p. 227).

Color is created by the visual system

For most of us, the visible world has several distinguishable hues: blue, green, yellow, red, and their intermediates. These hues appear different because the reflected light that reaches our eyes can vary in wavelength (Box 10.1), and we can detect some of these differences. For about 8% of human males and about 0.5% of females, however, some of these color distinctions are either absent or at least less striking.

Although the term *color blindness* is commonly used, most people with impaired color vision are able to distinguish some hues. Complete color blindness in humans is extremely rare, although it can be caused by brain lesions or by congenital absence of specialized receptors. Animals exhibit different degrees of color vision. Many species of birds, fish, and insects have excellent color vision. Humans and Old World monkeys also have an excellent ability to discriminate wavelengths, but many other mammals (e.g., cats) cannot discriminate wavelengths very well. We'll see more about the distribution of color vision among mammals later in this chapter.

A patch of light has other qualities besides hue. The color solid shown in Figure 10.5 illustrates the basic dimensions of our perception of light; the figure is deliberately asymmetrical, for reasons we will explain. The three dimensions of color are as follows:

1. **Brightness,** which varies from dark to light; it is the vertical dimension in Figure 10.5. The middle plane of the figure is tipped up for yellow and down for blue because yellow in the spectrum is perceived as lighter and blue as darker than the other hues.
2. **Hue,** which varies continuously around the color circle through blue, green, yellow, orange, and red. (Hue is what most people mean when they use the term *color.*)
3. **Saturation,** which varies from rich full colors at the periphery of the color solid to gray at the center. For example, starting with red at the periphery, the colors become paler toward the center, going through pink to gray. Yellow is shown closer to the central axis than the other saturated hues because yellow is perceived as less saturated than the other spectral hues.

It is important not to equate perception of a particular hue with a particular stimulus (a wavelength of light) because—depending on the intensity of illumination, the surrounding field, and prior exposure to a different stimulus—a patch illuminated by a particular wavelength is seen as various different hues. As illumination fades, the blues in a painting or a rug appear more prominent and the reds appear duller, even though the wavelength distribution in the light has not changed. In addition, the hue perceived at a particular point is strongly affected by the pattern of wavelengths and intensities in other parts of the visual field.

Brightness is created by the visual system

The brightness dimension of visual perception is also created by the visual system, not simply by the amount of light reflected. Figure 10.6 presents two examples. The enhancement of the boundaries of the bars in Figure 10.6a, each of which is uniformly gray but looks as though it varies in brightness, is based on a neural process called **lateral inhibition.**

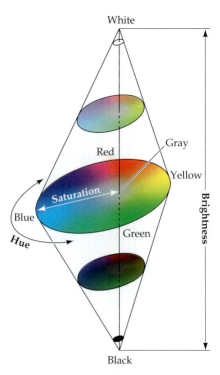

10.5 The Color Solid   The three basic dimensions of the perception of light are brightness, hue, and saturation.

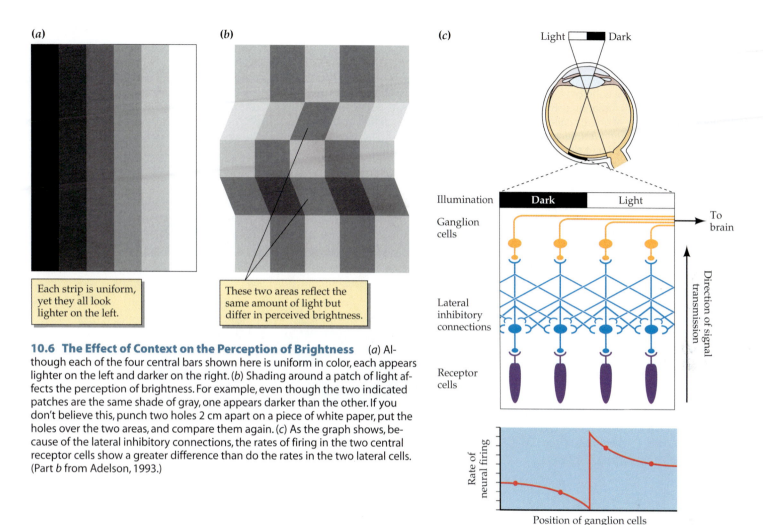

Each strip is uniform, yet they all look lighter on the left.

These two areas reflect the same amount of light but differ in perceived brightness.

10.6 The Effect of Context on the Perception of Brightness   (*a*) Although each of the four central bars shown here is uniform in color, each appears lighter on the left and darker on the right. (*b*) Shading around a patch of light affects the perception of brightness. For example, even though the two indicated patches are the same shade of gray, one appears darker than the other. If you don't believe this, punch two holes 2 cm apart on a piece of white paper, put the holes over the two areas, and compare them again. (*c*) As the graph shows, because of the lateral inhibitory connections, the rates of firing in the two central receptor cells show a greater difference than do the rates in the two lateral cells. (Part *b* from Adelson, 1993.)

Lateral inhibition occurs where the neurons in a region—in this case, retinal cells—are interconnected, either through their own axons or by means of intermediary neurons (interneurons), and each neuron tends to inhibit its neighbors (Figure 10.6*c*). Lateral inhibition occurs in the skin senses, too; if you press the end of a ruler against the skin of your forearm, for example, you will probably feel the pressure at the corners of the ruler more strongly than you feel the pressure along the line of contact.

In Figure 10.6*b*, two patches that clearly differ in brightness *reflect the same amount of light*. If you use your hands to cover the surrounding pattern to the left and right of the two patches, they appear the same. How are such puzzling effects produced? Although the contrast effect in Figure 10.6*a* is determined, at least in part, by interactions among adjacent retinal cells, the two areas indicated in Figure 10.6*b* are not adjacent, so the effect must be produced higher in the visual system (Adelson, 1993).

Motion can enhance the perception of objects

Movement enhances the visibility of objects, which is an important adaptation in the visual system because predators and prey both must be sensitive to moving objects in order to survive. In the periphery of our visual field, we may not be able to see stationary objects, but we can detect motion. We detect motion only within a range of speed that is appropriate to the locomotion of animals.

Anything that moves faster is a blur or may be invisible, as is a bullet speeding by. Anything that moves too slowly—such as the hour hand of a clock—is not seen as moving, although we can note from time to time that it has changed position. A

BOX 10.1   The Basics of Light

The physical energy to which our visual system responds is a band of electromagnetic radiation. This radiation comes in very small packets of energy called **quanta** (singular *quantum*). Each quantum can be described by a single number, representing its **wavelength** (the distance between two adjacent crests of vibratory activity).

The human visual system responds only to quanta whose wavelengths lie within a very narrow section of the total electromagnetic range, from about 400 to 700 nm, as the figure shows. Such quanta of light energy are called **photons** (from the Greek *phos*, "light"). The band of radiant energy visible to animals may be narrow, but it must provide for accurate reflection from the surface of objects in the size range that matters for survival. Radio waves are good for imaging objects of astronomical size; X-rays penetrate below the surface of objects.

Each photon is a very small amount of energy; the exact amount depends on the wavelength. A single photon of wavelength 560 nm contains only a tiny amount of energy. A 100-watt (W) light bulb gives off only about 3 W of visible light; the rest is heat. But even the 3 W of light amounts to 8 quintillion (8×10^{18}) photons per second. When quanta within the visible spectrum enter the eye, they can evoke visual sensations. The exact nature of such sensations depends both on the wavelengths of the quanta and on the number of quanta per second.

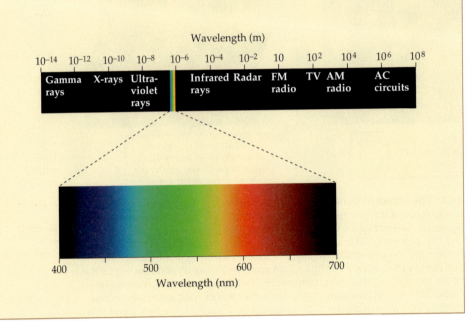

succession of still pictures, presented at the proper rate, can cause apparent motion, as in motion pictures. The investigation of apparent visual motion by psychologist Max Wertheimer in the 1920s led to the Gestalt movement in psychology. Perception of motion is analyzed by special areas of the brain, as we will see later in this chapter.

The Eye Is Both an Optical Device and a Neural Organ

The eye is an elaborate structure with optical functions (capturing light and forming detailed spatial images) and neural functions (transducing light into neural signals and processing these signals). Our examination of the eye will lead us to a discussion about how this elaborate organ evolved.

The vertebrate eye acts in some ways like a camera

Our ability to see depends on numerous structures and processes. First among these are the structures and processes that enable the eye to form relatively accurate optical images on the retina. Accurate optical images are necessary for us to be able to see the shapes of objects; that is, light from a point on a target object must end up as a point—rather than a blur—in the retinal image. Without optical images, light-sensitive cells would be able to detect only the presence or absence of light and would not be able to see forms, just as exposing photographic film to light outside a camera does not produce an image of the surroundings.

To produce optical images, the eye has many of the features of a camera, starting with the **cornea** and **lens** to focus light (see Figure 10.2). Light travels in a straight line until it encounters a change in the density of the medium, which causes light rays to bend. This bending of light rays, called **refraction,** is the basis of such in-

**Max Wertheimer
(1880–1943)**

struments as eyeglasses, telescopes, and microscopes. The cornea of the eye—the curvature of which is fixed—bends light rays and is primarily responsible for forming the image on the retina.

In a camera, the lens moves nearer to or farther from the film to adjust focus, and the same system is used in the eyes of fishes, amphibians, and reptiles. In mammals and birds, however, focus is adjusted by changes in the *shape* of the lens, which is controlled by the **ciliary muscles** inside the eye. As the degree of contraction of the ciliary muscles varies, the lens focuses images of nearer or farther objects so that they form sharp images on the retina; this process of focusing is called **accommodation.**

The cornea in aquatic animals has little or no refractive power because the indices of refraction of water and the cornea are very similar. For the same reason, human vision is fuzzy underwater, although acuity can be restored with goggles that re-create the air–cornea interface. In aquatic animals, the lens is responsible for almost all the refractive power of the eye, so the lens in a fish eye is nearly spherical.

In many people the eyeball is either too long or too short to allow the lens to bring images into sharp focus on the retina. Eyeglasses or contact lenses can correct such conditions. Near the end of this chapter we'll see that preventive steps can be taken during childhood to avoid overlengthening of the eyeball. As mammals age, their lenses become less elastic and therefore less able to change curvature to bring nearby objects into focus. Humans correct this problem by wearing reading glasses.

The amount of light that enters the eye is controlled by the size of the **pupil,** just as the aperture controls the light that enters a camera. The pupil is an opening in the structure called the **iris** (see Figure 10.2). In Chapter 2 we mentioned that dilation of the pupils is controlled by the sympathetic division of the autonomic system, and constriction by the parasympathetic division. Because usually both divisions are active, pupil size reflects a balance of influences.

During an eye examination, the doctor may use a drug to block acetylcholine transmission in the parasympathetic synapses of your iris; this drug relaxes the sphincter muscle fibers and permits the pupil to open widely. One drug that has this effect—belladonna (which is Italian for "beautiful lady")—got its name because it was thought to make a woman more beautiful by giving her the wide-open pupils of an attentive person. Other drugs, such as morphine, constrict the pupils.

The movement of the eyes is controlled by the **extraocular muscles,** three pairs of muscles that extend from the outside of the eyeball to the bony socket of the eye. Fixating still or moving targets requires delicate control of these muscles.

**EVOLUTION
AT WORK**

Visual processing begins in the retina

The first stages of processing visual information occur in the **retina,** the receptive surface inside the back of the eye (Figure 10.7*a*). The retina is only 200 to 300 μm thick—not much thicker than the edge of a razor blade—but it contains several types of cells in distinct layers (Figure 10.7*b*). The receptive cells are modified neurons; some are called **rods** because of their relatively long, narrow form, others are called **cones** (Figure 10.7*c*). The rods and cones release neurotransmitter molecules that control the activity of the **bipolar cells** that synapse with them (see Figure 10.7*b*). The bipolar cells in turn connect with **ganglion cells.** The axons of the ganglion cells form the **optic nerve,** which carries information to the brain.

Horizontal cells and **amacrine cells** are especially significant in interactions within the retina, such as lateral inhibition. The horizontal cells make contacts among the receptor cells; the amacrine cells contact both the bipolar and the ganglion cells.

The rods, cones, bipolar cells, and horizontal cells generate only graded local potentials; they do not generate or conduct action potentials. These cells affect each other through the graded release of neurotransmitters in response to graded changes in electrical potentials. The ganglion cells, on the other hand, do conduct action potentials. Because the ganglion cells have action potentials and are relatively large, they were the first retinal cells to have their electrical activity recorded. From the re-

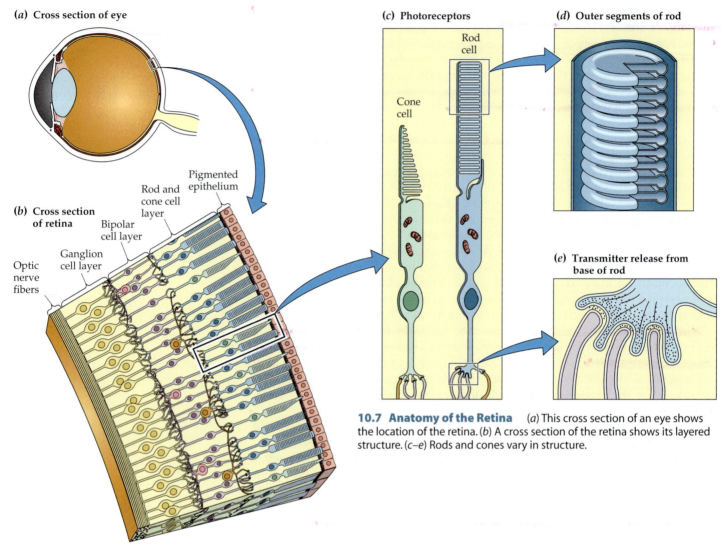

(a) Cross section of eye

(b) Cross section of retina

Optic nerve fibers

Ganglion cell layer

Bipolar cell layer

Rod and cone cell layer

Pigmented epithelium

(c) Photoreceptors

Cone cell

Rod cell

(d) Outer segments of rod

(e) Transmitter release from base of rod

10.7 Anatomy of the Retina (*a*) This cross section of an eye shows the location of the retina. (*b*) A cross section of the retina shows its layered structure. (*c–e*) Rods and cones vary in structure.

ceptive cells to the ganglion cells an enormous number of data converge and are compressed; the human eye contains about 100 million rods and 4 million cones, but there are only 1 million ganglion cells to transmit that information to the brain. Thus a great deal of information processing is done in the eye.

Two different functional systems correspond to the two different populations of receptors (rods and cones) in the retina. One system works in dim light and involves the rods and highly convergent neural processing; this system is called the **scotopic system** (from the Greek *skotos*, "darkness," and *ops*, "eye"). The scotopic system has only one receptor type (rods) and therefore does not respond differentially to different wavelengths, which is the basis for the saying "at night, all cats are gray."

The other system requires more light and involves much more detailed neural processing; in some species, it shows differential sensitivity to wavelengths, enabling color vision. This system involves the cones and is called the **photopic system** (which, like the term *photon*, comes from the Greek *phos*, "light").

At moderate levels of illumination, both rods and cones function, and some ganglion cells receive input from both types of receptors. Having these two systems is part of the reason we can see over a wide range of light intensities. Table 10.1 summarizes the characteristics of the photopic and scotopic systems.

The extraordinary sensitivity of rods and cones is the result of their unusual structure and biochemistry. A portion of their structure, when magnified, looks like a large stack of pancakes or discs (see Figure 10.7*d*). The stacking of discs increases the probability of capturing quanta of light, an especially important function because

TABLE 10.1 *Properties of the Human Photopic and Scotopic Visual Systems*

Property	Photopic system	Scotopic system
Receptors[a]	Cones	Rods
Approximate number of receptors per eye	4 million	100 million
Photopigments[b]	Three classes of cone opsins; the basis of color vision	Rhodopsin
Sensitivity	Low; needs relatively strong stimulation; used for day vision	High; can be stimulated by weak light intensity; used for night vision
Location in retina[c]	Concentrated in and near fovea; present less densely throughout retina	Outside fovea
Receptive field size and visual acuity	Small in fovea, so acuity is high; larger outside fovea	Larger, so acuity is lower
Temporal responses	Relatively rapid	Slow; long latency

[a]Cones and rods are illustrated in Figure 10.7c.
[b]Figure 10.24 shows the spectral sensitivities of the photopigments.
[c]See Figure 10.11.

light is reflected in many directions by the surface of the eyeball, the lens, and the fluid media inside the eye. The reflection and absorption of light at all these surfaces mean that only a fraction of the light that strikes the cornea actually reaches the retina.

The quanta of light that strike the discs are captured by special photopigment receptor molecules. In the rods this photopigment is **rhodopsin** (from the Greek *rhodon*, "rose," and *opsis*, "vision"). Cones use similar photopigments, as we will see later. The rod and cone photopigments in the eye consist of two parts: **retinal** (an abbreviated form of *retinaldehyde*, which is vitamin A aldehyde) and **opsin.** (From this point forward the noun *retinal*, standing for the molecule, will be printed in small capital letters—RETINAL—to distinguish it from the adjective *retinal*, meaning "pertaining to the retina.")

The pioneering studies of George Wald (1964) established the chemical structure of rhodopsin and related visual pigments, earning him the 1967 Nobel Prize in Physiology or Medicine. The visual receptor molecules span the membranes of receptor discs and have structures that are similar to those of the G protein–coupled neurotransmitter receptors that we discussed in Chapter 3.

When light activates a rhodopsin molecule (Figure 10.8a), the RETINAL dissociates rapidly from the opsin, revealing an enzymatic site on the opsin molecule. The activated opsin combines rapidly with many molecules of the G protein transducin (Figure 10.8c). Transducin in turn acts through an enzyme, phosphodiesterase (PDE), to transform cyclic GMP (cyclic guanosine monophosphate) to 5′-GMP. Cyclic GMP holds channels for sodium ions (Na$^+$) open; stimulation by light initiates a cascade of events that closes these channels. Capture of a single quantum of light can lead to the closing of hundreds of sodium channels in the photoreceptor membrane and block the entry of more than 1 million Na$^+$ ions (Schnapf and Baylor, 1987). Closing the Na$^+$ channels creates a hyperpolarizing generator potential (Figure 10.8b).

This change of potential represents the initial electrical signal of activation of the visual pathway. Stimulation of rhodopsin by light hyperpolarizes the rods, just as stimulation of the cone pigments by light hyperpolarizes the cones. And for rods and cones, the size of the hyperpolarizing photoreceptor potential determines the magnitude of the reduction in the release of synaptic transmitter (Figure 10.7e).

It may seem puzzling at first that stimulation by light *hyper*polarizes vertebrate retinal photoreceptors and causes them to release less neurotransmitter, since sensory stimulation depolarizes most other receptor cells. But remember that the visual system responds to *changes* in light. Either an increase or a decrease in the intensity

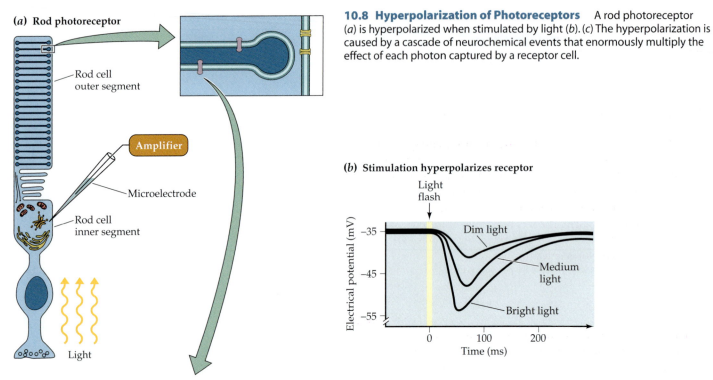

(a) Rod photoreceptor

Rod cell outer segment

Amplifier

Microelectrode

Rod cell inner segment

Light

10.8 Hyperpolarization of Photoreceptors   A rod photoreceptor (*a*) is hyperpolarized when stimulated by light (*b*). (*c*) The hyperpolarization is caused by a cascade of neurochemical events that enormously multiply the effect of each photon captured by a receptor cell.

(b) Stimulation hyperpolarizes receptor

Light flash

Dim light

Medium light

Bright light

Electrical potential (mV)

−35

−45

−55

0   100   200

Time (ms)

(c) Photochemical amplification of stimulus

1. Light stimulation of a molecule of rhodopsin activates about 500 molecules of the G protein transducin. This activation causes a GTP molecule to replace the GDP molecule that binds to a subunit of transducin.

2. The activated G protein activates a phosphodiesterase (PDE).

3. Each PDE molecule hydrolyzes more than 2000 molecules of cGMP, reducing its concentration.

5′–GMP

cGMP

Outer-segment membrane

Open Na⁺ channel

Na⁺

Na⁺

Closed Na⁺ channel

4. The reduction in cGMP leads to closure of Na⁺ channels and hyperpolarization of the receptor. One photon of light can block the entry of more than 1 million Na⁺ molecules.

Light

Rhodopsin

Disc

Disc membrane

Transducin

γ β α

GTP

GDP

α

GTP

PDE

Inside rod cell   Outside cell

of light can stimulate the visual system, and hyperpolarization is just as much a neural signal as depolarization is.

The cascade of processes required to stimulate the visual receptors helps account for three major characteristics of the visual system:

1. Its *sensitivity*, because weak stimuli are amplified to produce physiological effects

2. The *integration* of the stimulus over time, which makes vision relatively slow (compared, for example, to audition) but increases its sensitivity

3. The *adaptation* of the visual system to a wide range of light intensities, as we will discuss a little later

Photoreceptors excite some retinal cells and inhibit others

At their resting potentials, both rod and cone photoreceptors steadily release the synaptic neurotransmitter glutamate. Glutamate depolarizes one group of bipolar cells but hyperpolarizes another group.

The first group are called **off-center bipolar cells:** Turning *off* light in the center of an off-center bipolar cell's receptive field depolarizes the photoreceptor cells, causing them to release more glutamate, which depolarizes the off-center bipolar cell. The second group are called **on-center bipolar cells:** Turning *on* a light in the center of an on-center bipolar cell's receptive field hyperpolarizes the photoreceptor cells, causing them to release less glutamate, which depolarizes the on-center bipolar cell.

Each cone in the central retina connects to four types of bipolar cells (Figure 10.9): one on-center midget bipolar cell, one off-center midget bipolar cell, and several on-center and off-center diffuse bipolar cells (not shown in the figure). Whereas each **midget bipolar cell** in the central retina connects to just one cone, each **diffuse bipolar cell** collects signals from many cones.

Bipolar cells also release glutamate, but glutamate always depolarizes the ganglion cells. Therefore, when light is turned on, on-center bipolar cells depolarize (excite) **on-center ganglion cells;** and when light is turned off, off-center bipolar cells depolarize (excite) **off-center ganglion cells.** The stimulated on-center and off-center ganglion cells then fire nerve impulses and report "light" or "dark" to higher visual centers. Just as there are different types of bipolar cells—midget and diffuse—there are different types of ganglion cells, which we will describe shortly.

A small stimulus in a particular part of the visual field affects only those visual cells whose receptive fields are in the corresponding part of the retina. A mosaic of receptive fields covers the whole retina (except for the blind spot). This situation is similar to what occurs in the somatosensory system, where cells with different somatosensory receptive fields serve different parts of the body surface (see Figure 8.9) and the ensemble covers the whole body.

Different mechanisms enable the eyes to work over a wide range of light intensities

Many sensory systems have to work over wide ranges of stimulus intensity, as we learned in Chapter 8. This is certainly true of the visual system: A very bright light is about 10 billion times as intense as the weakest lights we can see (Figure 10.10). At any given time, however, we can discriminate over only a small fraction of this range of light intensity. Let's discuss the mechanisms by which the eye adapts to the prevailing level of illumination.

One way the visual system deals with a large range of intensities is by adjusting the size of the pupil. In bright light the pupil contracts quickly to admit only about one-sixteenth as much light as when illumination is dim. Although rapid, this pupil response cannot account for the billionfold range of visual sensitivity. Another mechanism for handling different light intensities is **range fractionation**; that is, different receptors—some with low thresholds (rods) and others with high thresholds (cones) handle different intensities (see Table 10.1). Figure 8.6 illustrated range fractionation for the somatosensory system.

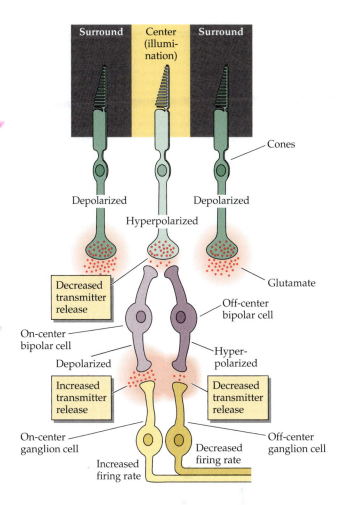

10.9 Connections of Cones to Bipolar Cells (After Purves et al., 2001.)

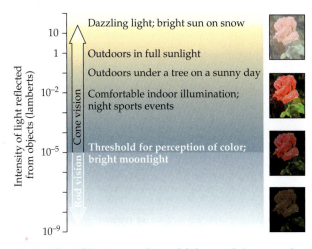

10.10 The Wide Range of Sensitivity to Light Intensity

Additional range fractionation would carry an unacceptable cost: If, at a particular light level, several sets of receptors were not responding, acuity would be impaired. If only a fraction of the receptors responded to the small changes in the intensity of light around a given level, the active receptors would be spaced apart from each other in the retina, and the "grain" of the retina would be coarse. The eye solves this problem by having receptors adapt to the prevailing level of illumination; that is, each receptor adjusts its sensitivity to match the average level of ambient illumination. Thus the visual system is concerned with differences, or changes, in brightness—not with the absolute level of illumination.

At any given time a photoreceptor operates over a range of intensities of about a hundredfold; that is, it is completely depolarized by a stimulus about one-tenth the ambient level of illumination, and a light ten times more intense than the ambient level will completely hyperpolarize it. The receptors can shift their whole range of response to work around the prevailing level of illumination. Further adaptation occurs in the ganglion cells and the lateral geniculate nucleus, and probably at higher levels too.

Three main factors help account for receptor adaptation in the visual system:

1. *The role of calcium.* Probably the most important factor is one shared by other sensory modalities: varying the concentration of calcium (Ca^{2+}) ions (E. N. Pugh and Lamb, 1990). When intracellular Ca^{2+} ions are bound experimentally and thus made unavailable for reactions, the visual system can no longer adapt to higher levels of illumination.

2. *The level of photopigment.* When the photoreceptor pigment is split apart by light, its two components—RETINAL and opsin—slowly recombine, so the balance between the rate of breakdown of the pigment and its rate of recombination determines how much photopigment is available at any given time to respond to stimulation by light. If you go from bright daylight into a dark theater, it takes several minutes until enough rhodopsin becomes available to restore your dark vision.

3. *The availability of retinal chemicals for transduction.* Several retinal chemicals are required for transduction. They tend to be abundant at low levels of illumination but increasingly rare at higher levels of illumination, so increasing numbers of photons are required to activate them and hyperpolarize the receptors (E. N. Pugh and Lamb, 1993).

Acuity is best in foveal vision because of the dense array of cones in the fovea

We noted early in this chapter that acuity is especially fine in the center of the visual field and falls off rapidly toward the periphery. Reasons for this difference have been found in the retina and successive levels of the visual system, each of which is a detailed map of the visible world. Although the neural maps preserve the order of the visual field, each map is topographic; that is, it enlarges some regions at the expense of others.

A photograph of the back of the eye, seen through the pupil, is shown in Figure 10.11*a*. The central region, called the **fovea** (Latin for "pit"), has a dense concentration of cones, and in this region light reaches the cone without having to pass through other layers of cells and blood vessels (Figure 10.12). The optic disc, to the nasal side of the fovea, is where blood vessels enter and leave the eye.

The high concentration of cones in the fovea accounts for high visual acuity in this region (Figure 10.11*b*). People differ in their concentrations of cones (Curcio et al., 1987), and this variation may be related to individual differences in visual acuity. Species differences in visual acuity also reflect the density of cones in the fovea. For example, hawks, which have an acuity much greater than that of humans, have much narrower and more densely packed cones in the fovea than humans do. In the human retina, both cones and rods increase their diameter toward the periphery.

The rods show a different distribution from the cones: They are absent in the fovea but more numerous than cones in the periphery of the retina (see Figure

EVOLUTION AT WORK

(a) Distributions of rods and cones across the retina

(b) Variation of visual acuity across the retina

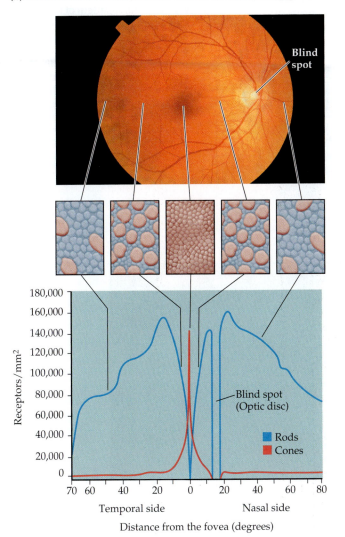

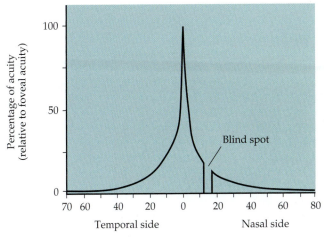

10.11 Frequencies of Retinal Receptors and Visual Acuity
(a) The photograph of the retina was taken through the pupil. The graph shows that rods and cones vary in size and distribution across the retina. (b) The variation of visual acuity across the retina reflects the distribution of cones.

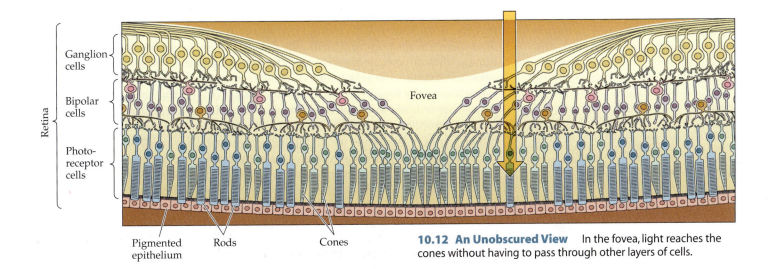

10.12 An Unobscured View
In the fovea, light reaches the cones without having to pass through other layers of cells.

(a) Monkey

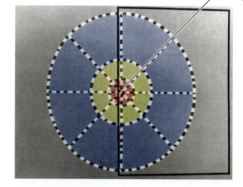

The small central region of the visual field projects to a large part of primary visual cortex.

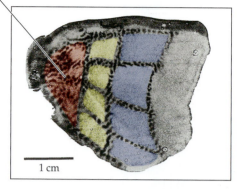

1 cm

(b) Human

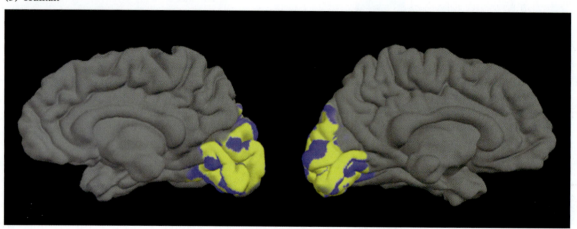

10.13 Location of the Primary Visual Cortex (*a*) A pattern of flickering lights (left) was shown in a monkey's visual field, and a map of the visual field was revealed by autoradiography in a flattened section of the primary visual cortex (*right*). (*b*) Maps of human visual cortex derived from functional-MRI measurements show primary visual cortex as the innermost yellow band on each medial view. (Part *a* from Tootell et al., 1988; *b* from Tootell et al., 1998; both courtesy of Roger Tootell.)

EVOLUTION AT WORK

10.11*a*). They are the most concentrated in a ring about 20° away from the center of the retina. That is why, if you want to see a dim star, you do best to search for it a little off to the side of your center of gaze. Not only are the rods more sensitive to dim light than the cones, but input from more rods converges on ganglion cells in the scotopic system, further increasing its sensitivity to weak stimuli.

A major part of the projection of visual space onto topographic brain maps is devoted to the foveal region (Figure 10.13*a*) (Tootell et al., 1982). Although the **primary visual cortex** (abbreviated **V1**) of the monkey is located on the lateral surface of the occipital area, human V1 is located mainly on the medial surface of the cortex (Figure 10.13*b*; see also Figure 10.19*d*). The fact that, as in the monkey, about half of the human V1 is devoted to the fovea and the retinal region just around the fovea does not mean that our spatial perception is distorted. Rather, this representation makes possible the great acuity of spatial discrimination in the central part of the visual field. Our acuity falls off about as rapidly in the horizontal direction as in the vertical direction, but species that live in open, flat environments (such as the cheetah and the rabbit) have fields of acute vision that extend farther horizontally than vertically.

Studying the regions of blindness caused by brain injuries reveals the extreme orderliness of the mapping of the visual field. If we know the site of injury in the visual pathway, we can predict the location of such a perceptual gap, or **scotoma** (plural *scotomata*), in the visual field. Although the word *scotoma* comes from the Greek *skotos,* meaning "darkness," a scotoma is not perceived as a dark patch in the visual field; rather it is a spot where nothing can be perceived, and usually rigorous testing is required to demonstrate its existence.

Within a scotoma, a person cannot perceive visual cues, but some visual discrimination in this region may still be possible; this paradoxical phenomenon has been called *blindsight*. In other cases, stimuli that cannot be seen within a scotoma affect judgments of stimuli outside it (Stoerig and Cowey, 1997). Blindsight may also be related to the phenomenon of *hemispatial neglect*—neglect of the side opposite to an injured cerebral hemisphere—which we will discuss in Chapter 19.

When we look at a complex organ like the eye of a mammal, an octopus, or a fly, it is hard at first to understand how it could have evolved. But inspection of different living species reveals a gradation from very simple light-sensitive cells to increasingly complex organs with focusing devices (Box 10.2), and each kind of photoreceptor confers benefits on the animal that possesses it.

Before ending our discussion of the retina, we should mention that some retinal ganglion cells possess a special photopigment that makes them sensitive to light (Hattar et al., 2002). As we will see in Chapter 14, these ganglion cells help control daily cycles of behavior called *circadian rhythms*, and they also inform the brain about the level of ambient light to control pupil diameter (Lucas et al., 2003).

Neural Signals Travel from the Retina to Several Brain Regions

The signals that result from visual processing in the retina converge on the ganglion cells, from which they then diverge to several brain structures (see Figure 3.17b). The optic nerves, which are made up of the axons of the ganglion cells in each eye, convey visual information to the brain (Figure 10.14). In all vertebrates, some or all of the axons of each optic nerve cross to the opposite cerebral hemisphere.

10.14 Visual Pathways in the Human Brain Visual fields are represented on the retinas and project to the cerebral hemispheres. The right visual field projects to the left cerebral hemisphere; the left visual field to the right cerebral hemisphere.

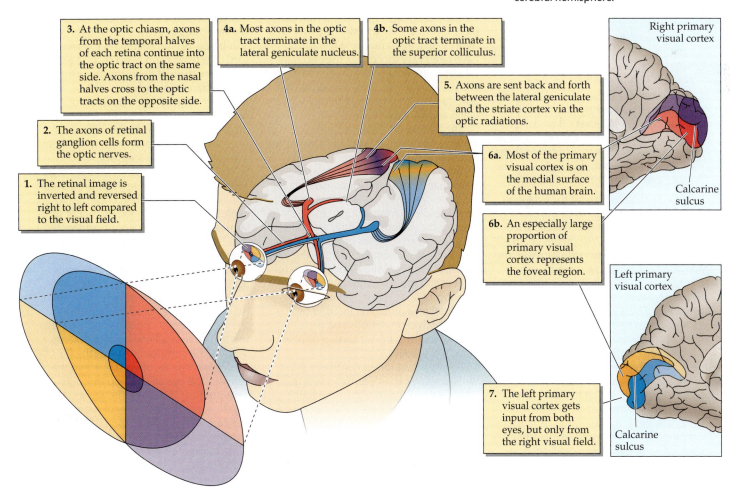

3. At the optic chiasm, axons from the temporal halves of each retina continue into the optic tract on the same side. Axons from the nasal halves cross to the optic tracts on the opposite side.

4a. Most axons in the optic tract terminate in the lateral geniculate nucleus.

4b. Some axons in the optic tract terminate in the superior colliculus.

5. Axons are sent back and forth between the lateral geniculate and the striate cortex via the optic radiations.

2. The axons of retinal ganglion cells form the optic nerves.

6a. Most of the primary visual cortex is on the medial surface of the human brain.

1. The retinal image is inverted and reversed right to left compared to the visual field.

6b. An especially large proportion of primary visual cortex represents the foveal region.

7. The left primary visual cortex gets input from both eyes, but only from the right visual field.

Right primary visual cortex

Calcarine sulcus

Left primary visual cortex

Calcarine sulcus

BOX 10.2 Eyes with Lenses Have Evolved in Several Phyla

Phylogenetic studies indicate that steps in the evolution of eyes with lenses, like those of a mammal or an octopus, included the following (Fernald, 2000):

1. Concentrating light-sensitive cells into localized groups that serve as photoreceptor organs (Figure A). Animals with such photoreceptor organs have better chances of surviving and reproducing than do similar animals with scattered receptor cells, because photoreceptor organs facilitate an ability to respond differently to stimuli that strike different parts of the body surface.

2. Clustering light receptors at the bottom of pitlike or cuplike depressions in the skin (Figure B). Animals with this adaptation can discriminate better among stimuli that come from different directions. They also perceive increased contrast of stimuli against a background of ambient light.

3. Narrowing the top of the cup into a small aperture so that, like a pinhole camera, the eye can focus well (Figure C).

4. Closing the opening with transparent skin or filling the cup with a transparent substance (Figure D). This covering protects the eye against the entry of foreign substances that might injure the receptor cells or block vision.

5. Forming a lens either by thickening the transparent skin or by modifying other tissue in the eye (Figure E). This adaptation improves the focusing of the eye while allowing the aperture to be relatively large to let in more light; thus vision can be acute even when light is not intense.

The only requirement for the evolution of eyes to begin appears to be the existence of light-sensitive cells. Natural selection then favors the development of auxiliary mechanisms needed to improve vision. Many kinds of cells show some sensitivity to light, and different phyla have modified different types of cells for specialized photoreceptors. The most common starting point has been cells of epidermal (skin) origin, but some lines (including that of our chordate vertebrate ancestors) derived their visual receptors from cells of neural origin. All known visual systems use a light-receptor molecule similar to rhodopsin, indicating a basic similarity among them.

Phylogenetic studies of the structure and development of eyes led investigators to conclude that eyes evolved independently in many different phyla

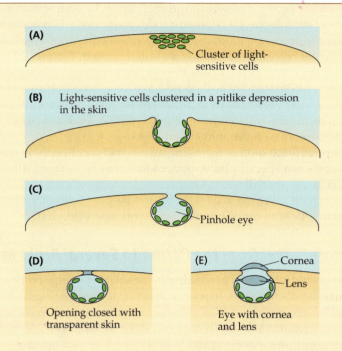

(A) Cluster of light-sensitive cells

(B) Light-sensitive cells clustered in a pitlike depression in the skin

(C) Pinhole eye

(D) Opening closed with transparent skin

(E) Cornea / Lens / Eye with cornea and lens

(Salvini-Plawen and Mayr, 1977). A competent optical system with a lens, however, has evolved in only 6 of the 33 phyla of multicellular animals. These few phyla have been very successful; they account for about 96% of known species of multicellular animals. An effective optical system may have contributed to this success (Land and Fernald, 1992).

The fact that the cephalopods (such as squid and octopuses) evolved a visual system that in many ways resembles that of vertebrates (from fish to humans) suggests that there are major constraints on the development of a visual system for a large, rapidly moving animal. Let's look at some of the major similarities and differences between the eyes of cephalopods and those of vertebrates. In both, the eyes are relatively large, allowing for many receptors and the ability to gather large amounts of light. The incoming light is regulated by a pupil and focused by a lens. In both cephalopods and vertebrates, three sets of extraocular muscles move the eyeballs.

An important difference in eye structure between cephalopods and vertebrates is the organization of the retina. In the vertebrate eye, light must travel through neurons and blood vessels to reach the receptors, and the area where the neural axons and blood vessels enter and leave the retina forms the blind spot.

In cephalopods the organization is more efficient in some respects: Light reaches the receptors directly, and the neurons and blood vessels lie behind the receptors; thus there is no blind spot. The detailed structure of the receptor cells is quite different in cephalopods and vertebrates. In addition, the visual stimulus causes depolarization of cephalopod (and most invertebrate) retinal receptor cells, but it causes hyperpolarization of fish and mammalian retinal receptors.

It is still uncertain whether eyes of all species evolved from a single progenitor or have arisen more than once during evolution (Fernald, 2000). The major similarities between cephalopod and vertebrate eyes have often been cited as examples of convergent evolution, showing ways in which similar functions can be achieved with different structures and processes, starting from different origins. However, the eyes of all seeing animals share at least two important genetic features: First, they all use opsin pigments. Second, the compound eye of the fruit fly *Drosophila,* the vertebrate eye, and the cephalopod eye all develop through genes of the *Pax* family. The finding that highly homologous molecules are key regulators of eye development in different phyla argues that eyes in all phyla share a common origin.

The optic nerves cross the midline at the **optic chiasm** (named for the Greek letter X [*chi*] because of its crossover shape), which is located just anterior to the stalk of the pituitary gland. In humans, axons from the half of the retina toward the nose (the nasal retina) cross over to the opposite side of the brain. The half of the retina toward the side of the head (the temporal retina) projects its axons to its own side of the head. After they pass the optic chiasm, the axons of the retinal ganglion cells are known collectively as the **optic tract.** Proportionally more axons cross the midline in animals, such as rodents, that have laterally placed eyes with little binocular overlap in their fields of vision.

Most axons of the optic tract terminate on cells in the **lateral geniculate nucleus (LGN),** which is the visual part of the thalamus. Axons of postsynaptic cells in the LGN form the **optic radiations,** which terminate in the visual areas of the **occipital cortex** at the back of the brain. The primary visual cortex is often called the **striate cortex** because a broad stripe, or *striation,* is visible in anatomical sections through this region; the stripe represents layer IV of the cortex, where the optic-radiation fibers arrive. Inputs from the two eyes converge on cells beyond layer IV of the primary visual cortex, making binocular and stereo vision possible.

In addition to the primary visual cortex (V1) shown in Figures 10.13 and 10.14, numerous surrounding regions of the cortex are also largely visual in function (see Figure 10.19c). Visual cortical areas outside the striate cortex are sometimes called **extrastriate cortex.** As Figure 10.14 shows, the visual cortex in the right cerebral hemisphere receives its input from the left half of the visual field, and the visual cortex in the left hemisphere receives its input from the right half of the visual field. Because of the orderly mapping of the visual field (known as *retinotopic mapping*) at the various levels of the visual system, damage to parts of the visual system can be diagnosed from defects in perception of the visual field.

Figure 10.14 shows that some retinal ganglion cells send their optic-tract axons to the superior colliculus in the midbrain. The superior colliculus helps coordinate rapid movements of the eyes toward a target.

Investigators have found several cortical areas for each sensory modality, and most of these areas are laid out in an orderly topographic map of the receptor surface (C. N. Woolsey, 1981a, 1981b, 1981c). Examination of the cortex of the macaque (an Old World monkey) reveals more than 30 visual areas, many of which contain a topographic representation of the retina (see Figure 10.19c). The different cortical regions work in parallel to process different aspects of visual perception, such as form, color, location, and movement, as we will discuss later in this chapter.

Investigators use a variety of techniques to map the visual system: anatomical tracing of fibers, electrophysiological recording of activity evoked by specific kinds of visual stimulation, PET (positron emission tomography) and other noninvasive measures of regional activity in the brain, and experimental and clinical lesions of the visual system. Integrating the findings from studies using these techniques provides us with our current understanding of the structure and functions of the visual system.

Neurons at different levels of the visual system have very different receptive fields

In the visual system, a neuron's **receptive field** consists of the stimuli in visual space that increase or decrease that neuron's firing. A small stimulus in a particular part of the visual field affects only those visual cells whose receptive fields are in the corresponding part of the retina. A mosaic of receptive fields covers the whole retina, except for the blind spot. Spots of light that are lighter or darker than surrounding areas are sufficient to activate cells in the retina or LGN, but many cells in the visual cortex are more demanding and respond only to more complicated stimuli.

The nature of the receptive field of a cell gives us good clues about its function(s) in perception. In the next sections we will see some cases in which neurons at lower levels in the visual system seem to account for particular perceptual phenomena and other cases in which solutions need to be sought at higher levels in the visual system.

IMPORTANT METHOD

(a) An on-center/off-surround cell

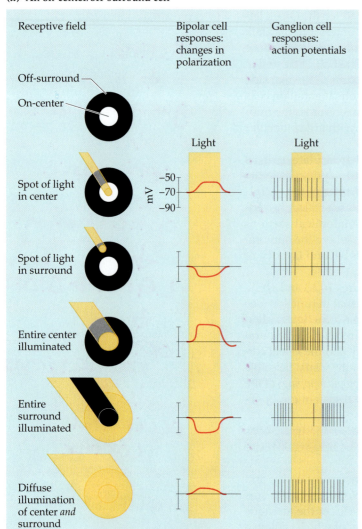

(b) An off-center/on-surround cell

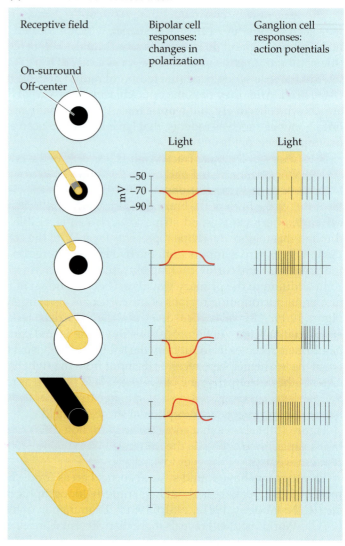

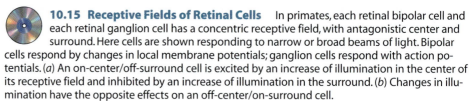

10.15 Receptive Fields of Retinal Cells In primates, each retinal bipolar cell and each retinal ganglion cell has a concentric receptive field, with antagonistic center and surround. Here cells are shown responding to narrow or broad beams of light. Bipolar cells respond by changes in local membrane potentials; ganglion cells respond with action potentials. (a) An on-center/off-surround cell is excited by an increase of illumination in the center of its receptive field and inhibited by an increase of illumination in the surround. (b) Changes in illumination have the opposite effects on an off-center/on-surround cell.

Stephen Kuffler (1913–1980)

Horace Barlow

Neurons in the retina and the LGN have concentric receptive fields

Two scientists discovered the main features of the receptive fields of vertebrate retinal ganglion cells independently within a few months of each other: Stephen Kuffler (1953), studying the cat; and Horace Barlow (1953), studying the frog. They recorded from single ganglion cells while they moved a small spot of light across the visual field, keeping the animal's eye still. Results showed that the receptive fields of retinal ganglion cells are concentric, consisting of a roughly circular central area and a ring around it.

Both bipolar cells and ganglion cells have two basic types of retinal receptive fields: **on-center/off-surround** (Figure 10.15a) and **off-center/on-surround** (Figure 10.15b). The center and its surround are always antagonistic. These antagonistic effects explain why uniform illumination of the visual field is less effective in activating a ganglion cell than is a well-placed small spot or a line or edge passing through the center of the cell's receptive field.

Investigators who study primate visual systems take the organization of the LGN as their key. The primate LGN has six main layers and some smaller layers intercalated between them (Figure 10.16). The structure is called *geniculate* because the layers are bent like a knee, for which the Latin word is *genu*. The smaller layers are called *koniocellular layers* because they contain very small neurons (the Greek root *koni* means "dust").

The four dorsal, or outer, layers of the primate LGN are called **parvocellular** (from the Latin *parvus*, "small") because their cells are relatively small. The two ventral, or inner, layers are called **magnocellular** (from the Latin *magnus*, "large") because their cells are large. Most of the neurons in the magnocellular layers have relatively large receptive fields, the input of which can be traced back to large ganglion cells, which receive their input from diffuse retinal bipolar cells that contact many neighboring receptor cells. Most magnocellular neurons do not show differential wavelength responses; that is, they cannot be involved in color discrimination.

The neurons of the parvocellular layers have relatively small receptive fields, the input of which can be traced back to small ganglion cells, which receive their input from midget bipolar cells, which

Coronal section

10.16 Cross Section of the Monkey Lateral Geniculate Nucleus

Lateral ventricle

Thalamus

Lateral geniculate nucleus

Hippocampus

Brainstem

Dorsal

Medial

In the four main dorsal layers (3–6), the cells are relatively small (parvocellular).

In the two main ventral layers (1–2), the cells are large (magnocellular).

Cells in layers 1, 4, and 6 (yellow) receive input from the eye on the opposite side of the body. Cells in layers 2, 3, and 5 (blue) receive input from the eye on the same side.

(in the central retina) are driven by single cones. These neurons discriminate wavelengths. The LGN cells of all six layers have concentric receptive fields.

There are two main types of ganglion cells (Leventhal, 1979; Perry et al., 1984), sometimes called *M* and *P* ganglion cells because they project their axons, respectively, to the magnocellular or parvocellular layers of the LGN. As noted already, M ganglion cells are relatively large cells with large dendritic fields and thus large receptive fields. M ganglion cells can detect stimuli with low contrast and are sensitive to rapid temporal change; they respond transiently, and they have large-diameter axons that conduct very rapidly. M ganglion cells make up about 10% of primate retinal ganglion cells.

About 80% of primate retinal ganglion cells are P cells projecting most of their axons to the P layers of the LGN and about 10% of their axons to the M layers. The P ganglion cells are relatively small and have small dendritic and receptive fields. The remaining 10% of the primate ganglion cells are konio (K) cells, which project in three different bands from the retina to the LGN and visual cortex.

David Hubel

Neurons in the visual cortex have varied and complicated receptive fields

The next level of the visual system, the primary visual cortex, provided a puzzle. Neurons from the LGN send their axons to cells in the primary visual cortex (V1), but the spots of light that are effective stimuli for LGN cells (Figure 10.17a) are not very effective at the cortical level. In 1959, David Hubel and Torsten Wiesel reported that visual cortical cells require more-specific, elongated stimuli than those that activate LGN cells. Most cells in area V1 respond best to lines or bars in a particular

Torsten Wiesel

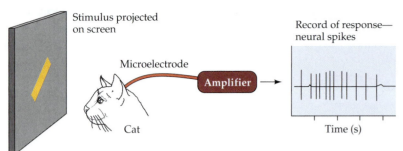

10.17 Receptive Fields of Cells at Various Levels in the Cat Visual System Microelectrode recordings reveal that cells differ greatly in their receptive fields. (a) Visual cells in the thalamus (LGN) have concentric receptive fields. (b) Visual cells in the cerebral cortex may show orientation specificity or respond only to motion, or (c) they may respond only to motion in a particular direction.

Examples of receptive fields of brain cells:

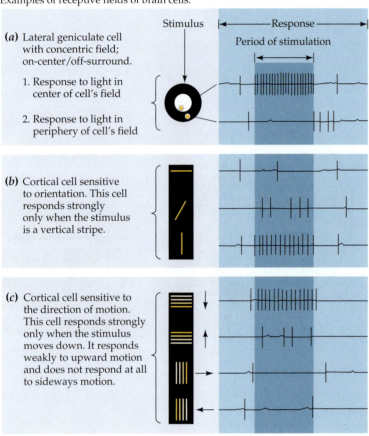

(a) Lateral geniculate cell with concentric field; on-center/off-surround.

1. Response to light in center of cell's field

2. Response to light in periphery of cell's field

(b) Cortical cell sensitive to orientation. This cell responds strongly only when the stimulus is a vertical stripe.

(c) Cortical cell sensitive to the direction of motion. This cell responds strongly only when the stimulus moves down. It responds weakly to upward motion and does not respond at all to sideways motion.

position and at a particular orientation in the visual field (Figure 10.17b). Some cortical cells also require movement of the stimulus to make them respond actively. For some of these cells, any movement in their field is sufficient; others are even more demanding, requiring motion in a specific direction (Figure 10.17c). For this and related research, Hubel and Wiesel were awarded the Nobel Prize in Physiology or Medicine in 1981.

Hubel and Wiesel categorized cortical cells into classes according to the types of stimuli required to produce maximum responses. So-called **simple cortical cells** responded best to an edge or a bar that had a particular width and a particular orientation and location in the visual field. These cells were therefore sometimes called *bar detectors* or *edge detectors*. Like the simple cells, **complex cortical cells** had elongated receptive fields, but they also showed some latitude for location; that is, they responded to a bar of a particular size and orientation anywhere within a larger area of the visual field.

Hubel and Wiesel's theoretical model can be described as hierarchical; that is, more-complex events are built up from inputs of simpler ones. For example, a simple cortical cell can be thought of as receiving input from a row of LGN cells, and a complex cortical cell can be thought of as receiving its input from a row of simple cortical cells.

Other theorists extrapolated from this model, suggesting that higher-order circuits of cells could detect any possible form. Thus it was suggested that by integration of enough successive levels of analysis, a unit could be constructed that would enable a person to recognize his or her grandmother, and such hypothetical "grandmother cells" were frequently mentioned in the literature. According to this view, any time such a cell was excited, up would pop a picture of one's grandmother. This hypothesis was given as a possible explanation for facial recognition.

COMPETING HYPOTHESES

Critics soon pointed out both theoretical and empirical problems with the hierarchical model. For one thing, a "grandmother-recognizing" circuit would require vast numbers of cells, perhaps even more than the number available in the cerebral cortex. At the same time that problems with this model were being shown, an alternative model was emerging, which we will describe next.

Most cells in the primary visual cortex are tuned to particular spatial frequencies

Concepts of pattern analysis in terms of lines and edges at various orientations have largely given way to what is known as the **spatial-frequency filter model**. To discuss this model, we must become familiar with a way of regarding spatial vision that is quite different from our intuitive thinking (F. W. Campbell and Robson, 1968; R. L. De Valois and De Valois, 1988). By *spatial frequency of a visual stimulus,* we mean the number of light–dark (or color) cycles that the stimulus shows per degree of visual space.

For example, Figure 10.18*a* and *b* differ in the spacing of the bars: Figure 10.18*a* has twice as many bars in the same horizontal space and is therefore said to have double the spatial frequency of Figure 10.18*b*. The spatial-frequency technique applies Fourier analysis (see Box 9.1) or linear systems theory, rather than analyzing visual patterns into bars and angles.

In Box 9.1 we saw that we can produce any complex, repeating auditory stimulus by adding together simple sine waves. Conversely, using Fourier analysis, we can determine which sine waves would be needed to make any particular complex waveform. The same principle of Fourier analysis can be applied to visual patterns. If the dimension from dark to light is made to vary according to a sine wave function, visual patterns like the ones in Figure 10.18*c* and *d* result. A series of dark and light stripes, like those in Figure 10.18*a* and *b,* can be analyzed into the sum of a visual sine wave and its odd harmonics—that is, multiples of the basic frequency.

A complex visual pattern or scene can also be analyzed by the Fourier technique; in this case, frequency components at different angles of orientation are also used.

(a) High-frequency square wave

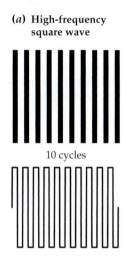

10 cycles

(b) Low-frequency square wave

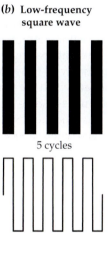

5 cycles

(c) High-contrast sinusoidal spatial grid

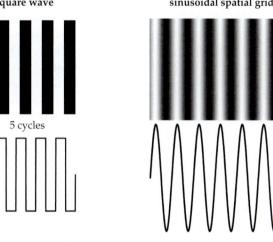
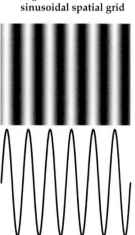
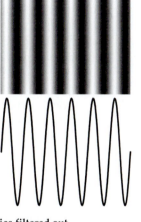

(d) Low-contrast sinusoidal spatial grid

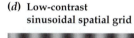

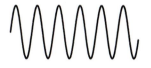

(e) Normal

(f) High frequencies filtered out

(g) Low frequencies filtered out

10.18 Spatial Frequencies (*a, b*) The spacing between dark and light stripes shows that part *a* has double the spatial frequency of part *b*. (*c, d*) These visual grids show sinusoidal modulation of intensity: (*c*) high contrast; (*d*) low contrast. (*e–g*) A photograph of Groucho Marx subjected to spatial filtering: (*e*) normal photograph; (*f*) high spatial frequencies filtered out; (*g*) low spatial frequencies filtered out. (Parts *e–g* courtesy of John Frisby.)

A given spatial frequency can exist at any level of contrast; Figure 10.18c and d show examples of high and low contrast, respectively.

To reproduce or perceive the complex pattern or scene accurately, the system has to handle all the spatial frequencies that are present in it. If the high frequencies are filtered out, the small details and sharp contrasts are lost; if the low frequencies are filtered out, the large uniform areas and gradual transitions are lost. Figure 10.18e–g show how the filtering of spatial frequencies affects a photograph. The photograph is still recognizable after the high visual frequencies are filtered out (Figure 10.18f) or when the low frequencies are filtered out (Figure 10.18g). (Similarly, speech is still recognizable, although it sounds distorted, after either the high audio frequencies or the low frequencies are filtered out.)

F. W. Campbell and J. G. Robson (1968) suggested that the visual system includes many channels that are tuned to different spatial frequencies, just as the auditory system has channels for different acoustic frequencies. The term channel is used here to mean a mechanism that accepts or deals with only a particular band or class of information. This concept is analogous to the transmission of information by a particular radio or television station, which uses an assigned channel, or band of wavelengths; to receive this information, you must tune your receiving device to the particular channel.

The suggestion that the nervous system has different spatial-frequency channels was soon supported by experiments on selective adaptation to spatial patterns (Blakemore and Campbell, 1969; Pantle and Sekuler, 1968). In these experiments a person spent a minute or more inspecting a visual grating with a given spacing (or spatial frequency), such as those in Figure 10.18a and b. Looking at the grating made the cells that are tuned to that frequency adapt (become less sensitive). Then the person's sensitivity to gratings of different spacings was determined.

The results showed that sensitivity to the subsequent gratings was depressed briefly at the particular frequency to which the person had adapted. The suggestion of multiple spatial-frequency channels

> had revolutionary impact because it led to entirely different conceptions of the way in which the visual system might function in dealing with spatial stimuli. It suggests that rather than specifically detecting such seminaturalistic features as bars and edges, the system is breaking down complex stimuli into their individual spatial frequency components in a kind of crude Fourier analysis. (R. L. De Valois and De Valois, 1988, p. 320)

The responses of cortical cells to spatial-frequency stimuli were found to be tuned more accurately to the dimensions of spatial-frequency grids than to the widths of bars (R. L. De Valois et al., 1977; Hochstein and Shapley, 1976; Maffei and Fiorentini, 1973). The receptive field of a cortical cell typically shows an excitatory axis and bands of inhibition on each side; the spacing of these components shows the frequency tuning. The spatial-frequency approach has proved useful in the analysis of many aspects of human pattern vision (K. K. De Valois et al., 1979) and provides the basis of high-definition television (HDTV).

Area V1 is involved in the formation of mental images

Neurons of V1 (the primary visual cortex) appear to be involved not only in perceiving objects and events, but also in forming mental images. For example, imagined objects activate regions that correspond to the retinotopic mapping of V1; when people imagined small letters (in order to be able to answer questions about them), PET recording showed activation of the foveal representation; when they imagined large letters, the parafoveal representation was activated (Kosslyn et al., 1993).

To obtain convergent evidence about the role of V1 in forming mental images, Kosslyn et al. (1999) used PET and also studied how impairing the function of V1 affected mental images. To impair function, they gave subjects repetitive transcranial magnetic stimulation (rTMS) directed to V1. Before each set of trials in which subjects formed and inspected mental images, rTMS was administered for 10 minutes; the effects were presumed to last for about 10 minutes after the conclusion of rTMS. This stimulation did not prevent the formation of images, but it significantly impaired the process, thus adding further evidence of the necessity of V1 for the formation of images.

Neurons in the visual cortex beyond area V1 have complex receptive fields and contribute to the identification of forms

Area V1 is only a small part of the portion of cortex that is devoted to vision. Area V1 sends axons to other visual cortical areas, including areas that appear to be involved in the perception of form: area V2, area V4, and the inferior temporal area (see Figure 10.19c). Some of these extrastriate areas also receive direct input from the LGN. The receptive fields of the cells in many of these extrastriate visual areas are

(*a*) **Macaque brain, lateral view**

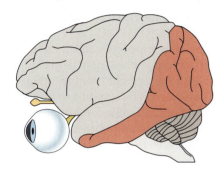

(*b*) **Macaque brain, medial view**

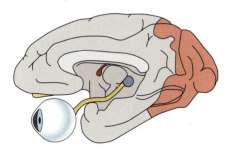

(*d*) **Visual areas in the human occipital cortex, "flattened" by computational techniques**

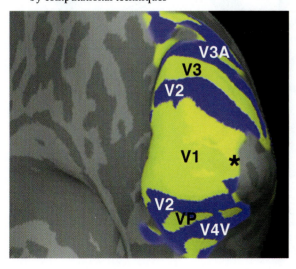

(*c*) **Visual areas in the macaque cortex, unfolded view**

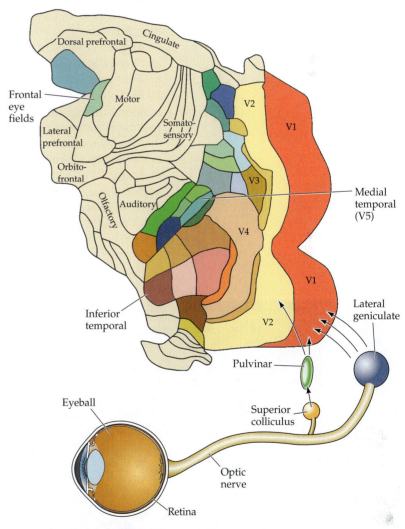

10.19 Main Visual Areas in Monkey and Human Brains (*a, b*) Macaque visual areas in occipital and temporal cortex are shown in pink. (*c*) All the known visual areas of the macaque on a flattened cortex in color. (*d*) Through computational techniques, the occipital regions of human brain shown in Figure 10.13*b* were "inflated," flattening the brain and bringing sulci in the cortex to the surface, which reveals the relative size and extent of various cortical visual areas. The asterisk identifies the representation of the center of the fovea. (Parts *a–c* after Van Essen and Drury, 1997; *d* from Tootell et al., 1998, courtesy of Roger Tootell.)

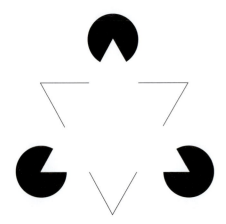

10.20 A Geometric Figure with "Illusory" or "Subjective" Contours Cells have been found in visual cortical areas that respond to illusory contours such as those of the upright triangle shown here. These contours thus have neurophysiological meaning.

even more complex than those in cells of area V1. As Figure 10.19*a–c* reflect, on the basis of anatomical, physiological, and behavioral investigations with macaque monkeys, we know that at least 32 distinct cortical areas are directly involved in visual function (Van Essen and Drury, 1997).

The visual areas of the human brain (Figure 10.19*d*) have been less thoroughly mapped than those of the monkey brain, and mainly by neuroimaging, which does not have as fine spatial resolution as the electrophysiological recording used in the monkey brain, but the general layout appears to be similar in the two species. However, the similarities are greatest for V1 and adjacent regions and fall off for other areas (Tootell et al., 2003).

In addition, the proportions of cortical areas between the two species show important differences. In macaque monkeys, the occipital lobe occupies about 32% of the isocortex (neocortex), and the frontal lobe about 26%; in humans, the occipital lobe occupies about 19%, and the frontal lobe about 36%. Whereas the 32 areas that are largely or entirely visual in function occupy about 55% of the surface of the macaque isocortex, the visual areas account for only about 30% of human isocortex (Tootell et al., 2003). We will discuss only a few of the main visual cortical areas and their functions.

Area V2 is adjacent to V1, and many of its cells show properties similar to those of V1 cells. Many V2 cells can respond to illusory contours, which may help explain how we perceive contours such as the boundaries of the upright triangle in Figure 10.20 (Peterhans and von der Heydt, 1989). Clearly such cells respond to complex relations among the parts of their receptive fields. Some V1 cells can also respond to illusory contours (Grosof et al., 1993), but this feature is more common in area V2.

Area V4 receives axons from V2 and has cells that give their strongest responses to the sinusoidal frequency gratings that we discussed earlier (see Figure 10.18*c* and *d*). Many V4 cells respond even better, however, to concentric and radial stimuli, such as those in Figure 10.21*a* (Gallant et al., 1993). Investigators have suggested that these V4 cells show an intermediate stage between the spatial-frequency processing in V1 and V2 cells and the recognition of pattern and form in cells of the inferior

(*a*)   (*b*)

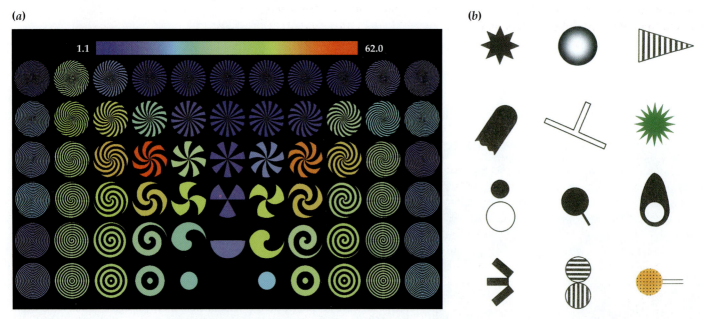

10.21 Complex Stimuli Evoke Strong Responses in Visual Cortex (*a*) These concentric and radial stimuli evoke maximal responses from some cells in visual cortical area V4. The stimuli that evoked the highest response rates (see scale bar) are shown in red and orange.

(*b*) These 12 examples illustrate the critical features of stimuli that evoke maximal responses from cells in the anterior inferior temporal area. (Part *a* from Gallant et al., 1993, courtesy of Jack Gallant; *b* from K. Tanaka, 1993, courtesy of Keiji Tanaka.)

temporal area. Area V4 also has many cells that respond most strongly to wavelength differences, as we will see later when we discuss color vision. Area V5, also called the *medial temporal (MT) area,* appears to be specialized for the perception of motion, as we will also discuss later in this chapter.

The inferior temporal (IT) visual cortex has many cells that respond best to particular complex forms, including forms that the subject has learned to recognize. Because many cells in IT cortex have highly specific receptive fields, it is hard to find the exact stimuli that can activate a particular cell. Experimenters start by presenting many three-dimensional animal and plant objects (Desimone et al., 1984; K. Tanaka, 1993). When a stimulus elicits a strong response, the experimenters then simplify the image by sequentially removing parts of the features to determine the necessary and sufficient features for maximal activation of the cell.

Most cells in IT cortex do not require a natural object such as a face to activate them; instead they require moderately complex shapes, sometimes combined with color or texture, such as those in Figure 10.21b. The complex receptive fields in IT cortex probably develop through experience and learning. After a monkey was trained for a year to discriminate a set of 28 moderately complex shapes, 39% of the cells in its anterior IT cortex responded significantly to some of these shapes. In control monkeys, on the other hand, only 9% of the cells responded strongly to these forms (Kobatake and Tanaka, 1994).

NEURAL PLASTICITY

The prefrontal cortex also contains a restricted region of neurons that are activated by faces but not by other visual stimuli, as found both by noninvasive recording of human subjects (Ungerleider et al., 1998) and by electrical recording of neurons in the monkey brain (Scalaidhe et al., 1997). These neurons receive connections from the superior temporal sulcus and adjacent cortex on the inferior temporal gyrus. These findings indicate that a ventral visual pathway that processes stimulus identification extends from the primary visual cortex through temporal cortical regions to the prefrontal cortex.

Area V1 Is Organized in Columns and Slabs

Area V1 is organized with a richness of representation. The primary visual cortex has separate representations for at least four dimensions of the visual stimulus: (1) location in the visual field, with larger, finer mapping of the central region of the visual field than of the periphery; (2) ocular dominance; (3) orientation; and (4) color.

Ocular dominance columns were first discovered by electrophysiological recording. Although the receptive field of an individual neuron is the same for vision through either eye, some cells are equally activated by the two eyes, but other cells respond preferentially (i.e., more strongly) to stimulation of one eye. However, all the cells in a vertical column of cells have the same ocular dominance. The vertical columns are arranged into **ocular dominance slabs** about 0.5 mm wide, all cells of which respond preferentially to stimulation of one eye. A given point in the visual field elicits responses in cells in adjacent left-eye-preferring and right-eye-preferring ocular dominance slabs.

Ocular dominance is especially clear in the broad layer IV, where each cell is monocular, responding to only one eye. Above and below the (monocular) ocular dominance stripes in layer IV, most of the cells respond to stimulation of both eyes. However, even though ocular dominance is expressed less strongly above and below layer IV, the cells in that slab still prefer one eye over the other.

Anatomical tracing techniques in the 1970s furnished additional information about the ocular dominance organization. For example, when a small dose of radioactive amino acid is injected into one eye, some of it is transported along neurons, crossing synapses and reaching layer IV of the primary visual cortex. Autoradiographic examination of the cortex then reveals parallel bands of radioactivity in layer IV that correspond to the ocular dominance stripes driven by the injected eye.

IMPORTANT METHOD

Techniques of optical imaging of cortical activity (T. Bonhoeffer and Grinvald, 1991; Ts'o et al., 1990) allow us to see the ocular dominance stripes in the primary

10.22 Visualization of Ocular Dominance Columns and Orientation Columns by Optical Imaging

(a) In this method for visualization of ocular dominance, a camera records changes in light reflected from the cortex when the monkey views a twinkling checkerboard with one eye. Small differences in reflected light are amplified, and intensity is coded by color (red for strong intensity, blue for weak). (b) After the recording is processed, regions activated by the active eye are seen as red stripes. (c) In this method for visualization of orientation preference, stimuli at different orientations (vertical, horizontal, diagonal) are presented to reveal groups of neurons that respond most strongly to a particular orientation. The stimuli are usually black or white, but here they are color-coded to correspond to color-coded responses to four different orientations combined into a single pattern. (d) Although the pattern at first seems disorderly, closer inspection reveals several regions at which all four orientations converge in a pinwheel pattern (inset). Note that the foci of pinwheels occur at regular intervals, that each orientation is represented only once within a pinwheel, and that the sequence of orientations is consistent across pinwheels. (After T. Bonhoeffer and Grinvald, 1991; b and d courtesy of A. Grinvald.)

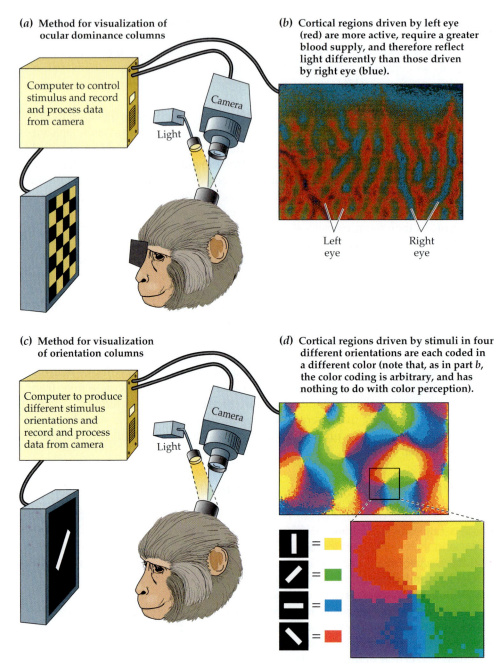

(a) Method for visualization of ocular dominance columns

Computer to control stimulus and record and process data from camera

Camera

Light

(b) Cortical regions driven by left eye (red) are more active, require a greater blood supply, and therefore reflect light differently than those driven by right eye (blue).

Left eye   Right eye

(c) Method for visualization of orientation columns

Computer to produce different stimulus orientations and record and process data from camera

Camera

Light

(d) Cortical regions driven by stimuli in four different orientations are each coded in a different color (note that, as in part b, the color coding is arbitrary, and has nothing to do with color perception).

visual cortex of an awake monkey when visual patterns are presented to one eye (Figure 10.22a and b). The imaging is based on small changes in the light reflected from the cortex during activity. These changes are of two types: (1) changes in blood volume, probably in the capillaries of the activated area; and (2) changes in cortical tissue, such as the movement of ions and water or the expansion and contraction of extracellular spaces. Experimenters can combine optical imaging with electrophysiological recording to obtain visual guidance for placing microelectrodes in particular parts of ocular dominance slabs. Figure 10.22b shows the ocular dominance slabs that were activated when one eye was stimulated. This recording technique may prove useful as a mapping tool in human neurosurgery.

Ocular dominance slabs develop during the first 4 months of life in the cat and during the first 6 months in the macaque monkey. As we saw in Chapter 7, both eyes must be exposed to the visual environment if each eye is to obtain its own cortical representation (see Figure 7.20). Up to the age of 3 or 4 months, human infants are unimpressed by stereograms (pairs of pictures showing somewhat different left-eye and right-eye views that most adult observers perceive as a three-dimensional view). Beginning at the age of 3 or 4 months, however, most infants are captivated by stereograms (Held, 1993). Presumably, before that age the cortex is unable to separate the information from the two eyes because the information reaches the same cortical neurons.

Primary visual cortex also has a columnar organization for stimulus orientation: A microelectrode that follows a path perpendicular to the surface records cells that all prefer the same stimulus orientation within the visual field (Figure 10.22c and d). As the recording electrode is moved from one **orientation column** to the next, the preferred axis of orientation shifts by a few degrees. That is, in one column all the cells may be "tuned" to upright stimuli (at an orientation of 0°); in an adjacent column, all cells may respond best to another orientation, perhaps at 10° from the vertical; in the next column, perhaps at 25°; and so forth.

In Figure 10.22d we see how these columns are organized parallel to the surface of the cortex. In this figure, optical recordings show the regions of primary visual cortex that respond best to stimuli of four different orientations. The columns are organized into slabs that run perpendicular to the borders of ocular dominance slabs. These slabs, however, stretch only from the center of one ocular stripe to the center of the adjacent stripe. Along the center of the ocular dominance stripes, preferred orientation shifts by 90°, creating regularly spaced "pinwheels" in which responses to the different stimulus orientations pivot around a center. A striking technical advance in the functional-MRI technique has made it possible to visualize individual orientation columns in the visual cortex of cats (D.-S. Kim et al., 2000), showing excellent agreement with data from electrical recording and optical imaging studies.

Also within the ocular dominance slabs of primate visual areas are vertical blobs (sometimes called *pegs*) that can be seen when the tissue is stained to reveal the enzyme cytochrome oxidase. Early experiments suggested that the blobs were related to color vision (Hendrickson, 1985; Livingstone and Hubel, 1984), but later work has cast doubt on this hypothesis. Quantitative studies show that neurons in the blobs cannot be readily distinguished from neurons outside the blobs on the basis of either chromatic tuning (Lennie et al., 1990) or orientation tuning (Leventhal et al., 1995). In addition, even nocturnal primates (whose retinas are poor in cones) and cats (which have little color vision) have blobs; and cone-rich rodents, such as ground squirrels, do not have blobs.

Blobs extend above and below layer IV but are not seen in layer IV itself. Figure 10.23 diagrams the organization of the primate primary visual cortex, including the large ocular dominance slabs, the orientation slabs, and the blobs. Along the centers of the ocular dominance slabs, the orientation slabs are arranged radially, like the "pinwheels" in Figure 10.22d, with blobs at the centers of the pinwheels; but else-

10.23 Organization of the Primate Primary Visual Cortex These two partial ocular dominance slabs represent the left and right eyes, respectively. Blobs extend vertically through layers I through III and V through VI, located in the centers of ocular dominance slabs. Small columns represent the preferred orientations of groups of cells; these orientation columns radiate from the centers of the blobs. The orientation is color-coded here as in Figure 10.22d. For simplification, this diagram does not represent spatial frequency (higher spatial frequencies are represented at the edges of the blocks and lower frequencies in the centers), nor does it represent the spectrally opponent cells (which we'll discuss shortly) that occur irregularly in the columns.

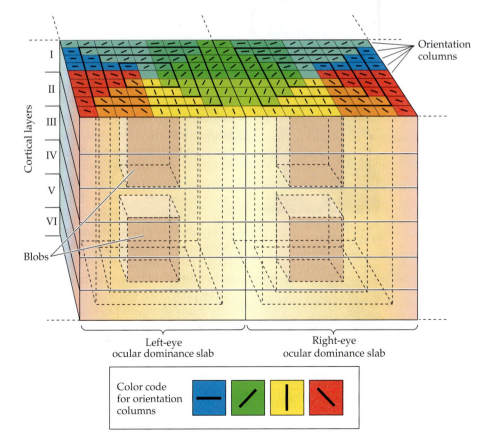

Color code for orientation columns

where the orientation slabs are laid out in a rectangular arrangement, like city blocks that cross the borders of the ocular dominance slabs.

Color Vision Depends on Special Channels from the Retinal Cones through Cortical Area V4

For most people, different hues are a striking aspect of vision. The system of color perception appears to have at least four stages. In the first stage the cones—the retinal receptor cells that are specialized to respond to certain wavelengths of light—receive visual information. In the second stage this information is processed by neurons in the local circuits of the retina, leading to retinal ganglion cells that are excited by light of some wavelengths and inhibited by light of other wavelengths. The ganglion cells send the wavelength information via their axons to the LGN, mainly in the parvocellular layers. From there this information goes to area V1, from which it is relayed to other visual cortical areas, where the third and fourth stages of color perception take place.

Color perception requires receptor cells that differ in their sensitivities to different wavelengths

Artists have long known that all the hues can be obtained from a small number of primary colors. On the basis of observations of mixing pigments and lights, scientists at the start of the nineteenth century hypothesized that three separate kinds of receptors in the retina provide the basis for color vision. This **trichromatic hypothesis** (from the Greek *tri-*, "three," and *chroma*, "color") was endorsed in 1852 by the great physiologist-physicist-psychologist Hermann von Helmholtz and became the dominant position.

COMPETING HYPOTHESES

Helmholtz predicted that blue-sensitive, green-sensitive, and red-sensitive receptors would be found, that each would be sharply tuned to its part of the spectrum, and that each type would have a separate path to the brain. The color of an object would be recognized, then, on the basis of which color receptor was activated. This system would be like the mechanisms for discriminating touch and temperature on the basis of which skin receptors and labeled neural lines are activated (see Chapter 8).

Later in the nineteenth century, physiologist Ewald Hering proposed a different explanation. He argued, on the basis of visual experience, that there are four unique hues and three opposed pairs of colors—blue versus yellow, green versus red, and black versus white—and that three physiological processes with opposed positive and negative values must therefore be the basis of color vision. As we will see, both this **opponent-process hypothesis** and the trichromatic hypothesis are encompassed in current color vision theory, but neither of the old hypotheses is sufficient by itself. Russell De Valois and Karen De Valois, whose results provide much of the information in this discussion, have been leaders in reconciling the trichromatic and opponent-process hypotheses.

Russell De Valois (1926–2003)

Measurements of photopigments in cones have borne out the trichromatic hypothesis in part. Each cone of the human retina has one of three classes of pigments. These pigments do not, however, have the narrow spectral distributions that Helmholtz predicted. The color system that Helmholtz postulated would have given rather poor color vision and poor visual acuity. Color vision would be poor because only a few different hues could be discriminated; within the long-wavelength region of the spectrum there would be only red, and not all the range of hues that we see. Acuity would be poor because the grain of the retinal mosaic would be coarse; a red stimulus could affect only one-third of the receptors. (In reality, though, acuity is as good in red light as it is in white light.)

The human visual system does not have receptors that are sensitive to only a narrow part of the visible spectrum. Two of the three retinal cone pigments show some response to light of almost *any* wavelength. The pigments have different *peaks* of sen-

Karen De Valois

sitivity, but the peaks are not as far apart as Helmholtz predicted. As Figure 10.24 shows, the peaks occur at about 420 nm (in the part of the spectrum where we usually see violet under photopic conditions), about 530 nm (where most of us see green), and about 560 nm (where most of us see yellow-green). Despite Helmholtz's prediction, none of the curves peak in the long-wavelength part of the spectrum, where most of us see red (about 630 nm).

Under ordinary conditions, almost any visual object stimulates at least two kinds of cones, thus ensuring high visual acuity and good perception of form. The spectral sensitivities of the three cone types differ from each other, and the nervous system detects and processes these differences to extract the color information. Thus, certain ganglion cells and certain cells at higher stations in the visual system are color-specific, even though the receptor cells are not. Similarly, visual receptors are not form-specific, but form is detected later in the visual centers by comparison of the outputs of different receptors.

Because the cones are not color detectors, the most appropriate brief names for them can be taken from their peak areas of wavelength sensitivity: *short* (S) for the receptor with peak sensitivity at about 420 nm, *medium* (M) at 530 nm, and *long* (L) at 560 nm (see Figure 10.24). There are typically twice as many L as M receptors, but far fewer S receptors (Brainard et al., 2000; Carroll et al., 2000; Hagstrom et al., 1998); this difference explains why acuity is much lower with short-wavelength illumination (blue light) than in the other parts of the visible spectrum.

The genes for wavelength-sensitive pigments in the retina have been analyzed, and the similarities in structure of the three genes suggest that they are all derived from a common ancestral gene (Nathans, 1987). In addition, the genes for the medium- and long-wavelength pigments occupy adjacent positions on the X chromosome and are much more similar to each other than either is to the gene for the short-wavelength pigment on chromosome 6.

The fact that humans and Old World monkeys have both M and L pigments, whereas most New World monkeys have only a single longer-wavelength pigment, suggests that the M and L pigments differentiated recently in evolutionary terms. Furthermore, the genes for the M and L pigments are variable among individuals, and particular variants in these pigment genes correspond to variants in color vision: so-called color blindness.

The fact that the genes for the M and L pigments are on the X chromosome explains why defects of red/green color vision are much more frequent in human males than in human females. Because males have only one X chromosome, a mutation in the genes for the M or L pigments can impair color vision. But if a female has a defective photopigment gene in one of her two X chromosomes, a normal copy of the gene on the other X chromosome can compensate. Only rarely do both of a female's X chromosomes have defective genes for color receptors.

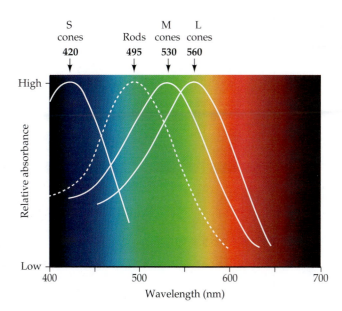

10.24 Spectral Sensitivities of Human Photopigments Each pigment has a peak sensitivity but responds to a wide range of wavelengths. S, short-wavelength; M, medium-wavelength; L, long-wavelength.

EVOLUTION AT WORK

GENES AND BEHAVIOR

Some retinal ganglion cells and parvocellular LGN cells show spectral opponency

Recordings made from retinal ganglion cells in Old World monkeys, which can discriminate colors as humans do, reveal the second stage of processing of color vision. Most ganglion cells and cells in the parvocellular layers of the LGN fire in response to some wavelengths and are inhibited by other wavelengths.

Figure 10.25*a* shows the response of a parvocellular LGN cell as a large spot of light centered on its receptive field is changed from one wavelength to another. Firing is stimulated by wavelengths above 600 nm, where the L cones are most sensitive, then inhibited below 600 nm, where the M cones are most sensitive. A cell exhibiting this response pattern is therefore called a *plus L/minus M cell* (+L/–M). This

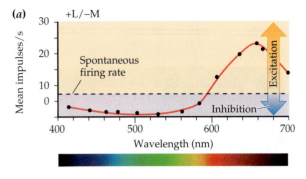

(a) +L/−M

Spontaneous firing rate

Excitation

Inhibition

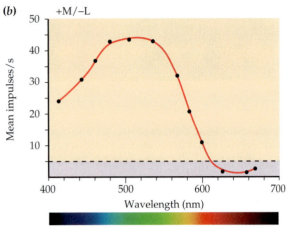

(b) +M/−L

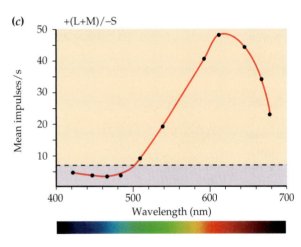

(c) +(L+M)/−S

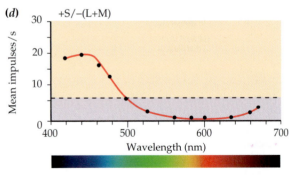

(d) +S/−(L+M)

10.25 Responses of the Four Main Types of Spectrally Opponent Cells in Monkey LGN   The four main types of spectrally opponent cells are (a) +L/−M, (b) +M/−L, (c) +(L+M)/−S, and (d) +S/−(L+M). Each type is excited by one band of wavelengths and inhibited by another.

is an example of a **spectrally opponent cell** because two regions of the spectrum have opposite effects on the cell's rate of firing. Figure 10.25 shows examples of responses of the four main kinds of spectrally opponent cells.

Each spectrally opponent ganglion cell receives input from two or three different kinds of cones through bipolar cells. The connections from at least one type of cone are excitatory, and those from at least one other type are inhibitory (Figure 10.26). The spectrally opponent ganglion cells thus record the difference in stimulation of different populations of cones. For example, a +M/−L cell responds to the difference in the excitation of M and L cones.

The peaks of the sensitivity curves of the M and L cones are not very different (see Figure 10.24). However, whereas the M-minus-L *difference* curve (Figure 10.25b) shows a clear peak at about 500 nm (in the green part of the spectrum), the L-minus-M difference function (see Figure 10.25a) shows a peak at about 650 nm (in the red part of the spectrum). Thus, +M/−L and +L/−M cells yield distinctly different neural response curves. LGN cells excited by the L and M cells, but inhibited by S cells (+(L +M)/− S) peak in the red range (Figure 10.25c), while cells excited by S, but inhibited by L and M (+S/−(L+M)) peak in the blue-violet range (Figure 10.25d).

Spectrally opponent neurons are the second stage in the system for color perception, but they still cannot be called *color cells*, for the following reasons: (1) They send their outputs into many higher circuits—for detection of form, depth, and movement, as well as hue; and (2) their peak wavelength sensitivities do not correspond precisely to the wavelengths that we see as the principal hues.

In addition to the four kinds of spectrally opponent ganglion cells, Figure 10.26 diagrams the presumed inputs of ganglion cells that detect brightness and darkness. The brightness detectors receive stimulation from both M and L cones (+M/+L); the darkness detectors are inhibited by both M and L cones (−M/−L).

In the monkey LGN, 70% to 80% of the cells are spectrally opponent; in the cat, very few spectrally opponent cells are found—only about 1%. This difference explains the ease with which monkeys discriminate wavelengths and the difficulty in training cats to discriminate even large differences in wavelength.

Some visual cortical cells and regions appear to be specialized for color perception

In the cortex, spectral information appears to be used for various kinds of information processing. Forms are segregated from their background by differences in color or intensity (or both). The most important role that color plays in our perception is to denote which parts of a complex image belong to one object and which belong to another. Some animals use displays of brightly colored body parts to call attention to themselves, but color can also be used as camouflage.

Some spectrally opponent cortical cells contribute to the perception of color, providing the third stage of the color vision system. R. L. De Valois and K. K. De Valois (1993) have suggested ways in which adding and subtracting the outputs of spectrally opponent ganglion cells could yield cortical cells that are perceptually opponent: red versus green, blue versus yellow, and black versus white. The spectral responses of these cells correspond to the wavelengths of the principal hues specified by human observers, and their characteristics also help explain other color phenomena.

10.26 A Model of the Connections of the Wavelength Discrimination Systems in the Primate Retina   The connections from the cones yield four kinds of spectrally opponent ganglion cells, as well as ganglion cells that detect brightness or darkness. (After R. L. De Valois and K. De Valois, 1980.)

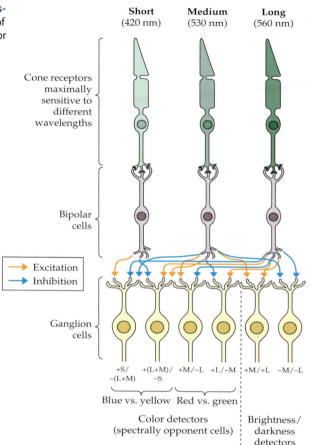

Visual cortical region V4 is particularly rich in color-sensitive cells. Electrophysiological recording in monkeys shows that only some V4 cells (probably a minority) are selective for color (Schein et al., 1982). Evidence that this area is normally involved in the perception of color comes from electrophysiological studies showing that some V4 cells respond best if the color outside the receptive field is different from the color preferred in the receptive field (Schein and Desimone, 1990). These cells provide a fourth stage of color perception that may be important for color constancy and for discrimination between a figure and background. Additional evidence of the role of V4 in color vision comes from PET studies in humans. Area V4 is activated when subjects view colored stimuli but not when they view black-and-white stimuli (Zeki et al., 1991).

It would probably be wrong to think of V4 as devoted exclusively to color perception. Cells in V4 are also tuned in the spatial domain, for orientation and for spatial frequency (Desimone and Schein, 1987). Schiller (1993) lesioned V4 in monkeys and found color vision relatively unaffected. V4 is the main pathway between the secondary visual area (V2) and the inferior temporal visual region, and it probably serves several aspects of visual perception.

Most mammalian species have some color vision

In 1942, Gordon Walls concluded from a survey that, among mammals, color vision is by no means widespread, and this conclusion has been repeated in many books and articles. A much more extensive survey by Gerald Jacobs (1993), however, indicates that almost all mammals probably have at least some degree of color vision. Among mammals, only certain primates have good trichromatic color vision (i.e., vision based on three classes of cone photopigments), but many species have dichromatic color vision (based on two classes of cone pigments). Many so-called color-blind humans (actually color-*deficient* humans) have dichromatic vision and can distinguish short-wavelength stimuli (blue) from long-wavelength stimuli (not blue).

On the basis of his survey, Jacobs (1993) suggested that it is better to think of a continuum of color capabilities than to use an all-or-none criterion, and he proposed that four categories cover all mammalian species:

Gerald Jacobs

1. *Excellent trichromatic color vision* is found in diurnal primates such as humans and the rhesus monkey (*Macaca mulatta*).
2. *Robust dichromatic color vision* is found in species that have two kinds of cone photopigments and a reasonably large population of cones. Examples of such species are the dog, the pig, and many male New World monkeys, such as the squirrel monkey (*Saimiri sciureus*) and the marmoset monkey (*Callithrix jaccus*). (The females may be trichromatic as a result of having genes that encode differing long-wavelength cones on their two X chromosomes.)
3. *Feeble dichromatic color vision* occurs in species that have two kinds of cone pigments but have very few cones. Examples are the domestic cat and the coati (*Nasua nasua*).
4. *Minimal color vision* is possessed by species that have only a single kind of cone pigment and that must rely on interactions between rods and cones to discriminate wavelength. Examples are the owl monkey (*Aotes trivirgatus*) and the raccoon (*Procyon lotor*).

When both diurnal and nocturnal species of a given taxonomic family have been tested for color vision (e.g., the coati and the raccoon), the diurnal species (in this case the coati) usually has the better color vision.

Perception of Visual Motion Is Analyzed by a Special System That Includes Cortical Area V5

Some retinal ganglion cells respond preferentially to a certain direction of motion of objects; for example, certain ganglion cells respond to stimuli that move to the left but not to stimuli that move to the right (Barlow and Levick, 1965). Investigators have hypothesized that the direction-selective responses require retinal circuits involving both excitation and inhibition: Whereas movement in the preferred direction stimulates excitatory units before inhibitory units, movement in the nonpreferred direction reaches inhibitory units first.

Motion is analyzed by the cortex, partly in regions close to those that control eye movements. All the neurons in area V5 (also called the *medial temporal area;* see Figure 10.19*c*) in the monkey respond to moving visual stimuli, but they do not respond differentially to the wavelength of stimulation. A variety of studies provide converging evidence that area V5 is specialized for the perception of motion and direction of motion. As mentioned previously, PET studies of human subjects show that moving stimuli, rather than colored stimuli, evoke responses in area V5.

When monkeys are trained to report the direction of perceived motion, experimental lesions of area V5 impair their performance, at least temporarily (Newsome et al., 1985). If experimenters electrically stimulated an area of V5 that normally responded to stimuli moving up in visual space, the monkeys reported that dots on the screen were moving up even when they were actually moving to the right.

CLINICAL ISSUE

One striking report described a woman who had lost the ability to perceive motion after a stroke that had damaged her area V5 (Zihl et al., 1983). The woman was unable to perceive continuous motion and saw only separate, successive positions. This impairment led to many problems in her daily life. She had difficulty crossing streets because she could not follow the positions of automobiles in motion: "When I'm looking at the car at first, it seems far away. But then when I want to cross the road, suddenly the car is very near." She complained of difficulties in following conversations because she could not see the movements of speakers' lips. Except for her inability to perceive motion, this woman's visual perception appeared normal.

The Many Cortical Visual Areas Are Organized into Two Major Systems

Many investigators have wondered why primate visual systems contain so many distinct regions. Certain regions specialize in processing different attributes or dimensions of visual experience (such as shape, location, color, motion, and orientation). But the number of visual fields—over 30—is larger than the number of basic attributes. Perhaps the reason that so many separate visual regions have been found is simply that investigators, being visually oriented primates themselves, have lavished special attention on the visual system.

Mortimer Mishkin

Other workers have suggested that the many cortical visual areas can be grouped into two major systems. Earlier work with hamsters led to the hypothesis that there are two visual systems: One, for *identification* of objects, involves especially the visual cortex; the other, for *location* of objects, involves especially the superior colliculus (G. E. Schneider, 1969).

This hypothesis was later extended to primates, on the basis of research on localized brain lesions in monkeys. Mortimer Mishkin and Leslie Ungerleider (1982) proposed that primates have two main cortical processing streams, both originating in primary visual cortex: a ventral processing stream responsible for visually *identifying* objects, and a dorsal stream responsible for appreciating the spatial *location*

Leslie Ungerleider

of objects and visual guidance of movement toward objects (Figure 10.27). These processing streams were called, respectively, the *what* and *where* streams.

PET studies, as well as brain lesions in patients, indicate that the human brain also possesses *what* and *where* visual processing streams similar to those found in monkeys (Ungerleider et al., 1998). In the ventral stream, including regions of the occipitotemporal, inferior temporal, and inferior frontal areas, information about faces becomes more specific as one proceeds farther forward. PET studies show that whereas general information about facial features and gender are extracted more posteriorly, the more anterior parts of the stream provide representations of individual faces (Courtney et al., 1996).

Discovery of these separate visual cortical streams helps us understand the case of patient D.F., described at the start of this chapter. Recall that after carbon monoxide poisoning, she lost the ability to perceive faces and objects while retaining the ability to reach and grasp under visual control. The investigators who studied her (A. D. Milner et al., 1991) hypothesized, from their observations and from findings such as those of Mishkin and Ungerleider, that D.F.'s ventral visual stream was devastated but that her dorsal stream was unimpaired. An opposite kind of dissociation had already been reported: Damage to the posterior parietal cortex often results in **optic ataxia** in which patients have difficulty in using vision to reach for and grasp objects, although some of these patients can still perceive objects correctly (Perenin and Vighetto, 1988).

Recent MRI imaging with D.F. supports the interpretation of impairment in her ventral stream with a relatively normal dorsal stream (T. W. James et al., 2003). High-resolution MRI of D.F.'s brain (Figure 10.28a) reveals diffuse damage with a concentration in the ventrolateral occipital cortex, including parts of Brodmann's areas

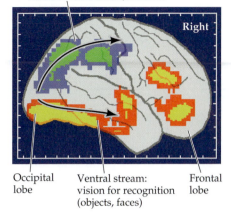

Dorsal stream:
vision for movement, location

Right

Occipital lobe Ventral stream: vision for recognition (objects, faces) Frontal lobe

10.27 Parallel Processing Pathways in the Visual System   The ventral (*what*) pathway shown in yellow and red, and the dorsal (*where*) pathway shown in green and blue, serve different functions. (Courtesy of Leslie Ungerleider.)

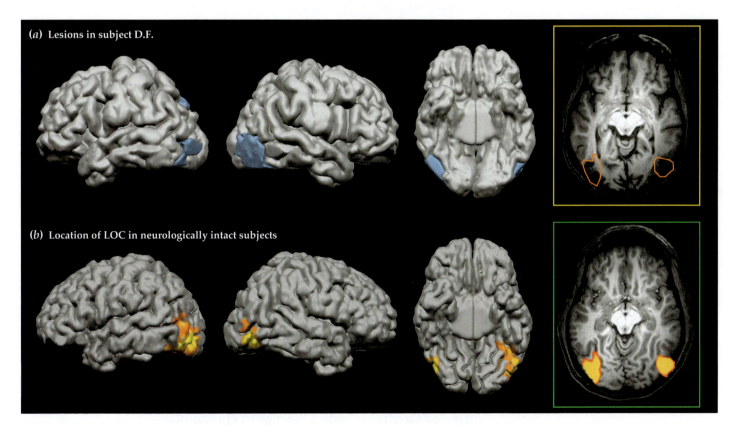

(*a*) Lesions in subject D.F.

(*b*) Location of LOC in neurologically intact subjects

10.28 Object Recognition Centers in the Brain   (*a*) In this reconstruction from MRI images, the brain region that was damaged in patient D.F. (blue) is seen from lateral views and from below (outlined in orange on the right). (*b*) In neurologically intact subjects, this same brain region is activated (yellow) when the subjects are looking at recogniz-ably intact pictures of various objects rather than scrambled pictures. D.F.'s inability to recognize the objects she sees appears to be due to the damage to this region on the border of occipital and temporal cortex. (From T. W. James et al., 2003; courtesy Thomas James).

18 and 19. Throughout the brain, there is evidence of atrophy, indicated by shrunken gyri and enlarged sulci.

Figure 10.28*b* shows the area activated in fMRI recordings when normal subjects viewed pictures of objects; it corresponds to D.F.'s lateral occipital lesion. When D.F. reached for and grasped objects, her fMRI activation in the parietal lobe was similar in location to that of normal subjects, indicating that D.F.'s dorsal stream is largely intact. D.F.'s intact dorsal pathway not only tells her where objects are but also guides her movements to use these objects properly.

It is still puzzling to understand how one part of D.F. knows exactly how to grasp a pencil while another part of her, the part that talks to you, has no idea whether it's a pencil, a ruler, or a bouquet of flowers. Imagining what this disjointed visual experience must be like for D.F. allows us to appreciate how effortlessly our brains seem to bind together information to give us the marvelous sense of sight.

Visual Neuroscience Can Be Applied to Alleviate Some Visual Deficiencies

Vision is so important that many investigators have sought ways to prevent impairment, to improve inadequate vision, and to restore sight to the blind. In the United States, half a million people are blind. Recent medical advances have reduced some causes of blindness but have increased blindness from other causes. For example, medical advances permit people with diabetes to live longer. But because we don't know how to prevent blindness associated with diabetes, that means there are more people alive today with diabetes-induced blindness. In the discussion that follows we will first consider ways of avoiding impairment of vision. Then we will take up ways of exercising and training that are designed to improve an impaired visual system.

Impairment of vision often can be prevented or reduced

CLINICAL ISSUE

Studies of the development of vision in children and other animals show that the incidence of **myopia** (nearsightedness) (from the Greek *myein*, "to be closed," and *ops*, "eye") can be reduced. Myopia develops if the eyeball is too long, forcing the eye to focus objects in front of the retina rather than on the retina. As a result, distant objects appear blurred. Considerable evidence suggests that myopia develops when children spend much time looking at targets close up rather than at objects far away (Marzani and Wallman, 1997).

Before civilization, most people spent most of their time looking at objects far away, such as predators, prey, sources of water, and so on. Thus they kept the eye relaxed most of the time. Now, however, people spend long periods of time gazing at objects close at hand, such as books and computer screens. This constant close focusing requires that the lens be kept thick (unrelaxed). The developing eyeball compensates by elongating to make focusing easier, thus causing progressive myopia. Preventive steps can be taken, especially during childhood and adolescence:

- Read only in adequate light—enough that you can hold the book as far away as possible and still discern the words.
- Avoid small type.
- If you already have a prescription for myopia but you can read without using glasses, do so, because reading with glasses force you to thicken your lens more, thus accelerating the problem.

Increased exercise can restore function to a previously deprived or neglected eye

In Chapter 7 we considered the misalignment of the two eyes (*lazy eye*), which can lead to the condition called **amblyopia** (from the Greek *amblys*, "blunt, dull"; and *ops,* "eye"), in which acuity is poor in one eye even though the eye and retina are normal. If the two eyes are not aligned properly during the first few years of life, the primary visual cortex of the child tends to suppress the information that arrives from one eye to the cortex, and that eye becomes functionally blind. Studies of the development of vision in children and other animals also show that most cases of amblyopia are avoidable.

The balance of the eye muscles can be surgically adjusted to bring the two eyes into better alignment. Alternatively, if the weak eye is given regular practice, with the good eye covered, then vision can be preserved in both eyes. Attempts to alleviate amblyopia by training, however, have produced mixed results and a great deal of controversy. The treatment recommended most often is, beginning at as early an age as possible, giving the weak eye extensive training and experience while obstructing the good eye (American Academy of Ophthalmology, 1994). (Although we follow the usual practice in referring to the "good eye" and the "weak eye," the difference lies not in the eyes but in the higher visual centers to which they send their neural messages. Even in an eye deprived of experience of visual patterns, the retinal cells often have normal receptive fields.) Children with amblyopia often wear a patch or opaque contact lens over the good eye to force use of the weak eye (Figure 10.29).

Some investigators (e.g., Epelbaum et al., 1993) have concluded that only treatment during the first few years of life can be effective. Others report considerable improvement, even with adults, if the eye is exercised sufficiently and if the amblyopia is not too severe. One study reported considerable recovery from long-standing amblyopia when the good eye was lost or severely damaged (Romero-Apis et al., 1982). In all eight patients in this study, aged 16 to 69 at the time they lost the good eye, the vision in the amblyopic eye improved markedly, thus revealing plasticity of the adult brain.

A remarkable study by Chow and Stewart (1972) encouraged much subsequent work on rehabilitation, even in adult people and other animals. Chow and Stewart studied kittens, depriving one or both eyes of pattern vision for about the first 20 months after birth—longer than the critical period for development of visual function (from about 3 to 12 weeks of age). When a unilaterally deprived kitten was then tested for pattern perception with the previously deprived eye, it showed almost no discrimination on formal tests and it was not able to guide its locomotion visually, although it performed well using its other eye.

The investigators then undertook an intensive program of rehabilitation with some of the kittens. They "gentled" and petted these animals frequently to keep them working on the demanding program. Over time the kittens developed some pattern discrimination with the previously deprived eye, and they could use it to guide their locomotion.

Furthermore, recovery of vision was accompanied by morphological changes in the LGN. After monocular deprivation, the LGN cells that had received input from the deprived eye were about one-third smaller than those that had been stimulated by pattern vision. When the previously deprived eye was retrained, the difference in size of LGN cells disappeared. Electrical recording showed that retraining also increased the number of binocular cells (those that respond to stimulation of either eye) in the visual cortex, in comparison with kittens that were not retrained. Such animal research, as well as research with human patients, provides encouraging examples for programs of rehabilitation (Bach-y-Rita, 1992). In Chapter 7 we saw that Michael May, who was blind from the age of 3 to 43, regained some aspects of vision quickly. Other aspects, such as the perception of faces and objects, remain severely impaired—but nevertheless show improvement with practice.

Most of us can expect our visual acuity to decline steadily, although not severely, after age 40. Recent research suggests that much of this decline is caused by changes in cortical visual pathways (Schmolesky et al., 2000). Investigators measured electrical responses of single neurons in the primary visual cortex of young adult or old macaque monkeys. The neurons of the old monkeys showed increased spontaneous

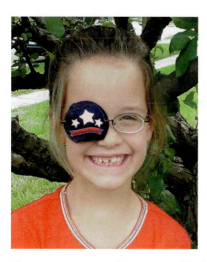

Figure 10.29 Hey There, You With the Stars in Your Eye   As a treatment for amblyopia, this girl is wearing a patch over her "good" eye—the one she has been relying upon while ignoring information from her other, "weak" eye. Visual experience through the weak eye will strengthen its influence on the cortex.

NEURAL PLASTICITY

Refer to the *Learning Biological Psychology CD* for study questions, animations, activities, and other study aids.

activity and decreased selectivity for orientation of stimuli, both of which may be caused by age-related degeneration of intracortical inhibition. Might visual exercise counteract these changes?

Frequent causes of visual impairment, especially with age, are diseases such as macular degeneration that damage the rods and cones. These diseases leave the ganglion cells and the higher neural pathways largely intact. Scientists at the Sandia National Laboratories and two universities are working on a 33-by-33 array of electrodes to be placed within the eye in contact with the ganglion cells. These electrodes would be stimulated by a small camera and radio frequency transmitter lodged in the patient's eyeglasses. The researchers hope to begin implanting the electrode array in patients in the next few years. (Note that a resolution of 33 by 33 pixels is, as illustrated in Figures 10.3 and 10.4, enough to recognize a face.) "The aim is to bring a blind person to the point where he or she can read, move around objects in the house, and do basic household chores," says Sandia project leader Kurt Wessendork. "They won't be able to drive cars, at least in the near future, because instead of millions of pixels, they'll see approximately a thousand … But people who are blind will see" (N. Singer, 2002, p. 1).

Summary

1. The perception of forms and the recognition of objects are complex accomplishments that require processing in many parts of the visual system.

2. The vertebrate eye is an elaborate structure that forms detailed and accurate optical images on the receptive cells of the retina.

3. Many different phyla have independently evolved photoreceptor organs; several have evolved eyes with lenses to focus light.

4. Visual-information processing begins in the retina, where cells that contain photopigments capture light and initiate neural activity. Two kinds of retinal receptor cells—rods and cones—represent the initial stages of two systems: the scotopic (dim light) and photopic (bright light) systems, respectively.

5. Each receptor reports only how strongly it has been excited, so at any given instant the visual nervous system receives an enormous array of quantitative information and has to determine what patterns in the outside world could have produced a particular set of "numbers." About one-third of the human isocortex is devoted to this computation.

6. Brain pathways of the visual system include the lateral geniculate nucleus (LGN) in the thalamus, the primary visual cortex (striate cortex, or V1), and other cortical regions. Some axons of retinal ganglion cells extend to the superior colliculus in the midbrain.

7. Recordings from cells at successively higher levels in the visual system reveal that the receptive fields change in two main ways: (1) They become larger (occupy larger parts of the visual field), and (2) they require increasingly specific stimuli to evoke responses.

8. The cortex contains several visual areas, each presenting a topographic map of the visual field, but each somewhat specialized for processing one or more different aspects of visual information, such as form, color, or movement.

9. For the perception of visual patterns and forms, the stimulus pattern is analyzed at the primary visual cortex according to the orientation and spatial frequency of stimuli, but further analysis at specialized cortical areas is required for recognition of objects, faces, and three-dimensional forms.

10. Like the somatosensory and auditory cortices, the primary visual cortex is organized in columns perpendicular to the surface. Columns, groups of columns, and slabs provide separate representations of the angular orientation of stimuli, of position in the visual field, of color, and of the two eyes.

11. In both cats and primates, parallel parvocellular, magnocellular, and koniocellular projective systems from the retina to the brain mediate different aspects of visual projection, but these systems show increasing overlap in the cortical visual areas.

12. The ability to locate visual stimuli in space is aided by detailed spatial maps in some regions of the visual system.

13. The discrimination of hue in Old World primates and in humans depends on the existence of three different cone photopigments and on the fact that retinal connections yield four different kinds of spectrally opponent retinal ganglion cells.

14. Clinical evidence supports the concept of parallel processing because genetic anomalies or injury to the brain may impair some aspects of visual perception while leaving others intact. An example is the impaired ability to detect direction of motion after injury to area V5.

15. The main pathways of the visual system appear to be determined genetically, but many aspects of the visual system develop in interaction with the environment and visual experience.

16. Visual cortical areas are organized into two main streams: a ventral stream that serves in the recognition of faces and objects and a dorsal stream that serves in location and visuomotor skills.

17. Attempts to treat amblyopia work best when retraining starts early in life, but success with some older patients demonstrates that the visual nervous system remains plastic even in adults.

Recommended Reading

Atkinson, J. (2000). *The developing visual brain.* Oxford, England: Oxford University Press.

De Valois, R. L., and De Valois, K. K. (1988). *Spatial vision.* New York: Oxford University Press.

Oyster, C. W. (1999). *The human eye: Structure and function.* Sunderland, MA: Sinauer Associates.

Palmer, S. E. (1999). *Vision science: Photons to phenomenology.* Cambridge, MA: MIT Press.

Purves, D., and Lotto, R. B. (2003). *Why we see what we do.* Sunderland, MA: Sinauer Associates.

Rodieck, R. W. (1998). *The first steps in seeing.* Sunderland, MA: Sinauer Associates.

Wandell, B. A. (1995). *Foundations of vision.* Sunderland, MA: Sinauer Associates.

11

Motor Control and Plasticity

Up, Up, and Away

He was Superman in the movies, flying around the world, using his great strength to save the helpless and thwart the wicked. In real life, too, actor Christopher Reeve was an exceptional, albeit human, athlete, riding horses in competitions around the country. In 1995 he was riding his thoroughbred, Eastern Express, in a competition when the horse balked at jumping a rail. Christopher was thrown forward, landing on his head and shattering the first two vertebrae of his spine. Immediate medical attention and surgery to stabilize the vertebrae saved his life, but the crushed segment of cervical spinal cord left his brain unable to communicate with his spinal cord. Forced to use a ventilator to breathe, Christopher could neither move nor feel his body below the shoulders.

Christopher's response to the devastating accident was remarkable for the resilience and willpower he wielded from his wheelchair. He appeared at the Academy Awards show the year after the accident; directed a film for HBO, In the Gloaming that garnered an Emmy nomination; and wrote a best-selling autobiography. In 1998, Christopher starred in a television remake of Alfred Hitchcock's Rear Window, portraying a nightmare aspect of his paralysis: the danger of suffocating if his respirator tube became dislodged.

His accomplishments were remarkable, but Christopher declared that his ultimate goals were to find a way to survive without his ventilator, and to walk on his own. Before his death in 2004, he had achieved one of these goals.

Christopher also left behind a foundation to further research so that someday people with injuries like his might recover full mobility. Can it be done?

Our emphasis shifts in this chapter to the motor system as we complete the circuit from sensory input to behavior. It is important to consider sensory and motor functions together. Just as we saw in Chapters 8 through 10 that motor activities are important for sensory and perceptual functions—movements of the fingers in active touch perception, sniffing in smell, and movements of the eyes and head in vision—so we will see in this chapter that sensory and perceptual processes set targets and goals for motor activities and help guide and correct our actions.

And just as our apparently effortless perception turns out to depend on intricate sensory mechanisms and perceptual processes, so, too, our apparently effortless adult motor abilities—such as reaching out and picking up an object, walking across the room, or even talking—require the development of complex muscular systems and their control and coordination by several parts and levels of the nervous system. Think, for example, of all the muscles involved when you say a single word. The tongue, larynx, throat, lips, chest, and diaphragm must work in a highly coordinated manner to produce even the simplest speech sound. And there is little room for error if you are to be understood.

We examine movements and their coordination from three different points of view—the behavioral view, the control systems view, and especially the neuroscience view.

The Behavioral View

By the early nineteenth century, scientists knew that the dorsal roots of the spinal cord serve sensory functions and that the ventral roots contain motor fibers; connections between the two seemed to provide the basis for simple movements. British physiologist Charles Sherrington conducted extensive studies of spinal animals (animals in which the spinal cord has been disconnected from the brain). He showed that skin stimulation, such as pinching, provokes simple acts such as limb withdrawal. Many such observations led him to argue that the basic units of movement are **reflexes**, which he defined as simple, highly stereotyped, and unlearned responses to external stimuli.

Francesco Clemente, *Twins*, 1978, gouache, ink, and colored pencil on four sheets of paper, mounted on linen, 93" × 59" (236.2 × 149.9 cm)

**Sir Charles Sherrington
(1857–1957)**

Sherrington showed that the magnitude of a reflex is directly related to the intensity of the stimulus. His work ushered in an era of intensive attempts to identify the different reflexes and to chart their pathways in the nervous system, particularly in the spinal cord. Some reflexes involve only short pathways in the spinal cord linking dorsal and ventral roots; others involve longer loops connecting spinal cord segments to each other, or to brain regions.

Are reflexes the basic units of more-complex movements and acts? Can every act be broken down into reflexes? No. For instance, Sherrington thought that complex acts were simply combinations of simpler reflexes stretched out in a particular temporal order. The limitations of this perspective become apparent when we think about complex sequences of behavior, such as speech, in reflex terms. For example, explanations of speech in terms of reflexes hold that the movements and sounds associated with each element of speech provide the stimuli for the next element. If this were true, speech would be a series of stimulus–response units chained together, each response triggering the next.

In reality, however, the speaker appears to have a plan in which several units (speech sounds and words) are placed in a larger pattern. Sometimes the units are misplaced, although the pattern is preserved: "Our queer old dean," said English professor William Spooner, when he meant, "Our dear old queen." Or "You hissed all my mystery lectures." (Spooner was so prone to mixing up the order of sounds in his sentences that this type of error is called a *spoonerism*.) Such mistakes reveal a plan: The speaker is anticipating a later sound and executing it too soon. A chain of reflexes would not be subject to such an error.

The concept of a **motor plan**, or *motor program*, holds that complex movements and acts are controlled and produced by a set of commands to muscles that is completely established *before* an act occurs. Feedback from movements may inform the motor program about how the execution is unfolding. Examples of behaviors that exhibit this kind of internal plan for action range from skilled acts, such as piano playing, to a wide repertoire of simple escape behaviors of animals such as crayfish.

It is common to distinguish between movements and acts. Simple reflexes include brief, unitary activities of muscle called **movements**. Movements are discrete, in many cases limited to a single part of the body, such as a limb. Complex, sequential behaviors, frequently oriented toward a goal, are considered **acts**, or *action patterns*. Different movements of several body parts might be included in such behaviors. You can think of an act as being made up of a particular sequence of movements.

Movements and acts can be analyzed and measured in a variety of ways

**IMPORTANT
METHOD**

Movements and acts are readily visible in motion pictures, and high-speed photography provides an intimate portrait of even the most rapid events. To deal with the large amounts of data furnished by high-speed photography, methods of simplification or numerical analysis have been devised. For example, sports trainers use detailed analyses of athletic acts based on time-lapse photographs or information derived from sensors attached at joints. Computer programs process digital photos to help quantify the performance, enabling detailed measurement of the positions of different body parts in successive instants. Other devices record the direction, strength, and speed of motions. Figure 11.1 illustrates the paths of normal and impaired reaching movements, a kind of movement considered at several points in this chapter.

Another approach to the fine-grained analysis of movements is to record the electrical activity of muscles, a procedure called **electromyography (EMG)**. As we'll see later in this chapter, like neurons, muscles produce action potentials when they contract. So, fine needle electrodes placed in a muscle, or electrodes placed on the skin over a muscle, detect electrical indications of muscle activity (Figure 11.2). If electrodes are placed over several different muscles, we get a record of the contraction of the muscles involved in an act, including the progressive buildup and decay of their activity (Hanakawa et al., 2003). In Figure 11.2 the EMGs show that a postural adjustment in the legs precedes the voluntary movement of the arm.

(a) Visually guided reaching task

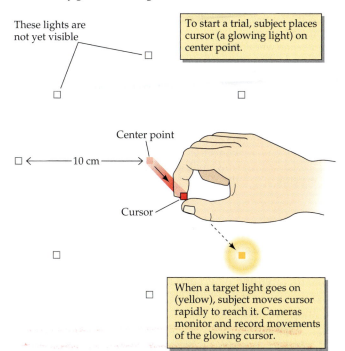

These lights are not yet visible

To start a trial, subject places cursor (a glowing light) on center point.

Center point

←—— 10 cm ——→

Cursor

When a target light goes on (yellow), subject moves cursor rapidly to reach it. Cameras monitor and record movements of the glowing cursor.

(b) Examples of arm movements after 200 practice trials

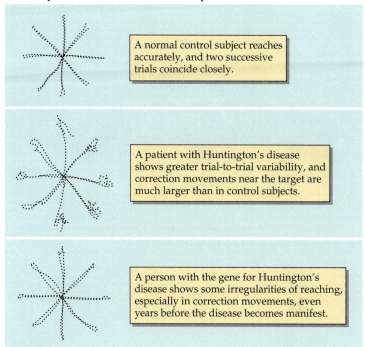

A normal control subject reaches accurately, and two successive trials coincide closely.

A patient with Huntington's disease shows greater trial-to-trial variability, and correction movements near the target are much larger than in control subjects.

A person with the gene for Huntington's disease shows some irregularities of reaching, especially in correction movements, even years before the disease becomes manifest.

11.1 Measurement of Reaching Movements   (a) An experimental setup to study reaching movements. (b) Recorded movement trajectories of normal subject (*top*), patient with Huntington's disease (*middle*), and a carrier of the gene for Huntington's disease (*bottom*). (Part *b* courtesy of Maurice R. Smith.)

The Control Systems View

Engineering descriptions of the regulation and control of machines provide a useful look at the mechanisms that regulate and control our movements. In designing machines, engineers commonly have two goals: (1) accuracy—to prevent or minimize error; and (2) speed—to accomplish a task quickly and efficiently. Usually it is difficult to pursue one of these goals without neglecting the other. Two forms of control mechanisms—closed-loop and open-loop—are commonly employed to optimize performance according to these criteria.

Closed-loop control mechanisms maximize *accuracy:* Information flows from whatever is being controlled back to the device that controls it. Driving a car is an example of a closed-loop motor system. In this case the variable being controlled is the position of an automobile on the road (Figure 11.3). Continuous information is provided by the driver's visual system, which guides corrections. Slow, sustained movements, sometimes called **ramp movements** (or *smooth movements*) are usually closed-loop in character, continuously guided by feedback.

The only way the car could stay on the road without feedback control (e.g., if you were driving with your eyes closed) would

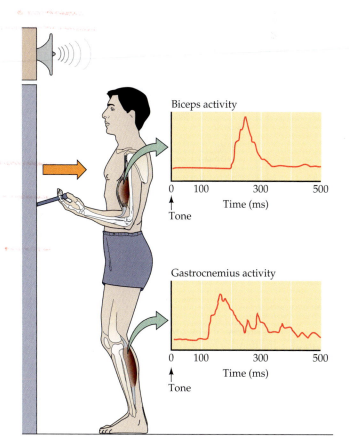

Biceps activity

0   100   300   500
Time (ms)
↑ Tone

Gastrocnemius activity

0   100   300   500
Time (ms)
↑ Tone

11.2 Electromyography   For these recordings made from biceps and gastrocnemius (calf) muscles, the subject was instructed to pull the handle as soon as a tone sounded. (After Purves et al., 2001.)

(a) Feedback control during driving

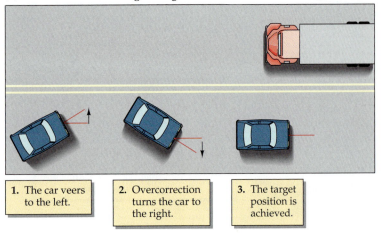

1. The car veers to the left.

2. Overcorrection turns the car to the right.

3. The target position is achieved.

(b) Schematic of closed-loop system

Control signal → Error detector → Error signal → Controller → Command → Controlled system → Output

Feedback signal

Transducer

11.3 A Closed-Loop System (*a*) Automobile driving provides an example of feedback control. (*b*) In the example in part *a*, the *controlled system* is the automobile. The input to the controlled system (i.e., the *control signal*) is the position of the steering wheel; the *output* is the position on the road. In any closed-loop system, the transducer is an element that measures output, and the error detector measures differences between actual output and desired output (control signal). In this example the *transducer* (the visual system), the *error detector* (the perceptual system), and the *controller* (the muscles) are all properties of the person driving the car. The driver compares the actual position of the car with its desired position on the road and makes corrections to minimize the discrepancy. Closed-loop systems emphasize accuracy and flexibility at the expense of speed.

be with the aid of accurate memory of all the turns and bends in the road. But the car would not be able to deal with anything new, such as other moving cars. Such a memory system could be considered a form of open-loop control.

Open-loop control mechanisms maximize speed; there are no external forms of feedback, the activity is preprogrammed. Open-loop controls are needed in systems that must respond so rapidly that there is no time to wait for a feedback pathway. For example, once a baseball pitcher begins throwing a fastball, the pitch will be completed no matter what sensory feedback is received. Such open-loop movements are called **ballistic movements**. Because there is **no feedback**, open-loop systems need other ways to reduce error and variability. They must anticipate potential error. As living systems, we learn how to accurately anticipate and avoid error when executing a rapid sequence of movements.

The Neuroscience View

The rest of this chapter offers the neuroscience view of motor behavior. Neuroscientists distinguish several different levels of hierarchically organized motor control systems:

- The *skeletal system* and the muscles attached to it determine which movements are possible.
- The *spinal cord* controls skeletal muscles in response to sensory information. In the simplest case, the response may be a reflex. The spinal cord also implements motor commands from the brain.
- The *brainstem* integrates motor commands from higher levels of the brain and transmits them to the spinal cord. It also relays sensory information about the body from the spinal cord to the forebrain.
- Some of the main commands for action are initiated in the *primary motor cortex*.
- The areas adjacent to the primary motor cortex, *nonprimary motor cortex*, initiate another level of cortical processing.
- Other brain regions—the *cerebellum and basal ganglia*—modulate the activities of these hierarchically organized control systems.

We will examine each of these levels of control in more detail. This organizational scheme, outlined in Figure 11.4, will guide the discussion.

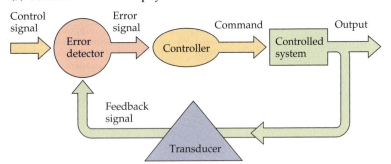

11.4 The Hierarchy of Movement Control The primary motor cortex receives information from other cortical areas and sends commands to the brainstem, which passes commands to the spinal cord. Both the cerebellum and the basal ganglia adjust these commands.

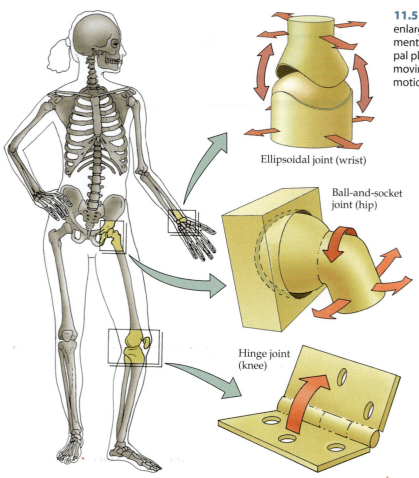

11.5 Joints and Movements Shown next to each joint is an enlarged mechanical model that indicates the kinds of movements the joint can perform. The wrist joint moves in two principal planes: lateral and vertical. The hip joint is a "universal" joint, moving in all three planes. The knee joint has a single plane of motion.

Ellipsoidal joint (wrist)

Ball-and-socket joint (hip)

Hinge joint (knee)

The skeletal system enables particular movements and precludes others

Some properties of behavior arise from physical characteristics of the skeleton. For example, the length, form, and weight of the limbs shape an animal's stride. The primary sites for bending are the joints, where bones meet. Figure 11.5 illustrates the human skeleton and shows examples of joints and their possible movements. Some joints, such as the hip, are almost "universal" joints, permitting movement in many planes. Others, like the elbow or knee, are more limited and tolerate little deviation from the principal axis of rotation.

Muscles control the actions of the skeletal system

Our bare skeleton must now be clothed with muscles. How a muscle attaches to bones is a direct indication of the movement it mediates. Muscles generate force only by contracting (shortening). Some muscles produce forces that maintain body posture; others produce movement around a joint. In contrast, some muscles do not act on the skeleton at all; examples include the muscles that move the eyes, lips, and tongue and those that contract the abdomen. Muscles have springlike properties that influence the timing of behavior and the forces that can be generated; the rate and force of muscular contractions limit some responses.

Muscles are connected to bone by **tendons.** Around a joint, different muscles are arranged in a reciprocal fashion: When one muscle group contracts, the other is extended; that is, the muscles are **antagonists.** Muscles that act together are said to be **synergists.** For example, four synergistic muscles act together to extend the leg at the knee. The three other muscles that flex the leg are antagonists to the four that ex-

11.6 The Arrangement of Muscles around the Elbow

Because muscles exert force only by contracting, muscle attachments determine the resulting movement. (*a*) The biceps muscle flexes the arm. (*b*) The triceps extends the arm. Because these two muscles mediate opposite movements, they are known as *antagonists*.

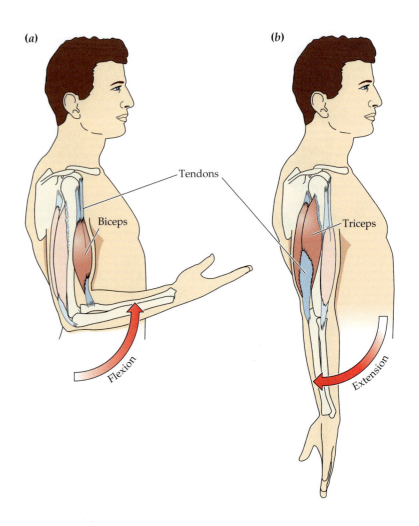

tend it. Coordinated action around a joint may require one set of motoneurons to be excited while the antagonistic set of motoneurons is inhibited (Figure 11.6). The limb can be locked in position by simultaneous contraction of opposing muscles.

The molecular machinery of muscles   A muscle is composed of thousands of individual **muscle fibers.** Each muscle fiber contains many filaments of two kinds arranged in a regular manner (Figure 11.7), giving the fibers a striped appearance. The thick and thin filaments (made up of the complex proteins **myosin** and **actin,** respectively) always overlap. Contraction of the muscle increases the overlap: The filaments slide past each other, shortening the overall length of the muscle fiber (see Figure 11.7).

Muscle types   Many of the muscles in your body, such as those in your stomach, are not under your direct control. Because of their appearance, these muscles are called **smooth muscle,** and because their contractions are regulated by the autonomic nervous system, we will not discuss them further. Rather, we will concern ourselves with a second class of muscle, called **striated muscles** (because they have a striped appearance), which are under voluntary control.

Because of the varying tasks they perform, different muscles require different speeds, precision, strength, and endurance. So there are two main types of striated muscle fibers: *fast-twitch* and *slow-twitch*. Eye movements, for example, must be quick and accurate so that we can follow moving objects and shift our gaze from one target to another. But fibers in the extraocular muscles do not have to maintain tension for long periods of time, because some fibers relax while others contract. The

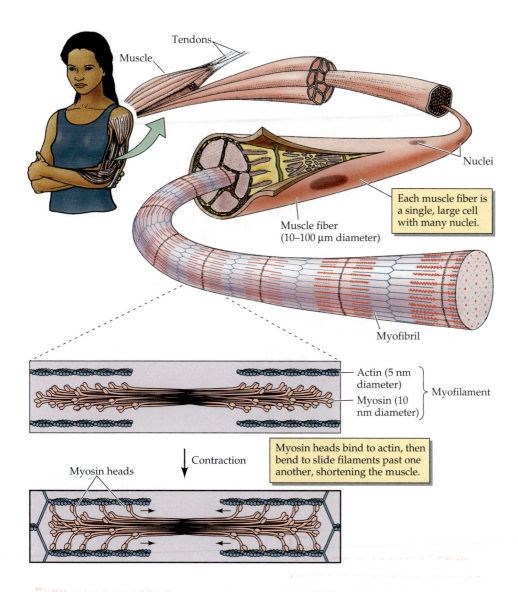

11.7 The Composition of Muscles and the Mechanism of Muscle Contraction Muscle fibers are shown here at progressively greater magnifications, from life size to 2 million times life size. The actions of myosin and actin cause muscle contraction.

Tendons

Muscle

Nuclei

Each muscle fiber is a single, large cell with many nuclei.

Muscle fiber (10–100 μm diameter)

Myofibril

Actin (5 nm diameter)

Myosin (10 nm diameter)

Myofilament

Contraction

Myosin heads

Myosin heads bind to actin, then bend to slide filaments past one another, shortening the muscle.

extraocular muscles are therefore made up of **fast-twitch muscle fibers.** In leg muscles, fast-twitch fibers react promptly and strongly but fatigue rapidly; they are used mainly for activities in which muscle tension changes frequently, as in walking or running. Mixed in with the fast-twitch muscle fibers are **slow-twitch muscle fibers,** which are not as fast but have greater resistance to fatigue; they are used chiefly to maintain posture. If you eat chicken or turkey you've already contrasted fast-twitch and slow-twitch muscles. The "white meats" of the breast were fast-twitch muscles for the rapid wing beats needed for flight. These birds fly only for short periods, so there's no need for these muscles to resist fatigue. In contrast, the "dark meats" of the leg are slow-twitch muscles, supporting the animal continuously as it walked about. They contracted slowly, but had lots of endurance. Most muscles consist of a mixture of slow-twitch and fast-twitch muscle fibers.

Neural messages reach muscle fibers at the neuromuscular junction

Once a motoneuron has integrated all the information bombarding it through hundreds or thousands of synapses, it may produce an action potential. As the axon splits into many branches near the target muscle, each branch carries an action potential to its terminal, which then (in vertebrates) releases the neurotransmitter **acetylcholine (ACh).** Then all the muscle fibers innervated by that motoneuron respond to the ACh by producing action potentials of their own (Figure 11.8*a* and *b*). The action potentials

(a)

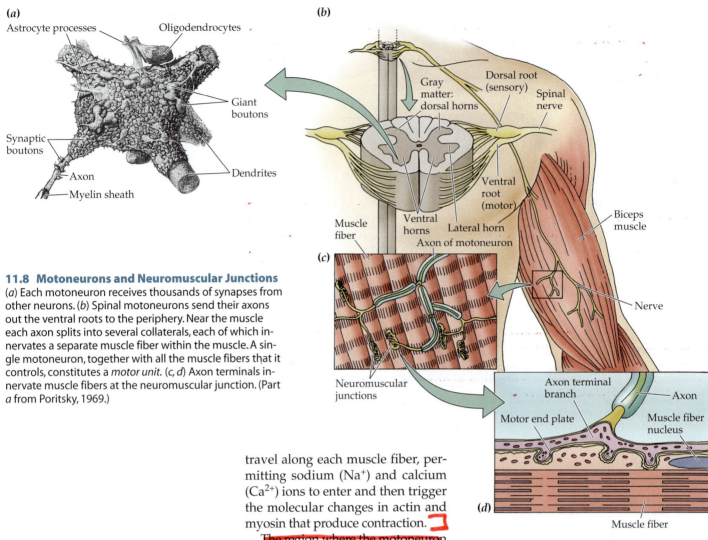

Astrocyte processes

Oligodendrocytes

Giant boutons

Synaptic boutons

Axon

Myelin sheath

Dendrites

(b)

Gray matter: dorsal horns

Dorsal root (sensory)

Spinal nerve

Ventral root (motor)

Biceps muscle

Ventral horns

Lateral horn

Axon of motoneuron

Muscle fiber

Nerve

(c)

Neuromuscular junctions

Axon terminal branch

Axon

Motor end plate

Muscle fiber nucleus

(d)

Muscle fiber

11.8 Motoneurons and Neuromuscular Junctions

(a) Each motoneuron receives thousands of synapses from other neurons. (b) Spinal motoneurons send their axons out the ventral roots to the periphery. Near the muscle each axon splits into several collaterals, each of which innervates a separate muscle fiber within the muscle. A single motoneuron, together with all the muscle fibers that it controls, constitutes a *motor unit*. (c, d) Axon terminals innervate muscle fibers at the neuromuscular junction. (Part *a* from Poritsky, 1969.)

NEURAL PLASTICITY

travel along each muscle fiber, permitting sodium (Na^+) and calcium (Ca^{2+}) ions to enter and then trigger the molecular changes in actin and myosin that produce contraction.

The region where the motoneuron terminal and the adjoining muscle fiber meet—and produce distinctive structures for communication—is called the **neuromuscular junction (NMJ)** (Figure 11.8c and d). The NMJ is large and very effective: Almost every action potential that reaches an axon terminal releases enough ACh to cause a depolarization in the innervated muscle fiber that is large enough to produce an action potential. Thus, every action potential in the motoneuron normally elicits a contraction in the postsynaptic muscle fiber.

In vertebrates, muscles can only be excited (by ACh), so the only way to prevent a muscle from contracting is to inhibit its motoneuron and prevent it from sending an action potential to the NMJ. Because it is large and accessible, the NMJ is a very well studied synapse, and much of what we know about synapses and synaptic plasticity (change in synaptic strength across time) was first established at the NMJ.

Even though the NMJ is a large and reliable synapse, its properties can change with use. All of us are familiar with muscle fatigue from extended use; some of the reduced responsiveness of the fatigued muscle is due to the diminished effectiveness of NMJs. Another well-studied example of neural plasticity is **posttetanic potentiation.** When a rapid series of action potentials (a *tetanus*) is induced in a motor nerve, the NMJs are altered for a while so that subsequent single action potentials cause a stronger end-plate potential in the muscle. This potentiation is caused by a buildup of Ca^{2+} ions in the presynaptic terminal and therefore the release of more ACh. The study of several types of NMJ plasticity led to other studies of synaptic plasticity that may underlie learning, as will be discussed in Chapter 18.

The ratio of motor axons to muscle groups affects the precision of the control of movements. Fine neural control results when each axon connects to only a few muscle fibers. The **motor unit** consists of a single motor axon and all the muscle fibers it innervates (see Figure 11.8*b*). The **innervation ratio** is the ratio of motor axons to muscle fibers. High innervation ratios characterize muscles involved in fine movements, like those of the eye—one motoneuron for every three fibers (a 1:3 ratio). Muscles that act on large body masses such as those of the leg have low innervation ratios of one neuron controlling several hundred muscle fibers (about 1:300), so the same call for contraction goes to hundreds of leg muscle fibers at the same time.

Motoneurons integrate information from the brain and spinal cord

Muscles contract because motoneurons of the spinal cord and cranial nerve nuclei send action potentials along motor axons to muscles. Thus, motoneurons are the **final common pathway** that links the activity of the rest of the spinal cord and brain to our many muscles. Because they respond to inputs from so many sources (see Figure 11.8*a*), motoneurons often have very widespread dendritic fields, and they are the largest cells in the spinal cord. Furthermore, motoneurons must respond to a tremendous variety of synaptic transmitters, both excitatory and inhibitory.

Motor cells of the spinal cord are not uniform in size or electrophysiological properties. Large motoneurons have axons of wide diameter and therefore conduct impulses faster. In general, small motoneurons innervate slow-twitch muscle fibers and are more easily excited by synaptic currents; therefore they are activated before large motoneurons are (Jones et al., 1994). Large motoneurons innervate fast-twitch muscle fibers and tend to respond after small cells do because, being large, they are less readily excited by synaptic currents. Their discharge characteristics are more phasic or abrupt.

In the 1960s Elwood Henneman (1991) found that muscle tension is increased by recruitment of increasing numbers of motor units in fixed order according to their size. Weak stimulation activates only small, low-threshold neurons for the slow-twitch muscle fibers defined earlier. Stronger stimulation excites larger, higher-threshold neurons that control fast-twitch muscle fibers. Evidence for the orderly recruitment of motor units has been found in a variety of voluntary and reflexive movements, and this systematic relationship is known as the **size principle.** It is similar to the principle of range fractionation for the coding of sensory intensity, which we discussed in Chapter 8 (see Figure 8.6).

Elwood Henneman

Sensory feedback from muscles, tendons, and joints monitors movements

To produce rapid coordinated movements of the body, the integrative mechanisms of the brain and spinal cord must continuously gather information about the state of the muscles, the positions of the limbs, and the instructions being issued by the motor centers. This collecting of information about body movements and positions is called **proprioception** (from the Latin *proprius,* "own," and *recipere,* "to receive").

The sequence and intensity of muscle activation are monitored by sensory receptors, which report the state of muscles and joints to the CNS. Two major kinds of receptors are muscle spindles and Golgi tendon organs. We'll discuss each in turn.

The muscle spindle   The **muscle spindle** of vertebrates is a complicated structure consisting of both afferent and efferent elements. The spindle gets its name from its shape: a sort of cylinder that is thicker in the middle and tapers at its two ends. The Latin for "spindle," *fusus,* is used to form adjectives referring to the muscle spindle; thus the small muscle fibers *within* each spindle are called **intrafusal fibers,** and the ordinary muscle fibers that lie *outside* the spindles are called **extrafusal fibers** (Figure 11.9*a* and *c*).

The muscle spindle contains two kinds of receptor endings: **primary sensory endings** (also called *annulospiral endings*) and **secondary sensory endings** (also called *flower spray endings*). These endings are related to different parts of the spindle (see

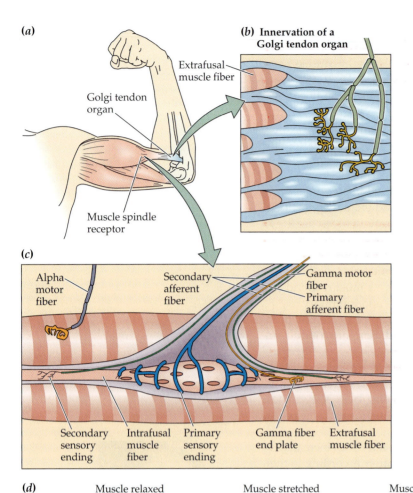

(a)

Extrafusal muscle fiber

Golgi tendon organ

Muscle spindle receptor

(b) Innervation of a Golgi tendon organ

(c)

Alpha motor fiber

Secondary afferent fiber

Gamma motor fiber
Primary afferent fiber

Secondary sensory ending

Intrafusal muscle fiber

Primary sensory ending

Gamma fiber end plate

Extrafusal muscle fiber

11.9 Muscle Receptors (*a*) The receptors in the body of the muscle are muscle spindles; those in the tendons are Golgi tendon organs. (*b*) This sensory ending is typical of a Golgi tendon organ. (*c*) A typical muscle spindle has two types of receptor endings: primary and secondary. Gamma motor fibers control a contractile portion of the spindle. (*d*) When a load is imposed on the muscle, muscle receptors are excited as shown here.

Figure 11.9*c*). The primary ending wraps in a spiral fashion around a region called the *nuclear bag* (the central region of the intrafusal fiber). The secondary endings terminate toward the thin ends of the spindle.

How do these elements become excited? Suppose a muscle is stretched, as when a load is placed on it. For example, if you were trying to hold your arm straight out in front of you, palm up, and someone put a book in your hand, that would put an additional load on your biceps. Your arm would move down briefly, stretching the biceps muscle. ~~The muscle spindle would also stretch, and the resulting deformation of the endings on the spindle would trigger nerve impulses in the afferent fibers. These afferents would inform the spinal cord, and the spinal cord would then inform the brain about the muscle stretch and therefore about the load imposed~~ (Figure 11.9*d*).

~~Two important factors affect~~ the stretch of the muscle. One is the *rate of change* of muscle length. In our example the rate of change is jointly a function of the weight of the load and the rate at which the load is applied. ~~The second factor is the *force you must continually exert with the muscle to prevent dropping the lo*~~ad. In our example this force is a function only of the weight of the book.

The different receptor elements of the muscle spindle are differentially sensitive to these two features of muscle length changes. The primary (central) endings show a maximum discharge early in stretch and then adapt to a lower discharge rate. In contrast, the secondary (distal) endings are maximally sensitive to maintained length and are slow to change their rate during the early phase of stretch. Because of this differential sensitivity, ~~the primary endings are called *dynamic* and the secondary endings are called *static* indicators of muscle length~~. This distinction arises from the difference in how these re-

(d)

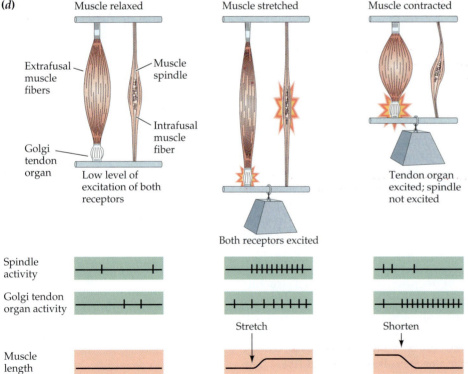

Muscle relaxed

Extrafusal muscle fibers

Muscle spindle

Golgi tendon organ

Intrafusal muscle fiber

Low level of excitation of both receptors

Muscle stretched

Both receptors excited

Muscle contracted

Tendon organ excited; spindle not excited

Spindle activity

Golgi tendon organ activity

Muscle length

Stretch

Shorten

ceptors are embedded in the spindle rather than from a difference in the nerve fibers themselves.

Regulation of muscle spindle sensitivity Muscle spindles not only help maintain posture; they also coordinate movement. A spindle is informed of planned and ongoing actions through innervation by a special motoneuron that alters the tension within the spindle and thus controls the sensitivity of its receptors. These motoneurons are called **gamma motoneurons,** or *gamma efferents,* to distinguish them from the faster-conducting **alpha motoneurons,** which go to extrafusal muscle fibers (see Figure 11.9*c*). The cell bodies of gamma motoneurons are found in the ventral horns of the spinal cord mixed in with the alpha motoneurons.

The gamma motoneuron axon fibers connect to a contractile region of the spindle. Activity in the gamma fibers causes a contraction in the length of the spindle, which modifies its sensitivity to changes in the length of adjacent extrafusal muscle fibers. Hence the number of impulses elicited in the spindle afferents is a function of two factors: (1) muscle stretch and (2) the resting tension in the muscle spindle.

How do the gamma motoneurons help coordinate movements? Suppose that instead of continuing to hold your arm out straight ahead, you move your forearm up and down. If the muscle spindle had only one fixed degree of internal tension, it would not be able to help monitor and coordinate this movement.

As the forearm moves up, both the extrafusal and the intrafusal fibers shorten. Shortening the spindle, as we have noted, removes the tension, so the sensory endings should no longer respond. But the real situation is more complicated and more effective: As the muscle shortens, the gamma efferents must correspondingly increase the tension on the intrafusal fibers if they are to maintain their sensitivity. One reflection of the importance of the gamma efferent system is the fact that about 30% of all efferent fibers are gamma motoneurons (the rest are alpha motoneurons).

The muscle spindles respond primarily to *stretch;* the other receptors that respond to muscle tension—Golgi tendon organs—are especially sensitive to muscle contraction, or shortening. **Golgi tendon organs** are rather insensitive to passive muscle stretch because they are connected in series with an elastic component (see Figure 11.9*a, b,* and *d*). They detect overloads that threaten to tear muscles and tendons. Stimulation of these receptors inhibits the motoneurons supplying the muscles that pull on the tendon and thus, by relaxing the tension, prevents mechanical damage.

Classic studies in physiology emphasized the importance of muscle spindles and Golgi tendon organs for movement. Mott (1895) and Sherrington (1898) showed that after they cut the afferent fibers from muscles, monkeys failed to use the deafferented limb, even if the efferent connections from motoneurons to muscles were preserved. The deafferented limb is not paralyzed, since it can be activated (the motoneurons still innervate the muscles), but lack of information from the muscle leads to relative disuse. When one limb is deafferented, the monkey makes do with the other, but when *both* are deafferented, the monkey has to learn to use them and is able to do so (Taub, 1976). Even if only one arm is deafferented, forced use of it can lead to the return of coordinated use of the two arms.

This effect was shown in experiments in which the hand of the intact limb was placed inside a ball, which prevented the monkey from grasping objects with the hand but allowed finger movements within the ball and thus prevented atrophy. Slowly the deafferented limb gained dexterity, and over several weeks fine movements returned. After several months the ball on the intact hand was removed, and the monkey made coordinated movements of both limbs. However, if the forced use lasted less than 4 months, movements of the deafferented limb subsequently regressed rapidly.

People who lose their proprioceptive sense (because of viral infections that destroy large myelinated sensory fibers from the body) can still control their muscles (because motor nerves are spared) but must compensate by using other sensory modalities for feedback. For example, two deafferented patients were found to rely heavily on visual feedback for walking and picking up objects (Nougier et al., 1996). In fact, there may be channels of visual information to the motor system of which we are unaware. Remember the young woman D.F. from Chapter 10? She could not report whether a slot was vertical or horizontal, yet when she was asked to insert a disk in the slot, she consistently rotated her hand to put it in smoothly. This finding suggests that even neurologically intact people use visual cues of which they are unaware to guide their movements (Goodale and Haffenden, 1998).

Movements Are Controlled at Several Nervous System Levels

The nerve cells directly responsible for excitation of muscle are the motoneurons in the ventral region of the spinal cord and in the brainstem nuclei of several cranial nerves. (See Figures 2.4 and 2.5 for the anatomy of the cranial nerves and spinal cord.) Firing patterns of these cells determine the onset, coordination, and termination of muscle activity. To understand the physiology of movement, we need to know the source of the inputs to motoneurons. A variety of influences from the brain and spinal cord converge on the motoneurons. This is another reason that motoneurons are called the *final common pathway.*

Spinal reflexes mediate "automatic" responses

One way to study spinal mechanisms is to sever the connections between the brain and the spinal cord, producing a *spinal animal,* and then observe the forms of behavior that can be elicited below the level of the cut. (All voluntary movements that depend on brain mechanisms are lost, of course, as is sensation from the regions below the cut.) Immediately after the cord is severed, the spinal cord neurons show decreased synaptic excitability. This condition, known as **spinal shock,** may last for months in humans, although for cats and dogs it may last only a few hours. During this period no reflexes mediated by the spinal cord can be elicited.

As spinal shock fades, various kinds of reflexes can be elicited, helping us understand the basic functional organization of the spinal cord. The spinal animal can show various stretch reflexes that may function well enough to support its weight standing for brief periods. Stimulation of the skin of a spinal animal can also elicit reflexes. Squeezing the toe pad triggers an abrupt withdrawal of the stimulated limb, called the **flexion reflex.** It is controlled by a multisynaptic pathway within the spinal cord. Other reflexes evident in the spinal animal include bladder emptying and penile erection. Thus, some very basic properties of movement are hardwired in the organization of the spinal cord itself and do not require the brain.

The behavior of the spinal animal also reveals the presence of pattern generator circuits in the spinal cord, which we'll describe later in this chapter. For example, mechanical stimulation of the feet or electrical stimulation of the spinal cord can elicit rhythmic movements of the legs. The alternating movements of the limbs are coordinated as in walking (P. Grillner et al., 1991).

The stretch reflex   A good example of automatic control at the spinal level is the **stretch reflex**—the contraction

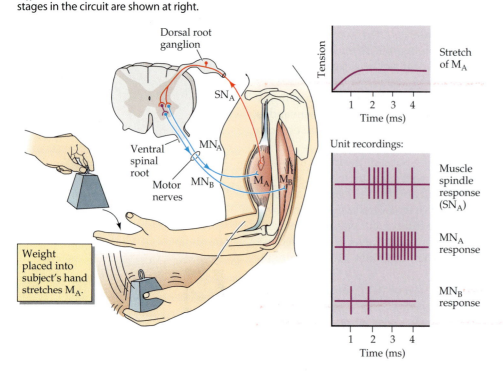

11.10 The Stretch Reflex Circuit
MN_A is the motor nerve to muscle A (M_A); MN_B is the motor nerve to muscle B (M_B), an antagonist to M_A. SN_A is the sensory nerve from the muscle spindle of M_A. Characteristic responses at different stages in the circuit are shown at right.

Dorsal root ganglion

SN_A

Ventral spinal root

MN_A

Motor nerves MN_B

M_A M_B

Weight placed into subject's hand stretches M_A.

Tension

Stretch of M_A

1 2 3 4
Time (ms)

Unit recordings:

Muscle spindle response (SN_A)

MN_A response

MN_B response

1 2 3 4
Time (ms)

that results when a muscle stretches. In Figure 11.10, a weight added to the hand imposes sudden stretch on muscle A (M$_A$). The circuit that keeps us from dropping the load is one that links muscle spindles and the relevant muscles:

1. A disturbance is imposed.
2. The muscle is stretched.
3. Afferents from the muscle spindle are excited.
4. The spindle afferents connect directly—that is, monosynaptically—to the motoneurons that control the stretched muscle, exciting them.
5. The motoneurons stimulate the muscle to oppose muscle stretch.

This sequence describes a simple negative feedback system that tends to restore the limb to its "desired" position. Muscle spindle afferents also inhibit the motoneurons that supply the antagonistic muscle (M$_B$ in Figure 11.10). Two synapses are required to inhibit the antagonistic motoneuron. Thus, in the situation illustrated in Figure 11.10, spindle information terminates on an interneuron, which inhibits the motoneuron that supplies M$_B$. The relaxation of antagonistic muscles ensures that they do not become injured by the sudden movement. A familiar example of the stretch reflex is the knee jerk used in medical examinations (see Figure 3.16). (Recall from Chapter 5 that the knee jerk reflex was abnormally slow in Chuck, who suffered from hypothyroidism.) Spinal reflexes are integrated and modulated by the activity of brain, which we consider next.

Pathways from the brain control different aspects of movements

There are many pathways from the brain to motoneurons. The two major divisions of the motor system are the pyramidal and extrapyramidal motor systems.

The pyramidal system (or corticospinal system) consists of neuronal cell bodies within the cerebral cortex and their axons, which pass through the brainstem, forming the pyramidal tract to the spinal cord (Figure 11.11). The pyramidal tract is seen the most clearly where it passes through the anterior aspect of the medulla. In a cross section of the medulla, the tract is a wedge-shaped anterior protuberance (pyramid) on each side of the midline. In the

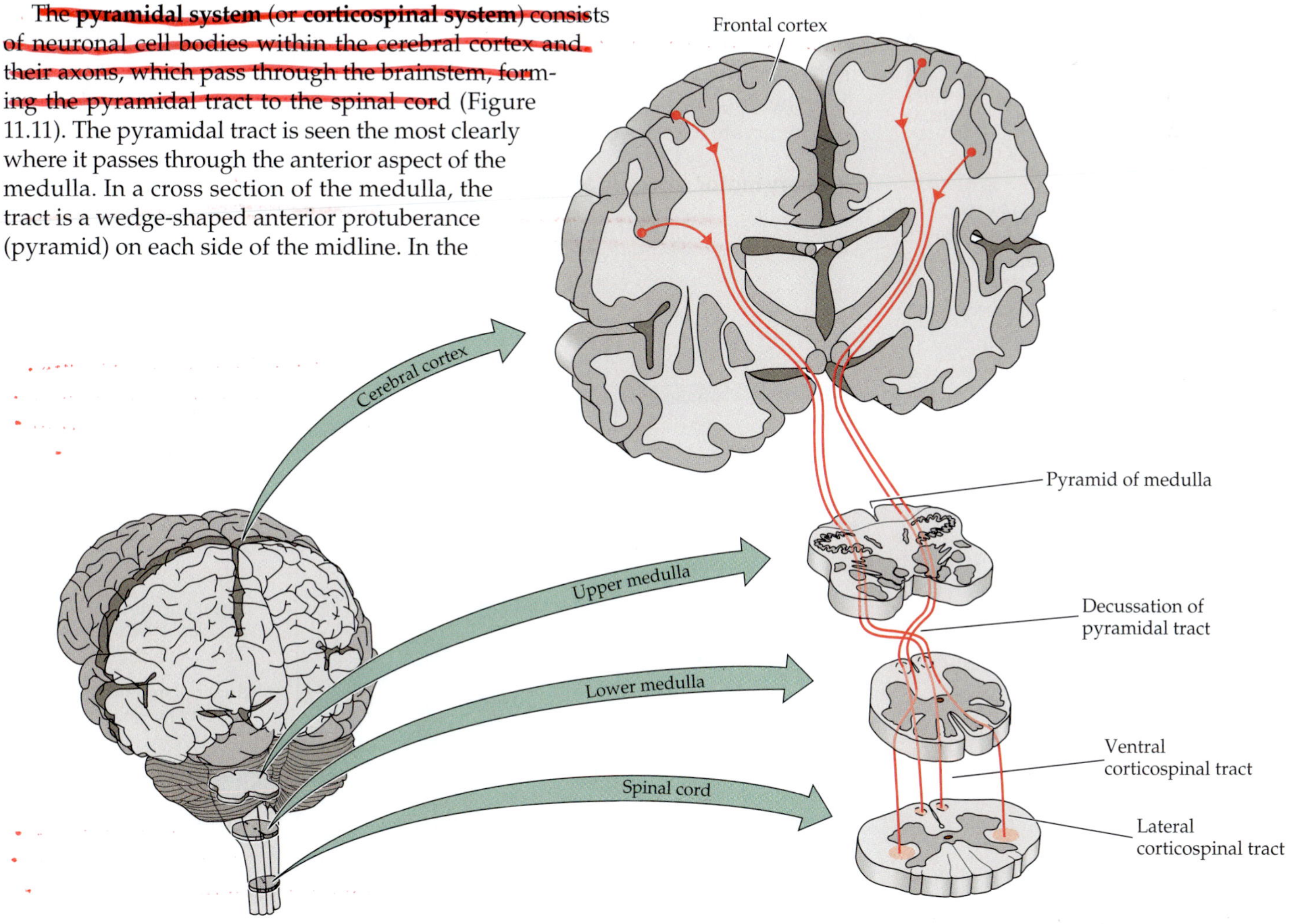

Figure 11.11 The Pyramidal System In the pyramidal (or corticospinal) motor system, most of the fibers cross to the opposite side in the medulla (at the decussation of the pyramidal tract) and descend the spinal corn in the lateral corticospinal tract.

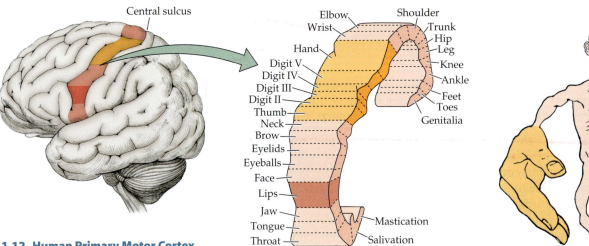

(a) Lateral view of brain showing location of primary motor cortex

Central sulcus

(b) Representation of the body in primary motor cortex

Elbow
Wrist
Hand
Digit V
Digit IV
Digit III
Digit II
Thumb
Neck
Brow
Eyelids
Eyeballs
Face
Lips
Jaw
Tongue
Throat
Shoulder
Trunk
Hip
Leg
Knee
Ankle
Feet
Toes
Genitalia
Mastication
Salivation

(c) Motor homunculus

11.12 Human Primary Motor Cortex

(a) This lateral view of the human brain shows the location of primary motor cortex (M1). (b) Regions controlling motor responses of different parts of the body are shown here in relative sequence and size. (c) The proportions of this homunculus show the relative sizes of primary-motor-cortex representations of parts of the body.

CLINICAL ISSUE

Figure 11.13 Motor Nuclei in the Brainstem   Shown here from the rear along with the reticular formation, control muscles of the head and neck. The cranial nerves corresponding to these muscles are shown in Figure 2.4.

medulla the pyramidal tract from the right hemisphere crosses the midline to innervate the left spinal cord, and vice versa.

Because the pyramidal tract crosses the midline (technically known as a *decussation*) in the medulla, the right controls the left side of the body while the left controls the right. Lesions of the pyramidal system deprive the patient of the ability to move individual joints and limbs.

Many of the axons of the pyramidal tract originate from neurons in the **primary motor cortex** (**M1**), or precentral gyrus, the cortical region just anterior to the central sulcus (Figure 11.12). Many of these cells are large neurons (called *Betz cells*) in layer V of the primary motor cortex. In the brainstem are cranial motor nuclei whose axons innervate muscles of the head and neck (Figure 11.13, and see Figure 2.4).

Primary motor cortex is an executive motor control mechanism—and more

In humans, brain damage to the primary motor cortex (M1) produces partial paralysis on the side of the body opposite the brain lesion (i.e., the *contralateral* side of the

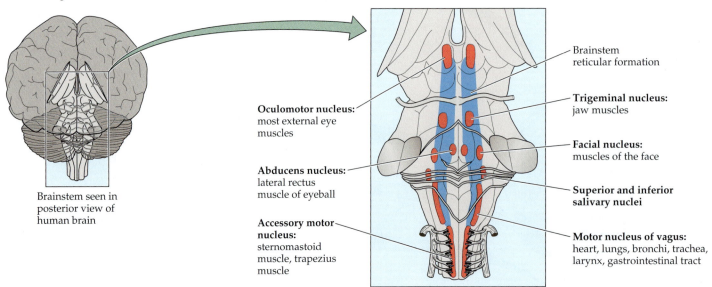

Brainstem seen in posterior view of human brain

Oculomotor nucleus: most external eye muscles

Abducens nucleus: lateral rectus muscle of eyeball

Accessory motor nucleus: sternomastoid muscle, trapezius muscle

Brainstem reticular formation

Trigeminal nucleus: jaw muscles

Facial nucleus: muscles of the face

Superior and inferior salivary nuclei

Motor nucleus of vagus: heart, lungs, bronchi, trachea, larynx, gastrointestinal tract

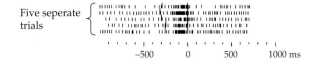

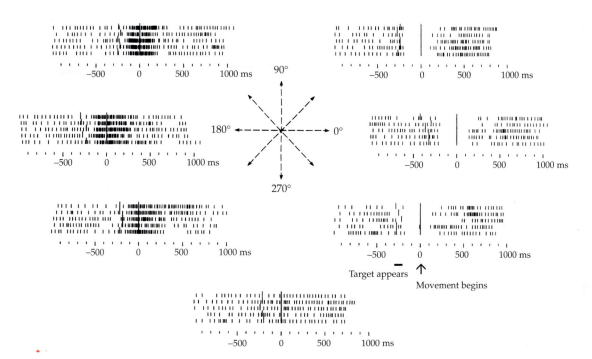

11.14 Directional Tuning of Motor Cortex Cells (a) Shown here is the activity of a single neuron during arm movement toward a target in eight different directions. Each horizontal record in the eight blocks of data represents one of five trials. Note that this cell consistently fires before the arm moves in the direction from 90° to 180° to 270°, and it is silent before movements in the other directions. (b) The average frequency of discharge during the interval before movement changed depending on the direction. (From Georgopoulos et al., 1982.)

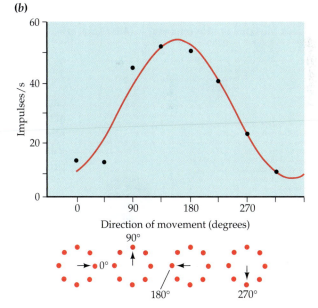

body). The disturbance is greatest in distal muscles, such as those of the hand. Humans with these lesions are generally disinclined to use the affected limb.

Early-twentieth-century researchers like Wilder Penfield, whom we discussed in the opening of Chapter 2, used electrical stimulation to develop functional maps of human primary motor cortex. Disproportionately large regions in the maps of M1 are devoted to the body parts involved in the most elaborate and complex movements in any species. For example, humans and other primates have extremely large cortical fields concerned with hand movements (see Figure 11.12). "Colonies" of cells are related to particular muscle groups, and they form vertical columns in the cortex (Ghez et al., 1991).

In primates the pyramidal tract has some monosynaptic connections with spinal motoneurons, but most pyramidal-tract neurons influence spinal motoneurons through polysynaptic routes and share control of these motor cells with other descending influences.

Apostolos Georgopoulos has focused on the properties of populations of motor cortex neurons (Georgopoulos et al., 1993). He recorded from M1 neurons of monkeys that were trained to make free arm movements in eight possible target directions (Figure 11.14a). Many cells changed their firing rates according to the direction of the movement, and for any one cell, discharge rates were highest in one particular direction (Figure 11.14b). Although different cells prefer different directions,

Apostolos Georgopoulos

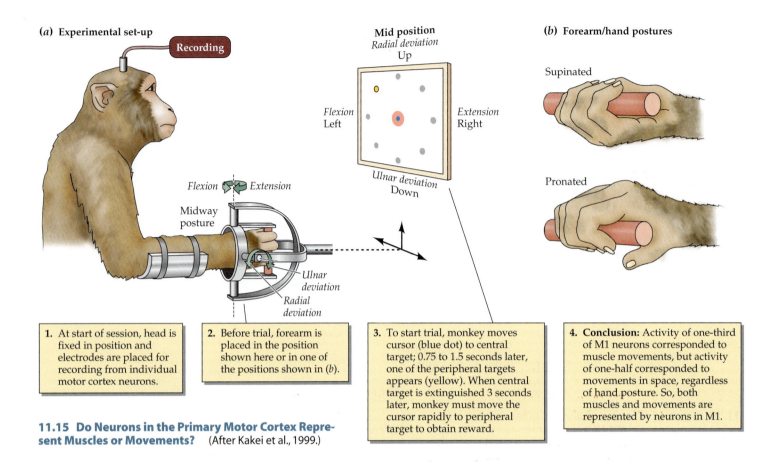

(a) Experimental set-up

Recording

Mid position
Radial deviation
Up

Flexion
Left

Extension
Right

Ulnar deviation
Down

Flexion ⚬ Extension

Midway
posture

Ulnar
deviation

Radial
deviation

(b) Forearm/hand postures

Supinated

Pronated

1. At start of session, head is fixed in position and electrodes are placed for recording from individual motor cortex neurons.

2. Before trial, forearm is placed in the position shown here or in one of the positions shown in (b).

3. To start trial, monkey moves cursor (blue dot) to central target; 0.75 to 1.5 seconds later, one of the peripheral targets appears (yellow). When central target is extinguished 3 seconds later, monkey must move the cursor rapidly to peripheral target to obtain reward.

4. **Conclusion:** Activity of one-third of M1 neurons corresponded to muscle movements, but activity of one-half corresponded to movements in space, regardless of hand posture. So, both muscles and movements are represented by neurons in M1.

11.15 Do Neurons in the Primary Motor Cortex Represent Muscles or Movements?   (After Kakei et al., 1999.)

each cell carries only partial information about the direction of reaching. When the activity of several hundred neurons is combined, the overall vector shows a good relation to the actual direction of the reaching arm. Given the millions of neurons in this region, a larger sampling would presumably provide an even more accurate prediction (Georgopoulos et al., 1993).

A long-standing controversy has raged over whether muscles or movements are represented in M1. That is, does activity of a cortical motor neuron encode a relatively simple parameter such as contraction of a particular muscle, or a more abstract parameter such as a particular movement of the hand through space? To address this controversy, experimenters trained a monkey to perform rapid tracking movements of the wrist to obtain liquid rewards (Kakei et al., 1999). As shown in Figure 11.15, the animal grasped a handle that could be rotated along the two axes of wrist motion: flexion–extension and radial–ulnar deviation. Movement of the handle controlled the position of a cursor on a computer screen. After much training (over 8 years!), the monkey performed well.

COMPETING HYPOTHESES

The experimenters then recorded the activity of single cells in M1 as the monkey performed from different starting positions. A substantial group of M1 neurons (28 of 88, or 32%) displayed changes in activity that corresponded to *muscle* movements, but an even larger group of neurons (44 of 88, 50%) showed activity that corresponded to *movement in space,* regardless of hand posture. In other words, these cells were active whenever the monkey moved its hand in a particular *direction,* no matter which muscles it needed to use to accomplish that movement. Thus, both movements and, to a lesser extent, muscles appear to be strongly represented in M1.

The role of primary motor cortex in learning   Several studies with both experimental animals and humans demonstrated that motor representations in M1 change as a result of training. Maps prepared from electrical stimulation in M1 show changes in relation to the acquisition of new skills: in monkeys, for example, a visually guided tracking movement with the arm (J. N. Sanes and Donoghue, 2000) or a precision grasping task (Nudo et al., 1996); in rats, a skilled reaching movement (Kleim et al., 1998).

In humans, the width of the precentral gyrus as seen with MRI offers an estimate of the size of M1. The gyrus is significantly wider in piano players, especially in the hand representation area (see Figure 11.12), than in nonmusician control subjects. The younger the musician was at the start of musical training, the larger the gyrus is in adulthood (Amunts et al., 1997).

Focal transcranial magnetic stimulation (fTMS) uses coils of wire placed near the head to induce a brief magnetic field that can stimulate neurons in the brain, beneath the skin and skull. Focal TMS was used in human volunteers to evoke isolated thumb movements in a particular direction. Then the subjects practiced moving the thumb in a different direction for 15 to 30 minutes. The same fTMS was then found to evoke thumb movement in the *new* direction for several minutes before the response reverted to the original direction (Classen et al., 1998). (This rapid change seems similar to the retuning of auditory cortical receptors during stimulation at another frequency, as noted in Chapter 9.)

Nonprimary motor cortex aids motor sequencing

Just anterior to M1 are cortical regions that are also important for motor control. Because they are *not* primary motor cortex, they are called (confusingly enough) *nonprimary motor cortex*. Nonprimary motor cortex consists of two main regions: the **supplementary motor area (SMA)**, which lies mainly on the medial aspect of the hemisphere, and the **premotor cortex**, which is anterior to the primary motor cortex (Figure 11.16). Patients with lesions of the premotor cortex retain fine motor control of the fingers but are impaired in the stability of stance and gait and in the coordination of the two hands. Patients with bilateral damage to the SMA are unable to move voluntarily, although some automatic and reflex movements remain, suggesting that this region is involved in the initiation of movement sequences (Tanji, 2001).

Studies of localized cerebral blood flow and metabolism reveal that in simple tasks, such as keeping a spring compressed between two fingers of one hand, blood flow increases markedly in the hand area of the opposite M1 (Roland, 1980, 1984). Increasing the complexity of motor tasks to a *sequence* of behaviors extends the area of blood flow increase to the SMA. Finally, when subjects mentally *rehearse* the complex movement sequence, the enhanced blood flow is restricted to just the SMA.

NEURAL PLASTICITY

CLINICAL ISSUE

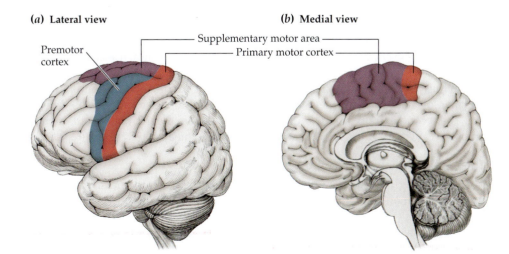

(a) Lateral view

Premotor cortex

Supplementary motor area
Primary motor cortex

(b) Medial view

Supplementary motor area
Primary motor cortex

11.16 Human Motor Cortical Areas
(*a*) The primary motor cortex (M1) lies just anterior to the central sulcus. Anterior to the primary motor cortex are the premotor cortex and the supplementary motor area (SMA), which together make up the nonprimary motor cortex. (*b*) The SMA lies mainly on the medial surface of the cerebral hemispheres.

Charles Gross

In contrast, the premotor cortex is activated when motor sequences are guided *externally* by stimuli (Halsband et al., 1994; Larsson et al., 1996) rather than generated internally.

A related distinction between SMA and premotor cortex is suggested by a study in which people learned the same sequence of finger movements under two conditions. In one condition the subjects soon became aware of the repeating sequence and began anticipating the next finger movement. In the other condition, subjects were distracted by another task and therefore never became aware of the repeating sequence, but nevertheless they learned it (as evidenced by their improved performance).

Both groups learned to perform the same sequence of finger movements, but different brain regions were activated in these two conditions. The undistracted subjects, explicitly aware of the sequence they were learning, showed activation of the premotor cortex, but the distracted subjects, unaware that they were (implicitly) learning the sequence, showed activation of the SMA (Hazeltine et al., 1997). Perhaps, then, the premotor cortex participates in *explicit* motor learning, while the SMA mediates *implicit* motor learning.

A subset of premotor neurons is also activated when objects are brought close to a monkey's face or hand. If the lights are then turned out, some of these neurons continue to fire even if the object is silently moved, suggesting to Charles Gross and colleagues (Graziano et al., 1997) that the cells are coding for where the monkey *thinks* the object is. When the lights are turned back on and the monkey sees that the object is gone, the neurons cease firing. Such neurons may help us reach out for objects that are no longer visible.

Distributed activity in motor areas   Motor areas of the cerebral cortex overlap in the control of muscular activity. Box 11.1 gives an example of this distributed control. Control of movements is not encoded in the successive or coordinated activation of individual neurons in M1; rather it emerges from the collective activation of a large distributed population of neurons—not only in M1 but also in the SMA and premotor cortex, and in the basal ganglia and cerebellum, to which we turn next.

Extrapyramidal Systems Also Modulate Motor Commands

In addition to the corticospinal outflow through the pyramidal tract, many other motor tracts run from the forebrain to the brainstem and spinal cord. Because these tracts are outside of the pyramids of the medulla, they and their connections are called the **extrapyramidal system** (Figure 11.17). In general, lesions of the extrapyramidal system do not prevent movement of individual joints and limbs, but they do interfere with spinal reflexes, usually exaggerating them.

The extrapyramidal system communicates to the spinal cord through two principal pathways: the reticulospinal and rubrospinal tracts. The extensive pool of interconnected neurons called the **reticular formation** modulates various aspects of movements. Some zones of the reticular formation facilitate movements; other zones are inhibitory. These effects are transmitted in descending tracts known as **reticulospinal tracts** that arise from the reticular formation and connect to spinal interneurons, where they influence the excitability of spinal motor circuitry. Some neurons of the reticular formation also help regulate the activation of muscles responsible for breathing. The second extrapyramidal outflow originates from the midbrain's **red nucleus** and so is called the **rubrospinal tract** (the Latin *ruber* means "red").

The basal ganglia modulate movements

The **basal ganglia** include a group of interconnected forebrain nuclei: the caudate nucleus, putamen, and globus pallidus. Closely associated with these structures are two nuclei in the midbrain: the substantia nigra and the subthalamic nucleus. Figure 11.17 shows the locations of these structures. The caudate nucleus and putamen together are referred to as the **striatum.**

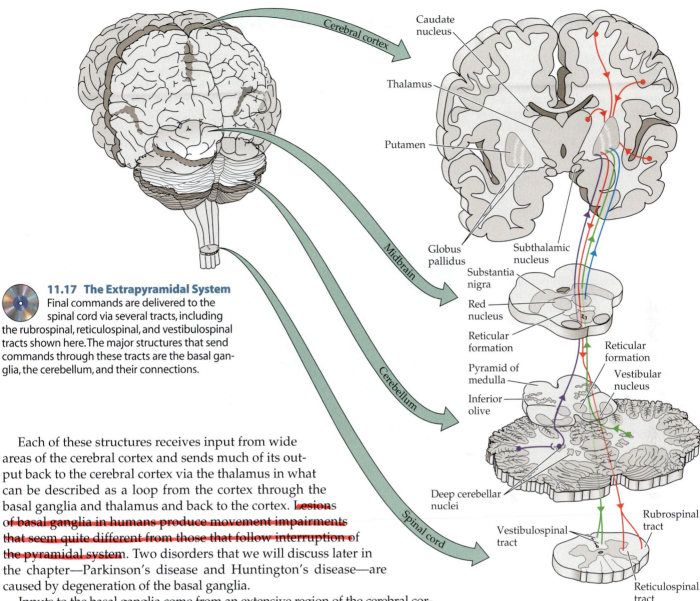

11.17 The Extrapyramidal System
Final commands are delivered to the spinal cord via several tracts, including the rubrospinal, reticulospinal, and vestibulospinal tracts shown here. The major structures that send commands through these tracts are the basal ganglia, the cerebellum, and their connections.

Each of these structures receives input from wide areas of the cerebral cortex and sends much of its output back to the cerebral cortex via the thalamus in what can be described as a loop from the cortex through the basal ganglia and thalamus and back to the cortex. Lesions of basal ganglia in humans produce movement impairments that seem quite different from those that follow interruption of the pyramidal system. Two disorders that we will discuss later in the chapter—Parkinson's disease and Huntington's disease—are caused by degeneration of the basal ganglia.

Inputs to the basal ganglia come from an extensive region of the cerebral cortex, as well as from thalamic nuclei and the substantia nigra. Lesions and recordings of single neurons during motor responses indicate that each structure of the basal ganglia contains a topographic representation of body musculature (DeLong et al., 1984). The basal ganglia play a role in determining the amplitude and direction of movement rather than the initiation of actions. The basal ganglia thus seem to modulate the patterns of activity initiated in other brain circuits that control movements, such as motor cortical systems (see Figure 11.4). The basal ganglia are especially important in the performance of movements influenced by memories, in contrast to those guided by sensory control (Evarts et al., 1984; Graybiel et al., 1994).

The cerebellum affects programs, timing, and coordination of acts

The cerebellum is a brain structure found in almost all vertebrates. In some vertebrate groups its size varies according to the range and complexity of movements. For example, the cerebellum is much larger in fish with extensive locomotor behavior than it is in less-active fish; it is also larger in flying birds than in bird species that do not fly.

Recall from Chapter 2 that the outer layers of the cerebellum are called the *cerebellar cortex* and are dominated by a sheet of large multipolar cells called *Purkinje*

BOX 11.1 Cortical Neurons Control Movements of a Robotic Arm

Signals from rat motor cortex can be used to control one-dimensional movements of a robotic arm, paralleling the movement of the rat's own arm (Chapin et al., 1999). If the rats receive visual feedback and are rewarded for successful movements of the robotic arm, they progressively cease to produce overt arm movements and let the robotic arm accomplish the task. This result suggests that paralyzed patients might learn to operate a robotic arm by cortical activity even though they can no longer move their own limbs.

Investigators have also used microwires implanted in two or more regions of the cortex of two owl monkeys to control a robotic arm in three dimensions, reproducing movements to reach for pieces of food placed in different positions, pick them up, carry them to the mouth, and return to the start position (Wessberg et al., 2000). In the first monkey, 16 microwires were implanted in each of the following areas: left dorsal premotor cortex (PMd), which is believed to plan the general temporal and spatial features of movements; left primary motor cortex (M1), which presides over the generation of movement commands for the right arm; left posterior parietal cortex (PP), which is thought to integrate visual, so-

matosensory, and motor information to determine the location of a movement target and how to reach it; and right PMd, M1, and PP. In the other monkey, 16 microwires were implanted in each of two areas: left PMd and M1.

Training and recording were continued for 12 months in the first monkey and for 24 months in the second. Algorithms were

Owl monkey perched atop a robotic arm

developed to predict the hand motions from the cortical signals, as well as to predict hand trajectories to other directions—for example, to the left instead of to the right. The algorithms were used to control movements of robotic arms in real time both locally and, over the Internet, at a distance.

Analysis of the effects of excluding particular neurons from the calculations showed, somewhat unexpectedly, that PMd neurons contributed the most to the predictions and, as expected, ipsilateral M1 neurons contributed the least. Each area could be used for accurate predictions, provided that enough neurons in that area were sampled.

The investigators suggest that this research could lead to voluntary control of prosthetic limbs in paralyzed patients. They note that implanted microwires yielded reliable recordings for at least 24 months. This result suggests that microwire arrays with implantable integrated circuits, designed to handle the signal processing and mathematical analysis, could form the basis of a brain–machine interface to control prosthetic devices (Carmena et al., 2003; Nicolelis, 2001). (Photograph courtesy of Miguel Nicolelis.)

Masao Ito

cells (see Figure 2.11). All output of the cerebellar cortex travels via the axons of Purkinje cells, all of which synapse with the deep cerebellar nuclei. At these synapses, Purkinje cells produce only inhibitory postsynaptic potentials. Hence all the circuitry of the extensive cortical portion of the cerebellum, which also includes 10 billion to 20 billion granule cells in humans, guides movement by inhibiting neurons.

Inputs to the cerebellar cortex come both from sensory sources and from other brain motor systems. Sensory inputs include the muscle and joint receptors, and the vestibular, somatosensory, visual, and auditory systems. Both pyramidal and nonpyramidal pathways contribute inputs to the cerebellum and in turn receive outputs from the deep nuclei of the cerebellum. It has been suggested that the cerebellum elaborates neural "programs" for the control of skilled movements, particularly rapid, repeated movements that become automatic. This role of the cerebellum in the acquisition and retention of learned motor responses will be discussed in Chapter 18.

Masao Ito (1987) described a long-term depression of Purkinje cell activity that occurs when two different kinds of inputs to these cells are stimulated together. The depression of firing can last as long as 1 hour. This kind of memory change in the cerebellar cortex might be important for adaptive changes in learning motor skills.

The cerebellum and the basal ganglia contribute differently to the modulation of motor functions

The foregoing discussion and Figure 11.4 indicate that the cerebellum and the basal ganglia occupy rather similar positions in modulating motor functions. However, Y. Liu et al. (1999) found differences in the activity of these brain regions when they

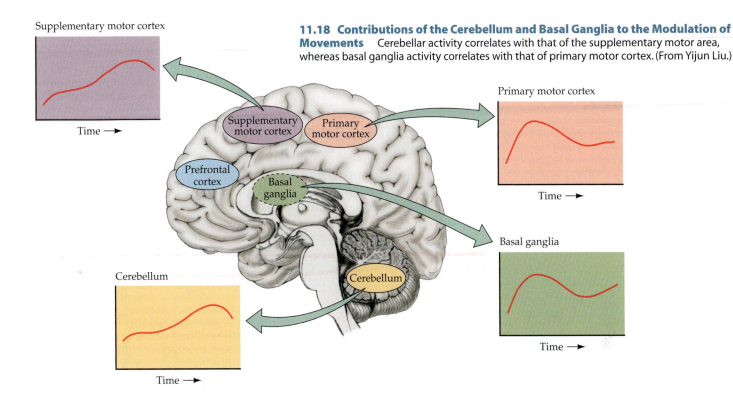

11.18 Contributions of the Cerebellum and Basal Ganglia to the Modulation of Movements Cerebellar activity correlates with that of the supplementary motor area, whereas basal ganglia activity correlates with that of primary motor cortex. (From Yijun Liu.)

examined fMRI responses of subjects performing a tactile discrimination task. The subjects were given two similarly shaped objects—one in each hand—and they had to decide by active touching whether the objects were the same or different.

Changing patterns of activity during this task were found in M1, the SMA, the cerebellum, and the basal ganglia. Cerebellar activity correlated significantly with activity of the SMA but not M1, whereas basal ganglia activity correlated more strongly with activity of M1 than of the SMA. Thus, although the task appears to require the activity of five brain regions (Figure 11.18), the cerebellum and basal ganglia show temporally and anatomically differentiated contributions.

The cerebellum and basal ganglia also contribute differently to the task of reaching. As we saw in Figure 11.1*b*, patients with Huntington's disease, who suffer from damage to the basal ganglia, show impairment especially toward the *end* of a reach, when corrections are made. In contrast, patients with cerebellar damage show errors especially in the *initial* direction of reach (M. A. Smith et al., 2000).

Endogenous oscillators drive many repetitive movements

However it is accomplished, most locomotion is rhythmic. For all animals, moving about consists of repetitive cycles of the same act, be it the beating of wings or the repetitive swinging of legs. In Chapter 3 we presented an example of a basic neural circuit that could act as an **endogenous oscillator** (see Figure 3.18*b*), generating regularly repeating sequences of behavior.

Many rhythmic movements are generated by mechanisms within the spinal cord. These endogenous rhythms are normally modulated by feedback, but they can function independently of brain influences or afferents. The term **central pattern generator** is used to refer to the neural circuitry responsible for generating rhythmic patterns of behavior as seen in walking. Typically neurons in a central pattern generator circuit display reciprocal inhibitory innervation. Electromyographic records of hindlimb muscles of cats with spinal cord section and dorsal root cuts reveal a "walking" pattern that lasts for seconds when a single dorsal root is briefly stimulated electrically (P. Grillner et al., 1991; S. Grillner, 1985).

Outputs from spinal motoneurons also show different types of coordination with different locomotor patterns, like galloping. Three intact adjacent spinal segments provide the minimal amount of spinal processing necessary for generating part of the locomotor rhythm. Thus the brain does not generate the essential rhythm in the spinal cord, but normally controls the onset of the rhythm and provides corrections as needed.

Disorders of Muscle, Spinal Cord, or Brain Can Disrupt Movement

Disorders at any level in the motor system—muscles, neuromuscular junctions, spinal cord, or brain regions—can impair movement. In the discussion that follows we will consider examples at each of these levels.

In muscular dystrophy, biochemical abnormalities cause muscles to waste away

Several muscle diseases involve biochemical abnormalities that lead to structural changes in muscle; these disorders are referred to as **muscular dystrophy.** As the name implies, a symptom that the various muscular dystrophies share is the wasting away of muscles (Blake et al., 2002).

CLINICAL ISSUE

Duchenne's muscular dystrophy strikes almost exclusively boys, beginning at the age of about 4 to 6 years and leading to death within a decade. Pedigrees have shown that the disorder is a simple Mendelian trait—caused by a single gene, in this case carried on the X chromosome. When the gene was identified, it was named *dystrophin.* In some ways the name is unfortunate because the dystrophin protein, when normal, does *not* lead to dystrophy. Dystrophin is normally produced in muscle cells and may play a role in regulating internal calcium (Ca^{2+}) stores. Because females have two X chromosomes, even if one carries the defective copy of the *dystrophin* gene, the other X chromosome can still produce normal dystrophin. But about half the sons of such females will receive the defective gene and will be afflicted with the disease.

The immune system may impair motor function by attacking neuromuscular junctions

Movement disorders involving neuromuscular junctions include a variety of reversible poison states. For example, snake bites can cause neuromuscular blocks because the venom of some highly poisonous snakes contains substances (such as bungarotoxin) that block postsynaptic acetylcholine receptors. If the neuromuscular junctions to the muscles for breathing are blocked, the victim suffocates.

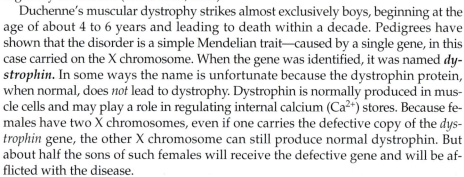

Studies of bungarotoxin led to an understanding of a debilitating neuromuscular disorder, **myasthenia gravis** (from the Greek *mys,* "muscle," and *asthenes,* "weak"; and the Latin *gravis,* "grave" or "serious"). This disorder is characterized by a profound weakness of skeletal muscles. The disease often first affects the muscles of the head, producing symptoms such as drooping of the eyelids, double vision, and slowing of speech. In later stages, paralysis of the muscles that control swallowing and respiration become life-threatening.

CLINICAL ISSUE

This is an instance of an *autoimmune* disorder, in which the patient's immune system attacks part of his own body and impairs function. Most cases of myasthenia gravis result from the patient developing antibodies that attack his own acetylcholine receptors, disrupting neuromuscular junctions. In other cases, the antibodies are directed toward other proteins that are associated with the acetylcholine receptor. Treatment often consists of drugs to suppress the immune system (Richman and Agius, 2003).

Motoneuron pathology causes some motor impairments

In the late 1930s the sad end of the brilliant baseball career of New York Yankees star Lou Gehrig brought public awareness to an unusual degenerative disorder in which the motoneurons of the brainstem and spinal cord are destroyed and their target muscles waste away. This syndrome is formally known as **amyotrophic lateral** sclerosis (ALS), commonly called *Lou Gehrig's disease*. The origins of the disease remain a mystery, but a wide range of causal factors are under investigation, including premature aging, toxic minerals, viruses, immune responses, and endocrine dysfunction.

About 10% of ALS cases are hereditary. The pedigrees of several afflicted families indicate that this rare form of ALS is a single-gene disorder. The particular gene has been isolated (Andersen et al., 1995) and found to encode an enzyme: copper/zinc superoxide dismutase. When scientists produced transgenic mice that, in addition to their own normal copies of the enzyme, carried a copy of the defective human gene, these animals displayed an ALS-like syndrome (Gurney et al., 1994). Their muscles wasted away and their motoneurons died, leading to an early death. These results suggest that the abnormal gene actively damages part of the neuromuscular system.

Spinal cord pathology causes some motor impairments

Pathological changes in motoneurons also produce movement paralysis or weakness. Virus-induced destruction of motoneurons—for example, by the disease polio—was once a frightening prospect around the world. Polioviruses destroy motoneurons of the spinal cord and, in more severe types of the disease, cranial motoneurons of the brainstem. Because the muscles can no longer be called on to contract, they atrophy.

Vehicular accidents, violence, falls, and sports injuries cause many human spinal injuries that result in motor impairment. Injuries to the human spinal cord commonly develop from forces to the neck or back that break bone and compress the spinal cord. If the spinal cord is severed completely, immediate paralysis results, and reflexes below the level of injury are lost—a condition known as **flaccid paralysis**. Flaccid paralysis generally results only when a considerable stretch of the spinal cord has been destroyed. When the injury severs the spinal cord without causing widespread destruction of tissue, reflexes below the level of injury frequently become excessive because the intact tissue lacks the dampening influence of brain inhibitory pathways.

An estimated 250,000 to 400,000 individuals in the United States have spinal cord injuries. We described the injury of actor Christopher Reeve (Figure 11.19) at the start of the chapter. He and his wife founded an organization to inform people about spinal cord injuries and mobilized research to repair such injuries (www.christopherreeve.org). With diligent training and physical therapy, he regained some sensation from his body and learned to move some of his fingers. Doctors regarded his progress as quite unusual. He also underwent special surgery that fulfilled one of his dreams: to breathe without a ventilator. A device monitored his blood oxygen levels and controlled a pacemaker with electrodes that stimulated his diaphragm to inhale. But his dream of walking on his own was never realized.

The hope of reconnecting the injured spinal cord no longer seems far-fetched. Months after the spinal cord is severed in lampreys, the fish can swim again without any therapeutic intervention (A. H. Cohen et al., 1989), but they seem unique among vertebrates in this regard. Four main strategies for reconnecting the brain and spinal cord in humans are being investigated (Figure 11.20):

1. One strategy is to provide stem cells that might differentiate into new neurons to send new axons across the break (Okano et al., 2003).
2. Another approach is to transplant glial cells that promote regeneration in the CNS. Recall from Chapter 9 that olfactory receptor neurons can be continuously produced throughout life and send out new axons. When Y. Li et al. (1997) took specialized glial cells (called *ensheathing cells*) from the olfactory bulb and used them as a bridge across spinal cord cuts in rats, the corticospinal axons regenerated across the injury, and the animals eventually regained use of their forepaws. Efforts are under way to genetically engineer ensheathing cells to make them

11.19 Leaders in the Campaign to Aid Victims of Spinal Paralysis Actor Christopher Reeve (1952–2004) and his wife Dana were guests of honor at a meeting held in 1999 by the Society for Neuroscience to mark the achievements of the Decade of the Brain. Reeve received the Special Achievement Award for his efforts to raise public awareness of spinal cord injury and for promoting research funding. (Courtesy of the Society for Neuroscience.)

11.20 Research Strategies for Reconnecting the Brain and Spinal Cord

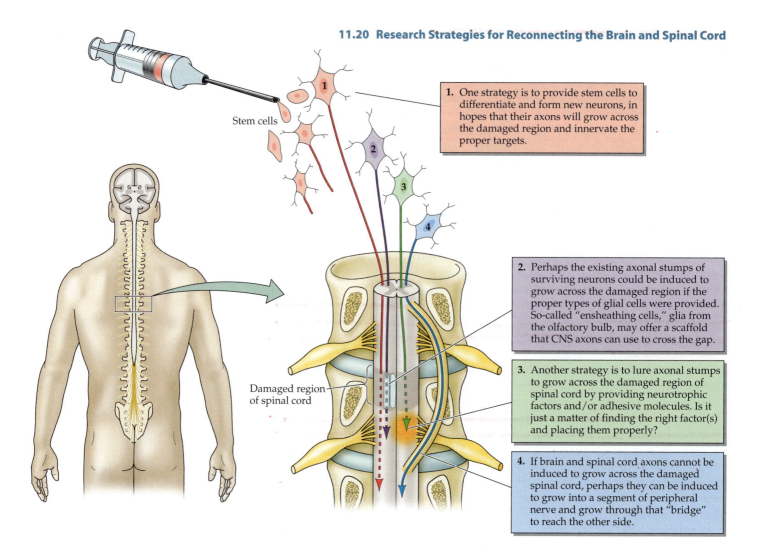

Stem cells

1. One strategy is to provide stem cells to differentiate and form new neurons, in hopes that their axons will grow across the damaged region and innervate the proper targets.

2. Perhaps the existing axonal stumps of surviving neurons could be induced to grow across the damaged region if the proper types of glial cells were provided. So-called "ensheathing cells," glia from the olfactory bulb, may offer a scaffold that CNS axons can use to cross the gap.

3. Another strategy is to lure axonal stumps to grow across the damaged region of spinal cord by providing neurotrophic factors and/or adhesive molecules. Is it just a matter of finding the right factor(s) and placing them properly?

4. If brain and spinal cord axons cannot be induced to grow across the damaged spinal cord, perhaps they can be induced to grow into a segment of peripheral nerve and grow through that "bridge" to reach the other side.

Damaged region of spinal cord

even more effective (L. Cao et al., 2003). These observations buoy the hope that regeneration in the injured spinal cord of humans will permit Christopher Reeve, and the many thousands who share his plight, to walk again someday.

3. A third strategy is to use neurotrophic factors and/or adhesive molecules (see Chapter 7) to entice the axons of surviving neurons to grow across the damaged region of spinal cord and reconnect to their targets (Cheng et al., 1996; Grill et al., 1997; Hendriks et al., 2004).

4. A final approach centers on the observation that axons in peripheral nerves, when cut by injury, will regrow and reconnect to their targets, yet cut axons in the CNS almost never accomplish this feat. No one really knows why peripheral and central axons differ in this regard, but it might be possible to exploit "regeneration-friendly" peripheral nerves by transplanting some to connect the brain and lower spinal cord, forming a "bridge" around the injured spinal cord (Bernstein-Goral and Bregman, 1993).

CLINICAL ISSUE

Cerebral cortex pathology causes some motor impairments

The most common motor impairments that follow strokes or injury to the human cerebral cortex are paralysis (**plegia**) or weakness (**paresis**) of voluntary movements on one side of the body. Usually the paralysis appears on the side of the body opposite the injured hemisphere. In addition, affected patients show some **spasticity**, especially increased rigidity in response to forced movement of the limbs.

Spasticity reflects the exaggeration of stretch reflexes that have been released from the inhibition they usually receive from the cortex. Abnormal reflexes occur, such as the flaring and extension of the toes elicited by stroking the sole of the foot (the *Babinski reflex*). In the months following cerebral cortical injury, the clinical picture changes. The initial paralysis slowly diminishes, and some voluntary movements of the proximal portion of limbs return, although fine motor control of fingers is seldom regained. As noted earlier, in humans the symptoms are more severe than in many other mammals.

Damage to nonmotor zones of the cerebral cortex, such as some regions of parietal or frontal association cortex, produces more-complicated changes in motor control. One such condition is **apraxia** (from the Greek *a*-, "not," and *praxis*, "action"), the inability to carry out certain acts even though paralysis or weakness is not evident and comprehension and motivation are intact. Apraxia is illustrated in the following example: When asked to smile, a patient is unable to do so, although he certainly attempts to. If asked to use a comb placed in front of him, he seems unable to figure out what to do. But things aren't as simple as they might appear. At one point in the discussion the patient spontaneously smiles, and at another point he retrieves a comb from his pocket and combs his hair with ease and accuracy.

Apraxia was first described by the nineteenth-century neurologist John Hughlings Jackson, who noted that some patients could not protrude the tongue on command even though they could use it in a variety of spontaneous acts, such as speech, licking their lips, and eating. Apraxia is a symptom of a variety of disorders, including stroke, Alzheimer's disease, and developmental disorders of children.

Neurologists studying patients who have suffered strokes have discovered several different types of apraxia. **Ideomotor apraxia** is characterized by the inability to carry out a *simple* motor activity in response to a verbal command (e.g., "smile," or "use this comb"), even though this same activity is readily performed spontaneously. **Ideational apraxia** is an impairment in carrying out a *sequence* of actions that are components of a behavioral script, although each element or step can be performed correctly (Kosslyn et al., 1992). Such patients have difficulty carrying out instructions for a sequence of acts—"Push the button, then pull the handle, then depress the switch"—but they can do each of these tasks in isolation. Apraxia does not seem to be related to language deficits; the patients may be perfectly good at naming objects (Rosci et al., 2003), yet they cannot perform the requested sequence of actions with those objects.

Parkinson's disease results from lack of stimulation of the basal ganglia

About 200 years ago, physician James Parkinson noted people in London who moved quite slowly, showed regular tremors of the hands and face while at rest, and walked with a rigid bearing. Another feature of what is now known as **Parkinson's disease** is a loss of facial muscle tone, which gives the face a masklike appearance. Patients who suffer from Parkinson's also show few spontaneous actions and have great difficulty in all motor efforts, no matter how routine. The hands may display tremors while at rest but move smoothly while performing a task. Parkinson's disease afflicts almost 1% of the U.S. population aged 65 and older, but it sometimes unaccountably occurs in younger people, such as actor Michael J. Fox.

CLINICAL ISSUE

Patients with Parkinson's show progressive degeneration of dopamine-containing cells in the **substantia nigra** that project to the striatum. The loss of cells in this area is continual, but symptoms appear only after a major loss. The discovery of a form of the disorder induced by illicit drugs (described in Box 11.2) has suggested that exposures to toxins over a prolonged period underlie the development of the disorder.

Most cases of Parkinson's disease are probably not inherited, but in one large Italian family, Parkinson's disease develops in members who inherit a defective copy of the gene that encodes **α-synuclein** (Polymeropoulos et al., 1997), a protein normally expressed in the basal ganglia. Another family with inherited Parkinson's dis-

GENES AND BEHAVIOR

BOX 11.2 The Frozen Addicts

Parkinson's disease has been difficult to study because until recently it was not possible to find or produce a similar disorder in laboratory animals. Sloppy synthesis of illegal drugs led to the first valuable model of Parkinson's disease. This saga began in 1982 when several drug addicts were admitted to a hospital in California with an unusual array of symptoms. Especially puzzling was the fact that although they were in their twenties, they presented an unmistakable portrait of Parkinson's disease, which is usually restricted to people 50 or older. The movements of these young patients were slow, they had tremors of the hands, and their faces were frozen without expression. In addition, the diagnosis of Parkinson's disease in these cases was confirmed by the therapeutic response to the drug L-dopa.

All of these drug addicts had recently used a "home-brewed" synthetic form of heroin. That fact, coupled with the recollection of a report of an unusual disorder that had arisen from a laboratory accident several years earlier, led to the conclusion that the synthetic heroin contained a neurotoxin that produced brain damage typical of Parkinson's disease (Kopin and Markey, 1988; Langston, 1985).

Moving step-by-step in a trail that resembles a detective story, researchers pieced together what had happened. Chemical studies led to the identification of a contaminant in the synthetic heroin now known as MPTP (an abbreviation of a much longer chemical name). Many addicts have been exposed to this substance, but relatively few exhibit this parkinsonian disorder. Patients with

symptoms show a decline in dopamine concentrations in the brain, as revealed by PET scans (W. R. Martin and Hayden, 1987).

The injection of MPTP into various research animals yielded a startling result: Although rats and rabbits showed only minimal and transient motor impairments, monkeys were as sensitive to the toxin as humans are, developing a permanent set of motor changes identical to those of humans with Parkinson's disease. Furthermore, the sites of damage in the brain were identical to those in the frozen addicts and in patients suffering from Parkinson's.

MPTP accumulates in the substantia nigra and caudate nucleus because it binds selectively to a form of the enzyme monoamine oxidase (MAO), which is plentiful in these regions. MPTP interacts with this enzyme to form a highly toxic metabolite: MPP+. Researchers have suggested that the natural pigment neuromelanin, found in the substantia nigra, accounts for the selectivity of damage produced by MPTP (S. H. Snyder and D'Amato, 1985). They have shown that MPP+ binds with special affinity to this pigment. Thus, cells with neuromelanin accumulate MPP+ to toxic levels, and because cells of the substantia nigra contain large amounts of the pigment, they are particularly vulnerable to the destructive impact of MPP+.

In other parts of the brain, MPP+ levels decline following exposure; in contrast, MPP+ levels in substantia nigra cells may continue to increase for some time following exposure. In view of this binding mechanism, the observed differences among species become more compre-

hensible: Nigral cells of monkeys and humans have pigment; those of rodents are unpigmented.

Monkeys can be protected against the toxic effects of MPP+ by oxidase inhibitors and certain other drugs (D'Amato et al., 1987). This drug model has already resulted in new drug treatments that hold considerable promise for human sufferers of Parkinson's disease. For example, the MAO inhibitor deprenyl slows progression of the disease. Discovering a primate model of this disease opened an exciting set of research opportunities that is removing the shroud of mystery around Parkinson's disease. Experiments with primates have also provided an opportunity to test other therapies, such as neural transplants. This research has led to successful transplants in human patients (see Figure 11.21), including some of the original frozen addicts.

Some researchers have speculated that Parkinson's disease in humans arises from exposure to an unknown toxin or toxins. In two cases involving laboratory workers, MPTP-induced disease arose from either inhalation of or skin contact with MPTP, suggesting that brief and almost trivial contact with MPTP is sufficient to begin the disease. Recent animal experiments indicate that some environmental toxins, such as certain herbicides (Betarbet et al., 2000) or combinations of herbicides (Thiruchelvam et al., 2000), may cause Parkinson's disease. The announcement of a *Drosophila* model of Parkinson's disease in 2000 may speed research toward prevention or alleviation of this disorder (Feany and Bender, 2000; Haass and Kahle, 2000).

ease turned out to have a defective copy of another gene, named *parkin* (Lucking et al., 2000).

The proteins that these genes produce, α-synuclein and parkin, normally interact with each other (Shimura et al., 2001). One theory is that defects in either protein can lead to abnormal accumulation of the α-synuclein into clumps called *Lewy bodies* in the dopaminergic cells. In the noninherited cases of Parkinson's, other factors such as toxins or brain injury may accelerate the formation of Lewy bodies that kill the dopaminergic cells. Thus, it might be possible someday to prevent Parkinson's by developing drugs to stop or reverse the accumulation of α-synuclein.

CLINICAL ISSUE

For years there was no treatment for Parkinson's disease, but a pharmacological therapy emerged from a discovery in the late 1960s. This treatment was the administration of a precursor to dopamine to enhance the dopamine levels of surviving cells. The substance, called L-dopa, markedly reduces symptoms in patients with Parkinson's; notably, it decreases tremors and increases the speed of movements.

Although L-dopa can reverse some symptoms of Parkinson's disease, nerve cell degeneration in the substantia nigra is relentless. Because the cell bodies in the brainstem degenerate, dopamine-containing terminals in the caudate nucleus and putamen also disappear. Eventually, too few dopamine-containing neurons remain in the substantia nigra to be influenced by the intake of L-dopa.

Electrical stimulation of particular sites within the basal ganglia can reduce the symptoms of Parkinson's disease, but such treatment requires the surgical implantation of electrodes into the brain. The electrical stimulation brings only temporary relief, so it must be repeated; but evidence suggests that the stimulation can also extend the effectiveness of L-dopa therapy (Nutt et al., 2001).

In the 1980s, researchers began to use transplants of dopamine-containing cells as a form of treatment in humans. The refinement of techniques led to the transplantation of human fetal cells, including stem cells, from the brainstem. Direct injection of these cells into the corpus striatum (Figure 11.21) has been reported to produce remarkable symptom relief in some patients with Parkinson's (Peschanski et al., 1994).

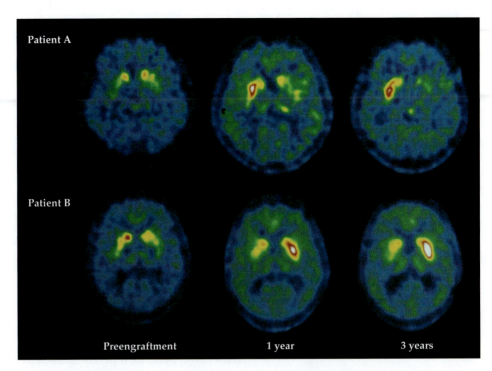

11.21 Brain Implants to Treat Parkinson's Disease The injection of human fetal cells into patients with Parkinson's disease led to increased dopamine receptors (coded in yellow and red) in the striatum 1 and 3 years later, as these PET scans reveal. (From Lindvall et al., 1994.)

Such transplants appear to have helped patients who suffer from drug-induced Parkinson's disease (see Box 11.2). In the first double-blind placebo-controlled clinical study of this procedure, the fetal cells produced dopamine in the brains of patients and improved the condition of some patients, but some other patients with grafts became afflicted with severe involuntary movements (Freed et al., 2001). Still, one analysis of the literature concluded that the transplants were effective in most patients (Isacson et al., 2001), so debate about this procedure continues.

An aspect of Parkinson's disease that may be independent of the degree of motor impairment is the appearance of cognitive and emotional changes. Some patients show marked cognitive decline during the course of their illness (Cummings, 1995). Depression in patients with Parkinson's is also common; some researchers have attributed such depression to the consequences of diminished movement capabilities and the general stress of such incapacity. Other researchers have attributed it to a diminished responsiveness of the serotonergic system (Sano et al., 1991).

Huntington's disease is characterized by excessive movement caused by deterioration of the basal ganglia

Whereas damage to the basal ganglia in Parkinson's disease *slows* movement, other kinds of basal ganglia disorders cause *excessive* movement. An example of the latter type was reported by George Huntington, a physician whose only publication (1872) described a strange motor affliction. He correctly deduced that this disorder was inherited, passed from generation to generation. **Huntington's disease** is transmitted by a single dominant gene, so each child of a victim has a 50% chance of developing the disease.

The first symptoms of this disease are subtle behavioral changes: clumsiness, and twitches in the fingers and face. Subtlety is rapidly lost as the illness progresses; a continuing stream of involuntary jerks engulfs the entire body. Aimless movements of the eyes, jerky leg movements, and writhing of the body turn the routine activities of the day into insurmountable obstacles. Worse yet, as the disease progresses,

(a) Control

Caudate nucleus   Putamen

(b) Patient with Huntington's disease

Lateral ventricles

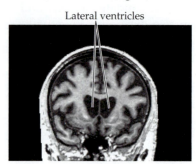

11.22 Neuropathology in Huntington's Disease   Compared with the control (a), coronal MRI section through the brain of a patient suffering from Huntington's disease (b) shows marked enlargement of the lateral ventricles, caused by atrophy of the neighboring caudate nucleus and putamen. Note also the shrunken cortical gyri and enlarged sulci of the patient compared with those of the brain of a healthy person. (MRI images courtesy of Terry L. Jernigan and C. Fennema Notestine.)

Nancy Wexler

GENES AND BEHAVIOR

marked behavioral changes include intellectual deterioration, depression, and in a minority of patients, a psychotic state that resembles schizophrenia. In some patients, cognitive and emotional changes may appear many years before obvious motor impairments do (Wexler et al., 1991). Huntington's disease usually develops over a period of 15 to 20 years.

The neuroanatomical basis of this disorder is the profound, progressive destruction of the basal ganglia, especially the caudate nucleus and the putamen (Figure 11.22), as well as impairment of the cerebral cortex. Several types of cells are particularly vulnerable, including neurons that contain the transmitter GABA. Acetylcholine-containing neurons are relatively spared.

Because the symptoms of Huntington's disease usually first appear between the ages of 30 and 45 years, many victims have children before knowing whether they will ultimately contract the disease. Until quite recently this uncertainty meant continuing generations of ravaged individuals. After losing her mother to this disease, psychologist Nancy Wexler organized a team of investigators that prepared a pedigree map of more than 10,000 individuals, including more than 300 patients with Huntington's disease, from a community in Venezuela where Huntington's disease is relatively common. The investigators were able to pinpoint the gene, on chromosome 4, that is responsible for the disorder (Gusella and MacDonald, 1993).

The gene is called *HD* (for *Huntington's disease*) and the protein that it encodes is called **huntingtin.** Within the *HD* gene is a series of three nucleotides—CAG—repeated over and over (see the appendix). This **trinucleotide repeat** can vary in length; if there are fewer than 30 repeats, no symptoms appear, but if there are 38 or more CAG trinucleotide repeats in the *HD* gene, the person will develop Huntington's disease (A. B. Young, 1993). Because the nucleotide triplet CAG codes for the amino acid glutamine, the huntingtin protein of people with the disorder has an overly long stretch of polyglutamines. One theory is that the polyglutamines are "sticky" and cause huntingtin proteins to attach to each other and to other proteins, somehow gumming up important cellular processes (Dunah et al., 2002; Panov et al., 2002).

The longer the string of glutamines in the huntingtin protein, the earlier in life Huntington's disease symptoms commence. When the repeats are carried by the mother, the gene with its CAG repeats is copied faithfully in eggs and transmitted to the offspring, but in the production of sperm, a father may transmit more or fewer repeats than he himself carries. Unfortunately, it is more common for the father to transmit more repeats than fewer repeats. Thus in some cases an asymptomatic father may transmit Huntington's disease to his offspring.

How does carrying a copy of *HD* with extended repeats cause degeneration of the striatum and the symptoms of Huntington's disease? One hypothesis was that only striatal cells normally make huntingtin, so only these cells die when it is defective. But huntingtin, whether normal or defective, is produced not just in the striatum, but throughout the brain, by both neurons and glial cells, as well as in muscles, liver, and testes (A. B. Young, 1993). Thus we still don't know why the defective huntingtin kills only striatal cells. Transgenic mice expressing the defective human *HD* gene develop a progressive syndrome with many of the characteristics of Huntington's disease (Mangiarini et al., 1996; Ona et al., 1999).

The example of Huntington's disease, with its increased movements, demonstrates the major role that inhibition plays in normal motor control. Without adequate inhibition, a person is compelled to perform a variety of unwanted movements. We saw in Figure 11.1*b* that patients with Huntington's disease are less accurate in reaching for a target. People whose genetic tests reveal that they will develop Huntington's disease show some impairment in accuracy of reaching several years before apparent onset of the disease (M. A. Smith et al., 2000).

Cerebellar damage leads to many motor impairments

Because the cerebellum modulates many aspects of motor performance, it is not surprising that its impairment leads to many abnormalities of behavior. These symptoms permit an examiner to identify with considerable accuracy the part of the cerebellum that is involved (Dichgans, 1984).

A relatively common lesion of the cerebellum results from a tumor that usually occurs in childhood. The tumor damages a part of the cerebellum—the vermis—that has close connections to the vestibular system and therefore causes disturbances of balance. The patient walks as if drunk and has difficulty even standing erect. Often patients afflicted in this way place their feet widely apart in an attempt to maintain balance.

Normally the world seems to hold still as we walk because movements of our eyes compensate for movements of the head. Some patients with lesions of the cerebellum, however, see the world around them move whenever they move their heads. If normal subjects wear prismatic lenses, they learn to compensate for the new relationship between movement of the eyes and perceived change of direction. Patients with lesions of the vestibular part of the cerebellum cannot make this adjustment, suggesting that this part of the cerebellum is important for such learning.

Some patients suffering from alcoholism show degeneration of the cortex of the anterior lobe of the cerebellum. When this region is damaged, abnormalities of gait and posture are common. The legs show **ataxia** (loss of coordination), but the arms do not. Loss of coordination and swaying indicate that the patient is not compensating normally for the usual deviations of position and posture.

Difficulties of motor coordination are common after damage to the lateral aspects of the cerebellum. One such problem is called **decomposition of movement** because gestures are broken up into individual segments instead of being executed smoothly. A patient who had this problem after damage to his right cerebellar hemisphere described his condition in this way: "The movements of my left hand are done subconsciously, but I have to think out each movement of my right arm. I come to a dead stop in turning and have to think it out before I start again." Thus the cerebellum is needed not to initiate acts or to plan the sequence of movements, but to facilitate activation and to "package" movements economically (V. B. Brooks, 1984).

We Can Trace a Choice Response from Input to Output

Now that we have reviewed the sensory and motor systems, it will be helpful to consider an example that includes sensory input, central processing, and a choice response. In Chapter 3 we considered the sequence and timing of events in a simple response, the knee jerk reflex (see Figure 3.16). Now let's consider the sequence and timing of events in a more complicated situation, in which a person is presented

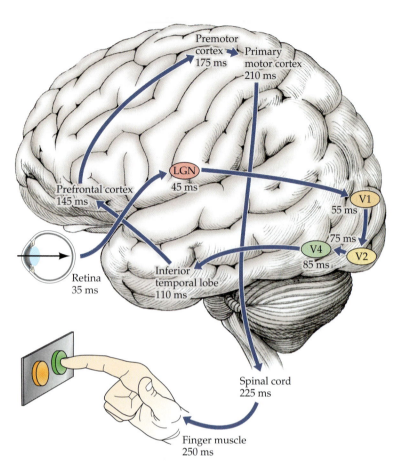

11.23 Input to Output The sequence and timing of brain events, from the presentation of visual stimuli to a discrimination response. Notice that it takes about 110 ms for the sensory system to recognize the stimulus (somewhere in the inferior temporal lobe), and about 35 ms more for that information to reach the prefrontal cortex, which then takes about 30 ms to determine which button to push. Then it takes about 75 ms for the movement to be executed (i.e., the time elapsed between the point at which the signal from the prefrontal cortex arrives in the premotor cortex and the point at which the finger pushes the button). LGN, lateral geniculate nucleus; V1, primary visual cortex; V2 and V4, extrastriate visual areas.

with two visual stimuli and has to signal, by pressing one of two buttons, whether the stimuli belong to the same category.

Reaction times in such an experiment averaged about 310 ms. A review of research suggests the sequence and timing of events at several stations in the nervous system for this task (Figure 11.23) (Thorpe and Fabre-Thorpe, 2001). The time shown at each station in Figure 11.22 is a typical average latency from the start of the stimulus. Activity proceeds from the primary visual cortex through the ventral *what* pathway (recall that this is the visual pathway that was damaged in patient D.F., impairing her ability to recognize objects; see Chapter 10) to prefrontal cortex, then through premotor and primary motor cortex, down to the spinal motoneurons, and out to the finger muscles.

Summary

Refer to the **Learning Biological Psychology CD** for study questions, animations, activities, and other study aids.

1. Two broad categories of motor activity—movements and acts—are divided into subcategories. Reflexes are movements; more-complex motor behaviors are acts. Complex acts suggest the existence of a motor plan.

2. Reflexes are patterns of relatively simple and stereotyped movements that are elicited by stimulation of sensory receptors; their amplitude is proportional to the intensity of the stimulation.

3. Many reflexes are controlled by closed-loop, negative feedback circuits. Some behaviors are so rapid, however, that they are controlled by open-loop systems; that is, the pattern is preset and does not respond to feedback.

4. Motor control systems are organized into a hierarchy that consists of the skeletal system and associated muscles, the spinal cord, the brainstem, and various parts of the brain, including the primary and nonprimary motor cortices, the cerebellum, and the basal ganglia.

5. Muscles around a joint work in pairs. Antagonists work in opposition; synergists work together.

6. Smooth muscles, such as those in the stomach, are under involuntary control; striated muscles are under voluntary control.

7. Action potentials travel over motor nerve fibers (axons from motoneurons) and reach muscle fibers at the neuromuscular junction, releasing acetylcholine to trigger muscle contraction.

8. The final common pathway for impulses to skeletal muscles consists of motoneurons whose cell bodies in vertebrates are located in the ventral horn of the spinal cord and within the brainstem. The motoneurons receive impulses from a variety of sources, including sensory input from the dorsal spinal roots, other spinal cord neurons, and descending fibers from the brain.

9. Muscle spindles and Golgi tendon organs—sensory receptors in the muscles and tendons, respectively—transmit a wide range of information about muscle activities to the central nervous system. The sensitivity of the muscle spindle can be adjusted by efferent impulses that control the length of the spindle. This adjustment allows flexible control of posture and movement.

10. When a muscle is stretched, a reflex circuit often causes contraction, which works to restore the muscle to its original length; this response is called the stretch reflex. The stretch of the muscle is detected by muscle spindles.

11. The pyramidal (corticospinal) tract is especially well developed in primates and is involved mainly in controlling fine movements of the extremities. Its fibers originate mainly in the primary motor cortex (M1) and adjacent regions, and they run directly to spinal motoneurons or to interneurons in the spinal cord. Nonprimary motor cortex helps control the sequence of movements.

12. Although the centers of representation of body parts are separated in an orderly fashion in M1, the subregional organization is broadly distributed, and each M1 neuron influences many muscles. M1 is involved in learning motor responses and in cognitive processes such as encoding serial order.

13. Control of movements involves the collective activation of a large distributed population of neurons in the different cortical motor areas.

14. Extrapyramidal brain regions that modulate movement include the basal ganglia (caudate nucleus, putamen, and globus pallidus), some major brainstem nuclei (substantia nigra, thalamic nuclei, and red nucleus), and the cerebellum.

15. Central pattern generators, such as endogenous oscillators, are responsible for generating rhythmic patterns of behavior in locomotion.

16. Movement disorders can result from impairment at any of several levels of the motor system: muscles, neuromuscular junctions, motoneurons, spinal cord, brainstem, cerebral cortex, basal ganglia, or cerebellum. The characteristics of these disorders depend on and permit diagnosis of the locus of impairment.

Recommended Reading

Georgopoulos, A. P. (1997). Voluntary movement: Computational principles and neural mechanisms. In M. D. Rugg (Ed.), *Cognitive neuroscience* (pp. 131–168). Cambridge, MA: MIT Press.

Purves, D., Augustine, G. J., Fitzpatrick, D., Katz, L., et al. (Eds.). (2004). *Neuroscience* (3rd ed.). Sunderland, MA: Sinauer Associates. (See Unit III: Movement and Its Central Control, Chapters 16–21.)

Sanes, J. N., and Donoghue, J. P. (2000). Plasticity and primary motor cortex. *Annual Review of Neuroscience, 23,* 393–415.

Stein, P. S. G., Grillner, S., and Selverston, A. I. (1998). *Neurons, networks, and motor behavior.* Cambridge, MA: MIT Press.

Vogel, S. (2002). *Prime mover: A natural history of muscle.* New York: Norton.

IV Regulation and Behavior

So far, we have reviewed the basic structure and function of the nervous system, the specialized organs that gather information about the environment, and the specialized motor systems that allow us to respond to that information. Which response should we make? The number of possible responses is infinite, but over the course of evolution, natural selection has shaped adaptive responses to particular situations. A hungry person should seek out and consume food; an animal that has lost water should drink; males and females should seek each other out in order to reproduce.

The brain plays a pivotal role in the decision about which response to make. To some extent we can identify the different brain regions that are involved in deciding whether to reproduce (Chapter 12); eat, drink, and seek shelter (Chapter 13); and sleep (Chapter 14). In each of these cases, we catalog the situations that usually elicit a particular response from members of a particular species, and we ask which brain regions are required for the response to be elicited, which brain regions are activated by the situation, and how various responses are integrated. As we'll see, many brain regions are involved in each of these responses. The involvement and integration of multiple brain regions is a recurring theme in this book, and in modern neuroscience in general.

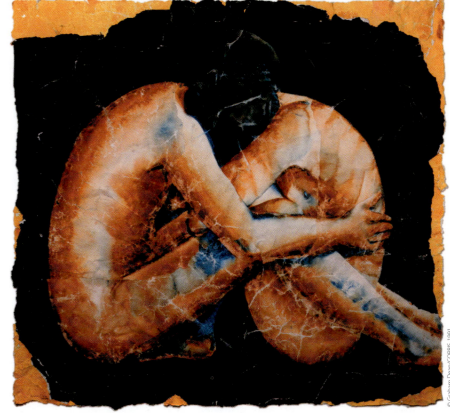

Graham Dean, *The Couple*

© Graham Dean/CORBIS, 1991

12

Sex: Evolutionary, Hormonal, and Neural Bases

Genitals and Gender: What Makes Us Male and Female?

Few aspects of human biology are as impressive and humbling as the making of a baby; it is a developmental ballet of staggering complexity and critical timing. With innumerable processes that must unfold perfectly and in precisely the right order, it is a marvel that in the great majority of cases gestation proceeds without a hitch. And inevitably, there are times when a crucial part of the program is derailed along the way, and a baby is born with a heartbreaking congenital deformity.

Such is the case with cloacal exstrophy, a developmental defect that affects about 1 in 400,000 live births. As a consequence of abnormal development of the pelvic organs, a genetic male with this condition is typically born with normal testes but lacking a penis. The parents of such an infant are faced with a terrible dilemma: Is it better to leave the child as it is and try to raise it as a boy without a penis, despite the emotional costs of the deformity? Or would the outcome be better if the child were unambiguously assigned to the female gender, underwent early surgery to remove the testes and fashion female-looking genitals, and were raised as a girl? Arguments for each course of action boil down to different opinions about the extent to which our gender identity is shaped through nurturing and socialization, rather than biological factors. What is the best choice?

Sexual behaviors are almost as diverse as the species that employ them. But in every case, males and females must produce a specific set of behaviors, in a precise and intricately coordinated sequence, in order to reproduce successfully. In this chapter we discuss our knowledge of these behaviors and their physiological underpinnings in three main sections:

1. First we'll review sexual behaviors, which include the sex act itself, copulation.
2. Next, the bewildering variety of sexual behaviors across species (and within our own species) will lead us to consider how and why sexual reproduction evolved in the first place. We'll find that sexual reproduction eventually gave rise to two distinct sexes, which can sometimes be remarkably divergent in structure and behavior.
3. The evolution of two different sexes will lead us to the final topic: sexual differentiation, the process by which an individual's body and brain develop in a male or female fashion.

SEXUAL BEHAVIOR

We wish we could explain exactly why and how humans and other animals engage in the three Cs—courting, copulating, and cohabiting—but very little practical knowledge of such matters exists, as James Thurber and E. B. White lamented in 1929 (Figure 12.1). You may feel that there has been little improvement in the years since. Two barriers have blocked our understanding of sexual behavior: (1) a deep-seated reluctance within our culture to disseminate knowledge about sexual behavior and (2) the remarkable variety of sexual behaviors in existence.

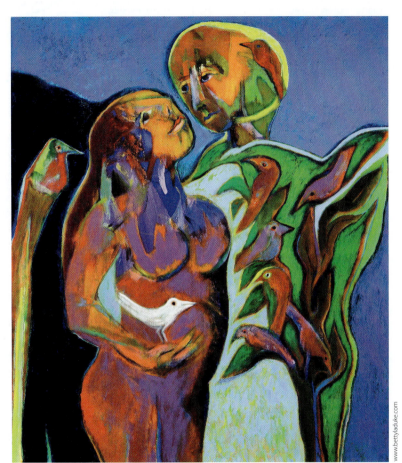

Betty LaDuke, *Oregon, Summer Joy*, 1972.

12.1 Sex According to Thurber and White In *Is Sex Necessary?* (1929), James Thurber and E. B. White explain, "It is customary to illustrate sexology chapters with a cross section of the human body. The authors have chosen to substitute in its place a chart of the North Atlantic, showing airplane routes. The authors realize that this will be of no help to the sex novice, but neither is a cross section of the human body." (If you insist on a cross section, see Figure 12.8.)

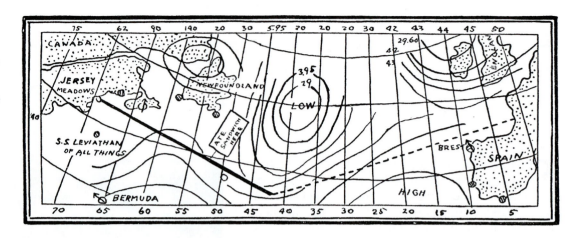

Reproductive Behavior Can Be Divided into Four Stages

There are four easily identifiable stages of reproductive behavior: (1) sexual attraction, (2) appetitive behavior, (3) copulation, and (4) postcopulatory behavior.

Sexual attraction is the first stage in bringing the male and female together (Figure 12.2). In many species, sexual attraction is closely synchronized with physiological readiness to reproduce. But it is important to recognize that, for a wide variety of species, attraction and sexual response are also strongly shaped by learned associations, varying from one individual to the next on the basis of experience (Pfaus et al., 2001).

Experimentally, an individual's attractiveness is gauged by observation of the responses of potential mates—how rapidly they approach, how hard they work to gain access, and so on. By manipulating the appearance of individuals, we can deduce which special features are most attractive. For example, males of many primate species are strongly attracted by the sight of a female's "sex skin," which swells when the ovaries are secreting estrogens. Most male mammals are attracted by particular female odors, which also tend to reflect estrogen levels.

Because estrogen secretion is associated with the release of eggs, these mechanisms tend to synchronize female sexual attractiveness with peak fertility. Of course, the female may find a particular male to be unattractive and refuse to mate with him. Although apparent rape has been described in some nonhuman species, including such close relatives of ours as the orangutans (Maggioncalda and Sapolsky, 2002), for most species copulation is not possible without the female's active cooperation.

If the animals are mutually attracted, they may progress to the next stage: **appetitive behaviors** (behaviors that establish, maintain, or promote sexual interaction). A female mammal that engages in such behaviors is said to be **proceptive:** She may approach males, remain close to them, or show alternating approach and retreat behavior. Proceptive female rats typically exhibit stereotyped "ear wiggling" and a hopping and darting gait in order to induce mounting by a male. Male appetitive behaviors usually consist of staying near the female. In many mammals the male may sniff around the female's face and vagina. Male birds may engage in elaborate songs or nest-building behaviors.

If both animals display appetitive behaviors, they may progress to the third stage of reproduction: **copulation,** also known as *coitus.* In many vertebrates, including all mammals, copulation involves one or more **intromissions,** in which the male inserts his penis into the female's vagina, followed by a variable amount of copulatory stimulation (usually through pelvic thrusting). When stimulation reaches a threshold level, the male ejaculates sperm-bearing **semen** into the female; the length of time and quantity of stimulation that are required vary greatly between species (and between individuals).

After one bout of copulation the animals will not mate again for a period of time, which is called the **refractory phase.** The refractory phase varies from minutes to months, depending on the species and circumstances. Many animals show a shorter refractory phase if they are provided with a new partner—a phenomenon known as the **Coolidge effect.**

The female often appears to be the one to choose whether or not copulation will take place; when she is willing to copulate she is said to be **sexually receptive,** in heat, or in **estrus.** In some species the female may show proceptive behaviors days before she will participate in copulation itself (see Figure 12.2). In most (but not all) species, females are receptive only when mating is likely to produce offspring. Usually this is when the female is ovulating or otherwise maximally fertile. Most species are seasonal breeders, with females that are receptive only during the breeding season; and some, like salmon, octopuses, and cicadas, reproduce only once, at the end of life.

Finally, the fourth stage of reproductive behavior consists of **postcopulatory behaviors.** These behaviors are especially varied across species. In some mammals—dogs and southern grasshopper mice, for example—the male's penis swells so much after ejaculation that he can't remove it from the female for a while (10 to 15 minutes in dogs), and the animals are said to be in a **copulatory lock** (Dewsbury, 1972). (Despite wild stories you may have heard or read, humans never experience copulatory lock, not even with VIAGRA.) Postcopulatory behaviors also include parental behaviors in many vertebrate species.

Copulation brings gametes together for reproduction

Successful reproduction requires that male and female **gametes**—**sperm** and **ovum** (plural *ova*), or **egg**—make contact and fuse in the process known as **fertilization.** If all goes well, the fertilized ovum, termed a **zygote,** will divide and grow to make a new individual.

For many vertebrates, fertilization takes place outside the female's body—a process known as **external fertilization.** In most fishes and frogs, for example, males and females release their gametes in water, where fertilization takes place. In some fishes, such as guppies and swordtails, the male uses a modified fin to direct his sperm to swim into the female's body, where the sperm fertilize the female's eggs. Such **internal fertilization,** a feature of all mammals, birds, and reptiles, allows the zygotes to remain moist even in a desert, and the resulting offspring may gain nutrients from the mother.

Birds use internal fertilization, even though most male birds do not have a penis. Semen is discharged and eggs are laid through the **cloaca** (plural *cloacae*), the same

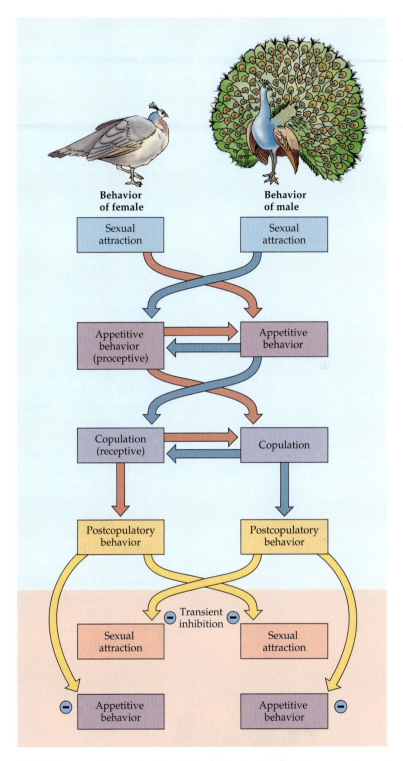

12.2 Stages of Reproductive Behavior Interaction between male and female partners in sexual reproduction is extensive, progressing in four stages: sexual attraction, appetitive behavior, copulation, and postcopulatory behavior. The postcopulatory phase (pink background) includes a temporary decrease in the sexual attractiveness of the partner and inhibition of appetitive behavior. (After Beach, 1977.)

TABLE 12.1 *Types of Sexual Reproduction in Animals*

Type	Examples of animals that follow this pattern
EXTERNAL FERTILIZATION (requires aquatic environment)	Many invertebrates, fishes, amphibians
INTERNAL FERTILIZATION	
Oviparity	Insects, birds, many reptiles, monotremes
Viviparity	Some fishes, reptiles, all mammals except monotremes

passage through which birds eliminate wastes. The female squats low; the male mounts her back, pushes his cloaca against hers, and squirts in the semen. After the sperm swim up the reproductive tract and fertilize an ovum, the female bird assembles rich nutrients and a tough shell around the zygote, which she later extrudes as an egg. Species that lay eggs are **oviparous** (from the Latin *ovum,* "egg," and *parere,* "to bring forth"), contrasting with **viviparous** species (the Latin *vivus* means "alive"), in which more-mature, live young are born.

All mammals use internal fertilization, and all but a few species (the monotremes—that is, the echidnas and the platypus of Australia—which are oviparous) give birth to live young. Table 12.1 summarizes the different types of sexual reproduction.

Copulation in rats is but a brief interlude

Like most other rodents, rats do not engage in lengthy courtship, nor do the partners tend to remain together after copulation. Rats are attracted to each other largely through odors. Females are spontaneous ovulators; that is, even when left alone they ovulate every 4 to 5 days. For a few hours during each cycle, the female seeks out a male and displays proceptive behaviors, and both animals produce vocalizations at frequencies too high for humans to detect but audible to each other.

These behaviors prompt the male to mount the female from the rear, grasp her flanks with his forelegs, and rhythmically thrust his hips. If she is receptive, the female adopts a stereotyped posture called **lordosis** (Figure 12.3) in which her rump is elevated and her tail is deflected to one side, allowing intromission. Once intromission has been achieved, the male rat makes a single deep thrust and then springs back off the female. During the next 6 to 7 minutes the male and female orchestrate seven to nine such intromissions; then, instead of springing away, the male raises the front half of his body up for a second or two while he ejaculates. Finally, he falls backward off the female.

After copulation the male and female separately engage in grooming their genitalia, and the male pays little attention to the female for the next 5 minutes or so, until, often in response to the female's proceptive behaviors, the two engage in another bout of intromissions and ejaculation. This pattern of multiple intromissions before ejaculation is an obligatory part of rat fertility: Only after repeated mechanical stimulation of the cervix and vagina will the female's brain cause the release of hormones to support pregnancy. In this instance, then, the behavior of one rat (the male) directly affects the hormonal secretions of its mate.

In other rodent species, intromission may be accompanied by more-prolonged thrusting, or the penis may swell to form a copulatory lock. The northern pygmy mouse has only a single ejaculation during a mating session (talk about pressure!). In some rodent species a male and a female live together before and long after copulation; such animals are said to form **pair bonds.**

Hormones play an important role in rat mating behaviors. Testosterone mediates the male's interest in copulation: If he is **castrated** (has his testes removed), he will stop ejaculating within a few weeks and will eventually stop mounting receptive females. Although testosterone disappears from the bloodstream within a few hours after castration, the hormone's effects on the nervous system take several days to dissipate. Treating a castrated male with testosterone eventually restores mating behavior; if the administration of testosterone is then stopped, the mating behavior fades again. This is an example of a hormone exerting an **activational effect:** The hormone

12.3 Copulation in Rats The raised rump and deflected tail of the female (the lordosis posture) make intromission possible. (After Barnett, 1975.)

12.4 Androgens Permit Male Copulatory Behavior
Although androgens have an effect, hormone level does not completely determine the amount of male sexual behavior, even in rodents. In the experiment whose results are shown here, after castration caused the sex activity of male guinea pigs to decrease, the same amount of testosterone was given to each animal, beginning at week 26. Each group returned to the level of sexual activity it had exhibited before castration. Doubling the amount of hormone at week 36 did not increase the mating activity of any group. (After Grunt and Young, 1953.)

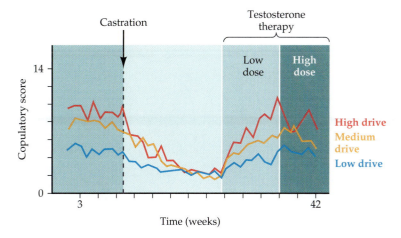

transiently influences behavior. In normal development, the rise of androgen secretion at puberty activates masculine behavior in males.

Interestingly, although individual male rats and guinea pigs differ considerably in the vigor with which they mate with a receptive female, blood levels of testosterone clearly are *not* responsible for these differences. For one thing, animals displaying different levels of sexual vigor do not show systematic differences in blood levels of testosterone. Furthermore, when these males are castrated and subsequently all treated with exactly the same doses of testosterone, their precastration differences in sexual activity persist (Figure 12.4).

Not only that, but it also turns out that a very small amount of testosterone—one-tenth the amount normally produced by the animals—is enough to fully maintain the mating behavior of male rats. Thus, since all rats make more testosterone than is required to maintain their copulatory behavior, some unknown factor must be responsible for individual differences in mating activity.

Estrogens secreted at the beginning of the 4- to 5-day **ovulatory cycle** facilitate the proceptive behavior of the female rat, and the subsequent production of progesterone increases proceptive behavior and activates receptivity (Figure 12.5). An adult female whose ovaries have been removed will show neither proceptive nor receptive behaviors. However, 2 days of estrogen treatment followed by a single injection of progesterone will, about 6 hours later, make the female rat proceptive and receptive for a few hours. Only the correct combination of estrogens and progesterone will fully activate copulatory behaviors in female rats. This is therefore another example of an activational effect of gonadal steroids.

The Neural Circuitry of the Brain Regulates Reproductive Behavior

Although most of our knowledge of the neural circuitry of reproductive behavior comes from rats, steroid receptors are consistently found in specific brain regions across a wide variety of vertebrate species. Steroid-sensitive regions include the isocortex, brainstem nuclei, medial amygdala, hippocampus, and many others. And as we'll see, steroid effects in the hypothalamus play a particularly important role in regulating copulatory behavior.

Steroids act on the hypothalamus to promote female receptivity

Donald Pfaff (1968, 1997) and colleagues have exploited the steroid sensitivity of the lordosis response to map out the neural centers

12.5 The Ovulatory Cycle of Rats Changes in hormone levels indicate when the female rat will display lordosis. This behavioral receptivity, or estrus, occurs after the animal has been exposed first to estrogens, then to progesterone. In spontaneous ovulators such as rats, the cycle of hormone secretion repeats unless eggs are fertilized. In that case, the embryos secrete hormones to interrupt the cycle and maintain pregnancy.

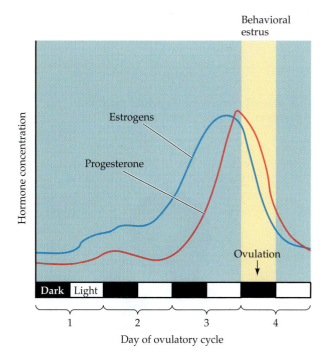

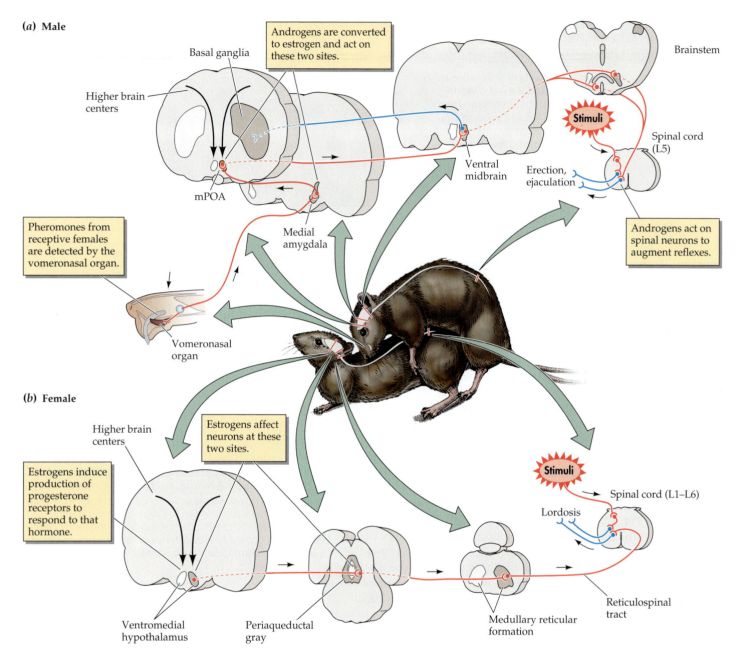

(a) Male

Basal ganglia

Higher brain centers

Androgens are converted to estrogen and act on these two sites.

Brainstem

mPOA

Ventral midbrain

Erection, ejaculation

Spinal cord (L5)

Stimuli

Androgens act on spinal neurons to augment reflexes.

Pheromones from receptive females are detected by the vomeronasal organ.

Medial amygdala

Vomeronasal organ

(b) Female

Higher brain centers

Estrogens affect neurons at these two sites.

Stimuli

Spinal cord (L1–L6)

Lordosis

Estrogens induce production of progesterone receptors to respond to that hormone.

Reticulospinal tract

Ventromedial hypothalamus

Periaqueductal gray

Medullary reticular formation

12.6 Neural Circuits for Reproduction in Rodents (Part *b* after Pfaff, 1980.)

Donald Pfaff

that mediate this behavior (Figure 12.6*b*). Using steroid autoradiography (see Box 2.3), investigators identified hypothalamic nuclei containing high densities of estrogen- and progesterone-sensitive neurons. In particular, the **ventromedial hypothalamus (VMH)** was found to be crucial for lordosis because lesions there abolish the response. Furthermore, tiny implants of estradiol in the brain can induce receptivity in females, but only if they are placed in the VMH region (Lisk, 1962; Pleim and Barfield, 1988).

One action of estrogen treatment is to increase the size of the dendritic trees of VMH neurons (Meisel and Luttrell, 1990). Another important action of estrogen is to stimulate the production of progesterone receptors so that the animal will respond to that hormone. Activated progesterone receptors in turn increase the production of proteins that must be present for lordosis to result (Mani et al., 2000).

The VMH sends axons to the **periaqueductal gray** region of the midbrain, where again, lesions greatly diminish lordosis. The periaqueductal gray neurons project to the **medullary reticular formation,** which in turn projects to the spinal cord via the **reticulospinal tract.** In the spinal cord the sensory information provided by the mounting male will now evoke the motor response of lordosis. Thus the role of the VMH is to monitor steroid hormone concentrations and, at the right time in the ovulatory cycle, activate a multisynaptic pathway that induces the spinal cord to contract back muscles, producing a lordosis response that is otherwise absent (Pfaff, 1997). Figure 12.6*b*, which is based on many studies, schematically represents this neural pathway and identifies the steroid-responsive components.

Androgens activate a neural system for male reproductive behavior

Steroid hormones also activate male copulatory behavior in rodents, and again the sites of steroid action provide important clues revealing the neural circuitry involved. The hypothalamic **medial preoptic area** (**mPOA**) is chock-full of steroid-sensitive neurons, and lesions of the mPOA abolish male copulatory behavior in a wide variety of vertebrate species (Meisel and Sachs, 1994). Furthermore, mating can be reinstated in castrated males by small implants of androgens in the mPOA but not in other brain regions.

Neurons in the mPOA send their axons to the ventral midbrain via the medial forebrain bundle. From the ventral midbrain, information goes to the basal ganglia (presumably to coordinate mounting behaviors) and then, via a multisynaptic pathway that involves several brainstem mechanisms, to the spinal cord (Hamson and Watson, 2004). The spinal cord, in turn, mediates various reflexes of copulation. Furthermore, a specialized set of lumbar spinothalamic (LSt) neurons acts as an ejaculation generator (Truitt and Coolen, 2002; Truitt et al., 2003); because of the location of the reflex circuits and ejaculation generator in the spinal cord, individuals with damage at higher levels of the spinal cord often remain capable of copulation and ejaculation.

We can gather information about male copulatory neural systems also by investigating a sensory system that activates male arousal in rodents—the vomeronasal system. The **vomeronasal organ** (see Chapter 9) consists of specialized receptor cells near but separate from the olfactory epithelium. These sensory cells detect chemicals called **pheromones** (see Chapters 5 and 9), which are released from one individual and detected by another. Vomeronasal receptor cells send electrical signals to the accessory olfactory bulb in the brain.

Receptive female rats release pheromones that can be detected by the male rat's vomeronasal organ and arouse the male, as evidenced by penile erections. The vomeronasal information from the accessory olfactory bulb projects to the **medial amygdala,** which depends on adult circulating levels of sex steroids to maintain a masculine form and function (Cooke et al., 1999, 2003). Lesions here will abolish penile erections in response to receptive females (Kondo et al., 1997). The medial amygdala in turn sends axons to the mPOA. So the mPOA appears to integrate hormonal and sensory information such as pheromones, and to coordinate the motor patterns of copulation. Figure 12.6*a* summarizes the neural circuitry for male rat copulatory behavior.

We will see later that androgens, acting perhaps on the hypothalamus and/or the medial amygdala, activate sexual arousal in humans as well.

Pheromones Guide Reproductive Behavior in Many Species

When steroid hormones from the gonads affect the brain to activate mating behavior, the activation is not absolute; individuals are simply more likely to engage in mating behaviors when gonadal steroid levels are adequate. This activation can be thought of as communication between the gonads and the brain: By producing steroids to make gametes, the gonads also inform the brain that the body is ready to mate. This signaling takes place inside the individual, but hormones can also provide information *between* animals.

For example, during ovulation, female goldfish produce a hormone called *F prostaglandin*. Some F prostaglandin escapes the female's body and passes through

EVOLUTION AT WORK

12.7 Prairie Voles

Alfred Kinsey

the water to a male. The F prostaglandin is detected by the male and stimulates his mating behavior (Sorensen and Goetz, 1993). The most likely scenario for the evolution of this relationship is that long ago, females released F prostaglandin only as a by-product of ovulation, but because the presence of the hormone conveyed important information about the female's condition, natural selection favored males who detected the hormone and began courting in response to the signal. Even very simple unicellular organisms, such as yeasts, prepare each other for mating by releasing and detecting chemicals (S. Fields, 1990).

Pheromones in the urine of male mice can also accelerate puberty in young females (Drickamer, 1992; M. A. Price and Vandenbergh, 1992) and can halt pregnancy in mature females (Brennan et al., 1990). Female mice can even identify an individual male by the particular mix of pheromones in his urine. When prairie voles mate (Figure 12.7), the female is exposed to pheromones from her mate's mouth and urine. If she is then isolated and has urine from that male or any other male applied to her snout, pregnancy will be blocked; the fetuses are resorbed by the female, and she is soon ready to mate again. Yet if the female remains with the original male from copulation on, pregnancy continues, apparently because the female is careful not to apply her mate's urine to her vomeronasal organ (Smale, 1988). Terminating pregnancy and absorbing the fetuses in the presence of a new male may be an attempt to make the best of a bad situation: If her original mate is gone, a female may be better off beginning a new litter with a different male.

Pheromones can also convey important information about reproductive status between individuals of the same sex. During *musth,* an annual period of increased sexual activity and intermale aggression, male elephants secrete a pheromone-laden liquid from specialized glands located on their temples, just behind their eyes. Among pubescent males, these secretions have a honeylike odor; in fact, they contain substances chemically similar to bee pheromones, and sometimes even attract bees. As male elephants mature, they produce a more malodorous liquid, containing increasing concentrations of a pheromone named *frontalin.* By broadcasting their low rank, and avoiding mature-smelling males, the honey-scented juveniles avoid needless aggressive encounters. And the secretions of the older bulls not only signal their rank to each other, but also appear to attract females that are ready to ovulate (L. E. Rasmussen and Greenwood, 2003; L. E. Rasmussen et al., 2002).

The Hallmark of Human Sexual Behavior Is Diversity

For as long as humans have written, they have written about sex. But little scientific information was available about human sexual behavior until the 1940s, when biology professor Alfred Kinsey began to ask friends and colleagues about their sexual histories. Kinsey constructed a standardized set of questions and procedures to obtain information for samples of the U.S. population categorized by sex, age, religion, and education. Eventually he and his collaborators were able to publish extensive surveys (based on tens of thousands of respondents) of the sexual behavior of American males (Kinsey et al., 1948) and females (Kinsey et al., 1953).

Controversial in their time, these surveys indicated that nearly all men masturbated, that college-educated people were more likely to engage in oral sex than were non-college-educated people, that many people had at one time or other engaged in homosexual behaviors, and that as much as 10% of the population preferred homosexual sex. Although it has since been suggested that the last figure is an overestimate, these surveys revealed much about human sexual behavior.

A further step is to make behavioral and physiological observations of people engaged in sexual intercourse or masturbation, but such studies are perilous for a scientist: John B. Watson, the founder of behaviorism, attempted such studies in the early 1920s, and the ensuing scandal cost him his professorship. After Kinsey's surveys were published, however, physician William Masters and psychologist Virginia Johnson began a large, well-known project of this kind (Masters and Johnson 1966, 1970; Masters et al., 1994), documenting the uniquely diverse sexuality of the human primate.

(a) Female

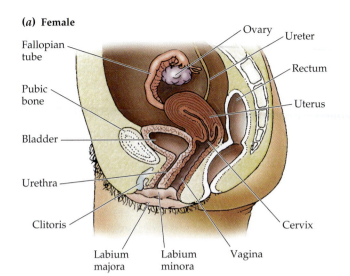

(b) Male

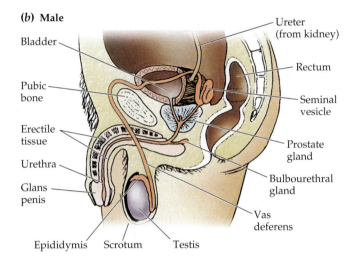

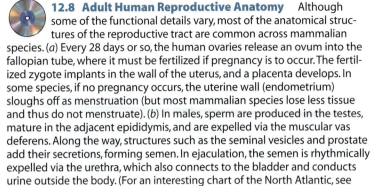

12.8 Adult Human Reproductive Anatomy Although some of the functional details vary, most of the anatomical structures of the reproductive tract are common across mammalian species. (*a*) Every 28 days or so, the human ovaries release an ovum into the fallopian tube, where it must be fertilized if pregnancy is to occur. The fertilized zygote implants in the wall of the uterus, and a placenta develops. In some species, if no pregnancy occurs, the uterine wall (endometrium) sloughs off as menstruation (but most mammalian species lose less tissue and thus do not menstruate). (*b*) In males, sperm are produced in the testes, mature in the adjacent epididymis, and are expelled via the muscular vas deferens. Along the way, structures such as the seminal vesicles and prostate add their secretions, forming semen. In ejaculation, the semen is rhythmically expelled via the urethra, which also connects to the bladder and conducts urine outside the body. (For an interesting chart of the North Atlantic, see Figure 12.1.)

Among most mammalian species, including nonhuman primates, the male mounts the female from the rear; but among humans, face-to-face postures are most common. A great variety of coital postures have been described, and many couples vary their postures from session to session or even within a session. It is this variety in reproductive behaviors, rather than differences in reproductive anatomy (Figure 12.8), that differentiates humans from most other species.

Masters and Johnson (1966) summarized the typical response patterns of men and women as consisting of four phases: increasing excitement, plateau, **orgasm** (the brief, extremely pleasurable sensations experienced by most men during ejaculation and by most women during copulation), and resolution (Figure 12.9). During the excitement phase, the **phallus** (plural *phalli*) (the penis in men, the clitoris in women) becomes engorged with blood, making it erect.

We now know some details about phallic erection. The **paragigantocellular nucleus (PGN)** in the pons sends serotonergic fibers down the spinal cord that inhibit erection (McKenna, 1999), and the sexually aroused forebrain inhibits the PGN, permitting erection. Antidepressant drugs that enhance the activity of brain serotonin receptors (see Chapter 16) can have side effects of difficulty achieving erection, ejaculation, and/or orgasm. These side effects may be due to enhancement of the effectiveness of PGN-released serotonin in spinal cord centers. (If you're wondering, the famous drug sildenafil [VIAGRA] acts directly on tissue in the penis to promote erection by inhibiting a second-messenger enzyme, phosphodiesterase-5 [Boolell et al., 1996].)

William Masters

Virginia Johnson

(a) Male

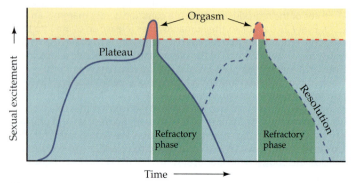

(b) Female

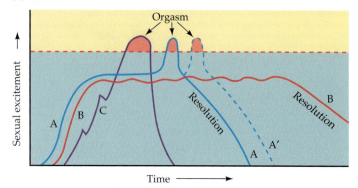

12.9 Human Sexual Response Cycles (a) The typical male pattern includes an absolute refractory phase after orgasm. (b) These three patterns are often observed in women. These diagrams are schematic and do not represent a particular physiological measure, although heart rate varies in roughly this manner. The patterns vary considerably from one individual to another. (After Masters and Johnson, 1966.)

In women, the excitement phase causes the vagina to secrete lubricating fluids that facilitate intromission. Stimulation of the penis and clitoris during rhythmic thrusting accompanying intromission may lead to orgasm. In both men and women, orgasm is accompanied by rhythmic contractions of genital muscles (mediating ejaculation in men and contracting the opening of the vagina in women).

In spite of the basic similarity, there are some typical differences between male and female sexual responses. One important difference is the greater variety of commonly observed copulatory sequences in women. Whereas men have only one basic pattern, women have three typical patterns (see Figure 12.9b). The second main difference between the sexes is that most men, but not most women, have an absolute refractory phase following orgasm (see Figure 12.9a). That is, most men cannot achieve full erection and another orgasm until some time has elapsed, the length of time varying from minutes to hours, depending on individual differences and other factors. Many women, on the other hand, can have multiple orgasms in rapid succession.

What about the broader experience of sexuality? In reviewing research on this topic, Peplau (2003) concludes that there are several distinct ways in which males and females differ as sexual beings. On many measures, males appear to experience greater sex drive than do females, engaging in more frequent masturbation, sexual fantasies, and pursuit of sexual contacts. Furthermore, sexuality and aggression are more closely linked in men, ranging from differences in sexual assertiveness to the most extreme manifestation: rape. Women, conversely, place greater emphasis than men on sexuality within the context of committed relationships. And women's sexuality can be characterized as being more plastic and adaptable over time, in response to new experiences and situations. To some extent, male and female sexuality may bear the imprint of our evolutionary history, but on an individual basis it is also shaped by sociocultural pressures and experience.

The similarities and differences in sexual responses exemplify the generalization of Chapter 1 that each person is in some ways like all other people, in some ways like some other people, and in some ways like no other person. Some behavioral differences are related to differences in genetic makeup; some may be related to differences in hormone levels. But some are certainly due to differences in experience and learning; sexual therapy, for example, usually consists of helping the person relax, recognize the sensations associated with coitus, and learn the behaviors that produce the desired effects in both partners. Masturbation during adolescence, rather than being harmful as suggested in previous times, may help avoid sexual problems in adulthood. As with other behaviors, practice, practice, practice helps.

Sexual behavior may also aid overall health; epidemiological studies indicate that men who have frequent sex tend to live longer than men who do not (Davey-Smith et al., 1997). Of course, given the risk of life-threatening sexually transmitted diseases, it is also important to one's health to take precautions to avoid the transmission of such diseases, such as by using latex condoms.

Hormones play only a permissive role in human sexual behavior

In male rodents a little bit of testosterone must be in circulation to activate male-typical mating behavior. The same relation seems to hold for human males. For example, boys who fail to produce testosterone at puberty show little interest in sex unless they are treated with synthetic androgens. These males, as well as men who have lost their testes as a result of cancer or accident, have made possible double-blind tests of whether androgens affect human copulatory behavior. (In *double-blind tests*, neither the subjects nor the investigator knows which subjects are receiving the drug and which are receiving a placebo until after the treatment is over.) In one double-blind study, Julian Davidson et al. (1979) demonstrated that androgens indeed stimulate sexual activity in men.

Recall that in rats, additional testosterone has no effect on the vigor of mating. Consequently, there is no correlation between the amount of androgens produced by an individual male rat and his tendency to copulate. In humans, too, testosterone levels below normal are sufficient to restore behavior, and there is no correlation between systemic androgen levels and sexual activity among men who have *some* androgen. In men over 60 years old, testosterone levels gradually decline as gonadotropin levels rise, indicating that the decline is in gonadal response to pituitary hormones.

Perhaps surprisingly, Barbara Sherwin and her collaborators have found that androgens may also activate sexual interest in women. Some women report reduced interest in sex after menopause. There are many possible reasons for such a change, including several hormonal changes. As mentioned earlier, estrogens increase a woman's ability to produce lubricants; and indeed, estrogen treatment of menopausal women aids lubrication, but it does not change their interest in sex. On the other hand, adding a very low-dose regimen of androgens can revive sexual interest in postmenopausal women (Sherwin, 1998, 2002).

There have been several attempts to determine whether women's interest or participation in sexual behavior varies with the menstrual cycle. Some researchers have found a slight increase in sexual behavior around the time of ovulation, but the effect is small, and several studies have failed to see any significant change in interest in sex across the menstrual cycle.

Do pheromones affect human reproductive function?

Martha McClintock (1971) reported that women residing together in a college dormitory were more likely to have their menstrual cycles in synchrony than would be expected by chance; that is, women who spend more time with each other are more likely to menstruate at the same time. McClintock hypothesized that pheromones passing between the women serve as a signal of the ovulatory cycle, enabling synchronization.

It has been difficult to prove that women show menstrual synchrony, but most studies confirm this idea (Weller and Weller, 1993). Whether the synchronization relies on social signals or pheromone signals between the women has been even more difficult to determine. However, women who have extracts of sweat from other women applied to their upper lip do display an acceleration or delay of their menstrual cycles, depending on where the donors were in their cycle (K. Stern and McClintock, 1998).

There is also some evidence that the body odors of men affect women's mate choices (and not just in the obvious way!). The **major histocompatibility complex** (**MHC**) is a group of immune-related genes that are so polymorphic—that is, they come in so many different forms, or *alleles*—that they encode millions of different overall combinations. The MHC is also a source of unique body odors, which therefore signal the individual's genotype. Women prefer the smell of men with MHCs that are not too similar to their own (Wedekind et al., 1995), but also not too dissimilar, and preferably containing some MHC alleles that are the same as those that the woman inherited from her father (but not from her mother) (Jacob et al., 2002). This may be an evolved mechanism for striking a balance between inbreeding and outbreeding. Whether or not MHC sensitivity requires a vomeronasal system is uncertain; recall from Chapter 9 that the vomeronasal organ may be a nonfunctional vestige in humans, and in any case, the main olfactory system is capable of discerning MHC-related odors.

Julian Davidson (1931–2001)

Barbara Sherwin

CLINICAL ISSUE

Martha McClintock

EVOLUTION AT WORK

WHY ARE THERE TWO SEXES?

Having talked about sex and some of its many complications, we may wonder how such an outlandish system ever got started, yet many animals come in two sexes. Author William Tenn (1968) imagined an exotic animal species that had seven different sexes. The sexes had wildly divergent bodies and behavior, allowing each to occupy a particular ecological niche, including both predator and prey. One problem with such an arrangement is reproduction: How do members of each of the seven sexes get together for mating when some are predators, some prey? In Tenn's scenario, one of the seven sexes was highly adapted for the tricky diplomacy of arranging suitable orgies.

In real life no creatures have more than two sexes, so perhaps even natural selection cannot solve diplomatic problems involving more than two parties. The discovery of a 425-million-year-old fossilized creature sporting a penis attests to the great antiquity of sexual reproduction (Siveter et al., 2003). But as we'll see next, species with only one sex reproduce perfectly well. Why should any species bother with two?

Sexual Reproduction Helps Combine Beneficial Mutations and Shed Harmful Ones

If, in a given population of animals, one individual has a very rare, *beneficial* mutation, the mutation can be spread to other individuals in only two ways. One way is for that individual to make clones of itself, to give birth to individuals that have only its genes, including the mutated one. In unicellular organisms this process is known as **fission,** the simple splitting of one individual cell into two. In multicellular animals this process is known as **parthenogenesis** (from the Greek *parthenos,* "virgin," and *genesis,* "production"; the Parthenon was a Greek temple to the virgin goddess Athena). If the mutation is especially useful, future generations will consist mostly of this individual's progeny. Eventually other beneficial mutations may arise. Thus it is possible for a species to evolve without sexual reproduction: Bdelloid rotifers, microscopic creatures living in ponds and marshes around the world, have been doing exactly that for at least 40 million years (Welch and Meselson, 2000).

EVOLUTION AT WORK

The other method of spreading new genes is sexual reproduction. In this process the original holder of a helpful new gene produces offspring that have both the new gene and genes from other individuals. Some of these other genes may also be beneficial. The *function of sexual reproduction* is to bring together, in a single individual, many beneficial mutations, each of which arose in different individuals. This mixing of beneficial genes certainly generates biological diversity. Experiments with fruit flies have confirmed that sexual reproduction provides a way for beneficial mutations to be separated from co-occurring harmful mutations, and thus accumulate rapidly (Rice and Chippindale, 2001). But evolutionary theorists still debate why any particular individual, if capable of either parthenogenesis or sexual reproduction, would benefit by producing offspring that carry only half of its genes (Peck and Waxman, 2000).

Some animals can reproduce by either method. Aphids, the small green insects that probably infest your garden every year, reproduce by parthenogenesis when the food supply is ample and the conditions are favorable for growth and unchecked reproduction. When conditions worsen, though, the aphids begin sexually reproducing, effectively swapping genes to produce hardier offspring that can migrate into other environments. So, despite halving each parent's genetic contribution to the next generation, the advantage of reproducing sexually may be that the new-and-improved gene combinations increase the probability that at least some offspring will survive.

12.10 Are Males Necessary? Whiptail lizards (*a*) and Amazon mollies (*b*) are two of the rare vertebrate species that reproduce by parthenogenesis. All individuals are females that produce daughters with only the mother's genes. Nevertheless, these animals exhibit mock mating behaviors (such as those displayed by the lizards shown here) that greatly resemble the mating behaviors of related species that reproduce sexually. (*c*) Clown fish are *protandrous* ("male first") sequential hermaphrodites, changing from male to female when they are large enough. Despite what you may see in the movies, a host anemone is generally occupied by a large and dominant female clown fish, a small male, and genderless juveniles. Sex change is fairly common among reef fishes; other species are *protogynous* ("female first") sequential hermaphrodites, and still others are simultaneous hermaphrodites (both sexes at once). (Part *a* by Patricia J. Wynne; *b* courtesy of Michael Ryan.)

Nevertheless, parthenogenesis has been documented to occur on rare occasions in some vertebrate species, such as chickens and turkeys; and in several species of whiptail lizards in the southwestern United States, all individuals are females that reproduce exclusively via parthenogenesis (Figure 12.10*a*) (Crews, 1994). Aquarium fanciers know a species of tropical fish, the Amazon molly (Figure 12.10*b*), that consists solely of females reproducing by parthenogenesis. Apparently, then, nothing inherent in the vertebrate body requires sexual reproduction, but this method of reproduction among vertebrates is so pervasive that it must convey some advantage.

Even sexual reproduction does not require that animals come in two different sexes. In many sexually reproducing species, each individual produces both sperm and eggs, and sex consists of donating sperm to a partner while accepting sperm in return. Individuals that can reproduce as either males or females are known as **hermaphrodites** (a term derived from the Greek *Hermaphroditos*—the son of the god Hermes and goddess Aphrodite—who, while bathing, became joined in one body with a nymph).

Simultaneous hermaphrodites, like slugs and snails and many other invertebrates, make both male and female gametes at the same time. Few vertebrates are simultaneous hermaphrodites, and all of them are fishes. **Sequential hermaphrodites** start out as one sex and then switch to the other sex when environmental conditions are right; again, vertebrate examples are primarily fishes, such as the clown fish shown in Figure 12.10*c*.

Mammals are **dioecious**—having distinct male and female sexes that specialize in making just one type of gamete—because early in the evolution of our ancestors, the male and female roles diverged until the sexes eventually split.

Males and Females Often Adopt Different Reproductive Strategies

When our ancestors began reproducing through separate male and female individuals, the two sexes came to diverge in form and behavior (Figure 12.11). Today many species are **sexually dimorphic,** the term that Darwin used to describe species in which males and females are visibly different. Species in which the sexes look very similar, such as the ringdoves pictured in Figure 12.11*c,* are referred to as sexually *monomorphic,* even though they are different internally—for example, in the production of eggs or sperm. Table 12.2 reviews the various reproductive strategies of animals.

The most obvious sexual dimorphism is the larger body size of males in many vertebrate species (see Figure 12.11*a* and *b*), but many other instances of sexual dimorphism are evident in the brains and bodies of rats, humans, and other vertebrates. One example of sexual dimorphism that appears to have had profound effects on vertebrate evolution is the difference in the size of male gametes (sperm) and female gametes (ova): The gametes of male vertebrates are small and cheap enough to produce by the millions; female gametes, on the other hand, are large, and producing them incurs high costs in nutrients and energy (Figure 12.12).

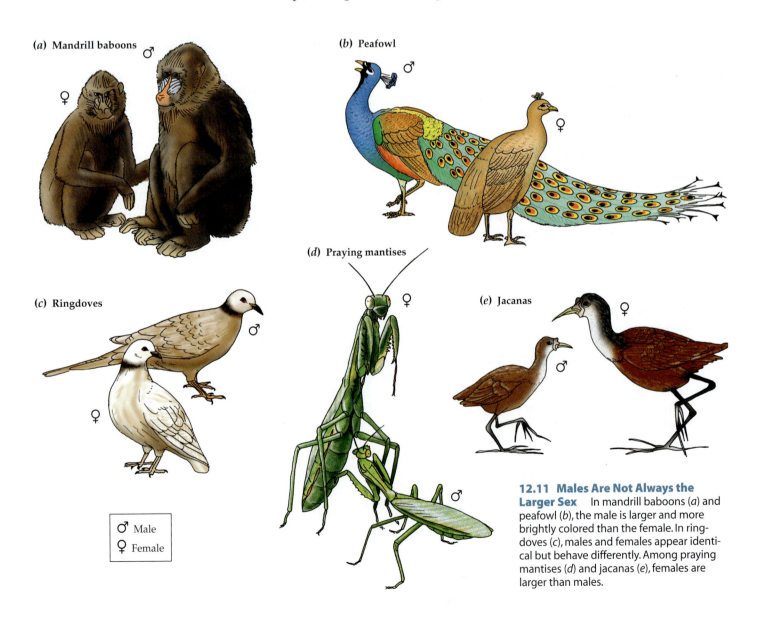

(a) Mandrill baboons

(b) Peafowl

(c) Ringdoves

(d) Praying mantises

(e) Jacanas

♂ Male
♀ Female

12.11 Males Are Not Always the Larger Sex In mandrill baboons (*a*) and peafowl (*b*), the male is larger and more brightly colored than the female. In ringdoves (*c*), males and females appear identical but behave differently. Among praying mantises (*d*) and jacanas (*e*), females are larger than males.

TABLE 12.2 *Reproductive Strategies of Animals*

Type of reproduction	Strategy	Examples of animals that use the strategy
Asexual	Fission	Unicellular animals
	Parthenogenesis (virgin birth)	
	Obligatory	Amazon mollies, some whiptail lizards
	Occasional	Aphids
Sexual	Hermaphroditism (each individual produces both sperm and eggs)	
	Simultaneous	Many invertebrates (e.g., *Aplysia*)
	Sequential	Some fishes
	Separate sexes (each individual produces either sperm or eggs)	
	Sexually monomorphic	Many birds (e.g., seagulls, ringdoves)
	Sexually dimorphic	Most mammals

Because of the low cost of producing sperm, a single male individual can gather enough energy and nutrients to produce sufficient sperm to inseminate many females—no need to be too choosy. Females, on the other hand, must be much more selective in order to reproduce successfully. In many cases, females that carefully nurture their costly eggs (in whatever manner is appropriate for that species) produce more surviving offspring, thereby passing on more of their genes (including the choosiness and parenting genes), which come to predominate in future generations.

One of the most important ways that females of any species can nurture their egg investments is to choose a mate carefully. Males that carry many beneficial genes are more likely to provide the female's offspring with beneficial genes. Therefore, the descendants of females that discover and mate with such males should come to predominate in future generations, while females that mate indiscriminately will have fewer descendants.

The difficulty for a female, of course, is determining whether a potential mate has beneficial genes. (Until recently, she could not count on training in molecular biology.) The female must closely observe the appearance and behavior of the male. A vigorous, healthy male must be doing something right, and in general, an unhealthy-looking male is more likely (although by no means certain) to carry harmful genes. On the other hand, inseminating a female is rarely dangerous to a male, and it is inexpensive. Even if the offspring do not survive, ample sperm will be left for the next female. The only real dangers for males come with mating in species such as black widow spiders and praying mantises in which the female kills the male afterward, and with contracting sexually transmitted diseases.

From this perspective, **courtship** is a period during which the female indirectly assesses the genetic makeup of a male to judge his suitability as a mate. For mammalian females, which carry their young in utero for a prolonged

12.12 Male Gametes Are Small and Cheap; Female Gametes, Large and Expensive Sperm cluster around a human ovum in this photo, magnified about 1000 times. Because they are so much smaller than ova, sperm are easier to produce.

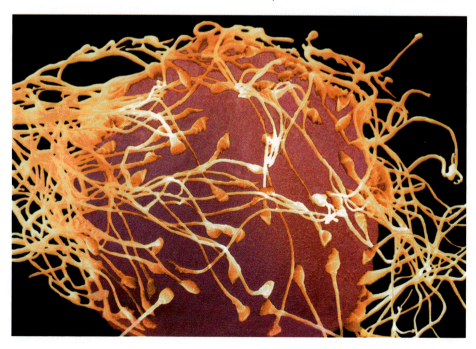

period and then provide milk for an additional time, the investment in each fertilized egg is tremendous, and therefore the pressure to select a good mate is intense. In most vertebrates, nearly all the females who reach reproductive age manage to mate, but only a minority of mature males ever persuade anyone to mate with them. Some interesting exceptions to this pattern are described in the next section.

Mating Systems Can Be Classified into Four Basic Types

EVOLUTION AT WORK

The mating strategies of males and females across species can be classified into four different mating systems: promiscuity, polygyny, polyandry, and monogamy. These different systems seem to be related to species differences in the investment of males and females in their offspring.

1. **Promiscuity.** For most species of mammals, females are very selective in mating and most males never mate. Thus a few males are doing most of the mating, and because the number of males and females is roughly equal, these males must be mating with more than one female. But most female mammals also mate with more than one male. Such a mating system, in which animals mate with several partners and do not establish long-lasting associations, is called *promiscuity*.

2. **Polygyny** (from the Greek *polys*, "many," and *gyne*, "woman"). With some animals, such as elephant seals and gorillas, a long-lasting association between mates develops—one male mating with a group of females (a harem). Each female mates with only one male, but that male mates with several females.

3. **Polyandry** (the Greek *andr-* means "man"). In this system, which is much rarer than polygyny, each female of the species mates with several males, but each male mates with only one female. The jacana (see Figure 12.11*e*) is an example of a polyandrous species; in this species the females compete for mates. The females are larger and more colorful than the males, and they defend the nest site from other females. Once the female jacana lays the eggs, she departs, leaving the male to incubate the eggs and raise the young. The term *polygamy* (literally "many spouses"; the Greek *gamos* means "marriage") is sometimes used to refer to polygyny and polyandry collectively. (*Bigamy* means "having two spouses.")

4. **Monogamy** (literally "having one spouse"). This mating system is characterized by one male and one female forming a breeding pair and mating exclusively (or almost exclusively) with one another. Monogamy is far more common among birds than among mammals (Figure 12.13). It has been suggested that because birds have a high metabolic rate and their young tend to be very immature at hatching, a single parent cannot provide enough food for the chicks to survive. In that case, males that did not care for eggs and chicks would make little or no contribution to the next generation; thus the development of monogamy would be expected. Yet there seems to be a distinction between social monogamy and sexual monogamy because even among birds thought to be monogamous, the chicks are not always genetically related to the male that is caring for them (Johnsen et al., 2000). So the adults sometimes copulate outside the pair.

The likelihood of extra-pair copulation may be higher for pairs that are more genetically similar than average (Blomqvist et al., 2002).

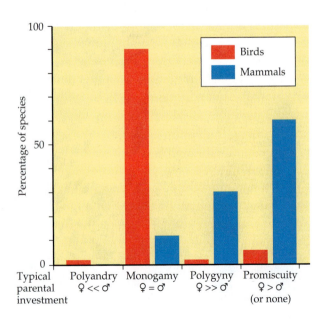

12.13 Mating Systems and Parental Investment in Offspring
These estimates of mating-system types show that birds are far more likely than mammals to be monogamous. Because monogamous species have the lowest uncertainty of paternity, paternal investment in their offspring is the highest. (Estimates for birds are based on data from Lack, 1968; estimates for mammals, on data from Daly and Wilson, 1978. Both should be regarded as only rough estimates.)

Why? In many species, individuals choose mates on the basis of similarity to themselves, a process called **phenotype matching.** The evolutionary logic is that a mate that is similar to you must carry many of the same genes that you carry, so your offspring will tend to carry more of your genes than would be the case if you had paired with a dissimilar mate. The problem is that for *very* similar pairs, the risk of accumulating harmful mutations through inbreeding increases. Extra-pair copulation provides some insurance against this outcome, for both sexes.

In species where both parents typically care for offspring, mothers and fathers again have conflicting evolutionary strategies. Whereas females can always be highly confident that they are caring for their own young (especially among mammals), males may be investing their resources in offspring sired by another male, at enormous cost to their own reproductive success. This *uncertainty of paternity* has prompted males of many species to evolve mechanisms to try to ensure paternity, and avoid investing in unrelated offspring. For example, among savannah baboons (Figure 12.14), in which a female typically mates with multiple males, males nonetheless can reliably identify their own offspring and intervene on their behalf (Buchan et al., 2003). Presumably, this ability of males to identify their own offspring is accomplished through a sensitive kind of phenotype matching.

12.14 Savannah Baboons

Sexual Selection Accentuates Differences between the Sexes

As we learned in Chapter 6, Charles Darwin was the first to recognize that competition between males and the tendency of females to be very selective in mating affect the course of natural selection. He coined the term **sexual selection** to refer to the selective pressures that each sex exerts on the other. Darwin regarded sexual selection as a special type of natural selection and used the concept to explain certain features that were not easy to explain on the basis of natural selection alone. For example, why do male lions have manes, male birds of paradise display elaborate tail feathers, and male moose sport enormous antlers? These features do not seem to help the animal gather food, elude predators, or find shelter. Indeed, in many cases such features seem to hinder those functions.

Darwin understood that the function of these features is to procure mates, simply because members of the other sex prefer mates with those features. Darwin also realized that sexual selection, by exerting *different* selective pressures on males and females, would impel the two sexes to diverge more and more in their appearance. This divergence can become extreme. The moa, an extinct flightless bird, exhibited a reversed sexual dimorphism in which males were so much smaller than females that until recently they were classified as belonging to different species (Bunce et al., 2003). Of course, there is a limit to the influence of sexual selection, because other selective pressures also apply. A male who is overly ornamented (Figure 12.15), for example, may be unable to find food or evade predators (R. Brooks, 2000)—activities that are crucial for survival.

12.15 A Result of Sexual Selection   The male Raggiana bird of paradise puts on a colorful tail display. Although such bright colors and elaborate feathers may interfere with the bird's ability to avoid predators, they definitely attract female birds of paradise.

Sexual reproduction provides pressure to select mates with advantageous genes. In sexual selection, individuals demanding that potential partners display certain characteristics or perform certain behaviors benefit by passing good genes to their offspring. At one level, the ornamentation or extravagant behavior indicates a generally healthy mate, likely to have pretty good genes. But once a particular species begins showing partiality for a specific trait—manes on male lions, elaborate tails on birds, men's beards, and so on—the prejudice tends to be self-perpetuating. For example, once a population of females comes to favor mating with maned lions, a female who mates with a male without a mane leaves her offspring (especially her sons) at a distinct disadvantage. Natural selection thus favors the maintenance of such mating preferences. There is considerable debate about the extent to which sexual selection has shaped human reproduction (see Box 12.1).

**EVOLUTION
AT WORK**

One interesting way in which females of several species enforce these demands is in the control of ovulation. In frogs, for example, exposure to courting males facilitates ovulation in the female; the more such behavior the males display, the more eggs are released and made available for fertilization. We saw earlier that a male rat must provide the female with several intromissions before ejaculation or she will not become pregnant; thus, female rats exert selective pressure on males to copulate a while before ejaculating. In other species, courtship and/or copulation is *required* for ovulation. In lions, only very vigorous copulation over several days induces the female to ovulate. The reproductive physiology of lionesses enforces strict evolutionary pressure on male behavior.

In an intriguing variant of this mechanism, both the parthenogenetic whiptail lizards and Amazon mollies discussed earlier display remnants of courtship-facilitated ovulation. In each case, there are closely related species that reproduce sexually; and in these sexual species, courtship and mating behaviors facilitate ovulation. The parthenogenetic females similarly release more eggs if they are courted and go through mating behavior. But with whom do you mate when your species consists of females only? With whiptail lizards, females take turns mating with one another, playing the role of a male one day, and the role of a female later (see Figure 12.10a). Such mock mating increases the number of eggs released and laid.

BOX 12.1   Evolutionary Psychology

Speculation about selective pressure on reproductive behavior in various animals leads inevitably to questions about the extent to which our own behaviors have been affected by the difference between male and female reproductive strategies:

- Are women inherently more selective than men about choosing mating partners? Such a difference could be a result of the tremendous investment of time, energy, and resources that a female mammal must make in each offspring.

- Are men more promiscuous than women? It's easy to imagine that the low cost of producing sperm (and the potential for a man to expend no energy on child rearing) might favor such behavior.

- Do romantic relationships tend to sour after about 7 years? If so, the reason for this tendency may be that in the ancestral environment in which hominids

evolved, periodically selecting a new mate provided insurance against genetic defects from any one mate affecting all of the offspring.

- Is there an "ideal" waist-to-hip ratio that indicates maximal fertility in women? Correlational studies suggest that a particular ratio is especially attractive to men, across different cultures and historical eras (Singh, 2002).

- Are women attracted to power, and men to youth, because natural selection favored these preferences?

Such speculations have given rise to a lively and controversial field called **evolutionary psychology** (Barkow et al., 1992; Buss, 2000). It's easy to spin plausible tales about how evolution might have shaped our behavior, but the challenge for theorists is to come up with ways to test (and potentially disprove) these hypotheses.

Such an enterprise is especially daunting when ethical considerations mean that the investigator can never manipulate the variables ("Let's see. I'd like you to marry that person over there, and then I'll ask you some questions 7 years from now."), but must rely on correlations and surveys.

Geoffrey Miller (2000) proposes that sexual selection was crucial for evolution of the human brain. If, among early hominids, people came to favor mates who sang, made jokes, or produced artistic works, then such high-order functioning would rapidly evolve in an arms race, as the ever more discriminating brains of one sex demanded ever more impressive performances from the brains of the other sex. Did humor, song, and art originate from the drive to be sexually attractive? And does sexual selection account for the large size of the human brain, as hypothesized by Miller (see Chapter 6)?

Amazon mollies "mate" not with one another, but with males of the closely related sailfin molly species. A male sailfin molly courts Amazon females, inserts his modified fin into the female, and deposits sperm. The sperm do not fertilize the eggs, but the Amazon releases more eggs and later gives birth to more daughters for having gone through the mock mating. Why should the male sailfins bother? Perhaps the cost to the male is very low, and perhaps the rehearsal improves later mating with a sailfin female. But another reason that has been suggested is that sailfin females, seeing the male mate with another female (of either species), may regard him as more attractive and may thus be more likely to mate with him (Schlupp et al., 1994).

In many species, males exert on each other a special kind of sexual selection pressure, called **sperm competition.** Because a fertile female may mate with multiple males, and thus have sperm from several sources in her reproductive tract, there is a distinct reproductive advantage for a male to produce sperm that can outperform those of his rivals. The effects of sperm competition are evident in the offspring produced—many a neighborhood cat has produced a litter of kittens that are a mix of colors and breeds—and also in the physiology of the sperm themselves. By producing sperm that swim farther and faster, in such high numbers that the ova are mobbed, a male maximizes the number of offspring he sires.

**EVOLUTION
AT WORK**

The swimming motion of sperm is powered by mitochondria in the sperm midpiece, and among primates, the size of the midpiece is greatest in the most promiscuous species (M. J. Anderson and Dixson, 2002). In one of the most extreme adaptations to sperm competition, the sperm of the European wood mouse work *cooperatively* to defeat rivals: Hundreds of sperm link together like microscopic freight trains, hurtling along twice as fast as individual sperm can swim. On reaching an ovum, trailing sperm sacrifice themselves to break up the train and advance a single sperm to fertilize the ovum (H. Moore et al., 2002).

SEXUAL DIFFERENTIATION

For species such as our own, in which the only kind of reproduction is sexual reproduction (so far), and in which sexual selection has generated sexual dimorphism, each individual must become either a male or a female to reproduce. **Sexual differentiation** is the process by which individuals develop either male or female bodies and behavior. In mammals this process begins before birth and continues into adulthood.

The Sex of an Individual Is Determined Early in Life

For mammals, the penetration of an egg by a sperm carrying either an X or Y chromosome is the key event in **sex determination**, the developmentally early event that decides whether the new individual will develop as a male or a female. From that point on, the path of sexual differentiation is set. We will describe that path and its occasional exceptions shortly. Mammals that receive an X chromosome from the father will become females; those that receive a Y chromosome will become males. (The mother always contributes an X chromosome.)

In vertebrates the first visible consequence of sexual determination is in the gonads. Very early in development each individual has a pair of **indifferent gonads,** glands that vaguely resemble both testes and ovaries. During the first month of gestation in humans, the indifferent gonads begin changing into either ovaries or testes.

Sex chromosomes direct sexual differentiation of the gonads

In mammals the Y chromosome contains a gene called the *SRY* **gene** (for *s*ex-determining *r*egion on the *Y* chromosome) that is responsible for the development of testes. If an individual has a Y chromosome, the cells of the indifferent gonad begin making the Sry protein. The Sry protein causes the cells in the core of the indifferent gonad to proliferate at the expense of the outer layers, and the indifferent gonad develops into a testis.

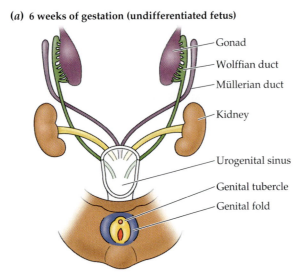

(a) 6 weeks of gestation (undifferentiated fetus)

Gonad
Wolffian duct
Müllerian duct
Kidney
Urogenital sinus
Genital tubercle
Genital fold

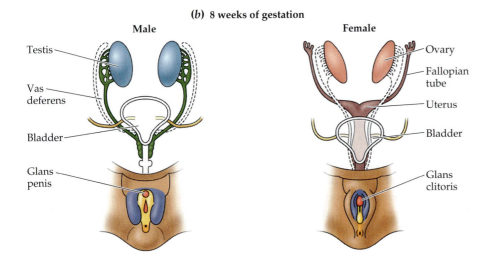

(b) 8 weeks of gestation

Male

Testis
Vas deferens
Bladder
Glans penis

Female

Ovary
Fallopian tube
Uterus
Bladder
Glans clitoris

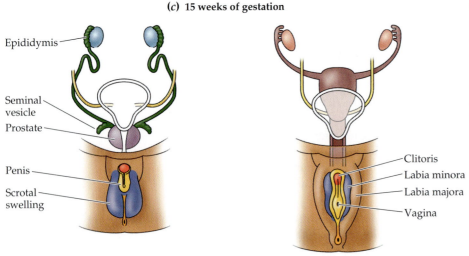

(c) 15 weeks of gestation

Epididymis
Seminal vesicle
Prostate
Penis
Scrotal swelling

Clitoris
Labia minora
Labia majora
Vagina

12.16 Sexual Differentiation in Humans (a) Undifferentiated fetus. (b, c) Male and female fetuses at 8 weeks (b) and 15 weeks (c) of gestation.

If the individual has no Y chromosome (or if it has a Y chromosome but the *SRY* gene is defective), no Sry protein is produced, and the indifferent gonad takes a different course: Cells of the outer layers of the gonad proliferate more than those of the inner core, and an ovary forms. This early decision of whether to form testes or ovaries has a domino effect, setting off a chain of events that usually results in either a male or a female.

Gonadal hormones direct sexual differentiation of the rest of the body

The most important way the gonads influence sexual differentiation is through their hormonal output. Whereas developing testes produce several hormones, early ovaries produce very little hormone. If other cells of the embryo receive the testicular hormones, they begin developing masculine characters; if the cells are not exposed to testicular hormones, they develop feminine characters.

We can chart masculine or feminine development by examining the structures that connect the gonads to the outside of the body. The conduits between the gametes and the exterior are quite different in males and females (see Figure 12.8), but at the embryonic stage all individuals have the precursor tissues of both systems. The early fetus has a genital tubercle that can form either a clitoris or a penis, as well as two sets of ducts that connect the indifferent gonads to the outer body wall: the **wolffian ducts** and the **müllerian ducts** (Figure 12.16a). In females, the müllerian ducts develop into the fallopian tubes, uterus, and inner vagina (Figure 12.16b and c, right), and only a remnant of the wolffian ducts remains. In males, hormones secreted by the testes orchestrate the converse outcome: The wolffian ducts develop into epididymis, vas deferens, and seminal vesicles (Figure 12.16b and c, left), while the müllerian ducts shrink to mere remnants.

The system is masculinized by two testicular secretions: testosterone, which promotes the development of the wolffian system, and **anti-mullerian hormone (AMH)**, which induces the regression of the müllerian system. In the absence of testes to produce testosterone and AMH, the genital tract develops by default in a feminine pattern, in which the wolffian ducts regress and the müllerian ducts develop into components of the female internal reproductive tract.

Testosterone also masculinizes other, non-wolffian-derived structures. Testosterone causes tissues around the urethra to form the prostate gland. Furthermore, testosterone acts on the epithelial tissues around the urethra to form a scrotum and penis. These effects are aided by the local conversion of testosterone into a more potent androgen, **dihydrotestosterone (DHT)**, accomplished by an enzyme that is found in the epithelial cells, **5α-reductase.** Androgens that are less potent than DHT are able to masculinize the genitalia only partially; and if androgens are absent altogether, the prostate fails to form and the external skin grows into the female labia and clitoris.

Departures from the orderly sequence of sexual differentiation result in predictable changes in development

Some people have only one sex chromosome: a single X. Such genetic makeup (referred to as XO) results in **Turner's syndrome:** an apparent female with poorly developed but recognizable ovaries, as you would expect because no *SRY* gene is available. In general, unless the indifferent gonad becomes a testis and begins secreting hormones, an immature mammal develops a female body. Immature ovaries, in Turner's syndrome the same as in normal females, produce few hormones. So the sex chromosomes determine the sex of the gonad, and gonadal hormones then drive sexual differentiation of the rest of the body (Figure 12.17*a*). Later in life, both hor-

(*a*)

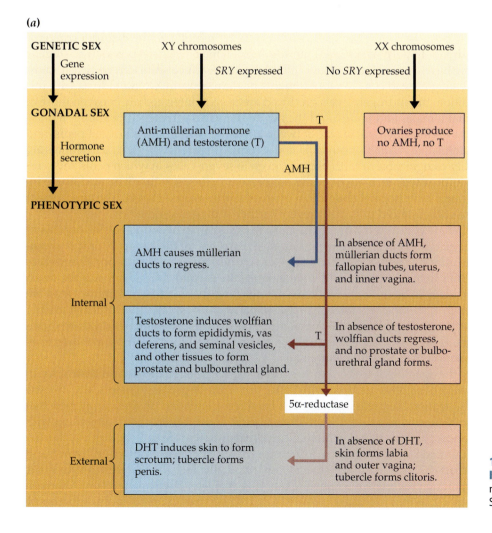

(*b*)

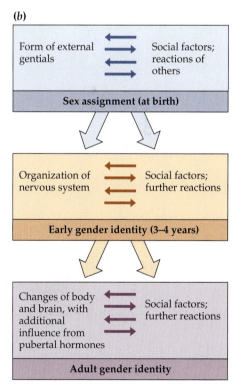

12.17 Sexual Differentiation and Gender Identity (*a*) Genetic and hormonal mechanisms of embryonic sexual differentiation. (*b*) Steps toward adult gender identity in humans.

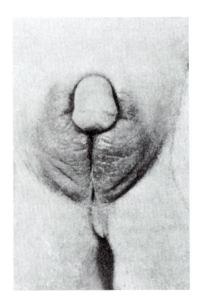

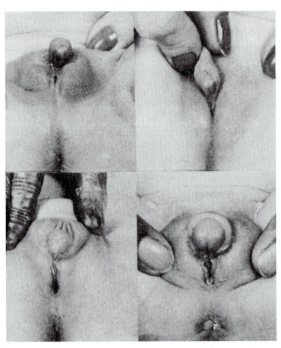

12.18 An Intersex Phenotype These genitalia are characteristic of newborn girls with congenital adrenal hyperplasia (CAH). (Courtesy of John Money.)

CLINICAL ISSUE

mones and experience guide sexual differentiation and the development of gender identity (Figure 12.17*b*).

Sometimes XX individuals with well-formed ovaries are exposed to androgens in utero, and depending on the degree of exposure, they may be masculinized. For example, most fetal rats develop in the uterus sandwiched between two siblings. If a female is surrounded by brothers, some of the androgen from the siblings must reach the female because, although her gross appearance will be feminine at birth, her anogenital distance (the distance from the tip of the phallus (penis or clitoris) to the anus) will be slightly greater (i.e., more malelike) than that of a female developing between two sisters (Clemens et al., 1978). In Chapter 9 we saw an example of a similar phenomenon in humans: Females who have a male twin produce otoacoustic emissions that are slightly more typical of males than of females.

In humans, the disorder **congenital adrenal hyperplasia** (**CAH**) can result in a female who is exposed to androgens before birth. In CAH, the adrenal glands fail to produce sufficient corticosteroids, producing instead considerable amounts of androgens. In XX individuals with this condition, the androgen levels produced are usually intermediate between those of normal females and males, and the newborn has an **intersex** appearance: a phallus that is intermediate in size between a normal clitoris and a normal penis, and skin folds that resemble both labia and scrotum (Figure 12.18). Such individuals are readily recognizable at birth because, even in severe cases in which penis and scrotum appear well formed, no testes are present in the "scrotum"; instead, these individuals have normal abdominal ovaries, as you would expect. The children are given corticosteroid pills that prevent further androgen production.

There is controversy over whether the best course of action for the parents of CAH girls is to opt for immediate surgical correction of the genitalia, or to wait until adulthood, when the CAH-affected individuals can decide for themselves whether to have surgery, and what gender role to follow. CAH females are much more likely to be described by their parents (and themselves) as tomboys than are other girls, and they exhibit enhanced spatial abilities on cognitive tests that usually favor males (Berenbaum, 2001). In adulthood, most CAH females describe themselves as heterosexual, but they are somewhat more likely to report a homosexual orientation than are other women.

At the opening of the chapter we discussed the dilemma of **cloacal exstrophy,** in which genetic boys are born with testes but without penises. Historically in these cases, neonatal sex reassignment has been recommended on the assumption that unambiguously raising these children as girls, and surgically providing them with the appropriate external genitalia, could produce a more satisfactory psychosexual outcome. In a long-term follow-up of 14 such cases, however, Reiner and Gearhart (2004) found that eight children eventually declared themselves to be male, even though several were unaware that they had ever been operated on. Although this indicates that prenatal exposure to androgens strongly predisposes subsequent male gender identity, five of the remaining six cases were apparently content with their female identities, suggesting that socialization can also play a strong role. In most people, gender is presumably established by nature and nurture working in conjunction.

A defective androgen receptor can block the masculinization of males

An interesting demonstration of the influence of androgens on sexual differentiation is provided by the condition known as **androgen insensitivity syndrome** (**AIS**). The gene for the androgen receptor is found on the X chromosome. An XY individual whose X chromosome has a defective androgen receptor gene is thus incapable of producing normal androgen receptors, and is therefore unable to respond to androgenic hormones. The gonads of such people develop as normal testes (as directed by Sry), and the testes produce AMH (which inhibits müllerian duct structures) and plenty of testosterone.

In the absence of working androgen receptors, however, the wolffian ducts fail to develop and the external tissue forms labia and a clitoris. Such individuals look like normal females at birth, and at puberty they develop breasts. (Breast development in humans appears to depend on the ratio of estrogenic to androgenic stimulation at puberty, and since androgen-insensitive individuals receive little androgenic *stimulation*, the functional estrogen-to-androgen ratio is high.)

Females with AIS may be recognized when their menstrual cycles fail to commence because neither ovaries nor uterus are present to produce menstruation. Such women are infertile and, lacking a müllerian contribution, have a shallow vagina, but otherwise they look like other women (Figure 12.19) and, as we'll see in the next section, behave like other women. At the end of this chapter we will describe another mutation that causes some people to appear to change their sex (without surgery) at adolescence.

How Should We Define Gender—by Genes, Gonads, Genitals, or the Brain?

Most humans are either male or female, and whether we examine their chromosomes, gonads, external genitalia, or internal structures, we see a consistent pattern: Each one is either feminine or masculine in character. Behavior is much more difficult than physical features to define as feminine or masculine. The only behavior displayed *exclusively* by one sex is childbirth. Even behaviors that are very rarely displayed by members of one sex or the other (e.g., sexual assault by women or breast-feeding by men) occur sometimes in the unexpected sex. As for behaviors that can be measured and made amenable to experimental study in humans or other animals, we have to resort to group means and statistical tests to see the differences. A given individual almost always displays some behaviors that are more common in the opposite sex.

Androgen-insensitive individuals show us that even morphological features can be confusing criteria by which to judge sex (see Figure 12.19). Androgen-insensitive humans have a male chromosome and testes. Like most males, they do not have fallopian tubes or a uterus, but they do have a vagina and breasts, and in many respects they behave like most females: They dress like females, they are attracted to and marry males, and perhaps most importantly, even after they learn the details of their condition they continue to regard themselves as women (Money and Ehrhardt, 1972).

As we will see next, there are also structural sex differences in parts of the central nervous system, in humans and other animals. In androgen-insensitive rats, some brain regions are masculine and others are feminine. Thus, from a scientific standpoint we cannot regard an animal, especially a human, as simply masculine or feminine. Rather we must specify which structure or behavior we mean when we say it is typical of females or of males.

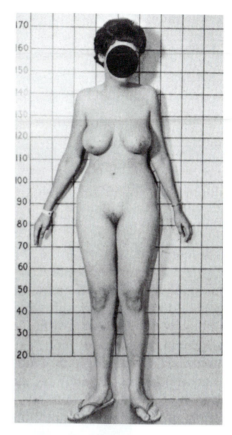

12.19 An Androgen-Insensitive Person Although this person has the male XY chromosome pattern and therefore testes (undescended), she also has complete androgen insensitivity. Therefore her body has developed in a feminine fashion. (Courtesy of John Money.)

COMPETING HYPOTHESES

Gonadal Hormones Direct Sexual Differentiation of the Brain and Behavior

As scientists began discovering that testicular hormones direct masculine development of the body, behavioral researchers found evidence for a similar influence on the brain (Phoenix et al., 1959). A female guinea pig, like most other rodents, normally displays the lordosis posture in response to male mounting for only a short period around the time of ovulation, when her fertility is highest. If a male mounts her at other times, she does not show lordosis. An experimenter can induce the female to display lordosis by injecting ovarian steroids in the sequence they normally follow during ovulation—giving her estrogens for a few days and then progesterone. A few hours after the progesterone injection, the female will display lordosis in response to male mounting.

Phoenix and collaborators exposed female guinea pigs to testosterone in utero. As adults, these females did not show lordosis. Even if their ovaries were removed and they were given the steroidal regimen that reliably activated lordosis in normal females, these fetally androgenized females did not show lordosis.

On the basis of these data, William C. Young and his colleagues inferred that the same testicular steroids that masculinize the genitalia also masculinize the developing brain, and thereby permanently alter behavior. This **organizational effect** of steroid hormones contrasts with the activational effects we mentioned earlier, such as the activation of lordosis in adult females in response to estrogens and progesterone.

Steroids have an organizational effect only when present during a **sensitive period** in early development. Unlike the transient nature of activational effects, the organizational effects of hormones tend to be permanent. The exact boundaries of the sensitive period of development depend on which behavior and which species is being studied. For rats, androgens given just after birth (the **neonatal** period) can affect later behavior. Guinea pigs, however, must be exposed to androgens before birth for adult behavior to be affected.

William C. Young (1899–1965)

Early testicular secretions result in masculine behavior in adulthood

The organizational hypothesis provides a unitary explanation for sexual differentiation: A single steroid signal (androgen) masculinizes the body, the brain, and behavior. From this point of view the nervous system is just another type of tissue listening for the androgenic signal that will instruct it to organize itself in a masculine fashion. If the nervous system does not detect androgens, it will organize itself in a feminine fashion. With their capacity to infiltrate the entire body, steroids have a unique ability to communicate a single message to disparate parts of the body to coordinate an integrated response.

What was demonstrated originally for the lordosis behavior of guinea pigs has been observed in a variety of vertebrate species and for a variety of behaviors. Exposing female rat pups to testosterone either just before birth or during the first 10 days after birth greatly reduces their lordosis responsiveness as adults. This explains the observation that adult male rats show very little lordosis even when given estrogens and progesterone. However, male rats that are castrated during the first week of life display excellent lordosis responses in adulthood if injected with estrogens and progesterone. In rats, many behaviors are now known to be consistent with the organizational hypothesis: Animals exposed to either endogenous or exogenous androgens early in life behave like males, whereas animals not exposed to androgens early in life behave like females.

Some sex differences in behavior seem indifferent to early exposure to androgens. For example, male rhesus monkeys yawn more often than females, but this behavior seems to be the result of adult exposure to androgens. If rhesus males are castrated in adulthood, they yawn about as rarely as normal females, and treating adult females with androgens activates yawning. Exposure to androgens during devel-

IMPORTANT METHOD

opment has no effect on later yawning behavior, so this sex difference in behavior seems to respond solely to activational rather than to organizational effects of androgens.

In other cases, androgens seem to be needed both in development (to organize the nervous system to enable the later behavior) and in adulthood (to activate that behavior). As we learned earlier, for example, the copulatory behavior of male rats can be quantified in terms of how often they mount a receptive female and how often such mounting results in intromission. Androgens must be present in adulthood to activate this behavior: Adult males that have been castrated stop mounting in a few weeks; injecting them with testosterone eventually restores masculine copulatory behavior. Such androgen treatment has some effect on adult female rats as well, causing them to mount other females more often, but they rarely manage intromission of their phallus (the clitoris) into the stimulus female's vagina.

Thus, masculine copulatory behavior in rats and several other rodent species seems to depend on both organizational and activational influences of androgens. An early criticism of this conclusion was offered by Frank Beach (1971), who pointed out that the failure of females and neonatally castrated male rats to achieve intromission could well be due to the small size of the phallus rather than any differences in the nervous system. Indeed, there is remarkable correlation between the size of the penis and intromission success in male rats castrated at various ages (Beach and Holz, 1946). Thus, although excellent evidence suggests that steroids present at birth masculinize the body, Beach found no proof that they also masculinize the brain. However, an unexpected development soon made it clear that steroids do indeed organize the developing nervous system of rodents to display male copulatory behavior, as we will see next.

**Frank Beach
(1911–1988)**

The estrogenic metabolites of testosterone masculinize the nervous system and behavior of rodents

Soon after the organizational hypothesis was published, some researchers reported a paradoxical finding: When newborn female rats were treated with estrogens, they failed to show lordosis behavior in adulthood (Feder and Whalen, 1965). In fact, researchers were very puzzled to find that neonatal treatment with a very small dose of estradiol, regarded at that time as a *female* hormone, could permanently *masculinize* these behaviors. The results were especially strange because during development, all rat fetuses are exposed to high levels of estrogens that originate in the mother and cross the placenta. If estrogens masculinize the developing brain, why aren't all females masculinized by maternal estrogens?

A closer look at the synthesis of steroid hormones reveals the explanation. Testosterone and estradiol molecules are very closely related in structure. In fact, testosterone is the precursor for the manufacture of estradiol in the ovary. In a single chemical reaction, called *aromatization,* the enzyme **aromatase** converts testosterone to estradiol (and other androgens to other estrogens). The ovaries normally contain a great deal of aromatase, and the brain was found to have high levels of aromatase as well. From this evidence arose the **aromatization hypothesis,** which suggested that testicular androgens enter the brain and are converted there into estrogens, and that these estrogens are what masculinize the developing rodent nervous system.

**COMPETING
HYPOTHESES**

Why, then, aren't the brains of females masculinized by maternal estrogens? A blood protein called **α-fetoprotein** binds estrogens and prevents them from entering the brain. Although both male and female fetuses produce α-fetoprotein, this protein does not bind androgens. The male rat's brain is masculinized when testosterone from his testes is conveyed by the bloodstream (unimpeded by α-fetoprotein) to his brain, where it is aromatized to estrogen. The estrogen binds to local estrogen receptors, and the steroid–receptor complex regulates gene expression to cause the brain to develop in a masculine fashion (Figure 12.20). If no androgens are present, there can be no estrogenic action in the brain (because α-fetoprotein has blocked estrogens of peripheral origin), so the fetus develops in a feminine fashion. A lack of

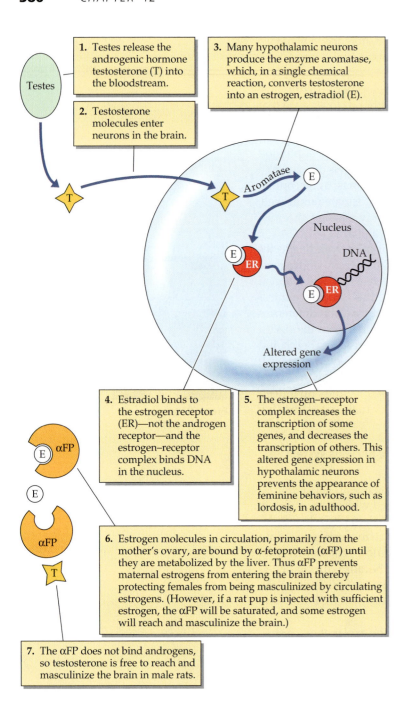

1. Testes release the androgenic hormone testosterone (T) into the bloodstream.

2. Testosterone molecules enter neurons in the brain.

3. Many hypothalamic neurons produce the enzyme aromatase, which, in a single chemical reaction, converts testosterone into an estrogen, estradiol (E).

Aromatase

Nucleus

DNA

Altered gene expression

4. Estradiol binds to the estrogen receptor (ER)—not the androgen receptor—and the estrogen–receptor complex binds DNA in the nucleus.

5. The estrogen–receptor complex increases the transcription of some genes, and decreases the transcription of others. This altered gene expression in hypothalamic neurons prevents the appearance of feminine behaviors, such as lordosis, in adulthood.

6. Estrogen molecules in circulation, primarily from the mother's ovary, are bound by α-fetoprotein (αFP) until they are metabolized by the liver. Thus αFP prevents maternal estrogens from entering the brain thereby protecting females from being masculinized by circulating estrogens. (However, if a rat pup is injected with sufficient estrogen, the αFP will be saturated, and some estrogen will reach and masculinize the brain.)

7. The αFP does not bind androgens, so testosterone is free to reach and masculinize the brain in male rats.

12.20 The Aromatization Hypothesis

aromatase seems to play a role in the unusual sexual differentiation of the spotted hyena (see Box 12.2).

The aromatization hypothesis, as investigated by Bruce McEwen, Frederick Naftolin, and their colleagues, was soon shown to be fully applicable to masculine copulatory behavior in rats. If a male rat was castrated at birth, he grew up to have a small penis and show few intromissions, even when given testosterone in adulthood. If a male was castrated at birth and given the androgen dihydrotestosterone (DHT), which cannot be aromatized into an estrogen, he grew up to have a penis of normal size, but still showed few or no intromissions when given testosterone. On the other hand, males castrated as newborns and treated with estrogens achieved intromission regularly when treated with androgens as adults, despite having very small penises (no larger than in untreated castrated males). Thus, Frank Beach's playful explanation of why female rats achieve few intromissions—"You can't be a carpenter if you don't have a hammer"—was disproved.

In primates, including humans, the importance of aromatization for masculinization of the nervous system is much less clear (Grumbach and Auchus, 1999). The human brain produces significant quantities of aromatase, but men who have mutations in the aromatase gene—and are thus unable to produce aromatase—nonetheless have masculine gender identities and sexual development. Estrogen resistance caused by mutations in the gene encoding the α-estrogen receptor (one of the two known isoforms of estrogen receptors) similarly lacks an effect on the development of masculine gender behavior. And androgen-insensitive XY individuals display very feminine behavior, even though they produce lots of testosterone and have functional estrogen receptors. The details of the masculinization of the primate nervous system, both nonhuman and human, thus remain to be worked out. Nevertheless, humans and a wide variety of other vertebrate species display distinct sexual dimorphisms in the nervous system.

Several regions of the nervous system display prominent sexual dimorphism

Bruce McEwen

Because male and female rats behave differently, researchers assumed that their brains were different, and the organizational hypothesis asserted that early androgens masculinize the developing brain. But these neural differences can be very subtle; the same basic circuit of neurons connected together will produce very different behavior if the strength of the myriad synapses varies. Sex differences in the number of synapses were identified in the preoptic area (POA) of the hypothalamus as early as 1971 (Raisman and Field, 1971). Later demonstrations of sexual dimorphism in the nervous system would include differences in the number, size, and shape of neurons, as well as the number of synapses. Let's discuss a few prominent models.

BOX 12.2 The Paradoxical Sexual Differentiation of the Spotted Hyena

Scientists of antiquity believed that spotted hyenas were hermaphrodites. The mistake is understandable because from birth the female hyena has a clitoris that is as large as the penis of males (as the photo shows), through which she urinates, receives semen, and gives birth. Females are also larger, more aggressive, and socially dominant over all males.

What is different about the hyena's prenatal development that causes this sexual monomorphism? In other mammals the placenta rapidly aromatizes androgens into estrogens; this conversion may be a way to protect the mother and fetal females from androgens produced by fetal males. (Remember that in many species a plasma protein—called *α-feto-protein*—prevents circulating estrogens from masculinizing the brain.) But the spotted hyena placenta is remarkably deficient in the aromatase enzyme (Licht et al., 1992).

Because the hyena mother produces large amounts of the androgen androstenedione (Glickman et al., 1987), and the placenta fails to convert the androstenedione to estrogens, all the fetuses receive considerable amounts of androgens, which may help account for their masculine appearance. Female hyenas that are treated prenatally with androgen-blocking drugs still develop masculinized exteriors (Drea et al., 1998), suggesting that a nonhormonal mechanism is involved. However, the pups of antiandrogen-treated females are much less likely to die during delivery (Drea et al., 2002), indicating that androgens must alter at

least some aspects of the genital tract of untreated females, and underscoring the costliness of the hyena's unusual mating system.

One remarkable finding from captive-bred hyenas is that female pups begin fighting immediately after birth. They are born with teeth and use them to attack their siblings. Female pups are very aggressive, especially toward a sister. In the laboratory, investigators intervene to prevent serious injury, but field studies indicate that in the wild it is very common for one pup to kill its sibling (Frank et al., 1991), at least during periods when food is scarce (Smale et al., 1999). It remains to be established that this extreme aggres-

sion is due to prenatal stimulation of the brain with androgens.

Even if the extreme aggressiveness of the female hyena is due to fetal androgens, females do mate with males, so their brains have not been made permanently unreceptive (as would happen in prenatally androgenized rats). Indeed, female hyenas seem to have a typically feminine SDN-POA (Fenstemaker et al., 1999) and SNB (Forger et al., 1996) (see the text). Just the same, mating in the spotted hyena is a tense affair: The female seems to just barely tolerate the male's proximity, and the male alternates between approaching and retreating from his more powerful mate. (Photograph courtesy of Stephen Glickman.)

Song control regions in male songbirds   While studying the brain regions involved in singing in canaries and zebra finches (see Chapter 19 for details of the song system), Fernando Nottebohm and Arthur Arnold (1976) noticed that the nuclei that control song are *much* larger in males than in females. In fact, the nuclei are five to six times larger in volume in males (which produce elaborate songs) than in females (which produce only simple calls).

Birds produce song through a specialized muscular organ called the **syrinx,** which controls the frequency of sounds produced by changing the tension of membranes around the air passage. The syrinx is controlled by the twelfth cranial nerve, which in turn is innervated primarily by a brain nucleus called the *robustus archistriatum (RA)*. Literally and figuratively higher still, the *higher vocal center (HVc)* exerts control over the RA. As we would expect, lesions of the RA or HVc disrupt singing, and electrical stimulation can elicit song snippets.

NEURAL PLASTICITY

Roger Gorski

As the organizational hypothesis would suggest, the early action of steroid hormone masculinizes the brains of zebra finches: Exposing a hatchling female to either testosterone or estradiol causes the HVc and the RA to be larger in adulthood. If such a female is also given testosterone as an adult, the nuclei become larger still, and she sings much like a male zebra finch does (Gurney and Konishi, 1979).

Female zebra finches treated with androgens only in adulthood do not sing. Thus, in zebra finches early hormone organizes a masculine song system, and adult hormone activates the system to produce song. In an interesting twist on the story, it has been difficult to determine the source of the steroidal signal; for example, inducing genetic females to develop with functional testes does not masculinize their song control nuclei, despite the presence of lots of testosterone (Wade and Arnold, 1996). Instead, it appears that the males' brains may locally manufacture the estradiol that masculinizes the system (Holloway and Clayton, 2001).

Singing in canaries, in contrast, relies only on adult effects of androgens; early exposure is unimportant. Adult female canaries will start singing after a few weeks of androgen treatment. The androgens cause the HVc and the RA to become larger, and their neurons grow and form new synaptic connections. This difference in hormonal control of song in zebra finches and canaries may be related to the ecological niche occupied by each.

Zebra finches are ready to breed at any time of the year, awaiting rainfall that will provide additional food. Canaries, however, are seasonal breeders whose reproductive tracts shut down in the fall. The male canary song system tracks this ebb and flow: The HVc and RA grow large in the spring, when the birds are singing and their testosterone levels are high, and shrink down again in the fall, as testosterone levels and singing decline.

The preoptic area of rats Where else might there be neural sex differences? The laboratory of Roger Gorski examined the preoptic area (POA) of the hypothalamus in rats because of an earlier report that the number of synapses in this region was different in males and females and because lesions of the POA disrupt ovulatory cycles in female rats and reduce copulatory behavior in males. Sure enough, the investigators found a nucleus within the POA that was much larger in volume in males than in females (Gorski et al., 1978).

This nucleus, dubbed the **sexually dimorphic nucleus of the POA (SDN-POA)**, is much more evident in male rats than in females (Figure 12.21). Like the song control nuclei in zebra finches, the SDN-POA conformed beautifully to the organizational hypothesis: Males castrated at birth had much smaller SDN-POAs in adulthood, while females androgenized at birth had large, malelike SDN-POAs as adults. Castrating male rats in *adulthood,* however, did not alter the size of the SDN-POA, and neither did treating adult females with androgens. Thus, testicular androgens somehow alter the development of the SDN-POA, resulting in a nucleus permanently larger in males than in females.

The function of the SDN-POA has been frustratingly elusive. Lesions of the SDN portion of the POA in rats cause only a slight, temporary decline in male copulatory behavior. A similar sexually dimorphic nucleus in gerbils appears to be involved in male-typical scent-marking behavior of that species (Yahr and Gregory, 1993). The

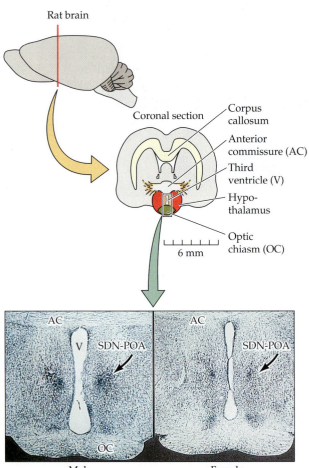

12.21 A Sex Difference in the Hypothalamus The sexually dimorphic nucleus of the preoptic area (SDN-POA) is much larger in male rats than in females. (Courtesy of Roger Gorski.)

association of sexual orientation and a human sexually dimorphic POA nucleus is discussed in Box 12.3.

In addition to fitting the organizational hypothesis, the SDN-POA conforms to the aromatization hypothesis: Testosterone is converted to an estrogen in the brain and binds estrogen receptors to masculinize the nucleus. For example, XY rats that are androgen-insensitive, like the people with AIS we discussed earlier (see Figure 12.19), have testes but a feminine exterior. These rats have a masculine SDN-POA because their *estrogen* receptors are normal. Androgen-insensitive rats also do not display lordosis in response to estrogens and progesterone, because the testosterone they secreted early in life was converted to an estrogen in the brain and masculinized their behavior (Olsen, 1979).

The spinal cord in mammals The birdsong work inspired a search for sexual dimorphism in the spinal cord, where neural elements controlling sexual response should be different for males and females. In rats, for example, the striated bulbocavernosus (BC) muscles (absent in adult females) that surround the base of the penis are innervated by motoneurons in the **spinal nucleus of the bulbocavernosus (SNB)** (Figure 12.22). Male rats have about 200 SNB cells, but females have far fewer motoneurons in this region of the spinal cord.

On the day before birth, female rats have BC muscles attached to the base of the clitoris that are nearly as large as those of males and that are innervated by motoneurons in the SNB region (Rand and Breedlove, 1987). In fact, a few days before birth, females have as many SNB cells as males do (Nordeen et al., 1985). In the days just before and after birth, however, many SNB cells die, especially in females, and the BC muscles of females die.

A single injection of androgens delivered to a newborn female rat permanently spares some SNB motoneurons and their muscles. Castration of newborn males, accompanied by prenatal blockade of androgen receptors, causes the BC muscles and SNB motoneurons to die as in females. Similarly, androgen-insensitive rats have very few SNB cells and no BC muscle, so aromatization seems to be unimportant for masculine development of this system.

Androgens act on the BC muscles to prevent their demise, and this sparing of the muscles causes the innervating SNB motoneurons to survive (Fishman et al., 1990; C. L. Jordan et al., 1991). Recall from Chapter 7 that about half of all the spinal motoneurons produced early in development normally die, that the death of the motoneurons can be prevented if they are provided with enough muscle target, and that the muscles are thought to provide a neurotrophic factor to keep the appropriate number of motoneurons alive into adulthood. For SNB motoneurons the neurotrophic factor may resemble ciliary neurotrophic factor (CNTF) because in mice with the receptor for CNTF knocked out, SNB motoneurons die in males, despite the presence of androgens (Forger et al., 1997).

The developmental rescue of SNB motoneurons is accomplished indirectly as a consequence of actions on muscle, but androgens can also directly affect the neurons themselves. SNB neurons contain androgen receptors and retain androgen sensitivity throughout life. In adulthood, androgen acts directly on the neurons to cause them to grow (Watson et al., 2001) and start producing substances to aid in the formation of new connections. For example, androgens directly stimulate SNB neurons to produce N-cadherin, a cell adhesion molecule that mediates the formation of new contacts between cells (Monks and Watson, 2001).

All male mammals have BC muscles, but in nonrodents the BC motoneurons are found in a slightly different spinal location and are known as **Onuf's nucleus.** Surprisingly, most female mammals retain a BC muscle into adulthood. For example, in women the BC surrounds the opening of

NEURAL PLASTICITY

(*a*) **Male rat**

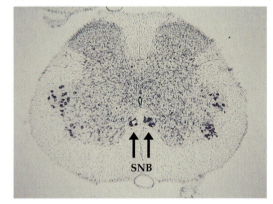

SNB

(*b*) **Female rat**

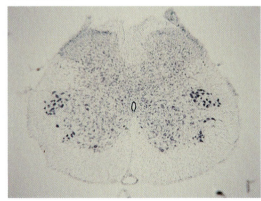

12.22 Sexual Dimorphism in the Spinal Cord
The spinal nucleus of the bulbocavernosus (SNB) consists of large, multipolar motoneurons. Male rats (*a*) have more SNB cells (arrows) than do females (*b*).

BOX 12.3 What Determines a Person's Sexual Orientation?

Some people develop romantic attachments to and yearn to have sex with a person of the same sex. Some researchers suggest that this sexual orientation is based on infants observing the adults around them and modeling their behavior on the behavior of the opposite sex, rather than their own. Others believe that something happens to the fetal brain to determine later orientation ("some people are born gay").

For the second group it is tempting to explain homosexual behavior as an example of the organizational action of early steroids that has been demonstrated in animals. If we deprive a male rat of androgens at birth, we can be sure that (with adult steroid treatment) he will display lordosis (a female behavior) in response to another male in adulthood. Superficially, the behavior of the male rat deprived of androgens at birth resembles homosexual behavior, but all we have measured is which sexual motor pattern the animal will display.

A neonatally androgenized animal mounts any rat—male or female. A female rat given estrogens and progesterone displays the lordosis posture in response to mounting by any rat—or even in response to the investigator's hand. In other words, the animals show these behaviors regard-

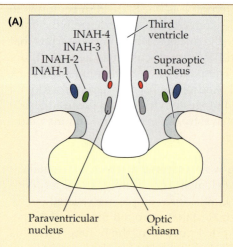

(A)

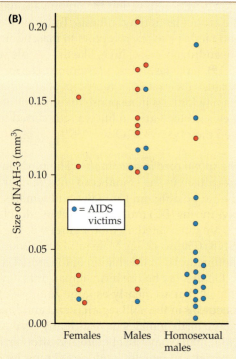

(B)

less of who or what their partner is. In contrast, we humans are more concerned about what sort of partner we have than about the particular sexual behavior we perform.

It is possible to measure what sort of rat companion a given rat prefers, but such studies paint a more complicated picture. There is more variability in steroid effects on a rat's partner preference than on lordosis or mounting behaviors. Homosexual behavior occurs in diverse wild species— mountain sheep, swans, gulls, dolphins, to name a few—but is not very amenable to

laboratory analysis (Bagemihl, 1999). Interestingly, homosexual behavior is noted widely among the anthropoid primates— apes and monkeys—but not among prosimian primates like lemurs and lorises. This division suggests that homosexuality

the vagina, and contractions of the BC slightly constrict the opening (hence in women the muscle is sometimes referred to as the *constrictor vestibule*).

Nevertheless, the BC is larger in men than in women, and men have more Onuf's motoneurons than women have (Forger and Breedlove, 1986), in keeping with the rat data. Motoneuron counts in the human spinal cord indicate that we all normally lose some of these motoneurons before the twenty-sixth week of gestation (see Figure 7.13) (Forger and Breedlove, 1987), a time during which male fetuses produce androgens.

Social Influences Affect Sexual Differentiation of the Nervous System

Environmental factors of many sorts, ranging from the temperature and chemical composition of the environment to the social contacts that an individual receives, can potently modulate the masculinization produced by steroids. A clear example of this is seen in the development of the SNB. Newborn rat pups can neither urinate nor defecate on their own; the mother (dam) must lick the anogenital region of each pup to elicit a spinal reflex to empty the bladder and colon. (Incidentally, the dam ingests at least some of the wastes and thereby receives pheromones from the pups that affect the composition of her milk as the pups mature. Another reason not to be a rat!)

BOX 12.3 *(continued)*

has a genetic basis in primates, emerging sometime around the Oligocene period (Vasey, 1995).

Simon LeVay (1991) performed postmortem examinations on the brains of homosexual men, heterosexual men, and women, and found that the POA (preoptic area) contains a nucleus (the third interstitial nucleus of the anterior hypothalamus, or INAH-3) (see Figure A) that is larger in men than in women and larger in heterosexual men than in homosexual men (Figure B). All but one of the gay men in the study had died of AIDS, and their sexual orientations were documented in their medical records. But the brain differences could not be due to AIDS pathology, because the straight men with AIDS had a significantly larger INAH-3 than did the gay men.

To the press and the public, this sounded like strong evidence that sexual orientation is "built in." It's possible, however, that early social experience affects the development of INAH-3 to determine later sexual orientation. Furthermore, sexual experiences as an adult could affect INAH-3 structure, so the smaller nucleus in some homosexual men may be the result of their homosexuality, rather than the cause. LeVay himself was careful to point out these alternatives, but most journalists never quite caught on.

In women, purported markers of fetal androgen exposure—otoacoustic emissions (McFadden and Pasanen, 1998) and finger length patterns (T. J. Williams et al., 2000)—suggest that lesbians, as a group, may have been exposed to slightly more fetal androgen than were heterosexual women. But these studies suggest considerable overlap between the two groups, indicating that fetal androgens cannot account fully for adult sexual orientation. Likewise, the finding that homosexual men and women are more likely to be left-handed than heterosexual men and women are (Lalumiere et al., 2000) suggests that androgens cannot be the whole story, because there is no known effect of early androgens on handedness. On the other hand, handedness does seem to be established early in life, so this correlation, too, indicates that early events influence adult orientation.

The reports that sexual orientation is heritable (J. M. Bailey and Bell, 1993) also do little to resolve the controversy. It appears that about 50% of variability in sexual orientation is accounted for by genetic factors, which leaves ample room for early social influences. Monozygotic twins, who have exactly the same genes, do not always have the same sexual orientation (Buhrich et al., 1991); and the likelihood

that a gay individual's monozygotic twin is also gay is about 50% (Bailey and Pillard, 1991; Bailey et al., 1993). In the unusual case of two nontwin brothers who are both homosexual, genetic evidence suggests that they are much more likely than by chance to have both inherited the same X chromosome region (called *Xq28*) from their mother (Hamer et al., 1993), but again the genetic explanation accounted for only some, not all, of the cases.

From a political viewpoint, the controversy—whether sexual orientation is determined before birth or determined by early social influences—is irrelevant. Many religions practiced in Western culture regard homosexuality as a sin that some people choose to commit, and this view forms the prime basis for laws and prejudices against homosexuality. But scientists representing each viewpoint agree that sexual orientation, especially in males, is set very early in life—by age 4 or so. Almost all homosexual and heterosexual men report that from the beginning, their interests and romantic attachments matched their adult orientation. Furthermore, despite extensive efforts, no one has come up with a reliable way to change sexual orientation (LeVay, 1996).

Celia Moore et al. (1992) noticed that dams spend more time licking the anogenital region of male pups than of females. If the dam is anosmic (unable to smell), she licks all the pups less and does not distinguish between males and females. Males raised by anosmic mothers thus receive less anogenital licking, and remarkably, fewer of their SNB cells survive the period around birth. The dam's stimulation of a male's anogenital region helps to masculinize his spinal cord.

NEURAL PLASTICITY

On the one hand, this masculinization is still an effect of androgens because the dam detects male pups by smelling androgen metabolites in their urine. On the other hand, this effect is clearly the result of a social influence: The dam treats a pup differently because he's a male and thereby masculinizes his developing nervous system. Perhaps this example illustrates the futility of trying to distinguish "biological" and "social" influences.

Attention from the dam has a different organizing effect on female rat pups. In adulthood, females who were licked frequently as pups show enhanced estrogen and oxytocin sensitivity in brain regions associated with maternal behavior, and they tend to be attentive mothers themselves. Females who are licked less as pups are less-attentive mothers later (Champagne et al., 2001).

What about humans? (No, no, not the licking part, the social influence part.) Humans are at least as sensitive to social influences as rats are. In every culture most people treat boys and girls differently, even when they are infants. Such differential treatment undoubtedly has some effect on the developing human brain and contributes to later sex differences in behavior. Of course, this is a social influence, but testosterone instigated the influence when it induced the formation of a penis.

If prenatal androgens have even a very subtle effect on the fetal brain, then older humans interacting with a baby might detect such differences and treat the baby differently. Thus, originally subtle differences might be magnified by early social experience. Such interactions of steroidal and social influences are probably the norm in the sexual differentiation of human behavior. Much controversy surrounds the debate over whether hormones or social influences determine sexual orientation (see Box 12.3).

Do Early Gonadal Hormones Masculinize Human Behaviors in Adulthood?

Since men and women behave differently, something about them, probably something about their brains, must be different. The remaining question is not *whether* steroids and social influences collaborate to produce sex differences in humans brains and behavior, but rather *how* they do so. For instance, does prenatal steroid exposure affect the adult behavior of humans? This is a tricky problem because, although prenatal androgens may or may not act on the human brain, they certainly act on the periphery.

If we expose a female fetus to enough androgen, she will look entirely male on the outside at birth and will be treated by family and society as a male. So if she(?) behaves in a male-typical fashion in adulthood, we won't know whether that behavior is due to what androgens did to the outside of the body or to the brain. We saw earlier that CAH females, exposed prenatally to androgens, play more like boys than normal females do. Is the reason for this difference in behavior the fact that androgens directly masculinized these females' brains or that, with their ambiguous genitalia, they or their parents had some doubts about their "real" gender?

Some people seem to change sex at puberty

We will close this chapter with a discussion of a fascinating phenomenon that demonstrates again the difficulty of distinguishing prenatal from social influences.

A rare genetic mutation affects the enzyme (5α-reductase) that converts testosterone to dihydrotestosterone (DHT). If an XY individual cannot produce this enzyme, the internal structures still develop in a masculine fashion. Testes develop, müllerian ducts regress, and wolffian duct structures, under the influence of testosterone, are masculinized. The genital epithelium, however, which normally possesses 5α-reductase, is unable to amplify the androgenic signal by converting the testosterone to the more active DHT. Consequently, the phallus is only slightly masculinized and resembles a large clitoris, and the genital folds resemble labia, although they contain the testes. Usually there is no vaginal opening.

(*a*) **Newborn**

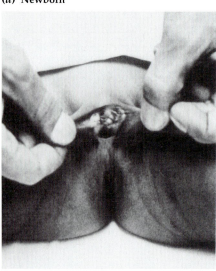

(*b*) **Adolescent**

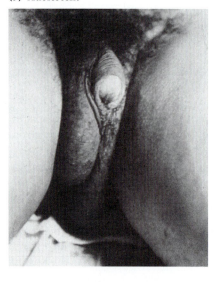

12.23 *Guevedoces*   In the Dominican Republic some individuals, called *guevedoces,* are born with ambiguous genitalia (*a*) and are raised as girls. At puberty, however, the phallus grows into a recognizable penis (*b*), and the individuals begin acting like young men. (Courtesy of Julianne Imperato-McGinley.)

Babies in a particular village in the Dominican Republic occasionally are born with this type of appearance (Figure 12.23). These children seem to be regarded as girls in the way they are dressed and raised (Imperato-McGinley et al., 1974). At puberty, however, the testes increase androgen production, and the external genitalia become more fully masculinized. The phallus grows into a recognizable penis; the body develops narrow hips and a muscular build, without breasts; and the individuals begin acting like young men. The villagers have nicknamed such individuals *guevedoces,* meaning "eggs (testes) at 12 (years)." These men never develop facial beards, but they usually have girlfriends, indicating that they are sexually interested in women.

There are two possible explanations for why these people raised as girls later behave as men. First, prenatal testosterone may have masculinized their brains; thus, despite being raised as girls, when they reach puberty their brains lead them to seek out females for mates. This explanation suggests that the social influences of growing up—assigning oneself to a gender and mimicking role models of that gender, as well as gender-specific playing and dressing—are unimportant for later behavior and sexual orientation.

An alternative explanation is that early hormones have no effect—that this culture simply recognizes and teaches children that some people can start out as girls and change to boys later. If so, then the social influences on gender role development might be completely different in this society from those in ours. In his Pulitzer Prize–winning novel *Middlesex* (2002), Jeffrey Eugenides describes the life of a baby born with 5α-reductase deficiency and raised as a girl in Detroit. It is interesting to see the novelist's conception of how masculine or feminine such a person would be.

The reports of sexual dimorphism in the adult human brain, often touted as proof of the predominance of "biological" influences, do not really address the issue. Nonetheless, across species the evidence suggests that hormones have at least some effect on the developing brain and that society reinforces and accentuates sex differences in humans.

Refer to the *Learning Biological Psychology CD* for study questions, animations, activities, and other study aids.

Summary

Sexual Behavior

1. Although reproductive behaviors vary widely in form between species, their ultimate goal is the successful fusion of male and female gametes, and the generation of a maximal number of viable offspring.

2. Reproductive behaviors are divided into four stages: sexual attraction, appetitive behavior, copulation, and postcopulatory behavior, including parental behaviors in some species.

3. The brain governs the time at which the organism should reproduce and uses protein hormones to induce the gonads to produce gametes and steroid hormones. Gonadal steroids activate the brain to increase the probability of reproductive behaviors.

4. Human copulatory behavior is remarkably varied. Most men show a single copulatory pattern; most women display one of three basic patterns of sexual response. For both sexes, the four basic stages of the sexual response pattern are (1) increasing excitement, (2) plateau, (3) orgasm, and (4) resolution. In general, men appear to experience greater sex drive than women; and whereas male sexuality is associated with feelings of power, female sexuality is more grounded in relationships and is more malleable. However, male and female sexuality overlap and are heavily influenced by sociocultural factors.

5. In humans, very low levels of testosterone are required for either men or women to display a full interest in mating, but additional testosterone has no additional effect. Therefore there is no correlation between circulating androgen levels and reproductive behaviors in men. Nor is there any strong correlation between copulatory behavior and stage of the menstrual cycle in women.

6. In many species, reproductive behaviors are organized by pheromones. Pheromones play a more subtle role, if any, in human sexuality.

Why Are There Two Sexes?

1. Sexual reproduction brings together in a single individual the beneficial mutations that have arisen in separate individuals, and it helps to shed harmful mutations.

2. In some species, sexual reproduction has led to the evolution of individuals specialized to reproduce as either a male or a female. Sexual differentiation during development then allows males and females to develop different bodies and brains.

3. Male and female vertebrates make different investments in their offspring; consequently, most males of most species are promiscuous, and most females of most species are very discriminating in choosing mates. This situation leads to sexual selection pressures that, over time, can exaggerate sexual dimorphism.

4. There are four different types of mating systems: (1) promiscuity (both sexes mate with multiple partners), (2) polygyny (each male mates with multiple females), (3) polyandry (each female mates with multiple males), and (4) monogamy (a single male and a single female form a lasting bond).

Sexual Differentiation

1. In birds and mammals, genetic sex determines whether testes or ovaries develop, and hormonal secretions from the gonads determine whether the rest of the body, including the brain, develops in a feminine or masculine fashion. In the presence of testicular secretions, a male develops; in the absence of testicular secretions, a female develops.

2. The brains of vertebrates are masculinized by the presence of testicular steroids during early development. Such organizational effects of steroids permanently alter the structure and function of the brain and therefore permanently alter the behavior of the individual.

3. Among the prominent examples of sexual dimorphism in the nervous system, gonadal steroids have been shown to alter characteristics such as neuronal survival, structure, and synaptic connections.

4. Several regions of the human brain are sexually dimorphic. However, we do not know whether these dimorphisms are generated by fetal steroid levels or by sex differences in the early social environment. Neither do we know whether any of the identified sex differences in neural structure are responsible for any sex differences in human behavior.

5. Although no reliable animal model of sexual orientation has been developed, all research indicates that sexual orientation is determined early in life and, especially in men, is not a matter of individual choice.

Recommended Reading

Becker, J. B., Breedlove, S. M., Crews, D., and McCarthy, M. M. (2002). *Behavioral endocrinology* (2nd ed.). Cambridge, MA: MIT Press.

Blum, D. (1997). *Sex on the brain.* New York: Viking Penguin.

Fausto-Sterling, A. (2000). *Sexing the body.* New York: Basic Books.

LeVay, S., and Valente, S. M. (2002). *Human sexuality.* Sunderland, MA: Sinauer Associates.

Miller, G. (2000). *The mating mind: How sexual choice shaped the evolution of human nature.* New York: Doubleday.

Nelson, R. J. (2000). *An introduction to behavioral endocrinology* (2nd ed.). Sunderland, MA: Sinauer Associates.

13

Homeostasis: Active Regulation of Internal States

A Pill to Make You Thin

In the mid-1990s, a 32-year-old woman was admitted to a cardiac care ward apparently suffering from acute heart failure. Clinical investigations revealed the root of her illness to be valvulopathy: The valves that usually keep the blood flowing in one direction through the heart had stiffened and failed. She thus joined a rapidly growing group of young women who had two things in common: a sudden, life-threatening heart valve disease, and a recent history of using the weight loss drug cocktail known as fen-phen (Connolly et al., 1997).

Faced with a mounting epidemic of obesity, physicians had welcomed the introduction of fen-phen—short for fenfluramine and phentermine—and wrote prescriptions by the millions for their often desperate patients. Previous drug treatments had proven ineffectual, and only a minority of dieters ever achieved significant long-term weight loss, but fen-phen yielded significant results quite rapidly. Tragically, epidemiological studies soon revealed that valvulopathy was evident in more than 30% of fen-phen users (Centers for Disease Control, 1997). The damage was linked specifically to fenfluramine, which was pulled from the market in 1997.

Although fenfluramine caused a lot of illness and suffering, the fact remains that it was an effective appetite suppressant. How did it work? Can we learn anything from the fen-phen disaster that will help us develop new treatments for tackling the obesity crisis?

S haped across innumerable millennia by the forces of evolution, our bodies contain a web of internal processes devoted to maintaining a constant bodily environment, and optimizing our acquisition and use of food energy. Body temperature, fluid balance, fat storage, nutrients—the conditions required for optimal cellular functioning—are carefully regulated, and although we are not normally aware of these processes, the nervous system is intimately involved in every stage.

Placed in the context of modern society, some of these ancient systems are creating new challenges for humankind to deal with. In particular, an epidemic of obesity is sweeping much of the First World, bringing with it a dramatic increase in associated diseases, such as diabetes, heart disease, and stroke. Identifying the cultural and physiological roots of this epidemic, and developing safe and effective methods for controlling it, is a major health concern. The physiological and behavioral processes governing the internal environment—and their role when things go wrong—are our topic in this chapter.

Starvos, *Solitary Figure*

Homeostasis Maintains Internal States within a Critical Range

Because warmth, water, and food are vital and scarce, elaborate physiological systems evolved to monitor and maintain them. One hallmark of these systems is **redundancy:** There are several different means of monitoring our stores, of conserving remaining supplies, and of shedding excesses. Therefore the loss of function of one part of the system can be compensated for by the remaining portions. This redundancy helps keep us alive, but it also makes it difficult for us to figure out how the body regulates temperature, water balance, and food intake. Another hallmark of these three regulatory, or **homeostatic,** systems is that each one exploits the organism's behavior to regulate and to acquire more heat, water, or food. The nervous system coordinates these regulatory systems.

If we are losing body heat, the nervous system directs us to seek warmth. When our internal water supplies are low, we seek water; and when our internal nutrient supplies are low, we seek food. Our conscious experience in each of these cases is that we feel cold, thirsty, or hungry, respectively. Other animals are unable to use words to tell us how they feel, so for the rest of this chapter we will assume that an animal seeking water is thirsty, that an animal seeking food is hungry, and that an animal seeking shelter has an internal drive to conserve heat.

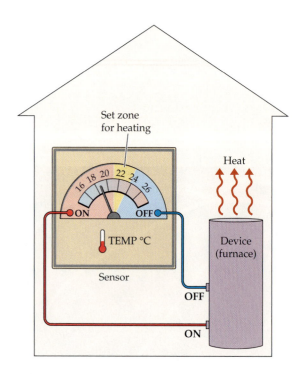

13.1 Negative Feedback   The thermostatically controlled heating system found in homes is an example of a negative feedback system. All such systems have a sensor (in this example a thermometer) to monitor the variable (in this case temperature), and a device (in this example the furnace) to change the variable (e.g., by heating the room). The changed variable (in this case, the heat) provides a negative feedback signal to the sensor, turning the system off.

The homeostatic mechanisms that regulate temperature, body fluids, and metabolism are primarily **negative feedback** systems. In each case, deviation from a desired value, called the **set point,** triggers a compensatory action of the system. A simple analogy is the setting of a household thermostat (Figure 13.1): A temperature drop below the set point activates the thermostat, which turns on the heating system. (We already discussed negative feedback systems in connection with neural circuits in Chapter 3, and with the regulation of hormone secretion in Chapter 5.) Note that in general there is a degree of tolerance in the feedback system equivalent to a small range between the "turn on" and "turn off" signals. Without this tolerance the system would be going on and off very frequently. So for most systems there is really a **set zone** rather than a set point.

The setting of the thermostat can be changed; for example, it can be turned down at night to save energy. Similarly, although the body temperature for most mammals is usually held within a narrow range—about 36°C to 38°C (97°F to 100°F)—most mammals reduce their temperature during sleep (rather like turning the thermostat down at night). Our bodies also integrate the demands for nutrients and water to result in a set range of body weight that is often remarkably narrow. Later in the chapter we will see examples of animals defending their body weight—that is, maintaining a particular weight in the face of physiological challenges.

Unavoidable losses require us to gain heat, water, and food

The regulation of internal resources is complicated by the fact that staying alive requires us to give up some of them. Because external temperatures rarely hover at 37°C (98.6°F) for long, we must actively heat or cool our bodies. We lose water vapor with each breath, as well as through sweating and, because various biochemical processes produce waste chemicals that can be eliminated only with a little water, through urination. Food provides us with energy and nutrients (chemicals needed for growth, maintenance, and repair of the body), but our behavior uses up energy and incurs wear and tear on the body, so more energy and nutrients are continuously needed. Our homeostatic mechanisms are continually challenged by these unavoidable losses (sometimes called *obligatory losses*), which require us to gain and conserve heat, water, and food constantly.

TEMPERATURE REGULATION

Why do we feel so uncomfortable when we're hot or cold? That's nature's way of telling us that body temperature is a vital concern.

Body Temperature Is a Critical Condition for All Biological Processes

The rate of chemical reactions is temperature-dependent. The enzyme systems of mammals and birds are most efficient within a narrow range around 37°C. At lower temperatures, reactions slow down, and some stop altogether. At higher temperatures, protein molecules fold together improperly and thus do not function as they should. At very high temperatures, tissue proteins break down and fuse together again in a haphazard manner, and if the tissue in question happens to be tasty, we say it is *cooked*. Brain cells are especially sensitive to high temperatures. A prolonged high fever can cause brain centers that regulate heart rate and breathing to die, immediately killing the rest of the patient too.

At very low temperatures, the lipid bilayers that make up cellular membranes become so disrupted by the formation of ice molecules that they cannot re-form

(a)

(b)

13.2 Braving the Cold   Mealworm beetles (*a*) and golden-mantled ground squirrels (*b*) are two species that sometimes have body temperatures below 0°C. The beetles produce an "antifreeze" in body fluids to prevent ice crystals from forming in their cell membranes.

when thawed. Some animals that cannot avoid subfreezing temperatures—for example, some species of fish and beetles (Figure 13.2*a*)—produce "antifreeze" consisting of special protein molecules that suppress the formation of ice crystals and prevent damage to membranes (Harding et al., 2003; Liou et al., 2000).

Some Animals Generate Heat; Others Must Obtain Heat from the Environment

Popular terminology distinguishes between *warm-blooded* animals (mainly mammals and birds) and *cold-blooded* animals (all the others). Unfortunately, this description is inaccurate. A hibernating ground squirrel (Figure 13.2*b*) may cool to less than 8°C, and a desert iguana, warmed by the sun, may have an internal temperature exceeding the mammalian norm of 37.8°C. Instead of these traditional categories, contemporary researchers favor a distinction between **endotherms** (from the Greek *endon,* "within"), which regulate their body temperature chiefly by internal metabolic processes, and **ectotherms** (from the Greek *ektos,* "outside"), which get most of their heat from the environment.

Ectotherms do regulate their body temperature, but through behavioral means, such as by moving to favorable sites or changing their exposure to external sources of heat. Endotherms also choose favorable environments, but primarily they regulate body temperature by making internal adjustments. Both endotherms and ectotherms seek out a preferred environmental temperature, which varies from species to species.

The advantages of endothermy come at a cost

No one knows whether endothermy arose in a common ancestor of the birds and mammals or arose separately in these two lines. What we do know is that endotherms pay substantial costs for maintaining a high body temperature and keeping it within narrow limits. Much food must be obtained and metabolized, and elaborate regulatory systems are required. Why evolve such a complicated and costly system, compared to the more economical and deviation-tolerant system of ectotherms?

One obvious advantage is greater independence from environmental conditions. As we've mentioned, enzyme systems are temperature-sensitive, so by producing a constant internal temperature, endothermy allows an animal to forage in a wider variety of environments. A second advantage of endothermy involves the use of oxygen. In order to stoke the chemical reactions through which they generate heat (discussed in the next section), endotherms evolved a greater capacity for oxygen uti-

EVOLUTION AT WORK

lization. This improved oxygen capacity brought with it the ability to sustain high levels of muscular activity over long periods of time.

Ectotherms are capable of bursts of intense muscular activity for only a few minutes, because anaerobic metabolism—metabolism consisting of chemical reactions that do not require oxygen—contributes most of the energy. After a few minutes, the animal must rest and repay the oxygen debt. In contrast, endotherms can employ primarily aerobic metabolism and thereby sustain long periods of muscular exertion (A. F. Bennett and Ruben, 1979). Ectotherms can escape from and sometimes even pursue endotherms over short distances, but in a long-distance race the endotherm will win.

Endotherms generate heat through metabolism

The utilization of food by the body is known as **metabolism.** Because the breaking of chemical bonds releases energy as heat, all living (and thus metabolizing) tissues produce heat. The unit of heat is a kilocalorie (kcal); 1 kcal is enough heat to raise the temperature of a liter of water 18°C. An adult human may generate 600 kcal per hour when exercising strenuously, but only 60 kcal per hour when resting.

When the human body is at rest, about a third of the heat it generates is produced by the brain. As body activity increases, the heat production of the brain does not rise much, but that of the muscles can increase nearly tenfold; so when we are active, our bodies produce a much higher percentage of the heat we generate. Like mechanical devices, muscles produce a good deal of heat while they are accomplishing work. Muscles and gasoline engines have about the same efficiency; each produces about four or five times as much heat as mechanical work. Some of the main ways the human body gains, conserves, and dissipates heat are shown in Figure 13.3.

The rate of heat production can be adjusted to suit conditions, particularly in certain organs. Deposits of brown adipose tissue (also called **brown fat**) are found especially around vital organs in the trunk and around the cervical and thoracic lev-

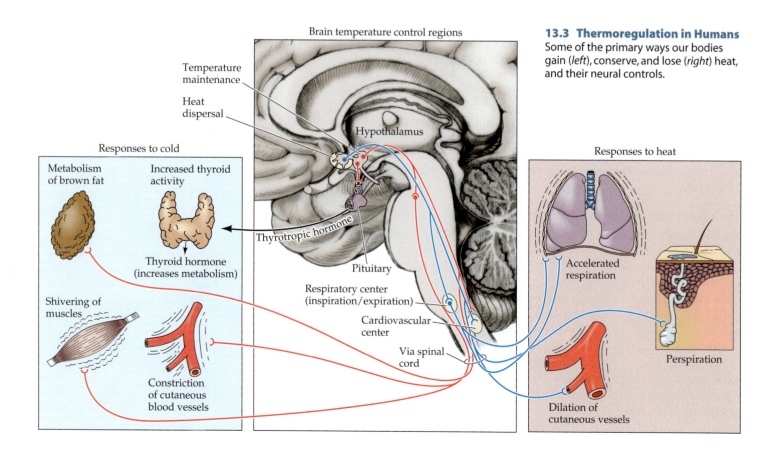

13.3 Thermoregulation in Humans Some of the primary ways our bodies gain (*left*), conserve, and lose (*right*) heat, and their neural controls.

Brain temperature control regions

Temperature maintenance
Heat dispersal
Hypothalamus
Thyrotropic hormone
Pituitary
Respiratory center (inspiration/expiration)
Cardiovascular center
Via spinal cord

Responses to cold
Metabolism of brown fat
Increased thyroid activity
Thyroid hormone (increases metabolism)
Shivering of muscles
Constriction of cutaneous blood vessels

Responses to heat
Accelerated respiration
Perspiration
Dilation of cutaneous vessels

TABLE 13.1 *Body Size and Heat Production of Some Birds and Mammals*

Species	Body weight (kg)	Body surface (m²)	Surface-to-weight ratio (m²/kg)	Energy output per day		
				Total (kcal)	Per unit of body weight (kcal/kg)	Per unit of body surface (kcal/m²)
Canary	0.016	0.006	0.375	5	310	760
Rat	0.2	0.03	0.15	25	130	830
Pigeon	0.3	0.04	0.13	30	100	670
Cat	3.0	0.2	0.07	150	50	750
Human	60	1.7	0.03	1500	25	850
Elephant	3600	24	0.007	47,000	13	2000

els of the spinal cord. These fat cells look brown because they are full of mitochondria that break down molecules and produce heat. Under cold conditions the sympathetic nervous system stimulates metabolism within the brown-fat cells, producing heat.

A more conspicuous way to generate heat is through muscular activity. At low temperatures, nerve impulses cause muscle cells to contract out of synchrony, producing shivering rather than coordinated movements. Humans start to shiver when the body temperature approaches 36.58°C. This response spreads from facial muscles to the arms and legs. The fivefold increase in oxygen uptake that accompanies extreme shivering shows how metabolically intense this response is.

The rate at which an animal loses heat is directly proportional to the ratio of its surface area to its volume or weight (Table 13.1). Small animals with large surface-to-volume ratios, such as the shrew, must eat nearly constantly and maintain high metabolic rates in order to maintain the target body temperature. A large animal, like an elephant, has a much lower surface-to-volume ratio, and because it loses heat more slowly, it can afford a lower metabolic rate per gram of body weight.

Across different climate zones, evolution has shaped the bodies of animals according to the thermoregulatory challenges they face (Figure 13.4); arctic animals tend to have blockier bodies with shorter appendages (to reduce surface area), along with

EVOLUTION AT WORK

(a)

(b)

(c)

13.4 Adaptations of Appendages to Climate   The external ears in foxes from tropical (*a*), temperate (*b*), and arctic (*c*) climates vary in size.

13.5 A Specialized Mechanism for Reducing Core Temperature Exercise produces heat, but some species, such as the dog, have a special heat exchange system to prevent the brain from overheating (*bottom right*). Human anatomy, lacking a carotid rete, is more like that of the rabbit (*bottom left*). (After Karasawa et al., 1997.)

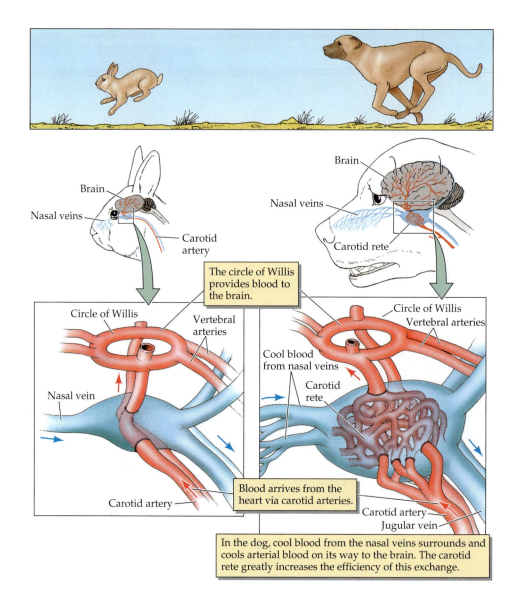

The circle of Willis provides blood to the brain.

Blood arrives from the heart via carotid arteries.

In the dog, cool blood from the nasal veins surrounds and cools arterial blood on its way to the brain. The carotid rete greatly increases the efficiency of this exchange.

increased insulation in the form of fur, feathers, or blubber. Equatorial and desert animals tend to have more-elongated bodies with enlarged appendages to increase surface area and, in some cases, like an elephant's ears, to act as radiators. Many species have specialized mechanisms for reducing core temperature (Figure 13.5).

Which Behaviors Can Adjust Body Temperature?

Ectotherms generate little heat through metabolism and therefore must rely heavily on behavioral methods to regulate body temperature. The marine iguana of the Galápagos Islands eats seaweed underwater for an hour or more at a time (occasionally coming up for air) in water that is 10°C to 15°C cooler than its preferred body temperature. After feeding, the iguana emerges and lies on a warm rock to restore its temperature. While warming up, it lies broadside to the sun to absorb as much heat as possible (Figure 13.6*a*). When its temperature reaches 37°C, the iguana turns to face the sun and thus absorb less heat, and it may extend its legs to keep its body away from warm surfaces (Figure 13.6*b*).

Many other ectotherms regulate body temperature in similar ways. Some snakes, for example, adjust their coils to expose more or less surface to the sun and thus keep their internal temperature relatively constant during the day. Bees regulate the temperature inside the hive by their behavior, keeping the temperature in the brood area

(a)
(b)

13.6 Behavioral Control of Body Temperature   (a) A Galápagos marine iguana, upon emerging from the cold sea, raises its body temperature by hugging a warm rock and lying broadside to the sun. (b) Once its temperature is sufficiently high, the iguana reduces its surface contact with the rock and faces the sun to minimize its exposure. These behaviors afford considerable control over body temperature. (Photographs by Mark R. Rosenzweig.)

at 35°C to 36°C. When the air temperature is low, the bees crowd into the brood area and shiver, thus generating heat. When the air temperature is high, the bees reduce the temperature in the brood area by fanning with their wings.

Even endotherms such as mammals and birds control their exposure to the sun and to hot or cold surfaces to avoid making excessive demands on their internal regulatory mechanisms. In hot desert regions, many small mammals, such as the kangaroo rat, remain in underground burrows during the day and appear above ground only at night, when the environment is relatively cool. And throughout history, of course, humans have devised many practices to adapt to conditions of cold or heat, ranging from the use of fans and swimming pools to the creation of heating systems and highly insulating clothing.

The behavioral thermoregulatory responses of ectotherms and endotherms are thus divided into three categories:

1. *Changing exposure of the body surface*—for example, by huddling or extending limbs
2. *Changing external insulation*—for example, by using clothing or nests
3. *Selecting a surrounding that is less thermally stressful*—for example, by moving to the shade or into a burrow

Humans seldom wait for the body to get cold before putting on a coat. We anticipate homeostatic signals on the basis of experience. As any parent will tell you, shivering reflects a lapse of intelligent behavior.

Young birds and mammals need help to regulate body temperature

Fetuses maintained in the mother's body rely on her to provide warmth and regulate temperature. Most birds keep their eggs warm by using a specially vascularized area of skin (the brood patch), which transfers heat efficiently to the eggs. Even after hatching or birth, the young of many species cannot regulate body temperature very well, mostly because they are small (and lose heat quickly) and have limited energy resources. So they must continue to be protected by their parents.

Because rat pups are born without hair, they have a hard time maintaining body temperature when exposed to cold. The rat mother keeps her pups protected in a warm nest, and warms them with her own body heat. As shown in Figure 13.7a, newborn rat pups are able to generate heat by using brown-fat deposits like the one between the shoulder blades (Blumberg et al., 1997).

(a)

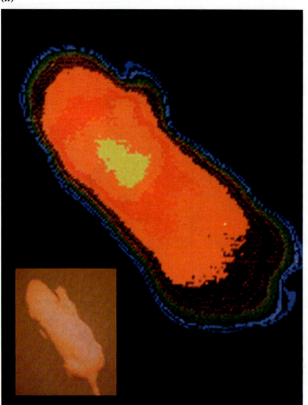

13.7 Physiological and Social Thermoregulation   (*a*) This infrared thermograph shows the dorsal surface of a 1-week-old rat pup oriented as shown in the inset. Areas of highest heat production are coded in orange and yellow, and the prominent yellow "hot spot" between the shoulder blades overlies a depot of brown fat, a thermogenic (i.e., heat-producing) organ. When rat pups are placed in a cold environment, they begin producing heat by using brown fat. (*b*) Rat pups also use behavioral mechanisms to conserve heat. Animals push to the center of a litter to gain heat and move to the periphery to cool off. Thus an anesthetized pup will be left in the center during high temperatures and pushed to the periphery when temperatures are low. (Part *a* courtesy of Mark S. Blumberg; *b* after Alberts, 1978.)

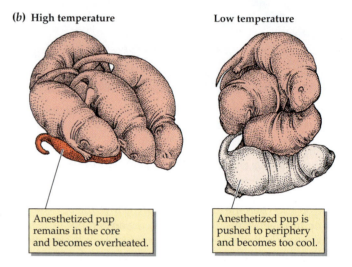

(*b*) **High temperature**   **Low temperature**

Anesthetized pup remains in the core and becomes overheated.

Anesthetized pup is pushed to periphery and becomes too cool.

Nonetheless, one problem for newborn rats is insulating their hairless bodies to conserve the heat they generate. To tackle this problem, they huddle together (Figure 13.7*b*). The effectiveness of this strategy is easily demonstrated: When isolated 5-day-old pups are placed in a cool chamber (23°C–24°C), their body temperature falls below 30°C in less than an hour, but when they are part of a group of four, the pups maintain their temperatures above 30°C for 4 hours or more (Alberts, 1978), and they consume less oxygen. Pups frequently change their positions in the huddle, regulating their temperature by moving to the inside or the outside of the clump. In effect, the pups share both the costs and the benefits of behavioral thermoregulation.

Some endotherms survive by letting their body temperature plummet

All endotherms show some variation in body temperature. There's usually a daily fluctuation in body temperature that constitutes a circadian rhythm, which we'll discuss in Chapter 14. When we are ill, we may have a fever. This fever is brought on by the body to help fight off infection.

But some endotherms occupy habitats with extreme seasonal variations in temperature. For example, golden-mantled ground squirrels in the far north survive long, cold winters by staying in their burrows, curling up in a tight ball, and allowing their body temperature to plummet. An animal in this state, called **torpor,** is cold to the touch and appears not to breathe, but it does take a breath every few moments or so. Its heart still beats, but only very slowly.

No one knows how these animals evolved the ability to survive this drop in body temperature, which would certainly kill a human, but it seems clear that they save a great deal of energy while in torpor. The state does not last the entire winter; once a week or so the animals arouse from torpor by raising their body temperature, move about the burrow, check on outside conditions, and if things look grim, reenter torpor. The arousal episode requires energy but lasts less than an hour, so the animals save a good deal of energy over the winter (Heldmaier and Ruf, 1992). Reduced glucose availability, which indicates a shortage of available energy, can trigger an episode of torpor (Dark et al., 1994).

The Brain Monitors and Regulates Body Temperature

The nervous system controls and regulates all the processes of heat production and heat loss, sometimes with assistance from the endocrine system. What parts of the nervous system are active in these processes?

In the 1880s, physiologists found that small lesions in the hypothalamus of dogs elevated body temperature. Barbour (1912) manipulated the temperature of the hypothalamus in dogs by implanting silver wires. When the wires were heated, body temperature fell; when the wires were cooled, body temperature rose. These results suggested that body temperature is monitored in the hypothalamus and that when temperature there departs in either direction from the desired level, compensatory actions are triggered. In the 1950s, electrical recording revealed that some neurons change their discharge rate in response to small increases or decreases of brain temperature; these cells are scattered throughout the preoptic area (POA) and the anterior hypothalamus.

Lesion experiments in mammals indicate that there are different sites for two kinds of regulation: (1) regulation by locomotor and other behaviors common to both endotherms and ectotherms, and (2) physiological regulation characteristic of endotherms. Lesions in the lateral hypothalamus of rats abolished *behavioral* regulation of temperature but did not affect the autonomic thermoregulatory responses such as shivering and vasoconstriction (Satinoff and Shan, 1971; van Zoeren and Stricker, 1977). On the other hand, lesions in the POA of rats impaired the *autonomic* responses but did not interfere with such behaviors as pressing levers to turn heating lamps or cooling fans on or off (Satinoff and Rutstein, 1970; van Zoeren and Stricker, 1977). This is a clear example of parallel circuits for two different ways of regulating the same variable.

Receptors at the surface of the body also monitor temperature. If you enter a cold room, you soon begin to shiver—long before your core temperature falls. If you enter a hot greenhouse or a sauna, you begin to sweat before your hypothalamic temperature rises. The skin provides information to central circuits, which promptly initiate corrective action in *anticipation* of a change in core temperature.

Does the body have a single master thermostat?

It would be simple to think that a single integrating center accounts for thermoregulation. However, evidence has accumulated to suggest that a single thermostat is inadequate to account for all the facets of thermoregulation. For one thing, as we saw in the previous section, there appear to be different brain sites for behavioral and autonomic regulation of temperature. Even two thermoregulatory circuits may not be sufficient.

A rat exposed to increasing heat normally shows a succession of three different responses: First it grooms, then it moves about actively, and finally it lies quietly in a sprawled-out position. Grooming allows the rat to lose heat by evaporation of saliva from the skin, activity normally helps the rat locate a cooler spot, and sprawling out helps the rat dissipate heat. Local heating of the brain does not produce this sequence; instead, each of these behaviors tends to be elicited by the heating of a different brain region (W. W. Roberts and Mooney, 1974). These observations are not consistent with the hypothesis of a single thermostat.

In addition, there seems to be a hierarchy of thermoregulatory circuits, some located at the spinal level, some centered in the midbrain, and others in the hypothalamus, including the POA. For example, spinal animals (in which the brain has been disconnected from the spinal cord) can regulate body temperature somewhat, indicating that a temperature monitor is available to the spinal cord and/or the body.

(a) Hypothalamus

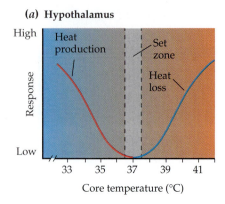

(b) Brainstem

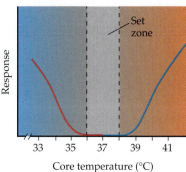

(c) Spinal cord

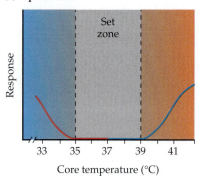

13.8 Multiple Thermostats in the Nervous System Thermoneutral zones of thermoregulatory systems are narrower at higher levels of the nervous system than at lower levels. (After Satinoff, 1978.)

Evelyn Satinoff

Such animals die in extended cold or heat, however, because they do not respond until body temperature deviates 2°C to 3°C from normal values.

Evelyn Satinoff (1978) suggested that the thermal set zones are broader in "lower" regions of the nervous system (Figure 13.8). The thermoregulatory systems at the "highest" level—the hypothalamus—have the narrowest neutral zones, and they normally coordinate and adjust the activity of the other systems. This arrangement can give the impression of a single system, although in reality there are multiple interlinked systems.

Figure 13.9 summarizes the basic thermoregulatory system: Receptors in the skin, body core, and hypothalamus detect temperature and transmit that information to three neural regions (spinal cord, brainstem, and hypothalamus). If the body temperature moves outside the set zone, each of these neural regions can initiate autonomic and behavioral responses to return it to the set zone.

FLUID REGULATION

The water that you drink on a hot day is carefully measured and partitioned by the nervous system. A precise balance of fluids and dissolved salts bathes the cells of the body and allows them to function.

EVOLUTION AT WORK

Our Cells Evolved to Function in Seawater

The first living creatures on Earth were single-celled organisms that arose in the sea. In this setting—a large body of water with fairly uniform concentrations of salts and minerals—most basic cellular reactions evolved, including DNA production and replication, the manufacture of proteins from amino acids, and the storing and harnessing of chemical energy from ATP. These various reactions evolved by natural selection to proceed efficiently only in a particular concentration of salt water. For these creatures, maintaining the proper concentration of salts in the water was effortless: They simply let seawater inside the cell membrane and let it out again. But when multicellular animals began coming out of the water onto land, they either had to evolve all new cellular processes to work without water, or they had to bring the water with them. Only the latter solution (no pun intended) was feasible.

Land animals had to prevent **dehydration** (excessive loss of water) so that their cells would work properly. Thus they needed a more or less watertight outer layer of cells, and they had to maintain the proper concentration of salts and other molecules in body fluids. The composition of the fluid inside your body, once proteins and the like have been removed, is still similar to that of seawater.

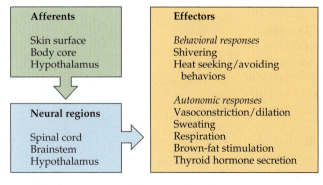

13.9 Basic Elements of Mammalian Thermoregulatory Systems

During evolution, diversity has arisen across species in the concentration of salt in plasma. For example, in closely related fish species, those that inhabit freshwater have a lower salt concentration in the plasma than those that inhabit seawater.

For a given species, if the concentration of molecules is altered even a small amount, the most basic cellular functions cease working properly and the animal dies. Only a few species can tolerate much variability in the distribution of salt in their environment; the salmon, for example, has unique adaptations that allow it to live in freshwater at hatching, to grow up in salt water, and to return again to freshwater to spawn.

Because we cannot seal our bodies from the outside world, we experience constant obligatory losses of water and salts. Many body functions require that we use up some water (and some salt molecules), as, for example, when we produce urine to rid ourselves of waste molecules. These losses necessitate active replenishment of the body's water and salts (Table 13.2), monitored and controlled by the nervous system, to maintain the precise composition of body fluids that cells require in order to function.

TABLE 13.2 *Average Daily Water Balance*

Source	Quantity (liters)
Approximate intake	
Fluid water	1.2
Water content of food	1.0
Water from oxidation of food	0.3
Total	**2.5**
Approximate output	
Urine	1.4
Evaporative loss	0.9
Feces	0.2
Total	**2.5**

Water in the human body moves back and forth between two major compartments

Most of our water is contained within the billions of cells that make up the body; this is the **intracellular compartment.** But some fluid is outside of our cells, in the **extracellular compartment.** The extracellular compartment can be subdivided into interstitial fluid (the fluid between cells) and blood plasma (the protein-rich fluid that carries red and white blood cells). Water is continually moving back and forth between these compartments, in and out of cells, via specialized water channels studding the cell membrane. These channels belong to a family of proteins called **aquaporins:** a single aquaporin-1 channel can selectively conduct about 3 *billion* molecules of water per second! (Agre et al., 2002). For the discovery and characterization of aquaporins, Peter Agre was awarded a Nobel Prize in Chemistry in 2003.

By convention, water in the stomach or elsewhere in the gastrointestinal tract is considered to be outside the body—in neither the intracellular nor the extracellular compartment. Water must leave the gastrointestinal tract and enter the body before we can make use of it. Similarly, water that has reached the bladder cannot be returned to the body, so it is effectively outside the body as well. Figure 13.10 presents a simplified version of the basic systems that regulate fluid intake.

To understand the forces driving the movement of water, we must understand osmosis. **Osmosis** is the passive movement of molecules from one place to another. The motive force behind osmosis is the constant vibration and movement of

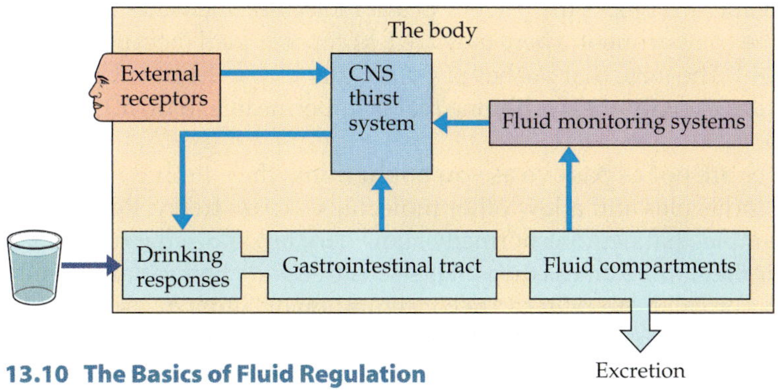

13.10 The Basics of Fluid Regulation

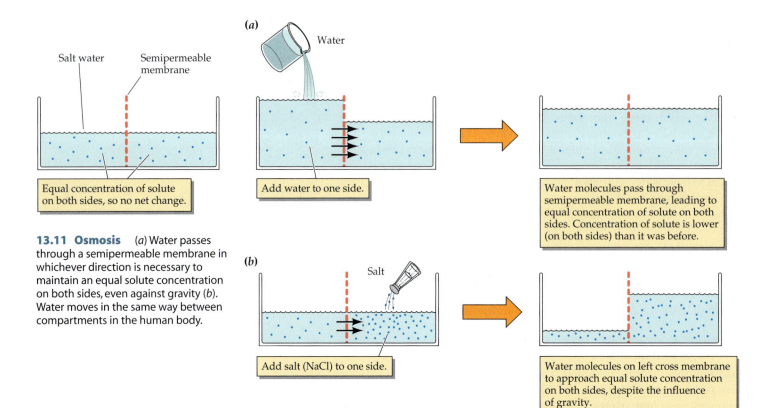

13.11 Osmosis   (a) Water passes through a semipermeable membrane in whichever direction is necessary to maintain an equal solute concentration on both sides, even against gravity (b). Water moves in the same way between compartments in the human body.

Within figure (a):

Salt water   Semipermeable membrane

Equal concentration of solute on both sides, so no net change.

Water

Add water to one side.

Water molecules pass through semipermeable membrane, leading to equal concentration of solute on both sides. Concentration of solute is lower (on both sides) than it was before.

Within figure (b):

Salt

Add salt (NaCl) to one side.

Water molecules on left cross membrane to approach equal solute concentration on both sides, despite the influence of gravity.

molecules. If we put a drop of food coloring (a **solute**) in a beaker of water (a **solvent**), the molecules of dye meander about because of this jiggling until they are more or less uniformly distributed throughout the beaker.

If we divide the beaker of water in half with a solid barrier that is impermeable to water and dye, and we put the dye in the water on one side, the molecules distribute themselves only within that half. If we divide the beaker with a barrier that impedes dye molecules only a little, then the dye first distributes itself within the initial half and then slowly invades and distributes itself across both halves. In this case we say that the barrier is permeable to the dye. A barrier such as a cell membrane that is permeable to some molecules but not others is referred to as *selectively permeable* or *semipermeable* (see Chapter 3). The osmotic movement of water across a semipermeable membrane is depicted in Figure 13.11.

Molecules have a tendency to spread out—to move *down* concentration gradients (from an area of higher concentration to an area of lower concentration). We mentioned this tendency in Chapter 3 in order to explain the movement of ions during generation of an action potential. In the case we have examined here, in which the semipermeable membrane blocks the passage of salt molecules, the water molecules are moving into the compartment where they are less concentrated (because the salt molecules are there). The force that pushes or pulls water across the membrane (the force that the solutes exert on the membrane that is impermeable to them) is called **osmotic pressure.**

Cell membranes are not as passive as you might think; they strongly resist the passage of some molecules and allow other molecules to pass freely. Recall from Chapter 3, for example, that neurons normally allow very few sodium ions (Na^+) to pass through their membrane unless the voltage-sensitive Na^+ channels are opened during the action potential. We refer to the concentration of solute in a solution as **osmolality.** Normally the concentration of NaCl in the extracellular fluid of mammals is about 0.9% (weight to volume, which means there's about 0.9 g of NaCl for every 100 mL of water). A solution with this concentration of salt is called *physio-logical saline* and is described as **isotonic,** having the same concentration of salt as mammalian fluids have. A solution with more salt is **hypertonic;** a solution lower in salt is **hypotonic.**

Drugs injected into the extracellular space of muscles are usually mixed in iso-tonic solution rather than in pure water because if pure water were injected, it would be pulled inside muscle cells (which are filled with ions) by osmotic pressure and would rupture them. At the other extreme, if hypertonic saline were injected, water would be pulled out of the cells, and that, too, could damage them. These fates could befall any cells bathed in fluid of the wrong tonicity, either too concentrated or too dilute. To prevent this from happening, the extracellular fluid serves as a *buffer*—a reservoir of isotonic fluid that provides and accepts water molecules so that cells can maintain proper internal conditions. The nervous system is responsible for ensur-ing that the extracellular compartment has about the right amount of water and solute to allow cells to absorb or shed water molecules readily, as conditions dictate.

Two Internal Cues Trigger Thirst

In addition to acting as a buffer, the extracellular fluid is an indicator of conditions in the intracellular compartment. In fact, the nervous system carefully monitors the extracellular compartment to determine whether we should seek water. Two dif-ferent states can signal that more water is needed: low extracellular volume (**hypo-volemic thirst**) or high extracellular solute concentration (**osmotic thirst**) (Figure 13.12). We'll consider each in turn.

Hypovolemic thirst is triggered by a loss of water volume

The example of hypovolemic thirst that is most easily understood is one we hope you never experience: serious blood loss (hemorrhage). Any animal that loses a sig-nificant amount of blood has a lowered total blood volume. In this condition, blood vessels that would normally be full and slightly stretched no longer contain their

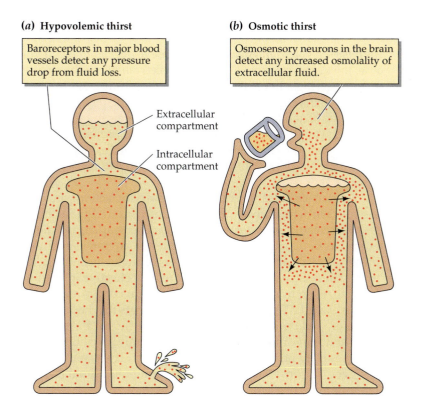

(a) Hypovolemic thirst

Baroreceptors in major blood vessels detect any pressure drop from fluid loss.

Extracellular compartment

Intracellular compartment

(b) Osmotic thirst

Osmosensory neurons in the brain detect any increased osmolality of extracellular fluid.

13.12 Two Kinds of Thirst (*a*) Hypovolemic thirst is trig-gered by the loss of blood or other body fluids (such as through diarrhea or vomiting) that contain both solutes and water. In this case, extracellular fluid is depleted without the solute concentration being changed in either the intracellular or the extracellular compartments, so there is no osmotic pressure to push water from one compartment to the other. (*b*) Osmotic thirst is triggered when the total volume of water is constant but a sudden increase in the amount of solute in the extracellular compartment (as after a very salty meal) ex-erts osmotic pressure that pulls water out of the intracellular compartment.

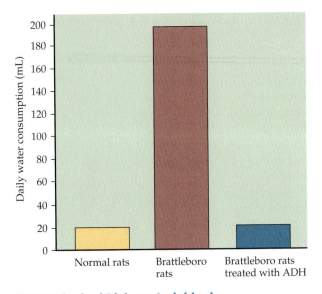

13.13 Inherited Diabetes Insipidus in Rats Unable to produce vasopressin (ADH), Brattleboro rats urinate profusely and so must drink a lot of water. Treatment with vasopressin corrects this condition, which is known as diabetes insipidus.

full capacity. Blood pressure drops, and the individual (unless unconscious) becomes thirsty.

Note that losing water from blood loss (or from diarrhea or vomiting) does not change the concentration of the extracellular fluid, because salts and other ions are lost along with the fluid. Rather, only the *volume* of the extracellular fluid is affected in these instances (see Figure 13.12*a*). However, continued loss in the extracellular compartment would lead to fluid passing out of the intracellular compartment. The initial drop in extracellular volume is detected by pressure receptors, termed **baroreceptors,** which are located in major blood vessels and in the heart. On receiving a signal from these baroreceptors via the autonomic nervous system, the brain activates several responses, such as thirst (to replace the lost water) and salt hunger (to replace the solutes that have been lost along with the water). Replacing the water without also replacing the salts would result in hypotonic extracellular fluid. The sympathetic portion of the autonomic nervous system also stimulates muscles in the artery walls to constrict, reducing the size of the vessels and partly compensating for the reduced volume.

The role of vasopressin An additional response to hypovolemia involves the release of the peptide hormone vasopressin from the posterior pituitary gland. Vasopressin induces additional constriction of blood vessels. Furthermore, vasopressin instructs the kidneys to reduce the flow of water to the bladder. For this reason, vasopressin is sometimes called *antidiuretic hormone* (*ADH*), as we saw in Chapter 5. (A diuretic is a substance that causes excessive urination.)

In the disease **diabetes insipidus,** the production of vasopressin ceases, and the kidneys retain less water; they send more urine to the bladder, and that urine is very pale and dilute (insipid). A consequence of all this urination is chronic thirst. Treatment with vasopressin relieves the symptoms. Diabetes insipidus has been modeled in rats with genetically defective vasopressin synthesis (Figure 13.13). (Note that when people talk about diabetes, they usually do not mean diabetes insipidus, but are referring to diabetes mellitus, which we'll discuss later in this chapter.)

The renin–angiotensin system In response to decreased blood volume, the kidneys release a hormone called *renin* into the circulation, triggering a hormonal cascade (Figure 13.14). Renin reacts with a protein called angiotensinogen to form angiotensin I, which is then converted to angiotensin II, which seems to be the active product. (The first demonstrated effect of this protein was to increase blood pressure, which is how it got its name: from the Greek *angeion,* "blood vessel," and the Latin *tensio,* "tension or pressure.")

Angiotensin II has several water-conserving actions. In addition to constricting blood vessels, angiotensin II triggers the release of two hormones: vasopressin, discussed earlier, and aldosterone, to be discussed shortly. However, angiotensin II also directly affects behavior: Very low doses of angiotensin II injected directly into the preoptic area are extremely effective in eliciting drinking, even in animals that are not deprived of water (A. N. Epstein et al., 1970). When administered to rats that had been deprived of food but not water, angiotensin II caused them to stop eating and start drinking; thus its effect is highly specific. It is clear from these and other studies that angiotensin II acts on the brain to trigger the sensation of thirst, prompting the animal to drink (Fitzsimmons, 1998).

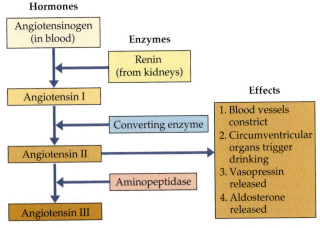

13.14 The Angiotensin Cascade A drop in blood volume is detected by the kidneys. The kidneys then release renin, which catalyzes the conversion of angiotensinogen (already present in blood) to angiotensin I. Angiotensin I is converted to angiotensin II (the most biologically active of the angiotensins).

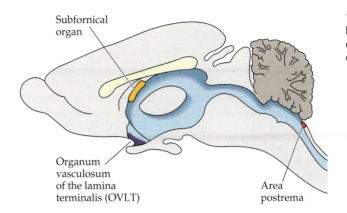

Subfornical organ

Organum vasculosum of the lamina terminalis (OVLT)

Area postrema

13.15 Circumventricular Organs The circumventricular organs, seen here in a midsagittal view of the rat brain, mediate between the brain and the cerebrospinal fluid (blue). The blood–brain barrier is weak in the subfornical organ and the OVLT, so neurons there can monitor the osmolality of blood.

Circulating angiotensin II may act via several other brain sites, particularly the **circumventricular organs.** As their name suggests, these organs lie in the walls encircling the cerebral ventricles (Figure 13.15). The blood–brain barrier is somewhat "leaky" in these regions, so the neurons here have enhanced access to proteins that are circulating in the blood or cerebrospinal fluid. Angiotensin II interacts with specific angiotensin receptors on the neurons of the circumventricular organs, producing a neural signal that is propagated to other sites in the brain.

The **subfornical organ** is a circumventricular organ that is particularly sensitive to angiotensin II: When angiotensin II is injected intravenously, neurons of the subfornical organ rapidly increase their metabolic activity (Kadekaro et al., 1989) and IEG (immediate early gene) expression (Lebrun et al., 1995) (see Box 2.3). However, the role of angiotensin II in "normal" thirst remains to be established; for example, modest reductions in blood volume can produce thirst independently of circulating angiotensin II levels (S. F. Abraham et al., 1975; Stricker, 1977). Perhaps the angiotensin II mechanism is just one of several redundant systems for provoking thirst, and is not active under all conditions (for a thorough review of the angiotensin system, see Fitzsimmons, 1998).

Osmotic thirst is triggered by a change in the concentration of extracellular fluid

Although hemorrhage is accompanied by powerful hypovolemic thirst, this is a relatively rare event. Thirst is more commonly triggered by obligatory water losses—recall that these include respiration, perspiration, and urination—in which more water is lost than salt. In this case, not only is the volume of the extracellular fluid decreased, triggering the responses described in the previous section, but also the solute concentration of the extracellular fluid increases. As a result of this increased saltiness of the extracellular fluid, water is pulled out of cells through osmosis.

Furthermore, the solute concentration of the extracellular fluid can be increased without any increase in volume—for example, by intake of salty food. In general, an increase in solute concentration of the extracellular fluid triggers a thirst that is independent of extracellular volume: osmotic thirst (see Figure 13.12b). Osmotic thirst causes us to seek water to protect the intracellular compartment from becoming so depleted of water that its cells are damaged.

In the 1950s it was shown that injecting a small amount of hypertonic (salty) solution into regions of the hypothalamus causes animals to start drinking. This observation suggested that some hypothalamic cells might be **osmosensory neurons**—that is, cells that respond to changes in osmotic pressure. Electrical recordings from single nerve cells have revealed osmotically responsive neurons spread widely throughout the preoptic area, the anterior hypothalamus, the supraoptic nucleus, and the organum vasculosum of the lamina terminalis (OVLT), a circumventricular organ (see Figure 13.15).

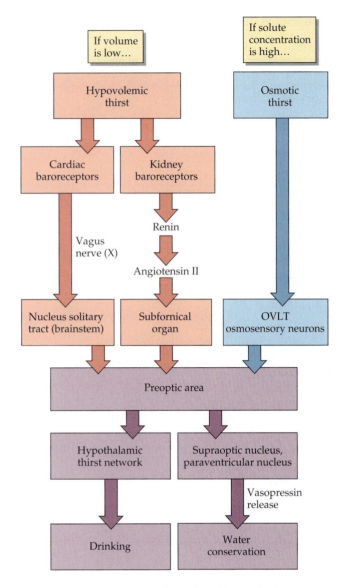

13.16 A More Complete View of Fluid Regulation This more detailed version of Figure 13.10 depicts the thirst signals and brain regions that regulate body fluids.

Osmosensory neurons have several key features that let them detect the concentration of extracellular fluid (Z. Zhang and Bourque, 2003). First, they are stretchy. Most cells of the body employ regulatory processes to try to maintain a constant volume in the face of osmotic challenges. Osmosensory neurons don't do this, and they will balloon or shrink to a greater extent than non-osmosensory neurons when the concentration of the extracellular fluid changes. Second, the cell membranes of osmosensory neurons are studded with mechanically gated ion channels—channels that open or close when the cell membrane is physically deformed. The stretching and shrinking of the cell membrane in these neurons opens and closes the mechanically gated channels, causing changes in cell membrane potentials that track the changes in extracellular concentration. This information is then relayed to other parts of the brain. The neural circuits that subsequently trigger drinking behavior are not yet fully described.

The two types of thirst (hypovolemic and osmotic), the two fluid compartments (extracellular and intracellular), and the multiple methods to conserve water make for a fairly complicated system. The current conceptualization of this system is depicted in Figure 13.16.

We don't stop drinking just because the throat and mouth are wet

Although plausible, the most obvious explanation of why we stop drinking—that a previously dry throat and mouth are now wet—is quite wrong. In one test of this hypothesis, thirsty animals were allowed to drink water, but the water they consumed was diverted out of the esophagus through a small tube. They remained thirsty and continued drinking. Moistening the mouth is not sufficient to stop the behavior of drinking or the sensation of thirst.

Furthermore, we stop drinking before water has left the gastrointestinal tract and entered the extracellular compartment. Somehow we monitor how much water we have ingested and stop in *anticipation* of correcting the extracellular volume and/or osmolality. Experience may teach us and other animals how to gauge accurately whether we've ingested enough to counteract our thirst (hypovolemic or osmotic). Normally all the signals—blood volume, osmolality, moisture in the mouth, estimates of the amount of water we have ingested that's "on the way"—register agreement, but the cessation of one signal alone will not stop thirst; in this way, animals ensure against dehydration.

Homeostatic Regulation of Salt Is Required for Effective Regulation of Water

Animals may travel great distances to eat salt, and the sodium ion (Na^+) is particularly important to fluid balance. The reason is that we cannot maintain water in the extracellular compartment without solutes; if the extracellular compartment contained pure water, osmotic pressure would drive it into the cells, killing them. The number of Na^+ ions we possess primarily determines how much water we can retain. Thus, thirsty animals may prefer slightly salty water (as long as it's hypotonic) over pure water, and this preference may be adaptive for conserving water. Some Na^+ loss is inevitable, as during urination. But when water is at a premium, the body tries to conserve Na^+ in order to retain water.

As noted earlier, low blood volume causes the kidneys to release renin, which makes angiotensin II available in circulation. In addition to its effects on thirst and vasopressin secretion, angiotensin II stimulates the release of **aldosterone** from the adrenal glands. Aldosterone, which is a steroid hormone classified as a mineralocorticoid, is crucial to Na^+ conservation. Aldosterone acts directly on the kidneys, inducing them to conserve Na^+, and thereby aiding water retention. Nonetheless, animals must find additional salt in their diets to survive.

Because some Na^+ aids water retention, you might think that seawater would quench thirst—but it doesn't. Seawater is hypertonic; it has too much Na^+. We lose some water each day without Na^+ (through our skin, with our breathing), and that sodium-free water must be replaced. Adding isotonic water will not help restore the water-to-sodium ratio. If we could excrete lots of sodium ions in our urine, we could drink seawater, use some of the water molecules to replace the day's loss, and excrete the excess salt. But our kidneys cannot excrete enough additional Na^+ in the urine to allow this.

Although we cannot survive on salt water, some species have evolved special adaptations that allow them to do so. Marine mammals have found a means of excreting excess salt, via kidneys that can produce very concentrated urine. Some desert rodents can also produce highly concentrated urine to help conserve water, and a rare variety of Bactrian camel found in Mongolia can meet its water requirements by drinking salt water, unlike its domesticated cousins, which require freshwater. Some seabirds, including gulls and petrels, have specialized salt glands near the nostrils that can excrete highly concentrated salt solutions (Figure 13.17) (Schmidt-Nielsen, 1960), so they can drink seawater.

13.17 Secretion of Excess Salt   Marine birds, such as this giant petrel, have only seawater to drink for long periods of time. To compensate, they have salt glands that pull salt out of plasma, releasing excess salt out the nostrils.

FOOD AND ENERGY REGULATION

Feast or famine—these are poles of human experience. Hunger for the food that we need to build, maintain, and fuel our bodies is a compelling drive, and flavors are powerful reinforcements. The behaviors involved in feeding ourselves shape our daily schedules and mold our activities. Our newspapers are full of food-related information: news of successes or failures of food crops; famines and droughts; laws and treaties governing the import and export of foods; hunger strikes; recipes and articles about food; advertisements for restaurants and kitchen appliances; effects of diet and obesity on health; clinics to treat weight problems.

Our basic reliance on food for energy and nutrition is shared with all other animals. In the remainder of this chapter we will look at the general needs and physiological regulation of feeding and energy expenditure, as well as some species-specific aspects of food-related behavior.

Nutrient Regulation Requires the Anticipation of Future Needs

The regulation of eating and of body energy is intimately related to the regulation of body temperature and water, which we have already considered, but it is more complicated. One reason for the greater complexity is that food is needed not only to supply energy but also to supply nutrients. **Nutrients,** in the technical meaning of the term, are chemicals that are not used as sources of energy but are required for the effective functioning of the body; for example, they are needed for the growth, maintenance, and repair of body structures.

We do not know all the nutritional requirements of the body—even for humans. Nine of the 20 amino acids found in our bodies are difficult or impossible for us to manufacture, so we must find these *essential amino acids* in our diet. We must also obtain a few fatty acids from food, as well as about 15 vitamins and a variety of minerals.

No animal can afford to run out of energy or nutrients; there must be a reserve on hand at all times. If the reserves are too large, though, mobility (for avoiding predators or securing prey) will be compromised. For this reason, the nervous system not only monitors nutrient and energy levels and controls the process of **digestion** (the process of breaking down ingested food), but also has complex mechanisms for *anticipating* future requirements.

Most of our food is used to provide us with energy

All the energy we need to move, think, breathe, and maintain body temperature is derived in the same way: It is released as the chemical bonds of complex molecules are broken to form smaller, simpler compounds. In a sense we "burn" food just as a car burns gasoline for energy. To raise body temperature, we release the bond energy as heat. For other bodily processes, such as those in the brain, the energy is utilized by more sophisticated biochemical processes.

The basic unit used for measuring food energy is properly called a **kilocalorie (kcal)**; in popular usage, this unit is often referred to by the more familiar but inaccurate term *calorie*. Studies of rat metabolism suggest that about one-third (33%) of the energy in food is lost in the process of digestion: Either it cannot be metabolized and is excreted, or it powers the digestive process itself. The majority (55%) of food energy in a meal is consumed by basal metabolic processes, such as heat production, maintenance of membrane potentials, and all the other basic life-sustaining functions of the body. The remainder, only about 12% of the total, is utilized for active behavioral processes, although this proportion is increased in more complex environments or during intense activity.

In general, the rate of basal metabolism follows a rule, devised by Max Kleiber (1947), that relates energy expenditure to body weight:

$$\text{kcal/day} = 70 \times \text{weight}^{0.75}$$

where weight is expressed in kilograms. This relationship applies across a wide range of body sizes, from the largest mammals to mice—a range in size greater than 3000 to 1 (Figure 13.18). Interestingly, at the population level Kleiber's equation holds across species, but it is not very accurate for *individuals* within a species, which warns us that body weight is only one factor affecting metabolic rate.

Within a species, an animal's basal metabolic rate may depart significantly from the value predicted by Kleiber's equation. For example, food-deprived people have a lower basal metabolism, as well as a lower weight. In fact, severe restriction of caloric intake affects metabolic rate much more than it affects body weight (Keesey and Corbett, 1984). Such adjustments in the rate of energy expenditure play a significant role in maintaining energy balance and in keeping an individual's body weight relatively constant (Keesey and Powley, 1986).

Because people and animals adjust their energy expenditures in response to under- or overnutrition, they tend to resist either losing or gaining weight (Figure 13.19). When a person begins dieting, his basal metabolic rate falls to *prevent* losing weight! Mice whose basal metabolic rate has been increased (by a transgenic increase in the energy used by mitochondria) eat more and weigh less than normal mice, without increased locomotor activity (Clapham et al., 2000). Perhaps someday a drug will be developed to exert this effect on human mitochondria, and produce such wonderful results.

However difficult dieting might be, the only known way to cause animals to live longer is to reduce their calorie intake to levels about 50% to 75% of what they would eat if food were always available (Weindruch and Walford, 1988), which may be related to the resulting decrease in basal metabolism. Both the body and

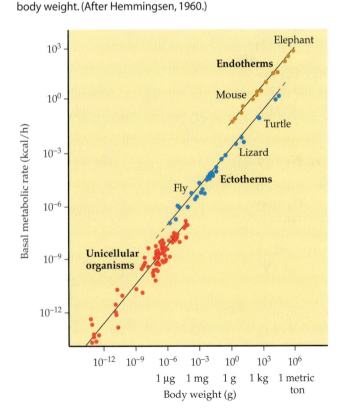

13.18 The Relation between Body Size and Metabolism Over a wide range of body weights, basal metabolic rate increases in a very regular, predictable fashion. However, endotherms have a higher metabolic rate than ectotherms of a similar body weight. (After Hemmingsen, 1960.)

the brain give evidence of slower aging with such caloric restriction (C.-K. Lee et al., 1999, 2000).

The mechanisms responsible for this enhanced longevity have not yet been fully described. Neurons of mice on restricted diets produce increased amounts of **brain-derived neurotrophic factor** (**BDNF**), which may promote their growth and survival (Anson et al., 2003) and contribute to the slowed aging of the brain. Mice that have been genetically engineered for decreased sensitivity to circulating **insulin-like growth factor** (**IGF**; associated with glucose homeostasis, among other functions) exhibit substantially increased life spans (Holzenberger et al., 2003). They also show increased resistance to oxidative stress—the cellular stress caused by interactions with oxygen free radicals, which may be a cause of physiological aging.

Carbohydrates provide energy for body and brain

Which molecules provide energy to the body, and how does the body regulate that energy? Large carbohydrate molecules can be broken down into simple carbohydrates, including sugars. The most important sugar used by our body is **glucose,** and this is the *only* fuel that the brain can use. Other cells of the body can use either glucose or other more complicated molecules, especially **ketones,** which are produced when fat is metabolized.

Because a constant supply of glucose is crucial for brain function and ultimate survival, it is stored by the liver and other tissues in the form of **glycogen.** This storage process is controlled by the pancreatic hormone **insulin;** another pancreatic hormone, **glucagon,** promotes the conversion of glycogen back into glucose when the concentration of glucose in the blood drops too low (Figure 13.20).

For long-term energy storage we use fat, maintained in fat cells; these fat cells form what is known as **adipose tissue.** Fat molecules are large and complicated. You may think of them as the result of the joining together of many sugars and other small molecules into a large molecule that is not soluble in water. Fat either comes directly from our food or is manufactured in the body from glucose and other nutrients. If the glycogen store becomes depleted, the body can convert fat into fatty acids to supply energy to itself, and into glucose to provide energy to the brain.

When a human or any other animal is deprived of food, little or no energy is stored in fat deposits. When an animal eats liberally, some of the energy is laid down in fat supplies so that it will be available in the future. Currently, there is vigorous debate about the most effective ways to decrease fat deposition through dieting. Although it is counterintuitive, evidence is accumulating to suggest that diets low in carbohydrates, and correspondingly high in proteins and fats (like the Atkins diet), are effective in helping people to lose weight and may increase serum levels of "good" cholesterol while decreasing fats (e.g., G. D. Foster et al., 2003; Samaha et al., 2003).

However, long-term studies will be required to establish the overall cardiovascular safety of low-carbohydrate diets; after all, plenty of evidence already indicates that people with diets low in fat have less heart disease. Furthermore, the long-term effects of

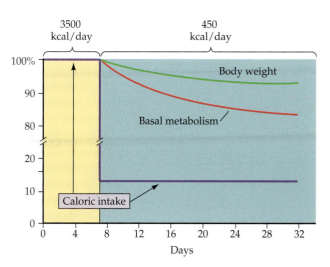

13.19 Why Losing Weight Is So Difficult   After 7 days on a diet of 3500 kcal/day, the intake of six obese subjects was restricted to a measly 450 kcal/day—a drop of 87%. However, basal metabolism also declined by 15%; so after 3 weeks, body weight had declined by only 6%. (After Bray, 1969.)

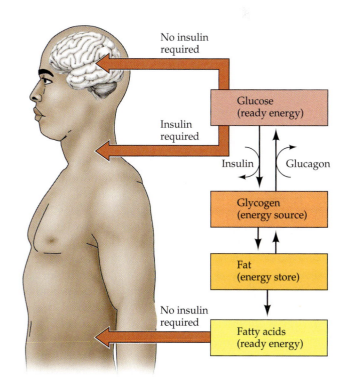

13.20 The Role of Insulin in Energy Utilization   The body can make use of either fatty acids or glucose for energy. The brain, however, can make ready use of only glucose; so the brain requires a constant supply of glucose, which it can use without the aid of insulin. On the other hand, the body can make use of glucose only with the aid of insulin; so in the absence of insulin, the body must use fatty acids for energy.

increased protein and fat loads on other organ systems—such as the liver and kidneys, which must work harder—remains to be established. So until longer-term data are available, perhaps the old adage "everything in moderation" remains sound advice. In any case, as we will see later, considerable evidence suggests that the body maintains its level of fat in the face of all but the most extreme diet restrictions, and regains fat after the surgical removal of fat stores.

Insulin Is Crucial for the Regulation of Body Metabolism

We have already mentioned the importance of insulin for converting glucose into glycogen. Another important role of insulin is enabling the body to use glucose. Most cells regulate the import of glucose molecules via **glucose transporters** that span the cell membrane and bring glucose molecules from outside the cell into the cell for use. The glucose transporters must interact with insulin in order to function. (Brain cells are an important exception; they can use glucose without the aid of insulin.)

Each time you eat a meal, the foods are broken down and glucose is released into the bloodstream. Most of your body requires insulin to make use of that glucose, so three different, sequential mechanisms stimulate insulin release:

1. The stimuli from food (sight, smell, and taste) evoke a conditioned release of insulin in anticipation of glucose arrival in the blood. This release, because it is mediated by the brain, is called the *cephalic phase* of insulin release.
2. During the *digestive phase,* food entering the stomach and intestines causes them to release gut hormones, some of which stimulate the pancreas to release insulin.
3. During the *absorptive phase,* glucose enters the bloodstream, and special cells in the liver, called **glucodetectors** (or *glucostats*), detect this circulating glucose and signal the pancreas to release insulin.

Terry Powley

The newly released insulin allows the body to make use of some of the glucose immediately, and other glucose is converted into glycogen. The liver and the pancreas communicate via the nervous system. Autonomic afferents from the liver deliver nerve impulses up the **vagus nerve** to synapse in the **nucleus of the solitary tract** (**NST**) in the brainstem, so information from glucodetectors in the liver travels up the vagus nerve to the NST. Terry Powley and colleagues (Powley, 2000) have mapped these vagal afferents to other brain regions, such as the hypothalamus, informing the brain of circulating glucose levels and contributing to hunger, as we'll discuss later. Efferent fibers carry signals from the brainstem back out the vagus nerve to the pancreas. These efferent fibers modulate insulin release from the pancreas.

CLINICAL ISSUE

Lack of insulin causes the disease **diabetes mellitus.** In *Type I* (or *juvenile-onset*) *diabetes mellitus,* the pancreas stops producing insulin. Although the brain can still make use of glucose from the diet, the rest of the body cannot and is forced to use energy from fatty acids. The result is that lots of glucose is left in the bloodstream because the brain cannot use it all, and the lack of insulin means there is no way to put it into glycogen storage. Some of the glucose is secreted into the urine, making the urine sweet, which is how we get the name *diabetes mellitus* (literally "passing honey"). In contrast, *diabetes insipidus* (literally "passing bland"), which we discussed earlier in the chapter, gets its name from the dilute urine that it produces.

An untreated person with diabetes eats a great deal and yet loses weight because the body cannot make much use of the ingested food and must derive energy solely from fatty acids, which causes damage to some tissues. People suffering from diabetes also drink and urinate copiously in an attempt to rid the body of the excess circulating glucose. Replacement of the missing insulin (via injection) allows the glucose to be utilized. Another, more common type of diabetes mellitus is called *Type II*, or *adult-onset, diabetes.* This milder version, caused either by gradually decreasing sensitivity to insulin or gradually decreasing insulin production, is particularly associated with obesity and often leads to further health problems.

Despite their importance, neither insulin nor glucose is the sole signal for either hunger or satiety

Given the crucial role of insulin in mobilizing and distributing food energy, you might think that the brain monitors circulating insulin levels to decide when it is time to eat and when it is time to stop eating. For example, if the insulin level is high, there must be food in the pipeline and the fat stores will be increased, so the brain might produce the sensation of **satiety** (feeling "full") so that we stop eating. If insulin levels are low, the brain might signal hunger to impel us to find food and eat. Indeed, lowering an animal's blood insulin levels causes it to become hungry and eat a large meal. If moderate levels of insulin are injected, the animal eats much less. These results suggest that insulin is a satiety signal.

Investigators tested this simple hypothesis by injecting a large amount of insulin into animals. But rather than appearing satiated, the animals responded by eating a large meal. High insulin levels direct much of the glucose into fat storage, which means that there is effectively less glucose in circulation for the brain. The brain learns of this functional glucose deficit from glucodetectors in the brain (probably in one or more of the circumventricular organs; see Figure 13.15) and the liver (which communicates to the NST via the vagus nerve). Is circulating glucose signaling satiety and hunger to the brain? Certainly this information plays a role normally, but it can't be the only source of information, because people with diabetes who remain untreated have very high levels of circulating glucose, yet they are chronically hungry.

Studies of diabetic rats provide more evidence that insulin is not the only satiety signal. Like untreated humans with diabetes, these rats eat a great deal. But if the rats are fed a high-fat diet, they eat normal amounts (M. I. Friedman, 1978), probably because their bodies can make immediate use of the fatty acids without the aid of insulin. Thus, circulating levels of insulin and glucose contribute to hunger and satiety, but they are not sufficient to explain those states entirely. Somehow the brain integrates insulin and glucose levels with other sources of information to decide whether to initiate eating. This seems to be the theme of hunger research—that the brain integrates many different signals rather than relying exclusively on any single signal to trigger hunger.

The Hypothalamus Coordinates Multiple Systems That Control Hunger

Although it appears that no single brain region has exclusive control of appetite, many findings demonstrate that the hypothalamus is critically important to the regulation of metabolic rate, food intake, and body weight. For example, functional MRI shows that drinking glucose after fasting affects the activity of the human medial hypothalamus (Figure 13.21; Y. Liu et al., 2000). Hypothalamic control of feeding appears to be quite complicated and, like other homeostatic systems, exhibits redundancy as a safety measure.

Early lesion studies suggested a simple hypothalamic system for feeding

An early theory of hypothalamic involvement, the *dual-center hypothesis* of eating, offered an overly simple model. According to this theory, the hypothalamus contained two control centers: a hunger center in the **lateral hypothalamus** (**LH**), and a satiety center in the **ventromedial hypothalamus** (**VMH**). Information from all the other brain regions, and from other factors (such as circulating hormones) that influence eating, was presumed to funnel into and act through these hypothalamic control centers.

The VMH satiety center Occasionally a person develops a pathologically voracious appetite and rapidly becomes obese. In the nineteenth century, physicians found that some such patients had tumors at the base of the brain. In 1940, Hetherington

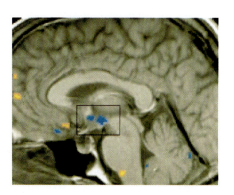

13.21 Sweet Spot Changes in hypothalamic activity following glucose ingestion are evident in this midsagittal fMRI image. (From Liu at al., 2000.)

13.22 Brain Regions Implicated in the Regulation of Eating

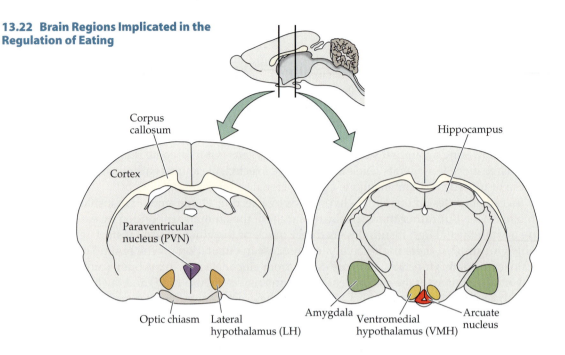

and Ranson reported that bilateral lesions of the ventromedial hypothalamus (Figure 13.22) cause rats to become obese. VMH lesions produced obesity in all the species that were tested—monkeys, dogs and cats, several species of rodents, and some species of birds.

The VMH was promptly called a satiety center because destroying it seemed to prevent animals from ever being satiated with food, but this characterization was soon found inadequate. Destruction of the VMH did not simply cause the rats to become feeding machines. Rather, the eating habits of VMH-lesioned rats were still controlled both by the palatability of food and by body weight, but these controls were no longer exerted in normal ways.

If palatable food of high caloric content was available, VMH-lesioned rats typically showed two phases of weight gain: (1) a *dynamic phase of weight gain*, marked by **hyperphagia** (a sharp increase in feeding; from the Greek, *hyper*, "over," and *phagein*, "to eat") and rapid weight gain; and (2) a *static phase of obesity*, in which weight stabilizes at an obese level, and food intake is not much above normal. Once animals have reached this new weight, they seem to display normal satiety in response to their food, and they regulate their weight at the new, higher level. Because the VMH is gone from these animals, it cannot be responsible for their satiety; therefore it seems likely that other brain regions normally contribute to satiety.

Further studies confirmed that the VMH could not be the only controller of satiety. For example, if an obese rat in the static phase is force-fed or food-deprived, its weight will change only temporarily, returning to the static-phase weight when normal feeding resumes (Figure 13.23). Furthermore, if VMH-lesioned rats are offered only a plain diet (rather than a high-fat diet), their weight does not rise much above that of control animals. And if they are offered food of low palatability, they may actually lose weight relative to controls (Sclafani et al., 1976). These results suggest that, in fact, VMH-lesioned rats are finicky eaters.

**COMPETING
HYPOTHESES**

The LH hunger center   In the 1950s it was reported that bilateral destruction of the lateral hypothalamus (LH) causes *aphagia* (refusal to eat) that may persist until the animal dies of starvation (Anand and Brobeck, 1951). This finding led investigators to propose that the LH contains a hunger center, and that the VMH normally acts as a brake on feeding by inhibiting the LH.

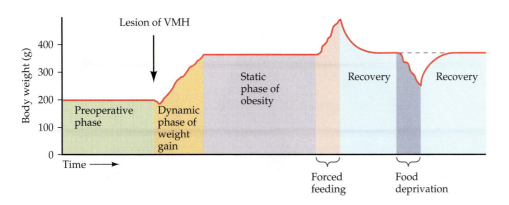

13.23 Lesion-Induced Obesity Rats in which the ventromedial hypothalamus (VMH) has been lesioned overeat and gain weight until they reach a new, higher body weight, which they defend in the face of either forced feeding or food deprivation. Thus they continue to regulate body weight, but at a higher set point. (After Sclafani et al., 1976.)

Studies soon cast doubt on this simple interpretation. For one thing, the effect of LH damage wasn't limited to hunger; the animals also displayed a refusal to drink (*adipsia*) (Teitelbaum and Stellar, 1954). Furthermore, the aphagia and adipsia were not necessarily permanent. If kept alive for about a week via a feeding tube, most LH-lesioned rats began to eat and drink spontaneously, implying that other brain regions must also be involved in feeding.

Recovered LH-lesioned rats regulate their new body weight with precision. As with VMH-lesioned animals, weight can be affected by manipulation of either the availability or the palatability of food (Figure 13.24), but when returned to a standard diet, the LH-lesioned animals return to this same (new) body weight (Keesey, 1980).

Human beings may become emaciated if they suffer from lesions or tumors of the lateral hypothalamus. Bilateral damage to the LH through accident or disease is rare, but even unilateral damage to the LH sometimes produces aphagia and adipsia. Cases of *anorexia* (absence of appetite) induced by LH lesions in humans are about one-fourth as frequent as cases of hypothalamic obesity (L. E. White and Hain, 1959).

Peripheral peptides drive a hypothalamic appetite controller

A spate of discoveries has greatly improved our understanding of the hypothalamic control of appetite. This evidence indicates that the **arcuate nucleus** of the hypothalamus contains a highly specialized appetite controller that is governed by circulating levels of several hormones. One of these hormones is insulin, which we have already discussed. The other three are more recently discovered peptides: leptin, ghrelin, and a hormone with the cumbersome name *Peptide YY*$_{3-36}$ (*PYY*$_{3-36}$). We

Phillip Teitelbaum

Eliot Stellar

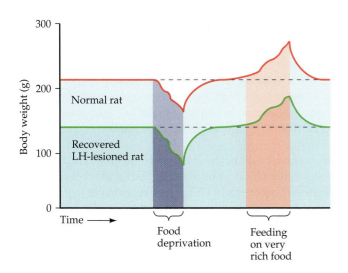

13.24 Lesion-Induced Weight Loss Both normal rats and rats that have recovered from lesions of the lateral hypothalamus (LH) regulate body weight quite well. The LH-lesioned rats regulate around a lowered target weight, but in parallel with normal rats. (After Keesey and Boyle, 1973.)

13.25 Inherited Obesity Both of these mice have two copies of the *obese* gene, which impairs the production of leptin by fat cells. The mouse on the left weighs about 67 g; a normal (wild-type) mouse at this age weighs about 25 g. The mouse on the right has been treated with leptin, and weighs about 35 g.

Jeffrey Friedman

will discuss each in turn, and then look at the organization of the hypothalamic appetite controller.

Leptin Mice that receive two copies of the gene called *obese* (abbreviated *ob*) regulate their body weight at a high level (Figure 13.25), as you might have guessed from the gene's name. These mice have larger and more numerous fat cells than their heterozygous littermates (*ob/+*; the plus sign indicates the wild-type, normal allele). The fat mice (*ob/ob*) maintain their obesity even when given an unpalatable diet or when required to work hard to obtain food (Cruce et al., 1974).

Jeffrey Friedman and coworkers found that *ob/ob* mice have defective genes for the peptide leptin (from the Greek *leptos*, "thin"). Fat cells produce leptin and then secrete the protein into the bloodstream (Y. Zhang et al., 1994). Leptin receptors (known as ObR because they are receptors to the obese gene product, leptin) have been identified in the choroid plexus, the cortex, and several hypothalamic nuclei (Hakansson et al., 1998), to be discussed shortly. Animals with defects in the gene that encodes ObR, such as Zucker rats (al-Barazanji et al., 1997; L. M. Zucker and Zucker, 1961) and diabetic mice (Coleman and Hummel, 1973), also become obese.

Thus the brain seems to monitor circulating leptin levels to measure and regulate the body's energy reserves in the form of fat. Defects in leptin production or leptin sensitivity cause a false underreporting of body fat, leading the animals to overeat, especially high-fat or sugary foods.

Ghrelin Discovered by Kenji Kangawa, Masayasu Kojima, and their colleagues, **ghrelin** is released into the bloodstream by endocrine cells of the stomach (Kojima et al., 1999). Ghrelin was named in recognition of its effects on growth hormone secretion (*GH-rel*easing), but we now know that ghrelin is a powerful appetite stimulant (Nakazato et al., 2001). Circulating levels of ghrelin rise during fasting and immediately drop on ingestion of a meal. Treating either rats or humans with exogenous ghrelin produces a rapid and large increase in appetite (Wren et al., 2000, 2001).

Curiously, obese subjects reportedly have lower baseline levels of ghrelin than lean subjects prior to eating, but following a meal their circulating levels of ghrelin do not drop (their leptin levels remain high too). So one mechanism of obesity may involve a ghrelin system that is unresponsive to feeding and thus always slightly elevated, prompting continual hunger (English et al., 2002).

PYY$_{3-36}$ Secreted into the circulation by cells of the small and large intestine, the small peptide PYY$_{3-36}$ is at a low level in the blood prior to eating, but that level rises rapidly on ingestion of a meal. Systemic injections of PYY$_{3-36}$ are reported to significantly curb appetite in both rats and humans, as do injections directly into the arcuate nucleus of the hypothalamus of rats (Batterham et al., 2002; Batterham and Bloom, 2003; but see also Tschöp et al., 2004 and Batterham et al., 2004 for ongoing debate). It therefore seems that PYY$_{3-36}$ may act in direct opposition to ghrelin, providing an appetite-

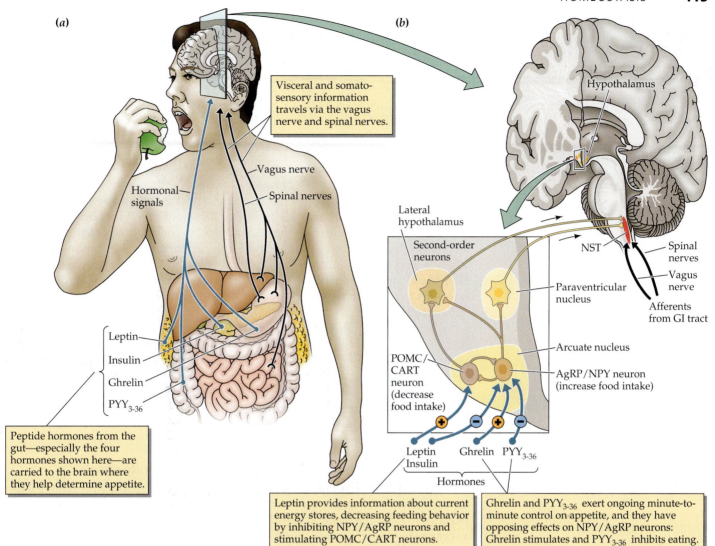

(a) Visceral and somato-sensory information travels via the vagus nerve and spinal nerves.

Vagus nerve

Hormonal signals

Spinal nerves

Leptin

Insulin

Ghrelin

PYY$_{3-36}$

Peptide hormones from the gut—especially the four hormones shown here—are carried to the brain where they help determine appetite.

(b) Hypothalamus

Lateral hypothalamus

Second-order neurons

NST

Paraventricular nucleus

Spinal nerves

Vagus nerve

Afferents from GI tract

POMC/CART neuron (decrease food intake)

Arcuate nucleus

AgRP/NPY neuron (increase food intake)

Leptin Insulin

Ghrelin

PYY$_{3-36}$

Hormones

Leptin provides information about current energy stores, decreasing feeding behavior by inhibiting NPY/AgRP neurons and stimulating POMC/CART neurons.

Ghrelin and PYY$_{3-36}$ exert ongoing minute-to-minute control on appetite, and they have opposing effects on NPY/AgRP neurons: Ghrelin stimulates and PYY$_{3-36}$ inhibits eating.

13.26 An Appetite Controller in the Hypothalamus
(a) The brain integrates a number of peripheral signals to determine appetite. Cardinal among these are four peptides secreted into the bloodstream: (1) leptin, secreted by fat cells; (2) insulin, secreted by the pancreas; (3) ghrelin, secreted by the stomach; and (4) PYY$_{3-36}$, secreted by the intestines. In addition, visceral and somatosensory information is transmitted via spinal nerves and the vagus. (b) Two types of neurons in the arcuate nucleus (ARC) are sensitive to peptides from the periphery: POMC/CART-synthesizing neurons signal a decrease in food intake; NPY/AgRP-synthesizing neurons promote increased feeding. Both types of arcuate neurons exert their effects via second-order neurons in the VMH and LH. POMC/CART neurons signal satiety by releasing α-MSH. NPY/AgRP neurons stimulate appetite through the release of NPY, but also by releasing AgRP, which directly competes for the melanocortin receptors, reducing the effectiveness of α-MSH in suppressing appetite.

suppressing stimulus to the hypothalamus. This discovery may represent an important missing piece of the appetite control puzzle, allowing us to construct a workable model of the arcuate nucleus appetite controller.

The organization of appetite control neurons of the arcuate nucleus is sketched in Figure 13.26. The appetite controller relies on two sets of arcuate neurons with opposing effects, which we can identify according to the types of neurotransmitters and hormones that they produce. One type of neuron produces the peptide neurotransmitters **neuropeptide Y** (**NPY**) and **agouti-related peptide** (**AgRP**). When activated, these NPY/AgRP neurons *stimulate* appetite while also reducing metabolism; both actions lead to weight gain. In contrast, activation of the other set of neurons—called POMC/CART neurons because they produce **pro-opiomelanocortin**

(POMC) and **cocaine- and amphetamine-regulated transcript (CART)**—*inhibit* appetite and increase in metabolism.

Projections from the POMC/CART neurons and NPY/AgRP neurons have two main functions. Some projections stay within the arcuate, allowing the two sets of neurons to influence each other's activity through reciprocal connections (see Figure 13.26*b*). Other projections leave the arcuate and make contact with neurons in other hypothalamic sites. It is through these projections that the arcuate system ultimately modulates food intake.

The arcuate appetite controller   Now let's consider how the peripheral peptide signals interact with this appetite controller. First, because it is made by fat cells, leptin (and to a lesser extent, insulin) conveys information about the body's energy reserves. Both types of neurons in the arcuate appetite controller have leptin receptors, but leptin affects them in opposite ways. High circulating levels of leptin *activate* the appetite-suppressing POMC/CART neurons but *inhibit* the appetite-increasing NPY/AgRP neurons, so in both systems leptin is working to suppress hunger. Leptin seems to have a long-term effect on the appetite controller, reflecting the body's current composition.

In contrast to leptin, ghrelin and PYY_{3-36} provide more acute, rapidly changing hour-to-hour hunger signals from the gut. Both peptides act primarily on the appetite-stimulating NPY/AgRP neurons of the arcuate nucleus. Ghrelin stimulates these cells, leading to a corresponding increase in appetite. PYY_{3-36} works in opposition, inhibiting the same cells to *reduce* appetite. Short-term control of appetite thus reflects a balance between ghrelin and PYY_{3-36} concentrations in circulation. The effects of the arcuate appetite controller on feeding behavior are mediated by other brain sites, which we will discuss in the next section.

Second-order hypothalamic mechanisms integrate appetite signals

Having identified the main components of the arcuate appetite controller, we can turn to the functional connections of these cells to "downstream" sites involved in feeding. Two hypothalamic sites—the **paraventricular nucleus (PVN)** and the LH—appear to be primary targets of projections from the arcuate (refer to Figure 13.26*b* for help in understanding this circuit).

The appetite-suppressing POMC/CART neurons of the arcuate project primarily to the lateral hypothalamus. Here they release **α-melanocyte-stimulating hormone (α-MSH)**, a peptide hormone belonging to a small family of substances, called **melanocortins,** that are derived from POMC. Acting via specific **melanocortin type-4 receptors (MC4Rs)** located on the LH neurons, α-MSH decreases the LH's appetite-stimulating activity, resulting in a net decrease in feeding.

The appetite-enhancing NPY/AgRP neurons exert their effects through both the PVN and the LH (see Figure 13.26*b*). Injecting NPY into the PVN stimulates feeding (Sarah Leibowitz, 1991), and NPY released by the NPY/AgRP neurons appears to provoke increased appetite. But what about that AgRP? We now know that AgRP is a competitive endogenous MC4R ligand. So when it is released in the LH, AgRP competes for MC4R binding. AgRP thus counters the appetite-suppressing effects of α-MSH that we just described and instead provokes an *increase* in feeding behavior via the LH.

The net result of all this is a constant balancing act between the appetite-stimulating effects of the NPY/AgRP system, and the appetite-suppressing effects of the POMC/CART system, spread across both the PVN and the LH.

Other systems also play a role in hunger and satiety

Appetite signals from the hypothalamus converge on the nucleus of the solitary tract (NST) in the brainstem (see Figure 13.26*b*). The NST can be viewed as part of a common pathway for feeding behavior, and it receives and integrates appetite signals from a variety of sources in addition to the hypothalamus. For example, the sensa-

Sarah Leibowitz

tion of hunger is affected by a wide variety of peripheral sensory inputs, transmitted via spinal and cranial nerves. The liver detects glucose levels and circulating levels of fatty acids, and it communicates both kinds of information through the vagus nerve to the NST. Cutting the vagus nerve disrupts feeding responses to manipulations of circulating glucose and fatty acids (Tordoff et al., 1991).

A variety of other brain locations also appear to participate in feeding behavior, either directly or through indirect effects on other processes. For example, as you might expect, the brain's reward system appears to be intimately involved with feeding. Activity of a circuit including the amygdaloid nuclei and the dopamine-mediated reward center in the nucleus accumbens (see Chapter 4) is hypothesized to mediate pleasurable aspects of feeding (Ahn and Phillips, 2002). Similarly, lesion studies indicate that feeding is impaired following destruction of regions within the amygdaloid nuclei, the frontal cortex, and the substantia nigra, to name but a few.

Obesity Is Difficult to Treat

Unfortunately, present-day dietary, surgical (Box 13.1), or pharmacological interventions seldom succeed in reliably reversing obesity for long periods of time. A few

BOX 13.1 Body Fat Stores Are Tightly Regulated, Even after Surgical Removal of Fat

As any dieter will attest, the body seems to know how much it wants to weigh, and it defies our efforts to change that value. As in other mammals, our homeostatic mechanisms defend a set value for weight. Perhaps the most striking demonstration of this phenomenon is exhibited by golden-mantled ground squirrels, which show an extreme seasonal variation in body weight, greatly fattening up in the spring.

When these squirrels are brought into the laboratory, they continue to show an annual rhythm in body weight, even when food is always available (Figure A) (I. Zucker, 1988). Force-feeding the squirrels or depriving them of food will cause a temporary increase or decrease in body weight, but as soon as food access returns to normal, body weight returns to the value that is normal for the season.

Even more impressive is the fact that if body fat is surgically removed, the animals will eat until they regain—with remarkable precision—the amount of fat that would be normal for the season (Figure B) (Dark et al., 1984). Needless to say, these results are not encouraging to humans considering liposuction. Usually the fat simply returns after the procedure.

In desperation, some people are turning to more extreme weight-loss surgeries: bariatric procedures that bypass part of the intestinal tract or stomach in order to reduce the volume and absorptive capacity of the digestive system. Although gastric bypass surgery can offer hope of substantial weight loss for the morbidly obese, it is accompanied by significant complications and risks, and it doesn't directly alter appetite. Less-invasive procedures are under study, such as the use of gastric stimulators that activate the gut's satiety signals to reduce appetite. Curiously, simply implanting inert weights into the abdominal cavities of mice causes them to lose a proportionate amount of weight, apparently by fooling the body into thinking it is fatter than it actually is (Adams et al., 2003). Perhaps some of us, someday, will be able to lose weight simply by taking on extra ballast!

(A) Annual body weight cycles of three ground squirrels with free access to food

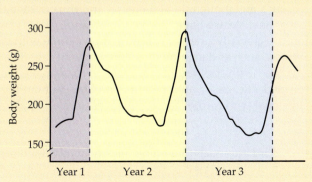

(B) Surgical fat removal has only a transient effect on body weight.

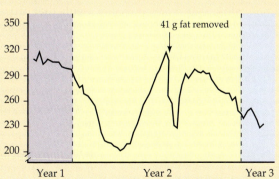

CLINICAL ISSUE

individuals improve; many others do not. Like it or not, our evolutionary history has optimized our bodies for obtaining and storing energy, and protecting against accumulating *too much* energy was not so much of a concern for our distant forebears (J. M. Friedman, 2003). The tendency to accumulate excess energy is probably exacerbated by our ever more sedentary lifestyles. The current epidemic of obesity is certainly a major health problem: Almost 65% of the adults in the United States are overweight, and about 31% qualify as obese (Flegal et al., 2002). The increased incidence of cardiovascular disease, diabetes, and other disorders that accompany obesity will be an increasingly heavy burden on health care services in the future.

In Lewis Carroll's *Alice's Adventures in Wonderland,* Alice quaffs the contents of a small bottle in order to shrink. The quest for a real-life shrinking potion—but one that makes you thin rather than short—is the subject of intense scientific activity, and several major strategies or targets are emerging, as described in the sections that follow.

Appetite control Hopes are high that drugs that modify the functioning of the hypothalamic appetite system will be safe and potent obesity treatments. Unfortunately, despite initial excitement, modifications of leptin signals have not proven to be very effective; only a tiny minority of obese people have abnormal leptin, and most have *higher* levels of circulating leptin than do thin people (Montague et al., 1997).

Interestingly, leptin appears to regulate endogenous cannabinoid levels in the hypothalamus (Di Marzo et al., 2001). Cannabinoids, such as anandamide, are endogenous substances that act much like the active ingredient in marijuana and that, like marijuana, can potently stimulate hunger. It follows that drugs that block cannabinoid receptors might be effective appetite suppressants.

Similarly, drugs can be targeted at some of the neurotransmitter systems integral to the appetite controller. For instance, given the efficacy of α-MSH transmission in reducing hunger, the MC4R melanocortin receptor will be an attractive target for drug development. In fact, we now know that the banned diet drug fenfluramine—discussed at the outset of this chapter—suppresses appetite by activating melanocortin pathways in the brain (Heisler et al., 2002). In light of the tragedies of the fen-phen story, an important issue will be to develop compounds that selectively affect appetite-related receptors, without significant side effects caused by acting elsewhere in the brain and periphery.

One especially promising treatment under development targets PYY_{3-36}. Recall that PYY_{3-36}, from the gut, acts on arcuate neurons to reduce appetite (see Figure 13.26a). Circulating PYY_{3-36} may be chronically low in obese people, and treatment with supplementary PYY_{3-36} reportedly reduces the intake of calories by about one-third (Batterham et al., 2003). A reduction of this magnitude would translate into a fairly rapid decrease in weight.

Increased metabolism An alternative approach to treating obesity involves treatments that cause the body's metabolic rate to increase, and thus release those extra calories in the form of heat. As we have discussed, metabolic rate is controlled by the thyroid hormones, especially thyroxine; but treating people with thyroxine has undesirable side effects, such as dangerously increased heart rate. The increase in heart rate may be avoided with compounds that selectively activate the thyroid hormone receptors (termed *TRb*) associated with metabolism, but not the thyroid hormone receptors associated with cardiovascular changes (termed *TRa*) (Grover et al., 2003).

Inhibition of fat tissue A third approach to treating obesity involves attempts to interfere with the formation of new fat tissue. For example, in order for fat tissue to grow, it must be able to recruit and develop new blood vessels. Drugs that inhibit the formation of blood vessels, termed *angiogenesis inhibitors,* may effectively block the formation of fat tissue (Rupnick et al., 2002). (Angiogenesis inhibitors are better known for their apparent effectiveness in slowing the growth of tumors.)

Reduced absorption Only a few drugs are currently approved for the treatment of obesity; most are still in development. One current obesity medication—orlistat (XENICAL)—works by interfering with the digestion of fat. However, this approach has generally produced only modest weight loss, and it often causes intestinal discomfort.

Reduced reward Finally, a different perspective on treating obesity focuses on the rewarding properties of food. Not only is food delicious, but "comfort foods" also directly reduce circulating stress hormones, thereby providing another reward. Chronic food restriction makes rewarding brain stimulations even more rewarding than usual, and this effect is reversed by treatment with leptin (Fulton et al., 2000). Drugs that affect the brain's reward circuitry (see Chapter 4), reducing the rewarding properties of food, may prove beneficial for weight loss.

Experience Protects Us from Toxins in Food

Learning has a profound effect on the feeding behavior of animals. We've already mentioned the cephalic phase of feeding, during which the stimuli of food evoke a conditioned release of insulin so that we will make quick use of the food. Another example of conditioning is the preference that many species show for foods to which they were exposed during development.

One can influence the food preferences of adult rats by exposing them to the food as nursing pups. Rats normally prefer plain water over garlic-flavored water, but if a rat mother has only garlic-flavored water to drink, she will drink it. Her offspring, nursing for the first 21 days of life, will grow up to prefer garlic water over plain. This preference is strengthened if the pups also are exposed to such water just after weaning (Capretta et al., 1975). Similarly, many adult humans prefer the cuisine they were fed by their parents while growing up.

Another important means by which experience shapes feeding is conditioned **taste aversion.** A young, inexperienced blue jay will readily snap up and eat a monarch butterfly. Score one for the blue jay. However, monarchs contain toxins, so a few minutes later the bird will vomit up the butterfly and wipe its bill repeatedly as if to remove any traces (Figure 13.27). That bird will eat other butterflies, but it will not eat another monarch (Wiklund and Sillén-Tullberg, 1985), even when hundreds are available. Score several hundred for the monarchs.

(*a*)

(*b*)

13.27 Taste Aversion A blue jay immediately before (*a*) and a few minutes after (*b*) eating a monarch butterfly and becoming sick from the toxins these butterflies contain. The animal regurgitates the butterfly, wipes its beak repeatedly, and will in the future avoid eating other monarchs. (Courtesy of Lincoln Brower.)

John Garcia

When first described by John Garcia (Garcia et al., 1955), the assertion that animals could learn with a single trial to avoid food associated with illness was a heresy, but it is now firmly established. The selective advantage of the "Garcia effect" seems obvious.

A related phenomenon is **flavor neophobia,** the avoidance of new things—in this case new foods. Rats are quite reluctant to eat any new food, and when they do, they tend to eat a small amount and wait a period before eating more. If they become ill after the first sample, conditioned taste aversion diverts them from taking more.

Eating Disorders Are Life-Threatening

Sometimes people shun food despite having no apparent aversion to it. These people, who are usually young, become obsessed with their body weight and become extremely thin—generally by eating very little and sometimes also regurgitating food, taking laxatives, over-exercising, or drinking large amounts of water to suppress appetite. This condition, which is more common in adolescent girls and women than in males, is called **anorexia nervosa.** The name of the disorder indicates (1) that the patients have no appetite (*anorexia*) and (2) that the disorder originates in the nervous system (*nervosa*). But the disorder is so poorly understood that both of these assumptions could be mistaken.

For example, people who suffer from anorexia nervosa sometimes think about food a good deal, and physiological evidence suggests that they respond even more than normal subjects to the presentation of food (Broberg and Bernstein, 1989), so their appetite may be normal or even exaggerated. Yet they deny themselves food. The idea that anorexia is primarily a nervous disorder stems from the distorted body image of the patients (they may consider themselves fat when others see them as emaciated) and from the fact that their diet is self-imposed.

Bulimia (or *bulimia nervosa,* from the Greek *boulimia,* "great hunger") is a related disorder. Like those who suffer from anorexia, people who are bulimic may believe themselves fatter than they are, but they periodically gorge themselves, usually with "junk food," and then either vomit the food or take laxatives to avoid weight gain. Also like sufferers of anorexia, people with bulimia may be obsessed with food and body weight, but not all of them become emaciated. Both anorexia and bulimia can be fatal because in each case the patient's lack of nutrient reserves damages various organ systems and/or leaves the body unable to battle otherwise mild diseases.

(a)

(b)

13.28 Changing Ideals of Female Beauty Actress Lara Flynn Boyle (*a*) and Helena Fourment, wife of the Flemish painter Paul Rubens, in *Helena Fourment as Aphrodite* (circa 1630) (*b*) exemplify ideal feminine forms of their respective eras. Some people have suggested that our modern weight-conscious notions of female beauty are responsible for some cases of anorexia nervosa and bulimia.

In **binge eating,** people spontaneously gorge themselves with far more food than is required to satisfy hunger, often to the point of illness. Such people are often obese, and the causes of the bingeing are not well understood. Mutation of the gene encoding the MC4R receptor is strongly associated with binge eating (Branson et al., 2003). Recall that α-MSH acts on MC4R to signal satiety; people with the mutation may be failing to receive the signal to stop eating.

Despite the epidemic of obesity that we described at the outset of the chapter, or perhaps because of it, our present culture emphasizes that women, especially young women, must be thin to be attractive (Figure 13.28*a*). This cultural pressure is widely perceived as one of the causes of eating disorders. In earlier times, however, when plump women were considered the most beautiful (witness Renaissance paintings, such as the one shown in Figure 13.28*b*), some women still fasted severely and may have suffered from anorexia. The origins of these disorders remain elusive, and to date, the available therapies cure only a minority of patients.

Refer to the *Learning Biological Psychology CD* for study questions, animations, activities, and other study aids.

Summary

1. The nervous system plays a crucial role in maintaining the homeostasis that the body requires for proper functioning. Temperature, fluid concentration, chemical energy, and nutrients must all be maintained within a critical range.

2. Several mechanisms that normally act in synchrony can be dissociated experimentally, revealing a redundancy of physiological methods that ensure homeostasis.

Temperature Regulation

1. Endotherms generate most of their body heat through the metabolism of food; ectotherms obtain most of their body heat from the environment. Both endotherms and ectotherms regulate body temperature, but ectotherms depend more on behaviors to capture heat than on internal heat-generating mechanisms.

2. Endotherms can remain active longer than ectotherms can, but endotherms are also obliged to gather more food than ectotherms do to generate their body warmth.

3. Body size and shape drastically affect the rate of heat loss. Small endotherms have a higher metabolic rate, using more energy (per gram of body weight) than large endotherms use.

4. Both endotherms and ectotherms use behavioral methods to help regulate body temperature at optimal levels. Young animals particularly depend on this form of thermoregulation.

5. Several regions of the nervous system monitor and help regulate body temperature, including the preoptic area of the hypothalamus, the brainstem, and the spinal cord.

Fluid Regulation

1. Our cells function properly only when the concentration of salts and other ions (the osmolality) of the intracellular compartment of the body is within a critical range. The extracellular compartment is a source of replacement water and a buffer between the intracellular compartment and the outside world.

2. Thirst can be triggered either by a drop in the volume of the extracellular compartment (hypovolemic thirst) or by an increase in the osmolality of the extracellular compartment (osmotic thirst). Either signal indicates that the volume or osmolality of the intracellular compartment may fall outside the critical range. Because of the importance of osmolality, we must regulate salt intake in order to regulate water balance effectively.

3. A drop in blood volume triggers at least three responses: (1) Baroreceptors in the major blood vessels detect any volume drop and signal the brain via the autonomic nervous system. (2) The brain in turn releases vasopressin from the posterior pituitary, and the vasopressin reduces blood vessel volume and the amount of water lost through urination. (3) The kidneys release renin, providing circulating angiotensin II, which reduces blood vessel volume to maintain blood pressure and may also signal the brain that the blood volume has dropped.

4. The hypothalamus contains osmosensory neurons that detect the concentration of extracellular fluid. Increased solute concentration of the extracellular fluid triggers an intake of water.

Food and Energy Regulation

1. Our digestive system breaks down food and uses most of it for energy, especially because we are endotherms. The brain must have glucose for energy; the body can use either glucose or fatty acids as fuel.

2. Although brain cells can use glucose directly, body cells can import glucose only with the assistance of insulin secreted by the pancreas. Insulin also promotes the storage of glucose as glycogen. Another pancreatic hormone, glucagon, catalyzes the conversion of glycogen back into glucose.

3. Manipulations of either glucose or insulin can affect whether an animal experiences hunger, but experimental studies have indicated that neither glucose nor insulin alone can be the single indicator of hunger or satiety.

4. An appetite controller located in the arcuate nucleus of the hypothalamus responds to levels of several peptide gut hormones. Leptin, providing a chronic signal about fat levels, stimulates arcuate POMC/CART neurons to release α-MSH in the lateral hypothalamus to decrease appetite via actions at MC4R receptors. Leptin inhibits arcuate NPY/AgRP neurons, decreasing their release of NPY and AgRP to suppress appetite further.

5. Ghrelin and PYY_{3-36} provide more-acute signals from the gut. Ghrelin stimulates, and PYY_{3-36} inhibits, the arcuate NPY/AgRP neurons, thereby stimulating or inhibiting hunger, respectively.

6. Within the nervous system are several regions that seem to contribute to the sensations of hunger or satiety, but an animal can regulate body weight reasonably well even when it lacks one of these regions. Thus there seems to be no single brain center for either satiety or hunger.

7. Obesity is a pervasive problem that is difficult to treat through diet, drugs, or surgery. Several drug strategies based on a new understanding of appetite control offer promise.

8. The major eating disorders are anorexia nervosa, bulimia, and binge eating. Although several cultural and physiological correlates of eating disorders have been indentified, the fundamental causes of these eating disorders remains a mystery.

Recommended Reading

Blatteis, C. M. (Ed.). (1998). *Physiology and pathophysiology of temperature regulation.* Singapore: World Scientific.

Bray, G. A., and Ryan, D. H. (Eds.). (1999). *Nutrition, genetics, and obesity.* Baton Rouge: Louisiana State University Press.

Cassell, D., and Gleaves, H. (2000). *The encyclopedia of obesity and eating disorders* (2nd ed.). New York: Facts On File.

Jessen, C. (2001). *Temperature regulation in humans and other mammals.* Berlin: Telos.

Ramsay, D. J., and Booth, D. (Eds.). (1991). *Thirst: Physiological and psychological aspects.* London: Springer.

Thompson, J. K. (2003). *Handbook of eating disorders and obesity.* New York: Wiley.

14

Biological Rhythms, Sleep, and Dreaming

When Sleep Gets Out of Control

Starting college always brings its share of new experiences and adjustments, but "Barry" knew something was wrong freshman year when he seemed to be sleepy all the time (S. Smith, 1997). Barry napped so often that his friends called him the hibernating bear. Of course, college can be exhausting, and many students seek refuge in long snooze sessions. But while he was camping with his pals, an even odder thing happened: "I laughed really hard, and I kind of fell on my knees. … After that, about every week I'd have two or three episodes where if I'd laugh … my arm would fall down or my muscles in my face would get weak. Or if I was running around playing catch and someone said something, I would get

weak in the knees. And there was a time there that my friends kinda used it as a joke. If they're going to throw me the ball and they didn't want me to catch it, they'd tell me a joke and I'd fall down and miss it."

It was as if any big surge in emotion in Barry could sometimes trigger a sudden, temporary paralysis lasting anywhere from a few seconds to a few minutes, affecting either a body part or his whole body. Sex became something of a challenge because sometimes during foreplay, Barry's body would just collapse. "Luckily, you're probably laying down, so it's not that big a deal. But it just puts a damper on the whole thing."

What's happening to Barry?

*He made the moon for the
    seasons*

The sun knows the place of its setting.

*Thou dost appoint darkness and it be-
    comes night*

*In which all the beasts of the forest
    crawl about*

The young lions roar after their prey

And seek their food from God.

When the sun rises they withdraw

And lie down in their dens.

— Psalm 104:19–23

Brett Bigbee, *Two Women*, 1990–1992

Courtesy of Alexandre Gallery, New York.

All living systems show repeating, pre-dictable changes over time. The fre-quency of these oscillations varies from rapid (e.g., brain potentials) to slow (e.g., annual changes like hibernation). Daily rhythms, the first topic of this chapter, have an intriguing clocklike regularity. Other rhythms range from minutes to seconds, and some extend from a month to years. One familiar daily rhythm is the sleep–waking cycle: By age 60, most humans have spent 20 years asleep. (Some, alas, on one side or the other of the classroom podium.)

Because sleep accounts for so large a slice of our lives, it is surprising that the behavioral and biological features of sleep remained unstudied for so long. Since the early 1960s, how-ever, sleep has been a major focus of investigation. Sleep is not just nonwaking, but rather the interlocking of elaborate cyclical processes, an alternation of several different states. The be-havioral correlates of these different sleep states range from tiny finger twitches to a galaxy of images and dreams. In this chapter we discuss biological rhythms and patterns of sleep in humans and other animals, and the physiological events of sleep.

BIOLOGICAL RHYTHMS

Biological rhythms range in length from minutes to seconds, and some extend from months to years. We discuss daily rhythms first because they have been studied the most.

Many Animals Show Daily Rhythms in Activity and Physiological Measures

Most functions of any living system display a rhythm of approximately 24 hours. Because these rhythms last about a day, they are called **circadian rhythms** (from the Latin *circa*, "about," and

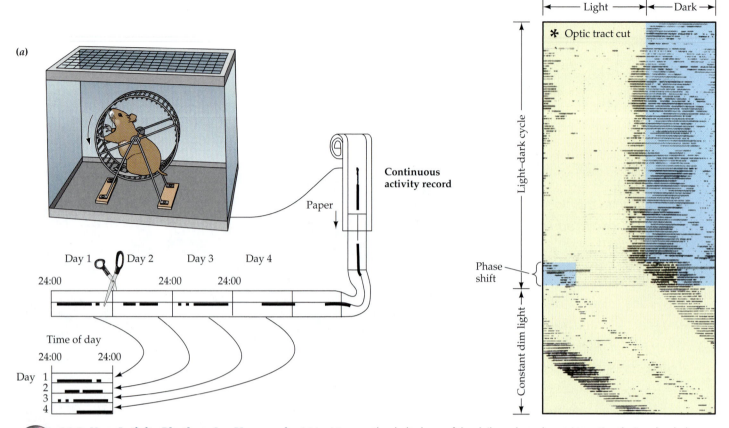

(a)

Day 1 Day 2 Day 3 Day 4

24:00 24:00 24:00

Time of day

Continuous
activity record

Paper

(b)

Light Dark

✱ Optic tract cut

Light–dark cycle

Phase
shift

Constant dim light

14.1 How Activity Rhythms Are Measured   *(a)* In this traditional setup for studying activity rhythms, a running wheel in a hamster's cage is monitored by an event recorder. Each revolution of the wheel produces a brief pen deflection, which forms a dark mark on a slowly moving roll of paper. The paper strips are cut apart, and each subsequent day's activity is aligned underneath. Computers have now replaced the moving-paper apparatus depicted here, but we have included it to explain the principles clearly. *(b)* A hamster's activity record shows that, normally, a hamster becomes active shortly after the start of the dark phase of the daily cycle and remains active during the dark period *(top)*. After several weeks the optic tract in such a hamster was severed (asterisk), but fibers from the eye to the hypothalamus were spared. The hamster was subsequently active earlier each day, but still in synchrony with the light–dark cycle, even if it was shifted. When placed in constant dim light *(bottom)*, the hamster became active a few minutes later each day. This *free-running* activity rhythm indicates that the hamster has an endogenous clock that has a period slightly greater than 24 hours. (After I. Zucker, 1976; based on Rusak and Zucker, 1979.)

**IMPORTANT
METHOD**

dies, "day"). By now circadian rhythms have been studied in a host of creatures at behavioral, physiological, and biochemical levels.

One favorite way to study circadian rhythms in the laboratory takes advantage of the penchant of rodents to run in activity wheels (Figure 14.1*a*). A switch attached to the wheel connects to a microcomputer that registers each revolution. The activity rhythm of a hamster in a running wheel is displayed in Figure 14.1*b*. Like most rodents, hamsters are **nocturnal**—active during the dark periods. Humans and most other primates are **diurnal**—active during the day. Almost all physiological measures—hormone levels, body temperature, drug sensitivity—change across the course of the day.

These circadian activities show extraordinary precision: The beginning of activity may vary only a few minutes from one day to another. For humans who attend to watches and clocks, this regularity may seem uninteresting, but other animals also display remarkable regularity. They are attending to a *biological clock.*

Circadian rhythms are generated by an endogenous clock

If a hamster is placed in a dimly lit environment, it continues to show a daily rhythm in wheel running and other measures, despite the absence of a light–dark cycle, suggesting that the animal has an internal clock to regulate these activities. On the other hand, even though the low level of light is constant, the animal may detect other external cues (e.g., outside noises, temperature, barometric pressure) that signal the time of day. Arguing for the internal clock, however, is the fact that the hamster shows a bit of imprecision in its cycle: Activity starts a few minutes later each day, so eventually the hamster is active while it is daytime outside (see Figure 14.1*b*, bottom). The animal is said to be **free-running,** maintaining its own cycle, which in the absence of external cues, is not exactly 24 hours long.

The free-running period is the animal's natural rhythm. (A **period** is the time between two similar points of successive cycles, such as sunset to sunset.) Because the animal's free-running period does not quite match the period of Earth's rotation, it cannot simply be reflecting an external cue but must be generated inside the animal. So the animal has some sort of endogenous oscillator, which we can call a clock, and in the hamster this clock runs a bit slow.

The internal clock can be set by light. If we expose a free-running nocturnal animal to periods of light and dark, the onset of activity soon becomes synchronized to the beginning of the dark period. The shift of activity produced by a synchronizing stimulus is referred to as a **phase shift** (see Figure 14.1*b*, middle), and the process of shifting the rhythm is called **entrainment.** Any cue that an animal uses to synchronize its activity with the environment is called a **zeitgeber** (German for "time giver"). Light acts as a powerful zeitgeber, and we can easily manipulate it in the laboratory. Because light stimuli can entrain circadian rhythms, the endogenous oscillatory circuit must have inputs from the visual system, as we'll discuss shortly. In humans, circadian rhythms can also be entrained by social stimuli (such as early-morning classes).

Circadian rhythms allow animals to anticipate changes in the environment

Why are circadian rhythms valuable to an organism? The major significance of circadian rhythms is that they synchronize behavior and body states to changes in the environment. The cycle of light and dark during the day has great significance for survival. For example, picture the small nocturnal rodent who can avoid many predators during the day by remaining hidden, and who moves about hurriedly in the dark.

An endogenous clock also allows animals to *anticipate* periodic events, such as the appearance of darkness, and to engage in appropriate physiological and behavioral preparations before conditions change. A snack in the den at the end of the day may prepare the animal for a long night of foraging. In other words, circadian rhythms provide the temporal organization of an animal's behavior. Diurnal animals are adapted for obtaining food during the daytime, and thus do not compete with nocturnal animals, whose adaptations favor activity during the night.

An Endogenous Circadian Clock Is Located in the Hypothalamus

Where in the body is the clock that drives circadian rhythms, and how does it work? One way to establish the locus of circadian oscillators is to remove different organs and examine behavioral or physiological systems for any changes in circadian organization. A pioneer in the field, Curt Richter, suggested that the biological clock is in the brain, because removing various endocrine glands had little effect on the free-running rhythm of rats, but large lesions of the hypothalamus interfered with circadian rhythms (Richter, 1967).

It was subsequently discovered that a small subregion of the hypothalamus—the **suprachiasmatic nucleus** (**SCN**), named for its location above the optic chiasm—serves as the biological clock. Lesions confined to the SCN portion of the hypothalamus interfere with circadian rhythms of drinking and locomotor behavior (Figure 14.2) (F. K. Stephan and Zucker, 1972), and daily rhythms of adrenal steroid secretion (R. Y. Moore and Eichler, 1972).

The clocklike activity of the SCN was also revealed in autoradiographic mapping of metabolic activity (Figure 14.3; see also Box 2.3). This circadian rhythm in metabolism can even be seen in SCN cells in a dish (Earnest et al., 1999; Yamazaki et al.,

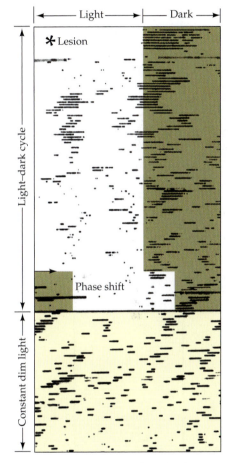

14.2 The Effects of Lesions in the SCN Circadian rhythms in the animal whose activity is plotted here were normal and synchronized to the light–dark period before an SCN lesion was made (asterisk). After the lesion the animal showed some daily rhythms in activity that were synchronous with the light–dark cycle, but when placed in continuous (dim) light, the animal's activity became completely random, indicating that the lesion had eliminated the endogenous rhythm. The lesioned animal does not show a free-running rhythm of activity but is arrhythmic, running at very different times each day. (From I. Zucker, 1976; based on Rusak and Zucker, 1979.)

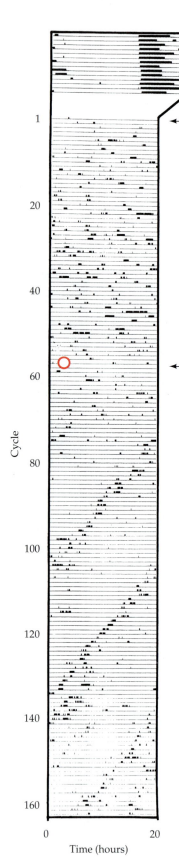

SCN removal

Transplant

Cycle

Time (hours)

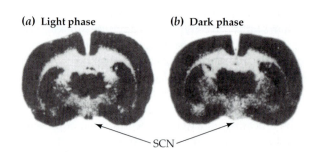

(a) Light phase   (b) Dark phase

SCN

14.3 The Circadian Rhythm of Metabolic Activity of the SCN   These autoradiograms are from coronal sections of rat brains. (a) In a section taken from an animal during a light phase, greater metabolic activity in the SCN is represented by the darkly stained regions at the base of the brain. (b) This dark staining is not evident in a section taken from an animal during a dark phase. (From W. J. Schwartz et al., 1979.)

2000). Electrical recordings from SCN **brain explants**—small pieces of brain tissue isolated from the body—show discharge rates that are synchronized to the light–dark cycle that the animal had previously experienced. This is striking evidence for the endogenous character of the circadian oscillators in the SCN. As we'll see next, however, transplants of the SCN from one animal to another conclusively prove that the SCN generates a circadian rhythm.

Transplants prove that the SCN produces a circadian rhythm

Ralph and Menaker (1988) found a male hamster that exhibited an unusually short free-running activity rhythm in constant conditions. As we have seen, normally hamsters free-run at a period slightly longer than 24 hours, but this male showed a period of 22 hours that was stable for 3 weeks. The researchers bred this male and, by studying his offspring, concluded that he possessed a mutation affecting the endogenous circadian rhythm. Animals with two copies of the mutation had an even shorter period: 20 hours. The mutation was named *tau*, after the Greek symbol used by scientists to represent the period of a rhythm. These animals could be entrained to a normal 24-hour light–dark period; only in constant conditions was their endogenous circadian periodicity revealed.

Dramatic evidence that this endogenous period is contained within the SCN was provided by transplant experiments. Nonmutant hamsters with a lesioned SCN were placed in constant conditions; and as expected, they showed arrhythmicity in activity (Figure 14.4, upper middle) (Ralph et al., 1990). Then the investigators transplanted into the hamsters an SCN taken from a fetal hamster with two copies of the mutant *tau* gene. About a week later the hamsters that had received the transplants began showing a free-running activity rhythm again, but the new rhythm matched that of the donor SCN: It was 19.5 hours rather than the original 24.05.

Reciprocal transplants gave comparable results: The endogenous rhythm always matched the genotype of the *donor* SCN, further demonstrating that the circuitry that produces this circadian rhythmicity is within the SCN itself. The SCN may enforce circadian periodicity through secretion of a particular chem-

14.4 Brain Transplants Prove That the SCN Contains a Clock   A wild-type hamster, when kept in constant dim light, displayed an endogenous circadian rhythm, 24.05 hours in duration (*top*). After the SCN was lesioned, the animal became arrhythmic. Later, an SCN from a fetal hamster with two copies of the *tau* mutation was transplanted into the adult hamster (circle). Soon thereafter the adult hamster began showing a free-running activity rhythm of 19.5 hours, matching the SCN of the donor animal. This response to the transplant showed that the period of the clock is determined within the SCN. (From Ralph et al., 1990.)

ical signal, since a transplanted SCN can restore circadian rhythms even if the tissue is encapsulated to prevent nerve connections but allow hormone release (Silver et al., 1996).

In mammals, light information from the eyes reaches the SCN directly

What pathways entrain circadian rhythms to light–dark cycles? The pathway varies depending on the species (Rusak and Zucker, 1979). Most vertebrates have photoreceptors outside the eye that are part of the mechanism of light entrainment. For example, the **pineal gland** of some amphibians is itself sensitive to light (Jamieson and Roberts, 2000) and helps entrain circadian rhythms to light. Because the skull over the pineal is especially thin in some amphibian species, we can think of them as having a primitive "third eye" in the back of the head. In birds, too, the pineal possesses photoreceptors that can detect daylight through the skull. In mammals, however, retinal pathways clearly mediate photoentrainment, because severing the optic nerves prevents circadian rhythms of all varieties from being entrained by light.

Robert Y. Moore (1983) established the existence of a direct **retinohypothalamic pathway**—retinal ganglion cells that project out of the optic chiasm to synapse within the SCN (Figure 14.5). This tiny pathway carries information about light to the hypothalamus to entrain behavior. Most of the retinal ganglion cells that extend their axons to the SCN do not rely on the traditional photoreceptors, rods and cones, to learn about light. Rather, these retinal ganglion cells themselves contain a special photopigment, called **melanopsin,** that makes them sensitive to light (Hattar et al., 2002). Even transgenic mice that lack rods and cones, and thus cannot detect images on the retina and are blind in every other respect, still entrain their behavior to light (Freedman et al., 1999) because the specialized melanopsin-containing ganglion cells still function.

Normally, the rods and cones also contribute to entrainment, because "knockout" mice lacking the gene for melanopsin, while notably impaired at entraining to light, can do so eventually (Ruby et al., 2002). If both traditional photoreceptors *and* melanopsin-containing ganglion cells are genetically disrupted, the mice are no longer able to entrain their behavior to the light cycle (Panda et al., 2003). The melanopsin-containing retinal ganglion cells also inform the brain about ambient light to control pupil diameter (R. J. Lucas et al., 2003).

Robert Y. Moore

(*a*)

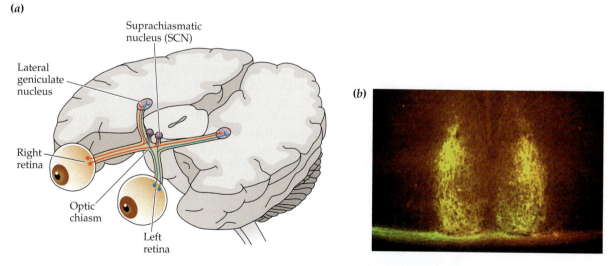

14.5 The Retinohypothalamic Pathway in Mammals   (*a*) This pathway carries information about the light–dark cycle in the environment to the SCN. For clarity of synaptic connections, the SCN is shown proportionately larger than other features. (*b*) Axons (seen at the bottom of this image) from the left eye are labeled green; those from the right are red. Both eyes project so diffusely to the two overlying SCNs that they are outlined in yellow. (Photograph courtesy of Andrew D. Huberman.)

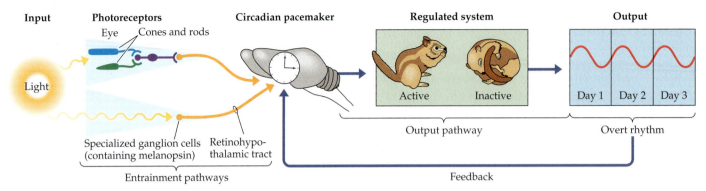

14.6 Schematic Model of the Components of a Circadian System

Figure 14.6 provides a schematic outline of the mammalian circadian system, including entrainment components.

Circadian rhythms have been genetically dissected in flies and mice

The fruit fly *Drosophila melanogaster* displays circadian rhythms in activity (they are diurnal). Flies with a mutation that disabled a particular gene failed to free-run when transferred to constant dim light, indicating that their internal clock was not running. Subtle mutations of the same gene could, depending on the exact change in the gene, cause the animals to have a free-running period that was longer or shorter than normal; thus the gene was dubbed *period* (Konopka and Benzer, 1971). Eventually several genes were discovered that affected the circadian cycle in *Drosophila*, and mammals were found to have homologs of each of them. Work in the fruit fly paved the way for understanding the molecular basis of the circadian clock in mammals.

Cells in the mammalian SCN make two proteins, named Clock and Cycle, that bind together to form a **dimer** (a pair of proteins attached to each other). The Clock/Cycle dimer then binds to the cell's DNA to promote the transcription of *period* (also called *per*) and another gene, called *cryptochrome* (*cry*). The resulting Per and Cry proteins then bind to each other and to a third protein, Tau (it was a mutation of the gene for this protein that resulted in hamsters with a shortened period for the brain transplants that we discussed earlier).

The Per/Cry/Tau protein complex then enters the nucleus to inhibit the ability of the Clock/Cycle dimer to promote transcription. This means that no new Per or Cry proteins are made for a while. But because the Per and Cry proteins degrade with time, eventually the Clock/Cycle dimer will be released from inhibition to start the whole cycle over again (Figure 14.7). The entire cycle takes about 24 hours to complete, and it is this 24-hour molecular cycle that drives the 24-hour activity cycle of SCN cells, which in turn synchronizes the body's various circadian cycles.

How does light synchronize the molecular clock? In fruit flies, one of the molecules involved in the clock is degraded by exposure to light. So outside light passes through the fly's body into brain cells to degrade the protein and synchronize the molecular clock. But things are different in mammals. We've already seen that the retinohypothalamic tract is needed to get light information to the SCN. When the retinal ganglion cells containing melanopsin detect light, they release the neurotransmitter glutamate in the SCN. The glutamate triggers a chain of events in SCN cells that promotes the production of Per protein. When the animal's photoperiod is shifted, this light-mediated boosting of Per production shifts the phase of the molecular clock and therefore the animal's behavior.

One indication of how important the molecular clock is to circadian behavior is the effect of mutations in the several genes involved in the clock. We've already seen that hamsters with a mutation in *tau* have a shorter free-running rhythm than nor-

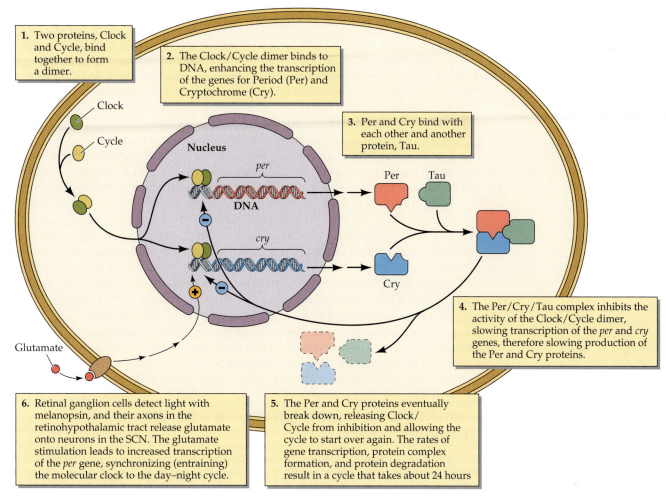

1. Two proteins, Clock and Cycle, bind together to form a dimer.

2. The Clock/Cycle dimer binds to DNA, enhancing the transcription of the genes for Period (Per) and Cryptochrome (Cry).

3. Per and Cry bind with each other and another protein, Tau.

4. The Per/Cry/Tau complex inhibits the activity of the Clock/Cycle dimer, slowing transcription of the *per* and *cry* genes, therefore slowing production of the Per and Cry proteins.

5. The Per and Cry proteins eventually break down, releasing Clock/Cycle from inhibition and allowing the cycle to start over again. The rates of gene transcription, protein complex formation, and protein degradation result in a cycle that takes about 24 hours

6. Retinal ganglion cells detect light with melanopsin, and their axons in the retinohypothalamic tract release glutamate onto neurons in the SCN. The glutamate stimulation leads to increased transcription of the *per* gene, synchronizing (entraining) the molecular clock to the day–night cycle.

14.7 A Molecular Clock in Flies and Mice This is a simplified view. In fact, two *per* genes and two *cry* genes are active in mammals, the protein called Tau here is more properly known as casein kinase I epsilon, and the mammalian version of Cycle is called Bmal1. (Based on Reppert and Weaver, 2002.)

mal hamsters have. Mice with both copies of their *Clock* gene disrupted show severe arrhythmicity in constant conditions (Figure 14.8). If only one copy of the gene is disrupted, the animals free-run for a few days but then suddenly stop showing any circadian rhythmicity. People who feel energetic in the morning ("larks") are likely to carry a different version of the *Clock* gene than "night owls" have (Katzenberg et al., 1998). Different alleles of the *per* gene are also associated with being a lark versus being a night owl (S. N. Archer et al., 2003).

14.8 When the Endogenous Clock Goes Kaput The homozygous *Clock/Clock* mouse whose activity is plotted here showed a normal circadian rhythm when given normal light cues (LD). When put in constant dim light conditions (DD), it maintained an activity period of 27.1 hours for the first 10 days but then lost circadian rhythmicity. Note, however, that an ultradian rhythm (i.e., a rhythm that has a frequency of more than once a day) with a period of just over 5 hours remains. (From J. S. Takahashi, 1995.)

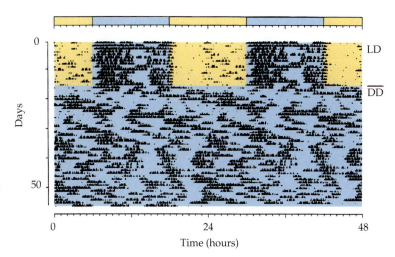

Many Biological Events Display Rhythms Shorter than a Day

Among the many diverse rhythmic biological events, a large group have periods that are shorter than those of circadian rhythms. Such rhythms are referred to as **ultradian** (designating a frequency greater than once per day; the Latin *ultra* means "beyond"), and their periods are usually from several minutes to hours. Ultradian rhythms are seen in such behaviors as bouts of activity, feeding, and hormone release. These ultradian rhythms may be superimposed on a circadian rhythm. Some more-complex human behaviors also display ultradian rhythms.

Human subjects isolated from cues about time of day, and even some in their normal environment, show a 90-minute cycle of daydreaming that is characterized by vivid sensory imagery (Lavie and Kripke, 1981). Ultradian rhythms in the performance of various tasks may reflect fluctuations in alertness, which may account for the ultradian rhythm in the performance of poorly motivated subjects (Broughton, 1985). The periods of ultradian rhythms seem to be correlated with measures such as brain and body size: More-rapid cycles are typical of smaller animals (Gerkema and Daan, 1985).

Destruction of the SCN in voles, which destroys the circadian timing of their activity, does not affect their ultradian feeding rhythms. Interestingly, an ultradian periodicity remains after loss of the circadian rhythm in *Clock/Clock* mice (see Figure 14.8). These findings indicate that separate clocks control circadian and ultradian rhythms. We still do not know whether all ultradian rhythms reflect the operation of a single clock, or many different oscillators separately control a variety of ultradian events. Sleep cycles show an ultradian character, as we'll see later in the chapter.

Animals Use Circannual Rhythms to Anticipate Seasonal Changes

Recall that many animals display a seasonal cycle in body weight (see Box 13.1). Many other behaviors of animals are also characterized by annual rhythms; for example, most animals breed only during a particular season. Some of these rhythms are driven by exogenous factors, such as food availability and temperature. But in the laboratory, animals exposed to short days and long nights (mimicking winter) will often change their phenotype to the nonbreeding condition (Figure 14.9). Furthermore, many annual rhythms, including body weight, persist under constant conditions in the lab. As with circadian rhythms in constant light, animals in isolation

14.9 A Hamster for All Seasons
Siberian hamsters in the wild suppress their reproductive systems and develop a silvery fur coat (*left*) for camouflage in the snow each fall. In the laboratory, they will undergo identical changes, despite warm temperatures and abundant food, if the lights are on for only 10 hours each day. They seem to interpret these short days as an indication that winter is coming. (Photo by Carol D. Hegstrom.)

show free-running annual rhythms of a period not quite equal to 365 days. Thus there also seems to be an endogenous **circannual** clock.

This realm of research obviously requires considerable patience. Such rhythms are sometimes called **infradian** because their frequency is less than once per day (the Latin *infra* means "below"). A familiar infradian rhythm is the 28-day human menstrual cycle. The relevance of annual rhythms to human behavior is becoming evident in striking seasonal disorders of behavior (see Chapter 16).

How does an animal know that a year has passed? Does it simply count the days being measured by the SCN until 365 have passed? No. Irving Zucker and colleagues (1983) measured activity rhythms, reproductive cycles, and body weight cycles of animals that were free-running in both their circadian and their circannual rhythms. SCN lesions clearly disrupted circadian activity cycles, but in at least some animals these lesions did *not* affect circannual changes in body weight and reproductive status.

Circannual cycles, then, do not arise from the circadian clock, and they seem to involve an oscillatory mechanism that is separate from the SCN. In the laboratory, animals born into a summerlike photoperiod (long days) reach puberty sooner than animals born into winterlike short days (Dark et al., 1990), indicating that the season of birth can affect development. Perhaps a similar mechanism is responsible for the greater risk of schizophrenia in people born in late winter (Mortensen et al., 1999).

Irving Zucker

SLEEPING AND WAKING

Most of us enjoy a single period of sleep starting late in the evening and lasting until morning. The onset and termination of sleep seem synchronized to many external events, including light and dark periods. What happens when all the customary synchronizing or entraining stimuli are removed? To investigate this question, volunteers spent weeks in a dark cave with all cues to external time removed. They displayed a circadian rhythm of the sleep–waking cycle, but the rhythm slowly shifted from 24 to 25 hours. In other words, people free-run just as a hamster does in constant dim light (Figure 14.10) (R. A. Wever, 1979). Because the free-running period is greater than 24 hours, some people in these studies are surprised when the experimenter comes in to say it's over. The subject may have experienced only 19 sleep–waking cycles during a 21-day study.

The free-running period of a little more than 24 hours (Czeisler et al., 1999) indicates that humans have an endogenous circadian clock that is very similar to the 24-hour clock in hamsters. External cues (lights, jobs, alarm clocks) then entrain our sleep cycle to a 24-hour period. You may think of sleep as a simple event in your life, but for biological psychologists sleep is a remarkably complex, multifaceted set of behaviors. For this reason we will devote the remainder of the chapter to this fascinating circadian phenomenon.

Human Sleep Exhibits Different Stages

Sleep seems to be characterized by the absence of behavior—a period of inactivity with raised thresholds to arousal by external stimuli. Sleep research gained momentum in the 1930s when experimenters found that brain potentials recorded from electrodes on the human scalp (by

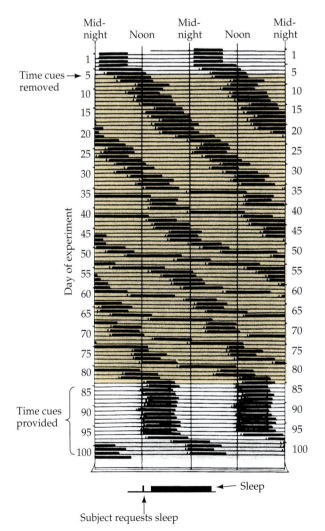

14.10 Humans Free-Run Too   These sleep–waking patterns were recorded in a subject who, after 5 days, was isolated from cues about the time of day. During this period the subject drifted away from a 24-hour daily cycle, getting the equivalent of 74 "nights" of sleep over the 77 days. (From Weitzman et al., 1981.)

**Eugene Aserinsky
(1921–1998)**

**Nathaniel Kleitman
(1895–1999)**

electroencephalography, or **EEG;** see Figure 3.19*a*) provided a way to define, describe, and classify levels of arousal and states of sleep. This measure of brain activity is usually supplemented with recordings of eye movements (**electro-oculography,** or **EOG**) and of muscle tension (**electromyography,** or **EMG**).

Nathaniel Kleitman and his student Eugene Aserinsky used these methods to discover two distinct classes of sleep: **slow-wave sleep (SWS)** and **rapid-eye-movement sleep,** or **REM sleep** (in pronunciation, *REM* rhymes with *gem*) (Aserinsky and Kleitman, 1953). In humans, slow-wave sleep can be divided further into four distinct stages, which we'll discuss next.

What are the electrophysiological distinctions that define different sleep states? To begin, the pattern of electrical activity in a fully awake, vigilant person is a mixture of many frequencies dominated by waves of relatively fast frequencies (greater than 15 to 20 cycles per second, or hertz [Hz]) and low amplitude, sometimes referred to as *beta activity.*

When you relax and close your eyes, a distinctive rhythm appears, consisting of a regular oscillation at a frequency of 9 to 12 Hz, known as the **alpha rhythm.** As drowsiness sets in, the time spent in the alpha rhythm decreases, and the EEG shows events of much smaller amplitude and irregular frequency, as well as sharp waves called **vertex spikes** (Figure 14.11). This is stage 1 sleep, which is accompanied by a slowing of heart rate and a reduction of muscle tension; in addition, under the closed eyelids the eyes may roll about slowly. Stage 1 sleep usually lasts several minutes and gives way to stage 2 sleep, which is defined by waves of 12 to 14 Hz called **sleep**

14.11 Electrophysiological Correlates of Waking and Sleep These are the characteristic EEG patterns seen during different stages of sleep in humans. The sharp wave called a *vertex spike* appears during stage 1 sleep. Brief periods of sleep spindles are characteristic of stage 2 sleep. Deeper stages of slow-wave sleep show progressively more of the large, slow delta waves. Note the similarity of EEG activity during waking, stage 1 sleep, and REM sleep. (After Rechtschaffen and Kales, 1968.)

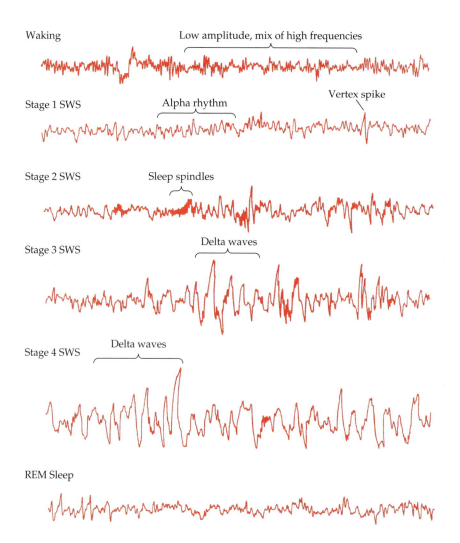

spindles that occur in periodic bursts (see Figure 14.11). If awakened during these first two stages of sleep, many subjects do not acknowledge that they have been asleep, even though they failed to respond to signals while in those stages.

In the early part of a night of sleep, stage 2 sleep leads to stage 3 sleep, which is defined by the appearance of large-amplitude, very slow waves (so-called **delta waves,** about one per second). Stage 4 sleep, which follows, is defined by more delta waves: present at least half the time.

After about an hour—the time usually required for progression through these stages, with a brief return to stage 2—something totally different occurs. Quite abruptly, scalp recordings display a pattern of small-amplitude, high-frequency activity similar in many ways to the pattern of an awake individual (see Figure 14.11, bottom), but the postural neck muscles and all the other skeletal muscles are completely relaxed and limp. The active-looking EEG coupled with deeply relaxed muscles is typical of REM sleep. If you see a cat sleeping in the sitting, *sphinx* position, it cannot be in REM sleep; in REM it will be sprawled limply on the floor.

As we'll see later, this flaccid muscle state appears despite intense brain activity because during this stage of sleep, brainstem regions are profoundly inhibiting motoneurons. Because of this seeming contradiction—the brain waves look awake, but the musculature is flaccid and unresponsive—another name for this state is *paradoxical sleep.* In addition to the rapid movements of the eyes under the closed lids that gives REM sleep its name, breathing and pulse rates become irregular. It is also during REM sleep that we experience vivid dreams, as we'll discuss in the next section.

The EEG portrait shows that sleep consists of a sequence of states instead of just an "inactive" period. Table 14.1 compares the properties of slow-wave sleep and

TABLE 14.1 *Properties of Slow-Wave and REM Sleep*

Property	Slow-wave sleep	REM sleep
AUTONOMIC ACTIVITIES		
Heart rate	Slow decline	Variable with high bursts
Respiration	Slow decline	Variable with high bursts
Thermoregulation	Maintained	Impaired
Brain temperature	Decreased	Increased
Cerebral blood flow	Reduced	High
SKELETAL MUSCULAR SYSTEM		
Postural tension	Progressively reduced	Eliminated
Knee jerk reflex	Normal	Suppressed
Phasic twitches	Reduced	Increased
Eye movements	Infrequent, slow, uncoordinated	Rapid, coordinated
COGNITIVE STATE	Vague thoughts	Vivid dreams, well organized
HORMONE SECRETION		
Growth hormone secretion	High	Low
NEURAL FIRING RATES		
Cerebral cortex (sustained) activity	Many cells reduced and more phasic	Increased firing rates; tonic
EVENT-RELATED POTENTIALS		
Sensory-evoked	Large	Reduced

14.12 A Typical Night of Sleep in a Young Adult   Note the progressive lengthening of REM episodes (blue) and the loss of stages 3 and 4 sleep as the night goes on. (After Kales and Kales, 1970.)

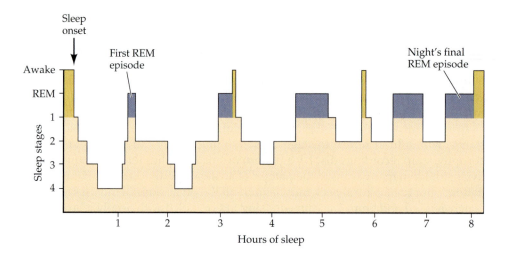

REM sleep. The total sleep time of young adults usually ranges from 7 to 8 hours, and 45% to 50% of sleep is stage 2 sleep. REM sleep accounts for about 20% of total sleep. A typical night of adult human sleep shows repeating cycles about 90 to 110 minutes long, recurring four or five times in a night (Figure 14.12). These cycles change in a subtle but regular manner through the night. Cycles early in the night are characterized by greater amounts of stages 3 and 4 SWS. The latter half of a typical night of sleep is bereft of stages 3 and 4. In contrast, REM sleep is typically more prominent in the later cycles of sleep. The first REM period is the shortest, sometimes lasting only 5 to 10 minutes; the last REM period, just before waking, may last up to 40 minutes.

Brief arousals (yellow bars in Figure 14.12) occasionally occur immediately after a REM period, and the sleeper may shift posture at this transition (Aaronson et al., 1982). The sleep cycle of 90 to 110 minutes has been viewed by some researchers as the manifestation of a basic ultradian rest–activity cycle (Kleitman, 1969); cycles of similar duration occur during waking periods, such as the cycles of daydreaming (Lavie and Kripke, 1981).

We do our most vivid dreaming during REM sleep

We can record the EEGs of subjects, awaken them at a particular stage—1, 2, 3, 4, or REM—and question them about thoughts or perceptions immediately prior to awakening. Early data from such studies strongly indicated that dreams were restricted largely to REM sleep. Subjects reported dreams 70% to 90% of the time when they were awakened in REM—in contrast to 10% to 15% for non-REM sleep periods.

Although all studies report a large percentage of dream reports upon waking from REM sleep, some investigators have increasingly questioned whether REM is the only sleep state associated with dreams. In response to careful, more-persistent questioning, subjects can report dreams upon waking from non-REM sleep, especially stage 2 sleep. Dream reports of REM sleep are characterized by visual imagery, whereas dream reports of non-REM sleep are of a more "thinking" type. REM dreams are apt to include a story that involves odd perceptions and the sense that "you are there" experiencing sights, sounds, smells, and acts. Subjects awakened from non-REM sleep report thinking about problems rather than seeing themselves in a stage presentation. Cartwright (1979) has shown that the dreams of these two states are so different that she could train people to predict with 90% accuracy whether a particular dream was from REM or SWS.

Terrifying dreams have been the subject of close scrutiny (Hartmann, 1984). **Nightmares** are defined as long, frightening dreams that awaken the sleeper from REM sleep. They are occasionally confused with **night terror,** which is a sudden

14.13 Night Terror   Although this 1791 painting by Henry Fuseli is called *The Nightmare,* it more aptly illustrates night terror, as the demon crushes the breath from his victim.

arousal from stage 3 or 4 SWS marked by intense fear and autonomic activation. In night terror the sleeper does not recall a vivid dream but may remember a sense of a crushing feeling on the chest, as though being suffocated (Figure 14.13). Night terrors, common in children during the early part of an evening's sleep, seem to be a disorder of arousal.

Nightmares are quite prevalent, and some people are especially plagued by them. At least 25% of college students report having at least one nightmare per month. (A common one, shared with Freud, is suddenly remembering a final exam that is already in progress.) Medications that enhance the activity of dopamine systems, such as L-dopa, also make nightmares more frequent (Hartmann, 1984).

The Sleep of Different Species Provides Clues about the Evolution of Sleep

Behavioral and EEG descriptions of sleep states let us make precise comparisons of different sleep stages in a variety of animals. As a result, investigators have been able to describe sleep in a wide assortment of mammals and to a lesser extent in reptiles, birds, and amphibians (S. S. Campbell and Tobler, 1984). Species differ widely in various measures of sleep, such as timing and periodic properties. In the sections that follow, we'll look at some of these factors.

REM sleep is evolutionarily ancient

The amount of daily life occupied by sleep and the percentage of sleep devoted to REM sleep for a variety of animals are shown in Figure 14.14. We can make several generalizations. All the mammals that have been investigated thus far display both REM and SWS, with the exception of the dolphin and the echidna (spiny anteater). The echidna is an egg-laying mammal, a **monotreme,** that shows prolonged SWS but no forebrain activation during sleep, so it is unclear whether it has REM sleep. The only other monotreme is the platypus (see Box 6.1), which displays the rapid

EVOLUTION AT WORK

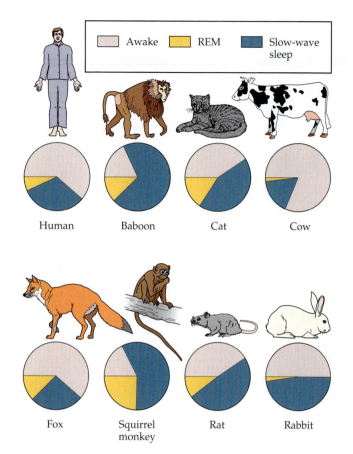

| Awake | REM | Slow-wave sleep |

Human   Baboon   Cat   Cow

Fox   Squirrel monkey   Rat   Rabbit

14.14 Amounts of Different Sleep States in Various Mammals

eye movements and twitching of REM sleep (J. M. Siegel et al., 1999). Among the other vertebrates, only birds display clear signs of both SWS and REM sleep. These comparisons suggest that SWS and REM sleep developed more than 150 million years ago in an ancestor common to birds and mammals.

We don't know why echidnas fail to show REM sleep, but the absence of REM sleep in dolphins is probably related to their continual need to emerge at the surface of the water to breathe. That requirement may be incompatible with the deep relaxation of muscles during REM sleep. In addition to lacking REM sleep periods, dolphins engage in SWS on only one side of the brain at a time (Mukhametov, 1984). It's as if one whole hemisphere is asleep while the other is awake (Figure 14.15). During these periods of "unilateral sleep," the animals continue to come up to the surface occasionally to breathe. Birds can also display unilateral sleep—one hemisphere sleeping while the other hemisphere watches for predators (Rattenborg et al., 1999).

Vertebrate species differ in their patterns and types of sleep

A **sleep cycle** is a period of one episode of SWS followed by an episode of REM sleep. For laboratory rats, one sleep cycle lasts an average of 10 to 11 minutes; for humans, one cycle lasts 90 to 110 minutes, as we said earlier. Across species, cycle duration is inversely related to metabolic rate; that is, small animals, which tend to have high metabolic rates (see Chapter 13), have short sleep cycles, and large species have long sleep cycles.

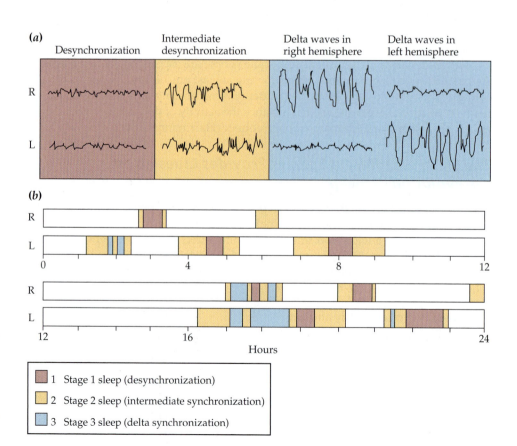

(a)   Desynchronization   Intermediate desynchronization   Delta waves in right hemisphere   Delta waves in left hemisphere

R

L

(b)

R

L

0   4   8   12

R

L

12   16   24

Hours

1	Stage 1 sleep (desynchronization)
2	Stage 2 sleep (intermediate synchronization)
3	Stage 3 sleep (delta synchronization)

14.15 Sleep in Marine Mammals
(*a*) EEG patterns in right (R) and left (L) brain hemispheres in a porpoise from recording of roughly symmetrical areas of the parietal cortex. (*b*) Diagrams of EEG stages in right and left brain hemispheres of a bottle-nosed dolphin during a 24-hour session. The two cerebral hemispheres seem to take turns sleeping. (From Mukhametov, 1984.)

Some birds sleep briefly while gliding. The swift spends almost all its time in the air, except during nesting season, and the sooty tern spends months flying or gliding above water, never alighting, catching fish at the surface. Of necessity, sleep cycles must be short in such birds, if they sleep at all.

Except for such birds, all vertebrates appear to show (1) a circadian distribution of activity, (2) a prolonged phase of inactivity, (3) raised thresholds to external stimuli during inactivity, and (4) a characteristic posture during inactivity. Many invertebrates also have clear periods of behavioral quiescence that include heightened arousal thresholds and distinctive postures (B. A. Klein, 2003; Shaw et al., 2000).

Our Sleep Patterns Change across the Life Span

In any mammal the characteristics of sleep–waking cycles change during the course of life. These changes are most evident during early development.

Mammals sleep more during infancy than in adulthood

A clear cycle of sleeping and waking takes several weeks to become established in human infants (Figure 14.16). A 24-hour rhythm is generally evident by 16 weeks of age. Infant sleep is characterized by shorter sleep cycles than those of adulthood. These features of the sleep of infants seem to be due to the relative immaturity of the brain. For example, premature infants have even shorter cycles than do full-term babies.

Infant mammals show a large percentage of REM sleep. In humans, for example, 50% of sleep in the first 2 weeks of life is REM sleep (Figure 14.17). The prominence of REM sleep is even greater in premature infants, accounting for up to 80% of total sleep. Unlike normal adults, human infants can move directly from an awake state to REM sleep. By about 4 months of age, REM sleep is entered through a period of SWS.

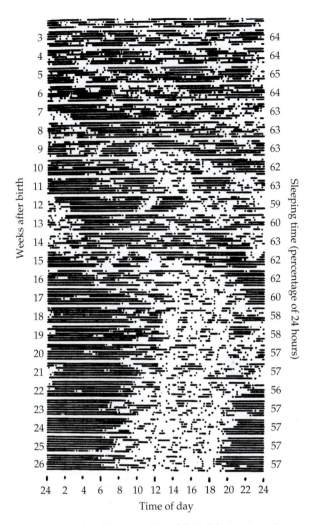

14.16 The Trouble with Babies   A stable pattern of sleep at night does not appear to be consolidated until about 16 weeks of age. The dark portions here indicate time asleep; the blank portions, time awake. (From Kleitman and Engelmann, 1953.)

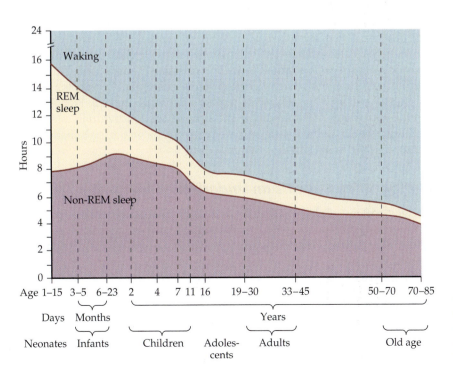

14.17 Human Sleep Patterns Change with Age Early in life we sleep a great deal, and about half of sleep time is spent in REM sleep. By adulthood, we average about 8 hours of sleep a night, 20% of which is REM sleep. (After Roffwarg et al., 1966.)

14.18 Typical Pattern of Sleep in an Elderly Person

Recordings of sleep in the elderly are characterized by frequent awakenings (yellow bars), the absence of stage 4 sleep, and a reduction of stage 3 sleep. Compare this recording with the young-adult sleep pattern shown in Figure 14.12. (After Kales and Kales, 1974.)

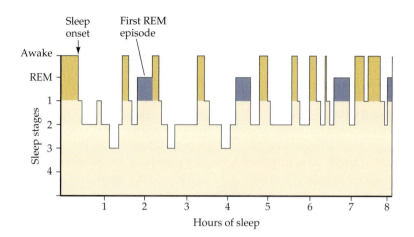

REM sleep of infants is quite active, accompanied by muscle twitching, smiles, grimaces, and vocalizations. The preponderance of REM sleep early in life suggests that this state provides stimulation that is essential to maturation of the nervous system. A hypothesis we'll consider shortly is that REM sleep is important for the consolidation of long-term memories. Because infancy is a time of much learning, this hypothesis may account for the large amount of REM sleep early in life.

Most people sleep appreciably less as they age

The parameters of sleep change more slowly in old age than in early development. Figure 14.18 shows the pattern of a typical night of sleep in an elderly person. A decline in the total amount of sleep is evident, as is an increase in the number of awakenings during a night (compare with Figure 14.12). Lack of sleep, or insomnia (which we will discuss at the end of this chapter), is a common complaint of the very elderly (Miles and Dement, 1980), although daytime naps may contribute to nighttime sleep difficulties.

The most dramatic progressive decline is in stages 3 and 4 sleep; people at age 60 spend only about half as much time in these stages as they did at age 20. Although gradual, the decline of stages 3 and 4 SWS starts quite early in life, as early as the third decade (Bliwise, 1989). By age 90, all sleep of stages 3 and 4 has disappeared. This decline in stages 3 and 4 sleep with age may be related to diminished cognitive capabilities, since an especially marked reduction of stages 3 and 4 SWS characterizes the sleep of aged humans who suffer from senile dementia. An age-associated decrease in stages 3 and 4 SWS is also seen in other mammals. Wilse B. Webb (1992) emphasized the wide range of variability in the sleep of aged individuals, although a central difference between the young and the old is the older person's inability to maintain sleep, causing sleep "dissatisfaction."

Manipulating Sleep Reveals an Underlying Structure

Sleep is affected by many environmental, social, and biological influences. From one viewpoint, though, sleep is an amazingly stable state: Major changes in our waking behavior have only a minor impact on subsequent sleep. But the effects of sleep deprivation on sleep are especially interesting because they give insight into the underlying mechanisms of sleep.

Sleep deprivation drastically alters sleep patterns

Most of us at one time or another have been willing or not-so-willing participants in informal **sleep deprivation** experiments. Thus most of us are aware of the effect of partial or total sleep deprivation: It makes us sleepy. The study of sleep deprivation is also a way to explore the potential regulatory mechanisms of sleeping and waking. Most of the studies concern **sleep recovery,** asking questions such as, Does a sleep-deprived organism somehow keep track of the amounts and types of lost sleep? When the organism is given the opportunity to compensate, is recovery partial or complete? Can you pay off sleep debts?

The effects of sleep deprivation Early reports from sleep deprivation studies emphasized a similarity between instances of "bizarre" behavior provoked by sleep deprivation and features of psychosis, particularly schizophrenia. A frequent theme in this work has been the functional role of dreams as a "guardian of sanity." But examination of schizophrenic patients does not confirm this view. For example, these patients can show sleep–waking cycles similar to those of normal adults, and sleep deprivation does not exacerbate their symptoms.

The behavioral effects of prolonged, total sleep deprivation vary appreciably and may depend on some general personality factors and on age. In several studies employing prolonged total deprivation—205 hours (8.5 days)—a few subjects showed occasional episodes of hallucinations. But the most common behavior changes noted in these experiments are increases in irritability, difficulty in concentrating, and episodes of disorientation. The subject's ability to perform tasks was summarized by L. C. Johnson (1969): "His performance is like a motor that after much use misfires, runs normally for a while, then falters again" (p. 216).

You don't need to resort to total sleep deprivation to see effects. Moderate sleep debt can accumulate with successive nights of little sleep. Volunteers who got 6 or 4 hours sleep per night for two weeks showed ever-mounting deficits in attention tasks and in speed of reaction compared to those sleeping 8 hours per night (Van Dongen et al., 2003). Interestingly, the sleep-deprived subjects often reported not feeling sleepy, yet they still exhibited behavioral deficits. By the end of the study, the subjects getting less than 8 hours of sleep per night had cognitive deficits equivalent to subjects who'd been totally sleep-deprived for 3 days!

Airline employees who had worked for 5 years on schedules that gave them little time to adapt to new time zones showed deficits in cognitive tasks of spatial memory and reduced volume of the brain's temporal lobe compared to employees on a schedule that permitted more time to recover from jet lag (K. Cho, 2001). Was it the disruption of circadian rhythms or accumulated sleep debt that caused the difference? We don't know.

Finally, it is clear that prolonged, total sleep deprivation in mammals compromises the immune system and leads to death (Box 14.1). Perhaps even fruit flies need sleep, since *Drosophila* with a particular mutation of the *cycle* gene (which is part of the circadian molecular clock; see Figure 14.7) die after only 10 hours of sleep deprivation (Shaw et al., 2002).

Sleep recovery Figure 14.19 provides data on sleep recovery in a young man following sleep deprivation for 11 days. No evidence of a psychotic state was noted, and the incentive for this unusually long act of not sleeping was simply the subject's own curiosity. Researchers got into the act only after the subject had started his deprivation schedule, which is the reason for the absence of predeprivation sleep data.

In the first night of sleep recovery, stage 4 sleep shows the greatest relative difference from normal. This increase in stage 4 sleep is usually at the expense of stage 2 sleep. However, the rise in stage 4 sleep during recovery never completely makes up for the deficit accumulated over the deprivation period. In fact, the amount is no greater than for deprivation periods half as long. REM sleep after prolonged sleep deprivation shows its greatest recovery during the second postdeprivation night. Eventually, the REM debt comes closer to being paid off. REM recovery may also involve another form of compensation—greater intensity: REM sleep in recovery nights is more "intense" than normal, with a greater number of rapid eye movements per period of time.

CLINICAL ISSUE

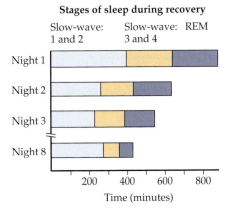

14.19 Sleep Recovery after 11 Days Awake (After Gulevich et al., 1966.)

BOX 14.1   Sleep Deprivation Can Be Fatal

*Sleep that knits up the
ravell'd sleave of care.*

—William Shakespeare, Macbeth,
Act II, Scene 2

Although some people seem to need very little sleep, most of us feel the need to sleep 7 to 8 hours a night. In fact, sustained sleep deprivation in rats causes them to increase their metabolic rate, lose weight, and within an average of 19 days, die (Everson et al., 1989). Allowing them to sleep prevents their death.

After the fatal effect of sleep deprivation had been shown, researchers undertook studies in which they terminated the sleep deprivation before the fatal end point and looked for pathological changes in different organ systems (Rechtschaffen and Bergmann, 1995). No single organ system seems affected in chronically sleep-deprived animals, but early in the deprivation they develop sores on their bodies. These sores seem to be the beginning of the end; shortly thereafter the rats' plasma reveals infections from a host of bacteria, which probably enter through the sores (Everson, 1993).

These bacteria are not normally fatal for rats because the rat's immune system and body defenses keep the bacteria in check, but severely sleep-deprived rats fail to develop a fever in response to these infections. (Fever helps the body fight infections.) In fact, the sleep-deprived animals show a drop in body temperature, which probably speeds bacterial infections, which in turn leads to diffuse organ damage.

The decline of these severely sleep-deprived rats is complicated, but if the sequence of events we have described is responsible for their death, then we should ask why the skin develops the sores that permit bacteria to enter. One observation is that the skin of these rats fails to show an inflammatory response to the infections. Inflammation is the local dilation of blood vessels, which enables greater blood flow and thus allows more immune cells to reach and attack an infection. Signs of inflammation include a reddening of the skin, a rise in local temperature, and swelling. We have no idea how sleep deprivation impairs the inflammatory response, but such response is crucial for maintaining the integrity of our skin. So perhaps Shakespeare's folk theory of the function of sleep, quoted above, isn't so far from the truth.

What about the rare humans who sleep only 1 or 2 hours a night? Why aren't their immune systems and inflammatory responses compromised? We don't know, but since the distinguishing trait of these people is that they don't need much sleep, perhaps their immune system and inflammatory response don't need much sleep either. Or perhaps the small amount of sleep they have almost every night is more efficient at doing whatever sleep does.

Some unfortunate humans inherit a defect in the gene for the prion protein (which can transmit mad cow disease, discussed in Chapter 16), and although they sleep normally at the beginning of life, in midlife they simply stop sleeping—with fatal effect. People with this disease, called *fatal familial insomnia*, die 7 to 24 months after the insomnia begins (Medori et al., 1992). In other people, the gene seems to mutate spontaneously, resulting in the same fatal insomnia (Mastrianni et al., 1999). Autopsy reveals degeneration of the thalamus; this lesion may be responsible for the insomnia (Manetto et al., 1992). (Electrical stimulation of the thalamus can induce sleep in animals.) As in sleep-deprived rats, sleep-deprived humans seem not to have obvious damage to any single organ system. Apparently these patients die because they are chronically sleep-deprived, and these results, combined with research on rats, certainly support the idea that prolonged insomnia is fatal.

Note that if you never quite recover all lost sleep time, that does not mean you shouldn't try to make up for lost sleep as soon as possible. The sooner you start making up for sleep loss, the more total sleep time you'll recover.

What Are the Biological Functions of Sleep?

Why do most of us spend one-third of our lifetime asleep? Furthermore, why is sleep divided into two dissimilar states with distinct physiological attributes? The functions of sleep are a subject of great debate; our discussion here emphasizes only the major ideas. Keep in mind that the proposed functions, or biological roles, of sleep are not mutually exclusive; sleep may play many roles. As with other processes, sleep may have acquired more than one function during evolution. The four functions most often ascribed to sleep are

1. Energy conservation
2. Predator avoidance
3. Body restoration
4. Memory consolidation

Sleep conserves energy

We consume less energy when we sleep. For example, SWS is marked by reduced muscular tension, lowered heart rate, reduced blood pressure, reduced body temperature, and slower respiration. This diminished metabolic activity during sleep suggests that one role of sleep is to conserve energy. From this perspective, sleep enforces the cessation of ongoing activities and thus ensures rest.

We can see the importance of this function by looking at the world from the perspective of small animals. Small animals have very high metabolic rates (see Chapter 13), so activity for them is metabolically expensive. Demand can easily outstrip supply. Periods of reduced activity can be especially valuable if they occur when food is scarce. Comparative sleep data offer some support for this view. There is a high correlation between total amount of sleep per day and waking metabolic rate: Small animals sleep more than large species (see Figure 14.14). The energy savings may not be as great as you might think, however, because at least some parts of sleep, such as the phasic events of REM sleep, are characterized by intense metabolic expenditure.

Sleep helps animals avoid predators

Intense evolutionary pressures have generated a variety of tactics for avoiding predators. Diurnal animals are well adapted to survive in the daytime; nocturnal animals are adapted for surviving at night. Meddis (1975) suggested that sleep helps animals stay out of harm's way during the part of the day when each is most vulnerable to predation. In this manner, sleep can enable effective sharing of an ecological niche—survival without becoming a meal. From a similar perspective, F. Snyder (1969) suggested that REM sleep is a periodic quasi-awakening to make sure the sleep site is still safe.

**EVOLUTION
AT WORK**

Sleep restores the body

If someone asked you why you sleep, chances are you would answer that you sleep because you're tired. Indeed, one of the proposed functions of sleep is simply the rebuilding or restoration of materials used during waking, such as proteins (Moruzzi, 1972). The release of growth hormone during SWS supports a restorative hypothesis. Hartmann (1973) suggested that there are two types of restorative needs that sleep deals with differently: physical tiredness and the tiredness associated with emotional activation.

Surprisingly, the restorative perspective is only weakly supported by research. A simple way to test this idea is to look at the effects of changes in presleep activity on the duration or cycle of sleep. Can intense metabolic expenditure during the day influence sleep duration? For most people, exercise may cause them to fall asleep more quickly, but not to sleep longer. On the other hand, we've seen that prolonged and total sleep deprivation—either forced on rats or, in humans, as a result of inherited pathology—interferes with the immune system and leads to death (see Box 14.1). So the widespread belief that sleep helps us recover from illness is well supported by animal research.

Does sleep aid memory consolidation?

Every now and then we are confronted with newspaper reports and advertisements that herald a new technique or gadget that will enable us to learn during sleep. The appeal of such possibilities is overwhelming to some people, including those who begrudgingly accept sleep as a necessary interference with the pursuit of knowledge and those who sport the fantasy that information can be transmitted by the deep embrace of a book.

More seriously, sleep is a state in which many neurons are active. Can we learn during this state? Apparently not. But even if we can't learn *during* sleep, can sleep help us consolidate what we learned beforehand? If so, then sleep deprivation may interfere with learning. Students participating in the ritual of overnight cramming for exams would want to know.

Only simple learning occurs during sleep   The idea that we can learn while sleeping is a controversial area beset with many conflicting claims (Aarons, 1976). The only overall conclusion one can confidently draw from a large range of studies is that if you are relying on acquiring and retaining complex information during sleep, you should find a backup system—it just doesn't work (Druckman and Bjork, 1994). Although nonhumans can acquire simple conditioned responses during various sleep stages, experiments that carefully monitor whether a person is truly asleep indicate that neither explicit nor implicit memories (see Chapter 17) for verbal material form during sleep (Wood et al., 1992).

A peculiar property of dreams is that unless we tell them to someone or write them down soon after waking, we tend to forget them (Dement, 1974), as though the brain refuses to consolidate information presented during REM sleep. It is probably beneficial that most dreams are not stored in long-term memory, because it would be counterproductive to squander permanent memory storage space on events that never happened.

Consolidation of material learned while awake   Even if we don't acquire new information presented *during* sleep, we may use sleep to consolidate information that we acquired while awake. In 1924, Jenkins and Dallenbach reported an experiment that continues to provoke research. They trained some subjects in a verbal learning task at bedtime and tested them 8 hours later on arising from sleep, and they trained other subjects early in the day and tested them 8 hours later (with no intervening sleep). The results showed better retention when a period of sleep intervened between a learning period and tests of recall. What accounts for such an effect?

NEURAL PLASTICITY

Several differing psychological explanations have been offered. One suggests that during the waking period between learning and recall, diverse experiences interfere with accurate recall. Sleep during this interval appreciably reduces interfering stimulation. A second explanation notes that memory tends to decay and that this relentless process is simply slower during sleep. These two explanations posit sleep as a passive process in consolidating memory. A third explanation emphasizes an active, functional contribution of sleep to learning. This view says that sleep includes processes that consolidate the learning of waking periods (Kavanau, 1997; C. Smith, 1985). Sleep is then seen as providing the conditions to allow a firm "printing" of enduring memory traces.

Humans learning a reaction-time task that activated certain brain regions showed, in a following REM period, increased activation of exactly those brain regions that had been exercised (Maquet et al., 2000), as if the regions used during the task were reviewing that task. Similarly, the patterned activity of neurons in birdsong nuclei while male zebra finches are learning to sing appears to be repeated during subsequent bouts of sleep (Dave and Margoliash, 2000).

The functional significance of REM sleep following learning has been explored by studies on REM sleep deprivation. As short a period as 3 hours of such deprivation retards the rate of learning in some cases (C. Smith, 1995). In humans, certain "perceptual" learning tasks, such as learning to discriminate different textures visually, show little improvement in a single training session but show considerable improvement 8 to 10 hours after the session. Karni et al. (1994) found that if people were deprived of REM sleep after a session, they failed to show improvement the next day.

In addition, several experiments have asked whether depriving animals of REM sleep interferes with their consolidation of previously learned tasks, but these studies offer inconsistent results. Sometimes REM deprivation interferes with memory consolidation, sometimes it does not (Vertes and Eastman, 2000). Jerome Siegel (2001) has pointed out that REM deprivation is necessarily accompanied by stress, which might be the cause of memory disruption. He also notes that there is no correlation across species between time spent in REM and obvious learning capacity. In humans, there is no correlation between the amount of REM sleep and either IQ or academic achievement (Borrow et al., 1980). Finally, one man who had brainstem injuries that seemed to eliminate REM sleep could still learn, and he completed his

Jerome M. Siegel

education (Lavie, 1996). So even if REM sleep *aids* learning, it is clear that it is not absolutely *necessary* for learning.

Some humans sleep remarkably little, yet function normally

One challenge to all of the theories about the function of sleep is the existence of a few people who seem perfectly normal and healthy, yet hardly sleep at all. These cases are more than just folktales. William Dement (1974) described a Stanford University professor who slept only 3 to 4 hours a night for more than 50 years and died at age 80. Sleep researcher Ray Meddis (1977) found a cheerful 70-year-old retired nurse who said she had slept little since childhood. She was a busy person who easily filled up her 23 hours of daily wakefulness. During the night she sat on her bed reading or writing, and at about 2:00 AM she fell asleep for an hour or so, after which she readily awakened.

William Dement

For her first 2 days in Meddis's laboratory, she did not sleep at all because it was all so interesting to her. On the third night she slept a total of 99 minutes, and her sleep contained both SWS and REM sleep periods. Later her sleep was recorded for 5 days. On the first night she did not sleep at all, but on subsequent nights she slept an average of 67 minutes. She never complained about not sleeping more, and she did not feel drowsy during either the day or the night. Meddis described several other people who sleep either not at all or for about 1 hour per night. Some of these people report having parents who slept little. Whatever the function of sleep is, these people possess some way of fulfilling it with a brief nap. They show less stage 1 and 2 sleep, so perhaps they are more efficient sleepers. Importantly, though, no person has ever been found who does not sleep at all.

At Least Four Interacting Neural Systems Underlie Sleep

At one time sleep was regarded as a passive state, as though most of the brain simply stopped working while we slept, leaving us unaware of events around us. We now know that sleep is an active state mediated by at least four interacting neural systems:

1. A *forebrain* system that by itself can display SWS
2. A *brainstem* system that activates the forebrain into wakefulness
3. A *pontine* system that triggers REM sleep
4. A *hypothalamic* system that affects the other three brain regions to determine whether the brain will be awake or asleep

The forebrain generates slow-wave sleep

The most straightforward evidence for the different sleep systems comes from experiments in which the brain is transected—literally cut into two parts, an upper part and a lower part. The entire brain can be isolated from the body by an incision between the medulla and the spinal cord. This preparation was first studied by the Belgian physiologist Frédéric Brémer (1938), who called it the *isolated brain,* or **encéphale isolé.**

**Frédéric Brémer
(1892–1959)**

The EEGs of such animals showed signs of waking that alternated with signs of sleeping (Figure 14.20*a*). During EEG-defined wakeful periods, the pupils were dilated and the eyes followed moving objects. During EEG-defined sleep, the pupils were small, as is characteristic of normal sleep. (Brémer did not distinguish between SWS and REM sleep; this distinction was not discovered until the 1950s. But we now know that REM sleep can also be detected in the isolated brain.) These results demonstrate that wakefulness, SWS and REM are all mediated by networks within the brain. But where in the brain are the centers that mediate wakefulness and sleep in the encéphale isolé?

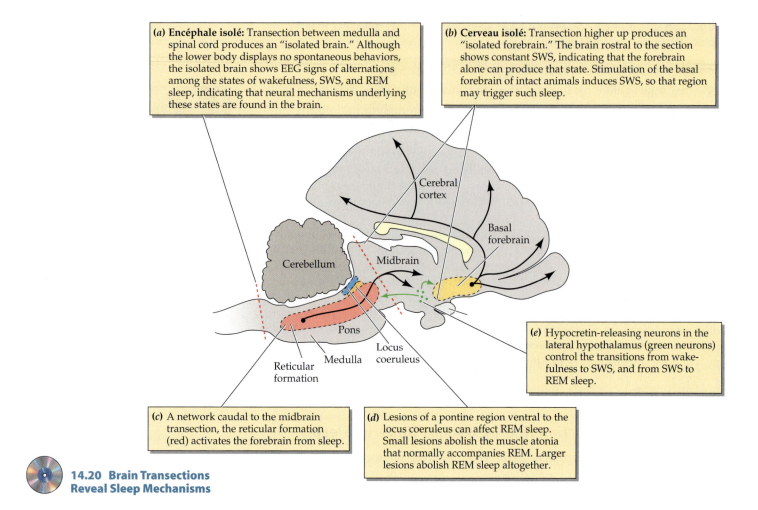

(a) Encéphale isolé: Transection between medulla and spinal cord produces an "isolated brain." Although the lower body displays no spontaneous behaviors, the isolated brain shows EEG signs of alternations among the states of wakefulness, SWS, and REM sleep, indicating that neural mechanisms underlying these states are found in the brain.

(b) Cerveau isolé: Transection higher up produces an "isolated forebrain." The brain rostral to the section shows constant SWS, indicating that the forebrain alone can produce that state. Stimulation of the basal forebrain of intact animals induces SWS, so that region may trigger such sleep.

(e) Hypocretin-releasing neurons in the lateral hypothalamus (green neurons) control the transitions from wakefulness to SWS, and from SWS to REM sleep.

(c) A network caudal to the midbrain transection, the reticular formation (red) activates the forebrain from sleep.

(d) Lesions of a pontine region ventral to the locus coeruleus can affect REM sleep. Small lesions abolish the muscle atonia that normally accompanies REM. Larger lesions abolish REM sleep altogether.

Cerebral cortex

Basal forebrain

Cerebellum

Midbrain

Pons

Locus coeruleus

Medulla

Reticular formation

14.20 Brain Transections Reveal Sleep Mechanisms

If the transection is made higher along the brainstem—in the midbrain—a very different result is achieved. Brémer referred to such a preparation as an *isolated forebrain,* or **cerveau isolé,** and he found that the EEG from the brain in front of the cut displayed constant SWS (see Figure 14.20*b*). We now know that the isolated forebrain does not show REM sleep, so it appears that the forebrain alone can generate SWS, with no contributions from the lower brain regions.

The constant SWS seen in the cortex of the cerveau isolé appears to be generated by the **basal forebrain** in the ventral frontal lobe and anterior hypothalamus. Lesions in that region can abolish SWS, and electrical stimulation of the basal forebrain can induce SWS activity (Clemente and Sterman, 1967). Neurons in this region become active at sleep onset, are inhibited by noradrenergic stimulation, and appear to use GABA for a neurotransmitter (Gallopin et al., 2000). To induce SWS, the basal forebrain neurons release GABA in the nearby tuberomammillary nucleus in the hypothalamus, effectively suppressing neural activity there.

Many **general anesthetics**—drugs such as barbiturates and anesthetic gases that render people unconscious during surgery—work by making $GABA_A$ receptors more sensitive to GABA. These drugs seem to induce an SWS-like state by activating the endogenous SWS system, exaggerating the GABA-ergic inhibition of the tuberomammillary nucleus (L. E. Nelson et al., 2002) to suppress wakefulness.

So the basal forebrain promotes SWS by releasing GABA into the nearby tuberomammillary nucleus, and left alone, this system would keep the cortex asleep forever. But as we'll see next, there is a brainstem system that arouses the forebrain from slumber.

CLINICAL ISSUE

The reticular formation wakes up the forebrain

In the late 1940s, electrical stimulation of an extensive region of the brainstem known as the **reticular formation** (Figure 14.21) was shown to activate the cortex. The reticular formation consists of a diffuse group of cells whose axons and dendrites course in many directions, extending from the medulla through the thalamus. Giuseppe Moruzzi and Horace Magoun (1949), pioneers in the study of the reticular formation, found that they could wake sleeping animals by electrically stimulating the reticular formation; the animals showed rapid awakening. Lesions of these regions produced persistent sleep in the animals (see Figure 14.20c).

The effects noted by Brémer were now interpreted as arising not from the loss of sensory input from the body, but from the interruption of an activating system within the brainstem. This mechanism remained intact in the encéphale isolé animal, but its output was prevented from reaching the cortex in the cerveau isolé animal. The "reticular formation" school argued that waking results from activity of brainstem reticular formation systems and that sleep is the passive result of a decline in activity in the reticular formation. As mentioned already, however, later studies revealed that the basal forebrain region actively imposes SWS on the brain. So

**Giuseppe Moruzzi
(1920–1986)**

**Horace Magoun
(1907–1991)**

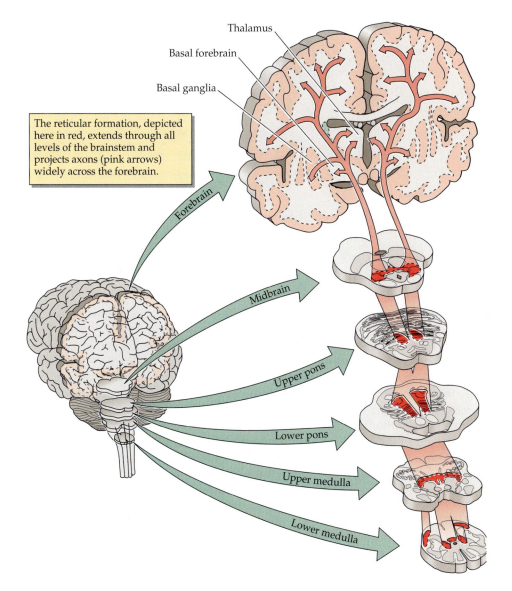

The reticular formation, depicted here in red, extends through all levels of the brainstem and projects axons (pink arrows) widely across the forebrain.

Thalamus

Basal forebrain

Basal ganglia

Forebrain

Midbrain

Upper pons

Lower pons

Upper medulla

Lower medulla

14.21 The Brainstem Reticular Formation   The reticular formation is thought to activate the rest of the brain.

14.22 The Raphe Nucleus, Locus Coeruleus, and Their Projections

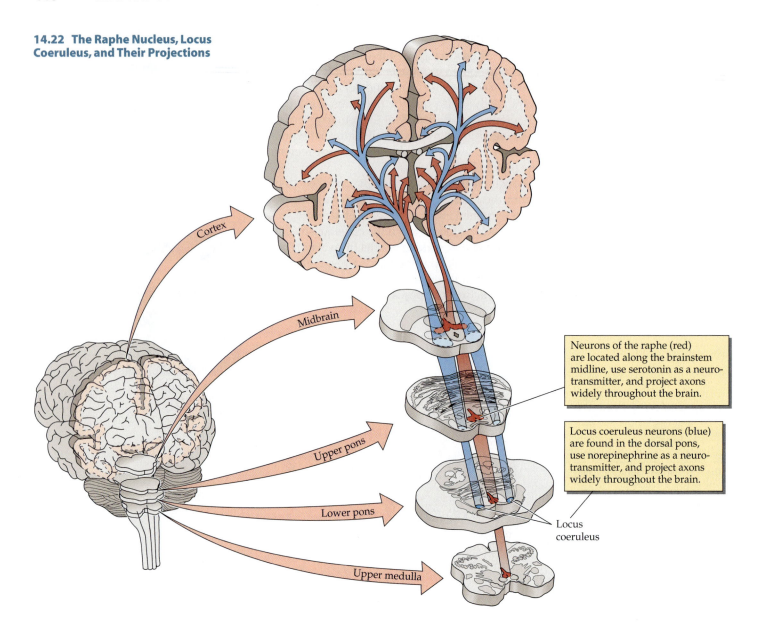

Neurons of the raphe (red) are located along the brainstem midline, use serotonin as a neurotransmitter, and project axons widely throughout the brain.

Locus coeruleus neurons (blue) are found in the dorsal pons, use norepinephrine as a neurotransmitter, and project axons widely throughout the brain.

Locus coeruleus

Cortex

Midbrain

Upper pons

Lower pons

Upper medulla

Michel Jouvet

the forebrain SWS system and the brainstem reticular formation seem to push the brain back and forth from SWS to wakefulness.

Michel Jouvet (1967) emphasized a system of neurons coursing in the midline of the brainstem called the **raphe** (pronouned "ra-FAY") **nucleus** (Figure 14.22). These neurons use the neurotransmitter serotonin, and Jouvet proposed that serotonin release throughout the brain promotes sleep, especially SWS. For example, the drug parachlorophenylalanine (PCPA) blocks the synthesis of serotonin, producing a decrease in transmitter levels and a reduction in sleep. Likewise, mice with the serotonin 1B receptor knocked out display less SWS than control mice (Boutrel et al., 1999). However, the broad controlling role once attributed to serotonin in neurochemical models of sleep must now be tempered by the recognition that other transmitters also seem to be part of the sleep story (Table 14.2).

The pons triggers REM sleep

Several methods have pinpointed the region of the pons that is important for REM sleep. Lesions of a small region just ventral to the locus coeruleus abolish REM sleep

TABLE 14.2 *Neural Activity of Neurotransmitter Systems during Sleep and Arousal*

Neurotransmitter	Site of cell bodies	Activity during		
		Wakefulness	SWS	REM
Serotonin	Raphe nuclei	High	Low	Very low
Norepinephrine	Locus coeruleus	High	Low	Very low
Acetylcholine	Brainstem	High	Low	High

(see Figure 14.20*d*) (L. Friedman and Jones, 1984). Electrical stimulation of the same region, or pharmacological stimulation of this region with cholinergic agonists, can induce or prolong REM sleep. Finally, monitoring of neuronal activity in this region reveals some neurons that seem to be active only during REM sleep (J. M. Siegel, 1994). So the pons seems to have a REM sleep center.

Small lesions that destroy only a part of this pontine REM center indicate that part of this region is specialized to produce the profound muscle atonia of REM. This motor inhibition depends on influences descending from the brain to the spinal cord. During REM sleep, the inhibitory transmitters GABA and glycine produce powerful inhibitory postsynaptic potentials (IPSPs) in spinal motoneurons that prevent them from reaching threshold and producing an action potential (Kodama et al., 2003). Thus the dreamer's muscles are not just relaxed, but flaccid. This loss of muscle tone during REM sleep can be abolished by small lesions ventral to the locus coeruleus, suggesting that this region plays a role in uncoupling the motor system during sleep (A. R. Morrison, 1983).

Cats with such lesions seem to act out their dreams. After a bout of SWS, EEGs of these cats become desynchronized as they do during waking and REM sleep, and the animals stagger to their feet. Are they awake or in REM sleep? They move their heads as though visually tracking moving objects (that aren't there), bat with their forepaws at nothing, and ignore objects that are present. In addition, the cat's *inner eyelid*, the translucent nictitating membrane, partially covers the eyes. Thus the cat appears to be in REM sleep, but motor activity is not being inhibited by the brain.

So far we've described three interacting brain systems controlling sleep: an SWS-promoting region in the forebrain, an arousing reticular formation in the brainstem, and a system in the pons that triggers paralysis of the body during REM. There is a fourth important system, in the hypothalamus, that seems to act as a "switch" among these three centers. To understand how we learned about this fourth system, we need to consider the rare but fascinating condition called *narcolepsy*.

A hypothalamic sleep center was revealed by the study of narcolepsy

You might not consider getting lots of sleep an affliction, but there are many people who are either drowsy all the time or suffer sudden attacks of sleep. At the extreme of such tendencies is **narcolepsy**, an unusual disorder in which the patient is afflicted by frequent, intense attacks of sleep, which last 5 to 30 minutes and can occur at any time during usual waking hours. Uncontrollable attacks of sleep occur several times a day—usually about every 90 minutes (Dantz et al., 1994).

CLINICAL ISSUE

Individuals with this sleep disorder are distinguished by the appearance of REM sleep in the first few minutes of sleep. At night, these individuals exhibit a relatively normal sleep pattern, but they seem to suffer abrupt, overwhelming sleepiness during their days. Many people with narcolepsy also show **cataplexy**, a sudden loss of muscle tone, leading to collapse of the body without loss of consciousness. Cataplexy can be triggered by sudden, intense emotional stimuli, including both laughter and anger. Narcolepsy usually manifests itself between the ages of 15 and 25 years and continues throughout life. Remember Barry from the start of this chapter? His narcolepsy symptoms began in his freshman year of college, when he started showing the classic signs of excessive daytime sleepiness and cataplexy.

(1)

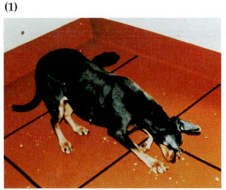

(2)

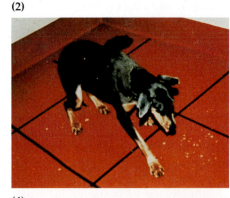

(3)

(4)

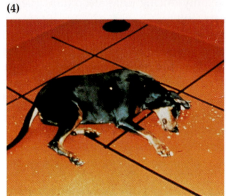

14.23 Narcolepsy in Dogs A narcoleptic dog that suffers cataplexy when excited is offered a food treat (1), becomes wobbly (2), lies down (3), and finally falls limply to the floor (4). (Courtesy of Seiji Nishino.)

Several strains of dogs exhibit narcolepsy (Aldrich, 1993), complete with sudden cataplexy and very short latencies to sleep onset (Figure 14.23). And just like humans who suffer from narcolepsy, they also often show REM immediately upon falling asleep. Cataplexy in these dogs is suppressed by the same drugs (discussed shortly) that are used to treat human cataplexy.

The mutant gene responsible for one of these narcoleptic strains of dogs was found to be a receptor for the neuropeptide hypocretin (this peptide is also known by the name *orexin*) (L. Lin et al., 1999). Mice with the *hypocretin* gene knocked out also display narcolepsy (Chemelli et al., 1999). Genetically normal rats can be made narcoleptic if injected with a toxin conjugated to molecules of hypocretin (Gerashchenko et al., 2001). The hypocretin–toxin complex destroys neurons that possess hypocretin receptors. No one knows why interfering with hypocretin signaling leads to narcolepsy, but the narcoleptic dogs show signs of neural degeneration in the amygdala and nearby forebrain structures (J. M. Siegel et al., 1999). This degeneration occurs about the time in development when symptoms of narcolepsy appear.

Similarly, humans with narcolepsy appear to have lost about 90% of their hypocretin neurons (Figure 14.24) (Thannicakal et al., 2000). This degeneration of hypocretin neurons seems to permit inappropriate activation of the cataplexy pathway that is normally at work during REM. So hypocretin normally keeps sleep at bay and prevents the transition from wakefulness directly into REM.

The neurons that normally produce hypocretin are found almost exclusively in the hypothalamus. Where do these neurons send their axons to release the hypocretin? Not so coincidentally, they send their axons to each of the three brain centers we mentioned before: the basal forebrain, the reticular formation, and the locus coeruleus (Sutcliffe and de Lecea, 2002). The hypocretin neurons also project axons to the tuberomammillary nucleus that is inhibited by the basal forebrain to induce SWS. Thus there is growing excitement that the hypothalamic hypocretin sleep center may act as a "switch," controlling whether we are awake, in SWS sleep, or in REM sleep (see Figure 14.20*e*).

(a) **Normal**

(b) **Narcoleptic**

14.24 Neural Degeneration in Humans with Narcolepsy   (*a*) Immunocytochemistry reveals hypocretin-containing neurons in the lateral hypothalamus of a person who does not have narcolepsy. (*b*) This same region of the brain from someone suffering from narcolepsy has far fewer hypocretin neurons. (Courtesy of Jerome Siegel.)

The traditional treatment for narcolepsy has been the use of amphetamines in the daytime. A more controversial treatment is the drug GHB (γ-hydroxybutyrate, trade name Xyrem), also known as a "date rape" drug, but there are concerns about potential abuse of this drug (Tuller, 2002). A newer drug, modafinil (PROVIGIL), is sometimes effective for preventing narcoleptic attacks and has been proposed as an "alertness drug" for people with attention deficit disorder. There is also debate about whether modafinil should be available to anyone who feels sleepy or needs to stay awake (Pack, 2003), but at least one study found the drug no more effective than caffeine in this regard (Wesensten et al., 2002). Now that narcolepsy is known to be caused by a loss of hypocretin signaling, there is hope of developing synthetic drugs to stimulate hypocretin receptors, both for the relief of symptoms in narcolepsy and to combat sleepiness in people without narcolepsy.

There is one common symptom of narcolepsy that many other people experience on occasion. **Sleep paralysis** is the (temporary) inability to move or talk either just before dropping off to sleep, or, more often, just after waking. In this state people may experience sudden sensory hallucinations (Cheyne, 2002). Sleep paralysis never lasts more than a few minutes, so it's best to relax and avoid panic. It is common: About 40% of both Canadian and Japanese university students have experienced this feeling (Fukuda et al., 1998). One hypothesis is that sleep paralysis is caused by the pontine center continuing to impose paralysis for a short while after awakening from a REM episode.

Sleep Disorders Can Be Serious, Even Life-Threatening

Narcolepsy is just one of several sleep disorders (Table 14.3) that have made sleep disorder clinics common in major medical centers. For some people, the peace and comfort of regular, uninterrupted sleep is routinely disturbed by the inability to fall asleep, prolonged sleep, or unusual awakenings.

Some minor dysfunctions are associated with sleep

Some dysfunctions associated with sleep are more common in children than in adults. Two sleep disorders in children—night terrors (described earlier) and **sleep enuresis** (bed-wetting)—are associated with SWS. Most people grow out of night terrors or sleep enuresis without intervention, but pharmacological approaches can be used to reduce the amount of stages 3 and 4 sleep (as well as REM time) while increasing stage 2 sleep. For sleep enuresis, some doctors prescribe a nasal spray of the hormone vasopressin (antidiuretic hormone) before bedtime, which decreases the amount of urine collecting in the bladder.

Somnambulism (sleepwalking) consists of getting out of bed, walking around the room, and appearing awake. It is more common in children than in adults. In most children these episodes last a few seconds to minutes, and the child usually does not remember the experience. Because such episodes occur during stages 3 and 4 SWS, they are more common in the first half of the night (when those stages predominate).

CLINICAL ISSUE

The belief that sleepwalkers are acting out a dream is not supported by data (Parkes, 1985). The main problem is the inability of sleepwalkers to wake into full contact with their surroundings. At least one person was acquitted of murder after suggesting that he had suffered from "homicidal somnambulism," but such claims are difficult to evaluate (Broughton et al., 1994). A male student who entered ten rooms in a women's dormitory one night, trying to remove the underwear from one woman and to cut off the shirt from another, was declared innocent of attempted sexual assault because he claimed to be sleepwalking.

Some people, however, do seem to be acting out their dreams during REM sleep. **REM behavior disorder** (**RBD**) is characterized by organized behavior—such as fighting an imaginary foe, eating a meal, acting like a wild animal—from a person who appears to be asleep (Schenck and Mahowald, 2002). Sometimes the person

TABLE 14.3 *Classification of Sleep Disorders*

DISORDERS OF INITIATING AND MAINTAINING SLEEP (INSOMNIA)

Ordinary, uncomplicated insomnia
  Transient
  Persistent
Drug-related insomnia caused by
  Use of stimulants
  Withdrawal of depressants
  Chronic alcoholism
Insomnia associated with psychiatric disorders
Insomnia associated with sleep-induced respiratory impairment
  Sleep apnea

DISORDERS OF EXCESSIVE DROWSINESS

Narcolepsy
Drowsiness associated with psychiatric problems
Drug-related drowsiness
Drowsiness associated with sleep-induced respiratory impairment

DISORDERS OF SLEEP–WAKING SCHEDULE

Transient disruption caused by
  Time zone change by airplane flight (jet lag)
  Work shift, especially night work
Persistent disruption
  Irregular rhythm

DYSFUNCTIONS ASSOCIATED WITH SLEEP, SLEEP STAGES, OR PARTIAL AROUSALS

Sleepwalking (somnambulism)
Sleep enuresis (bed-wetting)
Night terror
Nightmares
Sleep-related seizures
Teeth grinding
Sleep-related activation of cardiac and gastrointestinal symptoms

Source: After Weitzman, 1981.

remembers a dream that matches well with his behavior (C. Brown, 2003). This disorder usually begins after the age of 50 and is more common in men than in women. Individuals with RBD are reminiscent of the kittens with a lesion of the locus coeruleus region who were no longer paralyzed during REM and so acted out their dreams. Interestingly, the onset of RBD is often followed by the beginning symptoms of Parkinson's disease, suggesting that the disorder is caused by damage somewhere in the brain's motor systems. RBD is usually well controlled by antianxiety drugs (benzodiazepines) at bedtime.

Insomniacs have trouble falling asleep or staying asleep

Almost all of us experience an occasional inability to fall asleep, and a very few individuals die apparently because they stop sleeping altogether (see Box 14.1). But many people persistently find it difficult to fall asleep and/or stay asleep as long as they would like. Estimates of the prevalence of insomnia from surveys range from 15% to 30% of the adult population (Parkes, 1985). Insomnia is commonly reported by people who are older, female, or users of drugs like tobacco, coffee, and alcohol.

Insomnia seems to be the final common outcome for various situational, neurological, psychiatric, and medical conditions. It is not a trivial disorder; adults who regularly sleep for short periods show a higher mortality rate than those who regularly sleep 7 to 8 hours each night (Wingard and Berkman, 1983).

Sometimes there is a discrepancy between a person's reported failure to sleep and EEG indicators of sleep. This discrepancy has been labeled *sleep state misperception* (McCall and Edinger, 1992). People with this condition report that they did not sleep even when they showed EEG signs of sleep and failed to respond to stimuli during the EEG-defined sleep state.

Situational factors that contribute to insomnia include shift work, time zone changes, and environmental conditions such as novelty (that hard motel bed). Usually these conditions produce transient **sleep-onset insomnia,** a difficulty in falling asleep. Drugs and neurological and psychiatric factors seem to cause **sleep-maintenance insomnia,** a difficulty in remaining asleep. In this type of insomnia, sleep is punctuated by frequent nighttime arousals. This form of insomnia is especially evident in disorders of the respiratory system.

In some people, respiration becomes unreliable during sleep. Breathing may cease for a minute or so, or it may slow alarmingly; blood levels of oxygen drop markedly. This syndrome, called **sleep apnea,** arises either from the progressive relaxation of muscles of the chest, diaphragm, and throat cavity or from changes in the pacemaker respiratory neurons of the brainstem. In the former instance, relaxation of the throat obstructs the airway—a kind of self-choking. This mode of sleep apnea is common in very obese people, but it also occurs, often undiagnosed, in nonobese people. Sleep apnea is often accompanied by loud, interrupted snoring, so loud snorers should consult a physician about the possibility that they suffer from sleep apnea.

CLINICAL ISSUE

Each episode of apnea arouses the person enough to restore breathing, but the frequent nighttime arousals make such people sleepy in the daytime. Insertion of a removable tube in the throat can restore a normal sleep pattern and eliminate excessive daytime sleepiness. For others, breathing through a special machine (called a *continous positive airway pressure,* or *CPAP,* machine) maintains air pressure in their airways and prevents the collapse. Untreated sleep apnea appears to lead to several cardiovascular disorders, such as hypertension (Wolk and Somers, 2003).

Investigators have speculated that **sudden infant death syndrome** (**SIDS,** or *crib death*) arises from sleep apnea as a result of immature systems that normally pace respiration, or insufficient arousal mechanisms. Incidence of SIDS has been cut almost in half by the National Institute of Child Health and Human Development's "Back to Sleep" campaign, which urges parents to put infants to sleep on their backs rather than on their stomachs (Figure 14.25). Placing the baby face down may lead to suffocation if the baby does not arouse properly.

Although many drugs affect sleep, there is no perfect sleeping pill

Throughout recorded history humans have reached for substances to enhance the prospects of sleep. Early civilizations discovered substances in the plant world that induce sleep (Hartmann, 1978). Ancient Greeks used the juice of the poppy to obtain opium and used products of the mandrake plant that we recognize today as scopolamine and atropine. The preparation of barbituric acid in the mid-nineteenth century by the discoverer of aspirin, Adolph von Bayer, began the development of an enormous number of substances—*barbiturates*—that continue to be used for sleep dysfunctions. Unfortunately, none of these substances can provide a completely normal night of sleep in terms of time spent in various sleep states such as REM sleep, and none of them remain effective when used repeatedly.

Most modern sleeping pills—including the currently popular benzodiazepines triazolam (Halcion), zolpidem (AMBIEN), and zaleplon (SONATA)—activate GABA receptors, inhibiting broad regions of the brain. But reliance on sleeping pills poses many problems (Rothschild, 1992). Viewed solely as a way to deal with sleep problems, current drugs fall far short of being a suitable remedy for several reasons.

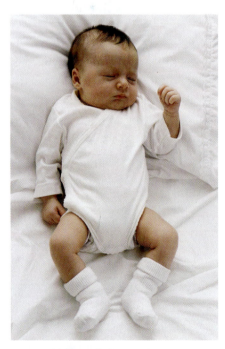

14.25 Back to Sleep
Placing infants on their backs for sleep reduces the risk of sudden infant death syndrome by half. Exposure to cigarette smoke increases the risk of crib death.

First, continual use of sleep medications causes them to lose their sleep-inducing properties, and this declining ability to induce sleep frequently leads to increased self-prescribed dosages that pose a health hazard.

A second major drawback in the use of sleeping pills is that they produce marked changes in the pattern of sleep, both during the period of drug use and for a period following drug use that may last for days. Most commonly, during the initial phase of drug use, REM sleep is reduced, especially during the first half of a night of sleep. A gradual adaptation to drug use is evident in the return of REM sleep with continued use of sleeping pills. Sudden withdrawal of sleeping pills results in a period of REM rebound with an intensity that many people experience as unpleasant nightmares, and that may lead to a return to reliance on sleeping pills.

A final major problem in the frequent use of sleeping pills is their impact on waking behavior. A persistent "sleep drunkenness" coupled with drowsiness, despite intense efforts at maintaining vigilance, may impair productive activity during waking hours.

These problems have led to the development of other biochemical approaches to the treatment of sleep disorders. Because the hormone melatonin is normally released from the pineal at night (see Figure 5.19b), the administration of exogenous melatonin has been suggested to aid the onset of sleep. In fact, melatonin does have a weak hypnotic effect soon after administration (Chase and Gidal, 1997), perhaps because it lowers body temperature, reducing arousal and causing drowsiness (Dawson and Encel, 1993). Mendelson (1997) remains unconvinced that melatonin really helps insomnia, but it does seem to reduce the effects of jet lag (Arendt et al., 1997).

Certainly the treatment for insomnia that has the fewest side effects, and that is very effective for many people, is not to use any drug, but to develop a regular routine to exploit the body's circadian clock. Thus, Wilse B. Webb (1992) advises insomniacs to use an alarm clock to wake up faithfully at the same time each day and then simply go to bed once they feel sleepy (Webb, 1992). Going through a bedtime routine of quiet activities can also help condition sleep onset. An important adjunct to this strategy is to ignore preconceived notions about how much sleep you "need." If you get out of bed every day at 6:00 AM and don't feel sleepy until midnight, then your body is telling you that you need only 6 hours of sleep, no matter what various pharmaceutical companies might say.

Wilse B. Webb

Summary

Biological Rhythms

1. Many living systems show circadian rhythms that can be entrained by environmental stimuli, especially light. These rhythms synchronize behavior and body states to changes in the environment.

2. Neural pacemakers in the suprachiasmatic nucleus (SCN) of the hypothalamus are the basis of many circadian rhythms. The basis of light entrainment is a specialized pathway from the retina to the SCN.

3. Rhythms shorter than 24 hours (ultradian rhythms) or longer than 24 hours (infradian rhythms) are evident in both behavior and biological processes. The underlying mechanism does not involve clocks in the SCN.

Sleep and Waking

1. During sleep, almost all mammals alternate between two main states: slow-wave sleep (SWS) and rapid-eye-movement (REM) sleep.

2. Human SWS shows four stages defined by EEG criteria that include bursts of spindles and persistent trains of large, slow waves. During SWS, muscle tension, heart rate, respiratory rate, and temperature decline progressively.

Refer to the *Learning Biological Psychology CD* for study questions, animations, activities, and other study aids.

3. REM sleep is characterized by a rapid EEG of low amplitude—almost like the EEG during active waking behavior—and intense autonomic activation, but the postural muscles are flaccid because of profound inhibition of motoneurons.

4. In adult humans, SWS and REM sleep alternate every 90 to 110 minutes. Smaller animals have shorter sleep cycles and spend more overall time asleep.

5. Mental activity does not cease during sleep. Subjects awakened from REM sleep frequently report vivid perceptual experiences (dreams); subjects awakened from SWS often report ideas or thinking.

6. The characteristics of sleep–waking cycles change during the course of life. Mature animals sleep less than the young, and REM sleep accounts for a smaller fraction of their sleep.

7. The prominence of REM sleep in infants suggests that REM sleep contributes to development of the brain and to learning.

8. Deprivation of sleep for a few nights in a row leads to impairment in tasks that require sustained vigilance. During recovery nights following deprivation, the lost SWS and REM sleep are partially restored over several nights.

9. Researchers have suggested several biological roles for sleep, including conservation of energy, avoidance of predators, restoration of depleted resources, and consolidation of memory.

10. Many brain structures are involved in the initiation and maintenance of sleep. (1) A basal forebrain system promotes SWS; (2) the brainstem reticular formation promotes arousal; (3) a pontine system appears to trigger REM sleep; and (4) a hypothalamic system of hypocretin-releasing neurons regulates these three centers to control the sleep–waking cycle.

11. Narcolepsy is the sudden, uncontrollable intrusion of sleep, which may be accompanied by cataplexy, during wakefulness. Disruption of hypocretin signaling, by lack of either hypocretin or hypocretin receptors, causes narcolepsy.

12. The fact that prolonged sleep deprivation can lead to death suggests that sleep promotes health. No pill can guarantee a normal night of sleep.

13. Sleep disorders fall into four major categories: (1) disorders of initiation and maintenance of sleep (e.g., insomnia); (2) disorders of excessive drowsiness (e.g., narcolepsy); (3) disorders of the sleep–waking schedule; and (4) dysfunctions associated with sleep, sleep stages, or partial arousals (e.g., sleepwalking).

Recommended Reading

Attarian, H. P. (Ed.). (2004). *Clinical handbook of insomnia.* Totowa, NJ: Humana.

Dement, W. C., and Vaughan, C. (1999). *The promise of sleep.* New York: Delacorte.

Dunlap, J. C., Loros, J. J., and DeCoursey, P. J. (2003). *Chronobiology: Biological timekeeping.* Sunderland, MA: Sinauer Associates.

Flanagan, O. J. (2000). *Dreaming souls: Sleep, dreams, and the evolution of the conscious mind.* New York: Oxford University Press.

Kryger, M. K., Roth, T., and Dement, W. C. (Eds.). (2000). *Principles and practice of sleep medicine* (3rd ed.). New York: Saunders.

Lavie, P. (2003). *Restless nights: Understanding snoring and sleep apnea.* New Haven, CT: Yale University Press.

Shneerson, J. M. (2000). *Handbook of sleep medicine.* Malden, MA: Blackwell Science.

Takahashi, J. S., Turek, F. W., and Moore, R. Y. (2001). *Handbook of behavioral neurobiology: Vol. 12, Circadian clocks.* New York: Kluwer.

V Emotions and Mental Disorders

So far in this text we have discussed a wide variety of behaviors that individuals display in particular circumstances, and in each case it has seemed rather straightforward that these behaviors are adaptive. It is clearly adaptive to be able to detect stimuli that surround us, to make coordinated movements, to drink when body fluids are low, to eat when energy supplies are low—or even to anticipate these needs—and to sleep at night (when moving about may be dangerous). It has been more difficult to understand in biological terms how it is that we are sometimes angry, terrified, or joyful, even though these emotions are clearly an important part of our experience.

Cheri, *Melancholy Face*

Chapter 15 takes up research that attempts to determine the roles that emotions play and the biological mechanisms of emotions. Just as other body systems may malfunction—we have seen examples in the cases of sensory, motor, and regulatory systems—so, too, may emotional systems. Hearing voices that are not present, persistently reliving dreadful memories, or being driven to suicide by depression do not help us survive and reproduce. Chapter 16 deals with dysfunctions that lead to mental illness and the still modest but growing means we have to combat them.

15

Emotions, Aggression, and Stress

Too Embarrassed to Work

Christine Drury had a great start on a career that was her dream: being anchorwoman of a television news program. She was only 26, but she was doing short, late-night news bulletins for an NBC affiliate in Indianapolis where David Letterman began as a weatherman. Christine was good at the job—not just being pretty and articulate in front of the camera, but writing the news scripts to make them direct and clear. Still she had a big problem—blushing. She had always blushed easily, and she had been teased about it often, sometimes by strangers.

Something about her job—perhaps the anxiety or concentration—started causing her to blush on camera, and because of her pale skin the blush was very visible to viewers. When Christine became self-conscious about it, the problem grew even worse, so that she was blushing during

almost every broadcast (Gawande, 2002). Wearing turtlenecks and really heavy makeup made the blushing harder to see, but she still experienced the blush, and she would visibly stiffen, her voice rising in pitch. A colleague felt she looked like a deer caught in the headlights when this happened. Christine was never going to be promoted unless she could look more relaxed on screen.

She tried breath control and giving up caffeine, but they didn't help. Neither did a variety of medicines: anxiolytic, antidepressant, sympathetic blocker. It looked like her young career was already over, when Christine learned of a clinic in Sweden that claimed to eliminate blushing—through surgery. The procedure would be expensive and, like all surgery, involved some risks. Would she go through with it?

The sound of unexpected footsteps in the eerie quiet of the night brings fear to many of us. But the sound of music we enjoy and the voice of someone we love summons feelings of warmth. For some of us, feelings and emotions can become vastly exaggerated; fears, for example, can become paralyzing attacks of anxiety and panic. No story about our behavior is complete without consideration of the many events in a single day that involve feelings.

The psychobiological study of emotions has progressed in several directions. One traditional area focuses on bodily responses during emotional states, especially changes in facial expression, and visceral responses such as changes in heart rate. The study of brain mechanisms related to emotional states has especially emphasized fear and aggression because both are important for human existence, so a special section of this chapter is devoted to aggression.

Another topic of research related to emotion is stress, such as the stress that accompanies some health impairments. Stress involves and affects not only the nervous and endocrine systems but also the immune system, so we also discuss the immune system in this chapter. In addition, the chapter emphasizes interrelations among the nervous, endocrine, and immune systems.

What Are Emotions?

The complicated world of emotions includes a wide range of observable behaviors, expressed feelings, and changes in body state. This diversity—that is, the many meanings of the word *emotion*—has made the subject hard to study. For many of us emotions are very personal states, difficult to define or identify except in the most obvious instances. Is the hissing cat afraid, angry, or just enjoying our frightened reaction? Moreover, many aspects of our emotions seem unconscious even to us. For these reasons, emotions were neglected as a field of study for many years, but there has been a significant renaissance in this fascinating subject.

Leonard Koscianski, *The Way It Is*, 1998

Emotions have four different aspects

There are at least four aspects to emotion:

1. *Feelings.* In many cases, emotions are feelings that are private and subjective. Humans can report an extraordinary range of states that they say they feel or experience.
2. *Actions.* Emotions can be actions commonly deemed "emotional," such as defending or attacking in response to a threat.
3. *Physiological arousal.* Emotions are states of physiological arousal—expressions or displays of distinctive somatic and autonomic responses. This emphasis suggests that emotional states can be defined by particular constellations of bodily responses that can also be examined in nonhuman animals.
4. *Motivational programs.* Emotions are motivational programs that coordinate responses to solve specific adaptive problems. We are motivated to seek pleasure and avoid pain.

Broad Theories of Emotion Emphasize Bodily Responses

In many emotional states we can sense the heart beating fast, hands and face feeling warm, palms sweating, and a queasy feeling in the stomach. Strong emotions are nearly inseparable from activation of the skeletal-muscle and/or autonomic nervous systems. Common expressions capture this association: "with all my heart," "hair standing on end," "a sinking feeling in my stomach."

Several theories have tried to explain the close ties between the subjective psychological phenomena that we know as emotions and the activity of visceral organs controlled by the autonomic nervous system, which we described in Chapter 2 (see Figure 2.6). Folk psychology suggests that the autonomic reactions are caused by the emotion: "I was so angry my stomach was churning," as though the anger produced the churning.

The James–Lange theory considers emotions to be the perception of bodily changes

COMPETING HYPOTHESES

William James, the leading figure in American psychology at about the start of the twentieth century, turned the folk psychology idea on its head, suggesting that the emotions we experience are caused by the bodily changes (Figure 15.1). From this perspective, we experience fear because we perceive the body activity triggered by particular stimuli.

About the same time that James was developing his theories of emotion, Danish physician Carl G. Lange (1834–1900) proposed a similar view, which emphasizes peripheral physiological events in emotion. Different emotions feel different because they are generated by a different constellation of physiological responses. The theory initiated many studies that attempted to link emotions to bodily responses, a focus of lasting interest in the field. Questions such as "What are the responses of the heart in love, anger, fear?" continue to form a prominent part of the biological study of emotions. Although the James–Lange theory initiated this research, it has not survived critical assessment.

The Cannon–Bard theory emphasizes central processes

**Walter Cannon
(1871–1945)**

The simplicity of the James–Lange theory presented ready opportunity for experimental assessment. Physiologists Walter Cannon and Philip Bard studied relations between emotion and the autonomic nervous system. They offered strong criticism of the James–Lange theory, claiming that the experience of emotion starts before the autonomic changes, which are relatively slow. In addition, autonomic changes accompanying strong emotions seemed very much the same, whether the emotion experienced was anger, fear, or great surprise. Cannon emphasized that these bodily reactions (increased heart rate, glucose mobilization, and other effects) are an emergency response of an organism to a sudden threatening condition, producing maximal activation of the sympathetic nervous system, readying the organism for fight or flight (W. B. Cannon, 1929). So the function of emotion is to help us deal with a changing environment.

In Cannon and Bard's view, however, it is the brain's job to decide what particular emotion is an appropriate response to the stimuli. According to this view, the cerebral cortex simultaneously decides on the appropriate emotional response and activates the sympathetic system so that the body is ready for appropriate action, as the brain decides. The Cannon–Bard theory provoked many studies of the effects of brain lesions and electrical stimulation on emotion.

Stanley Schachter proposed a cognitive interpretation of stimuli and visceral states

Like Cannon and Bard, Stanley Schachter (1975) emphasized cognitive mechanisms in emotion, suggesting that individuals interpret visceral activation in terms of the eliciting stimuli, the surrounding situation, their cognitive states, and experience. According to Schachter, emotional labels (e.g., anger, fear, joy) depend on the interpretations of a situation—interpretations that are controlled by internal cognitive systems.

**Philip Bard
(1898–1977)**

(*a*) **Folk psychology**

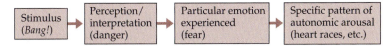

(*b*) **James–Lange theory**

(*c*) **Cannon–Bard theory**

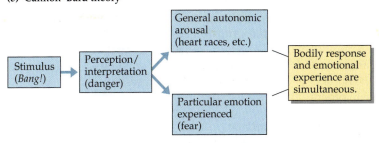

(*d*) **Schachter's cognitive theory**

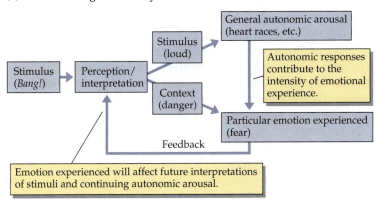

15.1 Different Views of the Chain of Events in Emotional Responses (*a*) Folk psychology suggests that emotions cause the body to react. (*b*) James and Lange suggested that the bodily response evokes the emotional experience. (*c*) Cannon and Bard insisted that the brain must interpret the situation to decide which emotion is appropriate. (*d*) Schachter attempted to reconcile these views by suggesting that the intensity of emotion can be affected by the bodily responses and that the brain continuously assesses the situation.

In a famous experiment (Schachter and Singer, 1962), people were injected with epinephrine (adrenaline) and told either that there would be no effect or that their heart would race. People who were warned of the reaction reported no emotional experience, but some people who were not forewarned experienced an emotion when their bodies responded to the drug, as would be predicted by the James–Lange theory (bodily reactions are experienced as emotion) but not the Cannon–Bard theory (the cortex separately activates emotion and the bodily reaction).

However, the particular emotion experienced could be affected by whether a confederate in the room acted angry or happy. The unsuspecting subjects injected with epinephrine were much more likely to report feeling angry when in the presence of an "angry" confederate, and more likely to report feeling elated when with a "happy" confederate. These findings contradict the James–Lange prediction that a different constellation of autonomic reactions would instigate feelings of anger or euphoria. Subjects injected with placebo were much less likely to report an emotional experience, no matter how the confederate behaved. Thus an emotional state is the result of an interaction between physiological activation and cognitive *interpretation* of that arousal.

Schachter's theory has its critics. For example, the theory asserts that physiological arousal is *nonspecific*, affecting only the intensity of a perceived emotion but not its quality, yet each different emotion exhibits a specific pattern of autonomic arousal (Cacioppo et al., 1993). When subjects were asked to pose facial expressions distinctive for particular emotions, autonomic patterns of the subjects were different for several emotions, such as fear and sadness (Levenson et al., 1990). Most researchers agree that emotions are complex, eliciting some actions and inhibiting others, depending on circumstances. Later in this chapter we'll see how certain stimuli, such as a sudden loud noise or the sight of a scorpion, may activate a more primitive fear pathway through the amygdala.

How Many Emotions Do We Experience?

An ongoing discussion about the study of human emotions focuses on whether there is a basic core set of emotions that underlies the more varied and delicate nuances of our world of feelings. Plutchik (1994) suggests that there are eight basic emotions, grouped in four pairs of opposites: (1) joy/sadness, (2) affection/disgust, (3) anger/fear, and (4) expectation/surprise. In Plutchik's view, all other emotions are derived from combinations of this basic array (Figure 15.2). But investigators do not yet agree about the number of basic emotions (six, seven, eight?). Although there is no way to determine once and for all the number of basic emotions, one clue comes from examining the number of different kinds of facial expressions that we produce and can recognize in others.

Facial expressions have complex functions in communication

Paul Ekman has provided rich insight into the properties of facial expressions. He and his collaborators have developed an array of analytical tools that enable objective description and measurement of facial expressions among humans of different cultures. How many different emotions can be detected in facial expressions? According to Keltner and Ekman (2000), there are distinctive expressions for anger, sadness, happiness, fear, disgust, surprise, contempt, and embarrassment (Figure 15.3). Facial expressions of these emotions are interpreted similarly across many cultures without explicit training. So they also suggest that there are eight different

Levels of intensity

15.2 Basic Emotions   In this proposed organizational scheme, the eight basic emotions are arrayed as four pairs of opposite emotions. Lower- and higher-intensity forms of each basic emotion appear at the bottom and top levels, respectively. (Modified from Plutchik, 1994.)

Anger

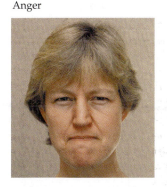

Sadness

Happiness

Fear

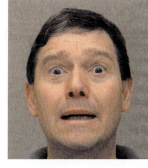

Disgust

Surprise

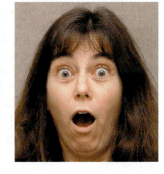

Contempt

15.3 Universal Facial Expressions of Emotion According to Paul Ekman and colleagues, the seven basic emotional facial expressions shown here are displayed in all cultures. Embarrassment has recently been proposed to be an eighth basic emotion.

emotions, but they are not quite the same as those proposed by Plutchik (see Figure 15.2). In case you're keeping track, whereas Plutchik included adoration and vigilance in his eight basic emotions, Keltner and Ekman include, instead, contempt and embarrassment. The other six emotions—anger, sadness, happiness, fear, disgust, and surprise—are the same in both schemes.

Cross-cultural similarity is also noted in the *production* of expressions specific to particular emotions. For example, people in a preliterate New Guinea society, when displaying particular emotions, show facial expressions like those of people in industrialized societies. However, this *universality* hypothesis of facial expression has come under criticism. Fridlund (1994) suggests that universal expressions do not account for the full complement of human facial expressions. Cultural differences may emerge in culture-specific display rules, which stipulate social contexts for facial expression. For example, Russell (1994) found significant agreement across cultures in the recognition of most emotional states from facial expressions, but isolated nonliterate groups did not agree with Westerners about recognizing surprise and disgust (Figure 15.4).

These subtle cultural differences suggest that cultures prescribe rules for facial expression, and control and enforce those rules by cultural conditioning. A model of this process is presented in Figure 15.5. Everyone agrees that cultures affect the facial display of emotion; the remaining controversy is over how extensive the cultural influence is.

According to Fridlund (1994), a major role of facial expression is *paralinguistic;* that is, the face is accessory to verbal communication, perhaps providing emphasis and direction in conversation. For example, Gilbert et al. (1986) showed that subjects display few facial responses to odor when smelling alone, but significantly more in a social setting. Similarly, bowlers seldom smile when making a strike, but they frequently smile when they turn around to meet the faces of onlookers (Kraut and Johnston, 1979). Sometimes we communicate our emotions *too* well, as we saw at the start of the chapter with Christine's tendency to blush when she didn't want to.

Paul Ekman

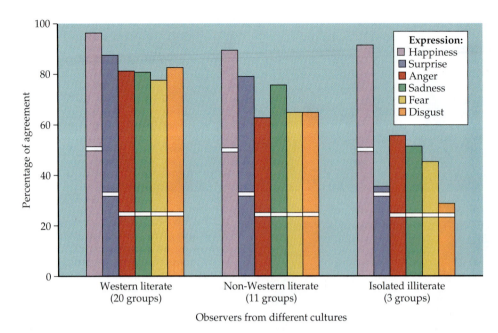

15.4 Cultural Differences in Recognizing Facial Expressions of Emotion   Within Western literate groups there is widespread agreement about the emotions represented by photographs of basic facial expressions (*left*). But people from isolated groups (*right*) are much less likely to agree with Western judgments of some facial expressions, especially those of surprise and disgust. The white horizontal bars indicate the percentage of agreement that would be expected by chance alone. (From Russell, 1994.)

Facial expressions are mediated by muscles, cranial nerves, and CNS pathways

How are facial expressions produced? Within the human face is an elaborate network of finely innervated muscles whose functional roles, in addition to facial expression, include the production of speech, eating, and respiration, among others. Facial muscles can be divided into two categories:

1. *Superficial facial muscles* attach to facial skin (Figure 15.6). They act as sphincters, changing the shape of the mouth, eyes, or nose, for example; or they pull on their attachment to the skin. One such muscle, the frontalis, wrinkles the forehead and raises the eyebrow.

2. *Deep facial muscles* attach to skeletal structures of the head. These muscles enable movements such as chewing. An example of a deep muscle is the masseter, a powerful jaw muscle.

Human facial muscles are innervated by two cranial nerves: (1) the facial nerve (VII), which innervates the superficial muscles of facial expression; and (2) the trigeminal nerve (V), which innervates muscles that move the jaw. Studies of the facial nerve reveal that the right and left sides are completely independent. As Figure 15.6 shows, the main trunk of the facial nerve divides into upper and lower divisions shortly after entering the face. These nerve fibers originate in the brainstem in a region called the nucleus of the facial nerve. Within the facial-nerve nucleus, cells that control the muscles of the lower face are clearly separated from those that control the muscles of the upper face.

The face areas of the human motor cortex are disproportionately large (see Figure 11.12), probably reflecting the ecological importance of facial expression in our species. The cerebral cortex innervates the facial nucleus both bilaterally and unilaterally: The lower two-thirds of the face receives input from the opposite side of the cortex; the upper third receives input from *both* sides. This is why most of us find it easier to produce one-sided movements of the lips than one-sided movement of an eyebrow.

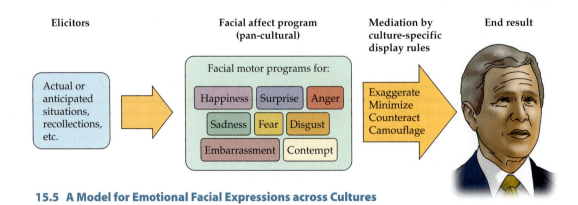

15.5 A Model for Emotional Facial Expressions across Cultures

In some conditions, facial musculature is inhibited selectively

Chronic selective inhibition of the facial musculature occurs in Parkinson's disease (which is discussed in Chapter 11), and recently it has been reported for patients with schizophrenia (Kring, 1999). Compared with nonpatients, patients with schizophrenia exhibit few outward signs of emotion, although recordings from facial muscles reveal very small, subtle facial activity characteristic of different emotions. In response to emotional stimuli, patients with schizophrenia report experiencing as much emotion as nonpatients. The social interactions of the patients are impaired by their lack of normal facial responses. Sometimes viruses infect the facial nerve and damage it enough to cause paralysis of facial muscles. This condition, known as **Bell's palsy,** usually affects just one side, resulting in a variety of symptoms, including drooping eyelid and mouth (Figure 15.7). Although pregnant women and people who suffer from diabetes are more likely to have Bell's palsy, it can apparently strike anyone. There is no standard treatment, but happily most people recover on their own within a few weeks and almost everyone recovers within 6 months.

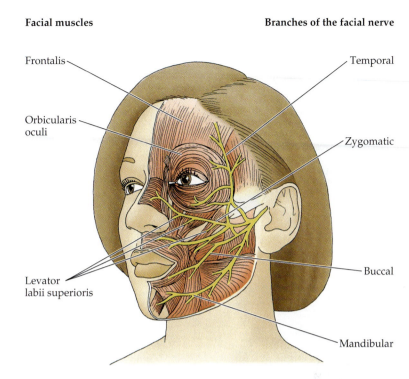

Facial muscles   Branches of the facial nerve

Frontalis

Orbicularis oculi

Levator labii superioris

Temporal

Zygomatic

Buccal

Mandibular

15.6 Superficial Facial Muscles and Their Neural Control

Emotions from the Comparative/Evolutionary Viewpoint

In his book *The Expression of the Emotions in Man and Animals* (1872), Charles Darwin presented evidence that expressions of emotions are universal among people of all regions of the world. He obtained anecdotal data from informants in different countries and analyzed observers' responses to different expressions, as a forerunner of the studies of facial expressions that we reviewed earlier (see Figure 15.4). But Darwin went further and attempted to determine whether humans and other animals share expressions of some emotions. Did these expressions and emotional mechanisms originate in a common ancestor to humans and other species?

Darwin not only reviewed reports of apparent expressions of emotion in various species of mammals (Figure 15.8), but he also considered information about the facial musculature and the nerves that innervate these muscles. Before Darwin, most investigators believed that the facial muscles were given uniquely to humans so that they could express their feelings. Darwin emphasized that nonhuman primates have the same facial muscles as humans. A century later, Redican (1982) described these distinctive primate expressions: (1) *grimace*, perhaps analogous to human expressions of fear or surprise; (2) *tense mouth*, akin to human expressions of anger; and (3) *play face*, homologous to the human laugh. Different facial expressions may represent different emotions across primate species (Figure 15.9). Jaak Panksepp (2000b) reviews the evidence that tickling in nonhuman primates, and even in rats, can elicit something like laughter, which may facilitate social learning through play.

How may emotion and emotional displays have evolved?

How do emotions help individuals survive and reproduce? Several benefits of emotions and their expression have been suggested. Darwin (1872) wrote about their benefits for communication:

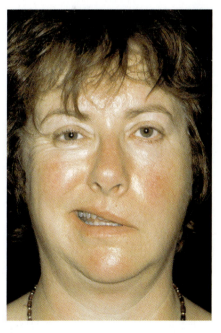

15.7 Bell's Palsy Leaves Half the Face Paralyzed This woman is smiling, but only the muscles on the right side of her face (left half of photograph) respond to her commands.

15.8 Emotional Expression in Animals
Crested black macaque monkey "in a placid condition" (*top*). "The same when pleased by being caressed " (*bottom*). (Darwin, 1872 [pg. 136].)

EVOLUTION AT WORK

The movements of expression in the face and body … are … of much importance for our welfare. They serve as the first means of communication between the mother and her infant; she smiles approval, and thus encourages her child on the right path, or frowns disapproval. We readily perceive sympathy in others by their expression; our sufferings are thus mitigated and our pleasure increased; and mutual good feeling is thus strengthened. The movements of expression give vividness and energy to our spoken words. They reveal the thoughts and intentions of others more truly than do words, which may be falsified (pg. 365).

Current proponents of **evolutionary psychology** point to additional ways in which emotions are adaptive and could have developed through natural selection (Cosmides and Tooby, 2000). They suggest that emotions are broad motivational programs that coordinate various responses to solve specific adaptive problems, including foraging for food, maintaining cooperative relations with members of one's group, choosing a mate, avoiding predators, and so forth.

For example, an ancestrally common situation that still recurs is that of being alone at night and perceiving that you are being stalked by a predator (human or nonhuman). As with most other kinds of behavior, individuals differ in their responses to this life-threatening situation. Some individuals make poor choices and are therefore less likely to survive and reproduce. Others make more-effective choices, and to the extent that this behavior is heritable, their descendants are also more likely to survive in similar situations. Thus, through natural selection, an effective program for dealing with this situation evolves. The emotion of fear calls forth shifts in perception, attention, cognition, and action that focus on avoidance of danger and seeking safety, as well as physiological preparations for fighting or flight. Other activities, such as seeking food, sleep, or mates, are suppressed. From an evolutionary perspective, in the face of an imminent threat to life it is better to be able to call on this recipe for action, developed and tested over the ages, than to ad-lib something. Similarly, feelings of disgust for body fluids may help us avoid exposure to germs (Curtis et al., 2004), and so it may be wise to recognize disgust in others.

Later in this chapter we will see that a stimulus that evokes fear activates a specific brain circuit that projects to three different brain regions, each of which produces a different component of the fear response: motor behavior, autonomic responses, and hormonal responses. Fear has been the emotion most frequently studied, but it seems likely that natural selection has also shaped other emotions.

Emotions develop in early childhood

Children show some emotions from the time of birth, and during the first 3 years of life they become capable of showing most of the emotions that adults display (M. Lewis, 2000). At birth, infants show both general distress and contentment or pleasure; interest or attention is classified by some as a third emotion present at birth. By the age of 3 months, infants also show evidence of joy; they start to smile and appear to show excitement and/or happiness in response to familiar faces. Sadness also emerges at this time, especially caused by the withdrawal of positive events. Disgust also appears, in the primitive form of spitting out distasteful objects placed in the mouth. Anger has been reported to appear between 4 and 6 months when babies are frustrated or restrained. Surprise first appears at about 6 months in response to violation of an expectation or to a discovery. Fearfulness first emerges at about 7 or 8 months. Thus, what some have called the primary or basic emotions are all present by 8 to 9 months after birth.

Between 18 and 24 months, the emergence of self-consciousness or self-awareness allows an additional group of emotions to develop, including embarrassment, empathy, and envy. Another milestone occurs sometime between 2 and 3 years of age when children become capable of evaluating their behavior against a standard. This ability allows the emergence of "self-conscious evaluative emotions" (pride, guilt, regret, shame), which Darwin (1872) characterized as unique to our species. Mark Twain (1897) agreed, saying, "Man is the only animal that blushes … Or needs to."

Blushing is caused by activation of sympathetic fibers that innervate the skin. Remember Christine at the start of the chapter? She elected to have the surgery to cut two nerves exiting from her sympathetic chain on each side (see Figure 2.6 *left*), losing sympathetic control of her entire face except for her pupils. Christine no longer blushes. She has no regrets and is working toward her dream. An interesting aspect of blushing is that it can be self-reinforcing: Christine's awareness of the problem made it happen more often. For the same reason, it's usually possible to trick people into blushing. Just look at someone closely and say, "Hey, you're blushing!"

Individuals Differ in Their Emotional Responsiveness

Even newborns show individual differences in emotional responsiveness. Responses of various body systems reveal distinct patterns that are characteristic of the individual. John and Beatrice Lacey (1970) referred to this characteristic as **individual response stereotypy.** Their work involved longitudinal (extending over many years) studies of people, from early childhood to adulthood. The stimuli they used to provoke autonomic responses included stress conditions such as immersion of the hand in ice-cold water, performance of rapidly paced arithmetic calculations, and exposure to intense stimuli on the skin. Across these conditions the investigators observed an individual profile of response that is evident even in newborns. For example, some newborns respond vigorously with heart rate changes, others with gastric contractions, and still others with blood pressure responses.

The response patterns are remarkably consistent throughout life. Jerome Kagan (1997) and colleagues have classified newborns on the basis of their behavioral responses to cues such as an alcohol-soaked cotton swab. About 20% of the infants were termed *high reactives* because they gave especially strong reactions to the stimuli. Later, many of these high reactives became extremely shy, and by the time they were old enough for school, about a third of them displayed extreme phobias (compared to fewer than 10% of the other children). In adulthood, high reactives show an exaggerated activation of the amygdala in response to photographs of strangers' faces (C. E. Schwartz et al., 2003). Because the amygdala has been implicated in fear (as we'll see later in this chapter), perhaps high reactives have a lifelong aversion to new acquaintances, which would certainly affect many aspects of life.

(a)

(b)

(c)

15.9 Facial Expression of Emotions in Non-human Primates   (a) An adult female chimpanzee screams at another female, who is pulling at her food. Screaming is used in submission and protest. (b) A juvenile chimpanzee shows a play face while being tickled. He also makes a guttural laughing sound. (c) A Tibetan macaque bares his teeth to signal submission to a dominant animal. In other primates, including humans, teeth baring has gained a different, friendlier meaning. (Photographs by Frans de Waal, from de Waal, 2003.)

Jerome Kagan

Autonomic Responses Are Elicited by Emotion-Provoking Stimuli

Although the changing expressions of the face are easy to see, the detection of visceral changes requires electronic devices. A subject who is connected to instruments that measure heart rate, blood pressure, stomach contractions, dilation or constriction of blood vessels, skin resistance, or sweating of the palms or soles exhibits many changes in response to emotional states. One device that measures several of these bodily responses is called a **polygraph,** popularly known as a *lie detector.* The use of polygraphs to try to detect lying in individuals who are accused of crimes is controversial; most psychophysiologists argue against such use (Box 15.1).

COMPETING HYPOTHESES

After reviewing a large array of data gathered in studies from the 1950s to the present, Cacioppo et al. (2000) state that most of the evidence on autonomic differentiation of emotions remains inconclusive. Distinct emotional stimuli do not invariably elicit a distinct pattern of autonomic responses. Positive emotions elicit a different array of autonomic responses than negative emotions do, but within those categories, different emotions elicit approximately the same autonomic profile.

Do Distinct Brain Circuits Mediate Emotions?

This question has been explored in studies involving either localized brain lesions or electrical stimulation. Taken together, these studies make it clear that particular brain regions are involved in emotions, but often the same regions seem to be involved in many emotions. In this section we will review these studies and then concentrate on the one emotion that may have a "dedicated" brain circuit: fear.

Brain lesions affect emotions

Decorticate rage   Surgical removal of the isocortex provided the oldest experimental demonstration of brain mechanisms and emotion. Early in the twentieth century, decorticate dogs (dogs from which the cortex has been removed) were shown to respond to routine handling with sudden intense rage—sometimes referred to as *sham rage* because it lacked well-directed attack. Snarling, barking, and growling were provoked by ordinary handling, and this behavior included strong visceral responses. Clearly, emotional behaviors of this type are organized at a subcortical level. These observations suggested that the cerebral cortex helps *inhibit* emotional responsiveness.

Papez's neural circuit   In 1937, James W. Papez (1883–1958), a neuropathologist, proposed a neural circuit of emotion. Papez (which rhymes with "capes") reached his conclusions from brain autopsies of humans with emotional disorders, including psychiatric patients. He also studied the brains of animal subjects such as rabid dogs. He noted the sites of brain destruction in these cases and concluded that destruction of a set of interconnected pathways in the brain would impair emotional processes.

These interconnected regions, known as the **Papez circuit,** include the mammillary bodies of the hypothalamus, the anterior thalamus, the cingulate cortex, the hippocampus, and the fornix. This circuit is schematically depicted with arrows in Figure 15.10. Later, Paul MacLean (1949) suggested that the amygdala and several other regions also interacted with the components of this circuit, and that the entire system be called the **limbic system.** Today, researchers seldom talk about the limbic system as a functional unit, but the term is still used to refer to these regions.

Klüver–Bucy syndrome   In 1938, psychologist Heinrich Klüver (1897–1979) and neurosurgeon Paul Bucy (1904–1993) described an unusual syndrome in primates following temporal lobe surgery. During studies on the cortical mechanisms of perception, they removed large portions of the temporal lobes of monkeys. The animals' behavior changed dramatically after surgery; the highlight was an extraordinary

BOX 15.1 Lie Detector?

One of the most controversial attempts to apply biomedical science is the so-called lie detector test. This test attempts to detect lying by measuring physiological responses during an interview. The use of polygraphs for lie detection is based on the assumption that people have emotional responses when lying because they fear detection and/or feel guilt about lying. Emotions are usually accompanied by bodily responses that are difficult for a person to control, such as changes in heart rate, respiration, and skin conductance (related to sweating). The name *polygraph* (from the Greek *polys*, "many," and *graphein*, "to write") reflects the use of several physiological measures. The modern form of the polygraph was introduced in 1917 by experimental psychologist William Marston, who coined the term *lie detector*.

Some proponents of polygraph examinations claim that they are accurate in 95% of tests, but the estimate from impartial research is an overall accuracy of about 65% (Nietzel, 2000). Even if the higher figure were correct, the fact that these tests are widely used means that thousands of truthful people could be branded as liars and fired, disciplined, or not hired. On the other hand, many criminals and spies have been able to pass the tests without detection. For example, long-time CIA agent Aldrich Ames, who

was sentenced in 1995 to life in prison for espionage, successfully passed polygraph tests after becoming a spy. Back in 1983, the Office of Technology Assessment concluded that polygraph tests are not an effective scientific method to check for breaches of security. In the wake of terrorist attacks, the National Research Council (2003) took up the question again and concluded that the polygraph test's "accuracy in distinguishing actual or potential security violators from innocent test takers is insufficient to justify reliance on its use in employee security screening."

It is difficult to do convincing research on lie detection because most studies involve only trivial attempts at deception that do not necessarily involve subjects emotionally. The U.S. Department of Defense has started a study with 120 volunteers, some trained to pretend that they have committed espionage. But Paul Ekman, a member of the National Academy of Sciences panel, said in a written statement that such research won't yield solid results unless the subjects are playing for "high stakes," such as loss of a job (Holden, 2001).

"Because of the controversies that surround the polygraph, most [American] courts do not allow testimony about it in trials. However, it is widely used in the initial stages of criminal investigations, often to convince suspects that they should

confess" (Nietzel, 2000, p. 225). Unfortunately, even innocent people may display emotional arousal when being questioned by the police. Polygraph testing was also widely used in U.S. businesses in the 1970s and 1980s, but in 1988, Congress passed the Employee Polygraph Protection Act, which, with some exceptions, prohibits the use of lie detectors by private businesses involved in interstate commerce. Even where such tests are permitted, employees are granted several rights (such as seeing the questions in advance), and the results of the lie detector test cannot be the sole basis for action against the employee.

Some scientists believe that modern neuroscience may provide new methods of lie detection someday. For example, psychologist Richard Davidson points to research on brain mechanisms of fear in the last decade. Fear results in activation of the amygdala (as we'll discuss later in this chapter) that might be visible with functional MRI (see Chapter 2) in the case of deception. Daniel Langleben et al. (2002) used fMRI to show that the anterior cingulate cortex (another region we'll discuss later in the chapter) became more active when subjects were lying. Even if brain imaging were found to be successful at detecting deception, such lie detectors would be more costly and less widely available than polygraphs.

---

taming effect. Animals that had been wild and fearful of humans prior to surgery became tame and showed neither fear nor aggression afterward. In addition, they showed strong oral tendencies, eating a variety of objects, including some that were inedible. Frequent mounting behavior was observed and was described as hypersexuality.

Because lesions restricted to the cerebral cortex did not produce these results, deeper regions of the temporal lobe, including sites within the limbic system (see Figure 15.10), were implicated, and more-detailed investigation focused on the amygdala. This syndrome has also been observed in humans following a variety of disorders that damage the temporal lobes, including degenerative hereditary disorders (Lanska and Lanska, 1994) and Alzheimer's disease (Forstl et al., 1993).

In many of the earlier studies, attempts to ablate the amygdala injured adjacent structures and interrupted fibers passing through the region, making it difficult to interpret results. A more modern study managed to destroy the amygdala bilaterally in monkeys without harming adjacent tissue or fibers of passage (Emery et al., 2001). The amygdalectomized monkeys demonstrated increased social affiliation, decreased anxiety, and increased confidence compared to control animals. The amygdala lesions led to a decrease in the usual reluctance of adult monkeys to engage a strange monkey in social behavior. In other words, the animals with amygdala lesions appeared to be much less fearful than control monkeys.

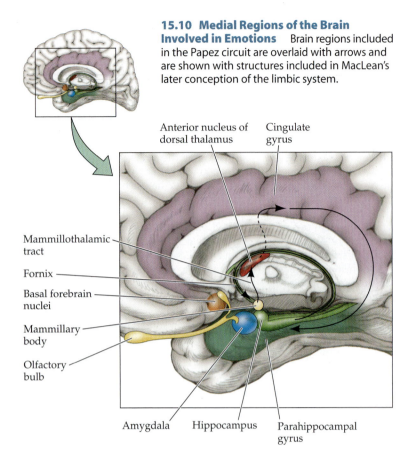

15.10 Medial Regions of the Brain Involved in Emotions Brain regions included in the Papez circuit are overlaid with arrows and are shown with structures included in MacLean's later conception of the limbic system.

Anterior nucleus of dorsal thalamus

Cingulate gyrus

Mammillothalamic tract

Fornix

Basal forebrain nuclei

Mammillary body

Olfactory bulb

Amygdala   Hippocampus   Parahippocampal gyrus

**James Olds
(1922–1976)**

Peter Milner

Electrical stimulation of the brain can produce emotional effects

Another productive approach to understanding the neuroanatomy of emotion is electrical stimulation of sites in the brains of awake, freely moving animals and observation of the effects on behavior. Such stimulation may produce either rewarding or aversive effects, or it may elicit sequences of emotional behavior.

Positive reinforcement and seeking behavior In 1954, psychologists James Olds and Peter Milner reported a remarkable experimental finding: Rats could learn to press a lever when the reward or reinforcement was a brief burst of electrical stimulation of the septal area within the limbic system. Another way to describe this phenomenon is **brain self-stimulation.** Heath (1972) reported that patients receiving electrical stimulation in this region feel a sense of pleasure or warmth, and in some instances stimulation in this region provokes sexual excitation.

The report of Olds and Milner (1954) is one of those rare scientific discoveries that starts a new field; many investigators have since employed techniques of brain self-stimulation, mapping the distribution of brain sites that yield self-stimulation responses (Figure 15.11). Animals will work to receive electrical stimulation of many different subcortical sites, but cerebral cortical stimulation usually does not have positive reinforcement properties. Positive brain sites are concentrated in the hypothalamus and extend into the brainstem. A large tract that ascends from the midbrain through the hypothalamus—the **medial forebrain bundle**—contains many sites that yield strong self-stimulation behavior. This bundle of axons is characterized by widespread origins and innervates an extensive set of forebrain regions. One important target for the axons is the nucleus accumbens that we discussed in Chapter 4. Dopaminergic stimulation of this site appears to be very pleasurable.

One theory, reviewed by N. M. White and P. M. Milner (1992), is that electrical stimulation taps into the circuits mediating more-customary rewards, such as the presentation of food to a hungry animal or water to a thirsty animal. As we discussed in Chapter 4, there is a growing belief that drugs of abuse are addictive because they activate these same neural circuits (P. L. Johnson and Stellar, 1994; Ranaldi and Beninger, 1994; Wise et al., 1992).

Electrical stimulation of some brain regions, including the amygdala, induces not pleasure but fear. These findings, coupled with the apparent loss of fear following amygdala lesions already discussed, bolster the idea that the amygdala mediates fear—an idea we will explore next.

Fear is mediated by circuitry that includes the amygdala

There is nothing subtle about fear. Many animals display similar behavior under conditions that provoke fear, such as danger to one's life posed by a predator. This lack of subtlety and the similarity of fear-related behavior across species may explain why we know much more about the neural circuitry of fear than about the circuitry of any other emotion (LeDoux, 1995). For example, it is very easy to reliably elicit fear by using classical conditioning (see Box 17.1), in which the person or animal is presented with a stimulus such as light or sound that is paired with a brief aversive stimulus such as mild electrical shock. After several such pairings, the response to the sound or light itself is the typical fear portrait, including freezing and autonomic signs such as cardiac and respiratory changes (Figure 15.12a).

Studies of such fear conditioning have provided a map of the neural circuitry that implicates the **amygdala** as a key structure in the mediation of fear (Figure 15.12b). The amygdala is located at the anterior medial portion of each temporal lobe and is composed of about a dozen distinct nuclei, each with a distinctive set of connections. Some of the connections with the rest of the brain include direct projections from sensory cortex. Recall that lesions of the entire amygdala seemed to abolish fear in monkeys with Klüver–Bucy syndrome. The same effect can be had from lesioning just the central nucleus of the amygdala, preventing blood pressure increases and freezing behavior in response to a conditioned fear stimulus.

Interconnections within the amygdala form an important part of the story. Information about the conditioned stimulus (the sound in Figure 15.12a) reaches the lateral portion of the amygdala first, is then transmitted to two other small subregions of the amygdala (the basolateral and basomedial portions), and then goes to the central nucleus. The central nucleus then transmits information to various brainstem centers to evoke three different aspects of emotional responses (see Figure 15.12b): Pathways through the central gray (periaqueductal gray) evoke emotional behaviors, those through the lateral hypothalamus evoke autonomic responses, and those through the bed nucleus of the stria terminalis evoke hormonal responses.

The data from this type of experiment fit well with observations that humans who experience temporal lobe seizures that include the amygdala commonly report intense fear as a prelude or warning about the immediate prospect of a seizure (Engel, 1992). Likewise, stimulation of various sites within the temporal lobe of humans—a procedure performed to identify seizure-provoking sites—elicits fear in some patients (Bancaud et al., 1994). Furthermore, when humans are shown a visual cue previously associated with shock, blood flow to the amygdala increases (LaBar et al., 1998). Pictures of fearful faces also elicit responses in the amygdala that are visible with functional MRI (see Chapter 2).

Patients with damaged amygdalas do poorly at using facial expression as indicators of trustworthiness, illustrating the role of this structure in mediating the *recognition* of fear in human facial expressions (Adolphs et al., 1994, 1998; A. W. Young et al., 1996). These patients suffer from a rare medical condition that results in the bilateral loss of the amygdala without damage to the surrounding hippocampus or overlying isocortex. When shown photos of facial expressions that represent six basic emotions—happiness, surprise, fear, disgust, sadness, and anger—they are markedly impaired in the recognition of fear, but they can select faces of people they know and learn the identities of new faces.

Neural circuitry has also been studied for other emotions

Disgust has been studied only in humans, where fMRI suggests that a region called the *insula* and the nearby putamen (part of the basal ganglia), but not the amygdala, are activated when we see or hear someone expressing disgust (M. L. Phillips et al., 1998). Confirming this idea is the report of a man whose head injury damaged these two regions: He was very poor at recognizing disgust in other people but was normal in recognizing other emotions (Calder et al., 2000).

Considerable progress has been made in identifying the neural circuits of other emotions in addition to fear. Table 15.1 presents some of this information, which comes from a review of the literature (Panksepp, 1998, 2000a). Much of this work used well-established techniques such as making localized brain lesions, transecting tracts, electrical stimulation, and electrical recording. Some investigators have visualized emotional circuits by seeing where immediate early genes (see Box 2.3) are expressed when an emotion is evoked (Kollack-Walker et al., 1999; Neophytou et al., 2000). Note in Table 15.1 that there is no one-to-one correspondence between an emotion and a brain region; that is, each emotion involves activity of more than one brain region, and some brain regions are involved in more than one emotion.

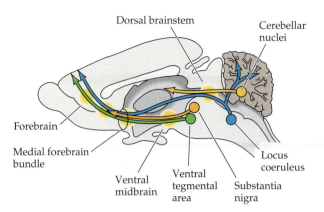

15.11 Self-Stimulation Sites in the Rodent Brain
Animals will work very hard pressing a bar in return for mild electrical stimulation at any of the sites indicated by large, orange circles.

CLINICAL ISSUE

(*a*) **Fear conditioning**

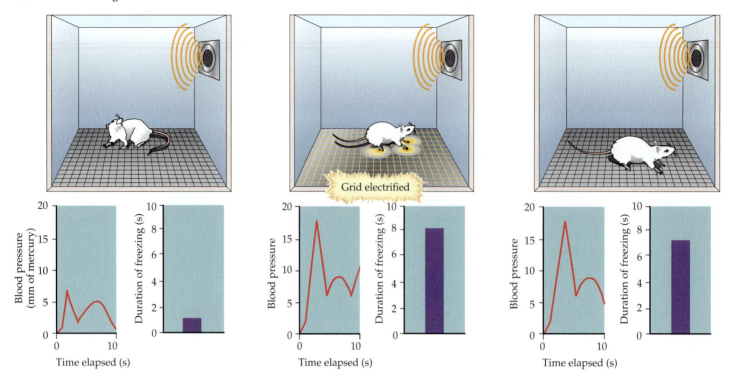

(*b*) **Fear circuitry**

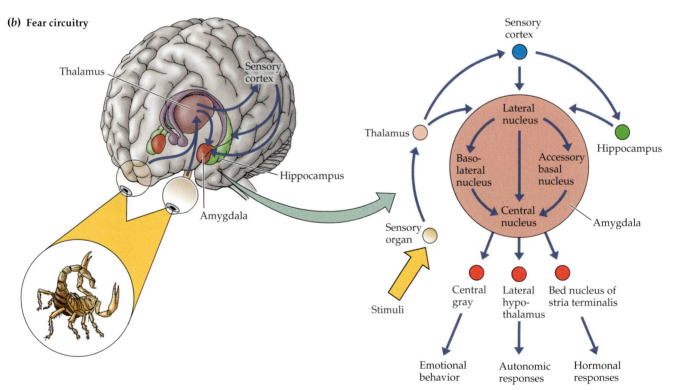

15.12 The Circuitry of Fear (*a*) In one classical-conditioning procedure to study fear, a tone is associated with a mild electrical shock, which causes increased blood pressure and "freezing" (*left* and *middle*); eventually the tone alone elicits these responses (*right*). (*b*) Proposed circuitry for the mediation of conditioned fear responses. A fear-inducing stimulus reaches the thalamus and is relayed to the cortex and hippocampus. All three regions project to the lateral nucleus of the amygdala. The information ultimately reaches the amygdala's central nucleus, which projects to three different brain nuclei, each of which seems to produce a different component of the fear response. (After LeDoux, 1994.)

TABLE 15.1 *Rodent Brain Regions Involved in Some Basic Emotions*

Basic emotion	Key brain areas
Seeking/expectancy	Nucleus accumbens–ventral tegmental area; mesolimbic mesocortical outputs (see Figure 4.3); lateral hypothalamus–periaqueductal gray
Fear	Central and lateral amygdala to medial hypothalamus and dorsal periaqueductal gray
Panic	Anterior cingulate; bed nucleus of stria terminalis; dorsomedial thalamus; dorsal periaqueductal gray
Happiness/play	Dorsomedial thalamus; parafascicular area; ventral periaqueductal gray

Source: Panksepp, 2000a.

The two cerebral hemispheres process emotion differently

The fact that the two cerebral hemispheres play different roles in cognitive processes in humans is well established by many experimental and clinical observations (see Chapter 19). Researchers have investigated the possibility that there are hemispheric differences in emotion processing. These studies indicate that the right hemisphere is specialized to discern other people's emotions, and that the left side of the face, which is controlled by the right hemisphere, is more expressive than the right (Fridlund, 1988).

Emotional syndromes   A major theme to emerge from studies of patients who have sustained injury or disease confined to one hemisphere is that the hemispheres differ in emotional tone. Patients who have suffered strokes involving the left anterior cerebral hemisphere have the highest frequency of depressive symptoms; the closer the lesion is to the frontal pole, the more intense is the depressive portrait. In these patients, injury-produced language deficits are not correlated with severity of depression (Starkstein and Robinson, 1994). In contrast, patients with right-hemisphere lesions are described as unduly cheerful and indifferent to their loss. Table 15.2 lists some of the clinical syndromes that include emotional changes following cerebrovascular disorders.

Results of unilateral injections of sodium amytal into a single carotid artery (the Wada test) offer additional data about hemispheric differences in emotion. This procedure, described in Box 19.1, is used to determine the hemisphere that is dominant for language. Generally, injection of sodium amytal into the left hemisphere produces a depressive aftereffect, whereas an identical injection into the carotid artery on the right side elicits smiling and a feeling of euphoria.

Richard J. Davidson (1994) has presented a different view of the role of the cerebral hemispheres in emotion processing. According to this view, anterior regions of

CLINICAL ISSUE

Richard J. Davidson

TABLE 15.2 *Some Clinical Syndromes Associated with Cerebrovascular Disease*

Syndrome	Clinical symptoms	Location of associated lesion
Indifference reaction	Undue cheerfulness or joking, loss of interest	Right parietal or temporal lobe
Major depression	Depressed mood, loss of energy, anxiety, restlessness, worry, social withdrawal	Left frontal lobe; left basal ganglia
Pathological laughing and crying	Frequent, usually brief laughing and/or crying; social withdrawal secondary to emotional outbursts	Bilateral hemispheric lesions, with almost any location
Mania	Elevated mood, increased energy, increased appetite, decreased sleep, feeling of well-being, flight of ideas	Right basotemporal or right orbitofrontal region

the left and right hemispheres are specialized for approach and withdrawal processes, respectively. Thus, damage to the left frontal region results in a deficit in approach, as is evident in the loss of interest and pleasure in other people and the difficulty in initiating behavior. The diminished activation of this area is associated with sadness and depression. In contrast, activation of the right anterior region is associated with withdrawal-related emotions, such as fear and disgust. Deficits in right anterior activation produced by lesions or injury will reduce withdrawal behavior and related negative emotions.

Processing of emotional stimuli Dichotic listening techniques (see Figure 19.14) have shown that the cerebral hemispheres may function differently in how they recognize emotional stimuli. Ley and Bryden (1982) presented normal subjects with brief sentences spoken in happy, sad, angry, and neutral voices. The sentences were presented through headsets—a different sentence in each ear. Subjects were instructed to attend to one ear and report both the content of the message and its emotional tone.

Subjects showed a distinct left-ear advantage for identifying the *emotional tone* of the voice and a right-ear advantage for understanding the *meaning* of the brief message. Because each ear projects more strongly to the opposite hemisphere (see Chapter 9), these results indicate that the right hemisphere is better than the left at interpreting emotional aspects of vocal messages.

The presentation of different stimuli to each eye also reveals hemispheric differences in the visual perception of emotional expressions. In a variety of tasks that emphasize either reaction time or identification, the common finding is that emotional stimuli presented to the left visual field (projecting to the right hemisphere) result in faster reaction times and more-accurate identification of emotional states (Bryden, 1982). Likewise, in one split-brain patient, in whom the corpus callosum connecting the two hemispheres had been surgically cut (see Chapter 19), the right cerebral hemisphere was much better than the left at discriminating emotional facial expressions (Stone et al., 1996).

Asymmetry of emotional facial expressions By cutting a photograph of the face of a person who is displaying an emotion down the exact middle of the face, we can create two new composite photos—one that combines two left sides of the face (one of which is printed in mirror image), and another that combines two right sides. The results reveal that facial expressions are not symmetrical (Figure 15.13). Furthermore, the two photos produced from the same original photo elicit different responses from people looking at them. In several studies, most subjects judged the left-sides photos as more emotional than the right-sides photos.

This composite-photo technique originated in 1902 (Hallervorden, 1902), but the main research has been conducted since the 1970s. A review of 49 experiments on facial asymmetry in emotional expression (Borod et al., 1997) concluded that the right cerebral hemisphere is dominant for the facial expression of emotion, and this is true for both posed and spontaneous faces, for pleasant and unpleasant emotions, and for both sexes and all ages.

Different emotions activate different regions of the human brain

What regions of the human brain are active during different emotions, and what does this information reveal about the emotions? Numerous studies have asked which brain regions become more active or less active during emotional experience (e.g., Canli et al., 2001; A. R. Damasio et al., 2000; Lane et al., 1999; Maddock, 1999; M. L. Phillips et al., 1998, 2000; Teasdale et al., 1999), and as we'll see, several forebrain areas are consistently implicated in emotion (Figure 15.14).

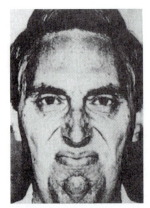

(a) Left sides

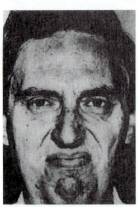

(b) Original

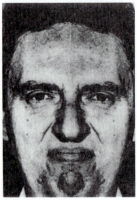

(c) Right sides

15.13 Emotions and Facial Asymmetry Composite faces reveal differences between right and left in the level of intensity of emotional expression. Photographs constructed from only the left side of the face (*a*) are judged to be more emotional than either the original face (*b*) or a composite based on just the right side of the face (*c*). (Courtesy of Ruben C. Gur.)

In Chapter 1 we mentioned a study conducted by Bartels and Zeki (2000), who recruited volunteers who professed to be "truly, deeply, and madly in love." Seventeen subjects were selected by means of written statements and interviews (11 female, 6 male; ages 21–37). Each subject furnished four color photographs: one of his or her boy- or girlfriend, and three of friends who were the same sex as the loved partner and were similar in age and length of friendship. Functional-MRI brain scans were taken while each subject was shown counterbalanced sequences of the four photographs. Brain activity elicited by viewing of the loved person was compared with that elicited by viewing of friends.

Love, compared with friendship, involved increased activity in the *insula* and *anterior cingulate cortex* (Figure 15.14*a* and *c*) and, subcortically, in the caudate and putamen, all bilaterally (see Figure 1.6). It also led to *reduced* activity in the *posterior cingulate* and *amygdala*, and in the right *prefrontal cortex* (Figure 15.14*a, b,* and *c*), as well as the parietal and middle temporal cortices. This combination of sites differs from those found in previous studies of other emotional states, suggesting that a unique network of brain areas is responsible for the emotion of love.

A study by Antonio Damasio et al. (2000) compared brain activation during four different kinds of emotion, and again the insula, cingulate cortex, and prefrontal cortex (Figure 15.14) were among the regions implicated. In a screening session, adults were asked to recall and attempt to reexperience episodes involving sadness, happiness, anger, or fear, as well as an equally specific but emotionally neutral episode. Measures were taken of skin conductance response (SCR) and heart rate (HR), and subjects rated the intensity of the experience on a scale of 0 to 4. During the experimental session, the subject was asked to signal as soon as the desired emotion was experienced. In each case the physiological responses (SCR and HR) preceded the signal, supporting the idea that at least some physiological responses precede the feeling of emotion. PET images were averaged for all subjects experiencing a given emotion, and activity during the neutral state was subtracted from activity during the emotion. Activity was altered in many brain regions during emotional experience, and even though we don't understand what role each region plays, it does appear that the four emotions were accompanied by significant differences in patterns of brain activity (Figure 15.15).

(a)   *(b)*   *(c)*

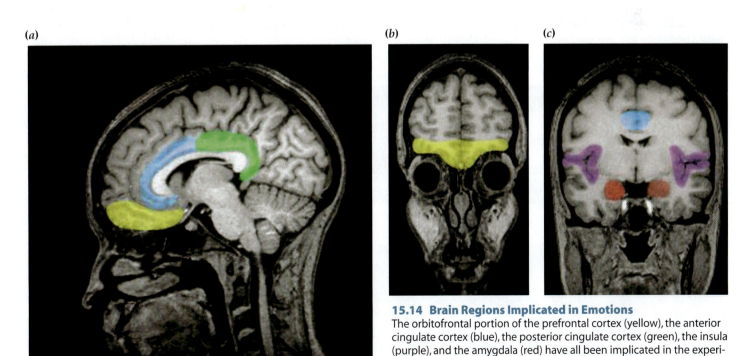

15.14 Brain Regions Implicated in Emotions
The orbitofrontal portion of the prefrontal cortex (yellow), the anterior cingulate cortex (blue), the posterior cingulate cortex (green), the insula (purple), and the amygdala (red) have all been implicated in the experience of emotion. They are depicted here in (*a*) midsagittal, (*b*) anterior coronal, and (*c*) posterior coronal sections. (From Dolan, 2002.)

Damasio and colleagues note that many of their observations are consistent with other studies. One notable exception is the lack of activation of the amygdala during fear and anger, which contradicts reports of others that the amygdala is involved in these emotions. In defense of their observations, Damasio et al. remark that most other reports show involvement of the amygdala during recognition or induction of an emotion by a visual stimulus, whereas their study emphasized the *feeling* phase. Future work could test whether there is a change from the amygdala to other areas in the transition from induction to feelings of fear or anger.

Imaging studies show that there is no simple, one-to-one relation between an emotion and changed activity of a brain region. There is no "happy center" or "sad center." Each emotion involves altered activity of several brain regions, and the same brain region may participate in more than one emotion. For example, activity of the cingulate cortex is altered in sadness, happiness, and anger; the left secondary somatosensory cortex is deactivated in both anger and fear.

Although different emotions appear to activate somewhat different patterns of responses, as we saw in Figure 15.15, there is a good deal of overlap among patterns for different emotions. Richard Lane (2000) suggests that four main regions are involved in different aspects of emotional responses:

1. The *anterior cingulate* and *medial prefrontal cortex,* for establishing a representation of the emotional state
2. The *anterior insula,* for processing visceral information
3. The *right temporal pole,* for performing complex sensory discrimination of emotional stimuli and perhaps also retrieving emotion-laden memories
4. The *posterior cingulate cortex,* for regulating autonomic responses

15.15 Brain Regions Involved in Four Emotions Red and yellow indicate areas of increased activity; purple indicates areas of decreased activity. For the identified sites, an upward arrow indicates increased activity; a downward arrow, decreased activity. (Courtesy of Antonio Damasio.)

(a) Sadness

↑Anterior cingulate cortex   ↓Posterior cingulate cortex   ↑Insula   ↑Dorsal pons

(b) Happiness

↑Right posterior cingulate cortex   ↑Left insula   ↓Left anterior cingulate cortex

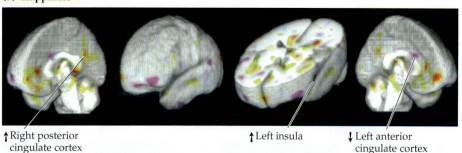

(c) Fear

↑Midbrain   ↓Orbitofrontal cortex

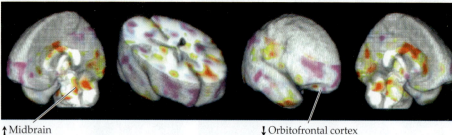

(d) Anger

↑Pons   ↑Left anterior cingulate cortex

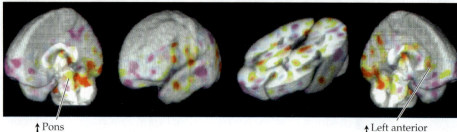

Neural Circuitry, Hormones, and Synaptic Transmitters Mediate Violence and Aggression

Violence, assaults, and homicide exact a high toll in many human societies; for example, homicide is the most prominent cause of death in young adults in the United States. Many different approaches have been used to investigate the psychological, anthropological, and biological dimensions of aggression.

What is aggression?

Surely we all know aggression. Consideration, however, suggests that this all-too-familiar term has many different meanings. In common usage, the term *aggression* refers to an emotional state that many humans describe as consisting of feelings of hate and a desire to inflict harm. This perspective emphasizes aggression as a powerful inner feeling. However, when we view aggression as an overt response—overt behavior that involves actual or intended destruction of another organism—we see several different forms.

Some investigators view the attack behavior of an animal directed at natural prey as *predatory aggression*. Comparative psychologists such as Stephen Glickman (1977), however, have argued that this behavior is more appropriately designated as *feeding behavior*. Aggression between males of the same species is observed in most vertebrates. The relevance to humans may be the fact that males are five times more likely than females to be arrested on charges of murder in the United States. Further, aggressive behavior between boys, in contrast to that between girls, is evident early, in the form of vigorous and destructive play behavior.

Stephen Glickman

Androgens seem to increase aggression

Male sex hormones play a major role in some forms of aggressive behavior, especially in social encounters between males (R. J. Nelson, 1995). One set of data relates levels of circulating androgens to different measures of aggressive behavior. At sexual maturity, intermale aggression markedly increases in many species. McKinney and Desjardins (1973) have shown changes in aggressiveness in mice that start at puberty, and immature mice treated with androgens display increased aggression. Levels of testosterone change seasonally in many species and seem related to variation in aggression in animals as diverse as birds and primates (Wingfield et al., 1987).

Observations of the behavioral effects of castration give additional evidence for the relation between hormones and aggression. Reductions in the level of circulating androgens produced following castration are commonly associated with a profound reduction in intermale aggressive behavior. Treating castrated animals with testosterone increases fighting behavior in mice (Figure 15.16).

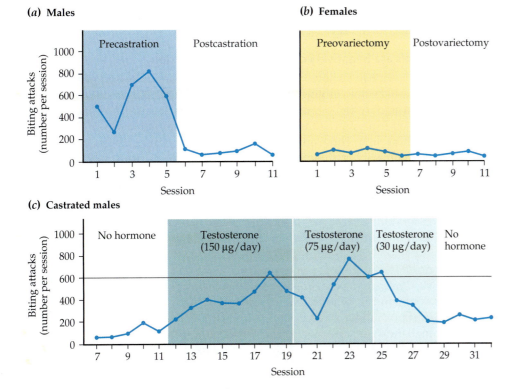

15.16 The Effects of Androgens on the Aggressive Behavior of Mice
Counts of the number of biting attacks initiated by males before and after castration (*a*) and by females before and after removal of the ovaries (*b*) reveal significantly higher aggression in males before castration. When castrated males are treated with testosterone (*c*), aggressive behavior is reinstated. (From G. C. Wagner et al., 1980.)

The idea of a relationship between hormones—especially androgens—and human aggression is controversial. Arguments summoned in legal briefs frequently cite the literature on nonhuman animals. Some human studies have shown a positive correlation between testosterone levels and the magnitude of hostility, as measured by behavior rating scales. Comprehensive studies of military veterans suggest that testosterone *is* related to antisocial behavior (Dabbs and Morris, 1990). Nonaggressive tendencies in males are associated with satisfaction in family functioning and with low levels of serum testosterone (Julian and McKenry, 1979). Among females, testosterone concentrations are highest in women prisoners convicted of unprovoked violence and lowest among women convicted of defensive violent crimes (Dabbs and Hargrove, 1997; Dabbs et al., 1988).

At least two variables seem to confound the correlations between testosterone and aggression. First is the observation that experience can affect testosterone levels. In mice and monkeys, the loser in aggressive encounters shows reduced androgen levels (I. S. Bernstein and Gordon, 1974; Lloyd, 1971), so low levels of testosterone in nonviolent prisoners may be a result, rather than a cause, of behavior. In men, testosterone levels rise in the winners and fall in the losers after sporting events or chess matches. Even male fans watching a sporting event respond with either an increase or a decrease in testosterone levels, depending on whether the team they are rooting for wins or loses, respectively (Bernhardt, 1997).

These observations suggest that a second confounding variable between testosterone and aggression is dominance, since most chess players could hardly be said to be aggressive. Despite the lack of a close relationship between aggression and androgens, people have tried to modify the behavior of male criminals by manipulating sex hormones. Studies of castration generally show that violence in sex offenders is reduced by this surgical procedure, especially where "excessive libido" is considered the instigator of sexual assaults (Brain, 1994). The administration of antiandrogen drugs such as cyproterone acetate, which exerts its impact by competing with testosterone for receptor sites, acts as reversible castration.

Several studies on criminals convicted of sexual assault have shown that administration of these antiandrogens reduces sexual drive and interest. However, some researchers have suggested that the effects of antiandrogens on aggressive behavior are less predictable than their effects on sexual behavior. Many ethical issues are involved in this approach to the rehabilitation of sex offenders, and the intricacies of such intervention have yet to be worked out.

COMPETING HYPOTHESES

Serotonin levels are negatively correlated with aggression

Aggressive behavior in various animals, including humans, may be connected to the synaptic transmitter serotonin. Studies show a negative correlation between brain serotonin activity and aggression. For example, Higley et al. (1992) studied 28 monkeys chosen from more than 4500 monkeys maintained on an island off the coast of South Carolina. These animals roamed freely, and researchers collected observations of aggressive behavior and noted body wounds from fights. Animals were ranked from least to most aggressive by researchers who knew nothing of the animals' neurochemical activity. Data from this study show a significant negative correlation between magnitude of aggression and serotonin activity. The investigators gauged serotonin activity by measuring a serotonin metabolite, 5-HIAA (5-hydroxyindoleacetic acid), in cerebrospinal fluid. The most aggressive animals had the lowest levels of serotonin metabolites, suggesting that they had the least serotonin being released at synapses in the brain. Mice with one of the serotonin receptor genes knocked out are hyperaggressive (Bouwknecht et al., 2001), as one would expect if serotonin normally inhibits aggression.

Diminished serotonin activity (as measured by low concentrations of 5-HIAA in cerebrospinal fluid) is seen in humans who become violent with alcohol use (Virkkunen and Linnoila, 1993), in U.S. marines expelled for excessive violence (G. L. Brown et al., 1979), in children who torture animals (Kruesi, 1979), and in children whose poor impulse control produces disruptive behavior.

We must caution that serotonin levels are not inflexible quantities that are indifferent to social stimuli and contexts. Serotonin is not the "antiaggression" transmitter. Other substances have been implicated in various forms of aggression in both humans and other animals. The list includes noradrenergic and GABA-ergic systems, as well as neuropeptides that might act as modulators of aggression. In addition, increased aggression is often seen in knockout mice (see Box 7.3), no matter which of several genes is deleted (R. J. Nelson et al., 1995). Clearly, aggression is regulated by many systems.

The neurology of human violence is a topic of controversy

Some forms of human violence are characterized by sudden intense physical assaults. In a controversial book, *Violence and the Brain,* Mark and Ervin (1970) suggested that some forms of intense human violence are derived from temporal lobe seizure disorders. They offered horrifying examples from newspaper accounts as preliminary evidence. For example, in 1966 Charles Whitman climbed a tower at the University of Texas and murdered, by random shooting, several passing individuals. Earlier he had killed family members, and letters he left behind revealed a portrait of a bewildered young man possessed by an intense need to commit violence. Postmortem analysis of Whitman's brain suggested the presence of a tumor deep in the temporal lobe.

Other, more-formal data cited by Mark and Ervin include the occurrence of aggression in temporal lobe seizure patients and the long-controversial claim that a large percentage of habitually aggressive criminals display abnormal EEGs that indicate likely temporal lobe disease. Mark and Ervin argued that temporal lobe disorders may underlie many forms of human violence and produce a disorder that they labeled **dyscontrol syndrome.**

CLINICAL ISSUE

Many other studies have linked violence in humans with some forms of seizure disorders or other clinical neurological pathology (D. O. Lewis, 1990). A high percentage of both juveniles and adults arrested for violent crimes have abnormal EEGs (D. O. Lewis et al., 1979; D. Williams, 1969). Devinsky and Bear (1984) examined a group of patients with seizures involving the limbic system. These patients showed aggressive behavior that occurred after an epileptic focus developed within this system. None of these patients had a history that included traditional sociological factors linked to aggression, such as parental abuse, poverty, or use of drugs. In these patients aggression was an event *between* seizures (Delgado-Escueta et al., 1981). But in another case—that of a babysitter who had killed the child in her charge in a most violent manner—the babysitter's violent response to the child was elicited *during* a temporal lobe seizure provoked by the child's laughter, which was a specific seizure-eliciting stimulus for this person (Engel, 1992).

Psychopaths are intelligent individuals with superficial charm who have poor self-control, a grandiose sense of self-worth, and little or no feelings of remorse (Hare et al., 1990), and who sometimes commit very violent acts. Compared to controls, psychopaths do not react as negatively to words about violence (Gray et al., 2003). PET studies suggest that psychopaths have reduced activity in the prefrontal cortex (Raine et al., 1998), and it is hypothesized that this may impair their ability to resist impulses. An MRI follow-up indicated that the prefrontal cortex of psychopaths is smaller than in controls (Raine et al., 2000)—another finding that is consistent with this hypothesis.

Undoubtedly human violence and aggression stem from many sources. Biological studies of aggression have been vigorously criticized by both politicians and social scientists. These critics argue that as a result of emphasizing biological factors such as genetics or brain mechanisms, the most evident origins of human violence and aggression might be overlooked, and odious forms of biological controls of social dysfunction might be instituted. However, the quality of life of some violent persons might be significantly improved if biological problems could be identified and addressed. For example, treatments that enhance serotonin activity in the brain may be an important addition to a social–environmental or psychotherapeutic intervention (Coccaro and Siever, 1995; Hollander, 1999).

**Hans Selye
(1907–1982)**

Stress Activates Many Bodily Responses

We all experience stress, but what is it? Attempts to define *stress* have not overcome a certain vagueness implicit in this term. Some researchers emphasize that **stress** is a multidimensional concept that includes the stress stimuli, the processing system (including the cognitive assessment of the stimuli), and the stress responses. The early use of the concept *stress* is closely identified with the work of Hans Selye, who popularized the term and defined it in a broad way as "the rate of all the wear and tear caused by life" (Selye, 1956). Experiencing negative emotions is one important source of that "wear and tear."

In many studies over almost 40 years, Selye described the impact of "stressors" on the responses of different organ systems of the body. He emphasized the connection between stress and disease in his "general adaptation syndrome." According to this scheme, the initial response to stress (called the **alarm reaction**) is followed by a second stage (the **adaptation stage**), which includes the successful activation of the appropriate response systems and the reestablishment of homeostatic balance. If stress is prolonged or frequently repeated, the **exhaustion phase** sets in, and it is characterized by increased susceptibility to disease.

This concept of stress and disease has been modified; some investigators note that the common ingredient of stressful stimuli is uncertainty or unpredictability about how to gain positive outcomes in response to these stimuli (S. Levine and Ursin, 1980). This model, which considers a broad array of factors relevant to stress and disease (including the roles of coping strategies and learning), emphasizes that stress per se does not inevitably lead to dysfunction or illness. The model thus helps account for the variability in health histories of humans exposed to similar stressful life experiences.

Ursin et al. (1978) studied a group of young recruits in the Norwegian military both before and during the early phase of parachute training, using a variety of psychological and physiological measures. In the training period, subjects were propelled down a long sloping wire suspended from a tower 12 m high. This parachute training evokes an experience somewhat like that of free fall. Initial apprehension is high, and at first the sense of danger is acute, even though recruits know that they are not likely to lose their lives in this part of the training.

On each jump day in this study, samples of blood revealed activation of tropic hormones from the anterior pituitary and of both the sympathetic and parasympathetic systems (Figure 15.17). Under stressful conditions the hypothalamus produces corticotropin-releasing hormone (CRH), which, as we saw in Chapter 5 (see Figure 5.15), causes the release of adrenocorticotropic hormone (ACTH) from the anterior pituitary. ACTH causes the release of corticosteroid hormones such as cortisol from the adrenal cortex.

Initially, cortisol levels were elevated in the blood, but successful jumps during training quickly led to a decrease in the pituitary–adrenal response. On the first jump, testosterone levels in the plasma fell below those of controls, but these levels returned to normal with subsequent jumps. Other substances that showed marked increases in concentration at the initial jump included growth hormone, which is also controlled by a tropic hormone from the anterior pituitary, and by epinephrine and norepinephrine from the adrenal medulla (see Figure 15.17*b*), whose release is mediated by the sympathetic nervous system.

Less-dramatic real-life situations also evoke clear endocrine responses, as shown by the research of Frankenhaeuser (1978). For example, riding in a commuter train was found to provoke the release of epinephrine; the longer the ride and the more crowded the train, the greater the hormonal response (Figure 15.18*a*). Factory work also leads to the release of epinephrine; the shorter the work cycle—that is, the more frequently the person has to repeat the same operations—the higher the levels of epinephrine. The stress of a PhD oral exam was shown to lead to a dramatic increase in both epinephrine and norepinephrine (Figure 15.18*b*).

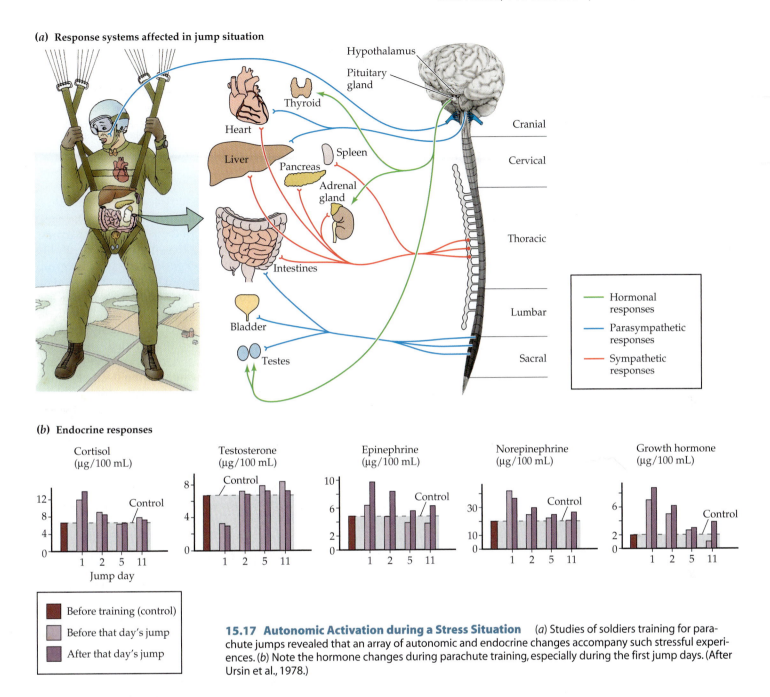

(a) Response systems affected in jump situation

(b) Endocrine responses

Legend:
- — Hormonal responses
- — Parasympathetic responses
- — Sympathetic responses

Graphs:
- Cortisol (µg/100 mL)
- Testosterone (µg/100 mL)
- Epinephrine (µg/100 mL)
- Norepinephrine (µg/100 mL)
- Growth hormone (µg/100 mL)

Jump day: 1 2 5 11

- Before training (control)
- Before that day's jump
- After that day's jump

15.17 Autonomic Activation during a Stress Situation (a) Studies of soldiers training for parachute jumps revealed that an array of autonomic and endocrine changes accompany such stressful experiences. (b) Note the hormone changes during parachute training, especially during the first jump days. (After Ursin et al., 1978.)

Stress experienced by animals in the wild has become an interesting area of study for investigators who are trying to understand the stress response of humans. Robert Sapolsky (2001) studied baboons living freely in a natural reserve in Kenya. At first appearance, these animals seem to have a good life: Food is abundant, predators are rare. The stresses they experience are the impacts they exert on each other. For males, this stress is the vigorous competition that surrounds courtship and the establishment of dominance hierarchies. An animal's place in the dominance hierarchy influences the physiology of the stress response, as seen in the animal's response to anesthesia produced by a dart gun syringe. In general, the testosterone levels of dominant males recover more rapidly after a stressful event than do those of subordinate males. Likewise, the subordinates display a more prolonged increase in levels of circulating cortisol.

Robert Sapolsky

(a)

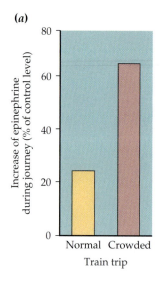

(b)

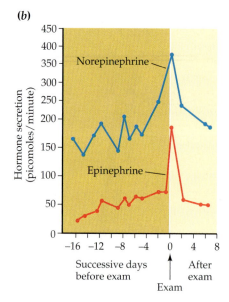

15.18 Hormone Changes in Humans in Response to Social Stresses (*a*) Small changes in crowding on a morning commuter train ride affect hormone levels in humans. A 10% increase in the number of passengers during a period of gasoline rationing (*right*) resulted in a much higher increase in epinephrine secretion. (*b*) Levels of epinephrine and norepinephrine in a graduate student during a 2-week period before, during, and after a thesis exam reflect levels of stress. (After Frankenhaeuser, 1978.)

Michael Meaney

Why do individuals differ in their response to stress? One hypothesis focused on early experience. Rat pups clearly find it stressful to have a human experimenter pick them up and handle them. Yet Seymour Levine et al. (1967) found that rats that had been handled as pups were less susceptible to adult stress than rats that had been left alone as pups. For example, the previously handled rats secreted less corticosteroid in response to a wide variety of adult stressors. This effect was termed **stress immunization** because a little stress early in life seemed to make the animals more resilient to later stress.

A follow-up study has suggested that there is more to the story. When pups are returned to their mother after a separation, she spends considerable time licking and grooming them. In fact, she will lick the pups much longer if they were handled by humans during the separation. Michael Meaney and colleagues suggest that this gentle tactile stimulation from Mom is crucial for the stress immunization effect. They found that, even among undisturbed litters, the offspring of mother rats that exhibited more licking and grooming behavior were more resilient in their response to adult stress than other rats were (D. Liu et al., 1997).

Stress and Emotions Are Related to Some Human Diseases

During the past 50 years, many psychiatrists and psychologists have strongly emphasized the role of psychological factors in disease. The field that developed out of this interest came to be known as **psychosomatic medicine** after an eminent psychoanalyst, Thomas French, suggested that particular diseases arise from distinctive sets of psychological characteristics or personality conflicts.

CLINICAL ISSUE

Emotional stimuli activate a diversity of neural and hormonal changes that influence pathological processes of body organs. Studies in psychosomatic medicine have broadened in scope and now range from evaluating emotions, stress, and sickness on a global scale to unraveling particular relations between emotions and bodily responses or conditions. A field called **health psychology** (or *behavioral medicine*) has developed from this interest (Baum and Posluszny, 1999; Schwartzer and Gutiérrez-Doña, 2000). Figure 15.19 shows how several factors that affect human health and disease interact.

One global approach to linking stress and human disease is to study the covariation between stressful life events and the incidence of particular diseases over a long period of time. Although many methodological problems complicate this approach, some consistent relations between stressful events and illness have been found (N. Adler and Matthews, 1994). For example, men who report frequent and severe stress in a period of 1 to 5 years prior to interviews are more likely to experience heart disease during a 12-year period following the interview than those who report little stress (Rosengren et al., 1991). The social network within which stress occurs may be a more important determinant of disease outcome than is stress itself (N. Adler and Matthews, 1994).

Emotions and stress influence the immune system

For a long while, researchers viewed the immune system as an automatic mechanism: A pathogen, such as a virus, arrived on the scene, and soon the defense mechanisms of the immune system went to work, usually prevailing with their armory of antibodies and other immunological devices. Few investigators thought of the nervous system as having an important role in this process, although the notion that the mind can influence well-being has been a persistent theme in human history.

In the 1980s a new field, **psychoneuroimmunology,** appeared; its existence signals a new awareness that the immune system—with its collection of cells that recognize intruders—interacts with other organs, especially hormone systems and the nervous system (Ader, 2001). Studies of both human and nonhuman subjects now clearly show psychological and neurological influences on the immune system. For example, people with happy social lives are less likely to develop a cold when exposed to the virus (S. Cohen et al., 2003). Likewise, people who tend to feel positive emotions will also produce more antibodies in response to a flu vaccination (Rosenkranz et al., 2003), which should help them fight off sickness. These interactions go in both directions: The brain influences responses of the immune system, and immune cells and their products affect brain activities.

The immune system   To understand this intriguing story, we need to note some of the main features of the immune system. In your blood are different classes of white blood cells (leukocytes). The **phagocytes** ("eating" cells, such as macrophages and neutrophils) are specialized to engulf and destroy invading germs. But phagocytes rely on other white blood cells (the lymphocytes) to tell them what to attack. **B lymphocytes** (or *B cells*, because they form in the bone marrow), produce proteins called **antibodies** (or *immunoglobulins*). Antibodies latch onto antigens (foreign molecules) such as viruses or bacteria and summon phagocytes and circulating proteins to destroy the invaders. **T lymphocytes** (*T cells*), so called because they form in the thymus gland, can act as *killer cells,* forming a strong part of the body's attack against foreign substances. In addition, special T lymphocytes called *helper T cells* secrete **cytokines,** cell signaling proteins such as the interleukins and lymphokines, which regulate the activity of B lymphocytes and phagocytes. Other T cells can selectively suppress B cells and/or phagocytes.

These immune system cells form in the thymus gland, bone marrow, spleen, and lymph nodes (Figure 15.20), which release the cells into the bloodstream.

Communication among the nervous, immune, and endocrine systems

The potential for interactions between the brain and the immune system is revealed in many anatomical and physiological studies (e.g., Ader and Cohen, 1993; Ader et al., 1990; Felten et al., 1993). For example, autonomic nerve fibers innervate immune system organs such as the spleen and thymus gland. These fibers are usually noradrenergic, sympathetic postganglionic axons that affect antibody production and immune cell proliferation (Bellinger et al., 1992).

The brain carefully monitors immune reactions to make sure they are not too extreme. If too much interleukin is released, immune cells might be overstimulated, attacking good cells as well as invading cells. Peripheral axons of the vagus nerve have receptors to detect high levels of cytokines such as interleukins and relay the information to the brain. Then brainstem neurons with axons that lead back out the vagus nerve release acetylcholine, which inhibits cytokine release from immune cells (H. Wang et al., 2003). Hypothalamic neurons also monitor interferons and interleukins in circulation (Bartfai, 2001; Samad et al., 2001). Thus the brain seems to be directly in-

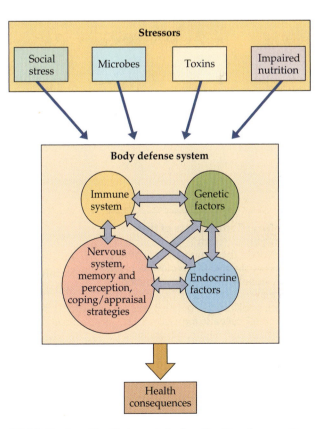

15.19 Factors That Interact during the Development and Progression of Disease

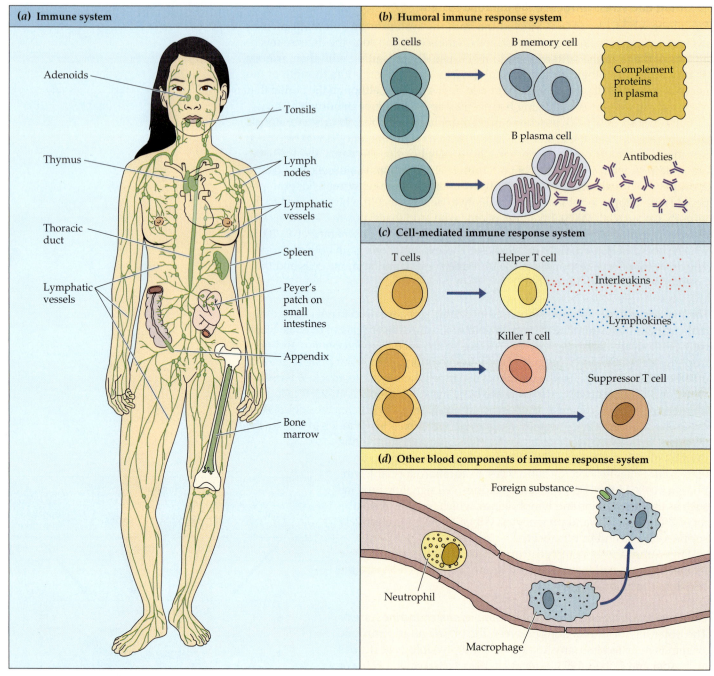

(a) Immune system

Adenoids

Tonsils

Thymus

Lymph nodes

Lymphatic vessels

Thoracic duct

Spleen

Lymphatic vessels

Peyer's patch on small intestines

Appendix

Bone marrow

(b) Humoral immune response system

B cells

B memory cell

Complement proteins in plasma

B plasma cell

Antibodies

(c) Cell-mediated immune response system

T cells

Helper T cell

Interleukins

Lymphokines

Killer T cell

Suppressor T cell

(d) Other blood components of immune response system

Foreign substance

Neutrophil

Macrophage

15.20 Main Components of the Human Immune System (a) The various components of the immune system protect us by means of three classes of white blood cells: B lymphocytes (b) produce antibodies to attack invading microbes. T lymphocytes (c) release cytokines to regulate B cells to divide or die. T cells also form killer cells that, together with neutrophils and macrophages (d), directly attack foreign tissues or microbes.

formed about the actions of the immune system. In fact, it has been suggested that the immune system serves as a kind of sensory receptor system (Besedovsky and del Rey, 1992), telling our brain when microbes have invaded the body.

There is an interesting theory about why our brains monitor the immune system so closely. Although that achy, lethargic feeling we have with the flu is unpleasant, it is also adaptive because it forces us to rest and keep out of trouble until we recover (Hart, 1988). Perhaps high levels of cytokines are what cause the brain to enforce that sick feeling. This idea has given rise to the idea that maybe some people are depressed because they have too high a level of circulating cytokines (Maes et al., 1991). Indeed, antidepressant drugs decrease cytokine production (Kenis and Maes, 2002).

The immune system and nervous system also interact extensively with the endocrine system. Some examples of these relationships are shown in Figure 15.21. All three systems interact reciprocally, so there is a constant state of flux, carefully tuning the immune system so that it vigorously attacks foreign cells but leaves the body's own cells alone.

Immunosuppression as a defense mechanism   Under stressful conditions, as noted earlier, a chain of processes starting with the production of corticotropin-releasing hormone causes the release of corticosteroid hormones from the adrenal cortex. One effect of these hormones is to suppress immunological responses by inhibiting the proliferation of some lymphocytes and triggering the death of others. You might ask why, during times of stress, the brain causes adrenal steroids to be released, if these steroids suppress the immune system. In a delightful book entitled *Why Zebras Don't Get Ulcers*, Robert Sapolsky (1994) considers a variety of evolutionary hypotheses about why immunity is suppressed during stress.

To the extent that stress might be a sudden emergency, the temporary suppression of immune responses makes some sense because the stress response demands a rapid mobilization of energy; immune responses extend longer than the immediacy of a demanding situation would require. A zebra wounded by a lion must first escape and hide, and only then does infection of the wound pose a threat. So the stress of the encounter first suppresses the immune system, saving resources until a safe haven is found. Later the animal can afford to mobilize the immune system to heal the wound. The adrenal steroids also suppress swelling (inflammation) of injuries, especially of joints, to help the animal remain mobile long enough to find refuge.

In the wild, animals are under stress for only a short while; an animal stressed for a prolonged period dies. So natural selection favored stress reactions as a drastic effort to deal with a short-term problem. What makes humans unique is that, with our highly social lives and keen analytical minds, we are capable of experiencing stress for prolonged periods—months or even years. The bodily reactions to stress, which evolved to deal with short-term problems, become a handicap when extended too long (Sapolsky, 1994). For example, long-term stress, lasting over a month, affects the probability that a person will catch a cold (S. Cohen et al., 1998). Sapolsky has compiled a list of stress responses that are beneficial in the short term but detrimental in the long term (Table 15.3).

Psychological stress and immunity
The anatomical and physiological data described in the previous section suggest some bases for the role of psychological factors in immune system responses. For example, several lines of evidence suggest that the competence of the immune system is decreased during depression (M. Stein et al., 1991). Such a compromise of the immune system would increase susceptibility to infectious diseases, cancer, and autoimmune disorders. Altered immune function is also observed in people who are grieving the death of a relative, especially a spouse (M. Stein and Miller, 1993).

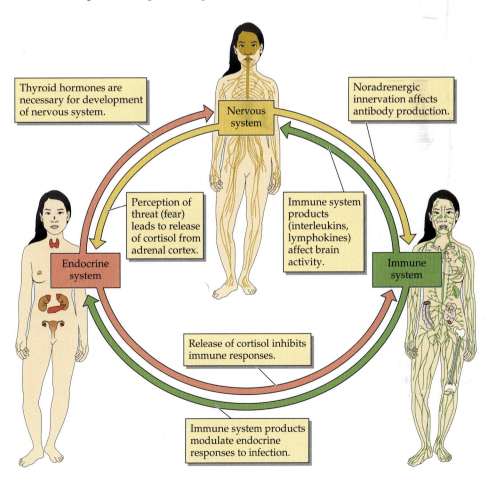

Thyroid hormones are necessary for development of nervous system.

Noradrenergic innervation affects antibody production.

Nervous system

Perception of threat (fear) leads to release of cortisol from adrenal cortex.

Immune system products (interleukins, lymphokines) affect brain activity.

Endocrine system

Immune system

Release of cortisol inhibits immune responses.

Immune system products modulate endocrine responses to infection.

15.21 Examples of Reciprocal Relations among the Nervous, Endocrine, and Immune Systems

TABLE 15.3 *The Stress Response and Consequences of Prolonged Stress*

Principal components of the stress response	Common pathological consequences of prolonged stress
Mobilization of energy at the cost of energy storage	Fatigue, muscle wasting, steroid diabetes
Increased cardiovascular and cardiopulmonary tone	Hypertension (high blood pressure)
Suppression of digestion	Ulcers
Suppression of growth	Psychogenic dwarfism, bone decalcification
Suppression of reproduction	Suppression of ovulation, impotency, loss of libido
Suppression of immunity and of inflammatory response	Impaired disease resistance
Analgesia	Apathy
Neural responses, including altered cognition and sensory thresholds	Accelerated neural degeneration during aging

Source: Sapolsky, 1992.

Stressful exam periods usually produce a decline in natural killer cell activity (Glaser et al., 1986) and γ-interferon, a glycoprotein that helps regulate the immune system. Of most importance, some studies have noted that the student's *perception* of the stress of the academic program is a predictor of the level of circulating antibody: Those who perceived the program as stressful showed the lowest levels. One experiment considered the effects of university examinations on wound healing in dental students (Marucha et al., 1998). Two small wounds were placed on the roof of the mouth of 11 dental students (sounds like revenge, doesn't it?). The first wound was timed during summer vacation; the second was inflicted 3 days before the first major examination of the term. Two independent daily measures showed that no student healed as rapidly during the exam period, when healing took 40% longer. A measure of immunological response declined 68% during the exam period. The experimenters concluded that even something as transient, predictable, and relatively benign (do students agree with this description?) as examination stress can have significant consequences for wound healing.

Another connection between the nervous and immune systems was described in Chapter 14, where we learned that sleep deprivation impairs the responsiveness of the immune system.

Emotions and stress influence cardiac function

Common views of causes of heart attacks emphasize the role of emotions. Many an excited person has heard the admonition, "Calm down before you blow a fuse!" M. Friedman and R. H. Rosenman (1974) focused on differences between two behavior patterns—type A and type B—in the development and maintenance of heart disease. *Type A* behavior is characterized by excessive competitive drive, impatience, hostility, and accelerated speech and movements; in short, life is hectic and demanding for such individuals. In contrast, *type B* behavior patterns are more relaxed, with little evidence of aggressive drive or emphasis on getting things done fast. Of course, this is a crude dichotomy; many individuals have some of each pattern in their characteristic style (Steptoe, 1993).

A strong association between hostility and heart disease has been noted in these studies (Almada et al., 1991). Excessive expression of hostility may also be related to social isolation, which has been implicated as a risk factor for heart disease in several studies. For example, men who are socially isolated and have experienced significant recent life stress, such as family separation, have a much higher mortality rate than do socially integrated controls (Ruberman et al., 1984). In normal young subjects, the presence of a friend during a demanding task lessens the magnitude of

Refer to the *Learning Biological Psychology CD* for study questions, animations, activities, and other study aids.

cardiovascular responses to this type of stress. So perhaps one of the best ways to deal with stress is to build strong friendships and a happy family.

Summary

1. The term *emotion* includes private subjective feelings, as well as expressions or displays of particular somatic and autonomic responses. The four main aspects of emotions are feelings, actions, physiological arousal, and motivational programs. Psychologists have generated different categorization systems to account for the varieties of emotions.

2. Whereas the James–Lange theory considered emotions to be the perceptions of stimulus-induced bodily changes, the Cannon–Bard theory emphasized the integration of emotional experiences and responses in the brain. A cognitive theory of emotions argues that activity in a physiological system is not enough to provoke an emotion; rather, the key feature in emotion is the interpretation of visceral activities.

3. Distinct facial expressions represent anger, contempt, happiness, sadness, disgust, fear, surprise, and embarrassment, and these expressions are interpreted similarly across many cultures. Facial expressions are controlled by distinct sets of facial muscles that in turn are controlled by the facial and trigeminal nerves.

4. Studies of brain lesions have revealed that particular brain circuits and interconnected regions mediate and control emotions. Relevant regions include limbic system sites described in Papez's neural circuit and other related regions, including the amygdala.

5. Emotions may have evolved as coordinated motivational programs that are useful in solving specific adaptive problems.

6. Electrical stimulation of some brain regions is rewarding.

7. The left and right cerebral hemispheres process emotions differently. In normal people the right hemisphere is better at interpreting emotional states or stimuli.

8. Fear is mediated by circuitry that involves the amygdala, which is directly connected to cortical sensory regions.

9. Aggressive behavior is increased by androgens. Brain regions of the limbic system and related sites differ in their relationship to aggressive behavior: Stimulation of some regions elicits a full, species-typical pattern of aggression. Serotonin levels are negatively correlated with aggression.

10. Assessment of stress in real-life situations shows that stress elevates the levels of several hormones (including cortisol, epinephrine, and norepinephrine) and suppresses other hormones (such as testosterone).

11. Stress affects human health and influences the outcome of disease. Incidence of illness tends to be higher in people who sustain prolonged stress, although constitutional factors, as well as strategies for coping with stress, are also important. The nervous system and immune system interact to monitor and maintain health.

12. Reciprocal relations are found among the nervous, endocrine, and immune systems.

Recommended Reading

Davidson, R. J., Scherer, K. R., and Goldsmith, H. H. (Eds.). (2002). *Handbook of affective sciences.* New York: Oxford University Press.

Frijda, N. H. (2000). Emotions. In K. Pawlik and M. R. Rosenzweig (Eds.), *International handbook of psychology* (pp. 207–222). London: Sage.

LeDoux, J. (2002). *The synaptic self: How our brains become who we are.* New York: Viking.

Lewis, M., and Haviland-Jones, J. M. (Eds.). (2000). *Handbook of emotions* (2nd ed.). New York: Guilford.

McEwen, B. S., and Lasley, E. N. (2002). *The end of stress as we know it.* Washington, DC: Joseph Henry Press.

Sapolsky, R. (1997). *The trouble with testosterone: And other essays on the biology of the human predicament.* New York: Scribner.

Stoff, D. M., and Cairns, R. B. (Eds.). (1996). *Aggression and violence: Genetic, neurobiological, and biosocial perspectives.* Mahwah, NJ: Erlbaum.

16

Psychopathology: Biological Basis of Behavioral Disorders

Twist and Shout

Sometimes his limbs would fling about unpredictably. Sometimes he would take to grunting or shouting for no apparent reason. Every movement that he attempted was a chaos of twitches, tics, and jerks so severe that he had to use a sippy cup to drink anything. At the age of 6, Jeff Matovic had been diagnosed with Tourette's syndrome, a disease characterized by uncontrollable movements and vocalizations, or tics. He had struggled valiantly with Tourette's for 25 years, overcoming ridicule, graduating from university, and marrying, but now the drugs that had given him partial relief from his symptoms had lost their effectiveness. Now that he was 31, Jeff's disorder had progressed to the point that daily life was exceptionally difficult. In desperation, Jeff was ready to try anything, no matter how experimental or extreme.

Sufferers of Tourette's syndrome tend to be of normal or above-normal intelligence and have normal cognitive and behavioral functioning—aside from their tics—making their plight all the more painful. People with this disorder often sense the buildup of an urge to emit tics; they report that only performing these acts can relieve this powerfully felt need. Tics can take a wide variety of forms, ranging from shouted obscenities to repeated movements or compulsions.

Professionals have long argued about whether this collection of symptoms is a psychiatric disturbance derived from the stresses of life or emerges from a fundamental disturbance in the brain. The same sort of discourse has informed the study of all the major categories of psychiatric disorders, but for Tourette's syndrome and many other disorders, major strides in neurobiological research are paving the way to improved understanding and treatment.

So how can an understanding of the brain help people like Jeff? What combinations of therapies, drugs, and even surgery can offer hope?

D ebilitating mental afflictions have plagued humankind throughout history, plunging their victims into an abyss of disordered thought, emotional chaos, and even the loss of a sense of self. Despite rapid advances in our understanding of zthe causes and treatment of illnesses such as schizophrenia, depression, and anxiety disorders, the need to reduce the emotional and economic costs of psychiatric illness remains great. Psychopathology affects hundreds of millions of people worldwide, not just an exotic few.

Our aim in this chapter is to survey the major categories of psychiatric disorders and explore their biological underpinnings. Although no single remedy has been found that cures all who suffer from any of these disorders, modern discoveries have restored millions of people to normal life.

The Toll of Psychiatric Disorders Is Huge

Although the classification of psychiatric disorders is an evolving science and subject to periodic revision, we know from psychiatric **epidemiology** (the scientific study of disease incidence) that psychiatric disorders are startlingly prevalent in modern society. About one-third of the U.S. population at some point in life reports symptoms that match the defining features of a major psychiatric disorder (Robins and Regier, 1991). Total rates for mental disorders in men and women are comparable, although the proportions of disorders are slightly different for the two sexes. Depression is more prevalent in females, and drug dependency and alcoholism are more frequent in males.

Certain psychiatric disorders—for example, drug abuse and schizophrenia—tend to appear relatively early in life. The age range 25 to 44 shows peaks for depression and antisocial personality, whereas cognitive impairment occurs especially in people older than 65. In a single year, as much as 19% of the adult population experiences psychiatric symptoms (Narrow et al., 2002). Clearly, mental disorders exact an enormous toll on our lives. Efforts to understand these disorders depend on research in diverse areas ranging from cell biology to sociology.

The seeds for a biological perspective in psychiatry were sown at about the beginning of the twentieth century. At that time, almost a quarter of the patient population in mental hospitals suffered from a type of psychosis characterized by profound delusions (false beliefs strongly held in spite of contrary evidence), grandiosity and euphoria, poor judgment, impulsive and capricious behavior, and fundamental changes in thought structure.

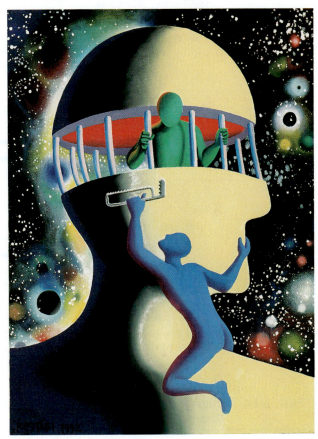

Mark Kostabi, *Mindscape*, 1992

Hideyo Noguchi
(1876–1928)

This disorder was known in all societies of the world and had been noted for centuries. Many people regarded it as a psychosis derived from the stresses and strains of personal and social interactions. But in 1911, microbiologist Hideyo Noguchi discovered that the brains of people suffering from this disorder had been extensively damaged by syphilis, a sexually-transmitted disease that has journeyed through history with humans and has appeared in almost all cultures. The subsequent discovery of antibiotics that are effective against *Treponema pallidum,* the spirochete bacterium that causes syphilis, brought to an end the misery of syphilitic psychosis. This success encouraged researchers to study other forms of psychopathology with renewed vigor and hopes for finding effective drug treatments.

Schizophrenia Is the Major Neurobiological Challenge in Psychiatry

Throughout the world, some persons are recognized as unusual because they hear voices that others don't, feel intensely frightened, sense persecution from unseen enemies, and act strangely. People with **schizophrenia** seem to have been a part of all the cultures of the world for centuries, although the historical origins of this disorder continue to be debated (Bark, 2002; Heinrichs, 2003). For many, this state lasts a lifetime; for others, it appears and disappears unpredictably. Of all the psychiatric disorders, schizophrenia has summoned the most intense public interest because it seems such a cruel exaggeration of the human condition. It is also a "public" disorder because many people who suffer from schizophrenia become homeless on our streets.

Epidemiological surveys of schizophrenia reveal a prevalence of 1% to 2% of the population: about 2.2 million people in the United States (Table 16.1). This disorder consumes a disproportionate share of community health resources because of its chronic and overwhelming character.

Schizophrenia is characterized by an unusual array of symptoms

Emil Kraepelin
(1856–1926)

The modern story of schizophrenia starts with Emil Kraepelin, a distinguished German psychiatrist whose book *Dementia Praecox and Paraphrenia* (1919) became the cornerstone of this field. Kraepelin described numerous clinical features common to the varied forms of schizophrenia: paranoia, grandiose delusions, auditory hallucinations, abnormal emotional regulation, and bizarre disturbances of thought. Kraepelin's use of the term *dementia praecox* embodied his view that this disorder begins during adolescence (*praecox* comes from the Latin for "early") and moves relentlessly to a chronic state of cognitive impairment (*dementia* comes from the Latin *de,* "away from," and *mens,* "mind"). Kraepelin believed the cause of the disease to be partly genetic.

The term *schizophrenia* (from the Greek *schizein,* "to split," and *phren,* "mind") was introduced by a contemporary of Kraepelin: Eugen Bleuler. In his monograph *Dementia Praecox; or, The Group of Schizophrenias* (Bleuler, 1950), which was originally published in 1911, Bleuler examined more closely the underlying psychological processes

TABLE 16.1 *Standardized Six-Month and Lifetime Prevalence of DIS[a]/DSM IV Disorders in Persons 18 Years and Older*

Disorders	Rate (%) Previous 6 months	Rate (%) Lifetime
Any psychiatric disorder covered	19.1	32.2
Substance use disorders	6.0	16.4
Alcohol abuse or dependence	4.7	13.3
Drug abuse or dependence	2.0	5.9
Schizophrenia	0.9	1.5
Affective disorders	5.8	8.3
Manic episode	0.5	0.8
Major depressive episode	3.0	5.8
Minor depression	—	3.3
Anxiety disorders	8.9	14.6
Phobia	7.7	12.5
Panic	0.8	1.6
Obsessive–compulsive disorder	1.5	2.5

Note: The rates are standardized to the age, sex, and race distribution of the 1980 noninstitutionalized population of the United States aged 18 years and older.

[a]Diagnostic Interview Schedule

TABLE 16.2 *Features of Schizophrenia*

Positive symptoms	Negative symptoms
Hallucinations, most often auditory	Social withdrawal
Delusions of grandeur, persecution, etc.	Flat affect (blunted emotional responses)
Disordered thought processes	Anhedonia (loss of pleasurable feelings)
Bizarre behaviors	Reduced motivation, poor focus on tasks
	Alogia (reduced speech output)
	Catatonia (reduced movement)

**Eugen Bleuler
(1857–1939)**

of schizophrenia. He identified the key symptom as **dissociative thinking**, a major impairment in the logical structure of thought. Bleuler also described a mix of accompanying symptoms, including loosened associations, autism, affective disturbance, delusions, and hallucinations.

More-modern researchers, starting with Kurt Schneider (1959), have worked toward more-objective and reliable definitions of the symptomatology of schizophrenia, and have tended to focus on first-rank symptoms, including (1) auditory hallucinations, (2) highly personalized delusions, and (3) changes in affect. Some investigators have proposed a major division of schizophrenic symptoms into two separate groups: positive and negative (Table 16.2) (Andreasen, 1991). The term **positive symptoms** refers to abnormal behavioral states that have been *gained;* examples include hallucinations, delusions, and excited motor behavior. The term **negative symptoms** refers to abnormality that results from normal functions that have been *lost*—for example, slow and impoverished thought and speech, emotional and social withdrawal, blunted affect. The blunted emotions of those who suffer from schizophrenia may be apparent only in how well they *express* themselves in facial and body signals because they report experiencing very strong emotions (Kring, 1999). Because positive and negative symptoms respond differently to drug treatments, they may arise from different neural abnormalities.

**COMPETING
HYPOTHESES**

Schizophrenia has a heritable component

For many years genetic studies of schizophrenia were controversial, although the notion of inheritance of mental illness is quite old. Some of the bickering related to a failure of early researchers to acknowledge that environmental influences are major modifiers of gene actions. For any genotype there is often a large range of alternative outcomes that are determined by both developmental and environmental factors.

The basic aim of studies in this area is to understand the role of genetic factors in causing and maintaining schizophrenic states, potentially allowing early identification and aid for the population at risk.

Family studies If schizophrenia is inherited, relatives of patients with schizophrenia should show a higher incidence of the disorder than is found in the general population. In addition, the risk of schizophrenia among relatives should increase with the closeness of the relationship because close relatives share a greater number of genes. In general, parents and siblings of people with schizophrenia have a higher risk of being or becoming schizophrenic than do individuals in the general population (Figure 16.1) (Gottesman, 1991). The risk is greater in cases of closer biological relatedness. However, the mode of inheritance of schizo-

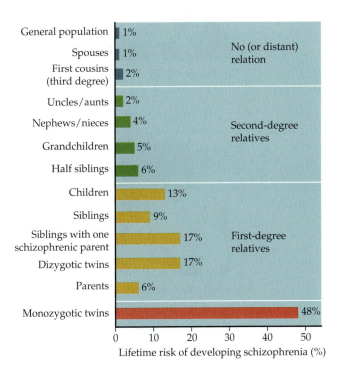

16.1 The Heritability of Schizophrenia The more closely related a person is to a patient with schizophrenia, the greater are his or her chances of also developing schizophrenia. (After Gottesman, 1991.)

**GENES AND
BEHAVIOR**

Irving Gottesman

E. Fuller Torrey

Elaine Walker

phrenia is not simple; that is, it does not involve a single recessive or dominant gene (Tamminga and Schulz, 1991). Most likely, multiple genes play a role in the emergence of schizophrenia.

It is easy to find fault with family studies. First, they confuse hereditary and experiential factors because members of a family share both. Second, the data usually depend on the recollections of relatives whose memories are likely to be clouded by zealous efforts to attribute blame for the disorder. "Funny" departed aunts and uncles are easily designated as the agents responsible for the mental disorder.

Twin studies   In twins, nature provides researchers with what seem to be the perfect conditions for a genetic experiment. Human twins from the same fertilized egg—called **monozygotic** (*identical*) twins—share an identical set of genes. Twins from two different eggs—**dizygotic** (*fraternal*) twins—like other full siblings, have only half of their genes in common.

When both individuals of a twin pair suffer from schizophrenia, they are described as being **concordant** for this trait. If only one member of the pair exhibits the disorder, the pair is described as **discordant.** Irving Gottesman and collaborators have shown that, whereas about 50% of monozygotic twin pairs who show schizophrenia are concordant for the disorder, the rate of concordance for dizygotic twins is only about 17% (see Figure 16.1) (Cardno and Gottesman 2000; Gottesman, 1991). The significantly higher concordance rate among monozygotic twins (who are twice as closely related genetically as dizygotic twins are) is strong evidence of a genetic factor. After all, environmental variables like family structure and socioeconomic stress would presumably be comparable for the two kinds of twins.

Even with identical twins, however, the concordance rate for schizophrenia is only about 50%. What accounts for the discordance of the other 50% of monozygotic twins? The answer to this question could provide crucial clues about the environmental and developmental determinants of schizophrenia, and factors that protect against its emergence in susceptible people. In studying discordant cases, E. Fuller Torrey noted that the twin who went on to develop schizophrenia tended to be the one who was more abnormal throughout life. The symptomatic twin frequently weighed less at birth and had an early developmental history that included more instances of physiological distress (Torrey et al., 1994; Wahl, 1976). During development, this twin was more submissive, tearful, and sensitive than the identical sibling, and he was often viewed by his parents as being more vulnerable.

During childhood the developmental difficulties of twins who later suffer from schizophrenia are reflected in behavioral, cognitive, and other neurological signs, such as impairments in motor coordination (Torrey et al., 1994). Elaine Walker found that these early signs are sufficiently evident that observers watching home films of children can pick out the child who went on to suffer from schizophrenia in adulthood with uncanny accuracy (Walker, 1991).

These sorts of behavioral distinctions can be objectively measured by means of various neuropsychological tests. For example, eye-tracking measurements, in which eye movements are recorded while following a moving target on a computer screen, are quite abnormal in patients with schizophrenia (Levy et al., 1993; Stuve et al., 1997). Patients with schizophrenia tend to be unable to use normal smooth movements of the eyes to follow the moving target, and instead show an intrusion of the rapid, jerky eye movements called *saccades* (Figure 16.2).

Adoption studies   Studies of adopted persons who have schizophrenia have confirmed the significance of genetic factors in the disorder. The biological parents of adoptees who suffer from schizophrenia are far more likely to have suffered from this disorder than are the adopting parents (Kety et al., 1975, 1994).

Studies of families, twins, and adoptees provide consistent evidence that genetics contributes to the incidence of schizophrenia. But many questions remain unanswered: (1) How is the disorder transmitted? (2) What is being inherited? (3) What

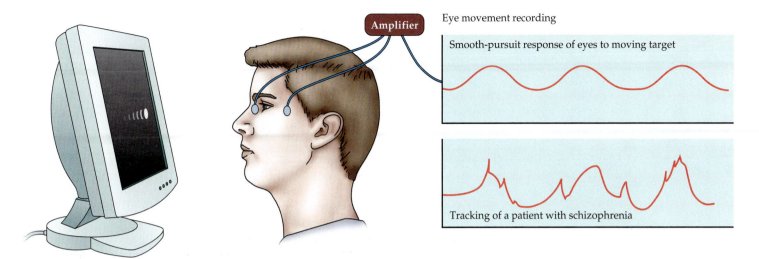

Eye movement recording

Smooth-pursuit response of eyes to moving target

Tracking of a patient with schizophrenia

16.2 Eye Tracking in Patients with Schizophrenia versus Normal People Patients with schizophrenia have greater difficulty making smooth pursuit movements with their eyes than normal people do. Eye movement recordings indicate that the eyes of people with schizophrenia move in jerky saccades rather than smoothly tracking the moving object.

genes are related to this disorder, and what processes do they control? It has proven difficult to identify any single gene that causes schizophrenia to develop (Faraone and Tsuang, 1985) or increases susceptibility (Brzustowicz et al., 2000; Levinson et al., 2002; Mowry et al., 2004). In fact, genetic analyses have suggested that genes influencing the development of schizophrenia are scattered across all but 8 of the 23 pairs of human chromosomes (Shastry, 2002). Nonetheless, a few genes have been identified that appear to be abnormal in a substantial proportion of cases of schizophrenia. These include the genes encoding neuregulin 1, which participates in NMDA, GABA, and ACh receptor regulation; dysbindin, which is implicated in synaptic plasticity; catechol-O-methyltransferase (COMT), which is involved in dopamine production; and G72, which is thought to contribute to glutamatergic activity (Kennedy et al., 2003). In the sections that follow we will discuss some of the systems in which these genes may exert their effects. But researchers speculate that many other genes may be involved in schizophrenia pathogenesis as well, including genes involved in myelination and glial cell functioning (Tkachev et al., 2003).

GENES AND BEHAVIOR

An interesting twist is the suggestion that paternal age is a risk factor in schizophrenia: Older fathers are more likely than younger men to have children with schizophrenia (Malaspina et al., 2002). It is thought that because the sperm of older men are the product of more cell divisions than the sperm of younger men, they have thus had more opportunity to accumulate mutations caused by errors in copying the chromosomes; these mutations may contribute to the development of schizophrenia in some cases.

The brains of some patients with schizophrenia show structural changes

Because in many patients the symptoms of schizophrenia are so marked and persistent, investigators hypothesized that the brains of people with this illness would show distinctive and measurable structural anomalies (Trimble, 1991). During the past century, postmortem studies have occasionally yielded exciting findings along these lines, but the brains used were usually from patients who had died at an advanced age, or who had been hospitalized and medicated for many years, so it was difficult to establish that any structural differences observed were exclusively due to the illness, rather than the result of normal aging or side effects of medication. The advent of CT and MRI scans has made it possible to study brain anatomy in liv-

(a) **Males**

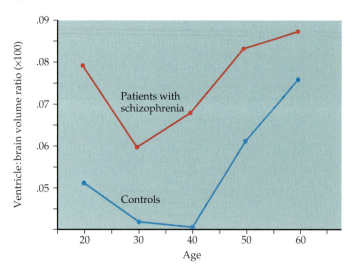

(b) **Females**

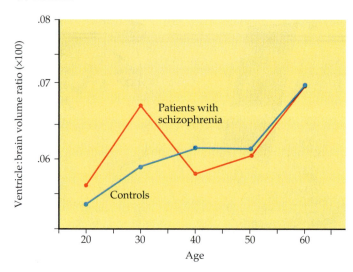

Nancy Andreasen

MRI brain images of twins discordant for schizophrenia

35-year-old female identical twins

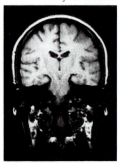

Well   Affected

28-year-old male identical twins

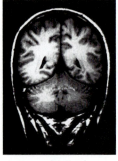
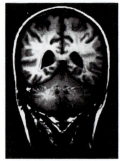

Well   Affected

16.3 Ventricular Enlargement in Schizophrenia   (a) The volume of the cerebral ventricles, relative to overall brain volume, is greater in male patients with schizophrenia than in control subjects. (b) This difference is also seen in some female patients. (After Hyde and Weinberger, 1990.)

ing patients at all stages of their illness (Hyde and Weinberger, 1990), and significant, consistent differences in brain structure have indeed been found in the brains of patients with schizophrenia, particularly in the size of the cerebral ventricles.

Ventricular abnormalities   Studies of patients with schizophrenia have consistently revealed an enlargement of cerebral ventricles, especially the lateral ventricles (Figure 16.3) (Hyde and Weinberger, 1990). Ventricular enlargement is not related to length of illness or to duration of hospitalization. Patients with this anatomical characteristic form a distinct subgroup, in which the extent of ventricular enlargement predicts responsiveness to antipsychotic drugs (Garver et al., 2000; D. R. Weinberger et al., 1980). Patients with more-enlarged ventricles tend to show poorer response to these drugs.

Neuropsychiatrist Nancy Andreasen found in MRI studies that enlargement of the ventricles is a static trait in patients, remaining for many years after the initial onset of the disease (Andreasen, 1994). Studies of identical twins discordant for schizophrenia have yielded startlingly clear results: Twins with schizophrenia have decidedly enlarged lateral ventricles compared to the well twins, in whom the ventricles are of normal size (Figure 16.4) (Torrey et al., 1994).

Limbic system abnormalities   Studying twins also revealed that more than 75% of discordant pairs show a marked difference in the size of the hippocampus and the amygdala. These structures are smaller in the twin with schizophrenia. This observation suggests that the ventricular enlargement in patients with schizophrenia arises from atrophy or destruction of adjacent neural tissue. When brain cells in the regions adjacent to the cerebral ventricles shrink or die, the ventricles expand to fill those regions. Some of

16.4 Identical Genes, Different Fates   Although each member of this pair of monozygotic twins has the same genes, only one of the twins (the one with larger ventricles) developed schizophrenia. (After Torrey et al., 1994; MRIs courtesy of Drs. E. Fuller Torrey and Daniel Weinberger.)

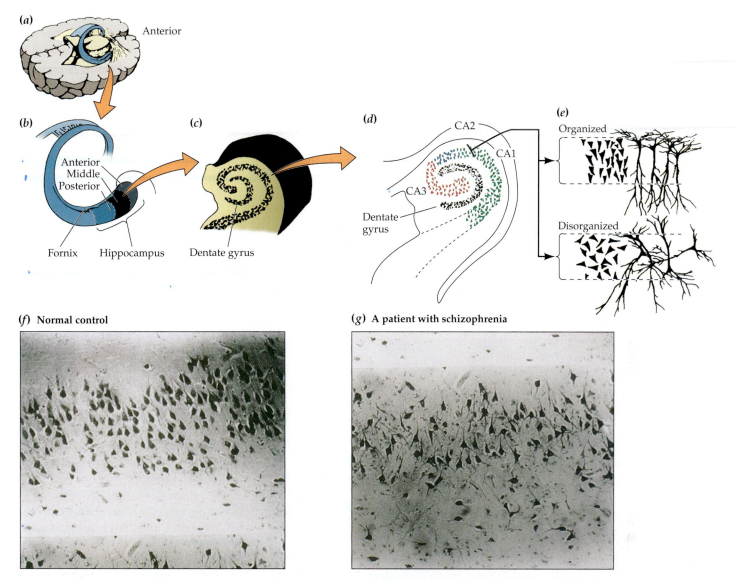

16.5 Cellular Disarray of the Hippocampus in Chronic Schizophrenia (*a*) This horizontal section of the cerebral hemispheres shows the location of the hippocampus. (*b*) Enlargements of the hippocampus and fornix show the location of anterior, middle, and posterior hippocampal segments. (*c*) The hippocampus and dentate gyrus are enlarged in this cross section. (*d*) The hippocampus is subdivided into three regions: CA1, CA2, and CA3. (*e*) Orientations of the pyramidal cells of a control subject (*upper*) and a patient with schizophrenia (*lower*) are compared in these hippocampal cross sections. (*f, g*) Histological cross sections show differences in tissue between a normal control (*f*) and a patient with schizophrenia (*g*). (After Kovelman and Scheibel, 1984; *f* and *g* courtesy of Arnold Scheibel.)

these changes might arise early in development, even in the prenatal period (Mednick et al., 1994).

Neuropathological studies of the limbic systems of patients with schizophrenia have revealed differences between patients and controls in several areas, including the hippocampus, amygdala, and parahippocampal regions. Kovelman and Scheibel (1984), comparing the brains of chronic sufferers of schizophrenia with those of medical patients of the same age that did not exhibit brain pathology, especially noted changes in the hippocampus of the former.

Figure 16.5 shows an example of these cellular differences. The hippocampal pyramidal cells of chronic sufferers of schizophrenia exhibit a characteristic disorientation (see Figure 16.5e), possibly resulting from abnormal synaptic arrangements of both the inputs and outputs of these cells. The degree of cellular disorientation reportedly reflects the severity of the disorder: The most impaired individuals exhibit the greatest disorganization (Conrad et al., 1991).

NEURAL PLASTICITY

The cellular derangement of schizophrenia probably arises during early cell development, and it has been hypothesized that maternal exposure to an influenza infection during the second trimester of pregnancy may be a root cause (Machón et al., 1997). These abnormalities of cellular arrangement in the hippocampus also are said to resemble those of mutant mice that show disordered neurogenesis in the hippocampus (A. B. Scheibel and Conrad, 1993). Given that we now know that humans make new neurons throughout life, especially in the hippocampus (see Chapter 7), abnormal neurogenesis or disordered integration of newly born cells could be a contributing factor in the development of schizophrenia in humans. Limbic system abnormalities are not limited to the hippocampus; other studies have noted differences between patients and controls in the entorhinal cortex, parahippocampal cortex, and cingulate cortex (Shapiro, 1993).

Regional anatomical abnormalities Several studies of long-term sufferers of schizophrenia have noted a marked shrinkage of the cerebellar vermis, and this finding cannot be explained by prolonged use of antipsychotic drugs (Heath et al., 1979; Loeber et al., 2001; Snider, 1982). Chronic sufferers of schizophrenia whose disorder started early in life also have a thicker corpus callosum, both in anatomical preparations and in some CT scans (Bigelow et al., 1983). One study, examining postmortem materials, found evidence that neuronal migration during the fetal period had been abnormal in the frontal cortex of patients with schizophrenia (Akbarian et al., 1996).

Numerous reports have indicated that patients with schizophrenia tend to be impaired on neuropsychological tests that are sensitive to frontal cortical lesions. These findings raise the possibility of frontal cortical abnormality as an important component of schizophrenia. Several studies have reported a loss of gray matter in schizophrenia patients (Suzuki et al., 2002; P. M. Thompson et al., 2001), with a wave of cortical gray matter loss occurring during adolescence in the case of early-onset schizophrenia (Figure 16.6).

Although some researchers have claimed that the frontal lobes are especially affected, other studies have failed to find major abnormalities of the frontal cortex (Highley et al., 2001; Wible et al., 1995), suggesting that structural differences in the frontal lobes, if present at all, must be quite subtle. So if the frontal lobes of people suffering from schizophrenia are not very different in their *structure*, what about the *activity* of the frontal cortex?

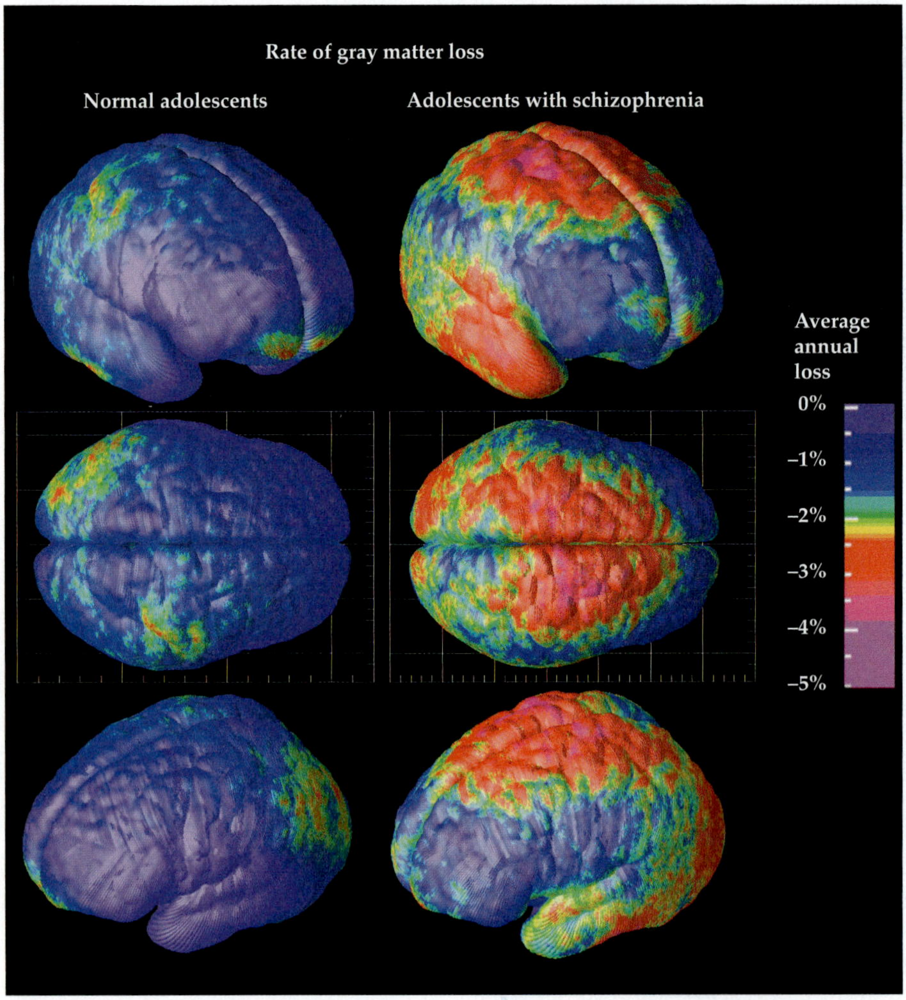

Rate of gray matter loss

Normal adolescents   **Adolescents with schizophrenia**

Average annual loss

0%
−1%
−2%
−3%
−4%
−5%

16.6 Accelerated Loss of Gray Matter in Adolescents with Schizophrenia Although neuron loss is a normal part of development, adolescents with schizophrenia (*right*) lose gray matter over wide regions at a faster rate than do unaffected adolescents (*left*). (From Thomson et al. 2001; courtesy of Paul Thomson.)

Functional maps reveal differences in schizophrenic brains

Functional-imaging technologies, such as positron emission tomography (PET) and functional magnetic resonance imaging (fMRI) (introduced in Chapter 2), allow researchers to visualize the activity of the living human brain with impressive clarity. Early observations using PET indicated that patients with schizophrenia show relatively less metabolic activity in the frontal lobes (compared with their posterior lobes) than do normal subjects (Buchsbaum et al., 1984). This observation, referred to as the **hypofrontality hypothesis,** generated controversy and fueled interest in the role of the frontal lobes in schizophrenia (D. R. Weinberger et al., 1994).

In discordant identical twins, frontal blood flow levels are low only in the twin who suffers from schizophrenia (Andreasen et al., 1986; Morihisa and McAnulty, 1985). Furthermore, functional-imaging studies suggest that in schizophrenia, the functional lateralization of the cerebral hemispheres may be altered, with the left hemisphere showing more activity than the right during resting states (Gur et al., 1987), at least in the frontal lobe (K. F. Berman and Weinberger, 1990).

Some experiments show the hypofrontality effect only during difficult cognitive tasks that particularly depend on the frontal lobes for accurate performance, such as the Wisconsin Card Sorting Task (Figure 16.7). Unlike control subjects, subjects with schizophrenia show no increase in their prefrontal activation above basal levels during the task (D. R. Weinberger et al., 1994). Treatment with drugs that alleviate symptoms of schizophrenia, discussed in the next section, is associated with increased activation of frontal cortex (Honey et al., 1999). Neurons in the frontal cortex of patients with schizophrenia have dendrites with a reduced density of synaptic spines compared to control subjects (L. A. Glantz and Lewis, 2000), which may contribute to a less active frontal cortex.

The brains of patients with schizophrenia show neurochemical changes

It is difficult to separate the neurochemical events that are primary causes of a psychiatric disorder from those that are secondary effects. Some secondary effects arise from the profound impairments of social behavior and may range from dietary limitations to prolonged stress. Treatment variables, especially the long-term use of antipsychotic drugs, can mask or distort primary causes because they frequently produce marked changes in the physiology and biochemistry of brain and body. Another major problem in neurochemical research of schizophrenia is the definition of schizophrenia itself. Is it a single disorder, or many disorders with different origins and outcomes?

Although drugs such as LSD and mescaline produce some perceptual, cognitive, and emotional changes that resemble psychosis in some ways, the resemblance is superficial at best. For instance, drug-induced psychoses often involve confusion, disorientation, and outright delirium; these are not typical symptoms of schizophrenia. And the hallucinations produced by these drugs are usually visual, in contrast to the predominantly auditory hallucinations of schizophrenia. Patients with schizophrenia who are given LSD report that the experience produced by the drug is very different from the experiences of their disorder. But one drug state—amphetamine psychosis—comes much closer than the rest to replicating the schizophrenic state.

The dopamine hypothesis As a consequence of the development of drug tolerance (see Chapter 4), some daily users of amphetamine reach a point at which they are taking astonishingly high doses—as much as 3000 mg per day—in order to experience the drug's euphoriant and stimulant effects. (Compare this with the normal 5 mg dose used to prolong wakefulness.) Many individuals taking these large doses

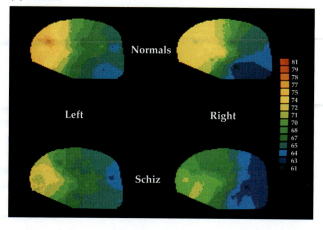

(a) At rest

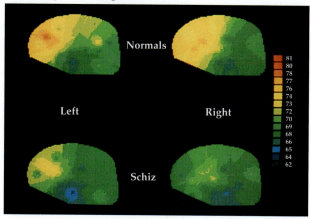

(b) During card-sorting task

16.7 Hypofrontality in Schizophrenia The frontal cortex is less activated in patients with schizophrenia ("Schiz") compared to their twins who don't have schizophrenia ("Normals") either at rest (*a*) or during the Wisconsin Card Sorting Task (*b*), a task that is very difficult for people with damage to the frontal lobes. Areas of high activation are shown in red and yellow. (Courtesy of Karen Berman.)

of amphetamine develop symptoms of paranoia, often involving delusions of persecution with auditory hallucinations, and exhibit suspiciousness and bizarre motor behavior. These phenomena bear a striking resemblance to the symptoms of schizophrenia and are referred to as **amphetamine psychosis.** Might there be an endogenous substance similar to amphetamine at play in schizophrenia? Several investigators have argued that phenylethylamine (PEA)—a substance with amphetamine-like properties—is produced in small quantities by the metabolism of norepinephrine in patients with schizophrenia.

Amphetamine also exacerbates the symptoms of schizophrenia. Neurochemically, amphetamine promotes the release of catecholamines, particularly dopamine, and prolongs the action of the released transmitter by blocking reuptake (see Chapter 4). Rapid relief from amphetamine psychosis is provided by injection of the dopamine antagonist **chlorpromazine** (trade name Thorazine), a substance that brings us to the second part of the story of the dopamine hypothesis.

Chlorpromazine is not just an antidote to amphetamine psychosis. Chlorpromazine and its family members—the **phenothiazines**—were the first identified class of effective antischizophrenic drugs (also known as *neuroleptic* or *antipsychotic* drugs). The introduction of chlorpromazine ushered in a neuropharmacological revolution during the 1950s, relieving symptoms for millions of sufferers and freeing them from long-term beds in psychiatric hospitals around the world. In the intervening years, researchers have learned that the phenothiazines exert their specific antipsychotic effects by blocking postsynaptic receptor sites for dopamine—specifically the dopamine D_2 receptor subtype—associated with the terminals of the mesolimbic dopamine system (see Chapter 4 for a review of the major dopaminergic projections of the brain).

We now know that all of the various antipsychotic drugs that are classified as **typical neuroleptics**—the phenothiazines, butyrophenones like haloperidol (Haldol), and others—feature this antagonist activity at D_2 receptors (Figure 16.8). In fact, the clinical

16.8 Antipsychotic Drugs That Affect Dopamine Receptors   Drugs vary widely in the affinity with which they bind to various neurotransmitter receptors. Drugs that block dopamine receptors, specifically the D_2 variety (purple), are more effective at combating symptoms of schizophrenia. Atypical neuroleptics such as clozapine tend to block $5HT_2$ receptors (green) more effectively than they block D_2 receptors. (After Seeman, 1990.)

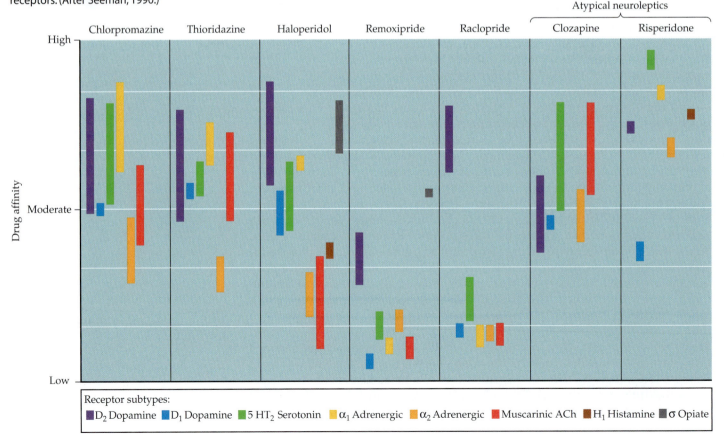

Receptor subtypes:
■ D_2 Dopamine   ■ D_1 Dopamine   ■ 5 HT_2 Serotonin   ■ $α_1$ Adrenergic   ■ $α_2$ Adrenergic   ■ Muscarinic ACh   ■ H_1 Histamine   ■ σ Opiate

potency of a typical neuroleptic can be predicted from its affinity for D_2 receptors, giving rise to the **dopamine hypothesis:** the idea that schizophrenia results from either excessive levels of synaptic dopamine, or from excessive postsynaptic sensitivity to dopamine. Over the years, many other clinical and experimental findings have bolstered the dopamine hypothesis; for example, treating patients who suffer from Parkinson's disease with L-dopa (the metabolic precursor of dopamine) may induce schizophrenia-like symptoms, presumably by boosting the synaptic availability of dopamine.

Criticisms of a dopamine model of schizophrenia began to emerge in the 1980s (Alpert and Friedhoff, 1980). Clinical observations revealed that some patients with schizophrenia show no changes when treated with drugs that affect dopamine. The subsequent development of a new generation of antischizophrenic drugs raised additional problems for the dopamine hypothesis. Called **atypical neuroleptics,** these drugs generally don't have the selective high affinity for dopamine receptors that is the hallmark of the typical neuroleptics. Atypical neuroleptic drugs such as **clozapine** selectively block serotonin receptors (especially $5HT_{2A}$ receptors), as well as other receptor types, including D_2 dopamine receptors (see Figure 16.8).

Atypical neuroleptics are just as effective as the older generation of drugs in relieving the positive symptoms of schizophrenia, but they are much more effective than the older drugs in relieving the negative symptoms of schizophrenia. Furthermore, the atypical neuroleptics are less likely to induce the troubling motor disorders that characterize long-term treatment with typical neuroleptics (see Box 16.1). An additional difficulty for the dopamine hypothesis is the report that clozapine can *increase* dopamine release in frontal cortex (Hertel et al., 1999)—hardly what we would expect if excess dopaminergic activity lies at the root of schizophrenia. In fact, it seems that supplementing neuroleptic treatments with L-dopa (thereby increasing dopaminergic activity) actually has a beneficial effect on schizophrenic symptoms (Jaskiw and Popli, 2004).

COMPETING HYPOTHESES

CLINICAL ISSUE

BOX 16.1 Long-Term Effects of Antipsychotic Drugs

Few people would deny that neuroleptic drugs have had a revolutionary impact on the treatment of schizophrenia. With such treatment, many people who might otherwise have been in mental hospitals their whole lives can take care of themselves in nonhospital settings. Drugs of this class can justly be regarded as "miracle drugs."

Unfortunately, traditional antipsychotic drugs can have other, undesirable effects. Soon after beginning to take these drugs, some users develop maladaptive motor symptoms (**dyskinesia,** from the Greek *dys,* "bad" and *kinesis,* "motion"). Although many of these symptoms are transient and disappear when the dosage of drug is reduced, some drug-induced motor changes emerge only after prolonged drug treatment—after months, sometimes years—and are effectively permanent. This condition, called **tardive dyskinesia** (the Latin *tardus* means "slow"), is characterized by repetitive, involuntary movements, especially involving the face, mouth, lips, and tongue. Elaborate uncontrollable movements of the tongue are

particularly prominent, including incessant rolling movements and sucking or smacking of the lips. Some patients show twisting and sudden jerking movements of the arms or legs (D. E. Casey, 1989).

The underlying mechanism for tardive dyskinesia continues to be a puzzle. Some researchers claim that it arises from the chronic blocking of dopamine receptors, which results in receptor site supersensitivity. Critics of this view, however, point out that tardive dyskinesia frequently takes a long time to develop and tends to be irreversible—a time course that is different from dopamine receptor supersensitivity. In addition, there is no difference in D_1 or D_2 receptor binding between patients with tardive dyskinesia and those without these symptoms.

A GABA deficiency hypothesis of tardive dyskinesia was offered by Fibiger and Lloyd (1984). They believed that tardive dyskinesia is the result of drug-induced destruction of GABA neurons in the corpus striatum. Neuroleptic-induced changes in enzymes related to GABA have

been observed in experimental animals. A noradrenergic hypothesis of this disorder has also been presented, on the basis of evidence that the concentration of norepinephrine in the cerebrospinal fluid is correlated with tardive dyskinesia (Kaufmann et al., 1986).

Long-term treatment with traditional antipsychotic drugs has another unusual effect: Prolonged blockage of dopamine receptors seems to increase the number of dopamine receptors and lead to receptor supersensitivity. In some patients, discontinuation of the drugs or a lowering of dosage results in a sudden, marked increase in positive symptoms of schizophrenia, such as delusions or hallucinations. This **supersensitivity psychosis** can often be reversed by administration of increased dosages of dopamine receptor–blocking agents. A newer generation of antipsychotic drugs, the atypical neuroleptics discussed in the text, have fewer side effects, which may make schizophrenia patients more likely to continue self-medication.

Studies of dopamine metabolites in blood, cerebrospinal fluid, and urine have provided inconsistent results regarding the possible hyperfunctioning of dopamine terminals. For example, many patients with schizophrenia have normal levels of dopamine metabolites in cerebrospinal fluid. Some postmortem and PET studies of schizophrenic brains reveal an increase in dopamine receptors, especially the D_2 type (Breier, Su, et al., 1997; K. L. Davis et al., 1991), even in patients who have been off of neuroleptic drugs for some time (Okubo et al., 1997). But PET studies of D_2 receptor density in people who suffer from schizophrenia are inconsistent, as are efforts to relate a D_2 receptor gene to schizophrenia.

Another problem with the dopamine hypothesis is the lack of correspondence between the time at which drugs block dopamine (quite rapidly, within hours) and the behavioral changes that signal the clinical effectiveness of the drug (usually on the order of weeks). Thus the relation of dopamine to schizophrenia may be more complex than is envisioned by the simple model of hyperactive dopamine synapses.

The glutamate hypothesis   Initially developed to produce a *dissociative* anesthetic state (one in which an animal is insensitive to pain but shows some types of arousal or responsiveness), **phencyclidine (PCP)** was soon found to be a potent **psychotomimetic;** that is, PCP produces phenomena strongly resembling both the positive and negative symptoms of schizophrenia. Users of PCP often experience auditory hallucinations, strange depersonalization, and disorientation; and they may commit intense assaultive behavior as a consequence of their drug-induced delusions. Prolonged psychotic states can develop with chronic use of this substance.

As illustrated in Figure 16.9, PCP acts as a noncompetitive NMDA receptor antagonist. PCP blocks the NMDA receptor's central calcium channel, thereby preventing the endogenous ligand—glutamate—from having its usual effects. Treating monkeys

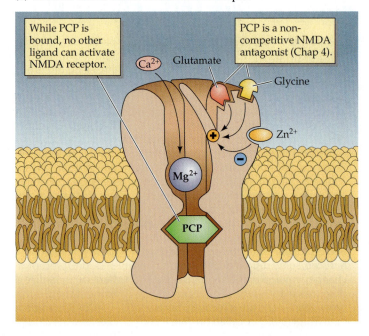

(a) Effects of PCP on various receptors

Serum PCP concentration (μM)	Mechanisms affected by PCP	Clinical effects
0.01		
	NMDA receptor	Psychosis
0.1		
	NE/DA/5-HT reuptake	Anesthesia
	σ Opiate receptor	
1.0		Coma
	K⁺ channel	
	Na⁺ channel	
	Nicotinic ACh receptor	
10.0		
	μ Opiate receptor	
	Muscarinic ACh receptor	
	Acetylcholinesterase	
100.0		
	GABA receptors	
1000.0		

(b) A model of PCP action on the NMDA receptor

16.9 The Effects of PCP on the NMDA Receptor   (*a*) The serum concentrations of PCP that elicit clinical effects are the same concentrations that result in PCP binding of the NMDA receptor. (*b*) PCP acts as a noncompetitive antagonist at NMDA receptors (see Chapter 4). This means that as long as PCP is bound to the receptor, the endogenous ligands may bind but can have no effect, rendering the receptor nonfunctional. The resemblance of PCP-induced psychosis to schizophrenia has prompted the development of a glutamate hypothesis of schizophrenia.

with PCP for 2 weeks produces a schizophrenia-like syndrome, including poor performance on a test that is sensitive to prefrontal damage (Jentsch et al., 1997). Other antagonists of NMDA receptors, such as ketamine, have similar effects. These and other observations therefore have prompted researchers to advance a **glutamate hypothesis of schizophrenia** (Moghaddam and Adams, 1998), proposing that schizophrenia results from an underactivation of glutamate receptors (Coyle et al., 2003).

Interestingly, differences in NMDA receptor understimulation produce a predictable range of phenomena that maps onto the spectrum of symptoms experienced by patients with schizophrenia of varying severity. These symptoms range from memory disturbances without frank psychosis when NMDA receptors are only mildly understimulated, to a clinical syndrome very much like acute schizophrenia in cases where NMDA receptor activation is more severely reduced. Neuropathological changes tend to appear when NMDA receptor underactivation is sustained over long periods (Farber, 2003).

If blockade or reduced activity of NMDA receptors is part of the pathogenesis of schizophrenia, you might ask, Would compounds that increase glutamatergic activity be effective antischizophrenic drugs? Although selective NMDA receptor agonists tend to produce seizures, other glutamatergic candidates are in development. In particular, drugs that modulate the activity of the metabotropic glutamate (mGlu) receptors may prove useful in schizophrenia (Chavez-Noriega et al., 2002; Moghaddam, in press). There are at least eight different subtypes of metabotropic receptors for glutamate, providing several promising targets for drug development. For example, it appears that some types of mGlu receptors can directly modulate NMDA receptor activity; alternatively, other mGlu receptors may interact with dopaminergic systems (Mueller et al., 2004).

**COMPETING
HYPOTHESES**

An integrative psychobiological model of schizophrenia emphasizes the interaction of multiple factors

In some ways, research on schizophrenia has given us many pieces of a large puzzle whose overall appearance is still unknown. Some efforts at integrating the many psychological and biological findings in the field have resulted in important views about the origins of schizophrenia. One influential model, presented by Mirsky and Duncan (1986), views schizophrenia as an outcome of the interaction of genetic, developmental, and stress factors. According to this model, at each life stage specific features contribute to an enhanced vulnerability to schizophrenia.

Genetic influences leading to "brain abnormalities" may provide the basic neurological substrate for schizophrenia. Birth complications that deprive the baby of oxygen—often evident in patients with schizophrenia (Rosso et al., 2000)—may exaggerate such abnormalities. Mirsky and Duncan suggested that through childhood and adolescence, neurological deficits are manifested by behaviors such as impaired cognitive skills, attention deficits, irritability, and delayed gross motor development.

According to this model, the emergence of schizophrenia and related disorders depends on whether the compromised brain is subjected to environmental stressors (Figure 16.10). For example, city life is considered more stressful than rural life, and people raised in a city are more likely to develop schizophrenia than are rural dwellers (Mortensen et al., 1999). The magnitude of brain abnormalities in vulnerable individuals determines how much stress is needed to produce a schizophrenic disorder. Schizophrenia emerges when the combination of stress and brain abnormalities exceeds a threshold value. People with many schizophrenic brain abnormalities may become symptomatic with relatively minor environmental stresses.

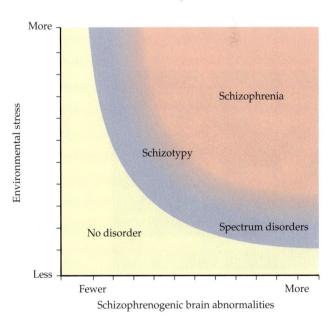

16.10 A Model of the Interaction of Stress and Brain Abnormalities in Schizophrenia Environmental stress and certain brain abnormalities may combine to produce a schizophrenic disorder. Disorders ranging from more mild to more severe are called, respectively, *spectrum disorders, schizotypy,* and *schizophrenia.* (After Mirsky and Duncan, 1986.)

Models like this one suggest the possibility of strategies for decreasing the likelihood of schizophrenia for a child at risk (Häfner, 1998). New biological aids, such as functional brain imaging and genetic tools, might help us identify and understand the at-risk child at a stage early in life, when interventions to reduce stress might avert schizophrenia later in life.

Mood Disorders Are a Major Psychiatric Category

It seems as though no person now alive nor any of our forebears has been a stranger to mood disorders. Many of us experience periods of unhappiness that we commonly describe as depression. In some people, however, an unhappy mood state is more than a passing malaise and occurs over and over with cyclical regularity. This condition is most common in people over 40 years of age, especially women, but can affect people of any age.

Depression is the most prevalent mood disorder

Clinically, **depression** is characterized not by sadness, but by an unhappy mood; loss of interests, energy, and appetite; difficulty in concentration; and restless agitation. Pessimism seems to seep into every act (A. Solomon, 2001). Periods of such **unipolar depression** (i.e., depression that alternates with normal emotional states) can occur with no readily apparent stress. Without treatment, the depression often lasts for several months. Depressive illnesses of this sort are estimated to afflict 13% to 20% of the population at any one time (Cassens et al., 1990). A second major type of mood disorder is **bipolar disorder** (formerly known as *manic–depressive illness*), characterized by repeated fluctuation between depressive periods and episodes of euphoric, sometimes grandiose, positive mood (or *mania*). We will return to discussion of the features of bipolar disorder a little later.

Depression can be lethal; it often leads to suicide. Most estimates indicate that about 80% of all suicide victims are profoundly depressed. Unlike the incidence of schizophrenia, suicide rates show great variability across time, age, and places in the world. Although the trend during the twentieth century in the United States and western Europe showed an overall progressive decline in the incidence of suicide, the great increase in pharmacological treatment of depression in the last two decades appears to have had little effect on suicide rates or the social and economic costs of depression (Greenberg et al., 2003).

Inheritance is an important determinant of depression

Genetic studies of depressive disorders reveal strong hereditary contributions (Moldin et al., 1991). The concordance rate (about 60%) for monozygotic twins is substantially higher than the concordance rate (about 20%) for dizygotic twins (Kendler et al., 1999). The concordance rates for monozygotic twins are similar whether the twins are reared apart or together. Adoption studies show high rates of affective illness in the biological parents compared to the foster parents. Although several early studies implicated specific chromosomes, subsequent linkage studies have failed to identify the locus of any relevant gene. There probably is no single gene for depression.

Functional maps of the brain show changes with depression

PET scans of depressed patients show increases in blood flow in the frontal cortex and the amygdala compared with controls (Figure 16.11) (Drevets, 1998). In addition to increasing in the frontal cortex, blood flow decreases in the parietal and posterior temporal cortex and in the anterior cingulate, systems that have been implicated in attentional networks and language. The increase in blood flow in the amygdala—a structure involved in mediating fear (see Chapter 15)—persists even after the alleviation of depression over time. Patients treated with antidepressants, however, show normal blood flow in the amygdala.

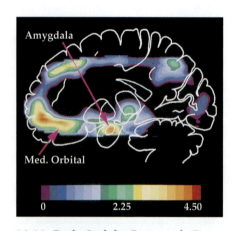

16.11 Brain Activity Patterns in Depression This PET scan reveals increased activity in the frontal cortex and the amygdala of depressed patients. This image is the result of the subtraction of brain scans of control subjects from those of depressed subjects. Areas of highest activation are shown in red and orange. (Courtesy of Wayne C. Drevets.)

Several neurochemical theories attempt to explain depression

Originally developed in response to experimental and clinical observations, the monoamine hypothesis of depression (Schildkraut and Kety, 1967) posits that depressive illness is associated with decreased activity of synapses employing the monoamine transmitters norepinephrine and serotonin.

Support for this hypothesis comes from the clinical effectiveness of two forms of treatment: antidepressant drugs and electroconvulsive shock therapy. Recall from our discussion of antidepressant drugs in Chapter 4 that some of the earliest effective antidepressants were compounds that inhibit **monoamine oxidase**—the type of enzyme that inactivates norepinephrine, dopamine, and serotonin—thus raising the level of monoamines present in synapses. In contrast, the drug **reserpine,** which reduces norepinephrine and serotonin release in the brain, can cause profound depression. But how do these findings relate to the effects of electrically shocking the brain?

Electroconvulsive shock therapy (**ECT**)—the intentional induction of seizures—was originally deployed during the 1930s in a desperate attempt to relieve the symptoms of schizophrenia, but clinical observations soon revealed that it could rapidly reverse severe depression. The advent of antidepressant drugs led to the temporary retirement of this clinical tool. But the need remained for a treatment for patients who don't respond to antidepressant drugs, or who are in imminent danger of committing suicide and need more-rapid relief than is provided by most antidepressant drugs. ECT fulfills these needs, and its use in limited cases of severe depression was resumed.

Although somewhat different from its original form, this treatment still elicits a large-scale seizure (Weiner, 1994). As you might guess, the beneficial effects of ECT appear to be related to its ability to induce the release of monoamine transmitters. As of the 1990s, transcranial magnetic stimulation (TMS; see Chapter 2) is also being touted as a treatment for depression (Gershon et al., 2003). Like ECT, TMS appears to be active in animal models of depression-like learned helplessness, and it appears to alter the metabolism of monoamine transmitters (Ben-Shachar et al., 1997).

CLINICAL ISSUE

The most recent class of antidepressants consists of the selective serotonin reuptake inhibitors (SSRIs), such as Prozac (Table 16.3) (see Chapter 4). In rats, such drugs increase neurogenesis in the hippocampus, which may mediate some of the mood effects of the drugs (Malberg et al., 2000). SSRI treatment also increases the production of brain steroids (Griffin and Mellon, 1999), such as allopregnanolone, which may contribute to the effectiveness of SSRIs by stimulating GABA receptors and producing an anxiolytic effect. Interestingly, psychotherapy and SSRI treatment together are more effective in combating depression than either one is alone (Keller et al., 2000).

Studies of suicide victims show lower concentrations of serotonin or its metabolites in the brain (Asberg et al., 1986). Suicide attempters who show lower levels of serotonin metabolites are ten times more likely to die of suicide later in their lives than are suicide attempters who show higher levels. In addition, a variant version of the gene for the $5HT_{2A}$ receptor is more common in suicide victims than in controls (Du et al., 2000).

TABLE 16.3 *Drugs Used to Treat Depression*

Drug class	Mechanism of action	Examples[a]
Monoamine oxidase inhibitors (MAOIs)	Inhibit the enzyme monoamine oxidase, which breaks down serotonin, norephinephrine, and dopamine	Marplan, Nardil, Parnate
Tricyclics and heterocyclics	Inhibit the reuptake of norepinephrine, serotonin, and/or dopamine	Elavil, Wellbutrin, Aventyl, Ludiomil, Norpramin
Selective serotonin reuptake inhibitors (SSRIs)	Block the reuptake of serotonin, having little effect on norepinephrine or dopamine synapses	Prozac, Paxil, Zoloft

[a]We give here the more commonly used trade names rather than chemical names.

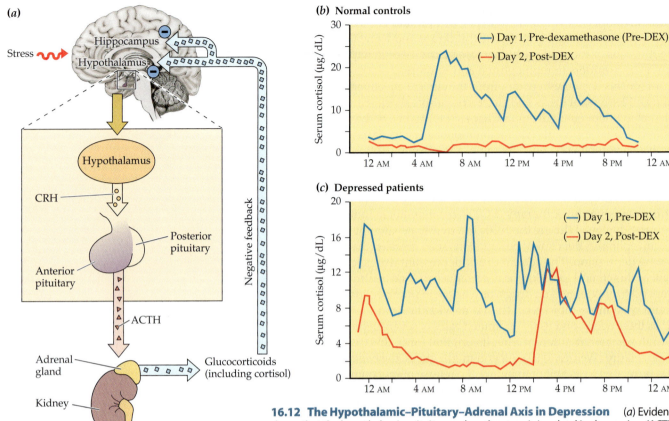

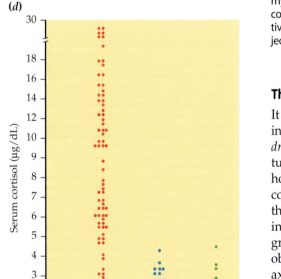

16.12 The Hypothalamic–Pituitary–Adrenal Axis in Depression (*a*) Evidence shows that the hypothalamic–pituitary–adrenal system is involved in depression. (ACTH, adrenocorticotropic hormone; CRH, corticotropin-releasing hormone.) (*b*) The normal circadian rhythm in the secretion of cortisol (day 1) is abolished by treatment with the synthetic glucocorticoid dexamethasone (DEX) (day 2). (*c*) The same dose of dexamethasone is far less effective in depressed patients. (*d*) Circulating cortisol levels are usually higher in depressed subjects than in psychiatric or normal controls. In this plot, each dot represents an individual case.

The hypothalamic–pituitary–adrenal axis is involved in depression

It has been known for some time that people with very high levels of circulating glucocorticoids are prone to depression. This condition, called *Cushing's syndrome*, may come about in several different ways: (1) as a consequence of pituitary tumors that produce excessive amounts of ACTH (adrenocorticotropic hormone), (2) from tumors of the adrenal glands resulting in hypersecretion of cortisol, or (3) from therapeutic treatments with corticosteroid drugs. In more than 85% of patients with Cushing's syndrome, depression appears quite early in the disorder, even before other typical signs, such as obesity or unusual growth and distribution of body hair (Haskett, 1985; Krystal et al., 1990). These observations suggest that dysfunction of the hypothalamic–pituitary–adrenal axis (Figure 16.12*a*) may be involved in depression, perhaps as part of a depression-inducing stress reaction (Heit et al., 1997).

Suicide victims show very high levels of circulating cortisol (Roy, 1992), and hospitalized patients with depression show elevated cortisol levels. These findings suggested that ACTH is released in excessive amounts by the anterior pituitary. It was eventually found that a standard method for assessing hypothalamic–pituitary–adrenal function—the **dexamethasone suppression test**—can double as a biological marker for depression.

Dexamethasone is a potent synthetic corticoid that ordinarily suppresses the early-morning rise in ACTH that is typical in normal people. Generally given late at night, dexamethasone seems to "fool" the hypothalamus into believing that there is a high level of circulating cortisol. In normal individuals, dexamethasone clearly suppresses cortisol release (Figure 16.12b), but in many depressed individuals it fails to have this effect (Figure 16.12c). As depression is relieved, dexamethasone again suppresses cortisol normally.

The normalization is claimed to occur no matter what the cause of relief—elapse of time, psychotherapy, pharmacotherapy, or electroconvulsive shock therapy. One possible mediating mechanism is that in depressed people the cells of the hypothalamus are subject to abnormal excitatory drive from limbic system regions, resulting in sustained release of ACTH. Some evidence suggests that depression causes a reduction of brain corticosteroid receptors, resulting in subnormal negative feedback in this system (Barden et al., 1995).

An intriguing proposal is that stress and the attendant release of glucocorticoids reduce the brain production of neurotrophic factors, such as brain-derived neurotrophic factor (BDNF; see Chapter 7), leading to neuronal atrophy and therefore depression (Duman et al., 1997). According to this hypothesis, drugs that increase serotonergic and/or noradrenergic activity cause an increase in cyclic AMP in the brain, which causes an increase in the production of cAMP responsive element–binding protein (CREB, which will be discussed in Chapter 18) leading to an increase in BDNF release. The BDNF then maintains other brain neurons to alleviate depression. Favoring this theory is evidence that stress reduces BDNF production in the rat hippocampus and that SSRI drugs block this effect. Furthermore, direct infusion of BDNF into the brains of rats provides a distinct antidepressant-like effect in animal models of depression (Shirayama et al., 2002).

COMPETING HYPOTHESES

Why do more females than males suffer from depression?

Studies all over the world show that more women than men suffer from major depression. Epidemiological studies of U.S. sites generally reveal a twofold difference for major depression (Robins and Regier, 1991). Some researchers suggest that the sex difference arises from patterns of help-seeking by males and females—notably, that women use health facilities more than men do. But sex differences in the incidence of depression also are evident in door-to-door surveys (Robins and Regier, 1991), which would appear to rule out the simple explanation that women seek treatment more often than men do.

CLINICAL ISSUE

Several psychosocial explanations have been advanced. One view emphasizes that depression in women arises from the social discrimination that prevents them from achieving mastery by self-assertion. According to this view, inequities lead to dependency, low self-esteem, and depression. Another psychosocial focus leans on the learned-helplessness model (which we will discuss shortly). According to this view, stereotypical images of men and women produce in women a cognitive set of classic feminine values, reinforced by societal expectations, of which helplessness is one dimension.

A genetic interpretation of the gender difference in depression might be that depression is an inherited disorder linked to the X chromosome. But relatives of male and female sufferers of depression show no differences in depression rates (which would be expected with X linkage). Thus, although there is a strong genetic determinant for depression in general, there does not seem to be a genetic basis for sex differences in depression.

COMPETING HYPOTHESES

Some researchers have emphasized gender differences in endocrine physiology. The occurrence of clinical depression often is related to events in the female reproductive cycle—for example, before menstruation, during use of contraceptive pills, following childbirth, and during menopause. Although several hormones have been linked to depression, there is little relation between circulating levels of hormones related to female reproductive physiology and measures of depression.

Epidemiological studies of Amish communities (Egeland and Hostetter, 1983) provide a different slant on the mystery of gender differences in depression. An exhaustive survey of this religious community, which prohibits the use of alcohol and

TABLE 16.4 *Characteristics of Animal Models of Depression*

Model	Activity change	Sensitivity to antidepressants	Decreased social contact
Stress models			
Learned helplessness	+	+	−
Chronic mild stress	−	+	−
Behaviorial despair separation models (e.g., primate separations)	+	+	+
Pharmacological models (e.g., reserpine reversal)	+	+	−
Anatomical models (e.g., olfactory bulbectomy)	+	+	−
Genetic models (e.g., Flinders-sensitive line)	+	+	−

IMPORTANT METHOD

CLINICAL ISSUE

shuns modernity, reveals no sex difference in major depression. One possibility is that in the general population, heavy use of alcohol masks depression in many males, making it appear as if fewer males than females suffer from depression. (Alcoholism is more common in males than in females.)

Animal models aid research on depression

Because a monkey or a cat or a rat can't tell us if it has delusions of persecution or if it hears voices telling it what to do, animal models of schizophrenia are limited. But many of the signs of depression are behaviorally overt—such as decreased social contact, problems with eating, and changes in activity. An animal model for the study of depression can provide the ability to evaluate proposed neurobiological mechanisms, a convenient way to screen potential treatments, and the ability to explore possible causes experimentally (Lachman et al., 1993). Table 16.4 lists the characteristics of animal models used in studies of depression.

In one type of stress model—**learned helplessness**—an animal is exposed to a repetitive stressful stimulus, such as an electrical shock, that it cannot escape. Like depression, learned helplessness has been linked to a decrease in serotonin function (Petty et al., 1994). Removing the olfactory bulb from rodents also creates a model of depression: The animals display irritability, hyperactivity, preferences for alcohol, elevated levels of corticosteroids, and deficiency in passive avoidance conditioning—all of which are reversed by many antidepressants. A genetically developed line of rats—the Flinders-sensitive line—has been proposed as a model of depression because these animals show reduced locomotor activity, reduced body weight, increased REM sleep, learning difficulties, and exaggerated immobility in response to chronic stress (Overstreet, 1993). These varied animal models may be useful in finding the essential mechanisms that cause and maintain depression.

Sleep characteristics change in affective disorders

The disturbance of sleep that accompanies depression is not news, but the character of the change and the fact that induced changes in sleep can influence depression are new pieces in the puzzle. Difficulty in falling asleep and inability to maintain sleep are common in major depression. In addition, EEG sleep studies of depressed patients show certain abnormalities that go beyond difficulty in falling asleep.

The sleep of patients with major depressive disorders is marked by a striking reduction in stages 3 and 4 of slow-wave sleep (SWS) and a corresponding increase in stages 1 and 2 (Figure 16.13a). Alterations of REM sleep patterns seem to have a special relationship with depression. Depressed patients enter REM sleep much sooner after sleep onset (Figure 16.13b)—the latency to REM sleep correlates with the severity of depression—and their REM sleep is unusually vigorous. Furthermore, the temporal distribution of REM sleep is altered, with an increased amount of REM sleep occurring during the first half of sleep, as though REM sleep were displaced toward an earlier period in the night (Wehr et al., 1985).

Sleep therapy can aid depression. Because people suffering from depression seem to have an overabundance of REM sleep, Vogel et al. (1980), hypothesized that selective REM sleep deprivation might relieve the symptoms of depression. A variety of studies have now confirmed a marked antidepressant effect of REM sleep depri-

(a) Sleep pattern of a patient with depression

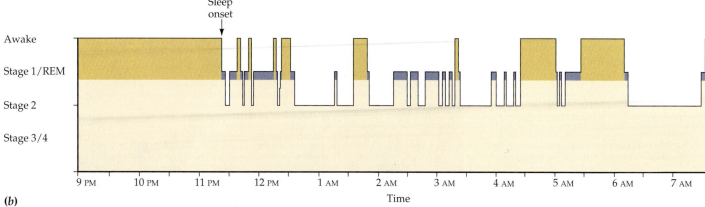

(b)

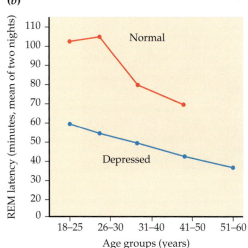

16.13 Sleep and Depression (a) Depressed subjects spend little or no time in sleep stages 3 and 4. (Compare with Figure 14.12.) (b) Patients suffering from depression also enter their first REM period earlier in the night. Thus, REM sleep seems to be distributed differently in people with depression.

Manic

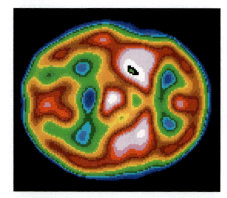

Depressive

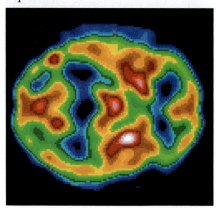

16.14 Functional Images of Bipolar Disorder Dramatic differences in brain activity are evident between the depressive and manic phases of this patient's bipolar illness. (Courtesy of Dr. Robert G. Kohn, Brain-Spect.com.)

vation. In one such procedure, patients repeatedly were awakened as they entered REM sleep, thereby reducing the overall amounts of REM sleep; the procedure was continued for 2 to 3 weeks. Control patients suffering from depression repeatedly were awakened from non-REM sleep. Depression was evaluated on the basis of a clinical rating scale. At the end of 3 weeks, the REM sleep–deprived group showed a significantly lower depression score than the non-REM sleep–deprived group. Three weeks later the treatments were reversed, and by the end of another 3 weeks, the effect had also switched. Several antidepressant drugs, such as monoamine oxidase inhibitors, suppress REM sleep for extended periods.

Other aspects of sleep and circadian rhythms also have been implicated in depression. Under some circumstances, body rhythms in hormone secretion and other activities can become desynchronized—an abnormality that is associated with depression. In an effort to resolve these irregularities, Wehr et al. (1982) had patients go to bed 6 hours before their usual time and reported that several patients showed a rapid improvement in their depression. In addition to these links between daily rhythms and depression, seasonal rhythms have been implicated in a particular depressive condition known as *seasonal affective disorder* (*SAD*), which is described in Box 16.2.

People with bipolar disorder show repeating mood cycles

Bipolar disorder is characterized by periods of depression alternating with periods of excessively expansive mood (or *mania*) that includes sustained overactivity, talkativeness, increased energy, and strange grandiosity (Figure 16.14). The rate at which the alternation occurs varies between individuals: Some patients exhibit *rapid-cycling* bipolar disorder, defined as consisting of four or more distinct cycles in one year (and some individuals have many more cycles than that; some may even show

BOX 16.2   The Season to Be Depressed

Seasonal rhythms characterize the behavior and physiology of many animals, including humans. For some unfortunate people, winter brings a low period that may become a profound depression. Sometimes the winter depression alternates with summertime mania (Blehar and Rosenthal, 1989). In wintertime, affected people feel depressed, slow down, generally sleep a lot, and overeat. Come summer, they are elated, energetic, and active, and they become thinner. This syndrome—called **seasonal affective disorder (SAD)**—appears predominantly in women and generally starts in early adulthood.

Some early reports suggested a positive correlation between latitude and the frequency of SAD: The farther from the equator, the more cases of SAD. But a study in a country at a far northern latitude—Iceland—where a relatively high rate of SAD would be expected, failed to confirm this relationship (Magnusson and Stefansson, 1993); and in general, a relationship between latitude and SAD has not been very evident (Mersch et al., 1999). Nevertheless, seasonal rhythms are controlled by the length of the day, so researchers asked if seasonal changes in exposure to sunlight might cause SAD.

To examine that prospect, researchers have treated SAD sufferers with doses of bright light, to see if it acts as an antidepressant. In one typical investigation (Rosenthal et al., 1985), patients with recurrent SAD received experimental treatments consisting of exposure to bright broad-spectrum light twice each day—5:00 AM to 8:00 AM, and 5:30 PM to 8:30 PM—for 2 weeks, thereby simulating the long daylight period that is characteristic of summer. The experimenters found that the light treatment had a significant antidepressant effect that reversed upon cessation of the light treatment. Control subjects exposed to dimmer light showed no such effect.

Light therapy for SAD

The efficacy of light therapy in SAD is now well established (Eastman et al., 1998), and in many ways light therapy resembles treatment with traditional antidepressant drugs; there is even a dose–response relationship for light therapy (T. M. Lee and Chan, 1999). Further studies have revealed that light therapy is most effective when administered immediately upon awakening in the morning (Lewy et al., 1998). A person receiving phototherapy is shown in the figure.

One important biological effect of light is that it suppresses melatonin, a hormone found in the pineal gland that affects gonadotropins and may be of importance in controlling sleep. Whereas exposure to darkness stimulates melatonin synthesis, light suppresses it. People with SAD have been shown to have a high threshold for melatonin suppression. However, oral administration of melatonin does not influence this disorder. Serotonin may be relevant because it has a marked seasonal rhythm in humans, with lower values in winter and spring than in summer or fall (Egrise et al., 1986). Consistent with this observation, SAD may respond to antidepressant medications that selectively block serotonin reuptake, such as sertraline (Zoloft) (A. Moscovitch et al., 2004).

Attention to seasonal affective disorder arose primarily because of animal research dealing with photoperiodic behavior and circadian control systems (see Chapter 14)—another example of basic research leading to alleviation of the distresses and diseases of humans. (Photo courtesy of Uplift Technologies.)

several cycles per *day*). Some people experience a milder, subclinical relative of bipolar disorder called *cyclothymia*, in which the patient experiences less-extreme moods, cycling between *dysthymia* (poor mood or mild depression) and *hypomania* (a state of increased energy and positive mood that lacks some of the bizarre aspects of frank mania).

Men and women are equally affected by bipolar disorder, and the age of onset is usually much earlier than that of unipolar depression. Bipolar disorder has a complex heritability: Genetic linkage analyses have revealed that there are loci on chromosomes 4, 11, 12, 16, 21, and X that are probably important (Craddock and Jones, 2001). Interestingly, the age of onset of bipolar disorder also appears to be partly heritable, governed by genes located on chromosomes 12, 14, and 15 (Faraone et al., 2004). As specific genes are identified within these chromosomal locations, rapid progress in understanding the basis of bipolar disorders can be expected. Although individual genes that cause the disorder have not been conclusively identified yet, several candidates are under study. For example, several studies have implicated the gene that encodes BDNF in bipolar disorder (E. Green and Craddock, 2003; Neves-Pereira et al., 2002); recall that BDNF has been associated with unipolar depression as well.

GENES AND BEHAVIOR

The neural basis of bipolar disorder is not fully understood, but since the 1980s it has been known that patients with bipolar disorder exhibit enlarged ventricles on CT or MRI scans. As in schizophrenia (see Figure 16.3), this enlargement probably indicates the presence of brain abnormalities, although the specific regions affected may differ. Ventricular enlargement is especially evident in people who have experienced repeated mood cycles (Strakowski et al., 2002), suggesting an accumulation of changes in the brain over time. These changes probably occur in subcortical limbic structures, like the amygdala, that have been implicated in emotion (DelBello et al., 2004).

Most people suffering from bipolar disorder benefit from treatment with mood-stabilizing drugs, such as the element **lithium** (Kingsbury and Garver, 1998). The mechanism by which this metal helps bipolar disorder is not understood; and because it has a narrow therapeutic index (the range of safe doses; see Chapter 4), care must be taken to avoid toxic side effects of an overdose. Nevertheless, well-managed lithium treatment produces marked relief for many patients and even has been reported to increase the volume of gray matter in the human brain (G. J. Moore et al., 2000).

Perhaps the fact that the manic phases blocked by lithium are so exhilarating is the reason that some bipolar clients stop taking the medication. Unfortunately, doing so means that the depressive episodes return as well. However, other drug treatments are available, and as in unipolar depression, it appears that transcranial magnetic stimulation may provide a nonpharmacological treatment alternative in difficult cases of bipolar disorder (Michael and Erfurth, 2004). Furthermore, evidence has accumulated that in both unipolar and bipolar depressive disorders, some forms of psychotherapy can be as effective as drug treatments (Hollon et al., 2002) and perhaps can be beneficially combined with other forms of treatment.

CLINICAL ISSUE

There Are Several Types of Anxiety Disorders

All of us have at times felt apprehensive and fearful. Some people experience this state with an intensity that is overwhelming and includes irrational fears, a sense of terror, unusual body sensations such as dizziness, difficulty breathing, trembling, shaking, and a feeling of loss of control. For some, anxiety comes in sudden attacks of panic that are unpredictable and last for minutes or hours. And anxiety can be lethal: A follow-up of patients with panic disorder revealed an increased mortality in men with this disorder resulting from cardiovascular disease and suicide (Coryell et al., 1986).

The American Psychiatric Association distinguishes several major types of anxiety disorders. **Phobic disorders** are intense, irrational fears that become centered on a specific object, activity, or situation that the person feels he or she must avoid. **Anxiety states** include *panic disorder,* characterized by recurrent transient attacks of intense fearfulness, as well as *generalized anxiety disorder,* in which persistent, excessive anxiety and worry is experienced for months. Other anxiety disorders include obsessive–compulsive disorder, posttraumatic stress disorder, and anxiety conditions induced by drugs, illnesses, or other causes.

Panic can be provoked chemically

Several decades ago, psychiatrists observed that some patients experience intense anxiety attacks during or after vigorous physical exercise. This effect was thought to be caused by a buildup of lactate in the blood. This observation inspired Pitts and McClure (1967) to administer sodium lactate to patients with a history of panic attacks. In some patients the infusions produced immediate panic attacks that resembled the naturally occurring episodes; this chemical treatment did not produce panic attacks in other people.

Margraf and Roth (1986) contested the study on the grounds that it failed to exclude confounding psychological factors: Patients showed a certain level of panic even when infused with placebo. However, PET scans (which we will discuss in the next section) do support the lactate induction effect. In an attempt to account for chemically induced panic, Liebowitz et al. (1986) suggested that the lactate-induced panic stimulates central noradrenergic mechanisms of the locus coeruleus and its outputs. This suggestion is partially supported by the observation that another locus coeruleus stimulant—inhaled 5% carbon dioxide—also produces panic in clinically vulnerable individuals.

Panic disorders are characterized by structural and functional changes in the temporal lobes

CLINICAL ISSUE

Many patients who suffer from recurrent panic attacks have temporal lobe abnormalities, according to MRI studies. Ontiveros et al. (1989) found temporal lobe abnormalities—including small lesions in white matter and dilation of the lateral ventricles—in 40% of patients with panic disorder. The magnitude of neuroanatomical anomalies correlated significantly with the total number of spontaneous attacks and the age of onset of panic (patients whose episodes of panic begin at an earlier age have more anomalies). Overall temporal lobe volumes tend to be lower in patients with panic disorder (Vythilingam et al., 2000), but hippocampal volumes tend to be normal. Instead, given the special role of the amygdala in mediating fear, it seems likely that changes may be especially evident in the amygdala and associated circuitry (Rauch et al., 2003). This function of the amygdala is discussed in detail in Chapter 15.

Functional-imaging technologies such as PET and fMRI (discussed in Chapter 2) have provided a graphic portrait of the anatomy of anxiety. It appears that metabolic abnormalities of the brain are present in the brains of people with panic disorder, even in the resting, nonpanic state. As you might expect, these abnormalities are especially evident in the temporal lobes. Increased activity of the parahippocampal gyrus, and decreased activity of the anterior temporal cortex and amygdala, especially on the right side (Boshuisen et al., 2002; H. Fischer et al., 1998; Reiman et al., 1986)—as well as changes in activity of the anterior cingulate gyrus and frontal cortex—are reliably observed. Gloor et al. (1982) reported that electrical stimulation of a region including the parahippocampus in awake patients commonly elicits sensations of strong fear and apprehension. In addition to this regional effect, lactate-vulnerable panic patients have abnormally high oxygen metabolism in the brain.

PET scan studies have repeatedly found systematic activation differences between patients who are vulnerable to lactate-induced panic and those not vulnerable to induced attacks. This distinction might reflect a fundamental difference in underlying biological mechanisms. Although not without their detractors (Posner and Raichle, 1994), functional-imaging studies generally indicate that temporal lobe structures play a key role in the elicitation and maintenance of a variety of anxiety states (Rauch et al., 1995).

Drug treatment of anxiety provides clues to the mechanisms of this disorder

Throughout history people have consumed all sorts of substances in the hopes of controlling anxiety. The list includes alcohol, bromides, scopolamine, opiates, and barbiturates. In the 1960s the tranquilizing agent meprobamate (Miltown) was introduced and became an instant best-seller, ushering in the modern age of anxiety pharmacotherapy. Spurred on by the promise of enormous profits, research aimed at discovering new drugs intensified and soon resulted in the introduction of the class of substances called **benzodiazepines,** which quickly became the favored drugs for treating anxiety. One type of benzodiazepine—diazepam (trade name Valium)—is one of the most prescribed drugs in history. Drugs that combat anxiety are commonly described as **anxiolytic** ("anxiety dissolving"), although at high doses they also have anticonvulsant and sleep-inducing properties. The anxiolytic drugs are also discussed in Chapter 4.

Early behavioral and electrophysiological data established that the anxiolytic benzodiazepines are associated in some way with the action of GABA synapses, where they act as agonists (recall from Chapter 4 that GABA is the most common inhibitory transmitter in the brain). This interaction with GABA receptors results in enhancement of GABA's action at inhibitory synapses in the brain. In other words, GABA-mediated postsynaptic inhibition is facilitated by benzodiazepines. Benzodiazepine receptors are a part of the GABA$_A$ receptor complex and are widely distributed throughout the brain. They are especially concentrated in the cerebral cortex and some subcortical areas, such as the hippocampus and the amygdala (Figure 16.15).

The ultimate function of the benzodiazepine–GABA$_A$ receptor complex is to regulate the permeability of neural membranes to chloride ions (Cl⁻). When GABA is released from a presynaptic terminal and activates postsynaptic receptors, chloride ions are allowed to move from the outside to the inside of the nerve cell, creating a local hyperpolarization (an inhibitory postsynaptic potential, or IPSP) and therefore inhibiting the neuron from firing. Benzodiazepines alone do little to change chloride conductance, but in the presence of GABA, they markedly enhance GABA-provoked increases in chloride permeability and thus potentiate the inhibitory effect of GABA. Interestingly, the brain probably makes its own anxiety-relieving substances that interact with the benzodiazepine-binding site; the neurosteroid allopregnanolone is a prime candidate for this function (see Chapter 4).

Although the benzodiazepines remain an important category of anxiolytics, other types of anxiety-relieving drugs have been developed. A notable example is the drug buspirone (Buspar), which we discussed in Chapter 4. Buspirone interacts with serotonin 5HT$_{1A}$ receptors to provide relief from anxiety. This observation is consistent with findings from functional-imaging research confirming that 5HT$_{1A}$ receptor density is abnormal in anxiety disorders (Neumeister et al., 2004). Selective serotonin reuptake inhibitors, such as paroxetine (Paxil) and fluoxetine (Prozac), also are widely used in the treatment of anxiety disorders.

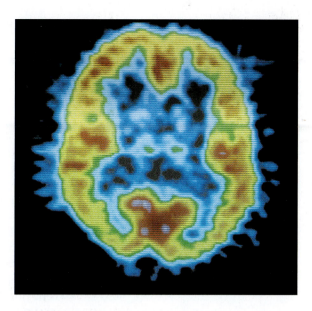

16.15 The Distribution of Benzodiazepine Receptors in the Human Brain   This PET scan of benzodiazepine receptors shows their wide distribution in the brain. Highest concentrations are shown in orange and red. (Courtesy of Goran Sedvall.)

In posttraumatic stress disorder, horrible memories won't go away

Some people experience some especially awful moments in life that seem indelible, resulting in vivid impressions that persist through the remainder of life. Persons exposed to sustained periods of unremitting horrors, such as the carnage of war, may find it extremely difficult to shut out these events, even long after they have passed. The kind of event that seems particularly likely to produce subsequent stress disorders is one that is intense and usually associated with witnessing abusive violence and/or death. Precipitating events may be the sudden loss of a close friend, rape, torture, kidnapping, and profound social dislocation, such as in forced migration.

In these cases, memories of horrible events intrude into consciousness and produce the same intense visceral arousal—the fear and trembling and general autonomic activation—that the original event caused. These traumatic memories are easily reawakened by stressful circumstances and even by seemingly benign stimuli that have somehow come to prompt recollection of the original event. An ever-watchful and fearful stance becomes the portrait of individuals afflicted with what is called **posttraumatic stress disorder** (**PTSD,** formerly called *combat fatigue, war neurosis,* or *shell shock*).

**GENES AND
BEHAVIOR**

Studies on risk factors associated with PTSD in Vietnam War veterans have clarified the interaction of genetic and environmental factors in this disorder. The disorder is particularly prevalent among those who served in the most intense combat areas (True et al., 1993). Familial factors also affect vulnerability, as shown in twin studies of Vietnam era veterans. Researchers compared twins—both monozygotic and dizygotic—who had served in combat zones with other veterans who had not served in Southeast Asia. Monozygotic twins were more similar than dizygotic twins, and the specific contribution of inheritance to PTSD is claimed to account for one-third of the variance.

A comprehensive psychobiological model of the development of PTSD draws connections among the symptoms and the neural mechanisms of fear conditioning, behavioral sensitization, and extinction (Charney et al., 1993). The investigators argue that patients learn to avoid a large range of stimuli associated with the original trauma. A kind of emotional numbing is the consequence of this avoidance, which can also be seen as a conditioned emotional response. Work in animals has revealed that this type of memory—**fear conditioning**—is very persistent and involves the amygdala and some brainstem pathways that are part of a circuit of startle response behavior (see Chapter 15). NMDA receptor–mediated mechanisms in the amygdala are important for the development of fear conditioning.

Behavioral sensitization—the second component of the model—enhances response magnitude after exposure to a stimulus. The fact that repeated stressors increase dopamine function in the forebrain suggests that the neural mechanisms involve dopamine.

Finally, the persistence of memory and fear in PTSD may depend on the failure or fragility of extinction mechanisms. In experimental animals, NMDA antagonists delivered to the amygdala prevent the extinction of fear-mediated startle. Sites projecting to the amygdala, such as the hippocampus and prefrontal cortex, may also lose their effectiveness in suppressing learned fear responses. Figure 16.16 presents this intriguing neural model. One important implication of this model is that it might direct clinical intervention. For example, it suggests a potentially important use for drugs that block conditioned responses.

Patients who display combat-related PTSD show (1) memory changes such as amnesia for some war experiences, (2) flashbacks, and (3) deficits in short-term memory (Bremner et al., 1993). Reports of such psychological changes have led to MRI studies of the brains of combat veterans with PTSD. Measurements of the right hippocampus re-

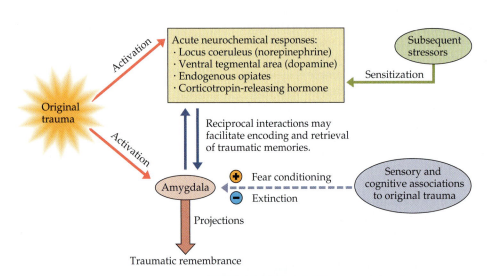

Symptom	Brain region
Flashbacks, intrusive memories	Cortex, hippocampus
Anxiety, fear, hypervigilance	Amygdala, locus coeruleus, ventral tegmental area
Facial expression of fear	Trigeminal, facial motor nuclei
Anhedonia, depression	Nucleus accumbens
Startle	Reticular formation
Hyperventilation	Medullary respiratory center
Sympathetic activation: rapid heart rate, increased blood pressure	Lateral hypothalamus
Parasympathetic activation: diarrhea, increased urination	Vagal nerve nucleus

16.16 A Neural Model of Posttraumatic Stress Disorder   The original trauma activates two systems: one in the brainstem, which sensitizes the subject to related stimuli in the future; and another in the amygdala, which conditions a long-lasting fearful reaction.

veal an 8% reduction in the volume of this structure, with no changes in other brain regions (Bremner et al., 1995).

Exposure to stress leads to high levels of circulating glucocorticoids, such as cortisol, which appears to cause cell loss and tissue shrinkage in the hippocampus (Sapolsky et al., 1990) and inhibits hippocampal neurogenesis (the birth of new neurons) (E. Gould et al., 1998). The pathological effects of high stress levels on the human brain have been well established in imaging studies (reviewed in Bremner, 2003). However, it is not clear that this stress-related pathology is simply attributable to high levels of circulating cortisol, because PTSD sufferers exhibit a paradoxical long term *reduction* in cortisol levels (Yehuda, 2002; Yehuda et al., 1995), even though levels of corticotropin-releasing hormone (CRH; see Chapter 5) are elevated in the cerebrospinal fluid (Baker et al., 1999). One possibility is that patients with PTSD have persistent increases in *sensitivity* to cortisol. In Chapter 17 we will discuss research-based methods that have been proposed to prevent or alleviate post-traumatic stress disorder.

COMPETING HYPOTHESES

In obsessive–compulsive disorders, thoughts and acts keep repeating

Neatness, orderliness, and similar traits are attributes we tend to admire, especially during those chaotic moments when we realize we have created another tottering pile of papers, bills, or the like. But when does orderliness and routine cross the line into pathology? People with **obsessive–compulsive disorder** (**OCD**) lead lives that are riddled with repetitive rituals and persistent thoughts that they are powerless to control or stop, despite recognizing that the behaviors are abnormal.

In OCD patients, routine acts that we all engage in, such as checking whether the door is locked when we leave our home, become *compulsions* that are repeated over and over. Recurrent thoughts, or *obsessions,* such as fears of germs or other potential harms in the world, invade the consciousness. Table 16.5 summarizes some of the symptoms of OCD. These symptoms progressively isolate a person from ordinary social engagement with the world. For many patients, hours of each day are consumed by compulsive acts such as repetitive hand washing.

Determining the number of persons afflicted with OCD is difficult, especially because many people with this disorder tend to hide their symptoms. It is estimated that more than 4 million people are affected by OCD in the United States (Rapoport, 1989). In many cases, the initial symptoms of this disorder appear in childhood; the peak age group for onset of OCD, however, is 25 to 44 years.

For a long time this disorder was thought of as a psychiatric dysfunction associated with psychological conflict. More recently, evidence has accumulated suggesting that this disorder is rooted in the neurobiology of the brain. Rapoport (1989) suggested that the features of this disorder reflect "subroutines" associated with species-typical grooming and territoriality that have evolved gradually. Symptoms are thought to arise when brain malfunction causes these programs to be

TABLE 16.5 *Symptoms of Obsessive–Compulsive Disorders*

Symptoms	Percentage of patients
OBSESSIONS	
Dirt, germs, or environmental toxins	40
Something terrible happening (fire, death or illness of self or loved one)	24
Symmetry, order, or exactness	17
Religious obsessions	13
Body wastes or secretions (urine, stool, saliva)	8
Lucky or unlucky numbers	8
Forbidden, aggressive, or perverse sexual thoughts, images, or impulses	4
Fear of harming self or others	4
Household items	3
Intrusive nonsense sounds, words, or music	1
COMPULSIONS	
Performing excessive or ritualized hand washing, showering, bathing, tooth brushing, or grooming	85
Repeating rituals (going in or out of a door, getting up from or sitting down on a chair)	51
Checking (doors, locks, stove, appliances, emergency brake on car, paper route, homework)	46
Engaging in miscellaneous rituals (such as writing, moving, speaking)	26
Removing contaminants from contacts	23
Touching	20
Counting	18
Ordering or arranging	17
Preventing harm to self or others	16
Hoarding or collecting	11
Cleaning household or inanimate objects	6

executed without the usual provoking stimuli—such as cleaning something that is already clean.

PET scan studies of patients with OCD have revealed some of the details of the neural mechanisms underlying the disorder. These studies consistently report increased metabolic rates in the orbitofrontal cortex, cingulate, and the caudate nuclei (Rauch et al., 1994; Saxena and Rauch, 2000; Saxena et al., 1998). This pattern of activation supports an anatomical model of obsessive–compulsive disorders proposed by Insel (1992) that emphasizes a circuit involving a loop among frontal, striatal, and thalamic structures.

Happily, OCD responds to drug treatment in most cases. What do effective OCD drugs—like fluoxetine (Prozac), fluvoxamine (Luvox), and clomipramine (Anafranil)—tend to have in common? Many studies have confirmed that the effective drugs share the ability to inhibit the reuptake of serotonin at serotonergic synapses, thereby increasing the synaptic availability of serotonin. This observation suggests that dysfunction of serotonergic neurotransmission plays a central role in OCD. Recall that we already discussed drugs that inhibit the reuptake of serotonin when we discussed treatments for depression. In fact, although OCD is classified as an anxiety disorder, some clinicians have long believed that this disorder is related to depression. For example, studies of the incidence of OCD and depression show some overlap between them. And like patients with depression, patients who suffer from OCD exhibit decreased REM sleep latency.

BOX 16.3   Tics, Twitches, and Snorts: The Unusual Character of Tourette's Syndrome

Their faces twitch in an insistent way, and every now and then, out of nowhere, they blurt out an odd sound or, quite suddenly, an obscene word. At times they fling their arms, kick their legs, or make violent shoulder movements. Sufferers of **Tourette's syndrome** also exhibit heightened sensitivity to tactile, auditory, and visual stimuli (A. J. Cohen and Leckman, 1992). Many patients also sense the buildup of an urge to emit verbal or phonic tics; they report that these acts relieve this powerfully felt need. Professionals have long argued about whether this collection of symptoms forms a psychiatric disturbance derived from the stresses of life or emerges from a disturbance in brain structures and/or function.

Tourette's syndrome begins early in life; the mean age of diagnosis is 6 to 7 years (de Groot et al., 1995), and the syndrome is three to four times more common in males than in females. Figure A draws a portrait of the chronology of symptoms. Associated behavioral disturbances include attention deficit hyperactivity disorder (ADHD), problems in school, and obsessive–compulsive disorder (Park et al., 1993).

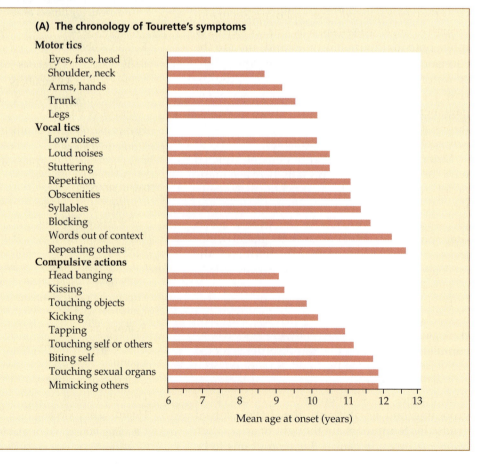

(A) The chronology of Tourette's symptoms

There is a heritable genetic component to OCD; initial results indicate that variations in several genes may contribute to susceptibility to this disorder (Grados et al., 2003). For example, the gene that encodes BDNF, which we have already discussed in the context of unipolar and bipolar depression, appears to be involved in OCD (Hall et al., 2003). The gene encoding the serotonin $5HT_{2A}$ receptor has also been implicated (Enoch et al., 1998).

Many researchers also believe that OCD and another disease involving repetitive behaviors, **Tourette's syndrome,** are part of a spectrum of related disorders. Jeff, the young man we described at the opening of the chapter, suffers from Tourette's. OCD and Tourette's are often **comorbid** (occurring together), and both disorders involve abnormalities of the basal ganglia. However, drug therapy in Tourette's syndrome has typically focused on modifying the actions of dopamine rather than serotonin. We discuss Tourette's syndrome in more detail in Box 16.3.

GENES AND BEHAVIOR

Neurosurgery Has Been Used to Treat Psychiatric Disorders

Through the ages, mentally ill people have been treated by methods limited only by the human imagination. Some methods have been gruesome, inspired by views that people with mental disorders are controlled by demonic forces. Disparate cultures have, for millennia, practiced *trephination* (drilling a hole through the skull) in the belief that this would allow the causative agents to escape from the brain of the

BOX 16.3 *(continued)*

Family studies have indicated that genetics appears to play an important role in this disorder. Twin studies of the disorder reveal a concordance rate among monozygotic twins of 53% to 77%, contrasted with a concordance rate among dizygotic twins of 8% to 23% (Hyde et al., 1992; R. A. Price et al., 1985). Among discordant monozygotic twin pairs, marked differences are seen in the density of dopamine D_2 receptors in the caudate nucleus of the basal ganglia (Wolf et al., 1996). This observation suggests that differences in the dopaminergic system, especially in the basal ganglia, may be important (D_2 receptor binding is illustrated in Figure B). The contemporary view is that Tourette's syndrome is mediated in a complex manner by one or more major genes and modified by other genes, but the precise genes that are involved have eluded identification so far (Pauls, 2003).

An unusual view of genetic factors in Tourette's is provided by a study of a set of triplets who were reared apart after the age of 2 months (Segal et al., 1990). The triplets consisted of a pair of monozygotic female twins and a dizygotic male. They were reunited when they were 47 years old. The male had a history of eye blinking, facial tics, and repetitive arm and finger movements that had begun at age 4. Eye blinking persisted into adulthood. The female twins showed a more severe set of symptoms: frequent motor and phonic tics, head jerks, shoulder jerks, and kicking leg movements.

Administration of haloperidol, a dopamine D_2 receptor antagonist that is better known as an effective antischizophrenic drug, significantly reduces tic frequency and is a primary treatment for Tourette's syndrome. Unfortunately, side effects limit the duration of this treatment. Behavior modification techniques that aim at reducing the frequency of some symptoms, especially tics, are claimed to help some patients (A. L. Peterson and Azrin, 1992). (Figure B courtesy of Steven Wolf.)

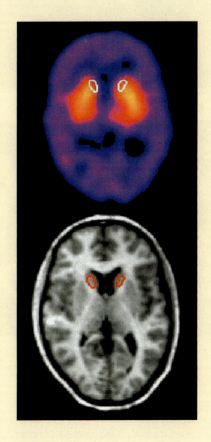

(B) D_2 binding in Tourette's syndrome. (*Top*) PET scan of D_2 receptor binding. (*Bottom*) MRI scan illustrating the location of the caudate nuclei.

Eliot Valenstein

afflicted. Although psychiatry largely was purged of such magical thinking by the twentieth century, until recently, treatment was a trial-and-error affair.

In the 1930s, experiments on frontal lobe lesions in chimpanzees inspired psychiatrist Egas Moniz to attempt similar operations in human patients. Moniz was intrigued by the report of a calming influence in nonhuman primates, and when he tried frontal surgery in people with severe mental illnesses, little else was available. His observations led to the beginning of **psychosurgery,** defined as the use of surgically produced brain lesions to modify severe psychiatric disorders. Eliot Valenstein (1986) reviewed the history of vigorous debate about psychosurgery, which continues to the present.

During the 1940s, **lobotomy** (disconnecting parts of the frontal lobes from the rest of the brain) was forcefully advocated by several neurosurgeons and psychiatrists. A presidential commission on psychosurgery estimated that during this period, 10,000 to 50,000 U.S. patients underwent this surgery (National Commission for the Protection of Human Subjects of Biomedical and Behavioral Research, 1978). During the most intense period of enthusiasm, patients of all diagnostic types were operated on, and different varieties of surgery were employed.

Follow-up assessments of the value of frontal lobe surgery revealed that outcomes were much less positive than originally claimed, and the procedure was widely abolished, except in cases of intractable pain. However, William Sweet (1973) and others argued that much-more-localized brain lesions—in contrast to the widespread damage caused by frontal lobotomy—might significantly relieve particular psychiatric disorders. Since the 1970s, a variety of experimental focal brain surgeries have been performed in severe cases of psychiatric illness, when all else has failed.

Positive results have been reported for several procedures. For example, Ballantine et al. (1987), reported beneficial effects of stereotaxic *cingulotomy* (lesions that interrupt pathways in the cingulate cortex) in the treatment of depression and anxiety disorders. Another follow-up study on a group of severely disabled OCD patients (Jenike et al., 1991) indicated that one-third of patients who underwent cingulotomy (Figure 16.17) benefited substantially from this intervention (Martuza et al., 1990). Patients who received ventromedial frontal lesions as a last-resort therapy for OCD showed significant improvement in obsessive–compulsive symptoms (Irle et al., 1998). This clinical improvement was sustained in some patients for 20 years. A different type of surgery, called *capsulotomy,* in which small, discrete lesions are placed in the anterior part of the internal capsule (the white matter projections underlying the cortex), reportedly is of long-lasting benefit in some cases of severe anxiety disorders (Ruck et al., 2003).

Psychosurgery need not always involve brain lesions; brain stimulation can also be beneficial in some cases. Jeff Matovic, whose situation we described at the opening of the chapter, turned to an experimental surgical procedure called *deep brain stimulation* in a desperate attempt to gain relief from the symptoms of his Tourette's syndrome. In Jeff's operation, announced in April 2004, neurosurgeons implanted bilateral stimulating electrodes within the thalamus, in regions associated with the control of movement. The stimulators are controlled by pacemakers and batteries implanted near Jeff's collarbone. Within hours of activation of the stimulators, Jeff's symptoms completely abated; and for the first time in 25 years he was free of the motor and vocal tics that had threatened to ruin his life. Although no information is yet available about long-term outcomes for this procedure, Jeff remains symptom-free.

Despite some apparently dramatic successes, like that of Jeff Matovic, psychosurgery remains a very uncommon treatment, limited to the most severe and unresponsive cases. The use of drugs has overshadowed psychosurgery, especially because most neurosurgical interventions are not reversible.

(a) Horizontal view

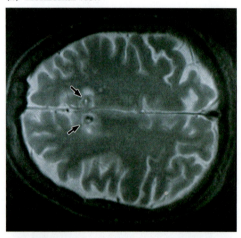

(b) Sagittal view

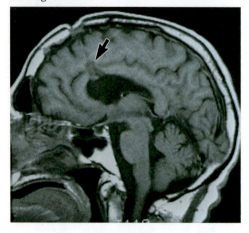

16.17 Neurosurgery to Treat Obsessive–Compulsive Disorder These horizontal (*a*) and sagittal (*b*) MRIs show the brain of a patient who underwent a cingulotomy—the disruption of cingulate cortex connections (arrows)—in an attempt to treat OCD. (From Martuza et al., 1990; courtesy of Robert L. Martuza.)

Prions, Mad Cows, and Creutzfeldt–Jakob Disease

Over two centuries ago shepherds in Europe recognized a fatal disease in sheep that was called *scrapie* because the animals "scraped" their skin, presumably in an attempt to relieve itching. The shepherds learned that the only way they could stop an outbreak was to kill all the sheep, burn the carcasses and the fields they had used, and keep new sheep away from those fields for years.

These drastic measures were needed because the disease is not transmitted by a virus or bacterium, which would rely on relatively fragile DNA or RNA for reproduction. Rather, scrapie is caused when a particular endogenous protein that normally takes one shape takes on a new, abnormal shape. Once one protein molecule does this, it induces the other molecules of that protein to also fold abnormally. The accumulation of abnormally folded proteins leads to brain degeneration. These infectious protein particles were named **prions** (pronounced "PREE-ons") by their discoverer, Stanley Prusiner, who was awarded the 1997 Nobel Prize in Physiology or Medicine for this research.

At some point, feed containing protein derived from sheep suffering from scrapie was fed to some cows in England and caused the cow version of the prion protein to fold abnormally. The result was a bovine version of scrapie called **bovine spongiform encephalopathy** (**BSE,** or *mad cow disease*) because of massive brain degeneration, leaving the brain "spongy" (Figure 16.18).

Unfortunately, before BSE was detected, infected cows provided beef for Britons and caused a similar disorder called **Creutzfeldt–Jakob disease** (**CJD**) in humans (technically, the form caused by eating contaminated beef is called *variant* CJD to distinguish it from other related forms). CJD is fatal, causing widespread brain degeneration and therefore dementia, sleep disorders (see Chapter 14), schizophrenia-like symptoms, and death. Although a few cases of BSE have now been detected in North American cattle, currently they are believed to pose little risk to human health because of changes in screening, processing, and feed production procedures.

Before "mad cows" introduced it in humans, CJD (the nonvariant form) was a very rare disease, and it cannot readily spread among humans because we aren't normally exposed to each other's brain tissue. (The human disease *kuru* is a related prion disease that was transmitted among the Fore people of New Guinea because of their cultural practice of consuming the bodies and brains of dead family members.) Neurosurgeons learned that instruments used on the brain of a CJD patient

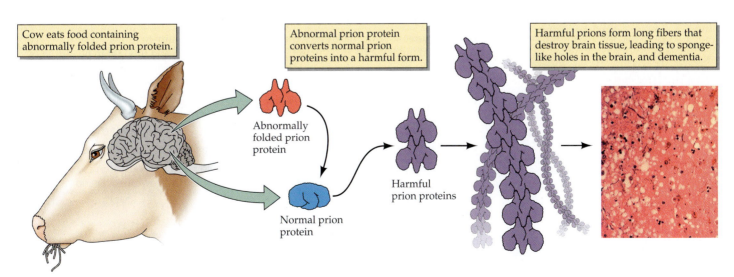

Cow eats food containing abnormally folded prion protein.

Abnormal prion protein converts normal prion proteins into a harmful form.

Harmful prions form long fibers that destroy brain tissue, leading to sponge-like holes in the brain, and dementia.

Abnormally folded prion protein

Normal prion protein

Harmful prion proteins

16.18 The Culprits of Mad Cow Disease Proteins that transmit disease, called *prions*, are the cause of bovine spongiform encephalopathy, also known as *mad cow disease*.

Refer to the *Learning Biological Psychology CD* for study questions, animations, activities, and other study aids.

must be destroyed because no sterilization procedure prevents them from infecting subsequent patients. It will be many years before we know the full extent of the mad cow problem, because prion-instigated symptoms arise years after infection, making it difficult to spot infected cows or people.

Summary

1. Mental disorders are common and exact enormous social and economic costs.

2. There is strong evidence for a genetic factor in the origin of schizophrenia. Consistent evidence comes from studies of the incidence of schizophrenia in families, twins, and adoptees. Several genes that may contribute to schizophrenia have been identified.

3. Structural changes in the brains of patients with schizophrenia—including enlarged ventricles, limbic system abnormalities, loss of gray matter, and abnormalities of other brain regions—may arise from early developmental problems. Functional-imaging studies indicate that in schizophrenia the frontal lobes are less active than normal.

4. Biochemical theories of schizophrenia especially emphasize the importance of the transmitters dopamine, glutamate, and serotonin.

5. According to an integrative psychobiological model, the emergence of schizophrenia depends on the interaction of a vulnerable biological substrate and environmental stressors.

6. Biological studies of depression reveal a strong genetic factor and the importance of levels of various neurotransmitters, including serotonin.

7. People suffering from depression show increased blood flow in the frontal cortex and the amygdala, and decreased blood flow in the parietal and posterior temporal cortex.

8. In the general population, females are more likely than males to suffer from depression. Various hypotheses have been proposed to explain this sex difference, but all of them remain inconclusive. Dysregulation of the hypothalamic–pituitary–adrenal axis is intimately associated with depression.

9. Changes in REM sleep that accompany depression include shortened onset to REM sleep and larger percentages of REM sleep in overall amounts of sleep. Some sleep treatments appear to act as antidepressants.

10. Bipolar disorder is characterized by extreme mood swings and subtle changes in the brain, and it has a complex genetic component.

11. Anxiety states are characterized by functional changes in the temporal lobes that can be revealed by PET scans.

12. Benzodiazepine antianxiety drugs affect receptors for the transmitter GABA. These drugs enhance the inhibitory influence of this neurotransmitter. Drugs that affect serotonergic transmission may also reduce anxiety.

13. Posttraumatic stress disorder is characterized by an inability to forget horrible experiences. Temporal lobe atrophy in this disorder is common and thought to be caused by exposure to glucocorticoids, but long-term PTSD sufferers have paradoxically low levels of glucocorticoids.

14. Obsessive–compulsive disorder is characterized by changes in basal ganglia and frontal structures and strongly linked to serotonin activities. It bears many similarities to Tourette's syndrome.

15. Neurosurgery continues to be used as a form of psychiatric treatment in severe cases.

16. Infectious proteins (prions) become concentrated in brain tissues, leading to damage and dementia in bovine spongiform encephalopathy (mad cow disease) and Creutzfeldt–Jakob disease.

Recommended Reading

Cichetti, D., and Walker, E. F. (Eds.). (2003). *Neurodevelopmental mechanisms in psychopathology.* Cambridge, England: Cambridge University Press.

Davis, K. L., Charney, D., Coyle, J. T., and Nemeroff, C. (Eds.). (2002). *Psychopharmacology: The fifth generation of progress.* New York: Lippincott, Williams & Wilkins.

Feldman, R. S., Meyer, J. S., and Quenzer, L. F. (1997). *Principles of neuropsychopharmacology.* Sunderland, MA: Sinauer Associates.

Fogel, B. S., Schiffer, R. B., Rao, S.M., and Anderson, S.C. (2003). *Neuropsychiatry: A comprehensive textbook* (2nd ed.). New York: Lippincott Williams and Wilkins.

Gottesman, I. I. (1995). *Schizophrenia genesis: The origins of madness.* New York: Freeman.

Huettel, S. A., Song, A. W., and McCarthy, G. (2004). *Functional magnetic resonance imaging.* Sunderland, MA: Sinauer Associates.

Leckman, J. F., and Cohen, D. J. (Eds.). (2001). *Tourette's syndrome—Tics, obsessions, compulsion* (2nd ed.). New York: Wiley.

Nathan, P. E., and Gorman, J. M. (Eds.). (1998). *A guide to treatments that work.* New York: Oxford University Press.

Solomon, A. (2001). *The noonday demon: An atlas of depression.* New York: Scribner.

Torrey, E. F., and Miller, J. (2002). *The invisible plague: The rise of mental illness from 1750 to the present.* Newark, NJ: Rutgers University Press.

Whybrow, P. C. (1997). *A mood apart.* New York: Basic Books.

VI Cognitive Neuroscience

*L*earning and memory, language, and cognition are the fascinating focal points of much current research. We start Part 6 with a top-down approach in Chapter 17, describing learning and memory in whole organisms and identifying the associated neural regions and systems. In Chapter 18 we investigate the neuronal and synaptic mechanisms and the neural networks that may underlie learning and memory. Chapter 19 focuses on the most elaborate products of brain function: the biology of language and cognitive states that are so distinctively human.

Striking cases of impaired memory start our discussion. We can discover a great deal about learning and memory by examining how they fail. Clinical cases show that memory can fail in quite different ways, and these observations demonstrate that there are different kinds of learning and memory. The clinical cases also provide clues about the brain regions that are especially involved in memory. Carefully designed animal research has delved deeper into this question. Noninvasive brain imaging is helping investigators acquire new evidence about the brain mechanisms of learning and memory. Together, these and other approaches are providing converging evidence to yield a comprehensive picture of the brain mechanisms.

Steve Dininno, *Letters And Numbers Out Of Head*

17

Learning and Memory: Biological Perspectives

Trapped in the Eternal Now

The man known in the neuroscience literature as patient H.M. suffered from epileptic seizures starting at the age of 16. His condition became steadily worse and could not be controlled by medication; he had to stop work at the age of 27. His symptoms indicated that the seizures began in both temporal lobes, so in 1953 a neurosurgeon removed most of the anterior temporal lobe, including much of the amygdala and hippocampus, on both sides. Similar operations had been performed earlier without harmful effects, although in those cases less tissue had been removed.

After H.M. recovered from the operation, his seizures were milder, and they could be controlled by medication. But this relief came at a terrible, unforeseen price: H.M. had lost the ability to form new memories (Scoville and Milner, 1957). Introduced to a new person, H.M. converses easily and pleasantly. But if the person leaves the room for 5 to 10 minutes and returns, H.M. has no recollection of having met her, and he may introduce himself all over again. More than 50 years after the surgery, H.M. retains a new fact only briefly; as soon as he is distracted, the newly acquired infor-

mation vanishes. He doesn't know his age or the current date, and he doesn't know that his parents (with whom he lived) died years ago. His IQ remains a little above average (Corkin et al., 1997) because most IQ tests monitor problem solving that doesn't require remembering new facts for more than a few minutes. H.M. recognizes that something is wrong with him because he has no memories of the past several years or even of what he did earlier in the same day.

> Every day is alone in itself, whatever enjoyment I've had, and whatever sorrow I've had. . . . Right now, I'm wondering, have I done or said anything amiss? You see, at this moment everything looks clear to me, but what happened just before? That's what worries me. It's like waking from a dream. I just don't remember. (B. Milner, 1970, p. 37)

H.M.'s inability to form new memories means that he can't construct a lasting relationship with another person. No matter what experiences he might share with someone today, H.M. will have to start over their acquaintance tomorrow. The study of H.M. and other people who share his predicament has taught us a great deal about learning and memory.

*I*nvestigating learning and memory and their biological mechanisms is one of the most active and exciting areas of biological psychology. All the distinctively human aspects of our behavior are learned: the languages we speak, how we dress, the foods we eat and how we eat them, and so on. Much of our own individuality depends on learning and memory. Research on learning and memory gives us a better understanding of almost all the topics we have taken up so far because almost every aspect of behavior and cognition requires learning: how we perceive, the skilled acts we perform, our motivations, and the ways we achieve our goals. Conditions that impair memory are particularly frightening; they make it impossible to take part in normal social life and can rob us of our identity.

Many Kinds of Brain Damage Can Impair Memory

The terms *learning* and *memory* are so often paired that it sometimes seems as if one necessarily implies the other. We cannot be sure that learning has occurred unless a memory can be elicited later. Here we are using *memory* in the common meaning of anything that shows that learning has occurred. Many kinds of brain damage, caused by disease or accident, impair learning and memory, and study of such cases is continuing to provide powerful lessons. We'll start by looking at some of these cases before progressing to newer brain-imaging techniques that provide novel information about the involvement of brain regions in learning and memory. Study of different types of memory impairment has revealed the existence of different classes of learning and memory, which we will discuss later in the chapter. First let's look at a few cases of memory impairment that have posed puzzles and have stimulated a great deal of controversy.

Rex Stevens, *Betsy (for Roy)*, 1997

For patient H.M., the present vanishes into oblivion

Patient H.M. suffers from **amnesia** (Greek for "forgetfulness"), a severe impairment of memory. In H.M.'s case, most old memories remain intact, but he has difficulty retrieving memories that had formed during the 10 years before the operation. Such memory loss is called **retrograde amnesia** (from the Latin *retro-*, "backward," and *gradi*, "to go"), the loss of memories formed *before* a particular event (in his case, the surgery). Retrograde amnesia after brain trauma or surgery is not rare. What is striking about H.M. is an unusual symptom: his apparent inability to retain *new* material for more than a brief period. When he meets someone new, almost as soon as that person leaves the room H.M. is unable to recall the person's name or even that he had met someone. The inability to form new memories *after* the onset of an illness is called **anterograde amnesia** (the Latin *antero-* means "forward").

There are a few indications that H.M. has formed some bits of long-term memory in the years since his operation. For example, when asked where he is, he sometimes guesses the Massachusetts Institute of Technology, the place where he has been interviewed and tested many times in the last 40 years (Hood et al., 1999; MacKay et al., 1998).

H.M.'s short-term memory is normal. For example, if he is given a series of digits and is asked to repeat the list immediately, like most people he can usually repeat a list of seven digits without error. But if he is given a list of words to study and is tested on them after other tasks have intervened, he cannot repeat the list; in fact, he does not even remember having studied the list. Thus, H.M. provides clear evidence that *short-term memory* (*STM*) differs from *long-term memory* (*LTM*).

Psychologists have recognized the distinction between STM and LTM on behavioral and cognitive grounds since the time of William James (1890). Short-term memory is usually considered to last only about 30 s, or as long as a person rehearses the material; it holds only a limited number of items (J. Brown, 1958; L. R. Peterson and Peterson, 1959). Long-term memory is an enduring form that lasts for hours, days, weeks, or more; it has a very large capacity. We will discuss long- and short-term memory in more depth later in this chapter.

Brenda Milner

After publication of H.M.'s case, similar cases were reported that resulted not from brain surgery but from disease. On rare occasions, herpes simplex virus destroys tissue in the medial temporal lobe. This destruction can produce a severe failure to form new long-term memories, although the acquisition of short-term memories is normal (A. R. Damasio, Eslinger, et al., 1985). An episode of reduced blood supply to the brain (**ischemia**), such as can be produced by a heart attack, can also damage the medial temporal lobe and memory formation. Within this general region of the brain, can we pinpoint a specific site as the cause of these memory problems?

H.M.'s surgery removed much of the amygdala and hippocampus from both sides of the brain (Figure 17.1). The memory deficit seemed to be caused by loss of the hippocampus because other surgery patients who had received the same type of damage to the amygdala, but less damage to the hippocampus, did not exhibit memory impairment. To test this hypothesis, investigators began to remove the hippocampus from experimental animals to reproduce H.M.'s deficit. But after a decade of research, brain scientists had to confess failure: Neither rats nor monkeys displayed widespread failure of memory consolidation after bilateral destruction of the hippocampus (Isaacson, 1972).

This puzzling discrepancy between humans and animals inspired more research, which produced major gains in knowledge—about amnesia in people and ways to test memory, about functions of the hippocampus and neighboring structures, and about brain mechanisms of memory. For example, scientists began to define more exactly what was impaired and what was spared in H.M.'s memory.

An early, incorrect hypothesis to explain why human results differed from those in other animals was that the impairment caused by damage to the medial temporal lobe in humans involves chiefly *verbal* material and animals, of course, cannot be tested for such deficits. An interesting finding suggested that H.M.'s memory deficit was restricted mainly to verbal material and might not hold for motor learning.

Brenda Milner (1965) presented a mirror-tracing task to H.M. (Figure 17.2a), and he showed considerable improvement over

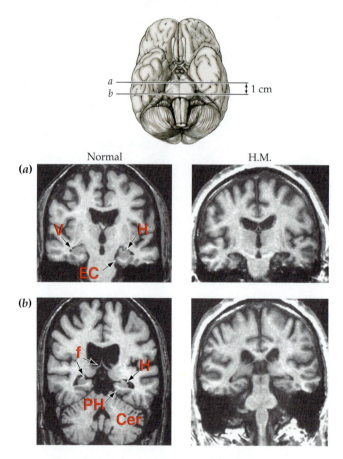

17.1 Brain Tissue Removed from Patient H.M.
(*a*) Approximately corresponding MRI scans of a normal subject (*left*) and patient H.M. (*right*) show that the hippocampus (H) and entorhinal cortex (EC), which are prominent in the normal scan, are absent bilaterally in H.M. (*b*) A more caudal scan (see the drawing at the top for planes of section) of a control patient (*left*) and H.M. (*right*) shows some of the hippocampus (H) intact in H.M., but the parahippocampus (PH) is absent. H.M.'s cerebellum (Cer) is so markedly shrunken that it does not appear in the scan. f, fornix; V, lateral ventricle. (From Corkin et al., 1997; courtesy of Suzanne Corkin.)

ten trials. The next day the test was presented again. When asked if he remembered it, H.M. said no, yet his performance was better than at the start of the first day (Figure 17.2*b*). Over three successive days, H.M. never recognized the problem, but his improved tracings showed evidence of memory. If an animal subject with the same type of brain damage showed similar proof of memory, we would have no doubt that the animal had normal memory because we do not ask animal subjects whether they *recognize* the test.

But the memory problems of H.M. and similar patients cannot be caused solely by difficulties with verbal material. First, such patients also have difficulty in reproducing or recognizing pictures and spatial designs that are not recalled in verbal terms. Second, although the patients have difficulty with the specific content of verbal material, they can learn some kinds of information *about* verbal material (N. J. Cohen and Squire, 1980).

For example, they can learn to read words printed mirror-reversed. The requirement for this task is not motor skill, but rather the ability to deal with abstract rules or procedures. If some words are used repeatedly, normal subjects come to recognize them and to read them easily. Patients of several kinds—those with temporal lobe amnesia, those who suffer from Korsakoff's syndrome (which we will describe shortly), and those who have recently received electroconvulsive shock therapy—learn the skill of mirror reading well but show impaired learning of the specific words.

Thus the important distinction is probably not between motor and verbal performances but between two kinds of memory: (1) **Declarative memory** is what we usually think of as memory: facts and information acquired through learning. It is memory we are aware of accessing. (2) **Procedural memory,** or **nondeclarative memory,** about perceptual or motor procedures is shown by *performance* rather than by *conscious recollection*. Examples of procedural memory are memory for the mirror-tracing task and for the skill of mirror reading, as we just described. The two kinds of memory can be distinguished as follows: Declarative memory deals with *what;* procedural memory deals with *how*. Thus an animal's inability to speak is probably not what accounts for its apparent immunity to the effects of medial temporal lesions on memory storage (Figure 17.3). Rather, the culprit is the difficulty in measuring declarative memory in animals.

Different types of tests measure declarative and procedural memories. Direct (explicit) tests of memory refer to a specific prior episode. Examples of direct tests include requests for information such as "Repeat the list of words you studied 10 minutes ago" or "What did you eat for dinner yesterday?" Direct tests also have been defined as requiring conscious recognition of the material. Indirect (implicit) tests of memory do not refer to a specific prior episode and do not require conscious recognition; the memory is inferred from performance. For example, memory for the recent presentation of certain words may be inferred from ease of recognizing them versus control words in blurred or very rapid presentation or from the probability of using them in a word completion test.

(a) The mirror-tracing task

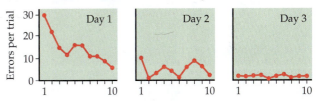

(b) Performance of H.M. on mirror-tracing task

17.2 H.M.'s Performance on a Mirror-Tracing Task (*a*) H.M. was given this mirror-tracing task to test motor memory. (*b*) His performance at this task on three successive days showed progressive improvement and thus long-term memory. (After B. Milner, 1965.)

17.3 Two Main Kinds of Memories

Long-term memories

Declarative:
Things you know that you can tell others

This type of memory can be tested readily in humans because they can talk. Patient H.M. seems to be unable to form new declarative memories.

Procedural (nondeclarative):
Things you know that you can show by doing

This type of memory can be tested readily in other animals as well as in humans. Patient H.M. can form new memories of this sort, such as the skill of mirror tracing.

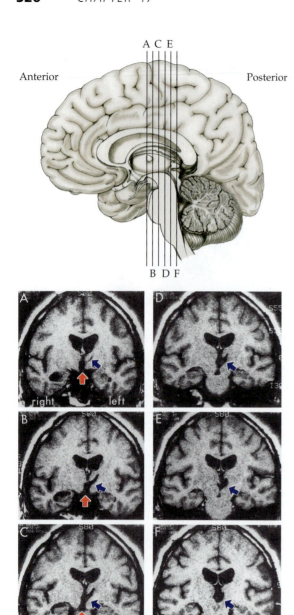

17.4 The Brain Damage in Patient N.A. Successive MRI scans were made through the diencephalic region (*top*); note that right and left are reversed in these scans, as if you were face-to-face with the patient. A prominent lesion on the left side of the brain is indicated by the purple arrows. The floor of the third ventricle also appears to be missing throughout much of the caudal two-thirds of the hypothalamus, as indicated by the red arrows in scans A through C. Where the mammillary nuclei should be present in B and C, there is no indication of intact tissue. (From Squire et al., 1989; MRI scans courtesy of Larry Squire.)

Damage to the medial diencephalon can also prevent the formation of new memories

The medial temporal lobe is not the only brain region involved in the formation of declarative memories. For example, the case of **patient N.A.** indicates that damage to the dorsomedial thalamus can also impair memory formation (Squire and Moore, 1979; Teuber et al., 1968). N.A. became amnesic as the result of a bizarre accident in which a miniature fencing foil injured his brain after entering through his nostril. N.A. is markedly amnesic, primarily for verbal material, and he can give little information about events since his accident in 1960, but he shows almost normal recall for earlier events (Kaushall et al., 1981).

An MRI study of N.A. (Figure 17.4) shows damage to the left dorsal thalamus, bilateral damage to the mammillary nuclei, and probable damage to the mammillothalamic tract (Squire et al., 1989). Like H.M., N.A. shows normal short-term memory but is impaired in forming declarative (but not procedural) long-term memories. The similarity in symptoms raises the question of whether the medial temporal region damaged in H.M. and the midline diencephalic region damaged in N.A. are normally parts of a larger memory system.

Patients with Korsakoff's syndrome show damage to midline diencephalic structures and to the frontal cortex

In 1887, Russian neurologist S. S. Korsakoff published a paper about a syndrome in which impaired memory was a major feature. This paper became a classic, and the syndrome was subsequently named after him: **Korsakoff's syndrome.** Sufferers of Korsakoff's syndrome fail to recall many items or events of the past; if such an item is presented again or if it happens to be recalled, the patient does not feel familiar with it. These patients frequently deny that anything is wrong with them. They often show disorientation to time and place, and they may **confabulate**—that is, fill a gap in memory with a falsification that they seem to accept as true.

The main cause of Korsakoff's syndrome is lack of the vitamin thiamine. Alcoholics who obtain most of their calories from alcohol and neglect their diet often exhibit this deficiency. Treating them with thiamine can prevent further deterioration of memory functions, but will not reverse the damage. Efforts to require manufacturers to add thiamine to alcoholic drinks, which would virtually eliminate any further cases of Korsakoff's syndrome, have repeatedly failed in the United States because political groups insist that such measures would encourage drinking.

Mair et al. (1979) examined the brains of two Korsakoff's patients whose behavior had been studied for several years. Temporal lobe structures, including the hippocampus, that were damaged in H.M., were normal in these patients. But the brains of the Korsakoff's patients showed shrunken, diseased mammillary bodies, as well as some damage in the dorsomedial thalamus. This damage is similar to that seen in N.A. Mair et al. (1979) characterize the mammillary bodies as a narrow funnel through which connections from the temporal lobe gain access to the frontal lobes. Damage to the basal frontal lobes, also found in patients suffering from Korsakoff's syndrome, probably causes the confabulation and denial that differentiates them from other patients who have amnesia, such as H.M.

Brain damage can destroy autobiographical memories while sparing general memories

One striking case of brain damage shows profound effects on memory and supports an important distinction between two subtypes of declarative memory that cognitive psychologist Endel Tulving (1972) has defined: semantic memory and episodic memory. **Semantic memory** is generalized memory, such as knowing the meaning of a word without knowing where or when you learned that word. **Episodic memory** is autobiographical memory that pertains to a person's particular history; you show episodic memory when you recall a specific episode or relate an event to a particular time and place (such as remembering where and when you last saw a certain friend).

Evidence for the distinction between semantic and episodic memory appeared in studies of **patient K.C.,** who had sustained brain injuries in a traffic accident. Brain scans revealed extensive damage to the left frontal-parietal and the right parietal-occipital cerebral cortex, and severe shrinkage of the hippocampus and parahippocampal cortex (R. S. Rosenbaum et al., 2000). K.C. can no longer retrieve any personal memory of his past, although his general knowledge remains good. He converses easily and plays a good game of chess, but he cannot remember where he learned to play chess or from whom. K.C. has difficulty acquiring new *semantic* knowledge, but he can acquire some, if care is taken to space out the trials to prevent interference among items (Tulving et al., 1991). But even with this method, K.C. cannot acquire new *episodic* knowledge.

The cortical damage, rather than impairment of the hippocampal region, appears to be responsible for the loss of episodic memory because other patients with hippocampal damage do not show this symptom. Studies of normal human subjects indicate increased blood flow in the anterior regions of the cortex during recall of episodic memories, so the anterior cortical damage may be what robs K.C. of episodic memory (Tulving, 1989).

**S. S. Korsakoff
(1853–1900)**

Endel Tulving

There Are Several Kinds of Memory and Learning

We have already mentioned the distinctions between declarative and procedural memories and between semantic and episodic memories. We will also be discussing some other kinds of memories and seeking to find the brain regions that are especially involved in them. Figure 17.5 presents a classification of some of the main kinds of long-term memory and gives an example of each. In addition, Box 17.1 reviews some basic definitions of learning.

In **skill learning,** subjects perform a challenging task on repeated trials in one or more sessions. The mirror-tracing task performed by H.M. (see Figure 17.2) is an example. Learning to read mirror-reversed text, also mentioned earlier, is a kind of perceptual skill learning.

Priming, also called *repetition priming*, is a change in the processing of a stimulus, usually a word or a picture, as a result of prior exposure to the same stimulus or related stimuli. For example, if a person is shown the word *stamp* in a list and later is asked to complete the word stem *STA-*, he or she is more likely to reply *stamp* than is a person who was not exposed to that word. Even patients like H.M., who do not recall being shown the list of words, nevertheless show the effect of priming.

Conditioning is defined in Box 17.1. Different brain areas are responsible for conditioning, depending on the complexity of the conditioning situation.

Do animals learn stimulus–response chains or form cognitive maps?

Many psychologists in the 1930s and 1940s were searching for the laws that govern all learning. Psychologists such as Clark L. Hull

17.5 Kinds of Long-Term Memory

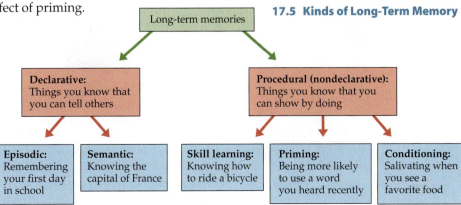

BOX 17.1 Learning and Memory: Some Basic Concepts and Definitions

Because you have probably studied learning and memory in one or more psychology courses, here we only briefly review some of the basic concepts and definitions. Basic experiments on learning and memory, as described for neuroscientists by Rescorla (1988), examine the organism's experience and behavior at two separate times. At the first time (t_1), the organism is exposed to a particular experience—a sensory stimulus or another opportunity to learn. At a later time (t_2), the investigator assesses the organism to determine whether the t_1 experience has modified its behavior.

The aim is to determine whether a particular t_1 experience produces an outcome at t_2 that would be absent without the t_1 experience. Therefore, studies of learning usually compare two organisms (or two groups of organisms) at t_2: those that were exposed to the t_1 experience and those that did not have that experience but instead had a "control" experience at t_1. The basic learning paradigms can be organized in terms of the different types of experiences provided at t_1 and the different techniques of assessment used at t_2.

Nonassociative learning involves only a single stimulus at t_1. Three kinds of nonassociative learning are habituation, dishabituation, and sensitization. **Habituation** is a decrease in response to a stimulus as the stimulus is repeated (when the decrement cannot be attributed to sensory adaptation or motor fatigue). Sitting in a café, you may stop noticing the door chime when someone enters; in this case you have habituated to the chime. When the response to a stimulus has become habituated, a strong stimulus (of the same sort or even in another sensory modality) will often cause the response to the habituated stimulus to increase sharply in amplitude; it may become even larger than the original response. The increase in response amplitude over the baseline level is called **dishabituation** (the habituation has been removed). If a loud firecracker is set off behind you, the next ring of the door chime may startle you; in this case you have become temporarily dishabituated to the chime. Even a response that has not been habituated may increase in amplitude after a strong stimulus. This effect is known as **sensitization:** The response is greater than the baseline level because of prior stimulation. After the firecracker, for example, you may overreact to someone standing up nearby. That horrible firecracker has sensitized you to many stimuli.

Learning that involves relations between events—for example, between two or more stimuli, between a stimulus and a response, or between a response and its consequence—is called **associative learning.** In one form, **classical conditioning** (also called *Pavlovian conditioning*), an initially neutral stimulus comes to predict an event. At the end of the nineteenth century, Ivan Pavlov (Figure A) found that a dog would salivate when

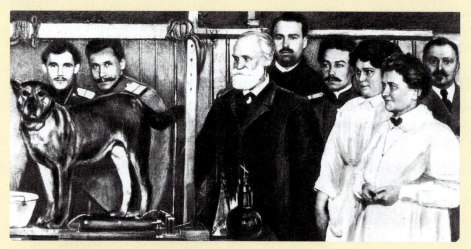

(A) Pavlov and spectators in his laboratory

**Edward C. Tolman
(1886–1959)**

held that animals form stimulus–response associations reinforced by rewards or punishments, and they attributed behavior such as that of rats in runways or mazes to this supposition (Hull, 1943). An opposing position was that of Edward C. Tolman (1949b), who held that when rats explore a maze, they do not learn a series of turns, but instead form a **cognitive map.** For example, after rats had run a maze several times, the experimenters removed a section of wall, thus opening up a shortcut to the goal area. Most rats took the shortcut as soon as it became available, thereby showing their knowledge of the overall layout of the maze.

Tolman and his students also demonstrated that rats' performance may not reveal all they know unless the test situation is appropriate to reveal the knowledge. One kind of evidence for this is the phenomenon called **latent learning,** which is described in the following experiment (Blodgett, 1929; Tolman and Honzik, 1930).

Rats were placed into two groups and allowed to gain experience in a maze. One group received food when they reached the goal area of the maze; they ran to that area more and more quickly in successive daily trials. Animals of the other group were allowed to explore the maze for a few daily sessions without receiving any re-

BOX 17.1 *(continued)*

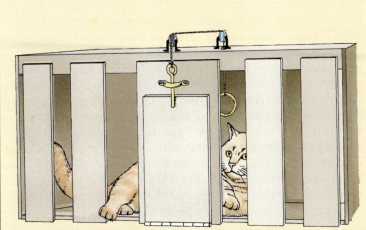

(B) Thorndike's puzzle box

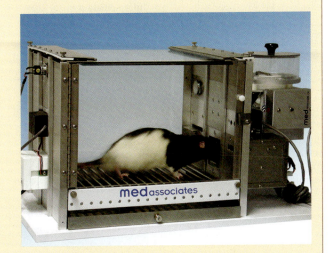

(C) A Skinner box

presented with an auditory or visual stimulus if the stimulus came to predict an event that normally caused salivation. If the experimenter rang a bell just before putting meat powder in the dog's mouth, repeating this sequence a few times would cause the dog to respond to the bell itself by salivating.

In this case the meat powder in the mouth is the *unconditioned stimulus* (*US*), which already evokes an unconditioned response (UR). The sound is the *conditioned stimulus* (*CS*), and the learned response to the CS alone (salivation in response to the bell in this example) is called the conditioned response (CR).

In **instrumental conditioning** (also called **operant conditioning**), an association is formed between the animal's behavior and its consequence(s). The first investigation of instrumental learning was Edward L. Thorndike's report (1898) of cats learning to escape from a puzzle box (Figure B). When placed in a small box with a latch inside, a cat would initially engage in a variety of behaviors and take quite a bit of time to free itself. But after several trial-and-error sequences, the cat learned to perform skillfully and economically the specific response (the conditioned instrumental response) that permitted escape (the reward). A modern example of an apparatus designed to study instrumental learning is an operant conditioning apparatus (Figure C), often called a *Skinner box* after its originator, B. F. Skinner. Here the conditioned instrumental response is pressing a bar to gain the reward of a food pellet.

Typical learning events have multiple dimensions or attributes. For example, Pavlov's dogs learned not only the relation between the conditioned auditory stimulus (the bell) and the meat powder, but also the location of the test and the rewarding features of the situation; so when they came into the test room, they would eagerly leap onto the test stand.

ward. Then, in one session they found food in the goal area. In the next trial they raced to the goal, reaching it just as rapidly as the rats that had been rewarded on every trial. If the experimenter hadn't offered the reward, he would not have realized that the previously unrewarded group had learned the maze as well as the uniformly rewarded rats; until the reward was introduced, the learning was latent, just as an image on photographic film is latent until the film is developed. Tolman (1949a) proposed that there are different kinds of learning and that each may have its own laws.

COMPETING HYPOTHESES

Memory Has Temporal Stages: Short, Intermediate, and Long

Even demonstrating that something has been learned does not guarantee that the memory for the learned material will be retrievable again in the future. A memory may later be absent for a variety of reasons: It may never have adequately formed, it may have decayed with time, it may have been impaired by injury to the brain, or it may be temporarily unretrievable because of the particular state of the subject.

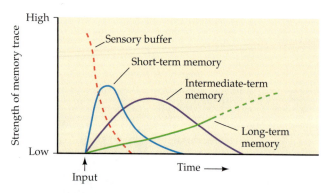

17.6 The Multiple-Trace Hypothesis of Memory According-ing to this hypothesis, an initial brief iconic memory (stored in a sensory buffer) is followed by a short-term memory trace, which may be followed by an intermediate-term memory trace. If the learning is sufficiently strong, a long-term memory trace may also result. (After McGaugh, 1968.)

Investigators often contrast short-term and long-term memories, but like many twofold distinctions, this differentiation is probably too simple. The **multiple-trace hypothesis** of memory classifies different types of memory by duration (Figure 17.6). The briefest memories are called **iconic memories** (from the Greek *eikon*, "image"). An example would be impressions of a scene that is illuminated for only an instant. You may be able to grasp one part of the display, but the rest vanishes from your memory in seconds. (A very brief auditory memory is called *echoic*, as if you could still hear it ringing in your ears.) These brief memories are thought to reflect the continuation of sensory neural activity—the so-called sensory buffers (see Figure 17.6).

Somewhat longer than iconic memories are **short-term memories (STMs)**. For example, suppose you want to telephone a person whose number you have never dialed before. You look up the number, and if nothing distracts or interrupts you, you call the number successfully, displaying an STM of the telephone number. If the line is busy, however, and you want to call back a minute later, you may have to look up the number again. If you rehearse or use the number, then it can remain in STM until you turn to another activity.

Unfortunately, the label *STM* is not used consistently among investigators from different fields. Cognitive psychologists, who first used the term, found that if subjects are not allowed to rehearse, STM lasts only about 30 s (J. Brown, 1958; L. R. Peterson and Peterson, 1959). Many biologists, however, define STM as memory that is not permanent but that lasts for minutes or hours, even up to a day. The lack of agreement on the duration of short-term and long-term memory undermines attempts to find biological mechanisms of the stages of memory.

Some memories last beyond the short term but fall short of long-term memories. For example, suppose you drive to school or work and park your car in a different place each day. If things go well, each afternoon you remember where you parked your car that morning, but you may not recall where you parked your car yesterday or a week ago. You are also likely to recall today's weather forecast, but not that of a few days ago. These are examples of what is sometimes called **intermediate-term memory (ITM)**—that is, a memory that outlasts STM but that is far from being permanent (McGaugh, 1966; Rosenzweig et al., 1993). Memories that last for days to years are called **long-term memories (LTMs)**.

There are good reasons—both clinical and experimental—to conclude that the cognitive processes and biological mechanisms that underlie STM storage are different from those that underlie LTM storage. Early behavioral evidence for differences between short-term and long-term memory stores came from the performance of subjects who learned lists of words or numbers. If you see or hear a list of ten words presented one at a time, and then 30 s later you try to repeat the list, you will probably remember best the first and the last items of the list.

Figure 17.7 shows typical results from such an experiment: a U-shaped serial position curve. The superior performance for the

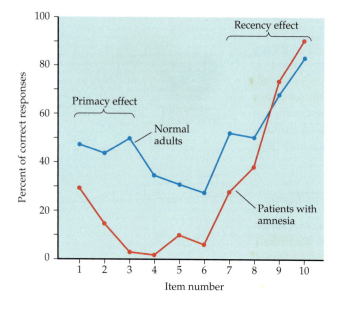

17.7 Serial Position Curves from Immediate-Recall Experiments These curves show the percentage of correct responses for immediate recall of a list of ten words. The patients with amnesia performed as well on the most recent items (8 through 10) as the normal adults did, but they performed significantly worse on earlier items. (After Baddeley and Warrington, 1970.)

start of the list is called the **primacy effect.** The superior performance for the end of the list is called the **recency effect.** If subjects try to recall the list a few minutes after having seen or heard the items, there is no recency effect; that is, it is short-lived and thus attributed to STM. The primacy effect, however, lasts longer and is usually attributed to LTM.

Experimental animals also show U-shaped serial position functions. These results provide one type of behavioral evidence to separate STM from longer-lasting memory stores in animal subjects, and they allow us to compare humans with other animals. A. A. Wright et al. (1985) gave similar recognition memory tests to pigeons, monkeys, and humans. For each test the material consisted of four sequentially presented color slides. Each slide was presented for 1 s to monkeys and humans and 2 s to pigeons, with a 1 s interval between items for all groups. After a delay, a probe item was presented; on half the trials the probe item matched one of the four test patterns. Subjects demonstrated their memory by making one response if the probe matched a test item and another response if it was new.

All three species showed primacy and recency effects in their serial position curves, differing only in the delays that reveal each effect (Figure 17.8). Thus, results for all three species provide evidence of two distinct memory processes: a transient STM that accounts for the short-lived recency effect, and a longer-lasting memory store that accounts for the primacy effect.

Brain lesion studies corroborate the parallel between humans and experimental animals: Rats with hippocampal lesions exhibit the recency but not the primacy effect, as though, like H.M., they cannot form new LTMs (Kesner and Novak, 1982). Similarly, patients with amnesia caused by impairment of the hippocampus show a reduced primacy effect but retain the recency effect (see Figure 17.7).

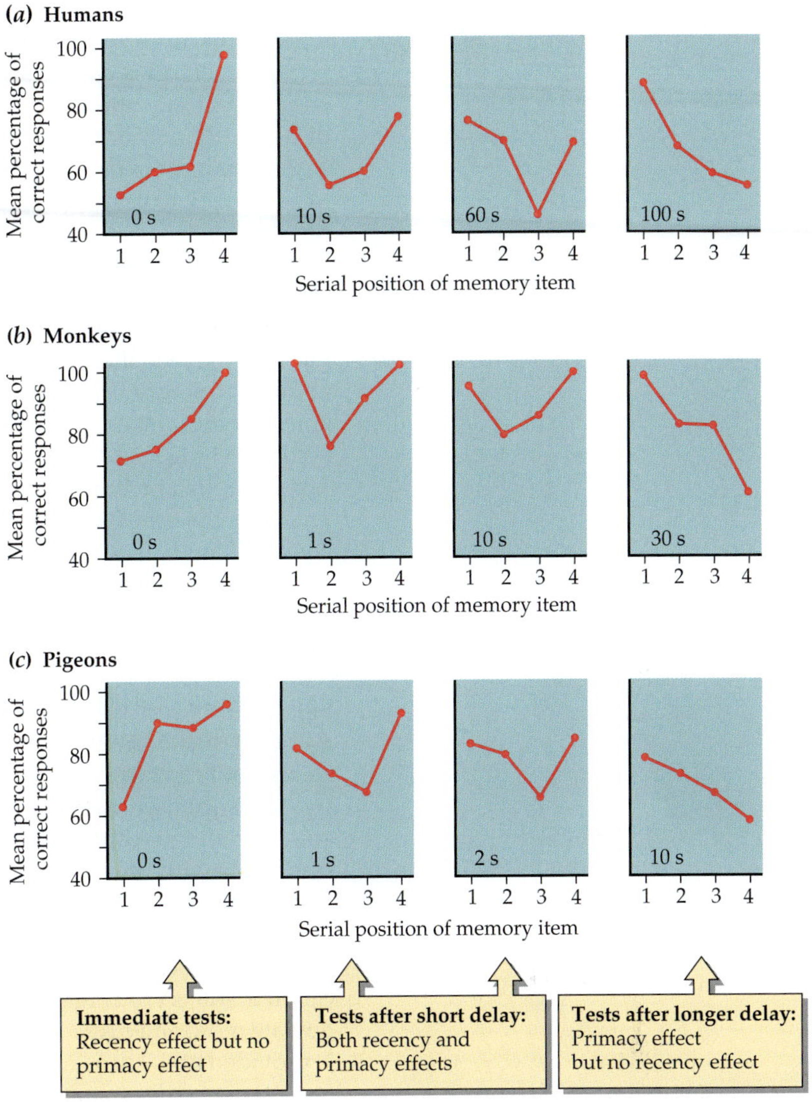

(a) Humans

(b) Monkeys

(c) Pigeons

Immediate tests: Recency effect but no primacy effect

Tests after short delay: Both recency and primacy effects

Tests after longer delay: Primacy effect but no recency effect

17.8 Recognition Memory Curves for Humans, Monkeys, and Pigeons These curves show the percentage of correct responses to a probe item for four positions in the stimulus series for humans (a), monkeys (b), and pigeons (c). (After A. A. Wright et al., 1985.)

The capacity of long-term memory is enormous

A fascinating case study of a man who remembered almost everything he had experienced from childhood on and was burdened by his total recall was presented by psychologist Alexander Luria in *The Mind of a Mnemonist* (1987). Even the fallible memory stores of most people hold huge numbers of memories and can acquire enormous amounts more. For example, American college students can recognize, on the average, about 50,000 different words. Many people who master several languages readily acquire even vaster vocabularies. Beyond the words, a language has grammar and grammatical forms, idioms, and familiar phrases; it is estimated that learning a language means acquiring on the order of 100,000 items of knowledge. Most of us recognize hundreds or thousands of faces and countless visual scenes and objects, hundreds of voices and many other familiar sounds, and hundreds of different odors. Depending on our interests, we may be able to recognize and sing

NEURAL PLASTICITY

or play many tunes and identify and supply information about a great many athletes, actors, or historical characters.

Such memories can be acquired rapidly and retained well. For example, psychologist Lionel Standing presented color slides to subjects for 5 s each in blocks of 20 to 1000 or more slides. A few days later he tested recognition memory by presenting pairs of slides, one previously seen and one new, and requiring subjects to indicate which of the pair they had seen before. After an early study showed 90% recognition for 2560 items, Standing increased the number of items to 10,000 and found little decrease in scores. He concluded that, for all practical purposes, "there is no upper bound to memory capacity" (Standing, 1973).

Of course, these results do not mean that the subjects learned all the details of the pictures; the two-alternative, forced-choice procedure guarantees only that *something* about the picture makes it more familiar than the paired item. Nevertheless, the amount of information acquired and the rapidity of acquisition are impressive. And accomplishing such a task doesn't require a human brain: Pigeons readily learned 320 slides in a picture recognition test, giving no indication that this amount approached their memory capacity, and they retained many of the discriminations for 2 years (Vaughan and Greene, 1984). An example of such memory retention in nature is displayed by Clark's nutcracker, a bird that can locate several thousand cache sites months after hiding food in them (Vander Wall, 1982). What kind of memory mechanisms provide for the enormous capacity of long-term memory?

Can memories be lost or distorted?

Although the capacity of long-term memory is enormous, we all experience instances of forgetting and inaccurate memory. Early in the twentieth century, investigators supposed that the **memory trace** (the record laid down in memory, presumably in the central nervous system, by a learning experience) decays or fragments with time. But then other workers studied how memories suffer interference from events before or after their formation, and many concluded that memories do not deteriorate with disuse.

Further research showed that each time a memory trace is activated during recall, it is subject to changes and fluctuations, so with successive activations it may deviate more and more from its original form. Furthermore, new information that is provided at the time of recall can add new aspects to the memory trace, so a later evocation of the memory is likely to reactivate the newer traces along with the older, and to produce distorted memories (Estes, 1997). Later in this chapter we will see that certain drugs given at the time of recall can significantly weaken a memory, although given at another time they do not affect memory.

Sometimes people can remember events that never happened. Psychologist Elizabeth Loftus (2003) has found that one way to create a false memory is to ask leading questions: "Did you see the broken headlight?" rather than "Was the headlight broken?" Another way to plant a false memory is to provide misinformation. In one study, for example, adults were read brief descriptions, provided by their family, of things that happened to them as children. One of these descriptions—getting lost in a shopping mall at 5 or 6 years of age—was a false event written by the experimenters. Yet about 25% of the subjects believed that they themselves had had this experience. Some, when questioned, even provided embellished details about the event (Loftus and Pickrell, 1995). Of course, some of these subjects may really have been lost in a mall once. But it is also easy to plant a memory of meeting a Bugs Bunny character at a Disney resort (Braun et al., 2002), something that could never happen in real life (because Bugs is a Warner Brothers character).

This possibility of planting false memories clouds the issue of "recovered memories" of childhood sexual or physical abuse. Controversial therapeutic methods such as hypnosis or guided imagery (in which the patient is encouraged to imagine "hypothetical" abuse scenarios) may inadvertently plant false memories. Indeed, one study found that people who had "recovered" memories of childhood sexual

Elizabeth Loftus

CLINICAL ISSUE

abuse, when brought to the laboratory and asked to remember lists of words, were more easily manipulated into falsely remembering a word than were control subjects or people who had always remembered their childhood abuse (McNally, 2003).

Different Regions of the Brain Process Different Aspects of Memory

In this section we will first consider the roles of different parts of the medial temporal lobe in the formation of declarative memory and then take up how other parts of the brain are involved in the formation of memories for specific aspects of experience.

The medial temporal lobe and declarative memory

As we saw earlier, the brain damage suffered by H.M. involved several parts of the medial temporal lobe. Investigators attempted to determine which parts were chiefly responsible for H.M.'s inability to form new declarative memories. Study of monkeys with experimental lesions of parts of the medial temporal region allowed the roles of the different structures to be examined systematically.

An important advance came when psychologists Brenda Spiegler and Mortimer Mishkin (1981) adopted a method for testing memory in monkeys that involved *declarative* memory—the kind of memory impaired in H.M. This is a test of object recognition memory known as the **delayed non-matching-to-sample** task (Figure 17.9). This method tested the ability of monkeys to recognize which of two objects had been seen, after delays ranging from 8 seconds to 2 minutes. Monkeys with extensive damage to the medial temporal lobe were severely impaired on this task, especially with the longer delays.

Other tests have also proved useful, for example, the **visual paired comparison** task. This task, originally devised for testing human infants, measures an individual's tendency to look at a novel object in comparison with a familiar object. Normal subjects prefer to inspect a novel object. Patients with amnesia are impaired on this task (McKee and Squire, 1993), and so are monkeys with lesions of the medial temporal lobe (Bachevalier et al., 1993).

After first lesioning various parts of the medial temporal region of monkeys, investigators used these and other tasks to test the monkeys' behavior. The amygdala (which had been lesioned in H.M.) was found not to be important for the formation

IMPORTANT METHOD

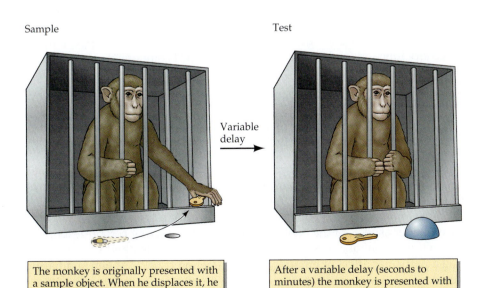

Sample	Test	Food found under the nonmatching object
The monkey is originally presented with a sample object. When he displaces it, he finds a pellet of food beneath.	After a variable delay (seconds to minutes) the monkey is presented with the original object and another object.	Over a series of trials with different pairs of objects, the monkey learns that food is present under the object that differs from the sample.

Variable delay

17.9 The Delayed Non-Matching-to-Sample Task

(a) **Ventral view of monkey brain showing areas of different medial temporal lesions**

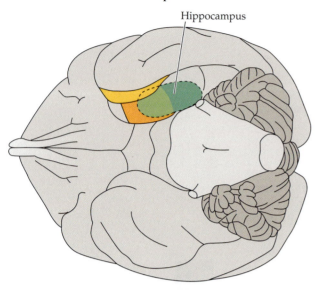

Hippocampus

(b) **Scores of groups with different lesions**

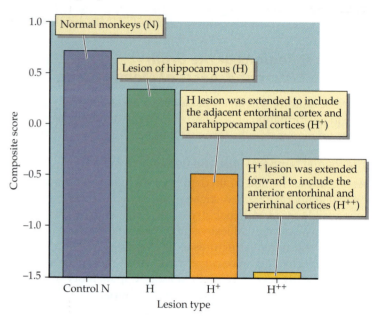

17.10 Behavioral Scores as a Function of Medial Temporal Lobe Lesions (a) In this ventral view of a monkey brain, the hippocampus is dorsal to the cross-hatched area. The parahippocampal cortex is shown in green, the entorhinal cortex in orange, and the perirhinal cortex in yellow. (After Squire and Zola-Morgan, 1991). (b) Different bilateral lesions of the medial temporal lobe yielded different results in tests of memory.

of declarative memories, although it is important in fear learning. A retrospective analysis of several studies, employing four different tests of memory with behavioral measures combined to provide composite scores, and lesions varying in size, yielded the results shown in Figure 17.10 (Zola-Morgan et al., 1994): Some impairment was produced by lesions that included the hippocampus proper, the dentate gyrus, and the subiculum; increased impairment was caused by lesions that included not only these regions but also the adjacent entorhinal cortex and the parahippocampal cortex; finally, the greatest impairment was caused by lesions that also included the anterior entorhinal and perirhinal cortices.

In human patients, too, damage restricted to only the hippocampus produces memory impairments similar to but not as severe as those seen with the more extensive damage in H.M. (Rempel-Clower et al., 1996; Zola-Morgan and Squire, 1986). Zola-Morgan and Squire (2001) concluded that the hippocampus is the final stage of convergence within the medial temporal lobe, combining operations of the adjacent, more specialized regions of cortex; even in the absence of the hippocampus, some memory function can be supported by the cortical components of the medial temporal system.

Different brain regions are involved in different attributes of memory

Any particular memory is composed of features or aspects that are specific and unique to that learning experience, as investigators of human memory noted decades ago (Spear, 1976; Underwood, 1969). Some of the main features (or attributes) of memories are space, time, sensory perception, response, and affect (i.e., emotional tone or content). For example, as you look at this book, you are aware of spatial aspects of your experience (where the book is in relation to you and where you are); you know the approximate or even the exact time; you perceive the color, shape, and other aspects of the book; you are aware of making certain responses, such as holding the book, turning the page, and writing notes; and you are experiencing a particular affect or emotional state—feeling content, eager, and happy (we hope).

Biological psychologists have tested whether the different attributes of memory are processed by different regions of the brain. Raymond Kesner (1980, 1991, 1998) designed a program of experiments with rats, as well as experimental and observational studies of people with various kinds of brain damage. Figure 17.11 shows some basic attributes of memory and the brain regions that are believed to process them.

In all of Kesner's tasks, only working, short-term memory was tested. Thus, for a *spatial recognition task*, Kesner et al. (1993) used the well-known eight-arm radial maze (Figure 17.12*a*). Appropriate pretraining taught the rat to expect to find a bit of food at the end of each arm of the maze. For this spatial recognition task, each trial consisted of a study phase and a test phase. In the study phase the rat was allowed to run down any arm. When it returned to the central platform, all doors to the arms were closed, confining the rat for a period of 1 to 30 s.

Next, two doors were opened, allowing the rat a choice between the arm it had recently entered and another arm; the rat found food only if it chose the arm it had entered in the study phase of the trial. In each of the four daily trials, different arms were used. Different groups of animals were tested after having received a sham lesion or a lesion in the hippocampus, the caudate nucleus, or the extrastriate cortex (visual cortex outside the primary visual area). The results of this experiment showed that only the animals with hippocampal lesions made more mistakes than the controls (the animals with sham lesions) on this predominantly spatial task.

To emphasize memory for the animal's own locomotor *response*, the investigators ran trials in a different apparatus (Figure 17.12*b*). In the study phase of a trial, the rat was placed in the middle arm on one side (e.g., 2), where it could make an initial turn to its left (3) or right (1). Then it was placed in a different starting location (5) and was rewarded only if it made a turn to the same side of its body as before, not to the same direction in space. Performance on this task, which depends on memory of the previous response, was impaired by lesions of the caudate nucleus but not by lesions of the other brain regions tested.

A task that emphasizes *sensory perception* is the object recognition (or non-matching-to-sample) test. In the study phase, the rat was first rewarded each time it pushed aside the sample object. In the test phase the rat was presented with two objects—one like the sample object that had been presented during the study phase and one novel object; the rat was rewarded only if it chose the object that did not match the sample (Figure 17.12*c*). Only lesions of the extrastriate visual cortex significantly impaired performance on this visual memory task.

Thus, Kesner et al. (1993) found a triple **dissociation** among brain regions and the tests. That is, lesions of each of three brain regions affected memory performance on only one of the three tests, and performance on each test was affected by lesions in only one of the three brain regions. This dissociation is good evidence that these different aspects of working memory are processed separately and, in part at least, by the brain regions indicated. Of course, an even more complete set of brain regions remains to be tested, if only to try to exclude them as important in processing these aspects of memory.

In Chapter 15 we learned that the amygdala plays a role in mediating emotional behavior, especially fear. Indeed, Kesner and Williams (1995) found that memory involving *affect* in rats is impaired by lesions of the amygdala, but not by lesions in the hippocampal formation or in the cerebral cortex dorsal to the hippocampus. Similarly, in humans who have sustained damage in the temporal lobe, the impairment in remembering emotionally charged words (e.g., *rape, terrorist*) is correlated with the extent of damage to the amygdala. Damage to the hippocampus impairs memory for both neutral words and emotional words (Richardson et al., 2004).

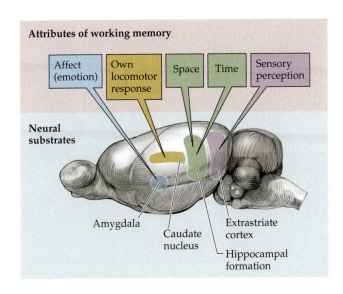

17.11 Basic Attributes of Memory and the Region of the Rat Brain That Is Thought to Process Each (After Kesner, 1980.)

(a) Spatial location recognition memory

In the study phase of each trial, the rat can choose any of the eight arms. In the test phase, doors block all but two arms: the arm entered on the study phase and one other. The rat obtains food only if it chooses the arm it entered on the study phase.

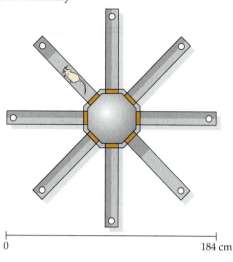

0   184 cm

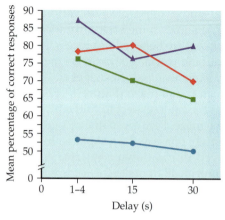

Brain region lesioned
- ● Hippocampus
- ■ Control
- ▲ Caudate nucleus
- ◆ Extrastriate visual cortex

Only rats with hippocampal lesions make significantly more errors than controls.

(b) Response recognition memory

In the first part of each trial, the rat is placed in the middle compartment on one side (2), and it finds food if it enters the compartment either to its right (1) or left (3). In the second part of the trial, it is placed in the middle compartment on the other side (5), and it finds food only if it turns to the same side of its body as it had in the first part.

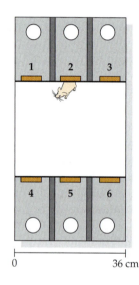

0   36 cm

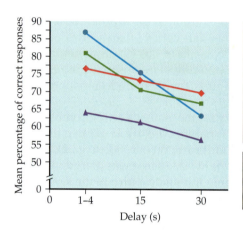

Brain region lesioned
- ● Hippocampus
- ■ Control
- ▲ Caudate nucleus
- ◆ Extrastriate visual cortex

Only rats with caudate nucleus lesions make significantly more errors than controls.

(c) Object recognition memory (non-matching-to-sample)

In the study phase of each trial, the rat obtains food by displacing a sample object over a small food well (top). In the test phase (bottom), the rat chooses between two objects and obtains food only if it chooses the object that does *not* match the sample.

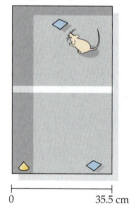

0   35.5 cm

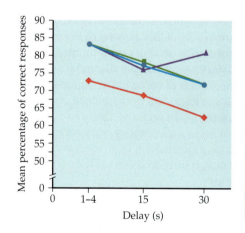

Brain region lesioned
- ● Hippocampus
- ■ Control
- ▲ Caudate nucleus
- ◆ Extrastriate visual cortex

Only rats with lesions of the extrastriate visual cortex make significantly more errors than controls.

17.12 Experiments to Test Specific Attributes of Animals' Memory Brain lesion experiments testing spatial location recognition (*a*), response recognition (*b*), and object recognition (*c*)—using the setups shown on the left—yielded the results shown on the right. (After Kesner et al., 1993.)

Place cells in the hippocampus process spatial memory

One of the clues that led investigators to test for the processing of spatial memory in the hippocampus was the discovery that some cells in the rat hippocampus seem to encode spatial location (O'Keefe and Dostrovsky, 1971). That is, these neurons produce action potentials preferentially when the rat is in a particular location or is moving toward that location, so they have been called **place cells.** This discovery led to a great deal of research to understand the properties of place cells and how they form.

The monkey hippocampus also contains some place cells that respond like those of rats, but monkeys have relatively fewer of these cells than rats have (Rolls and O'Mara, 1995). More cells in the monkey hippocampus respond to the part of the environment the monkey is looking at, so investigators researching them refer to them as *spatial view cells* and suggest that they reflect the importance of vision for monkeys. Perhaps there are place or spatial cells in the hippocampus of bird species that cache and retrieve food, since they have larger hippocampal formations than species that do not cache, as we reported in Chapter 6.

EVOLUTION AT WORK

Memory processes extend from acquisition to retrieval

Psychologists who study learning and memory suggest that several successive processes are necessary to guarantee recall of a past event: **encoding, consolidation,** and **retrieval** (Figure 17.13). The original information must enter sensory channels and then be *encoded* rapidly into a form that passes into short-term memory. Some of this information may then be *consolidated* in long-term storage. And in the final stage of processing, information that was stored earlier is *retrieved* for use.

There is both neurological and neurochemical evidence that the neural processes for short-term and long-term memory storage differ. For example, patients with brain damage like that of H.M. retain new items in short-term storage but show no long-term memory for them. With the three stages outlined here in mind, investigators have tried to determine whether particular examples of "forgetting" in normal subjects involve failure of encoding, of consolidation, or of retrieval, and whether pathological impairments of memory selectively involve one or another of these main processes. Performance on a memory test can be either enhanced or impaired, depending on the conditions of acquisition, of consolidation, or of retrieval.

Brain regions involved in encoding   Evidence that the activation of particular brain regions underlies the encoding of declarative memories comes from research in which separate activations are recorded for each stimulus in a series. When memory for the stimuli is tested later, the activations can be analyzed separately for stimuli remembered (and thus encoded successfully) and for stimuli forgotten (not encoded).

Beginning in the late 1990s, advances in functional MRI permitted the measurement of event-related brain responses to individual brief stimuli, such as a picture or a word presented for as short a time as 1 s

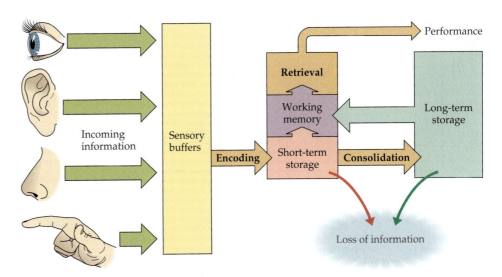

17.13 Hypothesized Memory Processes: Encoding, Consolidation, and Retrieval

(Buckner et al., 1996; B. R. Rosen et al., 1998). In one experiment, subjects looked at a series of photographs and classified each scene as indoors or outdoors; they were not told that they would be asked later to remember the pictures (Brewer et al., 1998). Thirty minutes later they were shown these pictures mixed with novel ones and were asked to identify which they had seen previously and which they had not. In a similar experiment, subjects saw words one at a time and were asked to classify them as abstract or concrete (A. D. Wagner et al., 1998).

When the activations elicited by individual stimuli were classified according to later success or failure of recognition, it was found that although the stimuli activated many brain areas, only a few brain areas predicted which stimuli would later be recognized. In the case of the pictures, the critical areas showing greater activation to correctly recalled stimuli were the right prefrontal cortex and the parahippocampal cortex in both hemispheres. In the case of the words, the critical areas were the *left* prefrontal cortex and the *left* parahippocampal cortex. These findings are compatible with results we will discuss in Chapter 19 showing that the right hemisphere is more involved in spatial perception, while the left hemisphere is mainly responsible for language.

Consolidating declarative information   Studies of patients with brain injury suggest that consolidation of declarative long-term memories takes considerable time and involves the hippocampus. To study this problem, four groups of investigators independently designed experiments in which animals learned equivalent material at various times before they sustained lesions of the hippocampal formation. These studies were done with rats (J. J. Kim and Fanselow, 1992; Winocur, 1990), mice (Y. H. Cho et al., 1993), and monkeys (Zola-Morgan and Squire, 1990). Psychologist-neuroscientist Larry Squire has studied this problem and many other aspects of memory with both human and nonhuman subjects.

Larry Squire

In the monkey experiment, animals learned to discriminate between two objects in 20 different pairs at each of 5 periods (16, 12, 8, 4, and 2 weeks before surgery)—a total of 100 pairs. Eleven of the monkeys were then given bilateral lesions of the hippocampal formation, including the subicular complex and the entorhinal cortex; seven monkeys formed the control group, receiving no lesions.

Two weeks after surgery the investigators showed the animals each of the 100 previously presented pairs in a mixed order. The control monkeys remembered more of what they had learned most recently than of what they had learned earlier (Figure 17.14). The lesioned monkeys, however, performed significantly worse than the controls on the object pairs they had learned 2 and 4 weeks before surgery; they did not differ from the controls for pairs learned earlier. Note also that the lesioned monkeys performed worse on items learned 2 and 4 weeks before surgery than on the items learned earlier.

These results show that the hippocampal system (i.e., the medial temporal region) is *not* a repository of long-term memory. In each of the animal experiments it was possible to identify a time after learning when damage to this system had no effect on memory. Thus the information that initially depends on the hippocampal system for processing does not depend on it for long-term (or permanent) storage. Permanent storage is thought to occur in regions of the cortex where the information is first processed and held in short-term memory; after further processing that involves the medial temporal region (and probably the midline diencephalic region as well), the permanent memory storage becomes independent of the medial temporal–diencephalic region.

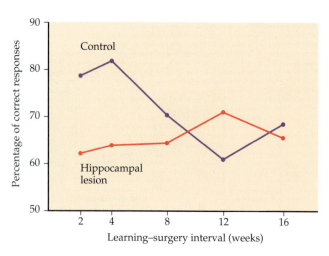

17.14 Retention by Monkeys of Object Discrimination Problems   An equal number of items was learned 2, 4, 8, 12, and 16 weeks before the experimental animals underwent hippocampal surgery. For the control animals, memory was best for the most recently learned items; for the lesioned animals, memory was significantly worse for the items learned 2 and 4 weeks prior to surgery. (After Zola-Morgan and Squire, 1990.)

The fact that memories require consolidation for long-term storage may help explain the retrograde amnesia that is common with injury to the brain. Memories that have not yet been completely consolidated in the cortex may be seriously impaired by interruption of processing. Conditions that follow learning can also modulate the strength of memory, as we will see in the next section.

CLINICAL ISSUE

Emotion can modulate memory formation

Most of us would agree that emotionally arousing experiences tend to be well remembered—sometimes too well. Descartes (1662) wrote, "The usefulness of all the passions [emotions] consists in their strengthening in the soul thoughts which are good for it to conserve… And all the harm they can do consists in their strengthening and prolonging these thoughts more than is necessary." Similarly, William James (1890) wrote, "An experience may be so exciting emotionally as almost to leave a scar on the cerebral tissues" (p. 670).

Recently investigators have found evidence that emotions can modulate memory formation in several ways. For example, emotions often enhance memory for aspects of an event or story that are closely tied to the emotional aspects, but they can also weaken memories that are not central to the emotional theme (Reisberg and Heuer, 1995).

An emotionally arousing story is remembered significantly better than a closely matched but more emotionally neutral story; this emotional enhancement of memory may be caused by activation of beta-adrenergic receptors by stress hormones from the adrenal glands (Cahill et al., 1994). Some subjects were told an emotional version of a story, and some were told a neutral version; both versions were accompanied by the same 12 slides. The first four items of both stories were identical, with four slides showing a mother and son going to visit the father's workplace in a hospital. In the second phase the two narratives differed, but the same five slides were shown: In the neutral version, the boy saw wrecked cars in a junkyard and then witnessed a disaster drill at the hospital; in the emotional version, the boy was badly injured in a traffic accident and was treated in the emergency room and in surgery. In the third phase (three slides), the mother went to pick up her other child at preschool.

The subjects heard the narratives and saw the slides while connected to heart rate and blood pressure monitors and were told that the study concerned physiological responses to different types of stimuli. One hour before the story presentation, all subjects received injections; some received a control injection of physiological saline solution; the others received propranolol, a beta-adrenergic receptor antagonist. (Propranolol and other so-called beta-blockers are used to combat high blood pressure.) A week later, without expecting any further contact with the stories, the subjects were asked to recall as many of the slides as possible and then took an 80-item multiple choice recognition memory test that assessed memory for both visual and narrative story elements.

Subjects who had received the control injection remembered the second, emotionally arousing phase of the story significantly better than the first or third phases. But subjects who had received the propranolol injection did not show better memory for the second, "emotional" phase than for the first and third phases. Control and propranolol-treated subjects scored about the same on the first and third phases of the story. Thus the drug did not affect memory in general but blocked only the enhancement caused by emotional arousal.

Did the propranolol affect memory strength by preventing the subjects from having an emotional reaction to the stories? To test this question, the investigators had each subject rate his or her degree of emotion in response to the story just after it was presented. The "emotional" version was rated significantly more arousing than the neutral version by subjects given the beta-blocker, as well as by subjects given the control injection, so it was not the failure to experience emotion that prevented the enhancement of memory.

The alternative hypothesis is that propranolol acted after training to block the enhancement of memory formation. This hypothesis is supported by animal research that we will review in Chapter 18.

Can modulation of learning help in understanding, alleviating, or preventing posttraumatic stress disorder?

CLINICAL ISSUE

What about cases when emotional experience causes us to remember something too well? Some people exposed to life-threatening events or other catastrophic experiences develop a syndrome known as **posttraumatic stress disorder** (**PTSD**), as discussed in Chapter 16. One set of symptoms is "reliving experiences such as intrusive thoughts, nightmares, dissociative flashbacks to elements of the original traumatic event, and … preoccupation with that event" (Keane, 1998, p. 398).

Perhaps people with PTSD are caught in a positive feedback loop in which each episode of reexperiencing (intrusive memory, flashback) produces a stress hormone response, which activates beta-adrenergic receptors that further reinforce the memory (Pitman, 1989). On the basis of this hypothesis, Cahill (1997) proposed a strategy to prevent PTSD formation by suppressing beta-adrenergic activity with drugs either shortly before a traumatic experience or as quickly as possible after it. For example, rescue workers could take an appropriate drug on their way to the scene of a disaster, and rape victims could be given an antiadrenergic drug such as propranolol as part of their treatment as soon as possible after the attack. This treatment would not delete memories of the event but might diminish the traumatic aspects.

It may be possible also to diminish some of the impact of already established traumatic memories. As noted earlier, a variety of treatments are **amnestic** (memory-impairing) if they are administered shortly before or shortly after original learning; such treatments include electroconvulsive shock and drugs, such as inhibitors of protein synthesis or NMDA receptor antagonists. A study with rats found that when a previously formed memory is reactivated, it can be weakened by administration of propranolol up to 2 hours after reactivation of the memory (Przybyslawski et al., 1999; Sara, 2000). Przybyslawski and colleagues suggest that if the drug is given when the memory is recalled, it might weaken the strength of the memory. Similarly, a study of fear conditioning in rats showed that when a consolidated fear memory was reactivated, it returned to a labile state that required protein synthesis for reconsolidation, just as new memories require protein synthesis for consolidation into long-term memories (Nader et al., 2000).

NEURAL PLASTICITY

Brain Imaging Provides Insights about Regions Involved in Different Kinds of Memories

Examination of brain-injured patients and animals with experimental lesions does not reveal what functions are served by the injured or missing tissue. Rather, the behavior shows what the surviving brain regions can accomplish after the lesion. Brain-imaging techniques are providing evidence about memory processes in the healthy brain.

The combination of lesion and neuroimaging studies helps overcome the limitations of each of these sources of evidence alone, and each provides constraints on data from the other source. For example, a memory task may activate several different brain regions, but some of these regions can be injured without performance on that task being affected. So some of the activations may represent *correlated* processes that are not *required* for the form of memory being measured. The lesion evidence makes it possible to discriminate between activations that are essential or nonessential for a specific form of memory. In the sections that follow, we will take up the kinds of memory shown in Figure 17.5.

Imaging studies of declarative memory

Imaging studies confirm and extend the conclusions from lesion studies that the medial temporal (hippocampal) and diencephalic systems are needed to form new declarative long-term memories. These regions are activated during both encoding of new material (C. E. Stern et al., 1996; Tulving et al., 1996) and retrieval (Schacter et al., 1996). A survey of 53 PET studies of memory revealed that encoding and retrieval activations are focused in somewhat different medial temporal brain regions (Figure 17.15) (Lepage et al., 1998).

Whereas the medial temporal region is necessary for processing information for long-term storage, the cortex has been considered to be the site of storage of long-term declarative memories. Patients like H.M., who no longer have a hippocampus, nevertheless retain memories that were stored before brain lesion. On the other hand, some patients with lesions of the cortex can no longer retrieve the names of specific categories of objects—for example, living things such as animals, manufactured things such as tools, or even more-specific categories, such as flowers or motor vehicles.

Neuroimaging studies of normal subjects provide data consistent with specific localizations for such categories. For example, asking subjects to name tools or animals yields cortical activations that overlap in some areas but differ in others (A. Martin et al., 1996). These results with normal subjects indicate that the surprising regional specificity of representations of knowledge in patients reflects the localized cortical geography of the normal brain (see Chapter 19).

The distinction between semantic (general) memory and episodic (autobiographical) memory is supported by the case of patient K.C., discussed earlier, who can no longer access any memories about his life, although he retains much general knowledge. But, as in many cases of brain lesions caused by accident or disease, the damage to K.C.'s brain was widespread and did not offer much information about the site(s) of episodic memories. In an attempt to localize episodic memory processes better, experimenters had subjects listen to autobiographical passages and to passages written by other people (Fink et al., 1996). The autobiographical passages, relative to the others, caused greater activation of right frontal and temporal lobe regions, as Figure 17.16 shows. Thus, autobiographical memories and semantic memories appear to be processed in different locations.

17.15 Encoding and Retrieval Activate Different Medial Temporal Regions of the Brain (*a*) This reference figure shows the position of a sagittal slice 25 mm from the midline. (*b*) Indicated here are the locations of peak activities in the hippocampal formation in 22 experiments on encoding (red) and 34 experiments on retrieval (blue). (Part *a* after Talairach and Tournoux, 1988; *b* after Lepage et al., 1998.)

Imaging studies of skill memory

Imaging studies have been conducted to investigate learning and memory for different kinds of skills:

- *Sensorimotor skills,* such as mirror tracing (see Figure 17.2) and rotary pursuit (in which the subject tries to maintain contact between a handheld stylus and a small target on a rotating disk)
- *Perceptual skills,* such as learning to read mirror-reversed text (mentioned earlier)
- *Cognitive skills,* such as tasks that require planning and problem solving (e.g., the Tower of Hanoi problem)

All three kinds of skill learning are impaired in patients with injury to the basal ganglia or with Huntington's disease, which attacks the basal ganglia. Other brain

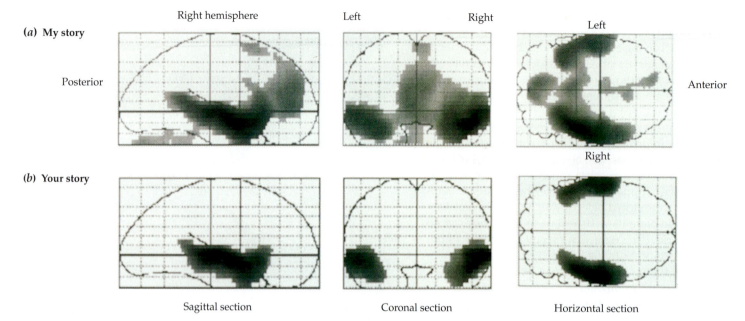

(a) **My story**

Right hemisphere   Left   Right   Left

Posterior   Anterior

Right

(b) **Your story**

Sagittal section   Coronal section   Horizontal section

17.16 My Story versus Your Story
Autobiographical passages (a) caused greater activation of the right frontal and temporal lobes than nonautobiographical passages (b). (After Fink et al., 1996; courtesy of Gereon Fink.)

regions, such as the motor cortex and the cerebellum, are involved in some examples of skill learning.

Neuroimaging studies support the importance of both the basal ganglia and the cerebellum, as well as of motor cortex, for sensorimotor skill learning. Rotary pursuit learning, in which subjects use a wand to track a spot on a rotating disk, activated the primary and secondary motor cortices (Grafton et al., 1992). Learning the specific sequences of finger movements activated the primary and secondary motor cortices and the basal ganglia (Doyon et al., 1996; Hazeltine et al., 1997). Some studies also show activation of the cerebellum, which appears to be related to the correction of errors in finger movements (Flament et al., 1996). Often the activations shift among brain regions as performance changes during the course of learning, so learning appears to involve a complex set of interacting neural networks.

Imaging studies of repetition priming

We mentioned earlier that priming is a change in processing of a stimulus due to prior exposure to the same or a related stimulus. Priming does not require declarative memory of the stimulus (H.M. and other patients with amnesia show priming for words they don't remember having seen), so it does not require the medial temporal or diencephalic regions. In addition, patients who suffer from Huntington's disease show normal priming, so intact basal ganglia are not required.

Priming tasks can be distinguished as perceptual or conceptual. *Perceptual* priming reflects prior processing of the *form* of the stimulus (you've been shown the word *pear* as part of a list; when asked to complete the word *pea-*, you're more likely to say "pear" than "peak"). *Conceptual* priming reflects the *meaning* of the stimulus (you've been shown the word *fruit* as part of a list and asked to complete the word *pea-*). Perceptual priming is related to *reduced* activity, relative to baseline activity during word stem completion, in bilateral occipitotemporal cortex (Schacter et al., 1996). Presumably the activity is reduced for the primed words because responding to them requires less effort than responding to nonprimed words does. Conceptual priming is related to reduced activity in left frontal cortex (Blaxton et al., 1996; Gabrieli et al., 1996; A. D. Wagner, Desmond, et al., 1997).

Imaging studies of conditioning

Research on brain circuits involved in classical conditioning will be taken up in Chapter 18. That work shows that cerebellar circuits are responsible for simple delay conditioning (in which there is no time gap between the conditioned stimulus and the unconditioned stimulus). Delay conditioning occurs normally even if the hippocampus has been lesioned, but for trace conditioning (in which the conditioned stimulus ends before the unconditioned stimulus starts), the hippocampus is required.

A PET study of human delay eye-blink conditioning used both behavioral intervention and the correlational approach (Logan and Grafton, 1995). During the first (control) session of the experiment, PET scans were made while subjects received an unpaired tone and puff of air to the right eye. In the second session, 1 to 6 days later, the stimuli were paired. In the third session, 2 to 7 days after the first, PET scans were made while the subjects received paired stimuli. Comparison of the scans from this third session with those from the first showed increased activity in several regions of the brain (Figure 17.17a). Activity in some of these regions correlated significantly with conditioning behavior (Figure 17.17b).

Thus the neural network activated during human delay eye-blink conditioning includes not only the cerebellar and brainstem regions found in animal research, but also the hippocampus, the ventral striatum, and regions of the cerebral cortex. But activity in these other areas may not be *essential* for eye-blink conditioning. For example, patients with hippocampal damage can acquire the conditioned eye-blink response, whereas patients with unilateral cerebellar damage can acquire a

CLINICAL ISSUE

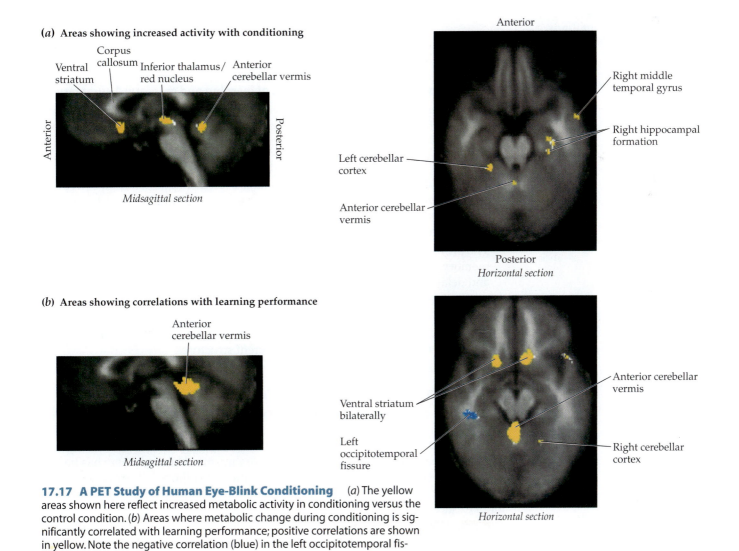

(a) **Areas showing increased activity with conditioning**

Midsagittal section

Anterior

Right middle temporal gyrus

Right hippocampal formation

Left cerebellar cortex

Anterior cerebellar vermis

Posterior
Horizontal section

(b) **Areas showing correlations with learning performance**

Anterior cerebellar vermis

Midsagittal section

Anterior cerebellar vermis

Ventral striatum bilaterally

Left occipitotemporal fissure

Right cerebellar cortex

Horizontal section

17.17 A PET Study of Human Eye-Blink Conditioning *(a)* The yellow areas shown here reflect increased metabolic activity in conditioning versus the control condition. *(b)* Areas where metabolic change during conditioning is significantly correlated with learning performance; positive correlations are shown in yellow. Note the negative correlation (blue) in the left occipitotemporal fissure. (From Logan and Grafton, 1995.)

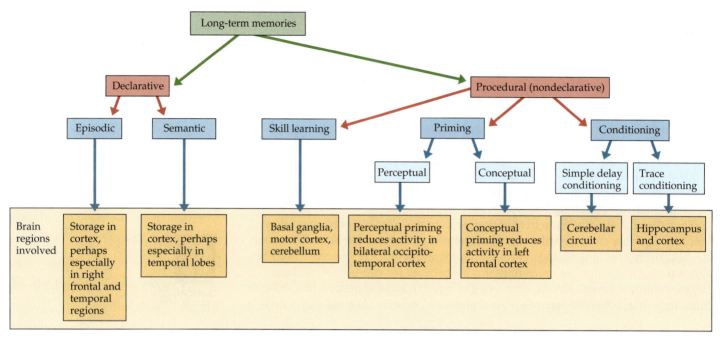

17.18 Brain Regions Involved in Different Kinds of Learning and Memory

conditioned eye-blink response only on the side where the cerebellum is intact (Papka et al., 1994).

Brain regions involved in different kinds of learning and memory: A summary

Figure 17.18 summarizes the findings we have reviewed about brain regions involved in different kinds of learning and memory. We can make several major conclusions:

- Many regions of the brain are involved in learning and memory.
- The kinds of learning and memory that have been distinguished from each other on cognitive grounds—such as declarative versus procedural, or semantic versus episodic—are mediated by different, or at least partially different, brain structures and regions.
- The same brain structure may be involved in different kinds of learning and memory; for example, the cerebellum is involved in both sensorimotor learning and delay conditioning.
- A given kind of learning may require activity of a circuit involving several different brain regions.
- Some kinds of learning that appear rather similar, such as delay and trace conditioning, may nevertheless involve different structures.

Comparative Approaches Yield Insights about the Evolution of Learning and Memory

Learning and memory exist throughout the animal kingdom, and some forms of short-term learning appear in single-celled organisms. Although there has been a good deal of speculation about the early evolution of abilities to learn and remember, we cannot research this subject directly because we cannot measure the behavior of extinct animals.

The fact that learning is so widespread suggests that it was an early evolutionary development, with changes occurring as organisms evolved to occupy new niches and meet new challenges. A fruitful approach is to compare the learning and memory of related species in which differences in ecological niche and lifestyle have caused different selection pressures for specific kinds of learning and therefore changes in brain structure.

As we consider attempts at comparing learning ability among existing species, we will see that it is not a simple matter. Just as it is difficult, perhaps impossible, to devise a "culture-free" intelligence test for human beings, so has it been difficult to devise tests for animals that do not favor the sensory and/or motor capacities of some species and work against those of others.

Learning abilities are widely distributed

Nonassociative learning appears to be very widespread among organisms. Simple animals with small nervous systems readily habituate to repeated mild stimuli and become sensitized to strong stimuli. Furthermore, the time courses and other features of habituation and sensitization are similar, whether studied in an earthworm, a mollusk, or a mammal. Some investigators have reported nonassociative learning even in paramecia and bacteria, single-celled organisms that do not have nervous systems.

**EVOLUTION
AT WORK**

Until recently, associative learning was believed to have a more restricted distribution than nonassociative learning in the animal kingdom. For example, *Aplysia* had been used for many years to investigate the neural mechanisms of habituation, but investigators had sought in vain for evidence of associative learning in *Aplysia* until it was discovered in 1980. Evidence for learning in the fruit fly *Drosophila* was long sought in order to try to relate learning to genetic factors, but only in 1974 did investigators first announce successful training in these animals.

Part of the difficulty in assessing the capacity of a species to learn and remember is that these capacities may be highly specific. Certain species can learn particular associations well, even though they are very poor at other tasks that do not seem more difficult to us. Evidence for specificity has accumulated since the 1960s and has led to two successive and quite different concepts.

First came the concept of **genetic constraints on learning** in the 1960s. This formulation held that species-typical genetic factors restrict the kinds of learning that a species can accomplish, or at least accomplish readily. For example, bees readily learn to come to a particular station to feed on a 24-hour schedule, which of course occurs in nature, but they cannot learn to come on an 8- or 12-hour schedule. Birds of some species do not learn the pattern of markings or even the color of their eggs even though they turn the eggs over frequently, yet they learn to recognize their young individually within 3 days after they hatch, just the time when the chicks begin to wander about.

The interpretation of such observations changed in the 1980s. Rather than supposing that the genes of certain species constrain those species' general ability to learn and thus make them selectively stupid, investigators now believe it more likely that **specific abilities to learn and remember** evolve in response to selective pressures in particular ecological niches (J. L. Gould, 1986; Sherry and Schacter, 1987). Let's consider an example of a specific learning ability.

**COMPETING
HYPOTHESES**

Selection for spatial memory is associated with increased hippocampal size in mammals and birds

A notable research program has used both naturalistic observations and experimental studies with birds and rodents to determine the effects that selection for spatial ability may have on brain measures. We saw one example of this research in Chapter 6: Species of birds that store (cache) food for retrieval days or weeks later have hippocampal regions larger than those of related species that do not cache food (see Figure 6.4). The differences in size of the hippocampus among these species could not be accounted for by other factors, including migratory behavior, social organization, diet, mode of development, nest dispersion, and habitat (Krebs et al., 1989; Sherry et al., 1989). Furthermore, surgical removal of the hippocampus in a

NEURAL PLASTICITY

food-storing species disrupts the birds' ability to retrieve cached food and to solve other spatial problems, without obvious effects on other behaviors (Sherry and Vaccarino, 1989). Thus the larger hippocampus in food-storing species of birds seems to be an adaptive modification that makes it possible for them to retrieve cached food.

Interestingly, the greater hippocampal size that is typical in food-storing species develops only if individual birds use spatial memory to retrieve stored food. Clayton and Krebs (1994) found this when they raised crows in the laboratory, giving some birds the chance to store and retrieve food while other birds ate from feeders and had no opportunity to store food. The birds that stored and retrieved food developed hippocampal formations that were larger than those of the birds that ate from feeders.

Comparison of two related species of kangaroo rats provided an independent test of this hypothesis. Both species are small, nocturnal, seed-eating, desert rodents from the same genus. One species, Merriam's kangaroo rat (*Dipodomys merriami*) hoards food in scattered locations and requires spatial memory to relocate its caches. In contrast, the bannertail kangaroo rat (*Dipodomys spectabilis*) hoards seeds in its burrow and thus needs no specialized spatial memory to retrieve them. As with food-storing versus non-food-storing birds, *D. merriami* has a significantly larger hippocampus than that of *D. spectabilis* (L. F. Jacobs and Spencer, 1994).

As another example, pigeons have been bred for their ability to fly rapidly and accurately to their home lofts. Pigeons of these strains have larger hippocampi than breeds of pigeons not selected for homing ability have (Rehkamper et al., 1988).

Investigators who test the spatial learning and memory of laboratory rats and mice have often observed that males perform better than females, and human males perform better than human females on many spatial tasks (D. F. Halpern, 1986). Some researchers have suggested that males in general are superior to females in spatial learning and memory, but others have hypothesized that the behavioral roles of the two sexes determine whether a sex difference in spatial memory exists in a given species and, if it does, which sex is superior in this behavior.

An instructive comparison has been made between two species of North American voles (Figure 17.19). Pine voles (*Microtus pinetorum*) are monogamous, and field observations show that the males and females travel over ranges that are equal in size. In contrast, meadow voles (*Microtus pennsylvanicus*) are highly polygynous (i.e., a male mates with several females), and the ranges of males are several times larger than those of females. In this polygynous mating system, males compete in order to include within their home range as many female ranges as possible.

The polygynous male meadow voles, in comparison with females of the same species, have significantly better scores on laboratory tests of spatial learning and memory. The monogamous pine voles show no sex differences on these tests. Furthermore,

(a) Sizes of home range

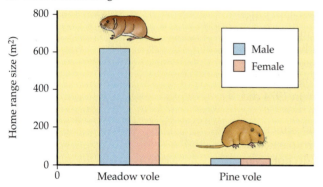

(b) Ranking in spatial learning

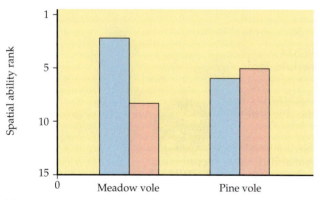

(c) Relative hippocampal size

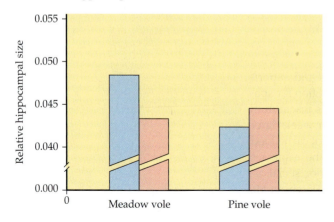

17.19 Sex, Memory, and Hippocampal Size   Males and females of two species of voles were compared on three variables: (*a*) size of home range, (*b*) score on a spatial learning task, and (*c*) hippocampal size divided by brain size. (After L. F. Jacobs et al., 1990.)

the polygynous male meadow voles have a significantly larger hippocampus than do the females, whereas among the monogamous pine voles, there is no significant difference in hippocampal size between the sexes (L. F. Jacobs et al., 1990).

When the size of the hippocampus differs between the sexes of a species, it is not invariably the male that shows the larger size. For example, the hippocampus of the female brown-headed cowbird (*Molothrus ater*) is significantly larger than that of the male, as investigators predicted on the basis of the breeding behavior of this species (Sherry et al., 1993). The female cowbird is parasitic: She lays her eggs in the nests of other species, which then do the work of hatching and feeding the cowbird chick. In order to do this, the female cowbird has to find and keep track of nests so that she can slip in and lay an egg when the other birds are away. The male cowbird does not participate in this spatial sleuthing and gets along with a smaller hippocampus. No sex difference in hippocampal size was found in two closely related species that are not parasitic.

EVOLUTION AT WORK

Recent research indicates that spatial learning can change the anatomy of the hippocampus in adult humans as well (Box 17.2).

Learning and Memory Change throughout Life

It is easier for us to form some kinds of new memories when we are in the middle of our lives, as young or mature adults, than when we are infants or elderly. Can these changes in ability over the life span be explained in neural terms? Do they provide clues about the neural mechanisms of learning and memory?

Many kinds of animals must be ready to learn as soon as they are born or hatched. For example, newly hatched chicks eagerly sample objects in their environment to find what is edible. Their yolk sacs provide nourishment, so they can sample small bits without having to ingest much. By the time the yolk sac is used up 3 to 4 days after hatching, the chicks need to have learned what is safe and good to eat. Young humans also learn what to eat (usually with vigorous suggestions from their parents), but there are other, more-complex cognitive skills that they must master.

Working memory requires brain development

Swiss psychologist Jean Piaget studied cognitive development in children. One of the tasks he devised was later found to require development of the dorsolateral prefrontal cortex in both children and monkeys. This "A not B" test requires an infant to uncover a toy that she sees hidden in one of two possible locations (A or B); both locations are used in a series of trials. After the toy is hidden, the infant's visual fixation is broken so that she cannot look at the location during the delay.

Human infants will not reliably reach for a hidden object until they are 7 to 8 months old. Before this age an infant will reach correctly to either location only if there is no delay (except for breaking visual fixation) between the hiding and the reaching. But with a delay of only 1 to 5 s during which the infant is prevented from reaching, she tends to reach for the object in the last location where she reached successfully, even if that is not the location where she just saw the toy hidden.

These observations suggest that with a short delay, the habit of successful reaching is stronger than the representational memory of the hidden object. No long-term memory is required in either case; only short-term working memories are involved. Testing of infants every 2 weeks shows a steady rise in their ability to perform successfully at longer delays. This improvement is due to maturation, not experience, because infants of a given age test equally well whether or not they've taken the test before. By age 8 to 12 months, most infants perform successfully with a delay of 10 s between seeing the object hidden and reaching for it. In the next section we'll see that some adult patients with amnesia fail the "A not B" test.

Adele Diamond and Patricia Goldman-Rakic (1989) confirmed these observations with human infants and also studied monkeys, using a similar test. Monkeys perform the test well by the age of 2 to 4 months. The investigators used both intact

Patricia Goldman-Rakic (1937–2003)

BOX 17.2 Mastering London Topography Changes Hippocampal Structure in Taxi Drivers

Can spatial training alter the anatomy of the hippocampus in humans as it does in animals? To test this idea, a group of investigators studied the brains of licensed London taxi drivers (Maguire et al., 2000). These drivers are very well suited for such a study because in order to obtain a license, they must undergo intensive training about London streets and locations (called colloquially "being on The Knowledge"). This training requires 2 years, on the average, and it is followed by a stringent set of police examinations.

In an earlier study using positron emission tomography (PET), the same investigators had found that having London taxi drivers recall complex routes around the city caused activation of a network of brain regions that included the right hippocampus; recall of landmarks for which the subjects had no knowledge of their location within a spatial framework activated similar brain regions, except for the right hippocampus (Maguire et al., 1997).

In the later study the experimental subjects were 16 right-handed men whose careers as licensed drivers ranged from 1.5 to 42 years; all had healthy general medical, neurological, and psychiatric profiles. Structural MRI scans of their brains were obtained and measured. For comparison, the investigators studied MRI scans of 50 healthy right-handed males with a similar age range and who did not drive taxis. The only brain regions that showed structural

differences between the taxi drivers and control subjects were the right and left hippocampi. The posterior part of the hippocampus was significantly larger in taxi drivers than in controls in both the right and the left hemispheres. In contrast, the anterior part of the hippocampus was significantly smaller in taxi drivers than in controls. There was no significant difference between taxi drivers and controls in either the midportion (body) or the overall size of the hippocampi.

Could these differences reflect an innate predisposition to learn to navigate the streets of London? To test this possibility, the investigators plotted the volume of the anterior and the posterior hippocampus against the number of months each person had spent as a taxi driver. The volume of the anterior right hippocampus correlated significantly negatively with the duration of taxi experience ($r = -0.6$, $p < 0.05$), and the volume of the posterior right hippocampus correlated significantly positively with the duration of taxi experience ($r = 0.6$, $p < 0.05$). Thus the greater the duration of taxi experience, the greater the anatomical effect in the right hippocampus. These correlations strongly indicate that experience alters the hippocampus, rather than initial hippocampal differences reflecting an innate disposition to acquire spatial knowledge. The left hippocampus did not show significant changes with duration of experience, suggesting that the left and right hippocampi participate differently in spatial navigation and memory.

Although this report offers surprising new information, like much innovative research it also raises many new questions. For example, is there a behavioral correlate to the reduction of size of the anterior hippocampus in taxi drivers? A report of this research in *The Economist* ("Neuroscience," 2000) comments ironically: "Whether the loss of frontal [hippocampal] tissue has any relationship with the robust political opinions for which London cabbies are renowned is an area that remains mercifully uninvestigated" (p. 83).

In a commentary on this study, Terrazas and McNaughton (2000) pointed out some surprises and some paths for future work. For example, they expressed surprise that changes in the brain with experience appear to accumulate for as long as 20 years; rather they expected the greatest changes to occur earlier, when knowledge acquisition was greatest. MRI measures can be done repeatedly in the same subjects, so these investigators would like to see longitudinal studies of some taxi drivers. To test whether it is only acquisition of spatial knowledge that produces localized effects in the hippocampus, they suggested comparable studies with groups that have similarly high demands of nonspatial learning, such as years of legal training and legal practice or medical studies and practice. Clearly the research by Maguire et al. has raised as many questions as it has solved. (Photos from Maguire et al. 1997; courtesy Eleanor Maguire.)

(A) Region including the hippocampus

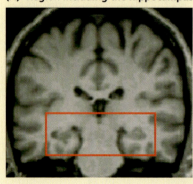

(B) Area that is larger in experienced drivers than in new drivers

monkeys and monkeys with lesions of dorsolateral prefrontal cortex or control lesions of inferior parietal cortex (Figure 17.20). Normal monkeys performed well on the test at delays of 10 s and more, as did monkeys with lesions of parietal cortex, but monkeys with lesions of *prefrontal cortex* made errors similar to those of 7- to

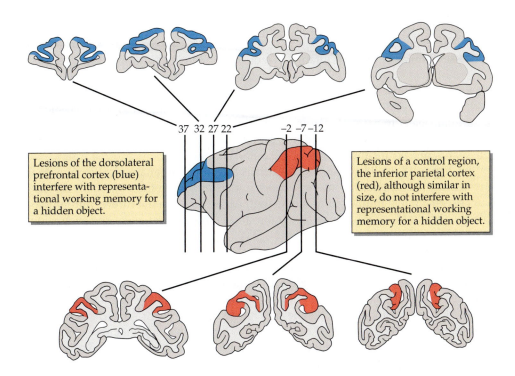

17.20 Cortical Regions Tested for Roles in Representational Memory
In monkeys, the brain sites shown here were lesioned for experiments on dorsolateral prefrontal cortex and inferior parietal cortex—regions known to be involved in representational memory. (After A. Diamond and Goldman-Rakic, 1989.)

Lesions of the dorsolateral prefrontal cortex (blue) interfere with representational working memory for a hidden object.

Lesions of a control region, the inferior parietal cortex (red), although similar in size, do not interfere with representational working memory for a hidden object.

8-month-old human infants. Thus a normal, relatively mature dorsolateral prefrontal cortex appears to be required for representational memory of the hidden object to be retained as long as 10 s. Further research on the roles of prefrontal cortex in memory will be discussed in Chapter 18.

Aging impairs some aspects of learning and memory

The capacity of older people to learn and remember has become a topic of heightened interest in recent years. This awareness stems in part from the growing proportion of elderly people in the populations of developed countries and the recognition that some reductions in performance accompany normal aging. It also reflects attention to pathological forms of cognitive impairment that are more likely to affect older people, such as Alzheimer's disease (see Chapter 7).

Older people and animals in normal health show some decrements in abilities to learn and remember (N. D. Anderson and Craik, 2000; Balota et al., 2000; Gallagher and Rapp, 1997; Gallagher et al., 1995; Kubanis and Zornetzer, 1981). Accurate comparisons of learning and memory in people of different ages are difficult because of confounding factors. For example, differences in learning ability may be caused not by age alone, but by other factors, such as educational level, how recently the subjects have experienced formal learning, or motivation. After experimenters correct for such factors, differences related to age usually accompany only some tasks, not all.

What kinds of tasks usually show decrements in performance with aging? Normal elderly people tend to show some memory impairment in tasks of conscious recollection that require effort (Hasher and Zacks, 1979) and that rely primarily on internal generation of the memory rather than on external cues (Craik, 1985). Giving elderly subjects easily organized task structures, or cues, can often raise their performance to the level of the young. Thus the type of task helps determine whether impairment is observed. Many elderly people take ginkgo biloba tablets (an herbal supplement) every day in an effort to boost their memory, but placebo-controlled studies indicate that the tablets have no effect on memory, attention, or other cognitive functions (P. R. Solomon et al., 2002).

In cases of pathological forms of aging, such as Alzheimer's disease, some memory systems deteriorate, and it has been suggested that what remains are memory processes similar to those of infants. In fact, testing the implications of this idea led Morris Moscovitch (1985) to discover a cognitive disability in patients with amnesia whose manifestation was similar to the failure on the "A not B" test that Piaget had described for 8-month-old infants. Most patients suffering from amnesia, shown a familiar object in a new location, B, continue to search for it at A, even passing by the object in plain sight in order to search for it at A. They appear to remember the search procedure and not the object being sought.

In Chapter 18 we'll learn about neurochemical and neuroanatomical changes that accompany learning and memory. A better understanding of these mechanisms may suggest effective therapies for patients with Alzheimer's in the future. But for people like patient H.M., whom we met at the start of this chapter, reversing such widespread loss of brain tissue may never be feasible. It will certainly never happen for H.M. himself.

Now in his late 70s, H.M. does not know his age or whether he has gray hair. Shown an old picture of himself with his mother, he doesn't recognize himself. He says that man looks like his father but can't be, because his father doesn't wear glasses. Yet H.M. does not act upset when he sees himself in the mirror, so perhaps over the past half-century he has learned to perceive his reflection as familiar. Asked what he thinks of his reflection, H.M. jokes, "I'm not a boy." He is courteous and concerned about other people. H.M. remembers the surgeon he met several times before his operation: "He did medical research on people... What he learned about me helped others too, and I'm glad about that" (Corkin, 2002, p. 158). He and his court-appointed guardian have already signed the forms to donate his brain for postmortem examination. But H.M. will never know how famous he is, or how much his dreadful condition taught us about learning and memory. Deprived of one of the most important characteristics of a human being, he has nevertheless held fast to his humanity.

Refer to the *Learning Biological Psychology CD* for study questions, animations, activities, and other study aids.

Summary

1. The abilities to learn and remember affect all behaviors that are characteristically human. Because every animal species appears capable of some learning and memory, the ability to learn must be required for survival. Whereas evolution by natural selection brings about adaptation over successive generations, learning permits prompt adaptation within the lifetime of the individual.

2. Individuals whose learning or memory capacities are impaired as a result of brain damage may provide valuable information about how different regions of the brain are involved in these processes.

3. Patients with Korsakoff's syndrome show gaps in memory, which they may attempt to fill by confabulation; this syndrome involves severe retrograde and anterograde amnesia, as well as impairment in encoding new information. Patients show damage to the mammillary nuclei, midline thalamus, and frontal cortex.

4. Some learning results in the formation of habits (gaining procedural, nondeclarative knowledge, or learning *how*); other learning results in the formation of representational memories (gaining declarative knowledge, or learning *what*). Abilities to form habits and memories appear to depend on different brain circuits.

5. Declarative memory tends to be flexible—accessible to many response systems. Procedural (nondeclarative) memory tends to be inflexible: The information is not readily expressed by response systems that were not involved in the original learning.

6. Learning includes both nonassociative forms such as habituation, dishabituation, and sensitization, and associative forms such as classical (Pavlovian) conditioning and instrumental conditioning.

7. Memories are often classified by how long they last. Frequently used classifications include iconic, short-term, intermediate-term, and long-term. Some disorders prevent the formation of long-term declarative memory while not impairing short-term memory.

8. Studies of people with brain damage in different locations and experiments with animals show that different attributes of memory are processed by different brain regions.

9. Although the capacity of long-term memory is huge, most of what we experience is not remembered. Attention, reinforcement, and emotional responses help determine what is held in memory beyond the short term.

10. Recall of a past event requires three memory processes: encoding, consolidation, and retrieval.

11. Memory strength can be modulated by emotional state and other conditions in the period following learning.

12. It may be possible to weaken traumatic memories by giving treatments that impair the consolidation of memory. Such treatments can be administered either shortly after the original experience or when the memory is reactivated.

13. Some patients with damage to the medial temporal lobe or medial diencephalon show particular impairment in the consolidation of long-term memories. Recent research has focused both on the type of memory test and on the sites of brain damage. Hippocampal lesions in people and animals impair the formation of representational long-term memories but spare the formation of habits (nondeclarative, or procedural, memories).

14. The hippocampal region is required for processing but not for storage of long-term declarative memory. Long-term (or permanent) memory is probably stored in the cortex.

15. Brain imaging is helping to identify brain regions involved in various aspects of learning and remembering. Encoding of information evokes greater activity in the left frontal region; information retrieval evokes greater activity in the right frontal region. Sensorimotor skill learning is accompanied by activation in the basal ganglia, the cerebellum, and the motor cortex. Delay conditioning is accomplished by a cerebellar circuit, but trace conditioning requires the hippocampus.

16. Abilities to learn and remember change throughout life. For some aspects of these changes, biological correlates have been found; other aspects continue to pose questions.

Recommended Reading

Eichenbaum, H. (2002). *The cognitive neuroscience of memory.* New York: Oxford University Press.

Gabrieli, J. D. E. (1998). Cognitive neuroscience of human memory. *Annual Review of Psychology, 49,* 87–115.

Luria, A. R. (1987). *The mind of a mnemonist.* Cambridge, MA: Harvard University Press.

McGaugh, J. L. (2003). *Memory and emotions: The making of lasting memories.* New York: Columbia University Press.

Squire, L. R., Clark, R. E., and Knowlton, B. J. (2001). Retrograde amnesia. *Hippocampus, 11,* 50–55.

Tulving, E., and Craik, F. I. M. (Eds.). (2000). *The Oxford handbook of memory.* Oxford, England: Oxford University Press.

Zola-Morgan, S., and Squire, L. R. (1993). Neuroanatomy of memory. *Annual Review of Neuroscience, 16,* 547–563.

18

Learning and Memory: Neural Mechanisms

Would You Drink from the River Lethe?

When Kathleen was knocked down by a bike messenger, lying in the middle of a busy Boston street, several thoughts ran through her head. "Oh, why did I wear a skirt today? Are these people all looking at my underpants?" And of course she worried that a car might run over her. But she also remembered an earlier, even more traumatic experience when an armed stranger forced his way into her car and tried to rape her. It had taken her over 8 months to stop having awful memories of that carjacking. Now she felt sure this less serious trauma would rekindle haunting memories of the earlier assault (Henig, 2004). Would she have to "forget" those horrible images all over again?

In Greek mythology, the spirits of people who died traveled to Hades, where they were required to drink from a river called Lethe. One drink from this "River of Oblivion" would cause them to forget everything about their lives on Earth. Characters in the movie Eternal Sunshine of the Spotless Mind are given a similar opportunity to forget at least some memories. It may seem silly to erase memories of a soon-to-be-ex-boyfriend, but Kathleen

had really suffered from anxiety and sleeplessness caused by her memories. She longed for a way to avoid going through that experience again.

In this chapter, we'll learn that it no longer seems far-fetched to think we might one day be able to erase unwanted memories. But is that a good idea? A person who survived the September 11 attacks or prolonged torture is most likely tormented by vivid, horrible memories. It is easy enough to say that such a person would be happier in the aftermath if it were possible to forget those memories. But would you take that option? What would it mean to no longer remember the last moments of a spouse or child who had died? Having survived a catastrophe, would you be willing to let those memories go so that you could be happier? And would you in fact be happier afterward? Would you still be you afterward? These questions seem to probe our very reason for living: Are we here to have, if possible, only good experiences? Again we find that the brain and its capacity for memories, good and bad, provides the core of human existence.

Whereas Chapter 17 stressed behavioral aspects of learning and memory and the general regions of the nervous system where plastic changes that underlie learning and memory occur, in this chapter we take up detailed sites and neural mechanisms. We focus on three main topics:

1. What are the basic biological mechanisms—at the molecular, synaptic, and cellular levels—for long-term storage of information in the nervous system?
2. At the level of neural circuits, how do the formation and modification of circuits function in memory?
3. What sequence of neurochemical events underlies the storage of long-term memory?

We will find that in some cases learning causes changes in the strength of existing synapses, and it is the change in synaptic strength that constitutes the animal's memory. In other cases, learning causes new synapses to form, and in some sense these new synapses are responsible for memory. There is also growing evidence that learning sometimes requires new neurons to be produced, even in adult brains. It seems that natural selection has exploited many different forms of neural plasticity because learning and memory are vital adaptations for survival and reproduction.

The combined use of somatic and behavioral interventions is yielding rapid progress in our understanding of the neural mechanisms of learning and memory. This approach is revealing how a brief experience can lead to a cascade of neurochemical events that may, in some cases, include protein synthesis and structural changes at synapses. Newer methods are also enabling investigators to determine how neural circuits are established or altered to serve memories.

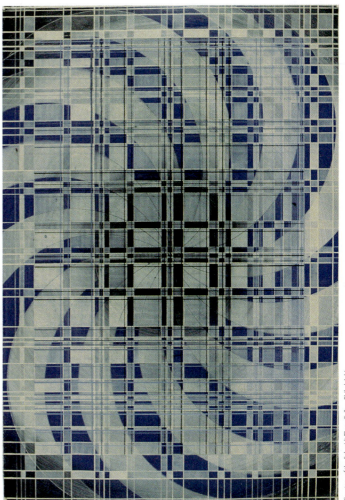

Robert Straight, *D-260*, 2000

Courtesy of the Schmidt/Dean Gallery, Philadelphia.

Changes in Synapses May Be Mechanisms of Memory Storage

Soon after experiments on memory began in the 1880s, and as information accumulated on the physiology and anatomy of the nervous system, investigators began to speculate that changes in synapses could be a mechanism to store memories. British neurophysiologist Charles S. Sherrington (1897), in the same publication in which he proposed the term *synapse*, stated that changes in neural connections were likely to be important for learning:

> Shut off from all opportunity of reproducing itself and adding to its number by mitosis or otherwise, the nerve cell directs its pent-up energy towards amplifying its connections with its fellows, in response to the events which stir it up. Hence, it is capable of an education unknown to other tissues. (p. 1117)

(a) Plasticity in a neural chain

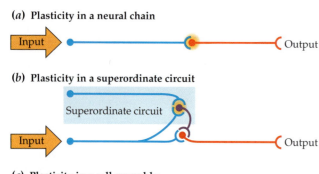

(b) Plasticity in a superordinate circuit

Superordinate circuit

Input ➜ Output

(c) Plasticity in a cell assembly

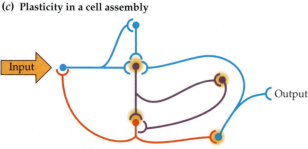

Input ➜ Output

18.1 Sites of Synaptic Plasticity in Neural Networks
Changes at sites of synaptic plasticity—such as the sites shown here (highlighted in orange) in a neural chain (a), a higher-order segment of a circuit (b), and a cell assembly (c)—may underlie memory storage.

NEURAL PLASTICITY

The great Spanish neuroanatomist Santiago Ramón y Cajal (1894) also suggested that neurons extend their axons and dendrites to make new connections with other neurons in both development and learning.

Early in the twentieth century, when Ivan Pavlov sought to explain conditioning in neural terms, it was natural to think that neurons in the sensory cortex, representing the conditioned stimulus (CS), developed or strengthened their connections to neurons in the motor cortex, where the unconditioned response (UR) is represented; thus CS–UR linkages would develop.

Different kinds of neural circuits can underlie memories

It will be helpful for us to organize the varied research on neural mechanisms of learning and memory according to the kinds of neural circuits that investigators consider, which range from simple neural chains to parallel distributed circuits. We will define each kind of circuit briefly here; these definitions will become more meaningful as we discuss research related to the different types of circuits. Most theorizing about circuits locates the site(s) of memory storage in one or more plastic synapses. A synapse is said to be plastic if it is capable of changing the strength with which it affects the postsynaptic target.

The neural chain (Figure 18.1a), at its simplest, can be a monosynaptic reflex arc, as in the knee jerk reflex (see Figure 3.16). Even a simple circuit such as this can show some learning because, as we will see a little later, some of the synapses within the circuit can be plastic. In this case, learning is said to cause intrinsic change in the circuit.

Many simple neural circuits also receive input from **superordinate circuits** (Figure 18.1b), also called *modulatory circuits*. We saw an example in the case of the motor system, where the activity of spinal reflex circuits is modulated by higher-order circuits at the level of the brainstem, basal ganglia, and motor cortex (see Chapter 11). In this chapter we will see an example (eye-blink conditioning) of plasticity in a superordinate circuit. In that case, plastic synapses in the superordinate circuit elicit the learned behavior, while the basic reflex circuit itself shows no change during training.

Many kinds of learning may require the establishment of relatively complex networks of neurons—**cell assemblies.** In Figure 18.1c, several plastic synapses help form a neural network.

Many current hypotheses suggest that a single group or ensemble of neurons can encode many different memories—each neuron participating to a greater or lesser extent in a particular memory, just as a person may belong to several different clubs or groups. In this case, each unit change may be too small to affect behavior significantly by itself, but the *aggregate* of changes in *many* neurons can produce large effects.

Let's examine the ways in which synapses can change and thereby store information.

The Nervous System May Form and Store Memories in Various Ways

As knowledge of synaptic anatomy and chemistry increased, hypotheses about plastic synaptic changes became more numerous and precise.

Physiological changes at synapses may store information

Some of the changes that may store information can be measured physiologically. The changes could be presynaptic, postsynaptic, or both (Figure 18.2a). Such changes

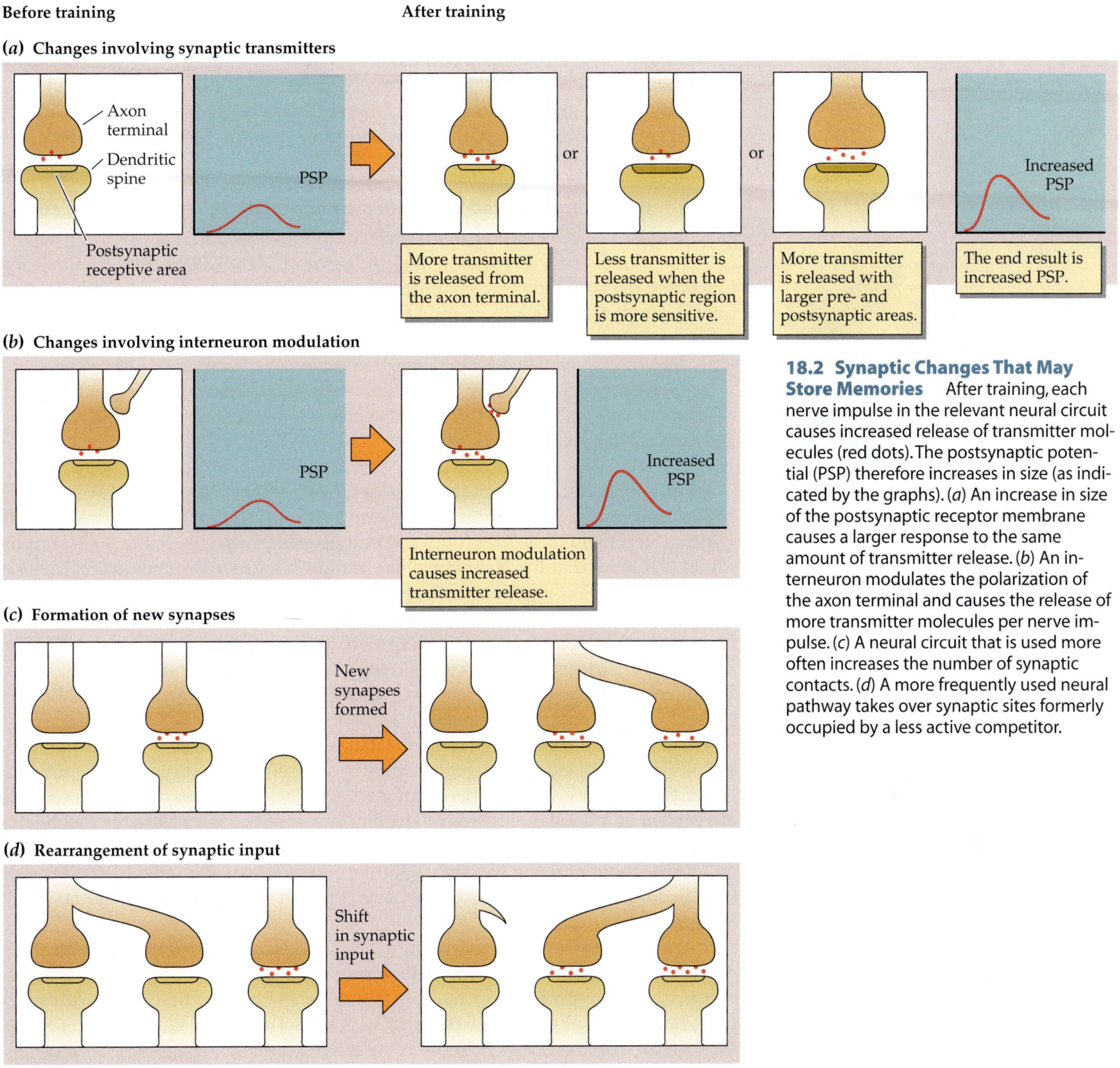

Before training   **After training**

(a) Changes involving synaptic transmitters

Axon terminal

Dendritic spine

PSP

Postsynaptic receptive area

More transmitter is released from the axon terminal.

or

Less transmitter is released when the postsynaptic region is more sensitive.

or

More transmitter is released with larger pre- and postsynaptic areas.

Increased PSP

The end result is increased PSP.

(b) Changes involving interneuron modulation

PSP

Increased PSP

Interneuron modulation causes increased transmitter release.

(c) Formation of new synapses

New synapses formed

(d) Rearrangement of synaptic input

Shift in synaptic input

18.2 Synaptic Changes That May Store Memories After training, each nerve impulse in the relevant neural circuit causes increased release of transmitter molecules (red dots). The postsynaptic potential (PSP) therefore increases in size (as indicated by the graphs). (a) An increase in size of the postsynaptic receptor membrane causes a larger response to the same amount of transmitter release. (b) An interneuron modulates the polarization of the axon terminal and causes the release of more transmitter molecules per nerve impulse. (c) A neural circuit that is used more often increases the number of synaptic contacts. (d) A more frequently used neural pathway takes over synaptic sites formerly occupied by a less active competitor.

include greater release of neurotransmitter molecules and/or greater effects when the receptor molecules become more numerous or more sensitive. The result of such changes would be an increase in the size of the postsynaptic potential. Changes in the rate of *inactivation* of the transmitter (through reuptake or enzymatic degradation) could produce a similar effect.

The amount of neurotransmitter released could also be affected by the influence of terminals from other neurons on the axon terminals (Figure 18.2b). That is, impulses from other neurons can alter the polarization of the axon terminals and thus affect the amount of neurotransmitter released.

Structural changes at synapses may provide long-term storage

Many investigators believe that long-term memories require changes in the nervous system so dramatic that they can be seen by microscope techniques. Structural changes resulting from use are apparent in other parts of the body. For example, exercise changes the mass and/or shape of muscles and bone. In a similar way, new synapses could form or synapses could be eliminated as a function of training (Figure 18.2*c*).

Training could also lead to reorganization of synaptic connections. For example, it could cause a more used pathway to take over sites formerly occupied by a less active competitor (Figure 18.2*d*).

What conditions are required to induce memory-related changes at synapses?

Psychologist Donald O. Hebb suggested conditions that could account for the development of the nervous system and for learning. Hebb (1949) proposed that the functional relationship between a presynaptic neuron (A) and a postsynaptic neuron (B) could change if A frequently took part in exciting B:

> When an axon of cell A is near enough to excite a cell B and repeatedly or persistently takes part in firing it, some growth process or metabolic change takes place in one or both cells such that A's efficacy, as one of the cells firing B, is increased. (p. 62)

**Donald O. Hebb
(1904–1985)**

Investigators testing Hebb's hypothesis have confirmed it in several systems, including the hippocampal formation (Kelso and Brown, 1986). **Hebbian synapses** grow stronger when the presynaptic terminal repeatedly causes the postsynaptic cell to fire. Note that the Hebbian synapse does not grow stronger just because it is often active, releasing transmitter. Rather, the synapse must be both *active* and *effective* at getting the postsynaptic cell to fire. So another formulation of Hebb's hypothesis is, "Neurons that fire together wire together" (Löwel and Singer, 1992, p. 211). Of course, learning could just as easily involve the *weakening* of synapses, so later theorists proposed that Hebbian synapses should also grow weaker if they repeatedly *fail* to drive the postsynaptic cell.

We discussed Hebbian synapses in Chapter 7 when we found that axonal projections from an open eye outcompete projections from a closed eye for synaptic control of visual cortex. Later in this chapter we will review the neurochemical cascade of events that are triggered when a Hebbian synapse becomes stronger. Hebb later expressed some amusement that his formulation had attracted so much attention, because he thought that it was only a formal expression of ideas that many theorists had held for years, and that other aspects of his theory were more original (P. M. Milner, 1993).

To explain how neural activity could lead to the formation of new synaptic connections as a result of experience, Hebb proposed the **dual-trace hypothesis.** According to this hypothesis, formation of a memory involves first a relatively brief transient process: Learning experience sets up activity that tends to reverberate through the activated neural circuits. This activity holds the memory for a short period. If sufficient, the activity helps build up a stable change in the nervous system—a long-lasting memory trace.

If learning induces long-term changes in either the strength or the number of synapses, then in theory it should be possible to detect physical alterations in the brain as a result of experience. By the 1960s, scientists began finding numerous instances in which learning experiences affected the brain.

Cerebral Changes Result from Training

The first demonstration that the brain can be altered by training or differential experience was made by an interdisciplinary team (Figure 18.3). They found that either formal training or informal experience in varied environments leads to measurable changes in the neurochemistry and neuroanatomy of the rodent brain (E. L. Bennett et al., 1964; Renner and Rosenzweig, 1987; Rosenzweig, 1984; Rosenzweig et al., 1961).

18.3 Pioneer Investigators of the Effects of Training and Differential Experience on Brain Chemistry and Anatomy Pictured from left to right are Edward L. Bennett, neurochemist; Marian C. Diamond, neuroanatomist; David Krech, biological psychologist; and Mark R. Rosenzweig, biological psychologist. (Photograph taken around 1965.)

In some experiments, animals were given different opportunities for informal learning. For example, littermates of the same sex were assigned by a random procedure to various laboratory environments. The following three environments were the most common:

1. **Standard condition (SC)**. Three animals were kept in a standard laboratory cage and provided with food and water (Figure 18.4*a*). This is the typical environment for laboratory animals.
2. **Impoverished** (or *isolated*) **condition (IC)**. A single animal was housed in an SC-sized cage (Figure 18.4*b*).
3. **Enriched condition (EC)**. A group of 10 to 12 animals was kept in a large cage containing a variety of stimulus objects, which were changed daily (Figure 18.4*c*). This environment is considered enriched because it provides greater opportunities for informal learning than does the SC.

At the end of the period of differential experience, each brain was dissected into standard samples for chemical analysis. In the initial experiments, animals in the enriched condition (EC) were found to have developed significantly greater activity of the enzyme acetylcholinesterase (AChE) in the cerebral cortex than their IC littermates had. (Recall that AChE breaks down the synaptic transmitter ACh and clears the synapse for renewed stimulation.) Control experiments showed that this effect could not be attributed to either

(*a*) **Standard condition**

(*b*) **Impoverished condition**

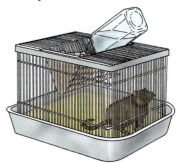

(*c*) **Enriched condition**

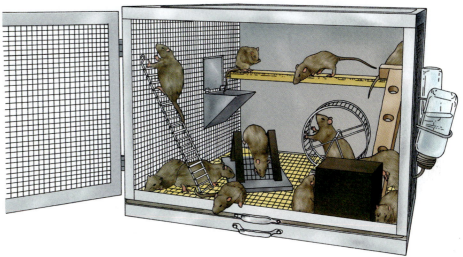

18.4 Experimental Environments to Test Effects of Enrichment on Learning and Brain Measures Interaction with an enriched environment has measurable effects on the brain, on stress reactions, and on learning.

greater handling of the EC animals or greater locomotor activity in the EC situation (Rosenzweig et al., 1961). Scrutiny of the data then revealed that the experimental groups differed not only in total enzymatic activity but also in *weight* of the cortical samples: The EC animals had developed a significantly heavier cerebral cortex than their IC littermates had (Rosenzweig et al., 1962).

This result was a real surprise because since the beginning of the twentieth century, brain weight had been considered a very stable characteristic and not subject to environmental influences. The differences in brain weight were extremely reliable, although small. Moreover, these differences were not distributed uniformly throughout the cerebral cortex. They were largest in the occipital cortex and smallest in the adjacent somesthetic cortex. Later experiments demonstrated that shorter periods could produce cerebral changes and that brains of adult rats also responded to differential experience.

The differences in cortical weights among groups were caused by differences in cortical thickness: Animals exposed to the EC environment developed slightly but significantly thicker cerebral cortices than their SC or IC littermates (M. C. Diamond, 1967; M. C. Diamond et al., 1964). More-refined neuroanatomical measurements were soon undertaken on pyramidal cells in the occipital cortex, including sizes of cell bodies, counts of dendritic spines, measurements of dendritic branching, and measurements of the size of synaptic contacts (Rosenzweig et al., 1972). Each of these measurements showed significant effects of differential experience, as we will see shortly.

Enriched experience has beneficial effects on brain anatomy, neurochemistry, and behavior

Experience in the EC environment promotes better learning and problem solving in a variety of tests. An enriched environment alters the expression of a large number of genes, many of which can be related to neuronal structure, synaptic plasticity, and transmission; some of these genes may play important roles in learning and memory (Rampon, Tang, et al., 2000). Enriched experience also aids recovery from or compensation for a variety of conditions, including malnutrition, thyroid insufficiency, and brain damage (Galani et al., 1997; Hamm et al., 1996; Johansson and Ohlsson, 1996; Rampon, Tang, et al., 2000; Will et al., 1977). An extensive review shows that, for recovery from brain injury in animals, environmental enrichment is more effective than either formal training or physical exercise (Will et al., in press). In some cases a combination of transplanting fetal cells and giving enriched experience is significantly more effective in restoring function after brain damage than either treatment is alone (Kelche et al., 1995). As we will see later in this chapter, enriched experience also appears to protect against age-related declines in memory, both in laboratory animals and in humans.

Because enriched experience has such widespread effects on brain anatomy, neurochemistry, and behavior, it appears that most experiments done with animals raised in standard, restricted laboratory environments are actually using animals with stunted brains.

Learning can produce new synaptic connections

The idea that enriched conditions could affect the number of synapses in the brain was slow to gain acceptance. In 1965, John C. Eccles, the neurophysiologist who shared the 1963 Nobel Prize in Physiology or Medicine, remained firm in his belief that learning and memory storage involve "growth just of bigger and better synapses that are already there, not growth of new connections" (p. 97). Not until the 1970s did experiments with laboratory rats assigned to enriched or impoverished environments provide evidence that learning can produce new synaptic connections.

When dendritic *spines* in the cerebral cortex were counted, the number of spines per unit of length of dendrite was found to be significantly greater in EC than in IC animals (Globus et al., 1973). Psychologist William Greenough also placed laboratory rats in SC, EC, and IC environments, and he quantified dendritic *branching* by

John C. Eccles (1903–1997)

COMPETING HYPOTHESES

(a)

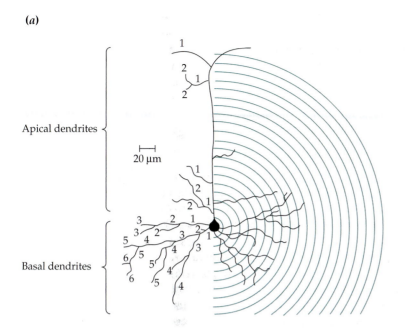

(b)

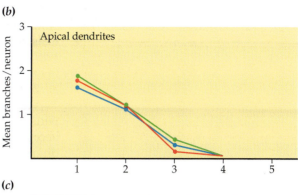

(c)

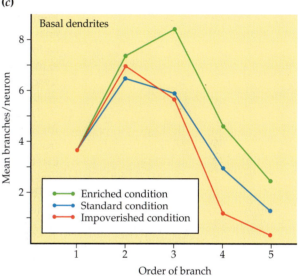

18.5 Measurement of Dendritic Branching   (a) An enlarged photograph of a neuron is used to quantify branching either by counts of the number of branches of different orders (*left*), or by counts of the number of intersections with concentric rings (*right*). (b, c) These results were obtained by counts of the number of branches on apical dendrites (b) and basal dendrites (c). There are significant differences in branching, especially in the basal dendrites, among rats kept for 30 days in enriched, standard, or impoverished environments. (From Greenough, 1976.)

the methods shown in Figure 18.5. The dendritic branching developed by EC animals was significantly greater than that of IC animals (Greenough and Volkmar, 1973; Volkmar and Greenough, 1972). The SC values fell between the IC and EC values and tended to be closer to the IC values. With enriched experience, each cell did not send its dendrites out farther, but instead tended to fill its allotted volume more densely with branches. These results, together with the dendritic spine counts, indicate that EC animals develop new synapses and more-elaborate information-processing circuits.

Several neuroanatomical studies confirm that dendritic morphology is constantly changing. Electrical activity of neurons promotes the growth of fine extensions from dendrites. These extensions, called **filopodia** (singular *filopodium*), occur not only during development, as mentioned in Chapter 7, but throughout the life span. They may become dendritic spines if they make contact with an axon (Maletic-Savatic et al., 1999; S. J. Smith, 1999), or form new dendritic branches for additional synapses (M. Fischer et al., 2000).

The *size* of existing synaptic contacts also changes as a result of differential experience. The mean length of the postsynaptic thickening in synapses of the occipital cortex is significantly greater in EC rats than in their IC littermates (M. C. Diamond et al., 1975; Greenough and Volkmar, 1973). Such increases in the size and number of synaptic contacts may increase the certainty of synaptic transmission in the circuits where changes occur. The fact that these changes, related to long-term memory, are found in the cerebral cortex is consistent with the hypothesis that much long-term memory is *stored* in the cortex, whereas information is *processed* for memory storage in other brain regions, such as the hippocampus, depending on the attributes of the particular memory (see Chapter 17).

William Greenough

NEURAL PLASTICITY

EC and IC environments affect both brain values and problem-solving behavior. Similar effects on brain measurements have been found in several species of mammals: mice, gerbils, ground squirrels, cats, and monkeys (Renner and Rosenzweig, 1987); effects of differential experience on brain measurements have also been found in birds, fish, and other vertebrate species (Rampon and Tsien, 2000; van Praag et al., 2000).

A few studies indicate similar plasticity of the human brain in response to experience. For example, we saw in Chapter 11 that the hand area of the motor cortex becomes larger in musicians, presumably because of their extensive practice. In addition, the occipital cortex of blind persons becomes sensitive to auditory stimuli, and transcranial magnetic stimulation of the occipital cortex can disrupt Braille reading, indicating that cross-modal neural reorganization can take place in the mature human brain (Kujala et al., 2000). A recent study assigned 100 children to a two-year enriched nursery school program at ages 3 to 5 while others received normal educational experience (Raine et al., 2001). When the children were tested at age 11, with skin conductance and electroencephalographic measures of arousal and attention, the children with early environmental enrichment showed increases in orienting and arousal.

Thus the cerebral effects of experience that were surprising when first reported for rats in the early 1960s are now seen to occur widely in the animal kingdom—from flies to philosophers (Mohammed, 2001). The finding that measurable changes can be induced in the brain by experience, even in adult animals, was one of several factors that led increasing numbers of investigators to ask in more detail how the brain reacts to training and how new information can be stored by the nervous system.

Invertebrate Nervous Systems Show Plasticity

One strategy for finding out how the nervous system is changed by a specific learning task is to exploit the relative simplicity of the central nervous systems of some invertebrates. Several investigators tried to find neural circuits necessary and sufficient for learning, with the goal of studying plastic synaptic changes in these circuits. Invertebrate preparations, such as the large sea slug *Aplysia* (Figure 18.6), offered certain advantages for this research:

- The number of nerve cells in an *Aplysia* ganglion is relatively small (though still on the order of a thousand) compared to the number in a mammalian brain.

- As we saw in Chapter 6, many individual cells in invertebrate ganglia can be recognized, both because of their shapes and sizes and because the cellular structure of the ganglion is uniform from individual to individual. Thus it is possible to identify certain cells and to trace their sensory and motor connections. The neurotransmitters in some of these large, identifiable cells are also known.

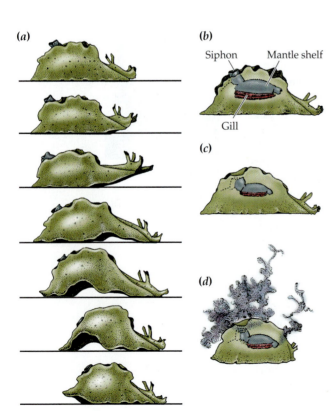

(a)

(b)
Siphon   Mantle shelf

Gill

(c)

(d)

18.6 Characteristic Behaviors of *Aplysia* (a) Locomotion. (b) In the usual posture, the siphon is extended and the gill is spread out on the back. Ordinarily only the tip of the siphon would be visible in a lateral view; here the rest of the siphon and the gill are shown as if the animal were transparent. (c) The siphon and the gill retract in response to light touch. (d) The head retracts and the animal releases ink in response to a strong stimulus. (After Kandel, 1976.)

A well-known program of research on neural plasticity in invertebrates was initiated by Eric R. Kandel, who was awarded the Nobel Prize in Physiology or Medicine in 2000 for research on neural mechanisms of learning and memory. Kandel investigated sites and mechanisms of plasticity for both nonassociative and associative learning in *Aplysia* (Kandel et al., 1987). One of his research programs focused on a relatively simple, nonassociative type of learning: habituation. If you direct a squirt of water onto an *Aplysia*—say, on the part of the body called the *siphon*—the animal quickly retracts its delicate gill (which is nearby) in case whatever hit the siphon might hit the gill. But with repeated stimulation of the siphon, the animal retracts the gill less and less as it habituates (in other words, it learns that the stimulation of the siphon represents no danger to the gill).

Kandel and associates demonstrated that this habituation is caused by changes in the synapse between the sensory cell that detects the squirt of water and the motoneuron that retracts the gill. As this synapse releases less and less transmitter, the gill slowly stops retracting in response to the stimulation (Figure 18.7a) (M. Klein et al., 1980). This is an instance in which the synaptic plasticity underlying learning is within the reflex circuit itself (see Figure 18.1a).

Both the number and the size of synaptic junctions have also been found to vary with training in *Aplysia*. For example, if an *Aplysia* is tested in the habituation paradigm over a series of days, each day the animal habituates

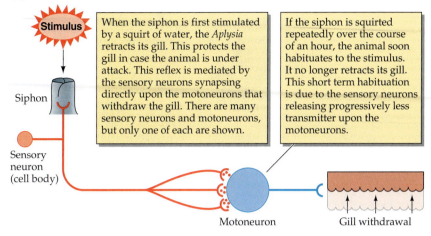

(a) **Short-term habituation**

Stimulus

Siphon

Sensory neuron (cell body)

When the siphon is first stimulated by a squirt of water, the *Aplysia* retracts its gill. This protects the gill in case the animal is under attack. This reflex is mediated by the sensory neurons synapsing directly upon the motoneurons that withdraw the gill. There are many sensory neurons and motoneurons, but only one of each are shown.

If the siphon is squirted repeatedly over the course of an hour, the animal soon habituates to the stimulus. It no longer retracts its gill. This short term habituation is due to the sensory neurons releasing progressively less transmitter upon the motoneurons.

Motoneuron   Gill withdrawal

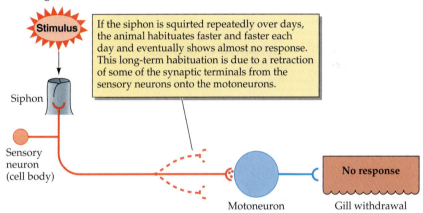

(b) **Long-term habituation**

Stimulus

Siphon

Sensory neuron (cell body)

If the siphon is squirted repeatedly over days, the animal habituates faster and faster each day and eventually shows almost no response. This long-term habituation is due to a retraction of some of the synaptic terminals from the sensory neurons onto the motoneurons.

Motoneuron   No response   Gill withdrawal

18.7 Synaptic Plasticity Underlying Habituation in *Aplysia*

faster than it did the day before. This response represents long-term habituation (as opposed to the short-term habituation we have already discussed), and in this case there is a reduction in the number of synapses between the sensory cell and the motoneuron (Figure 18.7b) (C. H. Bailey and Chen, 1983). This finding is similar to previous findings with mammals (M. C. Diamond et al., 1975; West and Greenough, 1972) and refutes the claim of Eccles and others that neurochemical events at existing synapses are sufficient to account for learning and long-term memory.

The similarity of results obtained with *Aplysia* and with rats indicates that over a wide range of species, information can be stored in the nervous system by changes in both strength and number of synaptic contacts, confirming the hypotheses diagrammed in Figure 18.2. Thus, even in a relatively simple animal like *Aplysia*, the structural remodeling of the nervous system early in development that we considered in Chapter 7 probably continues to some extent throughout life and can be driven by experience. Next we'll consider a neural circuit in the mammalian brain in which neural activity alters the strength of synaptic connections.

Eric R. Kandel

Could Long-Term Potentiation Be a Model for Studying Mechanisms of Learning and Memory?

Investigators have sought a way of isolating a vertebrate brain circuit in which learning occurs in order to study the mechanisms in detail, as in the "simple" inverte-

**IMPORTANT
METHOD**

brate systems. Long-term potentiation in the mammalian brain may be the answer. **Long-term potentiation (LTP)** is a stable and enduring increase in the effectiveness of synapses. To see LTP, we electrically stimulate axons in a circuit at a slow rate—say, once every second—and we find that the size of the response in the postsynaptic neurons is quite stable. But if we then stimulate the axons with a brief **tetanus** (a flurry of electrical stimulation triggering thousands of action potentials over 1 to 2 s), the size of the excitatory postsynaptic potential (EPSP) responses increases markedly and remains high throughout the recording period. This greater effectiveness of the synapses after the tetanus is the LTP (Figure 18.8a). Notice that the synapses in LTP behave like Hebbian synapses: (1) The tetanus drives a group of axons to fire repeatedly; (2) because the axon terminals are all firing at once, they succeed in causing the postsynaptic targets to fire repeatedly; and (3) the synapses are then stronger than they were before the tetanus.

LTP was first discovered in 1973 in the rabbit hippocampus by British neurophysiologist Timothy Bliss and Norwegian Terje Lømo, then a psychology student. The surprising aspect of their finding was the long-lasting nature of the increase in response magnitude. A shorter-term effect of this sort had long been known under the name of posttetanic potentiation, which occurs at neuromuscular junctions (see Chapter 11).

Soon after Bliss and Lømo reported their findings, other investigators demonstrated that LTP could also be studied in slices of rat hippocampus maintained in a tissue chamber (Schwartzkroin and Wester, 1975). LTP can be observed in awake and freely moving animals, in anesthetized animals, or in tissue slices, which is the focus of most current research. Although most of the work on LTP has been done in the hippocampus of the rat (Figure 18.8b), LTP has been observed in many other brain areas in several species of mammals, in fishes, and even in *Aplysia* (X. Y. Lin and Glanzman, 1994).

Bliss and Lømo (1973) were cautious about whether LTP bears any relation to normal behavior. However, LTP does resemble memory in several ways: LTP can be induced within seconds, it may last for days or weeks (Bliss and Gardner-Medwin, 1973), and it shows a labile consolidation period that lasts for several minutes after induction (Barrionuevo et al., 1980). Such properties have attracted many investigators to the study of LTP. After reviewing some other findings about LTP, we will consider more critically how well LTP may serve as a mechanism of memory. We'll follow our discussion of LTP by looking at an opposite phenomenon, the weakening of synaptic responses (or *long-term depression*), which may also be important as a mechanism of learning.

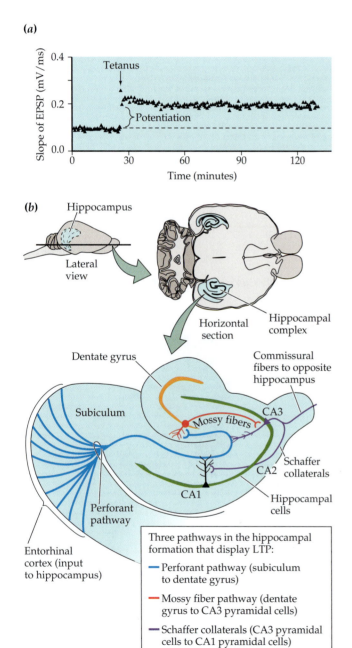

(a)

(b)

18.8 Long-Term Potentiation in the Hippocampus *(a)* If axons in the circuit are stimulated only once every second, the size of the response in the postsynaptic neurons is quite stable. However, after a brief tetanus (a burst of electrical stimulation triggering hundreds or thousands of action potentials over 1–2 seconds), the size of the excitatory postsynaptic potential (EPSP) responses increases markedly and remains high throughout the recording period. This greater responsiveness is called *long-term potentiation* (LTP). *(b)* *(Top)* This diagram shows the location of the hippocampal formation in whole rat brain and in a horizontal section. *(Bottom)* This diagram of the right hippocampal formation shows various neural pathways found in the hippocampal formation, many of which display LTP. (See the text for an explanation of CA1, CA2, and CA3.)

LTP occurs at several sites in the hippocampal formation

The *hippocampal formation* (see Figure 18.8*b*) consists of two interlocking C-shaped regions—the **hippocampus** itself and the **dentate gyrus**—and the adjacent **subiculum** (also called the *subicular complex* or *hippocampal gyrus*). The strange shapes of the structures in the hippocampal formation earned them picturesque names: *Hippocampus* itself comes from the Greek *hippokampos,* "seahorse," as we noted in Chapter 2. But other neuroanatomists called it by the Latin name *cornu ammonis* ("Ammon's horn"), referring to the horn of the ram that represented the Egyptian deity Ammon. One region where LTP is investigated is known as *CA1* (*cornu ammonis 1*), another as *CA3*. The dentate gyrus got its name from its toothlike projections (the Latin *dens* means "tooth"). The subiculum (from the Latin *subicere,* meaning "to raise or lift") can be seen as a support for the rest of the hippocampal formation.

Main inputs to the hippocampal formation come from the nearby entorhinal cortex via the axons of the perforant pathway that push through ("perforate") the subiculum (see Figure 18.8*b*). The site at which LTP was originally demonstrated consists of synapses from the perforant path to the dentate gyrus. But other pathways in the hippocampal formation also demonstrate LTP. For example, from the dentate gyrus, so-called mossy fibers run to the hippocampus, where they synapse in area CA3. As another instance, neurons in CA3 send their axons, called *Schaffer collaterals,* to area CA1; LTP has been studied intensively at these synapses. The CA1 and CA3 regions also receive inputs from the corresponding regions of the hippocampus in the other hemisphere of the brain via commissural fibers (fibers that cross over through the corpus callosum), but these connections will not concern us here.

In the 1980s, the discovery of selective agonists for different kinds of glutamate receptors allowed investigators to characterize the pharmacology of synaptic transmission in the hippocampus, and it turned out that these synapses use glutamate as a transmitter. The surprise came when investigators learned that LTP in area CA1 depends on a subclass of glutamate receptors that respond to the synthetic agonist *N*-methyl-D-aspartate (the NMDA receptors that we introduced in Box 4.2). Blocking of these receptors by antagonists of NMDA made it impossible to induce LTP in CA1, even though the NMDA antagonists did not affect other glutamate receptors, the AMPA receptors.

Although NMDA antagonists prevent the *induction* of LTP, they do not affect LTP that has already been established. Investigators learned that, under certain circumstances, activation of the NMDA-type glutamate receptors leads to an increase in the number of AMPA-type glutamate receptors. Let's discuss in some detail how this happens.

Timothy Bliss

Terje Lømo

NMDA receptors and AMPA receptors play separate roles in the induction of LTP in the CA1 region

When the neurotransmitter glutamate is released at a synapse that has both AMPA receptors and NMDA receptors, a moderate level of stimulation activates only the AMPA receptors, which handle most of the normal traffic of messages at these synapses. The NMDA receptors do not respond in this instance because magnesium ions (Mg^{2+}) block the NMDA receptor channel (Figure 18.9*a*), so few Ca^{2+} ions can enter the neuron. However, if AMPA receptors in the same neuron are stimulated enough, the postsynaptic neurons will be depolarized to a membrane potential of –35 mV or so. This partial depolarization removes the Mg^{2+} block (Figure 18.9*b*); the NMDA receptors now respond actively to glutamate and admit large amounts of Ca^{2+} through their channels. Thus the NMDA receptors are fully active only when they are gated by a combination of voltage (depolarization through other receptors) and the ligand (glutamate).

The large influx of Ca^{2+} at NMDA receptors leads to the next steps in the induction of LTP by activating some **protein kinases** (enzymes that catalyze phosphorylation, the addition of phosphate groups [PO_4] to protein molecules). Phosphorylation changes the properties of many protein molecules. Several protein kinases are

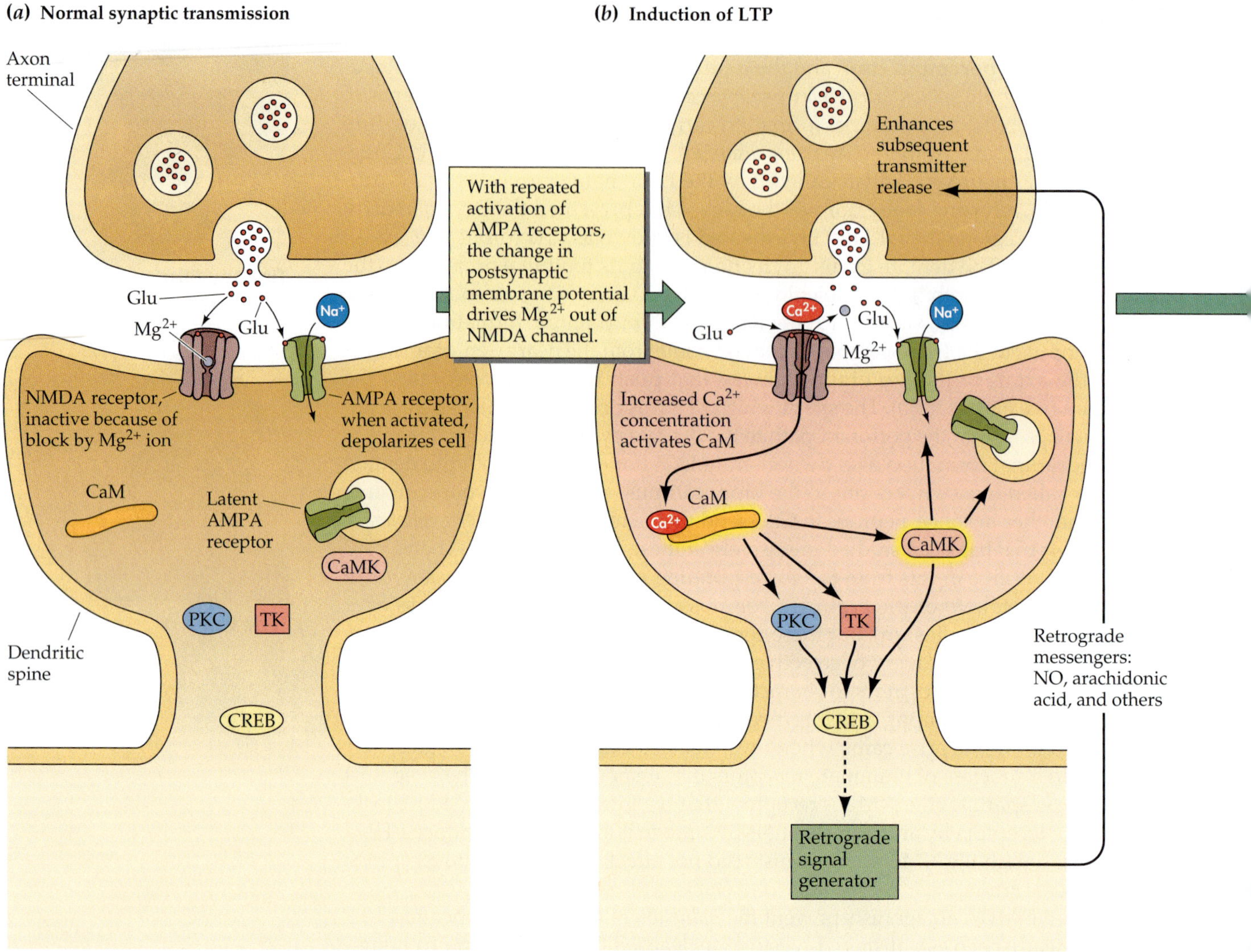

(a) Normal synaptic transmission

(b) Induction of LTP

With repeated activation of AMPA receptors, the change in postsynaptic membrane potential drives Mg²⁺ out of NMDA channel.

Axon terminal

Glu

Mg²⁺   Glu   Na⁺

NMDA receptor, inactive because of block by Mg²⁺ ion

AMPA receptor, when activated, depolarizes cell

CaM

Latent AMPA receptor

CaMK

PKC   TK

Dendritic spine

CREB

Enhances subsequent transmitter release

Ca²⁺   Glu   Na⁺

Glu   Mg²⁺

Increased Ca²⁺ concentration activates CaM

CaM

Ca²⁺   CaMK

PKC   TK

Retrograde messengers: NO, arachidonic acid, and others

CREB

Retrograde signal generator

18.9 Roles of the AMPA and NMDA Receptors in the Induction of LTP in the CA1 Region   (*a*) Normally the NMDA channel is blocked by a Mg²⁺ molecule, and only the AMPA channel functions in excitation of the neuron. (*b*) With repeated activation of AMPA receptors, depolarization of the neuron drives Mg²⁺ out of the NMDA channel, and Ca²⁺ ions enter. The rapid increase of Ca²⁺ ions triggers processes that lead to LTP. Activation of the protein CaM ki- nase (CaMK) increases the conductance of AMPA receptors already pres- ent in the membrane and promotes the movement of AMPA receptors from the interior of the spine into the membrane. (*c*) The synapse is en- hanced after induction of LTP. CaM, Calmodulin; CREB, cAMP responsive element–binding protein; Glu, glutamate; PKC, protein kinase C; TK, tyro- sine kinase.

present in relatively large amounts in neurons, including protein kinase A (PKA), protein kinase C (PKC), calcium–calmodulin kinase (CaM kinase, or CaMK), and tyrosine kinase (TK). Blockage of any of these kinases can prevent the induction of LTP.

CaM kinase affects AMPA receptors in two ways (Figure 18.9*c*) (Lisman et al., 2002). It phosphorylates AMPA receptors already present in the dendritic spine membrane, thus increasing their conductance to Na⁺ and K⁺ ions. It also promotes the movement of AMPA receptors from the interior of the spine into the membrane, making more receptors available to stimulate the spine. Additional steps in the neu- rochemical cascade underlying LTP will be described shortly.

In an attempt to test the importance of the NMDA receptor (NR) for LTP, Joe Z. Tsien and colleagues (Rampon, Jiang, et al., 2000) prepared genetically modified mice in which a major subunit of NR, the NR1 subunit, was prevented from ex-

(c) Enhanced synapse, after induction of LTP

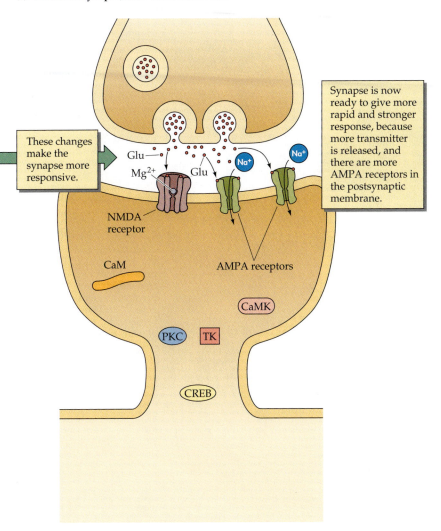

These changes make the synapse more responsive.

Glu
Mg²⁺   Glu   Na⁺   Na⁺

NMDA receptor

CaM   AMPA receptors

CaMK

PKC   TK

CREB

Synapse is now ready to give more rapid and stronger response, because more transmitter is released, and there are more AMPA receptors in the postsynaptic membrane.

pression in the brain. These knockout mice grew normally and appeared normal, but investigators were unable to induce LTP in their hippocampal slices. The knockout mice were also inferior to wild-type mice in several behavior tests known to involve the hippocampus. These results clearly supported the hypothesized importance of the NMDA receptors.

But then the researchers tried giving the knockout mice experience in an enriched environment like that shown in Figure 18.4c. To their surprise, they found that the enriched experience significantly improved the performance of the knockout mice, making them as good as the wild-type mice on some tests. At least for some types of learning and memory that are dependent on the hippocampus, NMDA receptors may play an important role normally, but they are not absolutely essential.

GENES AND BEHAVIOR

LTP is induced via a cascade of neurochemical steps

Several neurochemical steps have been identified in the induction of LTP, and we will see that some of these steps have also been implicated in other kinds of memory formation. In fact, many of these steps are seen whenever a signal leads cells to change the kinds of compounds they synthesize or the rate of synthesis. We have already seen that the entry of Ca^{2+} ions into neurons activates some protein kinases, which are essential for the induction and maintenance of LTP. These include PKA, PKC, and CaM kinase (Figure 18.10).

18.10 Steps in the Neurochemical Cascade during the Induction of LTP This illustration is based on LTP induction in the CA1 region of the hippocampus.

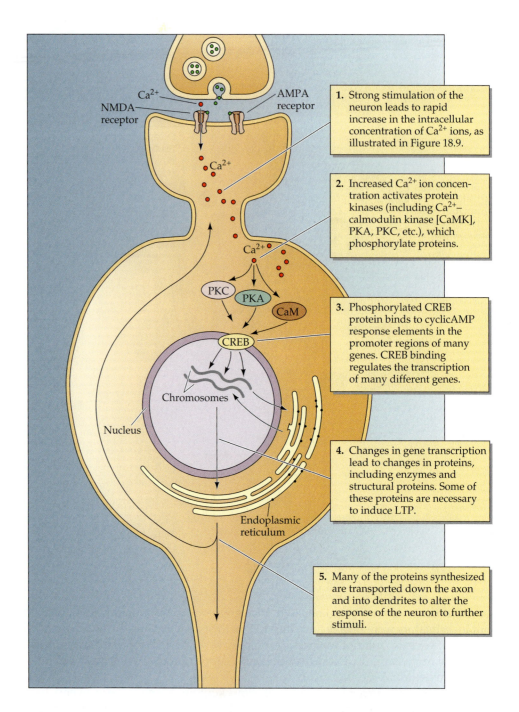

1. Strong stimulation of the neuron leads to rapid increase in the intracellular concentration of Ca^{2+} ions, as illustrated in Figure 18.9.

2. Increased Ca^{2+} ion concentration activates protein kinases (including Ca^{2+}–calmodulin kinase [CaMK], PKA, PKC, etc.), which phosphorylate proteins.

3. Phosphorylated CREB protein binds to cyclicAMP response elements in the promoter regions of many genes. CREB binding regulates the transcription of many different genes.

4. Changes in gene transcription lead to changes in proteins, including enzymes and structural proteins. Some of these proteins are necessary to induce LTP.

5. Many of the proteins synthesized are transported down the axon and into dendrites to alter the response of the neuron to further stimuli.

Drugs that inhibit CaM kinase interfere with the formation of intermediate-term memory (ITM), whereas inhibitors of PKC prevent the formation of long-term memory (LTM) (Rosenzweig et al., 1992, 1993; Serrano et al., 1994). Huang and Kandel (1994) reported a similar finding concerning LTP in the CA1 region of the hippocampus: One pattern of stimulation induces a form of LTP that is blocked by an inhibitor of CaM kinase; another pattern of stimulation induces a form of LTP that is blocked by inhibitors of PKA. Mice with one copy of the CaM kinase gene knocked out can still form short-term memories (STMs), but they cannot form LTMs (Frankland et al., 2001).

The activated protein kinases, in turn, not only catalyze the phosphorylation of proteins but also trigger the synthesis of proteins. First the kinases phosphorylate and activate **cAMP responsive element–binding protein (CREB)**. As its name indicates, CREB binds to *cAMP responsive elements;* these are particular sequences of nucleotides in the promoter regions of DNA adjacent to many genes. When CREB binds the cAMP responsive elements, it changes the rate of transcription of the adjacent gene. In this way CREB regulates the expression of over 100 genes and so occupies a strategic position in the neurochemical cascade underlying memory formation. CREB activation regulates the expression of many different genes that can alter the growth and differentiation of neurons. In mice, genetic deletion of CREB impairs LTM but not short-term memory (STM) for training involving both reward (Kogan et al., 1997) and punishment (Bourtchuladze et al., 1994). In humans, a mutation in the gene encoding the protein that CREB interacts with (called CREB binding protein, or CBP) results in a syndrome characterized by mental retardation (Petrij et al., 1995).

CLINICAL ISSUE

There are also proteins that regulate the ability of CREB to affect gene transcription. For example, a gene called *inducible cAMP early repressor* (ICER) can produce at least four different proteins that are endogenous CREB antagonists (Mioduszewska et al., 2003). Like CREB, these proteins bind to the cAMP responsive elements of various genes, but unlike CREB, they do not activate transcription of the genes. Thus they compete with CREB: If enough of these antagonists are present, CREB cannot work to form LTM (Yin et al., 1994). Perhaps synthetic CREB antagonists may one day be developed to prevent a person from making a permanent memory for traumatic experiences. Unlike drinking from the River Lethe, this mechanism would not affect memories that have already been encoded in LTM. Rather, the person would forget everything that had happened in the past day or so, which means that he or she would have to take the treatment soon after the traumatic event.

Note that for CREB to exert its full effects, the regulated genes must eventually produce proteins to affect synaptic function. This is one reason why the induction of LTP requires protein synthesis. The earlier stages of LTP, lasting an hour or so, appear not to require protein synthesis, but thereafter, inhibition of protein synthesis prevents longer-lasting LTP (Frey et al., 1993; Krug et al., 1984). Three hours after the induction of LTP, certain proteins increase while others decrease, indicating a complex pattern of changes in proteins (Fazeli et al., 1993). Evidence has accumulated that induction of LTP activates a **retrograde signal,** from the postsynaptic neuron to the presynaptic neuron (see Figure 18.9*b*), that instructs the presynaptic neuron to release more transmitter. (It's called a *retrograde signal* because it crosses the synaptic cleft in the opposite direction of the transmitter).

So LTP increases the effectiveness of synapses in two ways: by increasing the number of postsynaptic receptors *and* by increasing the release of transmitter. Thus, Colley and Routtenberg (1993) speak of the pre- and postsynaptic neurons as being engaged in a "synaptic dialogue" in forming LTP. Nitric oxide (NO), arachidonic acid, and nerve growth factor are among the 17 candidates proposed by different investigators as possible retrograde signals in LTP (J. R. Sanes and Lichtman, 1999).

Some of the complexity of and discrepancies in the results of experiments on LTP may come from the fact that several different phenomena seem to be involved. Reviews of the evidence suggest four or five overlapping but separable effects of prior stimulation on the amplitude of responses of hippocampal cells (W. C. Abraham and Goddard, 1985; Bliss and Collingridge, 1993). Depending on how and when the experimenter measures the responses and on which treatments are used to affect them, one or another phenomenon may predominate in the results. Further work is needed to sort out these complex phenomena and to decide the extent to which any of them can help us understand the mechanisms of various kinds of learning. We will also see significant differences between LTP induced in region CA1 and LTP induced in CA3.

Opioid peptides modulate the induction of LTP in the CA3 region

Although much research focuses on the role of the NMDA receptor in LTP, at the synapses between mossy fibers and CA3 neurons (see Figure 18.8*b*), LTP can be induced even in the presence of an NMDA antagonist, so NMDA receptors are not needed here (Harris and Cotman, 1986). On the other hand, the induction of LTP in region CA3 can be blocked by the presence of the opioid antagonist naloxone (Derrick and Martinez, 1994). In other parts of the brain, too, LTP can be induced without NMDA receptors being activated. For example, in the visual cortex of adult rats, LTP can be induced in the presence of a strong antagonist of NMDA (Aroniadou et al., 1993). But administering blockers of other Ca^{2+} channels prevents the induction of LTP. In cortex, NMDA receptors that regulate neural plasticity in development may become less important with maturity. Presumably other types of voltage-gated Ca^{2+} channels regulate synaptic plasticity in the adult cortex.

Long-term depression is the converse of LTP

We noted early in this chapter that negative as well as positive changes can store information in the nervous system. Several investigators have shown that **long-term depression (LTD)** may play a role in memory (Bear and Malenka, 1994; Linden, 1994). LTD is the converse of LTP: a lasting *decrease* in the magnitude of responses of neurons after afferent cells have been activated with electrical stimuli of relatively low frequency.

In the CA1 region of the hippocampus, the induction of LTD appears to require the entry of Ca^{2+} through NMDA receptors, just as the induction of LTP does. How can the entry of Ca^{2+} call for the induction of both LTP and LTD? The critical factor is the *amount* of change of Ca^{2+}. A large surge of Ca^{2+} in the postsynaptic neuron triggers the induction of LTP by activating Ca^{2+}-dependent protein kinases. In contrast, small increases of postsynaptic Ca^{2+} induce LTD by selectively activating the opposite kind of enzyme—protein phosphatases that catalyze dephosphorylation, which is the removal of phosphate groups (Lisman, 1989; Mulkey et al., 1993). Different sites on the AMPA receptor are phosphorylated or dephosphorylated in LTP and LTD, respectively (H.-K. Lee et al., 2000).

Is LTP a mechanism of memory formation?

Several reviewers (e.g., G. Lynch et al., 1991; Staubli, 1995; Teyler and DiScenna, 1986) assert that LTP and/or LTD are mechanisms of memory formation because of similarities between these changes in synaptic strength and examples of learning and memory. For example, LTP can be induced within seconds, it may last for days or weeks, and it shows a labile consolidation period that lasts for several minutes after induction. These properties of LTP have suggested to some investigators that LTP is a kind of synaptic plasticity that underlies certain forms of learning and memory. They have therefore sought to test this hypothesis by examining (1) whether other properties of LTP are reflected in properties of learning and memory, and vice versa; and (2) whether various treatments (e.g., drugs) have similar effects on LTP and on learning and memory.

COMPETING HYPOTHESES

Some scientists study both LTP and conditioning in the same neural circuit. One study recorded LTP while an *Aplysia* preparation was being conditioned (Murphy and Glanzman, 1999). The strength of responses was studied in the abdominal ganglion at a synapse between a sensory neuron from the siphon and a siphon motoneuron. For a cellular analog to classical conditioning, the conditioned stimulus (CS) was brief intracellular stimulation of the sensory siphon neuron, and the unconditioned stimulus (US) was extracellular stimulation of the nerve from the tail to the abdominal ganglion. Some preparations received a series of paired stimuli: CS followed immediately by US. Then, 60 minutes later, a test shock to the sensory neuron evoked a larger response in the motoneuron than a test shock before the pairing had. The larger response was evidence that LTP had been induced.

The same preparations also received a series of unpaired presentations of CS and US in another siphon neuron, and no enhancement occurred. In addition, if the pairing occurred when an NMDA antagonist was added to the solution bathing the preparation, no enhancement occurred, although synaptic transmission was not blocked (presumably because AMPA receptors continued to respond to the glutamate).

Fear conditioning in rats (Rogan et al., 1997) causes not only conditioning but also LTP. In a study by McKernan and Shinnick-Gallagher (1997), rats received an auditory tone as the CS paired with foot-shock, and a startle response was the conditioned response (CR). Twenty-four hours later, coronal slices through the amygdala were prepared from the brains. Slices were also prepared from animals given unpaired CS and US or given only noise stimuli. LTP was found in the amygdala slices from animals that had received paired training but not in slices from rats in the other conditions. Thus the experimenters were able to study and analyze the synaptic effects of whole-animal fear learning in an in vitro slice, employing the techniques traditionally used in the study of LTP. Potentiation was found only in synapses in the fear-conditioning circuit and not in other nearby synapses, providing additional evidence that LTP serves as a substrate for this kind of learning.

Other evidence for a similarity between LTP and learning comes from experiments in which a particular gene is disrupted to produce so-called knockout mice—mice in which one gene has been made nonfunctional (see Box 7.3). Kandel's group (Grant et al., 1992) disrupted four different kinases in four different groups of mice. They found that hippocampal LTP was reduced only in the mice missing the kinase gene *fyn*, and that these were the only mice that showed a deficit in maze learning.

GENES AND BEHAVIOR

This result strongly suggests that the fyn protein is important in both LTP and maze learning, and that the electrophysiological phenomenon of LTP is related to learning. Another group of investigators (A. J. Silva et al., 1992) produced knockout mice lacking the CaM kinase II gene; these mice were also slower at learning spatial relations. Interestingly, all of the knockout mice were able to learn the task eventually, indicating that none of these genes are absolutely necessary for learning.

Such findings support the idea that LTP is a kind of synaptic plasticity that underlies or is similar to certain forms of learning and memory and that it can therefore be used to investigate the mechanisms of those forms of learning and memory. As Box 18.1 describes, enhancing NMDA receptor activity by altering receptor subunits improves LTP and some kinds of learning and memory.

Glial cells may participate in learning and memory

Although most research on mechanisms of learning and memory concentrates on neurons, some investigators (e.g., Laming et al., 2000) are pointing to interactions of glial cells with neurons in learning and memory. For example, transgenic mice that overexpress an astrocytic calcium-binding protein were impaired in the Morris water maze, although they performed normally in nonspatial tasks (Gerlai et al., 1995). Experience in an enriched environment, which improves learning and memory formation, increases the production of new glial cells as well as new neurons (Nilsson et al., 1999), perhaps by inducing glial cells to provide neurotrophic factors (D. Young et al., 1999). Even in the hippocampal formation, the neural plasticity we discussed earlier can take place only as long as nearby glial cells provide a particular neurotrophic factor; blocking this neurotrophic factor reduces the insertion of AMPA-type glutamate receptors in response to neural activity (Beattie et al., 2002).

The Mammalian Cerebellum Houses the Brain Circuit for a Simple Conditioned Reflex

While many investigators studied learning in the apparently simpler nervous systems of invertebrates and others probed the phenomenon of LTP, some tried to define a circuit for learning in intact mammals. Psychologist Richard F. Thompson and his colleagues have been studying the neural circuitry of eye-blink conditioning in the rabbit since the 1970s (Lavond et al., 1993; R. F. Thompson, 1990; R. F. Thompson et al., 1998).

When a puff of air to the cornea (US) follows an acoustic tone (CS), a conditioned response (CR) develops rapidly: The rabbit comes to blink when the tone is sounded.

Richard F. Thompson

BOX 18.1 Modifying Brains for Better Learning and Memory

Now that investigators have found out quite a bit about both direct and modulatory processes involved in learning and memory, attempts are being made to improve some of these processes. Many changes *impair* learning and memory—for example, blockage of protein kinases, reduction in CREB, or inhibition of protein synthesis. Can other changes *improve* learning and memory? We'll consider an example of a change in the NMDA receptor that is implicated in some kinds of learning.

The NMDA receptor (NR) consists of the core NR1 subunit and NR2 subunits. The NR2 subunits determine the length of time that the NR channel is open to Ca^{2+} and thus the size of the excitatory postsynaptic potential (EPSP). Young animals express predominantly NR2B subunits, which allow longer Ca^{2+} conduction and thus larger EPSPs. The number of these subunits is down-regulated in the transition from juvenile to adult, and shorter-acting NR2A units come to predominate.

Joe Z. Tsien and coworkers (Y. P. Tang et al., 1999) prepared transgenic mice in which larger-than-normal numbers of juvenile NR2B subunits are expressed, especially in the cerebral cortex and the hippocampus. These animals showed normal growth and body weights and mated normally. Analysis of the hippocampal neurons in transgenic versus wild-type mice revealed that the transgenic mice had greater numbers of NR2B subunits per synapse and about fourfold greater flow of Ca^{2+} during activation. Hippocampal slices from transgenic mice showed enhanced LTP but no difference in LTD compared to wild-type mice.

At 3 to 6 months of age, transgenic mice were compared with wild-type mice in a variety of behavioral tasks. In examining a novel object rather than a familiar object (see the figure)—a test that requires the hippocampus—all mice showed equal amounts of initial exploration of the objects, and all showed equal preference for the novel object 1 hour later. When tested 1 day or 3 days later, however, transgenic mice exhibited significantly stronger preference for the novel object than did the wild-type mice, thus showing stronger long-term memory.

Presented with two objects, a smart mouse will spend more time investigating the one he hasn't seen before.

In two forms of associative emotional memory, the transgenic mice learned more strongly than the wild-type mice. The mice were tested for extinction of the fear response by repeated exposure to a neutral environment without shock. Although the transgenic mice showed greater fear responses early in the tests, they extinguished the fear responses more rapidly than the wild-type mice did. In the Morris hidden-platform water maze—a test known to require activation of NMDA receptors in the hippocampus—both the transgenic and wild-type mice learned, but the transgenic mice learned faster.

The investigators propose that their research indicates a potential new direction for treatment of disorders of learning and memory and "a promising strategy for creation of other genetically modified mammals with enhanced intelligence and memory" (Y. P. Tang et al., 1999, p. 69). They showed their enthusiasm by naming their transgenic mice *Doogies* after the teenage genius in the television show *Doogie Howser, M.D.*

These findings certainly indicate that the NMDA receptor is involved in several kinds of learning. Whether the findings will help treat disorders of learning and memory is less sure. Humans have an NR2B gene nearly identical to that in mice, but some neuroscientists worry that a drug that increases NMDA receptor activation could have undesirable side effects, such as increased risk of epilepsy or stroke. In fact, the genetic manipulation that made the Doogie mice smarter also caused them to experience chronic pain longer than control mice (Wei et al., 2001).

Others wonder whether general enhancement of learning and intelligence is a good idea socially. Tim Tully, a member of a group that in 1995 announced genetic improvement of long-term memory of *Drosophila* by inducing the activation of a form of CREB (Yin et al., 1995), suggested that we may have evolved to learn less rapidly in maturity to prevent overloading of the brain's memory capacity. Joe Tsien prefers to think that the decrease in learning with age is evolutionarily adaptive for the population because it reduces the possibility that older individuals—who may have already reproduced—will compete successfully against younger ones for resources such as food. This debate shows no prospects of early resolution.

(*a*) **Before**

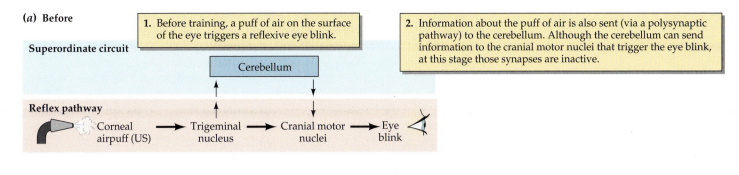

Superordinate circuit

1. Before training, a puff of air on the surface of the eye triggers a reflexive eye blink.

2. Information about the puff of air is also sent (via a polysynaptic pathway) to the cerebellum. Although the cerebellum can send information to the cranial motor nuclei that trigger the eye blink, at this stage those synapses are inactive.

Cerebellum

Reflex pathway

Corneal airpuff (US) → Trigeminal nucleus → Cranial motor nuclei → Eye blink

(*b*) **Training**

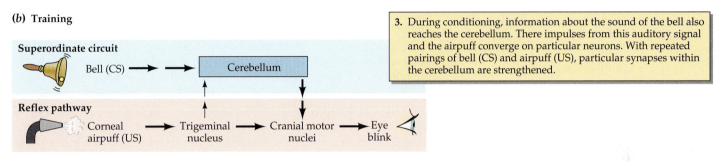

Superordinate circuit

Bell (CS) → → Cerebellum

3. During conditioning, information about the sound of the bell also reaches the cerebellum. There impulses from this auditory signal and the airpuff converge on particular neurons. With repeated pairings of bell (CS) and airpuff (US), particular synapses within the cerebellum are strengthened.

Reflex pathway

Corneal airpuff (US) → Trigeminal nucleus → Cranial motor nuclei → Eye blink

(*c*) **After**

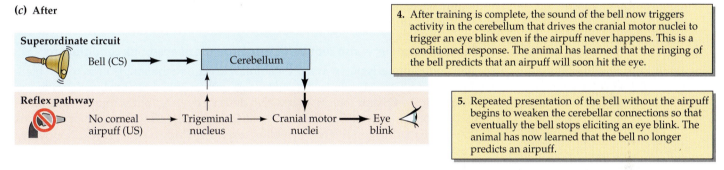

Superordinate circuit

Bell (CS) → → Cerebellum

4. After training is complete, the sound of the bell now triggers activity in the cerebellum that drives the cranial motor nuclei to trigger an eye blink even if the airpuff never happens. This is a conditioned response. The animal has learned that the ringing of the bell predicts that an airpuff will soon hit the eye.

Reflex pathway

No corneal airpuff (US) → Trigeminal nucleus → Cranial motor nuclei → Eye blink

5. Repeated presentation of the bell without the airpuff begins to weaken the cerebellar connections so that eventually the bell stops eliciting an eye blink. The animal has now learned that the bell no longer predicts an airpuff.

18.11 Sites in the Neural Circuit for Conditioning of the Eye-Blink Reflex (After R. F. Thompson and Krupa, 1994.)

The basic circuit of the eye-blink reflex is simple, involving cranial nerves and some interneurons that connect their nuclei (Figure 18.11*a*). Sensory fibers from the cornea run along cranial nerve V (the trigeminal nerve) to its nucleus in the brainstem. From there, some interneurons send axons to synapse upon other cranial nerve nuclei (VI and VII) in the brainstem. Motor fibers in the cranial nerves then activate the muscle fibers that cause the eyelids to close.

Thompson and colleagues found that destruction of the hippocampus has little effect on the acquisition or retention of the conditioned eye-blink response in rabbits (Lockhart and Moore, 1975). Therefore the hippocampus is *not* required for this conditioning. The team then searched further, mapping in detail the brain structures where neurons are electrically active during conditioning. They found that learning-related increases in the activity of individual neurons are prominent in the cerebellum (in both its cortex and deep nuclei) and in certain nuclei in the pons.

Deep cerebellar nuclei are necessary for eye-blink conditioning

The circuit of the conditioned reflex was mapped in detail by a combination of methods: electrophysiological recording, localized lesions, localized stimulation of neurons, localized infusion of small amounts of drugs, and tracing of fiber pathways. For example, prior work showed that the inhibitory synaptic transmitter GABA (gamma-aminobutyric acid) is the main transmitter in the deep cerebellar nuclei.

Using well-conditioned rabbits, the investigators injected a small amount of a blocking agent for GABA into the deep cerebellar nuclei. The injection resulted in the disappearance of the behavioral CR and of its electrophysiological neuronal replica. This effect was reversible: As the blocking agent wore off, the CR returned.

On the basis of these and other experiments, Thompson and his coworkers proposed a simplified schematic circuit for the conditioned eye-blink response. They concluded that the cerebellum is part of a superordinate circuit, and that training (the repeated pairing of CS and US) modifies synaptic strength within this superordinate circuit until the CS alone can elicit an eye blink (Figure 18.11b).

The trigeminal (V) pathway that carries information about the corneal stimulation (the US) to the cranial motor nuclei also sends axons to the brainstem (specifically a structure called the inferior olive). These brainstem neurons in turn send axons called *climbing fibers* to synapse upon cerebellar neurons. The same cerebellar cells also receive information about the auditory CS by a pathway through the auditory nuclei and other brainstem nuclei (see Figure 18.11b). After training, the information about the CS has a greater effect on cerebellar neurons so that they now trigger eye blink, even in the absence of an air puff (Figure 18.11c).

Studies on human subjects are consistent with the animal research on eye-blink conditioning. The role of the cerebellum in conditioning is not restricted to eye-blink conditioning. The cerebellum is also needed for the conditioning of leg flexion; in this task an animal learns to withdraw its leg when a tone sounds in order to avoid a shock to the paw (Donegan et al., 1983; Voneida, 1990). On the other hand, the cerebellum is not required for *all* forms of conditioning (L. Holt, M. D. Mauk, and R. F. Thompson, unpublished, cited in Lavond et al., 1993, p. 328).

The hippocampus is also required for some kinds of eye-blink conditioning

The hippocampus is not required for animals to acquire the simple form of eye-blink conditioning—specifically, *delay conditioning*—when little or no time passes between the end of the CS and the US, that we've described so far. But when the time intervals are longer (in what is called *trace conditioning*), animals without a hippocampus are unable to form conditioned eye-blink responses (Moyer et al., 1990). Removal of the hippocampus also prevents the formation of *discrimination reversal conditioning*—that is, conditioning in which the stimulus that previously served as CS now signals that no US is coming (Berger and Orr, 1983). So the neural plasticity underlying these more complicated forms of conditioning are still being actively investigated. For example, as we'll see next, it appears that the hippocampus may have to make new neurons in order for animals to learn trace conditioning.

Are new neurons required for some kinds of learning?

As we saw in Chapter 7, evidence since the 1990s has convinced neuroscientists that new nerve cells are generated in the adult brain, especially in the hippocampus. Adult mice living in an enriched environment produce additional cells in the hippocampus, compared to mice housed in standard cages (Kempermann et al., 1997). The production of new neurons in the hippocampus declines with age in the mouse, but even in senescent (20-month-old) mice, experience in an enriched environment resulted in a threefold increase in new neurons, as compared with animals in standard housing. New neurons also appear in the hippocampus of adult monkeys (E. Gould et al., 1998) and adult humans (Eriksson et al., 1998).

Now some of the investigators who have studied neurogenesis claim that new neurons in the hippocampus are required for trace conditioning (conditioning in which a time interval separates the CS from the US) of the eye-blink response (Shors et al., 2001). To test their hypothesis, Tracy Shors et al. injected rats with an agent, methyl-azoxymethanol (MAM), that kills proliferating cells. The agent was injected over 2 weeks at a carefully controlled dose that killed about 80% of new neurons in the hippocampus and impaired trace conditioning but had no apparent effect on overall health.

Rats given the effective treatment with MAM were still capable of delay conditioning, the simple type of conditioning that does *not* depend on the hippocampus. This is one of several indications that the deficit caused by MAM is specific to hippocampus-dependent learning. Although this is an important first step in testing the function(s) of newly generated neurons, it is not conclusive. Macklis (2001) points out that trace conditioning is more difficult than delay conditioning, so a level of stress that does not affect delay conditioning might nevertheless impair trace conditioning. We might also note that MAM kills proliferating glial cells as well as neurons, and this may play a role in the impairment caused by the drug treatment.

Memories of Different Durations Form by Different Neurochemical Mechanisms

Memories differ markedly in how long they last, from iconic and short-term memories to long-term and permanent memories, as we saw in Chapter 17. Behavioral evidence suggests that memories of different lengths reflect the operation of different neural processes. For example, individuals like H.M. (see Chapter 17), who have no trouble forming short-term memories, may have an impaired ability to form long-term memories. With habituation and sensitization, the formation of relatively short-term memories in *Aplysia* involves mainly neurochemical changes at existing synapses, whereas the formation of long-term memories also involves structural changes in existing synapses and changes in the number of synapses.

Drugs have been used extensively to study memory formation; this approach has led to many interesting discoveries and to new concepts. Unlike brain lesions or other permanent interventions, many chemical treatments are advantageous for this research because they are reversible. Drugs can produce relatively brief, accurately timed effects, and subjects can be tested in their normal state both before and after treatment.

Different agents appear to affect different stages of memory formation. This result has given rise to the concept of sequential neurochemical processes in memory formation. Since about 1960, much research on the formation of long-term memory (e.g., H. P. Davis and Squire, 1984; Flood et al., 1977; Rosenzweig, 1984) has centered on the hypothesis that long-term memory requires increased protein synthesis during the minutes (perhaps hours) that follow training. More recently, investigators have studied the neurochemical processes involved in earlier stages of memory formation—short-term and intermediate-term memories (Gibbs and Ng, 1977; Mizumori et al., 1985; Rosenzweig et al., 1992).

Australian psychologists Marie Gibbs and Kim Ng (1977) found evidence that short-term, intermediate-term, and long-term types of memory in chicks reflect three sequentially linked neurochemical processes. Their experiments studied chicks trained with a single-trial peck avoidance response: The chicks pecked at a small, shiny bead coated with an aversive liquid; after making a single peck, the chicks usually avoided a similar bead, whether it was presented minutes, hours, or even days later.

The formation of memory for the unpleasant experience could be impaired if an amnestic (amnesia-causing) agent was administered close to the time of training. Gibbs and Ng reported that different families of amnestic agents caused memory to fail at different times after training (Figure 18.12). The agents that caused memory failure by about 5 minutes after training were considered to prevent the formation of STM, those that caused failure about 15 minutes after training were thought to prevent the formation of ITM, and those that caused memory to fail by about 60 minutes after training were thought to be affecting LTM.

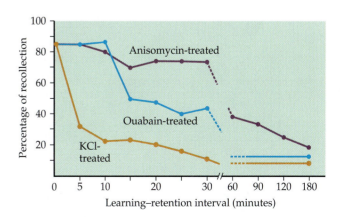

18.12 Timing of the Effects of Different Amnestic Agents Different amnestic agents are thought to impair different stages of memory. They therefore provide a means of observing the duration of each stage. (After Gibbs and Ng, 1977.)

Here are some examples of effects caused by different agents: Potassium chloride (KCl⁻), the NMDA receptor antagonist APV, and lanthanum chloride, each of which inhibits the influx of Ca^{2+} ions, prevent the formation of STM (and therefore of the succeeding ITM and LTM stages). Ouabain, which inhibits Na^+–K^+ ATPase, prevents the formation of ITM (and therefore also LTM). Protein synthesis inhibitors, such as anisomycin, prevent the formation of only LTM. Many agents have been used to disrupt memory at various stages, and although there are some inconsistencies, most of the data confirm at least three stages of memory formation.

The formation of long-term memory requires protein synthesis

Experiments to test the hypothesis that the formation of LTM requires protein synthesis have employed both behavioral intervention (in the form of training) and somatic intervention (in the form of agents that inhibit protein synthesis). Training increases the branching of dendrites and the number of synaptic contacts (Black and Greenough, 1998). The enlarged outgrowths of the neurons are made, in part, of proteins. Furthermore, direct measures of protein in the cerebral cortex of rats show a significant increase with enriched experience (E. L. Bennett et al., 1969).

IMPORTANT METHOD

The other side of the story is that inhibiting the synthesis of proteins in the brain at the time of training can prevent the formation of LTM, even though this inhibition does not interfere with acquisition or retrieval during tests of STM or ITM. The antibiotic anisomycin has been used extensively because at proper doses it is very effective at inhibiting protein synthesis without causing toxic side effects. For example, anisomycin treatment prevents LTM storage in mice, without affecting STM (E. L. Bennett et al., 1972; Flood et al., 1973). It may seem strange that the brain can get along with protein synthesis almost completely blocked for hours, but cells contain large supplies of proteins; existing enzymes, for example, can continue directing the cell's metabolism. With repeated administration of anisomycin, Flood et al. (1975, 1977) demonstrated that even relatively strong training could be overcome by inhibition of protein synthesis; the stronger the training, the longer the inhibition had to be maintained to cause amnesia.

Protein synthesis involved in the formation of LTM appears to occur in two successive waves—the first about 1 hour after training, the second about 5 to 8 hours after training (Matthies, 1989). Administering inhibitors of protein synthesis so that they were effective at either of these periods prevented the formation of LTM. One hypothesis is that protein synthesis is necessary to alter synaptic membranes to encode LTM.

Additional evidence supports the idea that memory forms in stages

Gibbs and Ng (1979) reported that chicks, untreated by any drug, showed dips in the strength of memory at about 15 minutes and 55 minutes after training. They suggested that the dips marked the times of transition between STM and ITM, and between ITM and LTM, respectively. They also found that preventing the formation of one stage of memory inhibited the formation of the following stage(s). These results support the concepts that memory forms in stages and that each stage of memory depends on the preceding one(s).

Further evidence for successive stages of memory formation comes from experiments by Diane Lee using relatively weak training. After weak training, achieved by use of a weak solution of the aversive substance, the retention function for control chicks (with no drug treatment) shows four components (Figure 18.13),

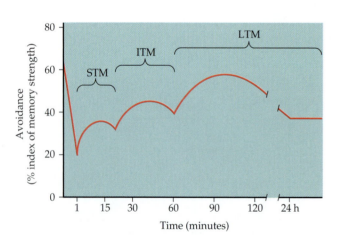

18.13 Four Components of Retention Strength after Weak Training in Chicks The components of this smoothed curve may reflect, successively, the sensory buffer, STM, ITM, and LTM. (After Rosenzweig et al., 1993.)

which may reflect, successively, the sensory buffer (the immediate continuation of sensory input; see Chapter 17), STM, ITM, and LTM (Rosenzweig et al., 1993).

If these components do represent successive stages, it should be possible to inhibit each of them with specific agents. The final rise in memory strength, beginning about 60 minutes after training and hypothesized to reflect LTM, was abolished by inhibitors of protein synthesis, in conformity with the hypothesis. Inhibitors of STM abolished all stages after the initial descending limb of the function (the presumptive sensory buffer), thus supporting the hypothesis that the stages are sequentially dependent.

In *Drosophila,* each stage in memory formation depends on a different gene

Because much is known about its genetics, the fruit fly *Drosophila* brings distinct advantages to the study of mechanisms of learning and memory, even though its central nervous system (which has about 100,000 very small neurons) is more complex than that of the mollusk *Aplysia.* Research with *Drosophila* has corroborated findings obtained with *Aplysia,* and it has added new information about stages of memory formation and the genetics of these stages.

Research on mechanisms of memory in *Drosophila* began when geneticist William Quinn et al. (1974) developed a method to condition groups of *Drosophila.* They put about 40 flies in a glass tube and let them move upward toward one of two odors that normally are equally attractive. Reaching the upper part of one tube brought an electrical shock; the other odor was not associated with shock. The group could then be tested after various time intervals for approach to each of the odors. As the procedure was refined, about 90% of the flies avoided the odor associated with shock (Jellies, 1981). The geneticists then tested mutant strains of *Drosophila.* In 1976 they announced the isolation of the first mutant that failed to learn to discriminate the odors, and they named it *dunce* (Dudai et al., 1976).

Tests showed that *dunce* had a real problem with learning; its deficiency was not in olfaction, locomotion, or general activity. Three more learning mutants were isolated and fondly named *cabbage, turnip,* and *rutabaga;* another mutant, *amnesiac,* learned normally but forgot more rapidly than normal flies (Quinn et al., 1979). Mutants found in other laboratories were also deficient in learning. Tests with other procedures showed that the failures of these mutants were not restricted to odor–shock training but occurred as well in other tests of associative learning, although the mutants appeared normal in nonlearning behaviors.

Further research showed that memory in *Drosophila* has four stages, which the investigators called *short-term memory, middle-term memory, anesthesia-resistant memory* (*ARM*), and *long-term memory* (Dubnau and Tully, 1998). Each stage can be canceled by deficiency in one or more genes specific to that stage. Thus, this genetic research provides independent support for the existence of separate stages of memory. Although ARM has not been reported in other animals, Dubnau and Tully (1998) suggested that, given the many similarities between learning in *Drosophila* and other animals, "it seems likely that ARM and LTM will be shown to exist as parallel forms of long-lasting memory in vertebrates as well" (p. 438).

We mentioned earlier in this chapter the cascade of neurochemical events that occur in LTP in the mammalian hippocampus. Recall that calcium ions activate protein kinases that bind to cAMP responsive element–binding protein (CREB) (see Figure 18.10). The CREB in turn binds to promoter regions adjacent to various proteins and regulates gene transcription to alter the cell's function. In *Drosophila,* genetic disruptions of the protein kinase A pathway impair memory (Tully, 1991), and repressing CREB before behavioral training prevents the formation of LTM without affecting the formation of other memory stages (Yin et al., 1994). Conversely, boosting expression of another protein kinase that activates CREB enhances memory in flies (Drier et al., 2002). Because genetic manipulation of CREB in both mammals

William Quinn

GENES AND BEHAVIOR

and flies affects LTM formation, this protein may have a long evolutionary history of participating in memory formation.

Memory Formation Can Be Modulated

Many agents and conditions in addition to those we have already discussed also affect the formation of memory. For example, the general state of arousal of an organism affects its ability to form memories; a moderate state of arousal is optimal (Bloch, 1976). Specific agents that affect memory formation include stimulants (such as amphetamine and caffeine), depressants (such as phenobarbital and chloral hydrate), neuropeptides, so-called neuromodulators that affect the activity or "gain" of neurons (including agents that elsewhere serve as neurotransmitters, such as acetylcholine and norepinephrine), drugs that affect the cholinergic transmitter system or the catecholamine transmitters, opioid peptides, and hormones.

Because many conditions or agents can either enhance or impair memory formation, it appears that some biological processes are essential in the formation of memories and that others are modulatory, superimposed on the basic processes. The variety of points in time at which treatments can affect memory formation also supports the idea that the cascade of events underlying memory formation takes considerable time.

Emotions can affect memory storage

Emotion appears to enhance the formation of memory, as we saw in Chapter 17. In research with humans, however, it is difficult to separate effects on memory formation from effects on attention at the time of learning or on rehearsal after the learning session. Research with animal subjects has clarified these effects and has investigated the neurochemical systems and the brain regions involved in the emotional enhancement of memory formation (see reviews by McGaugh et al., 1993, 1995). Substances effective in modulating memory storage include neurotransmitters and hormones such as acetylcholine, epinephrine, norepinephrine, vasopressin, the opioids, and GABA, as well as agonists and antagonists of these agents.

James L. McGaugh

Several lines of evidence suggest that epinephrine affects memory formation by influencing the amygdala. Posttraining electrical stimulation of the amygdala can enhance or impair memory formation, depending on the experimental conditions. Lesions of the amygdala block the memory-enhancing effects of systemic injections of epinephrine (Cahill and McGaugh, 1991). Injection of tiny doses of epinephrine into the amygdala enhances memory formation. This treatment appears to cause the release of norepinephrine within the amygdala, as do emotional experiences. Injections of propranolol, a blocker of beta-adrenergic receptors, into the amygdala block the memory-enhancing effects. Opioid peptides also block the release of norepinephrine (NE) in the amygdala and elsewhere in the brain.

On the basis of a variety of experimental findings on the effects and interactions of several families of agents—adrenergic, opioid, GABA-ergic, and cholinergic—on memory storage, James L. McGaugh (2003) proposes the following model: The amygdala influences memory formation in certain brain regions to which it sends axons, including the hippocampus and the caudate nucleus. The amygdala integrates the influences of several neuromodulatory systems that act on it, including adrenergic, opioid, GABA-ergic, and cholinergic systems.

Because several different neurotransmitter systems are involved in this model, multiple agents can affect the influences of emotion on memory formation; some of these agents and their synaptic sites of activity are shown in Figure 18.14. We learned in Chapter 17 that people who are exposed to a slide show of a distressing story (about a boy being hurt in an accident and rushed to a hospital for emergency surgery) tend to remember the story very well. But if they are given the beta-adrenergic blocker propranolol before seeing the emotional story, they don't remember the details as well. The theory is that blocking the stimulation of NE receptors in the

CLINICAL ISSUE

amygdala (see Figure 18.14) prevents the amygdala from strengthening the traumatic memory formation taking place elsewhere in the brain.

Remember Kathleen from the start of this chapter? After the bike messenger accident, her minor physical wounds were treated at a nearby emergency room. There she was also offered a chance to take part in a study in which people who had just had a traumatic experience would be given either propranolol or a placebo for a few weeks after the event. Knowing she was prone to posttraumatic stress, Kathleen enrolled in the study, but she felt sure that her blue pills were placebos because she felt no effect. In fact, she was taking propranolol. Months later, listening to a tape of their own recounting of the traumatic event, Kathleen and the other subjects given propranolol displayed fewer physiological signs of stress (heart rate, muscle tension, sweating) than did subjects getting the placebo (Pitman et al., 2002). Interestingly, when asked whether painful memories of the trauma were affecting their everyday life, the two groups of subjects seemed identical (Henig, 2004). So Kathleen may have benefited from the treatment, but only moderately so.

Perhaps it will one day be possible to selectively interfere with several of the neurotransmitters at work in the amygdala (see Figure 18.14) to provide more complete relief from traumatic memories. Even so, the treatment would probably have to be given soon after the accident to effectively dull the painful memories.

18.14 A Model of Neuromodulatory Interactions in the Regulation of Memory Storage   This diagram shows sites of activity of drugs that affect different neuromodulatory and neurotransmitter systems in the amygdala. Antagonists of the transmitters are italicized and indicated with blue circles; agonists are indicated by orange circles. ACh, acetylcholine; GABA, gamma-aminobutyric acid; NE, norepinephrine; OP, opioids. (After McGaugh, 1992.)

Some Brain Measures Correlate with Age-Related Impairments of Memory

Some measures of learning and memory decline with age, while others remain intact. Investigators are trying to find changes in the nervous system that may explain age-related declines in learning and memory. As we discussed in Chapter 7, several genes predispose people to Alzheimer's disease (Raber et al., 2000; Strittmatter and Roses, 1996).

In laboratory animals, both behavioral measures and brain measures can be obtained from the same individuals (Gallagher and Rapp, 1997). This method is more powerful than obtaining behavioral and brain measures in separate groups and trying to draw inferences from group means, as earlier studies had done. The animal research on aging also has the advantage that the life span of animals is shorter than that of humans.

IMPORTANT METHOD

Various mechanisms have been investigated to explain the decline of learning and memory with aging

In Chapter 17 we saw that, although many types of learning and memory remain rather stable during aging, impairments are seen especially in declarative memories that require organizational effort on the part of the person. Many investigators (e.g., Prull et al., 2000; Raz, 2000) have attempted to account for these age-related impairments. A variety of mechanisms have been examined as potential causes of declines in learning and memory during aging. They include loss of neurons and/or neural connections, impairment of the cholinergic system, and impaired representation of information by neural circuits. We'll consider each of these possible mechanisms in turn. Box 18.1 considers how age-related changes in NMDA receptors affect learning.

Impairment of the formation and retrieval of declarative memories   In brain-imaging studies, older subjects show less cortical activation, especially when encoding or re-

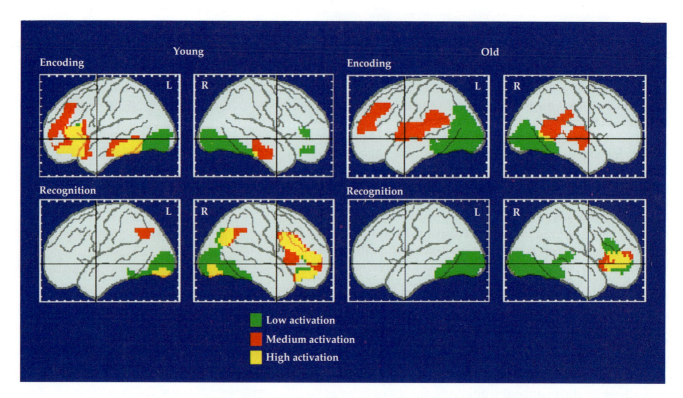

18.15 Active Brain Regions during Encoding and Recognition Tasks in Young and Old People   Lateral views of the cerebral hemispheres show regions of enhanced cerebral blood flow caused by encoding (*top*) and retrieving (*bottom*) information. (From Grady et al., 1995; courtesy of Cheryl Grady.)

trieval require self-initiated efforts. Thus, in Figure 18.15 the older subjects show less activation of frontal and temporal regions during the learning of new faces (Grady et al., 1995), a task in which encoding requires the subjects to organize the stimuli. The age difference is less noticeable for recognizing faces in this study because here the stimuli provide the organization. In fact, brain-imaging studies of recall yield a variety of effects, with older subjects showing less frontal activation in some studies but more in others.

Reviewing these reports, Grady and Craik (2000) noted that it is still unclear whether increased activation in elderly subjects represents recruitment of neurons to compensate for difficulty or just more-diffuse or nondifferentiated activity.

Loss of neurons and/or neural connections   Loss of neurons and/or neural connections with aging has been offered as a reason for impairment of learning and memory. The brain as a whole shows a gradual loss of weight after the age of 30 (see Figure 7.1), and some parts of the brain lose a larger proportion of weight or volume than other parts. We saw in Chapter 7 that shrinkage of the hippocampus in older people correlates significantly with impairment of memory (see Figure 7.26) (Golomb et al., 1994). Although not all investigators agree, most reports show age-related declines in both neuronal numbers (Simic et al., 1997) and synapses (Geinisman et al., 1995) in the hippocampus. Brain volume declines with age, especially in the frontal regions (Raz, 2000).

Decline in the acetylcholine system   Some studies of age-related changes focus on brain regions that provide inputs to the hippocampal formation. One such region is the **septal complex,** which provides input from subcortical structures to the hippocampus. The neurons of the septal complex are located in the medial septal nucleus and the vertical limb of the diagonal band (Figure 18.16). Many of these neurons use acetylcholine (ACh) as their transmitter. These regions of the septohippocampal pathway, along with neurons of the nucleus basalis, appear to be involved in the neuropathology of Alzheimer's disease (McGeer et al., 1984; Rossor et al., 1982).

Michela Gallagher et al. (1995) compared brain measures in two groups of aged rats: (1) those that perform about as well as young rats on tests of learning and memory, and (2) those that show impairment on these tests. Rats of three age groups—young (4–7 months), middle-aged (16–18 months), and aged (25–29 months)—were trained on a water maze (Figure 18.17). Most young rats reached criterion by the second trial, most middle-aged rats by the third trial, and most aged rats by the fourth trial. No young rat required more than four trials, but some aged rats did not reach criterion even by the sixth trial. However, more than one-fourth of the aged rats reached criterion by the second trial and thus performed as well as the young

The investigators then measured the activity of the enzyme choline acetyltransferase (ChAT) in the septal complex; this enzyme catalyzes the synthesis of ACh. ChAT activity in the septal complex was as high in aged rats that performed well as it was in young rats, but the aged rats that performed poorly showed significantly lower ChAT activity than the unimpaired aged rats or the young rats. ChAT activity did not decrease automatically with age, but only when aging was associated with impaired performance. This study thus suggests (but does not prove) that the decrease in ChAT is one cause of impaired performance with age.

Impaired coding by place cells Experiments on so-called place cells in the hippocampus (neurons that fire when the animal is in a particular location in its environment) show differences in the encoding of information related to aging in rats. In aged rats that showed poorer spatial learning in behavioral tests, the number of hippocampal neurons that responded to spatial cues did not appear to be different from that in young rats, but the neurons encoded a smaller amount of spatial information (Tanila, Shapiro, et al., 1997). When the visual cues surrounding a radial maze were changed, the spatial selectivity of place cells decreased considerably in memory-impaired aged rats, compared with that of young rats and that of aged rats with intact memory (Tanila, Sipila, et al., 1997). As noted earlier, the aged rats showed greater interindividual variability than the younger rats.

Can the effects of aging on memory be prevented or alleviated?

The hippocampus is more susceptible than most brain regions to some kinds of pathology. It can be attacked by certain kinds of encephalitis, and it is easily injured by hypoxia (lack of oxygen), which may occur during major surgery. In Chapter 16 we saw that

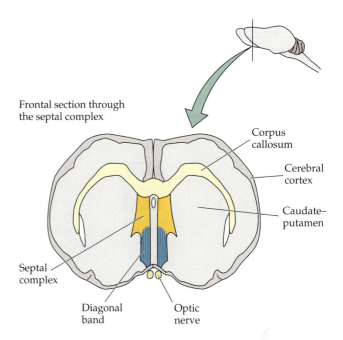

Frontal section through the septal complex

Corpus callosum

Cerebral cortex

Caudate–putamen

Septal complex

Diagonal band

Optic nerve

18.16 The Septal Complex in the Rat   The septal complex is a site at which changes related to defects in memory that occur with aging are studied. Cholinergic neurons here send axons widely through the forebrain.

Michela Gallagher

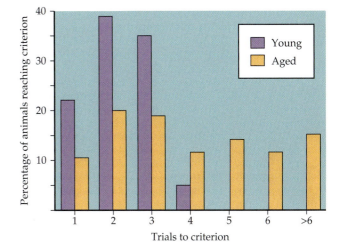

18.17 Performance of Young and Aged Rats in a Water Maze   All young rats learned the task by the fourth test trial; many aged rats required more trials to reach criterion, but some were as quick to learn as the young rats. (After Gallagher et al., 1995.)

glucocorticoids—adrenal hormones secreted during stress—can damage the hippocampus, which is particularly rich in glucocorticoid receptors.

Experiments with rats show that early handling, as opposed to isolation, lowers the concentration of glucocorticoids in adults and retards signs of aging of the hippocampus (Sapolsky, 1993). Rats raised in an enriched condition (EC), as opposed to those in an impoverished (isolated) condition (IC), have lower basal levels of corticosterone and, when challenged by a stressful situation, the EC rats show a more rapid return of glucocorticoids to low basal levels (Mohammed et al., 1993). Thus, adequate early experience may help protect the hippocampus.

CLINICAL ISSUE

Rats with enriched experience show greater expression of nerve growth factor (NGF) in the hippocampus than do IC rats (Mohammed et al., 1993; Ottoson et al., 1995). On the basis of these results, investigators in some clinical studies are infusing NGF into the brains of Alzheimer's patients (Nordberg, 1996; Seiger et al., 1993) in an attempt to prevent or alleviate impairment to the hippocampus and thus preserve memory.

Longitudinal research on humans indicates that enriched experience throughout life can help reduce the risk of cognitive decline in old age. Schaie (1994), summarizing a 35-year-long study of more than 5000 individuals, listed the following among seven factors that reduce the risk of "normal" cognitive decline:

- Living in favorable environmental circumstances (e.g., having received above-average education, pursuing occupations that involve high complexity and low routine, earning above-average income, and maintaining intact families).
- Being involved in activities typical of complex and intellectually stimulating environments (e.g., extensive reading, travel, attendance at cultural events, continuing-education activities, and participation in clubs and professional associations).
- "Being married to a spouse with high cognitive status" (p. 310).

Enriched experience may also cushion the brain and intellectual function against decline in old age. Masliah et al. (1991) report that the loss of synapses correlates strongly with the severity of symptoms in Alzheimer's disease. Enriched experience produces richer neural networks in the brains of all species that have been studied in this regard, as noted earlier in this chapter. If humans experience similar effects, as seems likely, then enriched experience may set up reserves of connections that help protect intellectual function from Alzheimer's.

Summary

1. Memory storage has long been hypothesized to involve changes in neural circuits. Research since the 1960s has demonstrated both functional and structural synaptic changes related to learning.

2. Much current research on neural changes related to learning and memory is based on a hypothesis stated by D. O. Hebb in 1949: The functional relationship between two neurons changes when one frequently takes part in exciting the other. These "Hebbian synapses" grow stronger when they successfully stimulate the postsynaptic neuron.

3. An early indication that training affects brain measures was the finding that formal training or enriched experience in rats leads to structural changes in the cerebral cortex, including alterations in the number and size of synaptic contacts and in the branching of dendrites.

4. Research on the mollusk *Aplysia* and other invertebrates has demonstrated the existence of plasticity in invertebrate nervous systems.

5. Long-term potentiation (LTP) of neural responses is a lasting increase in amplitude of the response of neurons caused by brief high-frequency stimulation of their afferents. In mammalian hippocampus, some forms of LTP depend on the activation of NMDA-type glutamate receptors, which induces an increase in the number of postsynaptic

Refer to the **Learning Biological Psychology CD** for study questions, animations, activities, and other study aids.

AMPA-type glutamate receptors and greater neurotransmitter release. Some of the many different forms of LTP may be components of or models for various kinds of learning. Long-term depression (LTD) may be a reversal of LTP.

6. Simple trace conditioning of the eye-blink response in the rabbit is crucially dependent on the cerebellum on the same side of the head. Information about the US and CS converge in the cerebellum and strengthen cerebellar synapses such that the CS alone comes to induce eye blink.

7. Neurochemical mechanisms mediate successive stages of memory formation: short-term memory (STM), intermediate-term memory (ITM), and long-term memory (LTM). Each stage appears to be linked to a different part of the cascade of neurochemical events that underlie memory formation. LTM appears to require protein synthesis in the posttraining period: Training induces increased synthesis of proteins in certain brain regions, and blocking protein synthesis prevents the formation of LTM, although it does not prevent learning or the formation of STM or ITM.

8. STM and ITM formation may depend on two different mechanisms. Different drugs that affect these mechanisms can cause specific failure at one or the other time period. The stages of memory formation appear to be sequentially linked, because failure of one stage causes failure of the succeeding stage(s).

9. Memory formation can be modulated (facilitated or impaired) by neural states and by a variety of agents, including stimulants, depressants, certain neurotransmitters, opioid peptides, hormones, and sensory stimulation.

10. Some neurochemical and neuroanatomical measures correlate with specific declines in learning and memory that occur in most elderly subjects. Some biological changes occur only in those subjects who show behavioral decline. The incidence of memory impairments in old age can be reduced by adequate early environment and continuing enriched experience.

Recommended Reading

Baddeley, A. D., Kopelman, M. D., and Wilson, B. A. (2002). *The handbook of memory disorders* (2nd ed.). New York: Wiley.

Gallagher, M., and Rapp, P. R. (1997). The use of animal models to study effects of aging on cognition. *Annual Review of Psychology, 48,* 339–370.

Lieberman, D. A. (2004). *Learning and memory: An integrative approach.* Belmont, CA: Thomson/Wadsworth.

Martinez, J. L., and Kesner, R. P. (Eds.). (1998). *Learning and memory: A biological view* (3rd ed.). New York: Academic Press.

McGaugh, J. L. (2003). *Memory and emotions: The making of lasting memories.* New York: Columbia University Press.

Prull, M. W., Gabrieli, J. D. E., and Bunge, S. A. (2000). Age-related changes in memory: A cognitive neuroscience perspective. In F. I. M. Craik and T. A. Salthouse (Eds.), *The handbook of aging and cognition* (pp. 91–153). Mahwah, NJ: Erlbaum.

Silva, A. J., Kogan, J. H., Frankland, P. W., and Kida, S. (1998). CREB and memory. *Annual Review of Neuroscience, 21,* 127–148.

19

Language and Cognition

How to Gain an Explosive Personality

Phineas P. Gage was a sober, efficient, capable young man, respected by the workmen he supervised as they cleared a path for a new railroad running from the village of Rutland, in the middle of Vermont, up to Burlington in the northwest corner of the state. But one day in 1848, something went wrong at their worksite near Cavendish. A hole had been drilled in the solid rock ground, and explosive materials were poured in. Gage himself was tamping the charge, making sure it was packed tight so that, when ignited, it would effectively blast the rock open. He was using an iron tamping rod that a local blacksmith had made for him: a cylinder an inch and a quarter in diameter, about three and a half feet long, flat at the bottom to tamp the charge, and tapered at the top.

The iron rod must have struck a spark from the surrounding rock because the charge went off unexpectedly, flinging the rod straight at Phineas's head. The rod pierced his left cheek, passed behind his left eye and out the top of his skull, landing some 60 feet away. Phineas was thrown onto his back, his limbs convulsing. Yet in a minute or two he spoke. With help from his men he walked to a wagon, where he sat for the ride to town. There Phineas walked upstairs unaided to a doctor's office to have his wounds cleaned and dressed. No one expected him to live; an undertaker made a coffin for him (Macmillan, 2000).

In fact, he worked at a series of menial jobs for another 12 years, but Gage was definitely a changed man. After the accident he was moody, stubborn, disrespectful of others, boastful, prone to cursing, and unable to stay focused on completing something. Despite the miracle of his physical health, "his mind was radically changed, so decidedly that his friends and acquaintances said that he was 'no longer Gage.'"

What happened to change his personality so drastically?

Inspection of the week's best-seller list confirms the impression that only humans write books, though chimps may dabble in paint and rats may occasionally eat books. By this and many other measures, human mental life is distinctive in the animal world, although it's increasingly clear that members of other species also communicate effectively with one another. In the mid-nineteenth century, the neurologist Paul Broca discovered that lesions in the left hemisphere impair speech and language. One of the most fascinating conclusions from this finding, and those that followed, is that the left and right sides of the brain perform different but complementary functions. In this chapter we survey the neuroscience of language, the role of the prefrontal cortex in planning behavior, the fascinating deficits in spatial perception that arise in some people, and the recovery of function following brain damage.

The Development and Evolution of Speech and Language Are Remarkable and Mysterious

There are an estimated 7000 languages in the world today, about 1000 of which have been studied by linguists (Wuethrich, 2000). All these languages have similar basic elements, and each is composed of a set of sounds and symbols that have distinct meanings. These elements are arranged in distinct orders according to rules characteristic of the particular language. Thus anyone who knows the sounds (**phonemes**), symbols, and rules (**grammar**) of a particular language can generate sentences that convey information to others who have similar knowledge of the language.

Children's acquisition of language is an incredible accomplishment because they do not need formal instruction, yet they discern the phonemes, vocabulary, and grammar rapidly. At birth, a baby can distinguish between sounds from Dutch and sounds from Japanese. Because adult monkeys can also make this discrimination (Ramus et al., 2000), this ability may reflect a basic property of the primate auditory system. But by attending to these sounds, the human baby, which began life babbling nearly all the phonemes found in any human language, soon comes to use only the subset of phonemes in use around her.

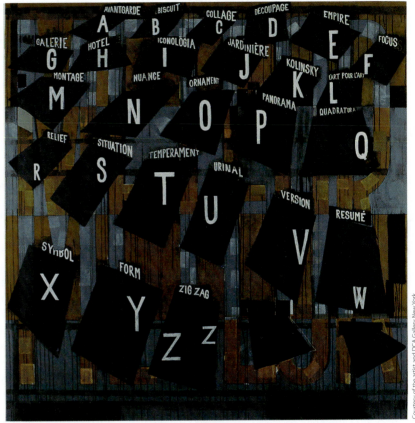

Jesper Christiansen, *Meteorpainting*, 1995, acrylic on canvas, 71" × 71"

**NEURAL
PLASTICITY**

**GENES AND
BEHAVIOR**

**EVOLUTION
AT WORK**

Peter Marler

By 7 months of age, infants pay more attention to sentences with unfamiliar structure than to sentences with familiar structure (Marcus et al., 1999), indicating that they have already acquired a sense of the rules of language being spoken around them and are actively looking out for exceptions. The rare children who are profoundly isolated develop little or no language (we discussed the famous case of Genie in Box 5.2), pointing to the importance of experience during a **sensitive period** early in life. Restoration of hearing in one adult who had been deaf most of her life also supports this hypothesis because even with her hearing restored, she did not learn to speak (Curtiss, 1989).

The notion of a sensitive period for language acquisition is also supported by the difficulty that postadolescents experience in learning a second language. Imaging studies indicate that people who learn a second language early in life activate the same brain region when using either language. But people learning a second language later than age 11 seem to use different brain regions for each language (K. H. Kim et al., 1997).

A gene has been identified that appears to be important for the normal acquisition of human language. People with a specific mutation of the gene *FOXP2* take a long time to learn to speak, and they display long-lasting difficulties with particular language tasks (such as learning verb tenses) (Lai et al., 2001). The pattern of brain activation in these individuals during performance of a language task is different from that seen in normal speakers (Liégeois et al., 2003). The *FOXP2* gene in the other great apes is quite different from that seen in humans (Enard et al., 2002), suggesting that this gene has been evolving rapidly in humans, presumably because language is so adaptive in our species. Recall that in Chapter 6 we asked how humans and chimps could differ so little in their total genome yet behave so differently. Perhaps major differences in a relatively few genes like *FOXP2* is enough to explain why we write books and chimpanzees do not.

Scholars have suggested that speech and language originally developed from gestures of the face and hands (Corballis, 2002; Hewes, 1973). Even today, hand movements facilitate speech: If you prevent people from gesturing, they make more slips and have more pauses in their speech (Krauss, 1998). Furthermore, people who have been blind from birth, and so have never seen the hand gestures of others, make hand gestures while they speak (Iverson and Goldin-Meadow, 1998). Later we'll see that deaf people who communicate exclusively with gestures use the same part of the brain that hearing people use while speaking and listening—further indication of a close link between gestures and speech.

In the sections that follow we'll examine communication in other species for clues to the evolution of language, then discuss the various human brain regions involved in language processes.

Some nonhumans engage in elaborate vocal behavior

Chirps, barks, meows, songs, and other sounds are among the many vocalizations produced by nonhuman animals. Many of these sounds seem to distinguish species, signal readiness to mate, or alert the group to danger. Whales sing and may imitate songs they hear from distant oceans (Noad et al., 2000), and some seal mothers recognize their pup's vocalizations even after 4 years of separation (Insley, 2000). Could the vocal behavior of nonhuman animals be related to the evolution of human language?

Birdsong   Many birds sing pleasant tunes, and these songs offer intriguing analogies to human speech. Birdsongs vary in complexity: Some repeat a simple basic unit; others are more elaborate (Figure 19.1). The principal roles of birdsong are territory defense and mate selection (Ball and Hulse, 1998). Although no investigator believes that birdsong is an evolutionary precursor to human speech, Peter Marler (1970) and other scientists have shown that birdsong provides an interesting analogy and experimental tool.

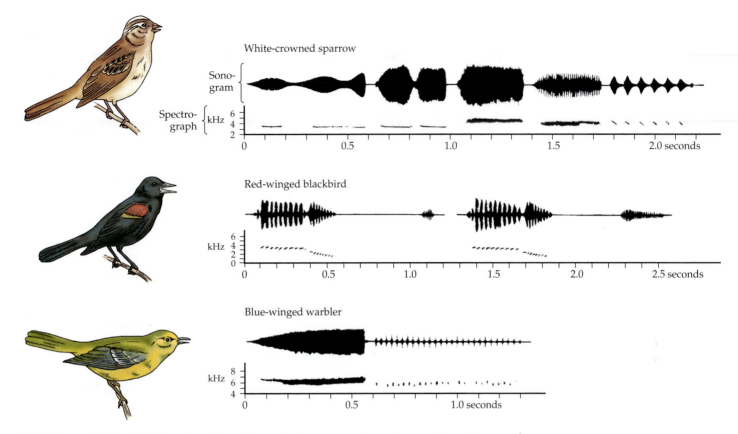

19.1 Songs of Three Bird Species For each species, the top trace shows the exact sound pattern detected by a sensitive microphone. The bottom trace shows the same pattern analyzed by a sound spectrograph, which reveals the amount of energy in different sound frequencies at each moment. (After Greenewalt, 1968.)

Some birds, such as chickens and ringdoves, have simple vocal behavior that is not affected by early deafening or by rearing in isolation (Baptista, 1996), but many birds must *learn* the appropriate song. For example, young canaries, zebra finches, and white-crowned sparrows learn the appropriate song from their elders—in the same way that humans learn language (DeVoogd, 1994). In these songbirds, only males of the species sing, and song is acquired in several distinct stages:

1. Initial exposure to the song of a male tutor, usually the father
2. A period of successive approximation of the produced song to the stored model
3. Fixing, or **crystallization,** of the song in a permanent form

Normally, song learning is complete by sexual maturity (90 days). We have seen already that human children must be exposed to language during an early sensitive period if they are ever to learn to speak. Likewise, male songbirds raised in acoustic isolation fail to develop normal song (Figure 19.2). However, if such isolated birds are exposed to tape recordings of species-typical vocalizations during an early sensitive period, they acquire normal song; if the birds are exposed to taped songs only later in life, they do not.

Masakazu Konishi (1985) demonstrated that songbirds show quite abnormal song if they are deafened during the second stage before they have learned how to produce the final song. So the male must first hear himself sing and compare his chirps with the memory of his father's song until he has replicated it. Deafening after the song has crystallized has very little effect on song production, as if the song has become fixed.

Masakazu Konishi

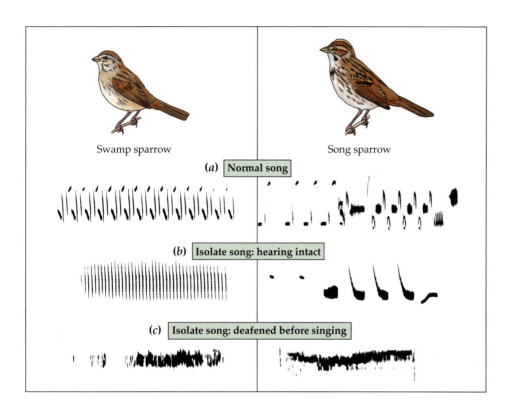

Swamp sparrow

Song sparrow

(a) Normal song

(b) Isolate song: hearing intact

(c) Isolate song: deafened before singing

19.2 Effects of Isolation on Birdsong Development (a) These sonograms show the typical adult song patterns of two sparrow species. The songs illustrated in (b) were produced by males reared in isolation; those in (c), by males deafened in infancy. Both early auditory isolation and deafening result in abnormal song, but the two species still produce different patterns. Deafening has a more profound effect because the animal is prevented from hearing its own song production, as well as that of other males. (After Marler and Sherman, 1983, 1985.)

When a bird is exposed to synthetic songs, composed of notes of both the same species and another species, it prefers to copy the song of its own species (Baptista, 1996; Marler, 1991; Marler and Peters, 1982; R. G. Morrison and Nottebohm, 1993), indicating a predisposition to learn the appropriate song. A bird is more likely to learn the song of another species if its tutor is a live bird rather than a recording, suggesting that social stimuli direct the attention of developing birds to an appropriate "mentor," whose song they copy (Baptista and Petrinovich, 1886).

The brain birdsong system is a series of brain nuclei and their connections that control the neural output to the vocal production organ, the **syrinx** (Figure 19.3) (Arnold and Schlinger, 1993; DeVoogd, 1994). A direct pathway, extending from the higher vocal center (HVc) to the nucleus robustus of the archistriatum (RA) to the brainstem twelfth-nerve nucleus, controls the vocal organ. Lesions along this direct pathway at any stage of development will disrupt song. A less direct pathway extends from the HVc to the brainstem, and early lesions of one of its components, the lateral magnocellular nucleus of the anterior neostriatum (LMAN), will stop song development; but LMAN lesions in adulthood do not affect song performance (Bottjer et al., 1984). Song learning is also accompanied by the generation in adulthood of new neurons (neurogenesis; see Chapter 7) in at least some birdsong regions (Scharff et al., 2000).

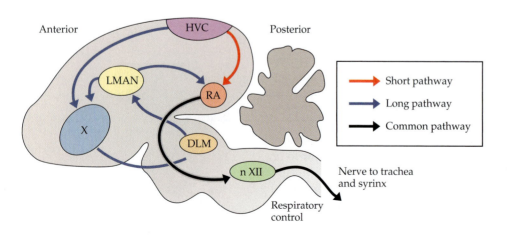

Anterior   HVC   Posterior

LMAN

RA

X

DLM

n XII

→ Short pathway
→ Long pathway
→ Common pathway

Nerve to trachea and syrinx

Respiratory control

19.3 Vocal Control Centers of the Songbird Brain Two neural pathways control birdsong. A direct route from the higher vocal center (HVc) to the nucleus robustus of the archistriatum (RA) to the nucleus of the twelfth cranial nerve (n XII) is crucial for song; lesions of any of these areas will disrupt song. The indirect path that includes the lateral magnocellular nucleus of the anterior neostriatum (LMAN) may play a role in song learning: Lesions of the LMAN halt the development of song in young birds, but lesions of the LMAN in adult zebra finches do not affect singing. The nucleus labeled X is called *area X of the paraolfactory lobe*. (After Arnold, 1980.)

A striking similarity between birdsong and human language involves the different contributions of the left and right cerebral hemispheres. We'll see later in this chapter that the left hemisphere plays a crucial role in language for most humans—strokes in the left hemisphere are much more likely to disrupt language than are strokes in the right hemisphere. Fernando Nottebohm (1980) found that lesions of the vocal control pathway in canaries impair song production, but only when made in the left hemisphere, not the right. We don't yet know of any anatomical differences between the two sides of the bird brain to explain why only the left hemisphere seems to control song (Ball and Hulse, 1998), but we'll see that brain regions involved in human language tend to be larger in the left hemisphere than the right.

Fernando Nottebohm

Vocalization in nonhuman primates   The calls of nonhuman primates have been examined intensively in both field and laboratory studies (Seyfarth and Cheney, 1997). Many nonhuman primate vocalizations seem preprogrammed, including infant crying and the emotional vocalizations of adults, such as shrieking in pain and moaning. Ploog (1992) cataloged the calls that squirrel monkeys make and the communication properties of those sounds in a social context. The monkeys' calls include shrieking, quacking, chirping, growling, and yapping sounds. Many of these calls can penetrate a forest for some distance, communicating alarm, territoriality, and other emotional statements.

Direct electrical stimulation of subcortical regions can elicit some calls (Figure 19.4), but stimulation of the cerebral cortex generally fails to elicit vocal behavior. Brain regions that elicit vocalizations also seem to be involved in defense, attack, feeding, and sex behaviors. These regions include sites in the limbic system and related structures. Just before vocalizing, monkeys display changes in electrical potential in cortical areas homologous to human speech areas (Gemba et al., 1995). Furthermore, monkeys, like people, are more likely to point the right ear (which has preferential connections with the left hemisphere) toward vocalizations from conspecifics (Ghazanfar and Hauser, 1999). This behavior suggests selective reliance on the left cerebral hemisphere to decode communication, an idea that has been amply confirmed in humans, as we'll see shortly.

Can nonhuman primates acquire language with training?

Throughout history people have tried to teach animals to talk. In most cases, however, any communication between animal and human resulted because the person learned to meow, grunt, or bark rather than because the animal learned to produce human speech. Since both the vocal tracts and the vocal repertoires of nonhuman primates are different from those of humans, scientists have given up attempting to train animals to produce human speech. But can nonhuman primates be taught other forms of communication that have features similar to those of human language, including the ability to represent objects with symbols and to manipulate these symbols according to rules of order? Can animals other than humans generate a novel string of symbols, such as a new sentence?

● Purring

Anterior coronal section

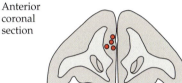

● Trilling

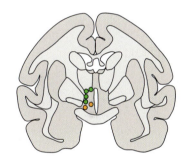

● Shrieking

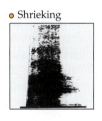

● Alarm peeping

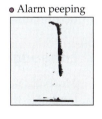

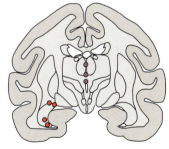

Posterior section

● Cackling

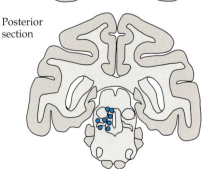

19.4 Elicitation of Vocalizations by Electrical Stimulation of the Monkey Brain   Stimulation at different sites in the monkey brain results in different, species-typical vocalizations. The left column shows spectrograms of different vocalizations, and the coronal sections in the right column show brain sites at which the different vocalizations are elicited. (After Ploog, 1992; spectrograms courtesy of Uwe Jürgens.)

19.5 Chimpanzee Using Symbols   Although there is no doubt that chimpanzees can learn to use arbitrary signs and/or symbols to communicate, some researchers still question whether this usage is equivalent to human language. (Photo courtesy of Sue Savage-Rumbaugh.)

**COMPETING
HYPOTHESES**

R. Allen Gardner and Beatrice Gardner (1969, 1984) taught chimpanzees American Sign Language (ASL), the sign language used in the United States by people who are deaf. The chimps mastered many signs and appeared to use them spontaneously and to generate new sequences of signs. Francine Patterson claimed to have taught a gorilla a vocabulary of several hundred ASL words (Patterson and Linden, 1981). David Premack (1971) used another approach. He taught chimpanzees a system based on an assortment of colored chips (symbols) that could adhere to a magnetic board. After extensive training, the chimpanzees could manipulate the chips in ways that seemed to reflect an acquired ability to form short sentences and to note various logical classifications.

At the Yerkes National Primate Research Center at Emory University, Project Lana has focused on teaching *Yerkish* to chimpanzees (Rumbaugh, 1977). Yerkish is a computer-based language in which different keys on a console represent words. Apes are quite good at acquiring many words in this language, and they appear to string together novel, meaningful chains (Figure 19.5). On the basis of studies such as these, Sue Savage-Rumbaugh et al. (1993) claimed that the ability to comprehend language preceded the appearance of speech by several million years.

One of the main critics of the conclusion that chimps can acquire language is Herbert Terrace (1979), who raised a young chimp and taught it many signs. Terrace tested carefully to see whether his chimp or others could construct sentences. According to linguists, grammar is the essence of language, so investigators look for the ability of sign-using chimps to generate meaningful and novel sequences of signs. As we have noted, the studies by Gardner and Gardner suggested that sign-using chimps made distinctive series of signs, just as though they were using words in a sentence. Terrace, however, argued that strings of signs were explicitly presented to the chimps and that the animals merely imitated rather than generating new combinations. He suggested that the imitation was quite subtle and might involve cuing practices not perceived by the experimenter.

Savage-Rumbaugh (1993) has responded that apes can comprehend spoken words, produce novel combinations of words, and respond appropriately to sentences arranged according to a syntactic rule. She believes that the ape's linguistic capacity has been underestimated. We'll see later in this chapter that several brain regions related to language are larger on the left than on the right in both humans and other great apes. This debate is far from settled, but the accomplishments of the trained chimpanzees have at least forced investigators to sharpen their criteria of what constitutes language (Fitch and Hauser, 2004; M. D. Hauser et al., 2002). Pinker (1994) insists, "Even putting aside vocabulary, phonology, morphology, and syntax, what impresses one the most about chimpanzee signing is that fundamentally, deep down, chimps just don't get it" (p. 349).

Language Disorders Result from Region-Specific Brain Injuries

Much of our early understanding of the relationship between brain mechanisms and language was derived from observation of language impairments following brain injury resulting from accidents, diseases, or strokes.

Several defining signs characterize aphasia

Early Egyptian medical records, written at least 3000 years ago, describe people who became speechless after blows to the temporal bone (Finger, 1994). In 1861, French neurologist Paul Broca examined a man who had lost the ability to speak. Postmortem study of this patient revealed damage to the left inferior frontal region—a region now known as **Broca's area** (Figure 19.6). In approximately 90% to 95% of the cases of language impairment due to brain injury—called **aphasia**—the damage is to the left cerebral hemisphere. This critical role of the left hemisphere is confirmed by techniques such as the Wada test (Box 19.1). We'll expand our discussion of the different functions of the two hemispheres later in this chapter.

The most prominent sign of aphasia is the substitution of a word by a sound, an incorrect word, or an unintended word. This characteristic is called **paraphasia.** At times an entirely novel word—called a **neologism**—may be generated by the substitution of a phoneme. Paraphasic speech in aphasic patients is evident both in spontaneous conversation and in attempts to read aloud from a text.

Conversation reveals another important aspect of speech: its fluency or ease of production. **Nonfluent speech** is talking with considerable effort, in short sentences, and without the usual melodic character of conversational speech.

Almost all patients with aphasia show some impairment in writing (**agraphia**) and disturbances in reading (**alexia**). Finally, the brain impairments or disorders that produce aphasia also produce a distinctive motor impairment called *apraxia* (see Chapter 11). Apraxia is characterized by impairment in the execution of complex sequential movements that is unrelated to paralysis, coordination problems, sensory impairments, or the comprehension of instructions. Patients suffering from apraxia are unable to imitate arbitrary sequences of movements or some common gestures, such as sticking out the tongue or waving goodbye, although these acts might appear in their spontaneous behavior. There seems to be one advantage to aphasia: Patients who suffer from this disorder are better than controls at detecting when someone is lying (Etcoff et al., 2000), presumably because they focus on facial features and are not distracted by the words being spoken.

Three major types of aphasia result from injury to particular brain regions

A prime concern has been the relation between the particular form of language disorder and the region of brain destruction or impairment. Figure 19.6 shows the main brain regions of the left hemisphere that are related to language abilities. Table 19.1

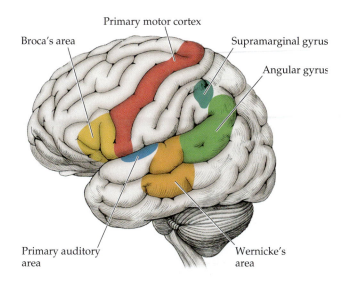

19.6 Cortical Speech and Language Areas in Humans Lesions in the anterior frontal region called *Broca's area* interfere with speech production; injury to an area of temporoparietal cortex called *Wernicke's area* interferes with language comprehension; injury to the supramarginal gyrus interferes with repetition of heard speech. For most individuals, these functional regions are found only in the left hemisphere.

**Paul Broca
(1824–1880)**

TABLE 19.1 *Language Symptomology in Aphasia*

Type of aphasia	Brain area affected	Spontaneous speech	Comprehension	Paraphasia	Repetition	Naming
Broca's aphasia		Nonfluent	Good	Uncommon	Poor	Poor
Wernicke's aphasia		Fluent	Poor	Common	Poor	Poor
Global aphasia		Nonfluent	Poor	Variable	Poor	Poor
Conduction aphasia		Fluent	Good	Common	Poor	Poor
Subcortical aphasia		Variable	Variable	Common	Good	Variable

summarizes the main features of various types of aphasia that we'll cover in this chapter. The sections that follow cover the three primary aphasias in more detail.

Broca's aphasia   As noted earlier, lesions in the left inferior frontal region (Broca's area) produce a type of aphasia known as **Broca's aphasia;** it this condition is also described as a *nonfluent aphasia.* Patients with Broca's aphasia have considerable difficulty producing speech, talking only in a labored and hesitant manner. Frequently they have lost the ability of readily naming persons or objects—an impairment referred to as **anomia.** Reading and writing are also impaired. The ability to utter automatic speech, however, is often preserved. Such speech includes greetings ("Hello"); short, common expressions ("Oh, my God!"); and swear words. Although these patients have difficulty *expressing* themselves, their *comprehension* remains relatively intact. Most people who suffer from Broca's aphasia have **hemiplegia**—partial paralysis involving one side of the body (usually the right, because the lesion often extends to the nearby motor cortex in the left hemisphere).

The CT scans in Figure 19.7*a* and *b* reveal lesion sites in patients with Broca's aphasia. Seven years after a stroke, one Broca's patient still spoke slowly, used mainly nouns and very few verbs or function words, and spoke only with great effort. When asked to repeat the phrase, "Go ahead and do it if possible," she could say only, "Go to do it," with pauses between each word. Broca's patients with brain lesions as extensive as hers show little recovery of speech with the passing of time.

Wernicke's aphasia   German neurologist Carl Wernicke described several syndromes of aphasia following brain lesions. The syndrome now known as **Wernicke's aphasia,** or *fluent aphasia,* includes a complex array of signs. Patients with this syndrome have very fluent verbal output, but

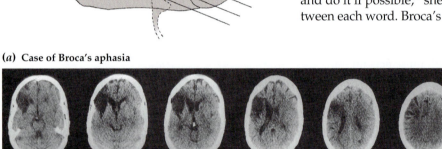

(a) Case of Broca's aphasia

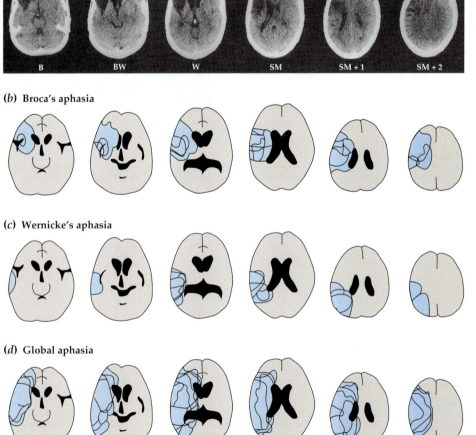

(b) Broca's aphasia

(c) Wernicke's aphasia

(d) Global aphasia

Slice B   Slice B/W   Slice W   Slice SM   Slice SM + 1   Slice SM + 2

19.7 Brain Lesions That Produce Aphasia   Levels of CT scan slices are labeled according to brain language regions shown by that slice: B, Broca's area; SM, supramarginal gyrus; W, Wernicke's area. (*a*) CT scans for one patient with Broca's aphasia, aged 51, 7 years after stroke. (*b*) Lesion sites for four cases of Broca's aphasia. (*c*) Lesion sites for four cases of Wernicke's aphasia. (*d*) Lesion sites for five cases of global aphasia. In *b*, large lesions (blue) were located in Broca's area on slices B and B/W, and the peak amount of tissue damage occurred in the frontal-parietal areas on slices SM and SM + 1. In *c*, lesions were located in Wernicke's area on slice W and in the supramarginal gyrus area on slice SM. In *d*, large lesions were present in every language area. (After Naeser and Hayward, 1978; CT scans courtesy of Margaret Naeser.)

their utterances contain many paraphasias that often make their speech unintelligible. Sound substitutions (e.g., "girl" becomes "curl") and word substitutions (e.g., *bread* becomes *cake*) are common, as are neologisms.

Word substitutions and speech errors occur in a context that preserves syntactical structure, although sentences seem empty of content. The ability to repeat words and sentences is impaired. Furthermore, patients have difficulty *understanding* what they read or hear. In some cases reading comprehension is more impaired than comprehension of spoken speech; in other cases the reverse is true. Unlike patients with Broca's aphasia, patients with Wernicke's aphasia usually do not display partial paralysis. Naturally, communication with people who have Wernicke's aphasia is difficult, often consisting of gestures and demonstration. This communication is facilitated by the patient's intact understanding of facial expressions.

In Wernicke's aphasia the most prominent brain lesions are in posterior regions of the left superior temporal gyrus and extend partially into adjacent parietal cortex, including the supramarginal and angular gyri (see Figure 19.7c) (H. Damasio, 1995). When *word deafness* (the inability to understand spoken words) is more evident than reading impairment, patients show greater involvement of the first temporal gyrus, especially tracts from the auditory cortex. In contrast, when *word blindness* (the inability to understand written words) predominates, greater destruction of the angular gyrus is evident.

Global aphasia   In some patients, brain injury or disease results in total loss of the ability to understand or produce language. This syndrome is called **global aphasia.** Patients suffering from global aphasia retain some ability for automatic speech, especially emotional exclamations. They can utter very few words, and no semblance of syntax is evident in their speech. In most cases, broad regions of the left hemisphere are damaged, encompassing frontal, temporal, and parietal cortex, including Broca's area, Wernicke's area, and the supramarginal gyrus (see Figure 19.7d). The prognosis for language recovery in these patients is quite poor.

The Wernicke–Geschwind model of aphasia represents some features of speech and language anatomically

One traditional approach to understanding aphasic disturbances, begun by Wernicke in the early twentieth century, uses a *connectionist* perspective. According to this view, deficits can be understood as breaks in an interconnected network of components, each of which is involved with a particular feature of language analysis or production.

Norman Geschwind (1972) developed this theory, often referred to as *disconnection theory*, to emphasize the symptoms of language impairment following the loss of *connections* among brain regions in a network. According to this perspective, when a word or sentence is heard, the auditory cortex transmits information about the sounds to Wernicke's area, where the sounds are analyzed to decode what they mean. For the word to be spoken, Wernicke's area must transmit this information to Broca's area, where a speech plan is activated. Broca's area then transmits this plan to adjacent motor cortex, which controls the relevant articulatory muscles.

The axons transmitting information from Wernicke's area to Broca's area form a bundle of nerve fibers called the **arcuate fasciculus** (from the Latin *arcuatus,* "bow-shaped," and *fasciculus,* "small bundle"). Patients with lesions of these axons have relatively fluent speech and comprehension of spoken words because Broca's and Wernicke's areas are intact. But they display **conduction aphasia,** a major impairment in the *repetition* of words and sentences (Figure 19.8a). When these patients attempt to repeat words, they produce incorrect phonemes substituting for correct sounds.

According to the Wernicke–Geschwind model, saying the name of a *seen* object or word involves the transfer of visual information to the **angular gyrus,** which then arouses the auditory pattern in Wernicke's area. From Wernicke's area the auditory

**Carl Wernicke
(1848–1905)**

**Norman Geschwind
(1926–1984)**

(*a*) Speaking a *heard* word

1. Information about the sound is analyzed by primary auditory cortex and transmitted to Wernicke's area.

2. Wernicke's area analyzes the sound information to determine the word that was said.

3. This information from Wernicke's area is transmitted through the arcuate fasciculus to Broca's area.

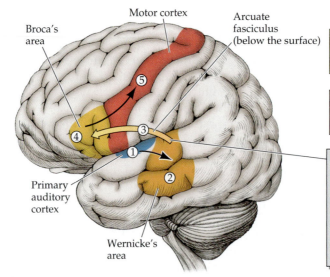

4. Broca's area forms a motor plan to repeat the word and sends that information to motor cortex.

5. Motor cortex implements the plan, manipulating the larynx and related structures to say the word.

Lesions of the arcuate fasciculus disrupt the transfer from Wernicke's area to Broca's area, so the patient has difficulty repeating spoken words (conduction aphasia), but may retain comprehension of spoken language (because of intact Wernicke's area) and may still be able to speak spontaneously (because of intact Broca's area).

(*b*) Speaking a *written* word

1. Visual cortex analyzes the image and transmits the information about the image to the angular gyrus.

2. The angular gyrus decodes the image information to recognize the word and associate this visual form with the spoken form in Wernicke's area.

3. Information about the word is transmitted via the arcuate fasciculus to Broca's area.

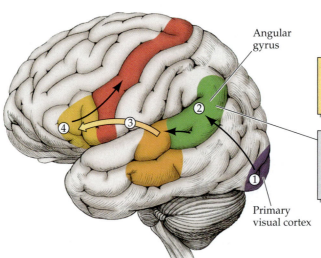

4. Broca's area formulates a motor plan to say the appropriate word and transmits that plan to motor cortex for implementation.

A lesion of the angular gyrus disrupts the flow of information from visual cortex, so the person has difficulty saying words he has seen but not words he has heard.

19.8 The Wernicke–Geschwind Connectionist Model of Aphasia (After Geschwind, 1976.)

form is transmitted via the arcuate fasciculus to Broca's area. There the model for the spoken form is activated and transmitted to the face area of the motor cortex, and the word is then spoken (Figure 19.8*b*). Thus, lesions involving the angular gyrus disconnect the systems involved in visual and auditory language; so patients with lesions in this region have difficulty reading aloud, but they are able to speak and understand speech.

Users of sign language show aphasia following brain injury

We have already noted how human hands and arms gesture during speech, and how spoken language may have evolved from such gestures. Formal hand and arm gestures with specific rules of arrangement form the basis of nonvocal languages of the deaf, such as American Sign Language (ASL). ASL consists of an elaborate code and grammar; Figure 19.9 shows some examples of ASL signs.

An exhaustive analysis of ASL by two linguists (Klima and Bellugi, 1979) clearly establishes this gesture-based set of symbols as a full-fledged language, as elaborate as its vocal counterparts. In fact, sign languages show features as subtle as dialect. Investigators have been interested in determining whether sign language is also similar to spoken language in its neural organization. Is there hemispheric specializa-

Feeling

Be quiet

Secret

19.9 American Sign Language   In ASL, letters, words, and concepts are communicated via different configurations (*signs*) of the hands and arms, as these three examples illustrate.

tion for a language system based on hand signals, most of which are formed by the right hand?

Meckler et al. (1979) described a young man who was raised by deaf–mute parents and who began to suffer from aphasia after an accident. Previously he had used both spoken and sign language for communication. After the accident, impairments in his spoken language and sign language were equally severe, as though the damaged brain region had subserved both languages. Chiarello et al. (1982) analyzed sign language deficits in an older deaf–mute person. She had well-developed sign language skills until, following a stroke in the left temporal cortex (including Wernicke's area), she became unable to generate hand signals with either hand. In another example, Bellugi et al. (1983) described aphasia in three deaf signers who had damage to the left hemisphere.

These cases indicate that the neural mechanisms of spoken and sign languages are similar. Cerebral injury in these cases interferes with the production of language movements, whether conveyed by speech or by hand. Deaf patients with damage to the *right* hemisphere, like hearing patients, tend to retain communication skills. They show impairments in various visuospatial tasks (described later in the chapter), but their signing is appropriate and includes all linguistic categories of expression.

Functional-imaging work shows that both hearing and deaf people activate the same areas of the left hemisphere during language tasks (Neville et al., 1998; Petitto et al., 2000). However, signers also show extensive activation of homologous areas of the right hemisphere, perhaps because some signs require the use of both hands.

Dyslexia is characterized by difficulty with reading

Some children seem to take forever to learn to read. Their efforts are laden with frustration, and prolonged practice produces only small improvements. The inability to read is called **dyslexia** (from the Greek *dys*, "bad," and *lexis*, "word"). Dyslexia is seen in nearly 5% of children in the general population; it is even more common in boys and in left-handed people. Some children with dyslexia have a high IQ; several have grown up to amass billion-dollar fortunes (B. Morris, 2002). So dyslexia seems to be a specific problem with language rather than a general cognitive deficit. Despite popular misconceptions, people who suffer from dyslexia do not "see letters backward" (Shaywitz, 2003). Although dyslexia is a fuzzy clinical category, it has been connected to interesting anatomical and physiological findings (Tallal et al., 1993).

Albert Galaburda (1994) conducted postmortem observations of four patients with dyslexia who had died from acute disease or trauma that did not involve the brain. All the brains showed striking anomalies in the arrangement of cortical cells, especially in areas of the frontal and temporal cortical regions.

CLINICAL ISSUE

Albert Galaburda

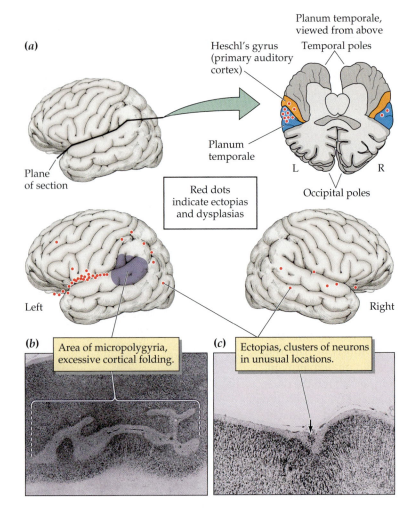

(a)

Heschl's gyrus (primary auditory cortex)

Planum temporale, viewed from above

Temporal poles

Planum temporale

Plane of section

L   R

Occipital poles

Red dots indicate ectopias and dysplasias

Left

Right

(b) Area of micropolygyria, excessive cortical folding.

(c) Ectopias, clusters of neurons in unusual locations.

19.10 Neural Disorganization in the Brain of a Patient with Dyslexia   *(a)* (*Top*) Drawings of the left and right planum temporale (see Figure 19.15) from the brain of a person suffering from dyslexia show these regions as nearly symmetrical; in most people the left planum temporale is considerably larger. The dots and the shaded area represent regions where microscopic anomalies called *ectopias, dysplasias,* and *micropolygyrias* have been found in the brains of individuals with dyslexia. (*Bottom*) Anomalies in patients with dyslexia are much more common in the left hemisphere, which is primarily responsible for language function. (*b, c*) These micrographs show (*b*) micropolygyria (literally, "many tiny gyri") and (*c*) ectopias, clusters of neurons in unusual locations, such as this cluster in cortical layer I (arrow), which is normally devoid of neuronal cell bodies. (After Galaburda, 1994; micrographs courtesy of Albert Galaburda.)

These anomalies consisted of unusual groupings of cells in outer layers of the cerebral cortex that distorted the normal layered arrangements and columnar organization (Figure 19.10). Some cells were disoriented, and excessive cortical folding (**micropolygyria**) was observed. Nests of extra cells, **ectopias,** were seen. The researchers argued that these anomalies of cerebral cortical cell arrangements probably arose quite early, perhaps during the middle of gestation, a period during which active cell migration occurs in cerebral cortex. The result of these deficits might be the production of unusual patterns of connectivity in language-related regions of the temporal cortex.

Shaywitz et al. (1998), using fMRI, found that the pattern of brain activation during a reading task was different between patients with dyslexia and controls. Subjects with dyslexia showed relatively little activation of the posterior regions, including Wernicke's area, while showing a relative overactivation of anterior regions. Compared to controls, the subjects with dyslexia also showed less activation of visual cortex (Demb et al., 1998) and a disruption of the spread of activation across the angular gyrus (K. R. Pugh et al., 2000) in response to written words. Perhaps such differences in brain activation will offer a less ambiguous diagnosis of dyslexia. Different genes have been proposed to affect the probability of developmental dyslexia (Fagerheim et al., 1999). One gene, called *DYXC1,* was isolated from a large Finnish family. The gene was disrupted only in those family members who had dyslexia, and it was also disrupted in 9% of individuals suffering from dyslexia in the general population (Taipale et al., 2003).

Sometimes people who learned to read just fine as children suddenly suffer from dyslexia in adulthood as a result of disease or injury, usually to the left hemisphere. This **acquired dyslexia** (or *alexia*) also tells us about how the brain processes language. One type of alexia, known as **deep dyslexia,** is characterized by errors in which patients read a word as another word that is related in meaning; for example, the printed word *cow* is read as *horse*. These patients are also unable to read aloud words that are abstract as opposed to concrete, and they make frequent errors in which they seem to fail to see small differences in words. It's as though they grasp words whole, without noting the details of the letters, so they have a hard time reading nonsense words.

In another acquired dyslexia, **surface dyslexia,** the patient makes different types of errors when reading. These patients can read nonsense words just fine, indicating that they know the rules of which letters make which sounds. But they find it difficult to recognize words in which the letter-to-sound rules are irregular. *The Tough*

GENES AND BEHAVIOR

CLINICAL ISSUE

Coughs as He Ploughs the Dough by Dr. Seuss (1987), for example, would confound them. In contrast to patients with deep dyslexia, those with surface dyslexia seem restricted to the details and sounds of letters.

These two kinds of dyslexia suggest that we have two different brain systems for reading: one focused on the sounds of letters, the other on the meanings of whole words (McCarthy and Warrington, 1990).

Electrical Stimulation Provides Information about the Organization of Language in the Brain

Electrical stimulation of the brain is used to explore language functions of the human cerebral cortex. Subjects in these studies are patients undergoing surgery for the relief of seizures. Electrical stimulation helps neurosurgeons locate—and thus avoid damaging—language-related cortical regions. By observing language interference produced by the electrical stimuli, the surgeon can identify these regions. Patients are given only local anesthesia, so that they can continue to communicate verbally.

Pioneering work by Penfield and Roberts (1959; discussed at the start of Chapter 2) provided a map of language-related zones of the left hemisphere (Figure 19.11*a*). Pooled data from many patients showed that stimulation anywhere within a large anterior zone stops speech. Other forms of language interference, such as misnaming or impaired repetition of words, were evident from stimulation of both this region and more-posterior temporoparietal cortex regions.

George Ojemann and collaborators (Calvin and Ojemann, 1994) examined the effects of electrical stimulation within a wide extent of cerebral cortex, focusing on the possible compartmentalization of linguistic systems such as naming, reading, speech production, and verbal memory. An interesting example of the effects of cortical stimulation on naming is shown in Figure 19.11*b*, which shows the different loci of naming errors in English and Spanish in a bilingual subject.

Ojemann and Mateer (1979) presented more-detailed cortical maps, which reveal several different systems. Stimulation of one system arrests speech and impairs all facial movements. This system, located in the inferior premotor frontal cortex, was regarded as the cortical, final motor pathway for speech. Stimulation of a second system alters sequential facial movements and impairs phoneme identification. This system includes sites in the inferior frontal, temporal, and parietal cortex. A third system is defined by stimulation-induced memory errors: It surrounds the sites of the systems that impair phoneme identification. Reading errors are elicited by stimulation of yet other cortical positions.

Functional Neuroimaging Portrays the Organization of the Brain for Speech and Language

A series of PET studies, summarized by Posner and Raichle (1994), examined brain activation during different levels of the processing of words. These levels include (1) passive exposure to visually presented words, (2) passive exposure to spoken words, (3) oral repetition of words, and (4) generation of a semantic association to a presented word. The successive levels of these experiments and the accompanying PET scans are presented in Figure 19.12.

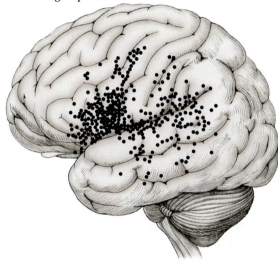

(a) Sites where stimulation interferes with speech in monolingual patients

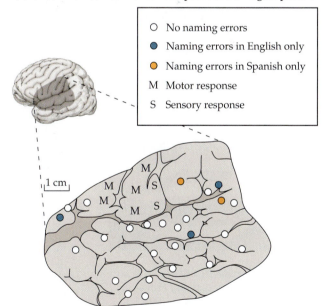

(b) Sites where stimulation affects speech in a bilingual patient

○ No naming errors
● Naming errors in English only
● Naming errors in Spanish only
M Motor response
S Sensory response

1 cm

19.11 Electrical Stimulation of Some Brain Sites Can Interfere with Language   (*a*) This summary of data obtained from many patients shows the brain sites where stimulation interferes with speech production. (*b*) This map shows stimulation sites that affected the speech of a patient who was bilingual—fluent in Spanish and English. Different regions interfere with either one language or the other, but not both. (Part *a* after Penfield and Roberts, 1959; *b* after Ojemann and Mateer, 1979.)

(*a*) **Passively viewing words**

(*b*) **Listening to words**

(*c*) **Speaking words**

(*d*) **Generating a verb associated with each noun shown**

19.12 Subtractive PET Scans of Brain Activation in Progressively More-Complex Language Tasks (*Left*) For clarity concerning the tasks, the subject is depicted here at a desk, but when the PET scans were made, the subjects reclined with their heads in a PET scanner and viewed a specially mounted display. (*Right*) These PET scans correspond to the tasks at left; see the text for details of these results. (After Posner and Raichle, 1994; PET scans courtesy of Marcus Raichle.)

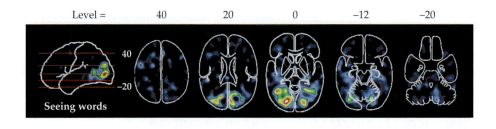
Seeing words

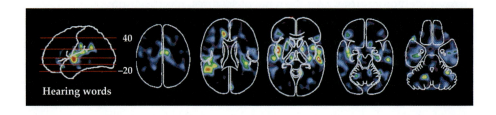
Hearing words

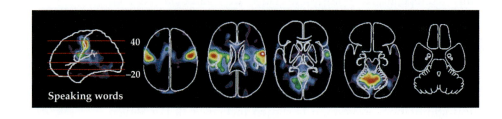
Speaking words

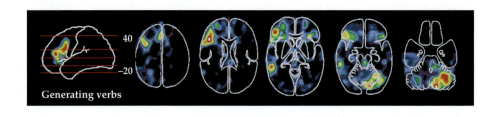
Generating verbs

Passive viewing of words activates a posterior area within the left hemisphere (Figure 19.12*a*). Passive hearing of words shifts the focus of maximum brain activation to the temporal lobes (Figure 19.12*b*). Repeating the words orally activates the motor cortex of both sides, the supplementary motor cortex, and a portion of the cerebellum and insular cortex (Figure 19.12*c*). During word repetition or reading aloud, activity was relatively absent in Broca's area. But when subjects were required to present a verb that was an appropriate semantic association for a presented noun, language-related regions in the left hemisphere, including Broca's area, were markedly activated (Figure 19.12*d*).

Interestingly, slightly different brain regions are activated when native speakers are reading Italian versus English (Paulesu et al., 2000). Perhaps the reason for this difference is that the sound associated with each letter is very regular in Italian, while in English, a given letter may have a very different sound in one word from the sound it has in another (to repeat the earlier example, compare the sounds of "ough" in the words *tough, cough, plough,* and *dough*).

Event-related potentials (ERPs; see Chapter 3) also confirm the activation of different brain regions depending on which aspect of language is being performed. Subjects are asked to read a sentence in which they encounter a word that is grammatically correct but, because of its meaning, doesn't fit. "The man started the car engine and stepped on the pancake." About 400 ms after the patient reads the word *pancake*, a negative wave is detected on the scalp (Kutas and Hillyard, 1980). Such "N400" responses (*N* denotes "negative," and the number represents the response time in milliseconds) to word meanings seem to be centered over the temporal lobe (Neville et al., 1992) and therefore may originate from Wernicke's area. But *grammatically* inappropriate words elicit a positive potential about 600 ms after they are encountered (a P600 response), as though it takes the brain 200 ms longer to detect this level of error (Osterhout, 1997).

IMPORTANT METHOD

This propensity for humans to use their left cerebral hemisphere for language processing can be seen quite early. Even 3-month-old infants, when exposed to speech, show more metabolic activity in the left hemisphere than the right (Dehaene-Lambertz et al., 2002), suggesting that we may be born with a predisposition to use our left brain for language. What functions, then, are fulfilled by our right cerebral hemisphere?

The Left Brain Is Different from the Right Brain

By the early twentieth century it was firmly established that the cerebral hemispheres are not equivalent in mediating language functions (Finger, 1994). The left hemisphere seemed to control this function and was commonly described as the dominant hemisphere. However, the right hemisphere does not just sit within the skull awaiting the call to duty when the left side of the brain is injured. In fact, many researchers have slowly drifted from notions of cerebral *dominance* to ideas of hemispheric *specialization,* or **lateralization.** This emphasis implies that some functional systems are connected more to one side of the brain than the other—that is, that functions become lateralized—and that each hemisphere is specialized for particular ways of working.

Lateralization of function is not a surprising idea; a broad look at body organs shows considerable asymmetry between the right and left sides. For example, in all vertebrates the heart is slightly to the left of the midline and the liver is on the right. Sometimes a person with a defect in one of the genes involved will develop the reverse pattern (B. Casey and Hackett, 2000).

Nevertheless, at the level of brain processing in normal individuals, the interconnections of the hemispheres ordinarily mask evidence of hemisphere specialization. But by studying patients whose interhemispheric pathways have been disconnected—**split-brain individuals**—researchers have been able to see cerebral hemispheric specialization in cognitive, perceptual, emotional, and motor activities.

Are there two minds in one head?

Starting in the 1930s, a small group of human patients underwent a surgical procedure designed to provide relief from frequent, disabling epileptic seizures (Bogen et al., 1988). In these patients, epileptic activity that was initiated in one hemisphere spread to the other hemisphere via the corpus callosum, the large bundle of fibers that connect the two hemispheres. Surgically cutting the corpus callosum appreciably reduces the frequency and severity of such seizures.

CLINICAL ISSUE

Studies at that time seemed to show that this remedy for seizures caused no apparent changes in brain function, as assessed by general behavior tests such as IQ tests. But the human corpus callosum is a huge bundle of more than a million axons, and it seemed strange that the principal connection between the cerebral hemispheres could be cut without producing detectable changes in behavior. The eminent physiological psychologist Karl Lashley, with characteristic sardonic humor, suggested that perhaps the only function of the corpus callosum was to keep the two hemispheres from floating apart in the cerebrospinal fluid. However, subsequent animal research with careful testing revealed deficits in behavior as consequences of hemispheric disconnection.

In one study on cats, for example, both the corpus callosum and the optic chiasm were sectioned, so that each eye was connected only to the hemisphere on its own side. Such cats learned with the left eye that a particular symbol stood for reward but that the inverted symbol did not, while with the right eye they were able to learn the opposite—that the inverted symbol was rewarded rather than the upright symbol. Thus each hemisphere was ignorant of what the other had learned (Sperry et al., 1956).

Beginning in the 1960s, Roger Sperry at the California Institute of Technology began using the behavioral techniques he had perfected in split-brain cats to study split-brain humans. In this group of patients, stimuli can be directed to either hemisphere. For example, objects that the patient feels with the left hand stimulate activity in nerve cells of the sensory regions in the right hemisphere. Because the corpus callosum is cut in these patients, most of the information sent to one half of the brain cannot travel to the other half. By controlling stimuli in this fashion—selectively presenting them to one hemisphere or the other—the experimenter can test the capabilities of each hemisphere.

In some of Sperry's studies, words were projected to either the left or the right hemisphere; that is, visual stimuli were presented in either the right or the left side of the visual field. Split-brain subjects can easily read and verbally communicate words projected to the left hemisphere, but no such linguistic capabilities were evident when the information was directed to the right hemisphere (Figure 19.13). Zaidel (1976) showed that the right hemisphere has a small amount of linguistic ability; for example, it can recognize simple words. In general, however, the vocabulary and grammatical capabilities of the right hemisphere are far less developed than they are in the left hemisphere.

19.13 Testing of a Split-Brain Individual Words or pictures projected to the left visual field activate the right visual cortex. (*a*) In normal individuals, activation of the right visual cortex excites corpus callosum fibers, which transmit verbal information to the left hemisphere, where the information is analyzed and language is produced. (*b*) In split-brain patients, the severing of callosal connections prevents language production in response to stimuli in the left visual field (*left*). However, split-brain individuals are able to respond verbally to stimuli in the right visual field (*right*).

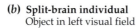

(a) Normal individual

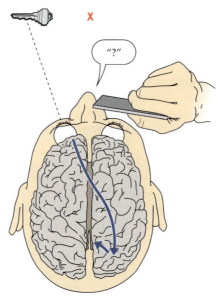

(b) Split-brain individual
Object in left visual field   Object in right visual field

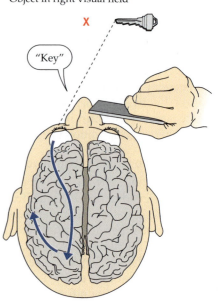

Sperry's findings not only confirmed the animal research, but they were more dramatic because they showed that only the processes taking place in the left hemisphere could be described verbally by the patients. Thus, in most people the left hemisphere possesses language and speech mechanisms. For our discussion here, the important result is that each hemisphere by itself can process and store information without any participation by the other hemisphere.

The ability of the "mute" right hemisphere had to be tested by nonverbal means. For example, a picture of a key might be projected to the left visual field and so reach only the right visual cortex. The subject would then be asked to touch several different objects that she could not see and hold up the correct one. Such a task could be performed correctly by the left hand (controlled by the right hemisphere) but not by the right hand (controlled by the left hemisphere). In such a patient, the left hemisphere literally does not know what the left hand is doing.

Whereas the left hemisphere controls speech, the right hemisphere seems to be somewhat better at processing spatial information, especially if the response is manual rather than simple recognition of a correct visual pattern.

The two hemispheres process information differently in normal humans

Almost all the research concerning differences between the hemispheres in the processing of information has concentrated on two modalities: hearing and vision. In each modality, psychologists can detect differences in behavioral response to confirm that, in most people, the left cerebral hemisphere has become specialized to process language.

The right-ear advantage   Through earphones, we can present different sounds to each ear at the same time; this process is called **dichotic listening.** The subject hears a particular speech sound in one ear and, at the same time, a different vowel, consonant, or word in the other ear. The task for the subject is to identify or recall these sounds.

Although this technique may seem to be a program designed to produce confusion, in general, data from dichotic listening experiments indicate that right-handed persons identify verbal stimuli delivered to the right ear more accurately than stimuli presented simultaneously to the left ear. This result is described as a right-ear "advantage" for verbal information. In contrast, about 50% of left-handed individuals reveal a reverse pattern, showing a left-ear advantage—more-accurate performance for verbal stimuli delivered to the left ear.

Doreen Kimura argues that auditory stimuli presented to the right ear produce stronger effects on the left auditory cortex than on the right auditory cortex, and vice versa (Figure 19.14). Thus, speech presented to the right ear exerts stronger control over lan-

19.14 Kimura's Model of the Right-Ear Advantage   (*a*) A word delivered to the left ear results in stronger stimulation of the right auditory cortex. (*b*) A word delivered to the right ear results in stronger input to the left hemisphere. (*c*) When words are delivered to both ears simultaneously, the one to the right ear is the one usually perceived because the right ear has more-direct connections to the left hemisphere. (After Kimura, 1973.)

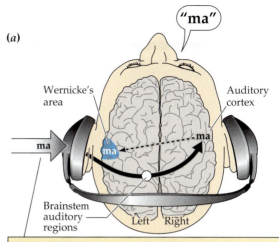

(*a*)

Information to the left ear goes to right auditory cortex and then to Wernicke's area in the left hemisphere. Subject repeats word.

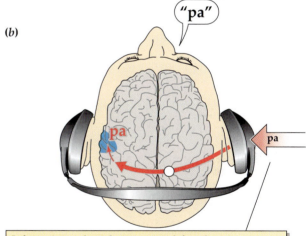

(*b*)

Information to the right ear goes to left auditory cortex, then to Wernicke's area. Subject repeats word.

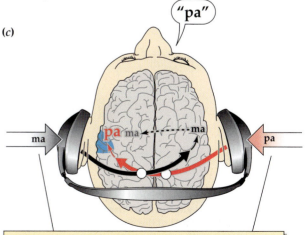

(*c*)

When conflicting information goes to both ears, that to the right ear reaches Wernicke's area first. Subject repeats only the right ear information.

Doreen Kimura

guage mechanisms in the left hemisphere than does speech presented to the left ear (Kimura, 1973). The right-ear advantage for speech sounds in right-handed individuals is restricted to particular kinds of speech sounds (Tallal and Schwartz, 1980), such as consonants like *b, d, t,* and *k,* but not vowel sounds.

Visual perception of linguistic stimuli We can study hemispheric specialization in normal humans by briefly exposing visual half-fields to stimuli (see Figures 10.14 and 19.13). If the stimulus exposure lasts less than 100 to 150 ms, input can be restricted to one hemisphere because this amount of time is not sufficient for the eyes to shift their direction. In intact humans, of course, further processing may involve the transmission of information through the corpus callosum to the other hemisphere.

Most studies show that verbal stimuli (words and letters) presented to the right visual field (going to the left hemisphere) are better recognized than the same input presented to the left visual field (going to the right hemisphere). On the other hand, nonverbal visual stimuli (such as faces) presented to the left visual field are better recognized than the same stimuli presented to the right visual field. Simpler visual processing, such as detection of light, hue, or simple patterns, is equivalent in the two hemispheres.

Does the left hemisphere hear words and the right hemisphere hear music?

The left and right auditory cortical areas appear to play somewhat different roles in human perception of speech and music. An early clue to this difference came from a study of the anatomy of the temporal lobes in adults (Geschwind and Levitsky, 1968): In 65% of the brains examined, the upper surface of the lobe—a region known as the **planum temporale**—was larger in the left hemisphere than in the right (Figure 19.15*a* and *b*). In only 11% of adults was the right side larger. The planum temporale includes part of the area known as *Wernicke's area,* where damage impairs the perception of speech. Perhaps the difference in size of this region between the two hemispheres reflects the left-hemisphere dominance.

We saw earlier that left-hemisphere dominance for speech is less common in left-handed people than in right-handed people, and MRI studies show that the asymmetry of the planum temporale is also reduced in left-handed people (Steinmetz et al., 1991), reinforcing the idea that the planum temporale is involved in speech. The difference in size of the planum temporale is even more evident in newborns than in adults; it appeared in 86% of the infant brains examined (Witelson and Pallie, 1973), and this difference may be related to the fact that speech

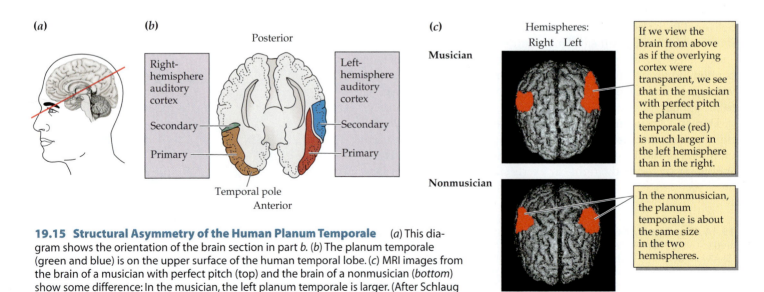

19.15 Structural Asymmetry of the Human Planum Temporale (*a*) This diagram shows the orientation of the brain section in part *b*. (*b*) The planum temporale (green and blue) is on the upper surface of the human temporal lobe. (*c*) MRI images from the brain of a musician with perfect pitch (top) and the brain of a nonmusician (bottom) show some difference: In the musician, the left planum temporale is larger. (After Schlaug et al., 1995; *c* courtesy of Gottfried Schlaug.)

activates the left cerebral hemisphere more than the right in 3-month-old infants (as discussed earlier).

This evidence suggests an innate basis for cerebral specialization for language and speech perception because the asymmetry is established before any experience with speech. The planum temporale tends to be larger on the left than on the right in chimpanzees too (Gannon et al., 1998). Similarly, Broca's area is larger on the left than on the right in chimps, bonobos, and gorillas as well as in humans (Cantalupo and Hopkins, 2001). Furthermore, just as our left hemisphere is more activated than the right when we hear speech rather than other sounds, the left hemisphere of monkeys is more activated than the right when they hear monkey vocalizations rather than human speech (Poremba et al., 2004). These results suggest that other primates already possess a precursor to language, as we discussed at the start of this chapter, and that the same brain regions mediate this language ability across primate species.

EVOLUTION AT WORK

In contrast, the auditory areas of the *right* hemisphere play a major role in the perception of music. Musical perception is impaired particularly by damage to the right hemisphere (Samson and Zatorre, 1994), and music activates the right hemisphere more than the left (Zatorre et al., 1994). But perfect pitch (the ability to identify any musical note without comparing it to a reference note) seems to involve the left rather than the right hemisphere.

Schlaug et al. (1995) made MRI measurements of the planum temporale in three kinds of subjects, all right-handed (because the larger size of the left planum temporale is seen especially in right-handed individuals): (1) musicians with perfect pitch, (2) musicians without perfect pitch, and (3) nonmusicians. The size of the left planum temporale was twice as large in musicians with perfect pitch than in nonmusicians (see Figure 9.15c). The size of the left planum temporale in musicians without perfect pitch was intermediate, but closer to that of nonmusicians. Because perfect pitch requires both verbal ability (to name the pitch) and musical ability, perhaps it is not surprising to find that, like language, perfect pitch is associated with the left hemisphere.

Despite these data, we cannot assign the perception of speech and pitch entirely to the left hemisphere and the perception of music entirely to the right hemisphere. We have seen that the right hemisphere can play a role in speech perception even in people in whom the left hemisphere is speech-dominant. Furthermore, although damage to the right hemisphere can impair the perception of music, it does not abolish it. Damage to *both* sides of the brain can completely wipe out musical perception (Samson and Zatorre, 1991). Thus, even though each hemisphere plays a greater role than the other in different kinds of auditory perception, the two hemispheres appear to collaborate in these as well as in many other functions.

Are left-handed people different?

Anthropologists speculate that the predominance of right-handedness goes back a long time into prehistory. People portrayed in cave paintings held things in their right hand, and Stone Age tools seem to be shaped for the right hand. Skull fractures of animals preyed on by ancient humans are usually on the animal's left side, so anthropologists conclude that most attackers held a club in the right hand.

Unusual attributes have been ascribed to the left-handed person—from an evil personality to an "abnormal" cortical organization of language. (Indeed, the Latin word for "left-handed" provides the root of not only the English term *sinistral* ("left-handed"), but also the negative word *sinister*.) Left-handed people make up a small percentage of human populations. A figure of about 10% is commonly reported, although this percentage may be lower in parts of the world where teachers actively discourage left-handedness. For example, there is a higher percentage of left-handed Chinese-Americans in U.S. schools, which are generally more tolerant of left-handedness, than among Chinese in China. Surveys of left-handed writing in American college populations reveal an incidence of 13.8% (Spiegler and Yeni-Komshian, 1983). This percentage is viewed as a dramatic increase over prior generations, perhaps re-

CLINICAL ISSUE

flecting a continuing decline in the social pressures toward right-handedness and an increase in the acceptability of left-handedness. Interestingly, other primates also show a preference for using the right hand (Westergaard et al., 1998).

Hardyck et al. (1976) examined more than 7000 children in grades 1 through 6 for school achievement, intellectual ability, motivation, socioeconomic level, and the like. A detailed analysis showed that left-handed children do not differ from right-handed children on any measure of cognitive performance. However, the idea that left-handed people are "damaged" humans has been common in the past and has even found occasional support in research.

CLINICAL ISSUE

D. A. Silva and Satz (1979) noted that several studies show a higher incidence of left-handedness in clinical populations than in the general population. They suggested that brain injury explains the high rate of left-handedness in this population. Early brain injury, these investigators argued, can cause a shift in handedness. Because most people are right-handed, early one-sided brain injury is more likely to effect a change from right-handedness to left-handedness than the reverse.

Geneticists have established that handedness is influenced by heredity, but it is not a simple, single-gene effect. According to Klar (2003), hair on the back of the scalp forms a clockwise whorl in 93% of right-handers but is a random mix of clockwise or anticlockwise among non-right-handers. Klar suggests that a single gene has a major (but not absolute) influence on asymmetries throughout the body.

How did hemispheric asymmetry and specialization evolve?

Some scientists believe that hemispheric specialization originated in the differential use of the limbs for many routine tasks. Picture early humans hunting. One hand holds the weapon and provides power; the other is used in more-delicate guidance or body balance. Other vertebrates—including toads (Vallortigara et al., 1999), crows (Hunt et al., 2001), walruses (Levermann et al., 2003), and chimpanzees (Corp and Byrne, 2004)—have been found to show preferences for using one limb or the other for particular behaviors, suggesting an adaptive advantage to handedness. In time the evolutionary successes offered by handedness might have been used in the emergence of language and speech.

EVOLUTION AT WORK

Arguments that propose a fundamental difference in cognitive style between the hemispheres suggest other connections to language and evolutionary advantages of cerebral specialization. According to this view, the left hemisphere provides processing that is analytical, and the right hemisphere offers a more holistic, general analysis of information (Table 19.2). Some theorists suggest that hemisphere specialization allows for separate cognitive modes that are mutually incompatible (Ivry and Robertson, 1998). But the notion, now common among the public, that the two hemispheres are so different that they need separate instruction, is not supported by the data. For example, although the left hand draws better than the right hand after the corpus callosum is cut, neither hand draws as well as before the surgery.

Williams Syndrome Offers Clues about Language

Williams syndrome, which occurs in approximately 1 out of 20,000 births (Bower, 2000), offers a fascinating dissociation between what we normally regard as intelligence and language. Individuals with **Williams syndrome** speak freely and fluently with a large vocabulary, yet they may be unable to draw simple images, to arrange colored blocks to match an example, or to tie shoelaces. The individuals are very sociable, ready to strike up conversation and smile. They may also display strong musical talent, either singing or playing an instrument.

GENES AND BEHAVIOR

The syndrome seems to be caused by the deletion of more than a dozen genes from one of the two chromosomes numbered 7 (de Luis et al., 2000). No one understands why the remaining copies of these genes, on the other chromosome 7, do not compensate for the lost copies. The absence of one copy of the gene called *elastin* (which encodes a protein important for connective tissue in skin and ligaments), leads to pixielike facial features (Figure 19.16). Several of the other missing genes are thought to lead to changes in brain development and to the behavioral features of the syndrome.

The psychological development of such individuals is complicated: As infants they may display a greater understanding of numerosity than other infants, but as adults they may show a poor grasp of numbers. Conversely, their language performance is poor in infancy but greatly improved by adulthood (Paterson et al., 1999). These findings suggest that the developmental process is distinctively altered in Williams syndrome.

TABLE 19.2 *Proposed Cognitive Modes of the Two Cerebral Hemispheres in Humans*

Left hemisphere	Right hemisphere
Phonetic	Nonlinguistic
Sequential	Holistic
Analytical	Synthetic
Propositional	Gestalt
Discrete temporal analysis	Form perception
Language	Spatial

The Frontal Lobes of Humans Are Related to Higher-Order Aspects of Cognitive and Emotional Functions

Because the complexity of human beings far exceeds that of other animals, researchers have sought characteristics of the brain that might account for human preeminence. As we noted in Chapter 6, among the most striking differences is the comparatively large size of the human prefrontal cortex. In part because of its size, the frontal region has been regarded as the seat of intelligence and abstract thinking. Adding to the mystery of frontal lobe function is the unusual assortment of behavioral changes that follows surgical or accidental lesions of this region.

The boundaries of the frontal lobes are not precisely defined, but the human frontal cortex occupies almost one-third of the entire cerebral cortical surface. The posterior portion of the frontal cortex includes motor and premotor regions (see Chapter 11). The anterior portion, usually referred to as **prefrontal cortex,** is a critical component of a widespread neuronal network, with extensive linkages throughout the brain (Fuster, 1990; Mega and Cummings, 1994). This prefrontal cortex was destroyed by lobotomy, the now discredited treatment for schizophrenia that we discussed in Chapter 16. The prefrontal cortex is further subdivided into a *dorsolateral* region and an *orbitofrontal* region (Figure 19.17*a*). The prefrontal cortex is especially prominent in humans and apes (Semendeferi et al., 2002), but it is a smaller portion of the cerebral cortex in other mammals (Figure 19.17*b*).

The study of prefrontal cortical function in animals began with the work of Carlyle Jacobsen in the 1930s. In his experiments with chimpanzees, Jacobsen employed delayed-response learning. The animals were shown where food was hidden, but they had to wait before being allowed to reach for it. This simple test situation re-

19.16 The Appearance of Williams Syndrome
Children with Williams syndrome often have a characteristic facial shape, caused by the loss of a copy of the *elastin* gene. The loss of copies of other nearby genes is thought to cause the mild mental retardation paired with verbal fluency. (Photo courtesy of the Williams Syndrome Association.)

(a) The prefrontal cortex in humans

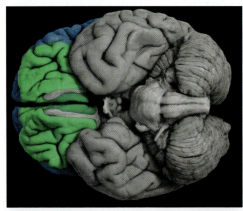
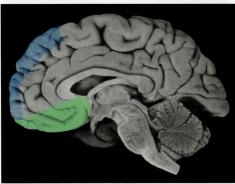

(b) Relative prefrontal cortex size in several mammals

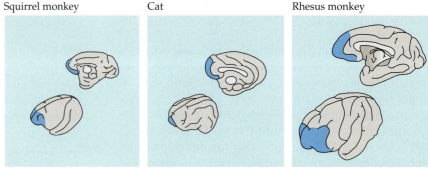

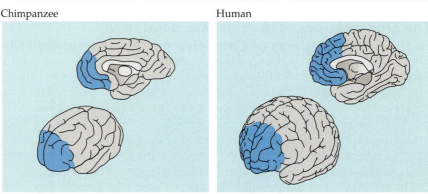

19.17 The Prefrontal Cortex (a) The human prefrontal cortex can be subdivided into a dorsolateral region (blue) and an orbitofrontal region (green). Lesions in these different areas of prefrontal cortex have different effects on behavior. (b) The relative percentage of prefrontal cortex is greatest in humans and other apes, such as the chimpanzee, but it decreases successively in monkeys, carnivores, and rodents (not shown). The brains here are drawn to different scales. (Photographs courtesy of S. Mark Williams and Dale Purves, Duke University Medical Center.)

vealed a remarkable impairment in chimpanzees with prefrontal lesions: These animals performed this task very poorly, in contrast with animals that sustained lesions in other brain regions. In interpreting this phenomenon, Jacobsen emphasized the memory function of the frontal cortex. However, in light of the effects of prefrontal damage in humans, which we take up next, it seems more likely that the chimpanzees were unable to direct their attention properly and/or to formulate a plan of which hiding place to examine when the time came.

Frontal lobe injury in humans leads to emotional, motor, and cognitive changes

The complexity of change following prefrontal damage is epitomized by the classic case of Phineas Gage, which we discussed at the start of this chapter. What happened to his brain to change his personality so radically that he was "no longer Gage"?

A century and a half after Phineas Gage's accident, measurement of his skull and modern imaging techniques indicate that his injury was probably confined to the orbitofrontal region of both frontal lobes, sparing the dorsolateral region (Figure 19.18). Having made these measurements, Hanna Damasio, Antonio Damasio, and colleagues searched their extensive roster of neurological cases and found that Gage's syndrome matches that of several other patients with damage to this brain region (H. Damasio et al., 1994).

The clinical portrait of humans with frontal lesions reveals an unusual collection of emotional, motor, and cognitive changes. The emotional reactivity of these patients shows a persistent strange apathy, broken by bouts of euphoria (an exalted sense of well-being). Ordinary social conventions are readily cast aside by impulsive activity.

Antonio Damasio

19.18 Phineas Gage Reconstructed   This computer reconstruction, based on measurements of Phineas Gage's skull, shows, from several different perspectives, the brain areas that are most likely to have been damaged in his famous accident. The red cylinder shows the path of the tamping iron, which entered the skull below the left eye and exited through the top of the head, severely damaging both frontal lobes. (From H. Damasio et al., 1994; courtesy of Hanna Damasio.)

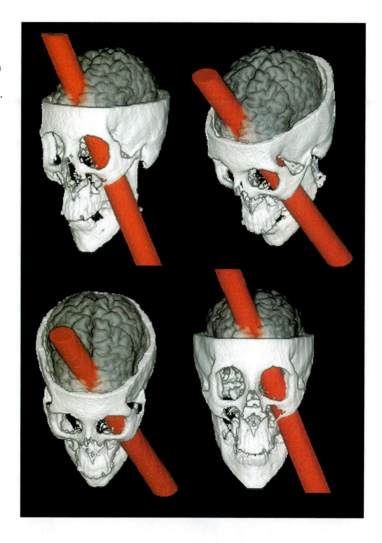

Concern for the past or the future is rarely evident (Duffy and Campbell, 1994; Petrides and Milner, 1982). Frontal patients show shallow emotions, even including reduced responsiveness to pain. Frequently, though, they exhibit episodes in which this apathy is replaced by boastfulness and silliness and, sometimes, unbridled sexual activity. Standard IQ test performance shows only slight changes after injury or stroke. Forgetfulness is shown in many tasks requiring sustained attention. In fact, some of these patients even forget their own warnings to "remember."

Clinical examination of patients with frontal lesions also reveals an array of strange impairments in motor activities, especially in the realm of "plans" for action. The patients seem to **perseverate** (continue beyond a reasonable degree) in any activity. For example, if the patient is asked to open and then close the fist, once the activity has begun (and it is difficult to initiate such acts in patients with frontal lesions) the patient continues a persistent sequence of fist opening and closing. The overall level of motor activity—especially ordinary, spontaneous movements—is quite diminished in these patients. For example, facial expression becomes blank, and head and eye movements are markedly reduced. Some reflexes that are evident only very early in life, such as the infantile grasp reflex of the hand, reappear in frontal cases.

One explanation for these disparate effects of prefrontal lesions is that this region of cortex may be important for goal-directed behavior, which requires prolonged attention and sensitivity to potential rewards and punishments. Patients with prefrontal lesions, like Gage, have an inability to plan acts and use foresight. They fail to realize that disrespectful behavior and dishonest bragging will come back to haunt them, and they are unable to stay focused on any but short-term projects. Table 19.3 lists the main clinical features of patients with lesions of various portions of the frontal lobes.

Examination of healthy subjects confirms the idea that prefrontal cortex is important for goal-directed behaviors. In humans performing a task in which some stimuli have more reward value than others, the level of activation in prefrontal cortex (as measured by fMRI) correlated with how rewarding the stimulus was (Gottfried et al.,

Hanna Damasio

TABLE 19.3 *Core Characteristics of the Regional Prefrontal Syndromes*

Dysexecutive type (dorsolateral)	Disinhibited type (orbitofrontal)	Apathetic type (mediofrontal)
Diminished judgment, planning, insight, and temporal organization	Stimulus-driven behavior	Diminished spontaneity
Cognitive impersistence	Diminished social insight	Diminished verbal output (including mutism)
Motor programming deficits (possibly including aphasia and apraxia)	Distractibility	Diminished motor behavior (including akinesis)
Diminished self-care	Emotional lability	Urinary incontinence
		Lower-extremity weakness and sensory loss
		Diminished spontaneous prosody
		Increased response latency

2003). In another testing situation that involved gambling, event-related potentials indicated that prefrontal cortex was especially active when people were making choices that could cost them money (Gehring and Willoughby, 2002). In monkeys, prefrontal cortex neurons become especially active when the animal has to make a decision that may provide a reward (Matsumoto et al., 2003), which also suggests that prefrontal cortex controls goal-directed behaviors.

Deficits in Spatial Perception Follow Some Types of Brain Injury

Injury to the parietal lobe can produce a variety of impairments such as the following: Faces cannot be recognized, spatial orientation is disturbed, objects placed in the hand cannot be recognized by touch alone, or one side of the body may be completely neglected, even to the point of being rejected as one's own.

The diversity of behavioral changes following injury to the parietal lobe is related partly to its large expanse and its critical position adjacent to occipital, temporal, and frontal regions. The anterior end of the parietal region includes the postcentral gyrus, which is the primary cortical receiving area for somatic sensation. Brain injury in this area does not produce numbness; rather, it produces sensory deficits on the opposite side that seem to involve complex sensory processing. For example, objects placed in the hand opposite the injured somatosensory area can be *felt* but cannot be identified by touch and active manipulation. This deficit is called **astereognosis** (from the Greek *a*, "not"; *stereos*, "solid"; and *gnosis*, "knowledge").

More-extensive injuries in the parietal cortex, beyond the somatosensory cortex, affect interactions between or among sensory modalities, such as visual or tactile matching tasks, which require the subject to identify visually an object that is touched or to reach for an object that is identified visually.

In prosopagnosia, faces are unrecognizable

Suppose one day you look in the mirror and you see someone who is not familiar to you. As incredible as this scenario might seem, some individuals suffer this fate after brain damage. This rare syndrome is called **prosopagnosia** (from the Greek *prosop-*, "face"; *a-*, "not"; and *gnosis*, "knowledge"). Such patients fail to recognize not only their own faces but also the faces of relatives and friends. No amount of remedial training restores their ability to recognize anyone's face. In contrast, the ability to recognize *objects* may be retained, and the patient readily identifies familiar people by the sounds of their voices.

Faces simply lack meaning in the patient's life. No disorientation or confusion accompanies this condition. There is no evidence of diminished intellectual abilities. Visual acuity is maintained, although most patients have a small visual-field defect—that is, an area of the visual field where they are "blind." Most research indicates that the right hemisphere is more important than the left for recognizing faces. For example, using the Wada test (see Box 19.1) to anesthetize the right hemisphere causes patients to have difficulty recognizing faces, whereas anesthetizing the left hemisphere has no effect on facial recognition (Figure 19.19). Similarly, split-brain patients do a better job of

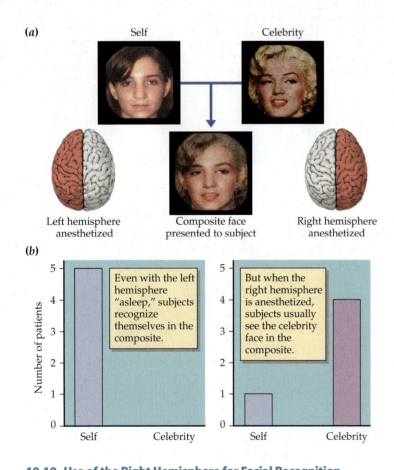

(a) Self / Celebrity

Left hemisphere anesthetized

Composite face presented to subject

Right hemisphere anesthetized

(b)

Even with the left hemisphere "asleep," subjects recognize themselves in the composite.

But when the right hemisphere is anesthetized, subjects usually see the celebrity face in the composite.

Number of patients

Self   Celebrity

Self   Celebrity

19.19 Use of the Right Hemisphere for Facial Recognition
Anesthetizing the left hemisphere in a Wada test (see Box 19.1) does not interfere with a subject's ability to recognize his own face in a picture "morphed" from his face and that of a celebrity. But when the right hemisphere is anesthetized, the subject interprets the morphed face as that of the celebrity. (From Keenan et al., 2001; courtesy of Julian Keenan.)

BOX 19.1 The Wada Test

Clinical observations of humans with brain injury indicate that about 95% of us show left-hemisphere specialization for verbal activities, but how can we determine which side of the brain mediates language in a person who is not ill? Wada and Rasmussen (1960) provided a technique to produce effects similar to those of brain injury without inflicting permanent damage. They injected a short-acting anesthetic (sodium amytal) into a single carotid artery—first on one side and then, several minutes later, on the other.

Recall from Chapter 2 that the circulation of the anterior two-thirds of the cerebral hemisphere comes from branches of the carotid artery. Most of the anesthetic in the first pass through the vascular system remains on the side of the brain where it was injected. The patient shows arrest of speech for a brief period when the anesthetic is injected in the hemisphere specialized for language processing. After a few minutes the effects wear off, so the injection is much like a reversible brain lesion.

The sodium amytal test (sometimes called the **Wada test**) confirms stroke data indicating that about 95% of humans have a left-hemisphere specialization for language. The Wada test also confirms that whereas most left-handed people show left dominance for language, the reverse pattern (right-hemisphere dominance for language) is more common in left-handed people than in right-handed people. A new variant of the Wada test is to use transcranial magnetic stimulation (TMS; see Chapter 2) in healthy subjects to disrupt electrical activity in the left hemisphere or the right, asking which interferes most with language function (Knecht et al., 2002). These studies again indicate that the left hemisphere is more important for language than the right in most people, but they also suggest that the right hemisphere does provide some contribution to language in many people.

recognizing faces if those faces are presented to the right hemisphere (Gazzaniga and Smylie, 1983). However, split-brain patients and functional imaging make it clear that both hemispheres have some capacity for recognizing faces. Thus, prosopagnosia is usually caused by *bilateral* damage to the **fusiform gyrus,** a region of cortex on the inferior surface of the brain where occipital and temporal cortex meet (Figure 19.20).

Prosopagnosia often involves other perceptual categories besides faces (Gauthier et al., 1999). Some patients suffering from prosopagnosia cannot recognize their own cars and do not recognize common makes of cars in general, although they can distinguish between cars and trucks. Bird-watchers are no longer able to recognize distinctive birds. Functional-MRI studies of healthy subjects also indicate that the fusiform gyrus is activated when people are identifying faces, birds, or cars (Gauthier et al., 2000). Thus this region seems to be responsible for identifying a particular instance from a large category (faces or birds or cars) in which all cases have many things in common. Different subregions may be specialized for one category or the other.

Neglect of one side of the body and space can result from parietal lobe injury

Brain damage involving the right inferior parietal cortex produces an unusual set of behavioral changes (Rafal, 1994). The key feature is neglect of the left side of both the body and space. A patient may fail to dress the left side of her body and may even disclaim "ownership" of her left arm or leg. "Well then, whose left arm is that, there in your bed?" "I don't know. My sister must have left that here. Wasn't that an awful thing to do!"

In some instances familiar people presented on the left side of the patient are completely neglected, although no visual-field defect is apparent. This phenomenon, called **hemispatial neglect,** can also be seen in simple test situations. A common test requires the patient to copy drawings of familiar objects. In a typical result, a patient who is asked to draw the face of a clock, for example,

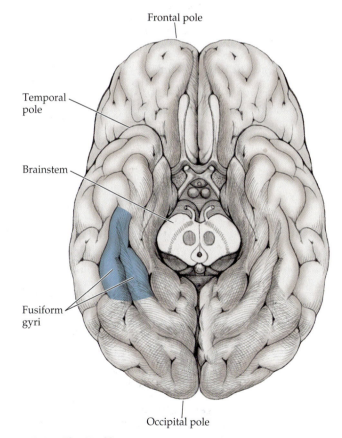

Frontal pole

Temporal pole

Brainstem

Fusiform gyri

Occipital pole

19.20 The Fusiform Gyrus   In this view from below the brain, the cerebellum has been removed to reveal the region of cortex that normally lies opposite the cerebellum. The fusiform gyrus, at the juncture of the temporal and occipital lobes, is active during discrimination of objects from a large category, such as faces or birds or cars. Bilateral destruction of this region leads to prosopagnosia, the inability to recognize individual faces.

Model   Patient's copy

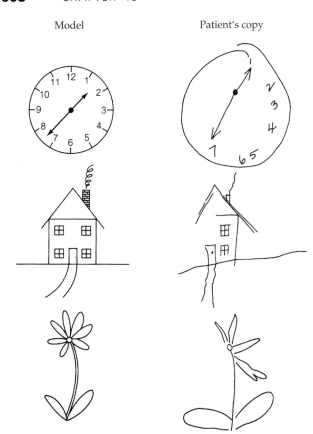

19.21 Diagnostic Test for Hemispatial Neglect When asked to duplicate drawings of common, symmetrical objects, patients suffering from hemispatial neglect ignore the left side of the model they are copying. (From Kolb and Whishaw, 1990.)

draws numbers only on the right side of the clock face (Figure 19.21) (Schenkerberg et al., 1980).

Associated with this dramatic change is a feature called *extinction of simultaneous double stimulation*. Most people can readily report the presence of two stimuli when those stimuli are presented simultaneously on both sides of the body. Patients with right inferior parietal lesions, however, are unable to note the double nature of the stimulation and usually report only the stimulus presented to the right side. This syndrome extends to visual imagery as well; when dreaming, for example, these patients scan only one side of dream scenes (Doricchi et al., 1991). Although many patients with injury to this region show recovery from unilateral neglect, the feature of extinction is quite persistent.

Yet another dramatic feature of this syndrome is the frequent *denial of illness* (*anosognosia*). Patients may adamantly maintain that they are capable of engaging in their customary activities and do not recognize the impressive signs of unilateral neglect. Remarkably, having these patients wear prisms to shift their visual field 10° to the right for a few minutes eases their symptoms: For a few hours they are less neglectful of the left visual field (Rossetti et al., 1998).

Many hypotheses have been offered to account for these symptoms. Some investigators have regarded the disorder as a consequence of loss of the ability to analyze spatial patterns; this hypothesis is consistent with the fact that unilateral neglect occurs with lesions of the right hemisphere but not with lesions of the left hemisphere. Others regard the syndrome as an attentional deficit (Mesulam, 1985).

Following Some Injuries, the Brain Can Recover Function

The course of behavior following brain injury often reveals conspicuous changes. Striking examples of language recovery following stroke have been observed in many adults. Amazing examples of language recovery have been described in children following the removal of a diseased cerebral hemisphere. Many theories are offered to describe the mechanisms mediating the **recovery of function** after lesions.

In spite of these encouraging developments, prevention is clearly better than the cure. Motor vehicle accidents, horseback riding, diving, and contact sports such as boxing are major causes of injuries to the brain and spinal cord. Box 19.2 describes the devastating effects of boxing on the brain.

Different strategies aim to reduce brain damage following injury or stroke

Most strokes are caused by a blood clot that blocks a blood vessel, cutting off the supply of oxygen and glucose to a brain region. In a minority of cases, the loss of blood flow to a brain region is caused by the rupture of a blood vessel. In either case, brain cells begin to die. At present, we don't know how to induce the adult brain to produce new neurons to replace those that die, so an important consideration in the management of stroke is to try to prevent as much neuronal death as possible.

One obvious strategy is to try to unblock the blood vessel as soon as possible, and various **thrombolytics** (literally "clot dissolvers"; from the Greek *thrombos*, "clot," and *lytikos*, "able to loosen") have been shown to be effective in restoring circulation. There is a growing consensus that part of the neuronal death following stroke is caused by neurons being overly excited, producing too many action potentials, leading to death (Lo et al., 2003; Rossi et al., 2000). Thus, new treatment strategies are being developed to suppress this **excitotoxicity** (Figure 19.22).

CLINICAL ISSUE

BOX 19.2 A Sport That Destroys the Mind

Boxing has a long history, much of it unpleasant. In ancient Greece and Rome, some boxers were admired for their courage and strength, but others, wearing leather wrappings studded with metal nuggets, bludgeoned each other to death for the entertainment of spectators. Although rules were developed during the eighteenth century in England, including the use of padded gloves, the goal of prizefighting has always been to knock the opponent out. A bout usually ends when one fighter has sustained a brief loss of consciousness.

To achieve that goal, boxers aim relentlessly at the head, which sustains blow after blow. The result of so many blows to the head has been called **dementia pugilistica** (the Latin *pugil* means "boxer"), a fancy term for the mental state commonly known as *punch-drunk* (Erlanger et al., 1999). Punch-drunk boxers have markedly impaired cognitive abilities. Even a boxer as formerly loquacious (and talented at dodging blows) as Muhammad Ali is, today, unable to utter more than a word or two at a time. Deaths in the ring are usually due to brain injuries, especially brain hemorrhage (Ryan, 1998). Several professional societies, as well as various medical and neurological societies, have urged the banning of this sport.

Brain scans indicate that very few boxers escape unscathed. Casson et al. (1982) studied ten active professional boxers who had been knocked out. The group included those of championship caliber, as well as mediocre and poor boxers. None of the knockouts sustained by the fighters involved a loss of consciousness lasting more than 10 s. Yet at least five of the group had definitely abnormal CT scans. The abnormalities included mild generalized cortical atrophy, which in some cases included ventricular dilation. Only one boxer had a clearly normal brain picture. The age of the boxers was not related to the degree of cortical atrophy.

Ironically, the most successful boxers were the ones with the most profound cortical atrophy. In fact, the total number of professional fights correlated directly with the magnitude of brain changes. During a career of boxing, a fighter accumulates many blows to the head; the most "successful" boxers thus frequently sustain the most punishment (A. H. Roberts, 1969) because they participate in more matches. A Parkinson's-like syndrome of tremors or paralysis may result from boxing. A large-scale CT study of 338 active boxers showed that scans were abnormal in 7% (showing brain atrophy) and borderline in 12% (B. D. Jordan et al., 1992).

Amateur soccer players may also suffer mild concussions, in their case from hitting the ball with their head, because they show slightly impaired memory and planning ability (Matser et al., 1999). But only in boxing is head trauma an explicit goal—no small reason that many believe boxing is a sport whose time has passed.

Sequence of damaging events with stroke:

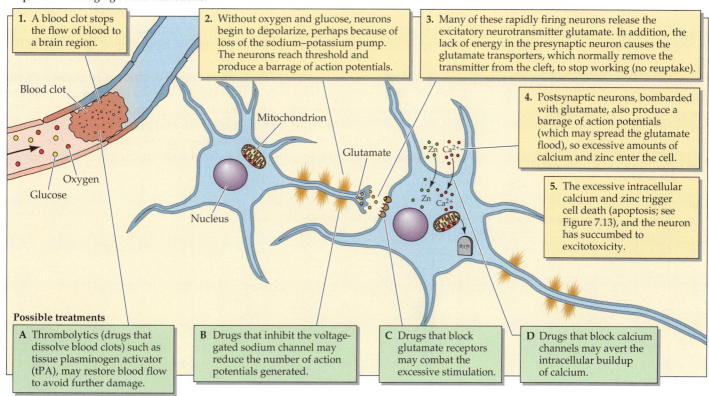

1. A blood clot stops the flow of blood to a brain region.

2. Without oxygen and glucose, neurons begin to depolarize, perhaps because of loss of the sodium–potassium pump. The neurons reach threshold and produce a barrage of action potentials.

3. Many of these rapidly firing neurons release the excitatory neurotransmitter glutamate. In addition, the lack of energy in the presynaptic neuron causes the glutamate transporters, which normally remove the transmitter from the cleft, to stop working (no reuptake).

4. Postsynaptic neurons, bombarded with glutamate, also produce a barrage of action potentials (which may spread the glutamate flood), so excessive amounts of calcium and zinc enter the cell.

5. The excessive intracellular calcium and zinc trigger cell death (apoptosis; see Figure 7.13), and the neuron has succumbed to excitotoxicity.

Blood clot
Oxygen
Glucose
Nucleus
Mitochondrion
Glutamate
Zn   Ca²⁺
Zn   Ca²⁺

Possible treatments

A Thrombolytics (drugs that dissolve blood clots) such as tissue plasminogen activator (tPA), may restore blood flow to avoid further damage.

B Drugs that inhibit the voltage-gated sodium channel may reduce the number of action potentials generated.

C Drugs that block glutamate receptors may combat the excessive stimulation.

D Drugs that block calcium channels may avert the intracellular buildup of calcium.

19.22 Strategies for Minimizing Brain Damage following Stroke or Injury

Some recovery from brain injury follows relief from generalized physiological abnormalities

Any brain injury destroys particular collections of nerve cells and produces more-generalized disturbances that temporarily affect the responsiveness of other nerve cells. In the region of a brain injury, for example, frequently the properties of the blood–brain barrier change. In time, the changes in the blood vessels around a site of injury reestablish the blood–brain barrier and increase blood flow to transiently distressed but intact tissue.

In addition, the brain tissue around the site of the stroke usually swells, as a result of **edema,** the buildup of intracellular fluid. The pressure from this swelling can mechanically damage nearby brain tissue, so physicians may administer drugs, such as glucocorticoids, to inhibit swelling. In cases of brain injury, a neurosurgeon may need to open the skull to relieve the brain from damaging pressure buildup within the skull. As recovery proceeds, the edema subsides and neurons that had been inhibited (but not killed) by the swelling resume function.

The anatomist Constantin von Monakow coined the term **diaschisis** to describe these distant inhibitory effects of brain lesions that seemed to be reversible (Monakow, 1914). With time, usage of this term has expanded to include a host of potentially reversible, nonspecific effects that make the immediate consequences of a brain lesion more intense than the persistent deficits.

The impairment caused by a brain lesion increases with the rate at which the lesion develops. Some investigators refer to this phenomenon as **lesion momentum,** or mass × velocity (Finger, 1978). A lesion in the brainstem that incapacitates animals when made all at one time may have only slight effect if done in two successive stages. The partial lesion may stimulate regrowth or relearning or both, so that some compensation has already been achieved by the time the rest of the tissue is removed.

Many aphasic patients show some recovery

Many people with brain disorders that produce aphasia recover some language abilities. For some people, language recovery depends on specific forms of speech therapy. The relative extent of recovery from aphasia can be predicted from several factors. For example, recovery is better in survivors of brain damage due to trauma, such as a blow to the head, than in those whose brain damage is caused by stroke. Patients with more-severe language loss recover less. Left-handed people show better recovery than those who are right-handed.

Kertesz et al. (1979) reported that the largest amount of recovery usually occurs during the initial 3 months following brain damage (Figure 19.23). In many instances, little further improvement is noted after 1 year, although this result may re-

Constantin von Monakow (1853–1930)

19.23 Courses of Recovery of Patients with Aphasia (a, b) The course of recovery from Broca's aphasia (a) differs from the course of recovery from Wernicke's aphasia (b). These graphs depict the aphasia quotient, a score derived from a clinical test battery. Higher scores indicate better language performance. (c) Here the course of recovery of the auditory comprehension of speech after a stroke in which Wernicke's area was damaged is compared with the course of recovery after a stroke in which Wernicke's area was spared. (Parts a and b after Kertesz et al., 1979; c after Naeser et al., 1990.)

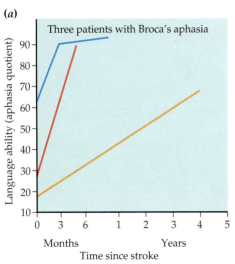
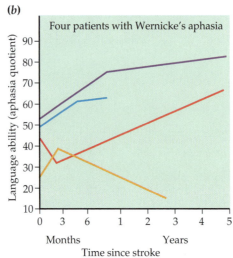
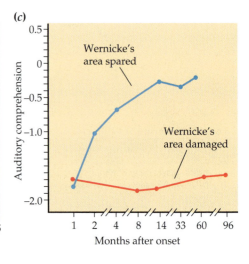

flect impoverished therapeutic tools rather than a property of neural plasticity. In general, patients suffering from Broca's aphasia have the highest rate of recovery.

One innovation, called *melodic intonation therapy,* draws attention to the differences between song and speech. Individuals suffering from aphasia can frequently sing words and phrases even though they show major handicaps in the ability to speak words. Melodic intonation therapy attempts to enhance communication by having patients sing sentences they would ordinarily attempt to deliver in conversational form.

Damage to the left hemisphere in children can also produce aphasia, but they often recover language. Language recovery is possible even after removal of the entire left hemisphere (Box 19.3). These observations show that the right hemisphere *can* take over the language functions of the left hemisphere if impairment occurs early in life. But as we grow older, the brain slowly loses the ability to compensate for injury.

The brain regrows and reorganizes anatomically after being injured

Anatomical dogma for many years declared that changes in the adult central nervous system are solely destructive. The intricate structure and connections of nerve cells were considered to be structurally fixed once adulthood was reached. Injury, it was thought, could lead only to the shrinkage or death of nerve cells. However, many impressive contemporary demonstrations to the contrary now emphasize the structural plasticity of nerve cells and their connections.

Regeneration of the axons of the peripheral nervous system has always been accepted, but comparable structural regrowth has been observed in the brain and spinal cord (Veraa and Grafstein, 1981). For example, injury to catecholamine-containing fibers in the medial forebrain bundle leads to regrowth of axonal portions connected to nerve cells. Dendrites in the brain may also grow back following injury. Figure 19.24 illustrates one form of regrowth after injury: **collateral sprouting.**

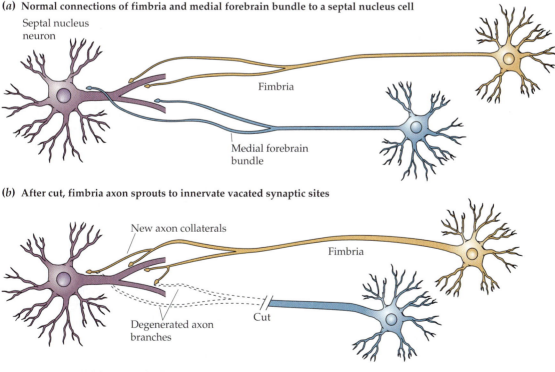

(*a*) **Normal connections of fimbria and medial forebrain bundle to a septal nucleus cell**

Septal nucleus neuron

Fimbria

Medial forebrain bundle

(*b*) **After cut, fimbria axon sprouts to innervate vacated synaptic sites**

New axon collaterals

Fimbria

Degenerated axon branches

Cut

19.24 Collateral Sprouting of a Brain Neuron (*a*) The septal nucleus is normally innervated by the fimbria and the medial forebrain bundle. (*b*) After the medial forebrain bundle has been severed, a fimbria axon develops sprouts that occupy synaptic sites formerly occupied by axon terminals from the medial forebrain bundle. (After Raisman, 1978.)

BOX 19.3 The Comparatively Minor Effects of Childhood Loss of One Hemisphere

During early development the brain is a vulnerable organ—a fact that is especially apparent when we look at the effect of a prolonged, difficult birth involving a period of oxygen loss: Some children born under such circumstances sustain lateralized brain injury involving a single cerebral hemisphere. Early in development such a child may show paralysis on one side of the body and frequent seizures. These seizures can be difficult to control with medication, and they may occur so often that they endanger life.

Surgical removal of the malfunctioning hemisphere reduces seizures. Although at first some severe effects of the surgery are evident, over a long period of time the restoration of behavior is practically complete. This result is strikingly illustrated in a case presented by A. Smith and O. Sugar (1975). The boy they described showed paralysis on his right side as an infant, and by 5 years of age he was experiencing 10 to 12 seizures a day. Although the boy's verbal comprehension was normal, his speech was hard to understand. To treat the problem, doctors removed all the cerebral cortex of the left hemisphere. At first, his language capacity worsened, but then it improved rapidly.

Long-term follow-up studies extended to age 26, when the patient had almost completed college. Tests revealed an above-normal IQ and superior language abilities; thus the early loss of most of the left hemisphere had not precluded language development. This patient also had remarkable development of nonverbal functions, including visuospatial tasks and manual tasks.

Whereas adult hemispherectomy of the left side usually results in drastic impairment of language, this case shows that childhood hemispherectomy can be followed by extensive functional recovery, demonstrating the additional plasticity of the young brain.

NEURAL PLASTICITY

In the peripheral nervous system, the story goes like this: If a peripheral sensory or motor fiber is injured, the terminal portions degenerate, and sensory or motor function in the affected region is immediately lost. Nerve fibers adjacent to the injured fibers recognize this injury (perhaps by a chemical signal delivered from the injured site), and they respond by developing sprouts or branches from intact axons. In time, usually weeks, these sprouts connect to denervated skin or muscle and acquire functional control of these regions on the periphery of the body (J. Diamond et al., 1976).

This mechanism seems to result in functional compensation for a loss of neuronal connections. The injured nerve fiber (axon) slowly regrows, and as it approaches the skin or muscles to which it had been connected, the sprouts retract. Again, chemical signals from the regrowing original fiber probably produce this change.

Demonstrations of collateral sprouting in the brain and spinal cord, once rarely observed, are now reported with regularity. A growing view is that injury of the nervous system might release neurotrophic factors (Nieto-Sampedro and Cotman, 1985).

Perhaps the most exciting prospect for brain repair following stroke or injury is the use of **embryonic stem cells.** These are cells, derived from embryos, that have not yet differentiated into specific roles and therefore seem to be able to develop, under local chemical cues, into the type of neuron needed. The finding that a limited number of new neurons are produced by the adult brain, which we have mentioned several times before, demonstrates that neurons can become integrated into functional brain circuits. Such cells even seem to migrate to the site of injury to take on their new roles (Björklund and Lindvall, 2000).

Although not all studies report encouraging results (Freed et al., 2001), in several studies implants of embryonic stem cells have been shown to reduce symptoms of Parkinson's disease (see Chapter 11) and stroke (Kondziolka et al., 2000). But great controversy surrounds the ethical issue of exploiting human embryos for such purposes. A limited number of embryonic stem cells can be harvested from the blood in the umbilical cord without harming the newborn or the mother, but another possible source of stem cells is genetic engineering. One goal is to harvest from a patient some cells—say, white blood cells—and induce them to revert to the state of embryonic stem cells. This approach might avoid problems of tissue rejection, because the implanted cells would be genetically identical to the patient.

Rehabilitation and retraining can help recovery from brain and spinal cord injury

Training can restore some functions after brain or spinal cord injury. For example, work with humans follows in the path of research on animals and shows some restoration of walking in spinal cord–injured humans following training (Barbeau et al., 1998).

Cognitive and/or perceptual handicaps that develop from brain impairments can also be modified by training. It is important at this point to distinguish between the role of experience in compensating for brain injury and its role in restoring behavior lost after injury. It is well known that experiences significantly reduce the impact of brain injury by fostering compensatory behavior. For example, vigorous eye movements can make up for large scotomata (blind spots in the visual field) that result from injury to the visual pathways. Behavior strategies can be changed after a brain injury to enable successful performance on a variety of tests.

The role of experience in the possible reorganization of pathways following a lesion was noted in Chapter 11, where we described how an individual whose arm afferents have been cut can recover control of the limbs. Some rehabilitation experts have questioned the wisdom of placing certain patients in sensory isolation (patients in coma, or patients kept in fixed positions in isolated rooms for intravenous therapy). Such patients, even if they cannot respond, might be aided by visitors, music, and changing visual stimuli. Some current programs of rehabilitation are putting these insights into effect.

CLINICAL ISSUE

Previous generations may have been too pessimistic about recovery from stroke, for now there's increasing evidence that people can regain considerable use of limbs affected by stroke if they are forced to. **Constraint-induced-movement therapy** persuades stroke patients to use the affected arm by simply tying the "good" arm to a splint for up to 90% of waking hours (Taub et al., 2002). But immobilizing the good arm isn't enough; such patients are subjected to rehabilitation therapy 6 hours a day to practice repetitively moving the affected limb (Figure 19.25). Most patients who received this treatment regained 75% of normal use of the paralyzed arm after only 2 weeks of this therapy, and there was evidence of a remapping of the motor cortex (Liepert et al., 2000).

Another surprising use of experience for rehabilitation involves a simple mirror. Altschuler et al. (1999) treated stroke patients who had reduced use of one arm by placing them before a mirror with only their "good" arm visible. To the patients, it looked as though they were seeing the entire body, but now both arms were the good arm. The patient was told to make symmetrical fluid motions with both arms. In the mirror, the motions looked perfectly symmetrical (of course), but surprisingly, most of the patients soon learned to use the "weak" arm more extensively. It was as though the visible feedback, indicating that the weak arm was moving perfectly, overcame the brain's reluctance to use that arm.

Perhaps the most important message to convey to victims of stroke is the encouragement that with effort and perseverance, their remarkably plastic brains can recover much of the lost behavioral capacity.

Figure 19.25 Constraint-Induced-Movement Therapy In this therapy, patients have their unaffected limb gently restrained (in this case in a white mitten) so that they must use the limb that was affected by the stroke in a series of repetitive tasks. (Photo courtesy of Edward Taub.)

Summary

1. Humans are distinct in the animal kingdom for their language and associated cognitive abilities. Possible evolutionary origins of human speech may be seen in aspects of gestures.

2. Studies of communication among nonhumans provide analogies to human speech. For example, the control of birdsong is lateralized in the brains of some species of songbirds. Further, in some of these species early experience is essential for proper song development.

3. Limitations of the vocal tract in nonhumans are proposed as one reason that they do not have speech, but nonhuman primates like the chimpanzee can learn to use signs of

Refer to the ***Learning Biological Psychology* CD** for study questions, animations, activities, and other study aids.

American Sign Language. However, controversy surrounds claims that these animals can arrange signs in novel orders to create new sentences.

4. Ninety to 95% of human language impairments involve injuries of the left cerebral hemisphere. Left anterior lesions produce an impairment in speech production called Broca's aphasia. More-posterior lesions, involving the temporoparietal cortex, affect speech comprehension, as seen in Wernicke's aphasia.

5. Left-hemisphere lesions in users of sign language produce impairments in the use of sign language that are similar to impairments in spoken language shown by nondeaf individuals suffering from aphasia.

6. Split-brain individuals show striking examples of hemispheric specialization. Most words projected only to the right hemisphere, for example, cannot be read, while the same stimuli directed to the left hemisphere can be read. Verbal abilities of the right hemisphere are also reduced; however, spatial-relation tasks are performed better by the right hemisphere than by the left.

7. Normal humans show many forms of cognitive specialization of the cerebral hemispheres, although these specializations are not as striking as those shown by split-brain individuals. For example, most normal humans show a right-ear advantage and greater accuracy for verbal stimuli in the right visual field.

8. Anatomical asymmetry of the hemispheres is seen in some structures in the human brain. Especially striking is the large size difference in the planum temporale (which is larger in the left hemisphere than in the right hemisphere of most right-handed individuals). Nevertheless, in most cases mental activity depends on interactions between the cerebral hemispheres.

9. The frontal lobes of humans are quite large compared with those of other animals. Injury in parts of this region produces an unusual syndrome of profound emotional changes, including reduced responsiveness to many stimuli. Tasks that require sustained attention show drastic impairment after frontal lesions.

10. In most patients, parietal cortex injuries produce perceptual changes. A dramatic example after bilateral damage is the inability to recognize familiar objects and the faces of familiar people. Some patients with right parietal injury neglect or ignore the left side of both the body and space.

11. Many functional losses following brain injury show at least partial recovery. Most recovery from aphasia occurs in the year following stroke, with fewer changes evident after that. Mechanisms of functional recovery may involve structural regrowth of cell extensions—dendrites and axons—and the formation of new synapses.

12. Retraining is a significant part of functional recovery and may involve both compensation, by establishing new solutions to adaptive demands, and reorganization of surviving networks. Greater recovery is evident in young individuals. Less impairment occurs when lesions are produced over a period of time—that is, when lesion momentum is reduced.

Recommended Reading

Bradbury, J. W., and Vehrencamp, S. L. (1998). *Principles of animal communication.* Sunderland, MA: Sinauer Associates.

Gazzaniga, M. S. (Ed.). (2000). *The new cognitive neurosciences* (2nd ed.). Cambridge, MA: MIT Press.

Hauser, M. (Ed.). (1999). *The design of animal communication.* Cambridge, MA: MIT Press.

Hillix, W. A., Rumbaugh, D. M., and Hillix, A. (2004). *Animal bodies, human minds: Ape, dolphin, and parrot language skills.* New York: Plenum.

Ivry, R. B., and Robertson, L. C. (1998). *The two sides of perception.* Cambridge, MA: MIT Press.

McManus, I. C. (2003). *Right hand, left hand: The origins of asymmetry in brains, bodies, atoms, and cultures.* Cambridge, MA: Harvard University Press.

Pinker, S. (1999). *Words and rules: The ingredients of language.* New York: Basic Books.

Rapp, B. (Ed.). (2001). *The handbook of cognitive neuropsychology: What deficits reveal about the human mind.* Philadelphia: Psychology Press.

Afterword

As a student, you are of course relieved to reach, at last, the final pages of a textbook. As authors, we, too, were relieved to arrive here. But we feel moved to have a final word with you to emphasize a theme that runs throughout the book and to discuss the importance of that theme explicitly before you go.

Plasticity Is a Defining Feature of the Brain

Sometimes in this book we have likened the brain to a machine, and that analogy is useful up to a point: The brain is a physical object whose parts must obey the laws of a material world. For example, in the early chapters we described how the various parts of the brain communicate by using physical media such as neurotransmitters, hormones, and action potentials. However, we have also described a nervous system that is remarkably plastic, and in a constant state of flux.

When we described psychological phenomena such as learning, perception, and cognition, it was implicit that these aspects of the mind are a product of the physical machine called the *brain*. But this machine is unlike any human-made machine because it is continually remodeling itself—rearranging the relationships between its parts—in a manner that (normally) improves its function. As you undoubtedly know from bitter experience, all human-made machines reach their peak performance once they are assembled, and simply tumble downhill after that. Computer scientists struggle and yearn to develop systems that can truly learn from experience—something that is accomplished quite easily when an egg and a sperm combine.

The study of behavior is the special domain of psychology, which has probed how behavior can change over time. Since the nineteenth century it has been understood that changes in behavior necessarily involve physical changes in the brain. (The only alternative would have been a regression to nonphysical explanations of behavior, such as the actions of spirits or demons.) But the complexity of the brain is so daunting that, until recently, few researchers even attempted to find out what part of the brain had been altered when behavior changed.

During the past few decades, however, psychologists and other neuroscientists have produced many concrete demonstrations that changes in behavior are due to brain changes. Indeed, it is now clear that constant remodeling is one of the brain's defining features. Just as important is the now abundant evidence that the relationship between changes in the brain and changes in behavior is bidirectional: Experience also can alter neural structure. This plasticity is a feature of the nervous system that persists throughout life, from embryonic development until old age.

Plasticity is prominent in neural development

The nervous systems of developing individuals are even more plastic than those of adults. That's why infants learn new languages and recover from brain injuries so much more readily than we adults do. In Chapter 7 we reviewed the many processes that occur as the brain puts itself together and showed how cell–cell interactions play a crucial role in all of those processes: The notochord induces cells to become motoneurons; targets secrete neurotrophic factors to attract and maintain neurons; radial glial cells guide migrating cells to their final destinations. The eventual form and function of developing cells is largely determined by the activities of their neighboring cells.

Thus the cells of the developing nervous system are in constant communication with one another, and they direct and constrain each other's fates. Because some of the neurons communicating these directions are sensory neurons that respond to stimuli in the environment, experience itself shapes the brain. The best-studied example of environmental effects on crucial aspects of development is in the visual system. Recall from Chapter 7 that early experience is crucial for maintaining the connections between the eye and brain that are needed to detect exactly the stimuli that surround us as adults.

Plasticity occurs at the molecular level

Even at the molecular level, plasticity and change are the norm. Remember from Chapters 3 and 4 that the number of neurotransmitter receptors in the postsynaptic region of a given synapse can increase or decrease depending on the amount of activity at that synapse. Usually this action serves to regulate the sensitivity of a particular pathway: Cells in the basal ganglia that receive too little dopamine stimulation start making more receptors to compensate, until they become supersensitive. Conversely, overstimulation leads to "down-regulation" of the receptors so that the signal is attenuated. Because experience clearly can affect which of our brain cells are firing, it must also indirectly affect the number and distribution of neurotransmitter receptors.

Endocrine regulation shows plasticity

Chapter 5 presented many examples of the complicated feedback systems in the endocrine system that regulate secretion to maintain relatively steady hormone levels. But experience also modulates patterns of hormone secretion: Winning an aggressive encounter can elevate testosterone levels, stress can augment ACTH secretion and kill hippocampal cells, and exposure to pheromones can accelerate or delay puberty. Although there are no data to indicate that pheromones play a role in human puberty, during the past century the average age at which individuals undergo puberty in our society has declined markedly, indicating that some environmental factors—perhaps better nutrition or greater exposure to sexual stimuli—have affected our reproductive systems too.

Sensory systems show plasticity

As noted already, research on sensory systems has been especially fruitful in demonstrating experiential effects on brain development and structure. In Chapter 8 we learned that changes in tactile stimulation, even in adulthood, can alter the projection patterns of information from the skin to the brain. This was first demonstrated in monkeys, and new, noninvasive techniques are now confirming that the same effects occur in humans.

For example, Yang et al. (1994) examined people who had lost a hand in an accident. On the side of the brain receiving information from the remaining hand, stimulation of that hand excited a region of the somatosensory cortex sandwiched between brain regions responding to the face and upper arm; as the map of primary somatosensory cortex in Figure 8.16 shows, this is normal. However, on the side of the brain that was no longer receiving information because of the lost hand, regions sensitive to the face and upper arm were found to be immediately adjacent to each other. Connections from the face and upper arm had shifted on that side of the brain to take over the region that had formerly been excited by stimuli from the hand (see Figure 8.19). Experimental manipulations of sensory inputs suggest that remapping of sensory cortex depends on extensive remodeling of synaptic contacts between the pyramidal neurons found in layer 2/3 of the sensory cortex (Petersen et al., 2004). It seems that sensory information is constantly competing not only for our attention, but for space in the brain—space to analyze and process the information that is most relevant to the business of surviving and reproducing.

Plasticity contributes to the causes and treatments of psychopathology

Our bodies and brains constantly make adjustments for the time of day and time of year, as detailed in Chapter 14. The waxing and waning of neural activity across these biological rhythms clearly influences behavior; in humans, for example, the short days of winter exacerbate certain forms of depression. Clearly, the ebb and flow of days and seasons is an environmental input that directly modulates the functioning of our nervous systems.

In Chapter 16 we saw that even severe psychopathologies such as schizophrenia are not entirely concordant in identical twins, so something other than genes must influence these disorders. The best candidate for that "something" is differences in experience.

Hopes are blossoming that recovery from brain accidents may be accomplished with grafts of genetically manipulated cells. These procedures clearly work in some cases, and they may be feasible one day in others. But to the extent that these transplants work at all, the success is due to the fact that the rest of the brain is capable of changing to integrate these new cells into an existing network. Thus the underlying plasticity of the brain will prove to be of vital practical importance in this arena.

Memory formation requires plasticity

In Chapters 17 and 18 we dealt with the phenomena that most explicitly depend on structural alterations in the adult nervous system: learning and memory. If our adult brains could not change, we would not be able to learn anything at all. But we *can* learn, and scientists have made remarkable progress in finding structural changes that may underlie learning and memory.

Recall that in a synapse that is activated in a particular way, the NMDA receptor allows ions to enter the postsynaptic cell; these ions then change the synapse so that it will transmit its signal more forcefully in the future. In other words, "neurons that fire together wire together." On the basis of inferences from behavior and what was known of neuroscience at the time, psychologist Donald Hebb predicted in 1949 that strengthening of synaptic action is the foundation of learning ("the Hebbian synapse"). Researchers are continuing to find evidence confirming Hebb's basic idea: that learning causes the number, pattern, and strength of synapses to change.

Neural prostheses exploit plasticity

Because the nervous system is very plastic, sometimes artificial devices—prostheses—can be integrated by the brain to improve functioning in cases of sensory or motor disabilities. For example, in Chapter 9 we discussed cochlear implants that afford partial hearing to many deaf people, and in Chapter 11 we discussed a robotic arm governed by brain activity. In the future, such devices may help paralyzed people move their limbs under the control of brain circuits.

Here we want to emphasize that, to be used successfully, most prostheses require learning. Cochlear implants are limited in the number of auditory frequencies to which they respond, and users have to learn how to interpret this information and to integrate it with other sensory input. The robotic arm controlled by brain activity similarly requires learning for successful use. So behavioral plasticity and underlying neural processes are necessary parts of any prosthetic program.

Temporal Constraints on Plasticity Are Diverse

Not only does neural plasticity take many different forms; it also takes many different time courses. Forms of learning and/or neural plasticity that seem to be similar may in fact follow different time courses over the life span. For example, LTP can be evoked in some layers of visual cortex of rats only until day 30, but it can be evoked in other cortical layers well into adulthood (Perkins and Teyler, 1988).

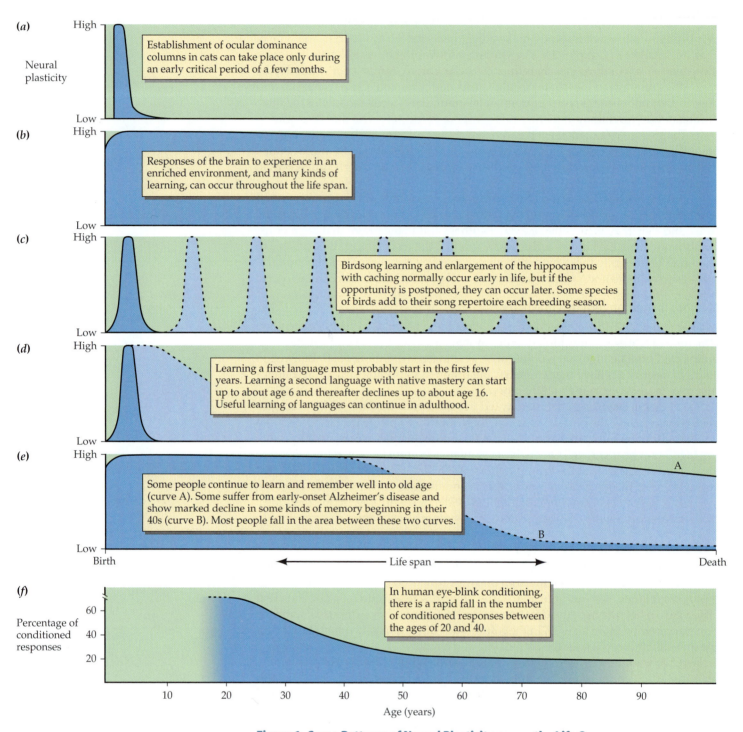

(a) Neural plasticity

Establishment of ocular dominance columns in cats can take place only during an early critical period of a few months.

(b)

Responses of the brain to experience in an enriched environment, and many kinds of learning, can occur throughout the life span.

(c)

Birdsong learning and enlargement of the hippocampus with caching normally occur early in life, but if the opportunity is postponed, they can occur later. Some species of birds add to their song repertoire each breeding season.

(d)

Learning a first language must probably start in the first few years. Learning a second language with native mastery can start up to about age 6 and thereafter declines up to about age 16. Useful learning of languages can continue in adulthood.

(e)

Some people continue to learn and remember well into old age (curve A). Some suffer from early-onset Alzheimer's disease and show marked decline in some kinds of memory beginning in their 40s (curve B). Most people fall in the area between these two curves.

Birth — Life span — Death

(f) Percentage of conditioned responses

In human eye-blink conditioning, there is a rapid fall in the number of conditioned responses between the ages of 20 and 40.

Age (years)

Figure 1 Some Patterns of Neural Plasticity across the Life Span

Plasticity can be limited to an early critical or sensitive period

Ocular dominance columns in the visual cortex form early and do not change later in life (Wiesel and Hubel, 1963). In cats, plasticity appears to be maximal at about 1 month of age and then declines over the next 3 months, after which time the visual pathways are virtually immutable (Figure 1a). During this plastic period, every major response property of cortical cells (ocular dominance, orientation selectivity, direction selectivity, disparity sensitivity) can be modified by manipulation of the visual environment (Mower et al., 1983). It is not clear what normally terminates plasticity in these aspects of the visual system.

Another example of learning that seems to be limited to an early critical period is learning of a first language with complete mastery. Investigators are not in complete agreement about the age limits, but such learning appears to be possible up to about 3 years of age, with a gradual falloff thereafter (Morford and Mayberry, 2000). Very few children with normal hearing are deprived of the possibility of acquiring speech in their first years, so most of the research in this area is based on acquisition of sign language by deaf children.

In Chapter 15 we saw that early handling by experimenters and early maternal stimulation help to make rat pups more resilient to stress later in life. Similarly, we saw in Chapter 18 that early handling or experience in a complex environment lowers the concentration of glucocorticoids in the rat brain and causes more-rapid return of glucocorticoids to the basal level, which protects the hippocampus from signs of aging.

Plasticity can extend over the life span

Although there is a great deal of interest in plasticity associated with early development of the nervous system, we must not lose sight of the fact that the nervous system remains plastic throughout life. Early findings of postweaning brain plasticity due to exposure to enriched environments, as discussed in Chapter 18, were subsequently extended to juvenile, adult, and aged animals (Figure 1*b*) (E. L. Bennett et al., 1964; Rosenzweig et al., 1961). Related results with aged rats were reported by Cummins et al. (1973) and by Greenough et al. (1986). Lifelong plasticity accounts for many of the learning experiences we have in life, such as learning a musical instrument as an adult, learning to use another language, and so forth.

Other experimental demonstrations of lifelong plasticity include remapping of the somatosensory cortex in adults by altering experience (Kaas, 1991), mentioned in Chapter 8, and remapping of auditory receptive fields (N. M. Weinberger, 1998), mentioned in Chapter 9. Sexual behavior can also leave its mark on the nervous system, even in adulthood (Figure 2) (Breedlove, 1997). Thus it is possible that structural differences between the sexes (or between people of differing sexual orientation) are the result of behavioral differences rather than the cause of them, as we discussed in Box 12.3.

Plasticity can occur at the first opportunity

Some kinds of plasticity develop as soon as the opportunity arises. For example, the critical period for plasticity of the visual system can be extended if cats are reared in the dark. Interestingly, however, if dark-reared cats are exposed to light for only 6 hours, the light exposure triggers the developmental process, and once triggered, the process runs to completion in the absence of further input (Mower et al., 1983).

Birdsong learning provides another example in which learning occurs at the first opportunity, as mentioned in Chapter 19. Normally a male bird learns its song from its father, but if a bird is prevented from hearing song at the usual age, it can still learn later, provided it is given an accurate model (Eales, 1985). For many years it was believed to be impossible for a bird to acquire a normal song after a critical period has passed—a conclusion that was based on experiments with a taped song tutor. However, when live tutors or naturalistic taped tutors are used, song can be acquired later. This finding fits in well with the observation that some species of songbirds add to their repertoire during each breeding season, which requires recurring periods of neural plasticity (Figure 1*c*).

In species of birds that cache food, such as nutcrackers, the hippocampus is larger than in related species that do not cache. If one of these birds is denied the opportunity to cache, the hippocampus does not show this size difference. The opportunity to cache can be postponed well beyond the usual age in laboratory-raised birds, but once the birds have the opportunity to cache, they do so promptly, and the hip-

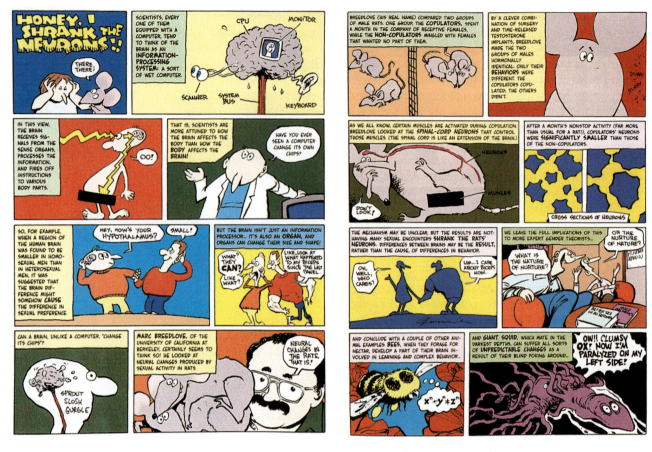

Figure 2 Sex on the Brain?   (From "Science Classics" by Larry Gonick; courtesy of Larry Gonick and *Discover* magazine.)

pocampus reflects this experience by enlarging (Clayton, 1995), as we mentioned in Chapter 17.

Some forms of plasticity are greatest at an early age but remain in later life in some form

Aligning the two eyes to prevent amblyopia ("lazy eye") is usually thought to be effective only for the first 5 to 6 years of life. But considerable improvement in amblyopia can be shown even by adults, if the condition is not too severe and if they exercise the weak eye sufficiently. As we mentioned in Chapter 10, one study reported considerable recovery from long-standing amblyopia after the normal eye was lost or severely damaged (Romero-Apis et al., 1982).

Chow and Stewart (1972) deprived cats of pattern vision in one eye for about 20 months after birth. When the kittens were tested for pattern perception with the previously deprived eye, they showed almost no discrimination on formal tests and were not able to guide locomotion with the previously deprived eye, although they performed well with the other eye. As we described in Chapter 10, the investigators then undertook an intensive program of rehabilitation with some of the cats, and over time the cats developed some pattern discrimination in the previously deprived eye, and they could use it to guide their locomotion. Furthermore, the cats' recovery was accompanied by morphological changes in the lateral geniculate nucleus, and electrophysiological recording showed increased numbers of binocular cells in the visual cortex. Here again, learning to see and plasticity of the visual system occurred after the usual developmental period had ended.

The literature on human recovery from congenital blindness is mixed, but it has been studied in people born with dense cataracts that were removed in adulthood. Gregory (1987) notes that "often the eye takes a long time to settle down after a cataract operation," which may partially explain why many of the historical cases show slow development of vision. A patient studied by Gregory and Wallace (1963) received corneal grafts that provided good retinal images immediately after the operation, and the patient could quickly recognize objects he already knew by touch, but his vision never became fully normal. We also met Michael May in Chapter 7, who is learning to use his vision, but very slowly compared to what infants accomplish. Transcranial magnetic stimulation experiments suggest that after years of visual deprivation, the visual cortex becomes substantially less responsive (Gothe et al., 2002).

In some cases, later plasticity depends on early training

Eric Knudsen has found that the development of auditory–visual neurons in the optic tectum of the barn owl can be finely manipulated in the young bird. In Chapter 9 we saw that a young owl equipped with prismatic lenses that displace the visual image learns to adapt to the lenses and locate objects accurately. If the prisms are fitted to an adult bird, the range of adjustment is normally quite restricted. However, subsequent work (Knudsen, 1998) has shown that if an owl learns an abnormal auditory–visual alignment as a juvenile and is then returned to the normal condition, it can easily reacquire the abnormal alignment as an adult. The early learning appears to leave a neural trace that, even if not used for an extended period, can be reestablished later, when needed.

The ability to learn a second language with native mastery is possible if the learner starts the second language by the age of 6 or 7, provided the first language was begun during the first year or two (Figure 1*d*). Mastery of the second language shows increasing departures from full native skill as the starting age increases from 7 to 16. Furthermore, people who started their second language in their teens form a second Broca's area adjacent to the Broca's area for their first language (K. H. Kim et al., 1997). Nevertheless, even people who start to learn a second (or third or fourth) language as an adult can gain conversational fluency, provided they work at it hard enough.

The decline in plasticity in the latter part of the life span takes many forms

As we noted in Chapters 7 and 18, abilities to learn and remember decline on the average in the latter part of the life span, but the amount of the decline varies with the type of learning. Let's consider the example of eye-blink conditioning, shown as a function of age in Figure 1*f*. Whereas panels *a* through *e* in Figure 1 are schematic, each summarizing multiple studies, Figure 1*f* in contrast is based on a single experiment that involved 150 healthy participants with ages ranging from 20 to 89 years (Woodruff-Pak and Jaeger, 1998).

The subjects were trained in delayed eye-blink conditioning and were given some other tests. Figure 1*f* shows the percentage of conditioned responses (CRs) during 72 trials in which a tone (the conditioned stimulus) was paired with an air puff to the eye. Note the rapid fall in the number of CRs over the first three decades (twenties through forties). After age 40, there was no further significant decline with age. The investigators found that the decline in conditioning with age paralleled a decline in accurately timed tapping and estimates of elapsed time, both of which, like eye-blink conditioning, are known to depend on cerebellar function.

On many other kinds of learning, some older people and animals perform as well as younger conspecifics (Figure 1*e,* curve A). On the other hand, some individuals suffer from early-onset Alzheimer's disease and show a marked decline in the formation of declarative memories in their forties (curve B). Most people fall into the area between these two curves as they age. In older individuals who show declines in ability with age, some studies show changes in neuroanatomy (such as shrinkage of the hippocampus) or in neurochemistry that may explain the decline. Perhaps all the observed declines in ability shown in Figure 1*e* are pathological rather than normal; if so, then we can hope for ways to prevent them.

It has been proposed that abilities to learn and remember in the latter part of the life span decline because there has been no evolutionary pressure to maintain them after the reproductive period (Baltes, 1997), which may indicate why special interventions are required to prevent such decline. In Chapter 18 we saw that enriched experience early in life and continued throughout the life span helps reduce the risk of cognitive decline in old age. At an international symposium on cognitive decline in old age, the research was summarized as follows (Rosenzweig and Bennett, 1996):

> It's a fortunate person whose brain
> Is trained early, again and again,
> And who continues to use it
> To be sure not to lose it,
> So the brain, in old age, may not wane. (p. 63)

Future Directions

To the extent that certain types of neural plasticity are limited to parts of the life span, it will be important to find the mechanisms that enable plasticity and those that inhibit it. Factors that inhibit continuing plasticity include declines in the production of neurotransmitters and nerve growth factors, age-related shrinkage of neural structures such as the hippocampus, and changes in receptor molecules. Other mechanisms remain to be identified, but identifying them will help us find ways to keep our brains malleable and our memory systems accurate well into old age.

The perspective we hope to have imparted to you concerning the neurosciences is that the brain is enormously changeable and adaptable. Of course, this emphasis reflects our view that neuroscience, at its core, is nothing less than the systematic investigation of the origins of behavior. We feel that what is most impressive about the behavior of both humans and other animals is its variety: Individuals of a given species use all sorts of different (sometimes bizarre) solutions to accomplish the same goals; they display different sets of behaviors across the span of their lifetimes; they develop unique strategies to solve life's basic problems of survival and reproduction. This diversity is the product of the individual's accumulated experiences, manifested in physical changes in the brain. The central remaining challenge—and it is a formidable one—is to try to understand exactly how experience molds the nervous system and exactly how neural changes govern subsequent behaviors. It is a challenge that engages us and thousands of other neuroscientists around the world. Perhaps you'll decide to join us. We have every expectation of fascinating and surprising stories yet to come.

Appendix

Molecular Biology: Basic Concepts and Important Techniques

Genes Carry Information That Encodes the Synthesis of Proteins

The most important thing about **genes** is that they are pieces of information, inherited from parents, that affect the development and function of our cells. It is very important to understand that information carried by the genes is a very specific sort: Each gene codes for the construction of a specific string of amino acids to form a **protein** molecule. This is *all* that genes do; they do not *directly* encode intelligence, or memories, or any other sort of complex behavior. The various proteins, each encoded by its own gene, make up the physical structure and most of the constituents of cells, such as enzymes. These proteins make complex behavior possible, and in that context they are also the targets upon which the forces of evolution act.

Enzymes are protein molecules that allow particular chemical reactions to occur in our cells. For example, only cells that have liver-typical proteins will look like a liver cell and be able to perform liver functions. Neurons are cells that make neuron-typical proteins so that they can look and act like neurons. The genetic information for making these sorts of proteins is crucial for an animal to live and for a nervous system to work properly.

One thing we hope this book will help you understand is that everyday experience can affect whether and when particular genetic recipes for making various proteins are used. But first let's review how genetic information is stored and how proteins are made. Our discussion will be brief because we assume that you've been exposed to some of this material before, in previous courses.

Genetic information is stored in molecules of DNA

The information for making all of our proteins could, in theory, be stored in any sort of format—on sheets of paper, magnetic tape, a CD-ROM—but all living creatures on this planet store their genetic information in a chemical called **deoxyribonucleic acid,** or **DNA.** Each molecule of DNA consists of a long strand of chemicals called **nucleotides** strung one after the other. There are only four nucleotides: guanine, cytosine, thymine, and adenine (abbreviated G, C, T, and A). The particular sequence of nucleotides (e.g., GCTTACC or TGGTCC or TGA) holds the information that will eventually make a protein. Because many millions of these nucleotides can be joined one after the other, a tremendous amount of information can be stored in very little space—on a single molecule of DNA.

A set of nucleotides that has been strung together can snuggle tightly against another string of nucleotides if it has the proper sequence: T nucleotides preferentially link with A nucleotides, and G nucleotides link with C nucleotides. Thus, T nucleotides are said to be complementary to A nucleotides, and C nucleotides are complementary to G nucleotides. In fact, most of the time our DNA consists not of a single strand of nucleotides, but of two complementary strands of nucleotides wrapped around one another.

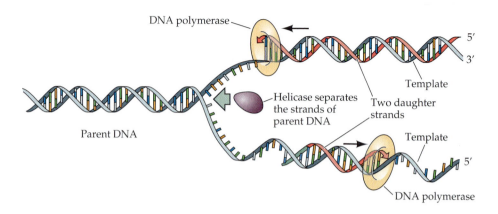

DNA polymerase

Helicase separates
the strands of
parent DNA

Parent DNA

Template

Two daughter
strands

Template

DNA polymerase

5′
3′

5′

A.1 Duplication of DNA   Before cell division, the genome must be duplicated as illustrated here so that each daughter cell has the full complement of genetic information.

The two strands of nucleotides are said to **hybridize** with one another, coiling slightly to form the famous double helix (Figure A.1). The double-stranded DNA twists and coils further, becoming visible in microscopes as **chromosomes,** which resemble twisted lengths of yarn. Humans and many other organisms are known as **eukaryotes** because we store our chromosomes in a membranous sphere called a **nucleus** (plural *nuclei*) inside each cell. You may remember that the ability of DNA to exist as two complementary strands of nucleotides is crucial for the duplication of the chromosomes, but that story will not concern us here. Just remember that, with very few exceptions, every cell in your body has a faithful copy of all the DNA you received from your parents.

DNA is transcribed to produce messenger RNA

The information from DNA is used to assemble another molecule—**ribonucleic acid, or RNA**—that serves as a template for later steps in protein synthesis. Like DNA, RNA is made up of a long string of four different nucleotides. For RNA, those nucleotides are G and C (which, you recall, are complementary to each other), and A and U (uracil), which are also complementary to each other. Note that the T nucleotide is found only in DNA, and the U nucleotide is found only in RNA.

When a particular gene becomes active, the double strand of DNA unwinds enough so that one strand becomes free of the other and becomes available to special cellular machinery (including an enzyme called *transcriptase*) that begins **transcription**—the construction of a specific string of RNA nucleotides that are complementary to the exposed strand of DNA (Figure A.2). This length of RNA, sometimes called the *message,* or **messenger RNA (mRNA)**, is also sometimes called a **transcript** because it contains a faithful transcript of the information in the DNA. Each DNA nucleotide encodes a specific RNA nucleotide (an RNA G for every DNA C, an RNA C for every DNA G, an RNA U for every DNA A, and an RNA A for every DNA T). This transcript is made in the nucleus where the DNA resides; then the mRNA molecule moves to the cytoplasm, where protein molecules are assembled.

RNA molecules direct the formation of protein molecules

In the cytoplasm are special organelles, called **ribosomes,** that attach themselves to a molecule of RNA, "read" the sequence of RNA nucleotides, and, using that information, begin linking together amino acids to form a protein molecule. The structure and function of a protein molecule depend on which particular amino acids are put together and in what order. The decoding of an RNA transcript to manufacture a particular protein is called **translation** (see Figure A.2), as distinct from *transcription*, the construction of the mRNA molecule.

Each trio of RNA nucleotides, or **codon**, encodes one of 20 different amino acids. Special molecules associated with the ribosome recognize the codon and bring a molecule of the appropriate amino acid so that the ribosome can fuse that amino acid to the previous one. If the resulting string of amino acids is short (say, 50 amino acids or so), it is called a **peptide;** if it is long, it is called a *protein.* Thus the ribosome assembles a very particular sequence of amino acids at the behest of a very particular sequence of RNA nucleotides, which were themselves encoded in the DNA inherited from our parents. In short, the secret of life is that DNA makes RNA, and RNA makes protein.

There are fascinating amendments to this short story. Often the information from separate stretches of DNA is spliced together to make a single transcript; so-called alternative splicing can create different transcripts from the same gene. Sometimes a protein is modified extensively after translation ends; special chemical processes can cleave long proteins to create one or several active peptides. But we will not consider those processes in this book.

Keep in mind that each cell has the complete library of genetic information (collectively known as the **genome**) but makes only a fraction of all the proteins encoded in that DNA. In modern biology we say that each cell **expresses** only some genes; that is, the cell transcribes certain genes and makes the corresponding gene products (protein molecules). Thus each cell must come to express all the genes needed to perform its function. Modern biologists refer to the expression of a particular subset of the genome as **cell differentiation:** The process differentiates the appearance and function of different types of cells. During development, individual cells appear to become more and more specialized, expressing progressively fewer genes. Many molecular biologists are striving to understand which cellular and molecular mechanisms "turn on" or "turn off" gene expression in order to understand development and pathologies such as cancer.

Molecular Biologists Have Craftily Enslaved Microorganisms and Enzymes

Many basic methods of molecular biology are not explicitly discussed in the text, so we will not describe them in detail here. However, you should understand what some of the terms *mean,* even if you don't know exactly how the methods are performed.

Molecular biologists have found ways to incorporate DNA from other species into the DNA of microorganisms such as bacteria and viruses. After the foreign DNA is incorporated, the microorganisms are allowed to reproduce rapidly, producing more and more copies of the (foreign) gene of interest. At this point the gene is said to be **cloned** because the researcher can make as many copies as she likes. To ensure that the right gene is being cloned, the researcher generally clones many, many different genes, each into different bacteria, and then "screens" the bacteria rapidly to find the rare one that has incorporated the gene of interest.

When enough copies of the DNA have been made, the microorganisms are ground up and the DNA extracted. If sufficient DNA has been generated, chemical steps can then determine the exact sequence of nucleotides found in that stretch of DNA—a process known as **DNA sequencing.** Once the sequence of nucleotides

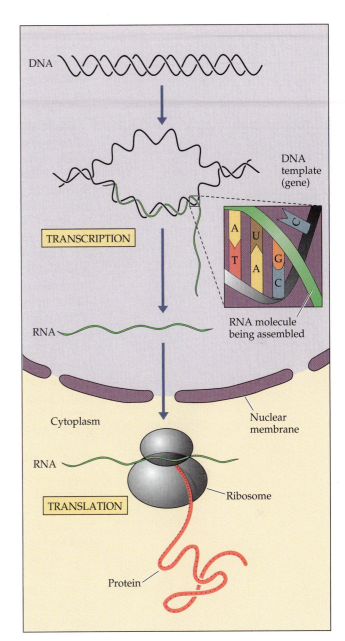

A.2 DNA Makes RNA, and RNA Makes Protein

has been determined, the sequence of complementary nucleotides in the messenger RNA for that gene can be inferred. The sequence of mRNA nucleotides tells the investigator the sequence of amino acids that will be made from that transcript because biologists know which amino acid is encoded by each trio of DNA nucleotides. For example, scientists have discovered the amino acid sequence of neurotransmitter receptors by this process.

The business of obtaining many copies of DNA has been boosted by a technique called the **polymerase chain reaction,** or **PCR.** This technique exploits a special type of polymerase enzyme that, like other such enzymes, induces the formation of a DNA molecule that is complementary to an existing single strand of DNA (see Figure A.1). Because this particular polymerase enzyme evolved in bacteria that inhabit geothermal hot springs, it can function in a broad range of temperatures. By heating double-stranded DNA, we can cause the two strands to separate, making each strand available to polymerase enzymes that, when the temperature is cooled enough, construct a new "mate" for each strand so that they are double-stranded again. The first PCR yields only double the original number of DNA molecules; repeating the process results in four times as many molecules as at first. Repeatedly heating and cooling the DNA of interest in the presence of this heat-resistant polymerase enzyme soon yields millions of copies of the original DNA molecule, which is why this process is also referred to as *gene amplification.*

With PCR, sufficient quantities of DNA are produced for chemical analysis or other manipulations, such as introducing DNA into cells. For example, we might inject some of the DNA encoding a protein of interest into a fertilized mouse egg (a zygote) and then return the zygote to a pregnant mouse to grow. Occasionally the injected DNA becomes incorporated into the zygote's genome, resulting in a **transgenic** mouse that carries and expresses the foreign gene.

Southern blots identify particular genes

Suppose we want to know whether a particular individual or a particular species carries a certain gene. Because all cells contain a complete copy of the genome, we can gather DNA from just about any kind of cell population: blood, skin, or muscle, for example. After the cells are ground up, a chemical extraction procedure isolates the DNA (discarding the RNA and protein). Finding a particular gene in that DNA just boils down to finding a particular sequence of DNA nucleotides. To do that, we can exploit the tendency of nucleic acids to hybridize with one another.

If we were looking for the DNA sequence GCT, for example, we could manufacture the sequence CGA (there are machines to do that readily), which would then stick to (hybridize with) any DNA sequence of GCT. The manufactured sequence CGA is called a **probe** because it is made to include some radioactive molecules so that we can follow the radioactivity to find out where the sequence goes. Of course, such a short length of nucleotides will be found in many genes. In order for a probe to recognize one particular gene, it has to be at least 15 nucleotides long.

When we extract DNA from an individual, it's convenient to let enzymes cut up the very long stretches of DNA into more manageable pieces of 1000 to 20,000 nucleotides each. A process called **gel electrophoresis** uses electrical current to separate these millions of pieces more or less by size. Large pieces move slowly through a tube of gelatin-like material, and small pieces move rapidly. The tube of gel is then sliced and placed on top of a sheet of paperlike material called *nitrocellulose.* When fluid is allowed to flow through the gel and nitrocellulose, DNA molecules are pulled out of the gel and deposited on the waiting nitrocellulose. This process of making a "sandwich" of gel and nitrocellulose and using fluid to move molecules from the former to the latter is called **blotting** (Figure A.3).

If the gene that we're looking for is among those millions of DNA fragments sitting on the nitrocellulose, our radiolabeled probe should recognize and hybridize to the sequence. The nitrocellulose sheet is soaked in a solution containing our ra-

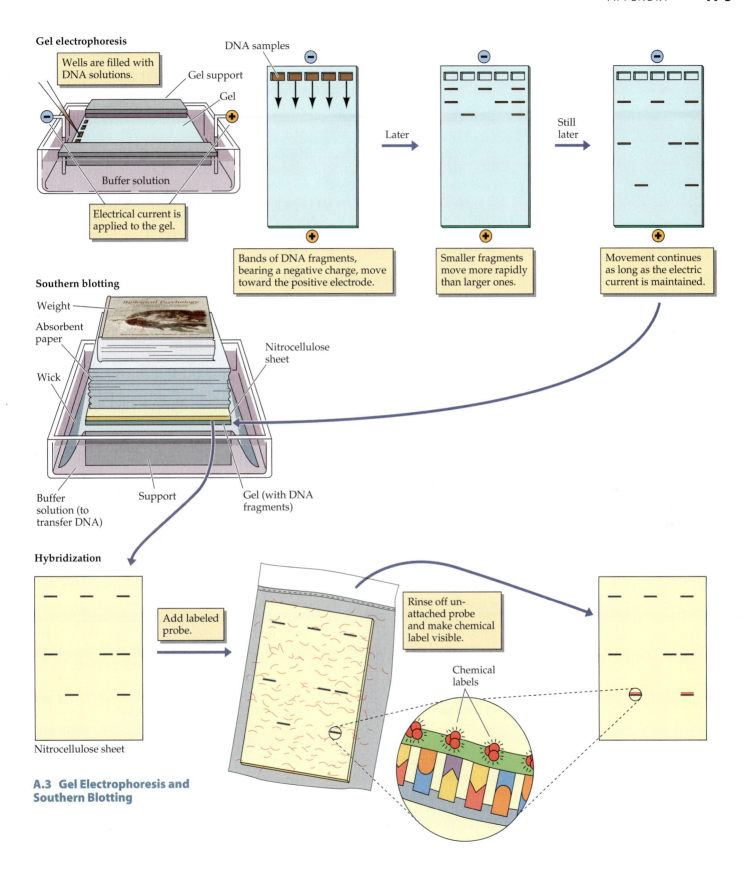

Gel electrophoresis

Wells are filled with DNA solutions.

Gel support

Gel

Buffer solution

Electrical current is applied to the gel.

DNA samples

Bands of DNA fragments, bearing a negative charge, move toward the positive electrode.

Later

Smaller fragments move more rapidly than larger ones.

Still later

Movement continues as long as the electric current is maintained.

Southern blotting

Weight

Absorbent paper

Wick

Nitrocellulose sheet

Buffer solution (to transfer DNA)

Support

Gel (with DNA fragments)

Hybridization

Nitrocellulose sheet

Add labeled probe.

Rinse off un-attached probe and make chemical label visible.

Chemical labels

A.3 Gel Electrophoresis and Southern Blotting

diolabeled probe; we wait for the probe to find and hybridize with the gene of interest (if it is present), and we rinse the sheet to remove probe molecules that did not find the gene. Then we place photographic film next to the nitrocellulose. The particles emitted by the radioactive probe molecule will expose the film just as light does. If the radiolabeled probe found the gene, the film will be dark in one particular band, corresponding to the size of DNA fragment that contained the gene (see Figure A.3).

This process of looking for a particular sequence of DNA is called **Southern blotting,** named after the man who developed the technique, Edward Southern, and the final film is called a *Southern blot.* Southern blots are useful for determining whether related individuals share a particular gene or for assessing the evolutionary relatedness of different species. The developed blots, with their lanes of exposed bands (see Figure A.3), are often seen in popular-media accounts of "DNA fingerprinting" of individuals.

Northern blots identify particular mRNA transcripts

A more relevant method for our discussions is the **Northern blot** (whimsically named as the opposite of a Southern blot). A Northern blot can identify which tissues are expressing a particular gene. If liver cells are making a particular protein, for example, then some transcripts for the gene that encodes that protein should be present. So we can take the liver, grind it up, and use chemical processes to isolate most of the RNA (discarding the DNA and protein). The resulting mixture consists of RNA molecules of many different sizes: long, medium, and short transcripts. Gel electrophoresis will separate the transcripts by size, and we can blot the size-sorted mRNAs onto nitrocellulose sheets; the process is very similar to the Southern blot procedure.

To see whether the particular transcript that we're looking for is among the mRNAs, we construct a radiolabeled probe (of either DNA nucleotides or RNA nucleotides) that is complementary to the mRNA transcript of interest and long enough that it will hybridize only to that particular transcript. We incubate the nitrocellulose in the probe, allow time for the probe to hybridize with the targeted transcript (if present), rinse off any unused probe molecules, lay the nitrocellulose next to photographic film, and wait a day or so. If the transcript of interest is present, we should see a band on the film (see Figure A.3). The presence of several bands indicates that the probe has hybridized to more than one transcript and we need to make a more specific probe or alter chemical conditions to make the probe less likely to bind similar transcripts.

Because different gene transcripts are of different lengths, the transcript of interest should have reached a particular point in the electrophoresis gel: Small transcripts should have moved far; large transcripts should have moved only a little. If our probe has found the right transcript, the single band of labeling should be at the point that is appropriate for a transcript of that length.

In situ hybridization localizes mRNA transcripts within specific cells

Northern blots can tell us whether a particular *organ* has transcripts for a particular gene product. For example, Northern blot analyses have indicated that thousands of genes are transcribed only in the brain. Presumably the proteins encoded by these genes are used exclusively in the brain. But such results alone are not very informative, because the brain consists of so many different kinds of glial and neuronal cells. We can refine Northern blot analyses somewhat, by dissecting out a particular part of the brain—say, the hippocampus—to isolate mRNAs. Sometimes, though, it is important to know *exactly which cells* are making the transcript. In that case we use **in situ hybridization.**

With in situ hybridization we use the same sort of labeled probe, constructed of nucleotides that are complementary to (and will therefore hybridize with) the targeted transcript, as in Northern blots. Instead of using the probe to find and hybridize with the transcript on a sheet of nitrocellulose, however, we use the probe to find the transcripts "in place" (*in situ* in Latin)—that is, on a section of tissue. After rinsing off the probe molecules that didn't find a match, we can use autoradiography (see Box 2.3) to look for the probe in the tissue section. Any cells in the section that were transcribing the gene of interest will have transcripts in the cytoplasm that should have hybridized with our labeled probe (Figure A.4; see also Box 2.3). In situ hybridization therefore can tell us exactly which cells are expressing a particular gene.

Western blots identify particular proteins

Sometimes we wish to study a particular protein rather than its transcript. In such cases we can use antibodies. **Antibodies** are large, complicated molecules (proteins, in fact) that our immune system adds to the bloodstream to identify and fight invading microbes, thereby arresting and preventing disease (see Figure 15.20). But if we inject a rabbit or mouse with a sample of a protein of interest, we can induce the animal to create antibodies that recognize and attach to that particular protein, just as if it were an infection.

Once these antibodies have been purified and chemically labeled, we can use them to search for the target protein. We grind up an organ, isolate the proteins (discarding the DNA and RNA), and separate them by means of gel electrophoresis. Then we blot these proteins out of the gel and onto nitrocellulose. Next we use the antibodies to tell us whether the targeted protein is among those made by that organ. If the antibodies identify only the protein we care about, there should be a single band of labeling (if there are two or more, then the antibodies recognize more than one protein). Because proteins come in different sizes, the single band of label should be at the position corresponding to the size of the protein that we're studying. Such blots are called **Western blots.**

To review, Southern blots identify particular DNA pieces (genes), Northern blots identify particular RNA pieces (transcripts), and Western blots identify particular proteins (sometimes called *products*).

Antibodies can also tell us which cells possess a particular protein

If we need to know which particular cells within an organ such as the brain are making a particular protein, we can use the same sorts of antibodies that we use in Western blots, but in this case directed at that protein in tissue sections. We slice up the brain, expose the sections to the antibodies, allow time for them to find and attach to the protein, rinse off unattached antibodies, and use chemical treatments to visualize the antibodies. Cells that were making the protein will be labeled from the chemical treatments (see Box 2.3).

Because antibodies from the *immune* system are used to identify *cells* with the aid of *chemical* treatment, this method is called **immunocytochemistry,** or **ICC.** This technique can even tell us where, within the cell, the protein is found. Such information can provide important clues about the function of the protein. For example, if the protein is found in axon terminals, it may be a neurotransmitter.

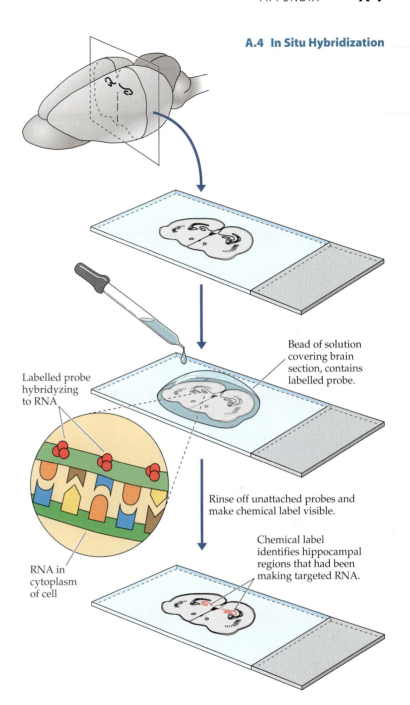

A.4 In Situ Hybridization

Bead of solution covering brain section, contains labelled probe.

Labelled probe hybridyzing to RNA

RNA in cytoplasm of cell

Rinse off unattached probes and make chemical label visible.

Chemical label identifies hippocampal regions that had been making targeted RNA.

Glossary

2-deoxyglucose (2-DG)   A molecule that resembles glucose. When injected into an animal, 2-DG accumulates more readily in active neurons than in inactive neurons, so it can indicate which parts of the brain are active during a given task.

5α-reductase   An enzyme that converts testosterone into dihydrotestosterone (DHT).

5-HT   See *serotonin*.

ABI   See *auditory brainstem implant*.

absolute refractory phase   See *refractory phase*.

abuse   In the context of substance-related disorders, a maladaptive pattern of substance usage that has lasted more than a month but does not fully meet the criteria for dependence.

accommodation   The process of focusing by the ciliary muscles and the lens to form a sharp image on the retina.

acetylcholine (ACh)   One of the best-known synaptic transmitters. Acetylcholine acts as an excitatory transmitter at synapses between motor nerves and skeletal muscles but as an inhibitory transmitter between the vagus nerve and the heart muscle.

acetylcholinesterase (AChE)   An enzyme that inactivates the transmitter acetylcholine both at synaptic sites and elsewhere in the nervous system.

ACh   See *acetycholine*.

AChE   See *acetylcholinesterase*.

acquired dyslexia   Dyslexia that occurs as a result of injury or disease. See also *alexia*.

acquired immune deficiency syndrome (AIDS)   A disease characterized by the loss of immune function that is spread by the human immunodeficiency virus (HIV).

act   Complex behavior, as distinct from a simple movement. Also called *action pattern*.

ACTH   See *adrenocorticotropic hormone*.

actin   A protein that, along with myosin, mediates the contraction of muscle fibers. See Figure 11.7.

action pattern   See *act*.

action potential   The propagated electrical message of a neuron that travels along the axon to adjacent neurons. Also called *nerve impulse*. See Figures 3.5, 3.6.

activational effect   A temporary change in behavior resulting from the administration of a hormone to an adult animal. Contrast with *organizational effect*.

active transport   The movement of cellular components and other substances via physiological processes that consume energy.

acupuncture   The insertion of needles at designated points on the skin to alleviate pain or neurological malfunction.

adaptation   In the context of sensory processing, the progressive loss of receptor sensitivity as stimulation is maintained. See Figure 8.7.

adaptation stage   The second stage in the stress response; it includes successful activation of the appropriate response systems and the reestablishment of homeostatic balance.

Aδ fiber   A moderately large, myelinated, and therefore fast-conducting axon, usually transmitting pain information. See Table 8.2. Contrast with *C fiber*.

adenohypophysis   See *anterior pituitary*.

adenosine   In the context of neural transmission, a neuromodulator that alters synaptic activity. Adenosine receptors are the site of action of caffeine. See Figure 4.9.

adequate stimulus   The type of stimulus for which a given sensory organ is particularly adapted. Light energy, for example, is the adequate stimulus for photoreceptors.

ADH   See *antidiuretic hormone*.

adipose tissue   Tissue made up of fat cells.

adipsia   A condition in which an individual refuses to drink.

adrenal cortex   The outer covering of the adrenal gland. Each of the three cellular layers of the adrenal cortex produces different hormones. See Figures 5.1, 5.14, Table 5.2.

adrenal gland   An endocrine gland adjacent to the kidney. See Figures 5.1, 5.15.

adrenal medulla   The inner core of the adrenal gland. The adrenal medulla secretes epinephrine and norepinephrine. See Figures 5.1, 5.15.

adrenaline   See *epinephrine*.

adrenocorticoids   A class of steroid hormones that are secreted by the adrenal cortex. Also called *adrenosteroids*.

adrenocorticotropic hormone (ACTH)   A tropic hormone secreted by the anterior pituitary gland that controls the production and release of hormones of the adrenal cortex. See Table 5.2, Figure 5.14.

adrenosteroids   See *adrenocorticoids*.

affective disorder   A disorder of mood, such as depression or bipolar disorder.

afferent   In reference to an axon, carrying nerve impulses from a sensory organ to the central nervous system, or from one region to another region of interest. Contrast with *efferent*.

affinity   See *binding affinity*.

afterpotential   The positive or negative change in membrane potential that may follow a nerve impulse.

agnosia   The inability to recognize objects, despite being able to describe them in terms of form and color; may occur after localized brain damage.

agonist   1. A molecule, usually a drug, that binds a receptor molecule and initiates a response like that of another molecule, usually a neurotransmitter. Contrast with *antagonist* (definition 1). 2. A muscle that moves a body part in the same general way as the muscle of interest; a synergistic muscle. Contrast with *antagonist* (definition 2). See also *synergist*.

agouti-related peptide (AGRP)   A peptide that is a naturally occurring antagonist to α-melanocyte stimulating hormone at melanocortin receptors.

agraphia   The inability to write.

AGRP   See *agouti-related peptide*.

AIDS   See *acquired immune deficiency syndrome*.

AIS   See *androgen insensitivity syndrome*.

alarm reaction   The initial response to stress.

aldosterone A mineralocorticoid hormone, secreted by the adrenal cortex, that helps maintain homeostasis in the concentrations of ions in blood and extracellular fluid by inducing the kidneys to conserve sodium.

alexia The inability to read.

alkaloids A class of chemicals, found in plants, that includes many psychoactive agents, such as curare, the opium alkaloids (morphine and codeine), and lysergic acid (to which LSD is related).

all-or-none property Referring to the fact that the amplitude of the nerve impulse is independent of the magnitude of the stimulus. See Table 3.1. Contrast with *graded potential.*

allele Any particular version of a gene.

allocortex Cortical tissue with three layers or unlayered organization.

allomone A chemical signal that is released outside the body by one species and affects the behavior of other species. See Figure 5.3. Contrast with *pheromone.*

allopregnanolone A naturally occurring steroid that modulates GABA receptor activity in much the same way that benzodiazepine anxiolytics do.

α-fetoprotein A protein found in the plasma of fetuses. In rodents, α-fetoprotein binds estrogens and prevents them from entering the brain.

α-melanocyte stimulating hormone (α-MSH) A peptide that binds the melanocortin receptor.

alpha motoneuron A motoneuron that controls the main contractile fibers (extrafusal fibers) of a muscle. See Figure 11.9.

α-MSH See *α-melanocyte stimulating hormone.*

alpha rhythm A brain potential that occurs during relaxed wakefulness, especially at the back of the head; its frequency is 8 to 12 Hz. See Figure 14.11.

α-synuclein A protein that has been implicated in Parkinson's disease.

ALS See *amyotrophic lateral sclerosis.*

altricial Referring to animals that are born in an undeveloped state and depend on maternal care, as human infants do. Contrast with *precocial.*

Alzheimer's disease A form of dementia that may appear in middle age but is more frequent among the aged.

amacrine cells A class of cells in the retina that contact both the bipolar cells and the ganglion cells, and are especially significant in inhibitory interactions within the retina.

amblyopia Reduced visual acuity that is not caused by optical or retinal impairments.

AMH See *anti-müllerian hormone.*

amine hormones A class of compounds, each composed of a single amino acid that has been modified into a related molecule, such as melatonin or epinephrine. Also called *monoamine hormones.*

amine neurotransmitter A neurotransmitter based on modifications of a single amino acid nucleus, such as acetylcholine, serotonin, or dopamine.

amino acid neurotransmitter A neurotransmitter that is itself an amino acid, such as GABA, glycine, or glutamate.

amnesia Severe impairment of memory.

amnestic Amnesia-causing.

AMPA α-Amino-3-hydroxy-5-methyl-4-isoxazole-propionic acid.

AMPA receptor A glutamate receptor that also binds the glutamate agonist AMPA. The AMPA receptor is responsible for most of the activity at glutaminergic synapses. See Box 4.2, Figure 18.9.

amphetamine A molecule that resembles the structure of the catecholamine transmitters and that enhances their activity.

amphetamine psychosis A delusional and psychotic state, closely resembling acute schizophrenia, that is brought on by repeated use of high doses of amphetamine.

amplitude Here, the distance of particle movement in a defined period of time, usually measured as dynes per square centimeter. See Box 9.1.

ampulla (pl. ampullae) An enlarged region of each semicircular canal that contains the receptor cells (hair cells) of the vestibular system. See Figure 9.14.

amygdala A group of nuclei in the medial anterior part of the temporal lobe. See Figure 2.10.

amyloid precursor protein (APP) A protein that, when cleaved by several enzymes, produces β-amyloid. Buildup of β-amyloid is thought to cause Alzheimer's disease.

amyotrophic lateral sclerosis (ALS) A disease in which motoneurons and their target muscles waste away.

analgesia Absence of or reduction in pain.

analgesic Referring to painkilling properties.

analogy Similarity of function, although the structures of interest may look different (e.g., the hand of a human and the trunk of an elephant).

anandamide An endogenous substance that binds the cannabinoid receptor molecule.

androgen insensitivity syndrome (AIS) A syndrome caused by a mutation of the androgen receptor gene that renders tissues insensitive to androgenic hormones like testosterone. Affected XY individuals are phenotypic females, but they have internal testes and regressed internal genital structures. See Figure 12.19.

androgens A class of hormones that includes testosterone and other male hormones. See Table 5.2, Figure 5.18.

androstenedione The chief sex hormone secreted by the human adrenal cortex. This hormone is responsible for the adult pattern of body hair in men and women.

angiogram A specialized X-ray image of the head, taken shortly after the cerebral blood vessels have been filled with a radiopaque dye by means of a catheter. This technique allows visualization of the major blood vessels and is used to assess stroke risk and other conditions.

angiotensin II A substance that is produced in the blood by the action of renin and that may be involved in the control of thirst.

angular gyrus A brain region in which strokes can lead to word blindness.

anion A negatively charged ion, such as a protein or chloride ion. Contrast with *cation.*

anomia The inability to name persons or objects readily.

anorexia Absence of appetite.

anorexia nervosa A syndrome in which individuals severely deprive themselves of food.

anosmia The inability to smell.

antagonist 1. A molecule, usually a drug, that interferes with or prevents the action of a transmitter. Contrast with *agonist* (definition 1). 2. A muscle that counteracts the effect of another muscle. Contrast with *synergist* or *agonist* (definition 2).

anterior Toward the front or head of an animal. Contrast with *posterior.*

anterior cingulate cortex A region of cortex curving just above the anterior corpus callosum; active during emotional processing, directing attention, and other cognitive processes. See Figures 15.14, 15.15.

anterior pituitary The front lobe of the pituitary gland; secretes tropic hormones. Also called *adenohypophysis.* See Figures 5.1, 5.13, Table 5.2.

anterograde amnesia The inability to form new memories beginning with the onset of a disorder. Contrast with *retrograde amnesia.*

anterograde degeneration The loss of the distal portion of an axon resulting from injury to the axon. Also called *wallerian degeneration.* See Box 7.1. Contrast with *retrograde degeneration.*

anterograde transport Movement of cellular substances away from the cell body toward the axon terminals. Contrast with *retrograde transport.*

anterolateral system A somatosensory system that carries most of the pain information from the body to the brain. Also called *spinothalamic system.* See Figure 8.24.

antibody A large protein that recognizes and permanently binds to particular shapes, normally as part of the immune system attack on foreign particles.

antidepressant drugs A class of drugs that relieve the symptoms of depression. Major categories include monoamine oxidase inhibitors, tricylics, and selective serotonin reuptake inhibitors.

antidiuretic hormone (ADH) See *arginine vasopressin.*

antigen A substance that stimulates the production of antibodies.

anti-müllerian hormone (AMH) A protein hormone secreted by the fetal testis that inhibits müllerian duct development. Also called *müllerian regression hormone.*

antipsychotic drugs A class of drugs that alleviate schizophrenia.

anxiety states A class of psychological disorders that include recurrent panic states, generalized persistent anxiety disorders, and posttraumatic stress disorders.

anxiolytics A class of substances that are used to combat anxiety; examples include

alcohol, opiates, barbiturates, and the benzodiazepines.

aphagia   The refusal to eat; often related to damage to the lateral hypothalamus.

aphasia   An impairment in language understanding and/or production that is caused by brain injury.

apical dendrite   The dendrite that extends from a pyramidal cell to the outermost surface of the cortex. Contrast with *basal dendrite*.

ApoE   Apolipoprotein E, a protein that may help break down amyloid. Individuals carrying the *ApoE4* allele are more likely to develop Alzheimer's disease.

apolipoprotein E   See *ApoE*.

apoptosis   See *cell death*.

APP   See *amyloid precursor protein*.

appetitive behavior   The second stage of mating behavior; helps establish or maintain sexual interaction. See Figure 12.2.

apraxia   An impairment in the ability to begin and execute skilled voluntary movements, even though there is no muscle paralysis.

aquaporins   Channels spanning the cell membrane that are specialized for conducting water molecules into or out of the cell.

arachnoid   The thin covering (one of the three meninges) of the brain that lies between the dura mater and pia mater.

arborization   The elaborate branching of dendrites of some neurons.

arcuate fasciculus   A tract connecting Wernicke's speech area to Broca's speech area. See Figure 19.8.

arcuate nucleus   An arc-shaped hypothalamic nucleus.

area 17   See *primary visual cortex*.

area postrema   One of the circumventricular nuclei that have weak blood–brain barriers. See Figure 13.15.

arginine vasopressin (AVP)   A peptide hormone from the posterior pituitary that promotes water conservation and increases blood pressure, controlling the removal of water from blood by the kidneys. Also called just *vasopressin* or *antidiuretic hormone*. See Table 5.2.

aromatase   An enzyme that converts many androgens into estrogens.

aromatization   The chemical reaction that converts testosterone to estradiol, and other androgens to other estrogens.

aromatization hypothesis   The hypothesis that testicular androgens enter the brain and are converted there into estrogens to masculinize the developing nervous system of some rodents.

aspartate   An amino acid transmitter that is excitatory at many synapses.

Asperger's syndrome   Sometimes called *high-functioning autism*, a syndrome characterized by difficulties in social cognitive processing; usually accompanied by strong language skills.

associative learning   A type of learning in which an association is formed between two stimuli or between a stimulus and a response; includes both classical and instrumental conditioning. Contrast with *nonassociative learning*.

astereognosis   The inability to recognize objects by touching and feeling them.

astrocyte   A star-shaped glial cell with numerous processes (extensions) that run in all directions. The extensions of astrocytes provide structural support for the brain and may isolate receptive surfaces. See Figure 2.20.

ataxia   An impairment in the direction, extent, and rate of muscular movement; often caused by cerebellar pathology.

attention   A state or condition of selective awareness or perceptual receptivity, possibly involving the activation of certain brain regions. See Figure 8.11.

atypical neuroleptics   A class of antischizophrenic drugs that have actions other than the dopamine D_2 receptor antagonism that characterizes the typical neuroleptics. These drugs often feature selective and high-affinity antagonism of serotonin $5HT_2$ receptors.

audiologist   A person who measures hearing abilities.

auditory brainstem implant (ABI)   A type of auditory prosthesis in which implanted microphones directly stimulate the auditory nuclei of the brainstem rather than the cochlea.

auditory cortex   A region of the temporal lobe that receives input from the medial geniculate nucleus. See Figure 9.6.

auditory-evoked potential   A change in EEG potential that follows presentation of an auditory stimulus.

auditory nerve   Cranial nerve VIII, which runs from the cochlea to the brainstem auditory nuclei. Also called *vestibulocochlear nerve*. See Figures 2.4, 9.1.

aura   In epilepsy, the unusual sensations or premonition that may precede the beginning of a seizure. See Box 3.2.

australopithecine   Of or related to *Australopithecus*, a primate genus, known only from the fossil record, thought to be an ancestor to humans. See Figure 6.15.

autism   A disorder arising during childhood, characterized by social withdrawal and stereotypy.

autocrine   Referring to a signal that is secreted by a cell into its environment and that feeds back to the same cell. See Figure 5.3.

autonomic ganglia   One of the three main divisions of the peripheral nervous system; includes the two chains of sympathetic ganglia and the more peripheral parasympathetic ganglia.

autonomic nervous system   The part of the peripheral nervous system that supplies neural connections to glands and to smooth muscles of internal organs. Its two divisions (sympathetic and parasympathetic) act in opposite fashion. See Figure 2.6.

autonomic response specificity   Patterns of bodily response governed by the autonomic nervous system that are characteristic of an individual.

autoradiography   A histological technique that shows the distribution of radioactive chemicals in tissues.

autoreceptor   A receptor for a synaptic transmitter that is located in the presynaptic membrane. Autoreceptors tell the axon terminal how much transmitter has been released.

autosome   One of a pair of chromosomes that are identical. All chromosomes except the sex chromosomes are autosomes.

AVP   See *arginine vasopressin*.

axo-axonic   Referring to a synapse in which a presynaptic axon terminal synapses onto another axon's terminal. Contrast with *axodendritic* and *dendro-dendritic*.

axo-dendritic   Referring to a synapse in which a presynaptic axon terminal synapses onto a dendrite of the postsynaptic neuron, either via a dendritic spine or directly onto the dendrite itself. Contrast with *axo-axonic* and *dendro-dendritic*.

axon   A single extension from the nerve cell that carries nerve impulses from the cell body to other neurons. See Figures 2.19, 2.22.

axon collateral   A branch of an axon from a single neuron.

axon hillock   A cone-shaped area from which the axon originates out of the cell body. Depolarization must reach a critical threshold at the axon hillock for the neuron to transmit a nerve impulse. See Figure 2.21.

axon terminal   The end of an axon or axon collateral, which forms a synapse on a neuron or other target.

axonal transport   The transportation of materials from the neuron cell body to distant regions in the dendrites and axons, and from the axon terminals back to the cell body.

B cell   See *B lymphocyte*.

B lymphocyte   An immune system cell that mediates humoral immunity. Also called *B cell*. See Figure 15.20.

ballistic movement   A rapid muscular movement that is thought to be organized or programmed by the cerebellum. Contrast with *ramp movement*.

barbiturates   A class of drugs that exert a tranquilizing effect by inhibiting the activity of neurons.

baroreceptor   A pressure receptor in the heart or a major artery that detects a fall in blood pressure and communicates that information to the brain via the autonomic nervous system.

basal dendrite   One of several dendrites on a pyramidal cell that extend horizontally from the cell body. Contrast with *apical dendrite*.

basal forebrain   A ventral region in the forebrain that has been implicated in sleep and Alzheimer's disease. See Figure 4.2.

basal ganglia   A group of forebrain nuclei (caudate nucleus, globus pallidus, and putamen) found deep within the cerebral hemispheres. See Figures 2.8, 2.10, 11.17.

basal metabolism   The rate of metabolism when a body is at rest.

basal nucleus of Meynert   See *magnocellular nucleus of the basal forebrain*.

base   A component of a DNA or RNA molecule. DNA contains four bases (adenine, thymine, cytosine, and guanine), a pair of which forms each rung of the molecule. The order of these bases determines the genetic information of a DNA molecule.

basic rest–activity cycle   A cycle of repeating periods of rest and activity that occur both in waking hours and during sleep.

basilar artery   An artery formed by the fusion of the vertebral arteries; its branches supply blood to the brainstem and to posterior portions of the cerebral hemispheres. See Figure 2.15.

basilar membrane   A membrane in the cochlea that contains the principal structures involved in auditory transduction. See Figures 9.1, 9.2.

Bcl-2   A family of genes, the protein products of which regulate apoptosis.

BDNF   See *brain-derived neurotrophic factor*.

BEAM   See *brain electrical activity mapping*.

behavioral intervention   An approach to finding relations between bodily variables and behavioral variables that involves intervening in the behavior of an organism and looking for resultant changes in body structure or function. See Figure 1.2. Contrast with *somatic intervention*.

behavioral neuroscience   Field of study concerned with the ways in which nervous system activity manifests in behavior.

behavioral sensitization   Exaggerated responsiveness to a seemingly benign environmental stimulus; associated with posttraumatic stress disorder.

behavioral teratology   The study of impairments in behavior that are produced by embryonic or fetal exposure to toxic substances.

Bell's palsy   A disorder, usually caused by viral infection, in which the facial nerve on one side stops conducting impulses, resulting in paralysis on one side of the face. See Figure 15.7.

benzodiazepines   A class of antianxiety drugs that bind with high affinity to receptor molecules in the central nervous system; one example is diazepam (Valium).

β-amyloid   A protein that accumulates in senile plaques in Alzheimer's disease.

β-secretase   An enzyme that cleaves amyloid precursor protein (APP), forming β-amyloid, which can lead to Alzheimer's disease.

bigamy   A mating system in which an individual has two mates or spouses. Contrast with *monogamy* and *polygamy*.

binaural   Pertaining to the two ears.

binaural detection   The detection of sound using two ears. See Figure 9.10. Contrast with *monaural detection*.

binaural interaction   The interaction of signals from two ears; especially important for localizing auditory stimuli.

binding affinity   Theoretically, the length of time that a transmitter or drug molecule binds to a receptor molecule. Practically, the concentration of transmitter or drug molecule that is required to bind half of the receptors at equilibrium.

binge eating   The paroxysmal intake of large quantities of food, often of poor nutritional value, and in the case of bulimia often followed by induced vomiting or diarrhea.

binocular deprivation   Depriving both eyes of form vision, as by sealing the eyelids. Contrast with *monocular deprivation*.

binocular disparity   The slight difference between the views from the two eyes; important in depth perception.

bioavailable   Referring to a substance, usually a drug, that is present in the body in a form that is able to interact with physiological mechanisms.

biological marker   A biological variable that accompanies a psychological disorder, irrespective of whether it directly causes the disorder.

biological psychology   Study of the biological bases of psychological processes and behavior.

biological rhythm   Any change in a biological measure that repeats periodically.

biotransformation   The process in which enzymes convert a drug into a metabolite that is itself active, possibly in ways that are substantially different from the actions of the original substance.

bipolar cells   A class of interneurons of the retina that receive information from rods and cones and pass the information to retinal ganglion cells. See Figure 10.7. See also *amacrine cells*.

bipolar disorder   A psychiatric disorder characterized by periods of depression that alternate with excessive, expansive moods. Also called *manic–depressive illness*. Contrast with *unipolar depression*.

bipolar neuron   A nerve cell that has a single dendrite at one end and a single axon at the other end; found in some vertebrate sensory systems. See Figure 2.19. Contrast with *multipolar neuron* and *monopolar neuron*.

blind spot   The place through which blood vessels enter the retina. Because there are no receptors in this region, light striking it cannot be seen. See Figure 10.1.

blob   A region of visual cortex distinguished by stains for the enzyme cytochrome oxidase. See Figure 10.23.

blood–brain barrier   The mechanisms that makes the movement of substances from capillaries into brain cells more difficult than exchanges in other body organs, thus affording the brain greater protection from exposure to some substances found in the blood.

blotting   Transferring DNA, RNA, or protein fragments to nitrocellulose following separation via gel electrophoresis. The blotted substance can then be labeled.

bouton   See *synaptic bouton*.

bovine spongiform encephalopathy (BSE)   Mad cow disease; a disorder caused by improperly formed prion proteins, leading to dementia and death. See also *Creutzfeldt–Jakob disease*.

brain-derived neurotrophic factor (BDNF)   A protein purified from the brains of many animals that can keep some classes of neurons alive; resembles nerve growth factor.

brain electrical activity mapping (BEAM)   A system of analysis and display of electrical brain signals.

brain explant   A piece of tissue taken out of the brain from one individual, to be either kept alive in a dish or transplanted into another individual.

brain self-stimulation   The process in which animals will work to provide electrical stimulation to particular brain sites, presumably because the experience is very rewarding.

brainstem   The region of the brain that consists of the midbrain, the pons, and the medulla.

Brattleboro rat   A rat that has a mutation in the gene for vasopressin that keeps the animal from producing functional hormone. Brattleboro rats show symptoms of diabetes insipidus.

brightness   One of the basic dimensions (along with hue and saturation) of light perception; varies from dark to light. See Figure 10.5.

Broca's aphasia   An impairment in speech production; related to damage in Broca's area. See Figure 19.7.

Broca's area   An area in the frontal region of the left hemisphere of the brain that is involved in the production of speech. See Figures 19.6, 19.7, 19.8.

Brodmann's areas   A classification of cortical regions based on subtle variations in the relative appearance of the six layers of isocortex.

brown fat   Tissue made up of fat cells that is found especially around vital organs in the trunk and around the cervical and thoracic levels of the spinal cord. Because it is capable of intense metabolism, brown fat can generate heat. Also called *brown adipose tissue*.

BSE   See *bovine spongiform encephalopathy*.

bulimia   A syndrome in which individuals believe themselves fatter than they are and periodically gorge themselves, usually with "junk food," and then either vomit or take laxatives to avoid weight gain. Also called *bulimia nervosa*.

bungarotoxin   A neurotoxin, isolated from the venom of the bungarus snake, that selectively blocks acetylcholine receptors.

C fiber   A small, unmyelinated axon that conducts pain information slowly and adapts slowly. See Table 8.2. Contrast with *Aδ fiber*.

c-fos   An immediate early gene, expressed by many neurons shortly after they have been activated. Identifying such cells through immunocytochemistry can provide a snapshot of brain regions active during a particular behavior. See Box 2.3.

caffeine   A stimulant compound found in coffee, cacao, and other plants that may have evolved to protect plants against insect predators. Caffeine stimulates and causes uncoordinated behavior in insects and inhibits their growth and reproduction.

CAH   See *congenital adrenal hyperplasia.*

calcitonin   A hormone released by the thyroid gland. See Table 5.2.

calorie   The amount of energy required to raise the temperature of 1 mL of water by 1°C.

CAM   See *cell adhesion molecule.*

cAMP   See *cyclic adenosine monophosphate.*

cAMP responsive element–binding protein (CREB)   A protein that is activated by cyclic AMP (cAMP) so that it now binds the promoter region of several genes involved in neural plasticity. See Figure 18.9.

cannabinoid receptor   A receptor that selectively binds substances that resemble the active ingredient in marijuana, THC. Two principal subtypes of cannabinoid receptors are known, identified as CB1 and CB2 receptors.

cannabinoids   A class of substances that bind the same endogenous receptors that are bound by the active ingredient in marijuana, Δ9-tetrahydrocannabinol (THC).

capsaicin   A compound synthesized by various plants, to deter predators, that mimics the experience of burning. Capsaicin is responsible for the burning sensation in chili peppers.

carotid arteries   The major arteries that ascend the left and right sides of the neck to the brain. The branch that enters the brain is called the *internal carotid artery.* See Figure 2.15.

CART   See *cocaine- and amphetamine-regulated transcript.*

caspases   A family of proteins that regulate cell death (apoptosis).

castration   Removal of the gonads, usually the testes.

CAT   See *computerized axial tomography.*

cataplexy   Sudden loss of muscle tone, leading to collapse of the body without loss of consciousness.

catecholamines   A class of monoamines that serve as neurotransmitters, including dopamine and norepinephrine. See Table 4.1.

cation   A positively charged ion, such as a potassium or sodium ion. Contrast with *anion.*

caudal   In the context of anatomy, referring to structures toward the tail end of an organism. Contrast with *rostral.*

caudate nucleus   One of the basal ganglia; it has a long extension or tail. See Figure 2.10.

CCK   See *cholecystokinin.*

cell adhesion molecule (CAM)   A protein found on the surface of a cell that guides cell migration and/or axonal pathfinding.

cell assembly   A large group of cells that tend to be active at the same time because they have been activated simultaneously or in close succession in the past.

cell-autonomous   Referring to cell processes that are directed by the cell itself rather than under the influence of other cells.

cell body   The region of a neuron that is defined by the presence of the cell nucleus. See Figures 2.19, 2.23. Also called *soma.*

cell–cell interactions   The general process during development in which one cell affects the differentiation of other, usually neighboring, cells.

cell death   The developmental process during which "surplus" nerve cells die. Also called *apoptosis.* See Figure 7.3.

cell differentiation   The developmental stage in which cells acquire distinctive characteristics, such as those of neurons, as the result of expressing particular genes. See Figure 7.3.

cell-mediated immunity   An immunological response that involves T lymphocytes. See Figure 15.20. Contrast with *humoral immunity.* See also *immune system.*

cell membrane   The lipid bilayer that ensheathes a cell, thus enveloping the cytoplasm and organelles of the cell.

cell migration   The movement of cells from site of origin to final location. See Figures 7.3, 7.4.

cell nucleus   The spherical central structure of a cell that contains the chromosomes of eukaryotic cells.

cell proliferation   The production of cells by mitotic division (mitosis). See Figure 7.4.

cellular fluid   See *intracellular fluid.*

central deafness   A hearing impairment that is related to lesions in auditory pathways or centers, including sites in the brainstem, thalamus, or cortex. Contrast with *conduction deafness, cortical deafness,* and *sensorineural deafness.*

central modulation of sensory information   The process in which higher brain centers, such as the cortex and thalamus, suppress some sources of sensory information and amplify others.

central nervous system (CNS)   The portion of the nervous system that includes the brain and the spinal cord. See Figures 2.3, 2.9.

central pattern generator   Neural circuitry that is responsible for generating a rhythmic pattern of behavior, such as walking.

central sulcus   A major groove that divides the frontal lobe from the parietal lobe. See Figure 2.7.

cephalic   See *rostral.*

cerebellar cortex   The outer surface of the cerebellum.

cerebellum (pl. cerebellums or cerebella)   A structure located at the back of the brain, dorsal to the pons, that is involved in the central regulation of movement. See Figures 2.7, 2.9, 2.11.

cerebral cortex   The outer covering of the cerebral hemispheres, which consists largely of nerve cell bodies and their branches. See Figure 2.12.

cerebral hemispheres   The right and left halves of the forebrain. See Figure 2.9.

cerebral ventricle   A cavity in the brain that contains cerebrospinal fluid. See Figure 2.14.

cerebrospinal fluid (CSF)   The fluid that fills the cerebral ventricles. See Figure 2.14.

cerveau isolé   An experimental preparation in which an animal's nervous system has been cut in the upper midbrain, dividing the brain from the brainstem. See Figure 14.20. Contrast with *encéphale isolé.*

cervical   Referring to the neck region. See Figures 2.5, 2.6.

cGMP   See *cyclic guanosine monophosphate.*

ChAT   See *choline acetyltransferase.*

chemical transmitter   See *neurotransmitter.*

chemoaffinity hypothesis   The notion that each cell has a chemical identity that directs it to synapse on the proper target cell during development. See Box 7.2.

chemoattractants   Compounds that attract particular classes of growth cones. Contrast with *chemorepellents.*

chemorepellents   Compounds that repel particular classes of growth cones. Contrast with *chemoattractants.*

chlorpromazine   An antipsychotic drug, one of the class of phenothiazines.

cholecystokinin (CCK)   A hormone that is released from the lining of the small intestine and that may be involved in the satiation of hunger. See Table 5.2.

choline acetyltransferase (ChAT)   An important enzyme involved in the synthesis of the neurotransmitter acetylcholine. See Box 4.1.

cholinergic   Referring to cells that use acetylcholine as their synaptic transmitter.

choreic movement   An uncontrollable, brief, and forceful muscular movement that is related to basal ganglia dysfunction.

choroid plexus   A highly vascular portion of the lining of the ventricles that secretes cerebrospinal fluid.

chromosome   A complex of condensed strands of DNA and associated protein molecules; found in the nucleus of cells.

ciliary muscle   One of the muscles that controls the shape of the lens inside the eye, focusing an image on the retina. See Figure 10.2.

cilium (pl. cilia)   A hairlike extension; the extensions in the hair cells of the cochlea, for example, are cilia. See Figure 9.1.

cingulate cortex   A region of medial cerebral cortex that lies dorsal to the corpus callosum. Also called *cingulum.* See Figures 2.10, 16.17.

cingulate gyrus   A cortical portion of the limbic system, found in the frontal and parietal midline. See Figure 2.7.

cingulum (pl. cingula)   See *cingulate cortex.*

circadian oscillator   A theoretical circuit with an output that repeats about once per day.

circadian rhythm   A pattern of behavioral, biochemical, and physiological fluctuation that has a 24-hour period.

circannual   Occurring on a roughly annual basis.

circle of Willis   A structure at the base of the brain that is formed by the joining of the carotid and basilar arteries. See Figure 2.15.

circuit   An assemblage that includes an arrangement of neurons and their interconnections. Circuits often perform a particular limited function. In a local circuit, all the neurons are contained within a level of brain organization of a particular region. Contrast with *system*.

circumvallate papillae One of three types of small structures on the tongue that contain taste receptors; the other two types are foliate and fungiform papillae. See Figure 9.16.

circumventricular organ An organ that lies in the wall of a cerebral ventricle. Circumventricular organs contain receptor sites that can be affected by substances in the cerebrospinal fluid. See Figure 13.15.

CJD See *Creutzfeldt–Jakob disease*.

classical conditioning A type of associative learning in which an originally neutral stimulus (the *conditioned stimulus*, or *CS*)—through pairing with another stimulus that elicits a particular response (the *unconditioned stimulus*, or *US*)—acquires the power to elicit that response when presented alone. A response elicited by the US is called an *unconditioned response* (*UR*); a response elicited by the CS alone is called a *conditioned response* (*CR*). Also called *Pavlovian conditioning*. Contrast with *instrumental conditioning*.

clitoris (pl. clitorides) A small mound of tissue just anterior to the vaginal opening. Stimulation of the clitoris produces orgasm in most women. See Figures 12.8, 12.16.

cloaca (pl. cloacae) The sex organ in many birds, through which sperm are discharged (in the male) and eggs are laid (in the female). This is the same passage through which wastes are eliminated.

cloacal exstrophy A rare medical condition in which XY individuals are born completely lacking a penis.

clones Asexually produced organisms that are genetically identical.

closed-loop control mechanism A control mechanism that provides a flow of information from whatever is being controlled to the device that controls it. See Figure 11.3. Contrast with *open-loop control mechanism*.

clozapine An antipsychotic drug.

CMR1 See *cool-menthol receptor 1*.

CNS See *central nervous system*.

CNV See *contingent negative variation*.

cocaine A drug of abuse, derived from the coca plant, that acts by potentiating catecholamine stimulation.

cocaine- and amphetamine-regulated transcript (CART) A peptide produced in the brain when an animal is injected with either cocaine or amphetamine. Associated with the appetite-control circuitry of the hypothalamus.

coccygeal Referring to the last, caudalmost, class of vertebrae in the spinal column. See Figure 2.6.

cochlea A snail-shaped structure in the inner ear that contains the primary receptor cells for hearing. See Figure 9.1.

cochlear amplifier The mechanism by which the cochlea is physically distorted by outer hair cells in order to "tune" the cochlea to be particularly sensitive to some frequencies more than others.

cochlear implant An electromechanical device that detects sounds and selectively stimulates nerves in different regions of the cochlea via surgically implanted electrodes.

cochlear nuclei Brainstem nuclei that receive input from auditory hair cells and send output to the superior olivary complex. See Figure 9.6.

coding The rules by which action potentials in a sensory system reflect a physical stimulus.

codon A set of three nucleotides that uniquely encodes one particular amino acid. A series of codons determines the structure of a peptide or protein.

cognitive map A mental representation of a spatial relationship.

coitus The sexual act. Also called *copulation*.

collateral sprouting The formation of a new branch on an axon, usually in response to the uncovering of unoccupied postsynaptic sites. See Figure 19.24.

colliculus (pl. colliculi) A small elevation. Two pairs of colliculi are found on the dorsal surface of the midbrain. See Figure 2.7. The rostral pair (the superior colliculi) receive visual information (see Figure 10.14); the caudal pair (the inferior colliculi) receive auditory information (see Figure 9.6).

colloid A large, gluelike molecule that cannot pass through the cell membrane. When injected into the peritoneum, colloids attract and retain water by osmotic pressure.

co-localization Here, the appearance of more than one neurotransmitter in a given presynaptic terminal.

commissural fiber An axon that crosses the sagittal midline.

comorbid Referring to the tendency of certain diseases or disorders to occur together in individuals.

competitive In the context of psychopharmacology, referring to a substance that directly competes with the endogenous ligand for binding to a receptor molecule. See Figure 4.7. Contrast with *noncompetitive*.

complex cortical cell A cell in the visual cortex that responds best to a bar of a particular size and orientation anywhere within a particular area of the visual field. See Figure 10.17. Contrast with *simple cortical cell*.

complex environment See *enriched condition*.

complex partial seizure In epilepsy, a type of seizure that doesn't involve the entire brain, and therefore can cause a wide variety of symptoms. See Box 3.2.

computerized axial tomography (CAT) A noninvasive technique for examining brain structure in humans through computer analysis of X-ray absorption at several positions around the head; affords a virtual direct view of the brain. The resulting images are referred to as *CAT scans* or *CT scans*. See Figure 2.16.

concentration gradient Variation of concentration of a substance within a region. See Figure 3.2.

concordant Referring to any trait that is seen in both individuals of identical twins. Contrast with *discordant*.

conditional learning A type of learning that teaches that a particular response to a particular stimulus is appropriate in one setting but not another.

conditioned response (CR) See *classical conditioning*.

conditioned stimulus (CS) See *classical conditioning*.

conditioned taste aversion The behavior in which an animal refuses to eat a food if it previously has become ill after eating that food.

conditioning A form of learning in which an organism comes to associate two stimuli, or a stimulus and a response. See Box 17.1. See also *classical conditioning* and *instrumental conditioning*.

condom A rubber sheath that is fitted over the penis to trap semen during sexual intercourse in order to prevent pregnancy and the transmission of disease.

conduction aphasia A language disorder in which comprehension remains intact but repetition of spoken language is impaired; related to damage of the pathways connecting Wernicke's area and Broca's area.

conduction deafness A hearing impairment that is associated with pathology of the external-ear or middle-ear cavities. Contrast with *central deafness*, *cortical deafness*, and *sensorineural deafness*.

conduction velocity The speed at which an action potential is propagated along the length of an axon (or section of peripheral nerve).

conduction zone The part of the neuron over which action potentials may be actively propagated. Usually corresponds to the cell's axon.

cone One class of receptor cells in the retina that are responsible for color vision. The three types of cones have somewhat different sensitivities to light of different wavelengths. See Figure 10.7. Contrast with *rod*.

confabulate To fill in a gap in memory with a falsification; often seen in Korsakoff's syndrome.

congenital Present at birth.

congenital adrenal hyperplasia (CAH) Any of several genetic mutations that can result in exposure of a female fetus to androgens, which results in a clitoris that is larger than normal at birth.

congenital insensitivity to pain The condition of being born without pain perception.

consciousness The state of awareness of one's own existence and experience.

conserved In the context of evolution, referring to a trait that is passed on from a common ancestor to two or more descendant species.

consolidation A stage of memory formation in which information in short-term or intermediate-term memory is transferred to long-term memory. See Figure 17.13.

consolidation hypothesis　The hypothesis that information passes through two stages in memory formation. During the first stage the memory is held by perseveration (repetition) of neural activity and is easily disrupted. During the second stage the memory becomes fixed, or consolidated, and is no longer easily disrupted.

constraint-induced-movement therapy　A therapy for recovery of movement after stroke or injury, in which the person's unaffected limb is constrained while he is required to perform tasks with the affected limb.

contingent negative variation (CNV)　A slow, event-related potential that is recorded from the scalp. A CNV arises in the interval between a warning signal and a signal that directs action.

contralateral　Pertaining to a location on the opposite side of the body. See Box 2.1. Contrast with *ipsilateral*.

convergence　The phenomenon of neural connections in which many cells send signals to a single cell. See Figure 3.17. Contrast with *divergence*.

convergent evolution　The evolutionary process by which responses to similar ecological features bring about similarities in behavior or structure among animals that are only distantly related (i.e., that differ in genetic heritage).

cool-menthol receptor 1 (CMR1)　A sensory receptor, found in some free nerve endings, that opens an ion channel in response to a mild temperature drop or exposure to menthol. See Figure 8.23.

Coolidge effect　The propensity of an animal that has appeared sexually satiated with a present partner to resume sexual activity when provided with a novel partner.

copulation　See *coitus*.

copulatory behavior　Coitus.

copulatory lock　Reproductive behavior in which the male's penis swells after ejaculation so that the male and female are forced to remain joined for 5 to 10 minutes; occurs in dogs and some rodents, but not in humans.

cornea　The transparent outer layer of the eye, whose curvature is fixed, bends light rays, and is primarily responsible for forming the image on the retina. See Figure 10.2.

coronal plane　The plane that divides the body or brain into front and back parts. Also called *frontal plane* or *transverse plane*. See Box 2.1.

corpus callosum　The main band of axons that connects the two cerebral hemispheres. See Figures 2.7, 2.13.

correlation　The covariation of two measures.

correlational approach　An approach to finding relations between bodily variables and behavioral variables that involves finding the extent to which a particular body measure covaries with a particular behavioral measure. See Figure 1.2.

cortex (pl. cortices)　Outer layers. 1. The cerebral cortex consists of the outer layers (gray matter) of the cerebral hemispheres.

See Figure 2.8. 2. The cerebellar cortex consists of the outer layers of the cerebellum. 3. The adrenal cortex consists of the outer layers of the adrenal gland. See Figure 5.14.

cortical barrel　A barrel-shaped portion of somatosensory cortex in rodents. Each barrel receives input from receptors of an individual whisker. See Figure 7.22.

cortical column　One of the vertical columns that constitute the basic organization of the isocortex. See Figure 8.17.

cortical deafness　A hearing impairment that is caused by a fault or defect in the cortex. Contrast with *central deafness, conduction deafness,* and *sensorineural deafness*.

cortical plate　A structure arising from the early proliferation of cells at the rostral end of the neural tube; the beginnings of the cerebral cortex.

corticospinal system　See *pyramidal system*.

corticosteroids　A class of steroid hormones secreted from the adrenal cortex, including glucocorticoids and mineralocorticoids.

corticotropin-releasing hormone (CRH)　A releasing hormone, produced by the hypothalamus, that controls the daily rhythm of adrenocorticotropic hormone release.

cortisol　A glucocorticoid hormone of the adrenal cortex.

courtship　The period during which two potential sexual partners increase their attractiveness toward each other.

CR　See *classical conditioning*.

cranial　Referring to the skull (cranium).

cranial nerves　One of the three main subdivisions of the peripheral nervous system, composed of a set of pathways concerned mainly with sensory and motor systems associated with the head. There are 12 cranial nerves, typically designated by Roman numerals I through XII. See Figure 2.4.

CREB　See *cAMP responsive element–binding protein*.

cretinism　Reduced stature and mental retardation caused by thyroid deficiency.

Creutzfeldt–Jakob disease (CJD)　A brain disorder in humans, leading to dementia and death, that is caused by improperly folded prion proteins. CJD is the human equivalent of bovine spongiform encephalopathy (BSE), or mad cow disease.

CRH　See *corticotropin-releasing hormone*.

crib death　See *sudden infant death syndrome*.

critical range　The range within which a particular biological measure must remain to ensure good health.

cross-tolerance　A condition in which the development of tolerance for an administered drug causes an individual to develop tolerance for another drug.

cryptochrome　A protein that participates in the molecular circadian clock.

crystallization　The final stage of birdsong formation, in which fully formed adult song is achieved.

CS　See *classical conditioning*.

CSF　See *cerebrospinal fluid*.

CT scan　See *computerized axial tomography*.

cupula (pl. cupulae)　A small gelatinous column that forms part of the lateral-line system of aquatic animals and also occurs

within the vestibular system of mammals. See Figure 9.14.

curare　An alkaloid neurotoxin that causes paralysis by blocking acetylcholine receptors in muscle.

Cushing's syndrome　A condition in which levels of adrenal glucocorticoids are high, often arising from pituitary tumors, adrenal tumors, or deliberate therapy involving corticosteroids.

cyclic adenosine monophosphate (cyclic AMP, or cAMP)　A second messenger that is involved in the synaptic activities of dopamine, norepinephrine, and serotonin.

cyclic AMP　See *cyclic adenosine monophosphate*.

cyclic GMP　See *cyclic guanosine monophosphate*.

cyclic guanosine monophosphate (cyclic GMP, or cGMP)　A second messenger that is common in postsynaptic cells.

cytoarchitectonics　The study of anatomical divisions of the brain based on the kinds and spacing of cells and the distribution of axons.

cytokine　A protein that induces the proliferation of other cells, as in the immune system. Examples include interleukins and interferons.

cytoskeleton　The lattice of specialized proteins that give a cell its shape. Changes in the cytoskeleton allow neurons to change their shape and form new connections; therefore the cytoskeleton plays an important role in neural plasticity. See Figure 2.22.

DA　See *dopamine*.

dB　See *decibel*.

deafferentation　The removal of sensory (afferent) input.

death gene　A gene that is expressed only when a cell becomes committed to natural cell death (apoptosis).

decibel (dB)　A measure of sound intensity. See Box 9.1.

declarative memory　A memory that can be stated or described. Contrast with *nondeclarative memory*.

decomposition of movement　Difficulty of movement in which gestures are broken up into individual segments instead of being executed smoothly; a symptom of cerebellar lesions.

deep dyslexia　Dyslexia in which the patient reads a word as another word that is semantically related. Contrast with *surface dyslexia*.

degradation　Here, the process by which neurotransmitter molecules are broken down into inactive metabolites.

dehydration　Excessive loss of water.

delayed non-matching-to-sample　A test in which the subject must respond to the unfamiliar stimulus of a pair. See Figure 17.9.

delta wave　The slowest type of EEG wave, characteristic of stages 3 and 4 slow-wave sleep. See Figure 14.11.

Δ9-tetrahydrocannabinol (THC) The major active ingredient in marijuana.

dementia Drastic failure of cognitive ability, including memory failure and loss of orientation.

dementia pugilistica The dementia that develops in boxers; it is especially prominent in successful boxers because they participate in more bouts.

dendrite One of the extensions of the cell body that are the receptive surfaces of the neuron. See Figures 2.19, 2.23.

dendrite thorn See *dendritic spine*.

dendritic branching The pattern and quantity of branching of dendrites. See Figure 18.5.

dendritic knob A portion of olfactory receptor cells present in the olfactory epithelium. See Figure 9.18.

dendritic spine An outgrowth along the dendrite of a neuron. Also called *dendrite thorn*. See Figures 2.21, 2.23.

dendritic tree The full arrangement of dendrites of a single cell.

dendro-dendritic Referring to a type of synapse in which a synaptic connection forms between the dendrites of two neurons. Contrast with *axo-axonic* and *axo-dendritic*.

denervation supersensitivity A condition in which target cells, upon losing neural input, produce more than the normal number of receptors, resulting in an exaggerated response when synaptic transmitter is applied.

dentate gyrus A strip of gray matter in the hippocampal formation. See Figure 18.8.

deoxyribonucleic acid (DNA) A nucleic acid that is present in the chromosomes of cells and codes hereditary information.

dependence In the context of substance-related disorders, the strong desire to self-administer a drug of abuse.

depolarization A reduction in membrane potential (the inner membrane surface becomes less negative in relation to the outer surface); caused by excitatory neural messages. See Figure 3.5. Contrast with *hyperpolarization*.

depressant A drug that acts to reduce neural activity.

depression A psychiatric condition characterized by such symptoms as an unhappy mood; loss of interests, energy, and appetite; and difficulty in concentration. See also *bipolar disorder* and *unipolar depression*.

dermatome A strip of skin innervated by a particular spinal root. See Figure 8.15.

dermis The layer of skin beneath the outermost layer (the epidermis). See Figure 8.4.

dexamethasone suppression test A test of pituitary–adrenal function in which the subject is given dexamethasone, a synthetic glucocorticoid hormone, which should cause a decline in the production of adrenal corticosteroids.

DHT See *dihydrotestosterone*.

diabetes insipidus Excessive urination, caused by the failure of vasopressin to induce the kidneys to conserve water.

diabetes mellitus Excessive glucose in the urine, caused by the failure of insulin to induce glucose absorption by the body.

Diablo A protein released by mitochondria, in response to high calcium levels, that activates apoptosis.

diaschisis A temporary period of generalized impairment following brain injury.

dichotic listening technique A test in which different sounds are presented to each ear at the same time; used to determine hemispheric differences in processing auditory information. See Figure 19.14.

dichotic stimuli Stimuli that differ at the two ears.

dichromat An organism that has only two classes of wavelength-sensitive light receptor cells.

diencephalon The posterior part of the forebrain, including the thalamus and hypothalamus. See Figure 2.9.

differential classical conditioning Classical conditioning in which two conditioned stimuli are used in the same animal; one (CS+) is paired with the unconditioned stimulus, and the other (CS–) is unpaired and has no consequence for the animal.

differentiation See *cell differentiation*.

diffuse bipolar cell A retinal bipolar cell that receives input from several receptors. Contrast with *midget bipolar cell*.

digestion The process by which food is broken down to provide energy and nutrients.

dihydrotestosterone (DHT) The 5α-reduced metabolite of testosterone; a potent androgen that is principally responsible for the masculinization of the external genitalia in mammalian sexual differentiation. See Figure 12.17.

dimer A complex of two proteins that have bound together.

dioecious The collective term for species of animals that consist of two distinct forms, each of which specializes in producing only one sort of gamete—either ova or sperm.

discordant Referring to any trait that is seen in only one individual of identical twins. Contrast with *concordant*.

dishabituation The restoration of response amplitude following habituation.

dissociation Here, the loss of one function with damage to brain region A but not B, and the loss of a different function with damage to brain region B but not A.

dissociation constant Theoretically, the length of time a transmitter or drug molecule binds to a receptor molecule. Practically, the concentration of transmitter or drug molecule that is required to bind half of the receptors at equilibrium.

dissociative thinking A condition, seen in schizophrenia, that is characterized by disturbances of thought and difficulty relating events properly.

distal In the context of anatomy, referring to structures toward the periphery or toward the end of a limb. See Box 2.1. Contrast with *proximal*.

diurnal Active during the day. Contrast with *nocturnal*.

divergence The phenomenon of neural connections in which one cell sends signals to many other cells. See Figure 3.17. Contrast with *convergence*.

dizygotic Referring to twins derived from separate eggs. Such twins are no more closely related genetically than are other full siblings. Contrast with *monozygotic*.

DNA See *deoxyribonucleic acid*.

dopamine (DA) A synaptic transmitter produced mainly in the basal forebrain and diencephalon that is active in the basal ganglia, the olfactory system, and limited parts of the cerebral cortex. See Table 4.1, Figure 4.3.

dopaminergic Referring to cells that use dopamine as their synaptic transmitter.

dorsal In the context of anatomy, referring to structures toward the back of the body or the top of the brain. See Box 2.1. Contrast with *ventral*.

dorsal column system A somatosensory system that delivers most touch stimuli via the dorsal columns of spinal white matter to the brain. See Figure 8.14.

dorsal raphe One of the midbrain nuclei that give rise to most of the serotonergic projections of the brain.

dorsal root See *roots*.

dose–response curve (DRC) A formal plot of a drug's effects (on the *y*-axis) versus the dose given (on the *x*-axis). Analysis of dose–response curves can provide a range of information about the drug, such as its efficacy, potency, and safety. See Figure 4.8.

double-blind test A test of a drug or treatment in which neither the subjects nor the attending researchers know which subjects are receiving the drug (treatment) and which are receiving the placebo (control).

double dissociation The phenomenon in which condition or treatment A causes impairment on behavioral test X but no impairment on test Y, whereas condition B causes impairment on test Y but not on test X.

down-regulation A compensatory reduction in receptor availability at the synapses of a neuron. For example, repeated exposure to an agonist drug may cause a neuron to produce fewer of the type of receptors to which that drug binds. Contrast with *up-regulation*.

Down syndrome Mental retardation that is associated with an extra copy of chromosome 21.

DRC See *dose–response curve*.

dual-trace hypothesis The hypothesis that the formation of a memory involves first a relatively brief transient memory storage process followed by a stable change in the nervous system, which is a long-lasting memory trace.

dualism The notion, promoted by Descartes, that the mind is subject only to spiritual interactions, while the body is subject only to material interactions.

ductus deferens See *vas deferens*.

duplex theory A theory of pitch perception that combines place theory and volley theory.

dura mater   The outermost of the three coverings (meninges) that embrace the brain and spinal cord. See also *pia mater* and *arachnoid*.

dynamic phase of weight gain   The initial period following destruction of the ventromedial hypothalamus, during which the animal's body weight increases rapidly. See Figure 13.22. Contrast with *static phase of obesity*.

dynein   A protein "motor" that moves substances in axonal transport. See Figure 2.22. See also *kinesin*.

dynorphins   One of three kinds of endogenous opioids. See Table 4.1.

dyscontrol syndrome   A condition consisting of temporal lobe disorders that may underlie some forms of human violence.

dyskinesia   See *tardive dyskinesia*.

dyslexia   A reading disorder attributed to brain impairment.

dystrophin   A gene product that is needed for normal muscle function. Dystrophin is defective in some forms of muscular dystrophy.

eardrum   See *tympanic membrane*.

EC   See *enriched condition*.

ecstasy   See *MDMA*.

ECT   See *electroconvulsive shock therapy*.

ectoderm   The outer cellular layer of the developing fetus. The ectoderm gives rise to the skin and the nervous system.

ectopia   Something out of place—for example, clusters of neurons seen in unusual positions in the cortex of someone suffering from dyslexia. See Figure 19.10.

ectotherm   An animal whose body temperature is regulated by, and that gets most of its heat from, the environment. Examples include snakes and bees. Contrast with *endotherm*.

ED$_{50}$ Effective dose 50%; the dose of a drug that is required to produce half of its maximal effect. See Figure 4.8.

edema   The swelling of tissue, especially in the brain, in response to injury.

EEG   See *electroencephalography*.

efferent   In reference to an axon, carrying information from the nervous system to the periphery. Contrast with *afferent*.

efficacy   The extent to which a drug activates a response when it binds to a receptor. Receptor antagonist drugs have low efficacy; receptor agonists have high efficacy. See Figure 4.8.

egg   See *ovum*.

ejaculation   The forceful expulsion of semen from the penis.

electrical force   Here, the tendency of like-charged particles to repel each other and opposite-charged particles to attract each other.

electrical synapse   The region between neurons where the presynaptic and postsynaptic membranes are so close that the nerve impulse can jump to the postsynaptic membrane without first being translated into a chemical message. See Box 3.1.

electroconvulsive shock therapy (ECT)   A last-resort treatment for intractable depression in which a strong electrical current is passed through the brain, causing a seizure. Rapid relief from depressive symptoms often results, associated with improved accumulation of monoamine neurotransmitters in the brain.

electroencephalography (EEG)   The recording and study of gross electrical activity of the brain recorded from large electrodes placed on the scalp. See Figures 3.19, 14.11.

electromyography (EMG)   The electrical recording of muscle activity. See Figure 11.2.

electro-oculography (EOG)   The electrical recording of eye movements, useful in determining sleep stages.

electroretinography (ERG)   The electrical recording of responses of the retina to flashes of different stimuli.

electrostatic pressure   The propensity of charged molecules or ions to move, via diffusion, toward areas with the opposite charge.

embryo   The earliest stage in a developing animal; humans are considered to be embryos until 8 to 10 weeks after conception.

embryonic stem cell   A cell, derived from an embryo, that has the capacity to form any type of tissue that a donor might produce.

EMG   See *electromyography*.

encéphale isolé   An experimental preparation in which an animal's brainstem has been separated from the spinal cord by a cut below the medulla. See Figure 14.20. Contrast with *cerveau isolé*.

encephalization factor   A measure of brain size relative to body size.

encoding   A stage of memory formation in which the information entering sensory channels is passed into short-term memory. See Figure 17.13.

end-plate potential   The action potential that is induced at the neuromuscular junction when the axon terminal releases its neurotransmitter, which in vertebrates is acetylcholine.

endocannabinoid   An endogenous ligand of cannabinoid receptors; thus, a homolog of marijuana that is produced by the brain.

endocast   A cast of the cranial cavity of a skull, especially useful for studying fossils of extinct species.

endocrine   Referring to glands that release chemicals to the interior of the body. These glands secrete the principal hormones. See Figure 5.3.

endocrine gland   A gland that secretes products into the bloodstream to act on distant targets. See Figure 5.1. Contrast with *exocrine gland*.

endogenous   Produced inside the body. Contrast with *exogenous*.

endogenous ligand   Any substance, produced within the body, that selectively binds to the type of receptor that is under study. Contrast with *exogenous ligand*.

endogenous opioids   A family of peptide transmitters that have been called the body's own narcotics. The three kinds of endogenous opioids are enkephalins, endorphins, and dynorphins. See Table 4.1.

endogenous oscillator   A circuit that generates regularly repeating sequences of neural activity or behavior.

endorphins   One of three kinds of endogenous opioids. See Table 4.1.

endotherm   An animal whose body temperature is regulated chiefly by internal metabolic processes. Examples include mammals and birds. Contrast with *ectotherm*.

enkephalins   One of three kinds of endogenous opioids. See Table 4.1.

enriched condition (EC)   A condition in which laboratory rodents are housed in a large cage with several conspecifics and a variety of stimulus objects. Also called *complex environment*. See Figure 18.4. Contrast with *impoverished condition* and *standard condition*.

enteric nervous system   An extensive mesh-like system of neurons that governs the functioning of the gut. This system is semi-autonomous but is generally considered to be part of the autonomic nervous system.

entrainment   The process of synchronizing a biological rhythm to an environmental stimulus. See Figure 14.1.

enzyme   A complicated protein whose action increases the probability of a specific chemical reaction.

EOAE   See *evoked otoacoustic emission*.

EOG   See *electro-oculography*.

ependymal layer   See *ventricular zone*.

epidemiology   The statistical study of patterns of disease in the population.

epidermis   The outermost layer of skin, over the dermis. See Figure 8.4.

epididymis   A crescent-shaped structure next to the testis in which sperm are stored. See Figures 12.8, 12.17.

epilepsy   A brain disorder marked by major sudden changes in the electrophysiological state of the brain that are referred to as seizures. See Box 3.2.

epinephrine   A compound that acts both as a hormone (secreted by the adrenal medulla) and as a synaptic transmitter. Also called *adrenaline*. See Table 4.1.

episodic memory   Memory of a particular incident or a particular time and place.

EPSP   See *excitatory postsynaptic potential*.

equilibrium   In chemistry, the point at which all ongoing reactions are canceled or balanced by others, resulting in a stable, balanced, or unchanging system.

equilibrium potential   The state in which the tendency of ions to flow from regions of high concentration is exactly balanced by the opposing potential difference across the membrane.

ERG   See *electroretinography*.

ERP   See *event-related potential*.

estradiol   The primary type of estrogen that is secreted by the ovary. See Table 5.2.

estrogens   A class of steroid hormones produced by female gonads. See Table 5.2, Figures 5.14, 5.18.

estrus   The period during which female animals are sexually receptive.

eukaryote   Any cell in which the genetic material is contained within a nuclear envelope.

event-related potential (ERP)   A large change in electrical potential in the brain that is elicited by a discrete sensory or motor event. Also called *evoked potential*. See Figure 3.19.

evoked otoacoustic emission (EOAE)   A sound produced by the cochlea in response to acoustic stimulation. Contrast with *spontaneous otoacoustic emission*.

evoked potential   See *event-related potential*.

evolution   The process by which a population of interbreeding individuals change over long periods of time.

evolution by natural selection   The Darwinian theory that evolution proceeds by differential success in reproduction.

evolutionary psychology   A field devoted to asking how natural selection has shaped behavior, especially reproductive behaviors in humans and other animals.

excitatory   Anything that depolarizes a neuron and/or increases the likelihood that it will produce an action potential. Contrast with *inhibitory*.

excitatory postsynaptic potential (EPSP)   A depolarizing potential in the postsynaptic neuron that is caused by excitatory presynaptic impulses. EPSPs increase the probability that the postsynaptic neuron will fire a nerve impulse. See Figure 3.11. Contrast with *inhibitory postsynaptic potential*.

excitotoxicity   The property by which neurons die when overstimulated, as with large amounts of glutamate.

exhaustion phase   A stage in the response to stress that is caused by prolonged or frequently repeated stress and is characterized by increased susceptibility to disease.

exocrine gland   A gland that secretes products through ducts to the site of action. Contrast with *endocrine gland*.

exogenous   Arising from outside the body. Contrast with *endogenous*.

exogenous ligand   Any substance, originating from outside the body, that selectively binds to the type of receptor that is under study. Contrast with *endogenous ligand*.

expression   In the context of genetics, the process by which a cell makes an mRNA transcript of a particular gene.

external capsule   A light-colored band of fibers in the brain lateral to the putamen.

external ear   The part of the ear that we readily see (the pinna) and the canal that leads to the eardrum. See Figure 9.1.

external fertilization   The process by which eggs are fertilized outside of the female's body, as in many fishes and amphibians. Contrast with *internal fertilization*.

extinction   In conditioning, a feature in which the learned response wanes when not reinforced.

extracellular compartment   The fluid space that exists outside of the cells of the body. See Figure 13.12.

extracellular fluid   The fluid in the spaces between cells (interstitial fluid) and in the vascular system.

extracellular space   The space between cells.

extrafusal fiber   One of the ordinary muscle fibers that lie outside the spindles and provide most of the force for muscle contraction. See Figure 11.9. Contrast with *intrafusal fiber*.

extraocular muscle   One of the muscles attached to the eyeball that control its position and movements.

extrapyramidal system   A motor system that includes the basal ganglia and some closely related brainstem structures. See Figure 11.17.

extrastriate cortex   Visual cortex outside of area 17 (which is primary visual cortex, or striate cortex).

extrinsic   Here, referring to the class of factors arising from outside the individual that influence development. Contrast with *intrinsic*.

facial nerve   Cranial nerve VII, which innervates facial musculature and some sensory receptors. See Figures 2.4, 15.6.

fallopian tube   The structure between the ovary and the uterus where fertilization takes place in humans. Also called *oviduct* or *uterine tube*. See Figures 12.8, 12.17.

FAS   See *fetal alcohol syndrome*.

fast-twitch muscle fiber   A type of striated muscle that contracts rapidly but fatigues readily. Contrast with *slow-twitch muscle fiber*.

fat   A large, complex carbohydrate that provides long-term energy storage. A lipid.

fatal familial insomnia   An inherited disorder in which humans sleep normally at the beginning of their life, but in midlife stop sleeping, and 7 to 24 months later die.

fear conditioning   A form of learning in which fear comes to be associated with a previously neutral stimulus.

feature detector model   A model of visual pattern analysis that emphasizes linear and angular components of the stimulus array. Contrast with *spatial-frequency filter model*.

feedback circuit   A circuit in which output information is used to modulate the input of that same circuit. See also *negative feedback* and *positive feedback*.

fertilization   The fusion of sperm and egg to produce a zygote.

fetal alcohol syndrome (FAS)   A disorder, including mental retardation and characteristic facial anomalies, that affects children exposed to alcohol (through maternal ingestion) during fetal development.

fetus   A developing individual after the embryo stage. Humans are considered to be fetuses from 10 weeks after fertilization until birth.

filopodium (pl. filopodia)   A very fine, tubular outgrowth from the growth cone.

final common pathway   The motoneurons, because they direct all the activity of the spinal cord and brain to the muscles.

fission   The process of splitting in two. Some unicellular organisms reproduce by fission; that is, they simply split into two daughter cells.

fixed action pattern   Complex preprogrammed, species-specific behavior that is triggered by particular stimuli and carried out without sensory feedback.

flaccid paralysis   A loss of reflexes below the level of transection of the spinal cord.

flavor neophobia   An adaptive shyness to new flavors that some species employ as a defense against consuming large quantities of foods of unknown safety.

flexion reflex   The abrupt withdrawal of a limb in response to intense stimulation of the foot.

fMRI   See *functional MRI*.

foliate papillae   One of three types of small structures on the tongue that contain taste receptors; the other two types are circumvallate and fungiform papillae. See Figure 9.16.

follicle-stimulating hormone (FSH)   A tropic hormone, released by the anterior pituitary, that controls the production of estrogens and progesterone. See Table 5.2, Figures 5.14, 5.18.

forebrain   The frontal division of the neural tube, containing the cerebral hemispheres, the thalamus, and the hypothalamus. Also called *prosencephalon*. See Figure 2.9.

fornix (pl. fornices)   A fiber tract that extends from the hippocampus to the mammillary body. See Figures 2.7, 2.10.

Fourier analysis   The analysis of a complex pattern into the sum of sine waves. See Box 9.1.

fourth ventricle   The passageway within the pons that receives cerebrospinal fluid from the third ventricle and releases it to surround the brain and spinal cord. See Figure 2.14.

fovea (pl. foveae)   A small depression in the center of the retina that has a dense concentration of cones and maximal visual acuity. See Figure 10.2.

fragile X syndrome   A condition that is a frequent cause of inherited mental retardation; produced by a fragile site on the X chromosome that seems prone to breaking because the DNA there is unstable.

free nerve ending   An axon that terminates in the skin without any specialized cell associated with it. See Figure 8.4.

free-running   Referring to a rhythm of behavior shown by an animal deprived of external cues about time of day. See Figure 14.1.

free-running period   The natural period of a behavior that is displayed if external stimuli do not provide entrainment. See Figure 14.1.

frequency   The number of cycles per second in a sound wave; measured in hertz (Hz). See Box 9.1.

frontal lobe   The most anterior portion of the cerebral cortex. See Figure 2.7.

frontal plane   See *coronal plane*.

FSH   See *follicle-stimulating hormone*.

functional MRI (fMRI)   Magnetic resonance imaging that detects changes in blood flow and therefore identifies regions of the brain that are particularly active during a given task.

functional tolerance   Decreased responding to a drug after repeated exposures, generally as a consequence of up- or down-regulation of receptors.

fundamental   Here, the predominant frequency of an auditory tone or a visual scene. Harmonics are multiples of the fundamental. See Box 9.1.

fungiform papillae   One of three types of small structures on the tongue that contain taste receptors; the other two types are circumvallate and foliate papillae. See Figure 9.16.

fusiform gyrus   A region on the inferior surface of the cortex, at the junction of temporal and occipital lobes, that has been associated with recognition of faces. See Figure 19.20.

G proteins   A class of proteins that reside next to the intracellular portion of a receptor and that are activated when the receptor binds an appropriate ligand on the extracellular surface.

GABA   See *gamma-aminobutyric acid.*

gamete   A sex cell (sperm or ovum) that contains only unpaired chromosomes and therefore has only half the total number of autosomal chromosomes.

gamma-aminobutyric acid (GABA)   Probably the major inhibitory transmitter in the mammalian nervous system; widely distributed in both invertebrate and vertebrate nervous systems. See Table 4.1.

gamma efferent   A motor neuron that controls muscle spindle sensitivity. See Figure 11.9.

gamma motoneuron   A motor neuron that innervates the contractile tissue in a muscle spindle.

ganglion (pl. ganglia)   A collection of nerve cell bodies outside the central nervous system. Contrast with *nucleus.*

ganglion cells   A class of cells in the retina whose axons form the optic nerve. See Figure 10.7. See also *amacrine cells* and *bipolar cells.*

gas neurotransmitter   A diffusible gas, such as nitric oxide or carbon monoxide, that is produced and released by a neuron to alter the functioning of another neuron. Usually, gas neurotransmitters act at retrograde synapses.

gated   Referring to the property by which an ion channel may be opened or closed by factors such as chemicals, voltage changes, or mechanical actions. See Figure 3.6.

gel electrophoresis   A method of separating molecules of differing size or electrical charge by forcing them to flow through a gel. See Figure A.3 in the appendix.

gender identity   The way that one identifies oneself, and is identified by others, as a male or a female.

gene   A length of DNA that encodes the information for constructing a particular protein.

gene amplification   See *polymerase chain reaction.*

general anesthetic   A drug that renders an individual unconscious.

generalized seizure   An epileptic seizure that arises from pathology at brain sites and projects to widespread regions of the brain. Generalized seizures include loss of consciousness and symmetrical involvement of body musculature. See Box 3.2. See also *grand mal seizure* and *petit mal seizure.*

generator potential   A local change in the resting potential of a receptor cell that mediates between the impact of stimuli and the initiation of nerve impulses.

genetic constraints on learning   The concept, prominent from the 1960s to the early 1980s, that species-typical factors restrict the kinds of learning that a species can accomplish readily. Contrast with *specific abilities to learn and remember.*

genetics   The study of inheritance, including the genes encoded in DNA.

genome   The total complement of genes that individuals of a given species carry on their chromosomes.

genotype   All the genetic information that one specific individual has inherited. Contrast with *phenotype.*

genus (pl. genera)   A group of species that resemble each other because of shared inheritance. See Figure 6.2, Table 6.1.

GH   See *growth hormone.*

ghrelin   A peptide hormone emanating from the gut that acts on the appetite controller of the hypothalamus to increase appetite. See Figure 13.24.

giant axon   A large-diameter axon; it is found in some invertebrates. The size of giant axons facilitates research on the properties of neural membrane structure and function.

glia   See *glial cells.*

glial cells   Nonneural brain cells that provide structural, nutritional, and other types of support to the brain. Also called *glia* or *neuroglia.* See Figure 2.20.

glioma (pl. gliomas or gliomata)   A brain tumor resulting from the aberrant production of glial cells.

global aphasia   The total loss of ability to understand language, or to speak, read, or write. See Figure 19.7.

globus pallidus   One of the basal ganglia. See Figure 2.10.

glomerulus (pl. glomeruli)   A complex arbor of dendrites from a group of olfactory cells.

glossopharyngeal nerve   Cranial nerve IX, which serves taste receptors in the tongue. See Figure 2.4.

glucagon   A hormone, released by alpha cells in the islets of Langerhans, that increases blood glucose. See Table 5.2.

glucocorticoids   A class of steroid hormones, released by the adrenal cortex, that affect carbohydrate metabolism.

glucodetector   A cell that detects and informs the nervous system about levels of circulating glucose. Also called *glucostat.*

glucose   An important sugar molecule used by the body and brain for energy.

glucose transporter   A molecule that spans the external membrane of a cell and transports glucose molecules from outside the cell to inside for use.

glucostat   See *glucodetector.*

glutamate   An amino acid transmitter, the most common excitatory transmitter. See Table 4.1.

glutaminergic   Referring to cells that use glutamate as their synaptic transmitter.

glycine   An amino acid transmitter, often inhibitory. See Table 4.1.

glycogen   A complex carbohydrate made by the combining of glucose molecules for a short-term store of energy.

GnRH   See *gonadotropin-releasing hormone.*

goiter   A swelling of the thyroid gland caused by iodide deficiency.

Golgi stain   A histological stain that fills a small proportion of neurons with a dark, silver-based precipitate. See Box 2.3.

Golgi tendon organ   One of the receptors located in tendons that send impulses to the central nervous system when a muscle contracts. See Figure 11.9.

Golgi type I cell   A type of large nerve cell. See Figure 2.11.

gonadotropin   An anterior pituitary hormone that selectively stimulates the cells of the gonads to produce sex steroids. See *luteinizing hormone* and *follicle-stimulating hormone.*

gonadotropin-releasing hormone (GnRH)   A hypothalamic hormone that controls the release of luteinizing hormone and follicle-stimulating hormone from the pituitary. See Figure 5.18.

gonads   The sexual organs (ovaries in females, testes in males), which produce gametes for reproduction. See Figure 5.1, Table 5.2.

graded potential   An electrical potential that is initiated at a postsynaptic site and can vary continuously in size. Also called *local potential* or *postsynaptic potential.* Contrast with *all-or-none property.*

graded response   A postsynaptic electrical potential that is formed by synaptic action and that spreads passively across the cell membrane, decreasing in strength with time and distance.

grammar   The rules for usage of a particular language.

grand mal seizure   A type of generalized epileptic seizure in which nerve cells fire in high-frequency bursts. Grand mal seizures cause loss of consciousness and sudden muscle contraction. See Box 3.2. Contrast with *petit mal seizure.*

grandmother cell   An extrapolation of the feature detector model suggesting that if there were enough levels of analysis, a unit could be constructed that would enable a person to recognize his or her grandmother.

granule cell   A type of small nerve cell. See Figure 2.11.

gray matter   Areas of the brain that are dominated by cell bodies and are devoid of myelin. See Figure 2.8. Contrast with *white matter.*

growth cone   The growing tip of an axon or a dendrite. See Figure 7.10.

growth hormone (GH)   A tropic hormone, secreted by the anterior pituitary, that influences the growth of cells and tissues. Also called *somatotropic hormone.* See Table 5.2, Figure 5.14.

guevedoces   Literally "eggs at 12" (in Spanish), a nickname for individuals who are raised as girls but at puberty change appearance and begin behaving as boys.

gustatory system   The taste system. See Figure 9.17.

gut hormone   A hormone that is released by the stomach or intestines, sometimes in response to food.

gyrus (pl. gyri)   A ridged or raised portion of a convoluted brain surface. See Figure 2.7. Contrast with *sulcus.*

habituation   A form of nonassociative learning in which an organism becomes less responsive following repeated presentations of a stimulus. See Box 17.1. Contrast with *sensitization* (definition 1).

hair cell   One of the receptor cells for hearing in the cochlea. Displacement of hair cells by sound waves generates nerve impulses that travel to the brain. See Figure 9.1.

hallucinogens   A class of drugs that alter sensory perception and produce peculiar experiences. See also *psychedelic.*

harmonics   Multiples of a particular frequency called the *fundamental.* See Box 9.1.

health psychology   A field that studies psychological influences on health-related processes, such as why people become ill or how they remain healthy.

Hebbian synapse   A synapse that is strengthened when it successfully drives the postsynaptic cell.

hemiplegia   Partial paralysis involving one side of the body.

hemispatial neglect   A syndrome in which the patient ignores objects presented to one side and may even deny connection with that side of the body.

hermaphrodite   An individual that can reproduce as either a male or a female.

heroin   Diacetylmorphine; an artificially modified, very potent form of morphine.

hertz (Hz)   Cycles per second, as of an auditory stimulus.

heterogametic   Referring to the sex that has two different sex chromosomes. Male mammals and female birds are heterogametic. Contrast with *homogametic.*

higher vocal center (HVc)   The highest-level neural structure in the song control circuitry of songbirds such as zebra finches and canaries.

hindbrain   The rear division of the brain; in the mature vertebrate, the hindbrain contains the cerebellum, pons, and medulla. Also called *rhombencephalon.* See Figure 2.9.

hippocampal gyrus   See *subiculum.*

hippocampus (pl. hippocampi)   A portion of the cerebral hemispheres found curled in the basal medial part of the temporal lobe that is thought to be important for learning and memory. See Figures 2.10, 17.1, 18.8.

histology   The study of tissue structure.

HIV   See *human immunodeficiency virus.*

homeostasis   The tendency for the internal environment to remain constant.

homeostatic   Referring to the process of maintaining a particular physiological measure relatively constant.

homeotherm   An older term, now considered inadequate, for an animal that maintains a relatively constant body temperature. Examples include birds and mammals. A more accepted term is *endotherm.* Contrast with *poikilotherm.*

hominid   A primate of the family Hominidae, of which humans are the only living species.

homogametic   Referring to the sex that has two similar types of sex chromosomes. Female mammals and male birds are homogametic. Contrast with *heterogametic.*

homology   A resemblance based on common ancestry, such as the similarities in forelimb structures of mammals. See Figure 6.3.

homoplasy   The similar appearance of features (e.g., the body forms of a tuna and a dolphin), often due to convergent evolution.

horizontal cells   Specialized retinal cells that contact both the receptor cells and the bipolar cells.

horizontal plane   The plane that divides the body or brain into upper and lower parts. See Box 2.1.

hormone   A chemical secreted by an endocrine gland that is conveyed by the bloodstream and regulates target organs or tissues. See Table 5.2.

horseradish peroxidase (HRP)   An enzyme found in horseradish and other plants that is used to determine the cells of origin of a particular set of axons. See Box 2.3.

HRP   See *horseradish peroxidase.*

hue   One of the basic dimensions (along with brightness and saturation) of light perception. Hue varies around the color circle through blue, green, yellow, orange, and red. See Figure 10.5.

human immunodeficiency virus (HIV)   The virus that can be passed through genital, anal, or oral sex and causes acquired immune deficiency syndrome (AIDS).

humoral immunity   An immunological response in which B lymphocytes produce antibodies that either directly destroy antigens, such as viruses or bacteria, or enhance the destruction of antigens by other cells. See Figure 15.20. Contrast with *cell-mediated immunity.* See also *immune system.*

hunger   The internal state of an animal seeking food. Contrast with *satiety.*

huntingtin   A protein produced by a gene (called *HD*) that, when containing too many trinucleotide repeats, results in Huntington's disease in a carrier.

Huntington's disease   A progressive genetic disorder characterized by choreic movements and profound changes in mental functioning. Also called *Huntington's chorea.*

HVc   See *higher vocal center.*

hybridize   Here, the process by which a string of nucleotides becomes linked to a complementary series of nucleotides.

hyperphagia   A condition involving increasing food intake, often related to damage to the ventromedial hypothalamus.

hyperpolarization   An increase in membrane potential (the inner surface of the membrane becomes more negative in relation to the outer surface); caused by inhibitory neural messages. See Figure 3.5. Contrast with *depolarization.*

hypertonic   Referring to a solution with a higher concentration of salt than that found in interstitial fluid and blood plasma (more than about 0.9% salt). Contrast with *hypotonic* and *isotonic.*

hypofrontality hypothesis   The hypothesis that schizophrenia may reflect underactivation of the frontal lobes.

hypothalamic–pituitary portal system   A system of capillaries that transport releasing hormones from the hypothalamus to the anterior pituitary. See Figure 5.13.

hypothalamus   Part of the diencephalon, lying ventral to the thalamus. See Figures 2.7, 2.9, Table 5.2.

hypotonic   Referring to a solution with a lower concentration of salt than that found in interstitial fluid and blood plasma (less than about 0.9% salt). Contrast with *hypertonic* and *isotonic.*

hypovolemic thirst   The response to a reduced volume of extracellular fluid. Contrast with *osmotic thirst.*

hypoxia   A transient lack of oxygen.

Hz   See *hertz.*

IAPs   See *inhibitor of apoptosis proteins.*

IC   See *impoverished condition.*

ICC   See *immunocytochemistry.*

iconic memory   A very brief type of memory that stores the sensory impression of a scene. Contrast with *short-term memory.*

ideational apraxia   An impairment in the ability to carry out a sequence of actions, even though each element or step can be done correctly.

identifiable neurons   Neurons that are large and similar from one individual to the next, enabling investigators to recognize them and give them code names. They occur especially in invertebrates. See Figure 6.8.

ideomotor apraxia   The inability to carry out a simple motor activity in response to a verbal command, even though this same activity is readily performed spontaneously.

IEGs   See *immediate early genes.*

IGF   See *insulin-like growth factor.*

IHC   See *inner hair cell.*

immediate early genes (IEGs)   A class of genes that show rapid but transient increases in response to extracellular signals such as neurotransmitters and growth factors. Examples include *c-fos* and *c-jun.*

immune system   The system that defends an organism from harmful foreign biological substances introduced into the body. It includes both cell-mediated immunity and humoral immunity. See Figures 15.20, 15.21.

immunocytochemistry (ICC)   A method for detecting a particular protein in tissues in which (1) an antibody recognizes and binds to the protein and (2) chemical methods are then used to leave a visible reaction product around each antibody. See Box 5.1.

impermeable   Referring to a barrier that does not allow a substance of interest to pass through.

impoverished condition (IC)   A condition in which laboratory rodents are housed singly in a small cage with adequate food and water but no complex stimulation. Also called *isolated condition*. See Figure 18.4. Contrast with *standard condition* and *enriched condition*.

imprinting   A form of learning in which young animals learn to follow the first relatively large moving object they see, usually their mother.

in estrus   Referring to a female animal that is receptive to copulation, usually as a result of steroid hormone exposure. Also called *in heat*.

in heat   See *in estrus*.

in situ hybridization   A method for detecting particular RNA transcripts in tissue sections by providing a nucleotide probe that is complementary to, and will therefore hybridize with, the transcript of interest. See Figure A.4 in the appendix.

in vitro   Literally "in glass," usually a laboratory dish; outside the body.

in vivo   Literally "in life"; within a living body.

incus (pl. incudes)   A middle-ear bone situated between the malleus (attached to the tympanic membrane) and the stapes (attached to the cochlea); one of the three ossicles that conduct sound across the middle ear. See Figure 9.1.

indifferent gonads   The undifferentiated gonads of the early mammalian fetus, which will eventually develop into either testes or ovaries. See Figure 12.16. See also *gonad*.

individual response stereotypy   The tendency of individuals to show the same response pattern to particular situations throughout their life span.

indoleamines   A class of monoamines that serve as neurotransmitters, including serotonin and melatonin. See Table 4.1.

induction   The process by which one set of cells influences the fate of neighboring cells, usually by secreting a chemical factor that changes gene expression in the target cells.

inferior colliculi   See *colliculus*.

infradian   Referring to a rhythmic biological event whose period is longer than that of a circadian rhythm—that is, longer than a day. Contrast with *ultradian*.

infrasound   Very low frequency sound energy, generally below the human auditory threshold of about 20 Hz.

infundibulum (pl. infundibula)   The stalk of the pituitary gland.

inhibitor of apoptosis proteins (IAPs)   A family of proteins that inhibit caspases and thereby stave off apoptosis.

inhibitory   Anything that hyperpolarizes a neuron and/or decreases the likelihood that it will produce an action potential. Contrast with *excitatory*.

inhibitory postsynaptic potential (IPSP)   A hyperpolarizing potential in the postsynaptic neuron that is caused by inhibitory connections. IPSPs decrease the probability that the postsynaptic neuron will fire a nerve impulse. See Figure 3.11. Contrast with *excitatory postsynaptic potential*.

inner ear   The cochlea and vestibular canals. See Figure 9.1.

inner hair cell (IHC)   One of the two types of receptor cells for hearing in the cochlea. See Figure 9.1. See also *outer hair cell*.

innervate   To provide neural input.

innervation   The supply of neural input to an organ or a region of the nervous system.

innervation ratio   The ratio expressing the number of muscle fibers innervated by a single motor axon. The fewer muscle fibers an axon innervates (i.e., the lower the ratio), the finer the control of movements.

input zone   The part of a neuron that receives information, from other neurons or from specialized sensory structures. Usually corresponds to the cell's dendrites. See Figure 2.19.

insomnia   Lack of sleep or of sufficient sleep.

instrumental conditioning   A form of associative learning in which the likelihood that an act (instrumental response) will be performed depends on the consequences (reinforcing stimuli) that follow it. Also called *operant conditioning*. Contrast with *classical conditioning*.

instrumental response   See *instrumental conditioning*.

insula   Region of cortical surface enfolded between the parietal and temporal lobes. See Figures 15.14, 15.15.

insulin   A hormone, released by beta cells in the islets of Langerhans, that lowers blood glucose. See Table 5.2.

insulin-like growth factor (IGF)   A member of the large family of growth factors that is associated, among other things, with glucose metabolism and longevity.

integration zone   The part of the neuron that initiates an action potential if the sum of all inhibitory and excitatory postsynaptic potentials exceeds a threshold value. Usually corresponds to the neuron's axon hillock, which is studded with voltage-gated sodium channels. See Figure 2.19.

intensity differences   Perceived differences in loudness between the two ears, which can be used to localize a sound source. Contrast with *latency differences*.

intermediate-term memory (ITM)   A form of memory that lasts longer than short-term memory, but does not last as long as long-term memory.

internal capsule   The fiber band in the basal ganglia that extends between the caudate

nucleus on its medial side and the globus pallidus and putamen on its lateral side.

internal carotid artery   See *carotid arteries*.

internal fertilization   The process by which sperm fertilize eggs inside of the female's body. All mammals, birds, and reptiles have internal fertilization. Contrast with *external fertilization*.

interneuron   A neuron that is neither a sensory neuron nor a motoneuron.

intersex   Referring to an individual with atypical genital development and sexual differentiation that generally resembles a form intermediate between typical male and typical female genitals.

intracellular compartment   The fluid space of the body that is contained within cells. See Figure 13.12.

intracellular fluid   Water within cells. Also called *cellular fluid*.

intrafusal fiber   One of the small muscle fibers that lie within each muscle spindle. See Figure 11.9. Contrast with *extrafusal fiber*.

intrinsic   Here, referring to factors arising within an individual that affect development. Contrast with *extrinsic*.

intrinsic activity   The ability of a drug, once bound to a receptor, to activate that receptor.

intromission   Insertion of the erect penis into the vagina during copulatory behavior.

inverse agonist   A substance that binds to a receptor and causes it to do the opposite of the naturally occurring transmitter.

ion   An atom or molecule that has acquired an electrical charge by gaining or losing one or more electrons.

ion channel   A pore in the cell membrane that permits the passage of certain ions through the membrane when the channels are open. See Figure 3.6.

ionotropic receptor   A receptor protein that includes an ion channel that is opened when the receptor is bound by an agonist. See Figures 3.15, 4.1. Contrast with *metabotropic receptor*.

ipsilateral   Pertaining to a location on the same side of the body. See Box 2.1. Contrast with *contralateral*.

IPSP   See *inhibitory postsynaptic potential*.

iris (pl. irides)   The circular structure of the eye that provides an opening to form the pupil. See Figure 10.2.

ischemia   The loss or reduction of blood circulation.

islets of Langerhans   Clusters of cells in the pancreas that release two hormones (insulin and glucagon) with opposite effects on glucose utilization. See Figure 5.1.

isocortex   Cerebral cortex that is made up of 6 distinct layers. Formerly referred to as *neocortex*. See Figure 2.12.

isolated condition   See *impoverished condition*.

isotonic   Referring to a solution with a concentration of salt that is the same as that found in interstitial fluid and blood plasma (about 0.9% salt). Contrast with *hypertonic* and *hypotonic.*

ITM   See *intermediate-term memory.*

kcal   See *kilocalorie.*

ketones   Breakdown products of fatty acids, which are generated in the metabolism of stored fat, and which the body can use as a metabolic fuel.

kilocalorie (kcal)   A measure of energy commonly applied to food; formally defined as the quantity of heat required to raise the temperature of 1 kg of water by 1°C.

kinases   A class of enzymes that catalyze the addition of a phosphate group to certain proteins.

kindling   A method of experimentally inducing an epileptic seizure by repeatedly stimulating a brain region. See Box 3.2.

kinesin   A protein "motor" that moves substances in axonal transport. See Figure 2.22. See also *dynein.*

knee jerk reflex   A variant of the stretch reflex in which stretching of the tendon beneath the knee leads to an upward kick of the leg. See Figure 3.16.

knockout organism   An individual in which a particular gene has been disabled by an experimenter. See Box 7.3.

Korsakoff's syndrome   A memory disorder, related to a thiamine deficiency, that is generally associated with chronic alcoholism.

L-dopa   The immediate precursor of the transmitter dopamine.

labeled lines   The concept that each nerve input to the brain reports only a particular type of information.

labia (sing. labium)   The folds of skin that surround the opening of the human vagina. See Figures 12.8, 12.17.

labile memory   An early stage of memory formation during which the formation of a memory can be easily disrupted by conditions that influence brain activity.

lamellipodium (pl. lamellipodia)   A sheetlike extension of a growth cone.

laminar organization   The horizontal layering of cells found in some brain regions. See Figures 2.12, 8.17.

latency   The time delay before a subject displays a behavior of interest.

latency differences   Differences between the two ears in the time of arrival of a sound, which can be employed by the nervous system to localize sound sources. Contrast with *intensity differences.*

latent learning   Learning that has taken place but has not (yet) been demonstrated by performance.

lateral   In the context of anatomy, referring to structures toward the side of the body. See Box 2.1. Contrast with *medial.*

lateral geniculate nucleus (LGN)   The part of the thalamus that receives information from the optic tract and sends it to visual areas in the occipital cortex. See Figure 10.16.

lateral hypothalamus (LH)   A hypothalamic region that may be involved in eating.

Lesions of the LH result in fasting and weight loss. See Figure 13.21.

lateral inhibition   The phenomenon by which interconnected neurons inhibit their neighbors, producing contrast at the edges of regions. See Figure 10.6.

lateral interaction   Especially in sensory systems, the phenomenon by which reciprocal connections among neurons at the same level in the hierarchy more sharply tune the responses of the system.

lateral-line system   A sensory system, found in many kinds of fish and some amphibians, that informs the animal of water motion in relation to the body surface.

lateral ventricle   A complexly shaped lateral portion of the ventricular system within each hemisphere of the brain. See Figure 2.14.

lateralization   The tendency for the right and left halves of a system to differ from one another.

learned helplessness   A learning paradigm in which individuals are subjected to inescapable, unpleasant conditions.

lens   A structure in the eye that helps form an image on the retina. The shape of the lens is controlled by the ciliary muscles inside the eye. See Figure 10.2.

lentiform nucleus   The lens-shaped region in the basal ganglia that encompasses the globus pallidus and the putamen. Also called *lenticular nucleus.* See Figure 2.10.

leptin   A protein, manufactured and secreted by fat cells, that may communicate to the brain the amount of body fat stored. Leptin is defective in obese mice.

lesion   Damage, as to a brain region, caused by disease or experimental design.

lesion momentum   The phenomenon in which the brain is impaired more by a lesion that develops quickly than by a lesion that develops slowly.

LGN   See *lateral geniculate nucleus.*

LH   1. See *lateral hypothalamus.* 2. See *luteinizing hormone.*

lie detector   See *polygraph.*

ligand   A substance that binds to receptor molecules, such as those at the surface of the cell.

ligand-gated ion channel   An ion channel that opens or closes in response to the presence of a particular chemical; an example is the ionotropic neurotransmitter receptor. Contrast with *voltage-gated ion channel.*

limbic system   A loosely defined, widespread group of brain nuclei that innervate each other to form a network; involved in mechanisms of emotion and learning. See Figure 2.10.

lipid bilayer   The structure of the neuronal cell membrane, which consists of two layers of lipid molecules, within which float various specialized proteins, such as receptors. See Figure 3.4.

lithium   An element that, administered to patients, often relieves the symptoms of bipolar disorder.

lobotomy   The detachment of a portion of the frontal lobe from the rest of the brain. Now largely discredited, lobotomy was

once a treatment for schizophrenia and many other ailments.

local circuit   See *circuit.*

local potential   See *graded potential.*

local potential change   A change in potential that is initiated at a postsynaptic site.

localization of function   The concept that specific brain regions are responsible for various types of experience, behavior, and psychological processes.

locus coeruleus   A small nucleus in the brainstem whose neurons produce norepinephrine and modulate large areas of the forebrain. See Figure 14.22.

long-term depression (LTD)   A lasting decrease in the magnitude of responses of neurons after afferent cells have been stimulated with electrical stimuli of relatively low frequency. Contrast with *long-term potentiation.*

long-term memory (LTM)   An enduring form of memory that lasts for days, weeks, months, or years and has a very large capacity. Contrast with *permanent memory.*

long-term potentiation (LTP)   A stable and enduring increase in the magnitude of responses of neurons after afferent cells have been stimulated with electrical stimuli of moderately high frequency. See Figures 18.8, 18.9, 18.10. Contrast with *long-term depression.*

lordosis   A female receptive posture in quadrupeds in which the hindquarter is raised and the tail is turned to one side, facilitating intromission by the male. See Figures 12.3, 12.6.

loudness   The subjective experience of the pressure level of a sound. See Box 9.1.

LSD   Lysergic acid diethylamide, a hallucinogenic drug.

LTD   See *long-term depression.*

LTM   See *long-term memory.*

LTP   See *long-term potentiation.*

lumbar   Referring to the lower part of the spinal cord or back. See Figures 2.5, 2.6.

luteinizing hormone (LH)   A tropic hormone, released by the anterior pituitary, that influences the hormonal activities of the gonads. See Table 5.2, Figures 5.14, 5.18.

lymphocytes   Immune system cells. Two different classes of lymphocytes (B and T) mediate two types of immunological responses. See Figure 15.20.

lymphokine   A secreted protein that induces immune system cells to divide.

lysergic acid diethylamide   See *LSD.*

M1   See *primary motor cortex.*

mad cow disease   See *bovine spongiform encephalopathy.*

magnetic resonance imaging (MRI)   A noninvasive technique that uses magnetic energy to generate images that reveal some structural details in the living brain. See Figures 1.6, 2.16.

magnocellular   Of or comprised of relatively large cells. Contrast with *parvocellular.*

magnocellular layers   The two ventral or inner layers of the lateral geniculate nucleus, so called because their cells are large.

See Figure 10.16. Contrast with *parvocellular layers*.

magnocellular nucleus of the basal forebrain A collection of neurons in the basal forebrain that modulates the activity of many areas of the cortex by providing cholinergic innervation and that is implicated in Alzheimer's disease. Also called *Meynert's nucleus, basal nucleus of Meynert,* or *nucleus basalis of Meynert.* See Figure 7.29.

magnocellular system The division of primate visual pathways that appears to be mainly responsible for the perception of depth and movement. See Figure 10.26. Contrast with *parvocellular system.*

major histocompatibility complex (MHC) A large and highly polymorphic family of genes that identify an individual's tissues (to aid in immune responses against foreign proteins).

malleus (pl. mallei) A middle-ear bone that is connected to the tympanic membrane; one of the three ossicles that conduct sound across the middle ear. See Figure 9.1.

mammillary body One of a pair of nuclei at the base of the brain that are slightly posterior to the pituitary stalk; a component of the limbic system. See Figure 2.7.

mammillothalamic tract The fiber bundle that connects the mammillary bodies to the thalamus.

manic–depressive illness See *bipolar disorder.*

MAO See *monoamine oxidase.*

MAO inhibitor See *monoamine oxidase inhibitor.*

MAOI See *monoamine oxidase inhibitor.*

marijuana A drug of abuse, usually smoked. The active ingredient is the chemical Δ9-tetrahydrocannabinol (THC).

marsupial An animal that is born at a very early developmental stage and that spends a period of its development in the maternal pouch.

MCR See *melanocortin receptor.*

MDMA A drug of abuse, 3,4-methylene-dioxymethamphetamine, also known as *ecstasy.*

medial In the context of anatomy, referring to structures toward the middle of an organ or organism. See Box 2.1. Contrast with *lateral.*

medial amygdala A portion of the amygdala that receives olfactory and pheromonal information.

medial forebrain bundle A collection of axonal tracts traveling in the midline region of the forebrain. See Figure 4.3.

medial geniculate nucleus A nucleus in the thalamus that receives input from the inferior colliculus and sends output to the auditory cortex. See Figure 9.6.

medial preoptic area (mPOA) A region of the anterior hypothalamus implicated in the regulation of many behaviors, including thermoregulation, sexual behavior, and gonadotropin secretion.

medulla (pl. medullas or medullae) The caudal part of the hindbrain. Also called *myelencephalon.* See Figures 2.7, 2.9.

medullary reticular formation The hindmost portion of the brainstem reticular formation, implicated in motor control and copulatory behavior. See Figure 12.6.

Meissner's corpuscle A skin receptor cell type. See Figures 8.4, 8.12.

melanocortin receptor A receptor that is activated by the α-melanocyte stimulating hormone (α-MSH) peptide.

melanopsin A photopigment found within particular retinal ganglion cells that project to the suprachiasmatic nucleus. See Figure 14.6.

melatonin An amine hormone that is released by the pineal gland. See Tables 4.1, 5.2.

melodic intonation therapy Therapy for aphasia patients that encourages them to sing, rather than merely speak, what they wish to say.

membrane potential A difference in electrical potential across the membrane of a nerve cell during an inactive period. Also called *resting membrane potential.* See Figures 3.1, 3.4.

memory A cognitive representation that is often acquired rapidly and that may last a long time.

memory trace A persistent change in the brain that reflects the storage of memory.

meninges (sing. meninx) The three protective sheets of tissue that surround the brain and spinal cord, called the dura mater, pia mater, and arachnoid.

meningitis An acute inflammation of the membranes covering the central nervous system—the meninges—usually caused by a viral or bacterial infection.

menstruation A visible flow of cells and blood that exits through the vagina between ovulations in some mammals, including humans and dogs.

Merkel's disc A skin receptor cell type. See Figures 8.4, 8.12.

mesencephalon See *midbrain.*

mesolimbocortical pathway A set of dopaminergic axons arising in the midbrain and innervating the limbic system and cortex. See Figure 4.3.

mesostriatal pathway A set of dopaminergic axons arising from the midbrain and innervating the basal ganglia, including those from the substantia nigra to the striatum. See Figure 4.3.

messenger RNA (mRNA) A strand of RNA that carries the code of a section of a DNA strand to the cytoplasm. See the appendix.

metabolic tolerance The form of drug tolerance that arises when the metabolic machinery of the body becomes more efficient at clearing the drug, as a consequence of repeated exposure.

metabolic rate The rate of the use of energy during a given period; measured in terms of kilocalories per day.

metabolism The breakdown of complex molecules into smaller molecules.

metabotropic receptor A type of transmitter receptor that does not contain an ion channel but may, when activated, use a G protein system to open a nearby ion channel. See Figures 3.15, 4.1. Contrast with *ionotropic receptor.*

metencephalon A subdivision of the hindbrain that includes the cerebellum and the pons. See Figure 2.9.

Meynert's nucleus See *magnocellular nucleus of the basal forebrain.*

MHC See *major histocompatibility complex.*

microelectrode An especially small electrode, such as the fine, fluid-filled glass electrodes used to record the membrane potential of neurons.

microfilament A very small filament (7 nm in diameter) found within all cells. Microfilaments determine cell shape.

microglial cells Extremely small glial cells that remove cellular debris from injured or dead cells. Also called *microglia.*

micropolygyria A condition of the brain in which small regions are characterized by more gyri than usual. See Figure 19.10.

microtubule A small hollow cylindrical structure (20–26 nm in diameter) in axons that is involved in axonal transport. See Figure 2.22.

midbrain The middle division of the brain. Also called *mesencephalon.* See Figure 2.9.

middle canal The central of the three spiraling canals inside the cochlea, situated between the vestibular canal and the tympanic canal. See Figure 9.1.

middle ear The cavity between the tympanic membrane and the cochlea. See Figure 9.1.

midget bipolar cell A retinal bipolar cell that connects to just one cone. Contrast with *diffuse bipolar cell.*

milk letdown reflex The reflexive release of milk in response to suckling, or to stimuli associated with suckling. The mechanism involves release of the hormone oxytocin. See Figure 5.11.

millivolt (mV) A thousandth of a volt.

mineralocorticoids A class of steroid hormones, released by the adrenal cortex, that affect ion concentrations in body tissues.

minimal discriminable frequency difference The smallest change in frequency that can be detected reliably between two tones.

mitochondrion (pl. mitochondria) A cellular organelle that provides metabolic energy for the cell's processes. See Figure 2.21.

mitosis (pl. mitoses) The process of division of somatic cells that involves duplication of DNA.

mitral cell Cells of the olfactory bulb that conduct smell information from the glomeruli to the rest of the brain. See Figure 9.18.

modulation of memory formation Facilitation or inhibition of memory formation by factors other than those directly involved in memory formation.

modulatory role The role that some hormones play in maintaining the sensitivity of neural circuits and other structures to hormonal influences.

modulatory site A portion of a receptor that, when bound by a compound, alters the receptor's response to its transmitter.

molecular layer The outermost layer of the cerebellum, containing the axons of neurons at deeper layers. See Figure 2.11.

monaural   Pertaining to one ear.

monaural detection   The detection of sound using only one ear. Contrast with *binaural detection*.

monoamine   A neurotransmitter based on either a catechol nucleus (such as dopamine and norepinephrine) or an indole nucleus (serotonin). See Table 4.1, Box 4.1.

monoamine hormones   See *amine hormones*.

monoamine hypothesis of depression   The hypothesis that depressive illness is associated with a decrease in the synaptic activity of connections that employ monoamine synaptic transmitters.

monoamine oxidase (MAO)   An enzyme that breaks down and thereby inactivates monoamine transmitters.

monoamine oxidase inhibitor (MAOI, or MAO inhibitor)   An antidepressant drug that blocks the breakdown of monoamine neurotransmitters by the enzyme monoamine oxidase, resulting in an accumulation of monoamine transmitters in synapses.

monoamines   A class of synaptic transmitters that contain a single amino group, NH_2. Examples include the catecholamines and indoleamines. See Table 4.1.

monocular deprivation   Depriving one eye of light. Contrast with *binocular deprivation*.

monogamy   A mating system in which a female and a male form a breeding pair that may last for one breeding period or for a lifetime. A durable and exclusive relation between a male and a female is called a *pair bond*. Contrast with *bigamy* and *polygamy*.

monopolar neuron   A nerve cell with a single branch that leaves the cell body and then extends in two directions: One end is the receptive pole, the other end the output zone. See Figure 2.19. Contrast with *multipolar neuron* and *bipolar neuron*.

monotreme   An egg-laying mammal belonging to an order that contains only two species: the echidna and the platypus.

monozygotic   Referring to twins derived from a single fertilized egg. Such individuals have the same genotype. Contrast with *dizygotic*.

morphine   An opiate compound derived from the poppy flower.

mossy fiber   One of the fibers that extend from the dentate gyrus to the hippocampus, where they synapse in area CA3. See Figures 2.11, 18.8.

motion sickness   The experience of nausea from unnatural passive movement, as in a car or boat.

motivated behavior   Behavior that an organism displays even in the face of barriers or contingencies.

motoneuron   A nerve cell in the spinal cord that transmits motor messages from the spinal cord to muscles. Also called *motor neuron*. See Figure 11.8.

motor cortex   A region of cerebral cortex that sends impulses to motoneurons. See Figures 11.12, 11.16.

motor neuron   See *motoneuron*.

motor plan   A plan for action in the nervous system.

motor unit   A single motor axon and all the muscle fibers that it innervates.

movement   A brief, unitary activity of a muscle or body part; less complex than an act.

mPOA   See *medial preoptic area*.

MRH   See *müllerian regression hormone*.

MRI   See *magnetic resonance imaging*.

mRNA   See *messenger RNA*.

müllerian duct   A primitive duct system in the embryo that will develop into female reproductive structures (fallopian tubes, uterus, and upper vagina) if testes are not present in the embryo. See Figure 12.17. Contrast with *wolffian duct*.

müllerian regression hormone (MRH)   See *anti-müllerian hormone*.

multiple sclerosis   Literally "many scars"; a disorder characterized by widespread degeneration of the white matter.

multiple-trace hypothesis   The hypothesis that a given memory is encoded in different ways at different times after a learning process. Implicit in this hypothesis is the idea that a memory must be transferred from one encoding scheme to another to become permanent. See Figure 17.6.

multipolar neuron   A nerve cell that has many dendrites and a single axon. See Figure 2.19. Contrast with *bipolar neuron* and *monopolar neuron*.

muscarinic   Referring to cholinergic receptors that respond to the chemical muscarine as well as to acetylcholine. Muscarinic receptors mediate chiefly the inhibitory activities of acetylcholine. Contrast with *nicotinic*.

muscle fiber   Large, cylindrical cells, making up most of a muscle, that can contract in response to neurotransmitter released from a motoneuron. See Figure 11.7. See also *extrafusal fiber* and *intrafusal fiber*.

muscle spindle   A muscle receptor that lies parallel to a muscle and sends impulses to the central nervous system when the muscle is stretched. See Figure 11.9.

muscular dystrophy   A disease that leads to degeneration of and functional changes in muscles.

musth   An annual period of heightened aggressiveness and sexual activity in male elephants.

mutant   An animal carrying a gene that differs from the norm or from the alleles carried by its parents.

mutation   A change in the nucleotide sequence of a gene as a result of unfaithful replication.

mV   See *millivolt*.

myasthenia gravis   A disorder characterized by a profound weakness of skeletal muscles; caused by a loss of acetylcholine receptors.

myelencephalon   See *medulla*.

myelin   The fatty insulation around an axon, formed by accessory cells. This myelin sheath improves the speed of conduction of nerve impulses. See Figures 2.20, 3.10.

myelination   The process of myelin formation. See Figures 2.20, 7.16.

myopia   "Nearsightedness"; the inability to focus the retinal image of objects that are far away.

myosin   A protein that, along with actin, mediates the contraction of muscle fibers. See Figure 11.7.

N-cadherin   A member of the superfamily of cadherins, which are cell adhesion molecules that mediate contact between neurons and contribute to their shape and functioning.

naloxone   A potent antagonist of opiates that is often administered to people who have taken drug overdoses. Naloxone binds to receptors for endogenous opioids.

narcolepsy   A disorder that involves frequent, intense episodes of sleep, which last from 5 to 30 minutes and can occur anytime during the usual waking hours.

natural selection   See *evolution by natural selection*.

NE   See *norepinephrine*.

negative feedback   The property by which some of the output of a system feeds back to reduce the effect of input signals. See Figure 3.18. Contrast with *positive feedback*.

negative polarity   A negative electrical-potential difference relative to a reference electrode. A neuron at rest exhibits a greater concentration of negatively charged ions in its interior than in its immediate surrounds; thus it is said to be negatively polarized. See Figure 3.1.

negative symptom   In psychiatry, a symptom that reflects insufficient functioning. Examples include emotional and social withdrawal, blunted affect, and slowness and impoverishment of thought and speech. Contrast with *positive symptom*.

neocortex   The relatively recently evolved portions of the cerebral cortex. All of the cortex seen at the surface of the human brain is neocortex. This term has been replaced by the term *isocortex*.

neologism   An entirely novel word, sometimes produced by patients with aphasia.

neonatal   Referring to newborns.

neophobia   The avoidance of new things.

Nernst equation   An equation used to calculate the equilibrium potential at a membrane.

nerve   A collection of axons bundled together outside the central nervous system. See Figures 2.3, 2.4. Contrast with *tract*.

nerve cell   See *neuron*.

nerve ending   In the periphery, an ending of a nerve thought to detect damage and transmit pain information.

nerve growth factor (NGF)   A substance that markedly affects the growth of neurons in spinal ganglia and in the ganglia of the sympathetic nervous system. See Figure 7.14.

nerve impulse   See *action potential*.

neural chain   A simple kind of neural circuit in which neurons are attached linearly, end to end. See Figure 3.17.

neural folds   In the developing embryo, ridges of ectoderm that form around the neural groove and come together to form the neural tube in the embryo. These neural folds will give rise to the entire nervous system.

neural groove   In the developing embryo, the groove between the neural folds. See Figure 7.2.

neural plasticity   The ability of the nervous system to change in response to experience or the environment. Also called *neuroplasticity*.

neural tube   An embryonic structure with subdivisions that correspond to the future forebrain, midbrain, and hindbrain. The cavity of this tube will include the cerebral ventricles and the passages that connect them. See Figure 7.2.

neurocrine   Referring to synaptic transmitter function. See Figure 5.3.

neuroendocrine cell   A neuron that releases hormones into local or systemic circulation. Also called *neurosecretory cell*.

neurofibrillary tangle   An abnormal whorl of neurofilaments within nerve cells. Neurofibrillary tangles are especially apparent in people suffering from dementia. See Figure 7.29.

neurofilament   A small rodlike structure found in axons. Neurofilaments are involved in the transport of materials. See Figure 2.22.

neurogenesis   The mitotic division of non-neuronal cells to produce neurons. See Figure 7.4.

neuroglia   See *glial cells*.

neurohypophysis   See *posterior pituitary*.

neuroleptics   A class of antipsychotic drugs, traditionally dopamine receptor blockers.

neuromodulator   A substance that influences the activity of synaptic transmitters.

neuromuscular junction (NMJ)   The region where the motoneuron terminal and the adjoining muscle fiber meet; the point where the nerve transmits its message to the muscle fiber.

neuromuscular synapse elimination   In postnatal development, the withdrawal by motoneurons of some of their terminal branches until every muscle fiber is innervated by only a single motoneuron.

neuron   The basic unit of the nervous system. Each neuron is composed of a cell body, receptive extension(s) (dendrites), and a transmitting extension (axon). Also called *nerve cell*. See Figures 2.18, 2.19.

neuron doctrine   The hypothesis that the brain is composed of separate cells that are distinct structurally, metabolically, and functionally.

neuronal cell death   The selective death (apoptosis) of many nerve cells.

neuropathic pain   Pain caused by damage to peripheral nerves; often difficult to treat.

neuropeptide   A peptide that is used by neurons for signaling.

neuropeptide Y (NPY)   A peptide neurotransmitter that may carry some of the signals for feeding.

neuropil   The conglomeration of dendrites and the synapses upon them.

neuroplasticity   See *neural plasticity*.

neuropsychopharmacology   The scientific field concerned with the discovery and study of compounds that selectively affect the functioning of the nervous system.

neuroscience   Study of the nervous system.

neurosecretory cell   See *neuroendocrine cell*.

neurotoxicology   The study of the effects of toxins and poisons on the nervous system.

neurotransmitter   The chemical in the presynaptic axon terminal (synaptic bouton) that serves as the basis of communication between neurons. The neurotransmitter travels across the synaptic cleft and reacts with the postsynaptic membrane when triggered by a nerve impulse. Also called *synaptic transmitter* or *chemical transmitter*. See Figure 3.13, Table 4.1.

neurotrophic factor   A target-derived chemical that acts as if it "feeds" certain neurons to help them survive.

neurotrophin   A chemical that prevents neurons from dying.

neutrophil   A type of phagocytic white blood cell. See Figure 15.20.

NGF   See *nerve growth factor*.

nicotine   A compound found in plants, including tobacco, that acts as an agonist on a large class of cholinergic receptors.

nicotinic   Referring to cholinergic receptors that respond to nicotine. Nicotinic receptors mediate chiefly the excitatory activities of acetylcholine, including at the neuromuscular junction. Contrast with *muscarinic*.

night terror   A sudden arousal from stage 3 or stage 4 slow-wave sleep that is marked by intense fear and autonomic activation. Contrast with *nightmare*.

nightmare   A long, frightening dream that awakens the sleeper from REM sleep. Contrast with *night terror*.

nigrostriatal bundle (NSB)   A dopaminergic tract that extends from the substantia nigra of the midbrain to the lateral hypothalamus, the globus pallidus, and the caudate putamen.

Nissl stain   A histological stain that outlines all cell bodies because the dyes are attracted to RNA, which encircles the nucleus.

NMDA receptor   A glutamate receptor that also binds the glutamate agonist NMDA (*N*-methyl-D-aspartate). The NMDA receptor is both ligand-gated and voltage-sensitive, so it can participate in a wide variety of information processing. See Box 4.2, Figure 18.9.

NMJ   See *neuromuscular junction*.

nociceptor   A receptor that responds to stimuli that produce tissue damage or pose the threat of damage.

nocturnal   Active during the dark periods of the daily cycle. Contrast with *diurnal*.

node of Ranvier   A gap between successive segments of the myelin sheath where the axon membrane is exposed. See Figures 2.20, 3.10.

nonassociative learning   A type of learning in which presentation of a particular stimulus alters the strength or probability of a response according to the strength and temporal spacing of that stimulus; includes habituation and sensitization. Contrast with *associative learning*.

noncompetitive   In the context of psychopharmacology, referring to a drug that affects a transmitter receptor while binding at a site other than that bound by the endogenous ligand. Contrast with *competitive*.

nondeclarative memory   A memory that is shown by performance rather than by conscious recollection. Also called *procedural memory*. Contrast with *declarative memory*.

nondirected synapse   A type of synapse in which the presynaptic and postsynaptic cells are not in close apposition; instead, neurotransmitter is released by axonal varicosities and diffuses away to affect wide regions of tissue.

nonfluent speech   Talking with considerable effort, short sentences, and the absence of the usual melodic character of conversational speech.

nongenomic effect   Here, an effect of a steroid hormone that is not mediated by direct changes in gene expression.

nonprimary motor cortex   Frontal lobe regions adjacent to the primary motor cortex that contribute to motor control and modulate the activity of the primary motor cortex. See Figure 11.16.

nonprimary sensory cortex   See *secondary sensory cortex*.

noradrenaline   See *norepinephrine*.

noradrenergic   Referring to systems using norepinephrine (noradrenaline) as a transmitter.

norepinephrine (NE)   A synaptic transmitter that is produced mainly in brainstem nuclei and in the adrenal medulla. Also called *noradrenaline*. See Table 4.1.

Northern blot   A method of detecting a particular RNA transcript in a tissue or organ, by separating RNA from that source with gel electrophoresis, blotting the separated RNAs onto nitrocellulose, and then using a nucleotide probe to hybridize with, and highlight, the transcript of interest.

notochord   A midline structure arising early in the embryonic development of vertebrates. See Figure 7.2.

NPY   See *neuropeptide Y*.

NSB   See *nigrostriatal bundle*.

NST   See *nucleus of the solitary tract*.

nucleotide   A portion of a DNA or RNA molecule that is composed of a single base and the adjoining sugar–phosphate unit of the strand. See Figure A.2 in the appendix.

nucleus (pl. nuclei)   1. Here, an anatomical collection of neurons within the central nervous system (e.g., the caudate nucleus). Contrast with *ganglion*. 2. See *cell nucleus*.

nucleus accumbens   A region of the forebrain that receives dopaminergic innervation from the ventral tegmental area. Dopamine release in this region may mediate the reinforcing qualities of many activities, including drug abuse.

nucleus basalis of Meynert See *magnocellular nucleus of the basal forebrain*.

nucleus of the solitary tract (NST) A brainstem nucleus that receives information from the parasympathetic vagus (tenth) cranial nerve. See Figure 13.16.

nucleus ruber See *red nucleus*.

nutrient A chemical that is needed for growth, maintenance, and repair of the body but is not used as a source of energy.

nystagmus An abnormal to-and-fro movement of the eye during attempts to fixate gaze.

ObR The receptor that binds leptin, the protein product of the *obese* (*ob*) gene.

obsessive–compulsive disorder (OCD) A syndrome in which the affected individual engages in recurring, repetitive acts that are carried out without rhyme, reason, or the ability to stop.

occipital cortex The cortex of the occipital lobe of the brain. Also called *visual cortex*. See Figure 10.14.

occipital lobes Large regions of cortex covering much of the posterior part of each cerebral hemisphere, and specialized for visual processing. See Figure 2.7.

OCD See *obsessive–compulsive disorder*.

ocular dominance column A region of cortex in which one eye or the other provides a greater degree of synaptic input. See Figure 10.22.

ocular dominance histogram A graph that portrays the strength of response of a brain neuron to stimuli presented to either the left eye or the right eye. Used to determine the effects of manipulating visual experience. See Figure 7.19.

ocular dominance slab A slab of visual cortex, about 0.5 mm wide, in which the neurons of all layers respond preferentially to stimulation of one eye. See Figure 10.23.

odorant A molecule that elicits a perceived odor.

off-center bipolar cell A retinal bipolar cell that is inhibited by light in the center of its receptive field and excited by light in the surround. See Figure 10.15. Contrast with *on-center bipolar cell*.

off-center ganglion cell A retinal ganglion cell that is activated when light is presented to the periphery, rather than the center, of the cell's receptive field. See Figure 10.15. Contrast with *on-center ganglion cell*.

off-center/on-surround Referring to a concentric receptive field in which the center inhibits the cell of interest while the surround excites it. See Figure 10.15. Contrast with *on-center/off-surround*.

OHC See *outer hair cell*.

olfaction The sense of smell.

olfactory bulb An anterior projection of the brain that terminates in the upper nasal passages and, through small openings in the skull, provides receptors for smell. See Figures 2.7, 9.18.

olfactory cilium Hairlike structure arising from the olfactory receptor cells. See Figure 9.18.

olfactory epithelium (pl. epithelia) A sheet of cells, including olfactory receptors, that lines the dorsal portion of the nasal cavities and adjacent regions, including the septum that separates the left and right nasal cavities. See Figure 9.18.

oligodendrocyte A type of glial cell that is commonly associated with nerve cell bodies. Some oligodendrocytes form myelin sheaths. See Figure 2.20.

on-center bipolar cell A retinal bipolar cell that is excited by light in the center of its receptive field and inhibited by light in the surround. See Figure 10.15. Contrast with *off-center bipolar cell*.

on-center ganglion cell A retinal ganglion cell that is activated when light is presented to the center, rather than the periphery, of the cell's receptive field. See Figure 10.15. Contrast with *off-center ganglion cell*.

on-center/off-surround Referring to a concentric receptive field in which the center excites the cell of interest while the surround inhibits it. See Figure 10.15. Contrast with *off-center/on-surround*.

ontogeny The process by which an individual changes in the course of its lifetime—that is, grows up and grows old.

Onuf's nucleus The human homolog of the spinal nucleus of the bulbocavernosus (SNB) in rats.

open-loop control mechanism A control mechanism in which feedback from the output of the system is not provided to the input control. Contrast with *closed-loop control mechanism*.

operant conditioning See *instrumental conditioning*.

opiate receptor A receptor that responds to endogenous and/or exogenous opiates.

opiates A class of compounds that exert an effect like that of opium, including reduced pain sensitivity. See Table 4.1 under "opioids."

opioid peptide A type of endogenous peptide that mimics the effects of morphine in binding to opiate receptors and producing marked analgesia and reward. See Table 4.1.

opioids A class of peptides produced in various regions of the brain that bind to opiate receptors and act like opiates. See Table 4.1.

opium A heterogeneous extract of the seedpod juice of the opium poppy, *Papaver somniferum*.

opponent-process hypothesis The theory that color vision depends on systems that produce opposite responses to light of different wavelengths. See Figures 10.25, 10.26.

opsin One of the two components of photopigments in the retina. The other component is RETINAL.

optic chiasm The point at which the two optic nerves meet. See Figures 2.7, 10.14.

optic disc The region of the retina devoid of receptor cells because ganglion cell axons and blood vessels exit the eyeball there. See Figure 10.2.

optic nerve Cranial nerve II; the collection of ganglion cell axons that extend from the retina to the optic chiasm. See Figure 2.4.

optic radiation Axons from the lateral geniculate nucleus that terminate in the primary visual areas of the occipital cortex. See Figure 10.14.

optic tectum (pl. tecta) The optical center of the midbrain. See Box 7.2.

optic tract The axons of retinal ganglion cells after they have passed the optic chiasm; most terminate in the lateral geniculate nucleus. See Figure 10.14.

optical imaging A method for visualizing brain activity in which near-infrared light is passed through the scalp and skull. The reflected light contains information about blood flow and electrical activity of the cortical surface.

oral contraceptive A birth control pill, typically consisting of steroid hormones to prevent ovulation.

orexins A group of proteins expressed in the lateral hypothalamus that trigger feeding; they have also been implicated in narcolepsy.

organ of Corti A structure in the inner ear that lies on the basilar membrane of the cochlea. It contains the hair cells and terminations of the auditory nerve. See Figure 9.1.

organizational effect A permanent alteration of the nervous system, and thus permanent change in behavior, resulting from the action of a steroid hormone on an animal early in its development. Contrast with *activational effect*.

organizational hypothesis The hypothesis that early testicular steroids masculinize the developing brain to alter behavior permanently.

organum vasculosum of the lamina terminalis (OVLT) One of the circumventricular organs. See Figure 13.15.

orgasm The climax of sexual experience, marked by extremely pleasurable sensations.

orientation column A column of visual cortex that responds to rod-shaped stimuli of a particular orientation. See Figure 10.23.

orphan receptor Any receptor for which no endogenous ligand has yet been discovered.

oscillator circuit A neural circuit that produces a recurring, repeating pattern of output. See Figure 3.18.

osmolality The number of solute particles per unit volume of solvent.

osmoreceptor One of the cells in the hypothalamus that are hypothesized to respond to changes in osmotic pressure.

osmosensory neuron A specialized type of balloonlike neuron that responds to the osmolality of the extracellular fluid by stretching or shriveling in hypotonic and hypertonic solutions, respectively. See Figures 13.12, 13.16.

osmosis The passive movement of molecules from one place to another. The motive force behind osmosis is the constant vibration and movement of molecules.

osmotic pressure   The force produced by osmosis.

osmotic thirst   The response to increased osmotic pressure in brain cells. Contrast with *hypovolemic thirst*.

ossicles   Three small bones (incus, malleus, and stapes) that transmit sound across the middle ear, from the tympanic membrane to the oval window. See Figure 9.1.

otolith   A small bony crystal on the gelatinous membrane in the vestibular system. See Figure 9.14.

otologist   A person who studies the outer, middle, and inner ear.

ototoxic   Toxic to the ears, especially the middle or inner ear.

outer hair cell (OHC)   One of the two types of receptor cells for hearing in the cochlea. See Figure 9.1. See also *inner hair cell*.

output zone   The part of a neuron, usually corresponding to the axon terminals, at which the cell's electrical activity is converted into a release of neurotransmitter. This secretory event conveys information to other neurons. See Figure 2.19.

oval window   The opening from the middle ear to the inner ear. See Figure 9.1.

ovaries   The female gonads, which produce eggs for reproduction. See Figures 5.1, 12.8, 12.17, Table 5.2.

overshoot   Here, the portion of the action potential during which the cell is transiently positive with relation to the extracellular medium. See Figures 3.5, 3.6. Contrast with *undershoot*.

oviduct   See *fallopian tube*.

oviparity   Reproduction through egg laying. Contrast with *viviparity*.

oviparous   Of or relating to oviparity. Contrast with *viviparous*.

OVLT   See *organum vasculosum of the lamina terminalis*.

ovulation   The production and release of an egg (ovum).

ovulatory cycle   The periodic occurrence of ovulation. See Figure 12.5.

ovum (pl. ova)   An egg, the female gamete.

oxytocin   A hormone, released from the posterior pituitary, that triggers milk letdown in the nursing female. See Table 5.2, Figures 5.10, 5.11.

Pacinian corpuscle   A skin receptor cell type. See Figures 8.4, 8.5, 8.12.

pain   The discomfort normally associated with tissue damage.

pair bond   See *monogamy*.

pancreas   An endocrine gland, located near the posterior wall of the abdominal cavity, that secretes insulin and glucagon. See Figure 5.1, Table 5.2.

papilla (pl. papillae)   A small bump that projects from the surface of the tongue. Papillae contain most of the taste receptor cells. See Figure 9.16.

paracrine   Referring to cellular communication in which a chemical signal diffuses to nearby target cells through the intermediate extracellular space. See Figure 5.3.

paradoxical sleep   See *rapid-eye-movement sleep*.

paragigantocellular nucleus (PGN)   A region of the brainstem reticular formation implicated in sleep.

parallel fiber   One of the axons of the granule cells that form the outermost layer of the cerebellar cortex. See Figure 2.11.

parallel processing   The use of several different circuits at the same time to process the same stimuli; a novelty in computers, but an ancient property of nervous systems.

paraphasia   A symptom of aphasia that is distinguished by the substitution of a word by a sound, an incorrect word, an unintended word, or a neologism (a meaningless word).

parasympathetic nervous system   One of the two systems that compose the autonomic nervous system. The parasympathetic division arises from both the cranial nerves and the sacral spinal cord. The other system is the sympathetic nervous system. See Figures 2.6, 2.9.

paraventricular nucleus (PVN)   A nucleus of the hypothalamus. See Figures 5.10, 13.21.

paresis (pl. pareses)   Partial paralysis.

parietal lobes   Large regions of cortex lying between the frontal and occipital lobes of each cerebral hemisphere. See Figure 2.7.

Parkinson's disease   A degenerative neurological disorder, characterized by tremors at rest, muscular rigidity, and reduction in voluntary movement, that involves dopaminergic neurons of the substantia nigra.

parthenogenesis   Literally "virgin birth"; the production of offspring without the contribution of a male or sperm.

partial agonist   A drug that, when bound to a receptor, has less effect than the endogenous ligand would. The term *partial antagonist* is equivalent. See Figure 4.8.

parvocellular   Of or consisting of cells that are relatively small. Contrast with *magnocellular*.

parvocellular layers   The four dorsal or outer layers of the primate lateral geniculate nucleus, so called because their cells are relatively small. See Figure 10.16. Contrast with *magnocellular layers*.

parvocellular system   The division of primate visual pathways that appears to be mainly responsible for analysis of color and form and for recognition of objects. Contrast with *magnocellular system*.

passive avoidance response   A response that an organism has learned not to make (e.g., not entering a compartment where it has been given a shock).

patch clamp technique   The use of very narrow pipette microelectrodes, clamped by suction onto tiny patches of the neural membrane, to record the electrical activity of a single square micrometer of membrane, including single ion channels.

patient H.M.   A patient who, because of damage to medial temporal lobe structures, is unable to encode new declarative memories. See Figure 17.1.

pattern coding   Coding of information in sensory systems based on the temporal pattern of action potentials.

Pavlovian conditioning   See *classical conditioning*.

PCP   See *phencyclidine*.

PCR   See *polymerase chain reaction*.

penis   The male genital organ, which enters the female's vagina to deliver semen. See Figure 12.8.

peptide   A short string of amino acids. Longer strings of amino acids are called *proteins*.

peptide neurotransmitters   A large family of neurotransmitters consisting of substances that are made up of short chains of amino acids. See Table 4.1.

perforant path   The route of axons that "perforate" the subiculum to provide the main inputs to the hippocampal formation. See Figure 18.8.

periaqueductal gray   The neuronal body–rich region of the midbrain surrounding the cerebral aqueduct that connects the third and fourth ventricles.

period   The interval of time between two similar points of successive cycles, such as sunset to sunset.

peripheral nervous system   The portion of the nervous system that includes all the nerves and neurons outside the brain and spinal cord. See Figure 2.9.

permanent memory   A type of memory that lasts without decline for the life of an organism. Contrast with *long-term memory*.

perseverate   To continue to show a behavior repeatedly.

PET   See *positron emission tomography*.

petit mal seizure   A type of generalized epileptic seizure that is characterized by a spike-and-wave electrical pattern. A person having a petit mal seizure is unaware of the environment and later cannot recall what happened. See Box 3.2. Contrast with *grand mal seizure*.

PGN   See *paragigantocellular nucleus*.

PGO wave   An EEG wave of activity from the pons (P) to the lateral geniculate (G) and on to the occipital cortex (O), usually seen only during REM sleep in cats.

phagocyte   An immune system cell that engulfs invading molecules or microbes.

phallus (pl. phalli or phalluses)   The clitoris or penis.

phantom limb   The experience of sensory messages that are attributed to an amputated limb.

pharmacodynamics   Collective name for the factors that affect the relationship between a drug and its target receptors, such as affinity and efficacy.

pharmacokinetics   Collective name for all the factors that affect the movement of a drug into, through, and out of the body.

phase shift   A shift in the activity of a biological rhythm, typically provided by a synchronizing environmental stimulus.

phasic receptor   A receptor that shows a rapid fall in nerve impulse discharge as stimulation is maintained.

phencyclidine (PCP)   An anesthetic agent that is also a psychedelic drug. Phencyclidine makes many people feel dissociated from themselves and their environment.

phenothiazines   A class of antipsychotic drugs that reduce the positive symptoms of schizophrenia.

phenotype   The sum of an individual's physical characteristics at one particular time. Contrast with *genotype*.

phenotype matching   In general, referring to processes by which an individual can assess the genetic relatedness of another individual on the basis of shared traits.

phenylketonuria (PKU)   An inherited disorder of protein metabolism in which the absence of an enzyme leads to a toxic buildup of certain compounds, causing mental retardation.

pheromone   A chemical signal that is released outside the body of an animal and affects other members of the same species. See Figure 5.3. Contrast with *allomone*.

phobic disorder   An intense, irrational fear that becomes centered on a specific object, activity, or situation that a person feels he or she must avoid.

phoneme   A sound that is produced for language.

phonemic paraphasia   A symptom of aphasia in which incorrect phonemes are substituted for correct sounds.

phosphoinositides   A class of common second-messenger compounds in postsynaptic cells.

phosphorylation   The addition of phosphate groups (PO_4) to proteins.

photon   A quantum of light energy.

photopic system   A system in the retina that operates at high levels of light, shows sensitivity to color, and involves the cones. See Table 10.1. Contrast with *scotopic system*.

phrenology   The belief that bumps on the skull reflect enlargements of brain regions responsible for certain behavioral faculties. See Figure 1.11.

phylogeny   The evolutionary history of a particular group of organisms. See Figure 6.1.

physical dependence   The state of an individual that has frequently taken high doses of a drug and will encounter unpleasant withdrawal symptoms if he or she stops.

physiological saline   A mixture of water and salt in which the concentration of salt is 0.9%, approximately equal in osmolarity to mammalian extracellular fluid. See also *isotonic*.

pia mater   The innermost of the three coverings (meninges) that embrace the brain and spinal cord. See also *dura mater* and *arachnoid*.

pineal gland   A secretory gland in the brain midline; the source of melatonin release. See Figures 2.7, 5.1, Table 5.2.

pinna (pl. pinnae)   See *external ear*.

pinocytosis   The process by which synaptic neurotransmitter is reabsorbed by the presynaptic axon terminal into specialized vesicles. See Figure 3.13.

pitch   A dimension of auditory experience in which sounds vary from low to high.

pituitary gland   A small, complex endocrine gland located in a socket at the base of the skull. The anterior pituitary and posterior pituitary are separate in function. See Figures 2.7, 5.10, 5.13.

PKU   See *phenylketonuria*.

place cell   A neuron within the hippocampus that selectively fires when the animal is in a particular location.

place theory   A theory of frequency discrimination stating that pitch perception depends on the place of maximal displacement of the basilar membrane produced by a sound. Contrast with *volley theory*.

placebo   A substance, given to a patient, that is known to be ineffective or inert but that sometimes brings relief.

placebo effect   A response to an inert substance (a placebo) that mimics the effects of an actual drug. For example, people suffering pain frequently experience relief from sugar tablets presented as medicine.

placenta (pl. placentas or placentae)   The specialized organ produced by the mammalian embryo that attaches to the walls of the uterus to provide nutrients, energy, and gas exchange to the fetus.

placental mammal   A mammal that produces a highly specialized placenta. All mammals except marsupials and monotremes are placental mammals.

planum temporale   A region of superior temporal cortex adjacent to the primary auditory area. See Figure 19.15.

plasticity   Malleability. See specifically *neural plasticity*.

poikilotherm   An older term, now considered inadequate, for an animal whose body temperature varies with the environment. Examples include reptiles. A more accepted term is *ectotherm*. Contrast with *homeotherm*.

polyandry   A mating system in which one female mates with more than one male. Contrast with *polygyny*.

polygamy   A mating system in which an individual mates with more than one other animal. Contrast with *monogamy* and *bigamy*.

polygraph   A device that measures several bodily responses, such as heart rate and blood pressure; popularly known as a *lie detector*.

polygyny   A mating system in which one male mates with more than one female. Contrast with *polyandry*.

polymerase chain reaction (PCR)   A method for reproducing a particular RNA or DNA sequence manyfold, allowing amplification for sequencing or manipulating the sequence. Also called *gene amplification*.

polymodal   Involving several sensory modalities.

POMC   See *pro-opiomelanocortin*.

pons (pl. pontes)   A portion of the metencephalon. See Figures 2.7, 2.9.

positive feedback   The property by which the output of a system feeds back to increase the input. A rarity in biological systems. Contrast with *negative feedback*.

positive reward model   A model of addictive behavior that emphasizes the rewarding attributes of drug ingestion.

positive symptom   In psychiatry, an abnormal state. Examples include hallucinations, delusions, and excited motor behavior. Contrast with *negative symptom*.

positron emission tomography (PET)   A technique for examining brain function in intact humans by combining tomography with injections of radioactive substances used by the brain. Analysis of the metabolism of these substances reflects regional differences in brain activity. See Figure 2.16.

postcentral gyrus   The strip of parietal cortex, just behind the central sulcus, that receives somatosensory information from the entire body. See Figure 2.7.

postcopulatory behavior   The final stage in mating behavior. Species-specific postcopulatory behaviors include rolling (in the cat) and grooming (in the rat). See Figure 12.2.

posterior   Toward the back or tail of an animal. Contrast with *anterior*.

posterior pituitary   The rear division of the pituitary gland. Also called *neurohypophysis*. See Figures 5.1, 5.10, Table 5.2.

postganglionic   "After the ganglion." In the autonomic nervous system, postganglionic neurons are the peripheral neurons that run from the autonomic ganglia to various targets in the body. See Figure 2.6. Contrast with *preganglionic*.

postganglionic cell   A cell in the autonomic nervous system that resides in the peripheral ganglia and sends its axons to innervate target organs. See Figure 2.6. Contrast with *preganglionic cell*.

postsynaptic   Referring to the region of a synapse that receives and responds to neurotransmitter. See Figure 2.21. Contrast with *presynaptic*.

postsynaptic membrane   The specialized membrane on the surface of the cell that receives information from a presynaptic neuron. This membrane contains specialized receptor proteins that allow it to respond to neurotransmitter molecules. See Figure 2.21. Contrast with *presynaptic membrane*.

postsynaptic potential   See *graded potential*.

posttetanic potentiation   A well-known example of neural plasticity in which a rapid series of action potentials (a tetanus) is induced in a nerve, with the result that subsequent single action potentials cause a stronger postsynaptic potential in the target.

posttraumatic stress disorder (PTSD)   A disorder in which memories of an unpleasant episode repeatedly plague the victim.

potassium equilibrium potential   See *equilibrium potential*.

precentral gyrus   The strip of frontal cortex, just in front of the central sulcus, that is crucial for motor control. See Figure 2.7.

precocial   Referring to animals that are born in a relatively developed state and that are able to survive without maternal care. Contrast with *altricial*.

preferred temperature　The environmental temperature at which an animal chooses to spend most of its time.

prefrontal cortex　The anteriormost region of the frontal lobe.

preganglionic　"Before the ganglion." In the autonomic nervous system, preganglionic neurons are the neurons that run from the central nervous system to the autonomic ganglia. See Figure 2.6. Contrast with *postganglionic*.

preganglionic cell　A cell of the autonomic nervous system that resides in the CNS and sends its axons to innervate autonomic ganglia. See Figure 2.6. Contrast with *postganglionic cell*.

premotor cortex　A region of nonprimary motor cortex just anterior to the primary motor cortex. See Figure 11.16.

prenatal　Before birth.

preoptic area　A region of the hypothalamus just anterior to the level of the optic chiasm.

presenilin　An enzyme that cleaves amyloid precursor protein (APP) to form β-amyloid, which can lead to Alzheimer's disease.

presynaptic　Referring to the region of a synapse that releases neurotransmitter. See Figure 2.21. Contrast with *postsynaptic*.

presynaptic membrane　The specialized membrane of the axon terminal of the neuron that is transmitting information in the form of a release of neurotransmitter. Vesicles bearing neurotransmitter can bind to this membrane and release their contents, thus affecting the postsynaptic membrane. See Figure 2.21.

primacy effect　The superior performance seen in a memory task for items at the start of a list; usually attributed to long-term memory. Contrast with *recency effect*.

primary motor cortex (M1)　The apparent executive region for the initiation of movement; primarily the precentral gyrus.

primary sensory cortex　For a given sensory modality, the region of cortex that receives most of the information about that modality from the thalamus or, in the case of olfaction, directly from the secondary sensory neurons.

primary sensory ending　The axon that transmits information from the central portion of a muscle spindle. See Figure 11.9.

primary somatosensory cortex (S1)　The gyrus just posterior to the central sulcus where sensory receptors on the body surface are mapped. Primary cortex for receiving touch and pain information, in the parietal lobe. Also called *somatosensory 1*. See Figures 8.14, 8.16.

primary visual cortex (V1)　The region of the occipital cortex where most visual information first arrives. Also called *striate cortex* or *area 17*. See Figures 10.13, 10.14, 10.19.

priming　1. In pheromones, the ability of a pheromone to slowly alter the physiology of a conspecific. 2. In memory, the phenomenon by which exposure to a stimulus facil-

itates subsequent responses to the same or a similar stimulus.

prion　A protein that can become improperly folded and thereby can induce other proteins to follow suit, leading to long protein chains that impair neural function.

procedural memory　See *nondeclarative memory*.

proceptive　Referring to a state in which an animal advertises its readiness to mate through species-typical behaviors, such as ear wiggling in the female rat. See Figure 4.2.

progesterone　The primary type of progestin secreted by the ovary. See Table 5.2, Figure 5.18.

progestins　A major class of steroid hormones that are produced by the ovary, including progesterone. See Table 5.2, Figure 5.14.

prolactin　A protein hormone, produced by the anterior pituitary, that promotes mammary development for lactation in female mammals. See Table 5.2, Figure 5.14.

promiscuity　A mating system in which animals mate with several members of the opposite sex and do not establish durable associations with sex partners.

pro-opiomelanocortin (POMC)　A prohormone that is characteristic of hypothalamic neurons participating in the appetite control system. POMC can be cleaved to produce the melanocortins, which also participate in feeding control. See Figure 13.24.

proprioception　Body sense; information about the position and movement of the body that is sent to the brain.

prosencephalon　See *forebrain*.

prosopagnosia　A condition characterized by the inability to recognize faces.

prostate gland　A male secondary sexual gland that contributes fluid to semen. See Figures 12.8, 12.17.

prosthetic device　An artificial replacement for a body part lost by accident or disease.

protein　A long string of amino acids. The basic building material of organisms. See also *peptide*.

protein hormones　A class of hormones that consists of protein molecules.

protein kinase　An enzyme that adds phosphate groups (PO_4) to protein molecules.

proximal　In the context of anatomy, referring to structures near the trunk or center of an organism. See Box 2.1. Contrast with *distal*.

psychedelic　Referring to a mental state with intensified sensory perception and distortions or hallucinations. Psychedelic drugs (also called *hallucinogens*) produce such states.

psychoneuroimmunology　The study of the immune system and its interaction with the nervous system and behavior.

psychopath　An individual incapable of experiencing remorse.

psychopharmacology　The study of the effects of drugs on the nervous system and behavior.

psychosocial dwarfism　Reduced stature caused by stress early in life that inhibits deep sleep. See Box 5.2.

psychosomatic medicine　A field of study that emphasizes the role of psychological factors in disease.

psychosurgery　Surgery in which brain lesions are produced to modify severe psychiatric disorders.

psychotogen　A substance that generates psychotic behavior.

PTSD　See *posttraumatic stress disorder*.

pupil　The aperture, formed by the iris, that allows light to enter the eye. See Figure 10.2.

pure tone　A tone with a single frequency of vibration. See Box 9.1.

Purkinje cell　A type of large nerve cell in the cerebellar cortex. See Figure 2.11.

pursuit movement　A type of eye movement in which the gaze smoothly and continuously follows a moving object.

putamen　One of the basal ganglia. See Figure 2.10.

PVN　See *paraventricular nucleus*.

pyramidal cell　A type of large nerve cell that has a roughly pyramid-shaped cell body; found in the cerebral cortex. See Figure 2.12.

pyramidal system　The motor system that includes neurons within the cerebral cortex and their axons, which form the pyramidal tract. Also called *corticospinal system*. See Figure 11.11.

pyramidal tract　The path of axons arising from the motor cortex and terminating in the spinal cord.

quantum (pl. quanta)　A unit of radiant energy.

RA　See *robustus archistriatum*.

radial glial cells　Glial cells that form early in development, spanning the width of the emerging cerebral hemispheres, and guide migrating neurons. See Figure 7.6.

radioimmunoassay (RIA)　A technique that uses antibodies to measure the concentration of a substance, such as a hormone in blood. See Box 5.1.

ramp movement　A slow, sustained motion that is thought to be generated in the basal ganglia. Also called *smooth movement*. Contrast with *ballistic movement*.

range fractionation　A hypothesis of stimulus intensity perception stating that a wide range of intensity values can be encoded by a group of cells, each of which is a specialist for a particular range of stimulus intensities. See Figure 8.6.

raphe nucleus　A group of neurons in the midline of the brainstem that contains serotonin and is involved in sleep mechanisms. See Figure 14.22.

rapid-eye-movement (REM) sleep　A stage of sleep characterized by small-amplitude, fast-EEG waves, no postural tension, and rapid eye movements. Also called *paradoxical sleep*. See Figure 14.11. Contrast with *slow-wave sleep*.

RBD See *REM behavior disorder.*

recency effect The superior performance seen in a memory task for items at the end of a list; attributed to short-term memory. Contrast with *primacy effect.*

receptive field The stimulus region and features that cause the maximal response of a cell in a sensory system. See Figures 8.9, 10.15, 10.17.

receptivity The state of sexual readiness in the female to show responses that are necessary for the male to achieve intromission.

receptor The initial element in a sensory system, responsible for stimulus transduction. Examples include the hair cells in the cochlea, and the rods and cones in the retina. See also *receptor molecule.*

receptor cell A specialized cell that responds to a particular energy or substance in the internal or external environment. The receptor cell converts this energy into a change in the electrical potential across its membrane.

receptor molecule A protein that captures and reacts to molecules of the transmitter or hormone. Also called *receptor.*

receptor site A region of specialized membrane that contains receptor molecules located on the postsynaptic surface of a synapse. Receptor sites receive and react with chemical transmitters.

receptor subtype Any type of receptor that has functional characteristics that distinguish it from other types of receptors for the same neurotransmitter. For example, at least 15 different subtypes of receptor molecules respond to serotonin.

recovery of function The recovery of behavioral capacity following brain damage from stroke or injury.

red nucleus A brainstem structure related to the basal ganglia. Also called *nucleus ruber.*

reductionism The scientific strategy of breaking a system down into increasingly smaller parts in order to understand it completely.

redundancy The property of having a particular process, usually an important one, monitored and regulated by more than one mechanism.

reflex A simple, highly stereotyped, and unlearned response to a particular stimulus (e.g., an eye blink in response to a puff of air). See Figures 3.16, 11.10.

refraction The bending of light rays by a change in the density of a medium, such as the cornea and the lens of the eyes.

refractory Transiently inactivated or exhausted.

refractory phase 1. A period during and after a nerve impulse in which the responsiveness of the axonal membrane is reduced. A brief period of complete insensitivity to stimuli (absolute refractory phase) is followed by a longer period of reduced sensitivity (relative refractory phase) during which only strong stimulation produces a nerve impulse. 2. A period following copulation during which an individual cannot recommence copulation. The

absolute refractory phase of the male sexual response is illustrated in Figure 12.9.

regulation An adaptive response to early injury, as when developing individuals compensate for missing or injured cells.

reinforcing stimulus See *instrumental conditioning.*

relative refractory phase See *refractory phase.*

releasing hormones A class of hormones, produced in the hypothalamus, that traverse the hypothalamic–pituitary portal system to control the pituitary's release of tropic hormones. See Figure 5.14.

REM behavior disorder (RBD) A sleep disorder in which a person physically acts out a dream.

REM sleep See *rapid-eye-movement sleep.*

renin A hormone released by the kidneys when they detect reduced blood flow.

repetitive transcranial magnetic stimulation See *transcranial magnetic stimulation.*

reserpine A drug that causes the depletion of monoamines and can lead to depression.

resting membrane potential See *membrane potential.*

reticular formation An extensive region of the brainstem (extending from the medulla through the thalamus) that is involved in arousal. See Figure 14.21.

reticulospinal tract A tract of axons arising from the brainstem reticular formation and descending to the spinal cord to modulate movement. See Figure 11.17.

retina The receptive surface inside the eye that contains the rods and cones. See Figures 10.2, 10.7.

RETINAL One of the two components of the photopigment found in the eye. The other component is opsin. (In this text, this term is printed in small capital letters—RETINAL—to distinguish it from the adjective *retinal,* meaning "pertaining to the retina.")

retinohypothalamic pathway The projection of retinal ganglion cells to the suprachiasmatic nuclei.

retrieval A process in memory during which a stored memory is used by an organism. See Figure 17.13.

retroactive amnesia A type of memory loss in which events immediately preceding a head injury are not recalled. See also *retrograde amnesia.*

retrograde amnesia Difficulty in retrieving memories formed before the onset of amnesia. Contrast with *anterograde amnesia.*

retrograde degeneration Destruction of the nerve cell body following injury to its axon. See Box 7.1. Contrast with *anterograde degeneration.*

retrograde messenger A substance, usually a gas neurotransmitter, that is released from a postsynaptic neuron in order to alter the functioning of a presynaptic neuron.

retrograde signal A signal that is thought to be released by the postsynaptic region that instructs the presynaptic neuron to increase subsequent transmitter release.

retrograde synapse A synapse in which a signal (usually a gas neurotransmitter) flows from the postsynaptic neuron to the presynaptic neuron, thus counter to the usual direction of synaptic communication. This mechanisms is thought to strengthen active synapses and may contribute to memory formation.

retrograde transport Movement of cellular substances toward the cell body from the axon terminals. See Figure 2.22. Contrast with *anterograde transport.*

reuptake The process by which released synaptic transmitter molecules are taken up and reused by the presynaptic neuron, thus stopping synaptic activity.

rhodopsin The photopigment in rods that responds to light.

rhombencephalon See *hindbrain.*

RIA See *radioimmunoassay.*

ribonucleic acid (RNA) A nucleic acid that implements information found in DNA. Two forms of RNA are transfer RNA and messenger RNA.

ribosomes Structures in the cell body where the translation of genetic information (the production of proteins) takes place.

RNA See *ribonucleic acid.*

robustus archistriatum (RA) One of the neural regions comprising the song control circuitry of songbirds, particularly implicated in song learning. See also *higher vocal center.*

rod One of the light-sensitive receptor cells in the retina that are most active at low levels of light. See Figure 10.7. Contrast with *cone.*

roots The two distinct branches of a spinal nerve, each of which serves a separate function. The dorsal root carries sensory information from the peripheral nervous system to the spinal cord. The ventral root carries motor messages from the spinal cord to the peripheral nervous system. See Figure 2.5.

rostral In the context of anatomy, referring to structures toward the head end of an organism. Also called *cephalic.* See Box 2.1. Contrast with *caudal.*

round window A membrane separating the cochlear duct from the middle-ear cavity. See Figure 9.1.

rTMS See *transcranial magnetic stimulation.*

rubrospinal tract Axons arising from the red nucleus in the midbrain and innervating neurons of the spinal cord. See Figure 11.17.

Ruffini's ending A skin receptor cell type. See Figures 8.4, 8.12.

S1 See *primary somatosensory cortex.*

S2 See *secondary somatosensory cortex.*

saccade A series of rapid movements of the eyes that occur regularly during normal viewing. Also called *saccadic movement.*

saccule A small, fluid-filled sac under the utricle in the vestibular system that responds to static positions of the head. See Figure 9.14.

sacral Referring to the lower part of the spinal cord or back. See Figures 2.5, 2.6.

SAD   See *seasonal affective disorder.*

sagittal plane   The plane that bisects the body or brain into right and left portions. See Box 2.1.

saltatory conduction   The form of conduction that is characteristic of myelinated axons, in which the nerve impulse jumps from one node of Ranvier to the next.

satiety   A feeling of fulfillment or satisfaction. Contrast with *hunger.*

saturated   Referring to the condition in which a maximal number of receptors of one type have been bound by molecules of a drug; additional doses of drug cannot produce additional binding.

saturation   One of the basic dimensions (along with brightness and hue) of light perception. Saturation varies from rich to pale (e.g., from red to pink to gray in the color solid of Figure 10.5).

saxitoxin (STX)   An animal toxin that blocks sodium channels when applied to the outer surface of the cell membrane.

SC   See *standard condition.*

Schaffer collateral   An axon branch from a neuron in area CA3 that projects to area CA1 in the hippocampus. See Figure 18.8.

schema (pl. schemata or schemas)   In terms of actions, a high-level program for movement.

schizophrenia   A severe psychopathology characterized by negative symptoms such as emotional withdrawal and impoverished thought, and by positive symptoms such as hallucinations and delusions.

Schwann cell   The accessory cell that forms myelin in the peripheral nervous system.

SCN   See *suprachiasmatic nucleus.*

scotoma (pl. scotomas or scotomata)   A region of blindness caused by injury to the visual pathway or brain.

scotopic system   A system in the retina that operates at low levels of light and involves the rods. See Table 10.1. Contrast with *photopic system.*

SDN-POA   See *sexually dimorphic nucleus of the preoptic area.*

seasonal affective disorder (SAD)   A putative depression brought about by the short days of winter.

second messenger   A slow-acting substance in the postsynaptic cell that amplifies the effects of nerve impulses and can initiate processes that lead to changes in electrical potential at the membrane.

secondary binding   Enhanced binding of a drug to lower-affinity receptors that occurs after the drug has saturated all of its highest-affinity receptors; secondary binding may cause side effects to become more pronounced. See Figure 4.8.

secondary sensory cortex   For a given sensory modality, the cortical regions receiving direct projections from primary sensory cortex for that modality. Also called *nonprimary sensory cortex.*

secondary sensory ending   The axon transmitting information from the ends of a muscle spindle.

secondary somatosensory cortex (S2)   The region of cortex that receives direct projec-

tions from primary somatosensory cortex. Also called *somatosensory 2.* See Figure 8.16.

secretin   A hormone that is released from the small intestine during digestion. See Table 5.2.

seizure   An epileptic episode. See Box 3.2.

selective permeability   The property of a membrane to allow some substances to pass through, but not others.

selective potentiation   The enhancement of the sensitivity or activity of certain neural circuits.

selective serotonin reuptake inhibitor (SSRI)   A kind of antidepressant drug that acts by selectively inhibiting the reabsorption of serotonin by presynaptic neurons, thereby increasing the concentration of serotonin in the synapse.

semantic memory   Generalized memory—for instance, knowing the meaning of a word without knowing where or when you learned that word.

semen   A mixture of fluid, including sperm, that is released during ejaculation.

semicircular canal   One of the three fluid-filled tubes in the inner ear that are part of the vestibular system. Each of the tubes, which are at right angles to each other, detects angular acceleration. See Figure 9.14.

seminal vesicle   A gland that stores fluid to contribute to semen. See Figures 12.8, 12.17.

semipermeable membrane   A membrane that allows some but not all molecules to pass through.

senile dementia   A neurological disorder of the aged that is characterized by progressive behavioral deterioration, including personality change and profound intellectual decline. It includes, but is not limited to, Alzheimer's disease.

senile plaques   A neuroanatomical change that correlates with senile dementia. Senile plaques are small areas of the brain that have abnormal cellular and chemical patterns. See Figure 7.28.

sensitive period   The period during development in which an organism can be permanently altered by a particular experience or treatment.

sensitization   1. A form of nonassociative learning in which an organism becomes more responsive to most stimuli after being exposed to unusually strong or painful stimulation. See Box 17.1. Contrast with *habituation.* 2. A process in which the body shows an enhanced response to a given drug after repeated doses. Contrast with *tolerance.*

sensorineural deafness   A hearing impairment that originates from cochlear or auditory nerve lesions. Contrast with *central deafness, conduction deafness,* and *cortical deafness.*

sensory conflict theory   A theory of motion sickness suggesting that discrepancies between vestibular information and visual information may simulate food poisoning and therefore trigger nausea.

sensory neuron   A neuron that is directly affected by changes in the environment, such as light, an odor, or a touch.

sensory pathway   The chain of neural connections from sensory receptor cells to the cortex.

sensory receptor organ   An organ specialized to receive particular stimuli; examples include the eye and the ear.

sensory–sensory conditioning   A form of learning in which two stimuli are presented in conjunction, and one stimulus comes to predict the occurrence of the other.

sensory transduction   The process in which a receptor cell converts the energy in a stimulus into a change in the electrical potential across its membrane.

septal complex   A brain region that provides subcortical input to the hippocampal formation.

sequencing   The process by which the order of nucleotides in a gene, or amino acids in a protein, is determined.

sequential hermaphrodites   Species in which individuals may be exclusively of one sex, and then switch to the other sex. See Figure 12.10.

serotonergic   Referring to neurons that use serotonin as their synaptic transmitter.

serotonin (5-HT)   A synaptic transmitter that is produced in the raphe nuclei and is active in structures throughout the cerebral hemispheres. See Table 4.1, Figures 4.5, 14.22.

set point   The point of reference in a feedback system. An example is the setting of a thermostat.

set zone   The range of a variable that a feedback system tries to maintain.

sex chromosome   One of a pair of chromosomes that in female mammals are identical (XX) but in males are different (XY). See also *autosome.*

sex determination   The process by which the decision is made for a fetus to develop as a male or a female. In mammals this is under genetic control, but in some groups of animals, environmental variables like incubation temperature determine the sex of the offspring.

sex-determining region on the Y chromosome   See *SRY gene.*

sex steroids   Steroid hormones secreted by the gonads: androgens, estrogens, and progestins.

sexual attraction   The first step in the mating behavior of many animals, in which animals emit stimuli that attract members of the opposite sex. See Figure 12.2.

sexual differentiation   The process by which individuals develop either malelike or femalelike bodies and behavior.

sexual dimorphism   A structural difference between the sexes.

sexual receptivity   See *receptivity* and *sexually receptive.*

sexual selection   Darwin's theoretical mechanism for the evolution of anatomical and behavioral differences between males and females.

sexually dimorphic Different between the two sexes; usually referring to a structure or behavior that is distinctly different in males and females.

sexually dimorphic nucleus of the preoptic area (SDN-POA) A region of the preoptic area that is five to six times larger in volume in male rats than in females. See Figure 12.21.

sexually receptive Referring to the state in which an individual (in mammals, typically the female) is willing to copulate. In many species, no sexual activity is possible other than during the period of sexual receptivity in the female, which generally corresponds to ovulation.

short-term memory (STM) A form of memory that usually lasts only for seconds, or as long as rehearsal continues. Contrast with *iconic memory.*

SIDS See *sudden infant death syndrome.*

simple cortical cell A cell in the visual cortex that responds best to an edge or a bar of a particular width and with a particular direction and location in the visual field. See Figure 10.17. Contrast with *complex cortical cell.*

simultaneous hermaphrodites Species in which individuals have both male and female reproductive organs at the same time.

sinistral Left-handed.

site-directed mutagenesis Technique in molecular biology that changes the sequence of nucleotides in an existing gene.

size principle The idea that as increasing numbers of motor neurons are recruited to produce muscle responses of increasing strength, small, low-threshold neurons are recruited first and then large, high-threshold neurons.

skill learning Learning to perform a task that requires motor coordination.

sleep apnea A sleep disorder that involves the slowing or cessation of respiration during sleep, which wakens the patient. Excessive daytime somnolence results from the frequent nocturnal awakening.

sleep cycle A period of slow-wave sleep followed by a period of REM sleep. In humans, a sleep cycle lasts approximately 90 minutes.

sleep deprivation The partial or total prevention of sleep.

sleep enuresis Bed-wetting.

sleep-maintenance insomnia Difficulty in staying asleep. Contrast with *sleep-onset insomnia.*

sleep-onset insomnia Difficulty in getting to sleep. Contrast with *sleep-maintenance insomnia.*

sleep paralysis A state during the transition to or from sleep, in which the ability to move or talk is temporarily lost.

sleep recovery The process of sleeping more than normally after a period of sleep deprivation, as though in compensation.

sleep spindle A characteristic 14 to 18 Hz wave in the EEG of a person said to be in stage 2 sleep. See Figure 14.11.

sleep state misperception Commonly, a person's perception that he has not been asleep when in fact he was. Common at the start of a sleep episode.

slow-twitch muscle fiber A type of striated muscle fiber that contracts slowly but does not fatigue readily. Contrast with *fast-twitch muscle fiber.*

slow-wave sleep (SWS) Sleep, divided into stages 1 through 4, that is defined by the presence of slow-wave EEG activity. See Figure 14.11. Contrast with *rapid-eye-movement (REM) sleep.*

SMA See *supplementary motor area.*

smooth movement See *ramp movement.*

smooth muscle A type of muscle fiber, as in the heart, that is controlled by the autonomic nervous system rather than by voluntary control. Contrast with *striated muscle.*

SNB See *spinal nucleus of the bulbocavernosus.*

SOAE See *spontaneous otoacoustic emission.*

sodium equilibrium potential See *equilibrium potential.*

sodium–potassium pump The energetically expensive mechanism that pushes sodium ions out of a cell, and potassium ions in.

solute The solid compound that is dissolved in a liquid. Contrast with *solvent.*

solvent The liquid (often water) in which a compound is dissolved. Contrast with *solute.*

soma (pl. somata) See *cell body.*

somatic intervention An approach to finding relations between bodily variables and behavioral variables that involves manipulating body structure or function and looking for resultant changes in behavior. See Figure 1.2. Contrast with *behavioral intervention.*

somatomedins A group of proteins, released from the liver in response to growth hormone, that aid body growth and maintenance.

somatosensory Referring to touch and pain sensation.

somatosensory 1 See *primary somatosensory cortex.*

somatosensory 2 See *secondary somatosensory cortex.*

somatosensory cortex The portion of parietal cortex that receives tactile stimuli from the body. See also *primary somatosensory cortex* and *secondary somatosensory cortex.*

somatotropic hormone See *growth hormone.*

somnambulism Sleepwalking.

Southern blot A method of detecting a particular DNA sequence in the genome of an organism, by separating DNA with gel electrophoresis, blotting the separated DNAs onto nitrocellulose, and then using a nucleotide probe to hybridize with, and highlight, the gene of interest. See Figure A.3 in the appendix.

spasticity Markedly increased rigidity in response to forced movement of the limbs.

spatial-frequency filter model A model of pattern analysis that emphasizes Fourier analysis of visual stimuli. Contrast with *feature detector model.*

spatial summation The summation at the axon hillock of postsynaptic potentials from across the cell body. If this summation reaches threshold, a nerve impulse is triggered. See Figure 3.12. Contrast with *temporal summation.*

species A group of individuals that can readily interbreed to produce fertile offspring. Individuals of different species produce either no offspring or infertile offspring. See Figure 6.2, Table 6.1.

specific abilities to learn and remember The concept that specific abilities to learn and remember evolve where needed. Contrast with *genetic constraints on learning.*

specific nerve energies The doctrine that the receptors and neural channels for the different senses are independent and operate in their own special ways, and can produce only one particular sensation each.

specific-pathway hypothesis The idea that each auditory input to the brain transmits information about only a narrow range of frequencies.

spectral filtering Alteration of amplitude of some, but not all, frequencies in a sound; when performed by the irregular shapes of the external ear, this process is a source of information that assists in the localization of sound sources.

spectrally opponent cell A visual receptor cell that has opposite firing responses to different regions of the spectrum. See Figures 10.25, 10.26.

sperm (pl. sperm) The gamete produced by males for fertilization of eggs (ova).

sperm competition The selective pressure that males of promiscuous species exert on each other to produce gametes that can outcompete the sperm of other males, because sperm from multiple males may be present in the genital tract of a single female.

spinal animal An animal whose spinal cord has been surgically disconnected from the brain to enable the study of behaviors that do not require brain control.

spinal nerve A nerve that emerges from the spinal cord. There are 31 pairs of spinal nerves. See Figure 2.5.

spinal nucleus of the bulbocavernosus (SNB) A group of motoneurons in the spinal cord of rats that innervate striated muscles controlling the penis. See Figure 12.22. See also *Onuf's nucleus.*

spinal root See *roots.*

spinal shock A period of decreased synaptic excitability in the neurons of the spinal cord after it has been isolated surgically from the brain.

spindle cell A type of small, rod-shaped nerve cell.

spinothalamic system See *anterolateral system.*

split-brain individual An individual whose corpus callosum has been severed, halting communication between the right and left hemispheres.

spontaneous otoacoustic emission (SOAE) A sound produced by the ears of many normal people. Contrast with *evoked otoa-coustic emission.*

SRY gene   A gene on the Y chromosome that directs the developing gonads to become testes. The name *SRY* stands for *sex-determining region on the Y chromosome.*

SSRI   See *selective serotonin reuptake inhibitor.*

stage 1 sleep   The initial stage of slow-wave sleep, which is characterized by small-amplitude EEG waves of irregular frequency, slow heart rate, and reduced muscle tension. See Figure 14.11.

stage 2 sleep   A stage of slow-wave sleep that is defined by bursts of regular 14 to 18 Hz EEG waves (called *sleep spindles*) that progressively increase and then decrease in amplitude. See Figure 14.11.

stage 3 sleep   A stage of slow-wave sleep that is defined by the spindles seen in stage 2 sleep, mixed with larger-amplitude slow waves. See Figure 14.11.

stage 4 sleep   A stage of slow-wave sleep that is defined by the presence of high-amplitude slow waves of 1 to 4 Hz. See Figure 14.11.

standard condition (SC)   The usual environment for laboratory rodents, with a few animals in a cage and adequate food and water, but no complex stimulation. See Figure 18.4. Contrast with *enriched condition* and *impoverished condition.*

stapedius   A middle-ear muscle that is attached to the stapes. See Figure 9.1.

stapes (pl. stapes or stapedes)   A middle-ear bone that is connected to the oval window; one of the three ossicles that conduct sounds across the middle ear. See Figure 9.1.

static phase of obesity   A later period following destruction of the ventromedial hypothalamus, during which an animal's weight stabilizes at an obese level and food intake is not much above normal. See Figure 13.22. Contrast with *dynamic phase of weight gain.*

stellate cell   A type of small nerve cell that has many branches. See Figure 2.11.

stem cell   A cell that is undifferentiated and therefore can take on the fate of any cell that the donor organism can produce.

stereocilium (pl. stereocilia)   A relatively stiff hair that protrudes from a hair cell in the auditory or vestibular system. See Figure 9.1.

stereopsis   The ability to perceive depth using the slight difference in visual information from the two eyes.

stereotypy   Excessive repetition of movements, ideas, patterns of speech, or other behaviors.

steroid hormones   A class of hormones, each of which is composed of four interconnected rings of carbon atoms.

steroid receptor cofactors   Proteins that affect the cell's response when a steroid hormone binds its receptor.

stimulation-elicited behavior   A motivational behavior, such as eating, drinking, or fearful escape, that is elicited by electrical stimulation of sites in the brain.

stimulus (pl. stimuli)   Physical event that triggers a sensory response.

STM   See *short-term memory.*

stress   Any circumstance that upsets homeostatic balance. Examples include exposure to extreme cold or heat or an array of threatening psychological states.

stress immunization   The concept that mild stress early in life makes an individual better able to handle stress later in life.

stretch reflex   The contraction of a muscle in response to stretch of that muscle. See Figure 11.10.

striate cortex   See *primary visual cortex.*

striated muscle   A type of muscle with a striped appearance, generally under voluntary control. Contrast with *smooth muscle.*

striatum   The caudate nucleus and putamen together.

stroke   A disorder of blood vessels—either a block or a rupture of a vessel—that destroys or cripples particular brain regions.

STX   See *saxitoxin.*

subcutaneous   Beneath the skin.

subfornical organ   One of the circumventricular organs. See Figure 13.15.

subiculum (pl. subicula)   A region adjacent to the hippocampus that contributes to the hippocampal formation. Also called *hippocampal gyrus.* See Figure 18.8.

substance P   A peptide transmitter implicated in pain transmission.

substance-related disorder   Drug addiction, either the abuse of drugs or the more serious dependence on drugs.

substantia nigra   A brainstem structure in humans that is related to the basal ganglia and named for its dark pigmentation. Depletion of dopaminergic cells in this region has been implicated in Parkinson's disease.

sudden infant death syndrome (SIDS)   The sudden, unexpected death of an apparently healthy human infant who simply stops breathing, usually during sleep. SIDS is not well understood. Also called *crib death.*

sulcus (pl. sulci)   A furrow of convoluted brain surface. See Figure 2.7. Contrast with *gyrus.*

superior colliculi   See *colliculus.*

superior olivary nuclei   A brainstem structure that receives input from both right and left cochlear nuclei, and provides the first binaural analysis of auditory information. See Figure 9.6.

superior olive   A distinctive brainstem nucleus that contributes to the binaural processing of sounds.

superordinate circuit   A neural circuit that is hierarchically superior to other, simple circuits.

supersensitivity psychosis   An exaggerated psychosis that may emerge when doses of antipsychotic medication are reduced, probably as a consequence of up-regulation of receptors that occurred during drug treatment.

supplementary motor area (SMA)   A region of nonprimary motor cortex that receives input from the basal ganglia and modulates the activity of the primary motor cortex. See Figure 11.16.

suprachiasmatic nucleus (SCN)   A small region of the hypothalamus above the optic chiasm that is the location of a circadian oscillator. See Figure 14.5.

supraoptic nucleus   A nucleus of the hypothalamus. See Figure 5.10.

surface dyslexia   A form of acquired dyslexia in which the patient seems to attend only to the fine details of reading. Contrast with *deep dyslexia.*

SWS   See *slow-wave sleep.*

Sylvian fissure   A deep fissure that demarcates the temporal lobe. See Figure 2.7.

sympathetic chain   A chain of ganglia that runs along each side of the spinal column; part of the sympathetic nervous system. See Figure 2.6.

sympathetic nervous system   One of two systems that compose the autonomic nervous system. The sympathetic nervous system arises from the thoracic and lumbar spinal cord. The other system is the parasympathetic nervous system. See Figure 2.6.

synapse   An area composed of the presynaptic (axonal) terminal, the postsynaptic (usually dendritic) membrane, and the space (or cleft) between them. The synapse is the site at which neural messages travel from one neuron to another. Also called *synaptic region.* See Figure 2.21.

synapse rearrangement   The loss of some synapses and the development of others; a refinement of synaptic connections that is often seen in development. See Figure 7.3.

synaptic bouton   The presynaptic swelling of the axon terminal from which neural messages travel across the synaptic cleft to other neurons. Also called simply *bouton.*

synaptic cleft   The space between the presynaptic and postsynaptic elements. This gap measures about 20 to 40 nm. See Figures 2.21, 3.13.

synaptic region   See *synapse.*

synaptic transmitter   See *neurotransmitter.*

synaptic vesicle   A small, spherical structure that contains molecules of synaptic transmitter. See Figure 2.21.

synaptogenesis   The establishment of synaptic connections as axons and dendrites grow. See Figure 7.3.

synergist   A muscle that acts together with another muscle. See also *agonist* (definition 2). Contrast with *antagonist* (definition 2).

synthetic   Here, referring to a chemical that is human-made.

syrinx (pl. syringes or syrinxes)   The vocal organ in birds.

system   A high level of brain organization that includes specialized circuits (e.g., the visual system). Contrast with *circuit.*

T cell   See *T lymphocyte.*

T lymphocyte   An immune system cell that attacks foreign microbes or tissue; "killer cell." Also called *T cell.* See Figure 15.20.

T1R   A family of taste receptor proteins that, when particular members heterodimerize, form taste receptors for sweet flavors and umami flavors.

T2R A family of bitter taste receptors.

tardive dyskinesia A disorder characterized by involuntary movements, especially involving the face, mouth, lips, and tongue; related to prolonged use of antipsychotic drugs, such as chlorpromazine. See Box 16.1.

tastant A substance that can be tasted.

taste aversion See *conditioned taste aversion*.

taste bud A cluster of 50 to 150 cells that detects tastes. Taste buds are found in papillae on the tongue. See Figure 9.16.

taste pore The small aperture via which tastant molecules are able to access the sensory receptors of the taste bud. See Figure 9.16.

tau 1. A protein associated with neurofibrillary tangles in Alzheimer's disease. 2. A mutation (*tau*) in hamsters that causes a shorter circadian period in free-running conditions.

taxonomy The classification of organisms. See Table 6.1 and Figure 6.2.

tectorial membrane A structure in the cochlear duct. See Figure 9.1.

tectum (pl. tecta) The dorsal portion of the midbrain, including the inferior and superior colliculi.

telencephalon The frontal subdivision of the forebrain that includes the cerebral hemispheres when fully developed. See Figure 2.9.

temporal lobes Large lateral cortical region of each cerebral hemisphere, continuous with the parietal lobe posteriorly, and separated from the frontal lobe by the Sylvian fissure. Contains the hippocampus and amygdala, and is involved in a variety of functions, including memory, emotional processing, and the olfactory and auditory senses. See Figure 2.7.

temporal summation The summation of postsynaptic potentials that reach the axon hillock at different times. The closer together the potentials are, the more complete the summation. See Figure 3.12. Contrast with *spatial summation*.

tendon Strong tissue that connects muscles to bone.

TENS See *transcutaneous electrical nerve stimulation*.

tensor tympani The muscle attached to the malleus and the tympanic membrane that modulates mechanical linkage to protect the delicate receptor cells of the inner ear from damaging sounds. See Figure 9.1.

testes (sing. testis) The male gonads, which produce sperm and androgenic steroid hormones. See Figures 5.1, 12.8, 12.16, Table 5.2.

testosterone A hormone, produced by male gonads, that controls a variety of bodily changes that become visible at puberty. See Figures 5.14, 5.18, Table 5.2.

tetanus An intense volley of action potentials. See Figure 18.8.

tetrahydrocannabinol (THC) See *Δ9-tetrahydrocannabinol*.

tetrodotoxin (TTX) A toxin from puffer fish ovaries that blocks the voltage-gated sodium channel, preventing action potential conduction.

thalamus (pl. thalami) The brain regions that surround the third ventricle. See Figures 2.7, 2.9.

THC See *Δ9-tetrahydrocannabinol*.

therapeutic index The margin of safety for a given drug, expressed as the distance between effective doses and toxic doses. See Figure 4.8.

third ventricle The midline ventricle that conducts cerebrospinal fluid from the lateral ventricles to the fourth ventricle. See Figure 2.14.

thirst The internal state of an animal seeking water.

thoracic Referring to the level of the chest—here, the vertebrae that have ribs attached and the spinal cord segments originating from those vertebrae. See Figures 2.5, 2.6.

threshold The stimulus intensity that is just adequate to trigger a nerve impulse at the axon hillock.

thrombolytic Of or related to dissolving of blood clots, as in a stroke. See Figure 19.22.

thyroid gland An endocrine gland located below the vocal apparatus in the throat that regulates metabolic processes, especially carbohydrate use and body growth. See Figure 5.1, Table 5.2.

thyroid-stimulating hormone (TSH) A tropic hormone, released by the anterior pituitary gland, that increases the release of thyroxine and the uptake of iodide by the thyroid gland. See Figures 5.9, 5.14.

thyrotropin-releasing hormone (TRH) A hypothalamic hormone that regulates the release of thyroid-stimulating hormone. See Figure 5.9.

thyroxine A hormone released by the thyroid gland. See Table 5.2.

timbre The relative intensities of the various harmonics, which gives each musical instrument its characteristic sound quality.

tinnitus A sensation of noises or ringing in the ears.

tip link A fine, threadlike fiber that runs along and connects the tips of stereocilia. See Figure 9.4.

TMS See *transcranial magnetic stimulation*.

tolerance A condition in which, with repeated exposure to a drug, an individual becomes less responsive to a constant dose. Contrast with *sensitization* (definition 2).

tomography A technique for revealing the detailed structure of a particular tissue using radiation. Examples include computerized axial tomography (CAT or CT) and positron emission tomography (PET).

tonic receptor A receptor in which the frequency of nerve impulse discharge declines slowly or not at all as stimulation is maintained.

tonotopic organization A major organizational feature in auditory systems in which neurons are arranged as an orderly map of stimulus frequency, with cells responsive to high frequencies located at a distance from those responsive to low frequencies.

torpor The condition in which animals allow body temperature to fall drastically. During torpor, animals are unresponsive to most stimuli.

Tourette's syndrome A heightened sensitivity to tactile, auditory, and visual stimuli that may be accompanied by the buildup of an urge to emit verbal or phonic tics.

toxin A poisonous substance, especially one that is produced by living organisms.

tract A bundle of axons found within the central nervous system. Contrast with *nerve*.

transcranial magnetic stimulation (TMS) Localized electrical stimulation of the brain through the skull caused by changes in the magnetic field in coils of wire around the head. Depending on the parameters, TMS may elicit a response or disrupt functioning in the region for a brief time. Also known as *repetitive TMS* or *rTMS*.

transcript The mRNA strand that is produced when a stretch of DNA is "read."

transcription The process during which mRNA forms bases complementary to a strand of DNA. The resulting message (called a *transcript*) is then used to translate the DNA code into protein molecules. See Figure A.2 in the appendix.

transcutaneous electrical nerve stimulation (TENS) The delivery of electrical pulses through electrodes attached to the skin, which excite nerves that supply the region to which pain is referred. TENS can relieve the pain in some instances.

transducer A device that converts energy from one form to another. Sensory receptor cells are one example.

transduction The conversion of one form of energy to another.

transgenic Referring to animals in which a new or altered gene has been deliberately introduced into the genome. See Box 7.3.

translation The process by which amino acids are linked together (directed by an mRNA molecule) to form protein molecules. See Figure A.2 in the appendix.

transmitter See *neurotransmitter*.

transneuronal degeneration The degeneration of neurons that formed synapses on, or received synapses from, a recently departed neuron.

transporters Specialized receptors in the presynaptic membrane that recognize transmitter molecules and return them to the presynaptic neuron for reuse.

transverse plane See *coronal plane*.

tremor A rhythmic, repetitive movement caused by brain pathology.

tremor at rest A tremor that occurs when the affected region, such as a limb, is fully supported; a symptom of Parkinson's disease.

TRH See *thyrotropin-releasing hormone*.

trichromatic hypothesis A hypothesis of color perception that there are three different types of cones, each excited by a different region of the spectrum and each having a separate pathway to the brain.

tricyclic antidepressants A class of compounds whose structure resembles that of chlorpromazine and of related antipsychotic drugs. Tricyclic antidepressants may relieve depression, but only after 2 to 3 weeks of daily administration.

trigger mechanism   A particular stimulus characteristic that is most effective in evoking responses from a particular cell.

triiodothyronine   A thyroid hormone. See Table 5.2.

trinucleotide repeat   Repetition of the same three nucleotides within a gene, which can lead to dysfunction, as in the cases of Huntington's disease and fragile X syndrome.

triplet code   A code for an amino acid specified by three successive bases of a DNA molecule.

tropic hormones   A class of anterior pituitary hormones that affect the secretion of other endocrine glands. See Figure 5.14.

TSH   See *thyroid-stimulating hormone*.

TTX   See *tetrodotoxin*.

tuning curve   A graph of the responses of a single auditory nerve fiber or neuron to sounds that vary in frequency and intensity.

turbinates   Complex shapes underlying the olfactory mucosa that direct inspired air over receptor cells. See Figures 9.18, 9.20.

Turner's syndrome   A condition seen in individuals carrying a single X chromosome but no other sex chromosome.

tympanic canal   One of three principal canals running along the length of the cochlea. The other two are the middle canal and the vestibular canal. See Figure 9.1.

tympanic membrane   The partition between the external ear and the middle ear. Also called *eardrum*. See Figure 9.1.

typical neuroleptics   A major class of antischizophrenic drugs that share an antagonist activity at dopamine D_2 receptors. Contrast with *atypical neuroleptics*.

ultradian   Referring to a rhythmic biological event whose period is shorter than that of a circadian rhythm, usually from several minutes to several hours. Contrast with *infradian*.

ultrasound   High-frequency sound; in general, beyond the threshold for human hearing, at about 20,000 Hz.

umami   A putative basic taste, probably mediated by the amino acid glutamate in foods.

unconditioned response (UR)   See *classical conditioning*.

unconditioned stimulus (US)   See *classical conditioning*.

undershoot   Here, the portion of the action potential when the membrane potential is transiently hyperpolarized relative to the resting potential. See Figures 3.5, 3.6. Contrast with *overshoot*.

unipolar depression   Depression that alternates with normal emotional states. Contrast with *bipolar disorder*.

unmyelinated axon   A fine-diameter axon that lacks a myelin sheath.

up-regulation   A compensatory increase in receptor availability at the synapses of a neuron. For example, repeated exposure to an antagonist drug may cause a neuron to produce more of the type of receptors to which that drug binds. Contrast with *down-regulation*.

UR   See *classical conditioning*.

urethra (pl. urethras or urethrae)   The duct that carries urine from the bladder to outside the body.

US   See *classical conditioning*.

uterine tube   See *fallopian tube*.

uterus (pl. uteri)   The organ in which the fertilized egg implants and develops in mammals. See Figures 12.8, 12.16.

utricle   A small, fluid-filled sac in the vestibular system above the saccule that responds to static positions of the head. See Figure 9.14.

V1   See *primary visual cortex*.

vagina   The opening in female genitalia that permits entry of the penis during copulation and later releases the fetus or egg. See Figures 12.8, 12.16.

vagus nerve   Cranial nerve X, which fulfills many functions, including innervation of many parasympathetic ganglia throughout the body and transmittal of information from various body organs to the brain. See Figures 2.4, 13.24.

vanilloid receptor 1 (VR1)   A receptor that binds capsaicin to transmit the burning sensation from chili peppers. It may be the receptor for detecting sudden increases in temperature. See Figure 8.23.

vanilloid receptor-like protein 1 (VRL1)   A receptor, found in some free nerve endings, that opens its channel in response to rising temperatures. See Figure 8.23.

varicosity   The axonal swelling from which neurotransmitter diffuses in a nondirected synapse.

vas deferens (pl. vasa deferentia)   A duct that connects the epididymis to the seminal vesicles. Also called *ductus deferens*. See Figures 12.8, 12.16.

vasopressin   See *arginine vasopressin*.

ventral   In the context of anatomy, referring to structures toward the belly or front of the body, or the bottom of the brain. See Box 2.1. Contrast with *dorsal*.

ventral root   See *roots*.

ventral tegmental area   A portion of the midbrain that projects dopaminergic fibers to the nucleus accumbens.

ventricle   See *cerebral ventricle*.

ventricular system   A system of fluid-filled cavities inside the brain. See Figure 2.14.

ventricular zone   A region lining the cerebral ventricles that displays mitosis, providing neurons early in development and glial cells throughout life. Also called *ependymal layer*. See Figure 7.6.

ventromedial hypothalamus (VMH)   A hypothalamic region involved in inhibiting eating, among other functions. See Figures 12.6, 13.21.

vertebral arteries   Arteries that ascend the vertebrae, enter the base of the skull, and join together to form the basilar artery. See Figure 2.15.

vertex spike   An EEG pattern seen during stage 1 slow-wave sleep. See Figure 14.11.

vestibular canal   One of three principal canals running along the length of the cochlea. The other two are the middle canal and the tympanic canal. See Figure 9.1.

vestibular nuclei   Brainstem nuclei that receive information from the vestibular organs through cranial nerve VIII (the auditory, or vestibulocochlear, nerve).

vestibular system   A receptor system in the inner ear that responds to mechanical forces, such as gravity and acceleration. See Figure 9.14.

vestibulocochlear nerve   See *auditory nerve*.

vestibulospinal tract   The group of axons, originating from the vestibular nuclei in the brainstem, that innervates neurons in the spinal cord. See Figure 11.17.

visual acuity   Sharpness of vision.

visual cortex   See *occipital cortex*.

visual field   The whole area that you can see without moving your head or eyes.

visual paired comparison   A task, originally devised for testing human infants, that measures an individual's tendency to look at a novel object in comparison with a familiar one.

viviparity   Literally "live birth"; reproduction in which the zygote develops extensively within the female until a well-formed individual emerges. Contrast with *oviparity*.

viviparous   Of or relating to viviparity. Contrast with *oviparous*.

VMH   See *ventromedial hypothalamus*.

VNO   See *vomeronasal organ*.

volley theory   A theory of frequency discrimination that emphasizes the relation between sound frequency and the firing pattern of nerve cells. For example, a 500 Hz tone would produce 500 neural discharges per second by a nerve cell or group of nerve cells. Contrast with *place theory*.

voltage-gated ion channel   An ion channel that opens or closes in response to the voltage difference across the membrane—for example, the voltage-gated Na^+ channel that mediates the action potential. Contrast with *ligand-gated ion channel*.

volt   A measure of the electrical-potential difference between two regions.

vomeronasal organ (VNO)   A collection of specialized receptor cells near but separate from the olfactory epithelium. These sensory cells detect pheromones and send electrical signals to the accessory olfactory bulb in the brain.

vomeronasal system   A specialized chemical detection system that detects pheromones and transmits information to the brain.

VR1   See *vanilloid receptor 1*.

VRL1   See *vanilloid receptor-like protein 1*.

vulva (pl. vulvae)   The region around the opening of the vagina.

Wada test A test in which a short-lasting anesthetic is delivered into one carotid artery to determine which cerebral hemisphere principally mediates language. See Box 19.1.

wallerian degeneration See *anterograde degeneration*.

wavelength Here, the length between two peaks in a repeated stimulus such as a wave, light, or sound. See Box 9.1.

Wernicke's aphasia A language impairment that is characterized by fluent, meaningless speech and little language comprehension; related to damage to Wernicke's area. See Figure 19.7.

Wernicke's area A region of the left hemisphere that is involved in language comprehension. See Figures 19.6, 19.7, 19.8.

Western blot A method of detecting a particular protein molecule in a tissue or organ, by separating proteins from that source with gel electrophoresis, blotting the separated proteins onto nitrocellulose, and then using an antibody that binds, and highlights, the protein of interest.

whisker barrel A barrel-shaped column of somatosensory cortex in rodents that receives information from a particular whisker. See Figure 7.22.

white matter A shiny layer underneath the cortex that consists largely of axons with white myelin sheaths. See Figure 2.8. Contrast with *gray matter*.

Williams syndrome A disorder characterized by largely intact, even fluent linguistic function, but clear mental retardation on standard IQ tests. Individuals suffering from this syndrome have great difficulty in copying a pattern of blocks, or assembling a picture from its parts. See Figure 19.16.

withdrawal symptom An uncomfortable symptom that arises when a person stops taking a drug that he or she has used frequently, especially at high doses.

wolffian duct A primitive duct system in the embryo that will develop into male structures (the epididymis, vas deferens, and seminal vesicles) if testes are present in the embryo. See Figure 12.16. Contrast with *müllerian duct*.

word blindness The inability to recognize written words.

word deafness The specific inability to hear words, although other sounds can be detected.

zeitgeber Literally "time-giver"; the stimulus (usually the light–dark cycle) that entrains circadian rhythms.

Zucker strain A strain of rats that display obesity.

zygote The fertilized egg.

References

Aarons, L. (1976). Sleep-assisted instruction. *Psychological Bulletin, 83*, 1–40.

Aaronson, S. T., Rashed, S., Biber, M. P., and Hobson, J. A. (1982). Brain state and body position. A time-lapse video study of sleep. *Archives of General Psychiatry, 39*, 330–335.

Abel, E. L. (1982). Consumption of alcohol during pregnancy: A review of effects on growth and development of offspring. *Human Biology, 54*, 421–453.

Abel, E. L. (1984). Prenatal effects of alcohol. *Drug and Alcohol Dependence, 14*, 1–10.

Abraham, S. F., Baker, R. M., Blaine, E. H., Denton, D. A., et al. (1975). Water drinking induced in sheep by angiotensin—A physiological or pharmacological effect? *Journal of Comparative and Physiological Psychology, 88*, 503–518.

Abraham, W. C., and Goddard, G. V. (1985). Multiple traces of neural activity in the hippocampus. In N. M. Weinberger, J. L. McGaugh, and G. Lynch (Eds.), *Memory systems of the brain* (pp. 62–76). New York: Guilford.

Adams, C. S., Korytko, A. I., and Blank, J. L. (2003). A novel mechanism of body mass regulation. *Journal of Experimental Biology, 206*, 2535–2536.

Adelson, E. H. (1993). Perceptual organization and the judgment of brightness. *Science, 262*, 2042–2044.

Ader, R. (2001). Psychoneuroimmunology. *Current Directions in Psychological Science, 10*, 94–98.

Ader, R., and Cohen, N. (1993). Psychoneuroimmunology: Conditioning and stress. *Annual Review of Psychology, 44*, 53–85.

Ader, R., Felten, D., and Cohen, N. (1990). Interactions between the brain and the immune system. *Annual Review of Pharmacology and Toxicology, 30*, 561–602.

Adler, E., Hoon, M. A., Mueller, K. L., Chandrashekar, J., et al. (2000). A novel family of mammalian taste receptors. *Cell, 100*, 693–702.

Adler, N., and Matthews, K. (1994). Health psychology: Why do some people get sick and some stay well? *Annual Review of Psychology, 45*, 229–259.

Adolphs, R., Tranel, D., and Damasio, A. R. (1998). The human amygdala in social judgment. *Nature, 393*, 470–474.

Adolphs, R., Tranel, D., Damasio, H., and Damasio, A. (1994). Impaired recognition of emotion in facial expressions following bilateral damage to the human amygdala. *Nature, 372*, 669–672.

Agmon-Snir, H., Carr, C. E., and Rinzel, J. (1998). The role of dendrites in auditory coincidence detection. *Nature, 393*, 268–272.

Agre, P., King, L. S., Yasui, M., Guggino, W. B., et al. (2002). Aquaporin water channels—From atomic structure to clinical medicine. *Journal of Physiology, 542*, 3–16.

Ahn, S., and Phillips, A. G. (2002). Modulation by central and basolateral amygdalar nuclei of dopaminergic correlates of feeding to satiety in the rat nucleus accumbens and medial prefrontal cortex. *Journal of Neuroscience, 22*, 10958–10965.

Akbarian, S., Kim, J. J., Potkin, S. G., Hetrick, W. P., et al. (1996). Maldistribution of interstitial neurons in prefrontal white matter of the brains of schizophrenic patients. *Archives of General Psychiatry, 53*, 425–436.

Albanese, A., Hamill, G., Jones, J., Skuse, D., Matthews, D. R., and Stanhope, R. (1994). Reversibility of physiological growth hormone secretion in children with psychosocial dwarfism. *Clinical Endocrinology (Oxford), 40*, 687–692.

al-Barazanji, K. A., Buckingham, R. E., Arch, J. R., Haynes, A., et al. (1997). Effects of intracerebroventricular infusion of leptin in obese Zucker rats. *Obesity Research, 5*, 387–394.

Alberts, J. R. (1978). Huddling by rat pups: Multisensory control of contact behavior. *Journal of Comparative and Physiological Psychology, 92*, 220–230.

Aldrich, M. A. (1993). The neurobiology of narcolepsy-cataplexy. *Progress in Neurobiology, 41*, 533–541.

Almada, S. J., Zonderman, A. B., Shekelle, R. B., Dyer, A. R., et al. (1991). Neuroticism and cynicism and risk of death in middle-aged men: The Western Electric Study. *Psychosomatic Medicine, 53*, 165–175.

Alpert, M., and Friedhoff, A. J. (1980). An undopamine hypothesis of schizophrenia. *Schizophrenia Bulletin, 6*, 387–390.

Altman, J. (1969). Autoradiographic and histological studies of postnatal neurogenesis. IV. Cell proliferation and migration in the anterior forebrain, with special reference to persisting neurogenesis in the olfactory bulb. *Journal of Comparative Neurology, 137*, 433–457.

Altschuler, E. L., Wisdom, S. B., Stone, L., Foster, C., et al. (1999). Rehabilitation of hemiparesis after stroke with a mirror. *Lancet, 353*, 2035–2036.

American Academy of Ophthalmology. (1994). Amblyopia: Etiology, diagnosis, and treatment. *Journal of Ophthalmic Nursing and Technology, 13*, 273–275.

American Psychiatric Association. (1994). *Diagnostic and statistical manual of mental disorders: DSM-IV* (4th ed.). Washington, DC: American Psychiatric Association.

Amos, L. A., and Cross, R. A. (1997). Structure and dynamics of molecular motors. *Current Opinion in Structural Biology, 7*, 239–246.

Amunts, K., Schlaug, G., Jaencke, L., Steinmetz, H., et al. (1997). Motor cortex and hand motor skills: Structural compliance in the human brain. *Human Brain Mapping, 5*, 206–215.

Anand, B. K., and Brobeck, J. R. (1951). Localization of a "feeding center" in the hypothalamus of the rat. *Proceedings of the Society for Experimental Biology and Medicine, 77*, 323–324.

Andersen, P. M., Nilsson, P., Ala-Hurula, V., Keranen, M. L., et al. (1995). Amyotrophic lateral sclerosis associated with homozygosity for an Asp90Ala mutation in CuZn-superoxide dismutase. *Nature Genetics, 10*, 61–66.

Anderson, M. J., and Dixson, A. F. (2002). Sperm competition: Motility and the midpiece in primates. *Nature, 416*, 496.

Anderson, N. D., and Craik, F. I. M. (2000). Memory in the aging brain. In E. Tulving and F. I. M. Craik (Eds.), *The Oxford handbook of memory* (pp. 411–425). Oxford, England: Oxford University Press.

Anderson, S. A., Eisenstat, D. D., Shi, L., and Rubenstein, J. L. (1997). Interneuron migration from basal forebrain to neocortex: Dependence on Dlx genes. *Science, 278*, 474–476.

Andreasen, N. C. (1991). Assessment issues and the cost of schizophrenia. *Schizophrenia Bulletin, 17*, 475–481.

Andreasen, N. C. (1994). Changing concepts of schizophrenia and the ahistorical fallacy. *American Journal of Psychiatry, 151*, 1405–1407.

Andreasen, N. C., Flaum, M., Swayze, V. O. D. S., Alliger, R., et al. (1993). Intelligence and brain structure in normal individuals. *American Journal of Psychiatry, 150,* 130–134.

Andreasen, N., Nassrallah, H. A., Dunn, V., Olson, S. C., et al. (1986). Structural abnormalities in the frontal system in schizophrenia. *Archives of General Psychiatry, 43,* 136–144.

Andrew, D., and Craig, A. D. (2001). Spinothalamic lamina I neurons selectively sensitive to histamine: A central neural pathway for itch. *Nature Neuroscience, 4,* 72–77.

Anson, R. M., Guo, Z., de Cabo, R., Iyun, T., et al. (2003). Intermittent fasting dissociates beneficial effects of dietary restriction on glucose metabolism and neuronal resistance to injury from calorie intake. *Proceedings of the National Academy of Sciences, USA, 100,* 6216–6220.

Archer, G. S., Friend, T. H., Piedrahita, J., Nevill, C. H., et al. (2003). Behavioral variation among cloned pigs. *Applied Animal Behaviour Science, 82,* 151–161.

Archer, S. N., Robilliard, D. L., Skene, D. J., Smits, M., et al. (2003). A length polymorphism in the circadian clock gene Per3 is linked to delayed sleep phase syndrome and extreme diurnal preference. *Sleep, 26,* 413–415.

Arendt, J., Skene, D. J., Middleton, B., Lockley, S. W., et al. (1997). Efficacy of melatonin treatment in jet lag, shift work, and blindness. *Journal of Biological Rhythms, 12,* 604–617.

Arnold, A. P. (1980). Sexual differences in the brain. *American Scientist, 68,* 165–173.

Arnold, A. P., and Schlinger, B. A. (1993). Sexual differentiation of brain and behavior: The zebra finch is not just a flying rat. *Brain, Behavior and Evolution, 42,* 231–241.

Aroniadou, V. A., Maillis, A., and Stefanis, C. C. (1993). Dihydropyridine-sensitive calcium channels are involved in the induction of N-methyl-D-aspartate receptor-independent long-term potentiation in visual cortex of adult rats. *Neuroscience Letters, 151,* 77–80.

Asberg, M., Nordstrom, P., and Traskman-Bendz, L. (1986). Cerebrospinal fluid studies in suicide. An overview. *Annals of the New York Academy of Sciences, 487,* 243–255.

Aserinsky, E., and Kleitman, N. (1953). Regularly occurring periods of eye motility, and concomitant phenomena, during sleep. *Science, 118,* 273–274.

Ashmore, J. F. (1994). The cellular machinery of the cochlea. *Experimental Physiology, 79,* 113–134.

Aungst, J. L., Heyward, P. M., Puche, A. C., Karnup, S. V., et al. (2003). Centre-surround inhibition among olfactory bulb glomeruli. *Nature, 426,* 623–629.

Avan, P., Loth, D., Menguy, C., and Teyssou, M. (1992). Hypothetical roles of middle ear muscles in the guinea-pig. *Hearing Research, 59,* 59–69.

Azar, B. (1995). NIAAA: 25 years of alcohol research. *American Psychological Association Monitor, 26,* 5, 23.

Bachevalier, J., Brickson, M., and Hagger, C. (1993). Limbic-dependent recognition memory in monkeys develops early in infancy. *Neuroreport, 4,* 77–80.

Bach-y-Rita, P. (1992). Recovery from brain damage. *Journal of Neurologic Rehabilitation, 6,* 191–199.

Bacskai, B. J., Hickey, G. A., Skoch, J., Kajdasz, S. T., et al. (2003). Four-dimensional multiphoton imaging of brain entry, amyloid binding, and clearance of an amyloid-beta ligand in transgenic mice. *Proceedings of the National Academy of Sciences, USA, 100,* 12462–12467.

Baddeley, A. D., and Warrington, E. K. (1970). Amnesia and the distinction between long- and short-term memory. *Journal of Verbal Learning and Verbal Behavior, 9,* 176–189.

Bagemihl, B. (1999). Biological exuberance: Animal homosexuality and natural diversity. New York: St. Martin's.

Bailey, C. H., and Chen, M. (1983). Morphological basis of long-term habituation and sensitization in *Aplysia. Science, 220,* 91–93.

Bailey, J. M., and Bell, A. P. (1993). Familiality of female and male homosexuality. *Behavior Genetics, 23,* 313–322.

Bailey, J. M., and Pillard, R. C. (1991). A genetic study of male sexual orientation. *Archives of General Psychiatry, 48,* 1089–1096.

Bailey, J. M., R. C. Pillard, M. C. Neale, and Y. Agyei. (1993). Heritable factors influence sexual orientation in women. *Archives of General Psychiatry, 50,* 217–223.

Baker, D. G., West, S. A., Nicholson, W. E., Ekhator, N. N., et al. (1999). Serial CSF corticotropin-releasing hormone levels and adrenocortical activity in combat veterans with post-traumatic stress disorder. *American Journal of Psychiatry, 156,* 585–588.

Ball, G. F., and Hulse, S. H. (1998). Birdsong. *American Psychologist, 53,* 37–58.

Ballantine, H. T., Bouckoms, A. J., Thomas, E. K., and Giriunas, I. E. (1987). Treatment of psychiatric illness by stereotactic cingulotomy. *Biological Psychiatry, 22,* 807–820.

Balota, D. A., Dolan, P. O., and Duchek, J. M. (2000). Memory changes in healthy older adults. In E. Tulving and F. I. M. Craik (Eds.), *The Oxford handbook of memory* (pp. 395–409). Oxford, England: Oxford University Press.

Baltes, P. B. (1997). On the incomplete architecture of human ontogeny: Selection, optimization, and compensation as foundation of developmental theory. *American Psychologist, 52,* 366–380.

Bancaud, J., Brunet-Bourgin, F., Chauvel, P., and Halgren, E. (1994). Anatomical origin of deja vu and vivid "memories" in human temporal lobe. *Brain, 117,* 71–90.

Bannon, A. W., Decker, M. W., Holladay, M. W., Curzon, P., et al. (1998). Broad-spectrum, non-opioid analgesic activity by selective modulation of neuronal nicotinic acetylcholine receptors. *Science, 279,* 77–81.

Bao, S., Chan, V. T., and Merzenich, M. M. (2001). Cortical remodelling induced by activity of ventral tegmental dopamine neurons. *Nature, 412,* 79–83.

Baptista, L. F. (1996). Nature and its nurturing in avian vocal development. In D. E. Kroodsma and E. H. Miller (Eds.), *Ecology and evolution of acoustic communication in birds* (pp. 39–60). Ithaca, NY: Cornell University Press.

Baptista, L., and Petrinovich, L. (1986). Song development in the white-crowned sparrow: Social factors and sex differences. *Animal Behaviour, 34,* 1359–1371.

Barasa, A. 1960. Forma, grandezza e densita dei neuroni della corteccia cerebrale in mammiferi di grandezza corporea differente. *Zeitschrift für Zellforschung, 53,* 69–89.

Barbeau, H., Norman, K., Fung, J., Visintin, M., et al. (1998). Does neurorehabilitation play a role in the recovery of walking in neurological populations? *Annals of the New York Academy of Sciences, 860,* 377–392.

Barbour, H. G. (1912). Die Wirkung unmittelbarer Erwärmung und Abkühlung der Warmenzentren auf die Korpertemperatur. *Archiv für Experimentalle Pathologie und Pharmakologie, 70,* 1–26.

Barden, N., Reul, J. M., and Holsboer, F. (1995). Do antidepressants stabilize mood through actions on the hypothalamic-pituitary-adrenocortical system? *Trends in Neurosciences, 18,* 6–11.

Bark, N. (2002). Did schizophrenia change the course of English history? The mental illness of Henry VI. *Medical Hypotheses, 59,* 416–421.

Barkow, J. H., Cosmides, L., and Tooby, J. (1992). *The adapted mind: Evolutionary psychology and the generation of culture.* New York: Oxford University Press.

Barlow, H. B. (1953). Summation and inhibition in the frog's retina. *Journal of Physiology (London), 119,* 69–88.

Barlow, H. B., and Levick, W. R. (1965). The mechanism of directionally selective units in rabbit's retina. *Journal of Physiology, 178,* 477–504.

Barnett, S. A. (1975). *The rat: A study in behavior.* Chicago: University of Chicago Press.

Baron-Cohen, S. (2003). *The essential difference: Men, women and the extreme male brain.* London: Allen Lane.

Barrionuevo, G., Schottler, F., and Lynch, G. (1980). The effects of repetitive low frequency stimulation on control and "potentiated" synaptic responses in the hippocampus. *Life Sciences, 27,* 2385–2391.

Bartels, A., and Zeki, S. (2000). The neural basis of romantic love. *Neuroreport, 11,* 3829–3834.

Bartfai, T. (2001). Telling the brain about pain. *Nature, 410,* 425–426.

Bartoshuk, L. M. (1993). Genetic and pathological taste variation: What can we learn from animal models and human disease? In D. Chadwick, J. Marsh, and J. Goode (Eds.), *The molecular basis of smell and taste transduction* (pp. 251–267). New York: Wiley.

Bartoshuk, L. M., and Beauchamp, G. K. (1994). Chemical senses. *Annual Review of Psychology, 45,* 419–449.

Basbaum, A., and Fields, H. L. (1978). Endogenous pain control mechanisms: Review and hypothesis. *Annals of Neurology, 4,* 451–462.

Basbaum, A., and Fields, H. L. (1984). Endogenous pain control systems: Brainstem spinal pathways and endorphin circuitry. *Annual Review of Neuroscience, 7,* 309–339.

Basil, J. A., Kamil, A. C., Balda, R. P., and Fite, K. V. (1996). Differences in hippocampal volume among food storing corvids. *Brain, Behavior and Evolution, 47,* 156–164.

Batterham, R. L., and Bloom, S. R. (2003). The gut hormone peptide YY regulates appetite. *Annals of the New York Academy of Sciences, 994,* 162–168.

Batterham, R. L., Cohen, M. A., Ellis, S. M., Le Roux, C. W., et al. (2003). Inhibition of food intake in obese subjects by peptide YY_{3-36}. *New England Journal of Medicine, 349,* 941–948.

Batterham, R. L., Cowley, M. A., Small, C. J., Herzog, H., et al. (2002). Gut hormone PYY_{3-36} physiologically inhibits food intake. *Nature, 418,* 650–654.

Batterham, R. L., Cowley, M. A., Small, C. J., Herzog, H., et al. (2004). Physiology: Does gut hormone PYY_{3-36} decrease food intake in rodents? *Nature, 430,* Brief Communications Arising (online only at www.nature.com).

Baum, A., and Posluszny, D. M. (1999). Health psychology: Mapping biobehavioral contributions to health and illness. *Annual Review of Psychology, 50,* 137–163.

Baumgardner, T. L., Green, K. E., and Reiss, A. L. (1994). A behavioral neurogenetics approach to developmental disabilities: Gene-brain-behavior associations. *Current Opinion in Neurology, 7,* 172–178.

Beach, F. A. (1971). Hormonal factors controlling the differentiation, development, and display of copulatory behavior in the ramstergig and related species. In E. Tobach, L. R. Aronson, and E. Shaw (Eds.), *The Biopsychology of Development* (pp. 249–296). New York: Academic Press.

Beach, F. A. (1977). *Human sexuality in four perspectives.* Baltimore: Johns Hopkins University Press.

Beach, F. A., and Holz, A. M. (1946). Mating behavior in male rats castrated at various ages and injected with androgen. *Journal of Experimental Zoology, 101,* 91–142.

Bear, M. F., and Malenka, R. C. (1994). Synaptic plasticity. *Current Opinion in Neurobiology, 4,* 389–399.

Beattie, E. C., Stellwagen, D., Morishita, W., Bresnahan, J. C., et al. (2002). Control of synaptic strength by glial TNFα. *Science, 295,* 2282–2285.

Beauchamp, G. K., Cowart, B. J., Mennella, J. A., and Marsh, R. R. (1994). Infant salt taste: Developmental, methodological, and contextual factors. *Developmental Psychobiology, 27,* 353–365.

Beggs, W. D., and Foreman, D. L. (1980). Sound localization and early binaural experience in the deaf. *British Journal of Audiology, 14,* 41–48.

Behl, C. (2002). Oestrogen as a neuroprotective hormone. *Nature Reviews. Neuroscience, 3,* 433–442.

Bellinger, D. L., Ackerman, K. D., Felten, S. Y., and Felten, D. L. (1992). A longitudinal study of age-related loss of noradrenergic nerves and lymphoid cells in the rat spleen. *Experimental Neurology, 116,* 295–311.

Bellugi, U., Poizner, H., and Klima, E. S. (1983). Brain organization for language: Clues from sign aphasia. *Human Neurobiology, 2,* 155–171.

Belluscio, L., Gold, G. H., Nemes, A., and Axel, R. (1998). Mice deficient in G(olf) are anosmic. *Neuron, 20,* 69–81.

Bennett, A. F., and Ruben, J. A. (1979). Endothermy and activity in vertebrates. *Science, 206,* 649–654.

Bennett, E. L., Diamond, M. L., Krech, D., and Rosenzweig, M. R. (1964). Chemical and anatomical plasticity of brain. *Science, 146,* 610–619.

Bennett, E. L., Orme, A. E., and Hebert, M. (1972). Cerebral protein synthesis inhibition and amnesia produced by scopolamine, cycloheximide, streptovitacin A, anisomycin, and emetine in rat. *Federation Proceedings, 31,* 838.

Bennett, E. L., Rosenzweig, M. R., and Diamond, M. C. (1969). Rat brain: Effects of environmental enrichment on wet and dry weights. *Science, 163,* 825–826.

Bennett, M. V. (2000). Electrical synapses, a personal perspective (or history). *Brain Research Reviews, 32,* 16–28.

Bennett, W. (1983). The nicotine fix. *Rhode Island Medical Journal, 66,* 455–458.

Ben-Shachar, D., Belmaker, R. H,. Grisaru, N., and Klein, E. (1997). Transcranial magnetic stimulation induces alterations in brain monoamines. *Journal of Neural Transmission, 104,* 191–197.

Benson, A. J. (1990). Sensory functions and limitations of the vestibular system. In R. Warren and A. H. Wertheim (Eds.), *Perception and control of self-motion* (pp. 145–170). Hillsdale, NJ: Erlbaum.

Benton, M. J., and Ayala, F. J. (2003). Dating the tree of life. *Science, 300,* 1698–1700.

Berenbaum, S. A. (2001). Cognitive function in congenital adrenal hyperplasia. *Endocrinology and Metabolism Clinics of North America, 30,* 173–192.

Berger, T. W., and Orr, W. B. (1983). Hippocampectomy selectively disrupts discrimination reversal conditioning of the rabbit nictitating membrane response. *Behavioural Brain Research, 8,* 49–68.

Berman, K. F., and Weinberger, D. R. (1990). The prefrontal cortex in schizophrenia and other neuropsychiatric diseases: *In vivo* physiological correlates of cognitive deficits. *Progress in Brain Research, 85,* 521–536.

Berneche, S., and Roux, B. (2001). Energetics of ion conduction through the K+ channel. *Nature, 414,* 73–77.Bernhardt, P. C. (1997). Influences of serotonin and testosterone in aggression and dominance: Convergence with social psychology. *Current Directions in Psychological Science, 2(6),* 44–48.

Bernhardt, P. C., Dabbs, J. M., Jr., Fielden, J. A., and Lutter, C. D. (1998). Testosterone changes during vicarious experiences of winning and losing among fans at sporting events. *Physiology & Behavior, 65,* 59–62.

Bernstein, I. S., and Gordon, T. P. (1974). The function of aggression in primate societies. *American Scientist, 62,* 304–311.

Bernstein, L. E., Auer, E. T., Jr., Moore, J. K., Ponton, C. W., et al. (2002). Visual speech perception without primary auditory cortex activation. *Neuroreport, 13,* 311–315.

Bernstein-Goral, H., and Bregman, B. S. (1993). Spinal cord transplants support the regeneration of axotomized neurons after spinal cord lesions at birth: A quantitative double-labeling study. *Experimental Neurology, 123,* 118–132.

Besedovsky, H. O., and del Rey, A. (1992). Immune-neuroendocrine circuits: Integrative role of cytokines. *Frontiers of Neuroendocrinology, 13,* 61–94.

Betarbet, R., Sherer, T. B., MacKenzie, G., Garcia-Osuna, M., et al. (2000). Chronic systemic pesticide exposure reproduces features of Parkinson's disease. *Nature Neuroscience, 3,* 1301–1306.

Bigelow, L., Nasrallah, H. A., and Rauscher, F. P. (1983). Corpus callosum thickness in chronic schizophrenia. *British Journal of Psychiatry, 142,* 284–287.

Binder, J. R., Rao, S. M., Hammeke, T. A., Yetkin, F. Z., et al. et al. (1994). Functional magnetic resonance imaging of human auditory cortex. *Annals of Neurology, 35,* 662–672.

Birnbaumer, L., Abramowitz, J., and Brown, A. M. (1990). Receptor-effector coupling by G proteins. *Biochimica et Biophysica Acta, 1031,* 163–224.

Björklund, A., and Lindvall, O. (2000). Cell replacement therapies for central nervous system disorders. *Nature Neuroscience, 3,* 537–544.

Black, J. E., and Greenough, W. T. (1998). Developmental approaches to the memory process. In J. L. Martinez, Jr., and R. P. Kesner (Eds.), *Neurobiology of learning and memory* (pp. 55–88). San Diego, CA: Academic Press.

Blake, D. J., Weir, A., Newey, S. E., and Davies, K. E. (2002). Function and genetics of dystrophin and dystrophin-related proteins in muscle. *Physiology Review, 82,* 291–329.

Blakemore, C. (1976). The conditions required for the maintenance of binocularity in the kitten's visual cortex. *Journal of Physiology (London), 261,* 423–444.

Blakemore, C., and Campbell, F. W. (1969). On the existence of neurones in the human visual system selectively sensitive to the orientation and size of retinal images. *Journal of Physiology (London), 203,* 237–260.

Blaxton, T. A., Bookheimer, S. Y., Zeffiro, T. A., Figlozzi, C. M., et al. (1996). Functional mapping of human memory using PET: Comparisons of conceptual perceptual tasks. *Canadian Journal of Experimental Psychology, 50,* 42–56.

Blehar, M. C., and Rosenthal, N. E. (1989). Seasonal affective disorders and phototherapy. Report of a National Institute of Mental Health-sponsored workshop. *Archives of General Psychiatry, 46,* 469–474.

Bleuler, E. (1950). *Dementia praecox; or, The group of schizophrenias* (translated by J. Zinkin). New York: International Universities Press.

Bliss, T. V. P., and Collingridge, G. L. (1993). A synaptic model of memory: Long-term potentiation in the hippocampus. *Nature, 361,* 31–39.

Bliss, T. V. P., and Gardner-Medwin, A. R. (1973). Long-lasting potentiation of synaptic transmission in the dentate area of the unanaesthetized rabbit following stimulation of the perforant path. *Journal of Physiology (London), 232,* 357–374.

Bliss, T. V. P., and Lømo, T. (1973). Long-lasting potentiation of synaptic transmission in the dentate area of the anaesthetized rabbit following stimulation of the perforant path. *Journal of Physiology (London), 232,* 331–356.

Bliwise, D. L. (1989). Neuropsychological function and sleep. *Clinics in Geriatric Medicine, 5,* 381–394.

Bloch, V. (1976). Brain activation and memory consolidation. In M. R. Rosenzweig and E. L. Bennett (Eds.), *Neural mechanisms of learning and memory* (pp. 583-590). Cambridge, MA: MIT Press.

Blodgett, H. C. (1929). The effect of the introduction of reward upon the maze performance of rats. *University of California Publications in Psychology, 4,* 113–134.

Blomqvist, D., Andersson, M., Kupper, C., Cuthill, I. C., et al. (2002). Genetic similarity between mates and extra-pair parentage in three species of shorebirds. *Nature, 419,* 613–615.

Blue, M. E., and Parnavelas, J. G. (1983). The formation and maturation of synapses in the visual cortex of the rat. II. Quantitative analysis. *Journal of Neurocytology, 12,* 697–712.

Blumberg, M. S., Sokoloff, G., and Kirby, R. F. (1997). Brown fat thermogenesis and cardiac rate regulation during cold challenge in infant rats. *American Journal of Physiology, 272,* R1308–R1313.

Bogen, J. E., Schultz, D. H., and Vogel, P. J. (1988). Completeness of callostomy shown by magnetic resonance imaging in the long term. *Archives of Neurology, 45,* 1203–1205.

Bonese, K. F., Wainer, B. H., Fitch, F. W., Rothberg, R. M., et al. (1974). Changes in heroin self-administration by a rhesus monkey after morphine immunisation. *Nature, 252,* 708–710.

Bonhoeffer, F., and Huf, J. (1985). Position-dependent properties of retinal axons and their growth cones. *Nature, 315,* 409–410.

Bonhoeffer, T., and Grinvald, A. (1991). Iso-orientation domains in cat visual cortex are arranged in pinwheel-like patterns. *Nature, 353,* 429–431.

Boolell, M., Gepi-Attee, S., Gingell, J. C., and Allen, M. J. (1996). Sildenafil, a novel effective oral therapy for male erectile dysfunction. *British Journal of Urology, 78,* 257–261.

Borod, J. C., Haywood, C. S., and Koff, E. (1997). Neuropsychological aspects of facial asymmetry during emotional expression: A review of the normal adult literature. *Neuropsychology Review, 7,* 41–60.

Borrow, S. J., Adam, K., Chapman, K., Oswald, I., et al. (1980). REM sleep and normal intelligence. *Biological Psychiatry, 15,* 165–169.

Boshuisen, M. L., Ter Horst, G. J., Paans, A. M., Reinders, A. A., et al. (2002). rCBF differences between panic disorder patients and control subjects during anticipatory anxiety and rest. *Biological Psychiatry, 52,* 126–135.

Bottjer, S. W., Miesner, E. A., and Arnold, A. P. (1984). Forebrain lesions disrupt development but not maintenance of song in passerine birds. *Science, 224,* 901–903.

Bourtchuladze, R., Frenguelli, B., Blendy, J., Cioffi, D., et al. (1994). Deficient long-term memory in mice with a targeted mutation of the cAMP-responsive element-binding protein. *Cell, 79,* 59–68.

Boutrel, B., Franc, B., Hen, R., Hamon, M., et al. (1999). Key role of 5-HT1B receptors in the regulation of paradoxical sleep as evidenced in 5-HT1B knock-out mice. *Journal of Neuroscience, 19,* 3204–3212.

Bouwknecht, J. A., Hijzen, T. H., van der Gugten, J., Maes, R. A., et al. (2001). Absence of 5-HT(1B) receptors is associated with impaired impulse control in male 5-HT(1B) knockout mice. *Biological Psychiatry, 49,* 557–568.

Bower, B. (2000). Genes to grow on. *Science News, 157*(9), 142.

Bower, B. (2003).Vision seekers. *Science News, 164,* 331–333.Brain, P. F. (1994). Neurotransmission, the individual and the alcohol/aggression link. Commentary on Miczek et al. "Neuropharmacological characteristics of individual differences in alcohol effects on aggression in rodents and primates." *Behavioural Pharmacology, 5,* 422–424.

Brainard, D. H., Roorda, A., Yamauchi, Y., Calderone, J. B. et al. (2000). Functional consequences of the relative numbers of L and M cones. *Journal of the Optical Society of America. Part A, Optics, Image Science and Vision, 17,* 607–614.

Branson, R., Potoczna, N., Kral, J. G., Lentes, K. U., et al. (2003). Binge eating as a major phenotype of melanocortin 4 receptor gene mutations. *New England Journal of Medicine, 348,* 1096–1103.

Braun, K. A., Ellis, R., and Loftus, E. F. (2002). Make my memory: How advertising can change our memories of the past. *Psychology and Marketing, 19,* 1–23.

Bray, G. A. (1969). Effect of caloric restriction on energy expenditure in obese patients. *Lancet, 2,* 397–398.

Breedlove, S. M. (1997). Sex on the brain. *Nature, 389,* 801.

Breier, A., Malhotra, A. K., Pinals, D. A., Weisenfeld, N. I., et al. (1997). Association of ketamine-induced psychosis with focal activation of the prefrontal cortex in healthy volunteers. *American Journal of Psychiatry, 154,* 805–811.

Breier, A., Su, T. P., Saunders, R., Carson, R. E., et al. (1997). Schizophrenia is associated with elevated amphetamine-induced synaptic dopamine concentrations: Evidence from a novel positron emission tomography method. *Proceedings of the National Academy of Sciences, USA, 94,* 2569–2574.

Breitner, J. C., Wyse, B. W., Anthony, J. C., Welsh-Bohmer, K. A., et al. (1999). APOE-epsilon4 count predicts age when prevalence of AD increases, then declines: The Cache County Study. *Neurology, 53,* 321–331.Bremer, F. (1938).

L'Activité électrique de l'écorce cérébrale. Paris: Hermann & Cie.

Bremner, J. D. (2003). Functional neuroanatomical correlates of traumatic stress revisited 7 years later, this time with data. *Psychopharmacology Bulletin, 37,* 6–25.

Bremner, J. D., Randall, P., Scott, T. M., Bronen, R. A., et al. (1995). MRI-based measurement of hippocampal volume in patients with combat-related posttraumatic stress disorder. *American Journal of Psychiatry, 152,* 973–981.

Bremner, J. D., Scott, T. M., Delaney, R. C., Southwick, S. M., et al. (1993). Deficits in short-term memory in posttraumatic stress disorder. *American Journal of Psychiatry, 150,* 1015–1019.

Brennan, P., Kaba, H., and Keverne, E. B. (1990). Olfactory recognition: A simple memory system. *Science, 250,* 1223–1226.

Brenowitz, E. A. (1991). Altered perception of species-specific song by female birds after lesions of a forebrain nucleus. *Science, 251,* 303–305.

Brewer, J. B., Zhao, Z., Desmond, J. E., Glover, G. H., et al. (1998). Making memories: Brain activity that predicts how well visual experience will be remembered. *Science, 281,* 1185–1187.

Brien, J. A. (1993). Oxtotoxicity associated with salicylates. A brief review. *Drug Safety, 9,* 143–148.

Broberg, D. J., and Bernstein, I. L. (1989). Cephalic insulin release in anorexic women. *Physiology and Behavior, 45,* 871–874.

Brook, J. S., Whiteman, M. M., and Finch, S. (1992). Childhood aggression, adolescent delinquency, and drug use: A longitudinal study. *Journal of Genetic Psychology, 153,* 369–383.

Brooks, R. (2000). Negative genetic correlation between male sexual attractiveness and survival. *Nature, 406,* 67–70.

Brooks, V. B. (1984). Cerebellar function in motor control. *Human Neurobiology, 2,* 251–260.

Brose, K., Bland, K. S., Wang, K. H., Arnott, D., et al. (1999). Slit proteins bind Robo receptors and have an evolutionarily conserved role in repulsive axon guidance. *Cell, 96,* 795–806.

Broughton, R. (1985). Slow-wave sleep awakenings in normal and in pathology: A brief review. In W. P. Koella, E. Ruther, and H. Schulz (Eds.), *Sleep '84* (pp. 164–167). Stuttgart, Germany: Gustav Fischer.

Broughton, R., Billings, R., Cartwright, R., Doucette, D., et al. (1994). Homicidal somnambulism: A case report. *Sleep, 17,* 253–264.

Brown, B. R. (2003). Sensing temperature without ion channels. *Nature, 421,* 495.

Brown, C. (2003, February 2). The man who mistook his wife for a deer. *The New York Times,* Section 6, p. 32.

Brown, G. L., Goodwin, F. K., Ballenger, J. C., Goyer, P. F., et al. (1979). Aggression in humans correlates with cerebrospinal fluid amine metabolites. *Psychiatry Research, 1,* 131–139.

Brown, J. (1958). Some tests of the decay theory of immediate memory. *Quarterly Journal of Experimental Psychology, 10,* 12–21.

Brown, W. A. (1998). The placebo effect. *Scientific American, 278*(1), 90–95.

Brown, R. E., and Milner, P. M. (2003). The legacy of Donald O. Hebb: More than the Hebb synapse. *Nature Review Neuroscience, 4 (12),* 1013–1019.

Brown, W. L. (1968). An hypothesis concerning the function of the metapleural gland in ants. *American Naturalist, 102,* 188–191.

Brownell, W. E., Bader, C. R., Bertrand, D., and de Ribaupierre, Y. (1985). Evoked mechanical

responses of isolated cochlear outer hair cells. *Science, 227,* 194–196.

Brownlee, S., and Schrof, J. M. (1997). The quality of mercy. Effective pain treatments already exist. Why aren't doctors using them? *U.S. News & World Report, 122,* 54–67.

Brunet, L. J., Gold, G. H., and Ngai, J. (1996). General anosmia caused by a targeted disruption of the mouse olfactory cyclic nucleotide-gated cation channel. *Neuron, 17,* 681–693.

Brunjes, P. C. (1994). Unilateral naris closure and olfactory system development. *Brain Research. Brain Research Reviews, 19,* 146–160.

Bryden, M. P. (1982). Laterality: Functional asymmetry in the intact brain. New York: Academic Press.

Brzustowicz, L. M., Hodgkinson, K. A., Chow, E. W., Honer, W. G., et al. (2000). Location of a major susceptibility locus for familial schizophrenia on chromosome 1q21-q22. *Science, 288,* 678–682.

Buchan, J. C., Alberts, S. C., Silk, J. B., and Altmann, J. (2003). True paternal care in a multi-male primate society. *Nature, 425,* 179–181.

Buchsbaum, M., Mirsky, A., DeLisi, L. E., Morihisa, J., et al. (1984). The Genain quadruplets: Electrophysiological, positron emission and X-ray tomographic studies. *Psychiatry Research, 13,* 95–108.

Buck, L., and Axel, R. (1991). A novel multigene family may encode odorant receptors: A molecular basis for odor recognition. *Cell, 65,* 175–187.

Buckner, R. L., Bandettini, P. A., O'Craven, K. M., Savoy, R. L., et al. (1996). Detection of cortical activation during averaged single trials of a cognitive task using functional magnetic resonance imaging. *Proceedings of the National Academy of Sciences, USA, 93,* 14878–14883.

Buhrich, N., Bailey, J. M., and Martin, N. G. (1991). Sexual orientation, sexual identity, and sex-dimorphic behaviors in male twins. *Behavior Genetics, 21,* 75–96.

Bullock, T. H. (1984). Comparative neuroscience holds promise for quiet revolutions. *Science, 225,* 473–478.

Bullock, T. H. (1986). Some principles in the brain analysis of important signals: Mapping and stimulus recognition. *Brain, Behavior and Evolution, 28,* 145–156.

Bunce, M., Worthy, T. H., Ford, T., Hoppitt, W., et al. (2003). Extreme reversed sexual size dimorphism in the extinct New Zealand moa *Dinornis. Nature, 425,* 172–175.

Buss, D. M. (2000). The dangerous passion: Why jealousy is as necessary as love and sex. New York: Free Press.

Cabelli, R. J., Hohn, A., and Shatz, C. J. (1995). Inhibition of ocular dominance column formation by infusion of NT-4/5 or BDNF. *Science, 267,* 1662–1666.

Cacioppo, J. T., Berntson, G. G., Larsen, J. T., Poehlmann, K. M., et al. (2000). The psychophysiology of emotion. In M. Lewis and J. M. Haviland-Jones (Eds.), *Handbook of emotions* (2nd ed., pp. 173–191). New York: Guilford.

Cacioppo, J. T., Klein, D. J., Berntson, G. G., and Hatfield, E. (1993). The psychophysiology of emotion. In M. Lewis and J. M. Haviland (Eds.), *Handbook of emotions* (pp. 119–142). New York: Guilford.

Cadoret, R. J., O'Gorman, T., Troughton, E., and Heywood, E. (1986). An adoption study of genetic and environmental factors in drug abuse. *Archives of General Psychiatry, 43,* 1131–1136.

Cahill, L. (1997). The neurobiology of emotionally influenced memory: Implications for understanding traumatic memory. In R. Yehuda and A. C. McFarlane (Eds.), *Annals of the New York Academy of Sciences: Vol. 41. Psychobiology of traumatic stress disorder* (pp. 238–246). New York: New York Academy of Sciences.

Cahill, L., and McGaugh, J. L. (1991). NMDA-induced lesions of the amygdaloid complex block the retention-enhancing effect of post-training epinephrine. *Psychobiology, 19,* 206–210.

Cahill, L., Prins, B., Weber, M., and McGaugh, J. L. (1994). Beta-adrenergic activation and memory for emotional events. *Nature, 371,* 702–704.

Calder, A. J., Keane, J., Manes, F., Antoun, N., et al. (2000). Impaired recognition and experience of disgust following brain injury. *Nature Neuroscience, 3,* 1077.

Calvert, G. A., Bullmore, E. T., Brammer, M. J., Campbell, R., et al. (1997). Activation of auditory cortex during silent lipreading. *Science, 276,* 593–596.

Calvin, W. H., and Ojemann, G. A. (1994). *Conversations with Neil's brain: The neural nature of thought and language.* Reading, MA: Addison-Wesley.

Campbell, F. W., and Robson, J. G. (1968). Application of Fourier analysis to the visibility of gratings. *Journal of Physiology (London), 197,* 551–566.

Campbell, S. S., and Tobler, I. (1984). Animal sleep: A review of sleep duration across phylogeny. *Neuroscience and Biobehavioral Reviews, 8,* 269–301.

Canli, T., Zhao, Z., Kang, E., Gross, J., et al. (2001). An fMRI study of personality influences on brain reactivity to emotional stimuli. *Behavioral Neuroscience, 115,* 33–42.

Cannon, S. C. (1996). Ion-channel defects and aberrant excitability in myotonia and periodic paralysis. *Trends in Neurosciences, 19,* 3–10.

Cannon, W. B. (1929). Bodily changes in pain, hunger, fear and rage. New York: Appleton.

Cantalupo, C., and Hopkins, W. D. (2001). Asymmetric Broca's area in great apes. *Nature, 414,* 505.

Cao, L., Liu, L., Chen, Z. Y., Wang, L. M., et al. (2003). Olfactory ensheathing cells genetically modified to secrete GDNF to promote spinal cord repair. *Brain* (Brain Advance Access published December 22, 2003, http://brain.oupjournals.org/cgi/content/abstract/awh072v1).

Cao, Y. Q., Mantyh, P. W., Carlson, E. J., Gillespie, A. M., et al. (1998). Primary afferent tachykinins are required to experience moderate to intense pain. *Nature, 392,* 390–394.

Capretta, P. J., Petersik, J. T., and Stewart, D. J. (1975). Acceptance of novel flavours is increased after early experience of diverse tastes. *Nature, 254,* 689–691.

Cardno, A. G., and Gottesman, I. I. (2000). Twin studies of schizophrenia: From bow-and-arrow concordances to star wars Mx and functional genomics. *American Journal of Medical Genetics, 97,* 12–17.

Carew, T. J. (2000). *Behavioral neurobiology: The cellular organization of natural behavior.* Sunderland, MA: Sinauer.

Carmena, J. M., Lebedev, M. A., Crist, R. E., O'Doherty, J. E., et al. (2003). Learning to control a brain–machine interface for reaching and grasping primates. *PLoS Biology, 1,* 1–16.

Carmichael, M. S., Warburton, V. L., Dixen, J., and Davidson, J. M. (1994). Relationships among cardiovascular, muscular, and oxytocin responses during human sexual activity. *Archives of Sexual Behavior, 23,* 59–79.

Carpenter, M. B., and Sutin, J. (1983). *Human neuroanatomy.* Baltimore: Williams & Wilkins.

Carroll, J., McMahon, C., Neitz, M., and Neitz, J. (2000). Flicker-photometric electroretinogram estimates of L:M cone photoreceptor ratio in men with photopigment spectra derived from genetics. *Journal of the Optical Society of America. Part A, Optics, Image Science, and Vision, 17,* 499–509.

Carter, C. S. (1992). Oxytocin and sexual behavior. *Neuroscience and Biobehavioral Reviews, 16,* 131–144.

Cartwright, R. D. (1979). The nature and function of repetitive dreams: A survey and speculation. *Psychiatry, 42,* 131–137.

Casey, B., and Hackett, B. P. (2000). Left-right axis malformations in man and mouse. *Current Opinion in Genetics and Development, 10,* 257–261.

Casey, D. E. (1989). Clozapine: Neuroleptic-induced EPS and tardive dyskinesia. *Psychopharmacology, 99,* S47–S53.

Cassens, G., Wolfe, L., and Zola, M. (1990). The neuropsychology of depressions. *Journal of Neuropsychiatry and Clinical Neurosciences, 2,* 202–213.

Casson, I. R., Sham, R., Campbell, E. A., Tarlau, M., et al. (1982). Neurological and CT evaluation of knocked-out boxers. *Journal of Neurology, Neurosurgery and Psychiatry, 45,* 170–174.

Catania, K. C. (2001). Early development of a somatosensory fovea: A head start in the cortical space race? *Nature Neuroscience, 4,* 353–354.

Caterina, M. J., Leffler, A., Malmberg, A. B., Martin, W. J., et al. (2000). Impaired nociception and pain sensation in mice lacking the capsaicin receptor. *Science, 288,* 306–313.

Caterina, M. J., Schumacher, M. A., Tominaga, M., Rosen, T. A., et al. (1997). The capsaicin receptor: A heat-activated ion channel in the pain pathway. *Nature, 389,* 816–824.

Centers for Disease Control. (1997). Cardiac valvulopathy associated with exposure to fenfluramine or dexfenfluramine: U.S. Department of Health and Human Services interim public health recommendations, November 1997. *MMWR Morbidity and Mortality Weekly Reports, 46,* 1061–1066.

Champagne, F., Diorio, J., Sharma, S., and Meaney, M. J. (2001). Naturally occurring variations in maternal behavior in the rat are associated with differences in estrogen-inducible central oxytocin receptors. *Proceedings of the National Academy of Sciences, USA, 98,* 12736–12741.

Chandrashekar, J., Mueller, K. L., Hoon, M. A., Adler, E., et al. (2000). T2Rs function as bitter taste receptors. *Cell, 100,* 703–711.

Chapin, J. K., Moxon, K. A., Markowitz, R. S., and Nicolelis, M. A. (1999). Real-time control of a robot arm using simultaneously recorded neurons in the motor cortex. *Nature Neuroscience, 2,* 664–670.

Chapman, C. R., Casey, K. L., Dubner, R., Foley, K. M., et al. (1985). Pain measurement: An overview. *Pain, 22,* 1–31.

Charney, D. S., Deutch, A. Y., Krystal, J. H., Southwick, S. M., et al. (1993). Psychobiologic mechanisms of posttraumatic stress disorder. *Archives of General Psychiatry, 50,* 295–305.

Chase, J. E., and Gidal, B. E. (1997). Melatonin: Therapeutic use in sleep disorders. *Annals of Pharmacotherapy, 31,* 1218–1226.

Chaudhari, N., Landin, A. M., and Roper, S. D. (2000). A metabotropic glutamate receptor variant functions as a taste receptor. *Nature Neuroscience, 3,* 113–119.

Chavez-Noriega, L. E., Schaffhauser, H., and Campbell, U. C. (2002). Metabotropic glutamate receptors: Potential drug targets for the treatment of schizophrenia. *Current Drug Targets, 1,* 261–281.

Chemelli, R. M., Willie, J. T., Sinton, C. M., Elmquist, J. K., et al. (1999). Narcolepsy in orexin knockout mice: Molecular genetics of sleep regulation. *Cell, 98,* 437–451.

Chen, M. S., Huber, A. B., Van Der Haar M. E., Frank, M., et al. (2000). Nogo-A is a myelin-associated neurite outgrowth inhibitor and an antigen for monoclonal antibody IN-1. *Nature, 403,* 434–439.

Cheng, H., Cao, Y., and Olson, L. (1996). Spinal cord repair in adult paraplegic rats: Partial restoration of hind limb function. *Science, 273,* 510–513.

Chenn, A., and Walsh, C. A. (2002). Regulation of cerebral cortical size by control of cell cycle exit in neural precursors. *Science, 297,* 365–369.

Cheyne, J. A. (2002). Situational factors affecting sleep paralysis and associated hallucinations: Position and timing effects. *Journal of Sleep Research, 11,* 169–177.

Chiarello, C., Knight, R., and Mundel, M. (1982). Aphasia in a prelingually deaf woman. *Brain, 105,* 29–52.

Cho, K. (2001). Chronic "jet lag" produces temporal lobe atrophy and spatial cognitive deficits. *Nature Neuroscience, 4,* 567–568.

Cho, Y. H., Berachochea, D., and Jaffard, R. (1993). Extended temporal gradient for the retrograde and anterograde amnesia produced by ibotenate entorhinal cortex lesions in mice. *Journal of Neuroscience, 13,* 1759–1766.

Chow, K. L., and Stewart, D. L. (1972). Reversal of structural and functional effects of long-term visual deprivation in cats. *Experimental Neurology, 34,* 409–433.

Christensen, D. (1999). Designer estrogens: Getting all the benefits, few of the risks. *Science News, 156,* 252–254.

Clapham, J. C., Arch, J. R. S., Chapman, H., Haynes, A., et al. (2000). Mice overexpressing human uncoupling protein-3 in skeletal muscle are hyperphagic and lean. *Nature, 406,* 415–418.

Clark, J. D., Beyene, Y., WoldeGabriel, G., Hart, W. K., et al. (2003). Stratigraphic, chronological, and behavioural contexts of Pleistocene *Homo sapiens* from Middle Awash, Ethiopia. *Nature, 423,* 747–752.

Classen, J., Liepert, J., Wise, S. P., Hallett, M., et al. (1998). Rapid plasticity of human cortical movement representation induced by practice. *Journal of Neurophysiology, 79,* 1117–1123.

Clayton, N. S. (1995). The neuroethological development of food-storing memory: A case of use it, or lose it. *Behavioural Brain Research, 70,* 95–102.

Clayton, N. S., and Krebs, J. R. (1994). Hippocampal growth and attrition in birds affected by experience. *Proceedings of the National Academy of Sciences, USA, 91,* 7410–7414.

Clemens, L. G., Gladue, B. A., and Coniglio, L. P. (1978). Prenatal endogenous androgenic influences on masculine sexual behavior and genital morphology in male and female rats. *Hormones and Behavior, 10,* 40–53.

Clemente, C. D., and Sterman, M. B. (1967). Limbic and other forebrain mechanisms in sleep induction and behavioral inhibition. *Progress in Brain Research, 27,* 34–37.

Clutton-Brock, T. H., and Harvey, P. H. (1980). Primates, brains and ecology. *Journal of Zoology, 190,* 309–323.

Coccaro, E. F., and Siever, L. J. (1995). Personality disorders. In F. E. Bloom and D. J. Kupfer (Eds.), *Psychopharmacology: The fourth generation of progress* (pp. 1567–1679). New York: Raven.

Coghill, R. C., McHaffie, J. G., and Yen, Y.-F. (2003). Neural correlates of interindividual differences in the subjective experience of pain. *Proceedings of the National Academy of Sciences, USA, 100,* 8538–8542.

Cohen, A. H., Baker, M. T., and Dobrov, T. A. (1989). Evidence for functional regeneration in the adult lamprey spinal cord following transection. *Brain Research, 496,* 368–372.

Cohen, A. J., and Leckman, J. F. (1992). Sensory phenomena associated with Gilles de la Tourette's syndrome. *Journal of Clinical Psychiatry, 53,* 319–323.

Cohen, N. J., and Squire, L. R. (1980). Preserved learning and retention of pattern-analyzing skill in amnesia: Dissociation of knowing how and knowing what. *Science, 210,* 207–210.

Cohen, S., Doyle, W. J., Turner, R., Alper, C. M., et al. (2003). Sociability and susceptibility to the common cold. *Psychological Science, 15,* 389–395.

Cohen, S., Frank, E., Doyle, W. J., Skoner, D. P., et al. (1998). Types of stressors that increase susceptibility to the common cold in healthy adults. *Health Psychology, 17,* 214–223.

Cohen, S., Lichtenstein, E., Prochaska, J. O., Rossi, J. S., et al. (1989). Debunking myths about quitting: Evidence from 10 perspective studies of persons who attempt to quit smoking by themselves. *American Psychologist, 44,* 1355–1365.

Colangelo, W., and Jones, D. G. (1982). The fetal alcohol syndrome: A review and assessment of the syndrome and its neurological sequelae. *Progress in Neurobiology, 19,* 271–314.

Coleman, D. L., and Hummel, K. P. (1973). The influence of genetic background on the expression of the obese (Ob) gene in the mouse. *Diabetologia, 9,* 287–293.

Colley, P. A., and Routtenberg, A. (1993). Long-term potentiation as synaptic dialogue. *Brain Research Review, 18,* 115–122.

Collings, V. B. (1974). Human taste response as a function of locus of stimulation on the tongue and soft palate. *Perception and Psychophysics, 16,* 169–174.

Conel, J. L. (1939). The postnatal development of the human cerebral cortex: Vol. 1. The cortex of the newborn. Cambridge, MA: Harvard University Press.

Conel, J. L. (1947). The postnatal development of the human cerebral cortex: Vol. 3. The cortex of the three-month infant. Cambridge, MA: Harvard University Press.

Conel, J. L. (1959). The postnatal development of the human cerebral cortex: Vol. 6. The cortex of the twenty-four-month infant. Cambridge, MA: Harvard University Press.

Connolly, H. M., Crary, J. L., McGoon, M. D., Hensrud, D. D., et al. (1997). Valvular heart disease associated with fenfluramine-phentermine. *New England Journal of Medicine, 337,* 581–588.

Conrad, A. J., Abebe, T., Austin, R., Forsythe, S., et al. (1991). Hippocampal pyramidal cell disarray in schizophrenia as a bilateral phenomenon. *Archives of General Psychiatry, 48,* 413–417.

Constantine-Paton, M., Cline, H. T., and Debski, E. (1990). Patterned activity, synaptic convergence, and the NMDA receptor in developing visual pathways. *Annual Review of Neuroscience, 13,* 129–154.

Cooke, B. M., Breedlove, S. M., and Jordan, C. L. (2003). Both estrogen receptors and androgen receptors contribute to testosterone-induced changes in the morphology of the medial amygdala and sexual arousal in male rats. *Hormones and Behavior, 43,* 336–346.

Cooke, B. M., Chowanadisai, W., and Breedlove, S. M. (2000). Post-weaning social isolation of male rats reduces the volume of the medial amygdala and leads to deficits in adult sexual behavior. *Behavioural Brain Research, 117,* 107–113.

Cooke, B. M., Tabibnia, G., and Breedlove S. M. (1999). A brain sexual dimorphism controlled by adult circulating androgens. *Proceedings of the National Academy of Sciences, USA, 96,* 7538–7540.

Corballis, M. C. (2002). From hand to mouth: The origins of language. Princeton, NJ: Princeton University Press.

Corkin, S. (2002). What's new with the amnesic patient H.M.? *Neuroscience, 3,* 153–159.

Corkin, S., Amaral, D. G., Gonzalez, R. G., Johnson, K. A., et al. (1997). H.M.'s medial temporal lobe lesion: Findings from magnetic resonance imaging. *Journal of Neuroscience, 17,* 3964–3979.

Corp, N., and Byrne, R. W. (2004). Sex difference in chimpanzee handedness. *American Journal of Physical Anthropology, 123,* 62–68.

Coryell, W., Noyes, R., Jr., and House, J. D. (1986). Mortality among outpatients with anxiety disorders. *American Journal of Psychiatry, 143,* 508–510.

Cosmides, L., and Tooby, J. (2000). Evolutionary psychology and the emotions. In M. Lewis and J. M. Haviland-Jones (Eds.), *Handbook of emotions* (2nd ed., pp. 91–115). New York: Guilford.

Costanzo, R. M. (1991). Regeneration of olfactory receptor cells. *CIBA Foundation Symposium, 160,* 233–242.

Courtney, S., Ungerleider, L., Keil, K., and Haxby, J. (1996). Object and spatial visual working memory activate separate neural systems in human cortex. *Cerebral Cortex, 6,* 39–49.

Cowan, W. M. (1979). The development of the brain. *Scientific American, 241*(3), 112–133.

Coyle, J. T., Tsai, G., and Goff, D. (2003). Converging evidence of NMDA receptor hypofunction in the pathophysiology of schizophrenia. *Annals of the New York Academy of Sciences, 1003,* 318–327.

Crabbe, J. C., Wahlsten, D., and Dudek, B. C. (1999). Genetics of mouse behavior: Interactions with laboratory environment. *Science, 284,* 1670–1672.

Craddock, N., and Jones, I. (2001). Molecular genetics of bipolar disorder. *British Journal of Psychiatry (Supplement), 41,* s128–s133.

Cragg, B. G. (1975). The development of synapses in the visual system of the cat. *Journal of Comparative Neurology, 160,* 147–166.

Craig, A. D., Reiman, E. M., Evans, A., and Bushnell, M. C. (1996). Functional imaging of an illusion of pain. *Nature, 384,* 258–260.

Craik, F. I. M. (1985). Paradigms in human memory research. In L.-G. Nilsson and T. Archer (Eds.), *Perspectives on learning and memory* (pp. 197–221). Hillsdale, NJ: Erlbaum.

Crasto, C., Singer, M. S., and Shepherd, G. M. (2001). The olfactory receptor family album. *Genome Biology, 2,* reviews1027.1–1027.4.

Crews, D. (1994). Temperature, steroids and sex determination. *Journal of Endocrinology, 142,* 1–8.

Crouch, R. (1997). Letting the deaf be deaf. Reconsidering the use of cochlear implants in prelingually deaf children. *Hastings Center Report, 27*(4), 14–21.

Cruce, J. A. F., Greenwood, M. R. C., Johnson, P. R., and Quartermain, D. (1974). Genetic versus hypothalamic obesity: Studies of intake and dietary manipulation in rats. *Journal of Comparative and Physiological Psychology, 87,* 295–301.

Cryns, K., and Van Camp, G. (2004). Deafness genes and their diagnostic applications. *Audiology and Neuro-otology, 9,* 2–22.

Cummings, J. L. (1995). Dementia: The failing brain. *Lancet, 345,* 1481–1484.

Cummins, R. A., Walsh, R. N., Budtz-Olsen, O. E., Reidel, J. C., et al. (1973). Environmentally-induced changes in the brains of elderly rats. *Nature, 243,* 516–518.

Curcio, C. A., Sloan, K. R., Packer, O., Hendrickson, A. E., et al. (1987). Distribution of cones in human and monkey retina: Individual variability and radial asymmetry. *Science, 236,* 579–582.

Curtis, V., Aunger, R., and Rabie, T. (2004, January 26). Evidence that disgust evolved to protect from risk of disease. *Biology Letters* (published online by FirstCite, http://www.pubs.royalsoc.ac.uk/firstcite_common.shtml).

Curtiss, S. (1989). The independence and task-specificity of language. In M. H. Bornstein and J. S. Bruner (Eds.), *Interaction in human development* (pp. 105–137). Hillsdale, NJ: Erlbaum.

Czeisler, C. A., Duffy, J. F., Shanahan, T. L., Brown, E. N., et al. (1999). Stability, precision, and near-24-hour period of the human circadian pacemaker. *Science, 284,* 2177–2181.

Dabbs, J. M., Jr., and Hargrove, M. F. (1997). Age, testosterone, and behavior among female prison inmates. *Psychosomatic Medicine, 59,* 477–480.

Dabbs, J. M., and Morris, R. (1990). Testosterone, social class, and antisocial behavior in a sample of 4,462 men. *Psychological Science, 1 (3),* 209–211.

Dabbs, J. M., Ruback, R. B., Frady, R. L., Hopper, C. H., et al. (1988). Saliva testosterone and criminal violence among women. *Personality and Individual Differences, 9,* 269–275.

Dalton, P., Doolittle, N., Nagata, H., and Breslin, P. A. (2000). The merging of the senses: Integration of subthreshold taste and smell. *Nature Neuroscience, 3,* 431–432.

Daly, M., and Wilson, M. (1978). *Sex, evolution and behavior.* North Scituate, MA: Duxbury Press.

Damak, S., Rong, M., Yasumatsu, K., Kokrashvili, Z., et al. (2003). Detection of sweet and umami taste in the absence of taste receptor T1r3. *Science, 301,* 850–853.

Damasio, A. R., Eslinger, P. J., Damasio, H., Van Hoesen, G. W., et al. (1985). Multimodal amnesic syndrome following bilateral temporal and basal forebrain damage. *Archives of Neurology, 42,* 252–259.

Damasio, A. R., Grabowski, T. J., Bechara, A., Damasio, H., et al. (2000). Subcortical and cortical brain activity during the feeling of self-generated emotions. *Nature Neuroscience, 3,* 1049–1056.

Damasio, H. (1995). *Human brain anatomy in computerized images.* New York: Oxford University Press.

Damasio, H., Grabowski, T., Frank, R., Galaburda, A. M., et al. (1994). The return of Phineas Gage: Clues about the brain from the skull of a famous patient. *Science, 264,* 1102–1105.

D'Amato, R. J., Alexander, G. M., Schwartzman, R. J., Kitt, C. A., et al. (1987). Evidence for neuromelanin involvement in MPTP-induced neurotoxicity. *Nature, 327,* 324–326.

Dantz, B., Edgar, D. M., and Dement, W. C. (1994). Circadian rhythms in narcolepsy: Studies on a 90 minute day. *Electroencephalography and Clinical Neurophysiology, 90,* 24–35.

Darian-Smith, I., Davidson, I., and Johnson, K. O. (1980). Peripheral neural representations of the two spatial dimensions of a textured surface moving over the monkey's finger pad. *Journal of Physiology (London), 309,* 135–146.

Dark, J., Forger, N. G., and Zucker, I. (1984). Rapid recovery of body mass after surgical removal of adipose tissue in ground squirrels. *Proceedings of the National Academy of Sciences, USA, 81,* 2270–2272.

Dark, J., Miller, D. R., and Zucker, I. (1994). Reduced glucose availability induced torpor in Siberian hamsters. *American Journal of Physiology, 267,* R496–R501.

Dark, J., Spears, N., Whaling, C. S., Wade, G. N., et al. (1990). Long day lengths promote brain growth in meadow voles. *Developmental Brain Research, 53,* 264–269.

Darwin, C. (1859). *On the origin of species by means of natural selection, or, The preservation of favoured races in the struggle for life.* London: J. Murray.

Darwin, C. (1871). *The descent of man, and selection in relation to sex.* London: J. Murray.

Darwin, C. (1872). *The expression of the emotions in man and animals.* London: J. Murray.

Darwin, C. (1887). *Life and letters of Charles Darwin: Vol. 3.* London: J. Murray.

Dave, A. S., and Margoliash, D. (2000). Song replay during sleep and computational rules for sensorimotor vocal learning. *Science, 290,* 812–816.

Davey-Smith, G., Frankel, S., and Yarnell, J. (1997). Sex and death: Are they related? Findings from the Caerphilly Cohort Study. *British Medical Journal (Clinical Research Edition), 315,* 1641–1644.

Davidson, J. M., Camargo, C. A., and Smith, E. R. (1979). Effects of androgen on sexual behavior in hypogonadal men. *Journal of Clinical Endocrinology and Metabolism, 48,* 955–958.

Davidson, R. J. (1994). Asymmetric brain function, affective style, and psychopathology: The role of early experience and plasticity. *Development and Psychopathology, 6,* 741–758.

Davies, M. J., Baer, D. J., Judd, J. T., Brown, E. D., et al. (2002). Effects of moderate alcohol intake on fasting insulin and glucose concentrations and insulin sensitivity in postmenopausal women: A randomized controlled trial. *Journal of the American Medical Association, 287,* 2559–2562.

Davis, H. P., and Squire, L. R. (1984). Protein synthesis and memory: A review. *Psychological Bulletin, 96,* 518–559.

Davis, K. L., Kahn, R. S., Ko, G., and Davidson, M. (1991). Dopamine in schizophrenia: A review and reconceptualization. *American Journal of Psychiatry, 148,* 1474–1486.

Dawson, D., and Encel, N. (1993). Melatonin and sleep in humans. *Journal of Pineal Research, 15,* 1–12.

Day, N. L., Leech, S. L., Richardson, G. A., Cornelius, M. D., et al. (2002). Prenatal alcohol exposure predicts continued deficits in offspring size at 14 years of age. *Alcoholism: Clinical and Experimental Research, 26,* 1584–1591.

Deacon, T. W. (1997). What makes the human brain different? In W. H. Durham (Ed.), *Annual Review of Anthropology: Vol. 26* (pp. 337–357). Palo Alto, CA: Annual Reviews Inc.

Dearborn, G. V. N. (1932). A case of congenital general pure analgesia. *Journal of Nervous and Mental Disease, 75,* 612–615.

De Felipe, C., Herrero, J. F., O'Brien, J. A., Palmer, J. A., et al. (1998). Altered nociception, analgesia and aggression in mice lacking the receptor for substance P. *Nature, 392,* 394–397.

de Groot, C. M., Janus, M. D., and Bornstein, R. A. (1995). Clinical predictors of psychopathology in children and adolescents with Tourette syndrome. *Journal of Psychiatric Research, 29,* 59–70.

Dehaene-Lambertz, G., Dehaene, S., and Hertz-Pannier, L. (2002). Functional neuroimaging of speech perception in infants. *Science, 298,* 2013–2015.

Dekaban, A. S., and Sadowsky, D. (1978). Changes in brain weights during the span of human life: Relation of brain weights to body heights and body weights. *Annals of Neurology, 4,* 345–356.

DelBello, M. P., Zimmerman, M. E., Mills, N. P., Getz, G. E., et al. (2004). Magnetic resonance imaging analysis of amygdala and other subcortical brain regions in adolescents with bipolar disorder. *Bipolar Disorder, 6,* 43–52.

Delgado-Escueta, A. V., Mattson, R. H., King, L., Goldensohn, E. S., et al. (1981). The nature of aggression during epileptic seizures. *New England Journal of Medicine, 305,* 711–716.

DeLong, M. R., Georgopoulos, A. P., Crutcher, M. D., Mitchell, S. J., et al. (1984). Functional organization of the basal ganglia: Contributions of single-cell recording studies. *CIBA Foundation Symposium, 107,* 64–82.

de Luis, O., Valero, M. C., and Jurado, L. A. (2000). WBSCR14, a putative transcription factor gene deleted in Williams-Beuren syndrome: Complete characterisation of the human gene and the mouse ortholog. *European Journal of Human Genetics, 8,* 215–222.

Demb, J. B., Boynton, G. M., and Heeger, D. J. (1998). Functional magnetic resonance imaging of early visual pathways in dyslexia. *Journal of Neuroscience, 18,* 6939–6951.

Dement, W. C. (1974). *Some must watch while some must sleep.* San Francisco: Freeman.

Dennis, S. G., and Melzack, R. (1983). Perspectives on phylogenetic evolution of pain expression. In I. Kitchell, H. H. Erickson, E. Carstens, and L. E. Davis (Eds.), *Animal pain* (pp. 151–161). Bethesda, MD: American Physiological Society.

Deol, M. S., and Gluecksohn-Waelsch, S. (1979). The role of inner hair cells in hearing. *Nature, 278,* 250–252.

de Paiva, A., Poulain, B., Lawrence, G. W., Shone, C. C., et al. (1993). A role for the interchain disulfide or its participating thiols in the internalization of botulinum neurotoxin A revealed by a toxin derivative that binds to ecto-acceptors and inhibits transmitter release intracellularly. *Journal of Biological Chemistry, 268,* 20838–20844.

Derrick, B. E., and Martinez, J. L. (1994). Frequency-dependent associative long-term potentiation at the hippocampal mossy fiber-CA3 synapse. *Proceedings of the National Academy of Sciences, USA, 91,* 10290–10294.

Descartes, R. (1662). *De homine.* Paris: Petrvm Leffen & Franciscvm Moyardvm.

Desimone, R., Albright, T. D., Gross, C. G., and Bruce, C. (1984). Stimulus-selective properties of inferior temporal neurons in the macaque. *Journal of Neuroscience, 4,* 2051–2062.

Desimone, R., and Schein, S. J. (1987). Visual properties of neurons in area V4 of the macaque: Sensitivity to stimulus form. *Journal of Neurophysiology, 57,* 835–868.

De Valois, K. K., De Valois, R. L., and Yund, E. W. (1979). Responses of striate cortex cells to grating and checkerboard patterns. *Journal of Physiology (London), 291,* 483–505.

De Valois, R. L., Albrecht, D. G., and Thorell, L. G. (1977). Spatial tuning of LGN and cortical cells in the monkey visual system. In H. Spekreijse and H. van der Tweel (Eds.), *Spatial contrast* (pp. 60–63). Amsterdam: Elsevier.

De Valois, R. L., and De Valois, K. K. (1980). Spatial vision. *Annual Review of Psychology, 31,* 309–341.

De Valois, R. L., and De Valois, K. K. (1988). *Spatial vision.* New York: Oxford University Press.

De Valois, R. L., and De Valois, K. K. (1993). A multi-stage color model. *Vision Research, 33,* 1053–1065.

Devane, W. A., Dysarz, F. A., Johnson, M. R., Melvin, L. S., et al. (1988). Determination and characterization of a cannabinoid receptor in rat brain. *Molecular Pharmacology, 34,* 605–613.

Devane, W. A., Hanus, L., Breuer, A., Pertwee, R. G., et al. (1992). Isolation and structure of a brain constituent that binds the cannabinoid receptor. *Science, 258,* 1946–1949.

Devinsky, O., and Bear, D. (1984). Varieties of aggressive behavior in temporal lobe epilepsy. *American Journal of Psychiatry, 141,* 651–656.

DeVoogd, T. J. (1994). Interactions between endocrinology and learning in the avian song system. *Annals of the New York Academy of Sciences, 743,* 19–41.

de Vries, H. (1901). Die Mutationen und die Mutationsperioden bei der Entstehung der Arten: Vortrag, gehalten in der allgemeinen Sitzung der Naturwissenschaftlichen Hauptgruppe der Versammlung Deutscher Naturforscher und Aerzte in Hamburg am 26. September 1901. Leipzig, Germany: Veit.

de Waal, F. B. M. (1999). Cultural primatology comes of age. *Nature, 399,* 635–636.

de Waal, F. B. M. (2003). Darwin's legacy and the study of primate visual communication. *Annals of the New York Academy of Sciences, 1000,* 7–31.

Dewsbury, D. A. (1972). Patterns of copulatory behavior in male mammals. *Quarterly Review of Biology, 47,* 1–33.

Diamond, A., and Goldman-Rakic, P. S. (1989). Comparison of human infants and rhesus monkeys on Piaget's AB task: Evidence for dependence on dorsolateral prefrontal cortex. *Experimental Brain Research, 74,* 24–40.

Diamond, J., Cooper, E., Turner, C., and Macintyre, L. (1976). Trophic regulation of nerve sprouting. *Science, 193,* 371–377.

Diamond, M. C. (1967). Extensive cortical depth measurements and neuron size increases in the cortex of environmentally enriched rats. *Journal of Comparative Neurology, 131,* 357–364.

Diamond, M. C., Krech, D., and Rosenzweig, M. R. (1964). The effects of an enriched environment on the histology of the rat cerebral cortex. *Journal of Comparative Neurology, 123,* 111–119.

Diamond, M. C., Lindner, B., Johnson, R., Bennett, E. L., et al. (1975). Differences in occipital cortical synapses from environmentally enriched, impoverished, and standard colony rats. *Journal of Neuroscience Research, 1,* 109–119.

Dichgans, J. (1984). Clinical symptoms of cerebellar dysfunction and their topodiagnostical significance. *Human Neurobiology, 2,* 269–279.

Di Chiara, G., Tanda, G., Bassareo, V., Pontieri, F., et al. (1999). Drug addiction as a disorder of associative learning. Role of nucleus accumbens shell/extended amygdala dopamine. *Annals of the New York Academy of Sciences, 877,* 461–485.

Diebel, C. E., Proksch, R., Green, C. R., Neilson, P., et al. (2000). Magnetite defines a vertebrate magnetoreceptor. *Nature, 406,* 299–302.

Di Marzo, V., Goparaju, S. K., Wang, L., Liu, J., et al. (2001). Leptin-regulated endocannabinoids are involved in maintaining food intake. *Nature, 410,* 822–825.

Dlugos, C., and Pentney, R. (1997). Morphometric evidence that the total number of synapses on Purkinje neurons of old f344 rats is reduced after long-term ethanol treatment and restored to control levels after recovery. *Alcohol and Alcoholism, 32*(2), 161–172.

Dohanich, G. (2003). Ovarian steroids and cognitive function. *Current Directions in Psychological Science, 12,* 57–61.

Dolan, R. J. (2002). Emotion, cognition, and behavior. *Science, 298,* 1191–1194.

Domjan, M., and Purdy, J. E. (1995). Animal research in psychology: More than meets the eye of the general psychology student. *American Psychologist, 50,* 496–503.

Donegan, N. H., Lowery, R. W., and Thompson, R. F. (1983). Effects of lesioning cerebellar nuclei on conditioned leg-flexion responses. *Society for Neuroscience Abstracts, 9,* 331.

Doricchi, F., Guariglia, C., Paolucci, S., and Pizzamiglio, L. (1991). Disappearance of leftward rapid eye movements during sleep in left visual hemi-inattention. *Neuroreport, 2,* 285–288.

Doyon, J., Owen, A. M., Petrides, M., Sziklas, V., et al. (1996). Functional anatomy of visuomotor skill learning in human subjects examined with positron emission tomography. *European Journal of Neuroscience, 8,* 637–648.

Drachman, D. A., and Leavitt, J. (1972). Memory impairment in the aged: Storage versus retrieval deficit. *Journal of Experimental Psychology, 93,* 302–308.

Drea, C. M., Place, N. J., Weldele, M. L., Coscia, E. M., et al. (2002). Exposure to naturally circulating androgens during foetal life incurs direct reproductive costs in female spotted hyenas, but is prerequisite for male mating. *Proceeding of the Royal Society of London. Series B: Biological Sciences, 269,* 1981–1987.

Drea, C. M., Weldele, M. L., Forger, N. G., Coscia, E. M., et al. (1998). Androgens and masculinization of genitalia in the spotted hyaena (*Crocuta crocuta*). 2. Effects of prenatal anti-androgens. *Journal of Reproduction and Fertility, 113,* 117–127.

Drevets, W. C. (1998). Functional neuroimaging studies of depression: The anatomy of melancholia. *Annual Review of Medicine, 49,* 341–361.

Drickamer, L. C. (1992). Behavioral selection of odor cues by young female mice affects age of puberty. *Developmental Psychobiology, 25,* 461–470.

Drier, E. A., Tello, M. K., Cowan, M., Wu, P., et al. (2002). Memory enhancement and formation by atypical PKM activity in *Drosophila melanogaster*. *Nature Neuroscience, 5,* 316–324.

Druckman, D., and Bjork, R. A. (1994). *Learning, remembering, believing: Enhancing human performance.* Washington, DC: National Academy Press.

Du, L., Bakish, D., Lapierre, Y. D., Ravindran, A. V., et al. (2000). Association of polymorphism of serotonin 2A receptor gene with suicidal ideation in major depressive disorder. *American Journal of Medical Genetics, 96,* 56–60.

Dubnau, J., and Tully, T. (1998). Gene discovery in *Drosophila:* New insights for learning and memory. *Annual Review of Neuroscience, 21,* 407–444.

Duchamp-Viret, P., Chaput, M. A., and Duchamp, A. (1999). Odor response properties of rat olfactory receptor neurons. *Science, 284,* 2171–2174.

Dudai, Y. (1988). Neurogenic dissection of learning and short term memory in *Drosophila*. *Annual Review of Neuroscience, 11,* 537–563.

Dudai, Y., Jan, Y.-N., Byers, D., Quinn, W. G., et al. (1976). Dunce, a mutant of *Drosophila* deficient in learning. *Proceedings of the National Academy of Sciences, USA, 73,* 1684–1688.

Duffy, J. D., and Campbell, J. J. (1994). The regional prefrontal syndromes: A theoretical and clinical overview. *Journal of Neuropsychiatry and Clinical Neurosciences, 6,* 379–387.

Dulac, C., and Torello, A. T. (2003). Molecular detection of pheromone signals in mammals, from genes to behaviour. *Nature Reviews. Neuroscience, 4,* 551–562.

Duman, R. S., Heninger, G. R., and Nestler, E. J. (1997). A molecular and cellular theory of depression. *Archives of General Psychiatry, 54,* 597–606.

Dunah, A. W., Hyunkyung, J., Griffin, A., Kim, Y.-M., et al. (2002). Sp1 and TAFII130 transcriptional activity disrupted in early Huntington's disease. *Science, 296,* 2238–2242.

Eales, L. A. (1985). Song learning in zebra finches (*Taeniopygia gyttata*): Some effects of song model availability on what is learnt and when. *Animal Behaviour, 33,* 1293–1300.

Earnest, D. J., Liang, F. Q., Ratcliff, M., and Cassone, V. M. (1999). Immortal time: Circadian clock properties of rat suprachiasmatic cell lines. *Science, 283,* 693–695.

Earnshaw, W. C., Martins, L. M., and Kaufmann, S. H. (1999). Mammalian caspases: Structure, activation, substrates, and functions during apoptosis. *Annual Review of Biochemistry, 68,* 383–424.

Eastman, C. I., Young, M. A., Fogg, L. F., Liu, L., et al. (1998). Bright light treatment of winter depression: A placebo-controlled trial. *Archives of General Psychiatry, 55,* 883–889.

Ebbinghaus, H. (1885). *Memory* (H. A. Ruger and C. E. Bussenius, Trans.). New York: Teachers College, 1913.

Eccles, J. C. (1965). Possible ways in which synaptic mechanisms participate in learning, remembering and forgetting. In D. P. Kimble (Ed.), *The anatomy of memory* (pp. 12–87). Palo Alto, CA: Science and Behavior Books.

Edwards, J. S., and Palka, J. (1991). Insect neural evolution—A fugue or an opera? *Seminars in the Neurosciences, 3,* 391–398.

Egaas, B., Courchesne, E., and Saitoh, O. (1995). Reduced size of corpus callosum in autism. *Archives of Neurology, 52,* 794–801.

Egeland, J. A., and Hostetter, A. M. (1983). Amish study, 1: Affective disorders among the Amish, 1976–1980. *American Journal of Psychiatry, 140,* 56–71.

Egrise, D., Rubinstein, M., Schoutens, A., Cantraine, F., and Mendlewicz, J. (1986). Seasonal variation of platelet serotonin uptake and 3H-imipramine binding in normal and depressed subjects. *Biological Psychiatry, 21,* 283–292.

Eisen, M. D., Duncan, R. K., and Saunders, J. C. (1999). The tip link's role in asymmetric stereocilia motion of chick cochlear hair cells. *Hearing Research, 127,* 14–21.

Elbert, T., Pantev, C., Wienbruch, C., Rockstroh, B., et al. (1995). Increased cortical representation of the fingers of the left hand in string players. *Science, 270,* 305–307.

Elster, A. D., and Burdette, J. H. (2001). *Magnetic resonance imaging.* Philadelphia: Mosby.

Emery, N. J., Capitanio, J. P., Mason, W. A., Machado, C. J., et al. (2001). The effects of bilateral lesions of the amygdala on dyadic social interactions in rhesus monkeys (*Macaca mulatta*). *Behavioral Neuroscience, 115,* 515–544.

Enard, W., Khaitovich, P., Klose, J., Zollner, S., et al. (2002). Intra- and interspecific variation in primate gene expression. *Science, 296,* 340–343.

Enard, W., Przeworski, M., Fisher, S. E., Lai, C. S., et al. (2002). Molecular evolution of FOXP2, a gene involved in speech and language. *Nature, 418,* 869–872.

Engel, J., Jr. (1992). Recent advances in surgical treatment of temporal lobe epilepsy. *Acta Neurologica Scandinavica. Supplementum, 140,* 71–80.

English, P. J., Ghatei, M. A., Malik, I. A., Bloom, S. R., et al. (2002). Food fails to suppress ghrelin levels in obese humans. *Journal of Clinical Endocrinology and Metabolism, 87,* 2984–2987.

Enoch, M. A., Kaye, W. H., Rotondo, A., Greenberg, B. D., et al. (1998). 5-HT2A promoter polymorphism -1438G/A, anorexia nervosa, and obsessive-compulsive disorder. *Lancet, 351,* 1785–1786.

Epelbaum, M., Milleret, C., Buisseret, P., and Dufier, J. L. (1993). The sensitive period for strabismic amblyopia in humans. *Ophthalmology, 100,* 323–327.

Epstein, A. N., Fitzsimons, J. T., and Rolls, B. J. (1970). Drinking induced by injection of angiotensin into the brain of the rat. *Journal of Physiology (London), 210,* 457–474.

Epstein, C. J. (1986). Developmental genetics. *Experientia, 42,* 1117–1128.

Erhardt, V. R., and Goldman, M. B. (1992). Adverse endocrine effects. In M. S. Keshavan and J. S. Kennedy (Eds.), *Drug-induced dysfunction in psychiatry.* New York: Hemisphere.

Erickson, J. T., Conover, J. C., Borday, V., Champagnat, J., et al. (1996). Mice lacking brain-derived neurotrophic factor exhibit visceral sensory neuron losses distinct from mice lacking NT4 and display a severe developmental deficit in control of breathing. *Journal of Neuroscience, 16,* 5361–5371.

Eriksson, P. S., Perfilieva, E., Bjork-Eriksson, T., Alborn, A. M., et al. (1998). Neurogenesis in the adult human hippocampus. *Nature Medicine, 4,* 1313–1317.

Erlanger, D. M., Kutner, K. C., Barth, J. T., and Barnes, R. (1999). Neuropsychology of sports-related head injury: Dementia pugilistica to post concussion syndrome. *Clinical Neuropsychologist, 13,* 193–209.

Ernst, T., Chang, L., Leonido-Yee, M., and Speck, O. (2000). Evidence for long-term neurotoxicity associated with methamphetamine abuse: A 1H MRS study. *Neurology, 54,* 1344–1349.

Estes, W. K. (1997). Processes of memory loss, recovery, and distortion. *Psychological Review, 104,* 148–169.

Etcoff, N. L., Ekman, P., Magee, J. J., and Frank, M. G. (2000). Lie detection and language comprehension. *Nature, 405,* 139.

Eugenides, J. (2002). *Middlesex: A novel.* New York: Farrar, Straus and Giroux.

Evans, C. J., Keith, D. E., Morrison, H., Magendzo, K., et al. (1992). Cloning of a delta opioid receptor by functional expression. *Science, 258,* 1952–1955.

Evans, P. D., Anderson, J. R., Vallender, E. J., Gilbert, S. L., et al. (2004). Adaptive evolution of *ASPM*, a major determinant of cerebral cortical size in humans. *Human Molecular Genetics, 13,* 489–494.

Evarts, E. V., Shinoda, Y., and Wise, S. P. (1984). *Neurophysiological approaches to higher brain functions.* New York: Wiley.

Everson, C. A. (1993). Sustained sleep deprivation impairs host defense. *American Journal of Physiology, 265,* R1148–R1154.

Everson, C. A., Bergmann, B. M., and Rechtschaffen A. (1989). Sleep deprivation in the rat: III. Total sleep deprivation. *Sleep, 12,* 13–21.

Eybalin, M. (1993). Neurotransmitters and neuromodulators of the mammalian cochlea. *Physiological Reviews, 73,* 309–373.

Fagerheim, T., Raeymaekers, P., Tonnessen, F. E., Pedersen, M., et al. (1999). A new gene (DYX3) for dyslexia is located on chromosome 2. *Journal of Medical Genetics, 36,* 664–669.

Falk, D. (1993). Sex differences in visuospatial skills: Implications for hominid evolution. In K. R. Gibson and T. Ingold (Eds.), *Tools, language and cognition in human evolution* (pp. 216–229). Cambridge, England: Cambridge University Press.

Faraone, S. V., Glatt, S. J., Su, J., and Tsuang, M. T. (2004). Three potential susceptibility loci shown by a genome-wide scan for regions influencing the age at onset of mania. *American Journal of Psychiatry, 161,* 625–630.

Faraone, S. V., and Tsuang, M. T. (1985). Quantitative models of the genetic transmission of schizophrenia. *Psychological Bulletin, 98,* 41–66.

Farber, N. B. (2003). The NMDA receptor hypofunction model of psychosis. *Annals of the New York Academy of Sciences, 1003,* 119–130.

Farbman, A. I. (1994). The cellular basis of olfaction. *Endeavour, 18,* 2–8.

Fay, R. R. (1988). *Hearing in vertebrates: A psychophysics databook.* Winnetka, IL: Hill-Fay Associates.

Fazeli, M. S., Corbet, J., Dunn, M. J., Dolphin, A. C., et al. (1993). Changes in protein synthesis accompanying long-term potentiation in the dentate gyrus *in vivo. Journal of Neuroscience, 13,* 1346–1353.

Feany, M. B., and Bender, W. W. (2000). A *Drosophila* model of Parkinson's disease. *Nature, 404,* 394–398.

Feder, H. H., and Whalen, R. E. (1965). Feminine behavior in neonatally castrated and estrogen-treated male rats. *Science, 147,* 306–307.

Felten, D. L., Felten, S. Y., Bellinger, D. L., and Madden, K. S. (1993). Fundamental aspects of neural-immune signaling. *Psychotherapy and Psychosomatics, 60,* 46–56.

Fenstemaker, S. B., Zup, S. L., Frank, L. G., Glickman, S. E., et al. (1999). A sex difference in the hypothalamus of the spotted hyena. *Nature Neuroscience, 2,* 943–945.

Ferguson, J. N., Young, L. J., Hearn, E. F., Matzuk, M. M., et al. (2000). Social amnesia in mice lacking the oxytocin gene. *Nature Genetics, 25,* 284–288.

Fernald, R. D. (2000). Evolution of eyes. *Current Opinion in Neurobiology, 10,* 444–450.

Fibiger, H. C., and Lloyd, K. G. (1984). The neurobiological substrates of tardive dyskinesia: The GABA hypothesis. *Trends in Neurosciences, 8,* 462.

Fields, R. D., and Stevens-Graham, B. (2002). New insights into neuron-glia communication. *Science, 298,* 556–562.

Fields, S. (1990). Pheromone response in yeast. *Trends in Biochemical Sciences, 15,* 270–273.

Finch, C. E., and Kirkwood, T. B. L. (2000). *Chance, development, and aging.* New York: Oxford University Press.

Fine, I., Wade, A. R., Brewer, A. A., May, M. G., Goodman, D. F., et al. (2003). Long-term deprivation affects visual perception and cortex. *Nature Neuroscience, 6,* 915–916.

Finger, S. (Ed.). (1978). Recovery from brain damage: Research and theory. New York: Plenum.

Finger, S. (1994). Origins of neuroscience: A history of explorations into brain function. New York: Oxford University Press.

Fink, G. R., Markowitsch, H. J., Reinkemeier, M., Bruckbauer, T., et al. (1996). Cerebral representation of one's own past: Neural networks involved in autobiographical memory. *Journal of Neuroscience, 16,* 4275–4282.

Finlay, B. L., and Darlington, R. B. (1995). Linked regularities in the development and evolution of mammalian brains. *Science, 268,* 1578–1584.

Fischer, C., Hatzidimitriou, G., Wlos, J., Katz, J., et al. (1995). Reorganization of ascending 5-HT axon projections in animals previously exposed to the recreational drug (+/–)3,4-methylenedioxymethamphetamine (MDMA, "ecstasy"). *Journal of Neuroscience, 15,* 5476–5485.

Fischer, H., Andersson, J. L., Furmark, T., and Fredrikson, M. (1998). Brain correlates of an unexpected panic attack: A human positron emission tomographic study. *Neuroscience Letters, 251,* 137–140.

Fischer, M., Kaech, S., Wagner, U., Brinkhaus, H., et al. (2000). Glutamate receptors regulate actin-based plasticity in dendritic spines. *Nature Neuroscience, 3,* 887–894.

Fishman, R. B., Chism, L., Firestone, G. L., and Breedlove, S. M. (1990). Evidence for androgen receptors in sexually dimorphic perineal muscles of neonatal male rats. Absence of androgen accumulation by the perineal motoneurons. *Journal of Neurobiology, 21,* 694–704.

Fitch, W. T., and Hauser, M. D. (2004). Computational constraints on syntactic processing in a nonhuman primate. *Science, 303,* 377–380.

Fitzsimmons, J. T. (1998). Angiotensin, thirst, and sodium appetite. *Physiological Reviews, 78,* 583–686.

Flament, D., Ellermann, J. M., Kim, S. G., Ugurbil, K., et al. (1996). Functional magnetic resonance imaging of cerebellar activation during the learning of a visuomotor dissociation task. *Human Brain Map, 4,* 210–226.

Flegal, K. M., Carroll, M. D., Ogden, C. L., and Johnson, C. L. (2002). Prevalence and trends in obesity among US adults, 1999–2000. *Journal of the American Medical Association, 288,* 1723–1727.

Flood, J. F., Bennett, E. L., Orme, A. E., and Rosenzweig, M. R. (1975). Relation of memory formation to controlled amounts of brain protein synthesis. *Physiology & Behavior, 15,* 97–102.

Flood, J. F., Bennett, E. L., Rosenzweig, M. R., and Orme, A. E. (1973). The influence of duration of protein synthesis inhibition on memory. *Physiology & Behavior, 10,* 555–562.

Flood, J. F., Jarvik, M. E., Bennett, E. L., Orme, A. E., et al. (1977). The effect of stimulants, depressants and protein synthesis inhibition on retention. *Behavioral Biology, 20,* 168–183.

Florence, S. L., Taub, H. B., and Kaas, J. H. (1998). Large-scale sprouting of cortical connections after peripheral injury in adult macaque monkeys. *Science, 282,* 1117–1121.

Forger, N. G., and Breedlove, S. M. (1986). Sexual dimorphism in human and canine spinal cord: Role of early androgen. *Proceedings of the National Academy of Sciences, USA, 83,* 7527–7531.

Forger, N. G., and Breedlove, S. M. (1987). Seasonal variation in mammalian striated muscle mass and motoneuron morphology. *Journal of Neurobiology, 18,* 155–165.

Forger, N. G., Frank, L. G., Breedlove, S. M., and Glickman, S. E. (1996). Sexual dimorphism of perineal muscles and motoneurons in spotted hyenas. *Journal of Comparative Neurology, 375,* 333–343.

Forger, N., Howell, M., Bengston, L., Mackenzie, L., et al. (1997). Sexual dimorphism in the spinal cord is absent in mice lacking the ciliary neurotrophic factor receptor. *Journal of Neuroscience, 17,* 9605–9612.

Forstl, H., Burns, A., Levy, R., Cairns, N., et al. (1993). Neuropathological correlates of behavioural disturbance in confirmed Alzheimer's disease. *British Journal of Psychiatry, 163,* 364–368.

Foster, G. D., Wyatt, H. R., Hill, J. O., McGuckin, B. G., et al. (2003). A randomized trial of a low-carbohydrate diet for obesity. *New England Journal of Medicine, 348,* 2082–2090.

Foster, N. L., Cahse, T. N., Mansi, L., Brooks, R., et al. (1984). Cortical abnormalities in Alzheimer's disease. *Annals of Neurology, 16,* 649–654.

Francis, D. D., Szegda, K., Campbell, G., Martin, W. D., et al. (2003). Epigenetic sources of behavioral differences in mice. *Nature Neuroscience, 6,* 445–446.

Frank, L. G., Glickman, S. E., and Licht, P. (1991). Fatal sibling aggression, precocial development, and androgens in neonatal spotted hyenas. *Science, 252,* 702–704.

Frankenhaeuser, M. (1978). Psychoneuroendocrine approaches to the study of emotion as related to stress and coping. *Nebraska Symposium on Motivation, 26,* 123–162.

Frankland, P. W., O'Brien, C., Masuo, O., Kirkwood, A., et al. (2001). α-CaMKII-dependent plasticity in the cortex is required for permanent memory. *Nature, 411,* 309–312.

Franz, S. I. (1902). On the functions of the cerebrum: I. The frontal lobes in relation to the production and retention of simple sensory-motor habits. *American Journal of Physiology, 8,* 1–22.

Frazier, W. T., Kandel, E. R., Kupfermann, l., Waziri, R., et al. (1967). Morphological and functional properties of identified neurons in the abdominal ganglion of *Aplysia californica. Journal of Neurophysiology, 30,* 1288–1351.

Fredriksson, R., Lagerstrom, M. C., Lundin, L.-G., and Schioth, H. B. (2003). The G-protein coupled receptors in the human genome form five main families. Phylogenetic analysis, paralogon groups and fingerprints. *Molecular Pharmacology, 63,* 1256–1272.

Freed, C. R., Greene, P. E., Breeze, R. E., Tsai, W.-Y., et al. (2001). Transplantation of embryonic dopamine neurons for severe Parkinson's disease. *New England Journal of Medicine, 344,* 710–719.

Freedman, M. S., Lucas, R. J., Soni, B., von Schantz, M., et al. (1999). Regulation of mammalian circadian behavior by non-rod, non-cone, ocular photoreceptors. *Science, 284,* 502–504.

Freitag, J., Ludwig, G., Andreini, P., Roessler, P., et al. (1998). Olfactory receptors in aquatic and terrestrial vertebrates. *Journal of Comparative Physiology, 183,* 635–650.

Frey, U., Huang, Y.-Y., and Kandel, E. R. (1993). Effects of cAMP simulate a late stage of LTP in hippocampal CA1 neurons. *Science, 260,* 1661–1664.

Fridlund, A. (1988). What can asymmetry and laterality in EMG tell us about the face and brain? *International Journal of Neuroscience, 39,* 53–69.

Fridlund, A. J. (1994). *Human facial expression: An evolutionary view.* San Diego, CA: Academic Press.

Fried, I., Wilson, C. L., MacDonald, K. A., and Behnke, E. J. (1998). Electric current stimulates laughter. *Nature, 391,* 650.

Fried, I., Wilson, C. L., Morrow, J. W., Cameron, K. A., et al. (2001). Increased dopamine release in the human amygdala during performance of cognitive tasks. *Nature Neuroscience, 4,* 201–206.

Friedman, J. M. (2003). A war on obesity, not the obese. *Science, 299,* 856–858.

Friedman, L., and Jones, B. E. (1984). Study of sleep-wakefulness states by computer graphics and cluster analysis before and after lesions of the pontine tegmentum in the cat. *Electroencephalography and Clinical Neurophysiology, 57,* 43–56.

Friedman, M., and Rosenman, R. H. (1974). *Type A behavior and your heart.* New York: Knopf.

Friedman, M. I. (1978). Hyperphagia in rats with experimental diabetes mellitus: A response to a decreased supply of utilizable fuels. *Journal of Comparative and Physiological Psychology, 92,* 109–117.

Fukuda, K., Ogilvie, R. D., Chilcott, L., Vendittelli, A.-M., et al. (1998). The prevalence of sleep paralysis among Canadian and Japanese college students. *Dreaming: Journal of the Association for the Study of Dreams, 8*(2), 59–66.

Fulton, S., Woodside, B., and Shizgal, P. (2000). Modulation of brain reward circuitry by leptin. *Science, 287,* 125–128.

Furukawa, S., Xu, L., and Middlebrooks, J. C. (2000). Coding of sound-source location by ensembles of cortical neurons. *Journal of Neuroscience, 20,* 1216–1228.

Fuster, J. M. (1990). Prefrontal cortex and the bridging of temporal gaps in the perception-action cycle. *Annals of the New York Academy of Sciences, 608,* 318–336.

Fuster, J. M., Bodner, M., and Kroger, J. K. (2000). Cross-modal and cross-temporal association in neurons of frontal cortex. *Nature, 405,* 347–351.

Gabrieli, J. D. E. (1998). Cognitive neuroscience of human memory. *Annual Review of Psychology, 49,* 87–115.

Gabrieli, J. D. E., Sullivan, E. V., Desmond, J. E., Stebbins, G. T., et al. (1996). Behavioral and functional neuroimaging evidence for preserved conceptual implicit memory in global amnesia. *Society for Neuroscience, 22,* 1449.

Gainetdinov, R. R., Wetsel, W. C., Jones, S. R., Levin E. D., et al. (1999). Role of serotonin in the paradoxical calming effect of psychostimulants on hyperactivity. *Science, 283,* 397–401.

Galaburda, A. M. (1994). Developmental dyslexia and animal studies: At the interface between cognition and neurology. *Cognition, 56,* 833–839.

Galani, R., Jarrard, L. E., Will, B. E., and Kelche, C. (1997). Effects of postoperative housing conditions on functional recovery in rats with lesions of the hippocampus, subiculum, or entorhinal cortex. *Neurobiology of Learning and Memory, 67,* 43–56.

Gallagher, M., Nagahara, A. H., and Burwell, R. D. (1995). Cognition and hippocampal systems in aging: Animal models. In J. L. McGaugh, N. M. Weinberger, and G. Lynch (Eds.), *Brain and memory: Modulation and mediation of neuroplasticity* (pp. 103–126). New York: Oxford University Press.

Gallagher, M., and Rapp, P. R. (1997). The use of animal models to study the effects of aging on cognition. *Annual Review of Psychology, 48,* 339–370.

Gallant, J. L., Braun, J., and Van Essen, D. C. (1993). Selectivity for polar, hyperbolic, and Cartesian gratings in macaque visual cortex. *Science, 259,* 100–103.

Gallopin, T., Fort, P., Eggermann, E., Cauli, B., et al. (2000). Identification of sleep-promoting neurons *in vitro. Nature, 404,* 992–995.

Gannon, P. J., Holloway, R. L., Broadfield, D. C., and Braun, A. R. (1998). Asymmetry of chimpanzee planum temporale: Humanlike pattern of brain language area homolog. *Science, 279,* 220–222.

Gaoni, Y., and Mechoulam, R. (1964). Journal of the American Chemical Society, 86, 1646.

Garavan, H., Morgan, R. E., Mactutus, C. F., Levitsky, D. A., and Strupp, B. J. (2000). Prenatal cocaine exposure impairs selective attention: Evidence from serial reversal and extradimensional shift tasks. *Behavioral Neuroscience, 114,* 725–738.

Garcia, J., Kimmeldorf, D. J., and Koelling, R. A. (1955). Conditioned aversion to saccharin resulting from exposure to gamma radiation. *Science, 122,* 157–158.

Gardner, L. I. (1972). Deprivation dwarfism. *Scientific American, 227*(1), 76–82.

Gardner, R. A., and Gardner, B. T. (1969). Teaching sign language to a chimpanzee. *Science, 165,* 664–672.

Gardner, R. A., and Gardner, B. T. (1984). A vocabulary test for chimpanzees (*Pan troglodytes*). *Journal of Comparative Psychology, 98,* 381–404.

Garver, D. L., Holcomb, J. A., and Christensen, J. D. (2000). Heterogeneity of response to antipsychotics from multiple disorders in the schizophrenia spectrum. *Journal of Clinical Psychiatry, 61,* 964–972.

Gauthier, I., Behrmann, M., and Tarr, M. J. (1999). Can face recognition really be dissociated from object recognition? *Journal of Cognitive Neuroscience, 11,* 349–370.

Gauthier, I., Skudlarski, P., Gore, J. C., and Anderson, A. W. (2000). Expertise for cars and birds recruits brain areas involved in face recognition. *Nature Neuroscience, 3,* 191–197.

Gawande, A. (2002). *Complications: A surgeon's notes on an imperfect science.* New York: Metropolitan Books.

Gazzaniga, M. S. (1992). Nature's mind: The biological roots of thinking, emotions, sexuality, language, and intelligence. New York: Basic Books.

Gazzaniga, M. S., and Smylie, C. S. (1983). Facial recognition and brain asymmetries: Clues to underlying mechanisms. *Annals of Neurology, 13,* 536–540.

Gehring, W. J., and Willoughby, A. R. (2002). The medial frontal cortex and the rapid processing of monetary gains and losses. *Science, 295,* 2279–2280.

Geinisman, Y., Detoledo-Morrell, L., Morrell, F., and Heller, R. E. (1995). Hippocampal markers of age-related memory dysfunction: Behavioral, electrophysiological and morphological perspectives. *Progress in Neurobiology, 45,* 223–252.

Gemba, H., Miki, N., and Sasaki, K. (1995). Cortical field potentials preceding vocalization and influences of cerebellar hemispherectomy upon them in monkeys. *Brain Research, 697,* 143–151.

Gendle, M. H., Strawderman, M. S., Mactutus, C. F., Booze, R. M., Levitsky, D. A., and Strupp, B. J. (2003). Impaired sustained attention and altered reactivity to errors in an animal model of prenatal cocaine exposure. *Developmental Brain Research, 147,* 85–96.

Georgopoulos, A. P., Kalaska, J. F., Caminiti, R., and Massey, J. T. (1982). On the relations between the direction of two-dimensional arm movements and cell discharge in primate motor cortex. *Journal of Neuroscience, 2,* 1527–1537.

Georgopoulos, A. P., Taira, M., and Lukashin, A. (1993). Cognitive neurophysiology of the motor cortex. *Science, 260,* 47–52.

Gerard, C. M., Mollereau, C., Vassart, G., and Parmentier, M. (1991). Molecular cloning of a human cannabinoid receptor which is also expressed in testis. *Biochemical Journal, 279,* 129–134.

Gerashchenko, D., Kohls, M. D., Greco, M. A., Waleh, N. S., et al. (2001). Hypocretin-2-saporin lesions of the lateral hypothalamus produce narcoleptic-like sleep behavior in the rat. *Neuroscience, 21,* 7273–7283.

Gerkema, M. P., and Daan, S. (1985). Ultradian rhythms in behavior: The case of the common vole (*Microtus arvalis*). In H. Schulz and P. Lavie (Eds.), *Ultradian rhythms in physiology and behavior* (pp. 11–32). Berlin: Springer.

Gerlai, R., Wojtowicz, J. M., Marks, A., and Roder, J. (1995). Overexpression of a calcium-binding protein, S100 beta, in astrocytes alters synaptic plasticity and impairs spatial learning in transgenic mice. *Learning and Memory, 2,* 26–39.

Gershon, A. A., Dannon, P. N., and Grunhaus, L. (2003). Transcranial magnetic stimulation in the treatment of depression. *American Journal of Psychiatry, 160,* 835–845.

Geschwind, N. (1972). Language and the brain. *Scientific American, 226*(4), 76–83.

Geschwind, N. (1976). Language and cerebral dominance. In T. N. Chase (Ed.), *Nervous system: Vol. 2. The clinical neurosciences* (pp. 433–439). New York: Raven.

Geschwind, N., and Levitsky, W. (1968). Human brain: Left-right asymmetries in temporal speech region. *Science, 161,* 186–187.

Ghazanfar, A. A., and Hauser, M. D. (1999). The neuroethology of primate vocal communication: Substrates for the evolution of speech. *Trends in Cognitive Sciences, 3,* 377–384.

Ghez, C., Hening, W., and Gordon, J. (1991). Organization of voluntary movement. *Current Opinion in Neurobiology, 1,* 664–671.

Gibbs, M. E., and Ng, K. T. (1977). Psychobiology of memory: Towards a model of memory formation. *Biobehavioral Reviews, 1,* 113–136.

Gibbs, M. E., and Ng, K. T. (1979). Neuronal depolarization and the inhibition of short-term memory formation. *Physiology & Behavior, 23,* 369–375.

Gibson, J. R., Beierlein, M., and Connors, B. W. (1999). Two networks of electrically coupled inhibitory neurons in neocortex. *Nature, 402,* 75–79.

Gilbert, A. N., and Wysocki, C. J. (1987). The smell survey results. *National Geographic, 172,* 514–525.

Gilbert, A. N., Yamazaki, K., Beauchamp, G. K., and Thomas, L. (1986). Olfactory discrimination of mouse strains (*Mus musculus*) and major histocompatibility types by humans (*Homo sapiens*). *Journal of Comparative Psychology, 100,* 262–265.

Gitelman, D. R., Alpert, N. M., Kosslyn, S., Daffner, K., et al. (1996). Functional imaging of human right hemispheric activation for exploratory movements. *Annals of Neurology, 39,* 174–179.

Glantz, L. A., and Lewis, D. A. (2000). Decreased dendritic spine density on prefrontal cortical pyramidal neurons in schizophrenia. *Archives of General Psychiatry, 57,* 65–73.

Glantz, M., and Pickens, R. (1992). *Vulnerability to drug abuse.* Washington, DC: American Psychological Association.

Glaser, R., Rice, J., Speicher, C. E., Stout, J. C., et al. (1986). Stress depresses interferon production by leukocytes concomitant with a decrease in natural killer cell activity. *Behavioral Neuroscience, 100,* 675–678.

Glickman, S. E. (1977). Comparative psychology. In P. Mussen and M. R. Rosenzweig (Eds.), *Psychology: An introduction* (2nd ed., pp. 625–703). Lexington, MA: Heath.

Glickman, S. E., Frank, L. G., Davidson, J. M., Smith, E. R., et al. (1987). Androstenedione may organize or activate sex-reversed traits in female spotted hyenas. *Proceedings of the National Academy of Sciences, USA, 84,* 344–347.

Globus, A., Rosenzweig, M. R., Bennett, E. L., and Diamond, M. C. (1973). Effects of differential experience on dendritic spine counts in rat cerebral cortex. *Journal of Comparative and Physiological Psychology, 82,* 175–181.

Gloor, P., Olivier, A., Quesney, L. F., Andermann, F., et al. (1982). The role of the limbic system in experiential phenomena of temporal lobe epilepsy. *Annals of Neurology, 12,* 129–144.

Glusman, G., Yanai, I., Rubin, I., and Lancet D. (2001). The complete human olfactory subgenome. *Genome Research, 11,* 685–702.

Golomb, J., de Leon, M. J., George, A. E., Kluger, A., et al. (1994). Hippocampal atrophy correlates with severe cognitive impairment in elderly patients with suspected normal pressure hydrocephalus. *Journal of Neurology, Neurosurgery and Psychiatry, 57,* 590–593.

Goodale, M. A., and Haffenden, A. (1998). Frames of reference for perception and action in the human visual system. *Neuroscience and Biobehavioral Reviews, 22,* 161–172.

Goodale, M. A., Milner, A. D., Jakobson, L. S., and Carey, D. P. (1991). A neurological dissociation between perceiving objects and grasping them. *Nature, 349,* 154–156.

Goodman, C. (1979). Isogenic grasshoppers: Genetic variability and development of identified neurons. In X. O. Breakefeld (Ed.), *Neurogenetics.* New York: Elsevier.

Goodman, C. S. (1996). Mechanisms and molecules that control growth cone guidance. *Annual Review of Neuroscience, 19,* 341–377.

Goodman, M., Tagle, D. A., Fitch, D. H., Bailey, W., et al. (1990). Primate evolution at the DNA level and a classification of hominoids. *Journal of Molecular Evolution, 30,* 260–266.

Gordon, N. S., Burke, S., Akil, H., Watson, S. J., et al. (2003). Socially-induced brain "fertilization": Play promotes brain derived neurotrophic factor transcription in the amygdala and dorsolateral frontal cortex in juvenile rats. *Neuroscience Letters, 341,* 17–20.

Gorelick, D. A., and Balster, R. L. (1995). Phencyclidine. In F. E. Bloom and D. J. Kupfer (Eds.), *Psychopharmacology: The fourth generation of progress* (pp. 1767–1776). New York: Raven.

Gorski, R. A., Gordon, J. H., Shryne, J. E., and Southam, A. M. (1978). Evidence for a morphological sex difference within the medial preoptic area of the rat brain. *Brain Research, 148,* 333–346.

Gothe, J., Brandt, S. A., Irlbacher, K., Roricht, S., et al. (2002). Changes in visual cortex excitability in blind subjects as demonstrated by transcranial magnetic stimulation. *Brain, 125,* 479–490.

Gottesman, I. I. (1991). Schizophrenia genesis: The origins of madness. New York: Freeman.

Gottfried, J. A., O'Doherty, J., and Dolan, R. J. (2003). Encoding predictive reward value in human amygdala and orbitofrontal cortex. *Science, 301,* 1104–1107.

Gottlieb, G. (1976). The roles of experience in the development of behavior and the nervous system. In G. Gottlieb (Ed.), *Studies on the development of behavior and the nervous system: Vol. 3. Neural and behavioral specificity.* New York: Academic Press.

Gould, E., Beylin, A., Tanapat, P., Reeves, A., et al. (1999). Learning enhances adult neurogenesis in the hippocampal formation. *Nature Neuroscience, 2,* 260–265.

Gould, E., Reeves, A. J., Graziano, M. S., and Gross, C. G. (1999). Neurogenesis in the neocortex of adult primates. *Science, 286,* 548–552.

Gould, E., Tanapat, P., McEwen, B. S., Flugge, G., et al. (1998). Proliferation of granule cell precursors in the dentate gyrus of adult monkeys is diminished by stress. *Proceedings of the National Academy of Sciences, USA, 95,* 3168–3171.

Gould, J. L. (1986). The biology of learning. *Annual Review of Psychology, 37,* 163–192.

Gould, S. J. (1981). *The mismeasure of man.* New York: Norton.

Grados, M. A., Walkup, J., and Walford, S. (2003). Genetics of obsessive-compulsive disorders: New findings and challenges. *Brain & Development, 25*(Suppl. 1), S55–S61.

Grady, C. L., and Craik, F. I. M. (2000). Changes in memory processing with age. *Current Opinion in Neurobiology, 10,* 224–231.

Grady, C. L., McIntosh, A. R., Horowitz, B., Maisog, J. M., et al. (1995). Age-related reductions in human recognition memory due to impaired encoding. *Science, 269,* 218–221.

Grafton, S. T., Mazziotta, J. C., Presty, S., Friston, K. J., et al. (1992). Functional anatomy of human procedural learning determined with regional cerebral blood flow and PET. *Journal of Neuroscience, 12,* 2542–2548.

Grant, S. G., O'Dell, T. J., Karl, K. A., Stein, P. L., et al. (1992). Impaired long-term potentiation, spatial learning, and hippocampal development in fyn mutant mice. *Science, 256,* 1903–1910.

Gratton, G., and Fabiani, M. (2001). Shedding light on brain function: The event-related optical signal. *Trends in Cognitive Sciences, 5,* 357–363.

Gray, N. S., MacCulloch, M. J., Smith, J., Morris, M., et al. (2003). Violence viewed by psychopathic murderers. *Nature, 423,* 497.

Graybiel, A. M., Aosaki, T., Flaherty, A. W., and Kimura, M. (1994). The basal ganglia and adaptive motor control. *Science, 265,* 1826–1831.

Graziano, M. S., Hu, X. T., and Gross, C. G. (1997). Coding the locations of objects in the dark. *Science, 277,* 239–241.

Green, E., and Craddock, N. (2003). Brain-derived neurotrophic factor as a potential risk locus for bipolar disorder: Evidence, limitations, and implications. *Current Psychiatry Reports, 5,* 469–476.

Green, W. H., Campbell, M., and David, R. (1984). Psychosocial dwarfism: A critical review of the evidence. *Journal of the American Academy of Child Psychiatry, 23,* 39–48.

Greenberg, P. E., Kessler, R. C., Birnbaum, H. G., Leong, S. A., et al. (2003). The economic burden of depression in the United States: How did it change between 1990 and 2000? *Journal of Clinical Psychiatry, 64,* 1465–1475.

Greenewalt, CH. (1968). *Bird song: Acoustics and physiology.* Washington, DC: Smithsonian Institution Press.

Greenough, W. T. (1976). Enduring brain effects of differential experience and training. In M. R. Rosenzweig and E. L. Bennett (Eds.), *Neural*

mechanisms of learning and memory (pp. 255–278). Cambridge, MA: MIT Press.

Greenough, W. T., McDonald, J. W., Parnisari, R. M., and Camel, J. E. (1986). Environmental conditions modulate degeneration and new dendrite growth in cerebellum of senescent rats. *Brain Research, 380,* 136–143.

Greenough, W. T., and Volkmar, F. R. (1973). Pattern of dendritic branching in occipital cortex of rats reared in complex environments. *Experimental Neurology, 40,* 491–504.

Greenspan, R. J., Finn, J. A., Jr., and Hall, J. C. (1980). Acetylcholinesterase mutants in *Drosophila* and their effects on the structure and function of the central nervous system. *Journal of Comparative Neurology, 189,* 741–774.

Gregory, R. L. (1987). Blindness, recovery from. In R. L. Gregory (Ed.), *The Oxford companion to the mind* (pp. 94–96). Oxford, England: Oxford University Press.

Gregory, R. L., and Wallace, J. G. (1963). *Recovery from early blindness: A case study.* Cambridge, England: Cambridge University Press.

Grevert, P., Albert, L. H., and Goldstein, A. (1983). Partial antagonism of placebo analgesia by naloxone. *Pain, 16,* 129–143.

Griffin, L. D., and Mellon, S. H. (1999). Selective serotonin reuptake inhibitors directly alter activity of neurosteroidogenic enzymes. *Proceedings of the National Academy of Sciences, USA, 96,* 13512–13517.

Grill, R., Murai, K., Blesch, A., Gage, F. H., et al. (1997). Cellular delivery of neurotrophin-3 promotes corticospinal axonal growth and partial functional recovery after spinal cord injury. *Journal of Neuroscience, 17,* 5560–5572.

Grillner, P., Hill, R., and Grillner, S. (1991). 7-Chlorokynurenic acid blocks NMDA receptor-induced fictive locomotion in lamprey—Evidence for a physiological role of the glycine site. *Acta Physiologica Scandinavica, 141,* 131–132.

Grillner, S. (1985). Neurobiological bases of rhythmic motor acts in vertebrates. *Science, 228,* 143–149.

Grosof, D. H., Shapley, R. M., and Hawken, M. J. (1993). Macaque V1 neurons can signal "illusory" contours. *Nature, 365,* 550–552.

Grothe, B. (2003). New roles for synaptic inhibition in sound localization. *Nature Reviews, 4,* 540–550.

Grover, G. J., Mellstrom, K., Ye, L., Malm, J., et al. (2003). Selective thyroid hormone receptor-beta activation: A strategy for reduction of weight, cholesterol, and lipoprotein (a) with reduced cardiovascular liability. *Proceedings of the National Academy of Sciences, USA, 100,* 10067–10072.

Grumbach, M. M., and Auchus, R. J. (1999). Estrogen: Consequences and implications of human mutations in synthesis and action. *Journal of Clinical Endocrinology and Metabolism, 84,* 4677–4694.

Grunt, J. A., and Young, W. C. (1953). Consistency of sexual behavior patterns in individual male guinea pigs following castration and androgen therapy. *Journal of Comparative and Physiological Psychology, 46,* 138–144.

Grutzendler, J., Kasthuri, N., and Gan, W.-B. (2002). Long-term dendritic spine stability in the adult cortex. *Nature, 420,* 812–816.

Gudermann, T., Schoneberg, T., and Schultz, G. (1997). Functional and structural complexity of signal transduction via G-protein-coupled receptors. *Annual Review of Neuroscience, 20,* 399–427.

Gulevich, G., Dement, W., and Johnson, L. (1966). Psychiatric and EEG observations on a case of prolonged (264 hours) wakefulness. *Archives of General Psychiatry, 15,* 29–35.

Gur, R. E., Resnick, S. M., Alavi, A., Gur, R. C., et al. (1987). Regional brain function in schizophrenia. I. A positron emission tomography study. *Archives of General Psychiatry, 44,* 119–125.

Gurney, M. E., and Konishi, M. (1979). Hormone induced sexual differentiation of brain and behavior in zebra finches. *Science, 208,* 1380–1382.

Gurney, M. E., Pu, H., Chiu, A. Y., Dal Canto, M. C., et al. (1994). Motor neuron degeneration in mice that express a human Cu,Zn superoxide dismutase mutation. *Science, 264,* 1772–1775.

Gusella, J. F., and MacDonald, M. E. (1993). Hunting for Huntington's disease. *Molecular Genetic Medicine, 3,* 139–158.

Haass, C., and Kahle, P. J. (2000). Parkinson's pathology in a fly. *Nature, 404,* 341–343.

Hadley, M. E. (2000). *Endocrinology* (5th ed.). Englewood Cliffs, NJ: Prentice-Hall.

Häfner, H. (1998). Neurodevelopmental disorder and psychosis: One disease or major risk factor? *Current Opinion in Psychiatry, 11,* 17–18.

Hagstrom, S. A., Neitz, J., and Neitz, M. (1998). Variations in cone populations for red-green color vision examined by analysis of mRNA. *Neuroreport, 9,* 1963–1967.

Hagstrum, J. T. (2000). Infrasound and the avian navigational map. *Journal of Experimental Biology, 203,* 1103–1111.

Hakansson, M. L., Brown, H., Ghilardi, N., Skoda, R. C., et al. (1998). Leptin receptor immunoreactivity in chemically defined target neurons of the hypothalamus. *Journal of Neuroscience, 18,* 559–572.

Hall, D., Dhilla, A., Charalambous, A., Gogos, J. A., et al. (2003). Sequence variants of the brain-derived neurotrophic factor (BDNF) gene are strongly associated with obsessive-compulsive disorder. *American Journal of Human Genetics, 73,* 370–376.

Hallervorden, J. (1902). Eine neue Methode experimenteller Physiognomik. *Psychiatrisch-Neurologische Wochenschrift, 28,* 309–311.

Halpern, D. F. (1986). A different answer to the question, "Do sex-related differences in spatial abilities exist?" *American Psychologist, 41,* 1014–1015.

Halpern, M. (1987). The organization and function of the vomeronasal system. *Annual Review of Neuroscience, 10,* 325–362.

Halsband, U., Matsuzaka, Y., and Tanji, J. (1994). Neuronal activity in the primate supplementary, pre-supplementary and premotor cortex during externally and internally instructed sequential movements. *Neuroscience Research, 20,* 149–155.

Hamburger, V. (1958). Regression versus peripheral control of differentiation in motor hypoplasia. *American Journal of Anatomy, 102,* 365–410.

Hamburger, V. (1975). Cell death in the development of the lateral motor column of the chick embryo. *Journal of Comparative Neurology, 160,* 535–546.

Hamer, D. H., Hu, S., Magnuson, V. L., Hu, N., et al. (1993). A linkage between DNA markers on the X chromosome and male sexual orientation. *Science, 261,* 321–327.

Hamm, R. J., Temple, M. D., O'Dell, D. M., Pike, B. R., et al. (1996). Exposure to environmental complexity promotes recovery of cognitive function after traumatic brain injury. *Journal of Neurotrauma, 13,* 41–47.

Hampton, R. R., Sherry, D. F., Shettleworth, S. J., Khurgel, M., et al. (1995). Hippocampal volume and food-storing behavior are related in parids. *Brain, Behavior and Evolution, 45,* 54–61.

Hamson, D. K., and Watson, N. V. (2004). Regional brainstem expression of Fos associated with sexual behavior in male rats. *Brain Research, 1006,* 233–240.

Hanakawa, T., Immisch, I., Toma, K., Dimyan, M. A., et al. (2003). Functional properties of brain areas associated with motor execution and imagery. *Journal of Neurophysiology, 89,* 989–1002.

Hanaway, J., Woolsey, T. A., Gado, M. H., and Roberts, M. P. (1998). *The brain atlas.* Bethesda, MD: Fitzgerald Science.

Harder, B. (2003). Unproven elixir: Hormone therapy tempts aging men, but its risks haven't yet been reckoned. *Science News, 163,* 296–301.

Harding, M. M., Anderberg, P. I., and Haymet, A. D. (2003). "Antifreeze" glycoproteins from polar fish. *European Journal of Biochemistry, 270,* 1381–1392.

Hardyck, C., Petrinovich, L., and Goldman R. (1976). Left-handedness and cognitive deficit. *Cortex, 12,* 226–279.

Hare, R. D., Harpur, T. J., Hakstian, A. R., Forth, A. E., et al. (1990). The revised psychopathy checklist: Descriptive statistics, reliability, and factor structure. *Psychological Assessment, 2,* 338–341.

Harris, E. W., and Cotman, C. W. (1986). Long-term potentiation of guinea pig mossy fiber responses is not blocked by N-methyl D-aspartate antagonists. *Neuroscience Letters, 70,* 132–137.

Hart, B. L. (1988). Biological basis of the behavior of sick animals. *Neuroscience and Biobehavioral Reviews, 12,* 123–137.

Hartmann, E. (1973). Sleep requirement: Long sleepers, short sleepers, variable sleepers, and insomniacs. *Psychosomatics, 14,* 95–103.

Hartmann, E. (1978). *The sleeping pill.* New Haven, CT: Yale University Press.

Hartmann, E. (1984). The nightmare: The psychology and biology of terrifying dreams. New York: Basic Books.

Harvey, P. H., and Krebs, J. R. (1990). Comparing brains. *Science, 249,* 140–146.

Harvey, P. H., and Pagel, M. D. (1991). *The comparative method in evolutionary biology.* New York: Oxford University Press.

Hasher, L., and Zacks, R. T. (1979). Automatic and effortful processes in memory. *Journal of Experimental Psychology: General, 108,* 356-358 .

Haskett, R. F. (1985). Diagnostic categorization of psychiatric disturbance in Cushing's syndrome. *American Journal of Psychiatry, 142,* 911–916.

Hattar, S., Liao, H.-W., Takao, M., Berson, D. M., et al. (2002). Melanopsin-containing retinal ganglion cells: Architecture, projections, and intrinsic photosensitivity. *Science, 295,* 1065–1070.

Hatten, M. E. (1990). Riding the glial monorail: A common mechanism for glial-guided neuronal migration in different regions of the developing mammalian brain. *Trends in Neurosciences, 13,* 179–184.

Hauser, M. D., Chomsky, N., and Tecumseh Fitch, W. (2002). The faculty of language: What is it, who has it, and how did it evolve? *Science, 298,* 1569–1579.

Hauser, P., Zametkin, A. J., Martinez, P., Vitiello, B., et al. (1993). Attention deficit-hyperactivity disorder in people with generalized resistance to thyroid hormone. *New England Journal of Medicine, 328,* 997–1001.

Hazeltine, E., Grafton, S. T., and Ivry, R. (1997). Attention and stimulus characteristics determine the locus of motor-sequence encoding. A PET study. *Brain, 120,* 123–140.

Heath, R. G. (1972). Pleasure and brain activity in man. *Journal of Nervous and Mental Diseases, 154,* 3–18.

Heath, R. G., Franklin, D. E., and Shraberg, D. (1979). Gross pathology of the cerebellum in patients diagnosed and treated as functional psychiatric disorders. *Journal of Nervous and Mental Disorders, 167,* 585–592.

Hebb, D. O. (1949). *The organization of behavior.* New York: Wiley.

Heffner, H. E., and Heffner, R. S. (1989). Unilateral auditory cortex ablation in macaques results in a contralateral hearing loss. *Journal of Neurophysiology, 62,* 789–801.

Heinrichs, R. W. (2003). Historical origins of schizophrenia: Two early madmen and their illness. *Journal for the History of Behavioral Sciences, 39,* 349–363.

Heisler, L. K., Cowley, M. A., Tecott, L. H., Fan, W., et al. (2002). Activation of central melanocortin pathways by fenfluramine. *Science, 297,* 609–611.

Heit, S., Owens, M. J., Plotsky, P., and Nemeroff, C. B. (1997). Corticotropin-releasing factor, stress, and depression. *Neuroscientist, 3,* 186–194.

Held, R. (1993). Binocular vision—Behavioral and neuronal development. In M. H. Johnson (Ed.), *Brain development and cognition: A reader* (pp. 152–166). Oxford, England: Blackwell.

Heldmaier, G., and Ruf, T. (1992). Body temperature and metabolic rate during natural hypothermia in endotherms. *Journal of Comparative Physiology. B, Biochemical, Systemic, and Environmental Physiology, 162,* 696–706.

Hemmingsen, A. M. (1960). Energy metabolism as related to body size and respiratory surfaces, and its evolution. *Reports of Steno Memorial Hospital, Copenhagen, 9,* 1–110.

Hendrickson, A. (1985). Dots, stripes and columns in monkey visual cortex. *Trends in NeuroSciences, 8,* 406–410.

Hendriks, W. T., Ruitenberg, M. J., Blits, B., Boer, G. J., et al. (2004). Viral vector-mediated gene transfer of neurotrophins to promote regeneration of the injured spinal cord. *Progress in Brain Research, 146,* 451–476.

Hendry, S. H. C., and Reid, R. C. (2000). The koniocellular pathway in primate vision. *Annual Review of Neuroscience, 23,* 127–153.

Henig, R. M. (2004, April 4). The quest to forget. *The New York Times,* Section 6, p. 32.

Henneman, E. (1991). The size principle and its relation to transmission failure in Ia projections to spinal motoneurons. *Annals of the New York Academy of Sciences, 627,* 165–168.

Herrada, G., and Dulac, C. (1997). A novel family of putative pheromone receptors in mammals with a topographically organized and sexually dimorphic distribution. *Cell, 90,* 763–773.

Hertel, P., Fagerquist, M. V., and Svensson, T. H. (1999). Enhanced cortical dopamine output and antipsychotic-like effects of raclopride by alpha-2 adrenoceptor blockade. *Science, 286,* 105–107.

Hetherington, A. W., and Ranson, S. W. (1940). Hypothalamic lesions and adiposity in the rat. *Anatomical Record, 78,* 149–172.

Hewes, G. (1973). Primate communication and the gestural origin of language. *Current Anthropology, 14,* 5–24.

Highley, J. R., Walker, M. A., Esiri, M. M., McDonald, B., et al. (2001). Schizophrenia and the frontal lobes: Post-mortem stereological study of tissue volume. *British Journal of Psychiatry, 178,* 337–343.

Higley, J. D., Mehlman, P. T., Taub, D. M., Higley, S. B., et al. (1992). Cerebrospinal fluid monoamine and adrenal correlates of aggression in free-ranging rhesus monkeys. *Archives of General Psychiatry, 49,* 436–441.

Hillis, D. M., Moritz, C., and Mable, B. K. (eds.). (1996). *Molecular systematics* (2nd ed.). Sunderland, MA: Sinauer.

Hingson, R., Alpert, J., Day, N., Dooling, E., et al. (1982). Effects of maternal drinking and marijuana use on fetal growth and development. *Pediatrics, 70,* 539–546.

Hippocrates. (1991). *On the sacred disease* (F. Adams, Trans.) [On-line, at www.soli.com]. (Library of the Future Series, 3rd ed., Version 4.5.) World Library. (Original work written in 400 B.C.E.)

Hiramoto, M., Hiromi, Y., Giniger, E., and Hotta, Y. (2000). The *Drosophila* Netrin receptor Frazzled guides axons by controlling Netrin distribution. *Nature, 406,* 886–889.

Hirsch, E., Moye, D., and Dimon, J. H. (1995). Congenital indifference to pain: Long-term follow-up of two cases. *Southern Medical Journal, 88,* 851–857.

Hirsch, H. V. B., and Spinelli, D. N. (1971). Modification of the distribution of receptive field orientation in cats by selective visual exposure during development. *Experimental Brain Research, 12,* 509–527.

Hochstein, S., and Shapley, R. M. (1976). Quantitative analysis of retinal ganglion cell classifications. *Journal of Physiology (London), 252,* 237–264.

Hodgkin, A. L., and Huxley, A. F. (1952). A quantitative description of membrane current and its application to conduction and excitation in nerve. *Journal of Physiology (London), 117,* 500–544.

Hodgkin, A. L., and Katz, B. (1949). The effect of sodium ions on the electrical activity of the giant axon of the squid. *Journal of Physiology (London), 108,* 37–77.

Hofmann, A. (1981). *LSD: My Problem Child.* New York: McGraw-Hill.

Holden, C. (2001). Panel seeks truth in lie detector debate. *Science, 291,* 967.

Hollander, E. (1999). Managing aggressive behavior in patients with obsessive–compulsive disorder and borderline personality disorder. *Journal of Clinical Psychiatry, 60*(Suppl.), 38–44.

Hollon, S. D., Thase, M. E., and Markowitz, J. C. (2002). Treatment and prevention of depression. *Psychological Science in the Public Interest, 3,* 39–77.

Holloway, C. C., and Clayton, D. F. (2001). Estrogen synthesis in the male brain triggers development of the avian song control pathway in vitro. *Nature Neuroscience, 4,* 170–175.

Holman, B. L., Mendelson, J., Garada, B., Teoh, S. K., et al. (1993). Regional cerebral blood flow improves with treatment in chronic cocaine polydrug users. *Journal of Nuclear Medicine, 34,* 723–727.

Holzenberger, M., Dupont, J., Ducos, B., Leneuve, P., et al. (2003). IGF-1 receptor regulates lifespan and resistance to oxidative stress in mice. *Nature, 421,* 182–187.

Honey, G. D., Bullmore, E. T., Soni, W., Varatheesan, M., et al. (1999). Differences in frontal cortical activation by a working memory task after substitution of risperidone for typical antipsychotic drugs in patients with schizophrenia. *Proceedings of the National Academy of Sciences, USA, 96,* 13432–13437.

Hood, K. L., Postle, B. R., and Corkin, S. (1999). An evaluation of the concurrent discrimination task as a measure of habit learning: Performance of amnesic subjects. *Neuropsychologia, 37,* 1375–1386.

Horai, S., Hayasaka, K., Kondo, R., Tsugane, K., et al. (1995). Recent African origin of modern humans revealed by complete sequences of hominoid mitochondrial DNAs. *Proceedings of the National Academy of Sciences, USA, 92,* 532–536.

Huang, Y. Y., and Kandel, E. R. (1994). Recruitment of long-lasting and protein kinase A-dependent long-term potentiations in the CA1 region of the hippocampus requires repeated tetanization. *Learning and Memory, 1,* 74–82.

Hubbard, A. (1993). A traveling-wave amplifier model of the cochlea. *Science, 259,* 68–71.

Hubel, D. H., and Wiesel, T. N. (1959). Receptive fields of single neurones in the cat's striate cortex. *Journal of Physiology (London), 148,* 573–591.

Hubel, D. H., and Wiesel, T. N. (1965). Binocular interaction in striate cortex kittens reared with artificial squint. *Journal of Neurophysiology, 28,* 1041–1059.

Hubel, D. H., Wiesel, T. N., and LeVay, S. (1977). Plasticity of ocular dominance in monkey striate cortex. *Philosophical Transactions of the Royal Society of London. Series B: Biological Sciences, 278,* 377–409.

Hudspeth, A. J. (1989). How the ear's works work. *Nature, 341,* 397–404.

Hudspeth, A. J. (1992). Hair-bundle mechanics and a model for mechanoelectrical transduction by hair cells. *Society of General Physiologists Series, 47,* 357–370.

Hudspeth, A. J. (1997). How hearing happens. *Neuron, 19,* 947–950.

Hudspeth, A. J., Choe, Y., Mehta, A. D., and Martin, P. (2000). Putting ion channels to work: Mechanoelectrical transduction, adaptation, and amplification by hair cells. *Proceedings of the National Academy of Sciences, USA, 97,* 11765–11772.

Huffman, K. J., Nelson, J., Clarey, J., and Krubitzer, L. (1999). Organization of somatosensory cortex in three species of marsupials, *Dasyurus hallucatus, Dactylopsila trivirgata,* and *Monodelphis domestica:* Neural correlates of morphological specializations. *Journal of Comparative Neurology, 403,* 5–32.

Hughes, J., Smith, T. W., Kosterlitz, H. W., Fothergill, L. A., et al. (1975). Identification of two related pentapeptides from the brain with potent opiate agonist activity. *Nature, 258,* 577–580.

Hull, C. L. (1943). *Principles of behavior.* New York: Appleton-Century.

Hunt, G. R., Corballis, M. C., and Gray, R. D. (2001). Laterality in tool manufacture by crows. *Nature, 414,* 707.

Huntington, G. (1872). On chorea. *Medical and Surgical Reporter, 26,* 317–321.

Huttenlocher, P. R., deCourten, C., Garey, L. J., and Van der Loos, H. (1982). Synaptogenesis in the human visual cortex-evidence for synapse elimination during normal development. *Neuroscience Letters, 33,* 247–252.

Hyde, T. M., and Weinberger, D. R. (1990). The brain in schizophrenia. *Seminars in Neurology, 10,* 276–286.

Hyde, T. M., Aaronson, B. A., Randolph, C., Rickler, K. C., et al. (1992). Relationship of birth weight to the phenotypic expression of Gilles de la Tourette's syndrome in monozygotic twins. *Neurology, 42,* 652–658.

Imperato-McGinley, J., Guerrero, L., Gautier, T., and Peterson, R. E. (1974). Steroid 5α-reductase deficiency in man: An inherited form of male pseudohermaphroditism. *Science, 86,* 1213–1215.

Indo, Y., Tsuruta, M., Hayashida, Y., Karim, M. A., et al. (1996). Mutations in the trka/ngf receptor gene in patients with congenital insensitivity to pain with anhidrosis. *Nature Genetics, 13,* 485–488.

Insel, T. R. (1992). Toward a neuroanatomy of obsessive-compulsive disorder. *Archives of General Psychiatry, 49,* 739–744.

Insley, S. J. (2000). Long-term vocal recognition in the northern fur seal. *Nature, 406,* 404–405.

Institute of Medicine. (1990). *Broadening the base of treatment for alcohol problems.* Washington, DC: National Academy Press.

Irle, E., Exner, C., Thielen, K., Weniger, G., et al. (1998). Obsessive-compulsive disorder and ventromedial frontal lesions: Clinical and neuropsychological findings. *American Journal of Psychiatry, 155,* 255–263.

Isaacson, R. L. (1972). Hippocampal destruction in man and other animals. *Neuropsychologia, 10,* 47–64.

Isacson, O., Bjorklund, L., and Sanchez Pernaute, R. (2001). Parkinson's disease: Interpretations of transplantation study erroneous. *Nature Neuroscience, 4,* 533.

Isles, A. R., Baum, M. J., Ma, D., Keverne, E. B., et al. (2001). Urinary odour preferences in mice. *Nature, 409,* 783–784.

Ito, J., Sakakibara, J., Iwasaki, Y., and Yonekura, Y. (1993). Positron emission tomography of auditory sensation in deaf patients and patients with cochlear implants. *Annals of Otology, Rhinology & Laryngology, 102,* 797–801.

Ito, M. (1987). Cerebellar adaptive function in altered vestibular and visual environments. *Physiologist, 30,* S81.

Iverson, J. M., and Goldin-Meadow, S. (1998). Why people gesture when they speak. *Nature, 396,* 228.

Ivry, R. B., and Robertson, L. C. (1998). *The two sides of perception.* Cambridge, MA: MIT Press.

Iwamura, Y., and Tanaka, M. (1978). Postcentral neurons in hand region of area 2: Their possible role in the form discrimination of tactile objects. *Brain Research, 150,* 662–666.

Jackson, H., and Parks, T. N. (1982). Functional synapse elimination in the developing avian cochlear nucleus with simultaneous reduction in cochlear nerve axon branching. *Journal of Neuroscience, 2,* 1736–1743.

Jacob, S., McClintock, M. K., Zelano, B., and Ober, C. (2002). Paternally inherited HLA alleles are associated with women's choice of male odor. *Nature Genetics, 30,* 175–179.

Jacobs, G. H. (1993). The distribution and nature of colour vision among the mammals. *Biological Reviews of the Cambridge Philosophical Society, 68,* 413–471.

Jacobs, L. F., Gaulin, S. J., Sherry, D. F., and Hoffman, G. E. (1990). Evolution of spatial cognition: Sex-specific patterns of spatial behavior predict hippocampal size. *Proceedings of the National Academy of Sciences, USA, 87,* 6349–6352.

Jacobs, L. F., and Spencer, W. D. (1994). Natural space-use patterns and hippocampal size in kangaroo rats. *Brain, Behavior and Evolution, 44,* 125–132.

Jacobson, M. (1991). *Developmental neurobiology.* New York: Plenum.

James, T. W., Culham, J., Humphery, G. K., Milner, A. D., et al. (2003). Ventral occipital lesions impair object recognition but not object-directed grasping: An fMRI study. *Brain, 126,* 2464–2475.

James, W. (1890). *Principles of psychology.* New York: Holt.

Jamieson, D., and Roberts, A. (2000). Responses of young *Xenopus laevis* tadpoles to light dimming: Possible roles for the pineal eye. *Journal of Experimental Biology, 203,* 1857–1867.

Jarvis, E. D., and Mello, C. V. (2000). Molecular mapping of brain areas involved in parrot vocal communication. *Journal of Comparative Neurology, 419,* 1–31.

Jaskiw, G. E., and Popli, A. P. (2004). A meta-analysis of the response to chronic L-dopa in patients with schizophrenia: Therapeutic and heuristic implications. *Psychopharmacology, 171,* 365–374.

Jauhar, S. (2003, July 15). A malady that mimics depression. *The New York Times,* p. F5.

Jellies, J. A. (1981). *Associative olfactory conditioning in Drosophila melanogaster and memory retention through metamorphosis.* Unpublished doctoral dissertation, Illinois State University, Normal, IL.

Jenike, M. A., Baer, L., Ballantine, T., Martuza, R. L., et al. (1991). Cingulotomy for refractory obsessive-compulsive disorder. A long-term follow-up of 33 patients. *Archives of General Psychiatry, 48,* 548–555.

Jenkins, J., and Dallenbach, K. (1924). Oblivescence during sleep and waking. *American Journal of Psychology, 35,* 605–612.

Jentsch, J. D., Redmond, D. E., Jr., Elsworth, J. D., Taylor, J. R., et al. (1997). Enduring cognitive deficits and cortical dopamine dysfunction in monkeys after long-term administration of phencyclidine. *Science, 277,* 953–955.

Jerison, H. J. (1991). *Brain size and the evolution of mind.* New York: American Museum of Natural History.

Jiang, Y., Ruta, V., Chen, J., Lee, A., et al. (2003). The principle of gating charge movement in a voltage-dependent K⁺ channel. *Nature, 423,* 42–48.Johansson, B. B., and Ohlsson, A. L. (1996). Environment, social interaction, and physical activity as determinants of functional outcome after cerebral infarction in the rat. *Experimental Neurology, 139,* 322–327.

Johnsen, A., Andersen, V., Sunding, C., and Lifjeld, J. T. (2000). Female bluethroats enhance offspring immunocompetence through extra-pair copulations. *Nature, 406,* 296–299.

Johnson, K. O., and Hsiao, S. S. (1992). Neural mechanisms of tactual form and texture perception. *Annual Review of Neuroscience, 15,* 227–250.

Johnson, L. C. (1969). Psychological and physiological changes following total sleep deprivation. In A. Kales (Ed.), *Sleep: Physiology and pathology.* Philadelphia: Lippincott.

Johnson, P. L., and Stellar, J. R. (1994). Effects of accumbens DALA microinjections on brain stimulation reward and behavioral activation in intact and 6-OHDA treated rats. *Psychopharmacology, 114,* 665–671.

Jones, K. E., Lyons, M., Bawa, P., and Lemon, R. N. (1994). Recruitment order of motoneurons during functional tasks. *Experimental Brain Research, 100,* 503–508.

Jordan, B. D., Jahre, C., Hauser, W. A., Zimmerman, R. D., et al. (1992). CT of 338 active professional boxers. *Radiology, 185,* 509–512.

Jordan, C. L., Breedlove, S. M., and Arnold, A. P. (1991). Ontogeny of steroid accumulation in spinal lumbar motoneurons of the rat: Implications for androgen's site of action during synapse elimination. *Journal of Comparative Neurology, 313,* 441–448.

Jouvet, M. (1967). Neurophysiology of the states of sleep. In G. C. Quarton, T. Melnechuk, and F. O. Schmitt (Eds.), *The neurosciences* (pp. 529–544). New York: Rockefeller University.

Julian, T., and McKenry, P. C. (1979). Relationship of testosterone to men's family functioning at mid-life: A research note. *Aggressive Behavior, 15,* 281–289.

Kaas, J. H. (1991). Plasticity of sensory and motor maps in adult mammals. *Annual Review of Neuroscience, 14,* 137–167.

Kaas, J. H. (2000). The reorganization of sensory and motor maps after injury in adult mammals. In M. S. Gazzaniga (Ed.), *The new cognitive neurosciences* (pp. 223–236). Cambridge, MA: MIT Press.

Kaas, J. H., and Hackett, T. A. (1999). "What" and "where" processing in auditory cortex. *Nature Neuroscience, 2,* 1045–1047.

Kaas, J. H., Nelson, R. J., Sur, M., Lin, C. S., et al. (1979). Multiple representations of the body within the primary somatosensory cortex of primates. *Science, 204,* 521–523.

Kaasinen, V., and Rinne, J. O. (2002). Functional imaging studies of dopamine system and cognition in normal aging and Parkinson's disease. *Neuroscience and Biobehavioral Reviews, 26,* 785–793.

Kadekaro, M., Cohen, S., Terrell, M. L., Lekan, H., et al. (1989). Independent activation of subfornical organ and hypothalamo-neurohypophysial system during administration of angiotensin II. *Peptides, 10,* 423–429.

Kafitz, K. W., Rose, C. R., Thoenen, H., and Konnerth, A. (1999). Neurotrophin-evoked rapid excitation through TrkB receptors. *Nature, 401,* 918–921.

Kagan, J. (1997). Temperament and the reactions to unfamiliarity. *Child Development, 68,* 139–143.

Kakei, S., Hoffman, D. S., and Strick, P. L. (1999). Muscle and movement representations in the primary motor cortex. *Science, 285,* 2136–2139.

Kales, A., and Kales, J. (1970). Evaluation, diagnosis and treatment of clinical conditions related to sleep. *JAMA, 213,* 2229–2235.

Kales, A., and Kales, J. D. (1974). Sleep disorders. Recent findings in the diagnosis and treatment of disturbed sleep. *New England Journal of Medicine, 290,* 487–499.

Kandel, E. R. (1976). *Cellular basis of behavior.* San Francisco: Freeman.

Kandel, E. R., Castellucci, V. F., Goelet, P., and Schacher, S. (1987). 1987 cell-biological interrelationships between short-term and long-term memory. *Research Publications—Association for Research in Nervous and Mental Disease, 65,* 111–132.

Kantak, K. M. (2003). Vaccines against drugs of abuse: A viable treatment option? *Drugs, 63,* 341–352.

Karasawa, J., Touho, H., Ohnishi, H., and Kawaguchi, M. (1997). Rete mirabile in humans—Case report. *Neurologia Medico-Chirurgica, 37,* 188–192.

Karlin, A. (2002). Emerging structure of the nicotinic acetylcholine receptors. *Nature Reviews. Neuroscience, 3,* 102–114.Karni, A., Tanne, D., Rubenstein, B. S., Askenasy, J. J., et al. (1994). Dependence on REM sleep of overnight improvement of a perceptual skill. *Science, 265,* 679–682.

Karp, L. E. (1976). *Genetic engineering, threat or promise?* Chicago: Nelson-Hall.

Katz, L. C., and Shatz, C. J. (1996). Synaptic activity and the construction of cortical circuits. *Science, 274,* 1133–1138.

Katzenberg, D., Young, T., Finn, L., Lin, L., et al. (1998). A CLOCK polymorphism associated with human diurnal preference. *Sleep, 21,* 569–576.

Kaufmann, C. A., Jeste, D. V., Shelton, R. C., Linnoila, M., et al. (1986). Noradrenergic and neuroradiological abnormalities in tardive dyskinesia. *Biological Psychiatry, 21,* 799–812.

Kaushall, P. I., Zetin, M., and Squire, L. R. (1981). A psychosocial study of chronic, circumscribed amnesia. *Journal of Nervous and Mental Disease, 169,* 383–389.

Kavanau, J. L. (1997). Memory, sleep and the evolution of mechanisms of synaptic efficacy maintenance. *Neuroscience, 79,* 7–44.

Kawamoto, K., Ishimoto, S., Minoda, R., Brough, D. E., et al. (2003). Math1 gene transfer generates new cochlear hair cells in mature guinea pigs in vivo. *Journal of Neuroscience, 23,* 4395–4400.

Keane, T. M. (1998). Psychological and behavioral treatments of post-traumatic stress disorder. In P. E. Nathan, and J. M. Gorman (Eds.), *A guide to treatments that work* (pp. 398–407). New York: Oxford University Press.

Keenan, J. P., Nelson, A., O'Connor, M., and Pascual-Leone, A. (2001). Self-recognition and the right hemisphere. *Nature, 409,* 305.

Keesey, R. E. (1980). A set-point analysis of the regulation of body weight. In A. J. Stunkard (Ed.), *Obesity.* Philadelphia: Saunders.

Keesey, R. E., and Boyle, P. C. (1973). Effects of quinine adulteration upon body weight of LH-lesioned and intact male rats. *Journal of Comparative and Physiological Psychology, 84,* 38–46.

Keesey, R. E., and Corbett, S. W. (1984). Metabolic defense of the body weight set-point. *Research Publications—Association for Research in Nervous and Mental Disease, 62,* 87–96.

Keesey, R. E., and Powley, T. L. (1986). The regulation of body weight. *Annual Review of Psychology, 37,* 109–133.

Kelche, C., Roeser, C., Jeltsch, H., Cassel, J. C., et al. (1995). The effects of intrahippocampal grafts, training, and postoperative housing on behavioral recovery after septohippocampal damage in the rat. *Neurobiology of Learning and Memory, 63,* 155–166.

Keller, M. B., McCullough, J. P., Klein, D. N., Arnow, B., et al. (2000). A comparison of nefazodone, the cognitive behavioral-analysis system of psychotherapy, and their combination for the treatment of chronic depression. *New England Journal of Medicine, 342,* 1462–1470.

Kelso, S. R., and Brown, T. H. (1986). Differential conditioning of associative synaptic enhancement in hippocampal brain slices. *Science, 232,* 85–87.

Keltner, D., and Ekman, P. (2000). Facial expression of emotion. In M. Lewis and J. M. Haviland-Jones (Eds.), *Handbook of emotions* (2nd ed., pp. 236–250). New York: Guilford.

Kemp, D. T. (1979). The evoked cochlear mechanical responses and the auditory microstructure—Evidence for a new element in cochlear mechanics. *Scandinavian Audiology. Supplementum, 9,* 35–47.

Kemp, J. A., and McKernan, R. M. (2002). NMDA receptor pathways as drug targets. *Nature Neuroscience, 5*(Suppl.): 1039–1042.

Kemp, M. (2001). The harmonious hand. Marin Mersenne and the science of memorized music. *Nature, 409,* 666.

Kempermann, G., Kuhn, H. G., and Gage, F. H. (1997). More hippocampal neurons in adult mice living in an enriched environment. *Nature, 386,* 493–495.

Kemppainen, N., Laine, M., Laakso, M. P., Kaasinen, V., et al. (2003). Hippocampal dopamine D2 receptors correlate with memory functions in Alzheimer's disease. *European Journal of Neuroscience, 18,* 149–154.

Kendler, K. S., Gardner, C. O., and Prescott, C. A. (1999). Clinical characteristics of major depression that predict risk of depression in relatives. *Archives of General Psychiatry, 56,* 322–327.

Kendler, K. S., Karkowski, L. M., Neale, M. C., and Prescott, C. A. (2000). Illicit psychoactive substance use, heavy use, abuse, and dependence in a US population-based sample of male twins. *Archives of General Psychiatry, 57,* 261–269.

Kenis, G., and Maes, M. (2002). Effects of antidepressants on the production of cytokines. *International Journal of Neuropsychopharmacology, 5,* 401–412.

Kennedy, J. L., Farrer, L. A., Andreasen, N. C., Mayeux, R., et al. (2003). The genetics of adult-onset neuropsychiatric disease: Complexities and conundra? *Science, 302,* 822–826.

Kertesz, A., Harlock, W., and Coates, R. (1979). Computer tomographic localization, lesion size, and prognosis in aphasia and nonverbal impairment. *Brain and Language, 8,* 34–50.

Kesner, R. P. (1980). An attribute analysis of memory: The role of the hippocampus. *Physiological Psychology, 8,* 189–197.

Kesner, R. P. (1991). Neurobiological views of memory. In J. L. Martinez and R. P. Kesner (Eds.), *Learning and memory: A biological view* (2nd ed., pp. 499–547). New York: Academic Press.

Kesner, R. P. (1998). Neurobiological views of memory. In J. L. Martinez, Jr., and R. P. Kesner (Eds.), *Neurobiology of learning and memory* (3rd ed., pp. 361–416). San Diego, CA: Harcourt Brace.

Kesner, R. P., Bolland, B. L., and Dakis, M. (1993). Memory for spatial locations, motor responses, and objects: Triple dissociation among the hippocampus, caudate nucleus, and extrastriate visual cortex. *Experimental Brain Research, 93,* 462–470.

Kesner, R. P., and Novak, J. M. (1982). Serial position curve in rats: Role of the dorsal hippocampus. *Science, 218,* 173–175.

Kesner, R. P., and Williams, J. M. 1995. Memory for magnitude of reinforcement: Dissociation between the amygdala and hippocampus. *Neurobiology of Learning and Memory, 64,* 237–244.

Kety, S., Rosenthal, D., Wender, P. H., Schulsinger, F., et al. (1975). Mental illness in the biological and adoptive families of adopted individuals who have become schizophrenic. A preliminary report based on psychiatric interviews. In R. R. Fieve, D. Rosenthal, and H. Brill (Eds.), *Genetic research in psychiatry.* Baltimore: Johns Hopkins University.

Kety, S. S., Wender, P. H., Jacobsen, B., Ingraham, L. J., et al. (1994). Mental illness in the biological and adoptive relatives of schizophrenic adoptees. Replication of the Copenhagen Study in the rest of Denmark. *Archives of General Psychiatry, 51,* 442–455.

Keynes, R. J., and Cook, G. M. (1992). Repellent cues in axon guidance. *Current Opinion in Neurobiology, 2,* 55–59.

Kiang, N. Y. S. (1965). Discharge patterns of single fibers in the cat's auditory nerve. Cambridge, MA: MIT Press.

Kim, D.-S., Duong, T. Q., and Kim, S.-G. (2000). High-resolution mapping of iso-orientation columns by fMRI. *Nature Neuroscience, 3,* 164–169 .

Kim, J. J., and Fanselow, M. S. (1992). Modality-specific retrograde amnesia of fear. *Science, 256,* 675–677.

Kim, K. H., Relkin, N. R., Lee, K. M., and Hirsch, J. (1997). Distinct cortical areas associated with native and second languages. *Nature, 388,* 171–174.

Kimmel, H. L., Gong, W., Vechia, S. D., Hunter, R. G., et al. (2000). Intra-ventral tegmental area injection of rat cocaine and amphetamine-regulated transcript peptide 55-102 induces locomotor activity and promotes conditioned place preference. *Journal of Pharmacology and Experimental Therapeutics, 294,* 784–792.

Kimura, D. (1973). The asymmetry of the human brain. *Scientific American, 228* (3),, 70-78.

Kingsbury, S. J., and Garver, D. L. (1998). Lithium and psychosis revisited. *Progress in Neuro-psychopharmacology & Biological Psychiatry, 22,* 249–263.

Kinsey, A. C., Pomeroy, W. B., and Martin, C. E. (1948). *Sexual behavior in the human male.* Philadelphia: Saunders.

Kinsey, A. C., Pomeroy, W. B., Martin, C. E., and Gebhard, P. H. (1953). *Sexual behavior in the human female.* Philadelphia: Saunders.

Klar, A. J. (2003). Human handedness and scalp hair-whorl direction develop from a common genetic mechanism. *Genetics, 165,* 269–276.

Kleiber, M. (1947). Body size and metabolic rate. *Physiological Reviews, 15,* 511–541.

Kleim, J. A., Barbay, S., and Nudo, R. J. (1998). Functional reorganization of the rat motor cortex following motor skill learning. *Journal of Neurophysiology, 80,* 3321–3325.

Klein, B. A. (2003). Signatures of sleep in a paper wasp. *Sleep, 26,* A115–A116.

Klein, M., Shapiro, K. M., and Kandel, E. R. (1980). Synaptic plasticity and the modulation of the Ca^{+2} current. *Journal of Experimental Biology, 89,* 117–157.

Kleitman, N. (1969). Basic rest-activity cycle in relation to sleep and wakefulness. In A. Kales (Ed.), *Sleep: Physiology and pathology.* Philadelphia: Lippincott.

Kleitman, N., and Engelmann, T. (1953). Sleep characteristics of infants. *Journal of Applied Physiology, 6,* 269–282.

Klima, E. S., and Bellugi, U. (1979). *The signs of language.* Cambridge, MA: Harvard University Press.

Klinke, R., Kral, A., Heid, S., Tillein, J., et al. (1999). Recruitment of the auditory cortex in congenitally deaf cats by long-term cochlear electrostimulation. *Science, 285,* 1729–1733.

Kluckhohn, C. (1949). *Mirror for man.* New York: Whittlesey House.

Klüver, H., and Bucy, P. C. (1938). An analysis of certain effects of bilateral temporal lobectomy in the rhesus monkey, with special reference to "psychic blindness." *Journal of Psychology, 5,* 33–54.

Knecht, S., Flöel, A., Dräger, B., Breitenstein, C., et al. (2002). Degree of language lateralization determines susceptibility to unilateral brain lesions. *Nature Neuroscience, 5,* 695–699.

Knibestol, M., and Valbo, A. B. (1970). Single unit analysis of mechanoreceptor activity from the human glabrous skin. *Acta Physiologica Scandinavica, 80,* 178–195.

Knudsen, E. I. (1982). Auditory and visual maps of space in the optic tectum of the owl. *Journal of Neuroscience, 2,* 1177–1194.

Knudsen, E. I. (1984). The role of auditory experience in the development and maintenance of sound localization. *Trends in Neurosciences, 7,* 326–330.

Knudsen, E. I. (1998). Capacity for plasticity in the adult owl auditory system expanded by juvenile experience. *Science, 279,* 1531–1533.

Knudsen, E., and Knudsen, P. (1985). Vision guides adjustment of auditory localization in young barn owls. *Science, 230,* 545–548.

Knudsen, E. I., Knudsen, P. F., and Esterly, S. D. (1984). A critical period for the recovery of sound localization accuracy following monaural occlusion in the barn owl. *Journal of Neuroscience, 4,* 1012–1020.

Knudsen, E. I., and Konishi, M. (1978). A neural map of auditory space in the owl. *Science, 200,* 795–797.

Kobatake, E., and Tanaka, K. (1994). Neuronal selectivities to complex object features in the ventral visual pathway of the macaque cerebral cortex. *Journal of Neurophysiology, 71,* 856–867.

Kodama, T., Lai, Y. Y., and Siegel, J. M. (2003). Changes in inhibitory amino acid release linked to pontine-induced atonia: An in vivo microdialysis study. *Journal of Neuroscience, 23,* 1548–1554.

Kogan, J. H., Frankland, P. W., Blendy, J. A., Coblentz, J., et al. (1997). Spaced training induces normal long-term memory in CREB mutant mice. *Current Biology, 7,* 1–11.

Kojima, M., Hosoda, H., Date, Y., Nakazato, M., et al. (1999). Ghrelin is a growth-hormone-releasing acylated peptide from stomach. *Nature, 402,* 656–660.

Kolb, B., and Whishaw, I. Q. (1990). *Fundamentals of human neuropsychology.* San Francisco: Freeman.

Kollack-Walker, S., Don, C., Watson, S. J., and Akil, H. (1999). Differential expression of c-fos mRNA within neurocircuits of male hamsters exposed to acute or chronic defeat. *Journal of Neuroendocrinology, 11,* 547–559.

Kondo, Y., Sachs, B. D., and Sakuma, Y. (1997). Importance of the medial amygdala in rat penile erection evoked by remote stimuli from estrous females. *Behavioural Brain Research, 88,* 153–160.

Kondziolka, D., Wechsler, L., Goldstein, S., Meltzer, C., et al. (2000). Transplantation of cultured human neuronal cells for patients with stroke. *Neurology, 55,* 565–569.

Konishi, M. (1985). Birdsong: From behavior to neuron. *Annual Review of Neuroscience, 8,* 125–170.

Konopka, R. J., and Benzer, S. (1971). Clock mutants of Drosophila melanogaster. Proceedings of the National Academy of Sciences, USA, 68, 2112–2116.

Koob, G. F. (1995). Animal models of drug addiction. In F. E. Bloom and D. J. Kupfer (Eds.), *Psychopharmacology: The fourth generation of progress* (pp. 759–772). New York: Raven.

Kopin, I. J., and Markey, S. P. (1988). MPTP toxicity: Implications for research in Parkinson's disease. *Annual Review of Neuroscience, 11,* 81–96.

Korsakoff, S. S. (1887). Disturbance of psychic functions in alcoholic paralysis and its relation to the disturbance of the psychic sphere in multiple neuritis of non-alcoholic origin. *Vestnik Psichiatrii 4*, fascicle 2.

Kosslyn, S. M., Alpert, N. M., Thompson, W. L., Maljkovic, V., et al. (1993). Visual mental imagery activates topographically organized visual cortex. *Journal of Cognitive Neuroscience, 5*, 263–287.

Kosslyn, S. M., Chabris, C. F., Marsolek, C. J., and Koenig, O. (1992). Categorical versus coordinate spatial relations: Computational analyses and computer simulations. *Journal of Experimental Psychology: Human Perception and Performance, 18*, 562–577.

Kosslyn, S. M., Pascual-Leone, A., Felician, O., Camposano, S., et al. (1999). The role of Area 17 in visual imagery: Convergent evidence from PET and RTMS. *Science, 208*, 167–170.

Kovelman, J. A., and Scheibel, A. B. (1984). A neurohistological correlate of schizophrenia. *Biological Psychiatry, 19*, 1601.

Kraepelin, E. (1919). *Dementia praecox and paraphrenia.* Edinburgh, Scotland: Livingstone.

Krauss, R. M. (1998). Why do we gesture when we speak? *Current Directions in Psychological Science, 7*(2), 54–60.

Kraut, R. E., and Johnston, R. E. (1979). Social and emotional messages of smiling: An ethological approach. *Journal of Personality and Social Psychology, 37*, 1539–1553.

Krebs, J. R., Sherry, D. F., Healy, S. D., Perry, V. H., et al. (1989). Hippocampal specialisation of food-storing birds. *Proceedings of the National Academy of Sciences, USA, 86*, 1388–1392.

Kril, J., Halliday, G., Svoboda, M., and Cartwright, H. (1997). The cerebral cortex is damaged in chronic alcoholics. *Neuroscience, 79*, 983–998.

Kring, A. M. (1999). Emotion in schizophrenia: Old mystery, new understanding. *Current Directions in Psychological Science, 8*(5), 160–163.

Krubitzer, L. A., Manger, P., Pettigrew, J. D., and Calford, M. B. (1995). The organization of neocortex in monotremes: In search of the prototypical plan. *Journal of Comparative Neurology 348*, 1–45.

Kruesi, M. J. (1979). Cruelty to animals and CSF 5HIAA. *Psychiatry Research, 28*, 115–116.

Krug, M., Lössner, B., and Ott, T. (1984). Anisomycin blocks the late phase of long-term potentiation in the dentate gyrus of freely moving rat. *Brain Research Bulletin, 13*, 39–42.

Krystal, A., Krishnan, K. R., Raitiere, M., Poland, R., et al. (1990). Differential diagnosis and pathophysiology of Cushing's syndrome and primary affective disorder. *Journal of Neuropsychiatry and Clinical Neurosciences, 2*, 34–43.

Kubanis, P., and Zornetzer, S. F. (1981). Age-related behavioral and neurobiological changes: A review with emphasis on memory. *Behavioral and Neural Biology, 31*, 115–172.

Kuffler, S. W. (1953). Discharge patterns and functional organization of mammalian retina. *Journal of Neurophysiology, 16*, 37–68.

Kuiper, G. G., Enmark, E., Pelto-Huikko. M., Nilsson, S., and Gustafsson, J. A. (1996). Cloning of a novel receptor expressed in rat prostate and ovary. *Proceedings of the National Academy of Sciences, USA, 93*, 5925–5930.

Kujala, T., Alho, K., and Naatanen, R. (2000). Cross-modal reorganization of human cortical functions. *Trends in Neurosciences, 23*, 115–120.

Kulkarni, A., and Colburn, H. S. (1998). Role of spectral detail in sound-source localization. *Nature, 396*, 747–749.

Kutas, M., and Hillyard, S. A. (1980). Reading senseless sentences: Brain potentials reflect semantic incongruity. *Science, 207*, 203–205.

LaBar, K. S., Gatenby, J. C., Gore, J. C., Ledoux, J. E., et al. (1998). Human amygdala activation during conditioned fear acquisition and extinction: A mixed-trial fMRI study. *Neuron, 20*, 937–945.

Lacey, J. I., and Lacey, B. C. (1970). Some autonomic-central nervous system interrelationships. In P. Black (Ed.), *Physiological correlates of emotion.* New York: Academic Press.

Lachman, H. M., Papolos, D. F., Boyle, A., Sheftel, G., et al. (1993). Alterations in glucorticoid inducible RNAs in the limbic system of learned helpless rats. *Brain Research, 609*, 110–116.

Lack, D. (1968). Ecological adaptations for breeding in birds. London: Methuen.

Lai, C. S. L., Fisher, S. E., Hurst, J. A., Vargha-Khadem, F., et al. (2001). A forkhead-domain gene is mutated in a severe speech and language disorder. *Nature, 413*, 519–523.

Lalumiere, M. L., Blanchard, R., and Zucker, K. J. (2000). Sexual orientation and handedness in men and women: A meta-analysis. *Psychological Bulletin, 126*, 575–592.

Laming, P. R., Kimelberg, H., Robinson, S., Salm, A., et al. (2000). Neuronal-glial interactions and behaviour. *Neuroscience and Biobehavioral Reviews, 24*, 295–340.

Land, M. F., and Fernald, R. D. (1992). The evolution of eyes. *Annual Review of Neuroscience, 15*, 1–29.

Landau, B., and Levy, R. M. (1993). Neuromodulation techniques for medically refractory chronic pain. *Annual Review of Medicine, 44*, 279–287.

Lane, R. D. (2000). Neural correlates of conscious emotional experience. In R. D. Lane (Ed.), *Cognitive neuroscience of emotion* (pp. 345–370). New York: Oxford University Press.

Lane, R. D., Chua, P. M., and Dolan, R. J. (1999). Common effects of emotional valence, arousal, and attention on neural activation during visual processing of picutres. *Neuropsychologia, 37*, 989–997.

Lange, C. G. (1887). Ueber Gemuthsbewegungen. In W. James and C. G. Lange (Eds.), *The emotions* (pp. 33–90). Baltimore: Williams & Wilkins.

Langleben, D. D., Schroeder, L., Maldjian, J. A., Gur, R. C., et al. (2002). Brain activity during simulated deception: An event-related functional magnetic resonance study. *Neuroimage, 15*, 727–732.

Langston, J. W. (1985). MPTP and Parkinson's disease. *Trends in Neurosciences, 8*, 79–83.

Lanska, D. J., and Lanska, M. J. (1994). Kluver-Bucy syndrome in juvenile neuronal ceroid lipofuscinosis. *Journal of Child Neurology, 9*, 67–69.

Larroche, J.-C. (1977). *Developmental pathology of the neonate.* Amsterdam: Excerpta Medica.

Larsson, J., Gulyas, B., and Roland, P. E. (1996). Cortical representation of self-paced finger movement. *Neuroreport, 7*, 463–468.

Lavie, P. (1996). *The enchanted world of sleep* (A. Berris, Trans.). New Haven, CT: Yale University Press.

Lavie, P., and Kripke, D. F. (1981). Ultradian circa 1 1/2 hour rhythms: A multioscillatory system. *Life Sciences, 29*, 2445–2450.

Lavond, D. G., Kim, J. J., and Thompson, R. F. (1993). Mammalian brain substrates of aversive classical conditioning. *Annual Review of Psychology, 44*, 317–342.

Laxova, R. (1994). Fragile X syndrome. *Advances in Pediatrics, 41*, 305–342.

Lazeyras F., Boex, C., Sigrist, A., Seghier, M. L., et al. (2002). Functional MRI of auditory cortex activated by multisite electrical stimulation of the cochlea. *Neuroimage, 17*, 1010–1017.

Leber, S. M., Breedlove, S. M., and Sanes, J. R. (1990). Lineage, arrangement, and death of clonally related motoneurons in chick spinal cord. *Journal of Neuroscience, 10*, 2451–2462.

Lebrun, C. J., Blume, A., Herdegen, T., Seifert, K., et al. (1995). Angiotensin II induces a complex activation of transcription factors in the rat brain: Expression of Fos, Jun and Krox proteins. *Neuroscience, 65*, 93–99.

Ledent, C., Valverde, O., Cossu, G., Petitet, F., et al. (1999). Unresponsiveness to cannabinoids and reduced addictive effects of opiates in CB_1 receptor knockout mice. *Science, 283*, 401–404.

LeDoux, J. E. (1994). Emotion, memory and the brain. *Scientific American, 270*(6), 50–57.

LeDoux, J. E. (1995). Emotion: Clues from the brain. *Annual Review of Psychology, 46*, 209–235.

Lee, C.-K., Klopp, R. G., Weindruch, R., and Prolla, T. A. (1999). Gene expression profile of aging and its retardation by caloric restriction. *Science, 285*, 1390–1393.

Lee, C.-K., Weindruch, R., and Prolla, T. A. (2000). Gene-expression profile of the ageing brain in mice. *Nature Genetics, 25*, 294–297.

Lee, H.-K., Barbarosie, M., Kameyama, K., Bear, M. F., et al. (2000). Regulation of distinct AMPA receptor phosphorylation sites during bidirectional synaptic plasticity. *Nature, 405*, 955–959.

Lee, T. M., and Chan, C. C. (1999). Dose-response relationship of phototherapy for seasonal affective disorder: A meta-analysis. *Acta Psychiatrica Scandinavia, 99*, 315–323.

Lefebvre, L., Whittle, P., Lascaris, E., and Finkelstein, A. (1997). Feeding innovations and forebrain size in birds. *Animal Behavior, 53*, 549–560.

Leggett, J. D., Aspley, S., Beckett, S. R., D'Antona, A. M., Kendall, D. A., and Kendall, D. A. (2004). Oleamide is a selective endogenous agonist of rat and human CB1 cannabinoid receptors. *British Journal of Pharmacology, 141*, 253–262.

Le Grand, R., Mondloch, C. J., Maurer, D., and Brent, H. P. (2001). Early visual experience and face processing. *Nature, 410, 890.*

Leibowitz, S. F. (1991). Brain neuropeptide Y: An integrator of endocrine, metabolic and behavioral processes. *Brain Research Bulletin, 27*, 333–337.

Leinders-Zufall, T., Lane, A. P., Puche, A. C., Ma, W., et al. (2000). Ultrasensitive pheromone detection by mammalian vomeronasal neurons. *Nature, 405*, 792–796.

Lennie, P., Krauskopf, J., and Sclar, G. (1990). Chromatic mechanisms in striate cortex of macaque. *Journal of Neuroscience, 10*, 649–669.

Lepage, M., Habib, R., and Tulving, E. (1998). Hippocampal PET activations of memory encoding and retrieval: The HIPER model. *Hippocampus, 8*, 313–322.

Leroi, I., Sheppard, J. M., and Lyketsos, C. G. (2002). Cognitive function after 11.5 years of alcohol use: Relation to alcohol use. *American Journal of Epidemiology, 156*, 747–752.

LeRoith, D., Shemer, J., and Roberts, C. T., Jr. (1992). Evolutionary origins of intercellular communication systems: Implications for mammalian biology. *Hormone Research, 38*, 1–6.

Lessard, N., Pare, M., Lepore, F., and Lassonde, M. (1998). Early-blind human subjects localize sound sources better than sighted subjects. *Nature, 395*, 278–280.

LeVay, S. (1991). A difference in hypothalamic structure between heterosexual and homosexual men. *Science, 253*, 1034–1037.

LeVay, S. (1996). Queer science: The use and abuse of research into homosexuality. Cambridge, MA: MIT Press.

Levenson, R. W., Ekman, P., and Friesen, W. V. (1990). Voluntary facial action generates emotion-specific autonomic nervous system activity. *Psychophysiology, 27,* 363–384.

Leventhal, A. G. (1979). Evidence that the different classes of relay cells of the cat's lateral geniculate nucleus terminate in different layers of the striate cortex. *Experimental Brain Research, 37,* 349–372.

Leventhal, A. G., Thompson, K. G., Liu, D., Zhou, Y., et al. (1995). Concomitant sensitivity to orientation, direction, and color of cells in layers 2, 3, and 4 of monkey striate cortex. *Journal of Neuroscience, 15,* 1808–1818.

Levermann, N., Galatius, A., Ehlme, G., Rysgaard, S., et al. (2003). Feeding behaviour of free-ranging walruses with notes on apparent dextrality of flipper use. *BMC Ecology, 3,* 9.

Levi-Montalcini, R. (1963). In J. Allen (Ed.), *The nature of biological diversity.* New York: McGraw-Hill.

Levi-Montalcini, R. (1982). Developmental neurobiology and the natural history of nerve growth factor. *Annual Review of Neuroscience, 5,* 341–362.

Levine, J. D., Gordon, N. C., and Fields, H. L. (1978). The mechanism of placebo analgesia. *Lancet, 2,* 654–657.

Levine, S., Haltmeyer, G. C., and Karas, G. G. (1967). Physiological and behavioral effects of infantile stimulation. *Physiology & Behavior, 2,* 55–59.

Levine, S., and Ursin, H. (1980). *Coping and health.* New York: Plenum.

Levinson, D. F., Holmans, P. A., Laurent, C., Riley, B., et al. (2002). No major schizophrenia locus detected on chromosome 1q in a large multi-center sample. *Science, 296,* 739–741.

Levinthal, F., Macagno, E., and Levinthal, C. (1976). Anatomy and development of identified cells in isogenic organisms. *Cold Spring Harbor Symposium on Quantitative Biology, 40,* 321–331.

Levy, D. L., Holzman, P. S., Matthysse, S., and Mendell, N. R. (1993). Eye tracking dysfunction and schizophrenia: A critical perspective. *Schizophrenia Bulletin, 19,* 461–536.

Lewin, G. R., and Barde, Y. A. (1996). Physiology of the neurotrophins. *Annual Review of Neuroscience, 19,* 289–317.

Lewis, D. O. (1990). Neuropsychiatric and experiential correlates of violent juvenile delinquency. *Neuropsychology Review, 1,* 125–136.

Lewis, D. O., Shankok, S. S., and Pincus, J. (1979). Juvenile male sexual assaulters. *American Journal of Psychiatry, 136,* 1194–1195.

Lewis, M. (2000). The emergence of human emotions. In M. Lewis and J. M. Haviland-Jones (Eds.), *Handbook of emotions* (2nd ed., pp. 265–280). New York: Guilford.

Lewis, R. (1998). Flies invade human genetics. *Scientist, 12,* 1, 4–5.

Lewy, A. J., Ahmed, S., Jackson, J. M., and Sack, R. L. (1992). Melatonin shifts human circadian rhythms according to a phase-response curve. *Chronobiology International, 9,* 380–392.

Lewy, A. J., Bauer, V. K., Cutler, N. L., Sack, R. L., et al. (1998). Morning vs evening light treatment of patients with winter depression. *Archives of General Psychiatry, 55,* 890–896.

Ley, R. G., and Bryden, M. P. (1982). A dissociation of right and left hemispheric effects for recognizing emotional tone and verbal content. *Brain and Cognition, 1,* 3–9.

Li, S., and Tator, C. H. (2000). Action of locally administered NMDA and AMPA/kainate receptor antagonists in spinal cord injury. *Neurological Research, 22,* 171–180.

Li, Y., Field, P. M., and Raisman, G. (1997). Repair of adult rat corticospinal tract by transplants of olfactory ensheathing cells. *Science, 277,* 2000–2002.

Licht, P., Frank, L. G., Pavgi, S., Yalcinkaya, T. M., et al. (1992). Hormonal correlates of "masculinization" in female spotted hyenas (*Crocuta crocuta*). 2. Maternal and fetal steroids. *Journal of Reproduction and Fertility, 95,* 463–474.

Lichtman, J. W., and Purves, D. (1980). The elimination of redundant preganglionic innervation to hamster sympathetic ganglion cells in early post-natal life. *Journal of Physiology (London), 301,* 213–228.

Liebenthal, E., Ellignson, M. L., Spanaki, M. V., Prieto, and T. E. (2003). Simultaneous ERP and fMRI of the auditory cortex in a passive oddball paradigm. *Neuroimage, 19,* 1395–1404.

Liebowitz, M. R., Gorman, J. M., Fryer, A., Dillon, D., et al. (1986). Possible mechanisms for lactate's induction of panic. *American Journal of Psychiatry, 143,* 495–502.

Liégeois, F., Baldeweg, T., Connelly, A., Gadian, D. G., et al. (2003). Language fMRI abnormalities associated with FOXP2 gene mutation. *Nature Neuroscience, 6,* 1230–1237.

Liepert, J., Bauder, H., Wolfgang, H. R., Miltner, W. H., et al. (2000). Treatment-induced cortical reorganization after stroke in humans. *Stroke, 31,* 1210–1216.

Lim, M. M., Wang, Z. X., Olazabal. D. E., Ren, X. H., et al. (2004). Enhanced partner preference in a promiscuous species by manipulating the expression of a single gene. *Nature, 429,* 754–757.

Lin, L., Faraco, J., Li, R., Kadotani, H., et al. (1999). The sleep disorder canine narcolepsy is caused by a mutation in the hypocretin (orexin) receptor 2 gene. *Cell, 98,* 365–376.

Lin, X. Y., and Glanzman, D. L. (1994). Long-term potentiation of *Aplysia* sensorimotor synapses in cell culture: Regulation by postsynaptic voltage. *Proceedings of the Royal Society of London. Series B: Biological Sciences, 255,* 113–118.

Lindemann, B. (1995). Sweet and salty: Transduction in taste. *News in Physiological Sciences, 10,* 166–170.

Linden, D. J. (1994). Long-term synaptic depression in the mammalian brain. *Neuron, 12,* 457–472.

Lindskog, M., Svenningsson, P., Pozzi, L., Kim, Y., et al. (2002). Involvement of DARPP-32 phosphorylation in the stimulant action of caffeine. *Nature, 418,* 774–778.

Lindvall, O., Sawle, G., Widner, H., Rothwell, J. C., et al. (1994). Evidence for long-term survival and function of dopaminergic grafts in progressive Parkinson's disease. *Annals of Neurology, 35,* 172–180.

Liou, Y.-C., Tocilj, A., Davies, P., and Jia, Z. (2000). Mimicry of ice structure by surface hydroxyls and water of a beta-helix antifreeze protein. *Nature, 406,* 322–324.

Lisk, R. D. (1962). Diencephalic placement of estradiol and sexual receptivity in the female rat. *American Journal of Physiology, 203,* 493–496.

Lisman, J. (1989). A mechanism for the Hebb and the anti-Hebb processes underlying learning and memory. *Proceedings of the National Academy of Sciences, USA, 86,* 9574–9578.

Lisman, J., Schulman, H., and Cline, H. (2002). The molecular basis of CAMKII function in synaptic and behavioural memory. *Nature Reviews. Neuroscience, 3,* 175–190.

Littlewood, E. A., and Muller, U. (2000). Stereocilia defects in the sensory hair cells of the inner ear in mice deficient in integrin alpha8beta1. *Nature Genetics, 24,* 424–428.

Liu, D., Diorio, J., Tannenbaum, B., Caldji, C., et al. (1997). Maternal care, hippocampal glucocorticoid receptors, and hypothalamic-pituitary-adrenal responses to stress. *Science, 277,* 1659–1662.

Liu, S., Qu, Y., Stewart, T. J., Howard, M. J., et al. (2000). Embryonic stem cells differentiate into oligodendrocytes and myelinate in culture and after spinal cord transplantation. *Proceedings of the National Academy of Sciences, USA, 97,* 6126–6131.

Liu, Y., Gao, J. H., Liotti, M., Pu, Y., et al. (1999). Temporal dissociation of parallel processing in the human subcortical outputs. *Nature, 400,* 364–367.

Liu, Y., Gao, J.-H., Liu, H.-L., and Fox, P. T. (2000). The temporal response of the brain after eating revealed by functional MRI. *Nature, 405,* 1058–1062.

Livingstone, M. S., and Hubel, D. (1984). Anatomy and physiology of a color system in the primate visual cortex. *Journal of Neuroscience, 4,* 309–356.

Lloyd, J. A. (1971). Weights of testes, thymi, and accessory reproductive glands in relation to rank in paired and grouped house mice (*Mus musculus*). *Proceedings of the Society for Experimental Biology and Medicine, 137,* 19–22.

Lo, E. H., Dalkara, T., and Moskowitz, M. A. (2003). Mechanisms, challenges and opportunities in stroke. *Nature Reviews. Neuroscience, 4,* 399–415.

Lockhart, M., and Moore, J. W. (1975). Classical differential and operant conditioning in rabbits (*Orycytolagus cuniculus*) with septal lesions. *Journal of Comparative and Physiological Psychology, 88,* 147–154.

Loconto, J., Papes, F., Chang, E., Stowers, L., et al. (2003). Functional expression of murine V2R pheromone receptors involves selective association with the M10 and M1 families of MHC class Ib molecules, *Cell, 112,* 607–618.

Loeb, G. E. (1990). Cochlear prosthetics. *Annual Review of Neuroscience, 13,* 357–371.

Loeber, R. T., Cintron, C. M., and Yurgelun-Todd, D. A. (2001). Morphometry of individual cerebellar lobules in schizophrenia. *American Journal of Psychiatry, 158,* 952–954.

Loehlin, J. C., and McFadden, D. (2003). Otoacoustic emissions, auditory evoked potentials, and traits related to sex and sexual orientation. *Archives of Sexual Behavior, 32,* 115–127.

Loewenstein, W. R. (1971). Mechano-electric transduction in the Pacinian corpuscle. Initiation of sensory impulses in mechanoreception. In *Handbook of sensory physiology: Vol. 1. Principles of receptor physiology* (pp. 269–290). Berlin: Springer.

Loftus, E. F. (2003). Make-believe memories. *American Psychologist, 58,* 867–873.

Loftus, E. F., and Pickrell, J. E. (1995). The formation of false memories. *Psychiatric Annals, 25,* 720–725.

Logan, C. G., and Grafton, S. T. (1995). Functional anatomy of human eyeblink conditioning determined with regional cerebral glucose metabolism and positron emission tomography. *Proceedings of the National Academy of Sciences, USA, 92,* 7500–7504.

Logothetis, N. K. (2003). The underpinnings of the BOLD functional magnetic resonance imaging signal. *Journal of Neuroscience, 23,* 3963–3971.

Löwel, S., and Singer, W. (1992). Selection of intrinsic horizontal connections in the visual cortex by correlated neuronal activity. *Science, 255,* 209–212.

Lucas, R. J., Hattar, S., Takao, M., Berson, D. M., et al. (2003). Diminished pupillary light reflex at high irradiances in melanopsin-knockout mice. *Science, 299,* 245–247.

Lucking, C. B., Durr, A., Bonifati, V., Vaughan, J., et al. (2000). Association between early-onset Parkinson's disease and mutations in the parkin gene. French Parkinson's Disease Study Group. *New England Journal of Medicine, 342,* 1560–1567.

Luria, A. R. (1987). *The mind of a mnemonist.* Cambridge, MA: Harvard University Press.

Lush, I. E. (1989). The genetics of tasting in mice. VI. Saccharin, acesulfame, dulcin and sucrose. *Genetical Research, 53,* 95–99.

Lynch, E. D., Lee, M. K., Morrow, J. E., Welcsh, P. L., et al. (1997). Nonsyndromic deafness DFNA1 associated with mutation of a human homolog of the *Drosophila* gene *diaphanous. Science, 278,* 1315–1318.

Lynch, G., Larson, J., Staubli, U., and Granger, R. (1991). Variants of synaptic potentiation and different types of memory operations in hippocampus and related structures. In L. R. Squire, N. M. Weinberger, G. Lynch, and J. L. McGaugh (Eds.), *Memory: Organization and locus of change* (pp. 330–363). New York: Oxford University Press.

Macagno, E., Lopresti, U., and Levinthal, C. (1973). Structural development of neuronal connections in isogenic organisms: Variations and similarities in the optic system of *Daphnia magna. Proceedings of the National Academy of Sciences, USA, 70,* 57–61.

Mace, G. M., Gittleman, J. L., and Purvis, A. (2003). Preserving the tree of life. *Science, 300,* 1707–1709.

Mace, G. M., Harvey, P. H., and Clutton-Brock, T. H. (1981). Brain size and ecology in small mammals. *Journal of Zoology, 193,* 333–354.

Machón, R. A., Mednick, S. A., and Huttunen, M. O. (1997). Adult major affective disorder after prenatal exposure to an influenza epidemic. *Archives of General Psychiatry, 54,* 322–328.

MacKay, D. G., Stewart, R., and Burke, D. M. (1998). H.M. revisited: Relations between language comprehension, memory, and the hippocampal system. *Journal of Cognitive Neuroscience, 10,* 377–394.

Macklis, J. D. (2001). New memories from new neurons. *Nature, 410,* 314–316.

MacLean, P. D. (1949). Psychosomatic disease and the "visceral brain": Recent developments bearing on the Papez theory of emotion. *Psychosomatic Medicine, 11,* 338–353.

Macmillan, M. (2000). *An odd kind of fame: Stories of Phineas Gage.* Cambridge, MA: MIT Press.

Madden, J. (2001). Sex, bowers and brains. *Proceedings of the Royal Society of London. Series B: Biological Sciences, 268,* 833–838.

Maddock, R. J. (1999). The retrosplenial cortex and emotion: New insights from functional imaging in the human brain. *Trends in Neurosciences, 22,* 310–316.

Maddox, B. (2002). *Rosalind Franklin: The dark lady of DNA.* London: Harper-Collins.

Maddox, B. (2003). The double helix and the "wronged heroine." *Nature, 421,* 407–408.

Madsen, K. M., Lauritsen, M. B., Pedersen, C. B., Thorsen, P., et al. (2003). Thimerosal and the occurrence of autism: Negative ecological evidence from Danish population-based data. *Pediatrics, 112,* 604–606.

Maes, M., Bosmans, E., Suy, E., Vandervorst, C., et al. (1991). Depression-related disturbances in mitogen-induced lymphocyte responses and interleukin-1 beta and soluble interleukin-2 receptor production. *Acta Psychiatrica Scandinavica, 84,* 379–386.

Maffei, L., and Fiorentini, A. (1973). The visual cortex as a spatial frequency analyser. *Vision Research, 13,* 1255–1267.

Magavi, S. S., Leavitt, B. R., and Macklis, J. D. (2000). Induction of neurogenesis in the neocortex of adult mice. *Nature, 405,* 951–955.

Maggioncalda, A. N., and Sapolsky, R. M. (2002). Disturbing behaviors of the orangutan. *Scientific American, 286*(6), 60–65.

Magnusson, A., and Stefansson, J. G. (1993). Prevalence of seasonal affective disorder in Iceland. *Archives of General Psychiatry, 50,* 941–946.

Maguire, E. A., Frackowiak, R. S. J., and Frith, C. D. (1997). Recalling routes around London: Activation of the right hippocampus in taxi drivers. *Journal of Neuroscience, 17,* 7103–7110.

Maguire, E. A., Gadian, D. G., Johnsrude, I. S., Good, C. D., et al. (2000). Navigation-related structural change in the hippocampi of taxi drivers. *Proceedings of the National Academy of Sciences, USA, 97,* 4398–4403.

Mair, W. G. P., Warrington, E. K., and Wieskrantz, L. (1979). Memory disorder in Korsakoff's psychosis. *Brain, 102,* 749–783.

Maki, P. M., and Resnick, S. M. (2000). Longitudinal effects of estrogen replacement therapy on pet cerebral blood flow and cognition. *Neurobiology of Aging, 21,* 373–383.

Malaspina, D., Corcoran, C., Fahim, C., Berman, A., et al. (2002). Paternal age and sporadic schizophrenia: Evidence for de novo mutations. *American Journal of Medical Genetics, 114,* 299–303.

Malberg, J. E., Eisch, A. J., Nestler, E. J., and Duman, R. S. (2000). Chronic antidepressant treatment increases neurogenesis in adult rat hippocampus. *Journal of Neuroscience, 20,* 9104–9110.

Maldonado, R., and Rodriguez de Fonseca, F. (2002). Cannabinoid addiction: Behavioral models and neural correlates. *Journal of Neuroscience, 22,* 3326–3331.

Maletic-Savatic, M., Malinow, R., and Svoboda, K. (1999). Rapid dendritic morphogenesis in CA1 hippocampal dendrites induced by synaptic activity. *Science, 283,* 1923–1927.

Manetto, V., Medori, R., Cortelli, P., Montagna, P., et al. (1992). Fatal familial insomnia: Clinical and pathologic study of five new cases. *Neurology, 42,* 312–319.

Manfredi, M., Bini, G., Cruccu, G., Accornero, N., et al. (1981). Congenital absence of pain. *Archives of Neurology, 38,* 507–511.

Manger, P. R., Collins, R., and Pettigrew, J. D. (1998). The development of the electroreceptors of the platypus (*Ornithorhynchus anatinus*). *Philosophical Transactions of the Royal Society of London. Series B: Biological Sciences, 353,* 1171–1186.

Mangiarini, L., Sathasivam, K., Seller, M., Cozens, B., et al. (1996). Exon 1 of the HD gene with an expanded CAG repeat is sufficient to cause a progressive neurological phenotype in transgenic mice. *Cell, 87,* 493–506.

Mani, S. K., Fienberg, A. A., O'Callaghan, J. P., Snyder, G. L., et al. (2000). Requirement for DARPP-32 in progesterone-facilitated sexual receptivity in female rats and mice. *Science, 287,* 1053–1056.

Manova, M. G., and Kostadinova, I. I. (2000). Some aspects of the immunotherapy of multiple sclerosis. *Folia Medica, 42*(1), 5–9.

Mantyh, P. W., Rogers, S. D., Honore, P., Allen, B. J., et al. (1997). Inhibition of hyperalgesia by ablation of lamina I spinal neurons expressing the substance P receptor. *Science, 278,* 275–279.

Maquet, P., Laureys, S., Peigneux, P., Fuchs, S., et al. (2000). Experience-dependent changes in cerebral activation during human REM sleep. *Nature Neuroscience, 3,* 831–836.

Marcus, G. F., Vijayan, S., Bandi Rao, S., and Vishton, P. M. (1999). Rule learning by seven-month-old infants. *Science, 283,* 77–80.

Margraf, J., and Roth, W. T. (1986). Sodium lactate infusions and panic attacks: A review and critique. *Psychosomatic Medicine, 48,* 23–50.

Mariani, J., and Changeaux, J.-P. (1981). Ontogenesis of olivocerebellar relationships. I. Studies by intracellular recordings of the multiple innervation of Purkinje cells by climbing fibers in the developing rat cerebellum. *Journal of Neuroscience, 1,* 696–702.

Mark, V. H., and Ervin, F. R. (1970). *Violence and the brain.* New York: Harper & Row.

Marler, P. (1970). Birdsong and speech development: Could there be parallels? *American Scientist, 58,* 669–673.

Marler, P. (1991). Song-learning behavior: The interface with neuroethology. *Trends in Neurosciences, 14,* 199–206.

Marler, P., and Peters, S. (1982). Developmental overproduction and selective attrition: New processes in the epigenesis of birdsong. *Developmental Psychobiology, 15,* 369–378.

Marler, P., and Sherman, V. (1983). Song structure without auditory feedback: Emendations of the auditory template hypothesis. *Journal of Neuroscience, 3,* 517–531.

Marler, P., and Sherman, V. (1985). Innate differences in singing behaviour of sparrows reared in isolation from adult conspecific song. *Animal Behavior, 33,* 57–71.

Marsicano, G., Goodenough, S., Monory, K., Hermann, H., et al. (2003). CB1 cannabinoid receptors and on-demand defense against excitotoxicity. *Science, 302,* 84–88.

Martin, A., Wiggs, C. L., Ungerleider, L. G., and Haxby, J. V. (1996). Neural correlates of category-specific knowledge. *Nature, 379,* 649–652.

Martin, W. R., and Hayden, M. R. (1987). Cerebral glucose and dopa metabolism in movement disorders. *Canadian Journal of Neurological Sciences, 14,* 448–451.

Martina, M., Vida, I., and Jonas, P. (2000). Distal initiation and active propagation of action potentials in interneuron dendrites. *Science, 287,* 295–300.

Martuza, R. L., Chiocca, E. A., Jenike, M. A., Giriunas, I. E., et al. (1990). Stereotactic radiofrequency thermal cingulotomy for obsessive compulsive disorder. *Journal of Neuropsychiatry and Clinical Neurosciences, 2,* 331–336.

Marucha, P. T., Kiecolt-Glaser, J. K., and Favagehi, M. (1998). Mucosal wound healing is impaired by examination stress. *Psychosomatic Medicine, 60,* 362–365.

Marzani, D., and Wallman, J. (1997). Growth of the two layers of the chick sclera is modulated reciprocally by visual conditions. *Investigative Ophthalmology and Visual Science, 38,* 1726–1739.

Masliah, E., Salmon, D. P., Butters, N., DeTeresa, R., et al. (1991). Physical basis of cognitive alterations in Alzheimer's disease: Synapse loss is the major correlate of cognitive impairment. *Annals of Neurology, 30,* 572–580.

Masters, W. H., and Johnson, V. E. (1966). *Human sexual response.* Boston: Little, Brown.

Masters, W. H., and Johnson, V. E. (1970). *Human sexual inadequacy.* Boston: Little, Brown.

Masters, W. H., Johnson, V. E., and Kolodny, R. C. (1994). *Heterosexuality.* New York: HarperCollins.

Masterton, R. B. (1993). Central auditory system. ORL; Journal of Oto-Rhino-Laryngology and Its Related Specialties, 55, 159–163.

Masterton, R. B. (1997). Neurobehavioral studies of the central auditory system. *Annals of Otology Rhinology Laryngology, Supplement, 168,* 31–34.

Mastrianni, J. A., Nixon, R., Layzer, R., Telling, G. C., et al. (1999). Prion protein conformation in a patient with sporadic fatal insomnia. *New England Journal of Medicine, 340,* 1630–1638.

Mateo, J. M., and Johnston, R. E. (2000). Kin recognition and the "armpit effect": Evidence of self-referent phenotype matching. *Proceedings of the Royal Society of London. Series B: Biological Sciences, 267,* 695–700.

Matser, E. J., Kessels, A. G., Lezak, M. D., Jordan, B. D., et al. (1999). Neuropsychological impairment in amateur soccer players. *JAMA, 282,* 971–973.

Matsumoto, K., Suzuki, W., and Tanaka, K. (2003). Neuronal correlates of goal-based motor selection in the prefrontal cortex. *Science, 301,* 229–232.

Matthews, G. (1996). Synaptic exocytosis and endocytosis: Capacitance measurements. *Current Opinion in Neurobiology, 6,* 358–364.

Matthies, H. (1989). Neurobiological aspects of learning and memory. *Annual Review of Psychology, 40,* 381–404.

Mattson, S. N., Riley, E. P., Gramling, L., Delis, D. C., et al. (1998). Neuropsychological comparison of alcohol-exposed children with or without physical features of fetal alcohol syndrome. *Neuropsychology, 12,* 146–153.

Mauch, D. H., Nägler, K., Schumacher, S., Göritz, C., et al. (2001). CNS synaptogenesis promoted by glia-derived cholesterol. *Science, 294,* 1354–1357.

Mayfield, R. D., Lewohl, J. M., Dodd, P. R., Herlihy, A., et al. (2002). Patterns of gene expression are altered in the frontal and motor cortices of human alcoholics. *Journal of Neurochemistry, 81,* 802–813.

McAllister, A. K., Katz, L. C., and Lo, D. C. (1997). Opposing roles for endogenous BDNF and NT-3 in regulating cortical dendritic growth. *Neuron, 18,* 767–778.

McAlpine, D., Jiang, D., and Palmer, A. R. (2001). A neural code for low-frequency sound localization in mammals. *Nature Neuroscience, 4,* 396–401.

McBurney, D. H., Smith, D. V., and Shick, T. R. (1972). Gustatory cross adaptation: Sourness and bitterness. *Perception & Psychophysics, 11,* 2228–2232.

McCall, W. V., and Edinger, J. D. (1992). Subjective total insomnia: An example of sleep state misperception. *Sleep, 15,* 71–73.

McCann, U. D., Seiden, L. S., Rubin, L. J., and Ricaurte, G. A. (1997). Brain serotonin neurotoxicity and primary pulmonary hypertension from fenfluramine and dexfenfluramine. A systematic review of the evidence. *JAMA, 278,* 666–672.

McCarthy, R. A., and Warrington, E. K. (1990). *Cognitive neuropsychology: A clinical introduction.* San Diego, CA: Academic Press.

McClintock, M. K. (1971). Menstrual synchrony and suppression. *Nature, 229,* 244–245.

McComb, K., Moss, C., Sayialel, S., and Baker, L. (2000). Unusually extensive networks of vocal recognition in African elephants. *Animal Behavior, 59,* 1103–1109.

McDonald, J. J., Teder-Sälejärvi, W. A., and Hillyard, S. A. (2000). Involuntary orienting to sound improves visual perception. *Nature, 407,* 906–908.

McFadden, D. (1993a). A masculinizing effect on the auditory systems of human females having male co-twins. *Proceedings of the National Academy of Sciences, USA, 90,* 11900–11904.

McFadden, D. (1993b). A speculation about the parallel ear asymmetries and sex differences in hearing sensitivity and otoacoustic emissions. *Hearing Research, 68,* 143–151.

McFadden, D., and Champlin, C. A. (1990). Reductions in overshoot during aspirin use. *Journal of the Acoustical Society of America, 87,* 2634–2642.

McFadden, D., and Pasanen, E. (1998). Comparison of the auditory systems of heterosexuals and homosexuals: Click-evoked otoacoustic emissions. *Proceedings of the National Academy of Sciences, USA, 95,* 2709–2713.

McGaugh, J. L. (1966). Time-dependent processes in memory storage. *Science, 153,* 1351–1358.

McGaugh, J. L. (1968). A multi-trace view of memory storage processes. In D. Bovet (Ed.), *Attuali orientamenti della ricerca sull' apprendimento e la memoria* (pp. 13-24). Rome: Academia Nazionale dei Lincei.

McGaugh, J. L. (1992). Neuromodulatory systems and the regulation of memory storage. In L. R. Squire and N. Butters (Eds.), *Neuropsychology of memory* (2nd ed., pp. 386–401). New York: Guilford.

McGaugh, J. L. (2003). *Memory and emotions: The making of lasting memories.* New York: Columbia University Press.

McGaugh, J. L., Introini-Collison, I. B., Cahill, L. F., Castellano, C., et al. (1993). Neuromodulatory systems and memory storage: Role of the amygdala. *Behavioural Brain Research, 58,* 81–90.

McGaugh, J. L., Weinberger, N. M., and Lynch, G. (Eds.). (1995). Brain and memory: Modulation and mediation of neuroplasticity. New York: Oxford University Press.

McGeer, P., McGeer, E., Suzuki, J., Dolman, C., et al. (1984). Aging, Alzheimer's disease, and the cholinergic system of the basal forebrain. *Neurology, 34,* 741–745.

McGue, M. (1999). The behavioral genetics of alcoholism. *Current Trends in Psychological Science, 8*(4), 109–115.

McKee, R. D., and Squire, L. R. (1993). On the development of declarative memory. *Journal of Experimental Psychology: Learning, Memory, and Cognition, 19,* 397–404.

McKenna, K. (1999). The brain is the master organ in sexual function: Central nervous system control of male and female sexual function. *International Journal of Impotence Research, 11*(Suppl. 1), S48–S55.

McKernan, M. G., and Shinnick-Gallagher, P. (1997). Fear conditioning induces a lasting potentiation of synaptic currents in vitro. *Nature, 390,* 607–611.

McKim, W. A. (1991). *Drugs and behavior: An introduction to behavioral pharmacology* (2nd ed.). Englewood Cliffs, NJ: Prentice Hall.

McKinney, T. D., and Desjardins, C. (1973). Postnatal development of the testis, fighting behavior, and fertility in house mice. *Biology of Reproduction, 9,* 279–294.

McLaughlin, S. K., McKinnon, P. J., Spickofsky, N., Danho, W., et al. (1994). Molecular cloning of G proteins and phosphodiesterases from rat taste cells. *Physiology & Behavior, 56,* 1157–1164.

McMahon, H. T., Foran, P., Dolly, J. O., Verhage, M., et al. (1992). Tetanus toxin and botulinum toxins type A and B inhibit glutamate, gamma-aminobutyric acid, aspartate, and met-enkephalin release from synaptosomes. Clues to the locus of action. *Journal of Biological Chemistry, 267,* 21338–21343.

McNally, R. J. (2003). Recovering memories of trauma: A view from the laboratory. *Current Directions in Psychological Science, 12,* 32–35.

McNamara, J. O. (1984). Role of neurotransmitters in seizure mechanisms in the kindling model of epilepsy. *Federation Proceedings, 43,* 2516–2520.

McNamara, J. O. (1999). Emerging insights into the genesis of epilepsy. *Nature, 399*(6738 Suppl.), A15–A22.

Meckler, R. J., Mack, J. L., and Bennett, R. (1979). Sign language aphasia in a non-deaf mute. *Neurology, 29,* 1037–1040.

Meddis, R. (1975). On the function of sleep. *Animal Behavior, 23,* 676–691.

Meddis, R. (1977). *The sleep instinct.* London: Routledge & Kegan Paul.

Mednick, S. A., Huttunen, M. O., and Machon, R. A. (1994). Prenatal influenza infections and adult schizophrenia. *Schizophrenia Bulletin, 20,* 263–267.

Medori, R., Montagna, P., Tritschler, H. J., LeBlanc, A., et al. (1992). Fatal familial insomnia: A second kindred with mutation of prion protein gene at codon 178. *Neurology, 42,* 669–670.

Mega, M. S., and Cummings, J. L. (1994). Frontal-subcortical circuits and neuropsychiatric disorders. *Journal of Neuropsychiatry and Clinical Neurosciences, 6,* 358–370.

Meisel, R. L., and Luttrell, V. R. (1990). Estradiol increases the dendritic length of ventromedial hypothalamic neurons in female Syrian hamsters. *Brain Research Bulletin, 25,* 165–168.

Meisel, R. L., and Sachs, B. D. (1994). The physiology of male sexual behavior. In E. Knobil and J. D. Neill (Eds.), *The physiology of reproduction* (2nd ed., Vol. 1, pp. 3–105). New York: Raven.

Mello, C. V., and Clayton, D. F. (1994). Song-induced ZENK gene expression in auditory pathways of songbird brain and its relation to the song control system. *Journal of Neuroscience, 14,* 6652–6666.

Melzack, R. (1984). Neuropsychological basis of pain measurement. *Advances in Pain Research,* 323–341.

Melzack, R. (1990). The tragedy of needless pain. *Scientific American, 262*(2), 27–33.

Melzack, R., and Wall, P. D. (1965). Pain mechanisms: A new history. *Science, 150,* 971–979.

Mendel, G. (1967). *Experiments in plant hybridisation* [Royal Horticultural Society of London, Trans.]. Cambridge, MA: Harvard University Press.

Mendelson, W. B. (1997). Efficacy of melatonin as a hypnotic agent. *Journal of Biological Rhythms, 12,* 651–656.

Mersch, P. P., Middendorp, H. M., Bouhuys, A. L., Beersma, D. G., et al. (1999). Seasonal affective disorder and latitude: A review of the literature. *Journal of Affective Disorders, 53,* 35–48.

Merzenich, M. M., and Jenkins, W. M. (1993). Reorganization of cortical representations of the hand following alterations of skin inputs induced by nerve injury, skin island transfers, and experience. *Journal of Hand Therapy, 6,* 89–104.

Merzenich, M. M., Schreiner, C., Jenkins, W., and Wang, X. (1993). Neural mechanisms underlying temporal integration, segmentation, and input sequence representation: Some implications for the origin of learning disabilities. *Annals of the New York Academy of Sciences, 682,* 1–22.

Meshberger F. L. (1990). An interpretation of Michelangelo's Creation of Adam based on neuroanatomy. *The Journal of the American Medical Association, 264,*1837–1841.

Mesulam, M.-M. (1985). Attention, confusional states and neglect. In M.-M. Mesulam (Ed.), *Principles of behavioral neurology.* Philadelphia: Davis.

Michael, N., and Erfurth, A. (2004). Treatment of bipolar mania with right prefrontal rapid transcranial magnetic stimulation. *Journal of Affective Disorders, 78,* 253–257.

Miles, L. E., and Dement, W. C. (1980). Sleep and aging. *Sleep, 3,* 1220.

Miller, G. F. (2000). The mating mind: How sexual choice shaped the evolution of human nature. New York: Doubleday.

Miller, J. M., and Spelman, F. A. (1990). *Cochlear implants: Models of the electrically stimulated ear.* New York: Springer.

Milner, A. D., Perrett, D. I., Johnston, R. S., Benson, P. J., et al. (1991). Perception and action in "visual form agnosia." *Brain, 114,* 405–428.

Milner, B. (1965). Memory disturbance after bilateral hippocampal lesions. In P. M. Milner and S. E. Glickman (Eds.), *Cognitive processes and the brain; An enduring problem in psychology.* Princeton, NJ: Van Nostrand.

Milner, B. (1970). Memory and the medial temporal regions of the brain. In D. H. Pribram and D. E. Broadbent (Eds.), *Biology of memory.* New York: Academic Press.

Milner, P. M. (1993). The mind and Donald O. Hebb. *Scientific American, 268*(1), 124–129.

Mioduszewska, B., Jaworski, J., and Kaczmarek, L. (2003). Inducible cAMP early repressor (ICER) in the nervous system—A transcriptional regulator of neuronal plasticity and programmed cell death. *Journal of Neurochemistry, 87,* 1313–1320.

Mirsky, A. F., and Duncan, C. C. (1986). Etiology and expression of schizophrenia: Neurobiological and psychosocial factors. *Annual Review of Psychology, 37,* 291–321.

Mishina, M., Kurosaki, T., Tobimatsu, T., Morimoto, Y., et al. (1984). Expression of functional acetylcholine receptor from cloned cDNAs. *Nature, 307,* 604–608.

Mishkin, M., and Ungerleider, L. (1982). Contribution of striate inputs to the visuospatial functions of parieto-preoccipital cortex in monkeys. *Behavioural Brain Research, 6,* 57–77.

Miyashita, Y. (1993). Inferior temporal cortex: Where visual perception meets memory. *Annual Review of Neuroscience, 16,* 245–263.

Mizumori, S. J. Y., Rosenzweig, M. R., and Bennett, E. L. (1985). Long-term working memory in the rat: Effects of hippocampally applied anisomycin. *Behavioral Neuroscience, 99,* 220–232.

Moghaddam, B. (In press). Targeting metabotropic glutamate receptors for treatment of the cognitive symptoms of schizophrenia. *Psychopharmacology.*

Moghaddam, B., and Adams, B. W. (1998). Reversal of phencyclidine effects by a group II metabotropic glutamate receptor agonist in rats. *Science, 281,* 1349–1352.

Mohammed, A. (2001). *Enrichment and the brain. Plasticity in the adult brain: From genes to neurotherapy.* 22nd International Summer School of Brain Research, Amsterdam, Netherlands.

Mohammed, A., Henriksson, B. G., Soderstrom, S., Ebendal, T., et al. (1993). Environmental influences on the central nervous system and their implications for the aging rat. *Behavioural Brain Research, 23,* 182–191.

Moldin, S. O., Reich, T., and Rice, J. P. (1991). Current perspectives on the genetics of unipolar depression. *Behavior Genetics, 21,* 211–242.

Monakow, C. von. (1914). Die Lokalisation im Grosshirn und der Abbau der Funktion durch kortikale Herde. Wiesbaden, Germany: Bergmann.

Money, J., and Ehrhardt, A. A. (1972). *Man and woman, boy and girl.* Baltimore: Johns Hopkins University Press.

Monks, D. A., and Watson N. V. (2001). N-cadherin expression in motoneurons is directly regulated by androgens: A genetic mosaic analysis in rats. *Brain Research, 895,* 73–79.

Monsonego, A., and Weiner, H. L. (2003). Immunotherapeutic approaches to Alzheimer's disease. *Science, 302,* 834–838.

Montague, C. T., Farooqi, I. S., Whitehead, J. P., Soos, M. A., et al. (1997). Congenital leptin deficiency is associated with severe early-onset obesity in humans. *Nature, 387,* 903–908.

Moore, C. L., Dou, H., and Juraska, J. M. (1992). Maternal stimulation affects the number of motor neurons in a sexually dimorphic nucleus of the lumbar spinal cord. *Brain Research, 572,* 52–56.

Moore, G. J., Bebchuk, J. M., Wilds, I. B., Chen, G., et al. (2000). Lithium-induced increase in human brain grey matter. *Lancet, 356,* 241-242.

Moore, H., Dvorakova, K., Jenkins, N., and Breed, W. (2002). Exceptional sperm cooperation in the wood mouse. *Nature, 418,* 174–177.

Moore, R. Y. (1983). Organization and function of a central nervous system circadian oscillator: The suprachiasmatic nucleus. *Federation Proceedings, 42,* 2783–2789.

Moore, R. Y., and Eichler, V. B. (1972). Loss of circadian adrenal corticosterone rhythm following suprachiasmatic lesions in the rat. *Brain Research, 42,* 201–206.

Morais-Cabral, J. H., Zhou, Y., and MacKinnon, R. (2001). Energetic optimization of ion conduction rate by the K⁺ selectivity filter. *Nature, 414,* 37–42.

Morford, J. P., and Mayberry, R. I. (2000). A reexamination of "early exposure" and its implications for language acquisition by eye. In C. Chamberlain, J. P. Morford, and R. I. Mayberry (Eds.), *Language acquisition by eye* (pp. 111-127). Mahwah, NJ: Erlbaum.

Morgan, D., Grant, K. A., Gage, H. D., Mach, R. H., et al. (2002). Social dominance in monkeys: Dopamine D2 receptors and cocaine self-administration. *Nature Neuroscience, 5,* 169–174.

Mori, K., Nagao, H., and Yoshihara, Y. (1999). The olfactory bulb: Coding and processing of odor molecule information. *Science, 286,* 711–715.

Morihisa, J., and McAnulty, G. B. (1985). Structure and function: Brain electrical activity mapping and computed tomography in schizophrenia. *Biological Psychiatry, 20,* 3–19.

Morrell, F. (1991). The role of secondary epileptogenesis in human epilepsy [Editorial]. *Archives of Neurology, 48,* 1221–1224.

Morris, B. (2002). Overcoming dyslexia. *Fortune, 145*(10), 1–7.

Morrison, A. R. (1983). A window on the sleeping brain. *Scientific American, 248*(4), 94–102.

Morrison, R. G., and Nottebohm, F. (1993). Role of a telencephalic nucleus in the delayed song learning of socially isolated zebra finches. *Journal of Neurobiology, 24,* 1045–1064.

Mortensen, P. B., Pedersen, C. B., Westergaard, T., Wohlfahrt, J., et al. (1999). Effects of family history and place and season of birth on the risk of schizophrenia. *New England Journal of Medicine, 340,* 603–608.

Moruzzi, G. (1972). The sleep-waking cycle. Ergebnisse der Physiologie, biologischen Chemie und experimentellen Pharmakologie, 64, 1–165.

Moruzzi, G., and Magoun, H. W. (1949). Brain stem reticular formation and activation of the EEG. *Clinical Neurophysiology, 1,* 455–473.

Moruzzi, G., and Magoun, H. W. (1995). Brain stem reticular formation and activation of the EEG. [1949 classic article.] *Journal of Neuropsychiatry and Clinical Neurosciences, 7,* 251–267.

Moscovitch, A., Blashko, C. A., Eagles, J. M., Darcourt, G., et al. (2004). A placebo-controlled study of sertraline in the treatment of outpatients with seasonal affective disorder. *Psychopharmacology, 171,* 390–397.

Moscovitch, M. (1985). Memory from infancy to old age: Implications for theories of normal and pathological memory. *Annals of the New York Academy of Sciences, 444,* 78–96.

Mott, F. W. (1895). Experimental inquiry upon the afferent tracts of the central nervous system of the monkey. *Brain, 18,* 1–20.

Mountcastle, V. B. (1979). An organizing principle for cerebral function: The unit module and the distributed system. In F. O. Schmitt and F. G. Worden (Eds.), *The neurosciences: Fourth study program* (pp. 21-24). Cambridge, MA: MIT Press.

Mountcastle, V. B. (1984). Central nervous mechanisms in mechanoreceptive sensibility. In I. Darian-Smith (Ed.), *Handbook of physiology, Section 1: Vol. 3. Sensory processes* (pp. 789–878). Bethesda, MD: American Physiological Society.

Mountcastle, V. B., Andersen, R. A., and Motter, B. C. (1981). The influence of attentive fixation upon the excitability of the light-sensitive neurons of the posterior parietal cortex. *Journal of Neuroscience, 1,* 1218–1235.

Movshon, J. A., and van Sluyters, R. C. (1981). Visual neural development. *Annual Review of Psychology, 32,* 477–522.

Mower, G. D., Christen, W. G., and Caplan, C. J. (1983). Very brief visual experience eliminates plasticity in the cat visual cortex. *Science, 221,* 178–180.

Mowry, B. J., Holmans, P. A., Pulver, A. E., Gejman, P. V., et al. (2004, March 24). Multicenter linkage study of schizophrenia loci on chromosome 22q. *Molecular Psychiatry,* advance online publication (http://www.nature.com/cgi-taf/DynaPage.taf?file=/mp/journal/vaop/ncurrent/abs/4001481a.html).

Moyer, J. R., Jr., Deyo, R. A., and Disterhoft, J. F. (1990). Hippocampectomy disrupts trace eyeblink conditioning in rabbits. *Behavioral Neuroscience, 104,* 243–252.

Mueller, H. T., Haroutunian, V., Davis, K. L., and Meador-Woodruff, J. H. (2004). Expression of the ionotropic glutamate receptor subunits and NMDA receptor-associated intracellular proteins in the substantia nigra in schizophrenia. *Brain Research: Molecular Brain Research, 121,* 60–69.

Mukamal, K. J., Conigrave, K. M., Mittleman, M. A., Camargo, C. A., Jr., et al. (2003). Roles of drinking pattern and type of alcohol consumed in coronary heart disease in men. *New England Journal of Medicine, 348,* 109–118.

Mukhametov, L. M. (1984). Sleep in marine mammals. In A. Borbely and J. L. Valatx (Eds.), *Experimental Brain Research. Supplementum: 8. Sleep mechanisms.* Berlin: Springer.

Mulkey, R. M., Herron, C. E., and Malenka, R. C. (1993). An essential role for protein phosphatases in hippocampal long-term depression. *Science, 261,* 1051–1055.

Münte, T. F. (2002). Brains out of tune. *Nature, 415,* 589–590.

Münte, T. F., Altenmüller, E., and Jäncke, L. (2002). The musician's brain as a model of neuroplasticity. *Nature Reviews. Neuroscience, 3,* 473–478.

Münte, T. F., Kohlmetz, C., Nager, W., and Altenmüller, E. (2001). Superior auditory spatial tuning in conductors. *Nature, 409,* 580.

Murphy, G. G., and Glanzman, D. L. (1999). Cellular analog of differential classical conditioning in *Aplysia:* Disruption by the NMDA receptor antagonist DL-2-amino-5-phosphonovalerate. *Journal of Neuroscience, 19,* 10595–10602.

Nader, K., Bechara, A., and Van Der Kooy, D. (1997). Neurobiological constraints on behavioral models of motivation. *Annual Review of Psychology, 48,* 85–114.

Nader, K., Schafe, G. E., and Le Doux, J. E. (2000). Fear memories require protein synthesis in the amygdala for reconsolidation after retrieval. *Nature, 406,* 722–726.

Naeser, M., Gaddie, A., Palumbo, C., and Stiassny-Eder, D. (1990). Late recovery of auditory comprehension in global aphasia. Improved recovery observed with subcortical temporal isthmus lesion vs. Wernicke's cortical area lesion. *Archives of Neurology, 47,* 425–432.

Naeser, M., and Hayward, R. (1978). Lesion localization in aphasia with cranial computed tomography and the Boston Diagnostic Aphasia Exam. *Neurology, 28,* 545–551.

Nakazato, M., Murakami, N., Date, Y., Kojima, M., et al. (2001). A role for ghrelin in the central regulation of feeding. *Nature, 409,* 194–198.

Narrow, W. E., Rae, D. S., Robins, L. N., and Regier, D. A. (2002). Revised prevalence estimates of mental disorders in the United States: Using a clinical significance criterion to reconcile 2 surveys' estimates. *Archives of General Psychiatry, 59,* 115–123.

Nastiuk, K. L., Mello, C. V., George, J. M., and Clayton, D. F. (1994). Immediate-early gene responses in the avian song control system: Cloning and expression analysis of the canary c-jun DNA. *Brain Research. Molecular Brain Research, 27,* 299–309.

Nathan, P. E., and Gorman, J. M. (1998). *A guide to treatments that work.* New York: Oxford University Press.

Nathans, J. (1987). Molecular biology of visual pigments. *Annual Review of Neuroscience, 10,* 163–194.

National Commission for the Protection of Human Subjects of Biomedical and Behavioral Research. (1978). Special study, implications of advances in biomedical and behavioral research: Report and recommendations of the National Commission for the Protection of Human Subjects of Biomedical and Behavioral Research (DHEW Publication No. OS 78-0015). Washington, DC: U.S. Department of Health, Education, and Welfare.

National Research Council. (2003). *The polygraph and lie detection.* Washington, D.C.: National Academic Press.

Neff, W. D., and Casseday, J. H. (1977). Effects of unilateral ablation of auditory cortex on monaural cat's ability to localize sound. *Journal of Neurophysiology, 40,* 44–52.

Nelson, G., Chandrashekar, J., Hoon, M. A., Feng, L., et al. (2002). An amino-acid taste receptor. *Nature, 416,* 199–202.

Nelson, G., Hoon, M. A., Chandrashekar, J., Zhang, Y., et al. (2001). Mammalian sweet taste receptors. *Cell, 106,* 381–390.

Nelson, L. E., Guo, T. Z., Lu, J., Saper, C. B., et al. (2002). The sedative component of anesthesia is mediated by GABA$_A$ receptors in an endogenous sleep pathway. *Nature Neuroscience, 5,* 979–984.

Nelson, R. J. (1995). *Introduction to behavioral endocrinology.* Sunderland, MA: Sinauer.

Nelson, R. J., Demas, G. E., Huang, P. L., Fishman, M. C., et al. (1995). Behavioural abnormalities in male mice lacking neuronal nitric oxide synthase. *Nature, 378,* 383–386.

Neophytou, S. I., Graham, M., Williams, J., Aspley, S., et al. (2000). Strain differences to the effects of aversive frequency ultrasound on behaviour and brain topography of c-fos expression in the rat. *Brain Research, 854,* 158–164.

Neumeister, A., Bain, E., Nugent, A. C., Carson, R. E., et al. (2004). Reduced serotonin type 1A receptor binding in panic disorder. *Journal of Neuroscience, 24,* 589–591.

Neuroscience: Taxicology. (2000). *Economist, 353,* 8162, 125.

Neves-Pereira, M., Mundo, E., Muglia, P., King, N., et al. (2002). The brain-derived neurotrophic factor gene confers susceptibility to bipolar disorder: Evidence from a family-based association study. *American Journal of Human Genetics, 71,* 651–655.

Neville, H. J., Bavelier, D., Corina, D., Rauschecker, J., et al. (1998). Cerebral organization for language in deaf and hearing subjects: Biological constraints and effects of experience. *Proceedings of the National Academy of Sciences, USA, 95,* 922–929.

Neville, H. J., Mills, D. L., and Lawson, D. S. (1992). Fractionating language: Different neural subsystems with different sensitive periods. *Cerebral Cortex, 2,* 244–258.

Newsome, W. T., Wurtz, R. H., Dursteler, M. R., and Mikami, A. (1985). Deficits in visual motion processing following ibotenic acid lesions of the middle temporal visual area of the macaque monkey. *Journal of Neuroscience, 5,* 825–840.

Nichols, M. J., and Newsome, W. T. (1999). The neurobiology of cognition. *Nature, 402,* C35–C38.

Nicolelis, M. A. (2001). Actions from thoughts. *Nature, 409,* 403–407.

Nieto-Sampedro, M., and Cotman, C. W. (1985). Growth factor induction and temporal order in central nervous system repair. In C. W. Cotman (Ed.), *Synaptic plasticity* (pp. 407–457). New York: Guilford.

Nietzel, M. T. (2000). Police psychology. In A. E. Kazdin (Ed.), *Encyclopedia of psychology* (Vol. 6, pp. 224–226). Washington, DC: American Psychological Association.

Nilsson, M., Perfilieva, E., Johansson, U., Orwar, O., et al. (1999). Enriched environment increases neurogenesis in the adult rat dentate gyrus and improves spatial memory. *Journal of Neurobiology, 39,* 569–578.

Nixon, K., and Crews, F. T. (2002). Binge ethanol exposure decreases neurogenesis in adult rat hippocampus. *Journal of Neurochemistry, 83,* 1087–1093.

Noad, M. J., Cato, D. H., Bryden, M. M., Jenner, M.-N., et al. (2000). Cultural revolution in whale songs. *Nature, 408,* 537–538.

Nobre, A. C., Sebestyen, G. N., Gitelman, D. R., Mesulam, M. M., et al. (1997). Functional localization of the system for visuospatial attention using positron emission tomography. *Brain, 120,* 515–533.

Noguchi, H. (1911). Serum diagnosis of syphilis and the butyric acid test for syphilis. Philadelphia: Lippincott.

Noguchi, Y., Watanabe, E., and Sakai, K. L. (2003). An event-related optical topography study of cortical activation induced by single-pulse transcranial magnetic stimulation. *Neuroimage, 19,* 156–162.

Nordberg, A. (1996). Functional studies of new drugs for the treatment of Alzheimer's disease. *Acta Neurologica Scandinavica. Supplementum, 165,* 137–144.

Nordeen, E. J., Nordeen, K. W., Sengelaub, D. R., and Arnold, A. P. (1985). Androgens prevent normally occurring cell death in a sexually dimorphic spinal nucleus. *Science, 229,* 671–673.

Norman, A. W., and Litwack, G. (1987). *Hormones.* Orlando, FL: Academic Press.

Norsell, U. (1980). Behavioral studies of the somatosensory system. *Physiological Reviews, 60,* 327–354.

Nottebohm, F. (1980). Brain pathways for vocal learning in birds: A review of the first 10 years. *Progress in Psychobiology and Physiological Psychology, 9.*

Nottebohm, F., and Arnold, A. P. (1976). Sexual dimorphism in vocal control areas of the songbird brain. *Science, 194,* 211–213.

Nougier, V., Bard, C., Fleury, M., Teasdale, N., et al. (1996). Control of single-joint movements in deafferented patients: Evidence for amplitude coding rather than position control. *Experimental Brain Research, 109,* 473–482.

NRC Commission on Life Science. (1988). *Use of laboratory animals in biomedical and behavioral research.* Washington, DC: National Academy Press. (ISBN 0-309-07878-4)

NRC Committee on Animals as Monitors of Environmental Hazards. (1991). *Animals as sentinels of environmental health hazards.* Washington, DC: National Academy Press.

Nudo, R. J., Milliken, G. W., Jenkins, W. M., and Merzenich, M. M. (1996). Use-dependent alterations of movement representations in primary motor cortex of adult squirrel monkeys. *Journal of Neuroscience, 16,* 785–807.

Nutt, J. G., Rufener, S. L., Carter, J. H., Anderson, V. C., et al. (2001). Interactions between deep brain stimulation and levodopa in Parkinson's disease. *Neurology, 57,* 1835–1842.

Obernier, J. A., White, A. M., Swartzwelder, H. S., and Crews, F. T. (2002). Cognitive deficits and CNS damage after a 4-day binge ethanol exposure in rats. *Pharmacology, Biochemistry and Behavior, 72,* 521–532.

Ojemann, G., and Mateer, C. (1979). Human language cortex: Localization of memory, syntax, and sequential motor-phoneme identification systems. *Science, 205,* 1401–1403.

Okano, H., Ogawa, Y., Nakamura, M., Kaneko, S., et al. (2003). Transplantation of neural stem cells into the spinal cord after injury. *Seminars in Cell and Developmental Biology, 14,* 191–198.

O'Keefe, J., and Dostrovsky, J. (1971). The hippocampus as a spatial map. Preliminary evidence from unit activity in the freely-moving rat. *Brain Research, 34,* 171–175.

Okubo, Y., Suhara, T., Suzuki, K., Kobayashi, K., et al. (1997). Decreased prefrontal dopamine D1 receptors in schizophrenia revealed by PET. *Nature, 385,* 634–636.

Olds, J., and Milner, P. (1954). Positive reinforcement produced by electrical stimulation of septal area and other regions of the rat brain. *Journal of Comparative and Physiological Psychology, 47,* 419–427.

Olsen, K. L. (1979). Androgen-insensitive rats are defeminised by their testes. *Nature, 279,* 238–239.

Ona, V. O., Li, M., Vonsattel, J. P., Andrews, L. J., et al. (1999). Inhibition of caspase-1 slows disease progression in a mouse model of Huntington's disease. *Nature, 399,* 263–267.

Ontiveros, A., Fontaine, R., Breton, G., Elie, R., et al. (1989). Correlation of severity of panic disorder and neuroanatomical changes on magnetic resonance imaging. *Journal of Neuropsychiatry and Clinical Neurosciences, 1,* 404–408.

Oppenheim, R. W. (1991). Cell death during development of the nervous system. *Annual Review of Neuroscience, 14,* 453–501.

Osterhout, L. (1997). On the brain response to syntactic anomalies: Manipulations of word position and word class reveal individual differences. *Brain and Language, 59,* 494–522.

Ottoson, D., Bartfai, T., Hokfelt, T., and Fuxe, K. (Eds.). (1995). *Wenner-Gren international series: Vol. 66. Challenges and perspectives in neuroscience.* Amsterdam: Elsevier.

Overstreet, D. H. (1993). The Flinders sensitive line rats: A genetic animal model of depression. *Neuroscience and Biobehavioral Reviews, 17,* 51–68.

Oyster, C. W. (1999). *The human eye: Structure and function.* Sunderland, MA: Sinauer.

Paabo, S. (2003). The mosaic that is our genome. *Nature, 421,* 409–412.

Pack, A. I. (2003). Should a pharmaceutical be approved for the broad indication of excessive sleepiness? *American Journal of Respiratory and Critical Care Medicine, 167,* 109–111.

Palmer, T. D., Schwartz, P. H., Taupin, P., Kaspar, B., et al. (2001). Progenitor cells from human brain after death. *Nature, 411,* 42–43.

Panda, S., Provencio, I., Tu, D. C., Pires, S. S., et al. (2003). Melanopsin is required for non-image-forming photic responses in blind mice. *Science, 301,* 525–527.

Panksepp, J. (1998). *Affective neuroscience.* New York: Oxford University Press.

Panksepp, J. (2000a). Emotions as natural kinds within the mammalian brain. In M. Lewis and J. M. Haviland-Jones (Eds.), *Handbook of emotions* (2nd ed., pp. 137–156). New York: Guilford.

Panksepp, J. (2000b). The riddle of laughter: Neural and psychoevolutionary underpinnings of joy. *Current Directions in Psychological Science, 9,* 183–186.

Panov, A. V., Gutekunst, C.-A., Leavitt, B. R., Hayden, M. R., et al. (2002). Early mitochondrial calcium defects in Huntington's disease are a direct effect of polyglutamines. *Nature Neuroscience, 5,* 731–736.

Pantev, C., Oostenveld, R., Engelien, A., Ross, B., et al. (1998). Increased auditory cortical representation in musicians. *Nature, 392,* 811–814.

Pantle, A., and Sekuler, R. (1968). Size detecting mechanisms in human vision. *Science, 162,* 1146–1148.

Papez, J. W. (1937). A proposed mechanism of emotion. *Archives of Neurology and Psychiatry, 38,* 725–745.

Papka, M., Ivry, R., and Woodruff-Pak, D. S. (1994). Eyeblink classical conditioning and time production in patients with cerebellar damage. *Society of Neuroscience Abstracts, 20,* 360.

Park, S., Como, P. G., Cui, L., and Kurlan, R. (1993). The early course of the Tourette's syndrome clinical spectrum. *Neurology, 43,* 1712–1715.

Parkes, J. D. (1985). *Sleep and its disorders.* Philadelphia: Saunders.

Paterson, S. J., Brown, J. H., Gsödl, M. K., Johnson, M. H., et al. (1999). Cognitive modularity and genetic disorders. *Science, 286,* 2355–2358.

Patterson, F., and Linden, E. (1981). *The education of Koko.* New York: Holt, Rinehart, and Winston.

Paulesu, E., McCrory, E., Fazio, F., Menoncello, L., et al. (2000). A cultural effect on brain function. *Nature Neuroscience, 3,* 91–96.

Pauls, D. L. (2003). An update on the genetics of Gilles de la Tourette syndrome. *Journal of Psychosomatic Research, 55,* 7–12.

Paulson, H. L., and Fischbeck, K. H. (1996). Trinucleotide repeats in neurogenetic disorders. *Annual Review of Neuroscience, 19,* 79–107.

Peck, J. R., and Waxman, D. (2000). Mutation and sex in a competitive world. *Nature, 406,* 399–404.

Pena, J. L., and Konishi, M. (2000). Cellular mechanisms for resolving phase ambiguity in the owl's inferior colliculus. *Proceedings of the National Academy of Sciences, USA, 97,* 11787–11792.

Penfield, W., and Rasmussen, T. (1950). *The cerebral cortex in man.* New York: Macmillan.

Penfield, W., and Roberts, L. (1959). *Speech and brain-mechanisms.* Princeton, NJ: Princeton University Press.

Pennisi, E. (1997). The architecture of hearing. *Science, 278,* 1223–1224.

Pennisi, E. (2003). Systems biology: Tracing life's circuitry. *Science, 302,* 1646–1649.

Peplau, L. A. (2003). Human sexuality: How do men and women differ? *Current Directions in Psychological Science, 12,* 37–40.

Perenin, M. T., and Vighetto, A. (1988). Optic ataxia: A specific disruption in visuomotor mechanisms. I. Different aspects of the deficit in reaching for objects. *Brain, 111,* 643–674.

Peretz, I., and Hyde, K. L. (2003). What is specific to music processing? Insights from congenital amusia. *Trends in Cognitive Science, 7,* 362–367.

Peris, J., Boyson, S. J., Cass, W. A., Curella, P., et al. (1990). Persistence of neurochemical changes in dopamine systems after repeated cocaine administration. *Journal of Pharmacology and Experimental Therapeutics, 253,* 38–44.

Perkins, A. T., and Teyler, T. J. (1988). A critical period for long-term potentiation in the developing rat visual cortex. *Brain Research, 439,* 222–229.

Perry, V. H., Oehler, R., and Cowey, A. (1984). Retinal ganglion cells that project to the dorsal lateral geniculate nucleus in the macaque monkey. *Neuroscience, 12,* 1101–1123.

Pert, C. B., and Snyder, S. H. (1973). Opiate receptor: Demonstration in nervous tissue. *Science, 179,* 1011–1014.

Pertwee, R. G. (1997). Pharmacology of cannabinoid CB1 and CB2 receptors. *Pharmacology and Therapeutics, 74(2),* 129–180.

Peschanski, M., Defer, G., N'Guyen, J. P., Ricolfi, F., et al. (1994). Bilateral motor improvement and alteration of L-dopa effect in two patients with Parkinson's disease following intrastriatal transplantation of foetal ventral mesencephalon. *Brain, 117,* 487–499.

Peter, M. E., Medema, J. P., and Krammer, P. H. (1997). Does the *Caenorhabditis elegans* protein CED-4 contain a region of homology to the mammalian death effector domain? *Cell Death and Differentiation, 4,* 51–134.

Peterhans, E., and von der Heydt, R. (1989). Mechanisms of contour perception in monkey visual cortex. II. Contours bridging gaps. *Journal of Neuroscience, 9,* 1749–1763.

Peters, A., Palay, S. L., and Webster, H. deF. (1991). *The fine structure of the nervous system: Neurons and their supporting cells* (3rd ed.). New York: Oxford University Press.

Petersen, C. C., Brecht, M., Hahn, T. T., and Sakmann, B. (2004). Synaptic changes in layer 2/3 underlying map plasticity of developing barrel cortex. *Science, 304,* 739–742.

Peterson, A. L., and Azrin, N. H. (1992). An evaluation of behavioral treatments for Tourette syndrome. *Behaviour Research and Therapy, 30,* 167–174.

Peterson, L. R., and Peterson, M. J. (1959). Short-term retention of individual verbal items. *Journal of Experimental Psychology, 58,* 193–198.

Petitto, L. A., Zatorre, R. J., Gauna, K., Nikelski, E. J., et al. (2000). Speech-like cerebral activity in profoundly deaf people processing signed languages: Implications for the neural basis of human language. *Proceedings of the National Academy of Sciences, USA, 97,* 13961–13966.

Petrides, M., and Milner, B. (1982). Deficits on subject-ordered tasks after frontal- and temporal-lobe lesions in man. *Neuropsychologia, 20,* 249–262.

Petrij, F., Giles, R., Dauwerse, H., Saris, J., et al. (1995). Rubinstein-taybi syndrome caused by mutations in the transcriptional co-activator cbp. *Nature, 376,* 348–351.

Petrovic, P., Kalso, E., Petersson, K. M., and Ingvar, M. (2002). Placebo and opioid analgesia imaging—A shared neuronal network. *Science, 295,* 1737–1740.

Pettigrew, J. D., and Freeman, R. D. (1973). Visual experience without lines: Effect on developing cortical neurons. *Science, 182,* 599–601.

Pettit, H. O., and Justice, J. B., Jr. (1991). Effect of dose on cocaine self-administration behavior and dopamine levels in the nucleus accumbens. *Brain Research, 539,* 94–102.

Petty, F., Kramer, G., Wilson, L., and Jordan, S. (1994). In vivo serotonin release and learned helplessness. *Psychiatry Research, 52,* 285–293.

Pfaff, D. W. (1968). Autoradiographic localization of radioactivity in rat brain after injection of tritiated sex hormones. *Science, 161,* 1355–1356.

Pfaff, D. W. (1980). Estrogens and brain function: Neural analysis of a hormone-controlled mammalian reproductive behavior. New York: Springer.

Pfaff, D. W. (1997). Hormones, genes, and behavior. *Proceedings of the National Academy of Sciences, USA, 94,* 14213–14216.

Pfaus, J. G., Kippin, T. E., and Centeno, S. (2001). Conditioning and sexual behavior: A review. *Hormones and Behavior, 40,* 291–321.

Pfefferbaum, A., Sullivan, E. V., Mathalon, D. H., Shear, P. K., et al. (1995). Longitudinal changes in magnetic resonance imaging brain volumes in abstinent and relapsed alcoholics. *Alcoholism: Clinical and Experimental Research, 19,* 1177–1191.

Pfrieger, F. W., and Barres, B. A. (1997). Synaptic efficacy enhanced by glial cells in vitro. *Science, 277,* 1684–1687.

Phillips, J. R., Johansson, R. S., and Johnson, K. O. (1990). Representation of braille characters in human nerve fibres. *Experimental Brain Research, 81,* 589–592.

Phillips, M. L., Marks, I. M., Senior, C., Lythgoe, D., et al. (2000). A differential neural response in obsessive-compulsive disorder patients with washing compared with checking symptoms to disgust. *Psychological Medicine, 30,* 1037–1050.

Phillips, M. L., Young, A. W., Scott, S. K., Calder, A. J., et al. (1998). Neural responses to facial and vocal expressions of fear and disgust. *Proceedings of the Royal Society of London. Series B: Biological Sciences, 265,* 1809–1817.

Phoenix, C. H., Goy, R. W., Gerall, A. A., and Young, W. C. (1959). Organizing action of prenatally administered testosterone propionate on the tissues mediating mating behavior in the female guinea pig. *Endocrinology, 65,* 369–382.

Pickens, R., and Thompson, T. (1968). Drug use by U.S. Army enlisted men in Vietnam: A followup on their return home. *Journal of Pharmacology and Experimental Therapeutics, 161,* 122–129.

Pierce, K., Müller, R.-A., Ambrose, J., Allen, G., et al. (2001). Face processing occurs outside the fusiform "face area": Evidence from functional MRI. *Brain, 124,* 2059–2073.

Pilla, M., Perachon, S., Sautel, F., Garrido, F., et al. (1999). Selective inhibition of cocaine-seeking behaviour by a partial dopamine D_3 receptor agonist. *Nature, 400,* 371–375.

Pines, J. (1992). Cell proliferation and control. *Current Opinion in Cell Biology, 4*(2), 144–148.

Pinker, S. (1994). *The language instinct.* New York: Morrow.

Pitman, R. K. (1989). Post-traumatic stress disorder, hormones, and memory. *Biological Psychiatry, 26,* 221–223.

Pitman, R. K., Sanders, K. M., Zusman, R. M., Healy, A. R., et al. (2002). Pilot study of secondary prevention of posttraumatic stress disorder with propranolol. *Biological Psychiatry, 51,* 189–192.

Pitts, J. W., and McClure, J. N. (1967). Lactate metabolism in anxiety neurosis. *New England Journal of Medicine, 277,* 1329–1336.

Pleim, E. T., and Barfield, R. J. (1988). Progesterone versus estrogen facilitation of female sexual behavior by intracranial administration to female rats. *Hormones and Behavior, 22,* 150–159.

Ploog, D. W. (1992). Neuroethological perspectives on the human brain: From the expression of emotions to intentional signing and speech. In A. Harrington (Ed.), *So human a brain: Knowledge and values in the neurosciences* (pp. 3–13). Boston: Birkhauser.

Plutchik, R. (1994). *The psychology and biology of emotion.* New York: HarperCollins.

Poinar, G. O., Jr. (1994). The range of life in amber: Significance and implications in DNA studies. *Experientia, 50,* 536–542.

Pollak, R. (1997). *The creation of Dr. B: A biography of Bruno Bettelheim.* New York: Simon & Schuster.

Polleux, F., Morrow, T., and Ghosh, A. (2000). Semaphorin 3A is a chemoattractant for cortical apical dendrites. *Nature, 404,* 567–573.

Polymeropoulos, M. H., Lavedan, C., Leroy, E., Ide, S. E., et al. (1997). Mutation in the alpha-synuclein gene identified in families with Parkinson's disease. *Science, 276,* 2045–2047.

Pope, H. G., Jr., Kouri, E. M., and Hudson, J. I. (2000). Effects of supraphysiologic doses of testosterone on mood and aggression in normal men: A randomized controlled trial. *Archives of General Psychiatry, 57,* 133–140.

Poremba, A., Malloy, M., Saunders, R. C., Carson, R. E., et al. (2004). Species-specific calls evoke asymmetric activity in the monkey's temporal poles. *Nature, 427,* 448–451.

Poritsky, R. (1969). Two and three dimenstional ultrastructure of boutons and glial cells on the motoneuronal surface in the cat spinal cord. *Journal of Comparative Neurology, 135,* 423–452.

Posner, M. I., and Raichle, M. E. (1994). *Images of mind.* New York: Scientific American Library.

Posthuma, D., De Geus, E. J. C., Baaré, W. F. C., Hulshoff Pol, H. E., et al. (2002). The association between brain volume and intelligence is of genetic origin. *Nature Neuroscience, 5,* 83–84.

Powley, T. L. (2000). Vagal circuitry mediating cephalic-phase responses to food. *Appetite, 34,* 184–188.

Praag, H. V., Schinder, A. F., Christie, B. R., Toni, N., et al. (2002). Functional neurogenesis in the adult hippocampus. *Nature, 415,* 1030–1034.

Premack, D. (1971). Language in a chimpanzee? *Science, 172,* 808–822.

Price, M. A., and Vandenbergh, J. G. (1992). Analysis of puberty-accelerating pheromones. *Journal of Experimental Zoology, 264,* 42–45.

Price, M. P., Lewin, G. R., McIlwrath, S. L., Cheng, C., et al. (2000). The mammalian sodium channel BNC1 is required for normal touch sensation. *Nature, 407,* 1007–1011.

Price, R. A., Kidd, K. K., Cohen, D. J., Pauls, D. L., et al. (1985). A twin study of Tourette syndrome. *Archives of General Psychiatry, 42,* 815–820.

Proksch, J. W., Gentry, W. B., and Owens, S. M. (2000). Anti-phencyclidine monoclonal antibodies provide long-term reductions in brain phencyclidine concentrations during chronic phencyclidine administration in rats. *Journal of Pharmacology and Experimental Therapeutics, 292,* 831–837.

Prull, M. W., Gabrieli, J. D. E., and Bunge, S. A. (2000). Age-related changes in memory: A cognitive neuroscience perspective. In F. I. M. Craik and T. A. Salthouse (Eds.), *The handbook of aging and cognition* (pp. 91-153). Mahwah, NJ: Erlbaum.

Przybyslawski, J., Roullet, P., and Sara, S. J. (1999). Attenuation of emotional and nonemotional memories after their reactivation: Role of beta adrenergic receptors. *Journal of Neuroscience, 19,* 6623–6628.

Pugh, E. N., Jr., and Lamb, T. D. (1990). Cyclic GMP and calcium: The internal messengers of excitation and adaptation in vertebrate photoreceptors. *Vision Research, 30,* 1923–1948.

Pugh, E. N., Jr., and Lamb, T. D. (1993). Amplification and kinetics of the activation steps in phototransduction. *Biochimica et Biophysica Acta, 1141,* 111–149.

Pugh, K. R., Mencl, W. E., Shaywitz, B. A., Shaywitz, S. E., et al. (2000). The angular gyrus in developmental dyslexia: Task-specific differences in functional connectivity within posterior cortex. *Psychological Science, 11*(1), 51–56.

Purves, D., Augustine, G. J., Fitzpatrick, D., Katz, L., et al. (Eds.). (2001). *Neuroscience* (2nd ed.). Sunderland, MA: Sinauer.

Purves, D., and Lotto, R. B. (2003). *Why we see what we do.* Sunderland, MA: Sinauer.

Quinn, W. G., Harris, W. A., and Benzer, S. (1974). Conditioned behavior in *Drosophila melanogaster. Proceedings of the National Academy of Sciences, USA, 71,* 708–712.

Quinn, W. G., Sziber, P. P., and Booker, R. (1979). The *Drosophila* memory mutant amnesiac. *Nature, 277,* 212–214.

Raab, D. H., and Ades, H. W. (1946). Cortical and midbrain mediation of a conditioned discrimination of acoustic intensities. *American Journal of Psychology, 59,* 59–83.

Raber, J., Wong, D., Yu, G. Q., Buttini, M., et al. (2000). Apolipoprotein E and cognitive performance. *Nature, 404,* 352–354.

Rafal, R. D. (1994). Neglect. *Current Opinion in Neurobiology, 4,* 231–236.

Raine, A., Reynolds, C., Venables, P. H., and Mednick, S. A. (2002). Stimulation seeking and intelligence: A prospective longitudinal study. *Journal of Personality and Social Psychology, 82,* 663–674.

Raine, A., Lencz, T., Bihrle, S., LaCasse, L., et al. (2000). Reduced prefrontal gray matter volume and reduced autonomic activity in antisocial personality disorder. *Archives of General Psychiatry, 57,* 119–127.

Raine, A., Meloy, J. R., Bihrle, S., Stoddard, J., et al. (1998). Reduced prefrontal and increased subcortical brain functioning assessed using positron emission tomography in predatory and affective murderers. *Behavioral Sciences & the Law, 16,* 319–332.

Raine, A., Venables, P. H., Dalais, C., Mellingen, K., et al. (2001). Early educational and health enrichment at age 3-5 years is associated with increased autonomic and central nervous system arousal and orienting at age 11 years: Evidence from the Mauritius Child Health Project. *Psychophysiology, 38,* 254–266.

Rainville, P., Duncan, G. H., Price, D. D., Carrier, B., et al. (1997). Pain affect encoded in human anterior cingulate but not somatosensory cortex. *Science, 277,* 968–971.

Raisman, G. (1978). What hope for repair of the brain? *Annals of Neurology, 3,* 101–106.

Raisman, G., and Field, P. M. (1971). Sexual dimorphism in the preoptic area of the rat. *Science, 173,* 731–733.

Rakic, P. (1971). Guidance of neurons migrating to the fetal monkey neocortex. *Brain Research, 33,* 471–476.

Rakic, P. (1985). Mechanisms of neuronal migration in developing cerebellar cortex. In G. M. Edelman, W. M. Cowan, and E. Gull (Eds.), *Molecular basis of neural development.* New York: Wiley.

Ralph, M. R., Foster, R. G., Davis, F. C., and Menaker, M. (1990). Transplanted suprachiasmatic nucleus determines circadian period. *Science, 247,* 975–978.

Ralph, M. R., and Menaker, M. (1988). A mutation of the circadian system in golden hamsters. *Science, 241,* 1225–1227.

Ramachandran, V. S., and Rogers-Ramachandran D. (2000). Phantom limbs and neural plasticity. *Archives of Neurology, 57,* 317–320.

Ramey, C. T., Campbell, F. A., Burchinal, M., Skinner, M. L., et al. (2000). Persistent effects of early childhood education on high-risk children and their mothers. *Applied Developmental Science, 4*(1), 2–14.

Ramón y Cajal, S. (1894). La fine structure des centres nerveus. Proceedings of the Royal Society of London. Series B: Biological Sciences, 55, 444–468.

Rampon, C., Jiang, C. H., Dong, H., Tang, Y. P., et al. (2000). Effects of environmental enrichment on gene expression in the brain. *Proceedings of the National Academy of Sciences, USA, 97,* 12880–12884.

Rampon, C., Tang, Y. P., Goodhouse, J., Shimizu, E., et al. (2000). Enrichment induces structural changes and recovery from nonspatial memory deficits in CA1 NMDAR1-knockout mice. *Nature Neuroscience, 3,* 238–244.

Rampon, C., and Tsien, J. Z. (2000). Genetic analysis of learning behavior-induced structural plasticity. *Hippocampus, 10,* 605–609.

Ramus, F., Hauser, M. D., Miller, C., Morris, D., et al. (2000). Language discrimination by human newborns and by cotton-top tamarin monkeys. *Science, 288,* 349–351.

Ranaldi, R., and Beninger, R. J. (1994). The effects of systemic and intracerebral injections of D1 and D2 agonists on brain stimulation reward. *Brain Research, 651,* 283–292.

Rand, M. N., and Breedlove, S. M. (1987). Ontogeny of functional innervation of bulbocavernosus muscles in male and female rats. *Brain Research, 430,* 150–152.

Randolph, M., and Semmes, J. (1974). Behavioral consequences of selective subtotal ablations in the postcentral gyrus of *Macaca mulatta. Brain Research, 70,* 55–70.

Rapin, I., and Katzman, R. (1998). Neurobiology of autism. *Annals of Neurology, 43,* 7–14.

Rapoport, J. L. (1989). The biology of obsessions and compulsions. *Scientific American, 260*(6), 82–89.

Rasmussen, L. E., and Greenwood, D. R. (2003). Frontalin: A chemical message of musth in Asian elephants (*Elephas maximus*). *Chemical Senses, 28,* 433–446.

Rasmussen, L. E., Riddle, H. S., and Krishnamurthy, V. (2002). Chemical communication: Mellifluous matures to malodorous in musth. *Nature, 415,* 975–976.

Rasmussen, P. (1996). The congenital insensitivity-to-pain syndrome (analgesia congenita): Report of a case. *International Journal of Paediatric Dentistry, 6,* 117–122.

Rattenborg, N. C., Lima, S. L., and Amlaner, C. J. (1999). Half-awake to the risk of predation. *Nature, 397,* 397–398.

Rauch, S. L., Jenike, M. A., Alpert, N. M., Baer, L., et al. (1994). Regional cerebral blood flow measured during symptom provocation in obsessive-compulsive disorder using oxygen 15-labeled carbon dioxide and positron emission tomography. *Archives of General Psychiatry, 51,* 62–70.

Rauch, S. L., Savage, C. R., Alpert, N. M., Miguel, E. C., et al. (1995). A positron emission tomographic study of simple phobic symptom provocation. *Archives of General Psychiatry, 52,* 20–28.

Rauch, S. L., Shin, L. M., and Wright, C. I. (2003). Neuroimaging studies of amygdala function in anxiety disorders. *Annals of the New York Academy of Sciences, 985,* 389–410.

Rauschecker, J. P. (1999). Making brain circuits listen. *Science, 285,* 1686–1687.

Rauschecker, J. P, and Shannon, R. V. (2002). Sending sound to the brain. *Science, 295,* 1025–1029.

Raz, N. (2000). Aging of the brain and its impact on cognitive performance: Integration of structural and functional findings. In F. I. M. Craik and T. A. Salthouse (Eds.), *The handbook of aging and cognition* (2nd ed., pp. 1–90). Mahwah, NJ: Erlbaum.

Reader, S. M., and Laland, K. N. (2002). Social intelligence, innovation, and enhanced brain size in primates. *Proceedings of the National Academy of Sciences, USA, 99,* 4436–4441.

Recanzone, G. H., Schreiner, D. E., and Merzenich, M. M. (1993). Plasticity in the frequency representation of primary auditory cortex following discrimination training in adult owl monkeys. *Journal of Neuroscience, 13,* 87–103.

Rechtschaffen, A., and Bergmann, B. M. (1995). Sleep deprivation in the rat by the disk-over-water method. *Behavioural Brain Research, 69,* 55–63.

Rechtschaffen, A., and Kales, A. (1968). *A manual of standardized terminology, techniques and scoring system for sleep stages of human subjects.* Bethesda, MD: U.S. National Institute of Neurological Diseases and Blindness, Neurological Information Network.

Redican, W. K. (1982). An evolutionary perspective on human facial displays. In P. Ekman (Ed.), *Emotion in the human face* (2nd ed., pp. 212–280). Elmsford, NY: Pergamon.

Reedy, F. E. J., Bartoshuk, L. M., Miller, I. J. J., Duffy, V. B., et al. (1993). Relationships among papillae, taste pores, and 6-n-propylthiouracil (prop) suprathreshold taste sensitivity. *Chemical Senses, 18,* 618–619.

Rehkamper, G., Haase, E., and Frahm, H. D. (1988). Allometric comparison of brain weight and brain structure volumes in different breeds of the domestic pigeon, *Columba livia* f. d. (fantails, homing pigeons, strassers). *Brain, Behavior and Evolution, 31,* 141–149.

Reichardt, L. F., and Tomaselli, K. J. (1991). Extracellular matrix molecules and their receptors: Functions in neural development. *Annual Review of Neuroscience, 14,* 531–570.

Reiman, E. M., Raichle, M., Robins, E., Butler, F. K., et al. (1986). The application of positron emission tomography to the study of panic disorder. *American Journal of Psychiatry, 143,* 469–477.

Reiner, W. G., and Gearhart, J. P. (2004). Discordant sexual identity in some genetic males with cloacal exstrophy assigned to female sex at birth. *New England Journal of Medicine, 350,* 333–341.

Reisberg, D., and Heuer, F. (1995). Emotion's multiple effects on memory. In J. L. McGaugh, N. M. Weinberger, and G. Lynch (Eds.), *Brain and memory: Modulation and mediation of neuroplasticity* (pp. 84–92). New York: Oxford University Press.

Rempel-Clower, N. L., Zola, S. M., Squire, L. R., and Amaral, D. G. (1996). Three cases of enduring memory impairment after bilateral damage limited to the hippocampal formation. *Journal of Neuroscience, 16,* 5233–5255.

Rende, R., and Plomin, R. (1995). Nature, nurture, and the development of psychopathology. In D. Cicccheti and D. J. Cohen (Eds.), *Developmental psychopathology: Vol. 1. Theory and methods* (pp. 291–314). New York: Wiley.

Renner, M. J., and Rosenzweig, M. R. (1987). Enriched and impoverished environments: Effects on brain and behavior. New York: Springer.

Reppert, S. M., Perlow, M. J., Tamarkin, L., and Klein, D. C. (1979). A diurnal melatonin rhythm in primate cerebrospinal fluid. *Endocrinology, 104,* 295–301.

Reppert, S. M., and Weaver, D. R. (2002). Coordination of circadian timing in mammals. *Nature, 418,* 935–941.

Rescorla, R. A. (1988). Behavioral studies of Pavlovian conditioning. *Annual Review of Neuroscience, 11,* 329–352.

Ressler, K. J., Sullivan, S. L., and Buck, L. B. (1994). A molecular dissection of spatial patterning in the olfactory system. *Current Opinion in Neurobiology, 4,* 588–596.

Ribeiro, R. C., Kushner, P. J., and Baxter, J. D. (1995). The nuclear hormone receptor gene superfamily. *Annual Review of Medicine, 46,* 443–453.

Rice, W. R., and Chippindale, A. K. (2001). Sexual recombination and the power of natural selection. *Science, 294,* 555–559.

Richardson, M., Strange, B. A., and Dolan, R. J. (2004). Encoding of emotional memories depends on amygdala and hippocampus and their interactions. *Nature Neuroscience, 7,* 278–284.

Richman, D. P., and Agius, M. A. (2003). Treatment of autoimmune myasthenia gravis. *Neurology, 61,* 1652–1661.

Richter, C. (1967). Sleep and activity: Their relation to the 24-hour clock. *Proceedings of the Association for Research in Nervous and Mental Diseases, 45,* 8–27.

Ridley, M. (2003). *Nature via nurture: Genes, experience, and what makes us human.* New York: Harper Collins.

Roberts, A. H. (1969). *Brain damage in boxers.* London: Pitman.

Roberts, W. W., and Mooney, R. D. (1974). Brain areas controlling thermoregulatory grooming, prone extension, locomotion, and tail vasodilation in rats. *Journal of Comparative and Physiological Psychology, 86,* 470–480.

Robins, L. N., and Regier, D. A. (1991). Psychiatric disorders in America: The epidemiologic catchment area study. New York: Free Press.

Rocca, W. A., Hofman, A., Brayne, C., Breteler, M. M., et al. (1991). The prevalence of vascular dementia in Europe: Facts and fragments from 1980–1990 studies. *Annals of Neurology, 30,* 817–824.

Rodier, P. M. (2000). The early origins of autism. *Scientific American, 282*(2), 56–63.

Roelink, H., Augsburger, A., Heemskerk, J., Korzh, V., et al. (1994). Floor plate and motor neuron induction by vhh-1, a vertebrate homolog of hedgehog expressed by the notochord. *Cell, 76,* 761–775.

Roffwarg, H. P., Muzio, J. N., and Dement, W. C. (1966). Ontogenetic development of the human sleep-dream cycle. *Science, 152,* 604–619.

Rogan, M. T., Staubli, U. V., and Ledoux, J. E. (1997). Fear conditioning induces associative long-term potentiation in the amygdala. *Nature, 390,* 604–607.

Roland, E., and Larson, B. (1976). Focal increase of cerebral blood flow during stereognostic testing in man. *Archives of Neurology, 33,* 551–558.

Roland, P. E. (1980). Quantitative assessment of cortical motor dysfunction by measurement of the regional cerebral blood flow. *Scandinavian Journal of Rehabilitation Medicine, 7,* 27–41.

Roland, P. E. (1984). Metabolic measurements of the working frontal cortex in man. *Trends in Neurosciences, 7,* 430–436.

Roland, P. E. (1993). *Brain activation.* New York: Wiley-Liss.

Rolls, E. T., and O'Mara, S. M. (1995). View-responsive neurons in the primate hippocampal complex. *Hippocampus, 5,* 409–424.

Romanski, L. M., Tian, B., Fritz, J., Mishkin, M., et al. (1999). Dual streams of auditory afferents target multiple domains in the primate prefrontal cortex. *Nature Neuroscience, 2,* 1131–1136.

Romero-Apis, D., Babayan-Mena, J. I., Fonte-Vazquez, A., Gutierrez-Perez, D., et al. (1982). Perdida del ojo fijador en adulto con ambliopia estrabica. *Anales Sociedad Mexicana de Oftalmologia, 56,* 445–452.

Rorabaugh, W. J. (1976). Estimated U.S. alcoholic beverage consumption, 1790–1860. *Journal of Studies on Alcohol, 37,* 357–364.

Rosci, C., Chiesa, V., Laiacona, M., and Capitani, E. (2003). Apraxia is not associated to a disproportionate naming impairment for manipulable objects. *Brain and Cognition, 53,* 412–415.

Rose, S. (2004, January 22). The code that must be cracked. *Guardian* (http://www.guardian.co.uk).

Rosen, B. R., Buckner, R. L., and Dale, A. M. (1998). Event-related functional MRI: Past, present, and future. *Proceedings of the National Academy of Sciences, USA, 95,* 773–780.

Rosenbaum, R. S., Priselac, S., Köhler, S., Black, S. E., et al. (2000). Remote spatial memory in an amnesic person with extensive bilateral hippocampal lesions. *Nature Neuroscience, 3,* 1044–1048.

Rosengren, A., Tibblin, G., and Wilhelmsen, L. (1991). Self-perceived psychological stress and incidence of coronary artery disease in middle-aged men. *American Journal of Cardiology, 68,* 1171–1175.

Rosenkranz, M. A., Jackson, D. C., Dalton, K. M., Dolski, I., et al. (2003). Affective style and in vivo immune response: Neurobehavioral mechanisms. *Proceedings of the National Academy of Sciences, USA, 100,* 11148–11152.

Rosenthal, N. E., Sack, D. A., Carpenter, C. J., Parry, B. L., et al. (1985). Antidepressant effects of light in seasonal affective disorder. *American Journal of Psychiatry, 142,* 606–608.

Rosenzweig, M. R. (1946). Discrimination of auditory intensities in the cat. *American Journal of Psychology, 59,* 127–136.

Rosenzweig, M. R. (1984). Experience, memory, and the brain. *American Psychologist, 39,* 365–376.

Rosenzweig, M. R., and Bennett, E. L. (1977). Effects of environmental enrichment or impoverishment on learning and on brain values in rodents. In A. Oliveno (Ed.), *Genetics, environment, and intelligence* (pp. 1–2). Amsterdam: Elsevier/North-Holland.

Rosenzweig, M. R., and Bennett, E. L. (1978). Experimental influences on brain anatomy and brain chemistry in rodents. In G. Gottlieb (Ed.), *Studies on the development of behavior and the nervous system: Vol. 4. Early influences* (pp. 289–327). New York: Academic Press.

Rosenzweig, M. R., and Bennett, E. L. (1996). Psychobiology of plasticity: Effects of training and experience on brain and behavior. *Behavioural Brain Research, 78,* 57–65.

Rosenzweig, M. R., Bennett, E. L., Colombo, P. J., Lee, D. W., et al. (1993). Short-term, intermediate-term, and long-term memory. *Behavioural Brain Research, 57,* 193–198.

Rosenzweig, M. R., Bennett, E. L., and Diamond, M. C. (1972). Brain changes in response to experience. *Scientific American, 226*(2), 22–29.

Rosenzweig, M. R., Bennett, E. L., Martinez, J. L., Colombo, P. J., et al. (1992). Studying stages of memory formation with chicks. In L. R. Squire and N. Butters (Eds.), *Neuropsychology of memory* (2nd ed., pp. 533–546). New York: Guilford.

Rosenzweig, M. R., Krech, D., and Bennett, E. L. (1961). Heredity, environment, brain biochemistry, and learning. *Current trends in psychological theory* (pp. 87–110). Pittsburgh, PA: University of Pittsburgh Press.

Rosenzweig, M., Krech, D., Bennett, E. L., and Diamond, M. (1962). Effects of environmental complexity and training on brain chemistry and anatomy: A replication and extension. *Journal of Comparative and Physiological Psychology, 55,* 429–437.

Roses, A. D. (1995). On the metabolism of apolipoprotein E and the Alzheimer diseases. *Experimental Neurology, 132,* 149–156.

Rossetti, Y., Rode, G., Pisella, L., Farné, A., et al. (1998). Prism adaptation to a rightward optical deviation rehabilitates left hemispatial neglect. *Nature, 395,* 166–169.

Rossi, D. J., Oshima, T., and Attwell, D. (2000). Glutamate release in severe brain ischaemia is mainly by reversed uptake. *Nature, 403,* 316–321.

Rosso, I. M., Cannon, T. D., Huttunen, T., Huttunen, M. O., et al. (2000). Obstetric risk factors for early-onset schizophrenia in a Finnish birth cohort. *American Journal of Psychiatry, 157,* 801–807.

Rossor, M., Garrett, N., Johnson, A., Mountjoy, C., et al. (1982). A post-mortem study of the cholinergic and GABA systems in senile dementia. *Brain, 105,* 313–330.

Rothschild, A. J. (1992). Disinhibition, amnestic reactions, and other adverse reactions secondary to triazolam: A review of the literature. *Journal of Clinical Psychiatry, 53,* 69–79.

Rothstein, J. D. (2000). Bundling up excitement. *Nature, 407,* 141, 143.

Roy, A. (1992). Hypothalamic-pituitary-adrenal axis function and suicidal behavior in depression. *Biological Psychiatry, 32,* 812–816.

Ruberman, W., Weinblatt, E., Goldberg, J. D., and Chaudhary, B. S. (1984). Psychosocial influences on mortality after myocardial infarction. *New England Journal of Medicine, 311,* 552–559.

Ruby, N. F., Brennan, T. J., Xie, X., Cao, V., et al. (2002). Role of melanopsin in circadian responses to light. *Science, 298,* 2211–2213.

Ruck, C., Andreewitch, S., Flyckt, K., Edman, G., et al. (2003). Capsulotomy for refractory anxiety disorders: Long-term follow-up of 26 patients. *American Journal of Psychiatry, 160,* 513–521.

Rumbaugh, D. M. (1977). Language learning by a chimpanzee: The LANA project. New York: Academic Press.

Rupnick, M. A., Panigrahy, D., Zhang, C. Y., Dallabrida, S. M., et al. (2002). Adipose tissue mass can be regulated through the vasculature. *Proceedings of the National Academy of Sciences, USA, 99,* 10730–10735.

Rusak, B., and Zucker, I. (1979). Neural regulation of circadian rhythms. *Physiological Reviews, 59,* 449–526.

Russell, J. A. (1994). Is there universal recognition of emotion from facial expressions? A review of the cross–cultural studies. *Psychological Bulletin, 115,* 102–141.

Ruthazer, E. S., Akerman, C. J., and Cline, H. T. (2003). Control of axon branch dynamics by correlated activity in vivo. *Science, 301,* 66–70.

Ryan, A. J. (1998). Intracranial injuries resulting from boxing. *Clinics in Sports Medicine, 17*(1), 155–168.

Rymer, R. (1993). Genie: An abused child's flight from silence. New York: HarperCollins.

Sack, R. L., Blood, M. L., and Lewy, A. J. (1992). Melatonin rhythms in night shift workers. *Sleep, 15,* 434–441.

Salvini-Plawen, L. V., and Mayr, E. (1977). On the evolution of photoreceptors and eyes. *Evolutionary Biology, 10,* 207–263.

Samad, T. A., Moore, K. A., Sapirstein, A., Billet, S., et al. (2001). Interleukin-1β-mediated induction of Cox-2 in the CNS contributes to inflammatory pain hypersensitivity. *Nature, 410,* 471–475.

Samaha, F. F., Iqbal, N., Seshadri, P., Chicano, K. L., et al. (2003). A low-carbohydrate as compared with a low-fat diet in severe obesity. *New England Journal of Medicine, 348,* 2074–2081.

Samson, S., and Zatorre, R. J. (1991). Recognition memory for text and melody of songs after unilateral temporal lobe lesion: Evidence for dual encoding. *Journal of Experimental Psychology; Learning, Memory, and Cognition, 17,* 793–804.

Samson, S., and Zatorre, R. J. (1994). Contribution of the right temporal lobe to musical timbre discrimination. *Neuropsychologia, 32,* 231–240.

Sandall, D. W., Satkunanathan, N., Keays, D. A., Polidano, M. A., et al. (2003). A novel α-conotoxin identified by gene sequencing is active in suppressing the vascular response to selective stimulation of sensory nerves in vivo. *Biochemistry, 42,* 6904–6911.

Sandler, A. D., Sutton, K. A., DeWeese, J., Girardi, M. A., et al. (1999). Lack of benefit of a single dose of synthetic human secretin in the treatment of autism and pervasive developmental disorder. *New England Journal of Medicine, 341,* 1801–1806.

Sanes, J. N., and Donoghue, J. P. (2000). Plasticity and primary motor cortex. *Annual Review of Neuroscience, 23,* 393–415.

Sanes, J. R., and Lichtman, J. W. (1999). Development of the vertebrate neuromuscular junction. *Annual Review of Neuroscience, 22,* 389–442.

Sano, M., Stanley, M., Lawton, A., Cote, L., et al. (1991). Tritiated imipramine binding. A peripheral marker for serotonin in Parkinson's disease. *Archives of Neurology, 48,* 1052–1054.

Sapolsky, R. M. (1992). Neuroendocrinology of the stress-response. In J. B. Becker, S. M. Breedlove, and D. Crews (Eds.), *Behavioral endocrinology,* pp. 287–324. Cambridge, MA: MIT Press.

Sapolsky, R. M. (1993). Potential behavioral modification of glucocorticoid damage to the hippocampus [Special issue: Alzheimer's disease: Animal models and clinical perspectives]. *Behavioural Brain Research, 57,* 175–182.

Sapolsky, R. M. (1994). *Why zebras don't get ulcers.* New York: Freeman.

Sapolsky, R. M. (2001). *A primate's memoir.* New York: Scribner.

Sapolsky, R. M., Uno, H., Rebert, C. S., and Finch, C. E. (1990). Hippocampal damage associated with prolonged glucocorticoid exposure in primates. *Journal of Neuroscience, 10,* 2897–2902.

Sara, S. J. (2000). Retrieval and reconsolidation: Toward a neurobiology of remembering. *Learning and Memory, 7,* 73–84.

Sartucci, F., Bonfiglio, L., Del Seppia, C., Luschi, P., et al. (1997). Changes in pain perception and pain-related somatosensory evoked potentials in humans produced by exposure to oscillating magnetic fields. *Brain Research, 769,* 362–366.

Satinoff, E. (1978). Neural organization and evolution of thermal regulation in mammals. *Science, 201,* 16–22.

Satinoff, E., and Rutstein, J. (1970). Behavioral thermoregulation in rats with anterior hypothalamic lesions. *Journal of Comparative and Physiological Psychology, 71,* 77–82.

Satinoff, E., and Shan, S. Y. (1971). Loss of behavioral thermoregulation after lateral hypothalamic lesions in rats. *Journal of Comparative and Physiological Psychology, 77,* 302–312.

Savage-Rumbaugh, E. S. (1993). *Language comprehension in ape and child.* Chicago: University of Chicago Press.

Savage-Rumbaugh, E. S., Murphy, J., Sevcik, R. A., Brakke, K. E., et al. (1993). *Monographs of the Society for Research in Child Development: Vol. 58, No. 3–4. Language comprehension in ape and child.* Chicago: University of Chicago Press.

Saxena, S., Brody, A. L., Schwartz, J. M., and Baxter, L. R. (1998). Neuroimaging and frontal-subcortical circuitry in obsessive-compulsive disorder. *British Journal of Psychiatry Supplement, 35,* 26–37.

Saxena, S., and Rauch, S. L. (2000). Functional neuroimaging and the neuroanatomy of obsessive-compulsive disorder. *Psychiatric Clinics of North America, 23,* 563–586.

Scalaidhe, S. P. O., Wilson, F. A. W., and Goldman-Rakic, P. S. (1997). Areal segregation of face-processing neurons in prefrontal cortex. *Science, 278,* 1135–1138.

Schachter, S. (1975). Cognition and peripheralist-centralist controversies in motivation and emotion. In M. S. Gazzaniga and C. Blakemore (Eds.), *Handbook of psychobiology.* New York: Academic Press.

Schachter, S., and Singer, J. (1962). Cognitive, social, and physiological determinants of emotional state. *Psychological Review, 69,* 379–399.

Schacter, D. L., Alpert, N. M., Savage, C. R., Rauch, S. L., et al. (1996). Conscious recollection and the human hippocampal formation: Evidence from positron emission tomography. *Proceedings of the National Academy of Sciences, USA, 93,* 321–325.

Schaie, K. W. (1994). The course of adult intellectual development. *American Psychologist, 49,* 304–313.

Scharff, C., Kirn, J. R., Grossman, M., Macklis, J. D., et al. (2000). Targeted neuronal death affects neuronal replacement and vocal behavior in adult songbirds. *Neuron, 25,* 481–492.

Scheibel, A. B., and Conrad, A. S. (1993). Hippocampal dysgenesis in mutant mouse and schizophrenic man: Is there a relationship? *Schizophrenia Bulletin, 19,* 21–33.

Scheibel, M. E., Tomiyasu, U., and Scheibel, A. B. (1977). The aging human Betz cells. *Experimental Neurology, 56,* 598–609.

Schein, S. J., and Desimone, R. (1990). Spectral properties of V4 neurons in the macaque. *Journal of Neuroscience, 10,* 3369–3389.

Schein, S. J., Marrocco, R. T., and de Monasterio, F. M. (1982). Is there a high concentration of color-selective cells in area V4 of monkey visual cortex? *Journal of Neurophysiology, 47,* 193–213.

Schenck, C. H., and Mahowald, M. W. (2002). REM sleep behavior disorder: Clinical, developmental, and neuroscience perspectives 16 years after its formal identification in *Sleep. Sleep, 25,* 120–138.

Schenkerberg, T., Bradford, D. C., and Ajax, E. T. (1980). Line bisection and unilateral visual neglect in patients with neurologic impairment. *Neurology, 30,* 509–518.

Schiffman, S. S., Simon, S. A., Gill, J. M., and Beeker, T. G. (1986). Bretylium tosylate enhances salt taste. *Physiology & Behavior, 36,* 1129–1137.

Schildkraut, J. J., and Kety, S. S. (1967). Biogenic amines and emotion. *Science, 156,* 21–30.

Schiller, P. H. (1993). The effects of V4 and middle temporal (MT) area lesions on visual performance in the rhesus monkey. *Visual Neuroscience, 10,* 717–746.

Schlaug, G., Jancke, L., Huang, Y., and Steinmetz, H. (1995). In vivo evidence of structural brain asymmetry in musicians. *Science, 267,* 699–701.

Schlupp, I., Marler, C., and Ryan, M. J. (1994). Benefit to male sailfin mollies of mating with heterospecific females. *Science, 263,* 373–374.

Schmidt-Nielsen, K. (1960). *Animal physiology.* Englewood Cliffs, NJ: Prentice-Hall.

Schmolesky, M. T., Wang, Y., Pu, M., and Leventhal, A. G. (2000). Degradation of stimulus selectivity of visual cortical cells in senes-

cent rhesus monkeys. *Nature Neuroscience, 3,* 384–390.

Schnapf, J. L., and Baylor, D. A. (1987). How photoreceptor cells respond to light. *Scientific American, 256*(4), 40–47.

Schnapp, B. J. (1997). Retroactive motors. *Neuron, 18,* 523–526.

Schneider, G. E. (1969). Two visual systems. *Science, 163,* 895–902.

Schneider, K. (1959). *Clinical psychopathology.* New York: Grune & Stratton.

Schneider, P., Scherg, M., Dosch, H. G., Specht, H. J., et al. (2002). Morphology of Heschl's gyrus reflects enhanced activation in the auditory cortex of musicians. *Nature Neuroscience, 5,* 688–694.

Schuckit, M. A., and Smith, T. L. (1997). Assessing the risk for alcoholism among sons of alcoholics. *Journal of Studies on Alcohol, 58,* 141–145.

Schuster, C. R. (1970). Psychological approaches to opiate dependence and self-administration by laboratory animals. *Federation Proceedings, 29,* 1–5.

Schwartz, C. E., Wright, C. I., Shin, L. M., Kagan, J., et al. (2003). Inhibited and uninhibited infants "grown up": Adult amygdalar response to novelty. *Science, 300,* 1952–1953.

Schwartz, M. W., Woods, S. C., Porte, D., Jr., Seeley, R. J., et al. (2000). Central nervous system control of food intake. *Nature, 404,* 661–671.

Schwartz, W. J., Smith, C. B., Davidsen, L., Savaki, H., et al. (1979). Metabolic mapping of functional activity in the hypothalamo-neurohypophysial system of the rat. *Science, 205,* 723–725.

Schwartzer, R., and Gutiérrez-Doña, B. (2000). Health psychology. In K. Pawlik and M. R. Rosenzweig (Eds.), *International handbook of psychology* (pp. 452–465). London: Sage.

Schwartzkroin, P. A., and Wester, K. (1975). Long-lasting facilitation of a synaptic potential following tetanization in the in vitro hippocampal slice. *Brain Research, 89,* 107–119.

Sclafani, A., Springer, D., and Kluge, L. (1976). Effects of quinine adulteration on the food intake and body weight of obese and nonobese hypothalamic hyperphagic rats. *Physiology & Behavior, 16,* 631–640.

Scoville, W. B., and Milner, B. (1957). Loss of recent memory after bilateral hippocampal lesions. *Journal of Neurology, Neurosurgery and Psychiatry, 20,* 11–21.

Seeman, P. (1990). Atypical neuroleptics: Role of multiple receptors, endogenous dopamine, and receptor linkage. *Acta Psychiatrica Scandinavica. Supplementum, 358,* 14–20.

Segal, N. L., Dysken, M. W., Bouchard, T. J., Jr., Pedersen, N. L., et al. (1990). Tourette's disorder in a set of reared-apart triplets: Genetic and environmental influences. *American Journal of Psychiatry, 147,* 196–199.

Seiger, A., Nordberg, A., von Holst, H., Backman, L., et al. (1993). Intracranial infusion of purified nerve growth factor to an Alzheimer patient: The first attempt of a possible future treatment strategy. *Behavioural Brain Research, 57,* 255–261.

Seil, F. J., Kelly, J. M., and Leiman, A. L. (1974). Anatomical organization of cerebral neocortex in tissue culture. *Experimental Neurology, 45,* 435–450.

Selkoe, D. J. (1991). Amyloid protein and Alzheimer's disease. *Scientific American, 265*(5), 68–71.

Selkoe, D. J. (1999). Translating cell biology into therapeutic advances in Alzheimer's disease. *Nature, 399*(6738 Suppl.), A23–A31.

Selye, H. (1956). *The stress of life.* New York: McGraw-Hill.

Semendeferi, K., and Damasio, H. (2000). The brain and its main anatomical subdivisions in living hominoids using magnetic resonance imaging. *Journal of Human Evolution, 38,* 317–332.

Semendeferi, K., Damasio, H., Frank, R., and Van Hoesen, G. W. (1997). The evolution of the frontal lobes: A volumetric analysis based on three-dimensional reconstructions of magnetic resonance scans of human and ape brains. *Journal of Human Evolution, 32,* 375–388.

Semendeferi, K., Lu, A., Schenker, N., and Damasio, H. (2002). Humans and great apes share a large frontal cortex. *Nature Neuroscience, 5,* 272–276.

Semple, D. M., Ebmeier, K. P., Glabus, M. F., O'Carroll, R. E., et al. (1999). Reduced in vivo binding to the serotonin transporter in the cerebral cortex of MDMA ("ecstasy") users. *British Journal of Psychiatry, 175,* 63–69.

Sendtner, M., Holtmann, B., and Hughes, R. A. (1996). The response of motoneurons to neurotrophins. *Neurochemical Research, 21,* 831–841.

Serrano, P. A., Beniston, D. S., Oxonian, M. G., Rodriguez, W. A., et al. (1994). Differential effects of protein kinase inhibitors and activators on memory formation in the 2-day-old chick. *Behavioral and Neural Biology, 61,* 60–72.

Serviere, J., Webster, W. R., and Calford, M. B. (1984). Isofrequency labelling revealed by a combined [14C]-2-deoxyglucose, electrophysiological, and horseradish peroxidase study of the inferior colliculus of the cat. *Journal of Comparative Neurology, 228,* 463–477.

Seuss, Dr. (1987). *The tough coughs as he ploughs the dough: Early writings and cartoons by Dr. Seuss.* New York: Morrow.

Seyfarth, R. M., and Cheney, D. L. (1997). Behavioral mechanisms underlying vocal communication in nonhuman primates. *Animal Learning & Behavior, 25,* 249–267.

Shapiro, R. M. (1993). Regional neuropathology in schizophrenia: Where are we? Where are we going? *Schizophrenia Research, 10,* 187–239.

Shastry, B. S. (2002). Schizophrenia: A genetic perspective (review). *International Journal of Molecular Medicine, 9,* 207–212.

Shaw, P. J., Cirelli, C., Greenspan, R. J., and Tononi, G. (2000). Correlates of sleep and waking in *Drosophila melanogaster. Science, 287,* 1834–1837.

Shaw, P. J., Tononi, G., Greenspan, R. J., and Robinson, D. F. (2002). Stress response genes protect against lethal effects of sleep deprivation in *Drosophila. Nature, 417,* 287–291.

Shaywitz, S. E. (2003). *Overcoming dyslexia.* New York: Random House.

Shaywitz, S. E., Shaywitz, B. A., Pugh, K. R., Fulbright, R. K., et al. (1998). Functional disruption in the organization of the brain for reading in dyslexia. *Proceedings of the National Academy of Sciences, USA, 95,* 2636–2641.

Sherrington, C. S. (1897). Part III. The central nervous system. In M. Foster (Ed.), *A textbook of physiology.* London: Macmillan.

Sherrington, C. S. (1898). Experiments in examination of the peripheral distribution of the fibres of the posterior roots of some spinal nerves. *Philosophical Transactions, 190,* 45–186.

Sherry, D. F. (1992). Memory, the hippocampus, and natural selection: Studies of food-storing birds. In L. R. Squire and N. Butters (Eds.), *Neuropsychology of memory* (2nd ed., pp. 521–532). New York: Guilford.

Sherry, D. F., Jacobs, L. F., and Gaulin, S. J. (1993). "The hippocampus and spatial memory": Reply. *Trends in Neurosciences, 16,* 57.

Sherry, D. F., and Schacter, D. L. (1987). The evolution of multiple memory systems. *Psychological Review, 94,* 439–454.

Sherry, D. F., and Vaccarino, A. L. (1989). Hippocampus and memory for food caches in black-capped chickadees. *Behavioral Neuroscience, 103,* 308–318.

Sherry, D. F., Vaccarino, A. L., Buckenham, K., and Herz, R. S. (1989). The hippocampal complex of food-storing birds. *Brain Behavior and Evolution, 34,* 308–317.

Sherwin, B. B. (1998). Use of combined estrogen-androgen preparations in the postmenopause: Evidence from clinical studies. *International Journal of Fertility and Women's Medicine, 43*(2), 98–103.

Sherwin, B. B. (2002). Randomized clinical trials of combined estrogen-androgen preparations: effects on sexual functioning. *Fertility and Sterility, 77*(Suppl. 4), 49–54.

Shimura, H., Schlossmacher, M. G., Hattori, N., Frosch, M. P., et al. (2001). Ubiquitination of a new form of α-synuclein by parkin from human brain: Implications for Parkinson's disease. *Science, 293,* 263–269.

Shingo, T., Gregg, C., Enwere, E., Fujikawa, H., et al. (2003). Pregnancy-stimulated neurogenesis in the adult female forebrain mediated by prolactin. *Science, 299,* 117–120.

Shirayama, Y., Chen, A. C., Nakagawa, S., Russell, D. S., et al. (2002). Brain-derived neurotrophic factor produces antidepressant effects in behavioral models of depression. *Journal of Neuroscience, 22,* 3251–3261.

Shors, T. J., Miesegaes, G., Beylin, A., Zhao, M., et al. (2001). Neurogenesis in the adult is involved in the formation of trace memories. *Nature, 410,* 372–376.

Siarey, R. J., Coan, E. J., Rapoport, S. I., and Galdzicki, Z. (1997). Responses to NMDA in cultured hippocampal neurons from trisomy 16 mice. *Neuroscience Letters, 232,* 131–134.

Sibley, C. G., and Ahlquist, J. E. (1987). DNA hybridization evidence of hominoid phylogeny: Results from an expanded data set. *Journal of Molecular Evolution, 26,* 99–121.

Sibley, C. G., and Ahlquist, J. E. (1990). *Phylogeny and classification of birds: A study in molecular evolution.* New Haven, CT: Yale University Press.

Sibley, C. G., Comstock, J. A., and Ahlquist, J. E. (1990). DNA hybridization evidence of hominoid phylogeny: A reanalysis of the data. *Journal of Molecular Evolution, 30,* 202–236.

Siegel, J. M. (1994). Brainstem mechanisms generating REM sleep. In M. H. Kryger, T. Roth, and W. C. Dement (Eds.), *Principles and practice of sleep medicine* (2nd ed., pp. 125–144). Philadelphia: Saunders.

Siegel, J. M. (2001). The REM sleep–memory consolidation hypothesis. *Science, 294,* 1058–1063.

Siegel, J. M., Manger, P. R., Nienhuis, R., Fahringer, H. M., et al. (1999). Sleep in the platypus. *Neuroscience, 91,* 391–400.

Siegel, J. M., Nienhuis, R., Gulyani, S., Ouyang, S., et al. (1999). Neuronal degeneration in canine narcolepsy. *Journal of Neuroscience, 19,* 248–257.

Siegel, R. K. (1989). Intoxication: Life in pursuit of artificial paradise. New York: Dutton.

Sillaber, I., Rammes, G., Zimmermann, S., Mahal, B., et al. (2002). Enhanced and delayed stress-induced alcohol drinking in mice lacking functional CRH1 receptors. *Science, 296,* 931–933.

Silva, A. J., Paylor, R., Wehner, J. M., and Tonegawa, S. (1992). Impaired spatial learning in alpha-calcium-calmodulin kinase II mutant mice. *Science, 257,* 206–211.

Silva, D. A., and Satz, P. (1979). Pathological left-handedness. Evaluation of a model. *Brain and Language, 7,* 8–16.

Silver, R., Lesauter, J., Tresco, P., and Lehman, M. (1996). A diffusible coupling signal from the transplanted suprachiasmatic nucleus controlling circadian locomotor rhythms. *Nature, 382,* 810–813.

Simic, G., Kostovic, I., Winblad, B., and Bogdanovic, N. (1997). Volume and number of neurons of the human hippocampal formation in normal aging and Alzheimer's disease. *Journal of Comparative Neurology, 379,* 482–494.

Singer, N. (2002). Ambitious plan to give sight to the blind. *Sandia Lab News, 54,* 19, 1.

Singer, P. (1975). *Animal liberation: A new ethics for our treatment of animals.* New York: New York Review.

Singh, D. (2002). Female mate value at a glance: Relationship of waist-to-hip ratio to health, fecundity and attractiveness. *Neuroendocrinology Letters, 23*(Suppl. 4), 81–91.

Siveter, D. J., Sutton, M. D., Briggs, D. E., and Siveter, D. J. (2003). An ostracode crustacean with soft parts from the Lower Silurian. *Science, 302,* 1749–1751.

Skinner, M., Holden, L., and Holden, T. (1997). Parameter selection to optimize speech recognition with the nucleus implant. *Otolaryngology and Head and Neck Surgery, 117,* 188–195.

Smale, L. (1988). Influence of male gonadal hormones and familiarity on pregnancy interruption in prairie voles. *Biology of Reproduction, 39,* 28–31.

Smale, L., Holekamp, K. E., and White, P. A. (1999). Siblicide revisited in the spotted hyaena: Does it conform to obligate or facultative models? *Animal Behaviour, 58,* 545–551.

Smith, A., and Sugar, O. (1975). Development of above normal language and intelligence 21 years after hemispherectomy. *Neurology, 25,* 813–818.

Smith, C. (1985). Sleep states and learning. A review of the animal literature. *Neuroscience and Biobehavioral Reviews, 9,* 157–169.

Smith, C. (1995). Sleep states and memory processes. *Behavioural Brain Research, 69,* 137–145.

Smith, C. M., and Luskin, M. B. (1998). Cell cycle length of olfactory bulb neuronal progenitors in the rostral migratory stream. *Developmental Dynamics, 213,* 220–227.

Smith, D. E., Roberts, J., Gage, F. H., and Tuszynski, M. H. (1999). Age-associated neuronal atrophy occurs in the primate brain and is reversible by growth factor gene therapy. *Proceedings of the National Academy of Sciences, USA, 96,* 10893–10898.

Smith, M. A., Brandt, J., and Shadmehr, R. (2000). Motor disorder in Huntington's disease begins as a dysfunction in error feedback control. *Nature, 403,* 544–549.

Smith, P. B., Compton, D. R., Welch, S. P., Razdan, R. K., et al. (1994). The pharmacological activity of anandamide, a putative endogenous cannabinoid, in mice. *Journal of Pharmacology and Experimental Therapeutics, 270,* 219–227.

Smith, S. (1997, September 2). Dreaming awake Part 1: Living with narcolepsy. *Minnesota Public Radio News* (http://news.minnesota.publicradio.org/features/199709/02_smiths_narcolepsy/narco_1.shtml).

Smith, S. J. (1999). Dissecting dendrite dynamics. *Science, 283,* 1860–1861.

Snider, S. R. (1982). Cerebellar pathology in schizophrenia—Cause or consequence? *Neuroscience and Biobehavioral Reviews, 6,* 47–53.

Snyder, F. (1969). Sleep and REM as biological enigmas. In A. Kales (Ed.), *Sleep: Physiology and pathology* (pp. 266–280). Philadelphia: Lippincott.

Snyder, S. H., and D'Amato, R. J. (1985). Predicting Parkinson's disease. *Nature, 317,* 198–199.

Sobel, N., Khan, R. M., Saltman, A., Sullivan, E. V., et al. (1999). The world smells different to each nostril. *Nature, 402,* 35.

Sobel, N., Prabhakaran, V., Desmond, J. E., Glover, G. H., et al. (1998). Sniffing and smelling: Separate subsystems in the human olfactory cortex. *Nature, 392,* 282–286.

Sobel, N., Prabhakaran, V., Zhao, Z., Desmond, J. E., et al. (2000). Time course of odorant-induced activation in the human primary olfactory cortex. *Journal of Neurophysiology, 83,* 537–551.

Solomon, A. (2001). *The noonday demon: An atlas of depression,* New York: Scribner.

Solomon, P. R., Adams, F., Silver, A., Zimmer, J., et al. (2002). Ginkgo for memory enhancement: A randomized controlled trial. *JAMA, 288,* 835–840.

Sorensen, P. W., and Goetz, F. W. (1993). Pheromonal and reproductive function of F prostaglandins and their metabolites in teleost fish. *Journal of Lipid Mediators, 6,* 385–393.

Spear, N. F. (1976). Retrieval of memories: A psychobiological approach. In W. K. Estes (Ed.), *Handbook of learning and cognitive processes: Vol. 4. Attention and memory.* Hillsdale, NJ: Erlbaum.

Sperry, R. W. (1974). Lateral specialization in the surgically separated hemispheres. In F. O. Schmitt and F. G. Worden (Eds.), *The neurosciences: Third study program* (pp. 5-16). Cambridge, MA: MIT Press.

Sperry, R. W., Stamm, J., and Miner, N. (1956). Relearning tests for interocular transfer following division of optic chiasma and corpus callosum in cats. *Journal of Comparative and Physiological Psychology, 49,* 529–533.

Spiegler, B. J., and Mishkin, M. (1981). Evidence for the sequential participation of inferior temporal cortex and amygdala in the acquisition of stimulus-reward associations. *Behavioural Brain Research, 3,* 303–317.

Spiegler, B. J., and Yeni-Komshian, G. H. (1983). Incidence of left-handed writing in a college population with reference to family patterns of hand preference. *Neuropsychologia, 21,* 651–659.

Squire, L. R., Amaral, D. G., Zola-Morgan, S., and Kritchevsky, M. P. G. (1989). Description of brain injury in the amnesic patient N.A. based on magnetic resonance imaging. *Experimental Neurology, 105,* 23–35.

Squire, L. R., and Kandel, R. R. (1999). *Memory: From mind to molecules.* New York: Scientific American Library.

Squire, L. R., and Moore, R. Y. (1979). Dorsal thalamic lesion in a noted case of chronic memory dysfunction. *Annals of Neurology, 6,* 503–506.

Squire, L. R., and Zola-Morgan, S. (1991). The medial temporal lobe memory system. *Science, 253,* 1380–1386.

Standing, L. G. (1973). Learning 10,000 pictures. *Quarterly Journal of Experimental Psychology, 25,* 207–222.

Starkstein, S. E., and Robinson, R. G. (1994). Neuropsychiatric aspects of stroke. In C. E. Coffey, J. L. Cummings, M. R. Lovell, and G. D. Pearlson (Eds.), *The American Psychiatric Press textbook of geriatric neuropsychiatry* (pp. 457–477). Washington, DC: American Psychiatric Press.

Staubli, U. V. (1995). Parallel properties of long-term potentiation and memory. In J. L. McGaugh, N. M. Weinberger, and G. Lynch (Eds.), *Brain and memory: Modulation and mediation of neuroplasticity* (pp. 303–318). New York: Oxford University Press.

Stein, B., and Meredith, M. A. (1993). *The merging of the senses.* Cambridge, MA: MIT Press.

Stein, M., and Miller, A. H. (1993). Stress, the hypothalamic-pituitary-adrenal axis, and immune function. *Advances in Experimental Medicine and Biology, 335,* 1–5.

Stein, M., Miller, A. H., and Trestman, R. L. (1991). Depression, the immune system, and health and illness. Findings in search of meaning. *Archives of General Psychiatry, 48,* 171–177.

Steinmetz, H., Volkmann, J., Jancke, L., and Freund, H. J. (1991). Anatomical left-right asymmetry of language-related temporal cortex is different in left- and right-handers. *Annals of Neurology, 29,* 315–319.

Stella, N., Schweitzer, P., and Piomelli, D. (1997). A second endogenous cannabinoid that modulates long-term potentiation. *Nature, 388,* 773–778.

Stephan, F. K., and Zucker, I. (1972). Circadian rhythms in drinking behavior and locomotor activity of rats are eliminated by hypothalamic lesions. *Proceedings of the National Academy of Sciences, USA, 69,* 1583–1586.

Stephan, H., Frahm, H., and Baron, G. (1981). New and revised data on volumes of brain structures in insectivores and primates. *Folia Primatologica, 35,* 1–29.

Steptoe, A. (1993). Stress and the cardiovascular system: A psychosocial perspective. In S. C. Stanford and P. Salmon (Eds.), *Stress: From synapse to syndrome* (pp. 119–141). London: Academic Press.

Stern, C. E., Corkin, S., Gonzalez, R. G., Guimaraes, A. R., et al. (1996). The hippocampal formation participates in novel picture encoding: Evidence from functional magnetic resonance imaging. *Proceedings of the National Academy of Sciences, USA, 93,* 8660–8665.

Stern, K., and McClintock, M. (1998). Regulation of ovulation by human pheromones. *Nature, 392,* 177–179.

Sternberg, R. J. (2000). Cognition. The holy grail of general intelligence. *Science, 289,* 399–401.

Stoerig, P., and Cowey, A. (1997). Blindsight in man and monkey. *Brain, 120,* 535–559.

Stone, V. E., Nisenson, L., Eliassen, J. C., and Gazzaniga, M. S. (1996). Left hemisphere representations of emotional facial expressions. *Neuropsychologia, 34,* 23–29.

Stowers L., Holy, T. E., Meister, M., Dulac, C., et al. (2002). Loss of sex discrimination and male-male aggression in mice deficient for TRP2. *Science, 295,* 1493–1500.

Strakowski, S. M., DelBello, M. P., Zimmerman, M. E., Getz, G. E., et al. (2002). Ventricular and periventricular structural volumes in first- versus multiple-episode bipolar disorder. *American Journal of Psychiatry, 159,* 1841–1847.

Stricker, E. M. (1977). The renin-angiotensin system and thirst: A reevaluation. II. Drinking elicited in rats by caval ligation or isoproterenol. *Journal of Comparative and Physiological Psychology, 91,* 1220–1231.

Strittmatter, W. J., and Roses, A. D. (1996). Apolipoprotein E and Alzheimer's disease. *Annual Review of Neuroscience, 19,* 53–77.

Stuve, T. A., Friedman, L., Jesberger, J. A., Gilmore, G. C., et al. (1997). The relationship between smooth pursuit performance, motion perception and sustained visual attention in patients with schizophrenia and normal controls. *Psychological Medicine, 27,* 143–152.

Substance Abuse and Mental Health Services Administration. (2003). *Results from the 2002 National Survey on Drug Use and Health: National Findings* (DHHS Publication No. SMA 03–3836, NHSDA Series H-22). Rockville, MD: Substance Abuse and Mental Health Services Administration, Office of Applied Studies.

Sunn, N., Egli, M., Burazin, T. C. D., Burns, P., et al. (2002). Circulating relaxin acts on subfornical organ neurons to stimulate water drinking in the rat. *Proceedings of the National Academy of Sciences, USA, 99,* 1701–1706.

Sutcliffe, J. G., and de Lecea, L. (2002). The hypocretins: Setting the arousal threshold. *Nature Reviews. Neuroscience, 3,* 339–349.Suzuki, M., Nohara, S., Hagino, H., Kurokawa, K., et al. (2002). Regional changes in brain gray and white matter in patients with schizophrenia demonstrated with voxel-based analysis of MRI. *Schizophrenia Research, 55,* 41–54.

Sweet, W. H. (1973). Treatment of medically intractable mental disease by limited frontal leucotomy—Justifiable? *New England Journal of Medicine, 289,* 1117–1125.

Szalavitz, M. (2004, March 25). The accidental addict: Clearing away the myths surrounding the OxyContin "epidemic." *Slate* (http://slate.msn.com/id/2097786).

Szente, M., Gajda, Z., Said Ali, K., and Hermesz, E. (2002). Involvement of electrical coupling in the in vivo ictal epileptiform activity induced by 4-aminopyridine in the neocortex. *Neuroscience, 115,* 1067–1078.

Taipale, M., Kaminen, N., Nopola-Hemmi, J., Haltia, T., et al. (2003). A candidate gene for developmental dyslexia encodes a nuclear tetratricopeptide repeat domain protein dynamically regulated in brain. *Proceedings of the National Academy of Sciences, USA, 100,* 11553–11558.

Takahashi, J. S. (1995). Molecular neurobiology and genetics of circadian rhythms in mammals. *Annual Review of Neuroscience, 18,* 531–554.

Talairach, J., and Tournoux, P. (1988). Co-planar stereotaxic atlas of the human brain: A 3-dimensional proportional system: an approach to cerebral imaging. Stuttgart, Germany: Thieme.

Tallal, P., Galaburda, A. M., Llinas, R. R., and von Euler, C. (1993). *Temporal information processing in the nervous system: Special reference to dyslexia and dysphasia.* New York: New York Academy of Sciences.

Tallal, P., and Schwartz, J. (1980). Temporal processing, speech perception and hemispheric asymmetry. *Trends in Neurosciences, 3,* 309–311.

Tamás, G., Lörincz, A., Simon, A., and Szabadics, J. (2003). Identified sources and targets of slow inhibition in the neocortex. *Science, 299,* 1902–1905.

Tamminga, C. A., and Schulz, S. C. (1991). *Schizophrenia research.* New York: Raven.

Tanaka, K. (1993). Neuronal mechanisms of object recognition. *Science, 262,* 685–688.

Tanaka, Y., Kamo, T., Yoshida, M., and Yamadori, A. (1991). "So-called" cortical deafness. Clinical, neurophysiological and radiological observations. *Brain, 114,* 2385–2401.

Tanda, G., Munzar, P., and Goldberg, S. R. (2000). Self-administration behavior is maintained by the psychoactive ingredient of marijuana in squirrel monkeys. *Nature Neuroscience, 3,* 1073–1074.

Tang, N. M., Dong, H. W., Wang, X. M., Tsui, Z. C., et al. (1997). Cholecystokinin antisense RNA increases the analgesic effect induced by electroacupuncture or low dose morphine: Conversion of low responder rats into high responders. *Pain, 71,* 71–80.

Tang, Y. P., Shimizu, E., Dube, G. R., Rampon, C., et al. (1999). Genetic enhancement of learning and memory in mice. *Nature, 401,* 63–69.

Tanila, H., Shapiro, M., Gallagher, M., and Eichenbaum, H. (1997). Brain aging: Changes in the nature of information coding by the hippocampus. *Journal of Neuroscience, 17,* 5155–5166.

Tanila, H., Sipila, P., Shapiro, M., and Eichenbaum, H. (1997). Brain aging: Impaired coding of novel environmental cues. *Journal of Neuroscience, 17,* 5167–5174.

Tanji, J. (2001). Sequential organization of multiple movements: Involvement of cortical motor areas. *Annual Review of Neuroscience, 24,* 631–651.

Taub, E. (1976). Movement in nonhuman primates deprived of somatosensory feedback. *Exercise and Sport Sciences Reviews, 4,* 335–374.

Taub, E., Uswatte, G., and Elbert, T. (2002). New treatments in neurorehabilitation founded on basic research. *Nature Reviews. Neuroscience, 3,* 228–235.

Teasdale, J. D., Howard, R. J., Cox, S. G., Ha, Y., et al. (1999). Functional study of the cognitive generation of affect. *American Journal of Psychiatry, 156,* 209–215.

Teitelbaum, P., and Stellar, E. (1954). Recovery from failure to eat produced by hypothalamic lesions. *Science, 120,* 894–895.

Tenn, W. (1968). *The seven sexes.* New York: Ballantine.

Terman, G. W., Shavit, Y., Lewis, J. W., Cannon, J. T., et al. (1984). Intrinsic mechanisms of pain inhibition: Activation by stress. *Science, 226,* 1270–1277.

Terrace, H. S. (1979). *Nim.* New York: Knopf.

Terrazas, A., and McNaughton, B. L. (2000). Brain growth and the cognitive map. *Proceedings of the National Academy of Sciences, USA, 97,* 4414–4416.

Tessier-Lavigne, M., and Placzek, M. (1991). Target attraction: Are developing axons guided by chemotropism? *Trends in Neurosciences, 14,* 303–310.

Tessier-Lavigne, M., Placzek, M., Lumsden, A. G., Dodd, J., et al. (1988). Chemotropic guidance of developing axons in the mammalian central nervous system. *Nature, 336,* 775–778.

Tetel, M. J. (2000). Nuclear receptor coactivators in neuroendocrine function. *Journal of Neuroendocrinology, 12,* 927–932.

Teuber, H.-L., Milner, B., and Vaughan, H. G. (1968). Persistent anterograde amnesia after stab wound of the basal brain. *Neuropsychologia, 6,* 267–282.

Tewksbury, J. J., and Nabhan, G. P. (2001). Directed deterrence by capsaicin in chillies. *Nature, 412,* 402–403.

Teyler, T. J., and DiScenna, P. (1986). Long-term potentiation. *Annual Review of Neuroscience, 10,* 131–161.

Thannickal, T. C., Moore, R. Y., Nienhuis, R., Ramanathan, L., et al. (2000). Reduced number of hypocretin neurons in human narcolepsy. *Neuron, 27,* 469–474.

Thaw, A. K., Frankmann, S., and Hill, D. L. (2000). Behavioral taste responses of developmentally

NaCl-restricted rats to various concentrations of NaCl. *Behavioral Neuroscience, 114,* 437–441.

Thiruchelvam, M., Richfield, E. K., Baggs, R. B., Tank, A. W., et al. (2000). The nigrostriatal system as a preferential target of repeated exposures to combined parquat and maneb: Implications for Parkinson's disease. *Journal of Neuroscience, 20,* 9207–9214.

Thompson, P. M., Giedd, J. N., Woods, R. P., MacDonald, D., et al. (2000). Growth patterns in the developing brain detected by using continuum mechanical tensor maps. *Nature, 404,* 190–193.

Thompson, P. M., Vidal, C., Giedd, J. N., Gochman, P., et al. (2001). Mapping adolescent brain change reveals dynamic wave of accelerated gray matter loss in very early-onset schizophrenia. *Proceedings of the National Academy of Sciences, USA, 98,* 11650–11655.

Thompson, R. F. (1990). Neural mechanisms of classical conditioning in mammals. Philosophical Transactions of the Royal Society of London. Series B: Biological Sciences, 329, 161–170.

Thompson, R. F., and Krupa, D. J. (1994). Organization of memory traces in the mammalian brain. *Annual Review of Neuroscience, 17,* 519–549.

Thompson, R. F., Thompson, J. K., Kim, J. J., Krupa, D. J., et al. (1998). The nature of reinforcement in cerebellar learning. *Neurobiology of Learning and Memory, 70,* 150–176.

Thompson, T., and Schuster, C. R. (1964). Morphine self-administration, food reinforced and avoidance behaviour in rhesus monkeys. *Psychopharmacologia, 5,* 87–94.

Thorndike, E. L. (1898). *Animal intelligence, an experimental study of the associative processes in animals.* New York: Macmillan.

Thorpe, S. J., and Fabre-Thorpe, M (2001). Seeking categories in the brain. *Science, 291,* 260–263.

Thurber, J., and White, E. B. (1929). *Is sex necessary? or, Why you feel the way you do.* New York: Harper and Bros.

Tissir, F., and Goffinet, A. M. (2003). Reelin and brain development. *Nature Reviews. Neuroscience, 4,* 496–505.

Tkachev, D., Mimmack, M. L., Ryan, M. M., Wayland, M., et al. (2003). Oligodendrocyte dysfunction in schizophrenia and bipolar disorder. *Lancet, 362,* 798–805.

Tobias, P. V. (1980). L'evolution du cerveau humain. *La Recherche, 11,* 282–292.

Tolman, E. C. (1949a). *Purposive behavior in animals and men.* Berkeley: University of California Press.

Tolman, E. C. (1949b). There is more than one kind of learning. *Psychological Review, 56,* 144–155.

Tolman, E. C., and Honzik, C. H. (1930). Introduction and removal of reward, and maze performance in rats. *University of California Publications in Psychology, 4,* 257–275.

Tomizawa, K., Iga, N., Lu, Y. F., Moriwaki, A., et al. (2003). Oxytocin improves long-lasting spatial memory during motherhood through MAP kinase cascade. *Nature Neuroscience, 6,* 384–390.

Tootell, R. B. H., Hadjikhani, N. K., Vanduffel, W., Liu, A. K., et al. (1998). Functional analysis of primary visual cortex (V1) in humans. *Proceedings of the National Academy of Sciences, USA, 95,* 811–817.

Tootell, R. B., Silverman, M. S., Hamilton, S. L., De Valois, R. L., et al. (1988). Functional anatomy of macaque striate cortex. III. Color. *Journal of Neuroscience, 8,* 1569–1593.

Tootell, R. B., Silverman, M. S., Switkes, E., and De Valois, R. L. (1982). Deoxyglucose analysis of retinotopic organization in primate striate cortex. *Science, 218,* 902–904.

Tootell, R. B., Tsao, D., and Vanduffel, W. (2003). Neuroimaging weighs in: Humans meet macaques in "primate" visual cortex. *Journal of Neuroscience, 23,* 3981–3989.

Tordoff, M., Rawson, N., and Friedman, M. (1991). 2,5-anhydro-d-mannitol acts in liver to initiate feeding. *American Journal of Physiology, 261,* R283–R288.

Torrey, E. F. (2002). Severe psychiatric disorders may be increasing. *Psychiatric Times, 19,* 1–6.

Torrey, E. F., Bowler, A. E., Taylor, E. H., and Gottesman, I. I. (1994). *Schizophrenia and manic depressive disorder.* New York: Basic Books.

Trachtenberg, J. T., Chen, B. E., Knott, G. W., Feng, G., et al. (2002). Long-term in vivo imaging of experience-dependent synaptic plasticity in adult cortex. *Nature, 420,* 788–794.

Travis, J. (1992). Can "hair cells" unlock deafness? *Science, 257,* 1344–1345.

Treisman, M. (1977). Motion sickness— Evolutionary hypotheses. *Science, 197,* 493–495.

Trimble, M. R. (1991). Interictal psychoses of epilepsy. *Advances in Neurology, 55,* 143–152.

True, W. R., Rice, J., Eisen, S. A., Heath, A. C., et al. (1993). A twin study of genetic and environmental contributions to liability for posttraumatic stress symptoms. *Archives of General Psychiatry, 50,* 257–264.

Truitt, W. A., and Coolen, L. M. (2002). Identification of a potential ejaculation generator in the spinal cord. *Science, 297,* 1566–1569.

Truitt, W. A., Shipley, M. T., Veening, J. G., and Coolen, L. M. (2003). Activation of a subset of lumbar spinothalamic neurons after copulatory behavior in male but not female rats. *Journal of Neuroscience, 23,* 325–331.

Tschöp, M., Castañeda, T. R., Joost, H. G., Thöne-Reinke, C., et al.(2004) Physiology: Does gut hormone PYY_{3-36} decrease food intake in rodents? *Nature, 430,* Brief Communications Arising (online only at www.nature.com).

Ts'o, D. Y., Frostig, R. D., Lieke, E. E., and Grinvald, A. (1990). Functional organization of primate visual cortex revealed by high resolution optical imaging. *Science, 249,* 417–420.

Tuller, D. (2002, January 8). A quiet revolution for those prone to nodding off. *The New York Times On the Web* (http://query.nytimes.com/gst/abstract.html?res=F70714FC3F5D0C7B8CDDA80894DA404482).

Tully, T. (1991). Physiology of mutations affecting learning and memory in *Drosophila*—The missing link between gene product and behavior. *Trends in Neurosciences, 14,* 163–164.

Tulving, E. (1972). Episodic and semantic memory. In E. Tulving and W. Donaldson (Eds.), *Organization of memory* (pp. 381–403). New York: Academic Press.

Tulving, E. (1989). Memory: Performance, knowledge, and experience. *European Journal of Cognitive Psychology, 1,* 3–26.

Tulving, E., Hayman, C. A., and Macdonald, C. A. (1991). Long-lasting perceptual priming and semantic learning in amnesia: A case experiment. *Journal of Experimental Psychology: Learning, Memory, and Cognition, 17,* 595–617.

Tulving, E., and Markowitsch, H. J. (1997). Memory beyond the hippocampus. *Current Opinion in Neurobiology, 7,* 209–216.

Tulving, E., Markowitsch, H. J., Craik, F. E., Habib, R., et al. (1996). Novelty and familiarity activations in PET studies of memory encoding and retrieval. *Cerebral Cortex, 6,* 71–79.

Twain, M. (1897). *Following the Equator: A journey around the world.* Hartford, CT: American.

Twain, M. (1990). *The autobiography of Mark Twain: Including chapters now published for the first time* (as arranged and edited, with an introduction and notes, by Charles Neider). New York: HarperPerennial. (Reprint; originally published: New York: Harper, 1959.)

Underwood, B. J. (1969). Attributes of memory. *Psychology Review, 76,* 559–573.

Ungerleider, L. G., Courtney, S. M., and Haxby, J. V. (1998). A neural system for human visual working memory. *Proceedings of the National Academy of Sciences, USA, 95,* 883–890.

Ungles, M. A., Whistler, J. L., Malenka, R. C., and Bonci, A. (2001). Single cocaine exposure in vivo induces long-term potentiation in dopamine neurons. *Nature, 411,* 583–586.

Ursin, H., Baade, E., and Levine, S. (1978). *Psychobiology of stress: A study of coping men.* New York: Academic Press.

Valbo, A. B., and Johansson, R. S. (1984). Properties of cutaneous mechanoreceptors in the human hand related to touch sensation. *Human Neurobiology, 3,* 3–15.

Valenstein, E. S. (1986). Great and desperate cures: The rise and decline of psychosurgery and other radical treatments for mental illness. New York: Basic Books.

Vallbona, C., Hazlewood, C., and Jurida, G. (1997). Response of pain to static magnetic fields in postpolio patients: A double-blind pilot study. *Archives of Physical Medicine and Rehabilitation, 78,* 1200–1203.

Vallortigara, G., Rogers, L. J., and Bisazza, A. (1999). Possible evolutionary origins of cognitive brain lateralization. *Brain Research. Brain Research Reviews, 30,* 164–175.

van Bergeijk, W. A. (1967). The evolution of vertebrate hearing. In W. D. Neff (Ed.), *Contributions to sensory physiology: Vol. 3.* New York: Academic Press.

Vander Wall, S. B. (1982). An experimental analysis of cache recovery in Clark's nutcracker. *Animal Behaviour, 30,* 84–94.

Van Dongen, H. P., Maislin, G, Mullington, J. M., and Dinges, D. F. (2003). The cumulative cost of additional wakefulness: Dose–response effects on neurobehavioral functions and sleep physiology from chronic sleep restriction and total sleep deprivation. *Sleep, 26,* 117–126.

VanDoren, M. J., Matthews, D. B., Janis, G. C., Grobin, A. C., et al. (2000). Neuroactive steroid 3alpha-hydroxy-5alpha-pregnan-20-one modulates electrophysiological and behavioral actions of ethanol. *Journal of Neuroscience, 20,* 1982–1989.

Van Essen, D. C., and Drury, H. A. (1997). Structural and functional analyses of human cerebral cortex using a surface-based atlas. *Journal of Neuroscience, 17,* 7079–7102.

van Praag, H., Kempermann, G., and Gage, F. H. (2000). Neural consequences of environmental enrichment. *Nature Reviews. Neuroscience, 1,* 191–198.

van Valen, L. (1974). Brain size and intelligence in man. *American Journal of Physical Anthropology, 40,* 417–423.

van Zoeren, J. G., and Stricker, E. M. (1977). Effects of preoptic, lateral hypothalamic, or dopamine-depleting lesions on behavioral thermoregulation in rats exposed to the cold. *Journal of Comparative and Physiological Psychology, 91,* 989–999.

Vasey, P. L. (1995). Homosexual behaviour in primates: A review of evidence and theory. *International Journal of Primatology, 16,* 173–204.

Vassar, R., Ngai, J., and Axel, R. (1993). Spatial segregation of odorant receptor expression in the mammalian olfactory epithelium. *Cell, 74,* 309–318.

Vaughan, W., and Greene, S. L. (1984). Pigeon visual memory capacity. *Journal of Experimental Psychology: Animal Behavior Processes, 10,* 256–271.

Veraa, R. P., and Grafstein, B. (1981). Cellular mechanisms for recovery from nervous system injury: A conference report. *Experimental Neurology, 71,* 6–75.

Verhagen, A. M., Ekert, P. G., Pakusch, M., Silke, J., et al. (2000). Identification of DIABLO, a mammalian protein that promotes apoptosis by binding to and antagonizing IAP proteins. *Cell, 102,* 43–53.

Vertes, R. P., and Eastman, K. E. (2000). The case against memory consolidation in REM sleep. *Behavioral and Brain Sciences, 23,* 867–876.

Villringer, A., and Chance, B. (1997). Non-invasive optical spectroscopy and imaging of human brain function. *Trends in Neurosciences, 20,* 435–442.

Virkkunen, M., and Linnoila, M. (1993). Brain serotonin, type II alcoholism and impulsive violence. *Journal of Studies on Alcohol (Supplement), 11,* 163–169.

Vogel, G. (1997). Cocaine wreaks subtle damage on developing brains. *Science, 278,* 38–39.

Vogel, G. (1999). Chimps in the wild show stirrings of culture. *Science, 284,* 2070–2073.

Vogel, G. W., Vogel, F., McAbee, R. S., and Thurmond, A. J. (1980). Improvement of depression by REM sleep deprivation: New findings and a theory. *Archives of General Psychiatry, 37,* 247–253.

Volkmar, F. R., and Greenough, W. T. (1972). Rearing complexity affects branching of dendrites in the visual cortex of the rat. *Science, 176,* 1445–1447.

Voneida, T. J. (1990). The effect of rubrospinal tractotomy on a conditioned limb response in the cat. *Society for Neuroscience Abstracts, 16,* 279.

Vythilingam, M., Anderson, E. R., Goddard, A., Woods, S. W., et al. (2000). Temporal lobe volume in panic disorder—A quantitative magnetic resonance imaging study. *Psychiatry Research, 99,* 75–82.

Wada, J. A., and Rasmussen, T. (1960). Intracarotid injection of sodium amytal for the lateralization of cerebral speech dominance: Experimental and clinical observations. *Journal of Neurosurgery, 17,* 266–282.

Wade, J., and Arnold, A. P. (1996). Functional testicular tissue does not masculinize development of the zebra finch song system. *Proceedings of the National Academy of Sciences, USA, 93,* 5264–5268.

Wagner, A. D., Desmond, J. E., Demb, J. B., Glover, G. H., et al. (1997). Semantic repetition priming for verbal and pictorial knowledge: A functional MRI study of left inferior prefrontal cortex. *Journal of Cognitive Neuroscience, 9,* 714–726.

Wagner, A. D., Schacter, D. L., Rotte, M., Koutstaal, W., et al. (1998). Building memories: Remembering and forgetting of verbal experiences as predicted by brain activity. *Science, 281,* 1188–1191.

Wagner, G. C., Beuving, L. J., and Hutchinson, R. R. (1980). The effects of gonadal hormone manipulations on aggressive target-biting in mice. *Aggressive Behavior, 6,* 1–7.

Wahl, O. F. (1976). Monozygotic twins discordant for schizophrenia: A review. *Psychological Bulletin, 83,* 91–106.

Wald, G. (1964). The receptors of human color vision. *Science, 145,* 1007–1016.

Walker, E. F. (1991). Schizophrenia: A life-course developmental perspective. San Diego, CA: Academic Press.

Walls, G. L. (1942). *The vertebrate eye: Vol. 1.* Bloomfield Hills, MI: Cranbrook Institute of Science.

Walsh, E. J., Wang, L. M., Armstrong, D. L., Curro, T., et al. (2003). Acoustic communication in *Panthera tigris:* A study of tiger vocalization and auditory receptivity. In Special Session on: Nature's orchestra: Acoustics of singing and calling animals—Production and reception of sound for communication by underwater and terrestrial animals. *Journal of the Acoustical Society of America, 113,* 2275.

Walters, R. J., Hadley, S. H., Morris, K. D. W., and Amin, J. (2000). Benzodiazepines act on $GABA_A$ receptors via two distinct and separable mechanisms. *Nature Neuroscience, 3,* 1273–1280.

Wang, F., Nemes, A., Mendelsohn, M., and Axel, R. (1998). Odorant receptors govern the formation of a precise topographic map. *Cell, 93,* 47–60.

Wang, H., Yu, M., Ochani, M., Amella, C. A., et al. (2003). Nicotinic acetylcholine receptor α7 subunit is an essential regulator of inflammation. *Nature, 421,* 384–388.

Wang, J. B., Imai, Y., Eppler, C. M., Gregor, P., et al. (1993). μ Opiate receptor: cDNA cloning and expression. *Proceedings of the National Academy of Sciences, USA, 90,* 10230–10234.

Wareing, M., Fisk, J. E., and Murphy, P. N. (2000). Working memory deficits in current and previous users of MDMA ("ecstasy"). *British Journal of Psychology, 91,* 181–188.

Watkin, P. M. (2001). Neonatal screening for hearing impairment. *Seminars in Neonatology, 6,* 501–509.

Watson, J. D., and Crick, F. H. C. (1953). A structure for deoxyribose nucleic acid. *Nature, 171,* 737.

Watson, N. V., Freeman, L. M., and Breedlove, S. M. (2001). Neuronal size in the spinal nucleus of the bulbocavernosus: Direct modulation by androgen in rats with mosaic androgen insensitivity. *Journal of Neuroscience, 21,* 1062–1066.

Webb, W. B. (1992). *Sleep, the gentle tyrant.* Bolton, MA: Anker.

Wedekind, C., Seebeck, T., Bettens, F., and Paepke, A. J. (1995). MHC-dependent mate preferences in humans. *Proceedings of the Royal Society of London. Series B: Biological Sciences, 260,* 245–249.

Wehling, M. (1997). Specific, nongenomic actions of steroid hormones. *Annual Review of Physiology, 59,* 365–393.

Wehr, T. A., Goodwin, F. K., Wirz-Justice, A., Breitmaier, J., et al. (1982). 48-hour sleep-wake cycles in manic-depressive illness: Naturalistic observations and sleep deprivation experiments. *Archives of General Psychiatry, 39,* 559–565.

Wehr, T. A., Sack, D. A., Duncan, W. C., Mendelson, W. B., et al. (1985). Sleep and circadian rhythms in affective patients isolated from external time cues. *Psychiatry Research, 15,* 327–339.

Wei, F., Wang G. D., Kerchner, G. A., Kim, S. J., et al. (2001). Genetic enhancement of inflammatory pain by forebrain NR2B overexpression. *Nature Neuroscience, 4,* 164–169.

Weinberger, D. R., Aloia, M. S., Goldberg, T. E., and Berman, K. F. (1994). The frontal lobes and schizophrenia. *Journal of Neuropsychiatry and Clinical Neurosciences, 6,* 419–427.

Weinberger, D. R., Bigelow, L. B., Kleinman, J. E., Klein, S. T., et al. (1980). Cerebral ventricular enlargement in chronic schizophrenia. An association with poor response to treatment. *Archives of General Psychiatry, 37,* 11–13.

Weinberger, N. M. (1998). Physiological memory in primary auditory cortex: Characteristics and mechanisms. *Neurobiology of Learning and Memory, 70,* 226–251.

Weindruch, R., and Walford, R. L. (1988). *The retardation of aging and disease by dietary restriction.* Springfield, IL: Thomas.

Weiner, R. D. (1994). Treatment optimization with ECT. *Psychopharmacology Bulletin, 30,* 313–320.

Weitzman, E. D. (1981). Sleep and its disorders. *Annual Review of Neurosciences, 4,* 381–417.

Weitzman, E. D., Czeisler, C. A., Zimmerman, J. C., and Moore-Ede, M. C. (1981). Biological rhythms in man: Relationship of sleep-wake, cortisol, growth hormone, and temperature during temporal isolation. In J. B. Martin, S. Reichlin, and K. L. Bick (Eds.), *Neurosecretion and brain peptides.* New York: Raven.

Welch, D. M., and Meselson, M. (2000). Evidence for the evolution of bdelloid rotifers without sexual reproduction or genetic exchange. *Science, 288,* 1211–1215.

Weller, L., and Weller, A. (1993). Human menstrual synchrony: A critical assessment. *Neuroscience and Biobehavioral Reviews, 17,* 427–439.

Wesensten, N. J., Belenky, G., Kautz, M.A., Thorne, D. R., et al. (2002). Maintaining alertness and performance during sleep deprivation: Modafinil versus caffeine. *Psychopharmacology, 159,* 238–247.

Wessberg, J., Stambaugh, C. R., Kralik, J. D., Beck, P. D., et al. (2000). Real-time predictions of hand trajectory by ensembles of cortical neurons in primates. *Nature, 408,* 361–365.

West, R. W., and Greenough, W. T. (1972). Effect of environmental complexity on cortical synapses of rats: Preliminary results. *Behavioral Biology, 7,* 279–284.

Westergaard, G. C., Kuhn, H. E., and Suomi, S. J. (1998). Bipedal posture and hand preference in humans and other primates. *Journal of Comparative Psychology, 112,* 55–64.

Wever, E. G. (1974). The evolution of vertebrate hearing. In W. D. Keidel and W. D. Neff (Eds.), Handbook of sensory physiology: Vol. 5. Auditory system. New York: Springer.

Wever, R. A. (1979). Influence of physical workload on freerunning circadian rhythms of man. *Pflugers Archiv. European Journal of Physiology, 381,* 119–126.

Wexler, N. S., Rose, E. A., and Housman, D. E. (1991). Molecular approaches to hereditary diseases of the nervous system: Huntington's disease as a paradigm. *Annual Review of Neuroscience, 14,* 503–529.

Whitaker, D., and McGraw, P. V. (2000). Long-term visual experience recalibrates human orientation perception. *Nature Neuroscience, 3,* 13.

White, L. E., and Hain, R. F. (1959). Anorexia in association with a destructive lesion of the hypothalamus. *Archives of Pathology, 68,* 275–281.

White, N. M., and Milner, P. M. (1992). The psychobiology of reinforcers. *Annual Review of Psychology, 43,* 443–471.

White, T. D., Asfaw, B., DeGusta, D., Gilbert, H., et al. (2003). Pleistocene *Homo sapiens* from Middle Awash, Ethiopia. *Nature, 423,* 742–747.

Whiten, A., Goodall, J., McGrew, W. C., Nishida, T., et al. (1999). Cultures in chimpanzees. *Nature, 399,* 682–685.

Wible, C. G., Shenton, M. E., Hokama, H., Kikinis, R., et al. (1995). Prefrontal cortex and schizophrenia. A quantitative magnetic resonance imaging study. *Archives of General Psychiatry, 52,* 279–288.

Wiesel, T. N., and Hubel, D. H. (1963). Single-cell responses in striate cortex of kittens deprived of vision in one eye. *Journal of Neurophsyiology, 26,* 1002–1017.

Wiesel, T. N., and Hubel, D. H. (1965). Extent of recovery from the effects of visual deprivation in kittens. *Journal of Neurophysiology, 28,* 1060–1072.

Wiklund, C., and Sillén-Tullberg, B. (1985). Why distasteful butterflies have aposematic larvae and adults, but cryptic pupae: Evidence from predation experiments on the monarch and the European swallowtail. *Evolution, 39,* 1155–1158.

Wildman, D. E., Uddin, M., Liu, G., Grossman, L. I., et al. (2003). Implications of natural selection in shaping 99.4% nonsynonymous DNA identity between humans and chimpanzees: Enlarging genus *Homo. Proceedings of the National Academy of Sciences, USA, 100,* 7181–7188.

Will, B., Galani, R., Kelche, C., and Rosenzweig, M. R. (In press). Recovery from brain injury in animals: Relative efficacy of environmental enrichment, physical exercise, or formal training (1990–2002). *Progress in Neurobiology.*

Will, B. E., Rosenzweig, M. R., Bennett, E. L., Hebert, M., et al. (1977). Relatively brief environmental enrichment aids recovery of learning capacity and alters brain measures after postweaning brain lesions in rats. *Journal of Comparative and Physiological Psychology, 91,* 33–50.

Williams, D. (1969). Neural factors related to habitual aggression. *Brain, 92,* 503–520.

Williams, S. R., and Stuart, G. J. (2003). Role of dendritic synapse location in the control of action potential output. *Trends in Neurosciences, 26,* 147–154.

Williams, T. J., Pepitone, M. E., Christensen, S. E., Cooke, B. M., et al. (2000). Finger-length ratios and sexual orientation. *Nature, 404,* 455–456.

Wilson, R. I., and Nicoll, R. A. (2002). Endocannabinoid signaling in the brain. *Science, 296,* 678–682.

Wilson, R. S., and Bennett, D. A. (2003). Cognitive activity and risk of Alzheimer's disease. *Current Directions in Psychological Science, 12,* 87–91.

Wingard, D. L., and Berkman, L. F. (1983). Mortality risk associated with sleeping patterns among adults. *Sleep, 6,* 102–107.

Wingfield, J. C., Ball, G. F., Dufty, A. M., Hegner, R. E., et al. (1987). Testosterone and aggression in birds. *American Scientist, 75,* 602–608.

Winocur, G. (1990). Anterograde and retrograde amnesia in rats with dorsal hippocampal or dorsomedial thalamic lesions. *Behavioural Brain Research, 38,* 145–154.

Winslow, J. T., and Insel, T. R. (2002). The social deficits of the oxytocin knockout mouse. *Neuropeptides, 36,* 221–229.

Wise, R. A. (1996). Neurobiology of addiction. *Current Opinion in Neurobiology, 6,* 243–251.

Wise, R. A., Bauco, P., Carlezon, W. A., Jr., and Trojniar, W. (1992). Self-stimulation and drug reward mechanisms. *Annals of the New York Academy of Sciences, 654,* 192–198.

Witelson, S. F., and Pallie, W. (1973). Left hemisphere specialization for language in the new-born. Neuroanatomical evidence of asymmetry. *Brain, 96,* 641–646.

Wolf, S. S., Jones, D. W., Knable, M. B., Gorey, J. G., et al. (1996). Tourette syndrome: Prediction of phenotypic variation in monozygotic twins by caudate nucleus D2 receptor binding. *Science, 273,* 1225–1227.

Wolinsky, E., and Way, J. (1990). The behavioral genetics of *Caenorhabditis elegans. Behavior Genetics, 20,* 169–189.

Wolk, R., and Somers, V. K. (2003). Cardiovascular consequences of obstructive sleep apnea. *Clinics in Chest Medicine, 24,* 195–205.

Wood, J. M., Bootzin, R. R., Kihlstrom, J. F., and Schacter, D. L. (1992). Implicit and explicit memory for verbal information presented during sleep. *Psychological Science, 3(_4),* 236–239.

Woodruff-Pak, D. S., and Jaeger, M. E. (1998). Predictors of eyeblink classical conditioning over the adult age span. *Psychology and Aging, 13,* 193–205.

Woolf, C. J., and Salter, M. W. (2000). Neuronal plasticity: Increasing the gain in pain. *Science, 288,* 1765–1769.

Woolsey, C. N. (1981a). Cortical sensory organization: Multiple auditory areas. Crescent Manor, NJ: Humana.

Woolsey, C. N. (1981b). Cortical sensory organization: Multiple somatic areas. Crescent Manor, NJ: Humana.

Woolsey, C. N. (1981c). Cortical sensory organization: Multiple visual areas. Crescent Manor, NJ: Humana.

Woolsey, T. A., Durham, D., Harris, R. M., Simous, D. T., et al. (1981). Somatosensory development. In R. S. Aslin, J. R. Alberts, and M. R. Peterson (Eds.), *Sensory and perceptual development: Influence of genetic and experiential factors.* New York: Academic Press.

Woolsey, T. A., and Wann, J. R. (1976). Areal changes in mouse cortical barrels following vibrissal damage at different postnatal ages. *Journal of Comparative Neurology, 170,* 53–66.

World Health Organization. (2001). *The World Health Report.* Geneva, Switzerland: World Health Organization.

Wren, A. M., Seal, L. J., Cohen, M. A., Brynes, A. E., et al. (2001). Ghrelin enhances appetite and increases food intake in humans. *Journal of Clinical Endocrinology and Metabolism, 86,* 5992–5995.

Wren, A. M., Small, C. J., Ward, H. L., Murphy, K. G., et al. (2000). The novel hypothalamic peptide ghrelin stimulates food intake and growth hormone secretion. *Endocrinology, 141,* 4325–4328.

Wright, A. A., Santiago, H. C., Sands, S. F., Kendrick, D. F., et al. (1985). Memory processing of serial lists by pigeons, monkeys, and people. *Science, 229,* 287–289.

Wuethrich, B. (2000). Learning the world's languages—before they vanish. *Science, 288,* 1156–1159.

Xerri, C., Coq, J., Merzenich, M., and Jenkins, W. (1996). Experience-induced plasticity of cutaneous maps in the primary somatosensory cortex of adult monkeys and rats. *Journal de Physiologie, 90,* 277–287.

Xu, L., Furukawa, S., and Middlebrooks, J. C. (1999). Auditory cortical responses in the cat to sounds that produce spatial illusions. *Nature, 399,* 688–691.

Yaffe, K., Lui, L. Y., Zmuda, J., and Cauley, J. (2002). Sex hormones and cognitive function in older men. *Journal of the American Geriatrics Society, 50,* 707–712.

Yahr, P., and Gregory, J. E. (1993). The medial and lateral cell groups of the sexually dimorphic area of the gerbil hypothalamus are essential for male sex behavior and act via separate pathways. *Brain Research, 631,* 287–296.

Yamazaki, S., Numano, R., Abe, M., Hida, A., et al. (2000). Resetting central and peripheral circadian oscillators in transgenic rats. *Science, 288,* 682–685.

Yanagisawa, K., Bartoshuk, L. M., Catalanotto, F. A., Karrer, T. A., et al. (1992). Anesthesia of the chorda tympani nerve: Insights into a source of dysgeusia. *Chemical Senses, 17,* 724.

Yang, T. T., Gallen, C. C., Ramachandran, V. S., Cobb, S., et al. (1994). Noninvasive detection of cerebral plasticity in adult human somatosensory cortex. *Neuroreport, 5,* 701–704.

Yasuda, K., Raynor, K., Kong, H., Breder, C., et al. (1993). Cloning and functional comparison of kappa and delta opioid receptors from mouse brain. *Proceedings of the National Academy of Sciences, USA, 90,* 6736–6740.

Yehuda, R. (2002). Post-traumatic stress disorder. *New England Journal of Medicine, 346,* 108–114.

Yehuda, R., Kahana, B., Binder-Brynes, K., Southwick, S., et al. (1995). Low urinary cortisol excretion in Holocaust survivors with posttraumatic stress disorder. *American Journal of Psychiatry, 152,* 982–986.

Yin, J. C., Del Vecchio, M., Zhou, H., and Tully, T. (1995). CREB as a memory modulator: Induced expression of a dCREB2 activator isoform enhances long-term memory in *Drosophila. Cell, 81,* 107–115.

Yin, J. C., Wallach, J. S., Del Vecchio, M., Wilder, E. L., et al. (1994). Induction of a dominant negative CREB transgene specifically blocks long-term memory in *Drosophila. Cell, 79,* 49–58.

Young, A. B. (1993). Role of excitotoxins in heredito-degenerative neurologic diseases. *Research Publications—Association for Research in Nervous and Mental Disease, 71,* 175–189.

Young, A. W., Hellawell, D. J., Van De Wal, C., and Johnson, M. (1996). Facial expression processing after amygdalotomy. *Neuropsychologia, 34,* 31–39.

Young, D., Lawlor, P. A., Leone, P., Dragunow, M., et al. (1999). Environmental enrichment inhibits spontaneous apoptosis, prevents seizures and is neuroprotective. *Nature Medicine, 5,* 448–453.

Young, L. J., Pitkow, L. J., and Ferguson, J. N. (2002). Neuropeptides and social behavior: Animal models relevant to autism. *Molecular Psychiatry, 7,* S38–S39.

Yu, S., Pritchard, M., Kremer, E., Lynch, M., et al. (1991). Fragile X genotype characterized by an unstable region of DNA. *Science, 252,* 1179–1181.

Zaidel, E. (1976). Auditory vocabulary of the right hemisphere following brain bisection or hemidecortication. *Cortex, 12,* 191–211.

Zatorre, R. J., Evans, A. C., and Meyer, E. (1994). Neural mechanisms underlying melodic perception and memory for pitch. *Journal of Neuroscience, 14,* 1908–1919.

Zecevic, N., and Rakic, P. (1976). Differentiation of Purkinje cells and their relationship to other components of developing cerebellar cortex in man. *Journal of Comparative Neurology, 167,* 27–48.

Zeki, S. (1993). *A vision of the brain.* London: Blackwell.

Zeki, S., Watson, J. D., Lueck, C. J., Friston, K. J., et al. (1991). A direct demonstration of functional specialization in human visual cortex. *Journal of Neuroscience, 11,* 641–649.

Zeman, A. (2002). *Consciousness: A user's guide.* New Haven, CT: Yale University Press.

Zhang, Y., Proenca, R., Maffei, M., Barone, M., et al. (1994). Positional cloning of the mouse obese gene and its human homologue. *Nature, 372,* 425–432.

Zhang, Z., and Bourque, C. W. (2003). Osmometry in osmosensory neurons. *Nature Neuroscience, 6,* 1021–1022.

Zheng, J. L., and Gao, W. Q. (2000). Overexpression of Math1 induces robust production of extra hair cells in postnatal rat inner ears. *Nature Neuroscience, 3,* 580–586.

Zheng, J., Shen, W., He, D. Z., Long, K. B., et al. (2000). Prestin is the motor protein of cochlear outer hair cells. *Nature, 405,* 149–155.

Zhou, Y., Morais-Cabral, J. H., Kaufman, A., and MacKinnon, R. (2001). Chemistry of ion coordination and hydration revealed by a K^+ channel-Fab complex at 2.0 A resolution. *Nature, 414,* 43–48.

Zihl, J., von Cramon, D., and Mai, N. (1983). Selective disturbance of movement vision after bilateral brain damage. *Brain, 106,* 313–340.

Zimmer, C. (2004). The soul made flesh: The discovery of the brain—and how it changed the world. New York: Basic Books.

Zola-Morgan, S., and Squire, L. R. (1986). Memory impairment in monkeys following lesions of the hippocampus. *Behavioral Neuroscience, 100,* 155–160.

Zola-Morgan, S. M., and Squire, L. R. (1990). The primate hippocampal formation: Evidence for a time-limited role in memory storage. *Science, 250,* 288–290.

Zola-Morgan, S., and Squire, L. R. (2001). Relationship between magnitude of damage to the hippocampus and impaired recognition memory in monkeys. *Hippocampus, 11*(2), 92–98.

Zola-Morgan, S., Squire, L. R., and Ramus, S. J. (1994). Severity of memory impairment in monkeys as a function of locus and extent of damage within the medial temporal lobe memory system. *Hippocampus, 4,* 483–495.

Zonta, M., Angulo, M. C., Gobbo, S., Rosengarten, B., et al. (2003). Neuron-to-astrocyte signalling is central to the dynamic control of brain microcirculation. *Nature Neuroscience, 6,* 43–49.

Zou, Z., Horowitz, L. F, Montmayeur, J. P., Snapper, S., et al. (2001). Genetic tracing reveals a stereotyped sensory map in the olfactory cortex. *Nature, 414,* 173–179.

Zucker, I. (1976). Light, behavior, and biologic rhythms. *Hospital Practice, 11,* 83–91.

Zucker, I. (1988). Seasonal affective disorders: Animal models non fingo. *Journal of Biological Rhythms, 3,* 209–223.

Zucker, I., Boshes, M., and Dark, J. (1983). Suprachiasmatic nuclei influence circannual and circadian rhythms of ground squirrels. *American Journal of Physiology, 244,* R472–R480.

Zucker, L. M., and Zucker, T. F. (1961). "Fatty," a mutation in the rat. *Journal of Heredity, 52,* 275–278.

Zurek, P. M. (1981). Spontaneous narrowband acoustic signals emitted by human ears. *Journal of the Acoustical Society of America, 69,* 514–523.

Author Index

Lucas, R. J., 297, 429
Lucking, C. B., 346
Ludwig, G., 273
Lueck, C. J., 313
Lui, L. Y., 145
Lukashin, A., 335, 336
Lumsden, A. G., 193
Lundin, L.-G., 82
Luria, A., 531
Luschi, P., 246
Lush, I. E., 272
Lutter, C. D., 150
Luttrell, V. R., 360
Lyketsos, C. G., 107
Lynch, E. D., 265
Lynch, G., 562, 568
Lynch, M., 208
Lyons, M., 329
Lythgoe, D., 474

M

Ma, D., 278
Ma, W., 278
Mable, B. K., 161
Macagno, E., 200
MacCulloch, M. J., 479
Macdonald, C. A., 527
MacDonald, D., 184
MacDonald, K. A., 8
MacDonald, M. E., 348
Mace, G. M., 162, 167
Mach, R. H., 117
Machado, C. J., 469
Machón, R. A., 495, 496
Macintyre, L., 612
Mack, J. L., 593
MacKay, D. G., 524
MacKenzie, G., 346
Mackenzie, L., 383
MacKinnon, R., 69
Macklis, J. D., 188, 573, 586
MacLean, P., 468
Macmillan, M., 582
Mactutus, C F., 112
Madden, J., 179
Madden, K. S., 483
Maddock, R. J., 474
Madsen, K. M., 210
Maes, M., 484
Maes, R. A., 478
Maffei, L., 304
Maffei, M., 414
Magavi, S. S., 188
Magee, J. J., 589
Magendzo, K., 109
Maggioncalda, A. N., 356
Magnuson, V. L., 385
Magnusson, A., 508
Magoun, H., 447
Maguire, E. A., 548
Mahal, B., 118
Mahowald, M. W., 451
Mai, N., 314
Maillis, A., 568
Mair, W. G. P., 526
Maislin, G., 441
Maisog, J. M., 578
Maki, P. M., 146
Malaspina, D., 493
Malberg, J. E., 503
Maldjian, J. A., 469
Maldonado, R., 109
Malenka, R. C., 117, 568

Maletic-Savatic, M., 559
Malhotra, A. K., 113
Malik, I. A., 414
Malinow, R., 559
Maljkovic, V., 304
Malloy, M., 601
Malm, J., 418
Malmberg, A. B., 239
Man, H., 568
Manes, F., 471
Manetto, V., 442
Manfredi, M., 237
Manger, P., 165
Manger, P. R., 165, 438
Mangiarini, L., 349
Mani, S. K., 360
Manova, M. G., 197
Mansi, L., 212
Mantyh, P. W., 241
Maquet, P., 444
Marcus, G. F., 584
Margoliash, D., 444
Margraf, J., 510
Mariani, J., 197
Mark, V. H., 479
Markey, S. P., 346
Markowitsch, H. J., 541, 542
Markowitz, J. C., 509
Markowitz, R. S., 340
Marks, A., 569
Marks, I. M., 474
Marler, C., 373
Marler, P., 584, 586
Marrocco, R. T., 313
Marsh, R. R., 270
Marsicano, G., 110
Marsolek, C. J., 345
Martin, A., 541
Martin, C. E., 362
Martin, N. G., 385
Martin, P., 254
Martin, W. D., 200
Martin, W. J., 239
Martin, W. R., 346
Martina, M., 69
Martinez, J. L., 530, 566, 568, 573
Martinez, P., 149
Martins, L. M., 194
Martuza, R. L., 517
Marucha, P. T., 486
Marzani, D., 316
Masliah, E., 580
Mason, W. A., 469
Massey, J. T., 335
Masters, W. H., 362, 363, 364
Masterton, R. B., 262
Mastrianni, J. A., 442
Masuo, O., 566
Mateer, C., 595
Mateo, J. M., 278
Mathalon, D. H., 108
Matser, E. J., 609
Matsumoto, K., 606
Matsuzaka, Y., 338
Matthews, D. B., 107
Matthews, D. R., 142
Matthews, G., 80
Matthews, K., 482
Matthies, H., 574
Matthysse, S., 492
Mattson, R. H., 479

Mattson, S. N., 209
Matzuk, M. M., 148
Mauch, D. H., 54
Mauk, M. D., 572
Maurer, D., 206
May, M. G., 286
Mayberry, R. I., 619
Mayeux, R., 493
Mayfield, R. D., 201
Mayr, E., 298
Mazziotta, J. C., 542
McAbee, R. S., 506
McAllister, A. K., 205
McAlpine, D., 261
McAnulty, G. B., 497
McBurney, D. H., 272
McCall, W. V., 453
McCann, U. D., 113
McCarthy, R. A., 595
McClintock, M., 278, 365
McClintock, M. K., 365
McClure, J. N., 510
McComb, K., 249
McCrory, E., 596
McCullough, J. P., 503
McDonald, B., 496
McDonald, J. J., 228
McDonald, J. W., 619
McEwen, B. S., 513, 572
McFadden, D., 256, 265, 385
McGaugh, J. L., 530, 539, 576, 577
McGeer, E., 579
McGeer, P., 579
McGoon, M. D., 390
McGraw, P. V., 206
McGrew, W. C., 177
McGuckin, B. G., 409
McGue, M., 108
McHaffie, J. G., 241
McIlwrath, S. L., 230
McIntosh, A. R., 578
McKee, R. D., 533
McKenna, K., 363
McKenry, P. C., 478
McKernan, M. G., 569
McKim, W. A., 116
McKinney, T. D., 477
McKinnon, P. J., 271, 272
McLaughlin, S. K., 271, 272
McMahon, C., 311
McMahon, H.T., 103
McNamara, J. O., 76
McNaughton, B. L., 548
Meador-Woodruff, J. H., 501
Meaney, M. J., 385
Mechoulam, R., 109
Meckler, R. J., 593
Meddis, R., 443, 445
Medema, J. P., 193–194
Mednick, S. A., 202, 495, 496
Medori, R., 442
Medori, T., 442
Mega, M. S., 603
Mehlman, P. T., 478
Mehta, A. D., 254
Meisel, R. L., 360, 361
Meister, M., 278
Mellingen, K., 560
Mello, C. V., 163
Mellon, S. H., 503

Mellstrom, K., 418
Meloy, J. R., 479
Meltzer, C., 612
Melvin, L. S., 110
Melzack, R., 237, 242
Menaker, M., 428
Mencl, W. E., 594
Mendel, G. J., 159
Mendell, N. R., 492
Mendelsohn, M., 276
Mendelson, J., 111
Mendelson, W. B., 454, 506
Mendlewicz, J., 508
Menguy, C., 252
Mennella, J. A., 270
Menoncello, L., 596
Meredith, M. A., 228
Mersch, P. P., 508
Merzenich, M., 234, 235
Merzenich, M. M., 234, 258, 264, 337
Meselson, M., 366
Mesulam, M. M., 228, 608
Meyer, E., 601
Michael, N., 509
Middendorp, H. M., 508
Middlebrooks, J. C., 262
Middleton, B., 454
Miesegaes, G., 572
Miguel, E. C., 510
Miki, N., 587
Mikami, A., 314
Miles, L. E., 440
Miller, A. H., 485
Miller, C., 583
Miller, D. R., 399
Miller, G., 179, 372
Miller, I. J. J., 272
Miller, J. M., 265
Milleret, C., 317
Milliken, G. W., 337
Mills, D. L., 597
Mills, N. P., 509
Milner, A. D., 282, 315
Milner, B., 522, 524, 525, 526, 605
Milner, P., 470
Milner, P. M., 22, 470, 556
Miltner, W. H., 613
Mimmack, M. L., 493
Miner, N., 598
Minoda, R., 265
Mioduszewska, B., 567
Mirsky, A., 496
Mirsky, A. F., 501
Mishina, M., 81
Mishkin, M., 262, 314, 533
Mitchell, S. J., 339
Mittleman, M. A., 107
Miyashita, Y., 227
Mizumori, S. J. Y., 573
Moghaddam, B., 501
Mohammed, A., 560, 580
Moldin, S. O., 502
Mollereau, C., 110
Monakow, C. von, 610
Mondloch, C. J., 206
Money, J., 377
Monks, D. A., 383
Monory, K., 110
Monsonego, A., 212
Montagna, P., 442
Montague, C. T., 418
Montmayeur, J. P., 277

Mooney, R. D., 399
Moore, C. L., 385
Moore, G. J., 509
Moore, H., 373
Moore, J. K., 258
Moore, J. W., 571
Moore, K. A., 483
Moore, R. Y., 427, 429, 450, 526
Moore-Ede, M. C., 433
Morais-Cabral, J. H., 69
Morford, J. P., 619
Morgan, D., 117
Morgan, R. E., 112
Mori, K., 276
Morihisa, J., 496, 497
Morimoto, Y., 81
Morishita, W., 569
Moritz, C., 161
Moriwaki, A., 148
Morrell, F., 76, 578
Morris, B., 593
Morris, D., 583
Morris, K. D. W., 106
Morris, M., 479
Morris, R., 478
Morrison, A. R., 449
Morrison, H., 109
Morrison, R. G., 586
Morrow, J. E., 265
Morrow, J. W., 95
Morrow, T., 193
Mortensen, P. B., 433, 501
Moruzzi, G., 443, 447
Moscovitch, A., 508
Moscovitch, M., 550
Moskowitz, M. A., 608
Moss, C., 249
Mott, F. W., 331
Motter, B. C., 228
Mountcastle, V. B., 42, 228, 232
Mountjoy, C., 579
Movshon, J. A., 206
Mower, G. D., 619
Mowry, B. J., 493
Moxon, K. A., 340
Moye, D., 237
Moyer, J. R., Jr., 572
Mueller, H. T., 501
Mueller, K .L., 272
Muglia, P., 509
Mukamal, K. J., 107
Mukhametov, L. M., 438
Mulkey, R. M., 568
Müller, R.-A., 210
Muller, U., 265
Mullington, J. M., 441
Mundel, M., 593
Mundo, E., 509
Münte, T. F., 234, 262, 263
Munzar, P., 116
Murai, K., 344
Murakami, N., 414
Murphy, G. G., 568
Murphy, J., 588
Murphy, K. G., 414
Murphy, P. N., 114
Muzio, J. N., 439

N

N'Guyen, J. P., 347
Naatanen, R., 560
Nabhan, G. P., 239

Subject Index

Illustration Credits

The following figures use elements originally rendered for *Neuroanatomy through Clinical Cases* by Hal Blumenfeld, M.D., Ph.D. (Blumenfeld, 2002): Figures 1.11*b*, 2.2, 2.4, 2.6, 2.10, 2.13, 2.14*a*, 2.15, Box 3.2*a*, 4.2, 4.3, 4.4, 4.5, 5.9, 5.10, 5.11, 5.15, 5.18, 5.19*a*, 6.6, 7.26, 7.28, 8.3, 8.5, 8.8, 8.10, 8.15*a*, 8.16*a*, 8.17, 8.22, 11.12*a*, 11.16, 11.18, 11.23, 13.3, 13.20, 15.10, 15.17, 16.12, 17.1, 17.4, 19.6, 19.8, 19.10, 19.11, 19.15*a*, 19.19*a*, 19.20.

Chapter 1
1.9: Reproduced with gracious permission of Her Majesty Queen Elizabeth II, copyright reserved. 1.10: Bettmann/Corbis. 1.11*a*: Bettmann/Corbis. Box 1.2 (A): Bettmann/Corbis.

Chapter 2
2.3*b*: From *Gray's Anatomy*, 35th ed., Figure 2.9, page 807. Reprinted with permission of the publisher, Churchill Livingstone. (Dissection by M. C. E. Hutchinson, photograph by Kevin Fitzpatrick, Guy's Hospital Medical School, London.) 2.16*a*: © Dan McCoy/Rainbow. 2.16*b*: © Hank Morgan, Science Source/Photo Researchers, Inc. 2.16*c*: Courtesy of Jamie Eberling. 2.17: Courtesy of Michael Leventon/MIT Artificial Intelligence Lab. 2.21*b*: © Dennis Kunkel Microscopy, Inc. Box 2.3 (F): From Sunn et al., 2002. *Penfield stamp*: © Canada Post Corporation, 1991, reproduced with permission.

Chapter 3
3.19*a*: Courtesy of Neuroscan Labs, a division of Neurosoft, Inc.

Chapter 4
4.12: © Biophoto Associates/Photo Researchers, Inc. 4.14: © Roger Ressmeyer/Corbis.

Chapter 5
5.17: Thomas & Pat Leeson/Photo Researchers, Inc.

Chapter 7
7.23*a*: Lauren Shear/SPL/Photo Researchers, Inc. 7.23*b*: Courtesy of the National Fragile X Foundation and the Fragile X Center of San Diego. *Michael May*: © Florence Low.

Chapter 8
8.1*a*: © Phil Savoie/naturepl.com. 8.1*b*: © Mike Hill/AGE Fotostock. 8.1*c*: © SuperStock/AGE Fotostock. 8.1*d*: © Stockbyte/PictureQuest.

Chapter 10
10.11*a*: © Paul Parker/SPL/Photo Researchers, Inc. 10.29: Courtesy of Patch Pals, www.PatchPals.com.

Chapter 12
12.7: Courtesy of Lisa Davis and Lowell Getz. 12.10*c*: © LogicStock/Painet Inc. 12.12: © Dr. David M. Phillips/Visuals Unlimited. 12.14: © Anup Shah/naturepl.com. 12.15: © Phil Savoie/naturepl.com. Box 12.2: © Laurence Frank, courtesy of Stephen Glickman.

Chapter 13
13.2*a*: David McIntyre. 13.2*b*: © Fredrick Sears/Painet, Inc. 13.4*a*: © Ken Lucas/Visuals Unlimited. 13.4*b*: © Patrick J. Endres/Visuals Unlimited. 13.4*c*: © Doug Allan/naturepl.com. 13.17: © Rod Planck/Photo Researchers, Inc. 13.26: © John Sholtis/Rockefeller University. 13.28*a*: © AP/Wide World Photos. 13.28*b*: Kunsthistorisches Museum, Vienna.

Chapter 14
14.25: © Royalty-Free/Corbis.

Chapter 15
15.3: © Sinauer Associates. 15.7: © Dr. P. Marazzi/SPL/Photo Researchers, Inc.

Chapter 16
16.18: Courtesy of the USDA Animal and Plant Health Inspection Service.

Chapter 17
Box 17.1 (A): Bettmann/Corbis. Box 17.1 (C): Courtesy of Med Associates.

Chapter 18
Box 18.1: Courtesy the Office of Communications, Princeton University.

Scientist Photographs

Chapter 2
Penfield: © Canada Post Corporation, 1991, reproduced with permission.

Chapter 3
Loewi: Courtesy Österreichische Gesellschaft für Zeitgeschichte, Wien—Bildarchiv.

Chapter 4
Hofmann: Courtesy of MCH Messe Basel AG.

Chapter 5
Bernard & Berthold: Courtesy of the National Library of Medicine.

Chapter 6
Bullock: Neuroscience History Archives, Brain Research Institute, University of California, Los Angeles. *Darwin:* Bettmann/Corbis. *Franklin:* © the Principal and Fellows of Newnham College, Cambridge. *Watson & Crick:* © A. Barrington Brown/Photo Researchers, Inc.

Chapter 7
May: © Florence Low.

Chapter 8
Müller: Courtesy of the National Library of Medicine. *Ramachandran:* Courtesy of Mr. Chetan Shah.

Chapter 9
Bartoshuk: Photo by Michael Marsland, courtesy of the Yale University Office of Public Affairs. *Bekesy:* Courtesy of Harvard Universty Press. *Buck:* Photo by Clay Eals, courtesy of the Fred Hutchinson Cancer Research Center.

Chapter 10
Wertheimer: Courtesy of the National Library of Medicine. *Wiesel:* Courtesy of Robert Reichert.

Chapter 11
Henneman: Courtesy of the Harvard University News Office. *Sherrington:* Neuroscience History Archives, Brain Research Institute, University of California, Los Angeles.

Chapter 12
Johnson: Becker Medical Library of Washington University, St. Louis. *Kinsey:* © William Dellenback/The Kinsey Institute for Research in Sex, Gender, and Reproduction. *Masters:* Becker Medical Library of Washington University, St. Louis. *McClintock:* Courtesy of the University of Chicago.

Chapter 13
Friedman: Courtesy of Rockefeller University. *Garcia:* Neuroscience History Archives, Brain Research Institute, University of California, Los Angeles.

Chapter 14
Aserinsky: Courtesy of Marshall University. *Kleitman:* Courtesy of the University of Chicago. *Webb:* Photo by Jeff Gage, courtesy of the University of Florida.

Chapter 15
Bard & Cannon: Courtesy of the National Library of Medicine. *Ekman:* © John McDermott. *Olds & Selye:* Neuroscience History Archives, Brain Research Institute, University of California, Los Angeles.

Chapter 16
Noguchi: Courtesy of the National Library of Medicine. *Walker:* Photo by Annemarie Poyo, © Emory University Photography.

Chapter 17
Korsakoff: Courtesy of the National Library of Medicine. *Tolman:* Department of Psychology, University of California, Berkeley.

Chapter 18
Eccles: Courtesy of the National Library of Medicine. *Greenough:* Courtesy of Kathy Bates. *Kandel:* Courtesy of Rene Perez. *Quinn:* Courtesy of the National Library of Medicine.

Chapter 19
Broca: Bettman/Corbis. *Geschwind:* Neuroscience History Archives, Brain Research Institute, University of California, Los Angeles. *Nottebohm:* Courtesy of Robert Reichert.

About the Book

Editor: Graig Donini

Project Editor: Kathaleen Emerson

Copy Editor: Stephanie Hiebert

Production Manager: Christopher Small

Book Production: Joan Gemme, Janice Holabird, Joanne Delphia, Michele Ruschhaupt, and Jefferson Johnson in QuarkXpress on the Macintosh

Art: Dragonfly Media Group

Photo Researcher: David McIntyre

Fine Art Consultant: Steven Diamond, Inc.

Book and Cover Design: Jefferson Johnson

Book and Cover Manufacturer: Courier Companies, Inc.